Level 4

Risks and Consequences

•

Dollars and Sense

•

From Mystery to Medicine

•

Survival

•

Communication

•

A Changing America

Level 4

— PROGRAM AUTHORS —

Carl Bereiter
Marilyn Jager Adams
Marlene Scardamalia
Marcy Stein
Anne McKeough
Michael Pressley
Marsha Roit
Jan Hirshberg
Joe Campione
Iva Carruthers
Gerald H. Treadway, Jr.

A Division of The McGraw·Hill Companies

Columbus, Ohio

Acknowledgments

Grateful acknowledgement is given to the following publishers and copyright owners for permissions granted to reprint selections from their publications. All possible care has been taken to trace ownership and secure permission for each selection included. In case of any errors or omissions, the Publisher will be pleased to make suitable acknowledgements in future editions.

RISKS AND CONSEQUENCES

"Mrs. Frisby and the Crow" reprinted with the permission of Atheneum Books for Young Readers, an imprint of Simon & Schuster Children's Publishing Division from MRS. FRISBY AND THE RATS OF NIMH by Robert C. O'Brien. Copyright © 1971 Robert C. O'Brien.

From TOTO by Marietta D. Moskin, text copyright © 1971 by Marietta Moskin. Used by permission of Coward-McCann, Inc., an imprint of Penguin Putnam Books for Young Readers, a division of Penguin Putnam Inc. From TOTO by Marietta D. Moskin, illustrated by Rocco Negri, illustrations copyright © 1971 by Rocco Negri. Used by permission of Coward-McCann, Inc., an imprint of Penguin Putnam Books for Young Readers, a division of Penguin Putnam Inc.

SARAH, PLAIN AND TALL COPYRIGHT © 1985 BY PATRICIA MACLACHLAN. Used by permission of HarperCollins Publishers.

"Escape" From CHARLOTTE'S WEB, COPYRIGHT 1952 BY E.B. WHITE RENEWED 1980 BY E.B. WHITE, ILLUSTRATIONS COPYRIGHT 1952 BY GARTH WILLIAMS RENEWED © 1980 BY GARTH WILLIAMS. Used by permission of HarperCollins Publishers.

"Hippo's Hope" from A LIGHT IN THE ATTIC by Shel Silverstein. COPYRIGHT © 1981 BY EVIL EYE MUSIC. Used by permission of HarperCollins Publishers.

From MAE JEMISON: SPACE SCIENTIST by Gail Sakurai, copyright © 1995 by Children's Press. All rights reserved. Reprinted by permission of Children's Press, an imprint of Scholastic Library Publishing.

From TWO TICKETS TO FREEDOM. Text © 1971 Florence B. Freedman, illustrations © 1971 Ezra Jack Keats. Reprinted with permission of Peter Bedrick Books, an imprint of the McGraw-Hill Companies. All rights reserved.

"Freedom" from COLLECTED POEMS by Langston Hughes. Copyright © 1994 by the Estate of Langston Hughes. Reprinted by permission of Alfred A Knopf, a Division of Random House Inc.

"Daedalus and Icarus" reprinted with the permission of Margaret K. McElderry Books, an imprint of Simon & Schuster Children's Publishing Division from GREEK MYTHS by Geraldine McCaughrean, illustrated by Emma Chichester Clark. Text copyright © 1992 Geraldine McCaughrean. Illustrations copyright © 1992 Emma Chichester Clark. From THE ORCHARD BOOK OF GREEK MYTHS by Geraldine McCaughrean first published in the UK by Orchard Books in 1992, a division of The Watts Publishing Group Limited, 96 Leonard Street, London EC2A 4XD.

DOLLARS AND SENSE

"Starting a Business" from THE KIDS' BUSINESS BOOK by Arlene Erlbach. Copyright 1998 by Arlene Erlbach. Published by Lerner Publications: A Division of Lerner Publishing Group. Used by permission of the publisher. All rights reserved.

"Henry Wells and William G. Fargo" from FAMOUS BUILDERS OF CALIFORNIA, copyright © 1987 by Edward F. Dolan, Jr. Reprinted with permission of Curtis Brown, Ltd. All rights reserved.

"Lemonade Stand" reprinted with the permission of Margaret K. McElderry Books, an imprint of Simon & Schuster Children's Publishing Division from WORLDS I KNOW AND OTHER POEMS by Myra Cohn Livingston. Text copyright © 1985 Myra Cohn Livingston.

"Elias Sifuentes, Restaurateur" Reprinted with the permission of Neil Johnson, c/o Mary Jack Wald Associates, Inc. from ALL IN A DAY'S WORK: Twelve Americans Talk About Their Jobs by Neil Johnson published by Joy Street Books/Little, Brown and Company, 1271 Avenue of the Americas, New York NY 10020. Copyright © 1989 by Neil Johnson.

From Business Is Looking Up by Barbara Aiello and Jeffrey Shulman. Copyright © 1988 by The Kids on the Block, Inc. Reprinted by permission of The Millbrook Press, Inc.

SALT by Harve Zemach, pictures by Margot Zemach. Copyright © 1965 by Margot Zemach. Reprinted by permission of Farrar, Straus & Giroux, LLC, on behalf of the Estate of Margot Zemach.

FROM MYSTERY TO MEDICINE

Maxine Kumin, "The Microscope." Copyright © 1968 by Maxine Kumin. Reprinted by permission of the author.

Adapted from Sure Hands, Strong Heart: The Life of Daniel Hale Williams by Lillie Patterson. Copyright © 1981 by Abingdon Press. Used by permission.

"Surgeons Must Be Very Careful" reprinted by permission of the publishers and the Trustees of Amherst College from THE POEMS OF EMILY DICKINSON, Thomas H. Johnson, ed., Cambridge, Mass.: The Belknap Press of Harvard University Press, Copyright © 1951, 1955, 1979, 1983 by the President and Fellows of Harvard College.

"The Germ" from VERSES FROM 1929 by Ogden Nash. Copyright © 1935 by Ogden Nash, renewed. Reprinted by permission of Curtis Brown, Ltd.

Carol Saller: THE BRIDGE DANCERS, by Carol Saller, text copyright 1991 by the author. THE BRIDGE DANCERS, illustrations copyright © 1991 by Gerald Talifero. Used by permission of the illustrator.

"Emily's Hands-On Science Experiment" from Current Science © 1998 by Weekly Reader Corp. All rights reserved!

"The New Doctor" from YOU CAN HEAR A MAGPIE SMILE, Copyright © 1980 by Paula Paul.

"The Story of Susan La Flesche Picotte" from Marion Marsh Brown's HOMEWARD THE ARROW'S FLIGHT © 1980. Revised edition 1995. © Field Mouse Productions, Grand Island, Nebraska.

Reprinted with the permission of Atheneum Books for Young Readers, an imprint of Simon & Schuster Children's Publishing Division from SHADOW OF A BULL by Maia Wojciechowska. Copyright © 1964 Maia Wojciechowska.

SURVIVAL

Chapter 10 from ISLAND OF THE BLUE DOLPHINS. Copyright © 1960, renewed 1988 by Scott O'Dell. Reprinted by permission of Houghton Mifflin Company. All rights reserved.

From The Arctic Explorer: The Story of Matthew Henson by Jeri Ferris, copyright 1989 by Jeri Ferris. Published by Carolrhoda Books, Inc. a Division of the Lerner Publishing Group. Used by permission of the publisher. All rights reserved.

MCBROOM AND THE BIG WIND by Sid Fleishman. TEXT COPYRIGHT © 1967 BY SID FLEISCHMAN. Used by permission HarperCollins Publishers. Illustrations copyright © 1982 by Walter H. Lorraine. By permission of the artist.

From ONE AT A TIME by David McCord. Copyright © 1952 by David McCord; copyright © renewed 1980 by David McCord. By permission of Little, Brown and Company (Inc.).

THE BIG WAVE by Pearl Buck COPYRIGHT © 1947 BY THE CURTIS PUBLISHING COMPANY; COPYRIGHT © 1948, 1976 BY PEARL S. BUCK. Used by permission of HarperCollins Publishers.

"Solitude", from NOW WE ARE SIX by A.A. Milne, illustrated by E.H. Shepard, copyright 1927 by E.P. Dutton, renewed © 1955 by A.A. Milne. Used by permission of Dutton Children's Books, A Division of Penguin Young Readers Group, A Member of Penguin Group (USA) Inc., 345 Hudson Street, New York, NY 10014. All rights reserved.

From THE DIARY OF A YOUNG GIRL THE DEFINITIVE EDITION by Anne Frank. Otto H. Frank & Mirjam Pressler, Editors, translated by Susan Massotty, copyright © 1995 by Doubleday, a division of Random House, Inc. Used by permission of Doubleday, a division of Random House, Inc.

"Many Thousand Gone" from I'M GOING TO SING: BLACK AMERICAN SPIRITUALS. Selected and illustrated by Ashley Bryan. Copyright © 1982 Ashley Bryan. Reprinted by permission of the author.

"Walk Together Children" from WALK TOGETHER CHILDREN: BLACK AMERICAN SPIRITUALS. Selected and illustrated by Ashley Bryan. Copyright © 1974 Ashley Bryan. Reprinted by permission of the author.

COMMUNICATION

"Messages by the Mile" from BEES DANCE AND WHALES SING: THE MYSTERIES OF ANIMAL COMMUNICATION, by Margery Facklam. Text copyright © 1992 by Margery Facklam. Reprinted by permission of Sierra Club Books for Children.

"Whalesong" © Judith Nicholls, 1990, from DRAGONSFIRE by Judith Nicholls, published by Faber & Faber. Reprinted by permission of the author.

From WE'LL BE RIGHT BACK AFTER THESE MESSAGES © Shelagh Wallace reprinted with permission of Annick Press.

From BREAKING INTO PRINT: *Before and After the Invention of the Printing Press* by Stephen Krensky, illustrated by Bonnie Christensen. Text copyright © 1996 by Stephen Krensky. Used by permission of Rosenstone/Wender. BREAKING INTO PRINT, illustrations copyright © 1996 by Bonnie Christensen. Published in the United States by Little, Brown and Co. All rights reserved. Used with permission.

KOKO'S KITTEN by Dr. Francine Patterson, photographs by Ronald H. Cohn. Copyright © 1985 by The Gorilla Foundation. Photographs copyright © Ronald Cohn/The Gorilla Foundation/National Geographic Society.

From LOUIS BRAILLE: THE BOY WHO INVENTED BOOKS FOR THE BLIND by Margaret Davidson. Copyright © 1971 by Margaret Davidson. Reprinted by permission of Scholastic Inc.

Text of "Connections" Copyright © 1996 by Diane Siebert. Reprinted by permission of S©ott Treimel New York. Aaron Meshon-illustrator.

Excerpt from THE LITTLE PRINCE, copyright © 1943 by Harcourt Inc., copyright renewed 1971 by Consuelo de Saint-Exupery, English translation copyright © 2000 by Richard Howard, reprinted with permission of Harcourt, Inc.

A CHANGING AMERICA

"The Voyage of the Mayflower" from COBBLESTONE's November 1989 issue: Pilgrims to a New World, © 1989, Cobblestone Publishing Company, 30 Grove Street, Suite C, Peterborough, NH 03458. All rights reserved. Reprinted by permission of the publisher.

"Pocahontas" text From THE VIRGINIA COLONY by Dennis B. Fradin, copyright © 1986 by Children's Press.

www.sra4kids.com

SRA/McGraw-Hill

A Division of The **McGraw-Hill** *Companies*

Send all inquiries to:
SRA/McGraw-Hill
8787 Orion Place
Columbus, Ohio 43240-4027

Printed in the United States of America.

ISBN 0-07-602696-5

4 5 6 7 8 9 RRW 10 09 08 07 06

— Program Authors —

Carl Bereiter, Ph.D.
University of Toronto

Marilyn Jager Adams, Ph.D.
BBN Technologies

Michael Pressley, Ph.D.
Michigan State University

Marsha Roit, Ph.D.
National Reading Consultant

Anne McKeough, Ph.D.
University of Calgary

Jan Hirshberg, Ed.D.
Reading Specialist

Marlene Scardamalia, Ph.D.
University of Toronto

Joe Campione, Ph.D.
University of California, Berkeley

Iva Carruthers, Ph.D.
Northeastern Illinois University

Gerald H. Treadway, Jr., Ed.D.
San Diego State University

Marcy Stein, Ph.D.
University of Washington, Tacoma

Table of Contents

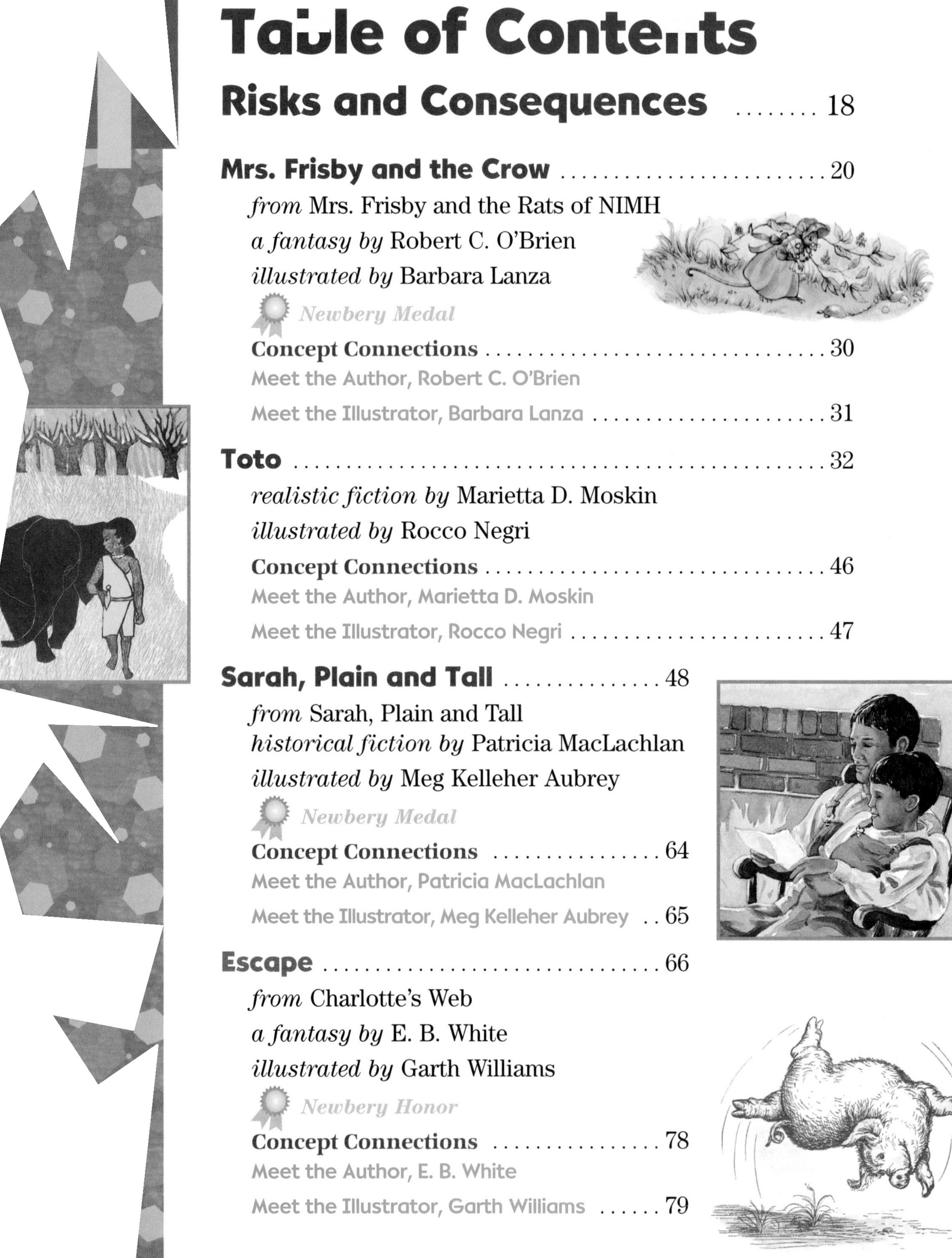

Table of Contents

UNIT 3

Table of Contents

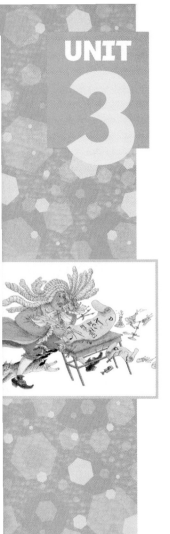

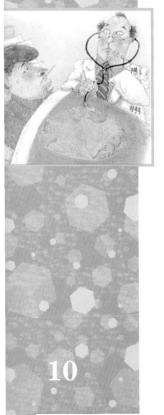

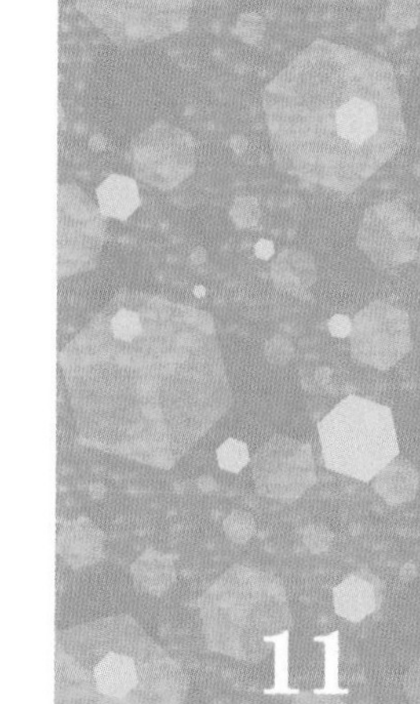

Table of Contents

あぁじゃがおきたわ、
いいゆめみてたの

Table of Contents

Table of Contents

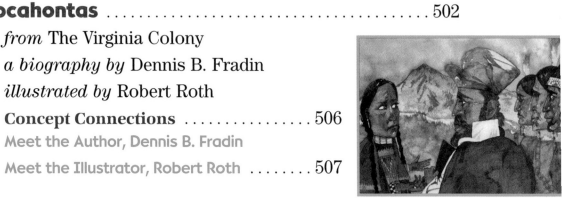

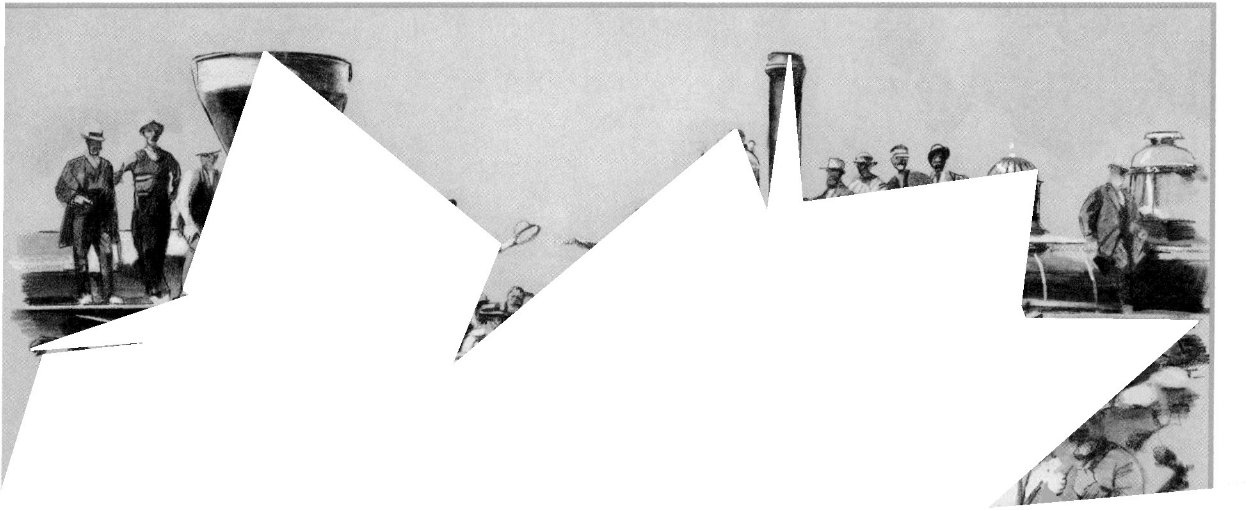

UNIT 1

Risks and Consequences

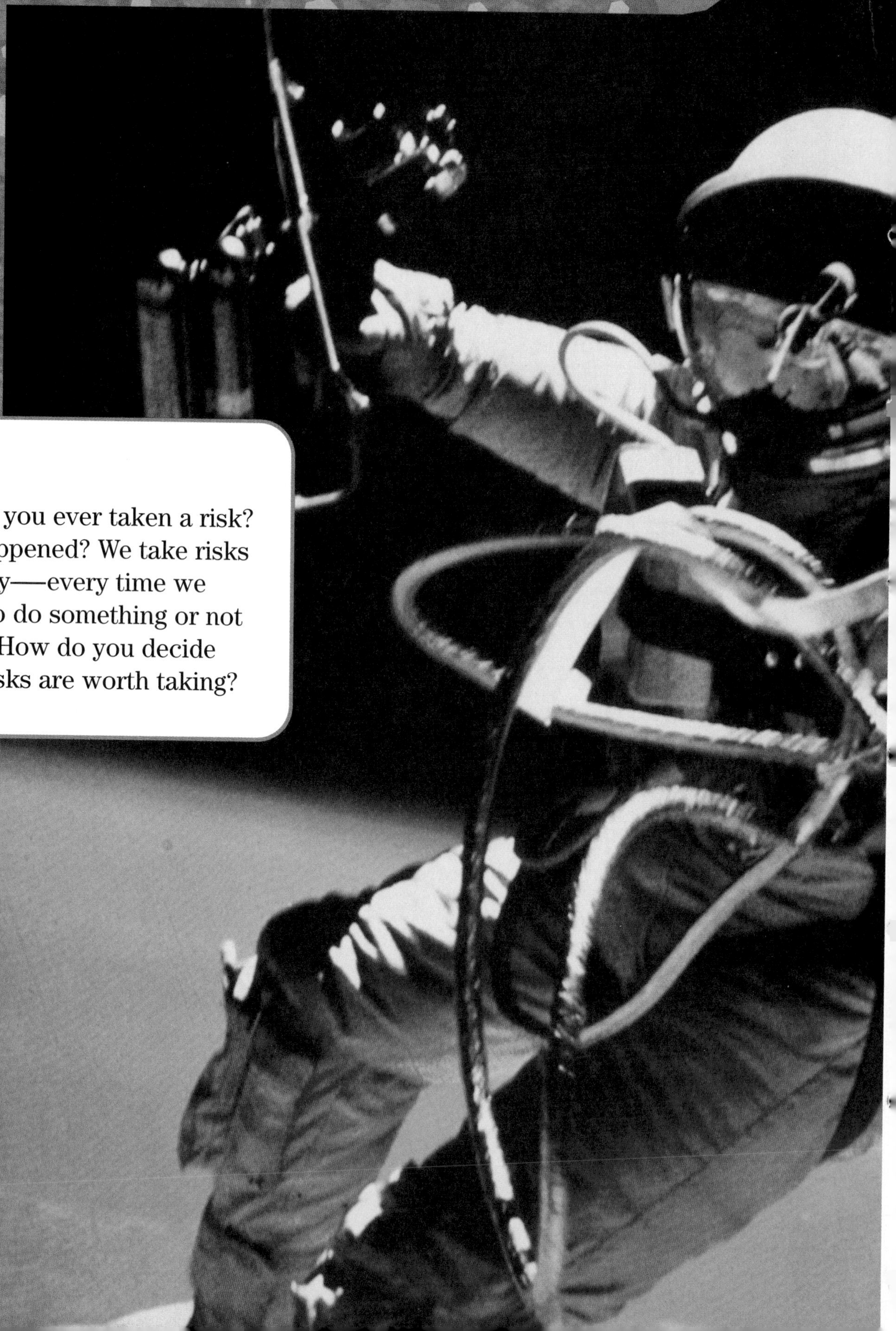

Have you ever taken a risk? What happened? We take risks every day—every time we decide to do something or not to do it. How do you decide which risks are worth taking?

Focus Questions Are there times when we must take a risk to help others? Can our own risks sometimes endanger others?

Mrs. Frisby and the Crow

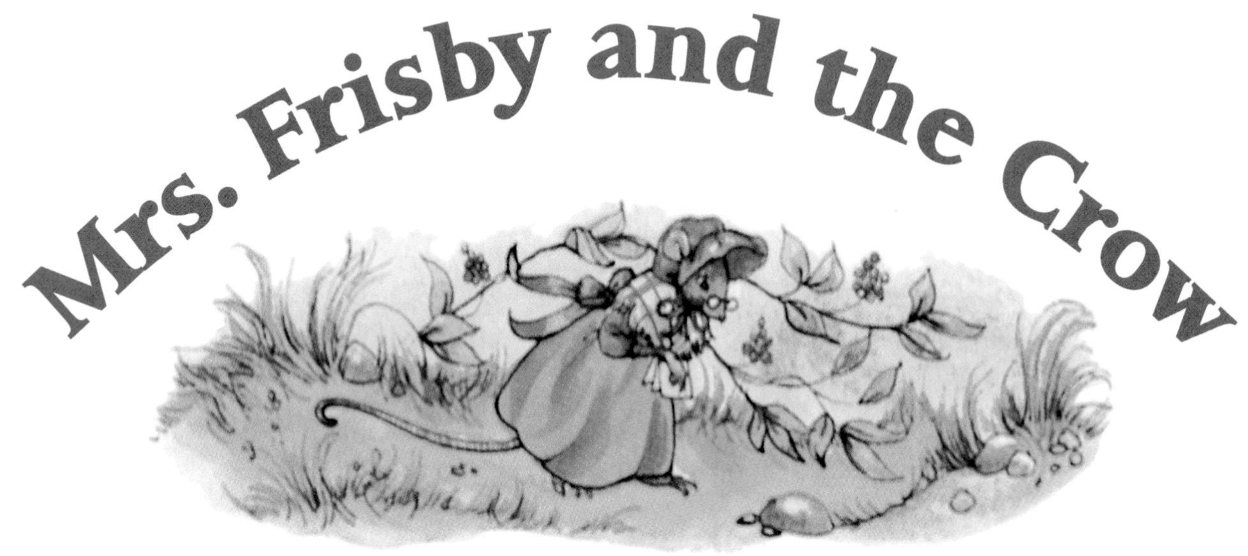

from ***Mrs. Frisby and the Rats of NIMH***
by Robert C. O'Brien
illustrated by Barbara Lanza

Mrs. Frisby is a mouse that lives with her children in a country garden. When her son Timothy becomes ill, she undertakes a treacherous journey to bring him some medicine.

Mrs. Frisby looked again at the sun and saw that she faced an unpleasant choice. She could go home by the same roundabout way she had come, in which case she would surely end up walking alone in the woods in the dark—a frightening prospect, for at night the forest was alive with danger. Then the owl came out to hunt, and foxes, weasels and strange wild cats stalked among the tree trunks.

The other choice would be dangerous, too, but with luck it would get her home before dark. That would be to take a straighter route, across the farmyard between the barn and the chicken house, going not too close to the house but cutting the distance home by half. The cat would be there somewhere, but by daylight—and by staying in the open, away from the shrubs—she could probably spot him before he saw her.

The cat: He was called Dragon. Farmer Fitzgibbon's wife had given him the name as a joke when he was a small kitten pretending to be fierce. But when he grew up, the name turned out to be an apt one. He was enormous, with a huge, broad head and a large mouth full of curving fangs, needle sharp. He had seven claws on each foot and a thick, furry tail, which lashed angrily from side to side. In color he was orange and white, with glaring yellow eyes; and when he leaped to kill, he gave a high, strangled scream that froze his victims where they stood.

But Mrs. Frisby preferred not to think about that. Instead, as she came out of the woods from Mr. Ages' house and reached the farmyard fence she thought about Timothy. She thought of how his eyes shone with merriment when he made up small jokes, which he did frequently, and how invariably kind he was to his small, scatterbrained sister Cynthia. The other children sometimes laughed at her when she made mistakes, or grew impatient with her because she was forever losing things; but Timothy never did. Instead, he would help her find them. And when Cynthia herself had been sick in bed with a cold, he had sat by her side for hours and entertained her with stories. He made these up out of his head, and he seemed to have a bottomless supply of them.

Taking a firm grip on her packets of medicine, Mrs. Frisby went under the fence and set out toward the farmyard. The first stretch was a long pasture; the barn itself, square and red and big, rose in the distance to her right; to her left, farther off, were the chicken houses.

When at length she came abreast of the barn, she saw the cattle wire fence that marked the other end of the pasture; and as she approached it, she was startled by a sudden outburst of noise. She thought at first it was a hen, strayed from the chicken yard—caught by a fox? She looked down the fence and saw that it was no hen at all, but a young crow, flapping in the grass, acting most odd. As she watched, he fluttered to the top wire of the fence, where he perched nervously for a moment. Then he spread his wings, flapped hard, and took off—but after flying four feet he stopped with a snap and crashed to the ground again, shedding a flurry of black feathers and squawking loudly.

He was tied to the fence. A piece of something silvery—it looked like wire—was tangled around one of his legs; the other end of it was caught in the fence. Mrs. Frisby walked closer, and then she could see it was not wire after all, but a length of silver-colored string, probably left over from a Christmas package.

The crow was sitting on the fence, pecking ineffectively at the string with his bill, cawing softly to himself, a miserable sound. After a moment he spread his wings, and she could see he was going to try to fly again.

"Wait," said Mrs. Frisby.

The crow looked down and saw her in the grass.

"Why should I wait? Can't you see I'm caught? I've got to get loose."

"But if you make so much noise again the cat is sure to hear. If he hasn't heard already."

"You'd make noise, too, if you were tied to a fence with a piece of string, and with night coming on."

"I would not," said Mrs. Frisby, "if I had any sense and knew there was a cat nearby. Who tied you?" She was trying to calm the crow, who was obviously terrified.

He looked embarrassed and stared at his feet. "I picked up the string. It got tangled with my foot. I sat on the fence to try to get it off, and it caught on the fence."

"*Why* did you pick up the string?"

The crow, who was very young indeed—in fact, only a year old—said wearily, "Because it was shiny."

"You knew better."

"I had been told."

Birdbrain, thought Mrs. Frisby, and then recalled what her husband used to say: The size of the brain is no measure of its capacity. And well she might recall it, for the crow's head was double the size of her own.

"Sit quietly," she said. "Look toward the house and see if you see the cat."

"I don't see him. But I can't see behind the bushes. Oh, if I could just fly higher . . . "

"Don't," said Mrs. Frisby. She looked at the sun; it was setting behind the trees. She thought of Timothy, and of the medicine she was carrying. Yet she knew she could not leave the foolish crow there to be killed—and killed he surely would be before sunrise—just for want of a few minutes' work. She might still make it by dusk if she hurried.

"Come down here," she said. "I'll get the string off."

"How?" said the crow dubiously.

"Don't argue. I have only a few minutes." She said this in a voice so authoritative that the crow fluttered down immediately.

"But if the cat comes . . ." he said.

"If the cat comes, he'll knock you off the fence with one jump and catch you with the next. Be still." She was already at work with her sharp teeth, gnawing at the string. It was twined and twisted and twined again around his right ankle, and she saw she would have to cut through it three times to get it off.

As she finished the second strand, the crow, who was staring toward the house, suddenly cried out:

"I see the cat!"

"*Quiet!*" whispered Mrs. Frisby. "Does he see us?"

"I don't know. Yes. He's looking at me. I don't think he can see you."

"Stand perfectly still. Don't get in a panic." She did not look up, but started on the third strand.

"He's moving this way."

"Fast or slow?"

"Medium. I think he's trying to figure out what I'm doing."

She cut through the last strand, gave a tug, and the string fell off.

"There, you're free. Fly off, and be quick."

"But what about you?"

"Maybe he hasn't seen me."

"But he will. He's coming closer."

Mrs. Frisby looked around. There was not a bit of cover anywhere near, not a rock nor a hole nor a log; nothing at all closer than the chicken yard—and that was in the direction the cat was coming from, and a long way off.

"Look," said the crow. "Climb on my back. Quick. And hang on."

Mrs. Frisby did what she was told, first grasping the precious packages of medicine tightly between her teeth.

"Are you on?"

"Yes."

She gripped the feathers on his back, felt the beat of his powerful black wings, felt a dizzying upward surge, and shut her eyes tight.

"Just in time," said the crow, and she heard the angry scream of the cat as he leaped at where they had just been. "It's lucky you're so light. I can scarcely tell you're there." Lucky indeed, thought

Mrs. Frisby; if it had not been for your foolishness, I'd never have gotten into such a scrape. However, she thought it wise not to say so, under the circumstances.

"Where do you live?" asked the crow.

"In the garden patch. Near the big stone."

"I'll drop you off there." He banked alarmingly, and for a moment Mrs. Frisby thought he meant it literally. But a few seconds later—so fast does the crow fly—they were gliding to earth a yard from her front door.

"Thank you very much," said Mrs. Frisby, hopping to the ground.

"It's I who should be thanking you," said the crow. "You saved my life."

"And you mine."

"Ah, but that's not quite even. Yours wouldn't have been risked if it had not been for me—me and my piece of string." And since this was just what she had been thinking, Mrs. Frisby did not argue.

"We all help one another against the cat," she said.

"True. Just the same, I am in debt to you. If the time ever comes when I can help you, I hope you will ask me. My name is Jeremy. Mention it to any crow you see in these woods, and he will find me."

"Thank you," said Mrs. Frisby. "I will remember."

Jeremy flew away to the woods, and she entered her house, taking the three doses of medicine with her.

Mrs. Frisby and the Crow

Concept Connections

Linking the Selection

Think about the following questions, and then record your responses in the Response Journal section of your Writer's Notebook.

- What risks did Mrs. Frisby have to choose between on her way home?
- Why did Mrs. Frisby risk her life to remove the string from the crow's leg?
- What risk did the crow take for Mrs. Frisby?

Exploring Concept Vocabulary

The concept word for this lesson is ***conscience.*** If you don't know what this word means, look it up in a dictionary. Answer these questions.

- How does a person's ***conscience*** affect his or her willingness to take a risk?
- How might this story be different if Mrs. Frisby didn't have a ***conscience?***

In the Vocabulary section of your Writer's Notebook, write a sentence that includes the word ***conscience*** as well as one of the selection vocabulary words.

Expanding the Concept

Think about the story "Mrs. Frisby and the Crow." What have you learned about risks from this story? What have you learned about consequences? Try to use the word ***conscience*** in your discussion of the story. Add new ideas about risks and consequences to the Concept/Question Board.

Meet the Author

Robert C. O'Brien could sing before he could talk. His favorite "toy" was the family's wind-up Victrola (music player), and he spent hours listening to music. He learned to play piano when he was very young, and he stayed with it all his life.

His other favorite thing to do was create splendid imaginary worlds, with himself in dazzling, heroic roles. In his forties he decided to share those worlds with others so he started writing books.

"When I get a story idea," he said, *"I write it down before I forget it. It isn't always for children, but those are the stories I most like to write."*

Meet the Illustrator

Barbara Lanza says that fantasy books are her favorite genre. *"I love doing fantasy. I've always loved little secret worlds, whether they are in the backyard or in outer space."*

Her parents and her high school art teacher encouraged Ms. Lanza to pursue a career in art. She says of her work, *"You really need to understand yourself and be very committed to bringing your feelings into your work. When you are an illustrator, you're illuminating something for someone else. By having a clear focus yourself, you can better describe things for others."*

Focus Questions When is a risk worth taking?
How can concern for others help us to overcome our own fears?

Toto

Marietta D. Moskin
illustrated by Rocco Negri

Deep in Africa, on the outer slopes of a gently rolling ring of hills, lived a timid young boy named Suku. His round thatched hut stood in a busy village where his tribe had always lived. Just a short distance away, on the other side of the blue and purple hills, was a quiet valley set aside for animals to live without fear of being hunted by men. Suku had often climbed to the top of the tallest hill and had watched the herds of animals moving through the grasslands far below. But that was as far as he ever went. His own world was outside the protected game reserve—with his family, in the safe, familiar village.

On a saucer-shaped plain sheltered by the ring of blue and purple hills lived a curious little elephant. His name was Toto—the little one—because he was the youngest and smallest elephant in the herd. With his large family he roamed across the silvery plains of his valley, feeding on the juicy grasses and bathing in the broad green river that twisted through the land. It was a good life for elephants and for the many other animals with whom they shared their peaceful valley.

Day by day the little elephant in the valley and the boy in the village grew stronger and bigger and learned the things they had to know.

Toto learned which berries and roots were good to eat and which ones would make him sick. He learned to recognize danger by smells in the air and sounds in the distance. He stood patiently while his mother doused him with water from her trunk, and he paid attention when she showed him how to powder himself with red dust to keep the insects away.

When his mother warned him never to stray outside their peaceful valley because there were dangers beyond the hills, Toto listened. Most of the time he was happy to play with his cousins among the thorn trees and with his friends, the antelope and the baby baboons. But sometimes Toto looked toward the blue and purple hills in the distance and wondered what lay behind their rounded crests.

Suku too learned a great many things a boy growing up in an African village had to learn. He carried water for his mother from the river and he collected dung to burn in the fire on which she cooked their midday meal. In the evening he helped his father and the other men to pen the tribe's cattle and goats within the village compound. But in the morning, when the boys and young men of the village went out to herd their cattle on the rich grazing lands in the valley, Suku did not go with them. He watched when the herd boys walked jauntily out of the village, brandishing their wooden staffs and shouting to their charges. At seven he was old enough to go, but Suku was frightened when he thought of the herd boys walking through the bush with nothing but a stick or crude iron spear to protect them from lions.

"Our ancestors were famous lion hunters," his mother scolded. "The men of our tribe have always walked fearlessly through the bush."

"Give Suku time," his father counseled. "Courage sometimes comes with need."

So Suku went on doing women's chores around the village and avoiding the boys who teased him.

And inside the ring of gently rolling purple hills, Toto, the little elephant, roamed with the herd across the grasslands. But whenever he saw the young weaverbirds flying from their hanging straw nests, he watched enviously as they sailed off into the sky far, far beyond the circle of hills.

One night Toto followed the elephant herd to the edge of their valley where the river flowed onto the plain through a gap in the hills. There, in a clearing between the trees, the young males of the herd fought mock battles with each other in the moonlight.

Sheltered by his mother's bulk, Toto watched for a while. Then, looking up at the velvety sky, he saw that the moon had traveled across the valley and was about to dip down below the highest hill.

I wonder where she goes, Toto thought. Perhaps I'll just follow the river a little ways and see. Not very far—just to where the river curves.

Slowly Toto moved away from the group of elephants. Nobody noticed. Not even his mother. But once he was in the shadows of trees, the moon was no longer there to guide him.

“Elephants have no enemies—Mother said so,” he told himself bravely. Only the lion might stalk an unprotected elephant child—but the lions had had their kill earlier that night. Toto had seen them at their meal.

Toto walked on through the darkness. Sometimes he could see the moon reflected on the river, and he hurried to catch up with it. But he didn’t look back, and so he didn’t realize that the hills lay behind him now. He didn’t notice either that he could no longer hear the loud trumpeting of the other elephants at play. He didn’t know that he was already in that mysterious world beyond the hills he had longed to discover.

Suddenly Toto felt a sharp pain in his right front leg. Something hard and sharp had fastened around his foot. Toto pulled and pulled, but he couldn't free his foot. Each time he pulled, the pain got sharper.

Nothing his mother had told him about danger had prepared Toto for this. In fear and pain he trumpeted loudly. But he had walked too far to be heard. There was no answering call from his mother or from any of the other elephants. For the first time in his life, Toto was alone.

In the round thatched hut in the village, Suku slept on a woven mat next to his parents. Suku was a sound sleeper, but something—some noise—awoke him before dawn. It sounded like an elephant trumpeting, Suku thought sleepily. But elephants rarely strayed this far out of the game reserve in the valley. He must have been dreaming, Suku told himself. He couldn't have heard an elephant this close.

But Suku could not go back to sleep. When the first sunshine crept through the chinks under the door, he got up and slipped into his clothes. He had promised his mother he would cut some papyrus reeds at the river today so that she could mend their torn sleeping mats. Now that he was awake he would do it before the day grew hot.

Quietly, so as not to waken the rest of his family, Suku tiptoed out of the hut. Outside, no one stirred. Even the cattle were still asleep.

Clutching his sharp reed knife, Suku followed the winding path down the hill to the riverbank, searching for a good stand of feathery papyrus.

Suddenly the silence at the river was broken by a loud rustling sound. The sound came again—not just a rustling this time, but a snapping of twigs and a swishing of the tall grasses. Carefully, and a little fearfully, Suku moved around the next curve in the path. And then he stopped again.

Before him, in the trampled grass, lay a very young elephant. Around one of the elephant's legs the cruelly stiffened rope of a poacher's trap had been pulled so tight that the snare had bitten deeply into the flesh. The elephant had put up a fierce struggle, but now he was exhausted. He lay quietly on his side, squealing softly from time to time.

Anger exploded inside Suku—anger at the cruel poachers who had set their cunning trap so close to the game reserve. He approached the trapped elephant carefully. His father had taught him to be aware of wounded animals who could be far more dangerous in fear and pain. But the little elephant seemed to sense that Suku wanted to help him, and he held very still. Grasping his knife, Suku slashed at the thick, twisted rope. It took time to free the elephant's leg, but finally the last strand of the rope gave way. The boy jumped out of the way quickly, and the small elephant slowly got to his feet. Then he just stood there on the path, staring at Suku.

"Shoo, shoo, little elephant—quickly, run back into the valley," Suku urged. The poachers who had set the trap could be back at any time. But Toto, who had spent the night by himself, would not leave that strange two-legged creature with the oddly dangerous smell but the warm, comforting sounds. When Suku turned to walk back to the village, Toto started after him.

"Please, little one, please, hurry home," Suku pleaded.

But the little elephant didn't budge.

"What are we going to do?" Suku asked in despair. "Will I have to lead you back to your family, you foolish little one?"

Suku didn't want to go into the bush. But he looked at the elephant baby and knew that there was no choice.

Suku began to walk, and the small elephant followed. He walked slowly and painfully, limping on the leg that had been cut so badly by the poacher's snare.

It was easy for Suku to find the way Toto had left the reserve. Trampled grass and elephant droppings formed a perfect track. After a while the boy and the elephant came to the clearing where the herd had watched the fight between the young bulls the night before. The clearing was empty, but a trail of droppings showed that the herd had moved on across the open bush.

Suku was so busy following the trail that he hadn't thought much about what he was doing. Suddenly he realized he was walking all by himself across the open grasslands. Just like the herd boys. And he didn't even have an iron spear for protection—nothing but a small reed cutting knife!

He walked on, trying not to think about the dangers. By now the sun was high in the sky, and at home they were surely wondering what had happened to him.

They walked and walked. Suku, who hadn't had any breakfast that morning, began to feel hungry and thirsty. Toto hadn't had breakfast either, but there was no time to stop and eat.

Suddenly Toto stopped. He raised his head and listened, trembling a little. Young as he was, Toto recognized the smells and sounds of danger.

Suku looked around to see what had frightened Toto. And then he saw the danger too. A few paces away, half-hidden in the silvery-tan grass, stood an enormous brown-maned lion.

The lion looked from the elephant to the boy, almost as if he were measuring which one would make the

easier victim. He looked haughty and strong and very big. Suku's fist tightened around the handle of his knife. He wasn't sure at all whether the knife would do him any good, but he was prepared to defend himself if the lion attacked. Behind him he could sense the little elephant stiffen. Even though the lion looked awfully big to him too, Toto had raised his trunk and spread his ears the way the big elephants did when they were ready to attack.

"Oh, please, make him go away, make him go away," Suku prayed silently. His hand around the knife handle felt clammy and stiff. It seemed to him that he and the elephant and the lion had stood there facing one another, forever.

It was Toto who broke the silence. He took a step toward the lion, and he trumpeted a warning.

The next moment—almost like an echo—another elephant call sounded across the bush. Then another and another. Turning his head, Suku saw a large herd of elephants advancing from behind a nearby stand of thorn trees. Toto's family had come to rescue their littlest one!

Then Suku heard another, more familiar sound. It was the rattling and roaring sound of a car traveling fast across rough ground. A second later the game warden's battered white Landrover appeared over the next small hill. Suku recognized the warden at the wheel, and next to the warden Suku saw his father standing up in the car with a gun in his hand.

"Stand still, Suku—just don't move," his father shouted. He aimed his gun at the lion, waiting to see what the lion would do.

The lion looked at his two young victims. Then he looked at the menacing group of elephants on his right and at the men in the car to his left. Mustering what dignity he could, he stalked slowly and deliberately away. Within moments he had disappeared into the tall dry grass.

Another loud, single call sounded from the elephant herd. Toto was being summoned. His mother was coming to take him back to the herd.

Slowly Toto raised his trunk to the boy who had brought him home. Then, still limping badly, he turned and followed his mother.

The warden had waited for the elephants to withdraw. Now he drove the Landrover over to where Suku stood.

"Get in, Suku—let's go," the warden said.

"You came just in time," Suku said.

"We found the cut snare and the elephant tracks—and someone in the village

had seen you going down to the river early this morning," his father explained.

"The poachers would have killed him for his hide," Suku said.

"You did right, Suku," the warden said. "I get so angry too when I catch these poachers. You would make a good game ranger some day, Suku. You love animals, and you are brave."

The warden's words made Suku feel good. He knew that he hadn't felt brave, but he had walked in the footsteps of his ancestors: he had gone into the bush, and he had faced a lion!

Now he would never feel shy of the village boys again. He knew he had earned his place in the tribe.

Under the leafy canopy of the forest, Toto nuzzled up close to his mother's flank. He had eaten his fill of crisp greens at the riverbank, and his mother had bathed his cut foot and smeared it with healing red mud. Now the herd was resting quietly in the shade near the river.

It was good to be back home, Toto thought contentedly. Let the moon and the sun and the birds travel beyond the hills if they wished. His place was here.

Concept Connections

Linking the Selection

Writer's Notebook

Think about the following questions, and then record your responses in the Response Journal section of your Writer's Notebook.

- What consequences did Toto face after straying outside the circle of hills?
- What risk did Toto take to save himself and Suku from the lion?
- How did Suku feel about himself after taking a risk and helping Toto?

Exploring Concept Vocabulary

The concept word for this lesson is ***dilemma.*** If you don't know what this word means, look it up in a dictionary. Answer these questions.

- How is a ***dilemma*** related to risks and consequences?
- What were some of the ***dilemmas*** faced by characters in this story?

In the Vocabulary section of your Writer's Notebook, write a sentence that includes the word ***dilemma*** as well as one of the selection vocabulary words.

Expanding the Concept

Think about the main characters in "Mrs. Frisby and the Crow" and "Toto." Compare the risks taken and consequences faced by the characters in the two stories. Try to use the word ***dilemma*** in your discussion as you compare characters from the stories. Add new ideas about risks and consequences to the Concept/Question Board.

Meet the Author

Marietta D. Moskin said, *"I can't remember a time when I didn't want to write poems or stories."* As soon as she could write, Ms. Moskin began to create fantasy worlds. During World War II, Ms. Moskin and her family spent several years in concentration camps. Even then, she hoarded scraps of paper so she could write her stories and poems.

"In my books," she once said, *"I have tried to draw as often as possible on my own experiences and remembered feelings."* "Toto" grew out of a family trip to East Africa (Kenya, Tanzania, and Uganda).

Meet the Illustrator

Rocco Negri for a time thought he wanted to become a writer. He once said, *"As far as I can remember, I was always very quiet. I communicated more in writing."* But then he got interested in art and decided it was something he would enjoy enormously. Art allowed him to live in two worlds at the same time—the real world and the world of make-believe.

"One of my greatest satisfactions in life is illustrating children's books, because children are so pure in appreciation and perception. They have no inhibition or discrimination to cloud their minds or hearts."

Focus Questions Can it be risky to make new friends?
What would make you risk leaving a place you love?

Sarah, Plain and Tall

from ***Sarah, Plain and Tall*** by Patricia MacLachlan
illustrated by Meg Kelleher Aubrey

"Did Mama sing every day?" asked Caleb. "Every-single-day?" He sat close to the fire, his chin in his hand. It was dusk, and the dogs lay beside him on the warm hearthstones.

"Every-single-day," I told him for the second time this week. For the twentieth time this month. The hundredth time this year? And the past few years?

"And did Papa sing, too?"

"Yes. Papa sang, too. Don't get so close, Caleb. You'll heat up."

He pushed his chair back. It made a hollow scraping sound on the hearthstones, and the dogs stirred. Lottie, small and black, wagged her tail and lifted her head. Nick slept on.

I turned the bread dough over and over on the marble slab on the kitchen table.

"Well, Papa doesn't sing anymore," said Caleb very softly. A log broke apart and crackled in the fireplace. He looked up at me. "What did I look like when I was born?"

"You didn't have any clothes on," I told him.

"I know that," he said.

"You looked like this." I held the bread dough up in a round pale ball.

"I had hair," said Caleb seriously.

"Not enough to talk about," I said.

"And she named me Caleb," he went on, filling in the old familiar story.

"*I* would have named you Troublesome," I said, making Caleb smile.

"And Mama handed me to you in the yellow blanket and said . . ." He waited for me to finish the story. "And said . . . ?"

I sighed. "And Mama said, 'Isn't he beautiful, Anna?'"

"And I was," Caleb finished.

Caleb thought the story was over, and I didn't tell him what I had really thought. He was homely and plain, and he had a terrible holler and a horrid smell. But these were not the worst of him. Mama died the next morning. That was the worst thing about Caleb.

"Isn't he beautiful, Anna?" Her last words to me. I had gone to bed thinking how wretched he looked. And I forgot to say good night.

I wiped my hands on my apron and went to the window. Outside, the prairie reached out and touched the places where the sky came down. Though winter was nearly over, there were patches of snow and ice everywhere. I looked at the long dirt road that crawled across the plains, remembering the morning that Mama had died, cruel and sunny. They had come for her in a wagon and taken her away to be buried. And then the cousins and aunts and uncles had come and tried to fill up the house. But they couldn't.

Slowly, one by one, they left. And then the days seemed long and dark like winter days, even though it wasn't winter. And Papa didn't sing.

Isn't he beautiful, Anna?

No, Mama.

It was hard to think of Caleb as beautiful. It took three whole days for me to love him, sitting in the chair by the fire, Papa washing up the supper dishes, Caleb's tiny hand brushing my cheek. And a smile. It was the smile, I know.

"Can you remember her songs?" asked Caleb. "Mama's songs?"

I turned from the window. "No. Only that she sang about flowers and birds. Sometimes about the moon at nighttime."

Caleb reached down and touched Lottie's head.

"Maybe," he said, his voice low, "if you remember the songs, then I might remember her, too."

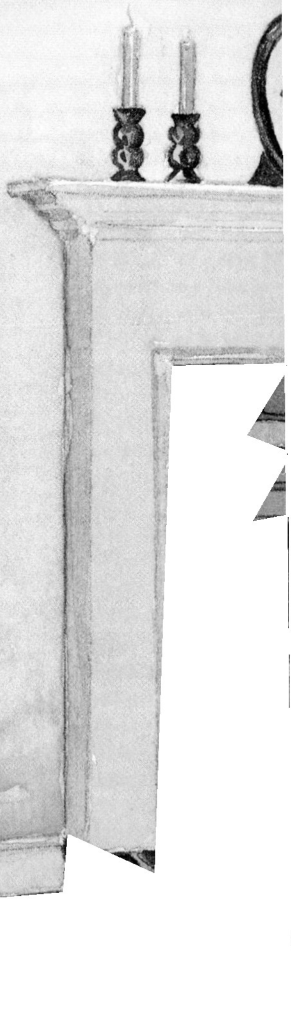

My eyes widened and tears came. Then the door opened and wind blew in with Papa, and I went to stir the stew. Papa put his arms around me and put his nose in my hair.

"Nice soapy smell, that stew," he said.

I laughed. "That's my hair."

Caleb came over and threw his arms around Papa's neck and hung down as Papa swung him back and forth, and the dogs sat up.

"Cold in town," said Papa. "And Jack was feisty." Jack was Papa's horse that he'd raised from a colt. "Rascal," murmured Papa, smiling, because no matter what Jack did Papa loved him.

I spooned up the stew and lighted the oil lamp and we ate with the dogs crowding under the table, hoping for spills or handouts.

Papa might not have told us about Sarah that night if Caleb hadn't asked him the question. After the dishes were cleared and washed and Papa was filling the tin pail with ashes, Caleb spoke up. It wasn't a question, really.

"You don't sing anymore," he said. He said it harshly. Not because he meant to, but because he had been thinking of it for so long. "Why?" he asked more gently.

Slowly Papa straightened up. There was a long silence, and the dogs looked up, wondering at it.

"I've forgotten the old songs," said Papa quietly. He sat down. "But maybe there's a way to remember them." He looked up at us.

"How?" asked Caleb eagerly.

Papa leaned back in the chair. "I've placed an advertisement in the newspapers. For help."

"You mean a housekeeper?" I asked, surprised.

Caleb and I looked at each other and burst out laughing, remembering Hilly, our old housekeeper. She was round and slow and shuffling. She snored in a high whistle at night, like a teakettle, and let the fire go out.

"No," said Papa slowly. "Not a housekeeper." He paused. "A wife."

Caleb stared at Papa. "A wife? You mean a mother?"

Nick slid his face onto Papa's lap and Papa stroked his ears.

"That, too," said Papa. "Like Maggie."

Matthew, our neighbor to the south, had written to ask for a wife and mother for his children. And Maggie had come from Tennessee. Her hair was the color of turnips and she laughed.

Papa reached into his pocket and unfolded a letter written on white paper. "And I have received an answer." Papa read to us:

"Dear Mr. Jacob Witting,

"I am Sarah Wheaton from Maine as you will see from my letter. I am answering your advertisement. I have never been married, though I have been asked. I have lived with an older brother, William, who is about to be married. His wife-to-be is young and energetic.

"I have always loved to live by the sea, but at this time I feel a move is necessary. And the truth is, the sea is as far east as I can go. My choice, as you can see, is limited. This should not be taken as an insult. I am strong and I work hard and I am willing to travel. But I am not mild mannered. If you should still care to write, I would be interested in your children and about where you live. And you.

"Very truly yours,
"Sarah Elisabeth Wheaton
"P.S. Do you have opinions on cats? I have one."

No one spoke when Papa finished the letter. He kept looking at it in his hands, reading it over to himself. Finally I turned my head a bit to sneak a look at Caleb. He was smiling. I smiled, too.

"One thing," I said in the quiet of the room.

"What's that?" asked Papa, looking up.

I put my arm around Caleb.

"Ask her if she sings," I said.

Caleb and Papa and I wrote letters to Sarah, and before the ice and snow had melted from the fields, we all received answers. Mine came first.

Dear Anna,

Yes, I can braid hair and I can make stew and bake bread, though I prefer to build bookshelves and paint.

My favorite colors are the colors of the sea, blue and gray and green, depending on the weather. My brother William is a fisherman, and he tells me that when he is in the middle of a fogbound sea the water is a color for which there is no name. He catches flounder and sea bass and bluefish. Sometimes he sees whales. And birds, too, of course. I am enclosing a book of sea birds so you will see what William and I see every day.

Very truly yours,
Sarah Elisabeth Wheaton

Caleb read and read the letter so many times that the ink began to run and the folds tore. He read the book about sea birds over and over.

"Do you think she'll come?" asked Caleb. "And will she stay? What if she thinks we are loud and pesky?"

"You *are* loud and pesky," I told him. But I was worried, too. Sarah loved the sea, I could tell. Maybe she wouldn't leave there after all to come where there were fields and grass and sky and not much else.

"What if she comes and doesn't like our house?" Caleb asked. "I told her it was small. Maybe I shouldn't have told her it was small."

"Hush, Caleb. Hush."

Caleb's letter came soon after, with a picture of a cat drawn on the envelope.

Dear Caleb,

My cat's name is Seal because she is gray like the seals that swim offshore in Maine. She is glad that Lottie and Nick send their greetings. She likes dogs most of the time. She says their footprints are much larger than hers (which she is enclosing in return).

Your house sounds lovely, even though it is far out in the country with no close neighbors. My house is tall and the shingles are gray because of the salt from the sea. There are roses nearby.

Yes, I do like small rooms sometimes. Yes, I can keep a fire going at night. I do not know if I snore. Seal has never told me.

Very truly yours,
Sarah Elisabeth

"Did you really ask her about fires and snoring?" I asked, amazed.

"I wished to know," Caleb said.

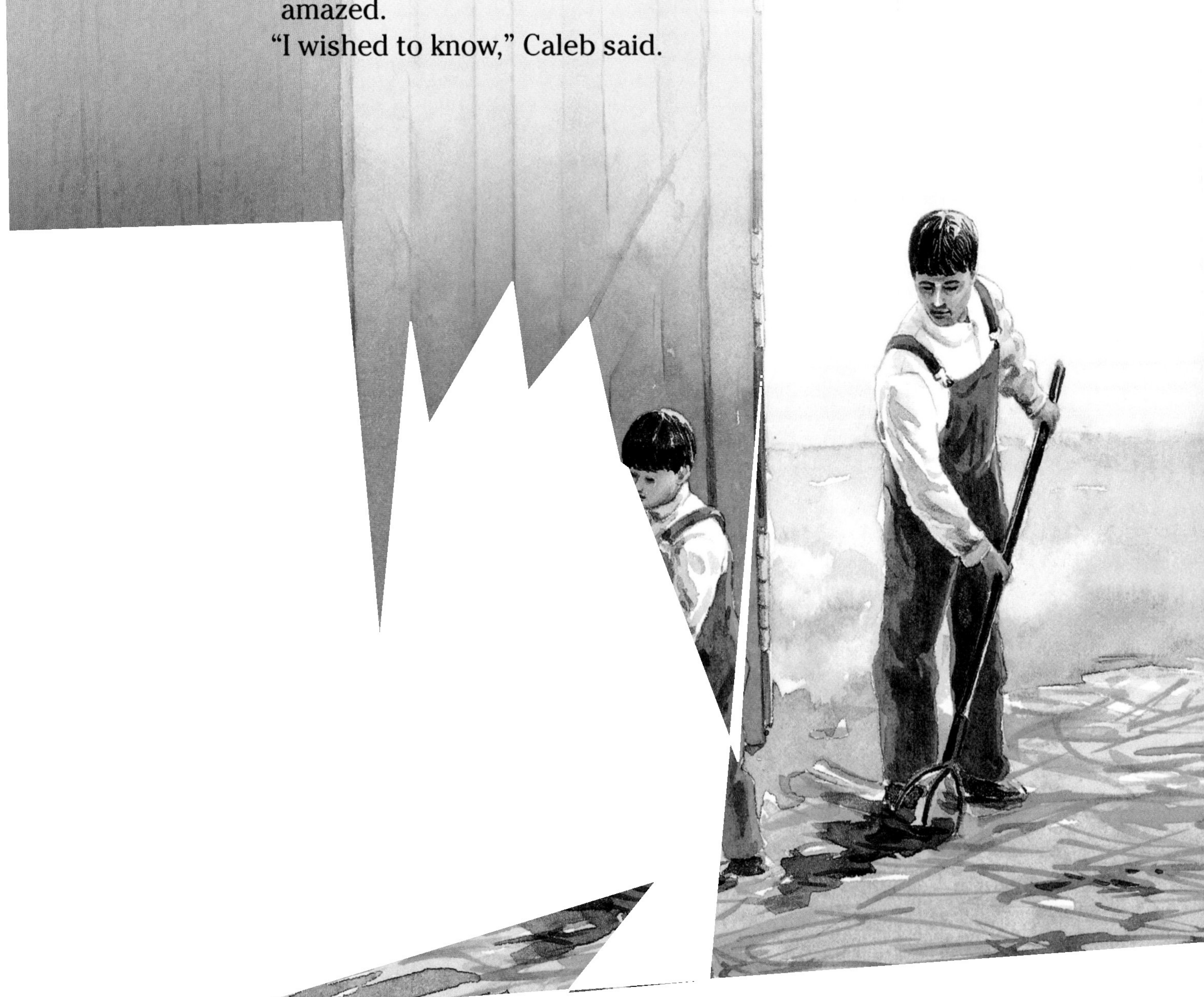

He kept the letter with him, reading it in the barn and in the fields and by the cow pond. And always in bed at night.

One morning, early, Papa and Caleb and I were cleaning out the horse stalls and putting down new bedding. Papa stopped suddenly and leaned on his pitchfork.

"Sarah has said she will come for a month's time if we wish her to," he said, his voice loud in the dark barn. "To see how it is. Just to see."

Caleb stood by the stall door and folded his arms across his chest.

"I think," he began. Then, "I think," he said slowly, "that it would be good—to say yes," he finished in a rush.

Papa looked at me.

"I say yes," I told him, grinning.

"Yes," said Papa. "Then yes it is."

And the three of us, all smiling, went to work again.

The next day Papa went to town to mail his letter to Sarah. It was rainy for days, and the clouds followed. The house was cool and damp and quiet. Once I set four places at the table, then caught myself and put the extra plate away. Three lambs were born, one with a black face. And then Papa's letter came. It was very short.

Dear Jacob,

I will come by train. I will wear a yellow bonnet. I am plain and tall.

Sarah

"What's that?" asked Caleb excitedly, peering over Papa's shoulder. He pointed. "There, written at the bottom of the letter."

Papa read it to himself. Then he smiled, holding up the letter for us to see.

Tell them I sing was all it said.

Sarah came in the spring. She came through green grass fields that bloomed with Indian paintbrush, red and orange, and blue-eyed grass.

Papa got up early for the long day's trip to the train and back. He brushed his hair so slick and shiny that Caleb laughed. He wore a clean blue shirt, and a belt instead of suspenders.

He fed and watered the horses, talking to them as he hitched them up to the wagon. Old Bess, calm and kind; Jack, wild-eyed, reaching over to nip Bess on the neck.

"Clear day, Bess," said Papa, rubbing her nose.

"Settle down, Jack." He leaned his head on Jack.

And then Papa drove off along the dirt road to fetch Sarah. Papa's new wife. Maybe. Maybe our new mother.

Gophers ran back and forth across the road, stopping to stand up and watch the wagon. Far off in the field a woodchuck ate and listened. Ate and listened.

Caleb and I did our chores without talking. We shoveled out the stalls and laid down new hay. We fed the sheep. We swept and straightened and carried wood and water. And then our chores were done.

Caleb pulled on my shirt.

"Is my face clean?" he asked. "Can my face be *too* clean?" He looked alarmed.

"No, your face is clean but not too clean," I said.

Caleb slipped his hand into mine as we stood on the porch, watching the road. He was afraid.

"Will she be nice?" he asked. "Like Maggie?"

"Sarah will be nice," I told him.

"How far away is Maine?" he asked.

"You know how far. Far away, by the sea."

"Will Sarah bring some sea?" he asked.

"No, you cannot bring the sea."

The sheep ran in the field, and far off the cows moved slowly to the pond, like turtles.

"Will she like us?" asked Caleb very softly.

I watched a marsh hawk wheel down behind the barn.

He looked up at me.

"Of course she will like us." He answered his own question. "We are nice," he added, making me smile.

We waited and watched. I rocked on the porch and Caleb rolled a marble on the wood floor. Back and forth. Back and forth. The marble was blue.

We saw the dust from the wagon first, rising above the road, above the heads of Jack and Old Bess. Caleb climbed up onto the porch roof and shaded his eyes.

"A bonnet!" he cried. "I see a yellow bonnet!"

The dogs came out from under the porch, ears up, their eyes on the cloud of dust bringing Sarah. The wagon passed the fenced field, and the cows and sheep looked up, too. It rounded the windmill and the barn and the windbreak of Russian olive that Mama had planted long ago. Nick began to bark, then Lottie, and the wagon clattered into the yard and stopped by the steps.

"Hush," said Papa to the dogs.

And it was quiet.

Sarah stepped down from the wagon, a cloth bag in her hand. She reached up and took off her yellow bonnet, smoothing back her brown hair into a bun. She was plain and tall.

"Did you bring some sea?" cried Caleb beside me.

"Something from the sea," said Sarah, smiling. "And me." She turned and lifted a black case from the wagon. "And Seal, too."

Carefully she opened the case, and Seal, gray with white feet, stepped out. Lottie lay down, her head on her paws, staring. Nick leaned down to sniff. Then he lay down, too.

"The cat will be good in the barn," said Papa. "For mice."

Sarah smiled. "She will be good in the house, too."

Sarah took Caleb's hand, then mine. Her hands were large and rough. She gave Caleb a shell—a moon snail, she called it—that was curled and smelled of salt.

"The gulls fly high and drop the shells on the rocks below," she told Caleb. "When the shell is broken, they eat what is inside."

"That is very smart," said Caleb.

"For you, Anna," said Sarah, "a sea stone."

And she gave me the smoothest and whitest stone I had ever seen.

"The sea washes over and over and around the stone, rolling it until it is round and perfect."

"That is very smart, too," said Caleb. He looked up at Sarah. "We do not have the sea here."

Sarah turned and looked out over the plains.

"No," she said. "There is no sea here. But the land rolls a little like the sea."

My father did not see her look, but I did. And I knew that Caleb had seen it, too. Sarah was not smiling. Sarah was already lonely. In a month's time the preacher might come to marry Sarah and Papa. And a month was a long time. Time enough for her to change her mind and leave us.

Papa took Sarah's bags inside, where her room was ready with a quilt on the bed and blue flax dried in a vase on the night table.

Seal stretched and made a small cat sound. I watched her circle the dogs and sniff the air. Caleb came out and stood beside me.

"When will we sing?" he whispered.

I shook my head, turning the white stone over and over in my hand. I wished everything was as perfect as the stone. I wished that Papa and Caleb and I were perfect for Sarah. I wished we had a sea of our own.

Sarah, Plain and Tall

Concept Connections

Linking the Selection

Writer's Notebook

Think about the following questions, and then record your responses in the Response Journal section of your Writer's Notebook.

- What risk did Sarah take by going to stay with Caleb, Anna, and Papa?
- What are the Wittings risking by inviting Sarah to stay with them?

Exploring Concept Vocabulary

The concept word for this lesson is ***unknown.*** If you don't know what this word means, look it up in a dictionary. Answer these questions.

- What feelings do you associate with trying things that are ***unknown?***
- How did the characters use letter-writing to help them deal with the ***unknown?***

In the Vocabulary section of your Writer's Notebook, write a sentence that includes the word ***unknown*** as well as one of the selection vocabulary words.

Expanding the Concept

Think about the expectations that Sarah and the Wittings might have had for their time together. Consider what the characters might gain or lose. Was any character risking more than the others? Try to use the word ***unknown*** in your discussion of the characters. Add new ideas about risks and consequences to the Concept/Question Board.

Meet the Author

Patricia MacLachlan grew up in Cheyenne, Wyoming, with parents who loved books and stories. *"We read them, discussed them, reread them, and acted out the parts."*

Ms. MacLachlan spent time writing about foster and adopted families for a family agency. When she decided to start writing books, she studied other writers first. She read 30 to 40 children's books each week.

Most of her books are about families, and her concern for families and for children has shaped her career. *"I write books about brothers and sisters, about what makes up a family, what works and what is nurturing."* Many of the characters she writes about are based on people in her own family.

Meet the Illustrator

Meg Kelleher Aubrey creates her work from photos she has taken. She loves to use her friends and family as models because, she says, *"Using familiar faces make[s] the project more personal and fun."* She received her degree in illustration from the Rhode Island School of Design and has won several awards for her art.

Focus Questions Have your friends ever urged you to take a risk? How does it feel to take a risk and realize that you wish you had not?

Escape

from ***Charlotte's Web***
by E. B. White
illustrated by Garth Williams

The barn was very large. It was very old. It smelled of hay and it smelled of manure. It smelled of the perspiration of tired horses and the wonderful sweet breath of patient cows. It often had a sort of peaceful smell—as though nothing bad could happen ever again in the world. It smelled of grain and of harness dressing and of axle grease and of rubber boots and of new rope. And whenever the cat was given a fish-head to eat, the barn would smell of fish. But mostly it smelled of hay, for there was always hay in the great loft up overhead. And there was always hay being pitched down to the cows and the horses and the sheep.

The barn was pleasantly warm in winter when the animals spent most of their time indoors, and it was pleasantly cool in summer when the big doors stood wide open to the breeze. The barn had stalls on the main floor for the work horses, tie-ups on the main floor for the cows, a sheepfold down below for the sheep, a pigpen down below for Wilbur, and it was full of all sorts of things that you find in barns: ladders, grindstones, pitch forks, monkey wrenches, scythes, lawn mowers, snow shovels, ax handles, milk pails, water buckets, empty grain sacks, and rusty rat traps. It was the kind of barn that swallows like to build their nests in. It was the kind of barn that children like to play in. And the whole thing was owned by Fern's uncle, Mr. Homer L. Zuckerman.

Wilbur's new home was in the lower part of the barn, directly underneath the cows. Mr. Zuckerman knew that a manure pile is a good place to keep a young pig. Pigs need warmth, and it was warm and comfortable down there in the barn cellar on the south side.

Fern came almost every day to visit him. She found an old milking stool that had been discarded, and she placed the stool in the sheepfold next to Wilbur's pen. Here she sat quietly during the long afternoons, thinking and listening and watching Wilbur. The sheep soon got to know her and trust her. So did the geese, who lived with the sheep. All the animals trusted her, she was so quiet and friendly. Mr. Zuckerman did not allow her to take Wilbur out, and he did not allow her to get into the pigpen. But he told Fern that she could sit on the stool and watch Wilbur as long as she wanted to. It made her happy just to be near the pig, and it made Wilbur happy to know that she was sitting there, right outside his pen. But he never had any fun—no walks, no rides, no swims.

One afternoon in June, when Wilbur was almost two months old, he wandered out into his small yard outside the barn. Fern had not arrived for her usual visit. Wilbur stood in the sun feeling lonely and bored.

"There's never anything to do around here," he thought. He walked slowly to his food trough and sniffed to see if anything had been overlooked at lunch. He found a small strip of potato skin and ate it. His back itched, so he leaned against the fence and rubbed against the boards. When he tired of this, he walked indoors, climbed to the top of the manure pile, and sat down. He didn't feel like going to sleep, he didn't feel like digging, he was tired of standing still, tired of lying down. "I'm less than two months old and I'm tired of living," he said. He walked out to the yard again.

“When I’m out here,” he said, “there’s no place to go but in. When I’m indoors, there’s no place to go but out in the yard.”

“That’s where you’re wrong, my friend, my friend,” said a voice.

Wilbur looked through the fence and saw the goose standing there.

“You don’t have to stay in that dirty-little dirty-little dirty-little yard,” said the goose, who talked rather fast. “One of those boards is loose. Push on it, push-push-push on it, and come on out!”

“What?” said Wilbur. “Say it slower!”

“At-at-at, at the risk of repeating myself,” said the goose, “I suggest that you come on out. It’s wonderful out here.”

“Did you say a board was loose?”

“That I did, that I did,” said the goose.

Wilbur walked up to the fence and saw that the goose was right—one board was loose. He put his head down, shut his eyes, and pushed. The board gave way. In a minute he had squeezed through the fence and was standing in the long grass outside his yard. The goose chuckled.

"How does it feel to be free?" she asked.

"I like it," said Wilbur. "That is, I *guess* I like it." Actually, Wilbur felt queer to be outside his fence, with nothing between him and the big world.

"Where do you think I'd better go?"

"Anywhere you like, anywhere you like," said the goose. "Go down through the orchard, root up the sod! Go down through the garden, dig up the radishes! Root up everything! Eat grass! Look for corn! Look for oats! Run all over! Skip and dance, jump and prance! Go down through the orchard and stroll in the woods! The world is a wonderful place when you're young."

"I can see that," replied Wilbur. He gave a jump in the air, twirled, ran a few steps, stopped, looked all around, sniffed the smells of afternoon, and then set off walking down through the orchard. Pausing in the shade of an apple tree, he put his strong snout into the ground and began pushing, digging, and rooting. He felt very happy. He had plowed up quite a piece of ground before anyone noticed him. Mrs. Zuckerman was the first to see him. She saw him from the kitchen window, and she immediately shouted for the men.

“Ho-*mer*!” she cried. “Pig’s out! Lurvy! Pig’s out! Homer! Lurvy! Pig’s out. He’s down there under that apple tree.”

“Now the trouble starts,” thought Wilbur. “Now I’ll catch it.”

The goose heard the racket and she, too, started hollering. “Run-run-run downhill, make for the woods, the woods!” she shouted to Wilbur. “They’ll never-never-never catch you in the woods.”

The cocker spaniel heard the commotion and he ran out from the barn to join the chase. Mr. Zuckerman heard, and he came out of the machine shed where he was mending a tool. Lurvy, the hired man, heard the noise and came up from the asparagus patch where he was pulling weeds. Everybody walked toward Wilbur and Wilbur didn’t know what to do. The woods seemed a long way off, and anyway, he had never been down there in the woods and wasn’t sure he would like it.

“Get around behind him, Lurvy,” said Mr. Zuckerman, “and drive him toward the barn! And take it easy—don’t rush him! I’ll go and get a bucket of slops.”

The news of Wilbur’s escape spread rapidly among the animals on the place. Whenever any creature broke loose on Zuckerman’s farm, the event was of great interest to the others. The goose shouted to the nearest cow that Wilbur was free, and soon all the cows knew. Then one of the cows told one of the sheep, and soon all the sheep knew.

The lambs learned about it from their mothers. The horses, in their stalls in the barn, pricked up their ears when they heard the goose hollering; and soon the horses had caught on to what was happening. "Wilbur's out," they said. Every animal stirred and lifted its head and became excited to know that one of his friends had got free and was no longer penned up or tied fast.

Wilbur didn't know what to do or which way to run. It seemed as though everybody was after him. "If this is what it's like to be free," he thought, "I believe I'd rather be penned up in my own yard."

The cocker spaniel was sneaking up on him from one side, Lurvy the hired man was sneaking up on him from the other side. Mrs. Zuckerman stood ready to head him off if he started for the garden, and now Mr. Zuckerman was coming down toward him carrying a pail. "This is really awful," thought Wilbur. "Why doesn't Fern come?" He began to cry.

The goose took command and began to give orders.

"Don't just stand there, Wilbur! Dodge about, dodge about!" cried the goose. "Skip around, run toward me, slip in and out, in and out, in and out! Make for the woods! Twist and turn!"

The cocker spaniel sprang for Wilbur's hind leg. Wilbur jumped and ran. Lurvy reached out and grabbed. Mrs. Zuckerman screamed at Lurvy. The goose cheered for Wilbur. Wilbur dodged between Lurvy's legs. Lurvy missed Wilbur and grabbed the spaniel instead. "Nicely done, nicely done!" cried the goose. "Try it again, try it again!"

"Run downhill!" suggested the cows.

"Run toward me!" yelled the gander.

"Run uphill!" cried the sheep.

"Turn and twist!" honked the goose.

"Jump and dance!" said the rooster.

"Look out for Lurvy!" called the cows.

"Look out for Zuckerman!" yelled the gander.

"Watch out for the dog!" cried the sheep.

"Listen to me, listen to me!" screamed the goose.

Poor Wilbur was dazed and frightened by this hullabaloo. He didn't like being the center of all this fuss. He tried to follow the instructions his friends were giving him, but he couldn't run downhill and uphill at the same time, and he couldn't turn and twist when he was jumping and dancing, and he was crying so hard he could barely see anything that was happening. After all, Wilbur was a very young pig—not much more than a baby, really. He wished Fern were there to take him in her arms and comfort him. When he looked up and saw Mr. Zuckerman standing quite close to him, holding a pail of warm slops, he felt relieved. He lifted his nose and sniffed. The smell was delicious—warm milk, potato skins, wheat middlings, Kellogg's Corn Flakes, and a popover left from the Zuckermans' breakfast.

"Come, pig!" said Mr. Zuckerman, tapping the pail. "Come pig!"

Wilbur took a step toward the pail.

"No-no-no!" said the goose. "It's the old pail trick, Wilbur. Don't fall for it, don't fall for it! He's trying to lure you back into captivity-ivity. He's appealing to your stomach."

Wilbur didn't care. The food smelled appetizing. He took another step toward the pail.

"Pig, pig!" said Mr. Zuckerman in a kind voice, and began walking slowly toward the barnyard, looking all about him innocently, as if he didn't know that a little white pig was following along behind him.

"You'll be sorry-sorry-sorry," called the goose.

Wilbur didn't care. He kept walking toward the pail of slops.

"You'll miss your freedom," honked the goose. "An hour of freedom is worth a barrel of slops."

Wilbur didn't care.

When Mr. Zuckerman reached the pigpen, he climbed over the fence and poured the slops into the trough. Then he pulled the loose board away from the fence, so that there was a wide hole for Wilbur to walk through.

"Reconsider, reconsider!" cried the goose.

Wilbur paid no attention. He stepped through the fence into his yard. He walked to the trough and took a long drink of slops, sucking in the milk hungrily and chewing the popover. It was good to be home again.

While Wilbur ate, Lurvy fetched a hammer and some 8-penny nails and nailed the board in place. Then he and Mr. Zuckerman leaned lazily on the fence and Mr. Zuckerman scratched Wilbur's back with a stick.

"He's quite a pig," said Lurvy.

"Yes, he'll make a good pig," said Mr. Zuckerman.

Wilbur heard the words of praise. He felt the warm milk inside his stomach. He felt the pleasant rubbing of the stick along his itchy back. He felt peaceful and happy and sleepy. This had been a tiring afternoon. It was still only about four o'clock but Wilbur was ready for bed.

"I'm really too young to go out into the world alone," he thought as he lay down.

Concept Connections

Linking the Selection

Think about the following questions, and then record your responses in the Response Journal section of your Writer's Notebook.

- Why did Wilbur decide to escape from his yard?
- Why was Wilbur at risk outside his pen?
- How did escaping lead to a positive consequence for Wilbur?

Exploring Concept Vocabulary

The concept term for this lesson is ***peer pressure.*** If you don't know what this term means, look it up in a dictionary. Answer these questions.

- How does ***peer pressure*** cause people to take risks they might not want to take?
- How was Wilbur affected by ***peer pressure*** from the other animals?

In the Vocabulary section of your Writer's Notebook, write a sentence that includes the term ***peer pressure*** as well as one of the selection vocabulary words.

Expanding the Concept

Think about the characters Sarah, from "Sarah, Plain and Tall," and Wilbur, from "Escape." What motivated these characters to leave their safe and familiar homes to have a new experience? Try to use the term ***peer pressure*** in your discussion of the characters. Add new ideas about risks and consequences to the Concept/Question Board.

Meet the Author

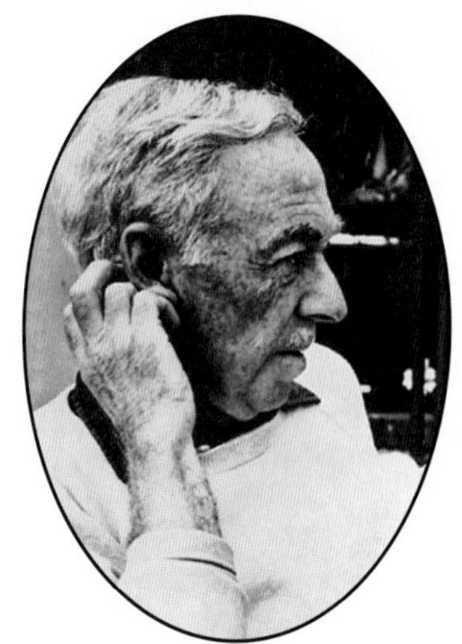

E. B. White E. B. White is best known for his classic children's books, *Stuart Little* and *Charlotte's Web*. He began to write his first book, *Stuart Little* after he had a vivid dream. Whenever one of his nieces or nephews wanted to be told a story, E. B. White would make up new adventures for his mouse-like hero whom he named Stuart Little. E. B. White began his writing career as a reporter, but his real passion was writing essays.

Meet the Illustrator

Garth Williams Garth Williams was born in New York City to parents who were both artists. "Everybody in my house was either painting or drawing," he said, "so I thought there was nothing else to do in life but make pictures." Later, Garth Williams wanted to become an architect, but he couldn't afford the cost of the college tuition. Instead, he won a painting scholarship to the Royal College of Art.

Williams tries to show humor, respect for others, and responsibility in his illustrations. He went on to illustrate many books, including *Stuart Little* and *Little House on the Prairie.*

Focus Questions Do you always think about the consequenses before you act? Are there risks too foolish to take?

Hippo's Hope

poem and drawings by Shel Silverstein

There once was a hippo who wanted to fly—
Fly-hi-dee, try-hi-dee, my-hi-dee-ho.
So he sewed him some wings that could flap through the sky—
Sky-hi-dee, fly-hi-dee, why-hi-dee-go.

He climbed to the top of a mountain of snow—
Snow-hi-dee, slow-hi-dee, oh-hi-dee-hoo.
With the clouds high above and the sea down below—
Where-hi-dee, there-hi-dee, scare-hi-dee-boo.

(Happy ending)
And he flipped and he flapped and he bellowed so loud–
Now-hi-dee, loud-hi-dee, proud-hi-dee-poop.
And he sailed like an eagle, off into the clouds–
High-hi-dee, fly-hi-dee, bye-hi-dee-boop.

(Unhappy ending)
And he leaped like a frog and he fell like a stone–
Stone-hi-dee, lone-hi-dee, own-hi-dee-flop.
And he crashed and he drowned and broke all his bones–
Bones-hi-dee, moans-hi-dee, groans-hi-dee-glop.

(Chicken ending)
He looked up at the sky and looked down at the sea–
Sea-hi-dee, free-hi-dee, whee-hi-dee-way.
And he turned and went home and had cookies and tea–
That's hi-dee, all hi-dee, I have to say.

Focus Questions What would the world be like if no one ever took a risk? Can you fulfill your dreams without taking some risks?

Mae Jemison

Space Scientist

by Gail Sakurai

THREE . . .

Two . . .

One . . .

Liftoff!

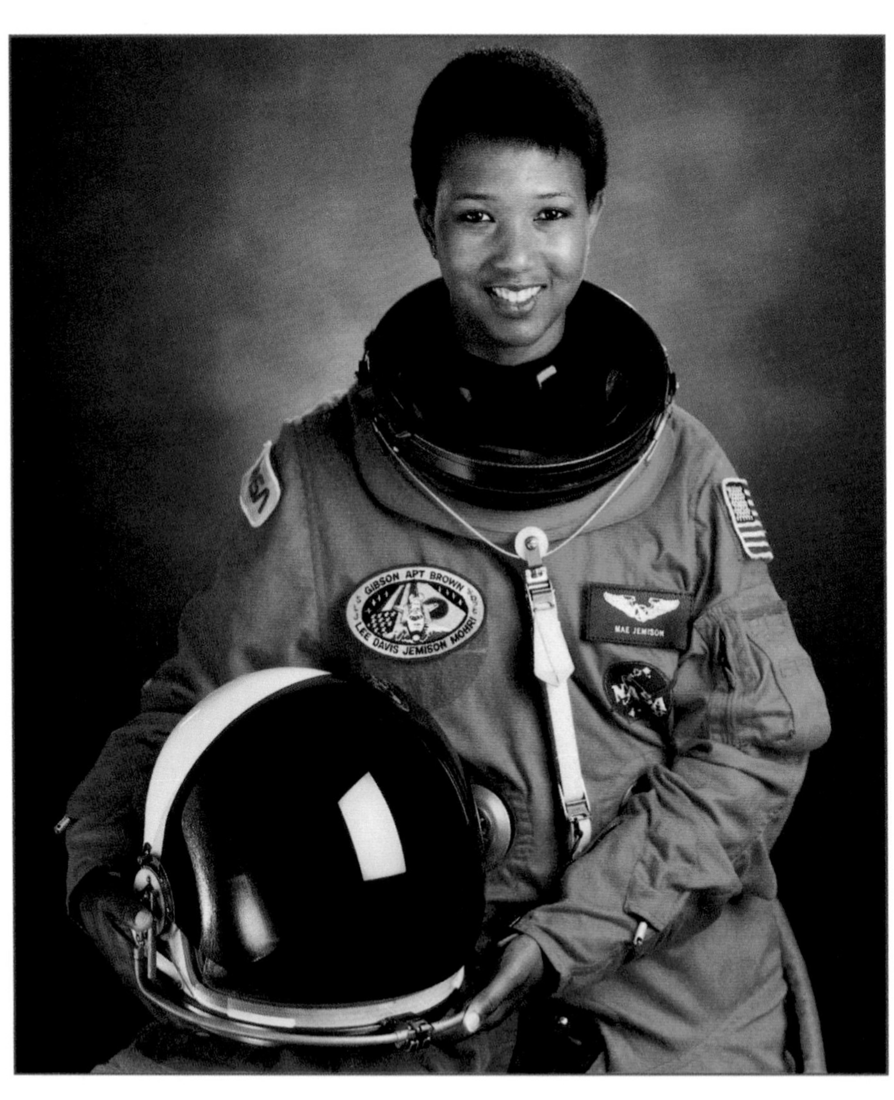

The space shuttle *Endeavour* thundered into the morning sky above Kennedy Space Center. Higher and higher it soared over the Atlantic Ocean. A few minutes later, *Endeavour* was in orbit around Earth.

Aboard the spacecraft, astronaut Mae Jemison could feel her heart pounding with excitement. A wide, happy grin split her face. She had just made history. She was the first African-American woman in space. The date was September 12, 1992.

The space shuttle *Endeavour* lifts off.

But Mae wasn't thinking about dates in history books. Her thoughts were of the wonder and adventure of space travel. "I'm closer to the stars—somewhere I've always dreamed to be," Mae said during a live television broadcast from space.

While in space, the *Endeavour* astronauts pose for a portrait.

Mae's dream didn't come true overnight. It happened only after many long years of hard work, training, and preparation. Her success

story began nearly thirty-six years earlier, in a small town in Alabama.

Mae Carol Jemison was born on October 17, 1956, in Decatur, Alabama. While she was still a toddler, Mae and her family moved to the big city of Chicago, Illinois. Mae considers Chicago her hometown because she grew up there.

Mae was the youngest child in her family. She had an older brother, Charles, and an older sister, Ada. Her parents, Charlie and Dorothy Jemison, were helpful and supportive of all of Mae's interests. "They put up with all kinds of stuff, like science projects, dance classes, and art lessons," Mae said. "They encouraged me to do it, and they would find the money, time, and energy to help me be involved."

Other adults were not as encouraging as Mae's parents. When Mae told her kindergarten teacher that she wanted to be a scientist, the teacher said, "Don't you mean a nurse?" In those days, very few African Americans or women were scientists. Many people, like Mae's teacher, couldn't imagine a little black girl growing up to become a scientist. But Mae refused to let other people's limited imaginations stop her from following her dreams.

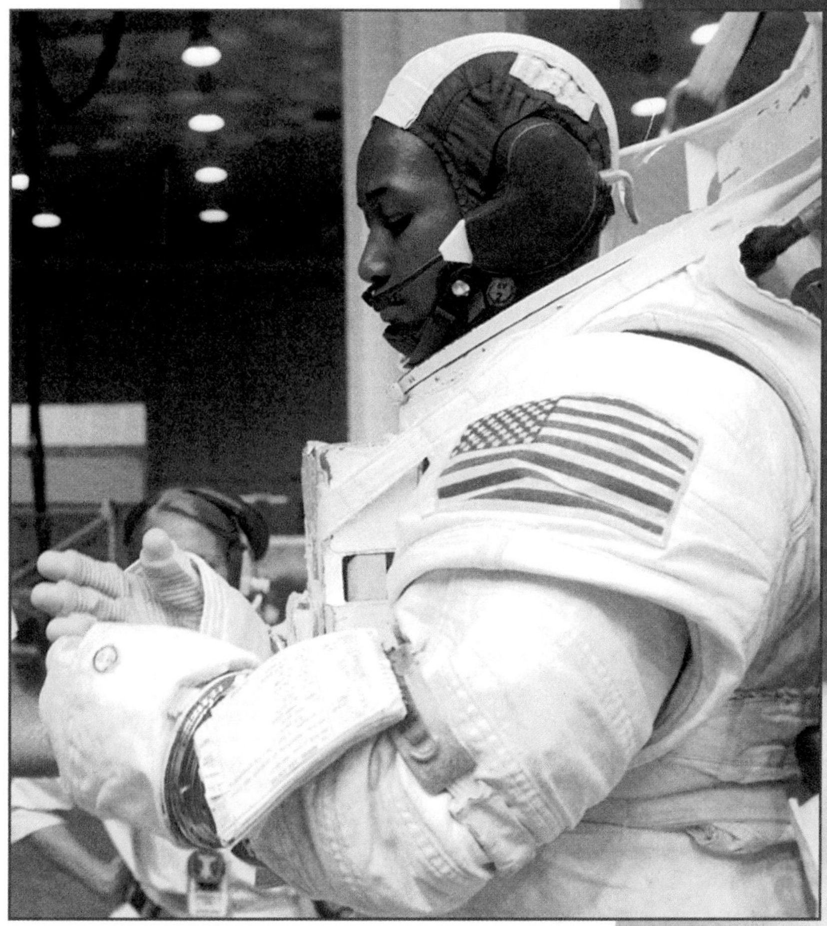

Mae had always dreamed of becoming an astronaut. Her dream came true in 1987.

Mae loved to work on school science projects. She spent many hours at the public library, reading books about science and space. On summer nights, she liked to lie outside, look up at the stars, and dream of traveling in space. Mae was fascinated by the real-life space flights and moon landings that she watched on television. Mae Jemison knew that she wanted to be an astronaut. Although all the astronauts at the time were white and male, Mae wasn't discouraged.

Science and space were not young Mae's only interests. She also loved to dance. Mae started taking lessons in jazz and African dance at the age of nine. By the time she was in high school, Mae was an accomplished dancer, and she frequently performed on stage. She was also skilled at choreography, the art of creating a dance.

Mae at Stanford University

In 1973, Mae graduated from Chicago's Morgan Park High School, where she was an honor-roll student and excelled in science and math. That fall, Mae entered Stanford University in California. At Stanford, she specialized in African and Afro-American studies, and chemical engineering. Mae continued her dancing and choreography. She also became involved with student organizations, and she was elected president of the Black Student Union.

After receiving her Bachelor of Science degree from Stanford, Mae enrolled at Cornell University Medical College in New York. She had decided to become a doctor. Medical school was demanding, but Mae still found time to participate in student organizations. She served as president of both the Cornell Medical Student Executive Council and the Cornell chapter of the National Student Medical Association.

Mae traveled to several countries as part of her medical training. She studied medicine in Cuba. She helped provide basic medical care for people in rural Kenya and at a Cambodian refugee camp in Thailand.

Mae received her Doctor of Medicine degree from Cornell University in 1981. Like all new doctors, she served an internship, a period of practicing under experienced doctors. Mae completed her internship at the Los Angeles County/University of Southern California Medical Center. Then she started working as a doctor in Los Angeles.

Mae was working as a doctor in this Los Angeles office when NASA selected her for its astronaut program.

Although she had settled into a career as a doctor, Mae wasn't finished traveling yet. She remembered the trips she had taken during medical school, and she still wanted to help people in other parts of the world. Mae decided to join the Peace Corps, an organization of volunteers who work to improve conditions in developing nations.

Mae spent more than two years in West Africa. She was the Area Peace Corps Medical Officer for Sierra Leone and Liberia. She was in charge of health care for all Peace Corps volunteers and U.S. embassy employees in those two countries. It was an important responsibility for someone who was only twenty-six years old.

"I learned a lot from that experience," Mae said. "I was one of the youngest doctors over there, and I had to learn to deal with how people reacted to my age, while asserting myself as a physician."

When her tour of duty in the Peace Corps was over, Mae returned to Los Angeles and resumed her medical practice. She also started taking advanced engineering classes.

Mae sits in the cockpit of a shuttle trainer.

Mae and her survival-training classmates watch a demonstration of how to build a fire.

Mae had not forgotten her dream of traveling in space. Now that she had the necessary education and experience, Mae decided to try and become an astronaut. She applied to the National Aeronautics and Space Administration (NASA), which is responsible for U.S. space exploration. After undergoing background checks, physical exams, medical tests, and interviews, Dr. Mae Jemison was accepted into the astronaut program in June 1987. She was one of only fifteen people chosen from nearly two thousand qualified applicants!

Mae didn't let success go to her head. "I'm very aware of the fact that I'm not the first African-American woman who had the skills, the talent, the desire to be an astronaut," she said. "I happen to be the first one that NASA selected."

Mae moved to Houston, Texas, where she began a year of intensive training at NASA's Johnson Space Center. She studied space shuttle equipment and operations. To learn how to handle emergencies and deal with difficult situations, Mae practiced wilderness- and water-survival skills. Survival training also helps teach cooperation and teamwork. These are important abilities for astronauts who must live and work together for long periods in a cramped space shuttle.

Mae took lessons on how to move her body and operate tools in a weightless environment. On Earth, the force of gravity keeps us from floating off the ground. But in space, there is less gravity, so people and objects drift about. Since there is no "up" or "down" in space, astronauts don't need to lie down to sleep. They can sleep in any position. To keep them from drifting while asleep, they zip themselves into special sleeping bags attached to the shuttle's walls.

During training, Mae got a preview of weightlessness. She flew in a special training jet that simulates zero gravity. The jet climbs nearly straight up, then loops into a steep dive. This is similar to the loop-the-loops on many roller coasters. For thirty seconds at the top of the loop, trainees feel weightless. Their feet leave the floor and they can fly around inside the padded cabin.

At the end of her training year, Mae officially became a mission specialist astronaut. "We're the ones people often call the scientist astronauts," Mae explained. "Our responsibilities are to be familiar with the shuttle and how it operates, to do the experiments once you get into orbit, to help launch the payloads or satellites, and also do extravehicular activities, which are the space walks."

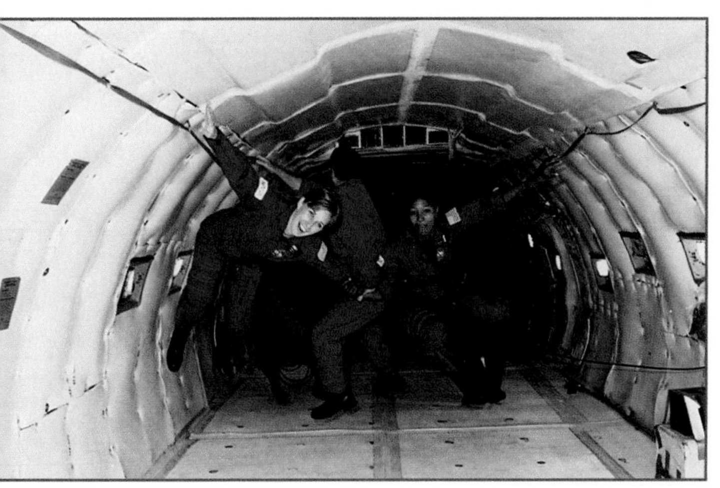

Mae in training (top) clinging to a life raft in water-survival training; (middle) practicing with the shuttle escape pole for emergency bailouts; (bottom) learning to use a parachute.

Bottom left: Mae and astronaut Jan Davis (left) hold onto each other in NASA's "zero-gravity" training aircraft.

This illustration shows how the space shuttle looks during flight. The cargo bay holds Spacelab, the science laboratory where *Endeavour*'s astronauts conducted most of their experiments.

In the 1970s, NASA designed the space shuttle as the first reusable spacecraft. A shuttle launches like a rocket, but it returns to Earth and lands on a runway like an airplane.

A space shuttle has many uses. It carries both equipment and people into space. Astronauts aboard a shuttle can capture, repair, and launch satellites. Shuttles are often used as orbiting laboratories, where space scientists conduct experiments in a zero-gravity environment. In the future, space shuttles might transport supplies and workers for building space stations.

The *Endeavour* crew on their way to the launch pad.

Although Mae was a full-fledged astronaut, she still had to wait four more years before she went into space. While she waited, Mae worked with the scientists who were developing experiments for her mission. She also trained with her fellow crew members. In her spare time, Mae liked to read, travel, ski, garden, dance, and exercise. She also enjoyed taking care of Sneeze, her white, gray, and silver African wildcat.

On September 12, 1992, the long wait was over. Space shuttle *Endeavour* perched on the launch pad like a great white bird waiting to take flight. Everything was ready for the liftoff.

Mae awoke early to shower and dress. She ate breakfast with the other astronauts. Then, Mae and the crew put on their orange space suits and boarded a van for the short drive to the launch pad. For two-and-a-half hours until liftoff, they lay on their backs, strapped into their seats, as the countdown progressed. At 10:23 A.M., precisely on time, *Endeavour* lifted off on its historic space journey.

Dr. Mae Jemison earned her place in the history books as the first African-American woman in space. Mae said, "My participation in the space shuttle mission helps to say that all peoples of the world have astronomers, physicists, and explorers."

Mae prepares to board the shuttle.

Mae injects liquid into a mannequin's hand. She is testing new medical equipment that is specially designed for a weightless environment.

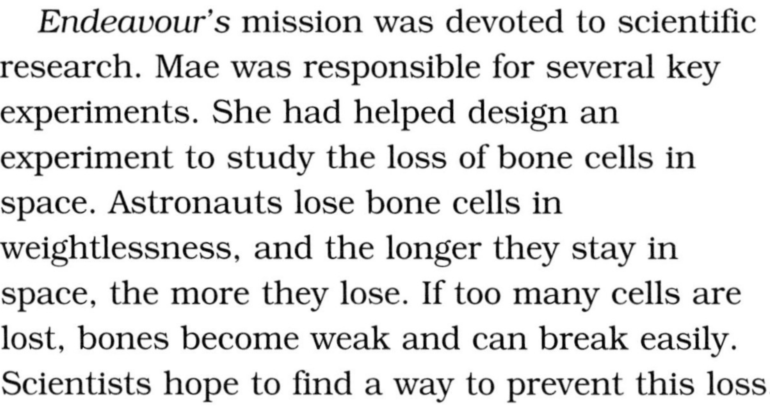

Endeavour's mission was devoted to scientific research. Mae was responsible for several key experiments. She had helped design an experiment to study the loss of bone cells in space. Astronauts lose bone cells in weightlessness, and the longer they stay in space, the more they lose. If too many cells are lost, bones become weak and can break easily. Scientists hope to find a way to prevent this loss. Mae explained, "The real issue is how to keep people healthy while they're in space."

Mae investigated a new way of controlling space motion sickness. Half of all astronauts experience space sickness during their first few days in space. They often feel dizzy and nauseated. Astronauts can take medicine to control space sickness, but the medicine can make them tired.

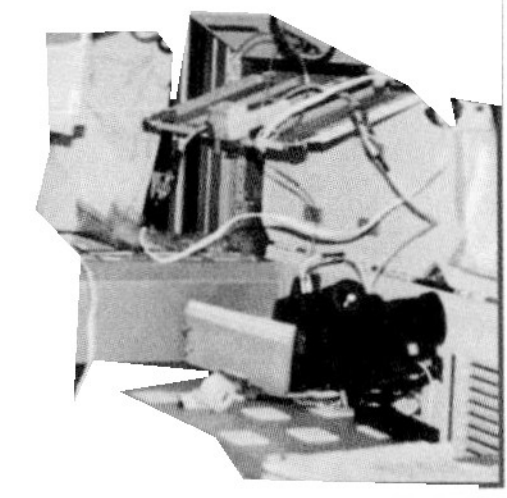

Mae and Jan Davis conduct a zero-gravity experiment. In space, a person's fluids shift toward the upper body. The device Mae is wearing simulates normal gravity and forces the fluids back to the lower body.

To carry out the space-sickness experiment, Mae had been trained in the use of "biofeedback" techniques. Biofeedback uses meditation and relaxation to control the body's functions. Mae wore special monitoring equipment to record her heart rate, breathing, temperature, and other body functions. If she started to feel ill, she would meditate. She concentrated intensely on bringing her body back to normal. The purpose of the experiment was to see if Mae could avoid space sickness without taking medication. The results of the experiment were not conclusive, but space researchers still hope to use biofeedback in the future.

Mae is all wired up for the biofeedback experiment.

Mae was also in charge of the frog experiment. Early in the flight, she fertilized eggs from female South African frogs. A few days later, tadpoles hatched. She then watched the tadpoles carefully. Her goal was to find out if the tadpoles would develop normally in the near-zero gravity of space. "What we've seen is that the eggs were fertilized and the tadpoles looked pretty good," said Mae. "It was exciting because that's a question that we didn't have any information on before."

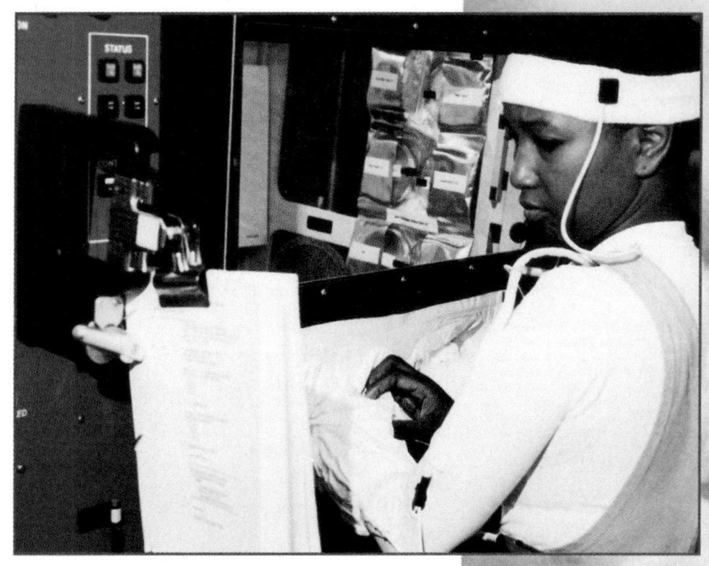
Mae works with the frog experiment.

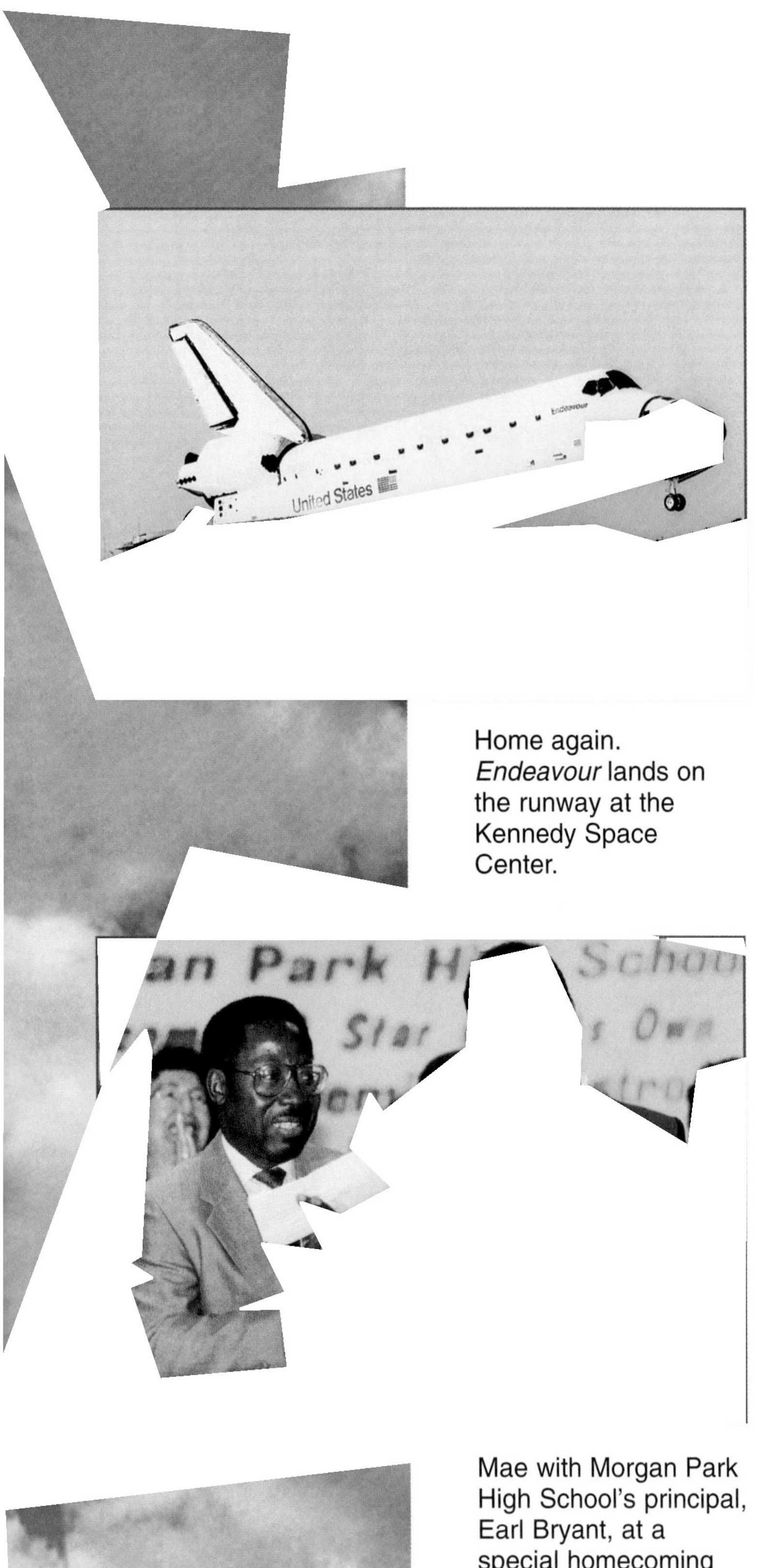

Home again. *Endeavour* lands on the runway at the Kennedy Space Center.

Mae with Morgan Park High School's principal, Earl Bryant, at a special homecoming ceremony in her honor.

On September 20, 1992, at 8:53 A.M., *Endeavour* landed at Kennedy Space Center. The crew had spent more than 190 hours (almost eight days) in space. They had traveled 3.3 million miles and had completed 127 orbits of Earth!

After her space mission, Mae returned home to Chicago. Her hometown welcomed her with six days of parades, speeches, and celebrations. Then she went to Hollywood to accept the American Black Achievement Awards' Trailblazer Award for being the first African-American woman in space. In 1993, Mae was inducted into the National Women's Hall of Fame in Seneca Falls, New York.

Mae Jemison had made her childhood dream come true. She was ready for new challenges. A few months after her space flight, Mae took a leave of absence from NASA to teach and to do research at Dartmouth College in New Hampshire. Then, on March 8, 1993, she permanently resigned from the astronaut corps.

Mae formed her own company called The Jemison Group, Inc. The Jemison Group's goal is to develop ways of using science and technology to improve the quality of life. Mae's company makes a special effort to improve conditions in poor and developing countries.

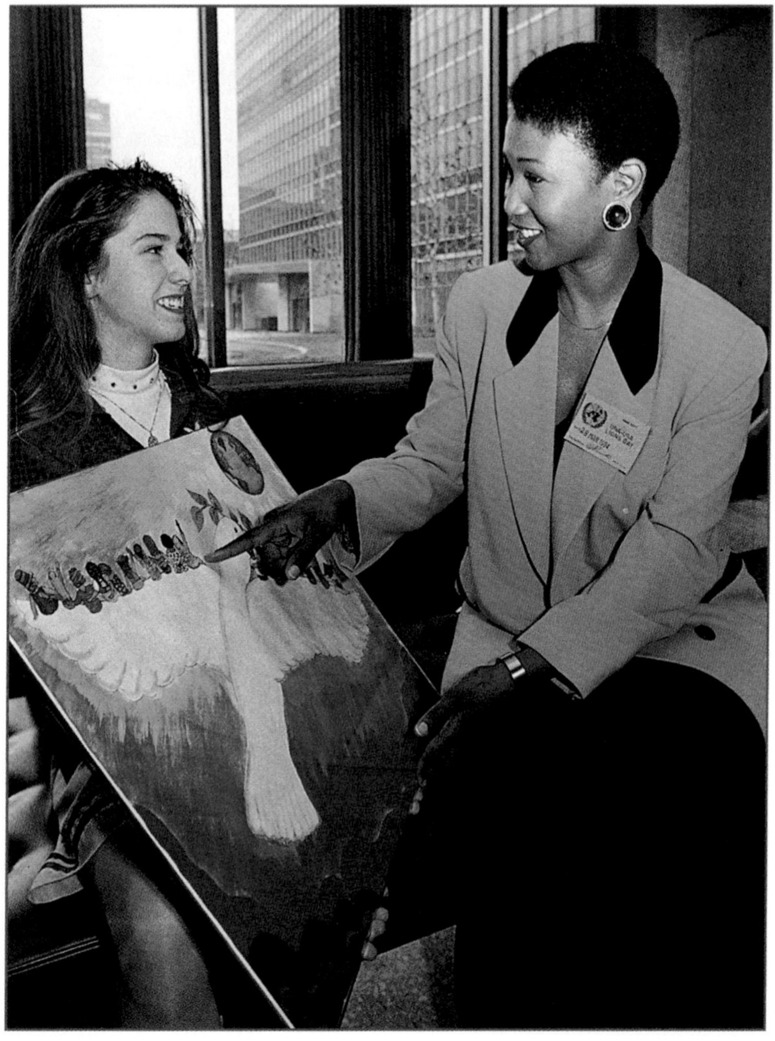

Mae encourages youngsters to follow their dreams. She is shown here with thirteen-year-old Jill Giovanelli, the winner of the International Peace Poster Contest.

The company's first project used satellite communications to provide better health care for people in West Africa. Mae also established an international summer science camp for young people.

Besides her work with The Jemison Group, Mae spends much of her time traveling around the country, giving speeches, and encouraging young people to follow their dreams. Mae Jemison believes in the motto:

"Don't be limited by others' limited imaginations."

Mae Jemison

Space Scientist

Concept Connections

Linking the Selection

Think about the following questions, and then record your responses in the Response Journal section of your Writer's Notebook.

- Why did Mae Jemison choose such a risky profession?
- How did Mae Jemison minimize the risks she faced in space?

Exploring Concept Vocabulary

The concept word for this lesson is ***challenge.*** If you don't know what this word means, look it up in a dictionary. Answer these questions.

- How are a ***challenge*** and a risk alike? How are they different?
- Why was Mae's age a ***challenge*** during her time as a Peace Corps volunteer?

In the Vocabulary section of your Writer's Notebook, write a sentence that includes the word ***challenge*** as well as one of the selection vocabulary words.

Expanding the Concept

Think about Mae Jemison and her accomplishments. What qualities make someone like Mae Jemison a successful risk-taker? Try to use the word ***challenge*** in your discussion of Mae Jemison. Add new ideas about risks and consequences to the Concept/Question Board.

Meet the Author

Gail Sakurai was born in Detroit, Michigan. As soon as she learned to read, she knew she wanted to be a writer.

Ms. Sakurai gets story ideas from the world around her. Her book about Dr. Mae Jemison, the first female African-American astronaut, grew out of a lifelong interest in space exploration. She says, *"I get the ideas for my books from everywhere—from things I read, from my children, and even from television. I have more ideas than I'll ever have time to use."*

Ms. Sakurai's advice to aspiring young writers is simple. *"Read. Read everything you can get your hands on!"*

Risks and Consequences

Saint George Killing the Dragon. 1430–35. **Bernardo Martorell.** Tempera on panel. 115.3 cm × 98 cm. The Art Institute of Chicago.

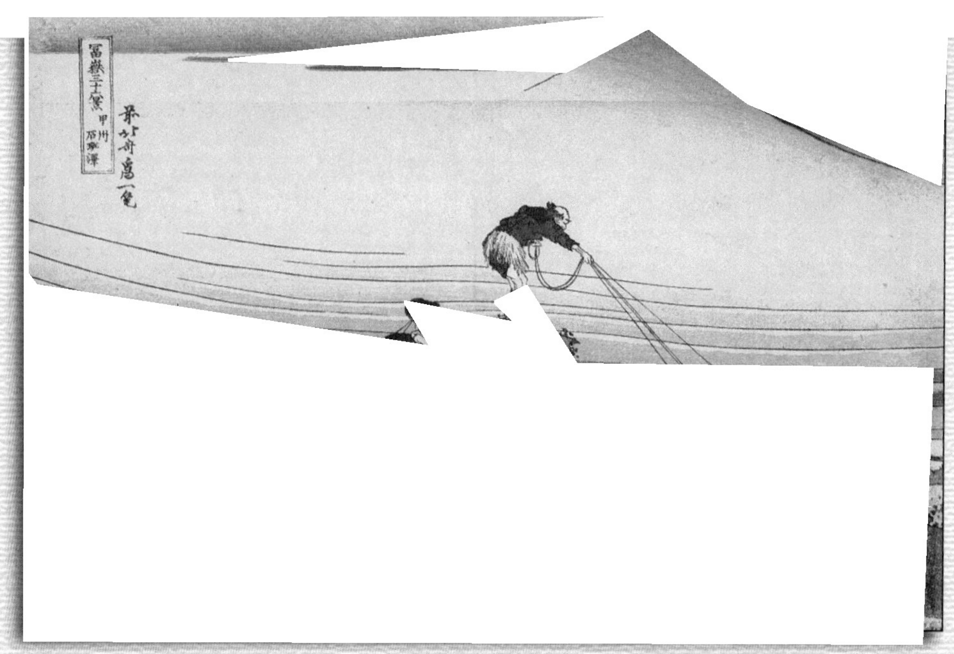

Kajikazawa in Kai Province. From the series Thirty-Six Views of Mount Fuji. 1823–29. **Katsushika Hokusai.** Woodblock print. $10 \times 15\frac{1}{8}$ in. The Metropolitan Museum of Art, New York, NY.

Margaret Bourke-White Atop the Chrysler Building. 1931–1933. Silver gelatin print.

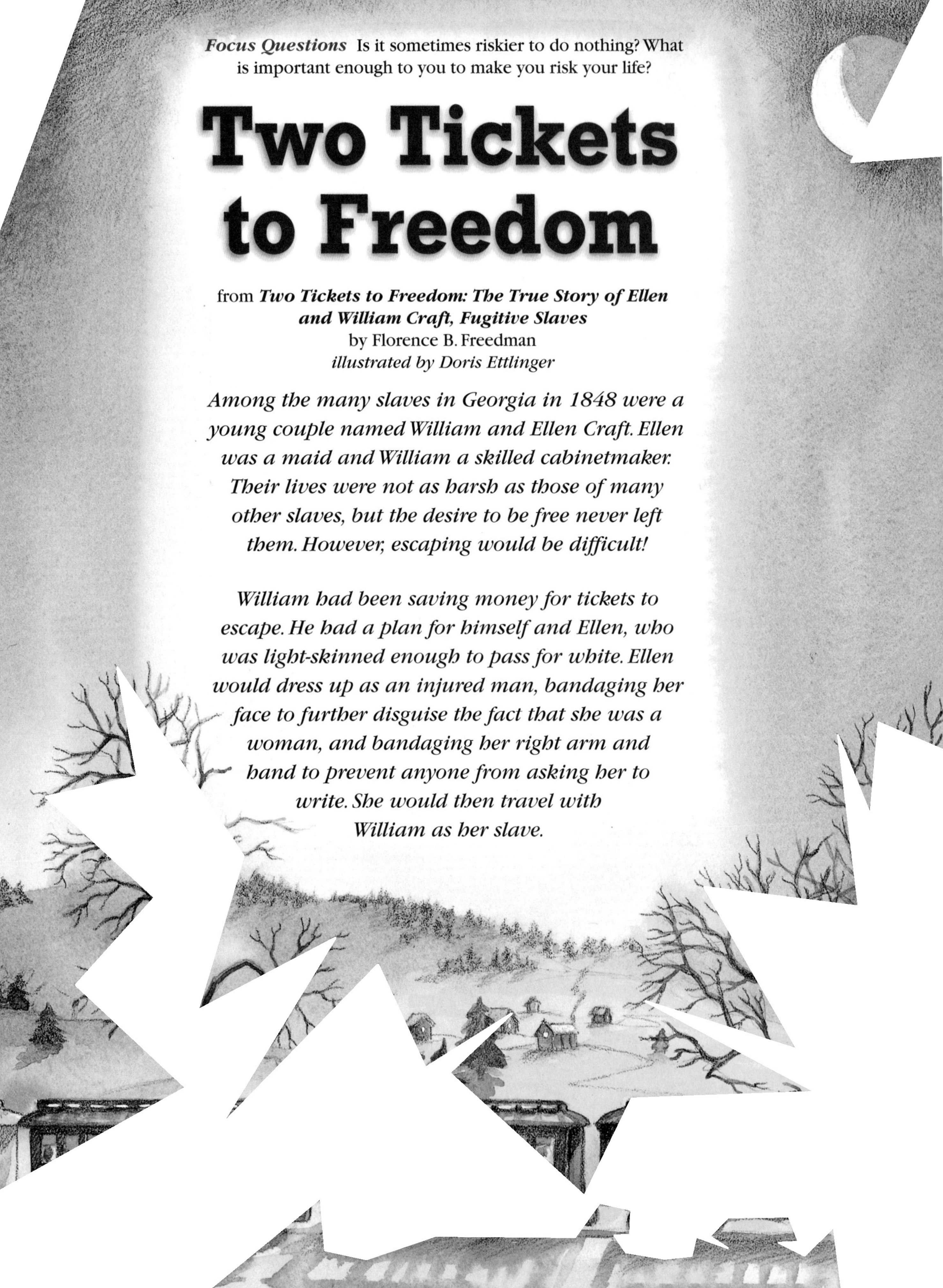

Focus Questions Is it sometimes riskier to do nothing? What is important enough to you to make you risk your life?

Two Tickets to Freedom

from ***Two Tickets to Freedom: The True Story of Ellen and William Craft, Fugitive Slaves***
by Florence B. Freedman
illustrated by Doris Ettlinger

Among the many slaves in Georgia in 1848 were a young couple named William and Ellen Craft. Ellen was a maid and William a skilled cabinetmaker. Their lives were not as harsh as those of many other slaves, but the desire to be free never left them. However, escaping would be difficult!

William had been saving money for tickets to escape. He had a plan for himself and Ellen, who was light-skinned enough to pass for white. Ellen would dress up as an injured man, bandaging her face to further disguise the fact that she was a woman, and bandaging her right arm and hand to prevent anyone from asking her to write. She would then travel with William as her slave.

Their journey would include a train ride to Fredericksburg, Virginia, followed by a boat trip to Washington, D.C., and finally a train ride to Philadelphia, the first stop on the Underground Railroad.

By the time they left the train in Fredericksburg and boarded a ship for Washington, D.C., William and Ellen felt sure they were safe. They were unaware that the most difficult part of their daring escape was just around the corner. Would they ever make it to Philadelphia?

In a few minutes, the ship landed at Washington, and there William and Ellen took a carriage to the train for Baltimore, the last slave port they were to see. They had left their cottage on Wednesday morning, the 21st of December. It was Christmas Eve, December 24, 1848, when they arrived in Baltimore.

William and Ellen were more tense than ever. They were so near their goal . . . yet they knew that officials in Baltimore were particularly watchful to prevent slaves from escaping across the border to Pennsylvania and freedom.

William settled his "master" in a first-class carriage on the train and went to the car in which blacks traveled. Before he entered, a Yankee officer stopped him, saying sternly, "Where are you going, boy?"

"Philadelphia, sir," William replied humbly.

"What are you going there for?" asked the officer.

“I am traveling with my master who is in another carriage, sir.”

“I think you had better get him out, and be quick about it, because the train will soon be starting,” the officer ordered. “It is against the rules to let any man take a slave past here unless he can satisfy them in the office that he has a right to take him along.” The officer moved on, leaving William on the platform.

William’s heart was beating furiously. To have come so far—and now this! How would Ellen be able to prove ownership? He consoled himself with the thought that God, who had been so good as to allow them to come this far, would not let them be turned aside now.

William hastened into the car to tell his master the bad news. "Mr. Johnson," seated comfortably in the railroad car, smiled at him. They were so near their destination.

"How are you feeling, sir?" asked William.

"Much better," answered his "master." "Thank God we are getting on so nicely."

"Not so nicely, sir, I am sorry to say," William said. "You must leave the train and convince the officials that I am your slave."

"Mr. Johnson" shuddered.

"Good heavens!" he whispered. "Is it possible that we will be sent back into slavery?"

They were silent for a few despairing moments. Then they left the train and made their way to the office.

Ellen summoned her last bit of courage.

"Do you wish to see me, sir?" "Mr. Johnson" asked the man who appeared to be the chief officer.

"Yes," he answered. "It is against our rules, sir, to allow any person to take a slave out of Baltimore into Philadelphia unless he can satisfy us that he has a right to take him along."

"Why is that?" asked "Mr. Johnson" innocently.

"Because, sir," the officer answered in a voice and manner that almost chilled the blood of the fugitives, "if we should allow any gentleman to take a slave past here into Philadelphia, and should the gentleman with whom the slave was traveling turn out to be not his rightful owner, and if the real owner should prove that his slave escaped on our railroad, we should have to pay for him."

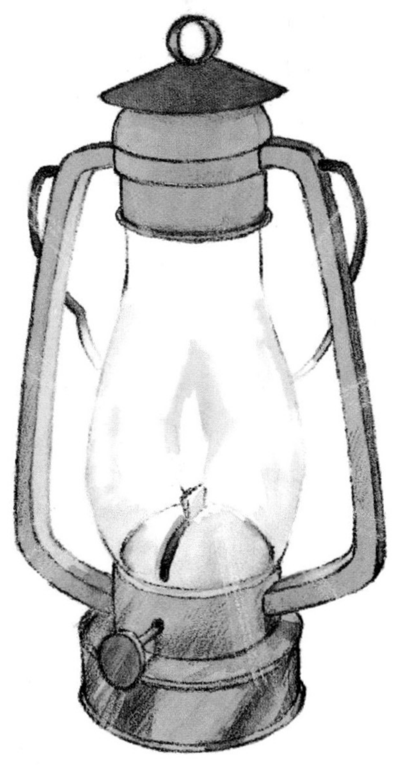

This conversation attracted the attention of a large number of curious passengers. They seemed sympathetic to "Mr. Johnson," because he was so obviously ill.

Seeing the sympathy of the other passengers, the officer asked, more politely, "Do you know someone in Baltimore who might vouch for you and assure us that you have a right to take this slave into Pennsylvania?"

"No, I do not," asserted "Mr. Johnson" regretfully. He then added more forcefully, "I bought tickets in Charleston to pass us through to Philadelphia, and you have no right to detain us here!"

The officer was firm. "Right or wrong, I shan't let you go."

William and Ellen looked at each other, but did not dare to say a word for fear they would give themselves away. They knew that, if the officer suspected them, he had the right to put them in prison. When their true identity became known, they would surely be sent back into slavery, and they knew they would rather be dead. They silently prayed to be delivered from this new danger.

Just then, the conductor of the train on which they had come from Washington, came in.

"Did this gentleman and his slave come on your train?" asked the official.

"They did," answered the conductor, and left.

Suddenly the bell rang for the train to leave. The other passengers fixed their eyes upon the officer, "Mr. Johnson," and his slave, their expressions showing their interest and concern.

The officer seemed agitated. Running his fingers through his hair, he finally said, "I don't know what to do." Then looking around, he added, "I calculate it is all right. Run and tell the conductor that it will be all right to let this gentleman and his slave proceed," he told one of the clerks. "Since he is not well, it is a pity to stop him here. We will let him go."

"Mr. Johnson" thanked him and stepped out, crossing the platform as quickly as possible, with his slave close behind. William escorted his master into one of the best carriages of the train and reached his own just as the train pulled out.

It was eight o'clock on Christmas Eve, just eight days after William had first thought of their plan. In the four days before they left Macon, he and Ellen had both been working; they had seen each other only at night, when they talked over each detail of their plan. They had had hardly any sleep for the four days of planning and the four days of the journey. Now that the last hurdle was passed, William realized how terribly tired he was. Knowing that they would be in Philadelphia in the morning, and that there were no important stations between Baltimore and Philadelphia, William relaxed his guard, and fell asleep. It proved to be the wrong time for sleeping.

When the train reached Havre-de-Grace, all the first-class passengers were told to get off the train and onto a ferryboat, to be ferried across the Susquehanna River to take the train again on the opposite side. This was to spare the passengers the jolting of rolling the cars onto the boat. The baggage cars, however, were rolled on the boat to be taken off on the other side. The sleeping William was near the baggage car, so they did not wake him.

When Ellen left the railroad carriage to get on the ferryboat, it was cold and dark and rainy. She was alone, without William, for the first time on the journey. She was frightened and confused.

"Have you seen my boy?" "Mr. Johnson" asked the conductor.

The conductor, who may well have been an abolitionist, thought he would tease this Southern slaveowner.

"No, I haven't seen anything of him for some time; no doubt he has run away and has reached Philadelphia long before now. He is probably a free man by now, sir."

"Mr. Johnson" knew better. "Please try to find him," he asked the conductor.

"I am no slave hunter," the conductor indignantly replied. "As far as I am concerned, everybody must look after his own slaves." With that, he strode away.

Ellen was frightened. She feared that William had been kidnaped into slavery, or perhaps killed on the train. She was in a predicament for another reason. She had no money at all. Although Ellen had been carrying the money up to then, she had given it all to William the night before after hearing that there were pickpockets in Philadelphia who preyed on travelers. A pickpocket would not think of a slave as a likely victim.

Ellen did have the tickets, however. Frightened and confused though she was, she realized that there was no use in her staying there at Havre-de-Grace. She must board the ferry and complete her journey, hoping and praying that she and William would find each other again in freedom.

The ferry ride over, the passengers went back on the train. After the train was well on its way to Philadelphia, the guard came to the car where William was sleeping and gave him a violent shake, saying, "Boy, wake up!"

William started, not knowing for a moment where he was.

"Your master is scared half to death about you," the guard continued. It was William's turn to be scared. He was sure that Ellen had been found out.

"What is the matter?" William managed to ask.

"Your master thinks you have run away from him," the guard explained.

Knowing that Ellen would never think any such thing, William felt reassured and went to his "master" immediately.

After talking with "Mr. Johnson" for a few minutes, William returned to his place, where the guard was talking with the conductor.

"What did your master want, boy?" asked the guard.

"He just wanted to know what had become of me."

"No," said the guard. "That's not it. He thought you had taken leave for parts unknown. I never saw a man so badly scared about losing his slave in my life. Now," continued the guard, "let me give you a little friendly advice. When you get to Philadelphia, run away and leave that cripple, and have your liberty."

"No, sir," replied William. "I can't promise to do that."

"Why not?" asked the conductor, evidently much surprised. "Don't you want your liberty?"

"Yes, sir," he replied, "but I shall never run away from such a good master as I have at present."

One of the men said to the guard, "Let him alone. I guess he'll open his eyes when he gets to Philadelphia."

In spite of William's seeming lack of interest, the men gave him a good deal of information about how to run away from his master in Philadelphia, information which he appeared not to be taking to heart, but which he found useful for both of them later.

On the train, William also met a free black man, who recommended to him a boardinghouse in Philadelphia kept by an abolitionist, where he would be quite safe if he decided to run away from his master. William thanked him, but did not let him know who he and his "master" really were.

Later on in the night, William heard a fearful whistling of the steam engine; he looked out the window and saw many flickering lights. A passenger in the next car also stuck his head out the window and called to his companion, "Wake up! We are in Philadelphia." The sight of the city in the distance and the words he heard made William feel as if a burden had rolled off his back; he felt really happy for the first time in his life.

As soon as the train reached the platform, he went to get "Mr. Johnson," took their luggage, put it into a carriage, got in and drove off to the abolitionist's boardinghouse recommended to him by the free black man.

No sooner had they left the station than Ellen, who had concealed her fears and played her part with so much courage and wit throughout the journey, grasped William's hand and said, "Thank God we are safe!" She burst into tears, and wept like a child.

When they reached the boardinghouse, Ellen was so weak and faint that she could scarcely stand alone. As soon as they were shown their room, William and Ellen knelt down and thanked God for His goodness in enabling them to overcome so many dangers in escaping from slavery to freedom.

That was Sunday, December 25, Christmas Day of 1848.

Ellen was twenty-two years old, and William a few years older. They thought all their troubles were over. They were young, strong, and in love. And they were free.

Philadelphia was the first stop on the Underground Railroad for William and Ellen. Eventually, they made their way to England, where their children were born. After the Civil War, they returned to Georgia with their family and bought a large plantation. There they established the Woodville Cooperative Farm School for poor families, to which they devoted the rest of their lives.

Two Tickets to Freedom

Concept Connections

Linking the Selection

Writer's Notebook

Think about the following questions, and then record your responses in the Response Journal section of your Writer's Notebook.

- Why were Ellen and William Craft willing to take such great risks on their journey?
- What were the possible consequences of their escape?

Exploring Concept Vocabulary

The concept word for this lesson is ***resolute.*** If you don't know what this word means, look it up in a dictionary. Answer these questions.

- What made Ellen and William Craft so ***resolute*** in their plan to escape?
- How did being ***resolute*** help Ellen and William escape?

In the Vocabulary section of your Writer's Notebook, write a sentence that includes the word ***resolute*** as well as one of the selection vocabulary words.

Expanding the Concept

Compare the risks Ellen and William Craft took with the risks taken by a character in another selection you have read. Try to use the word ***resolute*** in your discussion. Add new ideas about risks and consequences to the Concept/Question Board.

Meet the Author

Florence B. Freedman was born in Brooklyn, New York. She went to school at Columbia University and later became a teacher of English and Hebrew.

Many of Ms. Freedman's books are based on stories she heard or read when she was growing up. *Two Tickets to Freedom* is a true story. To write it, Ms. Freedman researched old newspaper articles, journals, and William Craft's own narrative of what happened.

Meet the Illustrator

Doris Ettlinger grew up in Staten Island, New York. She took painting lessons from local artists, read "How to Draw" books, and copied the comics from the newspaper. She studied illustration at the Rhode Island School of Design, graduating in 1973, and has illustrated professionally ever since. Today Ms. Ettlinger lives on the banks of the Musconetcong River in New Jersey with her husband and two children. Several days a week she teaches art to children and adults. She tells her students that *"drawing every day improves my skills, just as a musician practices an instrument or an athlete works out."*

Focus Questions What is freedom? Why did people risk their lives for freedom?

Freedom

Langston Hughes

illustrated by Tyrone Geter

Freedom will not come
Today, this year
        Nor ever
Through compromise and fear.

I have as much right
As the other fellow has
        To stand
On my two feet
And own the land.

I tire so of hearing people say,
Let things take their course.
Tomorrow is another day.
I do not need my freedom when I'm dead.
I cannot live on tomorrow's bread.
        Freedom
        Is a strong seed
        Planted
        In a great need.
        I live here, too.
        I want freedom
        Just as you.

Focus Questions Do we always recognize when we are taking a risk? Why do people take foolish risks?

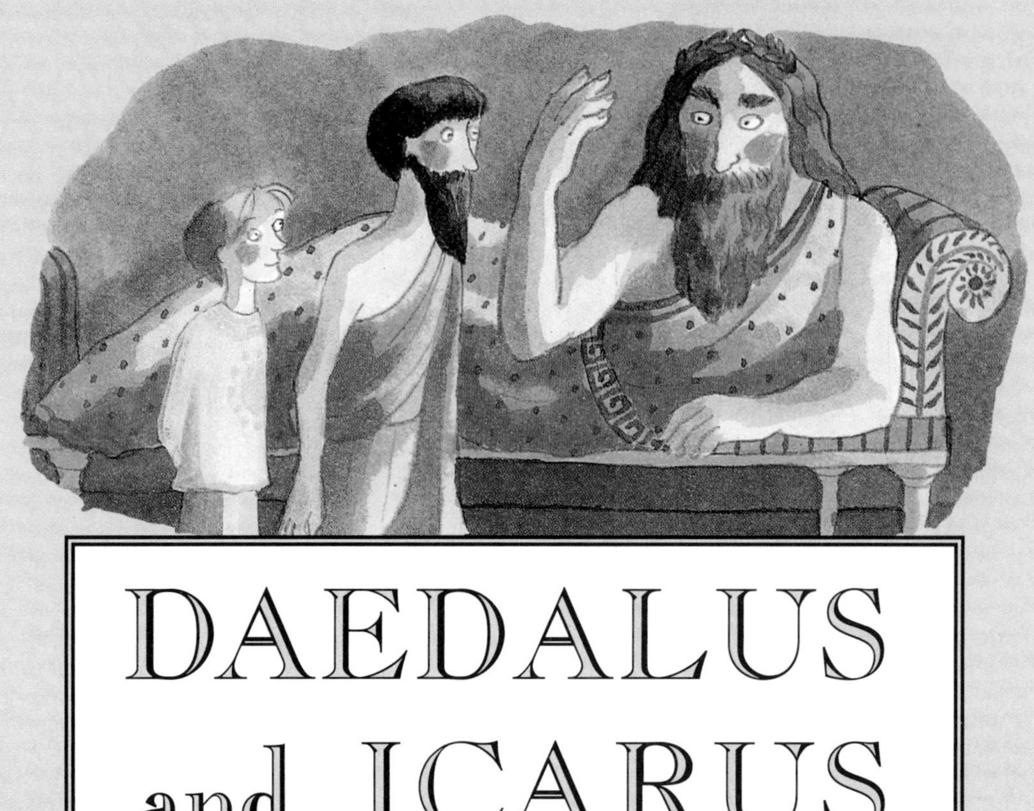

DAEDALUS and ICARUS

retold by Geraldine McCaughrean
illustrated by Emma Chichester Clark

Daedalus and Icarus lived in great comfort in King Minos's palace. But they lived the life of prisoners. Their rooms were in the tallest palace tower, with beautiful views across the island. They ate delectable food and wore expensive clothes. But at night the door to their fine apartment was locked, and a guard stood outside. It was a comfortable prison, but it was a prison, even so. Daedalus was deeply unhappy.

Every day he put seed out on the windowsill, for the birds. He liked to study their brilliant colors, the clever overlapping of their feathers, the way they soared on the sea wind. It comforted him to think that they at least were free to come and go. The birds had only to spread their wings and they could leave Crete behind them, whereas Daedalus and Icarus must stay forever in their luxurious cage.

Young Icarus could not understand his father's unhappiness. "But I like it here," he said. "The king gives us gold and this tall tower to live in."

Daedalus groaned. "But to work for such a wicked man, Icarus! And to be prisoners all our days!...We shan't stay. We shan't!"

"But we can't get away, can we?" said Icarus. "How can anybody escape from an island? Fly?" He snorted with laughter.

Daedalus did not answer. He scratched his head and stared out of the window at the birds pecking seed on the sill.

From that day onward, he got up early each morning and stood at the open window. When a bird came for the seed, Daedalus begged it to spare him one feather. Then each night, when everyone else had gone to bed, Daedalus worked by candlelight on his greatest invention of all.

Early mornings. Late nights. A whole year went by. Then one morning Icarus was awakened by his father shaking his shoulder. "Get up, Icarus, and don't make a sound. We are leaving Crete."

"But how? It's impossible!"

Daedalus pulled out a bundle from under his bed. "I've been making something, Icarus." Inside were four great folded fans of feathers. He stretched them out on the bed. They were wings! "I sewed the feathers together with strands of wool from my blanket. Now hold still."

Daedalus melted down a candle and daubed his son's shoulders with sticky wax. "Yes, I know it's hot, but it will soon cool." While the wax was still soft, he stuck the wings to Icarus's shoulder blades.

"Now you must help me put on my wings, Son. When the wax sets hard, you and I will fly away from here, as free as birds!"

"I'm scared!" whispered Icarus as he stood on the narrow window ledge, his knees knocking and his huge wings drooping down behind. The lawns and courtyards of the palace lay far below. The royal guards looked as small as ants. "This won't work!"

“Courage, Son!” said Daedalus. “Keep your arms out wide and fly close to me. Above all—are you listening, Icarus?”

“Y-y-yes, Father.”

“Above all, don’t fly too high! Don’t fly too close to the sun!”

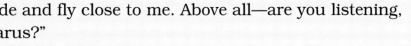

“Don’t fly too close to the sun,” Icarus repeated, with his eyes tight shut. Then he gave a cry as his father nudged him off the windowsill.

He plunged downward. With a crack, the feathers behind him filled with wind, and Icarus found himself flying. Flying!

“*I’m flying!*” he crowed.

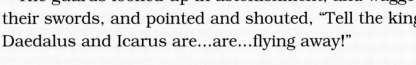

The guards looked up in astonishment, and wagged their swords, and pointed and shouted, “Tell the king! Daedalus and Icarus are...are...flying away!”

By dipping first one wing, then the other, Icarus found that he could turn to the left and the right. The wind tugged at his hair. His legs trailed out behind him. He saw the fields and streams as he had never seen them before!

Then they were out over the sea. The sea gulls pecked at him angrily, so Icarus flew higher, where they could not reach him.

He copied their shrill cry and taunted them: "You can't catch me!"

"Now remember, don't fly too high!" called Daedalus, but his words were drowned by the screaming of the gulls.

I'm the first boy ever to fly! I'm making history! I shall be famous! thought Icarus, as he flew up and up, higher and higher.

At last Icarus was looking the sun itself in the face. "Think you're the highest thing in the sky, do you?" he jeered. "I can fly just as high as you! Higher, even!" He did not notice the drops of sweat on his forehead: He was so determined to outfly the sun.

Soon its vast heat beat on his face and on his back and on the great wings stuck on with wax. The wax softened. The wax trickled. The wax dripped. One feather came unstuck. Then a plume of feathers fluttered slowly down.

Icarus stopped flapping his wings. His father's words came back to him clearly now: "*Don't fly too close to the sun!*"

With a great sucking noise, the wax on his shoulders came unstuck. Icarus tried to catch hold of the wings, but they just folded up in his hands. He plunged down, his two fists full of feathers—down and down and down.

The clouds did not stop his fall.

The sea gulls did not catch him in their beaks.

His own father could only watch as Icarus hurtled head first into the glittering sea and sank deep down among the sharks and eels and squid. And all that was left of proud Icarus was a litter of waxy feathers floating on the sea.

DAEDALUS and ICARUS

Concept Connections

Linking the Selection

Think about the following questions, and then record your responses in the Response Journal section of your Writer's Notebook.

- Why was Icarus less eager than Daedalus to take the risk of escaping?
- What was the consequence of Icarus ignoring his father's advice about flying too near the sun?

Exploring Concept Vocabulary

The concept word for this lesson is ***judgment.*** If you don't know what this word means, look it up in a dictionary. Answer these questions.

- What resources help you form a ***judgment*** about a risk you might take?
- Why does Daedalus make the ***judgment*** that trying to fly is a risk worth taking?

In the Vocabulary section of your Writer's Notebook, write a sentence that includes the word ***judgment*** as well as one of the selection vocabulary words.

Expanding the Concept

Think about the risks that were taken in the selections throughout this unit. Which risks had more positive outcomes than others? What conclusions can you draw about risks and consequences based on these outcomes? Try to use the word ***judgment*** in your discussion of the unit selections. Add new ideas about risks and consequences to the Concept/Question Board.

Meet the Author

Geraldine McCaughrean After Geraldine McCaughrean struggled with several unsuccessful and unpublished novels, she found that her true talent was in writing for children. In her retelling of both *The Odyssey* and *Greek Myths* she uses humor to create interest and excitement in age-old stories. McCaughrean has also translated several Japanese classics including *The Cherry Tree* and *Over the Deep Blue Sea*.

Meet the Illustrator

Emma Chichester Clark was born in London, England. She draws the eyes of most of her characters in a very distinctive way—as circles with pupil dots. This gives the character a childlike, curiously expressive appearance. Many of Emma Chichester Clark's books, such as *Tea At Aunt Agatha's*, show characters wearing wide-brimmed hats. Expressive eyes and wide-brimmed hats are the trademarks of Emma Chichester Clark.

UNIT 2 Dollars and Sense

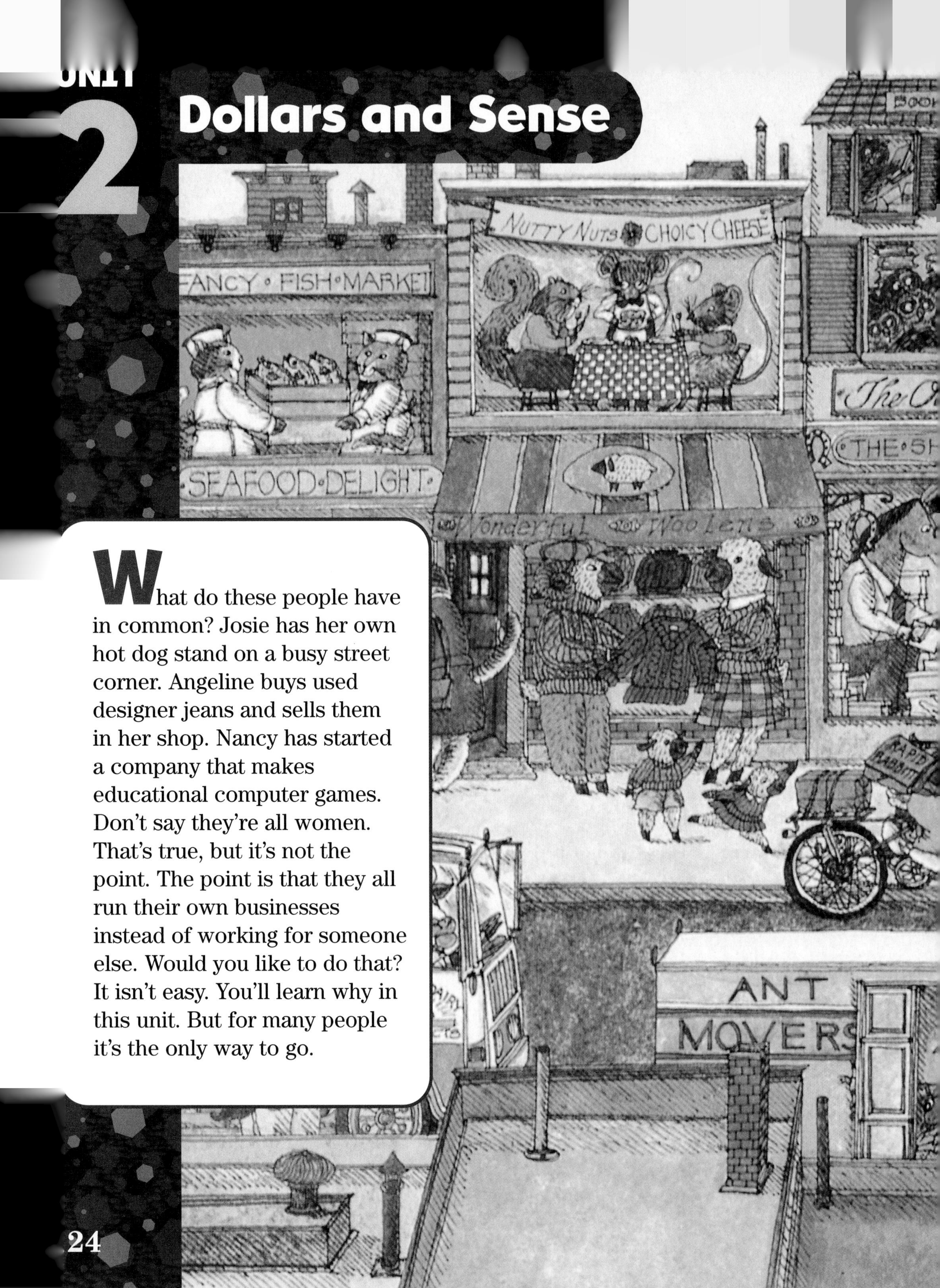

What do these people have in common? Josie has her own hot dog stand on a busy street corner. Angeline buys used designer jeans and sells them in her shop. Nancy has started a company that makes educational computer games. Don't say they're all women. That's true, but it's not the point. The point is that they all run their own businesses instead of working for someone else. Would you like to do that? It isn't easy. You'll learn why in this unit. But for many people it's the only way to go.

TORE
RAPID
RABBITT
MESSENGER SERVICE
POULTRY
HONEY & SWEET
SHOP
THE SPIDERS WEB
WEAVING
WEB-WOVEN
GIFTS
BUSY BEE
MOLE
MANHOLE
INC.
MOLES
WORKING
ANT
MOVERS
N
E
S
W

Focus Questions **Have you ever thought about starting your own business? What does it take to start a business?**

Starting a BUSINESS

by Arlene Erlbach

Good planners get ideas here...

Going into business means making lots of decisions and having a business plan. Successful entrepreneurs take time to plan their business before they start. They ask themselves many questions. You can answer questions about your business in a business journal or notebook.

Start by thinking about your business goals. Do you want a short term business that earns money for a specific item, like a new bike, musical instrument, or pet? Do you want an ongoing business that brings in steady money? Or maybe you'd like to only run your business during school vacations.

You'll also need to think about how much time you'll be able to spend on your business. Be realistic. If you already are expected to do lots of chores at home, you won't have as much time to devote to your business as a kid who has few family obligations. Ditto if you take lots of lessons or have the hardest teacher at school this year.

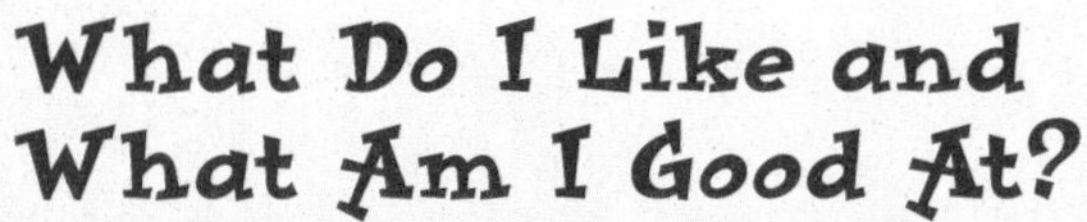

What Do I Like and What Am I Good At?

Most important, your business should be something you think is fun and something that's easy for you to do. To help you decide what kind of business to try, make a chart like the one below. Write down what you like to do and what you're good at. Then jot down businesses related to your likes and talents.

...and write them down here.

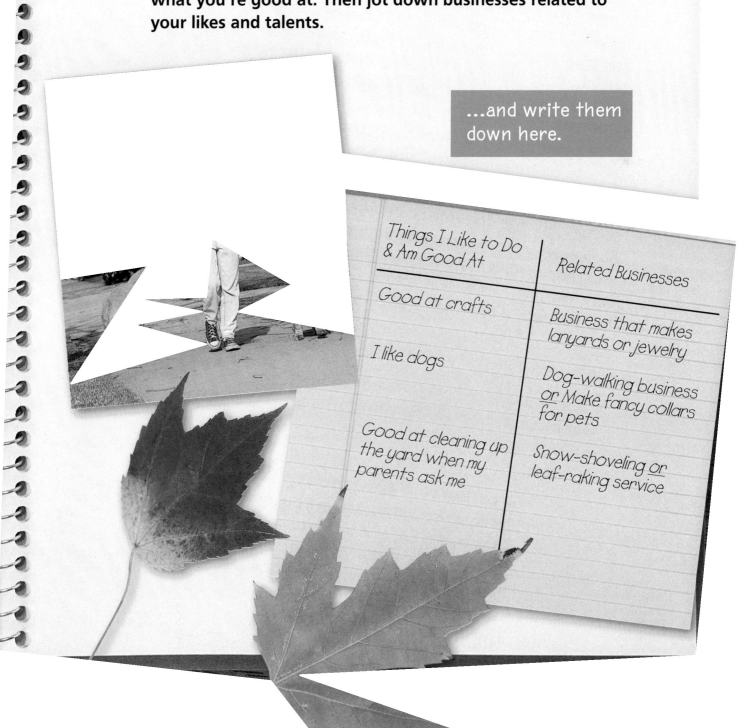

Things I Like to Do & Am Good At	Related Businesses
Good at crafts	Business that makes lanyards or jewelry
I like dogs	Dog-walking business or Make fancy collars for pets
Good at cleaning up the yard when my parents ask me	Snow-shoveling or leaf-raking service

Your manufacturing business could be making lanyards (also known as friendship bracelets).

Some businesses are <u>service</u> businesses. Others are manufacturing businesses. Service businesses provide care, maintenance, or repair to customers—such as dog walking, yard cleaning, or lawn mowing. Customers pay service businesses to do things they themselves don't have the time or desire to do. Most kids have service businesses, because they cost less to run than manufacturing businesses, and they are easier to start.

Manufacturing businesses make and sell products, such as jewelry, dog collars, or lanyards. Manufacturing businesses usually cost more than service businesses, and they require more preparation, but they can be very profitable as well as creative. Manufacturing businesses are especially good for artistic people.

What Is the Business Market?

Would enough customers need what your business offers? This is something very important to think about before you start.

Let's look back at your list. A snow shoveling business sounds great—if you live where it snows a lot, and if there are houses around you. But if you live in a neighborhood of condominiums or apartments, you might not get much business. The management for these buildings has probably made other arrangements for snow removal.

Is there another service you could offer in your community? In a neighborhood with lots of apartment buildings and condominiums, there may be a lot of older people. Maybe some of these people would like you to pick up their groceries, newspapers, or dry cleaning for them when the weather is cold and snowy. They may even need your services in good weather.

When you ask yourself these questions, you are analyzing the business market for an area. You are thinking about the people in that area, finding a need they have, and filling that need. Keeping your market in mind is a great start for brainstorming business ideas. Just follow these steps:

1. Think about items or services that might be needed in your neighborhood.
2. Think of a business that already exists in the area. Could you perform the same service, or provide a similar product, better or at a lower price?
3. Ask your family, neighbors, and friends what business they think is needed.
4. Make a list of the results, then ask yourself if the businesses are activities you would enjoy and be good at doing.

Businesses Needed in My Neighborhood	Would I Like To Do It?
Dog clean up	No!
Delivery service	Yes—but I'll need to buy a wagon.
Birthday party helper	Yes—I love birthday parties. Won't need to buy a wagon.

What do you like to do? Be honest!

Starting a BUSINESS

Concept Connections

Linking the Selection

Writer's Notebook

Think about the following questions, and then record your responses in the Response Journal section of your Writer's Notebook.

- What are some things to consider when creating a business plan?
- What is the most important thing to consider when starting a business?
- What is the difference between a manufacturing business and a service business?

Exploring Concept Vocabulary

The concept word for this lesson is ***market.*** If you don't know what this word means, look it up in a dictionary. Answer these questions.

- How does a ***market*** analysis let an entrepreneur know whether his or her business is likely to succeed?
- Why is the ***market*** important to a business?

In the Vocabulary section of your Writer's Notebook, write a sentence that includes the word ***market*** as well as one of the selection vocabulary words.

Expanding the Concept

Think about the ideas presented in "Starting a Business." Why do you think some people choose to start their own businesses instead of going to work for someone else? Try to use the word ***market*** in your discussion. Add new ideas about business to the Concept/Question Board.

Meet the Author

Arlene Erlbach has always loved to write. Mrs. Erlbach said, "When I was in grade school I'd make up stories about children while I lay in bed." In addition to being an author, Mrs. Erlbach is an elementary school teacher and is in charge of the school's Young Authors program. Mrs. Erlbach says she gets ideas for her writing "from my childhood, my son's experiences, the news, and the kids at the school where I teach."

Focus Questions What makes a good business partner? Why are some people better than others at spotting business opportunities?

Henry Wells and William G. Fargo

by Edward F. Dolan, Jr.

There is an odd fact about two of the most important men in California history. Neither ever lived in the state. Yet they gave California a giant company of stagecoaches, freight wagons, banking offices, and mail deliveries. The two men were Henry Wells and William G. Fargo, the founders of Wells Fargo & Company.

Henry Wells

Born December 12, 1805, Henry Wells was raised at Thetford, a small Vermont town. As a young man, he moved to New York State and went to work for Harnden's Express. In keeping with the word *express*—which means "rapid conveyance"—the company was in the business of making deliveries as swiftly as possible. It delivered all kinds of things, from letters and packages to merchandise and money.

Harnden's was just one of many such companies. They were all a great help to businesses and families in the time before today's systems of rapid communication and transportation came into being.

The slender Wells began as one of Harnden's deliverymen. He proved so good at his job that he was promoted to positions of greater responsibility. He also proved to be an ambitious man who wanted to be in business for himself. And so, in 1842, he formed his own express company with two friends. Close on its heels came a second firm, which he called Wells & Company. A third firm took shape in 1850—the American Express Company, today a giant operation doing business throughout the world.

By now, Wells was forty-five years old and a wealthy man. And, by now, he and William G. Fargo had been close friends for eight years.

William G. Fargo

William George Fargo was thirteen years younger than Wells. The date of his birth was May 20, 1818. His birthplace was the city of Albany, New York. After working as a railroad conductor, he took a job as an express company deliveryman. He went to work for Wells in 1842 when Wells formed his first company.

Fargo was a fine employee. His deliveries were very swift because he was an excellent horseman. He became such a valued worker that Wells made him a partner when Wells & Company was formed. Fargo became a high-ranking executive with American Express when that company took shape.

By 1852, the two friends were important businessmen in the East. They began to look to the West. Because of the gold rush that had started in 1848, northern California had become one of the busiest regions in the nation. Its many mining towns were all in need of food and supplies. They were being served by a number of express companies, some large and some small. But the region was so busy that the two men were certain it could use another. They decided that they must establish a company in the new state. On May 18, 1852, Wells Fargo & Company was established.

The California Visit

The company's main office was located in New York City. There, Wells and Fargo laid plans for their new venture.

First, they decided that the company would build offices in the many mining towns now dotting the Sierra Mountains. Then it would purchase gold from the miners, ship it down to San Francisco, and send it to New York. The company would make a profit by buying the gold for slightly less than it was worth in the East and then selling it or using it to make investments when it reached New York. Next, the company would provide a stagecoach service for travelers going to and from the gold fields. Finally, it would ship all types of needed goods from the East to San Francisco.

Two of the firm's top employees traveled to San Francisco in the spring of 1852. There, they opened the first Wells Fargo office in California. Henry Wells followed them a few weeks later. He wanted to visit

the Sierra mining towns so that he could learn firsthand the problems that working among them might bring. His trek into the mountains netted him a number of fine ideas for the company. One of the first had to do with mail from home for the miners.

Wells learned that nearly all of the miners had come west alone, leaving their families safe at home. Their hope had been to "strike it rich" fast and return to give their loved ones a better life. Now they yearned for news of family and friends. But mail delivery was a problem because the miners were constantly on the move. They were always moving to new diggings when the earth failed to reveal its hidden wealth. They were often impossible for the U.S. Postal Service to find.

Wells decided that his company would take on an extra job. It would start a mail service. The service would carry letters for a slightly higher fee than the Postal Service charged. He was sure no one would mind the fee because of a plan that had come to mind. It was a plan to make the miners easy to find and thus insure that their mail reached them.

The plan called for a miner to leave his name at the local Wells Fargo office whenever he came into a new town. The name would be placed on a card that would be sent to the San Francisco office. Then, when mail arrived in San Francisco, the employees there would look up the miner's latest card and forward the letter to its proper destination. The system worked beautifully. It was used by countless families everywhere.

Wells soon reached another decision. He knew that the offices in the mining towns would need rugged safes to hold the gold dust purchased by the company. There was no other way to protect the gold before it was shipped off to the East. Now he decided that the offices would have to be more than buildings with safes in them. They would have to be actual banks.

He knew that not all miners wanted to sell their gold to the company. Some planned to take all or a portion of their dust home for everyone to see. Until then, they needed a place where it could be safely stored. Wells said that each company office would hold the gold dust for them, just as banks held money for their customers. The company would charge a small monthly fee for this service.

The system worked this way: A miner could store his dust in any Wells Fargo office. In return, he was given a slip of paper with the exact amount of the deposit written on it. He could then hand the slip in at any Wells Fargo office at any time and receive a like amount in gold. The company promised that it would be completely responsible for the deposit. If the gold were misplaced or stolen, Wells Fargo would make good the loss. The system proved so popular that the company was soon providing all types of banking services.

Stolen Gold!

Those two words haunted Wells throughout his trip and brought him to yet another decision. The company planned to have its offices place its gold in boxes that would be shipped down to San Francisco aboard stagecoaches and wagons. For much of the time, the shipments would be moving along wilderness trails. Those trails would make fine places for robberies.

Wells had good reason to fear robberies. The gold rush had attracted all types of men from over the world—from the very finest to the very worst. Among the latter were cutthroats, burglars, shady gamblers, and bandits. They had already robbed and cheated miners everywhere. The rich gold shipments were bound to be their next prey.

Wells set down two rules concerning the robberies that were sure to come. First, since much of the gold was to be shipped aboard stagecoaches, he issued orders to his drivers. If they were held up by bandits while carrying passengers, they were not to put up a fight. They were to hand over their "treasure boxes" without a word. This would protect the passengers. The passengers must always know that they were safe when traveling with Wells Fargo.

Second, no matter how small the amount taken, the company was to spare no expense in tracking down the robbers. By letting highwaymen know that they would pay dearly for their crimes, Wells hoped to discourage at least some robbery attempts.

Throughout its history, Wells Fargo never strayed from these rules. They made the company one of the most trusted firms of the day.

FIVE HUNDRED DOLLARS
REWARD!
WELLS, FARGO & CO.
WILL PAY
FIVE HUNDRED DOLLARS,
For the arrest and conviction of the robber who stopped the Quincy Stage and demanded the Treasury Box, on Tuesday afternoon, August 17th, near the old Live Yankee Ranch, about 17 miles above Oroville. By order of
J. J. VALENTINE, Gen'l Supt.
RIDEOUT, SMITH & CO., Agents.
Oroville, August 18, 1875.

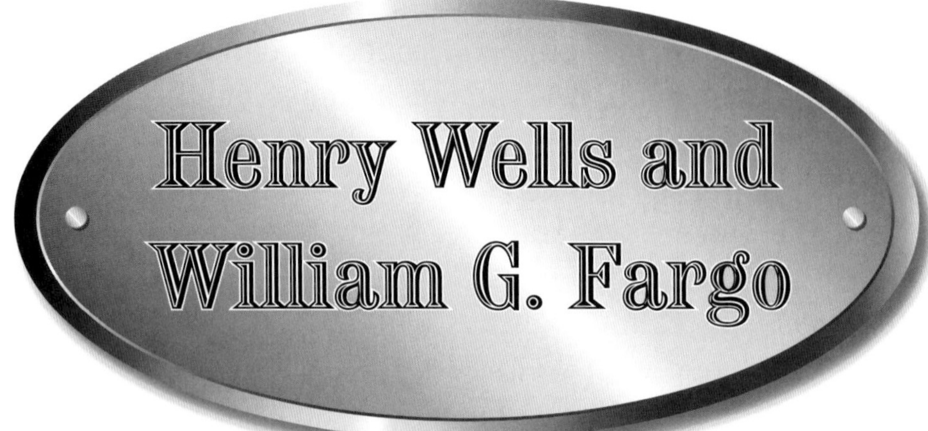

Concept Connections

Linking the Selection

Think about the following questions, and then record your responses in the Response Journal section of your Writer's Notebook.

- Why did Wells and Fargo decide to start a business in California?
- How did Wells and Fargo build trust with their customers?
- Why did Henry Wells think customers would be willing to pay for the mail and banking services offered by Wells Fargo?

Exploring Concept Vocabulary

The concept word for this lesson is ***opportunity.*** If you don't know what this word means, look it up in a dictionary. Answer these questions.

- What ***opportunity*** did the gold rush offer Wells and Fargo?
- How did Wells and Fargo take advantage of that ***opportunity?***

In the Vocabulary section of your Writer's Notebook, write a sentence that includes the word ***opportunity*** as well as one of the selection vocabulary words.

Expanding the Concept

Consider what you read about market analysis in "Starting a Business." How did Henry Wells and William Fargo analyze their market? What effect did this have on their business? Try to use the word ***opportunity*** in your discussion. Add new ideas about business to the Concept/Question Board.

Meet the Author

Edward F. Dolan, Jr. began writing when he was twelve. By the time he was sixteen years old, he had published his first story. Now he has written over seventy books! Many of his books are about history, social studies, the environment, health, and law. He has also written about explorers, sports, and mysteries of nature, such as the Bermuda Triangle.

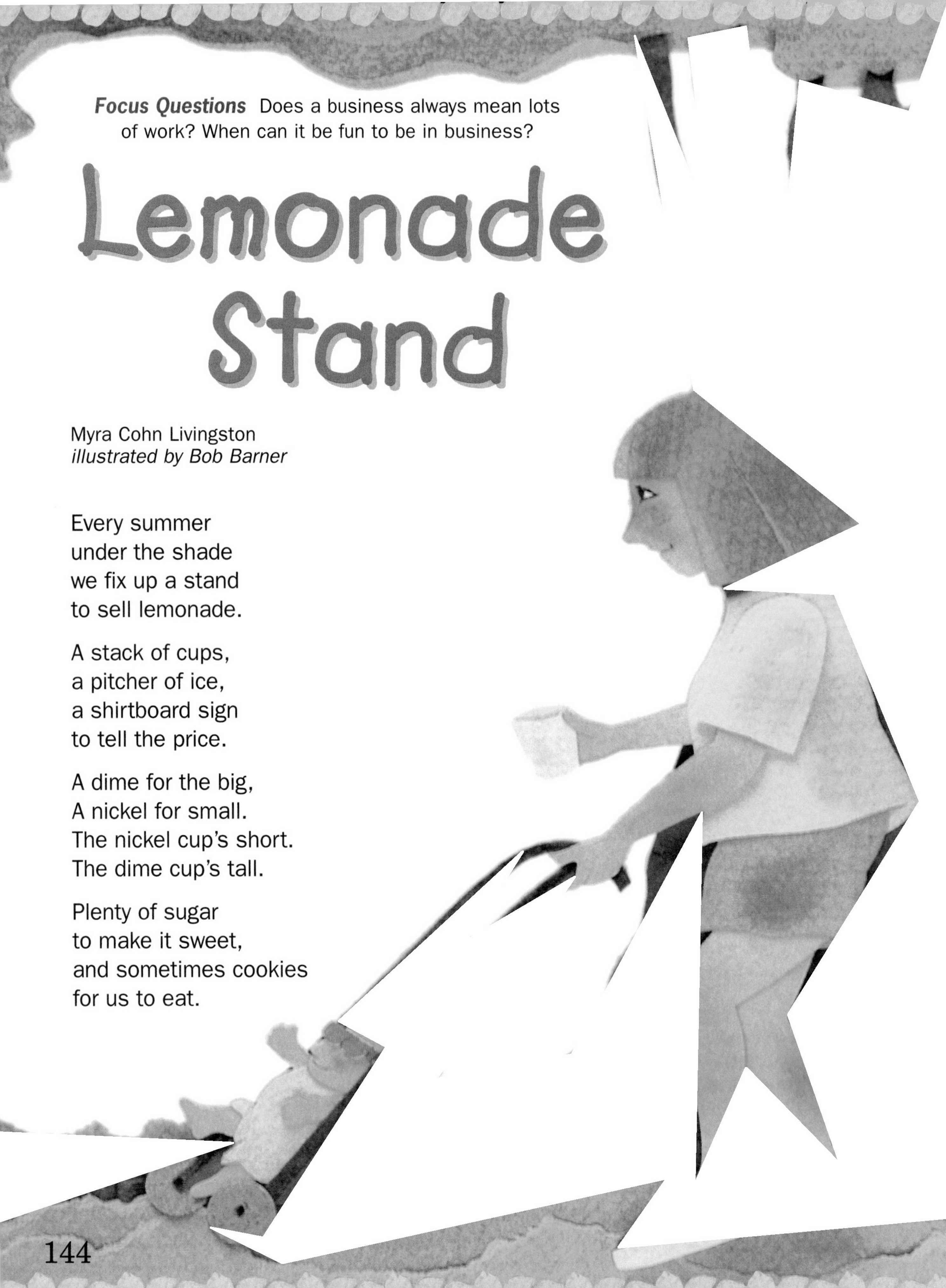

Focus Questions Does a business always mean lots of work? When can it be fun to be in business?

Lemonade Stand

Myra Cohn Livingston
illustrated by Bob Barner

Every summer
under the shade
we fix up a stand
to sell lemonade.

A stack of cups,
a pitcher of ice,
a shirtboard sign
to tell the price.

A dime for the big,
A nickel for small.
The nickel cup's short.
The dime cup's tall.

Plenty of sugar
to make it sweet,
and sometimes cookies
for us to eat.

But when the sun
moves into the shade
it gets too hot
to sell lemonade.

Nobody stops
so we put things away
and drink what's left
and start to play.

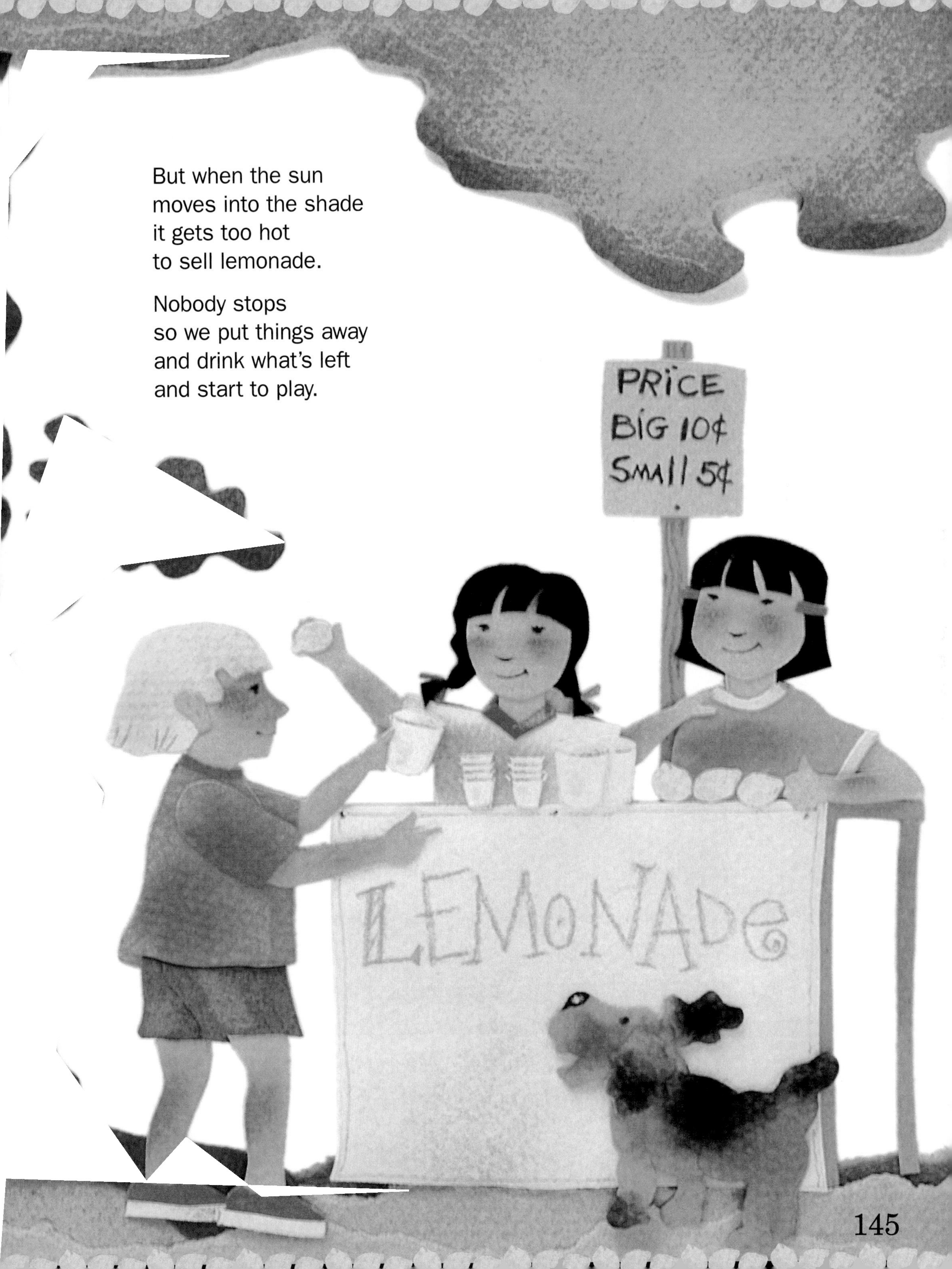

Focus Questions What makes a business successful? Does everyone have what it takes to run a business?

Elias Sifuentes

Restaurateur

from ***All in a Day's Work: Twelve Americans Talk About Their Jobs***

by Neil Johnson

I do it all. I open the restaurant in the morning and I close it up at the end of each day. From the minute that I open the door I do everything that has to be done until I close the door. There are a thousand things that have to be done in a restaurant.

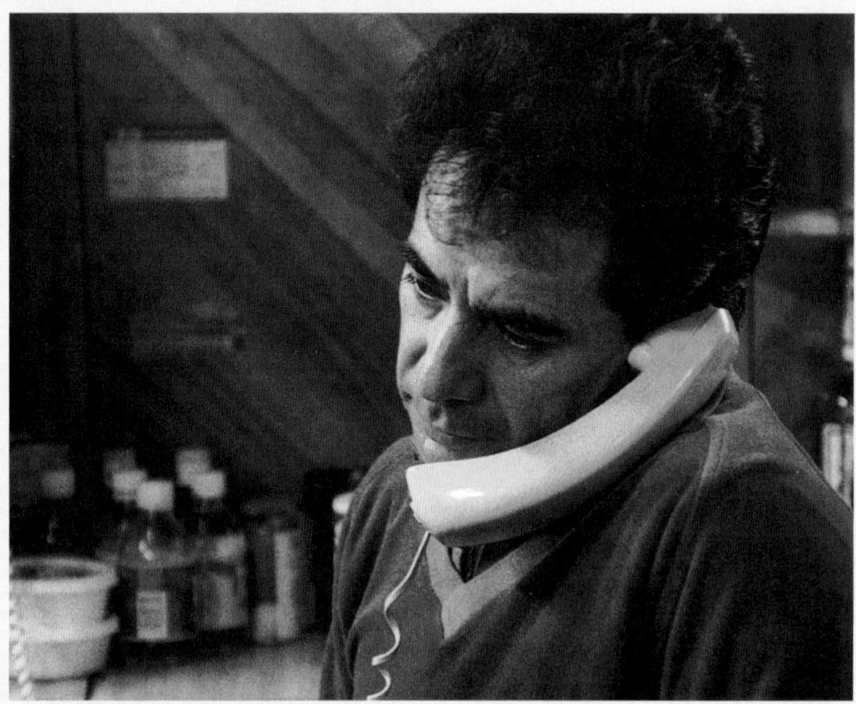

Elias Sifuentes has run a Mexican restaurant for almost ten years. After having other jobs and working part-time in Mexican restaurants for many years, he and a friend decided to start their own.

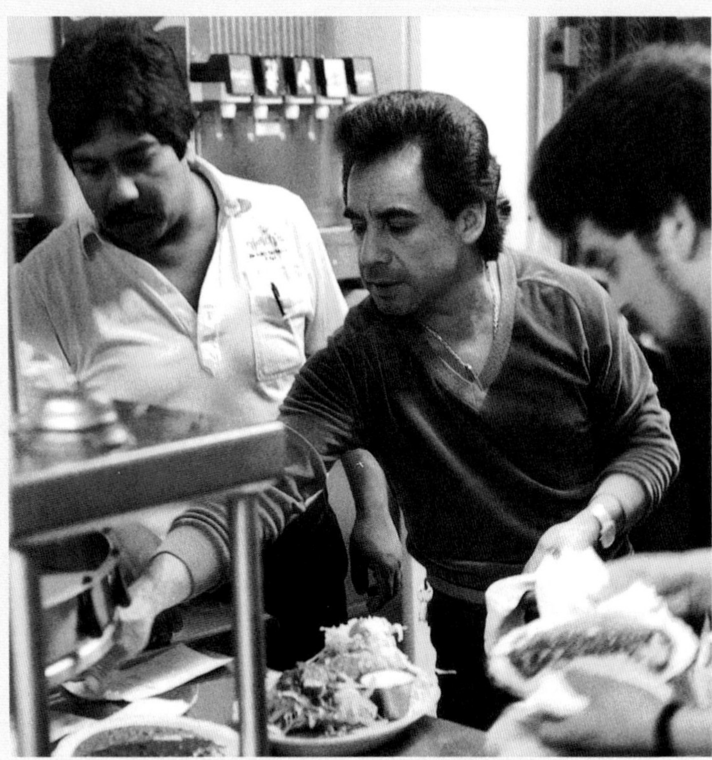

I used to work at a General Electric factory. I was a punch-press operator. I was making good money, but working there frustrated me because I like to work with people, talk to people. And there, there was nobody to talk to. The only time I got together with others was during lunch or during meetings. And I said to myself, "I like the money. I like the benefits. But this is not what I want to do all my life."

I've worked part-time in Mexican restaurants for most of my life being a waiter, cook, dishwasher. Not because I was hungry for money, but because I told myself, "Someday I'm going to do something for myself and I want to learn the whole trade." While I was at GE, the restaurant where I was working part-time was closed down. So my partner and I got together, and I said, "What are you going to do?" He said, "I don't know." I said, "Let's get a place of our own! I'll do the cooking. You be the front man. What else do we need?" He liked the idea, and so we put the idea to work, and it works.

We started from scratch. In the beginning, we didn't get a paycheck. The only money we got was to buy groceries. My partner was kind of frustrated. Whatever we were making was going to pay our bills. I told him, "That's what it is. That's the way it goes. I like to have a payday, but we just can't do it right now." When we expanded the place, we got more customers, more business. We felt better because it finally started to pay off. We were very pleased. We saw more traffic and we started putting money in our pockets. We felt better. One hundred percent. The success has continued ever since.

In the beginning I was kind of shaky and afraid because I knew very little spoken English. I could more or less write in English. And to learn all the trade—that's a big step. In Mexico I took a year of business administration in college, so I had my year's training. It's not a whole lot, but it helped me when I needed it. I learned about supervising, expenses, administration. How to buy, how to spend, how to control, all these kinds of things.

But now I am learning on the job. I believe you learn a lot better when you exercise what you are doing. To me, I have no other choice but to learn—be forced to learn to do the job. Until now, I have been fortunate to do a good job. There are a good number of people depending on me, and I haven't let them down yet. My twenty-eight employees depend on me to be smart enough to continue the business for all of us—so all of us can make a good living. A lot of places come and go. Even big companies with big money and good managers—they are gone. Fortunately we have managed to stay.

To stay in business, I have to be aggressive. I have to fight. If I go by another Mexican restaurant and I see a line of people, I say to myself, "They are doing something right." If I go to my place and see nobody there, I say, "I am doing something wrong." So then I have to do something different. I must be more conscious of my customers and give them more attention. That's what I do best—pay attention to my customers. Talk to them. Meet them. Let them know who I am.

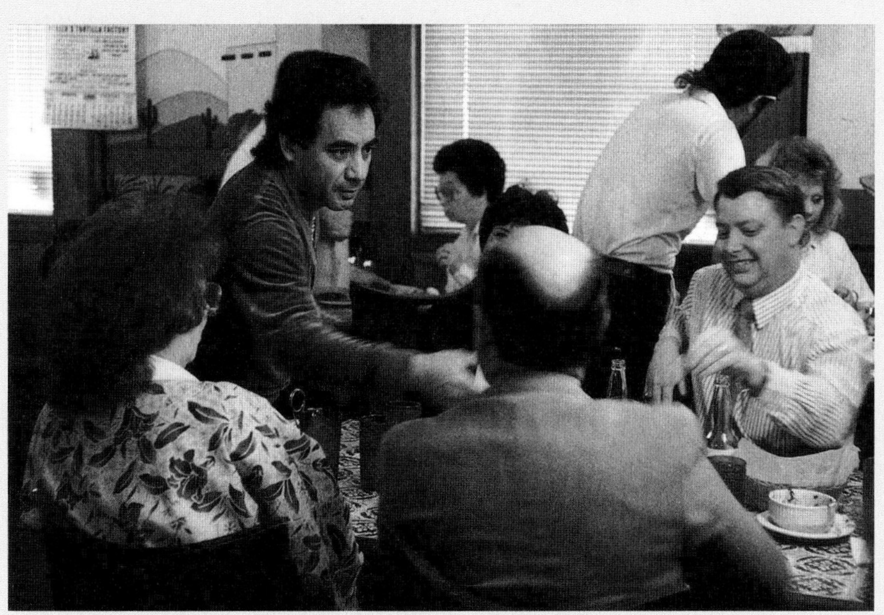

When customers complain, they keep me more aware. They open my eyes. I don't mind having a complaint once in a while. Nobody likes to have those, but if I do, I want to be sure that the same customer doesn't have the same complaint twice. I feel bad when a customer comes and tells me that he waited too long and never got service. I feel bad when a customer comes to tell me that a waiter has been rude. When a customer tells me that the food doesn't have enough seasoning, I feel bad. But I face the customer. It doesn't matter what happens, they always come to me. They say they want to see me. I say, "Fine, no problem." I take all kinds of complaints, which can get me down a lot.

I usually come to work at eight o'clock in the morning. Normally, I stay until two o'clock in the afternoon, doing the supervising, the purchasing, seeing the salesmen, seeing the advertisers. Then I go to my house to take a shower, and I come back at five o'clock. I stay until closing time at ten o'clock. We usually leave the place at eleven or twelve, after cleaning up.

When customers walk in my door, I receive them in the friendliest way I can. I see to it that they get service properly from my busboy, from my waitress, even from myself. If anything takes longer than it's supposed to, that is what I am there for—to take care of that kind of problem. Afterward, when the customer is finished, I come to the table again—maybe two, three more times. "Is everything OK? Everything satisfactory?" That's my job in the front of the restaurant. Then back in the kitchen, I see that everything comes out properly. I do that myself every morning. I taste everything, believe me! Chips, hot sauce, dressing, beans, Spanish rice, cheese sauce, you name it. I taste everything to see it is prepared right, before we open the doors. That keeps me going through lunchtime. Sometimes we stay so busy that I forget to sit down and have a meal.

A man who had come up from Mexico asked me the other day about opening a restaurant. He said to me, "If you did it, I can do it. " I said, "Yes, you can do it." Then he said, "You tell me how." I said, "Wait a minute. You just told me you can do it. You don't need my advice. You can do it! But if you don't have your heart in it, forget it."

Elias Sifuentes

Restaurateur

Concept Connections

Linking the Selection

Think about the following questions, and then record your responses in the Response Journal section of your Writer's Notebook.

- What experiences and skills did Elias Sifuentes have that helped him run his restaurant?
- How does Elias Sifuentes keep a high quality of food and service at his restaurant?

Exploring Concept Vocabulary

The concept word for this lesson is ***dedicated.*** If you don't know what this word means, look it up in a dictionary. Answer these questions.

- How does Elias Sifuentes show that he is ***dedicated*** to providing good service?
- Why do you think some people, like Elias Sifuentes, are ***dedicated*** to their work?

In the Vocabulary section of your Writer's Notebook, write a sentence that includes the word ***dedicated*** as well as one of the selection vocabulary words.

Expanding the Concept

Compare the businesses started by Wells and Fargo with Elias Sifuentes's business. Consider the customers as well as the services provided. Try to use the word ***dedicated*** in your discussion of the businesses. Add new ideas about business to the Concept/Question Board.

Meet the Author and Photographer

Neil Johnson lives in Shreveport, Louisiana. His articles and photographs have appeared in magazines and newspapers such as *Time, USA Today,* and *Louisiana Life.*

When Mr. Johnson decided to write about people at work, he looked for people who were enthusiastic, willing to talk, and didn't mind having their pictures taken. Elias Sifuentes fit all those things and more.

About photography, Mr. Johnson says, *"Photography . . . allows us to see things that cannot be put into words."*

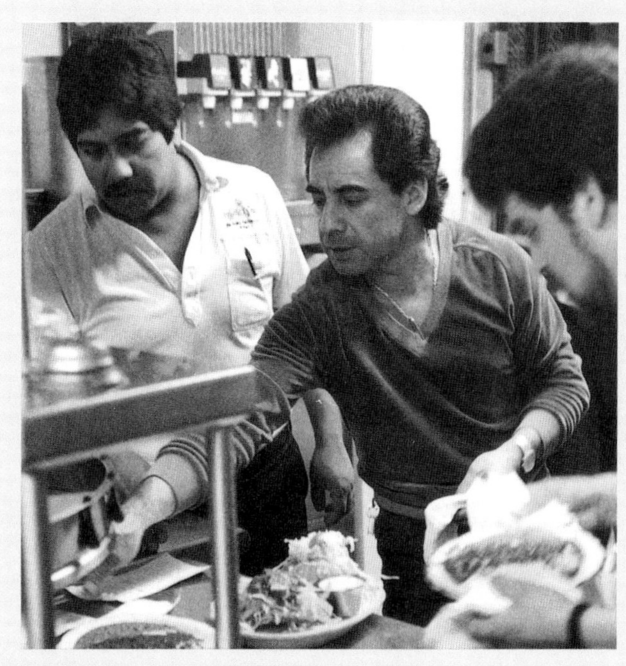

Dollars and Sense

Buffalo Newsboy. 1853. **Thomas LeClear.** Oil on canvas. 24 × 20 in. Albright-Knox Art Gallery, Buffalo, New York.

Poultry shop trade sign. Date unknown. Marble relief. Museo Ostiense, Ostia, Italy.

Incantation. 1946. **Charles Sheeler.** Oil on canvas. 24 × 20 in. The Brooklyn Museum, Brooklyn, New York.

Market Scene. Mid-20th century. **Rodrigue Mervilus.** Oil on canvas. Private Collection.

Focus Questions Are profits always the most important thing to a business? What business can you think of that could help your community?

Food from the 'Hood

A Garden of Hope

by Marlene Targ Brill

Sometimes horrible events turn into the most hopeful dreams. That's what happened to students at Crenshaw High School in South Central Los Angeles, California. In May 1992, riots destroyed the neighborhood surrounding their school. Businesses went up in flames. Hundreds of shopkeepers were left with nothing but ashes. Families, some too poor to afford gas money, were forced to travel from the city to the suburbs just to buy food.

Students in Tammy Bird's biology class felt awful. "This is where we all grew up," said Carlos Lopez. "The corner store in my neighborhood burned down. That was where we hung out."

Carlos and his classmates refused to let riots wreck their lives. They talked about different ways to help rebuild their community. Nothing seemed quite right. Then Ms. Bird remembered the weed-infested patch behind the football field. Perhaps the school would give them the quarter-acre plot of land for a garden. As a bonus, Ms. Bird offered extra credit to attract student gardeners.

Carlos and 38 of Ms. Bird's other students decided that planting was an important step toward restoring their neighborhood. The garden would be one green spot among the ashes. With Los Angeles's warm, sunny climate, crops could grow year round. Everyone agreed that their harvests should go to people unable to buy food.

Within weeks, the teenagers cleared the overgrown lot and planted seeds for collard greens, squash, tomatoes, and herbs. They grew vegetables organically, without chemicals that might hurt their bodies or the environment. Each day, they took turns watering and weeding the shoots during free time and before and after school. Adults from outside the community worked with the students as part of the city's overall plan to rebuild the riot-torn downtown.

The teenagers soon realized the community needed more than food to survive. It needed shops where people could easily buy everyday goods. Most of the burned-out stores had owners who lived outside the neighborhood. The money they made left South Central Los Angeles at the end of the workday. Students believed their community needed new business owners who were willing to put money back into the burned-out community. One adult volunteer, Melinda McMullen, suggested that the garden become that kind of business.

"We all wanted to give something back to the community, and this was a way to do it," Carlos remembered.

Melinda helped the students organize their business. First, they hunted for an office to house the company. They discovered an unused rabbit room behind the animal science lab and gave it a good scrubbing. Except for a few escaped rats eating electric wires, the room seemed perfect.

Then students met at lunchtime and after school to hammer out what the company would be like. Each volunteer became a student owner with an equal voice in making decisions. After several meetings, the owners agreed that the number-one reason for their business was to better their community. They wanted to prove that businesses could be kind and still make money, too. They pledged to create jobs for more teenagers. And they promised to use skills they learned from the garden to better the future for themselves and those around them.

Student owners named the company in much the same way as they planned—with respect for everyone's ideas. First, they brainstormed what the name should say about the business. They wanted a name that told people about the company's products in a general way. For now, products included organic foods. Who knew what the future would bring?

Everyone insisted that the name reflect who they were as people. This was a student-owned company, so the name should be catchy and fun. Moreover, students came from the inner city and were proud to live there. They represented many cultures, especially African-Americans, Latinos, and Asian Americans. The right name would celebrate these different groups working and living together.

For several hours, owners shouted out whatever name seemed to fit. Ms. Bird wrote 72 choices on the blackboard. Some sounded hip, such as *Food from the 'Hood,* and others unusual, such as *Straight Out 'the Garden.* Then everyone voted until five names remained. Over the next two weeks, students tested the five names on friends in class, at home, and throughout the neighborhood. They talked with strangers of all races, ages, and occupations.

Food from the 'Hood won thumbs-up. The name told about the products, which were different foods. And the name said where the company and its owners were from—the *'hood,* which was short for "inner-city neighborhood."

The only missing piece was the many cultures behind the business. To represent the different races, student artist Ben Osborne drew a company logo with white and brown hands reaching toward sun-lit buildings. He painted the logo and snappy name in bright colors on a mural behind the garden.

"People usually smile or laugh when they hear our company name," said student founder Ivan Lopez. "But they never forget us."

Slowly, a small garden turned into the nation's first student-run natural food company. Food from the 'Hood harvested its first crop two months after forming a business. They gave all the vegetables to a neighborhood homeless shelter. “Giving food to the needy really brought out the holiday spirit in us,” said student owner Jaynell Grayson.

Now Melinda had another idea. The student owners proved they could grow a healthy garden and brighten the community. Why not sell some of the vegetables to raise money to help owners pay for college?

“We found the best way to give back to our community was to get a higher education,” remembered Jaynell.

“We all got hooked on gardening. Then we decided to make money off of it. Then the scholarship idea kicked in,” Carlos added.

In the summer of 1993, students took a supply of vegetables to the Santa Monica, California, farmer’s market. Excited customers swarmed around the Food from the ’Hood table like bees. Customers couldn’t buy fast enough. Within 30 minutes, the company sold $150 worth of vegetables. Student owners were amazed at their easy success.

Making enough money to build a scholarship fund proved more difficult, however. After one year in business, sales totaled only $600. Three graduating owners split the sum, which was a good start but not nearly enough to send anyone to college. “That hardly covered college book fees,” Ben Osborne said.

After summer break, student owners met again. This time they talked about finding another way to raise money. A customer at a farmer’s market suggested that they offer a factory-made product with the company’s name on it. The product could sell more widely in stores than at a local farmer’s market.

One student studied what buyers liked and disliked in new products. He found that people were more willing to try new salad dressings than other new products. “We thought, since we already grow lettuce, why not sell the topping?" Jaynell said.

Students experimented with salad dressing recipes in Ms. Bird's science class. They tasted different mixes of ingredients for the right balance. The dressing had to include plenty of basil and parsley because these were grown in their garden. Then students sent the formulas to outside food labs to test the ingredients. "Our community has a problem with heart disease, so we wanted a healthy, low-salt choice," Jaynell said.

After six months of testing mixtures, students agreed on a creamy Italian recipe. Ben designed a colorful label modeled after the garden mural. Then everyone voted on the name for their new line of dressing. The winner, Straight Out 'the Garden Creamy Italian Dressing, combined the runner-up company name with the dressing flavor.

Ms. Bird continued to supervise Food from the 'Hood at school. Melinda kept her ears open for different sources of money and aid. Other adult help came from unusual places.

Norris Bernstein, who ran the successful Bernstein Salad Dressings, read about Food from the 'Hood. After talking with student owners, Bernstein became hooked on their strong sense of pride and independence. He helped students connect with large chain stores that would sell their dressing.

Another surprise visitor was Prince Charles from England. Carlos heard that the prince loved organic gardening, and he was visiting California. So Carlos wrote the British consul and asked if the prince would like to see Food from the 'Hood. "It was just something to do, just to see if it would really happen, and it really did," Carlos said later. The prince not only accepted, but he also ate lunch in the garden and later donated a van to help transport vegetables, herbs, and flowers to farmer's markets.

The city gave Food from the 'Hood $50,000. Some of the money went to supply an office to house the growing company. Students selected carpeting, a large meeting table, and furniture for five work stations. They ordered a telephone, answering machine, and computers.

Most money went toward making the first batch of salad dressing. Food from the 'Hood hired businesses to print labels, manufacture large amounts of salad dressing, and distribute the finished product to stores. "We wanted to work with other companies from poorer areas of Los Angeles. We especially looked for businesses run by minorities," student owner Mark Sarria said.

Food from the 'Hood chose women-owned company Sweet Adelaide to make and bottle the dressing. Skid Row Access, staffed by former homeless people of color, decorated banners. And herbs and spices came from small vendors rather than larger grocery store suppliers.

Some of the most difficult problems involved working together. Student owners took months to create a plan for dividing money the company earned. Finally, everyone agreed to a point system. Each owner earned points for hours spent in the garden and office.

Food from the 'Hood stands for good grades and going to college. Therefore, student owners received points for grades and for helping others improve their schoolwork. Owners learn to take care of each other. They share tips about how to study, complete college forms, and take college exams. For many, Food from the 'Hood is like family.

Although an adult watches over the office full-time now, student owners run every other part of the business. They produce and sell vegetables and salad dressing. They keep records, train new workers, pay bills, and answer telephones. Most importantly, they grow the garden, the heart of the business.

Hard work has paid off. Food from the 'Hood has added another salad dressing, Straight Out 'the Garden No-Fat Honey Mustard. More than 2,000 grocery stores carry the two dressings in 25 states. By 1996, the company awarded student owners a total of $27,000 to fund college.

Teachers claim that students improve in reading, writing, public speaking, and math after joining Food from the 'Hood. Many student owners discover talents they never knew they had. Sandra Raymond hated to talk in class before selling dressing and answering the office telephone. Now she feels confident enough to go into business. Similarly, Ben Osborne intends to study art in college as a result of designing the logo, mural, and salad dressing label.

"We showed that a group of inner-city kids can and did make a difference. We learn to take responsibility for our actions, how to sort out what's important, and how to be leaders instead of followers," Terie Smith, student founder, said.

Food from the 'Hood has become so successful that other schools asked to copy the program. In 1996 a high school group from Ithaca, New York, began using the name on applesauce. "We met with them in Washington, D.C., to talk about their applesauce idea, and we were very impressed," Terie said. Now three flavors of Food from the 'Hood East's Straight Out 'the Orchard are sold in Ithaca and are headed for New York City and other areas. Schools in Chicago, Illinois; Hawaii; and Oakland, California, hope to sell products that will help put kids through school.

The real success, however, is the garden, the center of giving. Half the total crop goes to community groups. Student owners vote which organizations receive the food. The idea is to help a balance of African-American, Latino, and Asian groups that reflects the company's—and community's—population.

New students apply to Food from the 'Hood each year. About 40 percent work other jobs in addition to going to school, but find time to garden. After more than five years, the business is here to stay. A small group of inner-city teenagers have proven that anyone can achieve success if they try.

"What comes from that garden is hope," said Carlos. "From anything—even the riots—amazing things can grow."

STATEMENT OF
PURPOSE
1.CREATE JOBS.
FOOD FROM THE HOOD

Food from the 'Hood

A Garden of Hope

Concept Connections

Linking the Selection

Think about the following questions, and then record your responses in the Response Journal section of your Writer's Notebook.

- How did students turn their garden into a business?
- Why were so many people included in choosing a name for the students' business?
- How does participating in the business help these students do better in school?

Exploring Concept Vocabulary

The concept word for this lesson is ***goals.*** If you don't know what this word means, look it up in a dictionary. Answer these questions.

- What are some ***goals*** that many businesses might have in common?
- What was the first ***goal*** of the students' business?

In the Vocabulary section of your Writer's Notebook, write a sentence that includes the word ***goal*** as well as one of the selection vocabulary words.

Expanding the Concept

What needs do you see in your community that you and other students could help with? What kind of business would meet those needs? Try to use the word ***goals*** in your discussion. Add new ideas about business to the Concept/Question Board.

Meet the Author

Marlene Targ Brill was born in Chicago, Illinois. She loved books from a very young age. Her parents read constantly, and she remembers being jealous of her older brother who had a room filled with books and records.

Ms. Brill had an active imagination. A favorite pastime was sitting in the window, watching people pass by, and making up stories about where they were going and what they were doing.

Brill says she loves all kinds and aspects of writing, especially research. She says, *"I feel like an explorer, delving into old newspapers, tracking down historical documents, and locating famous and not-so-famous people to interview. To me, research is an endless treasure hunt with many pots of gold."*

Focus Questions How do people get their ideas for new businesses? What are some things to think about before starting a business?

BUSINESS IS LOOKING UP

Barbara Aiello and Jeffrey Shulman
illustrated by Diane Paterson

Renaldo Rodriguez, a visually impaired eleven-year-old, needs money to buy a special type of calculator for the blind. He decides he can earn the money by starting a business and shares his idea with his best friend, Jinx.

"Jinx!" I shouted when she answered the phone. I sure was excited about my business idea. "It's me! Renaldo. Renaldo Rodriguez!"

"Renaldo, you're the only Renaldo I know," Jinx said. "And you don't have to holler! I can hear you."

I explained the whole idea to her—"R.R. Stepcards" I called it. That was a pretty clever name, even I have to admit. I told her how I would make and sell cards for people who had stepfamilies: birthday cards, get well cards, Valentine cards—the list was endless!

"What do you think, Jinx? Am I going to be Woodburn's first millionaire?"

There was silence on the other end. I could tell Jinx was thinking about it. She always thinks about things before she gives her opinion. And she always thinks about what other people might think. "Opposing viewpoints," she calls them. Jinx does a lot of thinking.

"Well," she finally asked, "have you done any marketing research?"

"Marketing research?"

"Have you thought about your investment?"

"Investment?"

Jinx was on a roll. I felt doomed.

"Oh, how will you advertise?"

I felt it coming, but I couldn't stop it. "Advertise?" I said. "Just listen to me," I thought to myself, "Renaldo Rodriguez, the human echo!"

Research? Investment? Advertising? "Jinx," I said, "this is starting to sound like work! Explain this stuff to me."

I knew Jinx was excited. I could hear the excitement in her voice. "Look," she began, "marketing research is the first thing you do. You find out if someone else has already thought of your idea. You find out if there's such a thing as a stepcard. If there's not, then you can figure out your investment. That's how much money you want to spend to get the business started."

"Spend?" I said. "But I want to *make* money, Jinx."

"I know," Jinx said in her most patient voice. "But you can't get something for nothing. We will have to buy markers and paper, maybe even paints and stencils, too. That's our investment."

"*Our* investment? When did it become *our* investment?"

"Renaldo, this is an excellent idea," Jinx continued. "But there's a lot to do. You're going to need a partner." And I didn't even have the time to say "A partner?" before Jinx jumped in again. "Hmmmm . . . I do like the sound of it," she said. "Yes, 'R.R. and J.B. Stepcards.' I like the sound of it very much."

And you know what? So did I. With J.B. as my partner, I was more excited than ever—so excited that I couldn't get to sleep that night. I turned my pillow to the cold side a hundred times until I gave up trying to sleep. I got out my stylus and slate and started to write: "R.R. and J.B. Stepcards. For Your Favorite Stepfriend." There were stepfathers, stepmothers, stepbrothers, stepsisters, stepgrandmothers—the list went on and on. "For All Occasions." There were birthdays,

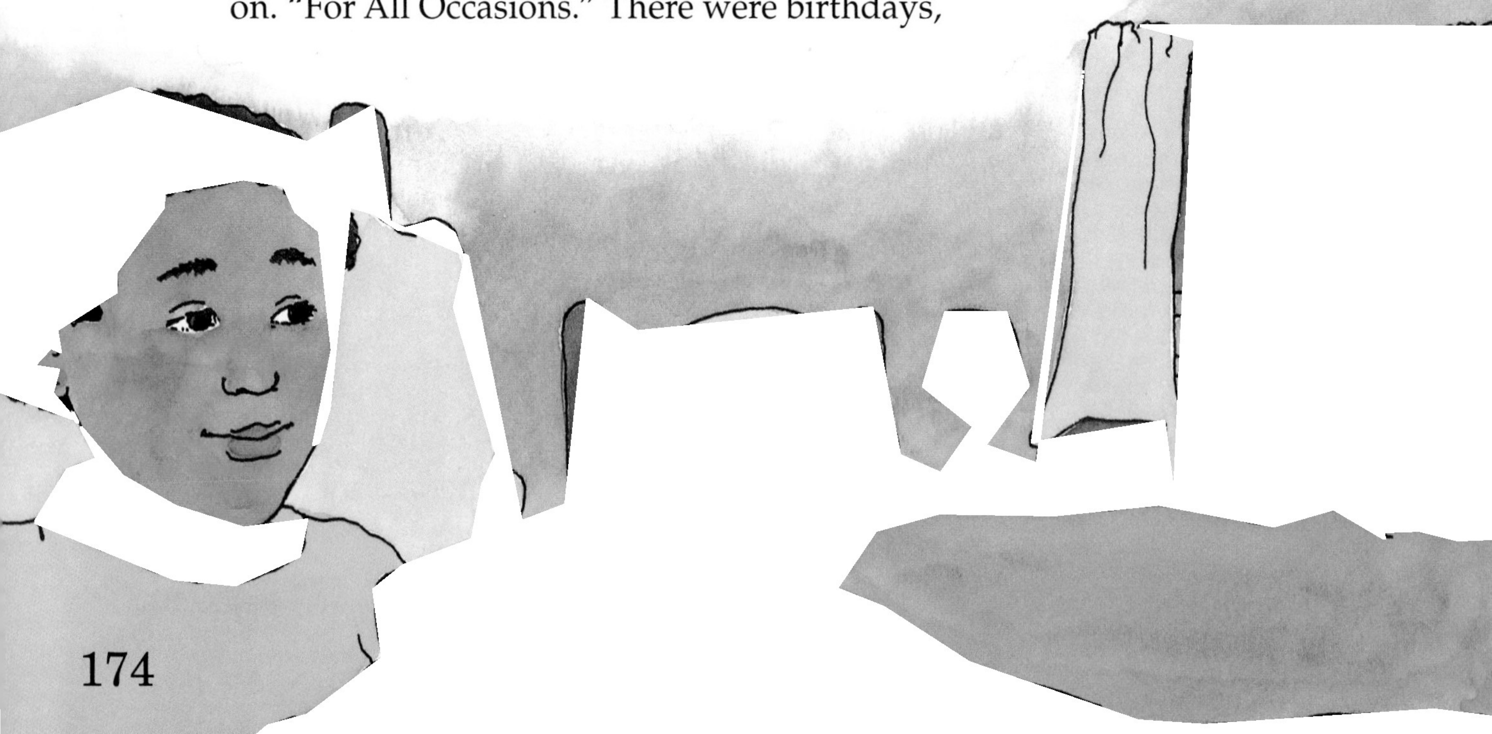

anniversaries, graduations, holidays—and so many more. I started counting our profits. I couldn't help it.

"Excuse me, Mr. Businessman," Josue said, hiding a big yawn. "Mom already came in here. She made me stop reading. We're supposed to be asleep, you know."

Josue was right. Mom doesn't let us read or write after lights out. But, you see, I don't have to sneak under the covers with a flashlight the way Josue does.

"I'm not reading," I told Josue. "This, my little brother, is marketing research—I think."

"It looks like reading to me. It's not fair. I ought to tell on you!" Josue climbed out of bed to get a better look. "Just what kind of business is this anyway?"

"None of *your* business," I said firmly. And I closed my slate. I wasn't taking any chances on someone stealing the business idea of the century, certainly not a nosy little brother. I turned my pillow over for the last time.

"Let's go to sleep."

The next day was Saturday, and with lots of kids from Woodburn, Jinx and I headed for the mall. We take turns delivering the "Woodburn Flyer" to the stores at the Woodburn Shopping Center. The "Flyer" is the free newspaper that tells about all the things happening at Woodburn. Then it's time for fun.

But this Saturday was different. Today, there were no video games, no french fries, no window-shopping. Today, we were all business.

I knew we were near Calloway's Cards and Gifts when I smelled the tempting aroma of cheese, tomato sauce, and special toppings. Polotti's Pizza Palace was just next door to the card store.

"I don't think I can do the marketing research on an empty stomach. How about a business lunch?" I was tapping my cane toward the sweet smell of Polotti's.

"Renaldo," Jinx said sternly, "we don't have much time."

"Okay. Okay," I said. "Give me your arm." Jinx was right. We really didn't have much time. "It will be faster for me to walk alongside you—and less temptation, too."

There must have been a thousand different kinds of cards in Calloway's, and each one was cornier or mushier than the last. One thing about those cards, though—they really cracked us up!

"Look at this one, Renaldo," Jinx said.

"To My Daughter and Her Husband on This Special Day," Jinx read. She described the card to me. "It's big," she said, passing it to me.

"It's almost the size of our spelling notebook," I said, feeling around the edges of the card.

"It has two pink hearts with bows on them. Two white doves are holding the ends of the ribbons in their mouths. It looks like the words *Happy Anniversary* are coming right out of their beaks," Jinx giggled.

I could feel the raised lines of the hearts, the bows, and the birds. "Yuk," I said, "it sounds pretty corny to me."

"Listen to this, Renaldo."

To My Daughter and Her Husband on This Special Day:
'Like two white doves are lovers true,
Like two pink hearts forever new.
I hope this day will always view
A ribbon of happiness just for you.'

"Double yuk," I said. "Who buys this mush?"

"Here's another one, Renaldo," Jinx said. "*Congratulations on Your New Baby!* It has a picture of a stork with a baby in a diaper hanging in its mouth."

"It must look so silly," I said, trying hard not to giggle too loudly.

"It gets worse." Jinx was cracking up. "When you open up the card, the stork drops the baby—plop!—right on somebody's doorstep!"

"It sounds like a wet diaper to me!" I squealed. Jinx was laughing, too. But then she suddenly stopped. I could tell she was really thinking.

"But, Renaldo," she said in a serious voice, "somebody buys these cards, and"—she was getting very excited—"there are no stepcards!"

Now I was getting excited, too. We did a high-five right there in Calloway's. "We're going to be rich!" we both shouted.

"C'mon, Renaldo," Jinx urged, "let's go home and get to work."

"Be sure to save an extra large pepperoni and sausage for Woodburn's youngest millionaires!" I shouted when we passed Polotti's.

Getting to work was not as easy as it sounded.

Jinx and I had to buy the paper for the cards. We put our money together for an investment of twelve dollars and thirty-two cents. ("That's a lot of french fries," I thought.) We had to decide what kind of cards to make. We had to think of designs for the front of the cards and messages to go inside. We had to find a way to let people know about "R.R. and J.B. Stepcards."

Let's face it: We had a lot to learn about starting a business.

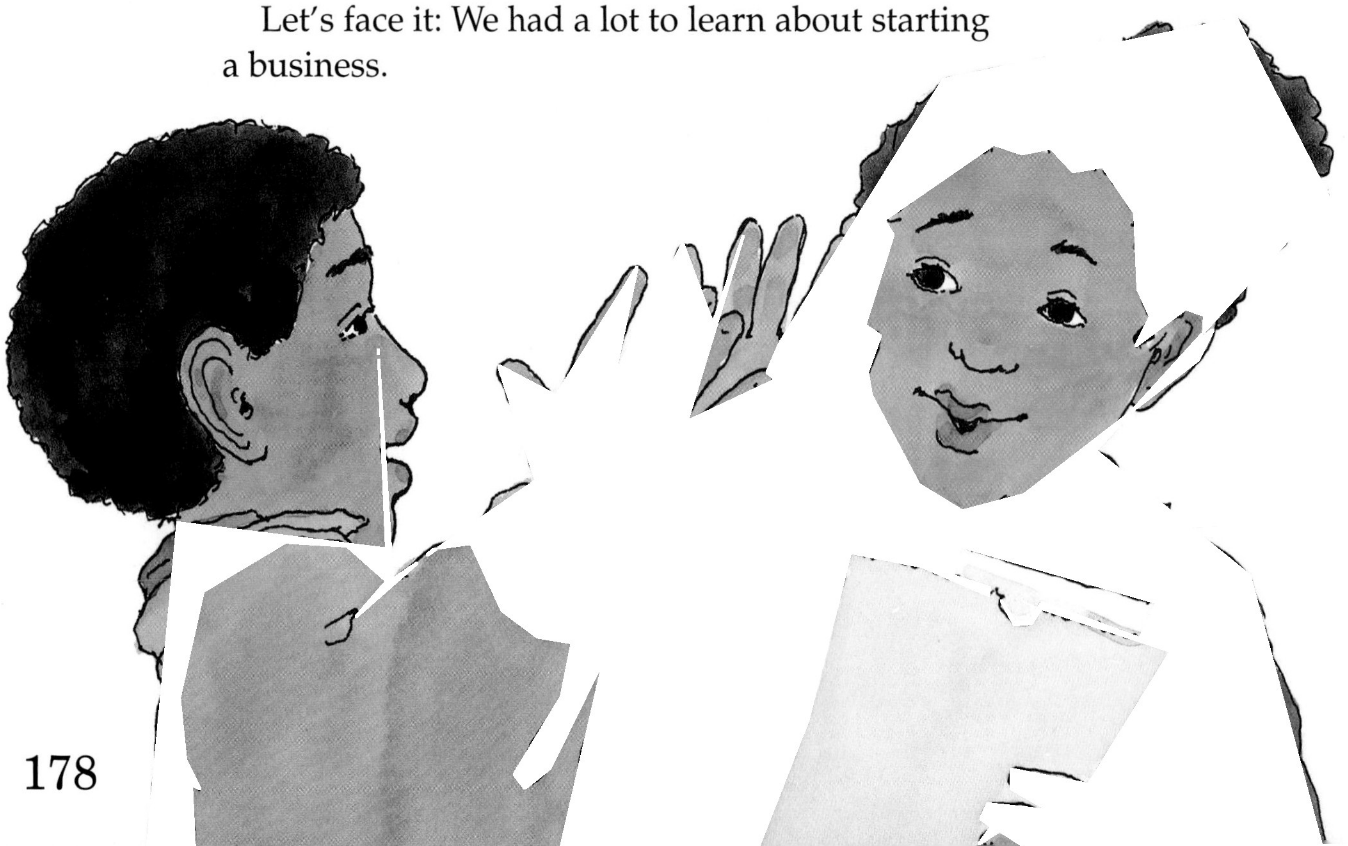

When I have more questions than answers, I always turn to the expert—my Mom. "Mom," I said when she got home from work, "Jinx and I need to speak to an old hand in the business world."

"Good luck finding one," she replied as she started to take off the running shoes she wears to work.

"No, Mom," I explained, "I meant you."

"Oh," she said, looking up. "What can this 'old hand' do for you?"

My Mom knows about business, especially bad businesses. She works in an office helping people who bought things that don't work or aren't safe. I figured if she knew all about bad businesses, she could tell us how to start a good one.

Jinx and I explained our business idea. "How do we get started?" Jinx asked.

"How do we make lots of money?" (I guess you can figure out who asked that one!)

Mom thought for a while. Then she spoke slowly. "Jinx, Renaldo, starting and running a business is not so easy. It's more than just making money. A successful business needs a good product to sell or a useful service to offer. And a successful businessman—or businesswoman—thinks about the customer all the time. Ask yourself: 'What do they want?' 'How can my product or my service help them?' "

Jinx and I were trying to listen to all of this, but it wasn't easy. We *did* have a lot to learn.

"Now, you two have a good product," Mom continued. "I'm proud of you for coming up with this idea. But a good idea is not enough. You need to plan carefully."

"What do we do, Mrs. Rodriguez?" Jinx asked.

"Well," Mom said, "you need to figure out how much money you'll need to get started and where the money will come from. You need to decide who will do the work and, believe me, a business *is* work. Now, if you're still interested in 'R.R. and J.B. Stepcards,' let's make a plan!"

"Always ask the expert," I shouted. I could hear the rubber soles of Mom's shoes make that familiar squeegy sound. Mom wears business suits and running shoes every day to work. Dad says she's dressed for success from her head to her knees—but her feet are dressed for failure! That always makes me laugh.

With Mom's help we really got started. Jinx and I used our "investment" to buy paper, paints, markers, and stencils. We worked every day after school. We took turns with the stencils to make the designs. We'd take a small roller and dip it into a bright color of paint. When we'd smooth the roller over the stencil, there was a butterfly or flower or other designs. Jinx said they looked great!

I liked making up the words for our stepcards. I thought of some pretty good ones, if I must say so myself.

To My Stepfather:
'Getting to know you hasn't been half bad.
I'm glad Mom picked you to be my Stepdad!'

Well, I didn't say they were great cards.

To My Stepsister:
'You have two families, I know that's true.
But I want you to know that I love you, too!'

All right, so Renaldo Rodriguez has a mushy side. Don't rub it in!

At the end of just one week, Jinx and I had 34 cards ready to go.

"To go where?" I asked.

"Where else?" Jinx said. "Why, the Woodburn School and Community Center!" It was time to advertise, and Woodburn was the place to start.

The Woodburn School was the oldest school building in the city. It almost closed the year before. There just weren't enough kids to fill it up, I guess. That's why the school board decided to add a Community Center. Now there was a day-care room for little kids and an activity center for older people, too. Woodburn is like a little city all its own.

The first thing on Monday morning Jinx and I marched down to Woodburn and showed our cards to Mr. Mohammadi, the assistant principal. Boy, was he excited!

"A sound idea," he said. "A very sound business idea. And you'll get a real education in the bargain. A real education. How can I help?"

We explained that advertising "R.R. and J.B. Stepcards" was the next part of our business plan.

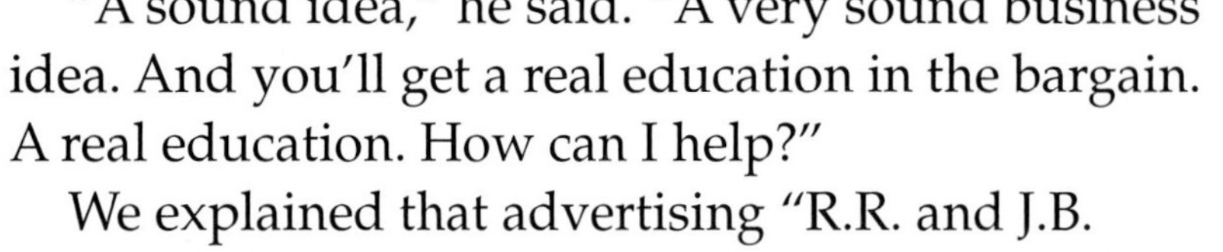

"Let's see now." Mr. Mohammadi was thinking out loud. "You can put advertisements in the school newspaper, posters in the Senior Center, flyers to go home. . . ." Mr. Mohammadi was pacing the floor and spouting new ideas faster than . . . faster than . . . well, faster than Jinx and I could write them down.

"This is going to be a snap," I predicted. "I should have started a business years ago. Think of all the time I've wasted in school!"

That stopped Mr. Mohammadi in his tracks. "Just a little business joke," I gulped.

If you want to start a business, take it from me: advertise! With Mr. Mohammadi's help, Jinx and I spread the word about "R.R. and J.B. Stepcards." Believe it or not, within one week, we sold 17 of our cards and had orders for 20 more. That's 37 cards! We'd make back all the money we spent on supplies. We'd even have some left over.

"Now that we'll have a little extra money, why not buy some stickers and glitter?" Jinx suggested. "Let's make the cards even prettier."

I was thinking about my calculator. I wanted to buy it as soon as I could. "But, Renaldo," Jinx said, "if we make our cards prettier, we'll sell more and make more money."

That made sense. Then I could buy the calculator and a new pair of soccer shoes.

"Don't forget," Jinx reminded me, "we have to pay to use the copying machine." We had to make copies of the advertisement Mr. Mohammadi was going to send home with the kids.

"And we need copies to take to the Senior Center, too," I told Jinx. I remember Mom saying, "You have to spend some money to make money." We thought that advertising was the best way to get more sales.

We thought right! Every day more orders came in the mail.

This was going to be a snap.

Jinx and I had to work every afternoon that week to fill the orders. And every day more orders came in.

Jeremy Kendall's stepsisters had their birthdays coming up, so he ordered two cards from "R.R. and

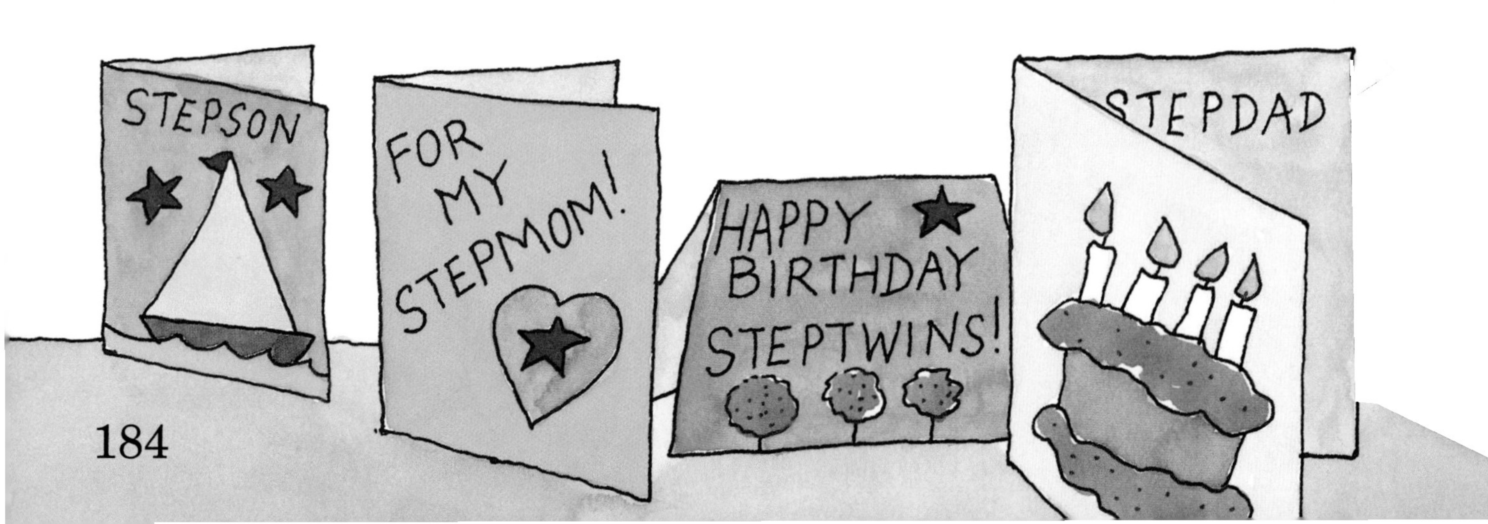

J.B. Stepcards," along with a special card for his stepmother. Mrs. Rothman (from the Senior Center) told us her son had just married a woman with twin boys, and she needed birthday cards for her stepgrandchildren. Roger Neville's stepfather was in the hospital, so he wanted a special get well card. And Joanne Spinoza's mother, Lena, wanted a stepcousin Valentine.

Phew! Jinx and I could hardly believe how well our business was going. We just didn't expect how happy people would be with our cards.

"You know, Jinx," I said, as I lined up the paint jars, "it's nice to give people something special."

Jinx agreed. "Jeremy told me that our card really helped him tell his stepmother how much he liked her."

"No kidding?"

"You know what else? He said she cried a little when she read it, and then she said she really liked him, too."

"Hey," I said, "making people happy is a pretty good way to make a living."

BUSINESS IS LOOKING UP

Concept Connections

Linking the Selection

Think about the following questions, and then record your responses in the Response Journal section of your Writer's Notebook.

- How did R.R. and J.B. Stepcards know there was a need for their product?
- In what ways did Renaldo and Jinx "spend money to make money?"

Exploring Concept Vocabulary

The concept word for this lesson is ***innovation.*** If you don't know what this word means, look it up in a dictionary. Answer these questions.

- Why might an ***innovation*** be easier to advertise than an existing product? Why might it be harder to advertise?
- Why did Mrs. Rodriguez tell Renaldo and Jinx that they needed more than just an idea to sell their ***innovation?***

In the Vocabulary section of your Writer's Notebook, write a sentence that includes the word ***innovation*** as well as one of the selection vocabulary words.

Expanding the Concept

Compare the business Renaldo and Jinx started with the business started by students in "Food from the 'Hood." Consider the size, goals, and products of the businesses. Try to use the word ***innovation*** in your discussion of the two businesses. Add new ideas about business to the Concept/Question Board.

Meet the Authors

Barbara Aiello was eight years old when her mother had to spend several weeks in a hospital. While she was away, Barbara made a magazine for her filled with neighborhood news, a short story, a pet column, and want ads. That was the beginning of her writing career. In addition to being a writer, Ms. Aiello is also a teacher who has spent many years working in special education.

Jeffrey Shulman teaches English at Georgetown University in Washington, D.C., and has been writing children's books since 1986. *Business Is Looking Up* is Mr. Shulman's first and favorite book. He enjoys telling his daughters stories. *"I like to make up the stories as I go along. It keeps my imagination pretty busy."*

Meet the Illustrator

Diane Paterson has illustrated several books for children, including *The Christmas Drum* and *Marmee's Surprise.* She has also illustrated several books she wrote herself, such as the children's books *Someday* and *Smile for Auntie.* Ms. Paterson lives in southwest Florida with her husband, her dog, and over 50 orchids.

Focus Questions How does a business build up a market?
What role does luck play in business success?

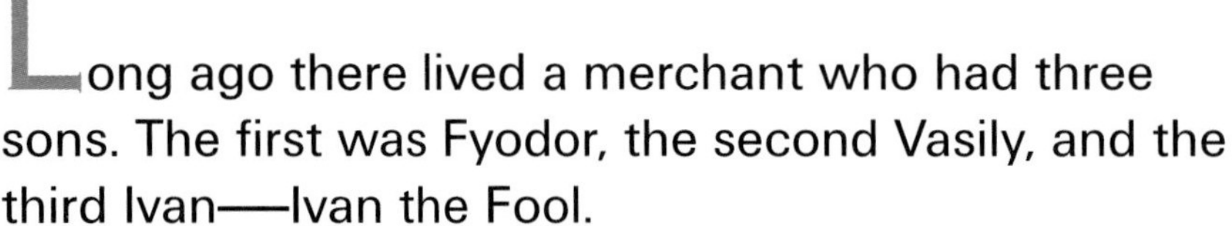

SALT

Harve Zemach
illustrated by Margot Zemach

Long ago there lived a merchant who had three sons. The first was Fyodor, the second Vasily, and the third Ivan—Ivan the Fool.

This merchant was rich. He sent his ships over the ocean in all directions to trade goods in foreign lands. Once he loaded two ships with precious furs, wax, and honey, and sent them sailing with his two elder sons. But when Ivan asked for the same, the merchant refused, saying: "You would do nothing but sing songs to the moon, and try to make the fishes dance, and come home without your head."

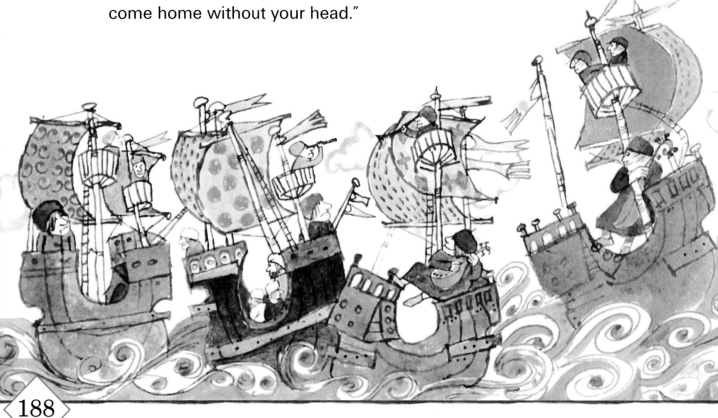

However, when he saw how much his son wanted to go, he gave him a ship with the very cheapest cargo of beams and boards.

Ivan prepared for the journey, set sail, and soon caught up with his brothers. They sailed together for a day or two, until a strong wind came up and blew Ivan's ship away into uncharted seas.

The wind blew Ivan and his crew to the north and to the south. At last they reached an island. Ivan stepped out upon the shore and found a path which led to the top of a mountain. There he discovered that this mountain was not made of rock, nor of sand, nor of stone, but of salt—pure Russian salt.

Without delay he ordered his sailors to throw away all the boards and beams, and to load the ship with salt. As soon as this was done, Ivan set forth once more.

After a long time or a short time, either nearby or far away, the ship arrived at a large city. Ivan went into the city to bow before the king and request permission to trade his merchandise. He took a bundle of the salt with him. The king greeted him in a friendly manner and heard his request.

"And what kind of goods do you sell?" asked the king.

"Russian salt, Your Majesty," said Ivan, showing him the contents of his bundle.

The king had never heard of salt. The people of his kingdom ate all their food without salt. When he saw what Ivan showed him, he thought it was only white sand.

"Well, little brother," he said to Ivan, "we have all we need of this. No one will pay you money for it."

Ivan turned away feeling very disappointed. Then he thought to himself: "Why don't I go to the king's kitchen and see how the cooks prepare the food and

what kind of salt they use." He went and watched the cooks running back and forth, boiling and roasting and pouring and mixing. But no one put a single grain of salt in the food.

Ivan waited his chance and then secretly poured the right amount of salt into all the stews and sauces.

When the first dish was served to the king, he ate of it and found it more tasty than ever before. The second dish was served, and he liked it even better.

Then the king called for his cooks and said to them: "In all the years that I have been king, you have never cooked me such a delicious meal. How did you do it?"

The cooks answered: "Your Majesty, we cooked the same as ever. But the merchant who asked your permission to trade was watching us. Perhaps he added something to the food."

"Send for him!" commanded the king.

Then Ivan, the merchant's son, was brought before the king. He fell on his knees and confessed his guilt.

"Forgive me, Your Majesty," he begged. "I put Russian salt in all the stews and sauces. That's the way we do it in my country."

"And what is the price of this salt?" asked the king.

Ivan realized his advantage and said: "Not very much—for two measures of salt, give me one measure of silver and one of gold."

The king agreed to this price and bought the entire cargo. Ivan filled his ship with silver and gold and made ready to sail for home.

Now the king had a daughter, a beautiful princess. Attended by her maidservants, she went down to the port to see the Russian ship. Ivan the Fool just then was strumming a tune. The melody reached the ears of the princess, and its sweetness entered her heart.

It was not long before Ivan and the beautiful princess stood together before the king to receive his blessing. To the sound of trumpets and the cheers of the king's subjects, Ivan and the princess departed from the city and sailed forth on a favorable wind.

For a long time, for a short time, Ivan and the princess sailed the sea. Then his elder brothers appeared across his path. They learned of his good luck and were very jealous.

They boarded his ship, seized him, and threw him into the sea. Then they divided the booty; Fyodor, the eldest brother, took the princess, and Vasily, the second brother, took the ship full of silver and gold.

Now it happened that when they flung Ivan from the ship, one of the boards that he himself had thrown into the sea was floating nearby. He grabbed hold of this board and for a long time was tossed upon the waves. Finally he was carried to an unknown island. No sooner had he landed on the shore than along came a gloomy giant with an enormous mustache, from which hung a huge pair of mittens, drying after the rain.

"What do you want here?" asked the giant. Ivan told him everything that had happened.

The gloomy giant sighed and said: "Come along, I will carry you home. Tomorrow your eldest brother is to marry the princess. Sit on my back."

The giant lifted Ivan, set him on his back, and raced across the sea. Soon Ivan could see his native land ahead, and moments later they arrived. The giant put him down, saying: "Now promise not to boast to anyone about riding on my back. Don't try to make fun of me. If you do, I shall grab you up and toss you back into the sea."

Ivan, the merchant's son, promised not to boast, thanked the giant, and went home.

He arrived just as the wedding procession was about to enter the church. When the princess saw him, she cried aloud and tore herself away from Fyodor, the eldest brother.

"This is the one I must marry," she said, "and not the other."

"What's that?" asked the father.

Ivan told him everything—how he had traded the salt, how he had won the favor of the princess, and how his brothers had thrown him into the sea.

The father got very angry at his elder sons, called them scoundrels, and married Ivan to the princess.

There now began a joyful feast. The guests ate and drank and made merry. The men began to boast, some

about their strength, some about their riches, some about their beautiful wives. And Ivan the Fool happily boasted too: "Listen to this! I really have something to boast about! A giant carried me piggyback across the sea!"

As soon as he said these words, the giant appeared at the gate.

"Ah, Ivan!" said the gloomy giant. "You promised not to boast about me. Now what have you done?"

"Forgive me!" cried Ivan. "It was not really I that boasted, but my happiness."

"Come, show me what you mean," said the giant. "What do you mean by happiness?"

Then Ivan took up his mandolin, and played and danced the best he knew how. And his playing and dancing was so filled with happiness that all the

guests danced and clapped their hands. And soon the gloomy giant let himself smile and kept time to the music with his feet.

"Well, Ivan," he said at last, "now I know what happiness is. You may boast about me all you like."

So the wedding feast continued, and the giant departed, and Ivan the Fool and the beautiful princess lived happily ever after.

SALT

Concept Connections

Linking the Selection

Think about the following questions, and then record your responses in the Response Journal section of your Writer's Notebook.

- How did Ivan convince the king that salt was valuable?
- Why did Ivan throw away the boards and beams on his boat to load the salt?

Exploring Concept Vocabulary

The concept word for this lesson is ***worth.*** If you don't know what this word means, look it up in a dictionary. Answer these questions.

- What did the king think salt was ***worth?***
- How did the ***worth*** of the beams change for Ivan?

In the Vocabulary section of your Writer's Notebook, write a sentence that includes the word ***worth*** as well as one of the selection vocabulary words.

Expanding the Concept

Compare the new products that are introduced in "Business Is Looking Up" and "Salt." Consider the demand for and value of the two products. Try to use the word ***worth*** in your discussion. Add new ideas about business to the Concept/Question Board.

Meet the Author

Harve Zemach was born in New Jersey. He was a philosopher and a social science teacher. While in college, he met Margot Zemach in Vienna, Austria, and they were married two years later.

Harve did not plan to be a writer. He was a teacher. But Margot really wanted to draw illustrations for children's books. She finally convinced him to write a book so she could illustrate it. He wrote a story about a boy in Vienna, and the book was a success. Harve kept teaching, but after that he also wrote a book every year for Margot to illustrate.

Meet the Illustrator

Margot Zemach was born in Los Angeles, California. By the time she was five, she was involved with the theater. Her mother was an actress and her stepfather was a director and dancer. Margot watched from backstage where she also drew pictures and made up stories.

"I have always drawn pictures, all my life. It seems necessary for me to draw. It really is where I live. I was a poor file clerk, a messy confused messenger girl, a very bad salesgirl, and I cannot add. Thank goodness I can draw."

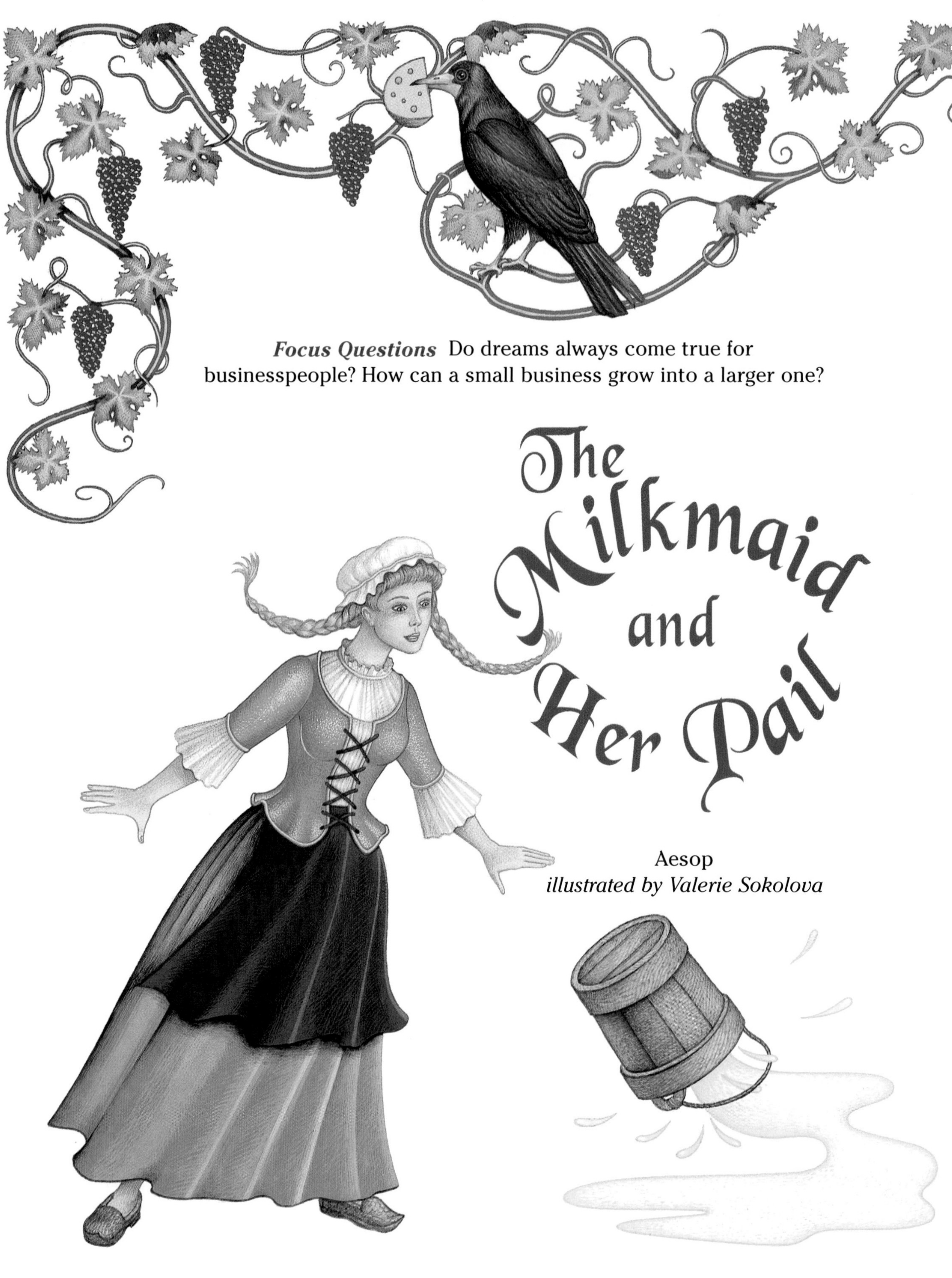

Focus Questions Do dreams always come true for businesspeople? How can a small business grow into a larger one?

The Milkmaid and Her Pail

Aesop
illustrated by Valerie Sokolova

A farmer's daughter finished milking the cows and was carrying her pail of milk upon her head. As she walked along, she started to daydream: "The milk in this pail will provide me with cream. I will make the cream into butter and take it to the market to sell. With the money, I will buy some eggs, and these will hatch into chickens. Then I'll sell some of the chickens, and with the money I'll buy myself a beautiful new dress, which I will wear to the dance. All the young fellows will admire me and want to dance with me, but I'll just toss my head and have nothing to say to them." At this, she forgot all about the pail on her head, and imagining herself at the dance, she tossed her head. Down went the pail, the milk spilled out all over the ground, and all her fine plans vanished in a moment!

Do not count your chickens before they are hatched.

Concept Connections

Linking the Selection

Think about the following questions, and then record your responses in the Response Journal section of your Writer's Notebook.

- What was the milkmaid's business plan?
- Why is the phrase "Do not count your chickens before they are hatched" good business advice?

Exploring Concept Vocabulary

The concept word for this lesson is ***profit.*** If you don't know what this word means, look it up in a dictionary. Answer these questions.

- How does the milkmaid plan to use the ***profits*** from the butter?
- Why might some goods or services not bring a ***profit?***

In the Vocabulary section of your Writer's Notebook, write a sentence that includes the word ***profit*** as well as one of the selection vocabulary words.

Expanding the Concept

Think about the businesses you read about throughout the unit. What conclusions can you draw about what makes a business successful? Try to use the term ***profit*** in your discussion of the unit selections. Add new ideas about business to the Concept/Question Board.

Meet the Author

Aesop lived, historians believe, sometime during the sixth century B.C. He was born a slave and, while working as a slave, began telling his stories. Because he was so witty and skillful with words, his master set him free. Many phrases from his stories are now widely used expressions such as "out of the frying pan and into the fire" and "actions speak louder than words."

Meet the Illustrator

Valerie Sokolova was born in Lvov, Ukraine, and later moved to Minsk, Belarus, where she graduated from the Belarus State Academy of Arts in 1986. She has illustrated more than thirty picture books in Russia, as well as a number of books in the United States, including *The Magic of Merlin* and *The Golden Books Treasury of Christmas Joy.* Ms. Sokolova presently lives in Brooklyn, New York.

UNIT 3

From Mystery to Medicine

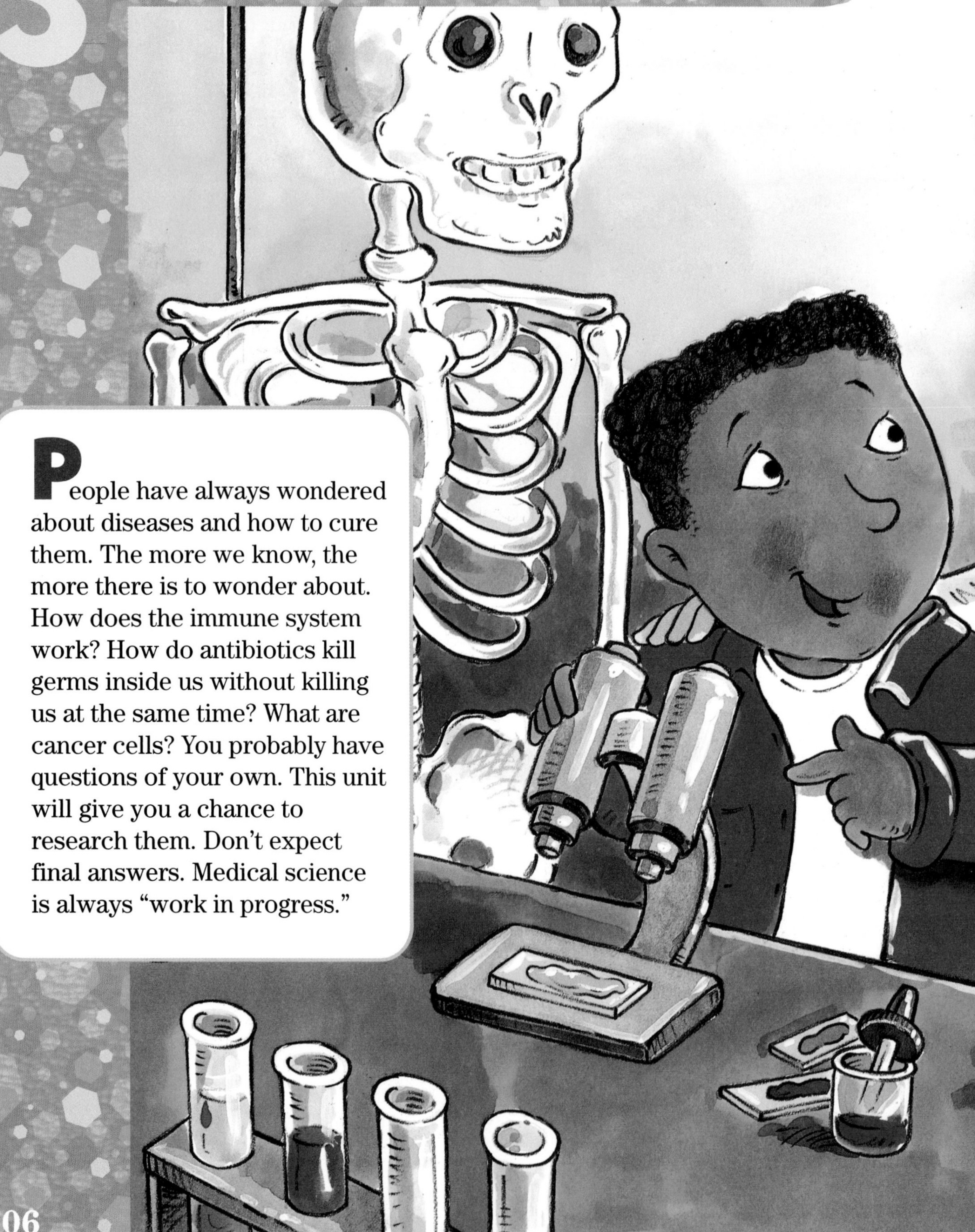

People have always wondered about diseases and how to cure them. The more we know, the more there is to wonder about. How does the immune system work? How do antibiotics kill germs inside us without killing us at the same time? What are cancer cells? You probably have questions of your own. This unit will give you a chance to research them. Don't expect final answers. Medical science is always "work in progress."

Focus Questions How do doctors know what makes us sick? Why can't doctors cure all the diseases in the world?

Medicine: Past and Present

André W. Carus

illustrated by Jim Roldan

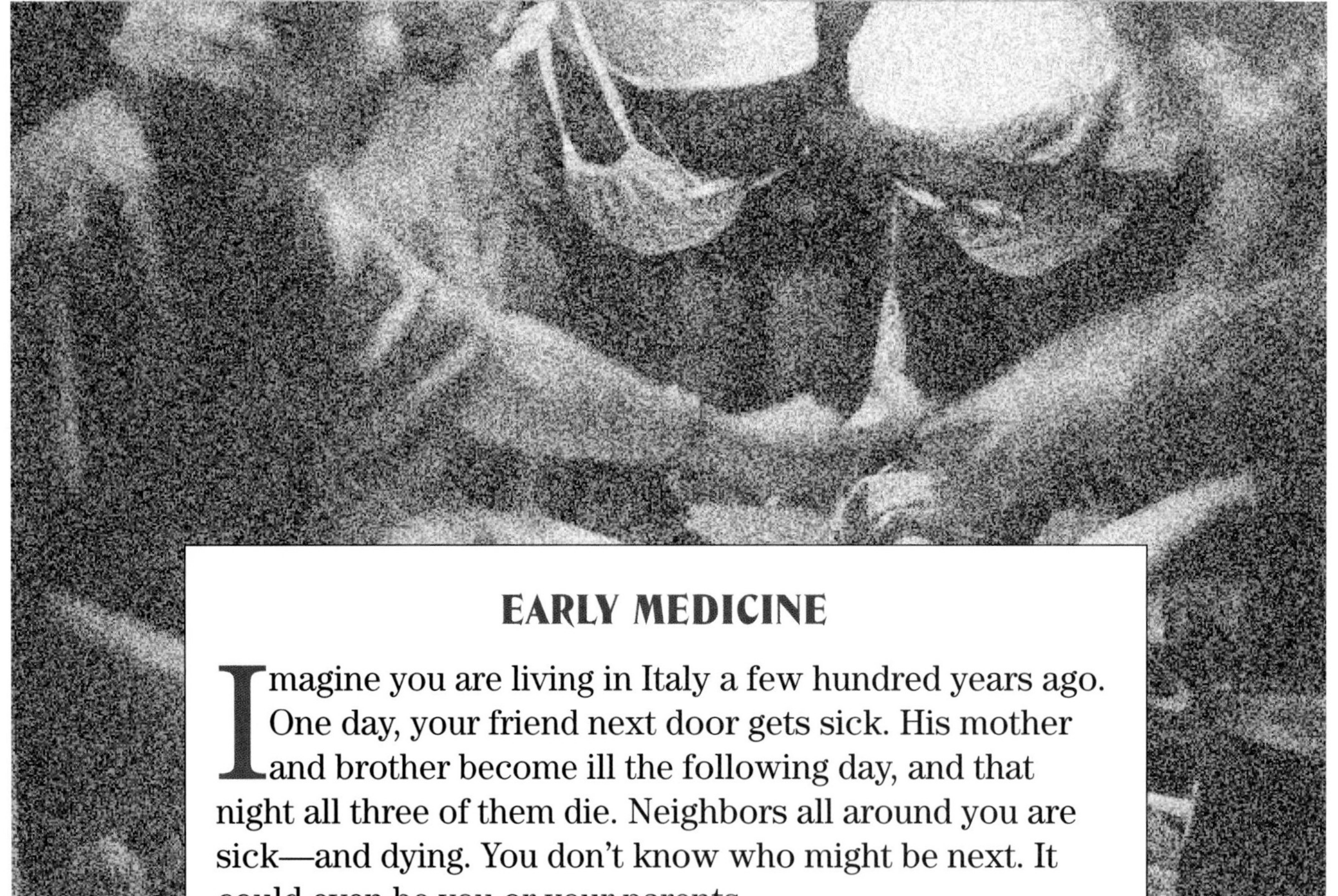

EARLY MEDICINE

Imagine you are living in Italy a few hundred years ago. One day, your friend next door gets sick. His mother and brother become ill the following day, and that night all three of them die. Neighbors all around you are sick—and dying. You don't know who might be next. It could even be you or your parents.

In those days, this nightmare is what life was like. In the middle of the fourteenth century, an epidemic called the Black Plague swept across Europe, Asia, and Africa. It killed about 75 million people, wiping out more than a third of Europe's population. While the disease spared some towns and villages, it killed nearly everyone in others. There was little warning, and those who caught the disease were dead within a few days.

Getting sick was always scary, not just during epidemics like the Black Plague. Death was never far away. People could fall ill and die at any moment, and no one would know why. Most people did not live to be very old. The average life expectancy was only thirty or forty years, about half what it is now in the United States.

For most of human history, people did not know what caused diseases. They could not see germs, so they didn't realize germs existed. Even after germs were discovered, it took a long time to connect them up with various diseases. It took even longer for people to understand how to keep germs from making people sick.

Before people knew about germs, they had other ideas about what caused diseases. Mostly, these ideas involved some kind of magical powers. It is easy to understand why people would believe such ideas. Diseases were terrifying and mysterious. Often there seemed to be no pattern to them. Why did some people die young and others get old? Why did some wounds get infected and others heal? Why did epidemics kill some people and not others? Without knowing about germs, it was easy to believe anything that might make a difference and possibly save a life.

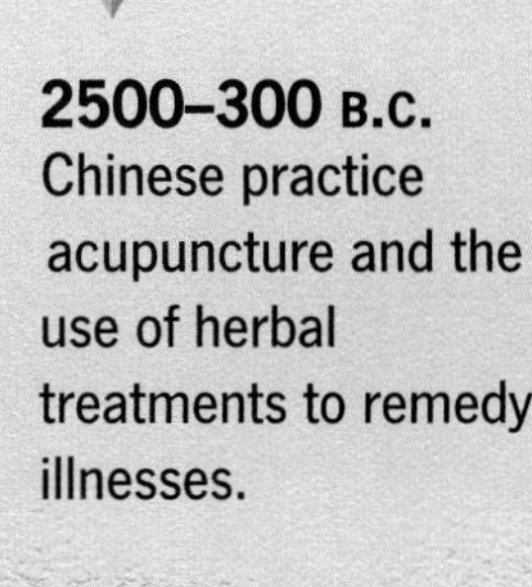

2500–300 B.C.
Chinese practice acupuncture and the use of herbal treatments to remedy illnesses.

So, it was a new idea when a few people suggested, in Greece about 2,500 years ago, that the human body is predictable and that diseases have natural causes and reasonable explanations. Hippocrates is the best known of these people. Because this basic idea is so important, he is called the Father of Medicine. Hippocrates was sure that he could find reasons for illness by closely studying the human body and observing diseases. He also thought that people could understand the way the body worked.

We now know that Hippocrates was on the right track. But when he lived, and for a long time afterwards, his idea was no more than a guess. And often it didn't seem like a very good guess (Hippocrates had lived nearly 2,000 years before the Black Plague and his beliefs still had very little support). So most people went on believing their old ideas and attempting to use magic to cure diseases. Sometimes the things they did had good results, even though the ideas about why these things worked were wrong. For example, when the ancient Chinese used herbs and the ancient Egyptians used moldy bread on wounds, they found that infections healed. Some Native-American people knew that chewing willow tree bark would help reduce pain. And many people knew that a doctor could help just by soothing patients and taking good care of them.

460–377 B.C.
Hippocrates learns through observation and examination of patients. Living in Greece, he is a great medical teacher and creates the Hippocratic oath, a code of medical ethics still in use today.

A.D. 1220–1280
Venetians first use eyeglasses to correct poor vision.

But Hippocrates' basic idea went on being not much more than a guess for a long time. Around 1600, things began to change. An Englishman named William Harvey discovered that blood in human and animal bodies doesn't just sit there. It moves, or circulates, all through the body every few minutes. And the heart is the pump that makes it move. This was an important breakthrough because it made sense of many things that had long been known about the heart and blood, but had never been pulled together. So it was an important step toward making Hippocrates' guess look more reasonable. A lot of seemingly mysterious and unrelated facts turned out to have a simple and natural explanation.

1334
The Plague spreads across Europe. Three fourths of the European and Asian populations die in a twenty-year period.

1628
The English doctor, William Harvey, discovers blood is circulated throughout the body by the heart. He realizes the heart works like a pump to keep the blood in constant motion.

DISCOVERING GERMS

The discovery of germs and how they cause diseases took much longer. The first step was to realize that there were animals so tiny that they couldn't be seen by the naked eye. This step was taken by a Dutchman named Anton van Leeuwenhoek in 1674. After he heard of microscopes that magnified small objects, he made himself a very powerful one. He used it to look at water from a nearby pond and was amazed to find tiny animals swimming around in it. No human being had ever seen them before! He found many different kinds of microbes, as these tiny animals are called today, and became famous for this discovery. Ever since 1300, people had sometimes thought that such tiny living things might cause diseases. But Leeuwenhoek did not know of this idea. He did not suspect that the microbes he saw could cause the diseases that kill people. But now people knew that microbes really existed.

1674
Anton van Leeuwenhoek studies life under the microscope and is able to achieve 160 times magnification.

1735
English surgeon Claudius Amyan successfully completes the first surgery to remove the appendix.

Another big step was taken around 1800 by an English doctor named Edward Jenner. He believed Hippocrates' guess; he was sure that diseases had natural causes. One particularly terrifying disease at that time was smallpox, which killed most people who got it. The few who recovered were left with scars on their faces and bodies but never got the disease again. Jenner guessed that the body developed some means to fight the disease, so that if it were invaded by smallpox again, the infection could not survive. He tried to think of a way of getting the body to develop these antibodies (as they are now called) to attack the disease without having to get smallpox first.

He knew that among cattle there was a disease called cowpox, which was similar to the human disease of smallpox. Humans could also get cowpox, but it rarely killed them and left no permanent scars. Jenner heard it said among country people in some parts of England that if you got cowpox, you would never get smallpox. Jenner

1753
James Lind discovers that lemons and limes can cure scurvy, a vitamin C deficiency. Sailors, who frequently suffer from this disease on long ocean voyages, welcome his findings and drink lime juice.

1780
Benjamin Franklin invents a bifocal lens.

decided to find out if this was true. He guessed that once the body developed antibodies to cowpox, the same antibodies would be able to fight off smallpox. He infected some people with cowpox, waited until they recovered, and then tried to infect them with smallpox. (This test was dangerous. Such experiments wouldn't be tried today!) The people didn't get ill. They had developed the antibodies, and they would not catch smallpox. They were immune to the disease.

So, Jenner had discovered a way of preventing smallpox. For the first time ever, doctors could do something to prevent a disease. And they had evidence that whatever caused smallpox could be defeated by something the body developed for itself. But they still didn't know what actually caused the disease. For centuries, people had been guessing that microbes, or germs, caused smallpox. No one made the actual connection between germs and disease until Louis Pasteur, a French chemist, conducted some experiments in the mid-1800s.

1796
Edward Jenner experiments with cowpox vaccinations against smallpox.

1860
The French scientist Louis Pasteur demonstrates the presence of airborne bacteria.

MAKING THE CONNECTION

While Pasteur was doing his experiments, other scientists were discovering many different microbes. One kind of very small microbe, shaped like a rod or stick, was called bacterium, after the Greek word for stick. Pasteur carefully followed these discoveries and learned a lot about different types of bacteria. But before he could make the connection between these bacteria (or germs) and diseases, he had a more difficult job. Pasteur had to dispel, or prove wrong, an old belief that was standing in the way of his research.

Many people believed that living things could grow from nonliving things. They thought that rats grew from pieces of cheese, rotting meat turned into worms, and animals grew out of water. This idea, called spontaneous generation, seems silly to us now. But, it is easy to see why people believed it. When Anton van Leeuwenhoek discovered microbes under his microscope, no one had an explanation for how they got into the water. So it seemed likely that the water must have turned into these animals. Pasteur thought this idea was wrong. He conducted several experiments to make sure.

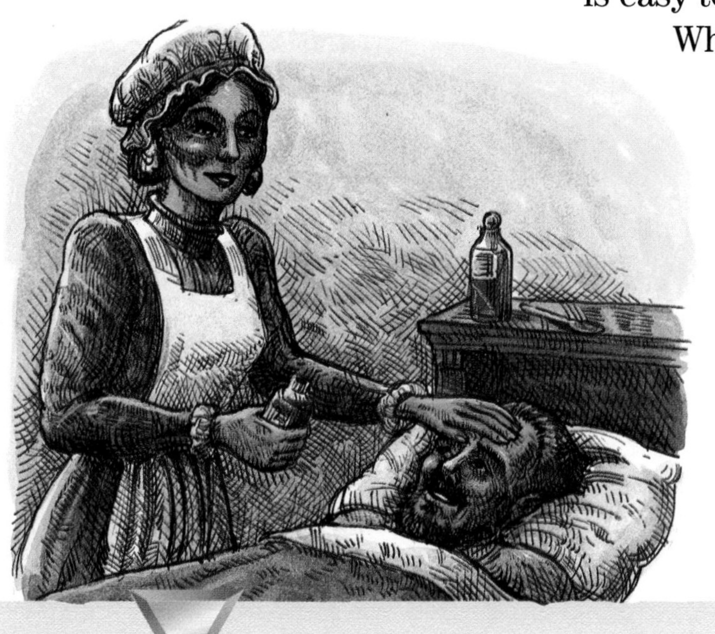

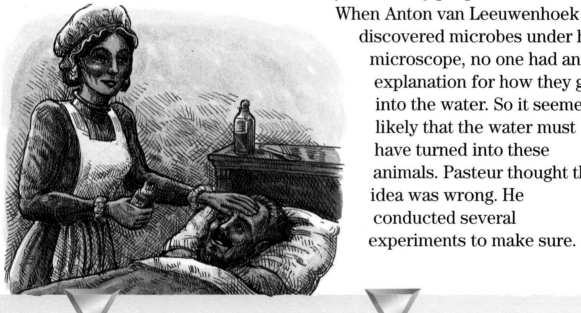

1860
Florence Nightingale establishes the Nightingale School for Nurses, the first of its kind in the world. An English nurse, Nightingale was the founder of modern nursing.

1881
Louis Pasteur vaccinates animals against anthrax.

In a previous series of experiments, Pasteur had learned that certain bacteria made wine spoil. When he heated the wine, the bacteria were killed. (This process of heating to kill bacteria became known as pasteurization.) In another set of experiments, Pasteur heated a flask of water to kill all the bacteria. He took samples of the water and showed under the microscope that the water contained no microbes. He then opened the flasks so that dust could get into the water. He took another sample of the water, looked at it under the microscope, and found bacteria in it. This proved that the bacteria was carried into the water by the dust particles. The bacteria had not grown out of the water.

Once people believed that all living things came only from other living things, it was easier for Pasteur to prove that diseases were caused by living things. While conducting his experiments on wine, Pasteur had wondered if bacteria might also cause diseases in humans.

1885
Louis Pasteur develops a vaccine for rabies.

1886
Louis Pasteur creates a process of sterilization known as pasteurization.

Pasteur began conducting experiments on animals with anthrax, a disease common in sheep and cattle. While looking under the microscope at blood samples from the sick animals, Pasteur discovered bacteria that were common to all of the infected animals. He knew that if he could inject healthy animals with this bacteria, and they got anthrax, it would prove that the bacteria caused the disease. Pasteur injected healthy rabbits and guinea pigs with a solution that contained the bacteria. All the animals became sick and died, proving the bacteria caused the disease. Using this information, Pasteur was able to develop a vaccine for anthrax.

1893
Daniel Hale Williams performs first successful heart surgery.

1895
Wilhelm Conrad Röntgen discovers X-rays.

FIGHTING GERMS

Pasteur's work made people aware that bacteria, or germs, caused diseases and infections. Joseph Lister, a Scottish surgeon who was a friend of Pasteur's, began to sterilize all his equipment before an operation to get rid of germs. He made sure that only clean gloves were used by his assistants. He disinfected wounds with carbolic acid to kill germs. Sure enough, his patients rarely died of infections, and other surgeons began to use his methods.

1899
The drug aspirin is first used to relieve pain.

1929
Alexander Fleming discovers mold contains a substance that will kill bacteria. He names it penicillin.

Although doctors could take steps to prevent germs on the outside of the body from spreading or infecting people, they had no way to kill the germs once they were inside the body. This important step in fighting diseases took place less than fifty years ago when Alexander Fleming discovered a substance that would kill bacteria. Quite by accident, Fleming noticed that one of his lab experiments on bacteria was contaminated with mold. Instead of just throwing the ruined experiment away, Fleming studied it carefully. What he found was extraordinary. The mold destroyed the bacteria. Fleming then tested the mold on other types of bacteria and found it had the same effect on many of them. Years of testing confirmed Fleming's observations. The substance Fleming found was penicillin, modern medicine's first antibiotic. Since its discovery, penicillin has saved hundreds of thousands of lives. Many infections that once killed people are now easily treated.

1939
Howard Florey uses penicillin, extracted from mold juice, to treat a patient for the first time.

1953
Jonas Salk develops a polio vaccine.

It is only within the last hundred years that most people in the United States have come to believe that Hippocrates' guesses are true. All medical research now assumes that the human body is part of nature, and that diseases have explanations just like everything else in nature. As the natural causes of diseases are discovered, scientists are able to find ways of stopping those diseases. More and more diseases can be prevented or cured. There has been tremendous progress in the last hundred years.

1958
Swedish doctor Ake Senning invents the first cardiac pacemaker.

1975
Smallpox is eliminated through a mass vaccination sponsored by the World Health Organization.

But there is a great deal that we don't know. We still cannot cure many diseases. We don't understand why some people get cancer or heart disease. Millions of people, however, are involved in research on these diseases and on the drugs to cure them. They all accept that Hippocrates was right. But, his idea is still just a guess. And while we think there must be natural causes for these diseases, we don't know what they are. When someone gets cancer today, we are almost as mystified and helpless as people were about any disease a few hundred years ago. If you become a doctor or a medical researcher you may be one of the heroes, like Jenner or Pasteur, who have dispelled some of that fear.

1985
"Keyhole" surgery is created, named so because it is less invasive.

1997
Stanley Prusiner is awarded a Nobel Prize for his discovery of prions, the cause of several serious brain diseases.

Medicine:
Past and Present

Concept Connections

Linking the Selection

Writer's Notebook

Think about the following questions, and then record your responses in the Response Journal section of your Writer's Notebook.

- Why were diseases mysterious to people who lived several hundred years ago?
- How did Louis Pasteur prove that bacteria cause disease?
- What are some mysteries that still exist in modern medicine?

Exploring Concept Vocabulary

The concept word for this lesson is ***breakthrough.*** If you don't know what this word means, look it up in a dictionary. Answer these questions.

- Why are many people interested in knowing about ***breakthroughs*** in the study of medicine?
- Why was the discovery of penicillin an important medical ***breakthrough?***

In the Vocabulary section of your Writer's Notebook, write a sentence that includes the word ***breakthrough*** as well as one of the selection vocabulary words.

Expanding the Concept

Based on the information you read in this selection, what do you think is the most important discovery in the history of medicine? Explain your choice. Try to use the word ***breakthrough*** in your discussion. Add new ideas about medicine to the Concept/Question Board.

Meet the Author

André W. Carus was the boss at the time the editors were putting together this book. They had trouble finding a short article about the history of medicine. The editors knew Mr. Carus had studied history, so they asked him to write an article. Said Mr. Carus, *"Writing is hard, but it's satisfying to get something down on paper. Running a company never gives you a sense of completion like that."*

Meet the Illustrator

Jim Roldan received a box of crayons, his first memorable gift as a child. He drew pictures of cartoon characters, animals, comic book heroes, dinosaurs and spaceships. He studied art at the Rhode Island School of Design. After a few years of working in a graphic design studio, Mr. Roldan started his own business illustrating advertisements, magazines, posters, books, and cartoon characters. He currently lives and works in New Hampshire, where he shares a house with his wife and their two cats.

Focus Questions What would medicine be like if everyone was too frightened to try new things? Why haven't people always known about microbes?

The Microscope

Maxine Kumin
illustrated by Robert Byrd

**Anton Leeuwenhoek was Dutch.
He sold pincushions, cloth, and such.
The waiting townsfolk fumed and fussed
As Anton's dry goods gathered dust.**

He worked, instead of tending store,
At grinding special lenses for
A microscope. Some of the things
He looked at were:

mosquitoes' wings,
the hairs of sheep, the legs of lice,
the skin of people, dogs, and mice;
ox eyes, spiders' spinning gear,
fishes' scales, a little smear
of his own blood,

and best of all,
the unknown, busy, very small
bugs that swim and bump and hop
inside a simple water drop.

Impossible! Most Dutchmen said.
This Anton's crazy in the head.
We ought to ship him off to Spain.
He says he's seen a housefly's brain.
He says the water that we drink
Is full of bugs. He's mad, we think!
They call him *Dummkopf,* which means dope.
That's how we got the microscope.

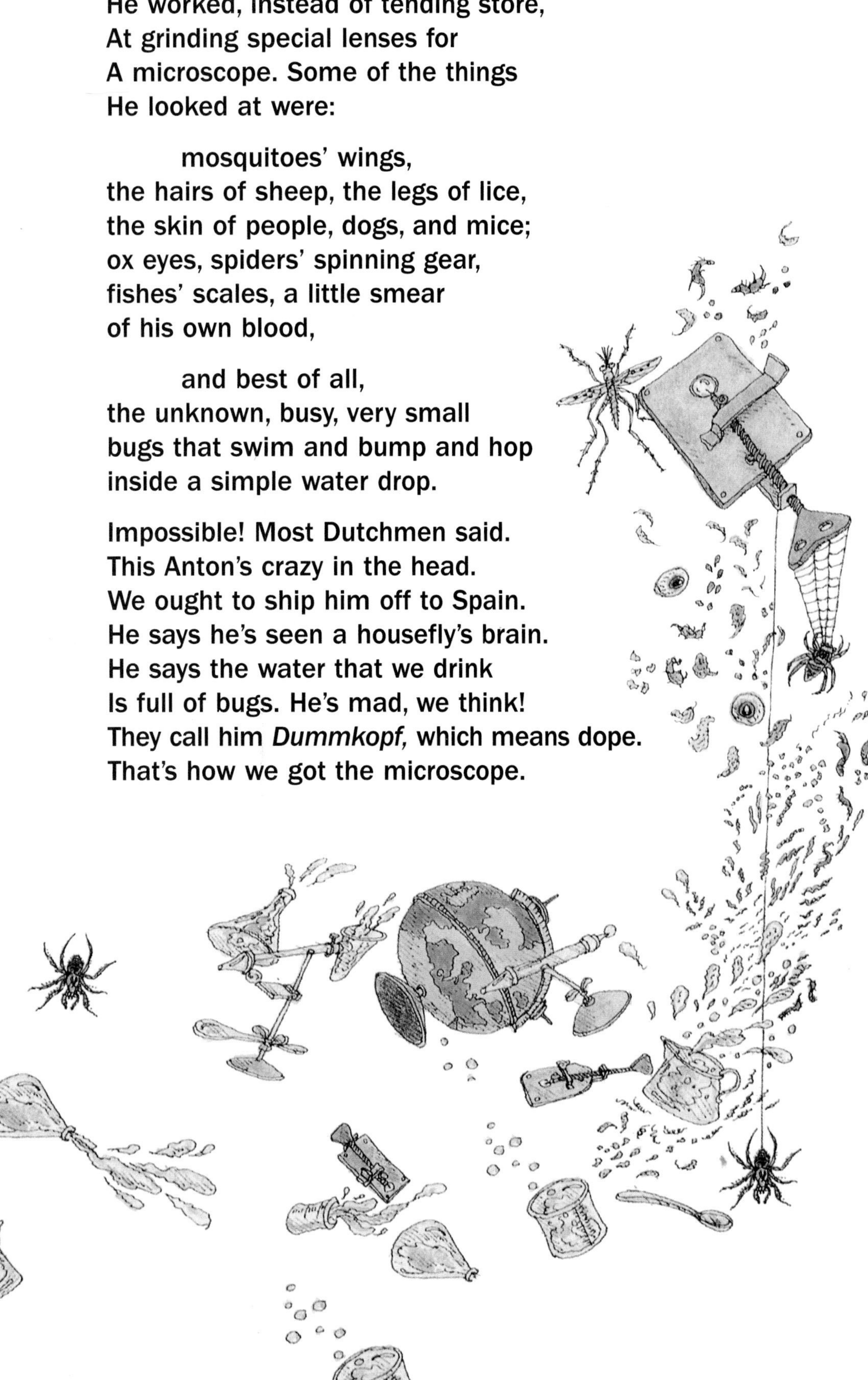

Focus Questions How do doctors decide when to operate? Do doctors ever get scared?

Sewed Up His Heart

from ***Sure Hands, Strong Heart: The Life of Daniel Hale Williams***
by Lillie Patterson
illustrated by Leslie Bowman

July 9, 1893, was hot and humid in Chicago. The scorching heat wave wrapped the city like a sweltering blanket and blistered the sidewalks. Rising temperatures sent thermometers zooming toward one hundred degrees.

The heat and high humidity took a heavy toll on young and old, animals and people. Horses pulling carts and streetcars dropped in their tracks. People fainted from heat prostration and sun strokes. No relief was in sight.

Doctors and hospitals were kept busy. The new Provident Hospital was no exception. Dr. Dan kept close watch on his patients. Making his rounds, he looked as immaculate as always, despite the heat. After his late-afternoon rounds were over, he retired to the closet-like room he used for his office.

Suddenly, a young student nurse burst into the room, her long starched skirt rustling as she ran.

"Dr. Dan!" she gasped. "An emergency! We need you."

Without a word Dr. Dan dropped the report he was reading and hurried to the room set aside for emergency cases. The lone hospital intern, Dr. Elmer Barr, came running to assist.

The emergency case was a young man. He had been brought in by his friend, who gave sketchy information. The patient's name: James Cornish. His age: twenty-four years. His occupation: laborer. The illness: he had been stabbed in the chest.

The frightened friend tried to explain what happened. James Cornish had stopped in a neighboring saloon on his way home from work. The heat and a few drinks caused an argument among the customers. A fight broke out. When it ended, Cornish lay on the floor, a knife wound in his chest.

"How long was the knife blade?" Dr. Dan asked as he began his examination. This would give a clue to the depth and seriousness of the wound.

The victim had not seen the knife blade. Nor had his friend. Action in the fight had been too fast and furious.

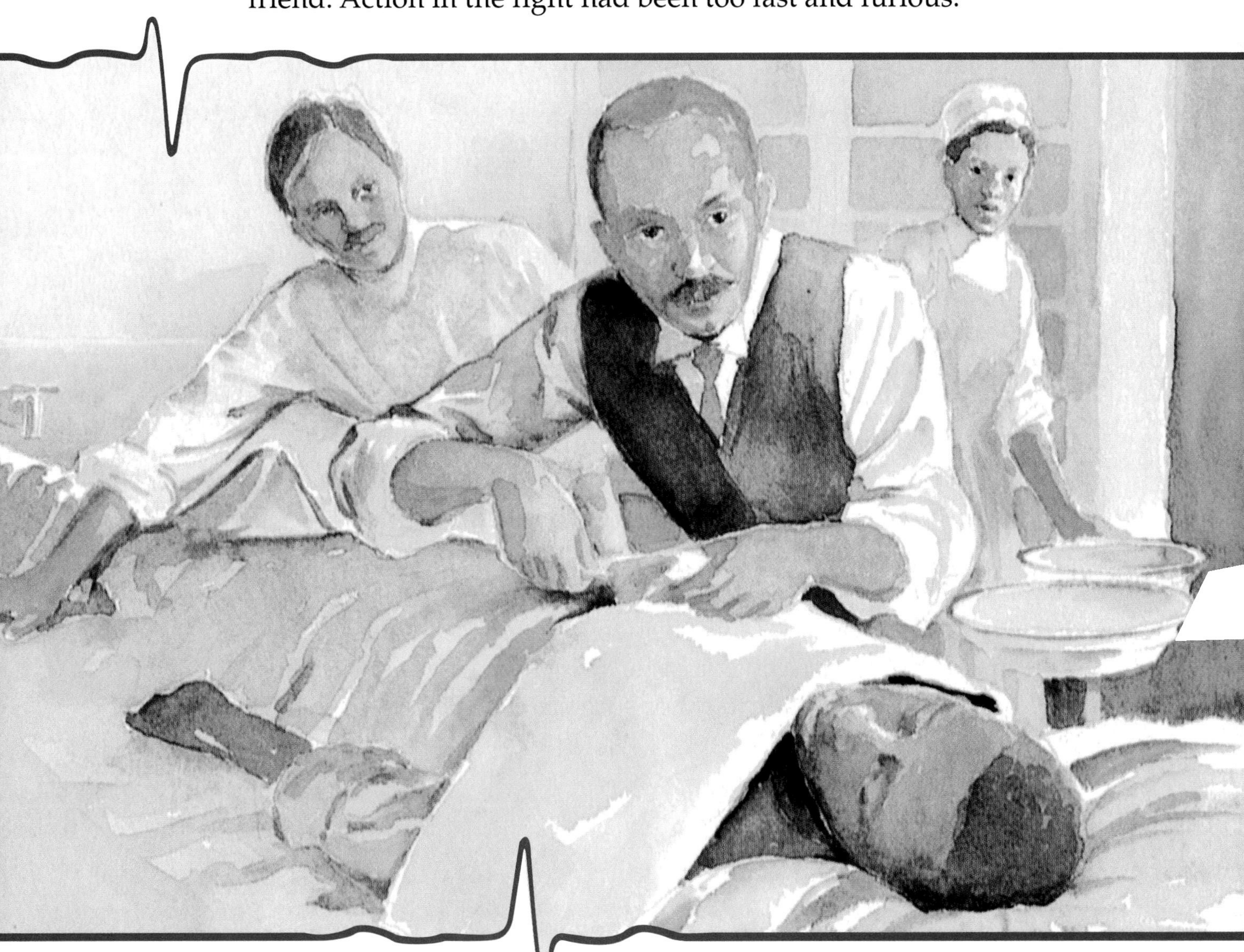

Dr. Dan discovered that the knife had made an inch-long wound in the chest, just to the left of the breastbone. There was very little external bleeding. Nevertheless, Cornish seemed extremely weak, and his rapid pulse gave cause for concern. The X ray had not yet been invented, so there was no way to determine what was happening inside the chest.

Dr. Dan knew from experience that such cases could develop serious complications. James Cornish must be kept in the hospital, he decided. And he must be watched closely.

That night Dr. Dan slept in the hospital. He did this often when there were serious cases. As he had feared, Cornish's condition worsened during the night. He groaned as severe chest pains stabbed the region above his heart. His breathing became labored. A high pitched cough wracked his sturdy frame. The dark face on the pillow was bathed in perspiration.

Dr. Dan watched the wounded man carefully all night. The next morning, as he took the patient's pulse, he voiced his concern to the intern. "One of the chief blood vessels seems to be damaged," he said to Dr. Barr. The knife must have gone in deep enough to cut the internal mammary artery, he explained. The heart itself might be damaged.

James Cornish showed symptoms of lapsing into shock.

Both doctors knew that something had to be done, and done quickly. Otherwise Cornish would surely die within a matter of hours.

But what?

The only way to know the damage done would be to open the chest and look inside. In 1893, doctors considered this highly impracticable. For surgery, the chest was still off limits.

Standing beside the patient's bed, the barber-turned-doctor faced the situation squarely. Later he would recall how he weighed the risks of that moment. Thoughts tumbled through his mind as furiously as flurries in a wintry Chicago snowstorm.

He knew that medical experts repeatedly warned against opening the thorax, the segment of the body containing the heart and lungs. Heart wounds were usually considered fatal. As a medical student, Dr. Dan had read a quote from an eminent physician-writer. "Any surgeon who would attempt to suture a wound of the heart," the surgeon wrote, "is not worthy of the serious consideration of his colleagues."

So far, doctors had followed this cautious advice.

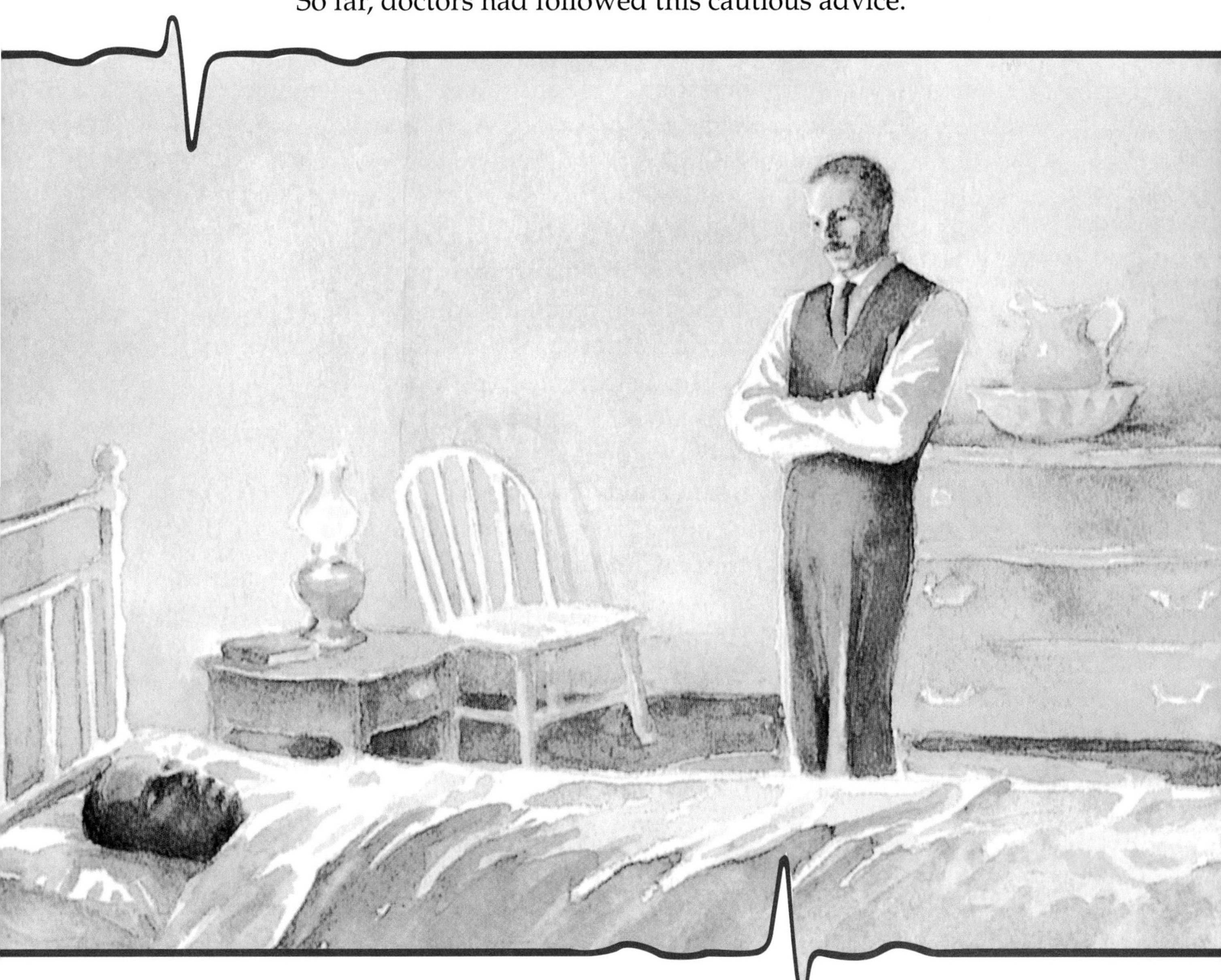

The risks were there for him and for Cornish. If he did not attempt an operation, Dr. Dan reasoned, the patient would die. Nobody would blame the doctor. Such cases often died.

On the other hand, if he opened the chest and Cornish died anyway, there would be certain condemnation from medical groups. His reputation as a surgeon would be questioned, perhaps lost.

The odds were against both him and Cornish. But Daniel Hale Williams had never allowed the odds to intimidate him.

Dr. Dan lifted his chin, the way he did when he faced a challenge. The storm of doubts suddenly swept away, leaving his mind clear and calm as a rain-washed April morning.

The surgeon quietly told his decision to the intern. Two words he spoke. "I'll operate."

The word spread quickly through Provident hospital. Like a small army alerted to do battle, student nurses rushed to get the operating room ready and prepare the patient. They knew Dr. Dan's strict rules regarding asepsis, or preventing infection. The instruments, the room, furniture; everything that came in contact with the patient must be free of microbes that might cause infection.

Meanwhile, Dr. Dan sent a hurried message to a few doctors who often came to watch him operate. The intern, a medical student, and four doctors appeared. Dr. George Hall of Provident's staff was there. So was Dr. Dan's friend, Dr. William Morgan. The circle of watchers gathered in the operating room; four white, two black.

Dr. Dan scrubbed his hands and arms thoroughly. Then, with a nod toward his colleagues, he walked over and looked down at Cornish, now under the effects of anesthesia. Strong shafts of sunlight slanted through a window, giving the doctor's curly red hair a glossy luster. His thin, sensitive mouth drew taut with concentration.

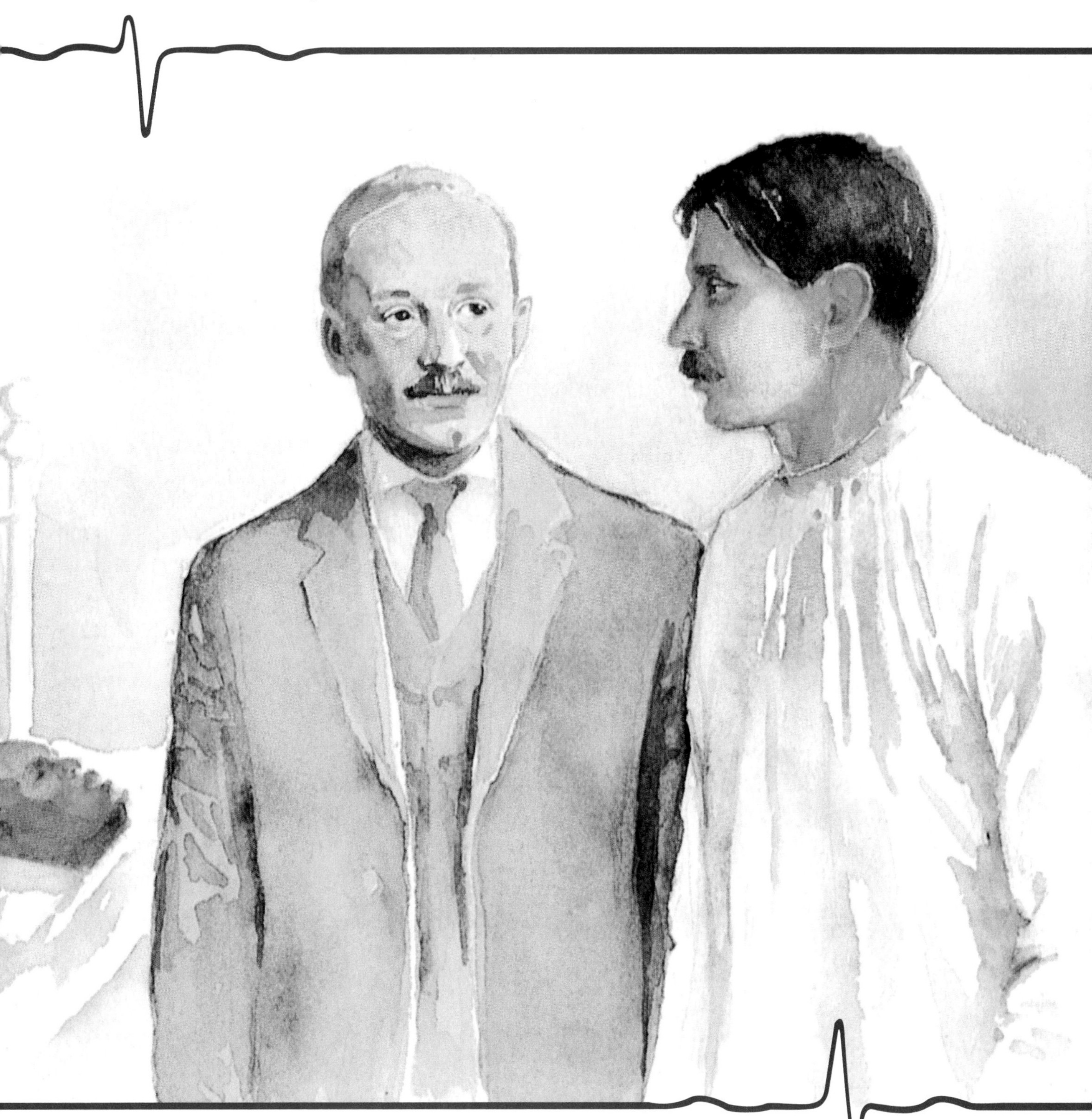

The surgical nurse, proud of her training, stood at attention.

Scalpel!

A loud sigh escaped one of the doctors when the light, straight knife touched Cornish's bare skin. After that there was silence from the onlookers.

None of them knew what would happen next. How would the body react when air suddenly hit the chest cavity? Would vital chest organs shift too far out of place? Dr. Dan could not benefit from the experiences of other doctors. No paper had been written, no lectures given to guide him. Dr. Dan was pioneering in an unexplored territory. He was on his own.

The surgeon worked swiftly. He had to. The surgeon of 1893 did not have a variety of anesthetics or artificial airways to keep the patient's windpipe open. Blood transfusion techniques were unknown. Penicillin and other infection-fighting drugs had not been discovered.

Quickly, Dr. Dan made the incision, lengthening the stab wound to the right. Expertly, he cut through the skin and the layers of fat beneath it. Now he could see the breastbone and the ribs. He made another cut to separate the rib cartilage from the sternum.

Long years of studying and teaching human anatomy gave his every movement confidence. Working with precision, he made his way through the network of cartilages, nerves, blood vessels. A few inches from the breastbone he cut through the cartilage to make a little opening, like a trapdoor.

Bending his head close to the patient's chest, he peered through the opening he had made. Now he could examine the internal blood vessels.

Now he could see the heart!

The tough bundle of muscles throbbed and jerked and pulsated, sending food and oxygen through the body. Dr. Dan examined the pericardium, the fibrous sac that protected the pear-shaped heart and allowed it to beat without rubbing against other parts of the body.

At each step, Dr. Dan reported his findings to the group of observers. The vital pericardium was cut—a tear of about an inch and a quarter in length. He probed further. Yes, there was another puncture wound, he reported, about one-half an inch to the right of the coronary artery. Had the knife moved a fraction of an inch, Cornish would have bled to death before he reached the hospital. Also—Dr. Dan paused—the left mammary artery was damaged.

As the problems were ticked off, the atmosphere in the room grew more tense. The temperature rose above one hundred degrees. Yet not one doctor reached to wipe the perspiration that poured down hands and faces. No one took note of the time. It seemed as though the moment were somehow suspended in history, awaiting results.

Dr. Dan kept on talking and working. The small wound in the heart itself should be left undisturbed, he advised. It was slight. The tear in the pericardium was a different matter. That had to be repaired.

Now the surgeon's hands moved with a rhythm born of knowledge, practice, and instinct. Strong hands; flexible enough to pluck tunes from guitars and violins. Sure hands; steady enough to string high telephone wires. Quick hands; made nimble from years of cutting hair and trimming beards and mustaches.

These hands now raced against time to save a life. Dr. Dan tied off the injured mammary artery to prevent bleeding.

Forceps!

Now he had to try to sew up the heart's protective covering. Meticulously, he irrigated the pericardial wound with a salt solution of one hundred degrees Fahrenheit. There must be no chance of infection after the chest was closed.

Using the smooth forceps, he held together the ragged edges of the wound. Against his fingers the fist-sized heart fluttered and thumped like a frightened bird fighting to fly free.

Sutures!

Despite the rapid heartbeats, the master surgeon managed to sew up the torn edges of the pericardium. For this he used a thin catgut. After that he closed the opening he had made, again using fine catgut.

Another kind of suture would be used for the skin and cartilages, he informed the circle of watchers. He changed to silkworm gut, using long continuous sutures. This allowed for quick entry if infection or hemorrhage developed later. Over the outer sutures he applied a dry dressing.

The operation was over. James Cornish was still alive.

Dr. Dan straightened his aching back. Only then did he stop to wipe the perspiration from his face.

Like figures in a fairy tale suddenly brought to life by magic, the circle of doctors began to move and talk. They rushed to congratulate the surgeon. "Never," said one, "have I seen a surgeon work so swiftly, or with so much confidence."

Each of them dashed from Provident to spread the news. Daniel Hale Williams had opened a man's chest, repaired the pericardium, closed the chest; and the patient's heart was still beating.

How long would Cornish live? Worried watchers waited in suspense. Had the doctor repaired the heart but killed the patient?

During the hours that followed the operation, Dr. Dan scarcely left Cornish's side. Alarming symptoms developed, and he made careful notes. The patient's body temperature rose to 103 degrees. His pulse raced at 134 beats a minute. Heart sounds became muffled and distant. Seizures of coughing shook his frame.

Dr. Dan shared his fears with Dr. Barr. Fluid had collected in the pleural cavity. This meant another operation.

He waited a few more days to give Cornish more time to gain strength. Three weeks after the first operation, Cornish was again rolled into the operating room. As before, Dr. Dan made an incision, this time between the seventh and eighth ribs. Through this opening he drew five pints of bloody serum.

Thanks to his careful adherence to antiseptic surgical techniques, there was no infection, and there were no further serious complications. Fifty-one days after James Cornish entered Provident with little chance of living, he was dismissed—a well man.

A news reporter from Chicago's *Inter Ocean* newspaper came to Provident to interview the surgeon and get the story first-hand. He found Dr. Dan more anxious to talk about his interracial hospital and the program for training nurses than to talk about the historic operation. The reporter had to coax details from him.

Nevertheless, the reporter's story came out with an eye-catching headline: "SEWED UP HIS HEART!" Another heading read: "DR. WILLIAMS PERFORMS AN ASTONISHING FEAT. . . ."

The *Medical Record* of New York later carried Dr. Dan's own scientific account of the techniques and procedures he had used during the operation. His case created worldwide attention, for it was the first recorded attempt to suture the pericardium of the human heart.

His pioneering operation gave courage to other doctors to challenge death when faced with chest wounds. Dr. Dan's techniques were copied by other surgeons, step by step.

The phrase "Sewed Up His Heart" became closely associated with the name of Daniel Hale Williams. The historic operation on James Cornish helped to advance the progress toward modern heart surgery.

Sewed Up His Heart

Concept Connections

Linking the Selection

Think about the following questions, and then record your responses in the Response Journal section of your Writer's Notebook.

- What risks did Dr. Dan face by performing the operation?
- Why was it a challenge for Dr. Dan to sew the patient's pericardium closed?
- Why did Dr. Dan have to perform the surgery quickly?

Exploring Concept Vocabulary

The concept word for this lesson is ***experimental.*** If you don't know what this word means, look it up in a dictionary. Answer these questions.

- Why are ***experimental*** procedures sometimes necessary in medicine?
- Why did Dr. Dan invite other doctors to come and watch the ***experimental*** surgery?

In the Vocabulary section of your Writer's Notebook, write a sentence that includes the word ***experimental*** as well as one of the selection vocabulary words.

Expanding the Concept

Consider what you learned about microbes in "Medicine: Past and Present." Why were microbes a concern for Dr. Dan, and what actions did he take as a result of this concern? Try to use the word ***experimental*** in your discussion. Add new ideas about medicine to the Concept/Question Board.

Meet the Author

Lillie Patterson grew up on Hilton Head, South Carolina. She spent most of her time with her grandmother who was a great reader and singer. *"From my grandmother I captured a sense of the power of words. It was natural that I would follow a career in library media services, and later in writing."*

Ms. Patterson became a children's librarian and a popular storyteller. She also helped to develop radio and television shows for children.

When she gets an idea for a book, Ms. Patterson spends a great deal of time doing research. She finds as much information as possible. Then she rereads everything until she feels she has captured "the spirit" of her subject.

Meet the Illustrator

Leslie Bowman grew up in Connecticut. She started drawing when she was about four years old. She says she never wanted to be anything but an artist. She got lots of encouragement, especially from her mother who was a painter herself.

Ms. Bowman started illustrating children's books in 1986. Since then she has illustrated several books and also worked for *Cricket Magazine.* She says, *"When I work on the illustrations for a book, I read the story over and over until I see the pictures in my head. Then I do sketches of what I see."* She does any research she needs, like finding out what clothes people wore at the time of the story. She adds these details to her sketches, and from these she produces her final illustrations.

Focus Question How hard is it to become a surgeon?

Surgeons Must Be Very Careful

Emily Dickinson

illustrated by Robert Byrd

Surgeons must be very careful
When they take the knife!
Underneath their fine incisions
Stirs the culprit,—Life!

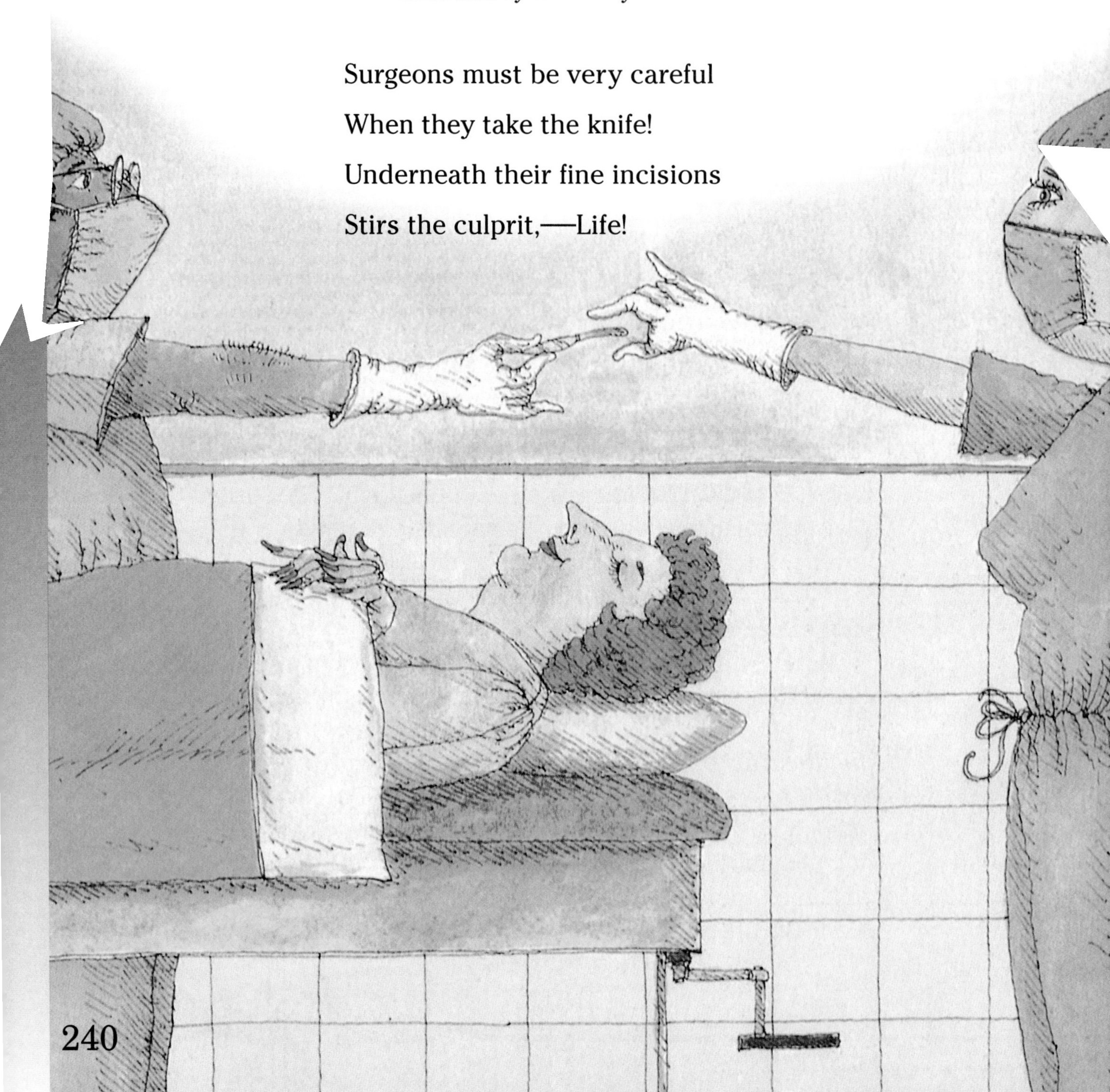

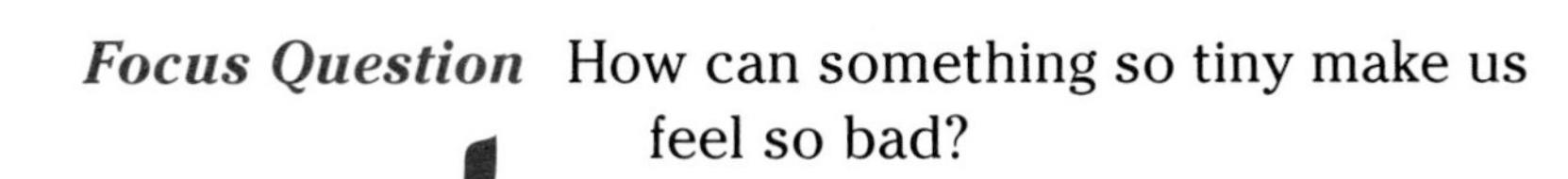

Focus Question How can something so tiny make us feel so bad?

The Germ

Ogden Nash

illustrated by Robert Byrd

A mighty creature is the germ,
Though smaller than the pachyderm.
His customary dwelling place
Is deep within the human race.
His childish pride he often pleases
By giving people strange diseases.
Do you, my poppet, feel infirm?
You probably contain a germ.

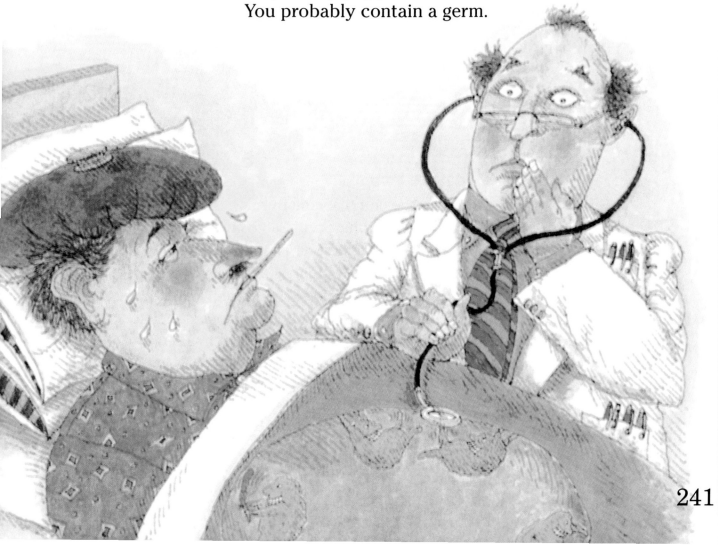

Focus Questions How do people know which plants are medicinal? What would you do if your friend got badly hurt, and you were the only one around?

The Bridge Dancers

Carol Saller

illustrated by Gerald Talifero

Mama gives the comb a yank through the mess of Callie's long, wild hair, and Callie gives a yell like you've never heard before. That's not to say I've never heard it before; I've heard it plenty. Callie says when she grows up she's going to the city to live, where she'll start a new style. All the ladies will come to her and pay a lot of money to get their hair tangled up in knots, and she'll get rich and never comb her hair again.

I'm not a lot like Callie. My hair doesn't fly around much, and I like it combed, and I don't often think about leaving this mountain. Callie's going to be thirteen soon. I'm only eleven, and I've never even been across the bridge.

When Callie's all combed, we go down the path to the bridge. It's our favorite place to play when our chores are done. The dirt path is steep from our house down the twisty old hill. We like to run down fast, bouncing off the little trees in a crazy zigzag, but when we reach the edge of the gorge, the path levels off and we run alongside it. To folks way down below on the river we must look like two little pokeberries, up high on the mountain's edge.

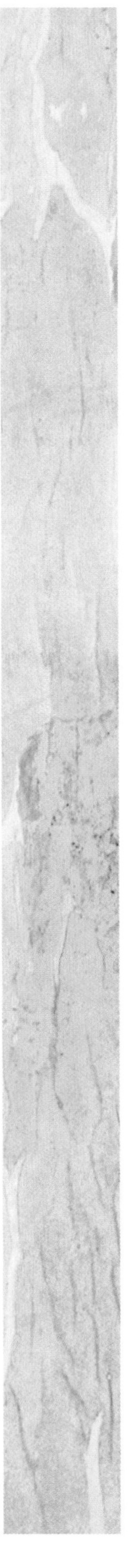

What we call the bridge isn't the real bridge, where horses and buggies can get across, that's a few miles off along the path. Our bridge is just a shaky old skeleton, a tangle of ropes and boards that ripples and swings in the breeze. Our house is the closest one to this bridge. The next nearest is the Ketchums' place, another mile up the mountain. Most of our neighbors live across the gorge; Mama says there are seven houses within the first half hour's walk. Mama often has to cross the bridge, but we're not allowed.

On this day, the wind is strong and the bridge is rocking like a boat in a storm. We make clover chains and toss them into the gorge, watching them blow away and then down, down. We count the seconds till they hit the water far below. Callie stays by the edge, but I spy some yellow-eyed daisies growing up the hill a ways, and I know Mama will want them. If you boil daisies—stalks, leaves, and all—it makes a tea that's good for coughs, or a lotion for bruises and sores. Mama doctors most of the folks on this mountain, and we always keep a store of dried plants for medicine. I pull the best ones and put them in my apron pocket.

Later, when the sun is behind the mountain and I'm getting cold and hungry, I start back up the path, but Callie doesn't want to go. "Maisie! I dare you to stand on the bridge!" she calls, just like she does every time we're here. I don't answer, but I stop and turn to look. She knows the thought of it scares me.

Now she skips up the hill a little ways and stands on her toes like a dancer, her skirt ballooning in the wind. In the gloomy light of sundown she is ghostlike and beautiful. "Announcing . . . Calpurnia the Great!" She twirls and leaps and strikes a pose with one toe pointed forward: "Calpurnia—the Daring Bridge Dancer!"

I laugh. I'm pretty sure she's only teasing. Callie dances toward the bridge, humming a tune that she imagines sounds like a circus. When she gets to the part of the bridge that sits on land, she holds onto one post and points her foot out

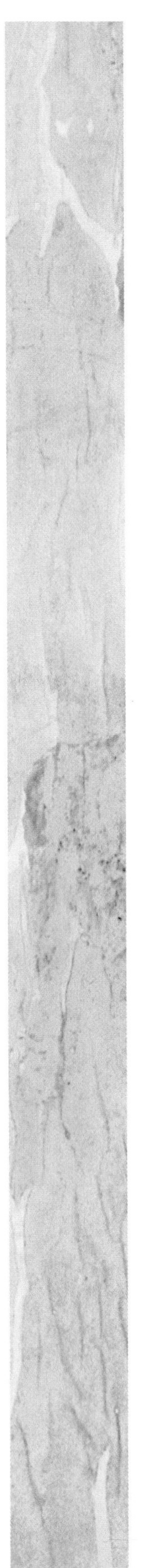

toward the gorge, leaning back in a swoop. Then she grabs both posts and slides both feet out onto the bridge. She starts to slip, but before I can cry out, she turns back, laughing. My heart is jumping. I'm getting ready to run and pull her away from the bridge when she skips aside quick as lightning and starts chewing a piece of clover. In a second I see why.

Mama is huffing down the path. She's lugging her doctoring bag and has to watch her step. If she'd seen Callie fooling around on the bridge we'd both have caught it. "Girls, I've got to attend to Mrs. Gainie," Mama says, putting her bag down for a rest. "She thought the baby would come last night, but tonight's the full moon. It'll come tonight." She looks us over and frowns across the gorge. "I might be gone till sunup, so get yourselves some supper, and don't forget to bolt the door, you hear?" She points at some dark clouds moving fast across the sky. "Hurry on up. I've already made a fire—there's a storm blowing." We nod. She starts for the bridge.

"Mama?" I call, and she stops and turns. "Is Mrs. Gainie going to be all right?" Mama nods. "She's a strong woman." She reaches for the bridge rail with one hand.

"Wait!" I call.

Mama stops again. "What is it, Maisie?"

"Have you got the tansy I picked?" I ask. Tansy is supposed to help a baby come, but if it doesn't do that, at least it keeps the bugs away.

Mama says, "I've got it, but I don't expect to need it this time." She smiles at me. "I'll mind my steps on the bridge, Maisie." Mama knows I'm afraid.

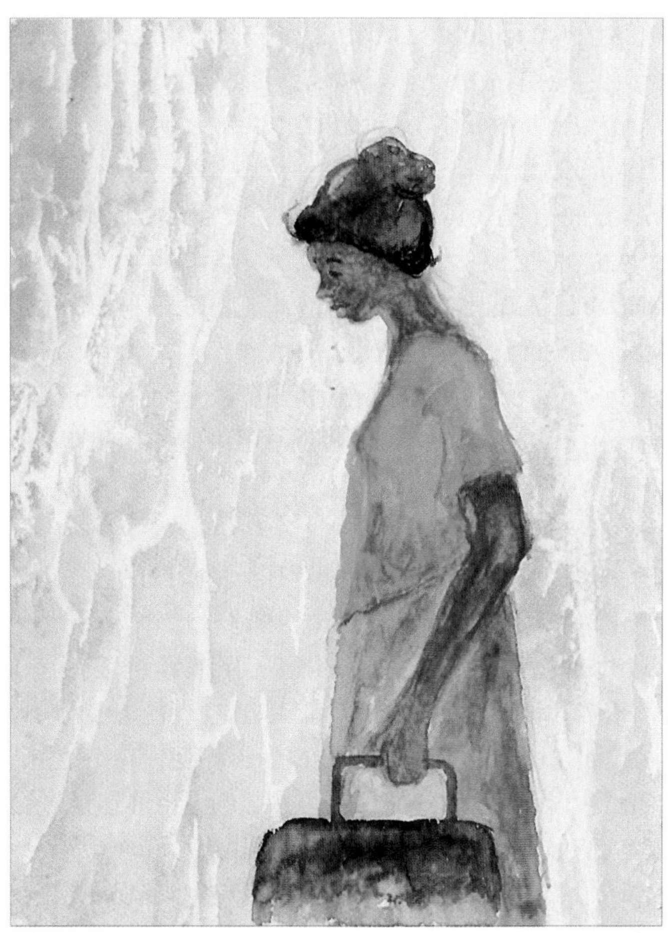

When Mama crosses the bridge, I never let go of her with my eyes. She's a big, heavy woman, and when she steps off the land part, the whole bridge from one side to the other dips into a sharp V with Mama at the bottom point. She goes slow, holding the ropes with one hand and her bag with the other, and she walks in a careful rhythm, giving the bridge time to bounce just right between steps. Callie says, "She won't fall if you look away," but I never look away. On the other side it's already dark, but we can just see Mama turn and wave. We wave back, and Mama disappears around the side of the mountain down the path to the Gainies'.

"Come on, Callie," I say, starting up the path. I know that there's supper to get and more wood to gather and plenty else to do. But Callie isn't of a mind to work. She throws her blade of grass to the wind and runs ahead of me, her arms flung wide. "Burst into jubilant song!" she cries. "The everlasting chains are loosed and we are free!" Callie gets a lot of big words from reading the Bible. "Let us soar into the heavens, never to be enchained again!"

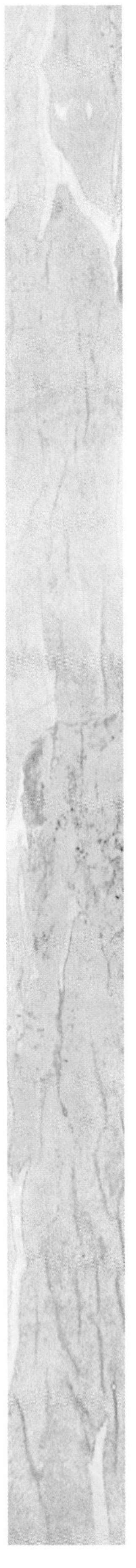

With that, she scampers off the path into the brush, and is soon just a flutter of white in the dusk, dancing and dodging among the trees. I feel the first drops of rain, and in a moment Callie is back.

"Maisie, I know what let's do," she says, blocking the path. She has to raise her voice now against the wind.

"What?" I ask with a frown. Callie's smile looks like it's hiding a bad idea, and I'm not sure I want to know.

"Let's get the ax and split a log for the fire," she says, wrapping her skirt around her and skipping along beside me. "There's a big storm coming. Let's have a fire that will last us all night."

I'm not sure. A fire would be good on a cold, stormy night, and I know there's only kindling left in the box. But Mama's the one who chops the wood. She takes down that big old ax from its pegs high on the wall and tells us to stand away. She's never told us not to touch it, but I have a feeling that we're not supposed to. I shake my head. "Callie, I don't hardly think you could even lift that ax. You're likely to get yourself killed." But my words blow away with the wind, and Callie is already halfway up to the house. I start to run, too, but I've never yet stopped Callie from doing what she wants to do. I figure the best I can do is be there when she needs help.

When I get to the door, Callie has the lantern lit and is dragging the rocking chair over to the wall. "Don't stand on that—it's too tottery!" I cry, and I run to hold the rocker while Callie climbs up and waits for the wobbling to stop. When the

chair is still, she reaches up both hands to lift the ax from its pegs. It's heavy, all right; I can see by the way Callie's muscles stand out on her arms. Just when she's got it lifted off the pegs, the wind blows the door shut with a powerful "bang!" and we both jump with fright. The rocker pitches, and Callie falls.

For a long moment it seems like nothing happens. My thoughts stop; even my heart seems to stop. Then Callie is crying out with pain and fear. It's her leg, cut deep by the ax. She clutches hold of my arm, tight, and gasps with the force of the pain. "Maisie, hurry and get Mama!" she whispers. "Callie . . ." I start to say, thinking about the wind, the dark, the bridge. Callie sees how I don't want to go, and she looks at me, begging with her eyes. "Maisie, I'm sorry—but you've got to go! You're the only one who can help me!"

I don't want to think about what Callie is saying. Instead I grab one of the clean cloths Mama uses for straining her herb medicines, and with shaky fingers, tie it tight around Callie's

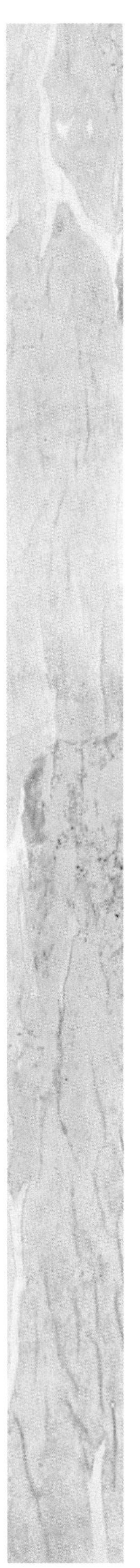

leg. I take a quilt from the bed and put it over her, then run to the kindling pile and throw an armload of sticks on the fire. Callie is crying; the wind is crying. I light another lantern and wonder how I can cross the bridge, in the night, in the storm.

Outside, the wind and trees are whipping at the sky. I hold my skirt in one hand, the lantern in the other, and stumble in the quivery light down the path to the bridge. With my whole heart I wish there was some other way to fetch Mama. I think of Mama with her jars and packets, her sure hands and her healing ways. She'll stop the bleeding with a poultice of yarrow; she'll make an herb tea that will help Callie sleep. But Mama is far across the valley—how will I ever cross that bridge . . . Near the bottom of the hill, I can hear it before I see it, ropes groaning and boards creaking, as it tosses in the storm.

I stand at the edge of the gorge, my lantern lighting the first few steps of the rain-slicked bridge. The fear in me is so powerful it stings my eyes, and I know I don't have the courage for even the first step. But I remember what Callie said—"Maisie, you're the only one who can help me"—and I step onto the bridge with both feet.

The bridge pitches and plunges. I grab for the ropes, and the lantern flies from my hands. "No!" I shriek, as it rolls away and drops into the darkness. On my hands and knees, I crawl back to the edge of the gorge, sobbing in the terrible black night, crying for Callie, crying for Mama. How can I cross the bridge . . . how can I help Callie . . . think what to do, Maisie, think what to do. With my face near the ground, I make myself take slow breaths. I can smell clover, damp with rain.

Suddenly, I know what to do. I pick myself up and start back up the path, feeling my way in the darkness, guided by the small light in the house at the top of the hill. I remember all the times I've watched Mama with her bag, with her poke leaves for burns, her chickweed for tummyache. It's the yarrow plant that stops someone bleeding, and I can make the poultice myself. Near the top I begin to run.

When I burst in through the door, I see that Callie's face is pale. "Maisie—Mama!" she says, weakly. "There, Callie, don't fret; it's going to be fine," I comfort her. "I know what to do. Mama will come later, but I know just what to do."

My hands shake a little as I set the kettle on to boil—the fire is still burning strong. Then I go to Mama's cupboard of crushed and dried plants. I find some yarrow and wrap it in a clean muslin cloth to make the poultice. My fingers are sure now—Mama does it exactly so. Then I take a handful of dried feverfew and put it in a pot, for tea. Callie is moaning, so I sit by her and talk. "Yarrow is just the thing—and I remember I picked this myself! It has such pretty little flowers, and so many funny names: thousand-leaf, angel flower, bunch-a-daisies, sneezewort. It won't take but a minute, once that water's boiled. Don't you worry, Callie. Maisie can take care of you."

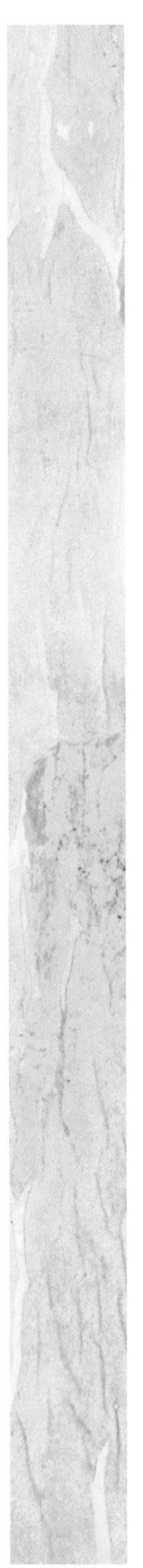

When the water is boiling, I pour some into the teapot with the feverfew and put it near the window to cool. Then I put the wrapped-up yarrow into the kettle and put the kettle back on the fire—not too long, just long enough for the water to soak in and soften the yarrow. Then I scoop out the poultice with a ladle, and after a minute, while it's still hot, I put it carefully on Callie's leg. I know it will hurt, so I keep talking. "Listen to that rain! It's really starting to pour now. You know, this is a pretty bad cut, Callie, and it hasn't stopped bleeding yet. This poultice will stop it. Can you smell how sweet?" But Callie yells when the poultice touches her leg.

When the tea is cool, I pour some into a cup, and hold up Callie's head for her to drink. "That's good," I tell her. "This will ease the pain. Maybe you can sleep a little; sleep till Mama comes." I rest her head in my lap, leaning my back against the wall. Rain thrashes the roof as I stroke her hair, all tangled and wild. I talk on and on, about ox-eye daisies and Queen Anne's lace, chickweed and tansy, the names like song words, lulling her to sleep at last.

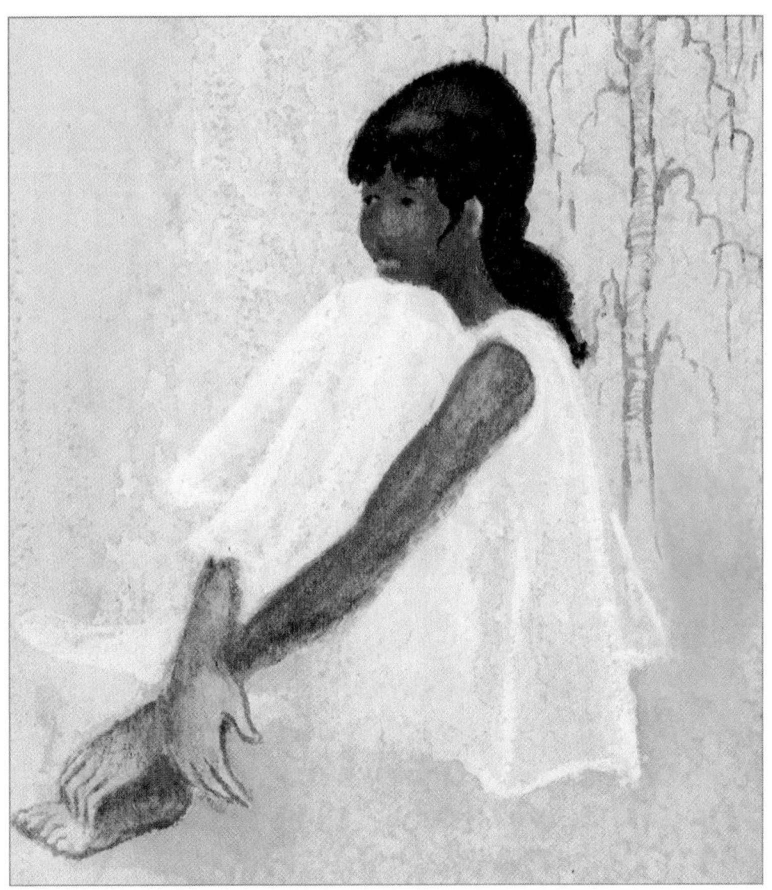

When Mama came home early the next morning, she found us sleeping on the floor. She unwrapped the cloths and washed out the cut—Callie hollered like anything—and said I'd done just what she'd have done herself. She never scolded about the ax—she knew there was no need—but she did ask why I hadn't come to fetch her. I was ashamed, telling Mama how I'd been too afraid to cross the bridge. "You've got good sense, Maisie," she answered. "I guess there's more than one way to cross a bridge."

It's been three months since Callie was hurt, and she's healed as much as she ever will. There's a fearsome scar on her leg, but Callie says that when she goes to live in the city she'll wear long pants like the men and no one will ever know.

Ever since I took care of Callie, Mama has let me help her with the doctoring. From the time I was little, I've helped her find and dry the flowers, but now I go along and watch when she tends to sick folks. When Callie talks about the city, I sometimes think I might visit her there. But for me, I think the mountain will always be my home. I like the way the mountain needs Mama. Someday I think it's going to need me, too.

The Bridge Dancers

Concept Connections

Linking the Selection

Think about the following questions, and then record your responses in the Response Journal section of your Writer's Notebook.

- What did Mama use for medicine?
- Why did Maisie take on the responsibility of treating her sister's wound?

Exploring Concept Vocabulary

The concept word for this lesson is ***remedy.*** If you don't know what this word means, look it up in a dictionary. Answer these questions.

- What did Maisie use as a ***remedy*** for Callie's pain?
- How did Maisie know which ***remedies*** to use for Callie's wounds?

In the Vocabulary section of your Writer's Notebook, write a sentence that includes the word ***remedy*** as well as one of the selection vocabulary words.

Expanding the Concept

Compare Dr. Dan from "Sewed Up His Heart" and Mama from "The Bridge Dancers." Consider the two characters' medical training as well as their roles in their communities. Try to use the word ***remedy*** in your discussion of the characters. Add new ideas about medicine to the Concept/Question Board.

Meet the Author

Carol Saller is a writer and editor who lives in Chicago, Illinois. She gets ideas for some of her stories from her two sons, John and Ben, who love to read.

When she's not working, Ms. Saller enjoys quilting and finding recipes for her husband to cook.

The Bridge Dancers is Ms. Saller's first book.

Meet the Illustrator

Gerald Talifero was born in Detroit, Michigan. Today he lives in Santa Barbara, California, where he works as an artist, designer, musician, and teacher.

Gerald Talifero is a multimedia artist who works in watercolor, pencil, and ink. In addition to art, he also works with troubled and disadvantaged children. His goal is to help children *"explore and develop their inner resources by outwardly coming in contact with nature."* Mr. Talifero and his "children" enjoy sailing, scuba diving, biking, and mountain climbing.

Fine Art

From Mystery to Medicine

Louis Pasteur in His Lab. 1885. **Albert Edelfelt.** Oil on canvas. Musée d'Orsay, Paris, France. Photo: ©Erich Lessing/Art Resource, NY.

Medicine, hexagonal relief from the Campanile. Mid-13th century. **Andrea Pisano.** Museo dell'Opera del Duomo, Florence, Italy. Photo: Nicolo Orsi Battaglini/Art Resource, NY.

***The Shop of the Druggist.* Pietro Longhi.** Accademia, Venice, Italy. Photo: SCALA/Photo Resource, NY.

***Interior of a Hospital with Doctors Tending Patients.* Gaddiano Manuscript 247.** Biblioteca Laurenziana, Florence, Italy. Photo: SCALA/Art Resource, NY.

Focus Questions How do scientists test what treatments work? How much more is there to learn about the human body?

Emily's Hands-On Science Experiment

by Hugh Westrup

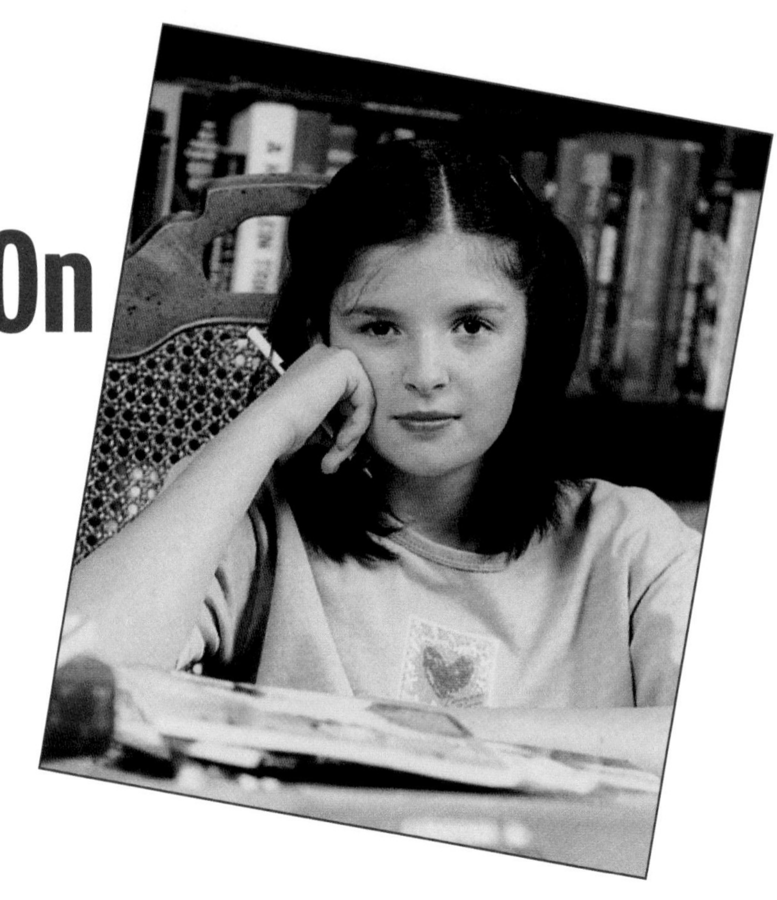

Emily Rosa looks nothing like what you would expect a scientist to look like. She doesn't carry around a calculator or wear a lab coat with a pocket protector. Still, the 11-year-old Colorado schoolgirl is the youngest person ever to publish the results of a scientific experiment in the *Journal of the American Medical Association*.

"Age doesn't matter," said George Lundberg, editor of the journal. "It's good science that matters, and this is good science."

Controversial science, too. Emily's experiment, a test of a widely used healing practice known as *therapeutic touch* drew angry responses when it was published in 1998.

Therapeutic touch (TT) doesn't actually involve touching. Instead, TT practitioners hold their hands several inches above a patient's body and move the hands back and forth.

The theory behind TT is that the practitioner's hands can sense a patient's energy field. That field, according to one longtime TT practitioner, feels to the touch like "warm gelatin or warm foam." By pushing the field around until it is in "balance," the therapist can supposedly make the patient feel better. Touch therapists claim they can treat cancer, ease asthma, and reduce pain and nausea, among other things.

One day, while Emily and her mother Linda were watching a videotape about therapeutic touch at home, an idea struck Emily: Why not do a scientific investigation of TT?

"My parents are skeptics, but I wanted to see for myself," said Emily.

Emily designed an experiment to test TT as a project for her school's annual science fair. She began by drawing up a *hypothesis*—an assumption that can be tested. Emily's hypothesis was this: If a human energy field exists, then trained touch therapists should be able to detect it.

Emily asked 21 practitioners of TT to be *subjects,* or participants in her experiment. She had them sit, one at a time, at a specially designed table. Positioned in the center of the table was an upright cardboard screen with two holes near the bottom. Each subject was asked to sit behind the screen and put his or her hands, palms up, through the holes.

Next, Emily flipped a coin and held one of her hands over the subject's left or right hand. The subject was then asked to identify which of his or her hands was near Emily's hand—in theory, by feeling her energy field.

In 280 *trials*, or repetitions of the experiment, the subjects correctly specified which hand Emily held above their own less than 44 percent of the time. In other words, the subjects performed no better than they would have simply by guessing.

When Emily's experiment was published in April 1998, the responses were sharp and immediate. "I do hope it's an April Fool's joke," said Dolores Krieger, a nursing professor at New York University. Krieger developed TT 26 years ago and says she has trained about 47,000 practitioners.

"The way [Emily's] subjects sat is foreign to TT, and our hands are moving, not stationary. You don't just walk into a room and perform—it's a whole *process,*" contended Krieger.

Several scientists praised Emily's work, however, and said that it cast doubt on the existence of a human energy field. *Journal* editor Lundberg urged touch therapists to reveal the results of Emily's study to potential patients. "Patients should save their money unless or until additional honest experimentation demonstrates an actual effect," said Lundberg.

Though Emily's experiment was a significant study, more work must be done to back up her findings. Like other first-time scientific experiments, Emily's must be *replicated*—done again by an independent investigator—to confirm or challenge her results. Further investigations could also modify Emily's experiment in various ways, in response to the criticisms of Krieger and other TT practitioners. A body of research on TT would then emerge.

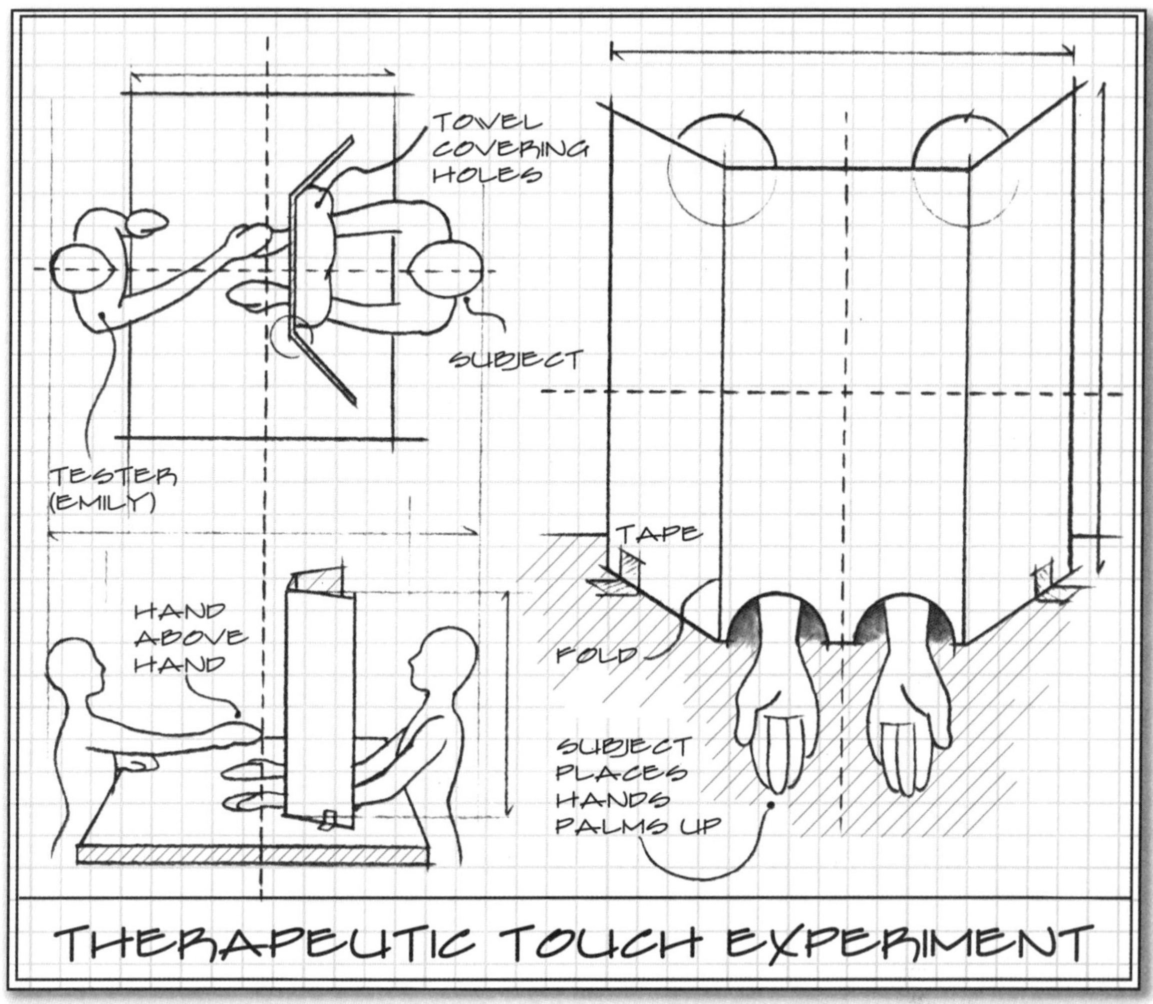

Because TT is a medical treatment, further *clinical trials* could also be conducted. A clinical trial is one that tests the effectiveness of a medical therapy on actual patients.

Numerous clinical studies of TT have actually been done already, said Donal O'Mathuna, a professor of bioethics and chemistry from Columbus, Ohio. Reviewing more than 100 clinical studies of TT, O'Mathuna found little evidence that TT helps patients.

Meanwhile, Emily continues her scientific pursuits. For her next experiment, she plans to test another popular form of alternative medicine: healing with magnets.

"Emily has always learned better by doing [things] herself," said Linda Rosa. "She is very curious, and it's a constant challenge to make sure she's involved in an active learning experience."

Emily's Hands-On Science Experiment

Concept Connections

Linking the Selection

Think about the following questions, and then record your responses in the Response Journal section of your Writer's Notebook.

- What was Emily's hypothesis?
- How did Emily test her hypothesis?
- Why were TT practitioners critical of Emily's experiment?

Exploring Concept Vocabulary

The concept word for this lesson is ***trial.*** If you don't know what this word means, look it up in a dictionary. Answer these questions.

- Why is it important to have more than one ***trial*** in a medical experiment?
- Why should more ***trials*** of Emily's experiment be conducted by another investigator?

In the Vocabulary section of your Writer's Notebook, write a sentence that includes the word ***trial*** as well as one of the selection vocabulary words.

Expanding the Concept

Compare Emily's experiment with one of Louis Pasteur's experiments. Consider the importance of the experiments to the field of medicine. Try to use the word ***trial*** in your discussion of the experiments. Add new ideas about medicine to the Concept/Question Board.

Meet the Author

Hugh Westrup was born and raised in Canada, receiving his Master's degree in psychology at York University. Mr. Westrup's scientific training helps him write nonfiction books for children. Some of the books he has written are *Maurice Strong: Working for Planet Earth*, *The Mammals*, *Bite Size Science*, and *Bite Size Geography*. He has also worked as an editor for *Current Science Magazine*, where his article about Emily's experiment was published.

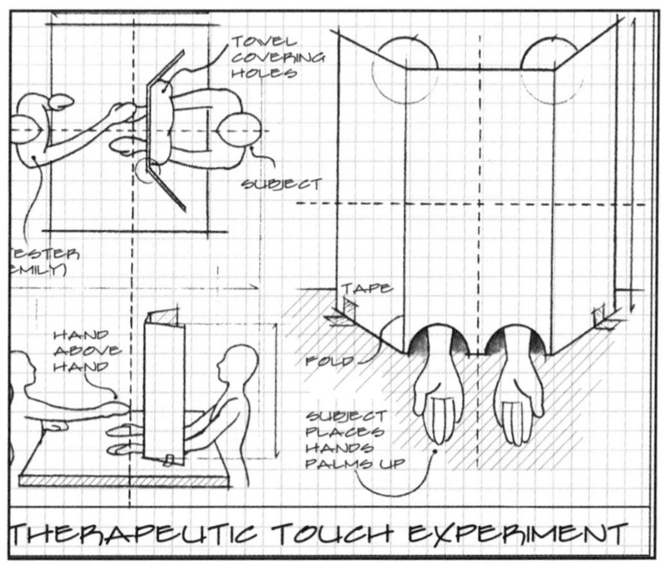

Focus Questions How does medicine differ from place to place? What are the most important qualities in a doctor?

The New Doctor

from ***You Can Hear a Magpie Smile***
by Paula G. Paul
illustrated by Roberta Collier-Morales

Manuelita's house seemed unusually quiet as Lupe approached it. She wasn't sure why at first, then she realized that it was because she did not hear Noche screeching, cawing, and chattering. Maybe Manuelita was not at home. Lupe ran the last few steps up to the front and knocked on the door.

Still no sounds came from inside the house, but soon the door opened noiselessly, and Lupe saw Manuelita standing in front of her. Noche was perched on her shoulder, his long tail hanging down her back. Manuelita said nothing, but stepped aside for Lupe to enter.

"I thought you weren't home," Lupe said.

"In a few more ticks of the clock, we would not have been," Manuelita said.

As Lupe walked into the kitchen, she saw several small cloth bags lying on the table and a large knapsack beside them. Manuelita began gathering up the bags and putting them inside the knapsack.

"You are going to gather herbs," Lupe said. She had seen Manuelita make these preparations before.

Manuelita nodded. She turned toward the cupboard to check the contents of a glass jar. Noche almost lost his balance with the turn and fluttered his wings to keep his position on Manuelita's shoulder. He seemed to know that Manuelita was

going out and was making sure he stuck close beside her so that she would not leave him behind.

"You will look for summer herbs along the river? May I go with you?" Lupe asked eagerly.

"No," Manuelita answered. "I am going into the mountains."

"The mountains?" Lupe asked puzzled. There was a bigger variety of herbs along the river than in the mountains.

"Yes," Manuelita answered. "I will need more osha."

"But I just brought you some. Remember? I gathered it when Maria and I were lost, and—"

"Yes," Manuelita said. "But I will need more. Much more. There is nowhere else in the whole country that osha is as plentiful and as strong as it is in these mountains here."

Lupe wondered why Manuelita thought she would need so much of the herb. She thought of all the things it was used for. The root could be boiled for upset stomach and headaches, or ground to a powder and mixed with flour to paste on the chest of someone who had a cold, or placed on a sore spot on the body to aid healing. The green leaves could be cooked with meat or beans and eaten regularly, just to stay healthy.

Maybe Manuelita thought there was going to be a lot of sickness in the village. But with the new doctor's popularity, many people would no doubt go to her with their complaints. Manuelita must know that, too. It didn't make sense.

Oh, well, Lupe thought, at least Manuelita doesn't seem unhappy. She is still going about her work as usual. She is being her old dependable self. Maybe that is a good sign.

Still, Lupe wanted to be with her friend.

"I will go with you into the mountains," she said. "I will have to ask Mama, of course, but I'm sure if she knows you are going, she will—"

"No." Manuelita's voice was firm. "I must go alone."

"But—"

Manuelita reached toward Lupe and held her shoulders. "I will go alone," she said, looking deep into Lupe's eyes, "but when I come back, you must come to me."

Lupe searched Manuelita's face, trying to understand. "Yes, of course, I will come," she said.

"Then go and play now. There is still time for that."

Lupe thought that was a strange thing for Manuelita to say, but Manuelita said many strange things. She didn't have time to ask her about it, however, because Manuelita had finished packing her knapsack and was ushering her out the door.

As Lupe started through the brush toward the village, she looked back to see Manuelita, carrying the knapsack and with Noche clinging to her shoulder. The bird was not making a sound but was acting as if he dared not be naughty for fear he would be left behind.

By the time Lupe reached the village, her friend Maria had found someone else to play hopscotch with her. They were too far along with the game to add a newcomer, so Lupe walked away from the sandy spot, looking for something else to do.

She walked past the school and saw several children on the playground, but she didn't feel like joining them. She just kept walking, and before she realized it, she found herself in front of the new temporary clinic building.

There didn't seem to be any cars around it, and the only activity going on was at the noisy construction site for the permanent building nearby. Lupe decided to walk up to the temporary building and peek inside for another look. Since the front door was open just a crack, she tried to see through it. At first, she couldn't see too clearly, so she leaned closer to the door. Just as she did, the door opened from the inside, and Lupe tumbled forward, sprawling on the floor and looking at a pair of sandals. The feet inside the sandals were webbed by gossamer-thin nylon hose.

"Well, what have we here?" said a voice from above. Lupe looked up and saw that both the feet and the voice belonged to Dr. Johnson. The doctor came down to her knees and looked at Lupe. "Are you hurt?" she asked.

"No!" Lupe said. She jumped up quickly and dusted herself off.

"I didn't mean to make you fall. I opened the door to get a breath of fresh air, and I had no idea you were leaning against it."

Lupe ducked her head to hide her burning cheeks.

"Oh, look," the doctor said. "You've scraped your knee on the threshold. Let's see what we can do about that."

Dr. Johnson led Lupe into the examination room. She took her to the sink and washed the knee with warm soapy water, then rinsed and dried it. Next, she took a bottle of red liquid from a shelf and dabbed some of the liquid on the scraped spot. The red medicine caused Lupe's knee to burn furiously, but she did not cry out, and she swallowed hard to keep the tears from her eyes.

The treatment was very much the same as Manuelita would have given. She would have washed the area and dried it. Sometimes she even used the fiery red medicine you could buy at the grocery store, but more often, she would dab on a plaster made from the osha.

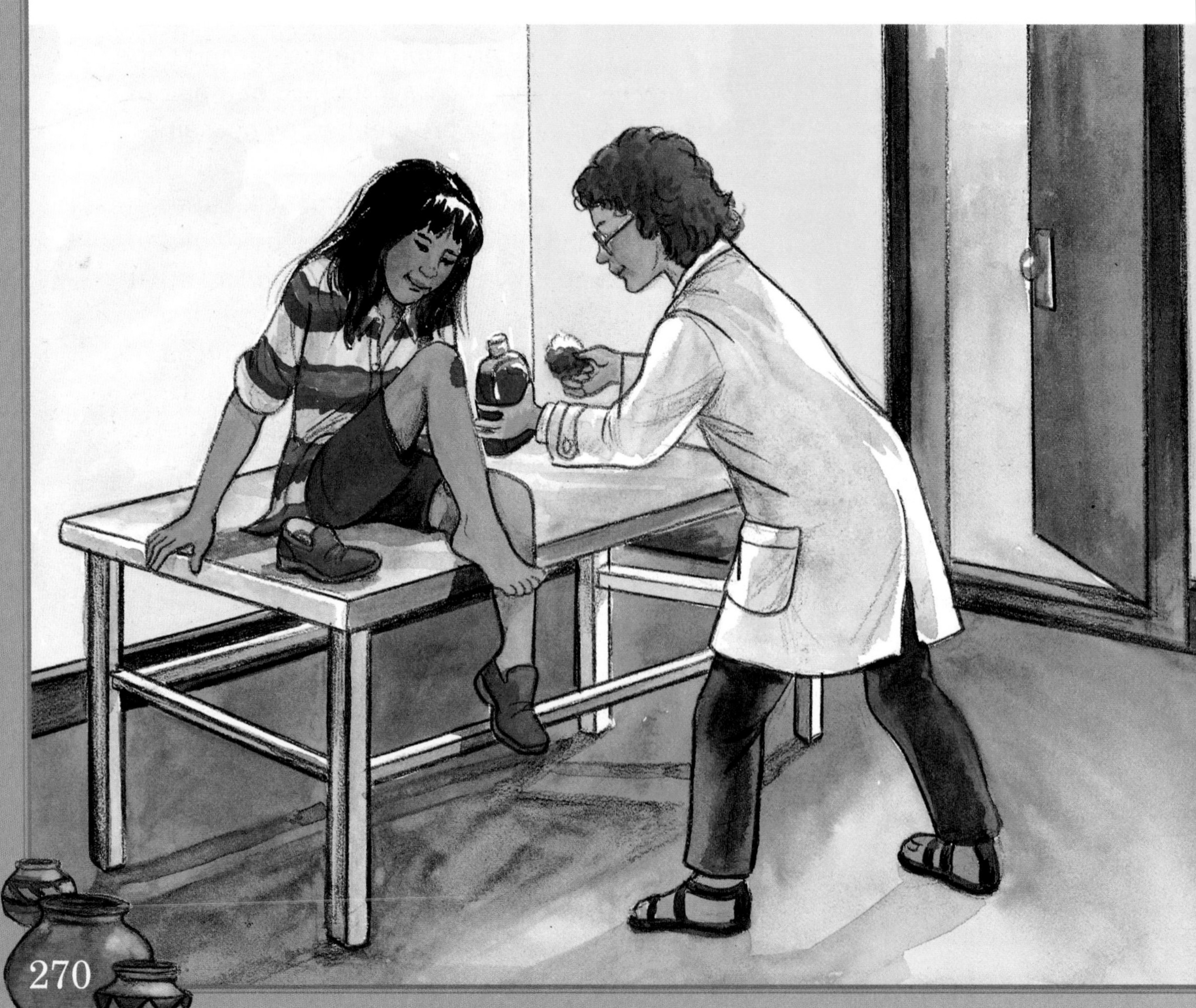

"There," Dr. Johnson said, putting the bottle of medicine away. "You have been my first patient, and you have come even before the clinic is officially open. It is to open tomorrow, you know. And I've spent all day today trying to get things organized and put away." The doctor sat down at her desk and faced Lupe. She smiled and said, "Now tell me, what can I do for you? Did you come for something special?"

"Nothing special," Lupe said, her voice very low.

"Perhaps you were just curious."

Lupe nodded her head.

"I can understand," Dr. Johnson said. "You have never had a clinic here before, and I suppose you wanted to see what it is like. I would have been the same way at your age. I was curious about just about everything—always poking my nose into something, and often getting into trouble."

Lupe looked up at the doctor, surprised. She was trying to imagine her as a little girl, poking her nose into things. The doctor was laughing at her memories, and the short curls on her head bounced as she laughed. Lupe found herself laughing with her.

"What is your name?" Dr. Johnson asked.

"Lupe Montano."

"I'm Dr. Eleanor Johnson. Did I meet you at the reception? I'm sorry I don't remember, but there were a lot of people there."

Lupe shook her head. "I wasn't there," she said. Lupe let her eyes roam around the room. Dr. Johnson had placed many things on the shelves and counters. There were bottles and jars which Lupe thought must contain medicines, but she didn't know what all the strange-looking tools were for.

"What are those for?" Lupe heard herself asking. She was surprised at her own question. She hadn't meant to ask anything, but her curiosity was stronger than her shyness.

This?" Dr. Johnson asked, picking up a piece of cloth attached to ropes and dials. "This is for taking blood pressure. Look, I'll show you how it works." The doctor wrapped the cloth around Lupe's arm. She put something in her own ears and placed the end of it to Lupe's arm also.

"When I listen here"—Dr. Johnson pointed to the thing in her ears—"and look at this" she pointed to the dial—"it helps me find out a little about your body, and maybe whether you are well or sick."

"What do you hear with that?" Lupe asked, pointing to the thing in the doctor's ears.

"This is a stethoscope, and I can hear your heartbeat," the doctor said, and she let Lupe listen to her own heartbeat.

"We will also have X rays, and on certain days of the week, we will have people come here to help me with them. An X ray takes pictures of the inside of your body."

Lupe had heard about X rays in school, although she had never seen one. Taking a picture, from the outside, of the inside of a person's body seemed more like witchcraft to her than anything Manuelita had ever done.

She looked up at the shelves full of bottles. "You have many remedies," she said. "It must have taken you a long time to mix them all."

"Oh, I didn't make them myself." The doctor laughed.

"Then where did you get them?" Lupe asked.

"Why, I bought them, from companies that sell medicines. There are many companies that know how to make medicines much better than I could."

Lupe looked at her silently. She wondered how she knew the medicines were good if she did not make them herself.

"I'll have a lot of advantages to share with you," Dr. Johnson said. "You won't have to travel all the way to Albuquerque when you are sick, or rely on home remedies you make yourself, that don't work most of the time. I'm looking forward to bringing that to all of you, and I'm looking forward to being your friend."

Dr. Johnson reached her hand toward Lupe's, but Lupe pulled her hand away and jumped up from her chair.

"I've got to go now," she said. "I forgot to tell my mother where I would be."

Lupe ran out of the building and down the road toward her house. She did not want to be friends with the new doctor, because the new doctor could not be Manuelita's friend. The new doctor would not want to have anything to do with a person who mixed her own medicines and did not know how to take pictures of people's insides.

Manuelita was gone for several days. Lupe began to worry about her. Manuelita had gone out searching for herbs and stayed far into the night and even overnight before, but never had she been gone this long. Lupe was also concerned because so many people had been going to the clinic. She was afraid they had abandoned Manuelita completely.

Worst of all, Lupe felt disloyal and guilty about the amount of time she, herself, had spent at the new clinic. She couldn't seem to help herself, though. She was fascinated by all the new medicines and strange instruments and, although she did not like to admit it, by the new doctor herself.

One day, when she couldn't talk Maria into going with her, Lupe decided to walk over to the clinic alone. She told herself she only wanted to see how the new building was coming along and perhaps catch a glimpse of Alonzo working with the big machines she'd heard him talk about. But before long, she was seated on the ground in front of the temporary mobile-home clinic, watching people coming and going. Occasionally, if it was someone she knew well enough, she would ask what their ailment was before they went in and what the treatment had been as they came out.

Manuelita had been right. The new doctor's medicine was often very different from hers.

Finally, when the sun was quite low on the horizon, Dr. Johnson herself came to the door. She took off her white coat and held it across her arm. She was wearing a summer dress made of a pretty blue material. It looked nice with her sandals.

"Hello, Lupe," she said. "Someone told me you were out here. Would you like to come in?"

Lupe shook her head.

"Oh, you needn't be shy," Dr. Johnson said. "You seem to be very interested in medicine. Wouldn't you like to talk? I enjoy talking to you."

"It's getting late. It will soon be time for supper," Lupe said, and she ran toward home.

The next time Lupe saw the doctor was in the grocery store. Lupe had gone there to get some flour for her mother to make *tortillas*. A few of the village men were standing around inside the store talking, and Dr. Johnson was talking to Mr. Baca, the owner of the store. She held a can of something in her hand and read the label.

"I don't know," she said. "I do hate to use this. I don't like these poisons, but the bugs are getting to be a problem at the clinic, and I've got to do something."

"You could try calabasilla leaves," Lupe blurted out.

"What?" Dr. Johnson turned around with a surprised look on her face. "Oh, hello, Lupe. I didn't know you were here. Seems you're always surprising me."

"I can bring you some leaves," Lupe said.

"Some what?"

"Leaves. Dried calabasilla leaves. If you sprinkle them around the edges of the rooms, it will keep the bugs out."

"Really? I've never heard of that."

"Works good," said one of the villagers in the store.

"Sure does," said another.

"Lupe knows," said still another.

"I'll bring you some tomorrow," Lupe said. She put the money for the flour on the counter.

Dr. Johnson had a funny look on her face, as if she didn't believe the dried leaves would work. But if she said anything in reply, Lupe didn't hear her over the noise of Mr. Baca's ancient cash register.

Lupe walked out of the store as quickly as she could. She would go back to the clinic just one more time, to deliver the leaves, she told herself. That would be her way of repaying Dr. Johnson for fixing her scraped knee. Every time Lupe thought of that incident, her heart sank. What would Manuelita think if she ever found out that her friend, Lupe Montano, had been the new doctor's first patient!

The day after Lupe had seen Dr. Johnson in the grocery store, she and Maria went down to the sandy spot to play hopscotch. While they were playing, Lupe heard a familiar cawing sound and looked up to see Manuelita walking through the brush toward her house. Noche, as usual, was perched on her shoulder.

"Manuelita's back!" Lupe said to Maria.

"Are you going to stop the game and go see her?" Maria asked, sounding disappointed.

"No," Lupe said. She stood on one foot and bent to pick up her pebble, then hopped to the end of the series of squares and circles. No matter how glad she was that Manuelita was back, she knew she wouldn't have time to go see her. It was getting late, and she still had to take the calabasilla leaves to Dr. Johnson.

When the game was over, Lupe went home to get the dried leaves. Maybe the doctor doesn't really want them, Lupe thought. She certainly didn't act as if she were anxious to have them. But Lupe was anxious to show her how well they worked, so she went to the pantry and took a jar from a shelf. It was too bad, she thought, to take the last jar, and one that Manuelita had given her family at that. But Lupe knew she could always gather the leaves from the sprawling gourd vines herself, when she found the time. They grew profusely along the river and on the mesas.

Lupe told her mother what she planned to do before she left the house.

"That's very nice of you, Lupe," Mama said. "It is always a good thing to welcome a newcomer with a gift."

When Lupe reached the clinic, there was no one in the waiting room. She was glad, because she didn't want to meet anyone who might say something to Manuelita about her being there. That was one of the reasons she had waited so late to come. She was surprised, however, to hear voices coming from inside the office as she walked up to the door. Two men's voices were speaking rapidly and excitedly in Spanish, and Dr. Johnson's voice was pleading in English.

"Please, please," Lupe could hear the doctor say. "Speak more slowly. My Spanish is not good. I can't understand you."

Lupe walked quietly into the office and saw Uncle Pedro and Cousin Josefa's husband.

"Lupe!" Dr. Johnson said as soon as she saw her. "Maybe you can help. Something's wrong, and these two men are too excited to speak English. Can you tell me what they're saying?"

Lupe questioned the men, who answered her in breathless Spanish. Lupe turned to the doctor.

"It is my Cousin Josefa," she said. "They want you to go to her."

"Josefa?" The doctor seemed puzzled for a moment. "Oh, yes. The woman who is going to have a baby!"

"Yes," Lupe answered. "The men say it is time. They are very excited."

"Of course," Dr. Johnson said with a little laugh. She gathered some things into a bag. "I daresay your cousin will be much calmer than these men are. Come on," she said, motioning to the men. "I'll have to go to her. I have no more facilities for delivering a baby in this temporary building than you'll have at home."

The men followed the doctor out to her car, and everyone, including Lupe, got in. No one seemed to expect Lupe not to go, and she certainly hated to miss the excitement. Maybe it was a good thing she did go along, she decided. She was the one who had to direct the doctor to her cousin's house.

When they arrived, the men took the doctor by one arm each and led her into the house. Cousin Josefa was in a bedroom near the front of the house. Lupe waited in the living room with the family while Dr. Johnson went inside to examine Josefa. That was exactly as Manuelita would have done it, Lupe thought. Soon, the doctor came out of the bedroom. She was smiling.

"Josefa is in fine shape," she said. "It will only be a short wait before the baby is born."

In a little while, Dr. Johnson went back to see about Josefa again.

"She is doing very well," the doctor said when she came out of the bedroom, but her smile had vanished.

The next time the doctor went in to examine Josefa, she looked even more concerned when she emerged.

"She is doing very well, physically, but something is making her unhappy. She kept asking for someone named Manuelita. Is that her friend? Or perhaps her mother?"

"I can get her for you," Lupe said quickly.

"No! No!" said Uncle Pedro.

Just then Josefa called from the bedroom. "Is that Lupe's voice I hear? Let me talk to her."

Dr. Johnson turned to Lupe. "I don't know," she said. "You really shouldn't. . . . "

"Lupe! Let me talk to Lupe!" Josefa called.

Dr. Johnson's brow wrinkled into a frown. She bit her lower lip. "Oh . . . very well," she said. "Come with me." She led Lupe into the bedroom.

"Lupe!" Cousin Josefa said happily from her bed. "The little curandera." She spoke to Lupe softly in Spanish. She could also speak English very well, as could her husband and Uncle Pedro, but, as with most people in the village, when she was excited or had something very special to say, Spanish seemed the best language for saying it. When she had finished talking, Lupe turned to the doctor and told her what Cousin Josefa had said.

"Josefa says that her father, my Uncle Pedro, wants you to help with the baby because he thinks only the new modern ways are good enough for his grandchild, but she says she wants Manuelita to help her, because she is sure Manuelita knows all the right things to do. She says perhaps you know too, but with Manuelita she is certain."

"Who is Manuelita?"

"A curandera."

"A what?"

"A curandera."

"Oh, yes," Dr. Johnson said. "I seem to remember . . . a healer. Yes, I've heard of them. Sometimes associated with witchcraft, aren't they? No, I won't have that."

"Manuelita does not use witchcraft," Lupe said. "That is what Uncle Pedro thinks, but it is not true."

Josefa, who had heard the conversation, began to cry.

"Now, now," Dr. Johnson said, turning to her. "You mustn't be upset."

"I have seen that your kind of medicine is good, but Manuelita's is good, too," Lupe said. "Perhaps you could learn from each other."

"Superstition has no place at a time like this," Dr. Johnson answered.

Josefa was crying softly. "Lupe is a little curandera," she said in English. "She knows the good way."

"You, a curandera?" Dr. Johnson asked. "What does she mean?"

"Manuelita has taught me many things," Lupe said.

"Well, I guess that explains your interest in medicine. Lupe, I welcome you to come talk to me as often as we can find the time. Maybe I can undo some of the wrong ideas you may have."

"But—" Lupe started to protest.

"We don't have time to talk about it now," Dr. Johnson said. "Josefa's baby will be here soon."

Josefa was still crying. "It is only that I want the best for my baby," she said.

"The best thing for you and the baby both is for you to remain calm."

But Josefa only cried harder and clutched at her middle. Dr. Johnson spoke as if she were talking to herself. "She was handling it so well at first."

"Maybe Manuelita could at least help you," Lupe insisted.

"I could use some help," Dr. Johnson said, "but a curandera . . . no." She looked again at the sobbing Josefa.

Dr. Johnson's not going to give in, Lupe thought. She watched as the doctor fussed around Josefa, holding her hand and talking to her softly.

"It's not going to be a good birth if she is so upset," Dr. Johnson said to no one in particular. She turned to Lupe. "Maybe it wouldn't hurt anything for this, this Manuelita just to be here. . . . All right, Lupe, go get the healer."

Lupe ran from the house as fast as she could, still clutching the jar of calabasilla leaves she had forgotten to give to Dr. Johnson. She was breathless when she reached Manuelita's house, but she managed to explain what was happening and to tell her that the new doctor was with Josefa.

She was surprised at how fast the elderly Manuelita was able to get to Josefa's home. Noche flew ahead, circling and returning to Manuelita and Lupe, screeching and talking nonsense. As usual, he was left outside when Manuelita entered the patient's house.

Uncle Pedro stood up to protest as soon as he saw Manuelita. "What's she doing here?" he asked.

Manuelita did not look at Uncle Pedro, or speak to him. He tried to follow Manuelita into the bedroom, but she slammed the door in his face, almost catching his nose between the door and the wall.

Lupe could hear many noises coming from the bedroom while she waited in the living room with the men.

"The doctor will see that it is done right," Uncle Pedro said, over and over again, to reassure both himself and his son-in-law.

The noises in the bedroom ceased. The silence was brief, interrupted by the cry of a tiny voice. Both of the men jumped from their seats. Dr. Johnson opened the bedroom door.

"Josefa and her husband have a beautiful daughter," she said.

She let everyone go into the room for a few minutes to see Josefa. First Josefa's husband went in, then Uncle Pedro, then Lupe.

Lupe saw Cousin Josefa holding her baby and smiling, and Manuelita standing beside them. Dr. Johnson walked toward Manuelita and held out her hand.

"Thank you," the doctor said. "I . . . I guess I have a lot to learn."

Manuelita took the doctor's hand in hers, but she did not speak.

The New Doctor

Concept Connections

Linking the Selection

Think about the following questions, and then record your responses in the Response Journal section of your Writer's Notebook.

- How was the treatment Lupe received from Dr. Johnson similar to the treatment she would have received from Manuelita?
- What did Lupe learn from visiting Dr. Johnson's office?

Exploring Concept Vocabulary

The concept word for this lesson is ***effective.*** If you don't know what this word means, look it up in a dictionary. Answer these questions.

- How did Dr. Johnson learn that natural medicine can be ***effective?***
- What did Lupe suggest to Dr. Johnson as an ***effective*** alternative to bug poison?

In the Vocabulary section of your Writer's Notebook, write a sentence that includes the word ***effective*** as well as one of the selection vocabulary words.

Expanding the Concept

In each of the selections you've read so far in this unit, people are learning from others about the practice of medicine. Discuss some of the ways this knowledge was shared and some of the things characters learned from one another. Try to use the word ***effective*** in your discussion of the selections. Add new ideas about medicine to the Concept/Question Board.

Meet the Author

Paula G. Paul grew up on a farm in Texas. Her family had no electricity, no television, no telephone, and the nearest town was 30 miles away. She was very good at entertaining herself and finding things that interested her. Even today she says, *"I am a person who is never bored."*

Ms. Paul says this about writing: *"The most important thing a person needs to be a good writer is perseverance, because it's not always easy. Even though we may be full of stories, what we need to learn is how to tell those stories in a way that is easy to read and understand. You have to learn how to tell the story. You have to believe in yourself."*

Meet the Illustrator

Roberta Collier-Morales admits that while she loved to draw, dance, sing, and play the piano as a child, she had a difficult time learning to read. She encourages others who are having problems with certain subjects to seek help and talk about what they are experiencing. *"The important thing is not to give up on yourself,"* she says. Ms. Collier-Morales studied art at Colorado State University, graduating in 1971. She is currently continuing her education in graduate school and lives with her two children, her parents, and her pets.

Focus Questions What makes some people decide to be doctors? How do doctors feel when they cannot help a patient get better?

The Story of Susan La Flesche Picotte

from ***Homeward the Arrow's Flight***
by Marion Marsh Brown
illustrated by Diane Magnuson

Susan La Flesche Picotte was the first female Native-American doctor in the United States. After completing medical school she returned to her home and began work as the doctor at the reservation school. In this excerpt, her first weeks as not only the school doctor but doctor for the whole reservation are told.

Susan wrote a letter of application on the very night that she told Rosalie, her sister, she wanted the position of reservation physician. Then she waited anxiously for a reply.

At last the letter arrived. She tore it open eagerly. "Well, finally," she sighed. She carried it to the kitchen where her mother was preparing supper. "I got the appointment," she said. "I don't get any more money though."

Her mother looked up. "So much more work and no more pay?" she asked.

"That's what the letter says: 'As there are no funds available except for your present salary as physician to the government school, we will be unable to pay any additional moneys for your additional services as reservation physician.' Well, anyway I have the title. Now to see what I can do with it."

That same night, the first snow of the winter fell. Susan was soon inundated with a siege of colds, grippe, and pneumonia. It was as if the first snowstorm had been a signal for winter illnesses to attack.

She had laid her plans carefully before entering into her new contract to do two jobs for the price of one. She would spend mornings at the school and would make house calls in the afternoons. The only problem, she soon discovered, was that there weren't enough hours in the day.

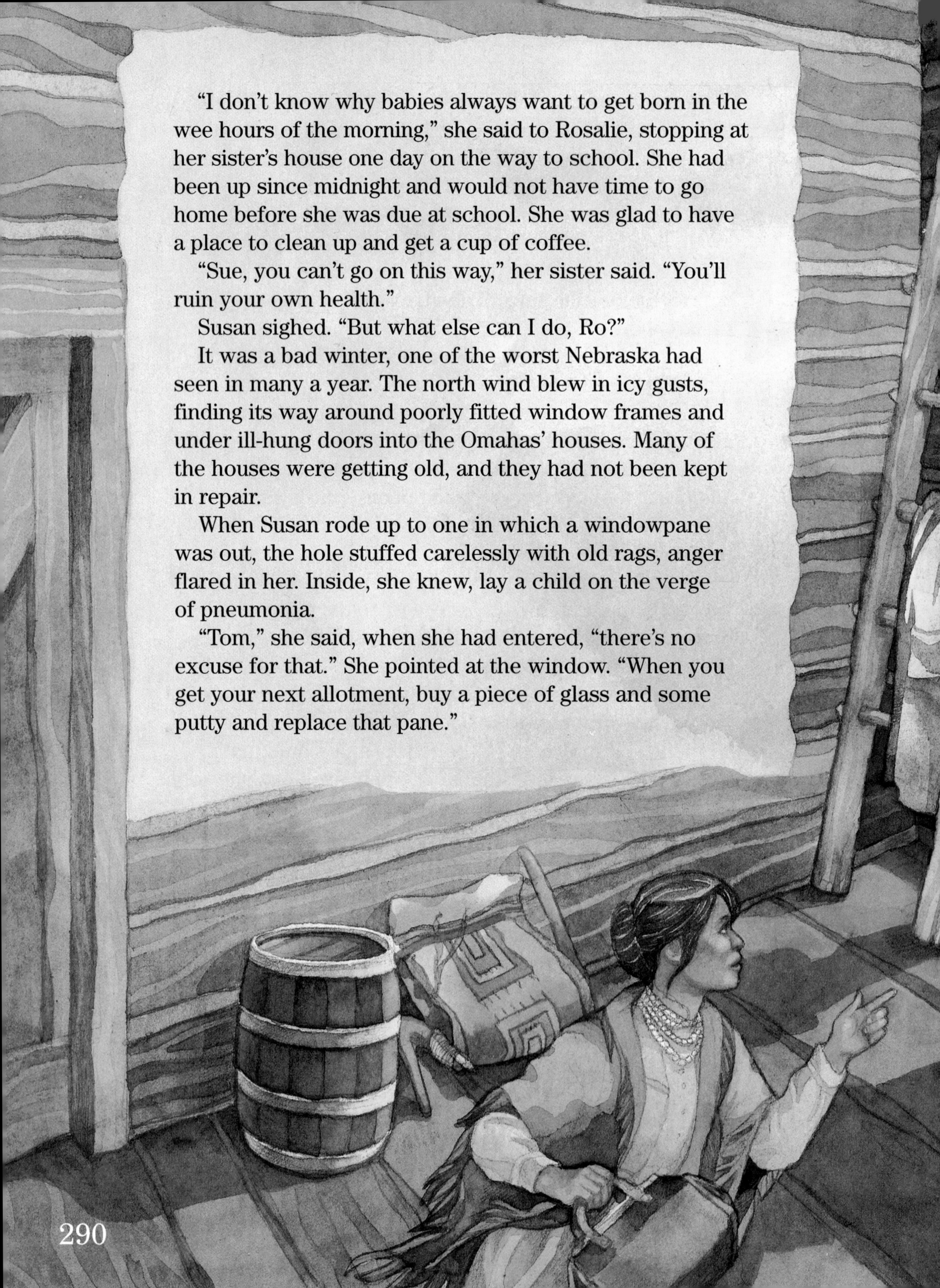

"I don't know why babies always want to get born in the wee hours of the morning," she said to Rosalie, stopping at her sister's house one day on the way to school. She had been up since midnight and would not have time to go home before she was due at school. She was glad to have a place to clean up and get a cup of coffee.

"Sue, you can't go on this way," her sister said. "You'll ruin your own health."

Susan sighed. "But what else can I do, Ro?"

It was a bad winter, one of the worst Nebraska had seen in many a year. The north wind blew in icy gusts, finding its way around poorly fitted window frames and under ill-hung doors into the Omahas' houses. Many of the houses were getting old, and they had not been kept in repair.

When Susan rode up to one in which a windowpane was out, the hole stuffed carelessly with old rags, anger flared in her. Inside, she knew, lay a child on the verge of pneumonia.

"Tom," she said, when she had entered, "there's no excuse for that." She pointed at the window. "When you get your next allotment, buy a piece of glass and some putty and replace that pane."

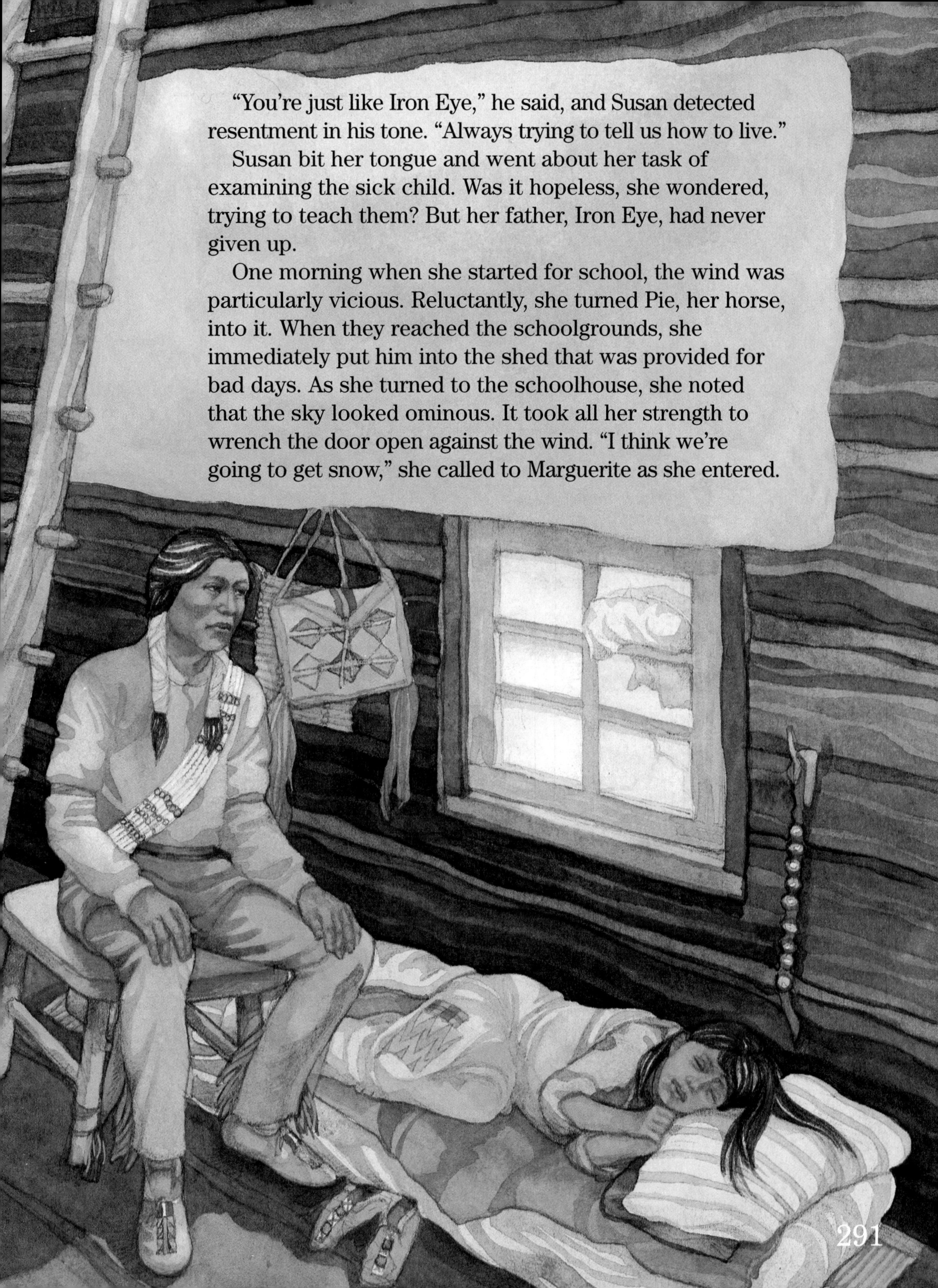

"You're just like Iron Eye," he said, and Susan detected resentment in his tone. "Always trying to tell us how to live."

Susan bit her tongue and went about her task of examining the sick child. Was it hopeless, she wondered, trying to teach them? But her father, Iron Eye, had never given up.

One morning when she started for school, the wind was particularly vicious. Reluctantly, she turned Pie, her horse, into it. When they reached the schoolgrounds, she immediately put him into the shed that was provided for bad days. As she turned to the schoolhouse, she noted that the sky looked ominous. It took all her strength to wrench the door open against the wind. "I think we're going to get snow," she called to Marguerite as she entered.

Marguerite turned back, and Susan saw the worried look on her face. "Oh, dear, I hope not. Charlie's sick again. He has an awful cough, Sue, and he was so hot last night. I know he has fever. And he went out to look after the stock this morning. I was hoping you could go by and see him this afternoon."

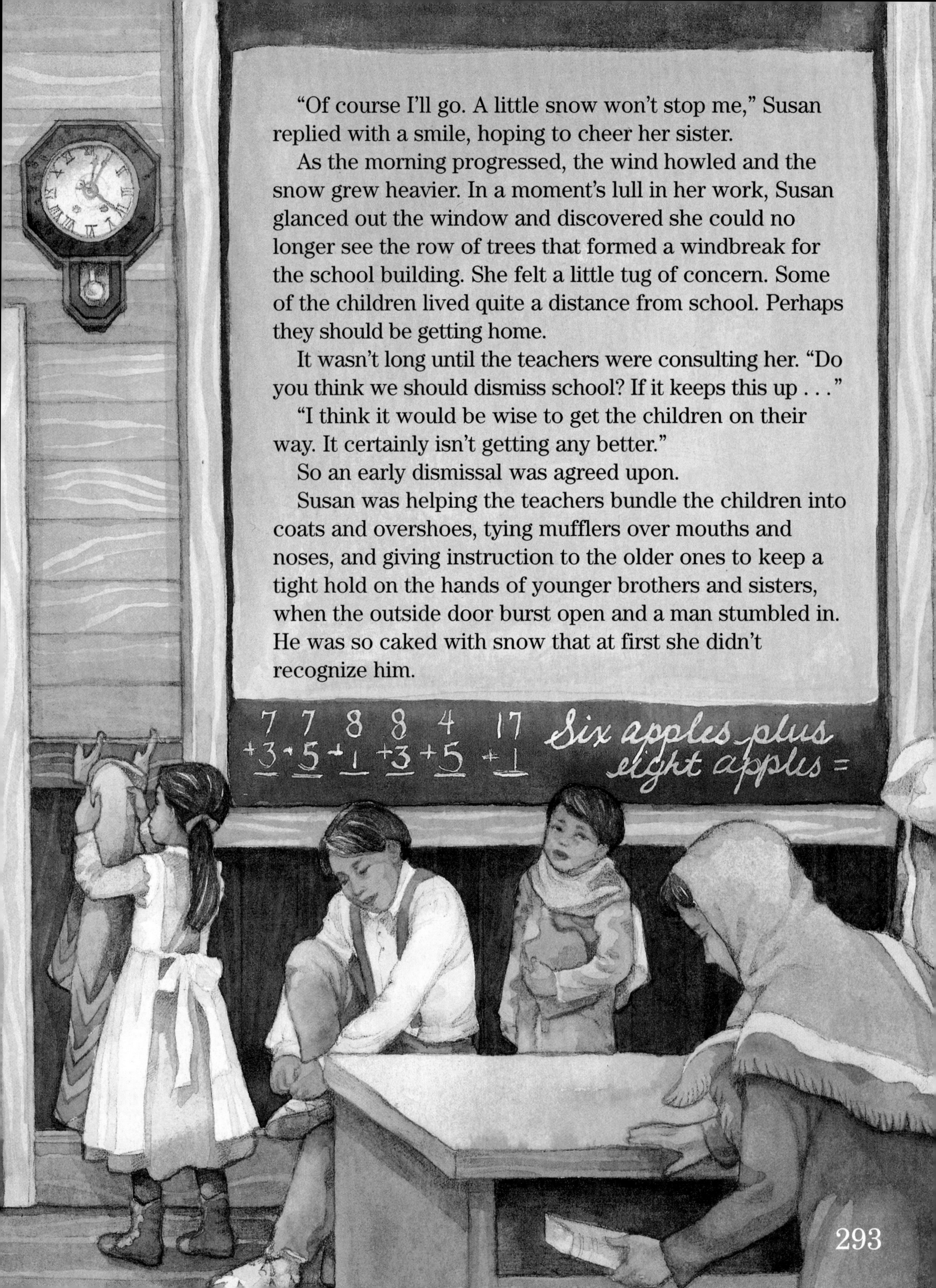

"Of course I'll go. A little snow won't stop me," Susan replied with a smile, hoping to cheer her sister.

As the morning progressed, the wind howled and the snow grew heavier. In a moment's lull in her work, Susan glanced out the window and discovered she could no longer see the row of trees that formed a windbreak for the school building. She felt a little tug of concern. Some of the children lived quite a distance from school. Perhaps they should be getting home.

It wasn't long until the teachers were consulting her. "Do you think we should dismiss school? If it keeps this up . . ."

"I think it would be wise to get the children on their way. It certainly isn't getting any better."

So an early dismissal was agreed upon.

Susan was helping the teachers bundle the children into coats and overshoes, tying mufflers over mouths and noses, and giving instruction to the older ones to keep a tight hold on the hands of younger brothers and sisters, when the outside door burst open and a man stumbled in. He was so caked with snow that at first she didn't recognize him.

"Dr. Susan!" he cried. "Come quick! My Minnie . . ."

"Oh, it's you, Joe," she said. "Has your wife started labor?"

He nodded. "But she's bad, Doctor. Not like before."

"Come on in and warm up, then go home and put lots of water on the stove to heat. I'll be along shortly."

Joe didn't linger. As soon as the children were on their way and she had straightened up her office, Susan sought out Marguerite. "I'll have to wait to see Charlie until after I deliver Minnie Whitefeather's baby. Joe says she's having a bad time, so I may be late."

"All right. Be sure to bundle up," Marguerite said. "It looks like the storm's getting worse."

"That I will. I always come prepared!" Susan assured her. She pulled her stocking cap down over her ears and donned the heavy wool mittens her mother had knit for her.

"I hope you'll be all right," Marguerite said. "It's a long way over there."

"Don't worry. You can depend on Pie!" Susan waved a cheery good-bye and plunged out into the storm. She had to fight her way to the shed. Already drifts were piling high. "I hope the children are all safely home by now," she thought. Her pony was nervous. "Good old Pie," she said, patting the sleek neck as she mounted. "When you were a young one and we went racing across the hills, you didn't think you were going to have to plow through all kinds of weather with me when you grew old, did you?"

The Whitefeathers lived on the northernmost edge of the reservation. Susan turned Pie onto the road, and he plodded into the storm. "Good boy!" she said encouragingly. But she couldn't hear her words above the violent shrieking of the wind. Nor, shortly, could she tell whether they were following the road; she could only trust Pie.

It seemed to her that the storm grew worse by the minute. Suddenly Pie stopped, turning his head back as if asking Susan what he should do. She tried to wipe the caked snow from her eyes to see what was wrong and found that her fingers were stiff. But she saw Pie's problem. A huge drift lay across their path. "We'll have to go around it, Pie." She pulled him to the left until they reached a point where the drift tapered off. Pie moved around it, and Susan thought, "Now can we find the road again—if we were on the road?" She pulled on the right rein. But she couldn't tell whether they were going north, for now the storm seemed to be swirling around them from all directions.

Soon another drift blocked their way. But this time Pie wallowed through with a strange, swimming motion. How did he know he could get through that one and not the

other, she wondered. Suddenly, having maneuvered the drift, the pony stopped.

"Get up, Pie! We have to go on!" she urged. He did not move. She slapped the stiff reins on his neck, but to no avail. She tried kicking his sides with feet she discovered were numb. "We'll freeze to death! Go *on!*" Still Pie refused to move.

At length she dismounted. If she could walk on her numb feet, perhaps she could lead him. Stumbling, she made her way to Pie's head.

Then she saw, and she caught her breath in terror. For Pie stood with his head directly over a bundle in the snow—a bundle that she knew instantly was a child.

"Oh, my!" she cried. She lifted the bundle into her arms. It was a boy, one of the little ones they had turned out of school to find his way home. "What were we thinking of?" Susan railed at herself. "Jimmy! Jimmy!" she cried, shaking the child. She scooped the snow off his eyelids. He stirred, and then his eyelids lifted. "Jimmy! It's Dr. Sue. You were asleep, Jimmy. You have to wake up now." She hoisted him in front of her on the pony, and, holding him close to give him warmth from her body, she beat on his arms.

The minute she was back in the saddle, Pie moved on. "Pie! Bless you. You probably saved Jimmy's life."

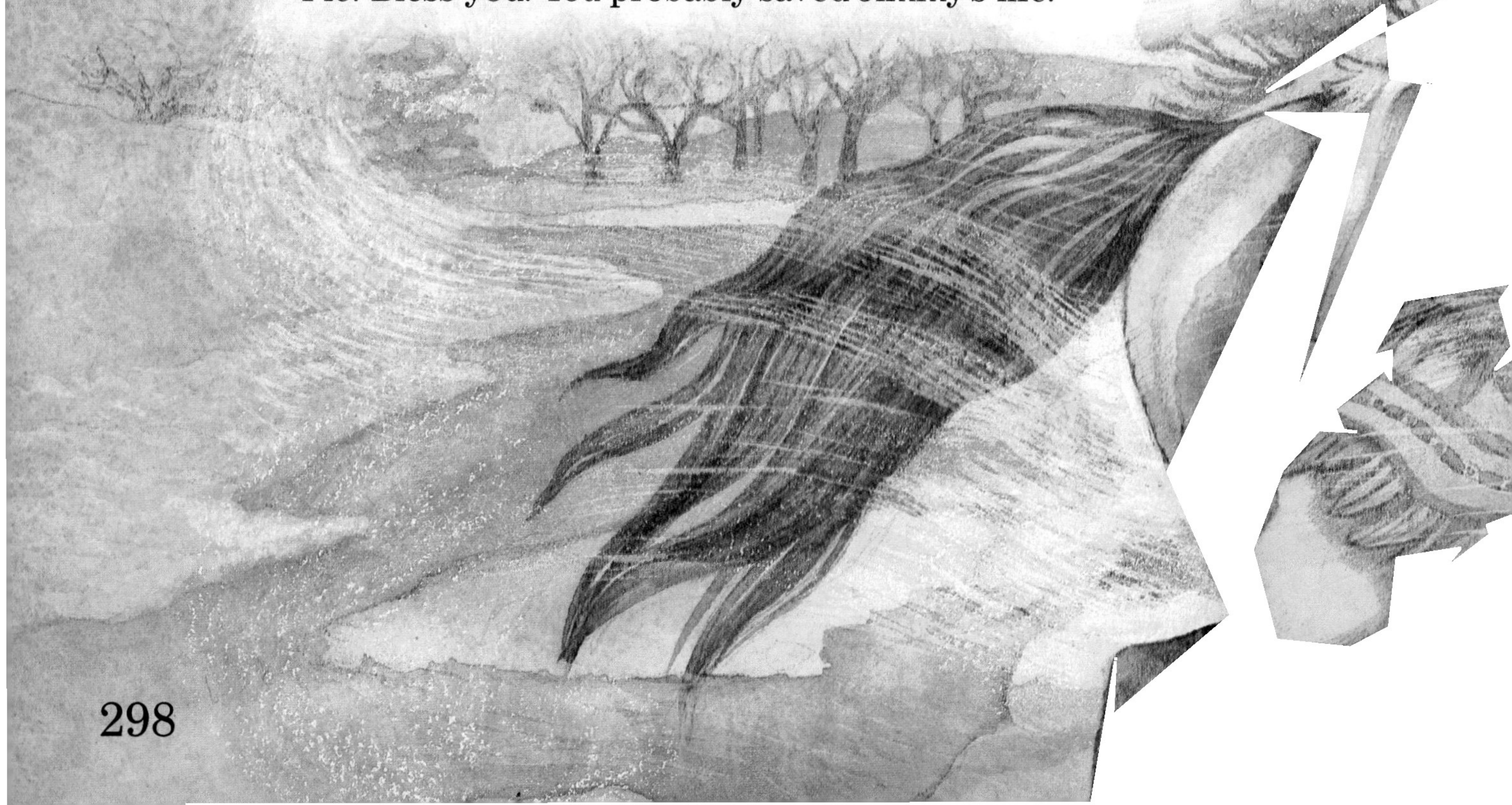

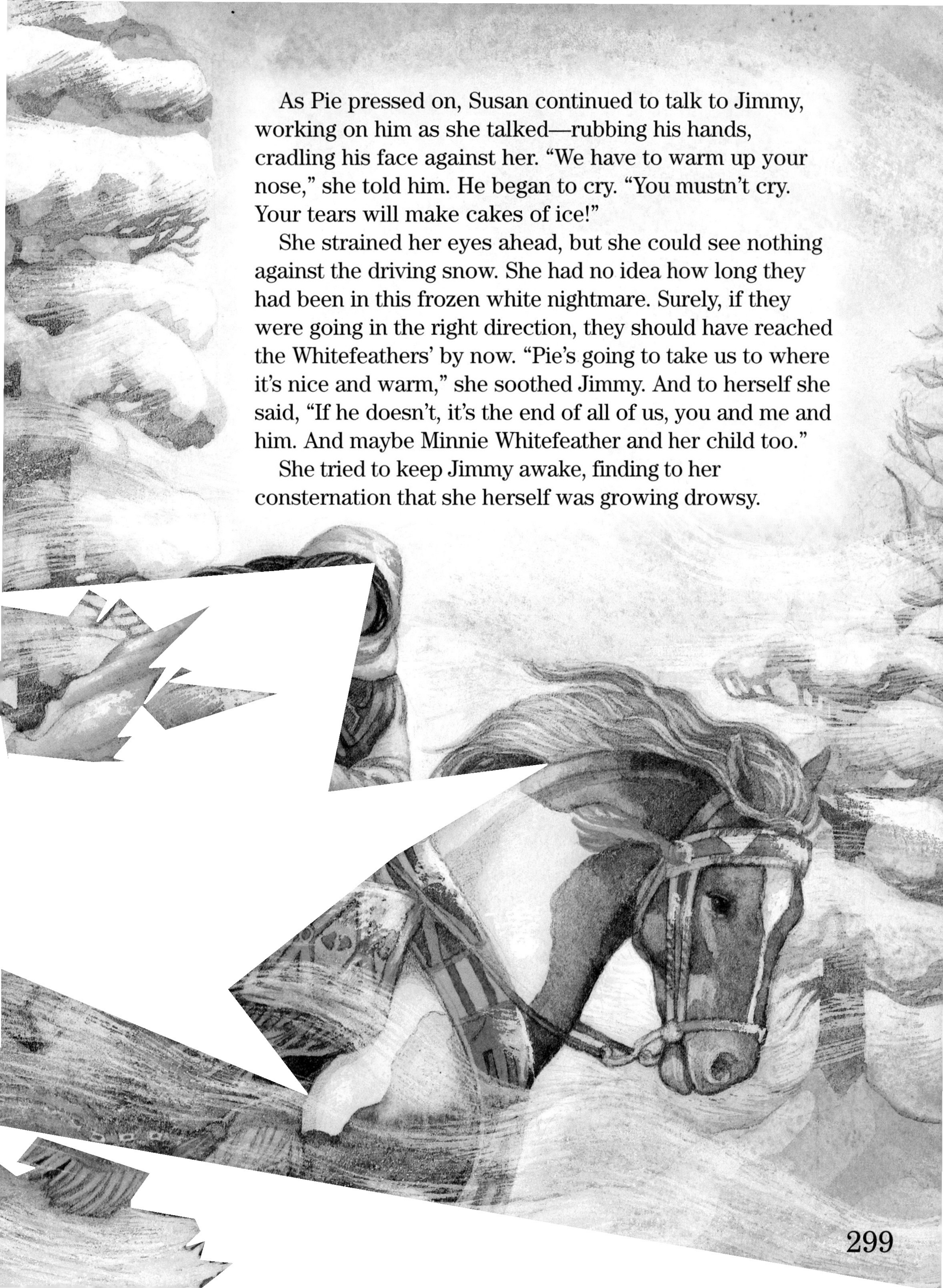

As Pie pressed on, Susan continued to talk to Jimmy, working on him as she talked—rubbing his hands, cradling his face against her. "We have to warm up your nose," she told him. He began to cry. "You mustn't cry. Your tears will make cakes of ice!"

She strained her eyes ahead, but she could see nothing against the driving snow. She had no idea how long they had been in this frozen white nightmare. Surely, if they were going in the right direction, they should have reached the Whitefeathers' by now. "Pie's going to take us to where it's nice and warm," she soothed Jimmy. And to herself she said, "If he doesn't, it's the end of all of us, you and me and him. And maybe Minnie Whitefeather and her child too."

She tried to keep Jimmy awake, finding to her consternation that she herself was growing drowsy.

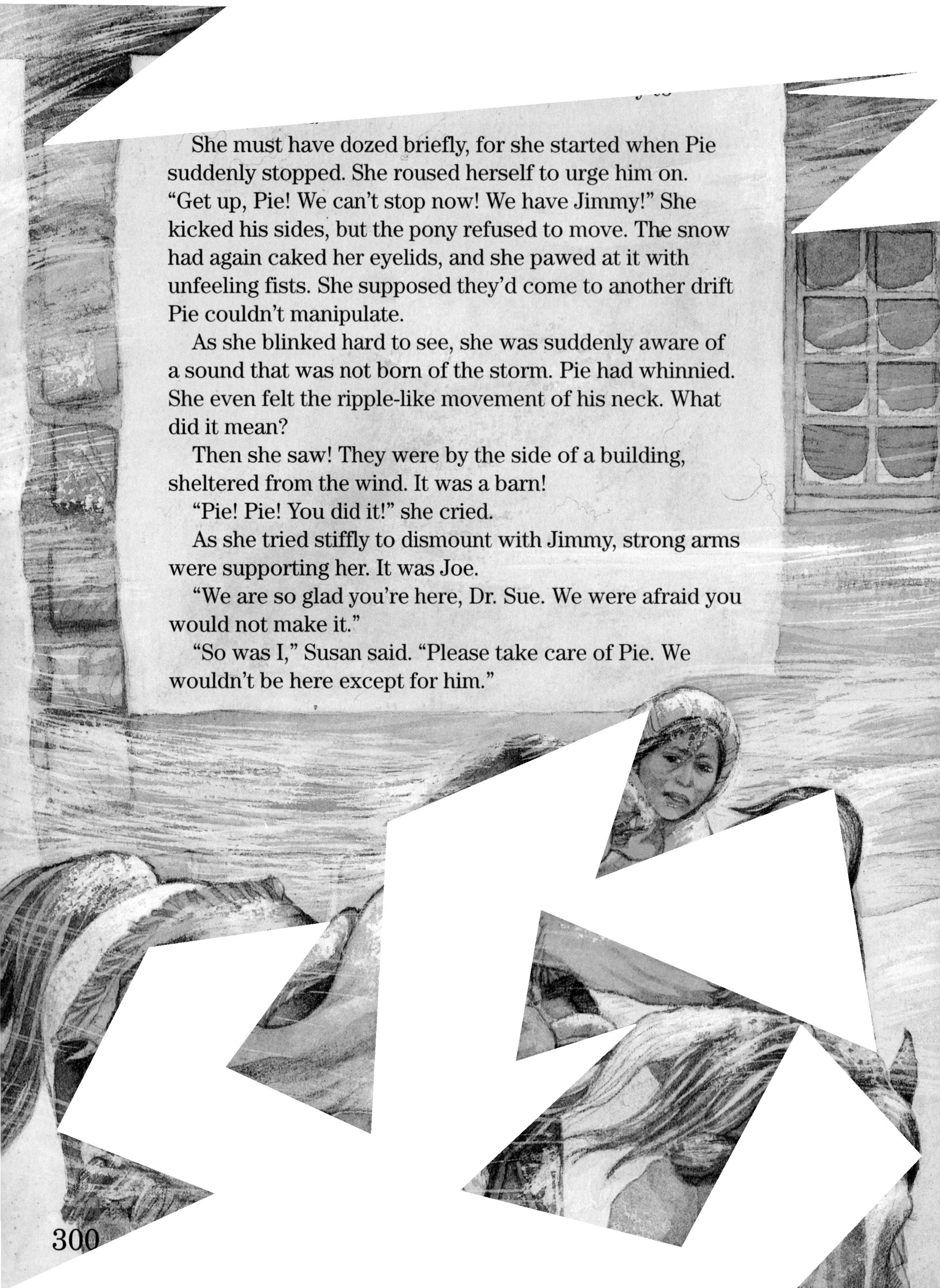

She must have dozed briefly, for she started when Pie suddenly stopped. She roused herself to urge him on. "Get up, Pie! We can't stop now! We have Jimmy!" She kicked his sides, but the pony refused to move. The snow had again caked her eyelids, and she pawed at it with unfeeling fists. She supposed they'd come to another drift Pie couldn't manipulate.

As she blinked hard to see, she was suddenly aware of a sound that was not born of the storm. Pie had whinnied. She even felt the ripple-like movement of his neck. What did it mean?

Then she saw! They were by the side of a building, sheltered from the wind. It was a barn!

"Pie! Pie! You did it!" she cried.

As she tried stiffly to dismount with Jimmy, strong arms were supporting her. It was Joe.

"We are so glad you're here, Dr. Sue. We were afraid you would not make it."

"So was I," Susan said. "Please take care of Pie. We wouldn't be here except for him."

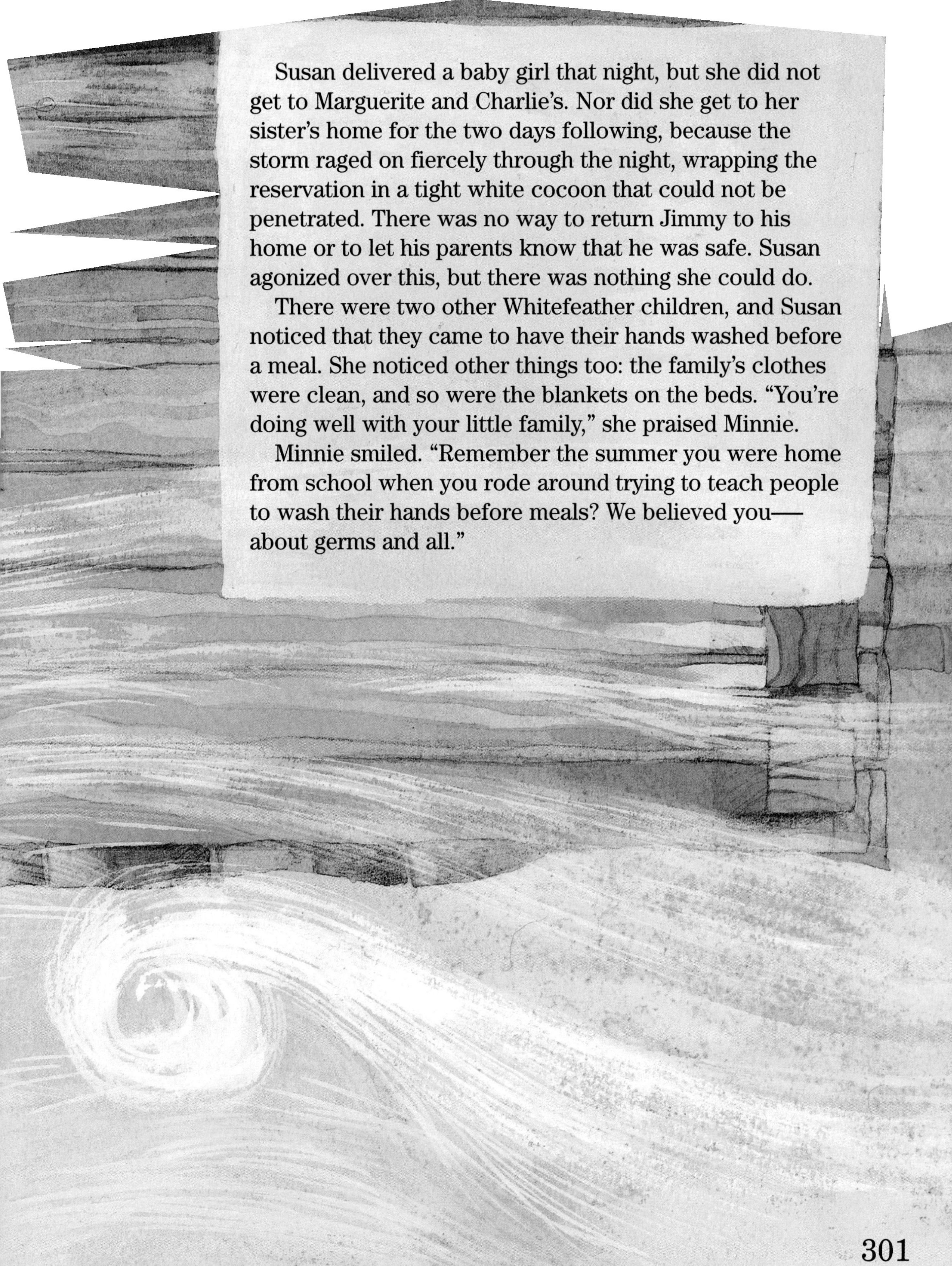

Susan delivered a baby girl that night, but she did not get to Marguerite and Charlie's. Nor did she get to her sister's home for the two days following, because the storm raged on fiercely through the night, wrapping the reservation in a tight white cocoon that could not be penetrated. There was no way to return Jimmy to his home or to let his parents know that he was safe. Susan agonized over this, but there was nothing she could do.

There were two other Whitefeather children, and Susan noticed that they came to have their hands washed before a meal. She noticed other things too: the family's clothes were clean, and so were the blankets on the beds. "You're doing well with your little family," she praised Minnie.

Minnie smiled. "Remember the summer you were home from school when you rode around trying to teach people to wash their hands before meals? We believed you—about germs and all."

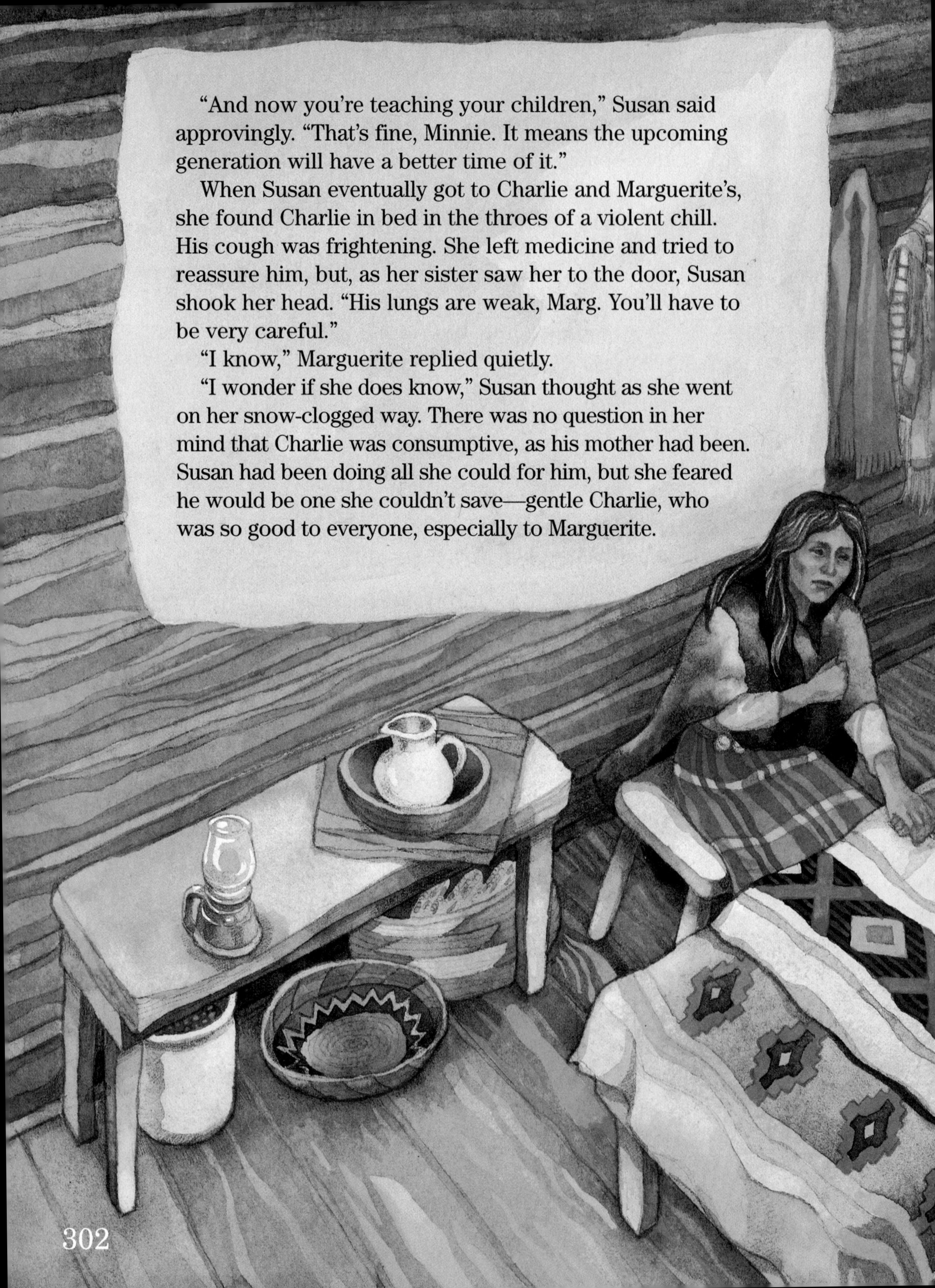

"And now you're teaching your children," Susan said approvingly. "That's fine, Minnie. It means the upcoming generation will have a better time of it."

When Susan eventually got to Charlie and Marguerite's, she found Charlie in bed in the throes of a violent chill. His cough was frightening. She left medicine and tried to reassure him, but, as her sister saw her to the door, Susan shook her head. "His lungs are weak, Marg. You'll have to be very careful."

"I know," Marguerite replied quietly.

"I wonder if she does know," Susan thought as she went on her snow-clogged way. There was no question in her mind that Charlie was consumptive, as his mother had been. Susan had been doing all she could for him, but she feared he would be one she couldn't save—gentle Charlie, who was so good to everyone, especially to Marguerite.

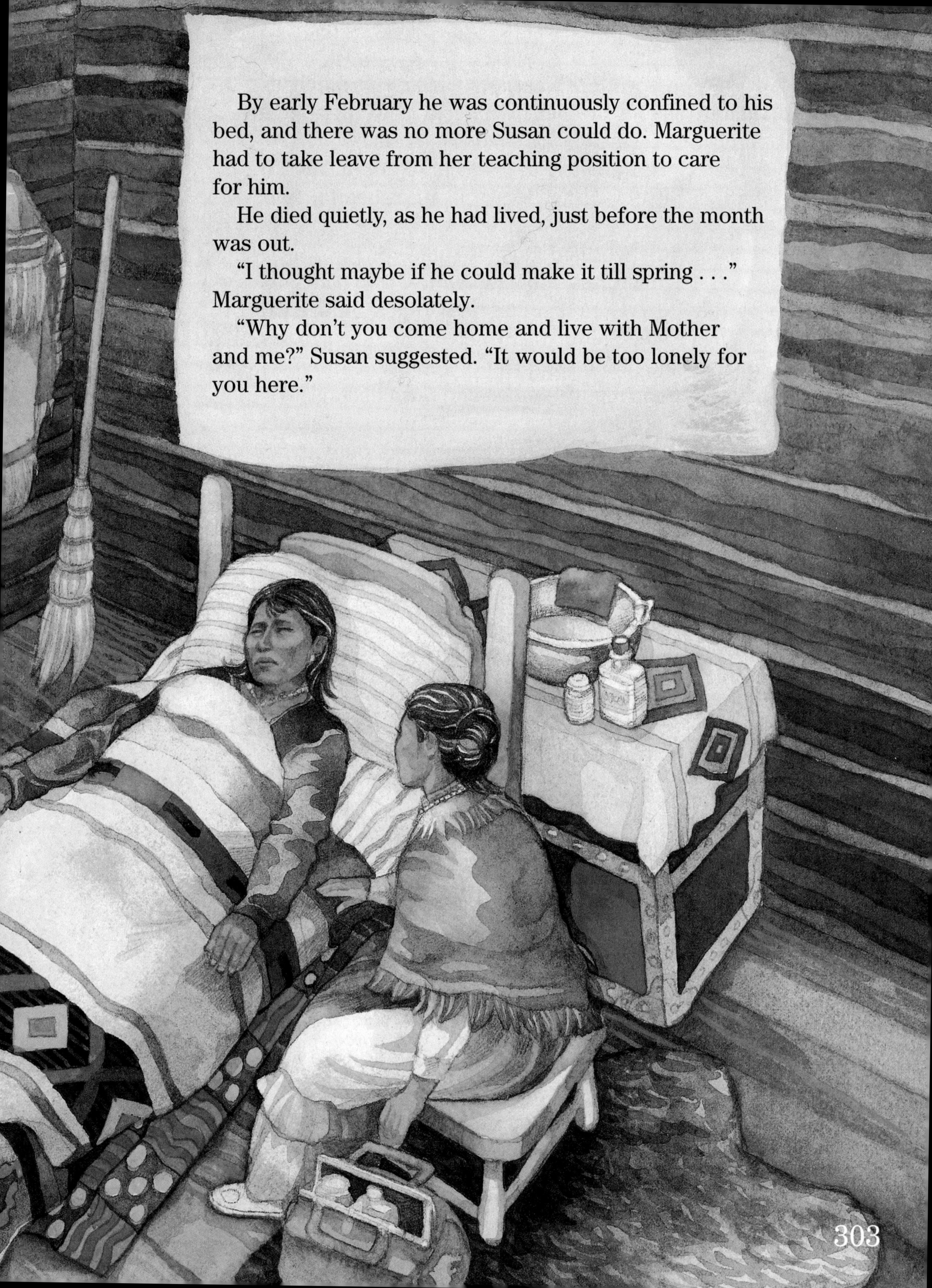

By early February he was continuously confined to his bed, and there was no more Susan could do. Marguerite had to take leave from her teaching position to care for him.

He died quietly, as he had lived, just before the month was out.

"I thought maybe if he could make it till spring . . ." Marguerite said desolately.

"Why don't you come home and live with Mother and me?" Susan suggested. "It would be too lonely for you here."

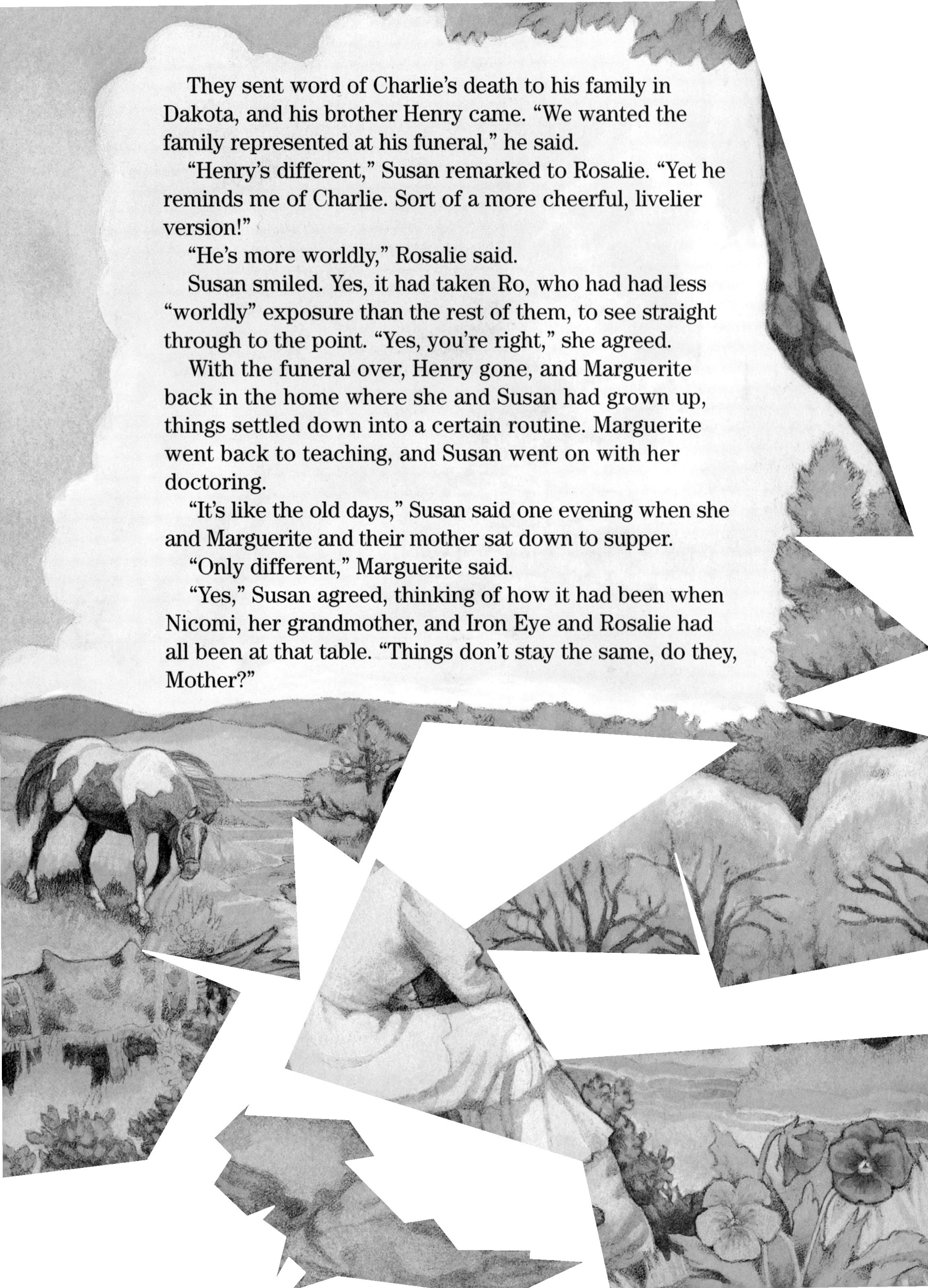

They sent word of Charlie's death to his family in Dakota, and his brother Henry came. "We wanted the family represented at his funeral," he said.

"Henry's different," Susan remarked to Rosalie. "Yet he reminds me of Charlie. Sort of a more cheerful, livelier version!"

"He's more worldly," Rosalie said.

Susan smiled. Yes, it had taken Ro, who had had less "worldly" exposure than the rest of them, to see straight through to the point. "Yes, you're right," she agreed.

With the funeral over, Henry gone, and Marguerite back in the home where she and Susan had grown up, things settled down into a certain routine. Marguerite went back to teaching, and Susan went on with her doctoring.

"It's like the old days," Susan said one evening when she and Marguerite and their mother sat down to supper.

"Only different," Marguerite said.

"Yes," Susan agreed, thinking of how it had been when Nicomi, her grandmother, and Iron Eye and Rosalie had all been at that table. "Things don't stay the same, do they, Mother?"

Her mother shook her head.

"We have to learn to accept change. That was one of the things Father tried to teach us long ago."

Spring was late that year, but when it finally came, it was so beautiful that Susan at times thought she couldn't bear it. Sometimes when she was riding home from a call in early evening, she would dismount and let Pie graze while she gazed down on the greening of the willows that fringed the river like a band of chartreuse lace. If it weren't too late, she would venture into the woods to look for wild flowers—violets and Dutchman's-breeches and the shy lady's-slipper.

"What a wonderful place to live," she thought. And more and more she could see that her work was bearing fruit. "I'm not accomplishing miracles," she told Rosalie one evening, "but I am beginning to see some of the results of better hygiene and health habits. And we're losing fewer babies and fewer cases to infection."

"You don't need to convince me," Rosalie said. "I can see it on every hand. How pleased Father would be."

The Story of Susan La Flesche Picotte

Concept Connections

Linking the Selection

Writer's Notebook

Think about the following questions, and then record your responses in the Response Journal section of your Writer's Notebook.

- What were some challenges Susan La Flesche Picotte faced in her work?
- What did Susan La Flesche Picotte try to teach members of her community in order to improve their health conditions?

Exploring Concept Vocabulary

The concept word for this lesson is ***hygiene.*** If you don't know what this word means, look it up in a dictionary. Answer these questions.

- How has knowledge about ***hygiene*** saved lives?
- What evidence is there that Susan La Flesche Picotte was succeeding in her efforts to teach about ***hygiene?***

In the Vocabulary section of your Writer's Notebook, write a sentence that includes the word ***hygiene*** as well as one of the selection vocabulary words.

Expanding the Concept

Like Maisie's mother in "The Bridge Dancers," Susan La Flesche Picotte was the only source of medical help in her community. Discuss the positive and negative sides of such a situation. Try to use the word ***hygiene*** in your discussion. Add new ideas about medicine to the Concept/Question Board.

Meet the Author

Marion Marsh Brown was born in Brownville, Nebraska. She grew up on a farm where she said she *"never lacked for interesting things to do."* She enjoyed riding horses, picking berries, climbing trees, swinging in a hammock, playing with the animals, and building tunnels through the haystack. Of all those things, reading was her favorite.

"I had to find out if I could write things too," she said. *"When I was ten, I saw my first story in print. It was on the children's page of the Sunday newspaper. I still remember the prize I received for it—a book called* I Wonder Why. *That was a good book for me to have, for I wondered 'Why?' about a lot of things then, and still do today, and I believe this is an essential trait for an author to have."*

Meet the Illustrator

Diane Magnuson has a degree in art and German and a master's degree in illustration. She has lived in many different places, but she began illustrating historical stories and Native American legends while living in the Northwest United States for 15 years. While they lived there, her husband was involved with Native American tribes, and his involvement in political issues brought many visitors and interesting discussions to their home.

Ms. Magnuson says of her work, *"Once the research and compositions are organized, I love to disappear into the painting, to become part of it and know the people in it."*

Focus Questions What would it be like if there were no doctors? How can doctors stay calm when someone is in great pain?

Shadow of a Bull

from ***Shadow of a Bull***
by Maia Wojciechowska
illustrated by Ramon Gonzalez Vicente

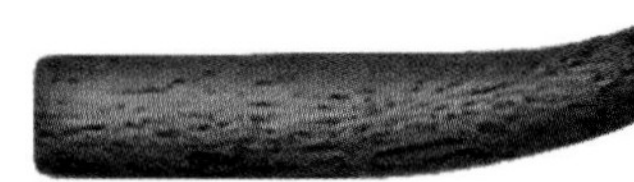

Manolo Olivar is the son of Spain's most famous bullfighter. Although his father died after being gored by a bull, Manolo is expected to follow in his father's footsteps. Everyone expects him to be Spain's next great bullfighter. But, Manolo lacks afición, *or desire. He knows he does not want to be a bullfighter, but he is unsure what he will become. One day while visiting a fighter who has been gored, Manolo realizes what he must do.*

On the way to the gored boy's house, Manolo listened to them tell about how bulls can hurt.

"The horn enters cleanly. If only it would exit that way. But either the man or the bull or both are moving at the time of the goring, and that's why the wounds are so bad."

"The horn tears into the body, ripping the muscles."

"And there is always the danger of infections. The horn is dirty, and before penicillin, it was almost always either amputation or death from infection."

"As far as the bullfighters are concerned, penicillin was the greatest invention of man."

"Poor devils! When they get gored in small towns there is never a doctor."

"And that's where they usually get gored."

"Even here in Arcangel, there is only one doctor who will touch a horn wound. Only one who knows anything about them, and he is getting old; when he is gone, maybe there will be no one."

"If you must get gored, be sure it's in Madrid."

"In Madrid they have a dozen doctors."

"I knew a doctor once who got rich on bullfighters. And then one day, he took his money and went to a printer and had millions of pamphlets printed. The pamphlet was called 'Stop the National Suicide'."

The men had never said anything before about pain, the amount of it a bullfighter had to endure. And Manolo had never thought before about pain. Now, listening to them, he thought that it would not be of dying that he would be afraid, but of the pain.

'El Magnifico,' lying on sheets that were as white as his face, looked to be about eighteen. The first thing Manolo noticed about him were his lips. They were pale, but he had been biting them. Drops of blood stood out in a row marking the places where the lips had been bitten. Without anyone having to tell him, Manolo knew that the boy was in great pain.

When they came into the room, 'El Magnifico' tried to hide his bloodied lips behind his hand. He did not say much, just that he was feeling all right. When he looked away from the men, he did not look out of the window, but at the wall where there was nothing but a stain. And when he turned back to them, his lips had fresh drops of blood on them.

"I was terrible," the boy said, trying to smile.

"You weren't there long enough," one of the men said, "to let us see how terrible."

"I would have been very bad," 'El Magnifico' said, fighting back tears.

"You might have been fine. It was a good little bull. You were too brave, and sometimes it's silly to be too brave. You don't let the people see how long your courage is, just how wide."

The boy's mother came into the room. She was a big woman with strong hands and a face that seemed carved from a rock.

"The doctor's coming," she said, not looking at the men but looking hard at her son. She waited for him to say something. He said nothing.

"Hasn't the doctor seen you?" one of the men asked.

The boy moaned and coughed to hide the sound of his pain.

"He was out of town," the mother said, looking now at them for the first time, her eyes accusing.

"The barber then, he took care of you in the infirmary?" the man wanted to know.

"Yes," the boy said, "he did the best he could."

"The barber's only a barber," the mother said angrily and left the room.

"He's in great pain. He doesn't show it, but he is in great pain," one of the men said softly to Manolo.

"It never hurts right after the goring. But when it starts hurting, it hurts for a long time," another added.

They heard footsteps outside. They were slow in reaching the door. The doctor was an old man. He shuffled when he moved from the door to the boy's bed. He looked tired. A shock of white hair fell listlessly over his wrinkled forehead as he bent over the boy.

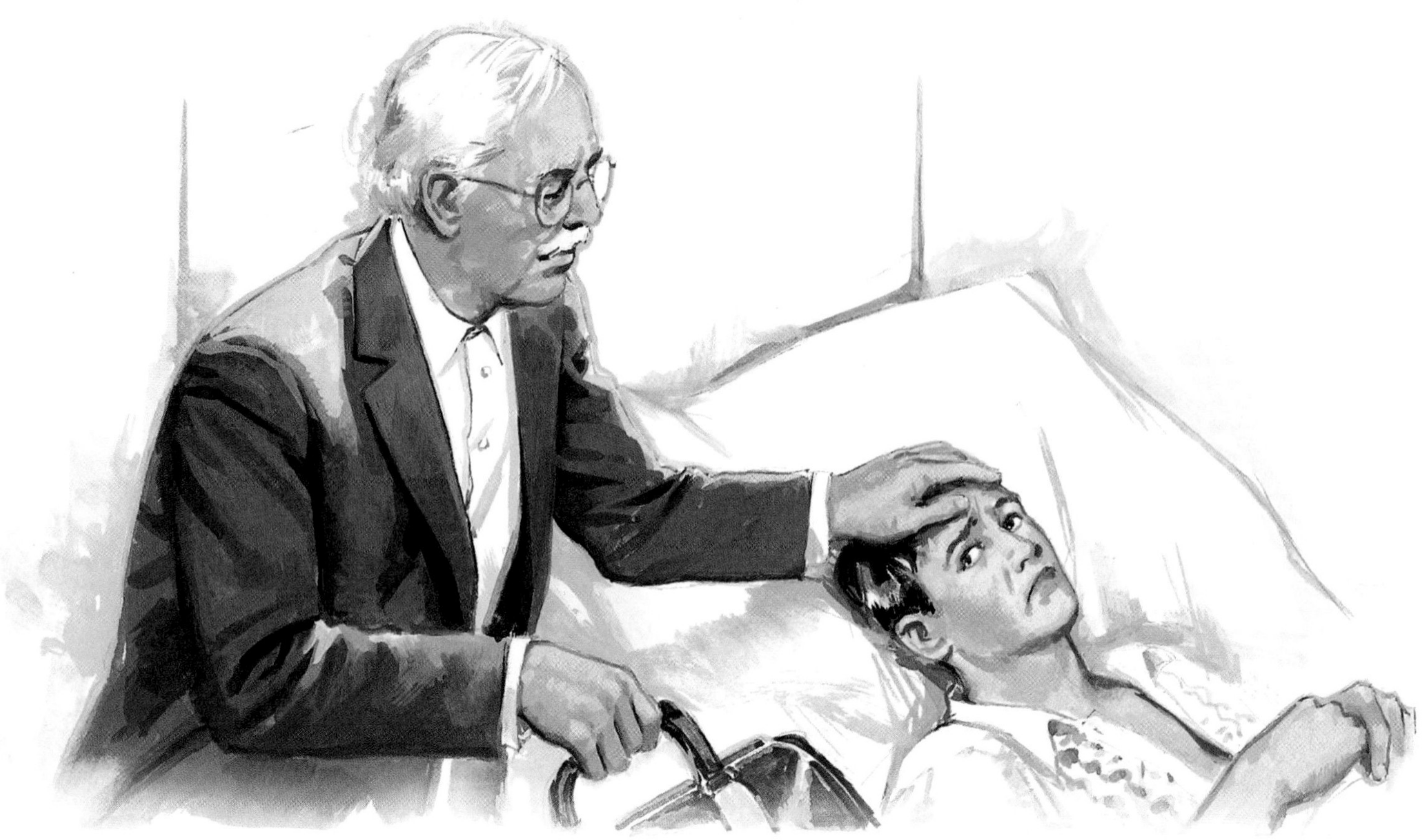

"*Olá*. How goes it?" He smiled at the boy and passed his hand over the boy's forehead. He did not greet the men, nor did he seem to notice Manolo.

"The barber cleaned it and bound it," the boy said feebly, raising on his elbow and then falling back on the pillows.

The men began to move towards the door.

"Stay," the doctor said not looking at them, taking the light blanket off the boy's bed and reaching into his bag for a pair of scissors. "I want Olivar's son to see what a goring looks like. Come here," he commanded, and Manolo moved closer, his heart beating loudly. "Look!" The doctor had cut the bandage and the gauze and pushed them aside. A flamelike, jagged tear, a foot long and several inches deep ran straight from the boy's knee up his thigh. Manolo caught his breath at the sight of it. "Bend down and look here," the doctor said. "Those are puddles of clotted blood. There are about seven different reds beside, all meat. The muscles are purple. The wound is always narrower where the horn enters and wider where it exits. Not pretty, is it?"

Manolo moved away feeling sick; but the voice of the doctor brought him back, and with its sound, so sure and matter of fact, the feeling of sickness left him.

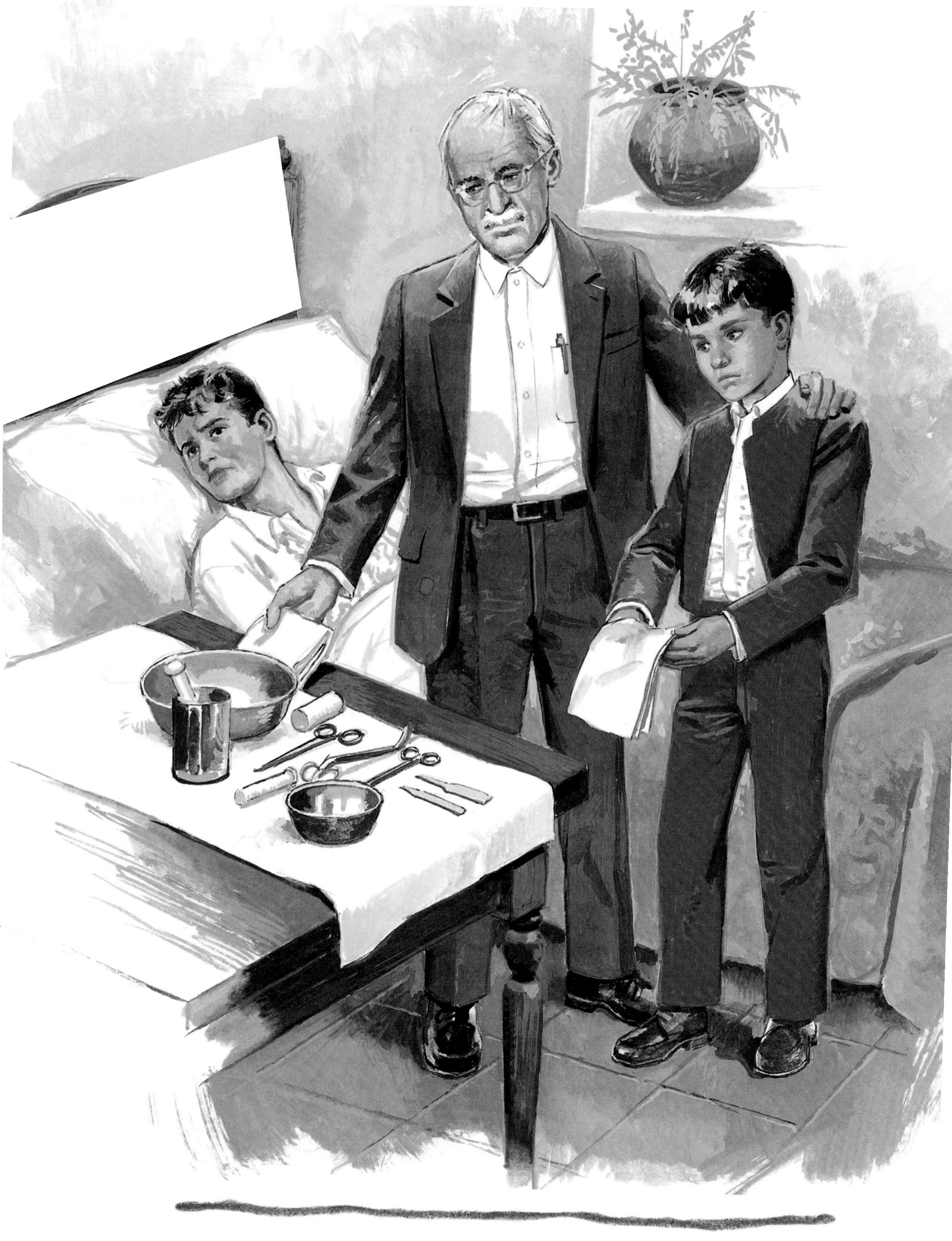

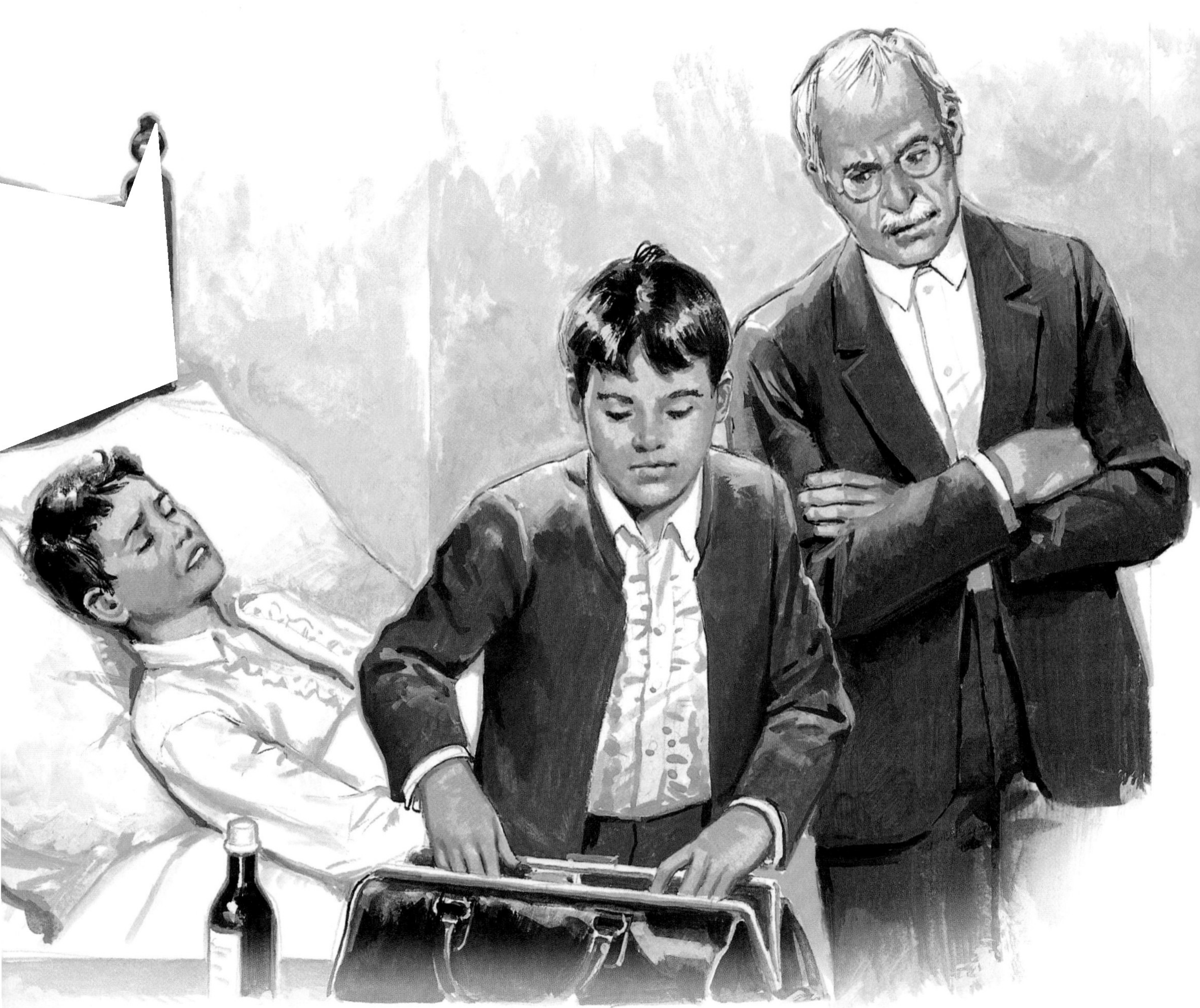

"I'll need your help," the doctor said, still looking at but not touching the wound. "It's a good, clean tear. The barber did his work well. He took the dirt out and cut off the dead flesh."

When he walked to the washbasin, his feet were not shuffling. He scrubbed his hands thoroughly. He put the surgical towel on the bedside table, took some instruments from the bag, put them on the towel, and then reached for a package of gauze pads and put those next to the instruments.

"Hand me those gloves," the doctor said to Manolo, pointing to a pair of rubber gloves in a plastic bag. "Let's see how good a nurse you'd make," he added. "Open the bag without touching the gloves and hold them out to me." Manolo did as he was told.

Manolo watched fascinated, as the doctor's hands moved surely into the wound, exploring the inside of it.

"The horn stayed away from the thigh bone," the doctor said. "He's a lucky boy. What I am doing now," he explained, speaking to Manolo, "is looking for foreign matter: dirt, pieces of horn, or dead flesh. But as I said before, the barber did a very good job of taking all those out of the wound. There is no danger of infection."

The admiration Manolo felt for the doctor was growing with each word, each gesture. No sound came from the pillow. With tenderness the doctor looked away from his work.

"He's fainted," he said with a smile. "Get the bottle of ammonia," he motioned towards the bag, "and a wad of cotton. Moisten the cotton and hold it under his nose."

Again Manolo did as he was told. When he opened the bottle, the strong odor of ammonia invaded his nostrils and spread through the entire room. He bent over the boy and passed the cotton directly under his nose. The boy coughed and jerked his head away.

"Good!" the doctor said watching, "he's not in shock. Just passed out from the pain. He will be fine. What he's got is one of those lucky gorings." His gloved hand pointed to the straight line of the torn flesh. "It's as good a goring as you could wish for, if you were wishing for a good goring. The bad ones are the ones that tear in and change angles. Those are the messy ones, the dangerous ones. But I don't want you to think this is nothing. It's the result of foolishness. Not the beast's, but the man's. The beast is led into the ring, the man walks in himself."

The doctor finished cleaning the wound and then stitched the flesh. Manolo was not asked again to help. He wished the doctor would once more request him to do something. As he watched the magic way the man's hands brought torn flesh together, he thought that what the doctor was doing and had done was the most noble thing a man could do. To bring health back to the sick, to cure the wounded, save the dying. This was what a man should do with his life; this, and not killing bulls.

"It will heal nicely. This one will. But then what?" The doctor walked to the wash basin and began washing the blood off the rubber gloves. "He," he pointed with his head to the boy, "will go on trying to prove that he can be good. And he isn't. But it's a point of honor with him. He will go on trying, and they will give him chances to try because he's fearless and the paying customers know that they will see a goring each time 'El Magnifico' is on the bill. But the tragedy is not that some people are bloodthirsty. The tragedy is that boys like him know of nothing else they want to do. I've grown old looking at wasted lives."

He walked over to Manolo and patted his head.

"The world is a big place," he said gently.

He seemed to want to add something, but he said nothing more. Silently, he put his instruments back in the bag and snapped it shut.

"Thank you for your help," the doctor said to Manolo, but his voice was tired now. The shuffle came back into his steps, and before he reached the door, he looked once again like a very old, very tired, man.

Walking back with the men, Manolo decided that if only he did not have to be a bullfighter he would be a doctor. He wanted to learn how to stop the pain and how to stop the fear of it. If only his father had been a doctor, a famous one, a bullfighters' doctor, then they would expect him to be one, too. And he would study hard. It would not be easy, but he would be learning to do something worthwhile.

He wondered if he were to tell the men, the six men, what he thought he would like to be, if they would listen to him. He looked at the men walking alongside him, talking once again about what they always talked about; and he knew that he would not tell them. He was who he was. A bullfighter's and not a doctor's son, and they expected him to be like his father. Maybe someday he could tell them.

Shadow of a Bull

Concept Connections

Linking the Selection

Think about the following questions, and then record your responses in the Response Journal section of your Writer's Notebook.

- Why did one of the men say that bullfighters think penicillin was the greatest invention?
- Why did Manolo decide that he wanted to become a doctor?

Exploring Concept Vocabulary

The concept word for this lesson is ***relief.*** If you don't know what this word means, look it up in a dictionary. Answer these questions.

- In what ways do doctors offer patients ***relief?***
- How was fainting a ***relief*** for El Magnifico?

In the Vocabulary section of your Writer's Notebook, write a sentence that includes the word ***relief*** as well as one of the selection vocabulary words.

Expanding the Concept

The selections throughout the unit presented doctors and other healers in a variety of times and places. What conclusions can you draw about the work doctors do and how their work has changed over time? Try to use the word ***relief*** in your discussion of the unit selections. Add new ideas about medicine to the Concept/Question Board.

Meet the Author

Maia Wojciechowska has lived an exciting, adventurous life. She was born in Warsaw, Poland, and came to the United States in 1942. Her jobs have included such things as detective, motorcycle racer, bullfighter, tennis player, and translator. In one year, she had 72 jobs!

Many of Ms. Wojciechowska's books are about the problem of trying to fit in with the rest of the world, but not fitting so well that you lose yourself. She said, "Shadow of a Bull *was mostly about pride and being locked in. . . . The word* pride *encompasses so much—honor and dignity and self-esteem. That sort of pride sometimes—most of the time—makes life harder than it needs to be. But without pride life is less."*

Meet the Illustrator

Ramon Gonzalez Vicente was born in Salamanca, Spain, where he also studied art. Later, he went to Barcelona, which is also in Spain, where he worked as an artistic director and illustrator for a publisher. Mr. Vicente has also illustrated for publishers in the United States, England, Germany, and other European countries. He has created illustrations for many books, but his favorite subject is children's literature.

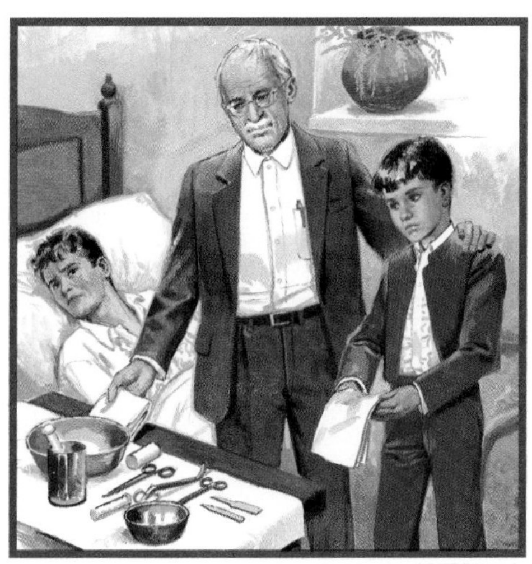

UNIT 4

Survival

Sometimes life gets very hard. People live through natural disasters and wars and terrible accidents. How do they do it? What helps them to survive all of these things?

lty
ood
pplies
ut it's
rain
up hope

Focus Questions **What basic needs must be met for people to survive? Why do some people try harder than others to survive?**

Island of the Blue Dolphins

from *Island of the Blue Dolphins*
by Scott O'Dell
illustrated by Russ Walks

With the help of the white man's ship, Karana's people have fled their island to escape the Aleuts, their enemies. In their haste Karana is left behind on the island. As she waits for a ship to return to rescue her, Karana's hopes begin to fade.

Summer is the best time on the Island of the Blue Dolphins. The sun is warm then and the winds blow milder out of the west, sometimes out of the south.

It was during these days that the ship might return and now I spent most of my time on the rock, looking out from the high headland into the east, toward the country where my people had gone, across the sea that was never-ending.

Once while I watched I saw a small object which I took to be the ship, but a stream of water rose from it and I knew that it was a whale spouting. During those summer days I saw nothing else.

The first storm of winter ended my hopes. If the white men's ship were coming for me it would have come during the time of good weather. Now I would have to wait until winter was gone, maybe longer.

The thought of being alone on the island while so many suns rose from the sea and went slowly back into the sea filled my heart with loneliness. I had not felt so lonely before because I was sure that the ship would return as Matasaip had said it would. Now my hopes were dead. Now I was really alone. I could not eat much, nor could I sleep without dreaming terrible dreams.

The storm blew out of the north, sending big waves against the island and winds so strong that I was unable to stay on the rock. I moved my bed to the foot of the rock and for protection kept a fire going throughout the night. I slept there five times. The first night the dogs came and stood outside the ring made by the fire. I killed three of them with arrows, but not the leader, and they did not come again.

On the sixth day, when the storm had ended, I went to the place where the canoes had been hidden, and let myself down over the cliff. This part of the shore was sheltered from the wind and I found the canoes just as they had been left. The dried food was still good, but the water was stale, so I went back to the spring and filled a fresh basket.

I had decided during the days of the storm, when I had given up hope of seeing the ship, that I would take one of the canoes and go to the country that lay toward the east. I remembered how Kimki, before he

had gone, had asked the advice of his ancestors who had lived many ages in the past, who had come to the island from that country, and likewise the advice of Zuma, the medicine man who held power over the wind and the seas. But these things I could not do, for Zuma had been killed by the Aleuts, and in all my life I had never been able to speak with the dead, though many times I had tried.

Yet I cannot say that I was really afraid as I stood there on the shore. I knew that my ancestors had crossed the sea in their canoes, coming from that place which lay beyond. Kimki, too had crossed the sea. I was not nearly so skilled with a canoe as these men, but I must say that whatever might befall me on the endless waters did not trouble me. It meant far less than the thought of staying on the island alone, without a home or companions, pursued by wild dogs, where everything reminded me of those who were dead and those who had gone away.

Of the four canoes stored there against the cliff, I chose the smallest, which was still very heavy because it could carry six people. The task that faced me was to push it down the rocky shore and into the water, a distance four or five times its length.

This I did by first removing all the large rocks in front of the canoe. I then filled in all these holes with pebbles and along this path laid down long strips of kelp, making a slippery bed. The shore was steep and once I got the canoe to move with its own weight, it slid down the path and into the water.

The sun was in the west when I left the shore. The sea was calm behind the high cliffs. Using the two-bladed paddle I quickly skirted the south part of the island. As I reached the sandspit the wind struck. I was paddling from the back of the canoe because you can go faster kneeling there, but I could not handle it in the wind.

Kneeling in the middle of the canoe, I paddled hard and did not pause until I had gone through the tides that run fast around the sandspit. There were many small waves and I was soon wet, but as I came out from behind the spit the spray lessened and the waves grew long and rolling. Though it would have been easier to go the way they slanted, this would have taken me in the wrong direction. I therefore kept them on my left hand, as well as the island, which grew smaller and smaller, behind me.

At dusk I looked back. The Island of the Blue Dolphins had disappeared. This was the first time that I felt afraid.

There were only hills and valleys of water around me now. When I was in a valley I could see nothing and when the canoe rose out of it, only the ocean stretching away and away.

Night fell and I drank from the basket. The water cooled my throat.

The sea was black and there was no difference between it and the sky. The waves made no sound among themselves, only faint noises as they went under the canoe or struck against it. Sometimes the noises seemed angry and at other times like people laughing. I was not hungry because of my fear.

The first star made me feel less afraid. It came out low in the sky and it was in front of me, toward the east. Other stars began to appear all around, but it was this one I kept my gaze upon. It was in the figure that we call a serpent, a star which shone green and which I knew. Now and then it was hidden by mist, yet it always came out brightly again.

Without this star I would have been lost, for the waves never changed. They came always from the same direction and in a manner that kept pushing me away from the place I wanted to reach. For this reason the canoe made a path in the black water like a snake. But somehow I kept moving toward the star which shone in the east.

This star rose high and then I kept the North Star on my left hand, the one we call "the star that does not move." The wind grew quiet. Since it always died down when the night was half over, I knew how long I had been traveling and how far away the dawn was.

About this time I found that the canoe was leaking. Before dark I had emptied one of the baskets in which food was stored and used it to dip out the water that came over the sides. The water that now moved around my knees was not from the waves.

I stopped paddling and worked with the basket until the bottom of the canoe was almost dry. Then I searched around, feeling in the dark along the smooth planks, and found the place near the bow where the water was seeping through a crack as long as my hand and the width of a finger. Most of the time it was out of the sea, but it leaked whenever the canoe dipped forward in the waves.

The places between the planks were filled with black pitch which we gather along the shore. Lacking this, I tore a piece of fiber from my skirt and pressed it into the crack, which held back the water.

Dawn broke in a clear sky and as the sun came out of the waves I saw that it was far off on my left. During the night I had drifted south of the place I wished to go, so I changed my direction and paddled along the path made by the rising sun.

There was no wind on this morning and the long waves went quietly under the canoe. I therefore moved faster than during the night.

I was very tired, but more hopeful than I had been since I left the island. If the good weather did not change I would cover many leagues before dark. Another night and another day might bring me within sight of the shore toward which I was going.

Not long after dawn, while I was thinking of this strange place and what it would look like, the canoe began to leak again. This crack was between the same planks, but was a larger one and close to where I was kneeling.

The fiber I tore from my skirt and pushed into the crack held back most of the water which seeped in whenever the canoe rose and fell with the waves. Yet I could see that the planks were weak from one end to the other, probably from the canoe being stored so long in the sun, and that they might open along their whole length if the waves grew rougher.

It was suddenly clear to me that it was dangerous to go on. The voyage would take two more days, perhaps longer. By turning back to the island I would not have nearly so far to travel.

Still I could not make up my mind to do so. The sea was calm and I had come far. The thought of turning back after all this labor was more than I could bear. Even greater was the thought of the deserted island I would return to, of living there alone and forgotten. For how many suns and how many moons?

The canoe drifted idly on the calm sea while these thoughts went over and over in my mind, but when I saw the water seeping through the crack again, I picked up the paddle. There was no choice except to turn back toward the island.

I knew that only by the best of fortune would I ever reach it.

The wind did not blow until the sun was overhead. Before that time I covered a good distance, pausing only when it was necessary to dip water from the canoe. With the wind I went more slowly and had to stop more often because of the water spilling over the sides, but the leak did not grow worse.

This was my first good fortune. The next was when a swarm of dolphins appeared. They came swimming out of the west, but as they saw the canoe they turned around in a great circle and began to follow me. They swam up slowly and so close that I could see their eyes, which are large and the color of the ocean. Then they swam on ahead of the canoe, crossing back and forth in front of it, diving in and out, as if they were weaving a piece of cloth with their broad snouts.

Dolphins are animals of good omen. It made me happy to have them swimming around the canoe, and though my hands had begun to bleed from the chafing of the paddle, just watching them made me forget the pain. I was very lonely before they appeared, but now I felt that I had friends with me and did not feel the same.

The blue dolphins left me shortly before dusk. They left as quickly as they had come, going on into the west, but for a long time I could see the last of the sun shining on them. After night fell I could still see them in my thoughts and it was because of this that I kept on paddling when I wanted to lie down and sleep.

More than anything, it was the blue dolphins that took me back home.

Fog came with the night, yet from time to time I could see the star that stands high in the west, the red star called Magat which is part of the figure that looks like a crawfish and is known by that name. The crack in the planks grew wider so I had to stop often to fill it with fiber and to dip out the water.

The night was very long, longer than the night before. Twice I dozed kneeling there in the canoe, though I was more afraid than I had ever been. But the morning broke clear and in front of me lay the dim line of the island like a great fish sunning itself on the sea.

I reached it before the sun was high, the sandspit and its tides that bore me into the shore. My legs were stiff from kneeling and as the canoe struck the sand I fell when I rose to climb out. I crawled through the shallow water and up the beach. There I lay for a long time, hugging the sand in happiness.

I was too tired to think of the wild dogs. Soon I fell asleep.

Island of the Blue Dolphins

Concept Connections

Linking the Selection

Think about the following questions, and then record your responses in the Response Journal section of your Writer's Notebook.

- How did the stars help Karana?
- What did Karana do to survive when her canoe began to leak?

Exploring Concept Vocabulary

The concept word for this lesson is ***endurance.*** If you don't know what this word means, look it up in a dictionary. Answer these questions.

- How did Karana display physical ***endurance?***
- Why will Karana need mental ***endurance*** to survive?

In the Vocabulary section of your Writer's Notebook, write a sentence that includes the word ***endurance*** as well as one of the selection vocabulary words.

Expanding the Concept

Discuss how Karana uses her physical and mental skills to survive on the island and in the canoe. Try to use the word ***endurance*** in your discussion. Add new ideas about survival to the Concept/Question Board.

Meet the Author

Scott O'Dell was born in Los Angeles, California. His father was a railroad worker and so the family moved often, but they always lived by the ocean. One of their homes was on Rattlesnake Island, near Los Angeles, where they lived in a house on stilts. From the house they could watch sailing ships go by.

Island of the Blue Dolphins is based on a true story. The rest of it, according to Mr. O'Dell, *"came directly from the memory of the years I lived at Rattlesnake Island and San Pedro. From the days when, with the other boys of my age, I voyaged out on summer mornings in search of the world."*

Focus Questions What makes it easier to survive in some places than in others? What steps would you take to survive in the Arctic?

Arctic Explorer:

The Story of Matthew Henson

by Jeri Ferris

Matthew Henson was the first African-American explorer to reach the North Pole. Before he made this famous expedition, he went on several trips to the arctic region with Robert Peary. During these trips, Henson learned the skills that would make him a great explorer. In this excerpt about Henson's first arctic journey, Peary has planned an expedition to North Greenland. He has little money and has asked Henson to help him without pay. Henson is eager to go. His job is to learn the survival techniques used by the Eskimos as they face the harsh, cold climate.

Members of the 1891–1892 North Greenland Expedition (left to right): Cook, Henson, Astrup, Verhoeff, and Gibson. Josephine and Robert Peary are standing in back. John Verhoeff fell into a crevasse in Greenland in the spring of 1892 while exploring and was never seen again.

"It was in June 1891," Matt Henson wrote, "that I started on my first trip to the Arctic regions, as a member of what was known as the 'North Greenland Expedition.' "

America's newspapers predicted disaster. A small group of inexperienced men trying to survive in a frozen place that had killed better men than they? Impossible. Then reporters learned that a woman was going too—the new Mrs. Peary. "Now we know he's crazy!" said one newspaper about Peary.

Josephine Peary listed the expedition members in her diary: "Dr. Cook, Mr. Gibson, Mr. Astrup, Mr. Verhoeff, and Mr. Peary's faithful attendant in his surveying labors in Nicaragua, Matt Henson." The ship, *Kite*, was so small that the people and supplies barely fit. They were going to be gone for a year and a half, so they needed a lot of supplies. There were crates of food (enough for two and a half years, just to be safe) and cans of pemmican, the beef-fat-raisin mixture that the men and dogs would eat while crossing the ice cap. There were skis and snowshoes, guns and ammunition, sledges, woolen clothing, a stove, pots and pans, and camera equipment. And after the last one hundred tons of coal was piled on deck, Matt could hardly find a place to set down his hammer and nails while he put together the wood frame for their base camp house.

The *Kite* plunged on through the Atlantic, rolling and pitching and sending all the passengers except Henson and Peary to bed seasick. On June 21 Matt saw Greenland for the first time. Its steep, wild cliffs rose straight up from the icy water. As the *Kite* steamed north through Baffin Bay, Matt saw hundreds of icebergs—gleaming blue and white chunks of ice—from the size of small sailboats to that of enormous floating mountains. In the valleys of Greenland, Matt saw glaciers that looked like thick flowing cream, frozen into white walls. And on the very top of Greenland lay the five hundred thousand square miles of silent ice cap. Matt couldn't see it yet, but he knew it was there, waiting.

The *Kite* pushed farther north into heavy ice, which floated on the water like a field of white. There were splits and cracks in the ice, and through these cracks (called leads) the *Kite* forced its way. Sometimes there were no leads at all, and the captain would shout for more steam power. The *Kite* would dash forward and smash against the ice. Sometimes the ice would break, and the ship could continue. Sometimes it would not, and the ship would have to back up and try another way.

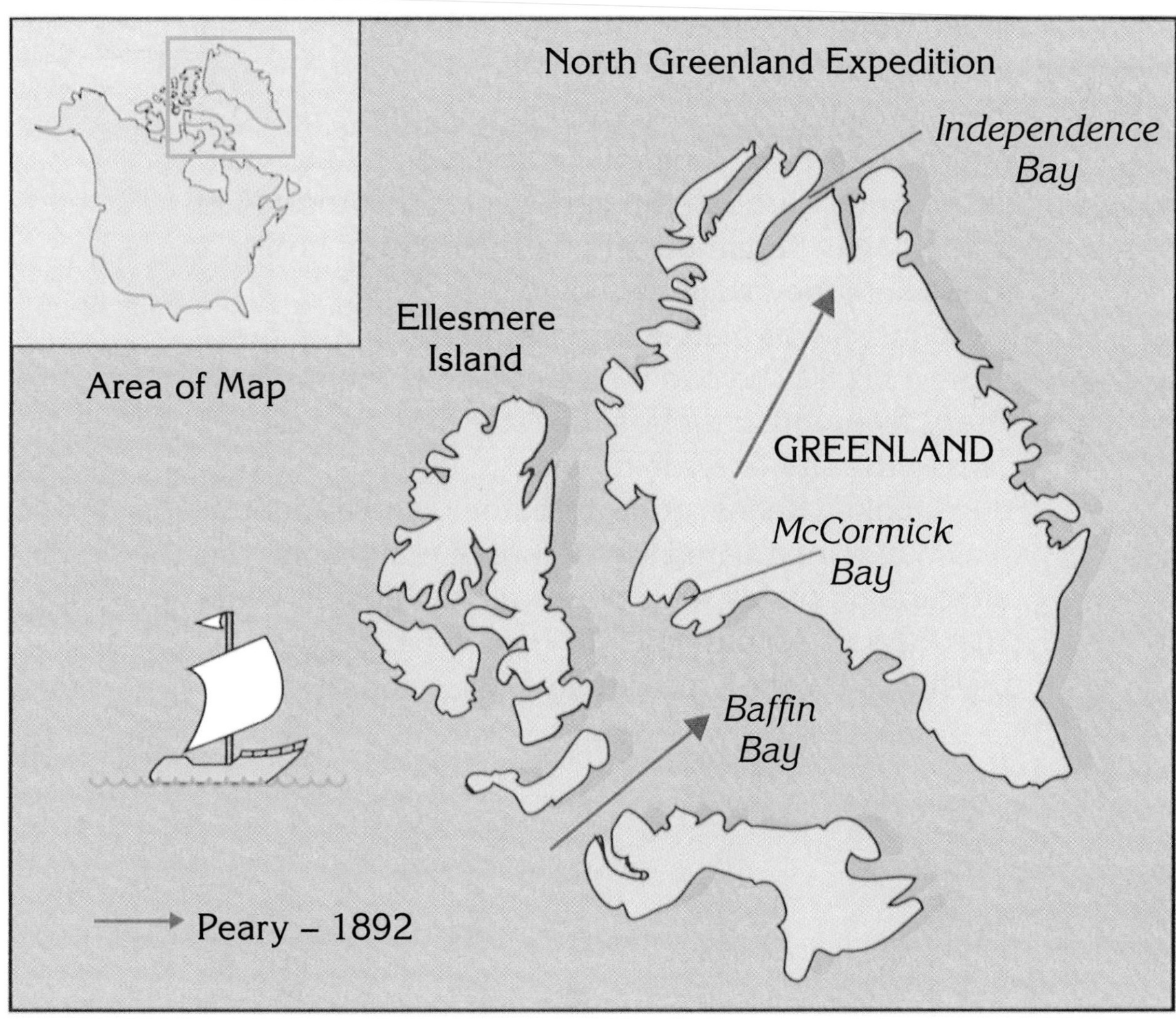

When the *Kite* was as far north as it could go, it dropped anchor in McCormick Bay, Greenland, and the crew unloaded the supplies. At the end of July, the *Kite* sailed for home, leaving Matthew Henson, the Pearys, and the other four men to survive the arctic winter. (A ship could only get through the ice in the summer, and the long, dangerous trip over the ice cap could only be started in the spring with the return of 24-hour sunlight. So the men had to wait in the Arctic through the dark winter months.) Matt immediately began putting up their sturdy house, to make sure they would survive.

August 8 was Matt's 25th birthday. For the first time in his life, he had a birthday celebration. Mrs. Peary fixed mock turtle soup, stew of little auk (a bird the size of a robin) with green peas, eider duck, baked beans, corn, tomatoes, and apricot pie. Matt remembered the delight of that dinner long after the tin plates were put away. Seventeen years later he said of that day, "To have a party given in my honor touched me deeply."

While Matt finished the small wooden house, the other men went to find Eskimos to join their group. (The men would have to use sign language because none of them spoke Eskimo.) Peary needed Eskimo men to help hunt polar bears and seals and walruses and reindeer and caribou and foxes for furs and meat. He needed Eskimo women to chew the furs and sew them into pants and coats. The thickest wool coat from home would be useless in the Arctic; they had to have clothing made of the same fur that kept the arctic animals warm. In exchange for their work, Peary would give the Eskimos pots and pans, needles, tools, and other useful items.

Matt and an Eskimo friend return from a hunting expedition.

On August 18 the men returned, and with them were four Eskimos: Ikwa, his wife, and their two children. The Eskimos walked slowly up to Matt and the Pearys. Then Ikwa stepped closer to Matt and looked at him carefully. His brown face lit up with excitement as he spoke rapidly to Matt in Eskimo.

Matt shook his head and tried to explain that he didn't understand, but Ikwa kept talking. Finally Ikwa took Matt's arm, pointed at the black man's skin, and said, "Inuit, Inuit!" Then Matt understood. "Inuit" must be what the Eskimos called themselves. Ikwa thought Matt was another Eskimo because he had brown skin, just as the Eskimos did. Matt looked down at the short fur-covered man, who smelled like seals and whale blubber. He looked into Ikwa's shining black eyes and smiled. From that moment on, the Eskimos called Matt "Miy Paluk," which meant "dear little Matthew," and they loved him as a brother.

In September Matt, Ikwa, Dr. Cook, and the Pearys took the whale boat and went to find more Eskimos. They didn't find a single Eskimo, but they did find some unfriendly walruses.

It began when the boat got mixed up with some walruses (250 walruses, Mrs. Peary said) that were peacefully fishing for clams. One after another the startled walruses poked their heads out of the water, spitting out clam shells and flashing their white tusks. Then an angry bull walrus roared, "Ook, ook, ook!" and headed straight for the boat. The water foamed and boiled as the rest of the herd charged right behind him, speeding along like torpedoes, all roaring their battle cry and tossing their enormous gray wrinkled heads. Matt and the others knew that just one tusk through the bottom of the boat would be the end of them. Ikwa shouted and pounded on the boat to frighten the walruses away, but the walruses weren't frightened. In fact, they were so angry that they tossed the boat up and down furiously. Bracing their feet, Matt and the others fired their guns while Mrs. Peary sat in the bottom of the boat and reloaded the guns as fast as she could. At last the walruses gave up. They dove to the bottom and disappeared, leaving a shaky group of explorers in a still-rocking boat.

Robert Peary

By the end of September, the dull red sun dipped lower each day and finally did not appear at all over the southern horizon. Every day was like a glorious sunset, with a golden, crimson glow on the mountain peaks. Then there was no sunset anymore, just one long night.

By the time the sun was gone, not to return until February, several Eskimo families were living at the camp in stone igloos (snow igloos were only used when the Eskimos traveled, following the animals whose meat and skins they needed).

That winter the men hunted by the full moon—by moonlight so bright that the blue-white ice sparkled. Peary planned for the spring trek. Astrup taught the men to ski. Gibson studied bird and animal life. Verhoeff studied rocks. Dr. Cook *wanted* to study the Eskimos by taking their pictures and measuring their bodies, but the Eskimos refused to let him near them. Finally Matt realized that they were afraid Dr. Cook would go home and make new people from the Eskimo pattern. So Matt got Ikwa to understand, and Dr. Cook got his pictures.

Meanwhile Matt studied with his Eskimo teachers. They taught him easy things, such as never to stand with his feet apart or his elbows sticking out, as this let the cold air close to his body. They taught him hard things, such as how to speak Eskimo. Matt learned, for example, that there is no Eskimo word for "hole." Instead there is a different word for "hole in igloo" or "hole in bear skin" or anything that has a hole.

Matt learned why the Eskimos smelled like walruses and seals and blubber—they *ate* walruses and seals and blubber. They also ate reindeer and polar bears and little auks. They ate the meat while it was still warm and raw and bloody; they ate it when it was frozen solid, by chipping off bite-size chunks; and sometimes they boiled it. They never ate carrots or beans or potatoes or apples or chocolate. In the Arctic the only food came from the bodies of the animals that lived there.

Matt learned how the Eskimos made the skin of a polar bear into clothing. Once the Eskimo man had killed the bear and removed its skin and scraped it as clean as he could, it was up to the Eskimo woman to finish. She had to chew the skin until all the fat was gone and it was completely soft. All day long the woman would fold the skin (with the fur folded inside), chew back and forth along the fold, make a new fold, and continue. It took two days to chew one skin. Then the woman would rest her jaws for one day before beginning on another skin. After the skin had dried, she would cut it up and sew it into a coat or pants. Her needle was made of bone, her thread was made from animal sinew, and her stitches had to be very, very tiny so not a whisper of wind could get through.

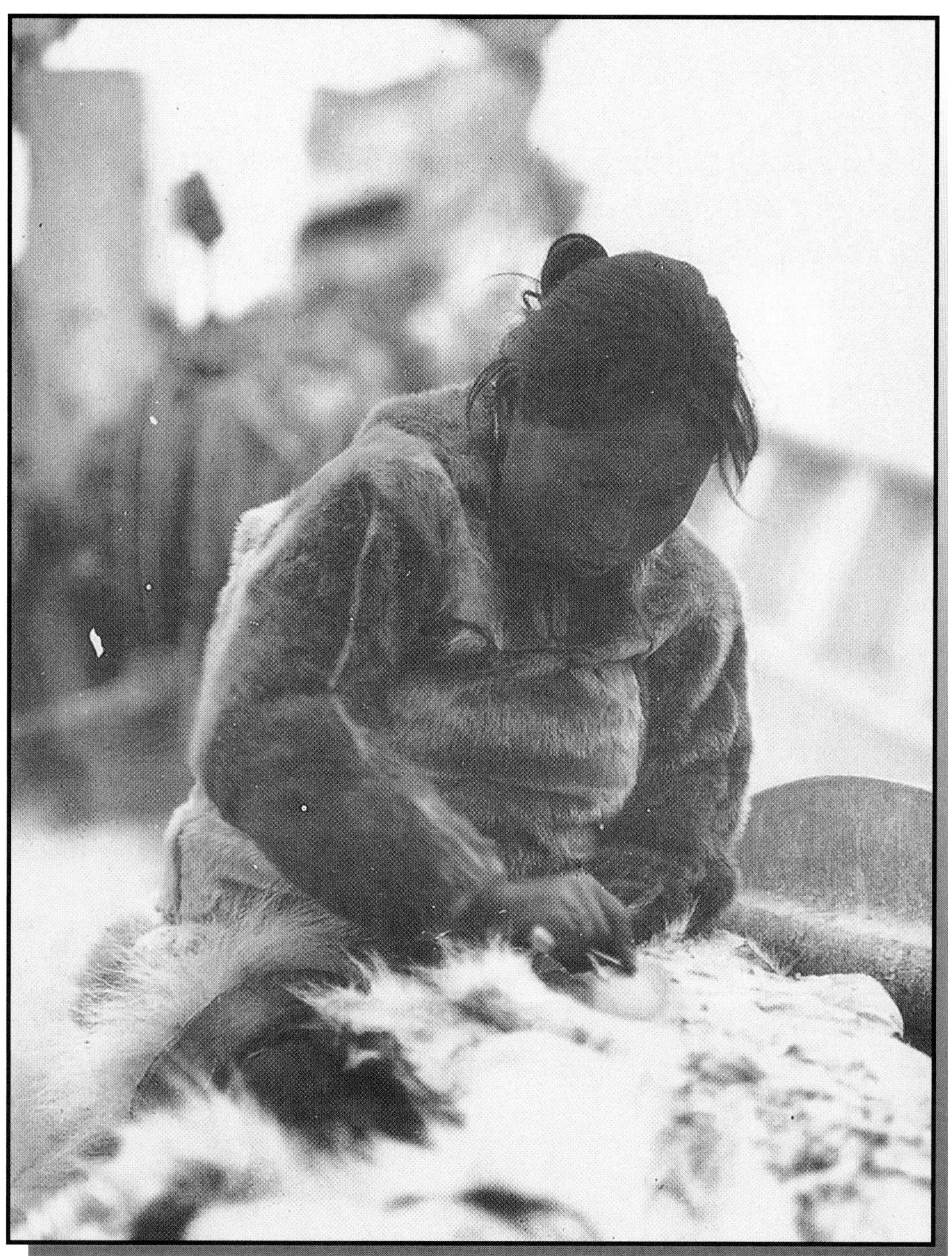

An Eskimo woman makes clothing out of an animal skin. Old Eskimo women had very short, flat teeth from chewing skins to soften them.

For Matt's winter outfit the women made stockings of arctic hare fur, tall boots of sealskin, polar bear fur pants, a shirt made of 150 auk skins (with the feathers next to Matt's skin), a reindeer fur jacket, and a white fox fur hood that went around his face. His mittens were made of bearskin with the fur inside.

But the piercing, freezing cold, colder than the inside of a freezer, took Matt's breath away, and the howling arctic wind drove needles of snow and ice into his face. Even his new sealskin boots felt terrible, until he learned to stand still after he put them on in the morning. Then they would freeze instantly to the shape of his feet and wouldn't hurt as much.

Once Matt had his fur clothes, cold or not, he was ready to learn how to drive a sledge pulled by the 80- to 120-pound Eskimo dogs. But first, if a dog got loose, Matt had to catch him. He would drop a piece of frozen meat on the snow and dive on top of the dog as the animal snatched the meat. Then he would "grab the nearest thing grabbable—ear, leg, or bunch of hair," slip the harness over the dog's head, push his front legs through, and tie him to a rock. Finally, Matt said, he would lick his dog bites.

When the dogs were in their traces, they spread out like a fan in front of the sledge. The king dog, who was the strongest and fiercest, led the way in the center. Matt had watched the Eskimos drive the dogs and knew that they didn't use the 30-foot sealskin whip *on* the dogs but *over* the dogs. The trick was to make the whip curl out and crack like a gunshot right over the ear of the dog who needed it. Matt stepped up behind the sledge, shouted, "Huk, huk!" and tried to crack the whip. The dogs sat down. Matt tried again and again and again. After many tries and lots of help from his Eskimo teachers, Matt learned how to snap the whip over the dogs' ears and make them start off at a trot. Then he had to learn how to turn them (they didn't have reins, as horses do), how to make them stop, and how to make them jump over open water with the sledge flying behind.

Dogs in their traces fan out in front of a sledge. If they are starving, the dogs will eat their traces, which are made of sealskin.

There were five Eskimo families at the camp, each family with its own stone igloo. At first it was hard for Matt to go inside the igloos because of their peculiar smell (Eskimos did not take baths, and Matt said that an Eskimo mother cleans her baby just as a mother cat cleans her kittens), but he didn't want to be rude, so he got used to it. Opposite the entrance hole was the bed platform, built of stone and covered with furs. At the end of the bed platform was a small stone lamp, filled with whale blubber for fuel, with moss for the wick. This little lamp was the light and heat and cook stove for the igloo. The Eskimo woman melted snow in a small pan over the lamp and used the water for cooking meat and for drinking. (Eskimos did not build fires for heating or cooking.)

Matt learned how to build a snow igloo when he hunted with the Eskimos, far from the camp. Two Eskimos could cut 50 to 60 snow blocks (each block 6-by-18-by-24-inches) with their long snow knives and build a whole igloo in just one hour. One man would stand in the center and place the blocks in an 8-foot circle around himself. He would add more blocks, spiraling round and round, with the blocks closing in on the center as they rose higher, until the top snow blocks fit perfectly against each other and the roof was complete. Then they would carry in the furs and cooking lamp, and it was home. A chunk of frozen meat, perhaps part of a walrus, might be in the middle of the igloo, handy for snacks and also a good footstool. Snow igloos even had shelves. The Eskimos would stick their snowshoes into the wall and lay mittens on the snowshoe shelf to dry.

The dogs, who had thick silver gray or white hair with a layer of short fine fur underneath to keep them warm, lived outdoors in the snow. They would curl into balls, cover their noses with their tails, and sleep, warm as muffins (usually), even if it was –50°F.

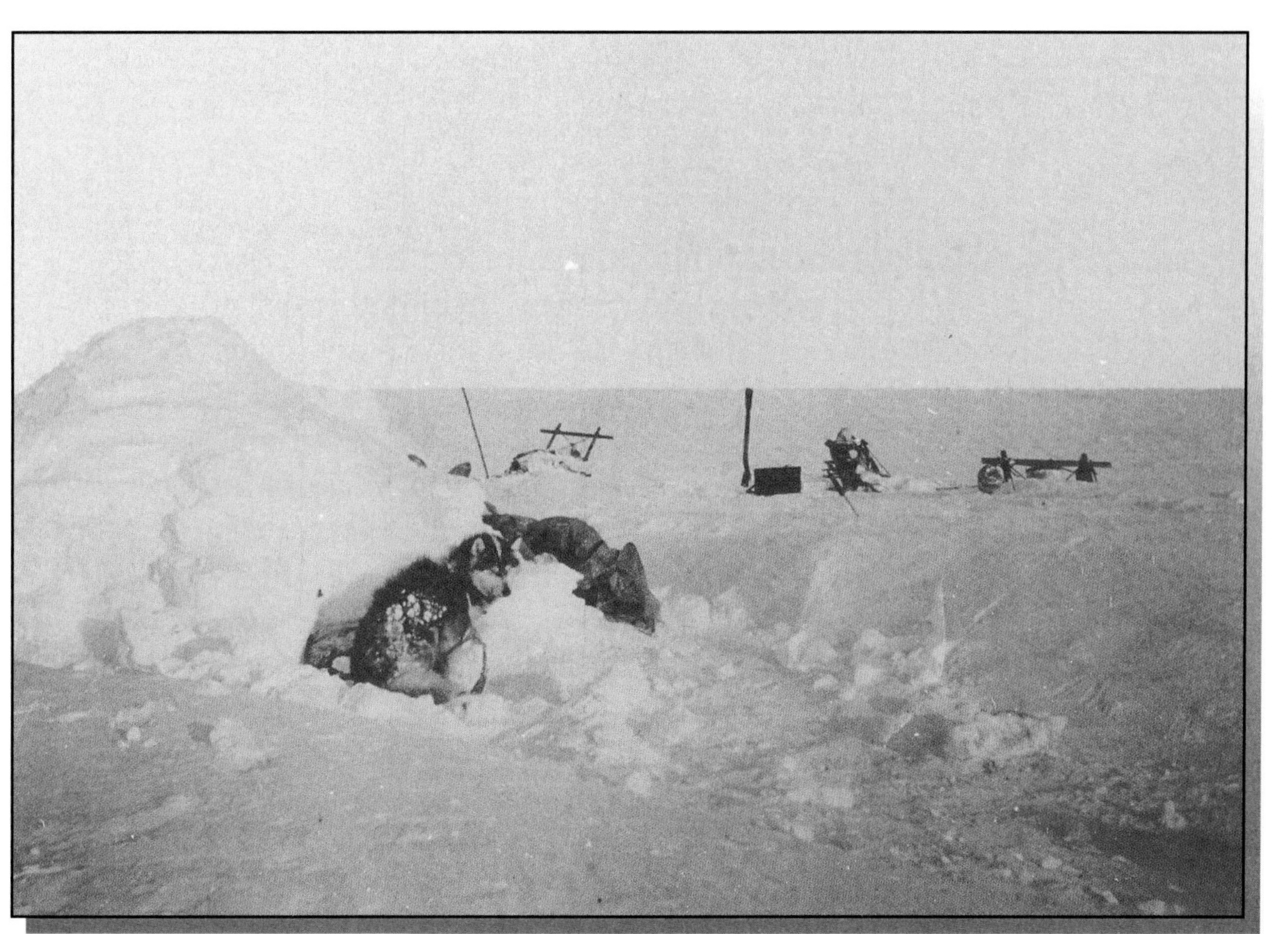

Dogs curl up outside Peary's igloo.

During the full moons Matt and the Eskimos hunted reindeer and arctic hares. The large pure white hares themselves could not be seen against the white snow, only their black shadows. They were like an army of frozen or leaping ghosts. And in the deep blackness of the arctic night, Matt saw hundreds of shooting stars, so thick and close they seemed to burst like rockets. While he watched the stars, the Eskimos explained that what Matt called the Big Dipper was really seven reindeer eating grass, and the constellation he called the Pleiades was really a team of dogs chasing a polar bear.

The Eskimos had no tables or chairs, no books or paper or writing, no money or bills to pay, no king or chief, no doctors or dentists, no schools or churches, no laws, and no wars. They needed shelter from the cold, strong dogs to pull their sledges, and animals they could hunt for furs and meat. Several families usually lived close together to help each other. If one man killed a walrus, he would share it with everyone. Perhaps in a few days another man would kill a bear or a reindeer; then that man would share it too.

Meanwhile in the wooden house, there was more to eat than raw meat, and there was a new cook. Mrs. Peary wrote in her diary for November 17, 1891, "Matt got supper tonight, and will from now until May 1 prepare all the meals under my supervision." For Christmas, at least, he didn't do all the cooking. Mrs. Peary prepared arctic hare pie with green peas, reindeer with cranberry sauce, corn and tomatoes, plum pudding, and apricot pie. Then, wrote Mrs. Peary, "Matt cleared everything away."

In February the sun returned. For days and days before it actually appeared, the sky was a magnificent dawn of pink, blue, crimson, and deep yellow, with rosy clouds. Then the sun appeared in the south at noon, but just for a moment the first day. Each day it rose a little higher. The crystal

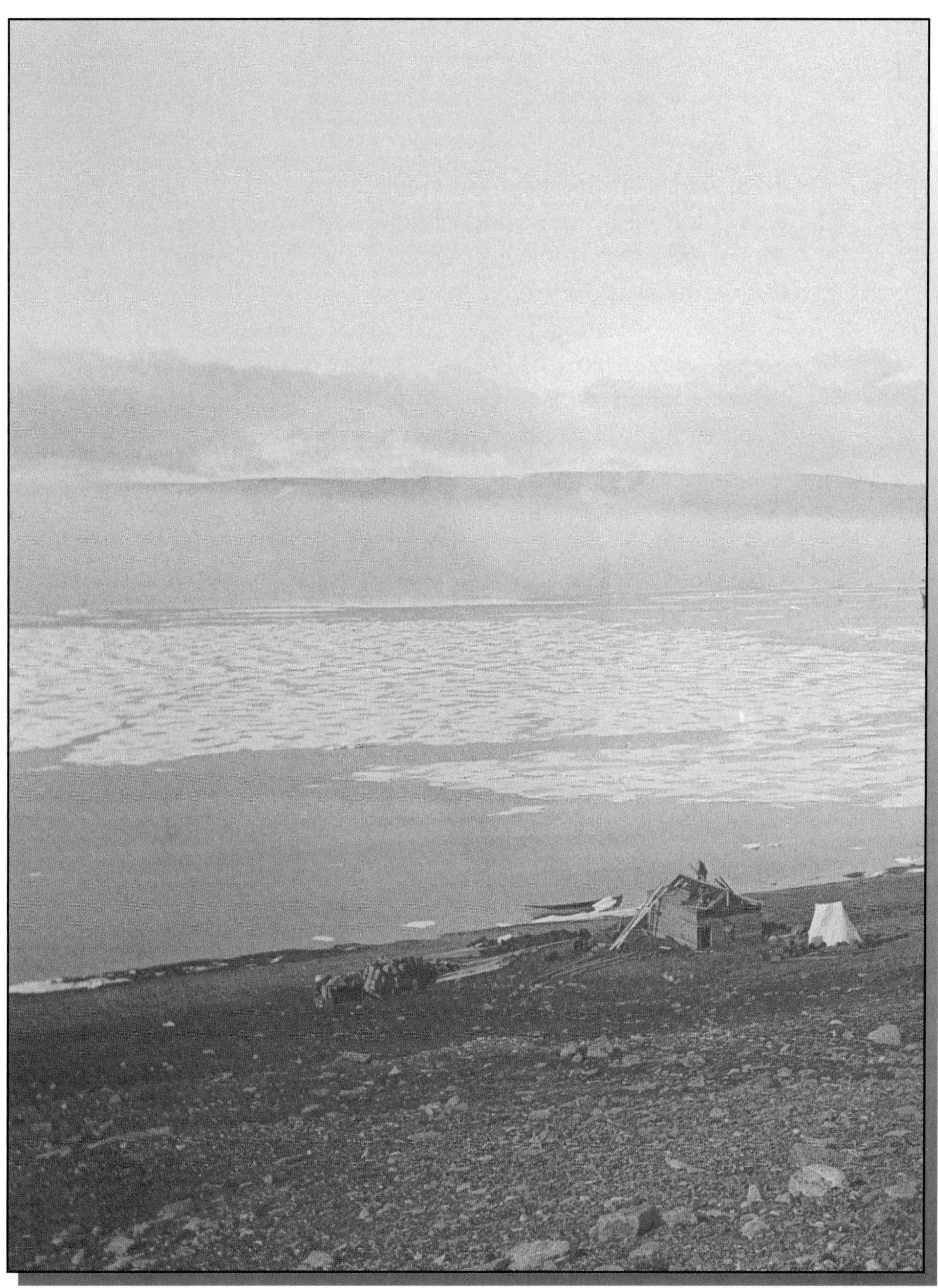

Robert Peary's house on McCormick Bay.

clear water in the bay was deep blue, and the air was thick with the sound of wings and songs as thousands of birds swooped and swarmed over the water and up the cliffs.

But Greenland's ice cap, which Matt intended to cross, was a frozen, lifeless desert of snow and howling wind and glaciers and deep crevasses. Even though Matt always covered the inside of his boots with soft dried moss for insulation, his heel froze when he helped haul boxes of pemmican and biscuits up to the ice cap in the beginning of May. (Freezing is very serious. The blood stops moving in the frozen part, and the skin and muscle can soon die.) Matt, who was the best at driving the dogs and at speaking the Eskimo language, had planned to be one of the first men to cross the ice cap, but Peary sent him back to the base camp. There were three reasons: one was the frozen heel; another was that someone had to protect Mrs. Peary at the camp; and the third was that Peary believed an explorer should have a college education in order to know what to do in an emergency.

During the short summer, while the others were gone, Matt went hunting so everyone would have plenty of fresh meat; he learned more of the Eskimo language; his foot healed; and he protected Mrs. Peary from danger.

In the end only Peary and Astrup actually crossed the ice cap. All the others turned back. The Eskimos, who feared Kokoyah, the evil spirit of the ice cap, refused to go at all. Peary did discover a large bay at the northeast corner of Greenland, which he named Independence Bay, but he did not find out if there was a way to get to the North Pole by land. He would have to try again. He asked Matt to come along again too.

Arctic Explorer:

The Story of Matthew Henson

Concept Connections

Linking the Selection

Think about the following questions, and then record your responses in the Response Journal section of your Writer's Notebook.

- In what ways did Matthew Henson help the members of his expedition survive?
- How do animals help Eskimos survive in the arctic?

Exploring Concept Vocabulary

The concept word for this lesson is ***adapt.*** If you don't know what this word means, look it up in a dictionary. Answer these questions.

- Who helped Matthew Henson learn to ***adapt*** to the cold?
- What are some ways in which Matthew ***adapted*** to life in the arctic?

In the Vocabulary section of your Writer's Notebook, write a sentence that includes the word ***adapt*** as well as one of the selection vocabulary words.

Expanding the Concept

Discuss whether you agree or disagree with Robert Peary's belief that an explorer should have a college education in order to deal with emergencies. Consider the knowledge Matthew Henson gained from his experience with Eskimos. Try to use the word ***adapt*** in your discussion. Add new ideas about survival to the Concept/Question Board.

Meet the Author

Jeri Ferris grew up on a small Nebraska farm, with her own horse at home and a library nearby. She once said she had *"the ideal writer's childhood."*

Ms. Ferris taught for several years. When she realized how hard it was to find biographies of great and brave people, she began writing them herself. *"My goal is to make these determined men and women inescapably alive, to make their deeds inescapably real, and to plant the seeds of similar determination and self-confidence in the children who read about them. My goal is that children, no matter their ethnic and social backgrounds and despite the obstacles, will say to themselves, 'I, too, can make a difference.'"*

Focus Questions What are some things you can do to prepare for a natural disaster? Have you ever been frightened by the weather?

McBroom and the Big Wind

Sid Fleischman
illustrated by Walter Lorraine

I can't deny it—it does get a mite windy out here on the prairie. Why, just last year a blow came ripping across our farm and carried off a pail of sweet milk. The next day it came back for the cow.

But that wasn't the howlin', scowlin', almighty *big* wind I aim to tell you about. That was just a common little prairie breeze. No account, really. Hardly worth bragging about.

It was the *big* wind that broke my leg. I don't expect you to believe that—yet. I'd best start with some smaller weather and work up to that bonebreaker.

I remember distinctly the first prairie wind that came scampering along after we bought our wonderful one-acre farm. My, that land is rich. Best topsoil in the country. There isn't a thing that won't grow in our rich topsoil, and fast as lightning.

The morning I'm talking about our oldest boys were helping me to shingle the roof. I had bought a keg of nails, but it turned out those nails were a whit short. We buried them in our wonderful topsoil and watered them down. In five or ten minutes those nails grew a full half-inch.

So there we were, up on the roof, hammering down shingles. There wasn't a cloud in the sky at first. The younger boys were shooting marbles all over the farm and the girls were jumping rope.

When I had pounded down the last shingle I said to myself, "Josh McBroom, that's a mighty stout roof. It'll last a hundred years."

Just then I felt a small draft on the back of my neck. A moment later one of the girls—it was Polly, as I recall—shouted up to me. "Pa," she said, "do jackrabbits have wings?"

I laughed. "No, Polly."

"Then how come there's a flock of jackrabbits flying over the house?"

I looked up. Mercy! Rabbits were flapping their ears across the sky in a perfect V formation, northbound. I knew then we were in for a slight blow.

"Run, everybody!" I shouted to the young'uns. I didn't want the wind picking them up by the ears. "Will*jill*hester*chester*peter*polly*tim*tom*mary*larry*and-little*clarinda*—in the house! Scamper!"

The clothesline was already beginning to whip around like a jump rope. My dear wife, Melissa, who had been baking a heap of biscuits, threw open the door. In we dashed and not a moment too soon. The wind was snapping at our heels like a pack of wolves. It aimed to barge right in and make itself at home! A prairie wind has no manners at all.

We slammed the door in its teeth. Now, the wind didn't take that politely. It rammed and battered at the door while all of us pushed and shoved to hold the door shut. My, it was a battle! How the house creaked and trembled!

"Push, my lambs!" I yelled. "Shove!"

At times the door planks bent like barrel staves. But we held that roaring wind out. When it saw there was no getting past us, the zephyr sneaked around the house to the back door. However, our oldest boy, Will, was too smart for it. He piled Mama's heap of fresh biscuits against the back door. My dear wife, Melissa, is a wonderful cook, but her biscuits *are* terribly heavy. They made a splendid door stop.

But what worried me most was our wondrous rich topsoil. That thieving wind was apt to make off with it, leaving us with a trifling hole in the ground.

"Shove, my lambs!" I said. "Push!"

The battle raged on for an hour. Finally the wind gave up butting its fool head against the door. With a great angry sigh it turned and whisked itself away, scattering fence pickets as it went.

We all took a deep breath and I opened the door a crack. Hardly a leaf now stirred on the ground. A bird began to twitter. I rushed outside to our poor one-acre farm.

Mercy! What I saw left me popeyed. "Melissa!" I shouted with glee. "Will*jill*hester*chester*peter*polly*-tim*tom*mary*larry*andlittle*clarinda*! Come here, my lambs! Look!"

We all gazed in wonder. Our topsoil was still there—every bit. Bless those youngsters! The boys had left their marbles all over the field, and the marbles had grown as large as boulders. There they sat, huge agates and sparkling glassies, holding down our precious topsoil.

But that rambunctious wind didn't leave empty-handed. It ripped off our new shingle roof. Pulled out the nails, too. We found out later the wind had shingled every gopher hole in the next county.

Now that was a strong draft. But it wasn't a *big* wind. Nothing like the kind that broke my leg. Still, that prairie gust was an education to me.

"Young'uns," I said, after we'd rolled those giant marbles down the hill. "The next uninvited breeze that comes along, we'll be ready for it. There are two sides to every flapjack. It appears to me the wind can be downright useful on our farm if we let it know who's boss."

The next gusty day that came along, we put it to work for us. I made a wind plow. I rigged a bedsheet and tackle to our old farm plow. Soon as a breeze sprung up I'd go tacking to and fro over the farm, plowing as I went. Our son Chester once plowed the entire farm in under three minutes.

On Thanksgiving morning Mama told the girls to pluck a large turkey for dinner. They didn't much like that chore, but a prairie gust arrived just in time. The girls stuck the turkey out the window. The wind plucked that turkey clean, pinfeathers and all.

Oh, we got downright glad to see a blow come along. The young'uns were always wanting to go out and play in the wind, but Mama was afraid they'd be carried off. So I made them wind shoes—made 'em out of heavy iron skillets. Out in the breeze those shoes felt light as feathers. The girls would jump rope with the clothesline. The wind spun the rope, of course.

Many a time I saw the youngsters put on their wind shoes and go clumping outside with a big tin funnel and all the empty bottles and jugs they could round up. They'd cork the containers jam full of prairie wind.

Then, come summer, when there wasn't a breath of air, they'd uncork a bottle or two of fresh winter wind and enjoy the cool breeze.

Of course, we had to windproof the farm every fall. We'd plant the field in buttercups. My, they were slippery—all that butter, I guess. The wind would slip and slide over the farm without being able to get a purchase on the topsoil. By then the boys and I had reshingled the roof. We used screws instead of nails.

Mercy! Then came the *big* wind!

It started out gently enough. There were a few jackrabbits and some crows flying backward through the air. Nothing out of the ordinary.

Of course the girls went outside to jump the clothesline and the boys got busy laying up bottles of wind for summer. Mama had just baked a batch of fresh biscuits. My, they did smell good! I ate a dozen or so hot out of the oven. And that turned out to be a terrible mistake.

Outside, the wind was picking up ground speed and scattering fence posts as it went.

"Will*jill*hester*chester*peter*polly*tim*tom*mary*larry*and-little*clarinda*!" I shouted. "Inside, my lambs! That wind is getting ornery!"

The young'uns came trooping in and pulled off their wind shoes. And not a moment too soon. The clothesline began to whip around so fast it seemed to disappear. Then we saw a hen house come flying through the air, with the hens still in it.

The sky was turning dark and mean. The wind came out of the far north, howling and shrieking and shaking the house. In the cupboard, cups chattered in their saucers.

Soon we noticed big balls of fur rolling along the prairie like tumbleweeds. Turned out they were timber wolves from up north. And then an old hollow log came spinning across the farm and split against my chopping stump. Out rolled a black bear, and was he in a temper! He had been trying to hibernate and didn't take kindly to being awakened. He gave out a roar and looked around for somebody to chase. He saw us at the windows and decided we would do.

The mere sight of him scared the young'uns and they huddled together, holding hands, near the fireplace.

I got down my shotgun and opened a window. That was a *mistake!* Two things happened at once. The bear was coming on and in my haste I forgot to calculate the direction of the wind. It came shrieking along the side of the house and when I poked the gunbarrel out the window, well, the wind bent it like an angle iron. That buckshot flew due south. I found out later it brought down a brace of ducks over Mexico.

But worse than that, when I threw open the window such a draft came in that our young'uns *were sucked up through the chimney!* Holding hands, they were carried away like a string of sausages.

Mama near fainted away. "My dear Melissa," I exclaimed. "Don't you worry! I'll get our young'uns back!"

I fetched a rope and rushed outside. I could see the young'uns up in the sky and blowing south.

I could also see the bear and he could see me. He gave a growl with a mouthful of teeth like rusty nails. He rose up on his hind legs and came toward me with his eyes glowing red as fire.

I didn't fancy tangling with that monster. I dodged around behind the clothesline. I kept one eye on the bear and the other on the young'uns. They were now flying over the county seat and looked hardly bigger than mayflies.

The bear charged toward me. The wind was spinning the clothesline so fast he couldn't see it. And he charged smack into it. My, didn't he begin to jump! He jumped red-hot pepper, only faster. He had got himself trapped inside the rope and couldn't jump out.

Of course, I didn't lose a moment. I began flapping my arms like a bird. That was such an enormous *big* wind I figured I could fly after the young'uns. The wind tugged and pulled at me, but it couldn't lift me an inch off the ground.

Tarnation! I had eaten too many biscuits. They were heavy as lead and weighed me down.

The young'uns were almost out of sight. I rushed to the barn for the wind plow. Once out in the breeze, the bedsheet filled with wind. Off I shot like a cannonball, plowing a deep furrow as I went.

Didn't I streak along, though! I was making better time than the young'uns. I kept my hands on the plow handles and steered around barns and farmhouses. I saw haystacks explode in the wind. If that wind got any stronger it wouldn't surprise me to see the sun blown off course. It would set in the south at high noon.

I plowed right along and gained rapidly on the young'uns. They were still holding hands and just clearing the tree tops. Before long I was within hailing distance.

"Be brave, my lambs!" I shouted. "Hold tight!"

I spurted after them until their shadows lay across my path. But the bedsheet was so swelled out with wind that I couldn't stop the plow. Before I could let go of the handles and jump off I had sailed far *ahead* of the young'uns.

I heaved the rope into the air. "Will*jill*hester*chester*-peter*polly*tim*tom*mary *larry*andlittle*clarinda*!" I shouted as they came flying overhead. "Hang on!"

Hester missed the rope, and Jill missed the rope, and so did Peter. But Will caught it. I had to dig my heels in the earth to hold them. And then I started back. The young'uns were too light for the wind. They hung in the air. I had to drag them home on the rope like balloons on a string.

Of course it took most of the day to shoulder my way back through the wind. It was a mighty struggle, I tell you! It was near suppertime when we saw our farmhouse ahead, and that black bear was still jumping rope!

I dragged the young'uns into the house. The rascals! They had had a jolly time flying through the air, and wanted to do it again! Mama put them to bed with their wind shoes on.

The wind blew all night, and the next morning that bear was still jumping rope. His tongue was hanging out and he had lost so much weight he was skin and bones.

Finally, about midmorning, the wind got tired of blowing one way, so it blew the other. We got to feeling sorry for that bear and cut him loose. He was so tuckered out he didn't even growl. He just pointed himself toward the tall timber to find another hollow log to crawl into. But he had lost the fine art of walking. We watched him jump, jump, jump north until he was out of sight.

That was the howlin', scowlin' all mighty *big* wind that broke my leg. It had not only pulled up fence posts, but the *holes* as well. It dropped one of those holes right outside the barn door and I stepped in it.

That's the bottom truth. Everyone on the prairie knows Josh McBroom would rather break his leg than tell a fib.

Concept Connections

Linking the Selection

Think about the following questions, and then record your responses in the Response Journal section of your Writer's Notebook.

- How did the McBroom family survive the first windstorm on their farm?
- How did Josh McBroom survive his encounter with the bear?
- What did Mr. and Mrs. McBroom invent to protect their children from the wind?

Exploring Concept Vocabulary

The concept word for this lesson is ***resourcefulness.*** If you don't know what this word means, look it up in a dictionary. Answer these questions.

- Why would ***resourcefulness*** be important for surviving in a remote area?
- How did the McBrooms show ***resourcefulness*** in using the wind?

In the Vocabulary section of your Writer's Notebook, write a sentence that includes the word ***resourcefulness*** as well as one of the selection vocabulary words.

Expanding the Concept

Compare the efforts of the McBroom family with those of the crew in "Arctic Explorer: The Story of Matthew Henson." Consider how each group worked together to survive harsh conditions. Try to use the word ***resourcefulness*** in your discussion of the characters. Add new ideas about survival to the Concept/Question Board.

Meet the Author

Sid Fleischman worked as a reporter after he graduated from college. He also wrote novels, suspense stories, and screenplays. Years later, he wrote his first children's book—it was for his own children.

Mr. Fleischman's interest in tall tales grew out of a keen interest in folklore. His McBroom books are filled with exaggeration and humor, characteristics common to tall tales.

Mr. Fleischman writes at a big table cluttered with library books, pens, pencils, letters, notes, and projects. He has been a full-time freelance writer since 1952.

Meet the Illustrator

Walter Lorraine was born in Worcester, Massachusetts, on February 3, 1929. He studied art at the Rhode Island School of Design. Later he was a book designer for a large publishing company and worked with children's book illustrators. Eventually, he started illustrating books himself. Mr. Lorraine says, *"Good illustrators have something to say. Whatever their techniques or styles, they always make a particular individual statement. Whether to convey fact or fiction, they are essentially storytellers who use pictures instead of words."*

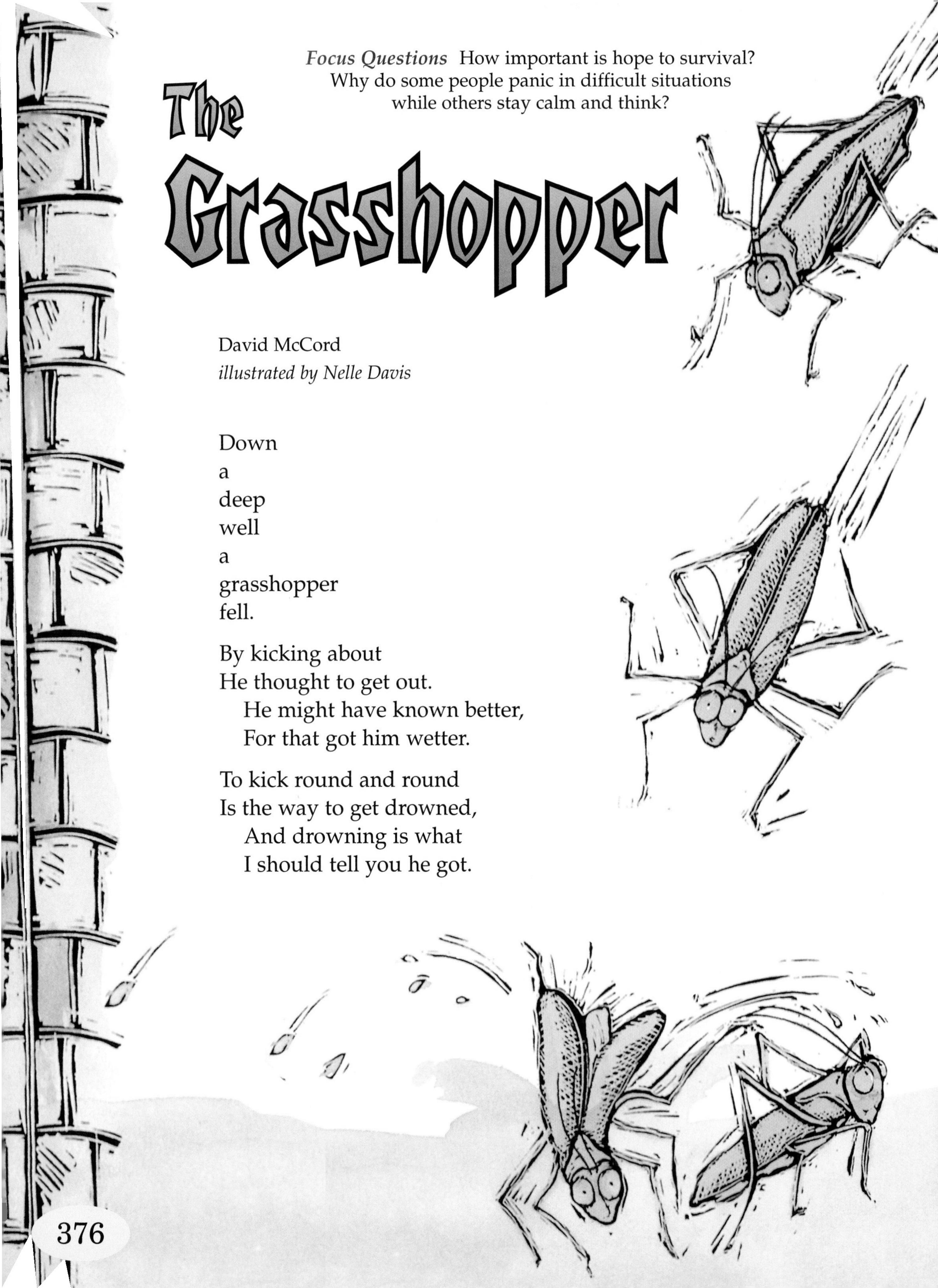

Focus Questions How important is hope to survival? Why do some people panic in difficult situations while others stay calm and think?

The Grasshopper

David McCord
illustrated by Nelle Davis

Down
a
deep
well
a
grasshopper
fell.

By kicking about
He thought to get out.
    He might have known better,
    For that got him wetter.

To kick round and round
Is the way to get drowned,
    And drowning is what
    I should tell you he got.

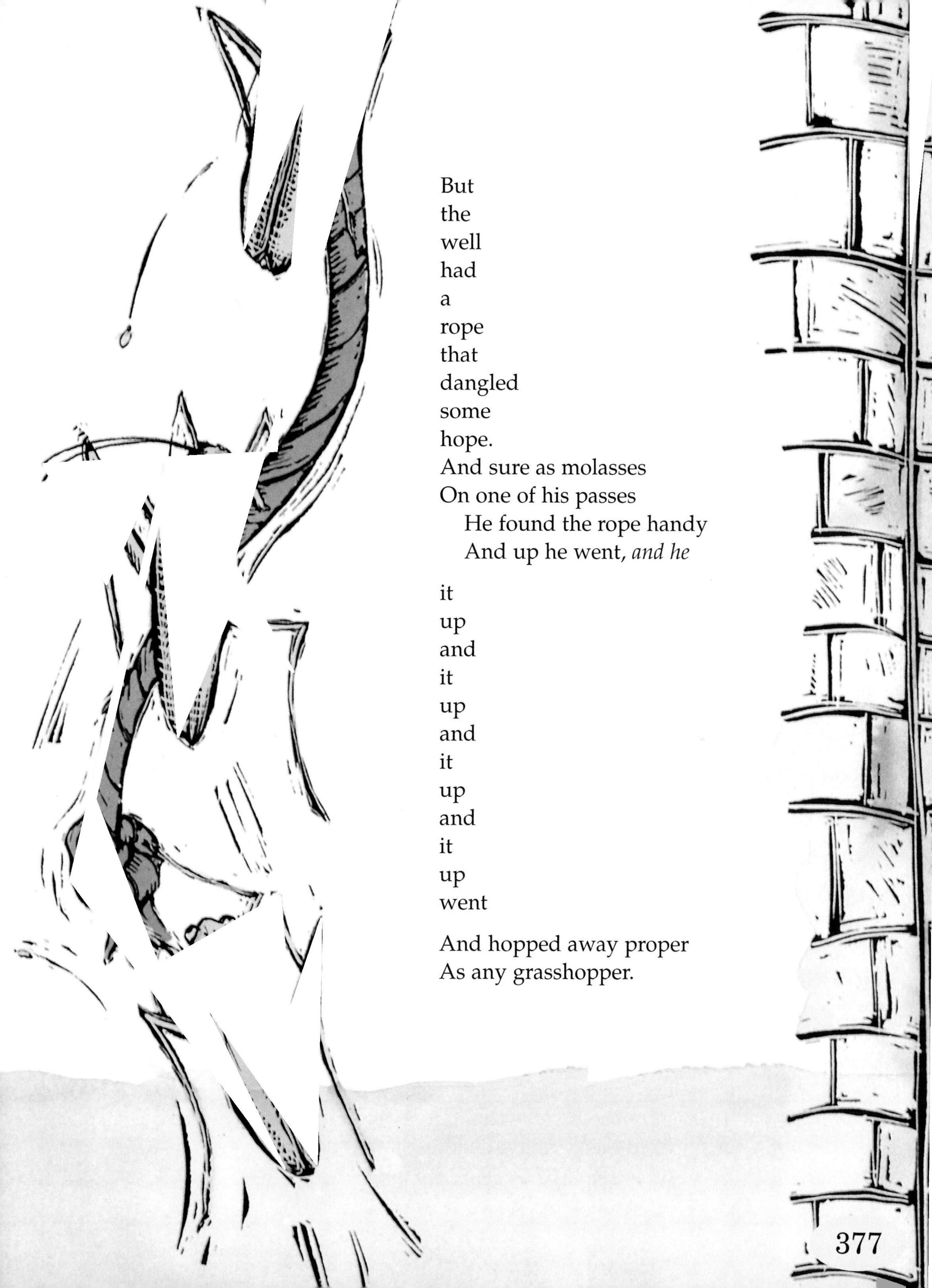

But
the
well
had
a
rope
that
dangled
some
hope.
And sure as molasses
On one of his passes
He found the rope handy
And up he went, *and he*

it
up
and
it
up
and
it
up
and
it
up
went

And hopped away proper
As any grasshopper.

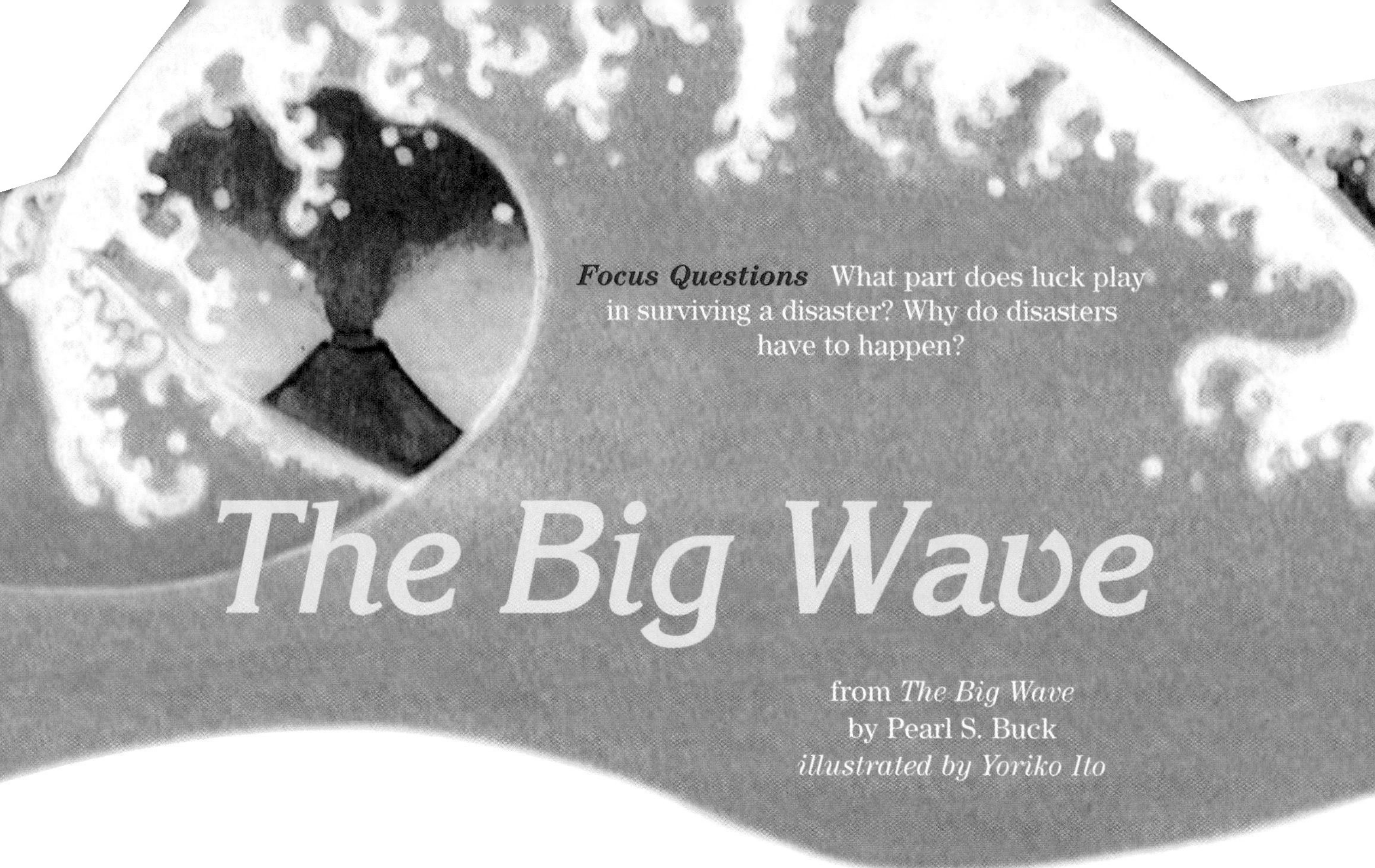

Focus Questions What part does luck play in surviving a disaster? Why do disasters have to happen?

The Big Wave

from *The Big Wave*
by Pearl S. Buck
illustrated by Yoriko Ito

Jiya and his family live in a small Japanese fishing village. When a distant volcano erupts, it causes a tidal wave. As the giant wave approaches the village, Jiya's father forces him to climb to safety on a nearby mountain. He climbs to the terraced farm of his friend Kino's family. The rest of Jiya's family stays behind. From the mountaintop, Jiya watches as the wave hits.

Upon the beach where the village stood not a house remained, no wreckage of wood or fallen stone wall, no little street of shops, no docks, not a single boat. The beach was as clean of houses as if no human beings had ever lived there. All that had been was now no more.

Jiya gave a wild cry and Kino felt him slip to the ground. He was unconscious. What he had seen was too much for him. What he knew, he could not bear. His family and his home were gone.

Kino began to cry and Kino's father did not stop him. He stooped and gathered Jiya into his arms and carried him into the house, and Kino's mother ran out of the kitchen and put down a mattress and Kino's father laid Jiya upon it.

"It is better that he is unconscious," he said gently. "Let him remain so until his own will wakes him. I will sit by him."

"I will rub his hands and feet," Kino's mother said sadly.

Kino could say nothing. He was still crying and his father let him cry for a while. Then he said to his wife:

"Heat a little rice soup for Kino and put some ginger in it. He feels cold."

Now Kino did not know until his father spoke that he did feel cold. He was shivering and he could not stop crying. Setsu came in. She had not seen the big wave, for her mother had closed the windows and drawn the curtains against the sea. But now she saw Jiya lying white-pale and still.

"Is Jiya dead?" she asked.

"No, Jiya is living," her father replied.

"Why doesn't he open his eyes?" she asked again.

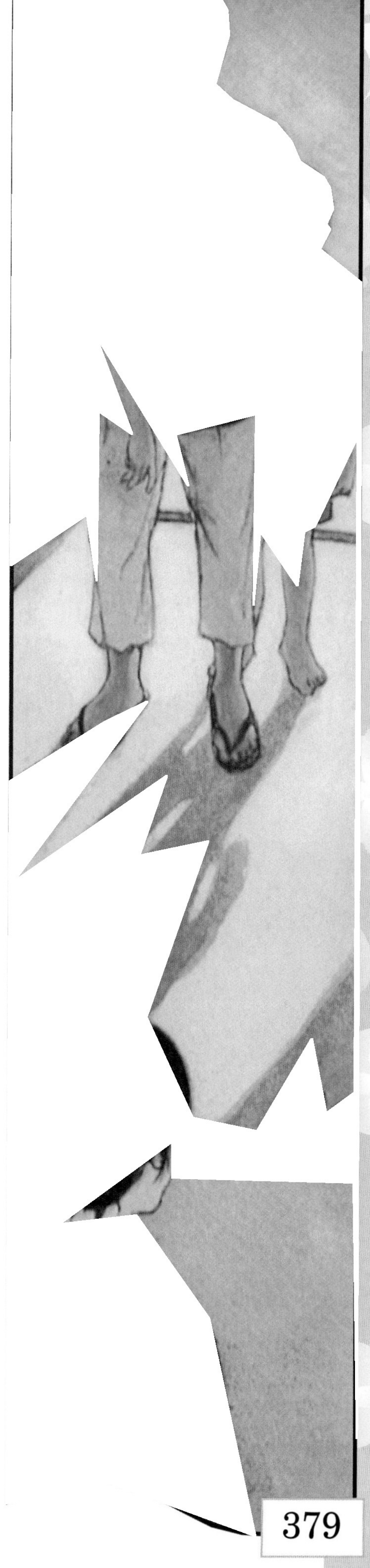

"Soon he will open his eyes," the father replied.

"If Jiya is not dead, why does Kino cry?" Setsu asked.

"You are asking too many questions," her father told her. "Go back to the kitchen and help your mother."

So Setsu went back again, sucking her forefinger, and staring at Jiya and Kino as she went, and soon the mother came in with the hot rice soup and Kino drank it. He felt warm now and he could stop crying. But he was still frightened and sad.

"What will we say to Jiya when he wakes?" he asked his father.

"We will not talk," his father replied. "We will give him warm food and let him rest. We will help him to feel he still has a home."

"Here?" Kino asked.

"Yes," his father replied. "I have always wanted another son, and Jiya will be that son. As soon as he knows that this is his home, then we must help him to understand what has happened."

So they waited for Jiya to wake.

"I don't think Jiya can ever be happy again," Kino said sorrowfully.

"Yes, he will be happy someday," his father said, "for life is always stronger than death. Jiya will feel when he wakes that he can never be happy again. He will cry and cry and we must let him cry. But he cannot always cry. After a few days he will stop crying all the time. He will cry only part of the time. He will sit sad and quiet. We must allow him to be sad and we must not make him speak. But we will do our work and live as always we do. Then

one day he will be hungry and he will eat something that our mother cooks, something special, and he will begin to feel better. He will not cry any more in the daytime but only at night. We must let him cry at night. But all the time his body will be renewing itself. His blood flowing in his veins, his growing bones, his mind beginning to think again, will make him live."

"He cannot forget his father and mother and his brother!" Kino exclaimed.

"He cannot and he should not forget them," Kino's father said. "Just as he lived with them alive, he will live with them dead. Someday he will accept their death as part of his life. He will weep no more. He will carry them in his memory and his thoughts. His flesh and blood are part of them. So long as he is alive, they, too, will live in him. The big wave came, but it went away. The sun shines again, birds sing, and earth flowers. Look out over the sea now!"

Kino looked out the open door, and he saw the ocean sparkling and smooth. The sky was blue again, a few clouds on the horizon were the only sign of what had passed—except for the empty beach.

"How cruel it seems for the sky to be so clear and the ocean so calm!" Kino said.

But his father shook his head. "No, it is wonderful that after the storm the ocean grows calm, and the sky is blue once more. It was not the ocean or the sky that made the evil storm."

"Who made it?" Kino asked. He let tears roll down his cheeks, because there was so much he could not understand. But only his father saw them and his father understood.

"Ah, no one knows who makes evil storms," his father replied. "We only know that they come. When they come we must live through them as bravely as we can, and after they are gone, we must feel again how wonderful is life. Every day of life is more valuable now than it was before the storm."

"But Jiya's family—his father and mother and brother, and all the other good fisherfolk, who are lost—" Kino whispered. He could not forget the dead.

"Now we must think of Jiya," his father reminded him. "He will open his eyes at any minute and we must be there, you to be his brother, and I to be his father. Call your mother, too, and little Setsu."

Now they heard something. Jiya's eyes were still closed, but he was sobbing in his sleep. Kino ran to fetch his mother and Setsu and they gathered about his bed, kneeling on the floor so as to be near Jiya when he opened his eyes.

In a few minutes, while they all watched, Jiya's eyelids fluttered on his pale cheeks, and then he opened his eyes. He did not know where he was. He looked from one face to the other, as though they were strangers. Then he looked up into the beams of the ceiling and around the white walls of the room. He looked at the blue-flowered quilt that covered him.

None of them said anything. They continued to kneel about him, waiting. But Setsu could not keep quiet. She clapped her hands and laughed. "Oh, Jiya has come back!" she cried. "Jiya, did you have a good dream?"

The sound of her voice made him fully awake. "My father—my mother—" he whispered.

Kino's mother took his hand. "I will be your mother now, dear Jiya," she said.

"I will be your father," Kino's father said.

"I am your brother now, Jiya," Kino faltered.

"Oh, Jiya will live with us," Setsu said joyfully.

Then Jiya understood. He got up from the bed and walked to the door that stood open to the sky and the sea. He looked down the hillside to the beach where the fishing village had stood. There was only beach, and all that remained of the twenty and more houses were a few foundation posts and some big stones. The gentle

little waves of the ocean were playfully carrying the light timber that had made the houses, and throwing it on the sands and snatching it away again.

The family had followed Jiya and now they stood about him. Kino did not know what to say, for his heart ached for his friend-brother. Kino's mother was wiping her eyes, and even little Setsu looked sad. She took Jiya's hand and stroked it.

"Jiya, I will give you my pet duck," she said.

But Jiya could not speak. He kept on looking at the ocean.

"Jiya, your rice broth is growing cold," Kino's father said.

"We ought all to eat something," Kino's mother said. "I have a fine chicken for dinner."

"I'm hungry!" Setsu cried.

"Come, my son," Kino's father said to Jiya.

They persuaded him gently, gathering around him, and they entered the house again. In the pleasant cosy room they all sat down about the table.

Jiya sat with the others. He was awake, he could hear the voices of Kino's family, and he knew that Kino sat beside him. But inside he still felt asleep. He was very tired, so tired that he did not want to speak. He knew that he would never see his father and mother any more, or his brother, or the neighbors and friends of the village. He tried not to think about them or to imagine their quiet bodies, floating under the swelling waves.

"Eat, Jiya," Kino whispered. "The chicken is good."

Jiya's bowl was before him, untouched. He was not hungry. But when Kino begged him he took up his porcelain spoon and drank a little of the soup. It was hot and good, and he smelled its fragrance in his nostrils. He drank more and then he took up his chopsticks and ate some of the meat and rice. His mind was still unable to think, but his body was young and strong and glad of the food.

When they had all finished, Kino said, "Shall we go up the hillside, Jiya?"

But Jiya shook his head. "I want to go to sleep again," he said.

Kino's father understood. "Sleep is good for you," he said. And he led Jiya to his bed, and when Jiya had laid himself down he covered him with the quilt and shut the sliding panels.

"Jiya is not ready yet to live," he told Kino. "We must wait."

The body began to heal first, and Kino's father, watching Jiya tenderly, knew that the body would heal the mind and the soul. "Life is stronger than death," he told Kino again and again.

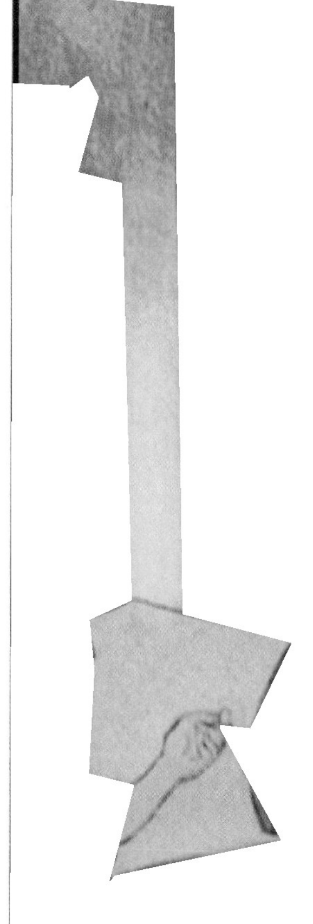

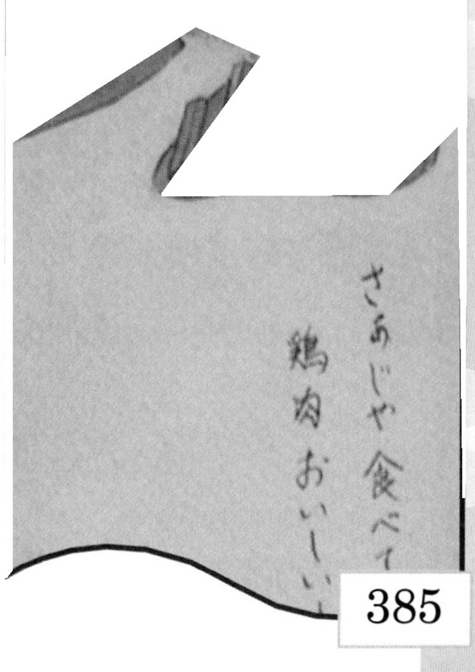

But each day Jiya was still tired. He did not want to think or to remember—he only wanted to sleep. He woke to eat and then to sleep. And when Kino's mother saw this she led him to the bedroom, and Jiya sank each time into the soft mattress spread on the floor in the quiet, clean room. He fell asleep almost at once and Kino's mother covered him and went away.

All through these days Kino did not feel like playing. He worked hard beside his father in the fields. They did not talk much, and neither of them wanted to look at the sea. It was enough to look at the earth, dark and rich beneath their feet.

One evening, Kino climbed the hill behind the farm and looked toward the volcano. The heavy cloud of smoke had long ago gone away, and the sky was always clear now. He felt happier to know that the volcano was no longer angry, and he went down again to the house. On the threshold his father was smoking his usual evening pipe. In the house his mother was giving Setsu her evening bath.

"Is Jiya asleep already?" Kino asked his father.

"Yes, and it is a good thing for him," his father replied. "Sleep will strengthen him, and when he wakes he will be able to think and remember."

"But should he remember such sorrow?" Kino asked.

"Yes," his father replied. "Only when he dares to remember his parents will he be happy again."

They sat together, father and son, and Kino asked still another question. “Father, are we not very unfortunate people to live in Japan?”

“Why do you think so?” his father asked in reply.

“Because the volcano is behind our house and the ocean is in front, and when they work together for evil, to make the earthquake and the big wave, then we are helpless. Always many of us are lost.”

“To live in the midst of danger is to know how good life is,” his father replied.

“But if we are lost in the danger?” Kino asked anxiously.

“To live in the presence of death makes us brave and strong,” Kino’s father replied. “That is why our people never fear death. We see it too often and we do not fear it. To die a little later or a little sooner does not matter. But to live bravely, to love life, to see how beautiful the trees are and the mountains, yes, and even the sea, to enjoy work because it produces food for life—in these things we Japanese are a fortunate people. We love life because we live in danger. We do not fear death because we understand that life and death are necessary to each other.”

The Big Wave

Concept Connections

Linking the Selection

Think about the following questions, and then record your responses in the Response Journal section of your Writer's Notebook.

- How did Jiya survive the tidal wave?
- Why does Kino's father think living in danger is beneficial?

Exploring Concept Vocabulary

The concept word for this lesson is ***disaster.*** If you don't know what this word means, look it up in a dictionary. Answer these questions.

- What are some examples of natural ***disasters?***
- How did Kino's family help Jiya deal with the ***disaster*** that took his family?

In the Vocabulary section of your Writer's Notebook, write a sentence that includes the word ***disaster*** as well as one of the selection vocabulary words.

Expanding the Concept

Compare Jiya with Karana from "Island of the Blue Dolphins." Consider each character's relationship with the sea. Try to use the word ***disaster*** in your discussion of the characters. Add new ideas about survival to the Concept/Question Board.

Meet the Author

Pearl S. Buck was three months old when her parents took her to China, where she grew up. She wrote her first story at age nine. It was published in an English-language newspaper there. Afterward the newspaper printed many of her stories and even paid her for them. She decided then that one day she would be a real writer.

Growing up in China with American parents, Buck saw how people from different backgrounds separated themselves from each other. Because she had both Chinese and American friends, she often felt as though she lived in two worlds. And she realized early that the worlds were not the same. She made it her life's work to try and bring the cultures together and to speak out against every kind of bigotry.

Meet the Illustrator

Yoriko Ito grew up in Japan. When she was a little girl, she knew she wanted to paint. It wasn't until after she came to San Francisco at age 21 that she knew she wanted to study art. However, she says she became a children's book illustrator by accident. She showed her portfolio to some authors at a librarians' conference, and an author introduced her to a publisher. *"I was really lucky,"* says Ms. Ito.

Now Ms. Ito works at the Dreamworks film company. She painted backgrounds for movie animation for *The Prince of Egypt* and *El Dorado.* Ms. Ito advises young artists, *"You have to do your best always. If you believe in something, don't doubt your ability. . . . Remember, you can't please everybody. Trust yourself."*

Focus Questions What helps you survive those times when you feel unhappy? How long can a person survive with no one else to talk to?

Solitude

A. A. Milne
illustrated by Ernest H. Shepard

I have a house where I go
  When there's too many people,
I have a house where I go
  Where no one can be;
I have a house where I go,
Where nobody ever says "No";
Where no one says anything—so
  There is no one but me.

Focus Questions Why do some people risk their own safety to help others survive? What can we learn from people who have survived terrible events?

Anne Frank:

The Diary of a Young Girl

Anne Frank
translated from the Dutch
by B. M. Mooyaart-Doubleday
illustrated by Susan Keeter

During World War II, many Jewish families in Germany and elsewhere in Europe hid to avoid being sent to concentration camps. Anne Frank and her family moved to Holland to escape the Nazis. When the Nazis came to Holland, the Franks hid for two years in a secret annex in Mr. Frank's office building. During this time, Anne kept a diary of her daily thoughts, feelings, and activities. Her father found these diaries after her death in a concentration camp in 1945 and had them published. These are a few of her first diary entries.

I hope I shall be able to confide in you completely, as I have never been able to do in anyone before, and I hope that you will be a great support and comfort to me.
Anne Frank, 12 June 1942.

Wednesday, 8 July, 1942

Dear Kitty,

Years seem to have passed between Sunday and now. So much has happened, it is just as if the whole world had turned upside down. But I am still alive, Kitty, and that is the main thing, Daddy says.

Yes, I'm still alive, indeed, but don't ask where or how. You wouldn't understand a word, so I will begin by telling you what happened on Sunday afternoon.

At three o'clock (Harry had just gone, but was coming back later) someone rang the front doorbell. I was lying lazily reading a book on the veranda in the sunshine, so I didn't hear it. A bit later, Margot appeared at the kitchen door looking very excited. "The S.S. have sent a call-up notice for Daddy," she whispered. "Mummy has gone to see Mr. Van Daan already." (Van Daan is a friend who works with Daddy in the business.) It was a great shock to me, a call-up; everyone knows what that means. I picture concentration camps and lonely cells—should we allow him to be doomed to this? "Of course he won't go," declared Margot, while we waited together. "Mummy has gone to the Van Daans to discuss whether we should move into our hiding place tomorrow. The Van Daans are going with us, so we shall be seven in all." Silence. We couldn't talk any more, thinking about Daddy, who, little knowing what was going on, was visiting some old people in the Joodse Invalide; waiting for Mummy, the heat and suspense, all made us very overawed and silent.

Suddenly the bell rang again. "That is Harry," I said. "Don't open the door." Margot held me back, but it was not necessary as we heard Mummy and Mr. Van Daan downstairs, talking to Harry, then they came in and closed the door behind them. Each time the bell went, Margot or I had to creep softly down to see if it was Daddy, not opening the door to anyone else.

Margot and I were sent out of the room. Van Daan wanted to talk to Mummy alone. When we were alone together in our bedroom, Margot told me that the call-up was not for Daddy, but for her. I was more frightened than ever and began to cry. Margot is sixteen; would they really take girls of that age away alone? But thank goodness she won't go, Mummy said so herself; that must be what Daddy meant when he talked about us going into hiding.

Into hiding—where would we go, in a town or the country, in a house or a cottage, when, how, where . . . ?

These were questions I was not allowed to ask, but I couldn't get them out of my mind. Margot and I began to pack some of our most vital belongings into a school satchel. The first thing I put in was this diary, then hair curlers, handkerchiefs, schoolbooks, a comb, old letters; I put in the craziest things with the idea that we were going into hiding. But I'm not sorry, memories mean more to me than dresses.

At five o'clock Daddy finally arrived, and we phoned Mr. Koophuis to ask if he could come around in the evening. Van Daan went and fetched Miep. Miep has been in the business with Daddy since 1933 and has become a close friend, likewise her brand-new husband, Henk. Miep came

and took some shoes, dresses, coats, underwear, and stockings away in her bag, promising to return in the evening. Then silence fell on the house; not one of us felt like eating anything, it was still hot and everything was very strange. We let our large upstairs room to a certain Mr. Goudsmit, a divorced man in his thirties, who appeared to have nothing to do on this particular evening; we simply could not get rid of him without being rude; he hung about until ten o'clock. At eleven o'clock Miep and Henk Van Santen arrived. Once again, shoes, stockings, books, and underclothes disappeared into Miep's bag and Henk's deep pockets, and at eleven-thirty they too disappeared. I was dog-tired and although I knew that it would be my last night in my own bed, I fell asleep immediately and didn't wake up until Mummy called me at five-thirty the next morning. Luckily it was not so hot as Sunday; warm rain fell steadily all day. We put on heaps of clothes as if we were going to the North Pole, the sole reason being to take clothes with us. No Jew in our situation would have dreamed of going out with a suitcase full of clothing. I had on two vests, three pairs of pants, a dress, on top of that a skirt, jacket, summer coat, two pairs of stockings, lace-up shoes, woolly cap, scarf, and still more; I was nearly stifled before we started, but no one inquired about that.

Margot filled her satchel with schoolbooks, fetched her bicycle, and rode off behind Miep into the unknown, as far as I was concerned. You see I still didn't know where our secret hiding place was to be. At seven-thirty the door closed behind us. Moortje, my little cat, was the only creature to whom I said farewell. She would have a good home with the neighbors. This was all written in a letter addressed to Mr. Goudsmit.

There was one pound of meat in the kitchen for the cat, breakfast things lying on the table, stripped beds, all giving the impression that we had left helter-skelter. But we didn't care about impressions, we only wanted to get away, only escape and arrive safely, nothing else. Continued tomorrow.

Yours, Anne

Thursday, 9 July, 1942

Dear Kitty,

So we walked in the pouring rain, Daddy, Mummy, and I, each with a school satchel and shopping bag filled to the brim with all kinds of things thrown together anyhow.

We got sympathetic looks from people on their way to work. You could see by their faces how sorry they were they couldn't offer us a lift; the gaudy yellow star spoke for itself.

Only when we were on the road did Mummy and Daddy begin to tell me bits and pieces about the plan. For months as many of our goods and chattels and necessities of life as possible had been sent away and they were sufficiently ready for us to have gone into hiding of our own accord on July 16. The plan had had to be speeded up ten days because of the call-up, so our quarters would not be so well organized, but we had to make the best of it. The hiding place itself would be in the building where Daddy has his office. It will be hard for outsiders to understand, but I shall explain that later on. Daddy didn't have many people working for him: Mr. Kraler, Koophuis, Miep, and Elli Vossen, a twenty-three-year-old typist who all knew of our arrival. Mr. Vossen, Elli's father, and two boys worked in the warehouse; they had not been told.

I will describe the building: there is a large warehouse on the ground floor which is used as a store. The front door to the house is next to the warehouse door, and inside the front door is a second doorway which leads to a staircase. There is another door at the top of the stairs, with a frosted glass window in it, which has "Office" written in black letters across it. That is the large main office, very big, very light, and very full. Elli, Miep, and Mr. Koophuis work there in the daytime. A small dark room containing the safe, a wardrobe, and a large cupboard leads to a small somewhat dark second office. Mr. Kraler and Mr. Van Daan used to sit here, now it is only Mr. Kraler. One can reach Kraler's office from the passage, but only via a glass door which can be opened from the inside, but not easily from the outside.

From Kraler's office a long passage goes past the coal store, up four steps and leads to the showroom of the whole building: the private office. Dark, dignified furniture, linoleum and carpets on the floor, radio, smart lamp, everything first-class. Next door there is a roomy kitchen with a hot-water faucet and a gas stove. Next door the W.C. [water closet]. That is the first floor.

A wooden staircase leads from the downstairs passage to the next floor. There is a small landing at the top. There is a door at each end of the landing, the left one leading to a storeroom at the front of the house and to the attics. One of those really steep Dutch staircases runs from the side to the other door opening on to the street.

The right-hand door leads to our "Secret Annexe." No one would ever guess that there would be so many rooms hidden behind that plain gray door. There's a little step in front of the door and then you are inside.

There is a steep staircase immediately opposite the entrance. On the left a tiny passage brings you into a room which was to become the Frank family's bed-sitting-room, next door a smaller room, study and bedroom for the two young ladies of the family. On the right a little room without windows containing the washbasin and a small W.C. compartment, with another door leading to Margot's and my room. If you go up the next flight of stairs and open the door, you are simply amazed that there could be such a big light room in such an old house by the canal. There is a gas stove in this room (thanks to the fact that it was used as a laboratory) and a sink. This is now the kitchen for the Van Daan couple, besides being general living room, dining room, and scullery.

A tiny little corridor room will become Peter Van Daan's apartment. Then, just as on the lower landing, there is a large attic. So there you are, I've introduced you to the whole of our beautiful "Secret Annexe."

Yours, Anne

Friday, 10 July, 1942

Dear Kitty,

I expect I have thoroughly bored you with my long-winded descriptions of our dwelling. But still I think you should know where we've landed.

But to continue my story—you see, I've not finished yet—when we arrived at the Prinsengracht, Miep took us quickly upstairs and into the "Secret Annexe." She closed the door behind us and we were alone. Margot was already waiting for us, having come much faster on her bicycle. Our living room and all the other rooms were chock-full of rubbish, indescribably so. All the cardboard boxes which had been sent to the office in the previous months lay piled on the floor and the beds. The little room was filled to the ceiling with bedclothes. We had to start clearing up immediately, if we wished to sleep in decent beds that night. Mummy and Margot were not in a fit state to take part; they were tired and lay down on their beds, they were miserable, and lots more besides. But the two "clearers-up" of the family—Daddy and myself—wanted to start at once.

The whole day long we unpacked boxes, filled cupboards, hammered and tidied, until we were dead beat. We sank into clean beds that night. We hadn't had a bit of anything warm the whole day, but we didn't care; Mummy and Margot were too tired and keyed up to eat, and Daddy and I were too busy.

On Tuesday morning we went on where we left off the day before. Elli and Miep collected our rations for us, Daddy improved the poor blackout, we scrubbed the kitchen floor, and were on the go the whole day long again. I hardly had time to think about the great change in my life until Wednesday. Then I had a chance, for the first time since our arrival, to tell you all about it, and at the same time to realize myself what had actually happened to me and what was still going to happen.

Yours, Anne

Anne Frank:

The Diary of a Young Girl

Concept Connections

Linking the Selection

Think about the following questions, and then record your responses in the Response Journal section of your Writer's Notebook.

- What did Anne Frank and her family do to try to avoid being sent to a concentration camp?
- Why did Anne become more frightened when she learned the call-up had been for her sister instead of her father?

Exploring Concept Vocabulary

The concept word for this lesson is ***fortitude.*** If you don't know what this word means, look it up in a dictionary. Answer these questions.

- How might ***fortitude*** help a person survive a difficult situation like the one the Franks faced?
- How did Anne show her ***fortitude*** after arriving at the "Secret Annexe?"

In the Vocabulary section of your Writer's Notebook, write a sentence that includes the word ***fortitude*** as well as one of the selection vocabulary words.

Expanding the Concept

Compare the family in this selection with Kino's family in "The Big Wave." Discuss how families helped others survive. Try to use the word ***fortitude*** in your discussion. Add new ideas about survival to the Concept/Question Board.

Meet the Author

Anne Frank was four when her family fled to Amsterdam, Holland, to escape the Nazis. The Nazis eventually came to Holland, so the Franks went into hiding. They moved into the attic of her father's warehouse, a place they called the "Secret Annexe." For two years, they did not leave the attic. Anne wrote in her diary about everything that happened there.

Anne's parents had given her the small, clothbound book for her thirteenth birthday. She wrote inside, *"I want to write, but more than that, I want to bring out all kinds of things that lie buried deep in my heart . . . . I want this diary itself to be my friend, and I shall call my friend Kitty."*

In 1944 the Franks were discovered and taken to concentration camps. Of the eight people in the secret annex, only Anne's father survived. When he returned to Amsterdam, Miep and Elli gave him the diary they had found in the annex.

Meet the Illustrator

Susan Keeter has art degrees from Syracuse University. Ms. Keeter's mother and stepfather ran an art school in their home so Ms. Keeter had access to art materials and instruction throughout her childhood.

This story particularly affected Ms. Keeter because her mother was born the same year as Anne Frank. She says, *"I look at my mother, her friends, her work, the beauty she creates and wonder what Anne Frank would have accomplished—how she would have changed the world—if she had been allowed to live a full life."*

Minamoto no Yorinobu Swimming across a bay to attack the rebellious Tadatsune. 1879. **Tsukioka Yoshitoshi.** Woodblock print. Vincent van Gogh Museum, Rijsmuseum, Amsterdam.

Choctaw Removal. 1966. **Valjean McCarthy-Hessing.** Watercolor on paper. The Philbrook Museum of Art, Tulsa, Oklahoma.

Buchenwald Concentration Camp Survivors. 1945. **Margaret Bourke-White.** Photograph.

The Old Plantation. c.1790–1800. **Artist unknown.** Watercolor on laid paper. Abby Aldrich Rockefeller Folk Art Center.

Focus Questions Can people make a difficult situation easier to survive? How do survivors pass on their stories to others?

Music & Slavery

Wiley Blevins

illustrated by Ashley Bryan

Mother was let off some days at noon to get ready for spinning that evening. She had to portion out the cotton they was gonna spin and see that each got a fair share. When mother was going round counting the cards each had spun she would sing this song:

Keep your eye on the sun.
See how she run.
Don't let her catch you with your work undone.
I'm a trouble, I'm a trouble.
Trouble don't last always.

That made the women all speed up so they could finish before dark catch 'em, 'cause it be mighty hard handlin' that cotton thread by firelight.

Bob Ellis
slave in Virginia

The life of many slaves in the United States was often full of fear and misery. Long hours were often spent picking cotton in the hot summer sun. At night, the slaves ate what little food their owners had given them and frequently slept on dirt floors. The slaves lived in run-down, overcrowded cabins and owned only the few clothes and possessions their masters had given them. They lived in fear of being beaten if they did not work hard enough or disobeyed their owners. They were not paid, and they were not allowed to leave their homes without special permission.

These terrible living conditions and lack of freedoms made many slaves want to escape. For most, however, there was no real hope of escape. Each day was a struggle to survive. One way the slaves dealt with these hardships was through music. It was a way to express both their sadness and their hope.

The slaves brought with them from Africa a strong tradition of music. Song and dance were an important part of their daily lives. They sang as they worked. They sang to celebrate. They sang when they were sad. They continued this tradition in the new world.

Slaves also brought instruments with them. The drum was the most important instrument used by them in Africa. However, many slave owners believed drums were being used to send secret messages. Therefore, drums were forbidden on most plantations. Instead, slaves kept the strong rhythms of their songs by clapping their hands, stomping their feet, swaying their bodies, and using other instruments such as the banjo. The banjo, developed by the slaves, became a commonly used instrument and is still in use today.

Many of the songs the slaves sang were developed as they worked in the fields. Singing helped take their minds off the difficulties of their work. These songs often changed over time. Many songs required a leader who would sing one line of the song while the others sang the response. These "call and response" chants were unique to slave music. Some songs that survived have become well-known spirituals, or religious songs. These songs, including "Swing Low Sweet Chariot" and "Go Down Moses," are based on stories in the Bible in which people were kept as slaves. Slaves were punished, often severely beaten, if they spoke against slavery. Through the spirituals, they could sing about the brutality of slavery without fear of being punished. Many of these songs are still sung today and are a tribute to the rich musical heritage of the slaves.

MANY THOUSAND GONE

illustrated by Ashley Bryan

No more auc-tion block for me, No more, No more,

No more auc-tion block for me, Ma - ny thou-sand gone.

No more peck of corn for me,
No more,
No more,
No more peck of corn for me,
Many thousand gone.

No more hundred lash for me,
No more,
No more,
No more hundred lash for me,
Many thousand gone.

Walk Together Children

illustrated by Ashley Bryan

O, Walk to-geth-er child-ren, Don't you get wea-ry,
Sing to-geth-er child-ren, Don't you get wea-ry,

Walk to-geth-er child-ren, Don't you get wea-ry,
Sing to-geth-er child-ren, Don't you get wea-ry,

Walk to-geth-er child-ren, Don't you get wea-ry, There's a
Sing to-geth-er child-ren, Don't you get wea-ry, There's a

great camp meet-ing in the Prom-ised Land.

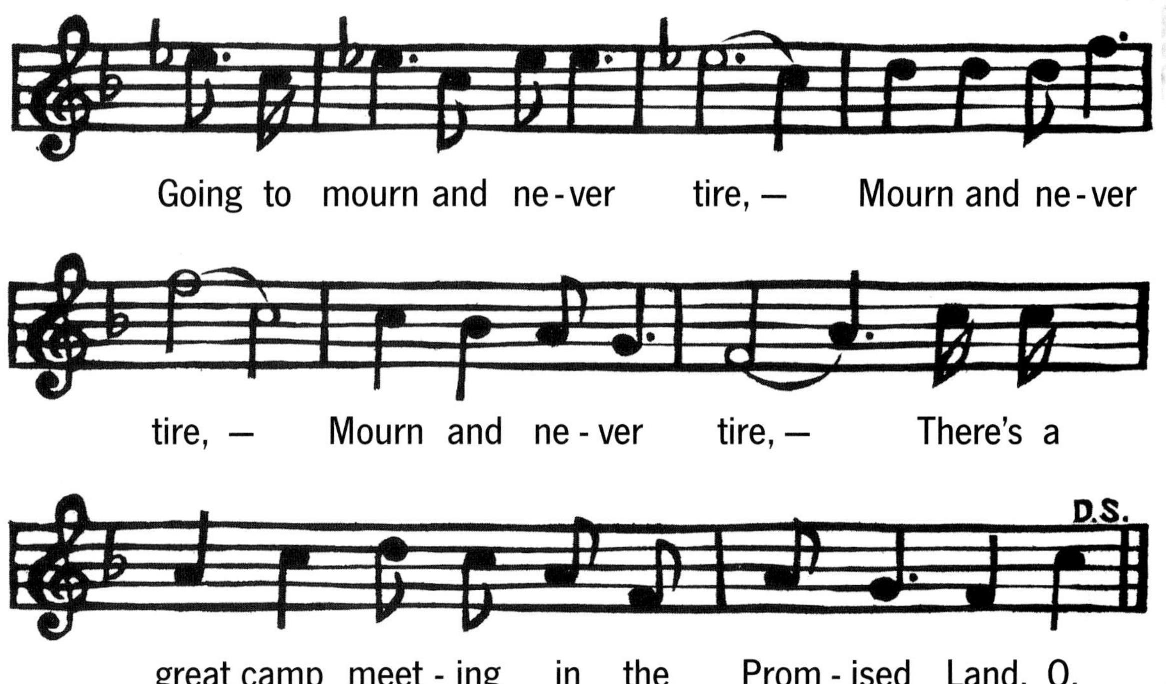
Going to mourn and ne-ver tire, — Mourn and ne-ver
tire, — Mourn and ne-ver tire, — There's a
D.S.
great camp meet-ing in the Prom-ised Land. O,

Music & Slavery

Concept Connections

Linking the Selection

Think about the following questions, and then record your responses in the Response Journal section of your Writer's Notebook.

- How did slaves keep the strong rhythms of their songs alive after their drums were taken away?
- How can you tell from their songs that a sense of community was important to slaves?

Exploring Concept Vocabulary

The concept word for this lesson is ***persevere.*** If you don't know what this word means, look it up in a dictionary. Answer these questions.

- How did songs help the slaves ***persevere*** despite their hardships?
- In what other selection did art help someone ***persevere?***

In the Vocabulary section of your Writer's Notebook, write a sentence that includes the word ***persevere*** as well as one of the selection vocabulary words.

Expanding the Concept

The selections in this unit have told about people surviving a variety of dangers and challenges. Based on what you have read, what do you think are the most important character traits in a survival situation? Try to use the word ***persevere*** in your discussion. Add new ideas about survival to the Concept/Question Board.

Meet the Author

Wiley Blevins grew up in West Virginia. During his childhood, he heard stories about his grandfather's life on a Virginia plantation. The stories were often about the music and celebrations of the slaves. Mr. Blevins always wondered, *"How could slaves spend so much time singing and celebrating?"*

Mr. Blevins began to study slavery and music further. He says, *"It became clear to me how the music of slaves was a way for them to cope with their brutal living conditions. It was one of their survival mechanisms."*

Meet the Illustrator

Ashley Bryan started writing and illustrating his own books in kindergarten. He bound them and gave them away as gifts for his friends and family. By the time he was in fourth grade, he had already created hundreds of books.

Mr. Bryan now lives in Isleford, Maine, on an island off the coast. He carries a sketchbook to draw people he meets and interesting places he sees as he travels. When he's not traveling, he paints at home during the day and works on his books at night.

UNIT 5

Communication

How do you let other people know what you want? Do you have a baby sister or brother? How does the baby tell others what he or she wants? Can you tell what your pet dog or cat or bird wants? How? It's all communication, and it takes as many forms as there are people and animals that need to communicate.

Focus Questions How is animal communication similar to human communication? Do you think people will ever learn to understand what animals are saying?

MESSAGES BY THE MILE

by Margery Facklam

Fin whales swim fast and travel alone, but they stay in touch with other fin whales hundreds of miles away. You might think the world's second-largest animal (only the blue whale is larger) would have the loudest voice, but we can't hear even a trace of the fin whale's long-distance song. Its sound is *infrasonic,* meaning it is *below* the level humans can hear. The rumblings of earthquakes, volcanoes, and severe thunderstorms are also infrasonic as they are building. We may feel them before they erupt, but we don't hear them. Divers swimming near big whales say they can feel the sound tingle right through their bodies. In the days before the churning engines of big ships filled the oceans with noise, the songs of fin whales may have carried for two or three thousand miles.

How whales make their sounds is still a mystery. They have no vocal cords. As one scientist put it, whales have a lot of complicated "plumbing" in their heads, and we don't know how it all works. Whales often sing near canyons on the ocean bottoms. Sounds echo from these deep hollows and trenches. Musicians say the songs sound as if they've been amplified in a recording studio.

Dr. Roger Payne and Dr. Katherine Payne, a husband-and-wife team, studied whale songs for twenty years. They began by recording the sounds made by the humpback whales feeding in the cold waters of the Arctic and Antarctic oceans in the spring. They could hear long, low rumbles, shrill whistles, grunts, eerie groans, and high squeaks like a door opening on a rusty hinge (much like the sounds of the dolphins). Some noises were used when whales met. Perhaps they were asking, "Who are you?" or warning others to stay away; perhaps the sounds were simply a form of greeting. All the "conversations" were short.

It wasn't until the humpback whales had migrated to breeding grounds in warm seas—around Hawaii, California, Bermuda, or Africa—that the Paynes heard the male humpback's beautiful, long melody. The humpback sings this song only when he is alone. His tune is the most complicated of all animal songs, with many notes in different patterns. Most humpback songs last an hour or two, interrupted only when the whale comes up for air. But one scientist taped a song that went on for more than twenty-two hours. The whale was still singing when the scientist got tired and packed up his equipment to go home.

The humpback's songs change each season. At the beginning of the spring migration, the males in one part of the ocean pick up the old melody and begin to make changes in it. They improvise. The song may drop in pitch, or one part may be speeded up while another slows down. As soon as one whale sings a new song, the other whales learn it. We depend on rhymes and repeating choruses to help us remember long songs and poems. Whales do, too. They repeat rhythms and patterns of notes.

Whales from the Pacific Ocean sing a different song from those in the Atlantic. In twenty years of study, the North Atlantic humpbacks have never gone back to an old version of a song after they have changed it. Does an old song go out of style? Is it a message they no longer need? Are they now telling a "story" of things that happened during the most recent migration? Nobody knows.

Some years after the whale studies, Dr. Katherine Payne was watching a group of elephants at the Washington Park Zoo, in Portland, Oregon. The elephants were separated by thick concrete walls, but they called back and forth with their usual trumpetings, snorts, barks, and rumbles. For centuries, people who lived near elephants have heard such rumblings. Some claimed it was only the elephants' stomachs digesting food. But at the zoo that day, Dr. Payne felt a strange throbbing in the air every ten or fifteen seconds.

Later, back in her office at Cornell University, she kept thinking about that feeling. It reminded her of when she was a young girl, singing in the church choir. She had felt the same throbbing from the lowest notes of the big pipe organ. It also felt like the vibrations from the whales' infrasonic songs. Could the elephants be sending infrasonic messages?

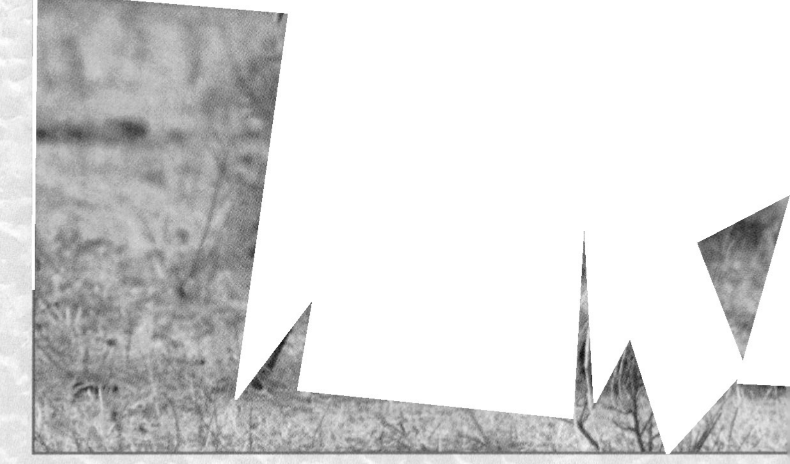

Infrasonic calls would explain how herds stay in touch, even though they are separated by thick forests. Infrasonic communication might also help explain some of the elephants' behavior. For example, a group of grandmother and mother elephants traveling with babies, aunts, and baby-sitters sometimes stops suddenly. For a minute or two, they stand still as statues, with their ears fanned out. Then, just as suddenly, they change direction and march away. How do two or three groups of elephants manage to arrive at a waterhole at the same time? They run from different directions and greet each other as old friends. How does a male elephant traveling alone find a female for a mate? If we found that elephants sent infrasonic messages, that would answer a lot of our questions.

Dr. Payne and her team went back to the zoo with recording equipment that could pick up the sounds we can't hear. When the tapes were played back at higher speed, the sounds were clear. There's a spot on an elephant's forehead that trembles when the animal makes the deep rumbling or purring sounds that we hear. But whenever the taping equipment registered the low-level "silent" sounds, the elephant's forehead also fluttered. Dr. Payne knew she was right. The elephant's secret language wasn't secret anymore. Like fin whales, elephants communicated with infrasound.

MESSAGES BY THE MILE

Concept Connections

Linking the Selection

Think about the following questions, and then record your responses in the Response Journal section of your Writer's Notebook.

- How is communication among fin whales similar to the way elephants communicate?
- How did Dr. Payne realize that elephants might communicate with infrasonic sound?

Exploring Concept Vocabulary

The concept word for this lesson is ***meaningful.*** If you don't know what this word means, look it up in a dictionary. Answer these questions.

- What are some examples of noises that are not ***meaningful*** communication?
- What makes scientists think that humpback whale songs are ***meaningful?***

In the Vocabulary section of your Writer's Notebook, write a sentence that includes the word ***meaningful*** as well as one of the selection vocabulary words.

Expanding the Concept

Compare whale songs with the songs you like to listen to. What "messages" are communicated in the different types of songs? Try to use the word ***meaningful*** in your discussion. Add new ideas about communication to the Concept/Question Board.

Meet the Author

Margery Facklam says she loves to be a writer because she is never bored. There are always new ideas to develop or research for her to do. Her interest in science began as a child. Growing up, Mrs. Facklam spent every Saturday at the Buffalo Museum of Science. When she was in high school, she worked in the reptile house at the Buffalo Zoo. Later, Mrs. Facklam became a high school science teacher.

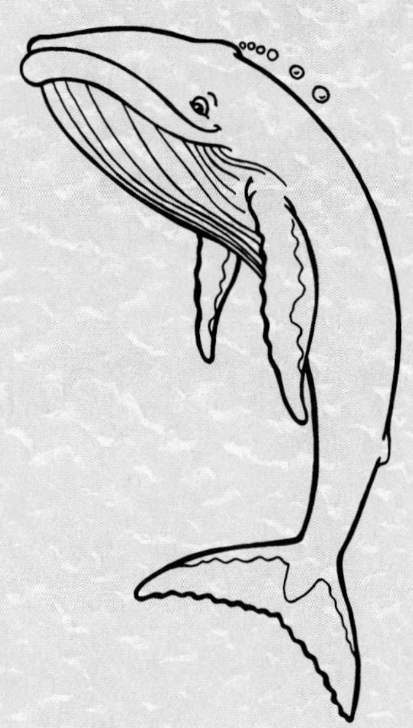

Focus Questions Why do poems communicate emotions so well?
Do animals have their own forms of poetry?

Whalesong

by Judith Nicholls

I am
ocean voyager,
sky-leaper,
maker of waves;
I harm no man.

I know
only the slow tune
of turning tide,
the heave and sigh
of full seas meeting land
at dusk and dawn,
the sad whale song.
I harm no man.

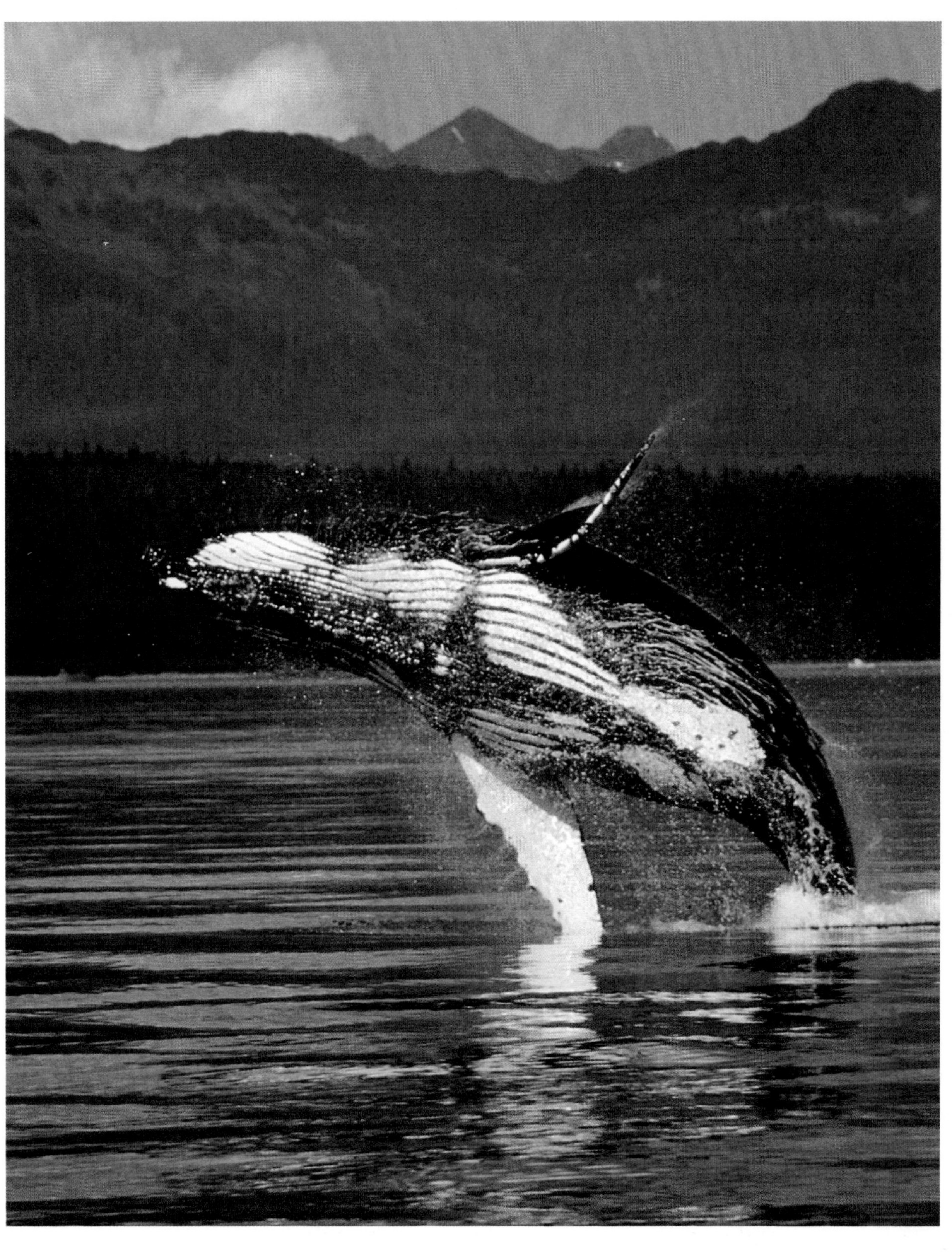

Focus Questions How can we find out if what we see on TV is true? Could mass communications (TV, radio) exist without commercials?

"We'll Be Right Back after These Messages"

by Shelagh Wallace
illustrated by Tony Caldwell

You're watching your favorite show, it's just getting to a really good part and then . . . a commercial. What do you do? Go to the kitchen? Press the mute button? Watch the commercial?

If you're an average TV viewer, you'll find yourself in this situation many, many times—during a year, you see (or perhaps choose not to see) at least 20,000 commercials. Commercials pay for most of the programs you watch: networks charge advertisers to air the advertisers' ads, then use the money they receive to cover the costs of producing the shows. But TV advertising isn't limited to just commercials. There are other kinds of ads on TV as well.

Sometimes you watch an ad on TV without even knowing that's what it is. A well-known soft drink prominently displayed during a prime-time TV show, a Saturday morning cartoon with popular characters that are also toys you can buy, "infomercials," and even music videos are, in fact, advertisements. They're all intended to persuade you to buy something, whether it's a can of cola, an action toy, an amazing new mop, or a compact disc.

How effective are these kinds of ads at convincing you to buy their products? When an American music video channel started showing videos in 1981, music sales boomed. Record companies found that actually being able to see bands perform their songs made people more likely to buy the group's records and concert tickets. The constantly changing camera shots, unusual camera angles and, of course, memorable music are exactly the same things advertisers use in "regular" commercials to get your attention and make sure you remember their ad.

Advertisers use other techniques, as well, to get your attention and hold it for the entire length of a commercial. Here are just some of those techniques:

- Repeating the ad over and over again. Studies show that, if you have a choice, many people are more likely to buy an advertised brand instead of an unadvertised brand, even an unadvertised brand that's cheaper. One reason you're familiar with the advertised brand name is that you've heard the ad for it over and over again.
- Using camera effects and special effects. Close-ups can make products look larger than they are. Computer-generated special effects can make toys appear to do something, such as move by themselves, that they won't actually do when you get them home.

- Emphasizing "premiums," the toys or prizes that come with certain products. The "special gift inside" may be the only reason you buy the cereal.
- Showing or saying words such as "free," "new," "amazing," and "improved" to get everyone's attention. (Did someone say "free"?)
- Hiring famous people to tell you to buy a certain product. Advertisers conduct surveys to find out which celebrities you trust and like the most, then use those people to promote their products.

There are limits, however, to the extent advertisers can use these techniques to convince you to buy their products. Your government—the Canadian Radio-Television and Telecommunications Commission (CRTC) in Canada and the Federal Communications Commission (FCC) in the U.S.—has hundreds of rules to guarantee that the television industry serves you and the "public interest." As a Canadian or American citizen, you literally own the airwaves that the TV networks use for broadcasting. The networks are allowed to "borrow" the airwaves provided that what they broadcast meets the needs of the public.

The networks, governments, and advertisers agree that children are a special part of the TV audience. Kids under five years of age don't understand that commercials are there to sell them something. (To them, ads are just shorter programs.) And it isn't until kids are about eight years of age that they understand that commercials aren't always literally true. Because of this, the advertising industries in both Canada and the U.S. must obey special rules that restrict what can be advertised to kids under twelve and how it can be advertised to them.

According to the rules, advertisers can't take advantage of you by having a baseball player tell you how great a particular brand of bat is, for example. He can endorse a sports drink, but not a bat or a baseball. What's the difference? Bats and baseballs are too closely identified with what the player does for a living. Seeing him advertise either a bat or a baseball could leave you with the impression that you'll play like him if you buy one, too. Computer-generated effects in commercials are okay, as long as there's at least one part of the ad that shows the product as it actually is. If a toy plane can't fly on its own, the ad has to show someone's hand holding the plane.

"We'll Be Right Back after These Messages"

Concept Connections

Linking the Selection

Think about the following questions, and then record your responses in the Response Journal section of your Writer's Notebook.

- Why do advertisers repeat their messages again and again?
- How can television viewers see an advertisement without even knowing it?

Exploring Concept Vocabulary

The concept word for this lesson is ***mass media.*** If you don't know what this word means, look it up in a dictionary. Answer these questions.

- Why is advertising important to the ***mass media?***
- What evidence does the selection offer that advertising in the ***mass media*** works?

In the Vocabulary section of your Writer's Notebook, write a sentence that includes the word ***mass media*** as well as one of the selection vocabulary words.

Expanding the Concept

Discuss the advantages and disadvantages for society of the ***mass media*** as a means of communication.

Add new ideas about communication to the Concept/Question Board.

Meet the Author

Shelagh Wallace was born and raised in Burlington, Ontario. After working for several years in book publishing, Ms. Wallace began writing books herself. She credits her grandfather with encouraging her to write. *"Everyone in my family [is a great reader], but it was my grandfather who wrote stories and encouraged all his grandchildren to write stories as well."* When asked to give advice to aspiring writers, Ms. Wallace replies, *"Read. Read a lot. Read a wide variety of books by many different authors."*

Meet the Illustrator

Tony Caldwell creates his wonderful art from Breckinridge, Colorado, where he is a ski instructor, mountain biker, and rider of horses. A graduate of Maryland Institute College of Art in Baltimore, Tony enjoys assignments which are festive and challenging in color or black and white.

Focus Questions How did the printing press change the way people communicate? How would your life be different if there were no books?

Breaking into Print

Before and After the Invention of the Printing Press

Stephen Krensky

illustrated by Bonnie Christensen

In a long room with seven tables and seven windows, a French monk sat hunched over a parchment page. He dipped a goose quill in some ink and began to write. The quill made a scratching sound, like a cat clawing at a closed door.

The monk worked six hours almost every day for many months. He hoped to finish before the first snow fell.

The monk was making a book.

The monastery was a small part of a great empire, an empire with far more soldiers than books. Its emperor, Charlemagne, both read and spoke Latin, but he could write little more than his name.

His scribes, however, created a new script that made writing easier to understand.

Parchment was made from a specially prepared animal skin, usually from sheep or goats. The best parchment, called vellum, was made from calfskin. Monks worked only in natural light. The risk of fire from candles posed too great a danger to their precious manuscripts.

Under Charlemagne's rule (800–814 A.D.) Latin was firmly established as the language of the court and education. Charlemagne's scribes also pioneered leaving spaces between words and starting phrases with capital letters.

In the Middle Ages, people believed in superstitions and magic to explain things such as thunderstorms and diseases. Rome had a population of about 500,000 in 300 A.D. After the fall of its empire, no European city had more than 20,000 people for hundreds of years.

Across the countryside, reading and writing counted for little. Few roads were free of robbers or wolves. In the villages, warring peasants lived and died without ever seeing a book.

In time, the villages knew longer periods of peace. The peasants began to eat better and made goods to trade on market day. Successful merchants learned to read and write so that they could keep records of their business. Sometimes their children were taught as well.

More books were now needed, more than the monks could manage alone. In the new book-making guilds, many hands worked together.

Many such books were made with a new material called paper. It was much cheaper than parchment and especially useful for wood or metal block printing.

Block printing was first developed in Asia in the eighth century. No press was used for the printing process. After the blocks were etched and inked, paper was rubbed on them to make a print.

In faraway China, printers had been using paper for centuries. And around 1050, the Chinese printer Pi Sheng had invented movable type using baked clay tablets. Yet few Chinese printers were excited about the invention. Their alphabet has thousands of characters. Only in a dream could printers create so much type. And even if they managed this feat, organizing the type would turn the dream into a nightmare.

The Koreans made further progress. They were actually printing books with movable type around 1400. But their written language is as complicated as Chinese, which discouraged them from making too much of the process.

In the German town of Mainz, one young man knew nothing of Chinese or Korean printing methods. But he was interested in the idea and process of printing. His name was Johannes Gensfleisch, but he followed the old custom of taking his mother's name: Gutenberg.

As a young goldsmith and gem cutter, Gutenberg had learned how to cut steel punches and cast metal in molds. He knew which metals were hard and which were soft, which melted easily and which could take great heat without melting. Over the next few years, Gutenberg tinkered with the printing process.

Gutenberg cast 290 different letters, numbers, punctuation marks, and other symbols in preparation to printing his first book.

Although he had a simpler alphabet than the Chinese or Koreans, he still faced many obstacles. There was no room for sloppy or careless design. Printed letters had to fit as closely together as handwritten ones. Printed words had to fall in a straight line. Printed lines had to leave even spaces above and below.

Gutenberg also had to find the proper metal to cast letters and the right ink to use. If the metal was too hard, it would break too easily. If the metal was too soft, it would lose its shape too quickly. As for the ink, it could not be too thick or too thin or likely to fade over time.

Gutenberg was very practical. He did not believe in reinventing things that already worked fine. So he adapted a winepress for printing. He made it taller, so that the work could be done at waist height, and he created a rolling tray for sliding the paper in and out.

Gutenberg spent almost twenty years building and tinkering. He invented adjustable molds to make letters in different widths. He found the right alloy for casting his letters. He built the upper and lower type cases for storing capital and small letters. He even created the long, grooved composing stick for quickly assembling lines of print.

Gutenberg's great project was a two-column Bible.

It reflected everything he knew of the art of printing.

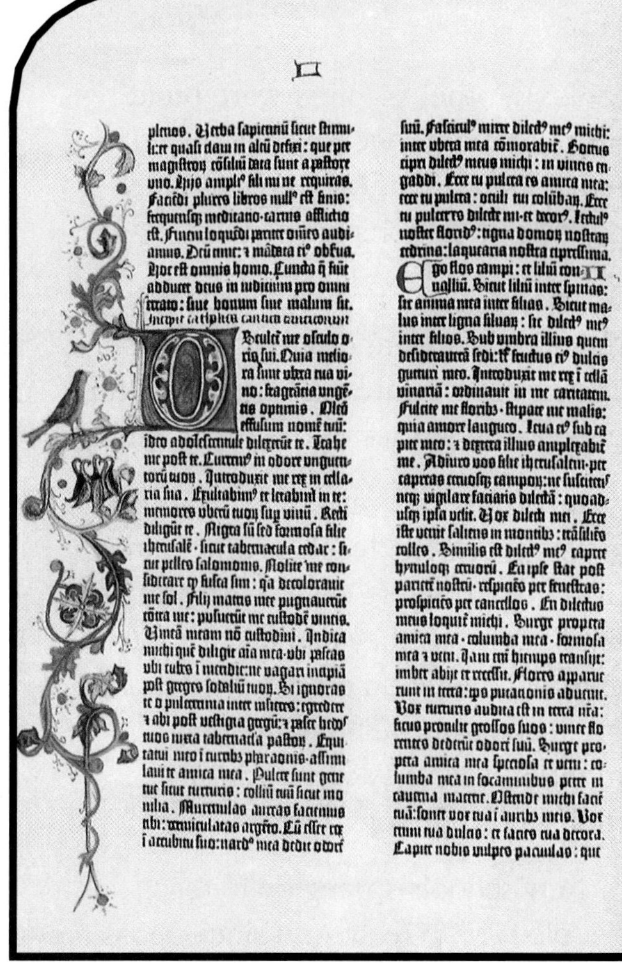

Gutenberg began working on the Bible project in 1452. It took more than three years to complete. The Gutenberg Bible, published in 1456, was printed in a run of 200 copies. Though it was started with two presses, six presses were eventually used together. As many as 50 copies were printed on vellum, requiring up to 5,000 animal skins.

Soon, other printers were building on Gutenberg's work. They added more than one ink to a page. They added illustrations to the text.

They began printing more than religious works and public notices. They began printing philosophy and poetry and stories of the imagination.

In almost no time at all, printing grew beyond the reach of one man or firm. New printers were setting up shop as fast as they could learn the craft. A generation earlier, printers had produced a single book in a few months. Now they were printing thousands of books a year.

New schools sprang up to teach people how to read. And since books were no longer rare or costly, students as well as teachers could own them.

Lower costs played a great part in the success of printing. By 1463, ten printed Bibles sold for the price of one manuscript copy. By the year 1500, there were more than 1,000 printers in Europe, and they had printed millions of books.

Despite the success of printed books, some wealthy people looked down on them as plain and coarse. Although many schools were for rich students, some poor students were educated for free.

This freed the students from memorizing so much and gave them more time to think.

There were geography books for Christopher Columbus and science books for Nicolaus Copernicus. And there were art and science and engineering and many other books for Leonardo da Vinci, who studied almost everything.

Reading and writing were no longer just for studious monks or highborn lords and ladies. Books were no longer chained up in private libraries or boldly sold for a king's ransom.

The printing press took learning and knowledge from just a privileged few and shared them with everyone else. And that change, more than any other act, set the stage for the modern world to come.

Breaking into Print

Before and After the Invention of the Printing Press

Concept Connections

Linking the Selection

Think about the following questions, and then record your responses in the Response Journal section of your Writer's Notebook.

- Why wasn't the early printing press more successful in China and Korea?
- How did the printing press change the way people gained information?

Exploring Concept Vocabulary

The concept word for this lesson is ***literacy.*** If you don't know what this word means, look it up in a dictionary. Answer these questions.

- What effect did the printing press have on ***literacy*** rates?
- Why is ***literacy*** important to society?

In the Vocabulary section of your Writer's Notebook, write a sentence that includes the word ***literacy*** as well as one of the selection vocabulary words.

Expanding the Concept

Compare books and television as methods of communication. Consider the availability and audience of each. Try to use the word ***literacy*** in your discussion. Add new ideas about communication to the Concept/Question Board.

Meet the Author

Stephen Krensky was always interested in fiction and illustrating, but he never thought of becoming a writer. He didn't write down his stories. He made them up in his head at night, using characters from stories he had read.

In college, Mr. Krensky became interested in writing and illustrating stories for children. Since then he has written over 60 books on subjects including dinosaurs, soccer, George Washington, Paul Revere, Native American children, and teachers.

"People often ask me how I can write something that twelve-year-olds or nine-year-olds or six-year-olds will want to read. I'm not sure, but I do know that the part of me that was once twelve and nine and six is not neatly boxed and tucked away in some dusty corner of my mind."

Meet the Illustrator

Bonnie Christensen studied at the Center for Book Arts and Parsons School of Design.

Her first book was an alphabet book she was going to print by hand on a press more than 170 years old. But an editor saw samples of her work and bought the book for her publishing company to print.

"I love books," Ms. Christensen says, *"both for children and adults, antique and new, short and long, with or without illustrations, and so I've come to love the book arts, which include printing, papermaking, book-binding and wood engraving."*

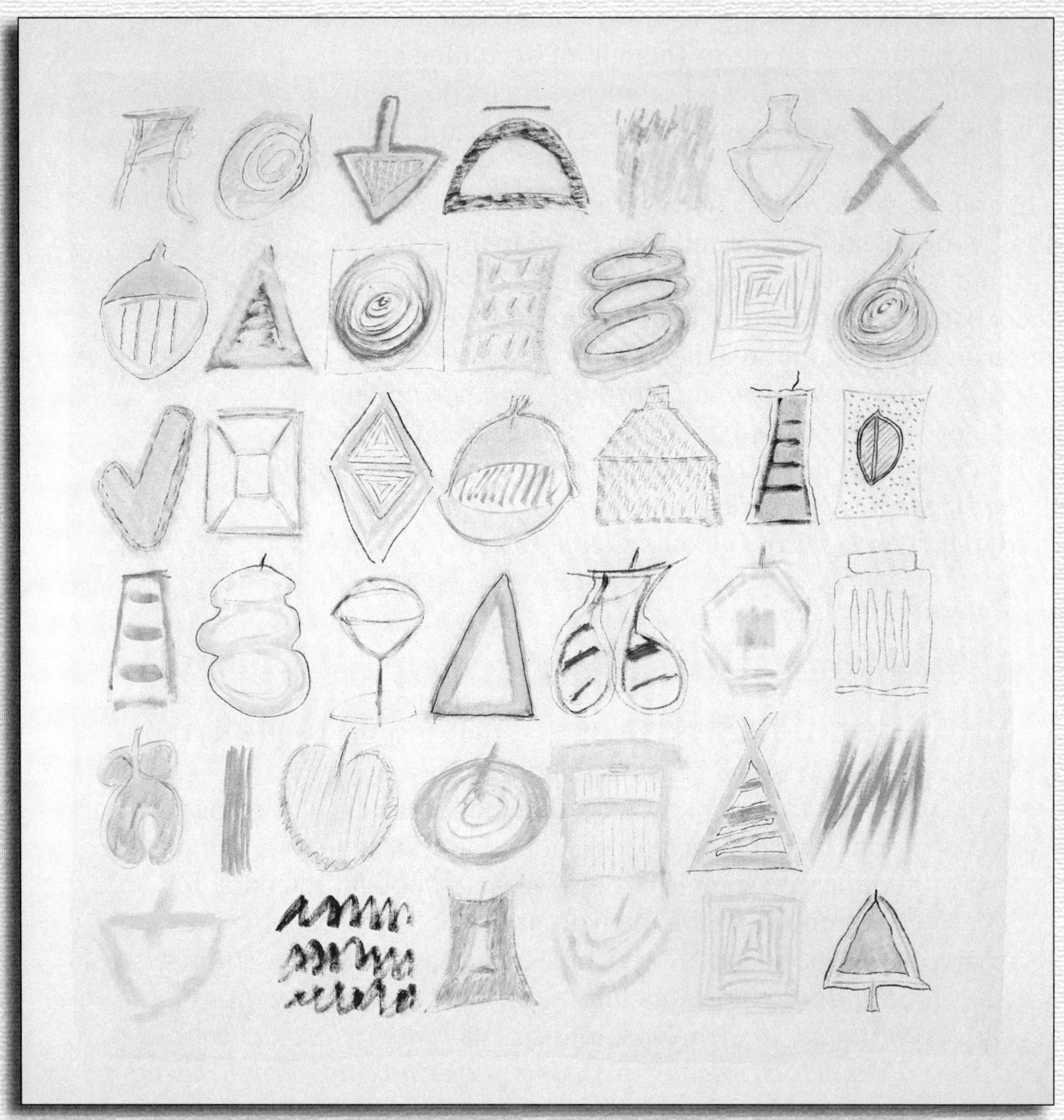

Symbols. 1984. **Ida Kohlmeyer.** Oil, graphite, and pastel on canvas. $69\frac{1}{2} \times 69$ in. The National Museum of Women in the Arts, Washington, D.C., gift of Wallace and Wilhelmina Holladay.

Young Girl Writing a Love Letter. **Johan G. Meyer Von Bremen.** Josef Mensing Gallery, Hamm-Rhynern, Germany. Photo: SuperStock.

The News Room. **Jane Wooster Scott.** Collection of Vernon Scott IV. Photo: SuperStock.

Focus Questions Could all animals learn to communicate with people? What would you ask Koko if you had the chance to communicate with her?

Koko's Kitten

from ***Koko's Kitten***
by Dr. Francine Patterson
photographs by Ronald H. Cohn

Koko's full name is Hanabi-Ko, which is Japanese for Fireworks Child. She was born on the Fourth of July. Every year, I have a party for Koko with cake, sparkling apple cider, and lots of presents.

Koko knows what birthdays are. When asked what she does on her birthday, Koko answered, "Eat, drink, (get) old."

Three days before Koko's party, I said, "I'm going shopping today. What do you want for your birthday?"

"Cereal there. Good there drink," Koko signed.

"But what presents do you want?" I asked.

"Cat," answered Koko.

Later, she repeated, "Cat, cat, cat."

I wasn't surprised that Koko asked for a cat. I have been reading to Koko for many years and two of her favorite stories have been "Puss in Boots" and "The Three Little Kittens."

Koko gets very involved in the stories I read her. When reading the story of the three little kittens who lose their mittens, Koko sees that their mother is angry and that the kittens are crying.

"Mad," Koko signs.

Koko loves picture books. Gorilla books are her favorites. Cat books are next. She likes to go off on her own with a book to study the pictures and sign to herself.

On her birthday, I gave Koko the usual assortment of presents—apple juice, some special fruits and nuts, and a baby doll. I didn't want to give Koko a stuffed toy because I knew she'd eventually destroy it.

The only durable toy cat I could find was in a mail order catalogue and I ordered it right away. It was made of cement and covered with vinyl and black velvet. I chose it because it looked real and it was sturdy—gorilla-proof. The toy cat didn't arrive in time for Koko's birthday, so I decided to save it for Christmas.

In December, I made a list for Koko. I drew about twenty pictures—fruits, vegetables, nuts, dolls, combs, and blankets. Every year, Koko gets a stocking and lots of presents. She loves Christmas.

"What do you want for Christmas?" I asked as I showed Koko the pictures.

Koko carefully studied the booklet. Then she pointed to a doll, nuts—and a cat.

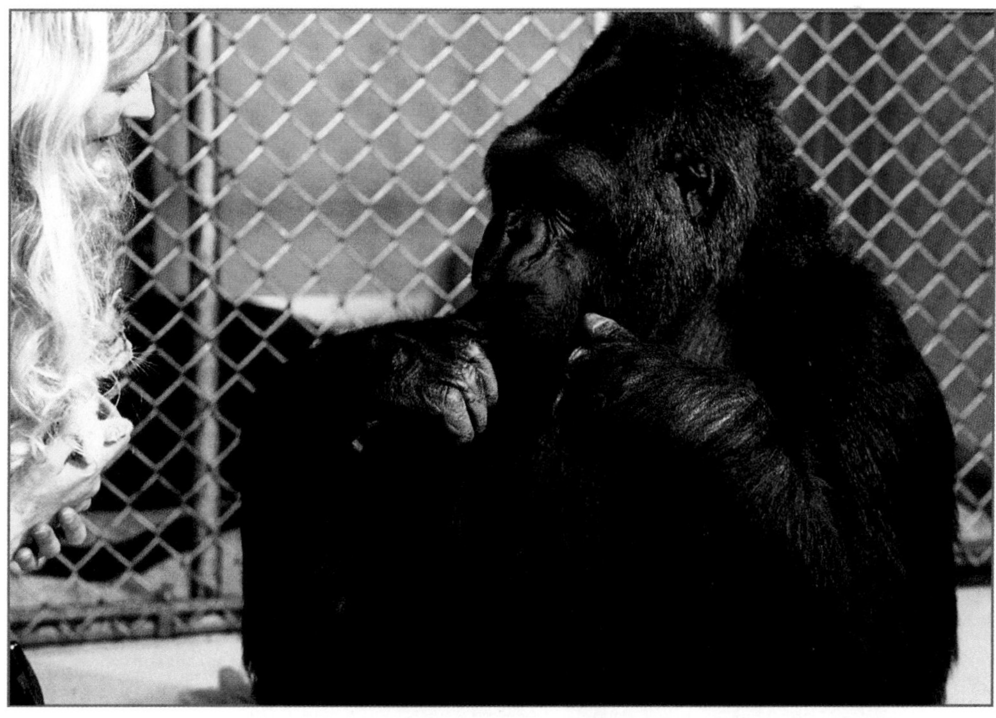

Koko signs "cat"

I bought Koko some nuts and a new doll. I wrapped the toy cat and put it with the rest of her presents.

On Christmas morning, Koko ate her cereal and opened her stocking. It was filled with nuts. Koko threw the nuts aside and went to her next present.

Koko unwrapped a doll.

"That stink," Koko signed.

Then came the velvet cat.

"That red," she signed.

Koko often uses the word red to express anger. Koko was very upset. She started running back and forth, banging on her walls. She was doing display charges past me. They were angry, angry charges.

It is natural for gorillas to display when frightened or in great danger. They run sideways, pound their chests, then go down on all fours, and run back and forth.

But this was Christmas, usually a happy day for Koko, and she was with people she loved.

Later in the day, Barbara, a friend who had known Koko since she was a baby gorilla, arrived.

"That looks like a black cat," Barbara said to Koko. "Would you show it to me?"

Koko signs "mad"

Koko did not answer. She pulled a blanket over her head.

"Could I see it?" Barbara asked.

Koko pulled a rag over the toy cat, then tossed it in the air. "Cat that," Koko signed.

"Please let me see it," said Barbara.

Koko gave her a toy dinosaur instead.

I finally understood Koko's strange behavior. She was unhappy with her Christmas present. I had made a mistake. Koko did not want a cement and velvet toy cat. Koko wanted a real cat. Koko wanted a pet.

Things don't always happen quickly where we live. Every day is full of its own activities. So it was almost six months later when Karen, one of my assistants, arrived with three kittens. The kittens had been abandoned by their mother and raised by a dog, a Cairn terrier.

Karen showed the kittens to Koko.

"Love that," Koko signed.

As we showed Koko the kittens, she gave each one her blow test. When Koko meets a new animal or person, she blows in their face. I think she is trying to get a better scent. When she blows at a person, she expects them to blow back. Maybe she expected the kittens to blow back, too.

The first kitten was smoky gray and white. Koko's blow test took him by surprise. The second kitten was a tailless gray tabby. He was also startled by the blow test. The third kitten, a brown tabby, did not react at all.

After the blow test, Koko seemed to have made some judgments about the kittens.

"Which one do you want?" we asked.

"That," signed Koko, pointing to the tailless tabby.

Koko chooses the tabby

I am not sure why Koko picked the gray tabby as her favorite. I never asked her. Perhaps it was because he didn't have a tail—a gorilla has no tail.

That night, all three kittens went home with Karen. Two days later, the kittens came back for another visit. Koko was happy to see them.

"Visit love tiger cat," Koko signed.

First she picked up the smoky gray and white one. Then Koko took the tailless tabby and carried him on her thigh. After a while, she pushed him up onto the back of her neck.

"Baby," Koko signed.

She cradled the tabby in her legs and examined its paws. Koko squeezed, and the tabby's claws came out.

"Cat do scratch," Koko signed. "Koko love."

"What will you name the kitty?" I asked.

"All Ball," Koko signed.

"Yes," I said. "Like a ball, he has no tail."

Ball stayed overnight as a visiting kitten. By the end of the week, Ball was a permanent member of our household.

Koko had her kitten at last.

For the first few weeks, Ball lived in my house. Every evening at six o'clock, I would take Ball to Koko's trailer for an evening visit. I carried the kitten in my pocket as I prepared Koko for bed. Koko soon grew accustomed to this routine.

"What happens at night?" I asked.

"All Ball," signed Koko.

"Right," I said. "Ball visits you at night."

When he was older, Ball snuck into Koko's trailer by himself. It worried me in the beginning. I did not know how Koko would treat the kitten unsupervised. As it turned out, Koko was always gentle. Ball was never afraid of her.

Kittens should not be separated from their mothers until they are at least six weeks old. Poor Ball was abandoned by his mother at birth, which might have accounted for some of his faults.

Ball was an unusual cat. He was very aggressive. He would go up to people and bite them for no reason. He would bite Koko, too.

"Cat bite. Obnoxious," Koko signed, but she never struck back.

Koko did not like to be scratched or bitten, but she loved Ball in spite of his naughty behavior.

"Tell me a story about Ball," I said.

"Koko love Ball," she signed.

Koko treated Ball as if he were her baby.

The very first time she picked him up, she tried to tuck him in her thigh. That's where mother gorillas put their infants. Older babies are carried on their mothers' backs. Koko tried this with Ball, too.

Koko was a good gorilla mother. She combed and petted Ball to keep him clean. She also examined his eyes, ears, and mouth to make sure he was healthy. It was Koko who discovered Ball's ear mites.

Ball was often a topic of conversation during Koko's lessons.

"Love visit," Koko signed when Ball and I arrived for a morning lesson.

"Ball," I said.

"Trouble," signed Koko. "Love."

Koko seemed to enjoy conversations about her kitten. This dialogue took place between Koko and a research assistant named Janet.

Koko signs "love"

"I'll give you some grapes if you tell me about Ball, the cat," Janet said.

"Soft," Koko signed.

"What kind of animal is he?" Janet asked.

"Cat, cat, cat," Koko answered.

"Do you love Ball?"

"Soft, good cat cat," Koko signed.

In addition to sign language, art is another way I test Koko's perceptions. Ball lay with a green toy on an orange towel. I gave Koko a canvas and some paints and asked her to draw Ball. Koko had ten colors to choose from. First she picked black for Ball's body. Next she picked orange for the towel and green for the toy.

"What about Ball's eyes?" I asked.

Koko picked tan.

Koko loves to play games. Her favorites are "chase," "blow-it," and "tickle."

Koko likes to be tickled, and she thinks that others will like it, too.

"Tickle," Koko signed to Ball when they were lying on the floor together.

Ball was not a good tickler, nor did he like to be tickled. So Koko and I pretended. I tickled Koko while carrying the kitten in my hand. Koko thought this was very funny.

"Chase, blow-it. Enjoy," Koko signed to Ball.

In blow-it, Koko blows as hard as she can into the face of her playmate. It's not hard to understand why this game was not one of Ball's favorites.

Chase is similar to tag. Players run back and forth and chase each other. This is a popular game among gorillas in the wild. But Ball never quite caught on to chase.

"Ball" sitting on Koko's back

Koko did not realize that kittens don't necessarily enjoy gorilla games. Koko did understand that kittens like warmth, affection, and attention. And Koko supplied plenty.

On a foggy December morning, one of the assistants told me that Ball had been hit by a car. He had died instantly.

I was shocked and unprepared. I didn't realize how attached I had grown to Ball, and I had no idea how the news would affect Koko. The kitten meant so much to her. He was Koko's baby.

I went to Koko at once. I told her that Ball had been hit by a car; she would not see him again.

Koko did not respond. I thought she didn't understand, so I left the trailer.

Ten minutes later, I heard Koko cry. It was her distress call—a loud, long series of high-pitched hoots.

I cried, too.

Three days later, Koko and I had a conversation about Ball.

"Do you want to talk about your kitty?" I asked.

"Cry," Koko signed.

"Can you tell me more about it?" I asked.

"Blind," she signed.

"We don't see him anymore, do we? What happened to your kitty?" I asked.

"Sleep cat," Koko signed.

A few weeks later, Koko saw a picture of a gray tabby who looked very much like Ball. She pointed to the picture and signed, "Cry, sad, frown."

It was an unhappy time.

News of All Ball's death traveled quickly. We received thousands of letters. People of all ages wrote to us and expressed their sympathy. Some sent cards, others sent photographs, and many children created pictures. They all had one message: that Koko should have a new kitten.

As we approached Christmas, I wanted to get Koko a new kitten. I had no idea how difficult that would turn out to be.

On December 20, Barbara asked Koko, "What would you like for Christmas?"

"Cat cat tiger cat," was Koko's reply.

We heard of a Manx who was soon expecting a litter. We waited weeks until we discovered that the cat was just getting fat. Christmas came and went.

In January I showed Koko a picture of three kittens. One had a long tail, one had a short tail, and one was tailless.

"When you get another kitty, what kind would you like?" I asked.

"That," Koko signed as she pointed to the tailless cat.

"We'll get you a kitty like that," I said. "Is that okay?"

"Good. Nice," Koko answered.

"How do you feel about kitties?" I asked.

"Cat gorilla have visit," she signed. "Koko love."

Koko was ready for a new kitten if only I could find one.

More time went by. I called the Humane Society. They had no kittens at all—let alone a rare, tailless Manx. I called many other places and was disappointed again and again. I was told that not many kittens were born during that time of year.

The worst part of this period was my feeling that I was letting Koko down. I'd watch as someone would ask Koko, "Where's your cat?" And she would look around almost as if she were doing a double take, as if she were looking for Ball.

Then our luck changed. We received a letter from a breeder of Manx cats who wanted to help. He didn't have any kittens then, but he called other Manx breeders nearby until he located a litter of Manx kittens in Southern California. They were just about ready to leave their mother.

We set the date for March 17. The day before, I told Koko she was getting a new kitty—a red kitty. Red is Koko's favorite color. She was very excited.

Then, another delay.

The breeder called. "I'm sorry," he said. "The kitten is not coming today."

Koko was upset. I was disappointed.

"Trouble," she signed.

"We are having trouble getting you a new kitty. We have been trying very hard," I explained.

Finally, on March 24, a red, tiger-striped Manx was brought to our home. Seeing the kitten, Koko purred with pleasure. It was a wonderful moment. She placed him on her chest and petted him.

"Let me hold the kitty," I said.

But Koko would not let go. She kissed and cradled her kitten.

"Baby," she signed.

Koko was happy. Her new kitten had come to stay.

"Lipstick" playing with Koko

Koko's Kitten

Concept Connections

Linking the Selection

Think about the following questions, and then record your responses in the Response Journal section of your Writer's Notebook.

- How does Koko communicate with Dr. Patterson?
- What kinds of things can Koko communicate to Dr. Patterson?

Exploring Concept Vocabulary

The concept word for this lesson is ***convey.*** If you don't know what this word means, look it up in a dictionary. Answer these questions.

- What means can Koko use to ***convey*** information to Dr. Patterson?
- How did Koko ***convey*** to Dr. Patterson her anger over receiving a toy cat, rather than the real cat she had hoped for?

In the Vocabulary section of your Writer's Notebook, write a sentence that includes the word ***convey*** as well as one of the selection vocabulary words.

Expanding the Concept

Compare Koko's communication skills with those of a young human child. Consider the ideas and emotions Koko expresses as well as her way of communicating them. Try to use the word ***convey*** in your discussion. Add new ideas about communication to the Concept/Question Board.

Meet the Author

Dr. Francine Patterson (known as Penny to her friends) has been teaching Koko since the gorilla was one year old. Since she taught Koko sign language, the gorilla easily communicates with humans.

Dr. Patterson has written articles for numerous periodicals including *National Geographic* and *Science.* She has also contributed to several books. She has written two children's books about Koko: *Koko's Kitten* and *Koko's Story.*

Meet the Photographer

Ronald H. Cohn grew up in Chicago, Illinois, within walking distance of the Museum of Science and Industry. He spent all his weekends there. *"That really did it for me,"* he says. *"I had some curiosities, and they were satisfied there. My visits there gave me a very broad interest in all kinds of science."*

Mr. Cohn has been working with Dr. Patterson and Koko from the beginning of the project. *"Koko is like my daughter,"* he says. *"I see her every day."*

Mr. Cohn has this advice for students: *"If you are interested in something, read about it. Try to fulfill your curiosities and find a way to do what you want to do."*

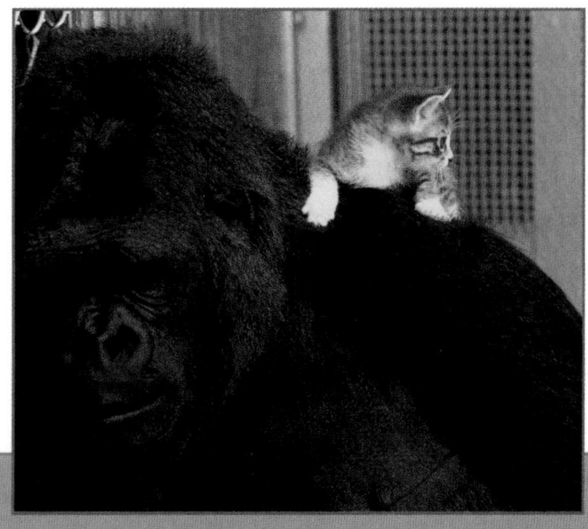

Focus Questions Why is written communication so important to society? Have you ever tried to learn a new form of communication?

Louis Braille

The Boy Who Invented Books for the Blind

from ***Louis Braille: The Boy Who Invented Books for the Blind***
by Margaret Davidson
illustrated by Bob Dorsey

It's Just a Show-off Trick!

So the busy months passed. And Louis grew happier and happier with his life at school. Only one thing was wrong—but it was the most important thing of all.

Louis was taking reading lessons. But it wasn't anything like what he had dreamed of for so long. In 1820 there was only one way for the blind to read. It was called *raised-print.* Each letter of the alphabet was raised from the page. It stood up from the paper background so it could be felt with the fingers. This sounded easy. But it wasn't.

Some of the letters were simple to feel. But others were almost impossible to tell apart. The *Q*'s felt like *O*'s. The *O*'s felt like *C*'s. The *I*'s turned out to be *T*'s and the *R*'s were really *B*'s.

But Louis was determined. Again and again his fingers traced the raised letters until he could tell them apart—most of the time. Then letter by letter he began to feel out words.

But it was so slow! Louis was one of the brightest boys in the school. But often even he forgot the beginning of a sentence before he got to the end of it. Then he had to go back the whole way and start over again.

It would take months to read a single book this way! "This isn't really reading," Louis cried one day. "It's just a show-off trick!"

"It's the best we can do," a teacher answered. "People have tried to find a better way for years."

Louis knew this was true. He knew that people had tried so many things—raised letters, lowered letters, letters of stone and letters of string, letters of wax and letters of wood. One man had even made an alphabet of pins. Louis tried to imagine how it would feel to read a page of pins. Ouch!

Besides, Louis soon learned that in the entire school library there were just fourteen books. Just fourteen! And there were good reasons for this. The raised-print books were very expensive to make. Each one had to be made by hand. They were also big and hard to store. Each letter had to be at least three inches from top to bottom—or blind fingers could not feel it. So only a few words could fit on a page.

No. Louis knew now that there would never be many books for the blind. Not the raised-print way. Then there must be another, better way! There just had to be! Soon that was all Louis could think—or talk—about. And his friends got good and tired of it.

"Do shut up, Louis," they begged.

"But it's so important!" Louis tried to explain. "Don't you see? Without books we can never really learn! But just think what we could grow up to be if only we could read. Doctors or lawyers or scientists. Or writers even! *Anything* almost."

"All right," one of the boys snapped. "We want to read too. Find us a way, if you're so smart."

"I can't," Louis cried. "I'm blind!"

Then one day in the spring of 1821 Captain Charles Barbier came to the Institute. Captain Barbier had worked out a way for his soldiers to send messages to each other in the dark. He called it nightwriting. The Captain thought it might work for the blind too.

Nightwriting used raised dots. A word was broken down into sounds. Each sound was given a different pattern of raised dots. The dots were pushed—or punched—into heavy sheets of paper with a long pointed tool called a *stylus*. When the paper was turned over, raised dots could be felt on the other side.

Dots! At first the blind boys were very excited. There were so many things right about dots! They were so small—just feel how many fit under a single fingertip. And they were so easy to feel!

But before long the boys knew that many things were wrong with Captain Barbier's nightwriting, too. There were so many things it would not do. There was no way to make capital letters or write numbers. There was no way to make periods or commas or exclamation points. It took up far too much room. But most of all it was so hard to learn and hard to feel.

Nightwriting might work well enough for soldiers to send simple notes like "advance" or "enemy is behind you." But it was no way to read or write many words. It was no way to make many books for the blind.

So nightwriting was a failure. Did that mean dots were a failure too? Louis didn't think so. As the days passed it was all he could think of. He even dreamed of dots at night.

And before long Louis made up his mind. He was going to do it himself. He was going to work out a way for the blind to *really* read and write with dots! Quickly and easily. At least he was going to try with all his heart and mind.

Louis set right to work. He was almost never without his tools now. Wherever he went he took heavy sheets of paper, a board to rest them on, and his stylus—the long, thin tool for punching dots. (The stylus was shaped almost exactly like an *awl*—the tool that had made Louis blind.)

Captain Barbier soon heard that someone was trying to make his nightwriting better. He hurried to the Institute to see who it was.

Louis was excited when he learned he was going to meet Captain Barbier, the man who had invented nightwriting. It was Captain Barbier who had worked with dots in the first place! Would the Captain like his ideas? Louis hoped so!

But things went wrong from the start. Captain Barbier's eyebrows rose with surprise as Louis tapped into the room. He had been expecting a man. Not a twelve-year-old boy! Louis couldn't see the look on Captain Barbier's face. But he could hear the chill in his voice.

"I hear you think you have worked out some improvements on my system," the Captain said.

"Yes . . . yes, sir," Louis answered.

"Well?"

"Sir . . . ?" said Louis, confused.

"Explain, explain!"

Louis tried. But the more he talked, the more he could tell that Captain Barbier wasn't really listening.

But Louis kept trying. "S . . . sir. One thing that must be worked out. We must find a way for words to . . . to be spelled the same way again and again."

"Why?" said the Captain. His voice was cold as ice.

"So . . . so we can have books—many books."

"Why?" the Captain asked again. Captain Barbier was like many other people in Louis's day. He felt sorry for blind people. He would never be cruel to them. But he did not think they were as smart as other people—people who could see. He thought blind people should be satisfied with simple things—like being able to read short notes and signs and directions. He certainly didn't think they needed many books!

"Is that all?" said the Captain.

"Yes . . ." Louis was almost whispering now.

"Very interesting," Captain Barbier snapped. "I will think about it." But Louis knew he would not. Captain Barbier was a proud man—too proud. He was used to giving orders and having them obeyed. He might have been able to accept these ideas from another man. But from a boy? A half-grown child? No, he didn't like it. He didn't like it at all!

Captain Barbier said a few more stiff words. Then with a bang of the door he was gone.

Louis sighed. He knew he would get no help from the Captain. He would have to work alone.

The Alphabet of Dots

Louis tried not to waste a single minute. Even when he was home on vacation, he worked on his dots. Often his mother would pack him a lunch of bread and cheese and fruit, and he would wander out to sit on some sunny hillside. Other times he sat by the side of the road, bent over his paper and board. "There is Louis, making his pinpricks," the neighbors said with a smile as they passed. What was he doing? Was it some kind of a game the blind boy was playing to keep himself busy? Louis didn't try to explain. He just went on punching patterns of dots.

At home in Coupvray Louis had plenty of free time to work on his experiments. At school it was not nearly so easy. There were so many other things to do. Louis had to go to class. He had to spend an hour or two in one of the workshops every day. He had to practice his music and do his homework. He had to eat meals with the rest of the boys—or someone would come looking for him.

But Louis still found time to work on his ideas. He worked in bits and pieces. He worked before breakfast. And between classes. He worked after dinner. And late at night.

That was the best time of all. The boys were all asleep, and everything was quiet. Hour after hour Louis bent over his board, experimenting with different patterns of dots.

Sometimes he got so tired he fell asleep sitting up. Sometimes he became so excited he forgot what time it was and worked until he heard the milk wagons rattling by under his window. Louis would raise his head with surprise then. For he knew it was early morning. He had worked the whole night through again! Then Louis would crawl into bed to nap for an hour or two—before he had to get up yawning for breakfast and his first class.

Louis's friends became more and more worried about him.

"You never sleep!"

"Half the time you forget to eat!"

"And for what?" a third boy snapped. "A wild goose chase! That's what!"

"Maybe you're right," Louis always answered them softly. And he kept on working.

Three years went by—three years of hard work and trying and not quite succeeding.

Sometimes Louis got so tired he could hardly lift his hand. And sometimes he became very, very discouraged.

Again and again Louis had simplified Captain Barbier's patterns of dots. But still they were not simple enough. No, reading with dots was still too hard.

Were the boys right? Was this a wild goose chase? Men had been working on this problem for hundreds of years—smart men, important men, older men. And one after another *they* had failed. Who did he think he was? What right did he have to think he could do better than they? "Sometimes I think I'll kill myself if I don't succeed," Louis said to Gabriel.

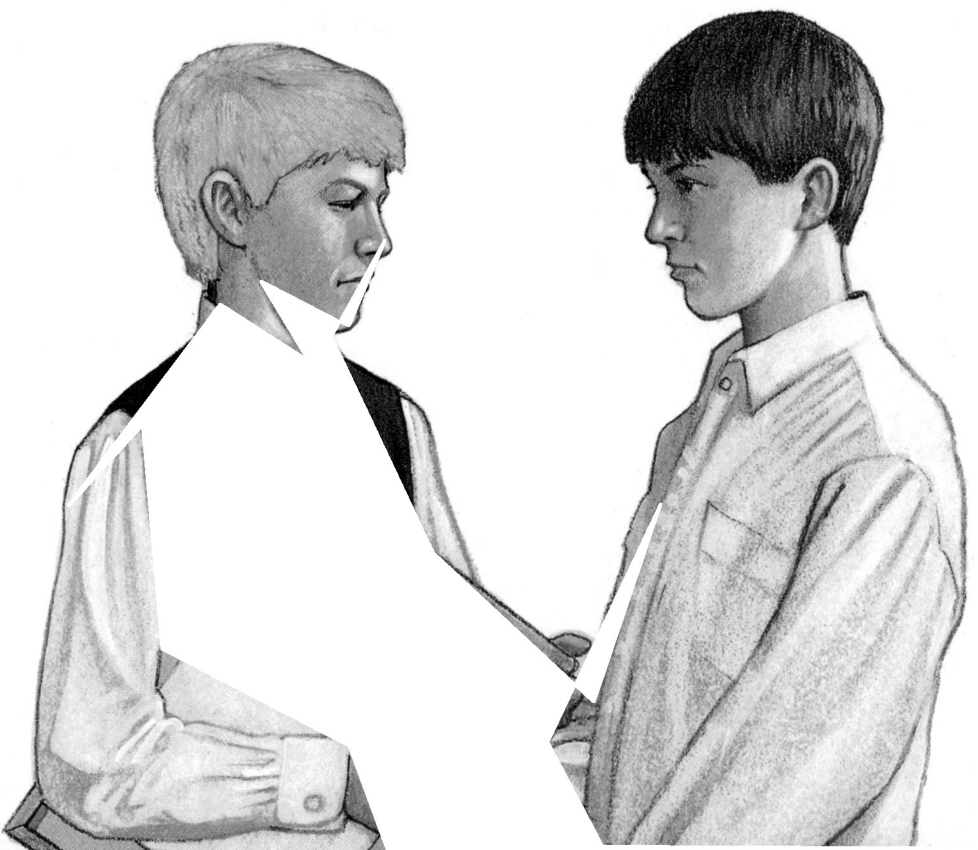

Then Louis had a new and very different idea. It seemed so simple—after he'd had it. Captain Barbier's nightwriting had been based on *sounds*. But there were so many sounds in the French language. Sometimes it took almost a hundred dots to write out a simple word. This was far, far too many to feel easily with the fingertips. But what if he used dots in a different way? What if the patterns of dots didn't stand for sounds at all? What if they stood for the letters of the alphabet instead? There were only twenty-six of them, after all!

Louis was filled with excitement. He was sure he was right! Now he worked even harder. And everything began to fall into place.

First Louis took a pencil and marked six dots on a heavy piece of paper. He called this six-dot pattern a *cell*. It looked like this:

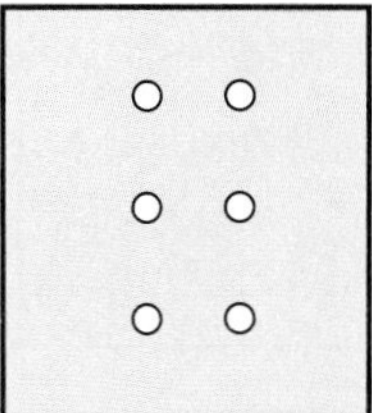

He numbered each dot in the cell:

1 ○ ○ 4
2 ○ ○ 5
3 ○ ○ 6

Then he took his stylus and raised dot number one—that would stand for *A*:

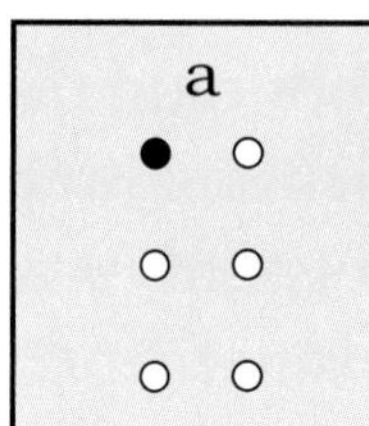

He raised dots number one and two—and that would stand for *B*:

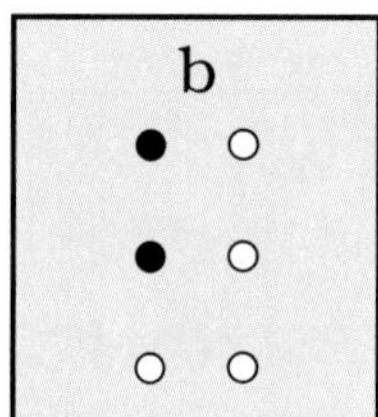

Raised dots number one and four would be *C*:

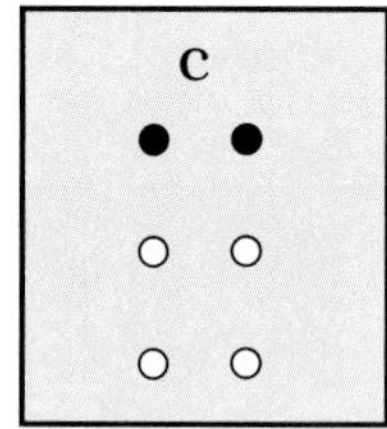

Louis made letter after letter. And when he was finished Louis Braille's alphabet of dots looked like this:

a	b	c	d	e	f	g
●○ ○○ ○○	●○ ●○ ○○	●● ○○ ○○	●● ○● ○○	●○ ○● ○○	●● ●○ ○○	●● ●● ○○
h	**i**	**j**	**k**	**l**	**m**	**n**
●○ ●● ○○	○● ●○ ○○	○● ●● ○○	●○ ○○ ●○	●○ ●○ ●○	●● ○○ ●○	●● ○● ●○
o	**p**	**q**	**r**	**s**	**t**	**u**
●○ ○● ●○	●● ●○ ●○	●● ●● ●○	●○ ●● ●○	○● ●○ ●○	○● ●● ●○	●○ ○○ ●●
v	**w**	**x**	**y**	**z**		
●○ ●○ ●●	○● ●● ○●	●● ○○ ●●	●● ○● ●●	●○ ○● ●●		

Louis ran his fingers over his alphabet. It was so simple! So simple! Fifteen-year-old Louis Braille felt like shouting or crying or laughing out loud. All the letters of the alphabet had been made out of the same six dots—used over and over again in different patterns! He knew it wouldn't look like much of anything to people who could see. But it wasn't supposed to! It was meant to be felt! Quickly. Easily. And it worked!

Louis Braille

The Boy Who Invented Books for the Blind

Concept Connections

Linking the Selection

Think about the following questions, and then record your responses in the Response Journal section of your Writer's Notebook.

- Why did Louis Braille think having books for the blind was so important?
- What did Louis like about Captain Barbier's nightwriting system?

Exploring Concept Vocabulary

The concept word for this lesson is ***decipher.*** If you don't know what this word means, look it up in a dictionary. Answer these questions.

- Why was it important to Louis Braille that his code be easy to ***decipher?***
- Why were books made with raised-print difficult to ***decipher?***

In the Vocabulary section of your Writer's Notebook, write a sentence that includes the word ***decipher*** as well as one of the selection vocabulary words.

Expanding the Concept

Compare Louis Braille's invention with that of Johannes Gutenberg from "Breaking into Print: Before and After the Invention of the Printing Press." How did each of these people advance human communication? Try to use the word ***decipher*** in your discussion. Add new ideas about communication to the Concept/Question Board.

Meet the Author

Margaret Davidson has written several biographies for children. Some of her books have been written under the names Mickie Compere and Mickie Davidson.

Ms. Davidson says about writing books, *"I've been asked [how I came to write books], and the only valid answer I've been able to scare up is that I loved to read when I was a child. It was a whole world to me."*

When she's not writing, Ms. Davidson enjoys art, reading, and visiting museums.

Meet the Illustrator

Bob Dorsey has been a professional illustrator for 17 years, working with a wide range of media and a variety of subjects. Some of his favorite projects include portraits, wildlife, children, and sports. Mr. Dorsey is well known for the many portraits that he has done for the National Baseball Hall of Fame in Cooperstown, New York. His paintings have been exhibited throughout the United States.

Focus Questions How would the world be different without telephones? Might the birds be thinking that we build phone lines just for their use?

Connections

Diane Siebert
illustrated by Aaron Meshon

Extending high above the ground,
They stretch forever, wrapped around
The voices sent to rendezvous
With other voices passing through.

And as they travel far away,
The wind-blown conversations sway
As rows and rows of resting birds
Perch happily on miles of words.

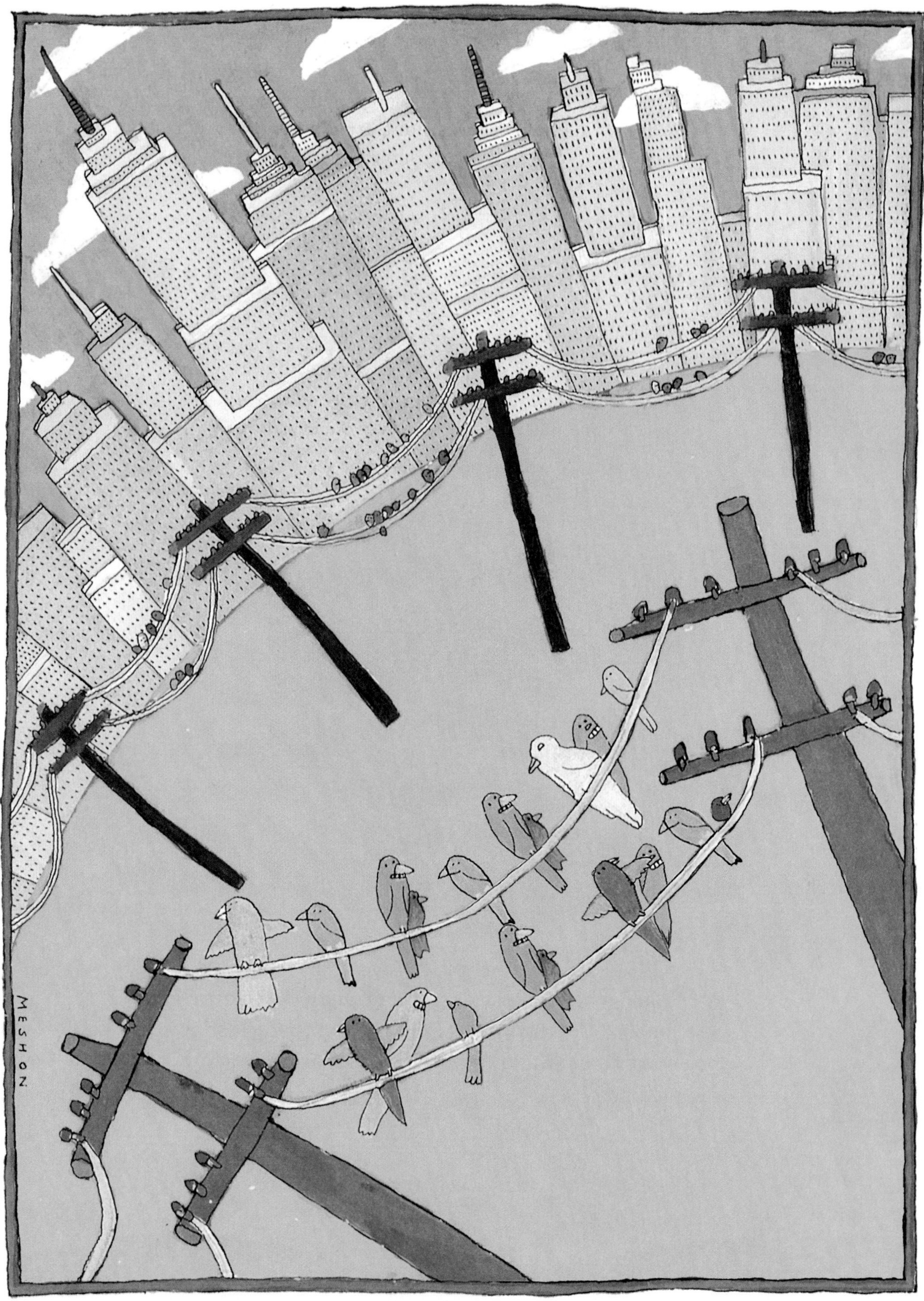
MESHON

Focus Questions What can keep people from communicating? Why do we find it so important to find someone with whom we can communicate?

My Two Drawings

from *The Little Prince*
written and drawn by **Antoine de Saint-Exupéry**
translated from the French by Richard Howard

Once when I was six I saw a magnificent picture in a book about the jungle, called *True Stories*. It showed a boa constrictor swallowing a wild beast. Here is a copy of the picture.

In the book it said: "Boa constrictors swallow their prey whole, without chewing. Afterward they are no longer able to move, and they sleep during the six months of their digestion."

In those days I thought a lot about jungle adventures, and eventually managed to make my first drawing, using a colored pencil. My drawing Number One looked like this:

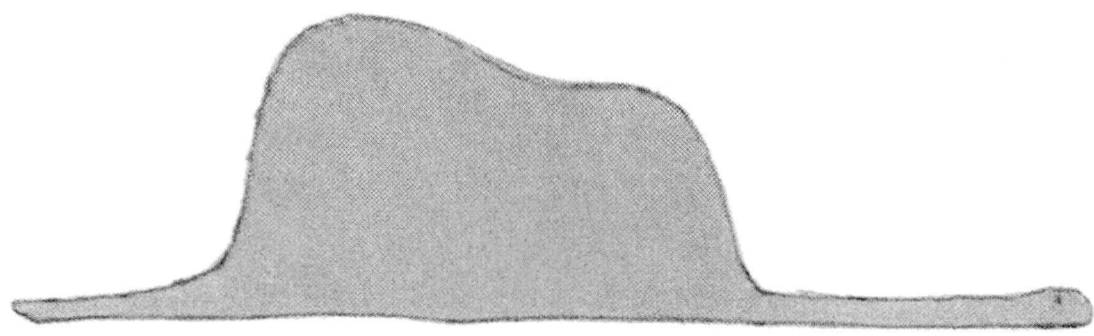

I showed the grown-ups my masterpiece, and I asked them if my drawing scared them.

They answered, "Why be scared of a hat?"

My drawing was not a picture of a hat. It was a picture of a boa constrictor digesting an elephant. Then I drew the inside of the boa constrictor, so the grown-ups could understand. They always need explanations. My drawing Number Two looked like this:

The grown-ups advised me to put away my drawings of boa constrictors, outside or inside, and apply myself instead to geography, history, arithmetic, and grammar. That is why I abandoned, at the age of six, a magnificent career as an artist. I had been discouraged by the failure of my drawing Number One and of my drawing Number Two. Grown-ups never understand anything by themselves, and it is exhausting for children to have to provide explanations over and over again.

So then I had to choose another career, and I learned to pilot airplanes. I have flown almost everywhere in the world. And, as a matter of fact, geography has been a big help to me. I could tell China from Arizona at first glance, which is very useful if you get lost during the night.

So I have had, in the course of my life, lots of encounters with lots of serious people. I have spent lots of time with grown-ups. I have seen them at close range...which hasn't much improved my opinion of them.

Whenever I encountered a grown-up who seemed to me at all enlightened, I would experiment on him with my drawing Number One, which I have always kept. I wanted to see if he really understood anything. But he would always answer, "That's a hat." Then I wouldn't talk about boa constrictors or jungles or stars. I would put myself on his level and talk about bridge and golf and politics and neckties. And my grown-up was glad to know such a reasonable person.

My Two Drawings

Concept Connections

Linking the Selection

Think about the following questions, and then record your responses in the Response Journal section of your Writer's Notebook.

- How did the pilot change his drawing Number One to better communicate his message?
- Why did the pilot continue to show grown-ups his drawing Number One?

Exploring Concept Vocabulary

The concept word for this lesson is ***comprehend.*** If you don't know what this word means, look it up in a dictionary. Answer these questions.

- In the pilot's opinion, what subjects could grown-ups ***comprehend?***
- In the pilot's opinion, what subjects could grown-ups not ***comprehend?***

In the Vocabulary section of your Writer's Notebook, write a sentence that includes the word ***comprehend*** as well as one of the selection vocabulary words.

Expanding the Concept

In this unit you have read about many different ways of communicating. What conclusions can you draw about the importance of understanding others and of being understood? Try to use the word ***comprehend*** in your discussion. Add new ideas about communication to the Concept/Question Board.

Meet the Author/Illustrator

Antoine de Saint-Exupéry loved aviation. He joined the French Army Air Force and later became a commercial pilot. As a writer he combined his thrill for flying with adventure to create exciting adult novels and of course the story of *The Little Prince. The Little Prince* happened by accident. One day while Saint-Exupéry was at lunch with his publisher, he began to doodle on his napkin. His publisher saw the drawing of what Saint-Exupéry called "just a little fellow I carry around in my heart" and suggested the author create a children's book. Writing *The Little Prince* was a joyful task for Saint-Exupéry.

Meet the Translator

Richard Howard is an American poet and translator. He has translated over 100 books from French to English, including modern French fiction and poetry from the nineteenth century. Richard Howard uses his poems to bring past artists, writers, and musicians to life. In each poem, he has a historical character speak about their life and times.

UNIT 6

A Changing America

First were the Native Americans. Different tribes and societies occupied parts of North America. Then the Europeans came and began to set up colonies. That was more than 150 years before the United States came into being. What was life like during those years? It wasn't all log cabins and teepees and battles over territory. A complex society grew up that led to the America we know today. So it's *your* history—even if your ancestors didn't come over on the *Mayflower*!

altimore
adelphia
erdam
IROQUOIS LONGHOUSE
TIP PEKOE*
Sedition in BOSTON
PENNSYLVANIA
FREEDMAN
BLACKSMITH
in ye
COLONIES
COLONIAL TRAD

Focus Questions Would you have liked to be one of the first people to colonize America? Why did the Native Americans help the first colonists?

Early America

by Trevor Matheney

When the colonists arrived in America, they were beginning a new life in what to them was a "new world." They weren't completely aware of the long and varied history of the place they called the Americas.

There is evidence that long before Columbus in 1492 or John Cabot in 1497 ever set foot in the Americas, nomadic groups had traveled from Asia and spread out through what is now the United States and South America. These people formed tribes such as the Hopewell and Powhatan and great civilizations such as the Aztec and Inca. In addition, artifacts that have been found suggest visits by the Japanese, Chinese, and Phoenicians.

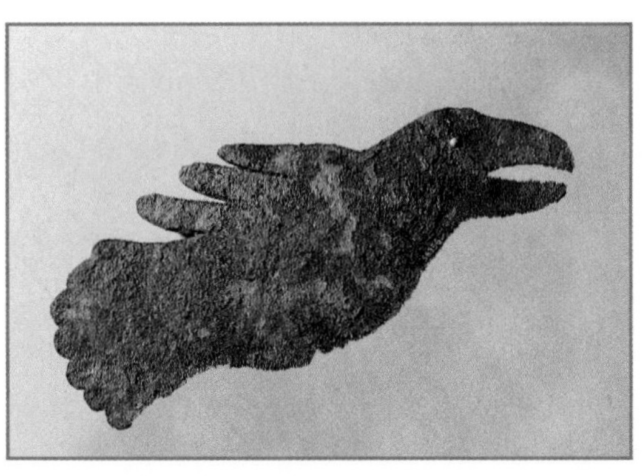

Hopewell Culture (300 B.C.–A.D. 500), Ohio: Raven or crow with a pearl eye cut from a sheet of copper

By the early 1500s many Spanish, English, French, and Portuguese explorers, fishermen, and traders were traveling to the Americas and returning with tales of giant forests, huge stretches of land, and plenty of clear blue waters.

This was particularly interesting to European men. For the most part in Europe at that time, only the oldest son could inherit the land of his father. Thus, for many younger sons the only way to have land of their own was to leave Europe. The idea of settling in the New World of the Americas became very attractive.

Other people wanted to escape some of the problems they faced in Europe. In many places in Europe, people were not allowed religious freedom. Some of these people felt they would be able to worship as they pleased in the New World.

Spain and England were the first countries to build settlements in the Americas. These settlements were called colonies. The first Spanish settlement was established at St. Augustine, Florida, in 1565.

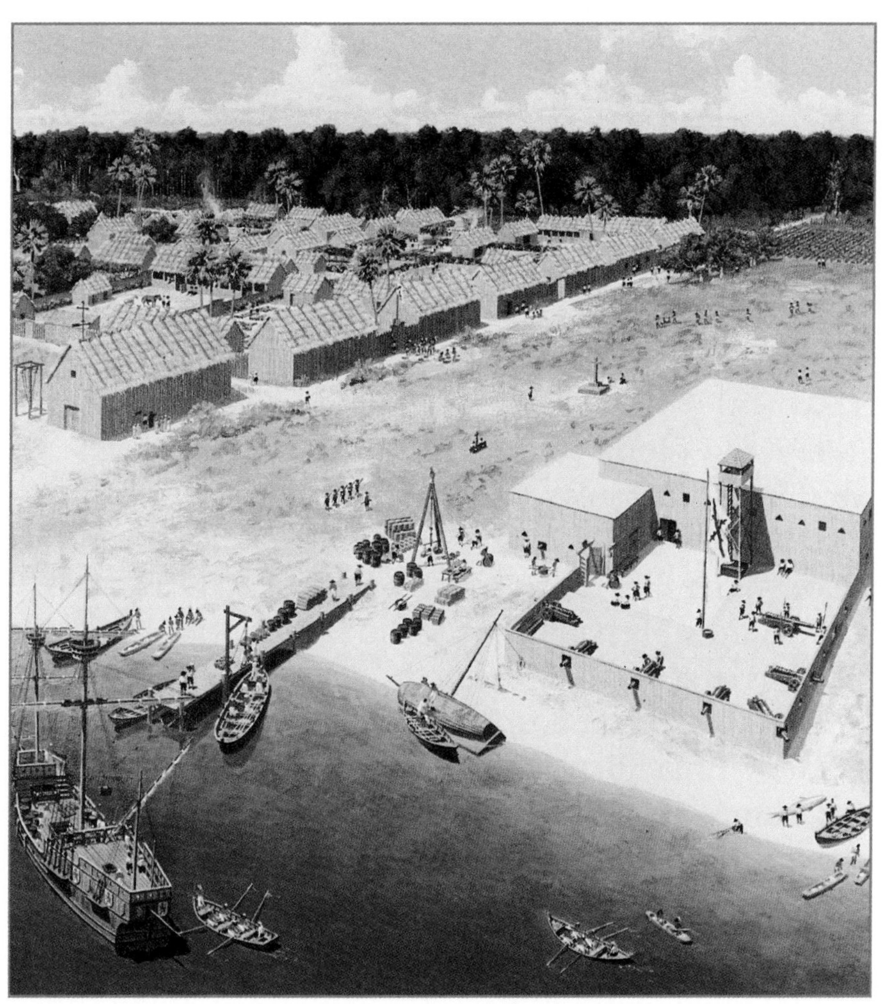

Spanish settlement at St. Augustine, Florida

Sir Walter Raleigh's expedition to Roanoke Island, 1585

In 1585, the English began a colony on Roanoke Island off the coast of what is now North Carolina. This colony failed. However, another attempt to colonize Roanoke Island was made in 1587. It was here that Virginia Dare, the first English child born in America, was born. In 1590, when supply ships returned from England to the Roanoke Colony, everyone had disappeared. No one knows what happened to these early colonists. Because of this, the Roanoke Colony has become known as the Lost Colony.

The Jamestown Colony, founded in 1607, and the Plymouth Colony, founded in 1620, were the first two English colonies that survived. The Jamestown Colony grew into what was called the Virginia Colony. The Plymouth Colony was located in what is now Massachusetts and is where the Pilgrims first settled.

The colonists had to face the hardships of living in a new, unfamiliar land. Many died of disease or starvation. Most of the early colonists were farmers, growing corn, beans, and other food and raising their own animals. They made their own clothes, built their own homes, and worked long, hard days. Few colonial children went to school. Often parents used the Bible to teach their children to read. A few colleges were eventually started for men only. The first college in the colonies was Harvard, founded in 1636 in Massachusetts.

The Native Americans helped these early colonists survive their first years in the New World. However, some Native American groups were upset at having their lands taken by these new people who often brought with them unfriendly ways and diseases deadly to the Native Americans. As more and more colonists arrived, they began taking land from these groups. Several wars were fought between the colonists and the Native Americans. In 1675, a Native American leader named King Philip led the Wampanoag and Narragansett tribes in a war against the colonists in Massachusetts and Rhode Island. These were the same tribes who had helped the colonists survive their first years in the New World. Now, they were angry. Both tribes were nearly destroyed in this war. Clashes between the colonists and the Native Americans continued throughout the colonial period.

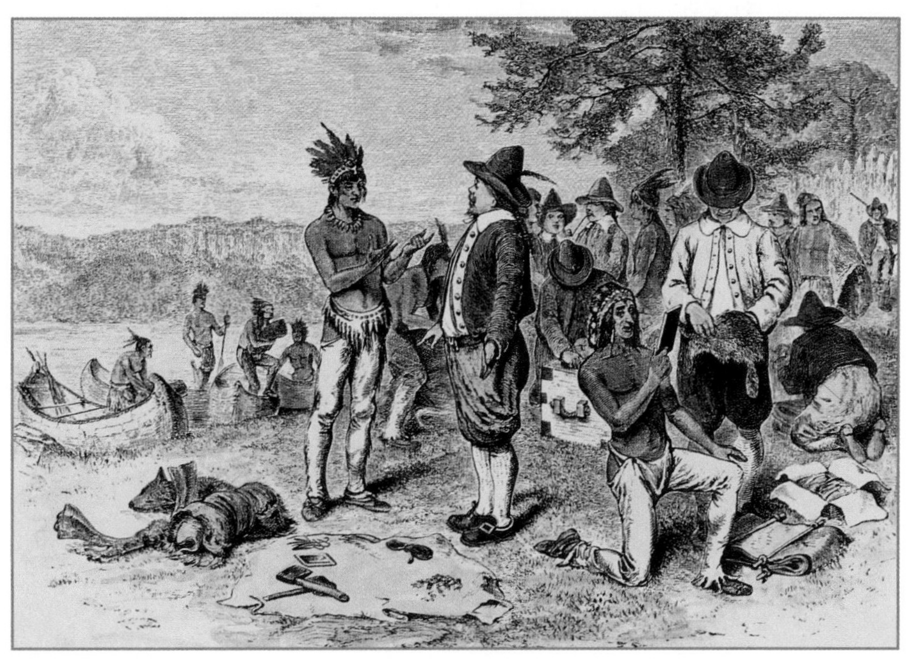

Native Americans helping English: Dutch fur trader

Although the colonies were governed by England, not all colonists were English. Many were from Germany, France, the Netherlands, Sweden, Ireland, and Scotland. Others were brought from Africa as indentured servants and later, slaves. By 1700 there were about 250,000 colonists living in the thirteen English colonies in America.

The colonies were different in many ways. For example, in Massachusetts, many of the colonists came as families looking for land to settle. The Rhode Island and Pennsylvania colonies were settled by religious groups in search of freedom to worship as they pleased. The New York Colony became a very culturally and ethnically diverse colony. People from all countries began to settle there.

Many early colonists were unmarried men under the age of twenty-five. In the Maryland Colony, most colonists were single men who arrived as indentured servants. They would work for a period of time, up to seven years, before being given their freedom. In exchange, they received food and shelter, and often learned a trade. Over half of these Maryland colonists died of starvation and disease within a few years of arriving in the colonies.

As the number of indentured servants decreased, there was a shortage of workers in the colonies. To fill this shortage, the colonists turned to slavery. In some colonies, over one-fourth of the population consisted of African slaves. However, not all colonial Africans were slaves. Some had come to America as indentured servants and when their indenture was served they were free to work as they saw fit.

England was not the only country to own land in America. Spain owned what is now Florida, and France owned much of the land west of the thirteen English colonies. This prevented the English colonists from spreading out. Because of this, the population in the English colonies became more concentrated. Cities and towns grew out of the early settlements.

The colonists began to feel they lived in a country so different from England that English law and the English government no longer served them well. These ideas would lead to the Revolutionary War, in which the thirteen English colonies would become the United States of America.

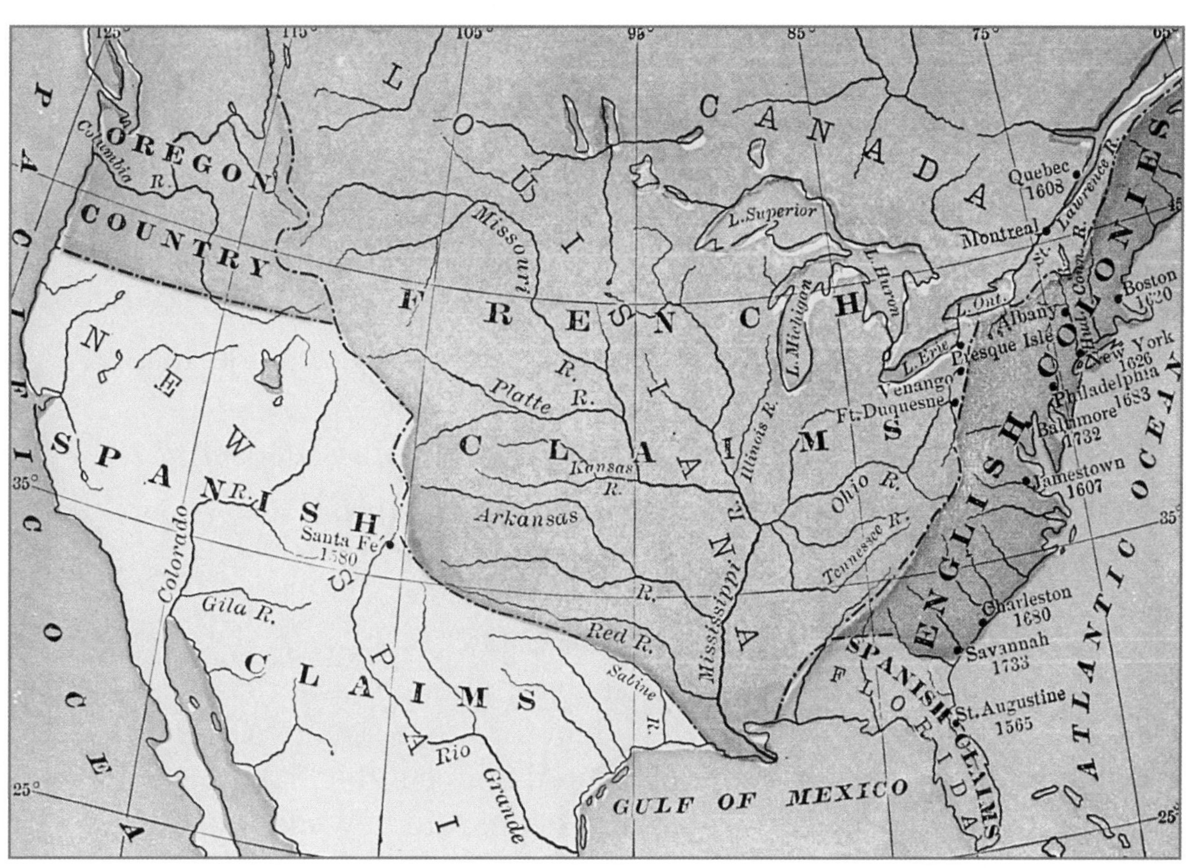

Early America

Concept Connections

Linking the Selection

Think about the following questions, and then record your responses in the Response Journal section of your Writer's Notebook.

- What are some of the reasons people settled in Colonial America?
- How did the colonists' relations with Native Americans change over time?

Exploring Concept Vocabulary

The concept word for this lesson is ***establish.*** If you don't know what this word means, look it up in a dictionary. Answer these questions.

- When was the Spanish settlement at St. Augustine, Florida, ***established?***
- What was the first colony ***established*** in Massachusetts?

Write a sentence that includes the word ***establish*** as well as one of the selection vocabulary words.

Expanding the Concept

Think about the colonists' reasons for going to America. Discuss whether the hope they had for life in America still exists for people living in the United States today. Try to use the word ***establish*** in your discussion. Add new ideas about the theme A Changing America to the Concept/Question Board.

Meet the Author

Trevor Matheney is a pen name of Wiley Blevins, who wrote "Music and Slavery" from Unit 4. Mr. Blevins grew up in the South and eventually became a teacher. He has taught both in the United States and in Ecuador. Currently Mr. Blevins lives in New York City, where he is a writer and an editor.

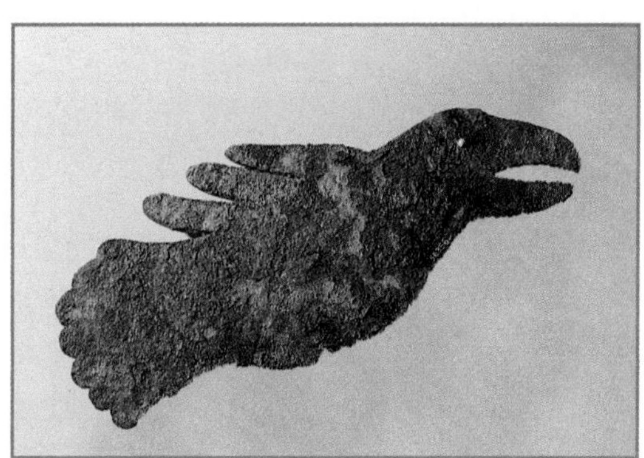

Focus Questions Why would people take such a risky journey to go live in America? Were the children aboard the Mayflower very different from children now?

The Voyage of the Mayflower

Patricia M. Whalen
illustrated by James Watling

Pelted by rain under a black sky, the ninety-foot *Mayflower* rolled and pitched on mountainous waves. Its masts were bare because during a storm, a sailing ship must lower all its sails and drift with the wind to avoid capsizing or breaking apart.

Below the main deck, the passengers huddled in the dark. They could hear the wind howling and the waves thudding against the vessel's wooden sides and washing over the deck. Seawater dripped down on them through the canvas covering the deck gratings and seeped through the seams in the planking. The passengers were soaked and shivering; several were seasick besides. As frightened adults tried to comfort terrified children, they prayed for safety in the storm and an end to the long, terrible voyage.

Suddenly, above the din of the storm, they heard the noise of splitting timber. One of the beams supporting the deck had cracked! The ship was in danger of sinking. Then someone remembered a great iron screw brought from Holland. Carefully, the ship's carpenter positioned it beneath the beam and braced it. It would hold; the passengers and crew could reach land safely.

Crossing the Atlantic in 1620 was extremely risky. A wooden ship could leak or break apart in a storm. Since the sails could be raised only in fair weather, it was impossible to predict how long a voyage would last. To avoid the stormy autumn months, ships usually made the crossing in spring or summer. They almost never sailed alone.

Aware of these dangers, the Pilgrims had planned to cross the ocean in two ships in the summer of 1620. The English Separatists from Holland (who called themselves Saints) borrowed money from London businessmen and purchased a small ship, the *Speedwell*. For the Separatists' safety, and to help them establish a profitable colony, the businessmen recruited additional volunteers in London. The

businessmen rented the *Mayflower*, a ship three times the size of the *Speedwell*, for these recruits, whom the Separatists called Strangers. The Saints and Strangers met for the first time in Southampton, England, a few days before the ships sailed on August 5.

The tiny *Speedwell* had been refitted with taller masts and larger sails so it could keep up with the *Mayflower*. These changes, however, caused the ship to leak badly at sea. On August 12, the ships put into Dartmouth. After the *Speedwell* was examined and repaired, they set off again on August 23. Two days later, the *Speedwell* began to leak again, and the vessels headed for Plymouth, England. There the ships' masters, carpenters, and principal passengers agreed that the *Speedwell* could not make the crossing.

Over the next few days, the sixty-seven Strangers on the *Mayflower* made room for thirty-five of the Saints from the *Speedwell*, along with their belongings and provisions. On September 6, the *Mayflower* set out from Plymouth alone. The one hundred two passengers, including thirty-four children, would not see land for sixty-six days.

The *Mayflower*, like all ships of the time, was built to carry cargo, not passengers. A few families crowded into the "great cabbin" in the stern. Most of the passengers, however, traveled in bunks or tiny "cabbins" below the main deck and above the hold, where cargo was stored. In this "'tween decks" area, they had only five feet of head room. Each person's living space was smaller than the mattress of a modern twin bed.

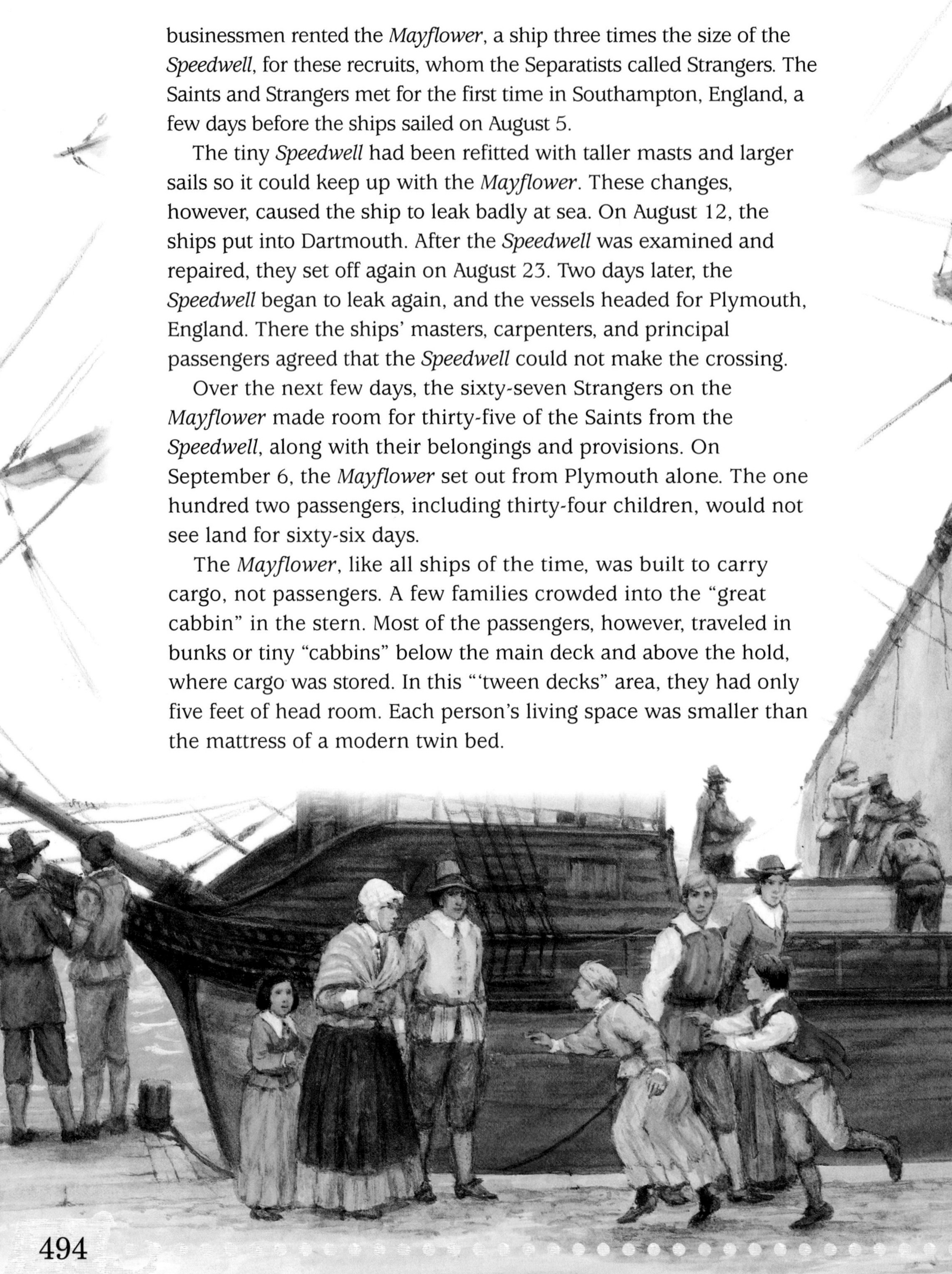

The Pilgrims suffered other discomforts. Many were seasick, particularly at the beginning of the voyage. In storms, they were constantly wet and cold. They could not bathe or wash and dry their clothes and bedding. For toilet purposes, they used buckets.

In fair weather, the adults and children who had recovered from seasickness could leave their dim, foul-smelling quarters for the wind and spray of the main deck. The adults took deep breaths of the cold, tangy air and stretched cramped muscles. The younger children, forbidden to run around, played quiet games. Damaris Hopkins, age three, and Mary and Remember Allerton, ages four and six, "tended the baby" (played with dolls). Six- and nine-year-old brothers Wrestling and Love Brewster played "I Spy" and "Hunt the Slipper" with six- and seven-year-old Jasper and Richard More. Finger games such as cat's cradle and paper, scissors, stone were popular with eight-year-old Humility Cooper, Ellen More, John Cooke, John Billington, and Bartholomew Allerton. Elizabeth Tilley, age fourteen, and Mary Chilton and Constance Hopkins, both fifteen, helped prepare the meals.

For cooking, the passengers built charcoal fires in metal braziers set in sandboxes. There was so little space, however, that only a few people could cook at once. When storms made lighting fires dangerous, everyone ate cold meals.

After morning prayers, they ate a simple breakfast of cheese and ship's biscuit (hard, dry biscuit). If cooking was allowed, they might have porridge. Their midday meal might consist of ship's biscuit and cheese or, in fair weather, cooked "pease pottage," boiled salt fish, pork, or beef and any freshly caught bonito or porpoise. Before retiring, they had a light supper. Everyone, even the children, drank beer with their meals because it was preferred to water.

Not until December 11, more than a month after first sighting land, did the Pilgrims decide where they would build their colony. One day, before an exploring party left the *Mayflower,* the

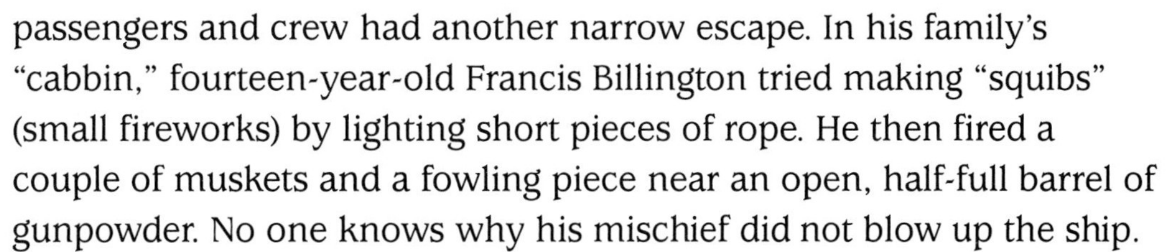

passengers and crew had another narrow escape. In his family's "cabbin," fourteen-year-old Francis Billington tried making "squibs" (small fireworks) by lighting short pieces of rope. He then fired a couple of muskets and a fowling piece near an open, half-full barrel of gunpowder. No one knows why his mischief did not blow up the ship.

The *Mayflower* remained anchored offshore during the winter while the Pilgrims built their new homes. On April 5, 1621, the ship set sail for England. With the prevailing winds and currents, it made the return trip in only thirty-one days.

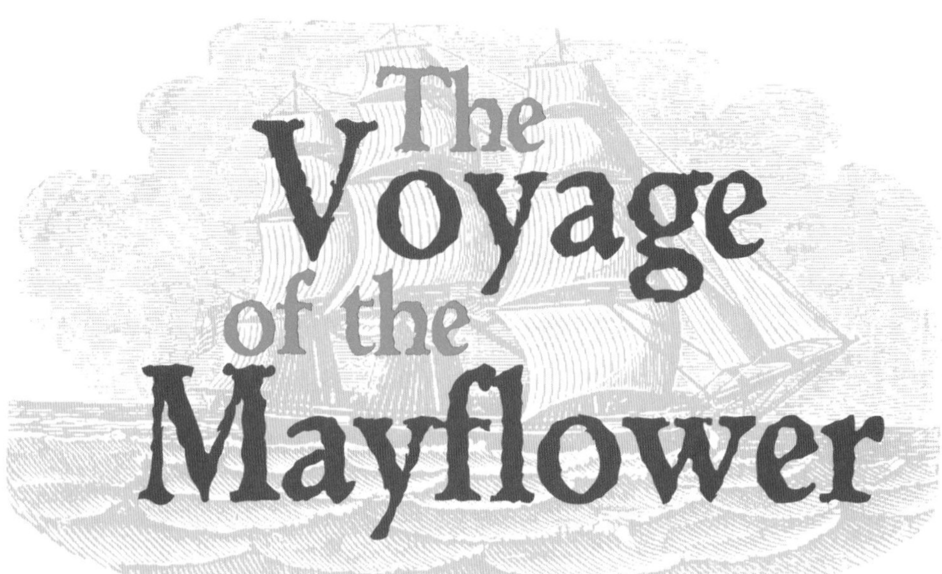

Concept Connections

Linking the Selection

Think about the following questions, and then record your responses in the Response Journal section of your Writer's Notebook.

- Why was the *Mayflower's* journey so risky and so lengthy?
- How did their crossing prepare the Pilgrims for hardships they might face in their new land?

Exploring Concept Vocabulary

The concept word for this lesson is ***voyage.*** If you don't know what this word means, look it up in a dictionary. Answer these questions.

- Why did the Pilgrims undertake the ***voyage?***
- Why did the *Mayflower* make the ***voyage*** alone?

Write a sentence that includes the word ***voyage*** as well as one of the selection vocabulary words.

Expanding the Concept

In what ways did the Pilgrims show determination? Is there anything that would cause you to undertake such a journey? Try to use the word ***voyage*** in your discussion. Add new ideas about the theme A Changing America to the Concept/Question Board.

Meet the Illustrator

James Watling was educated at the Barron School of Art and Leeds College of Art. He began teaching in 1954, first in secondary schools, then at McGill University in Montreal after he moved to Canada from England. He retired as an Associate Professor in Art Education in 1995. Some of Mr. Watling's interests include gardening, woodworking, nature, and wildlife. He has been illustrating since the 1960s and continues this today.

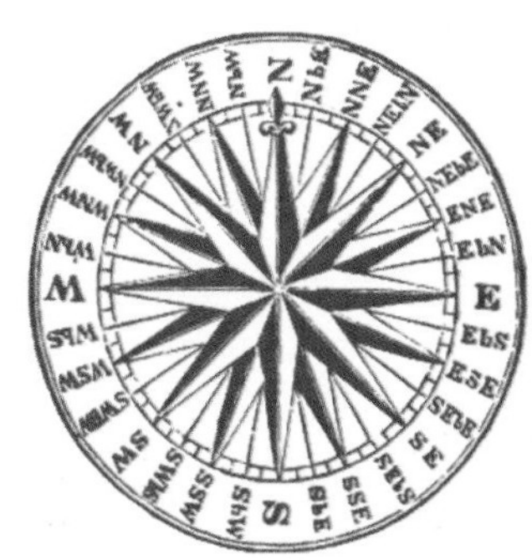

Fine Art

A Changing America

Sampler. c.1792. **Patty Coggeshall.** Linen embroidered with silk thread. 19 $\frac{1}{2}$ × 16 $\frac{5}{8}$ in. The Metropolitan Museum of Art, New York, NY.

The Mason Children: David, Joanna, and Abigail. 1670. **Attributed to the Freake-Gibbs Painter.** Fine Arts Museum of San Francisco.

Quilled Buckskin Robe. National Museum of the American Indian, Smithsonian Institution.

Focus Questions What was it like for the Native Americans to see the colonists arriving? Can we call Pocahontas a "colonist"?

Pocahontas

from *The Virginia Colony*

by Dennis B. Fradin

illustrated by Robert Roth

This painting of Pocahontas, done while she was touring England shortly before her death, shows her in English clothing.

Exactly when and where the Native American girl named Matoaka was born is not known, but it probably was in eastern Virginia around 1595. When the Jamestown colonists arrived in 1607, Matoaka was about twelve years old. Little is known about Matoaka's life away from the colonists, but when she was with them, she lived up to her nickname, Pocahontas, which means "The Playful One."

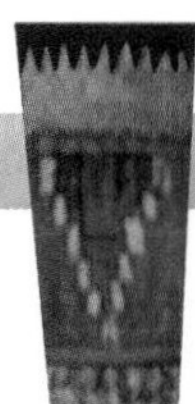

After Pocahontas saved John Smith's life in early 1608, there was a short time of peace between the colonists and the Native Americans. During this time Pocahontas often came to Jamestown, where she would challenge the young men to compete with her at performing handsprings and running races. The English youths taught her a phrase: "Love you not me?" which Pocahontas would repeat to them. In return, Pocahontas taught Captain Smith and the other colonists some Native American words.

In the spring of 1608, John Smith got into an argument with Pocahontas's people during a bargaining session and took seven of them captive. Powhatan tried to get the prisoners released, but nothing worked until he sent Pocahontas to Jamestown as his agent. Captain Smith and the other leaders of Jamestown let the prisoners go for the sake of Pocahontas.

About a year after this incident, Smith left Virginia, and relations between the Native Americans and the colonists worsened. Those few times when the Native Americans and the colonists met peacefully, Pocahontas and her people asked what had become of Captain Smith. The colonists always said that he was dead.

In 1613 Pocahontas was staying in a Native American village along the Potomac River when she was kidnapped and taken first to Jamestown and then to Henrico. In Henrico she was given fancy English petticoats and dresses to replace her deerskin clothes, taught the English language, and renamed Rebecca. How Pocahontas felt about this we do not know. We do know, however, that Pocahontas met the tobacco planter John Rolfe in the summer of 1613 and that the next spring the two were married in a ceremony that was Jamestown's big social event of the year.

In 1616 Pocahontas and her husband went with their year-old son, Thomas, and several other Native Americans to England. She was introduced to royalty and invited to balls and banquets. In England, Pocahontas also learned a startling piece of news: John Smith was still alive! One day in the fall of 1616 Captain Smith called at the house where she was staying near London.

Pocahontas, who by this time was ill because of England's damp and chilly weather, was both pleased and upset at the sight of Smith. "They did tell us always you were dead," she said. Pocahontas then teased Smith for having forgotten her, reminded him that she had adopted

him long ago, and called him "Father." When Smith said that she should not call him "Father," Pocahontas answered, "I tell you then I will, and I will be forever and ever your countryman."

A few minutes later Captain Smith left, and the two never met again. In March of 1617, just as the Rolfes were about to sail home to Virginia, Pocahontas died of smallpox. The woman who had saved John Smith's life and who had once performed handsprings in Jamestown was only twenty-two years old when she died. Thomas Rolfe, her son, was educated in England. At age twenty he returned to Virginia, where he became a popular citizen and even helped defend the colony against the Native Americans.

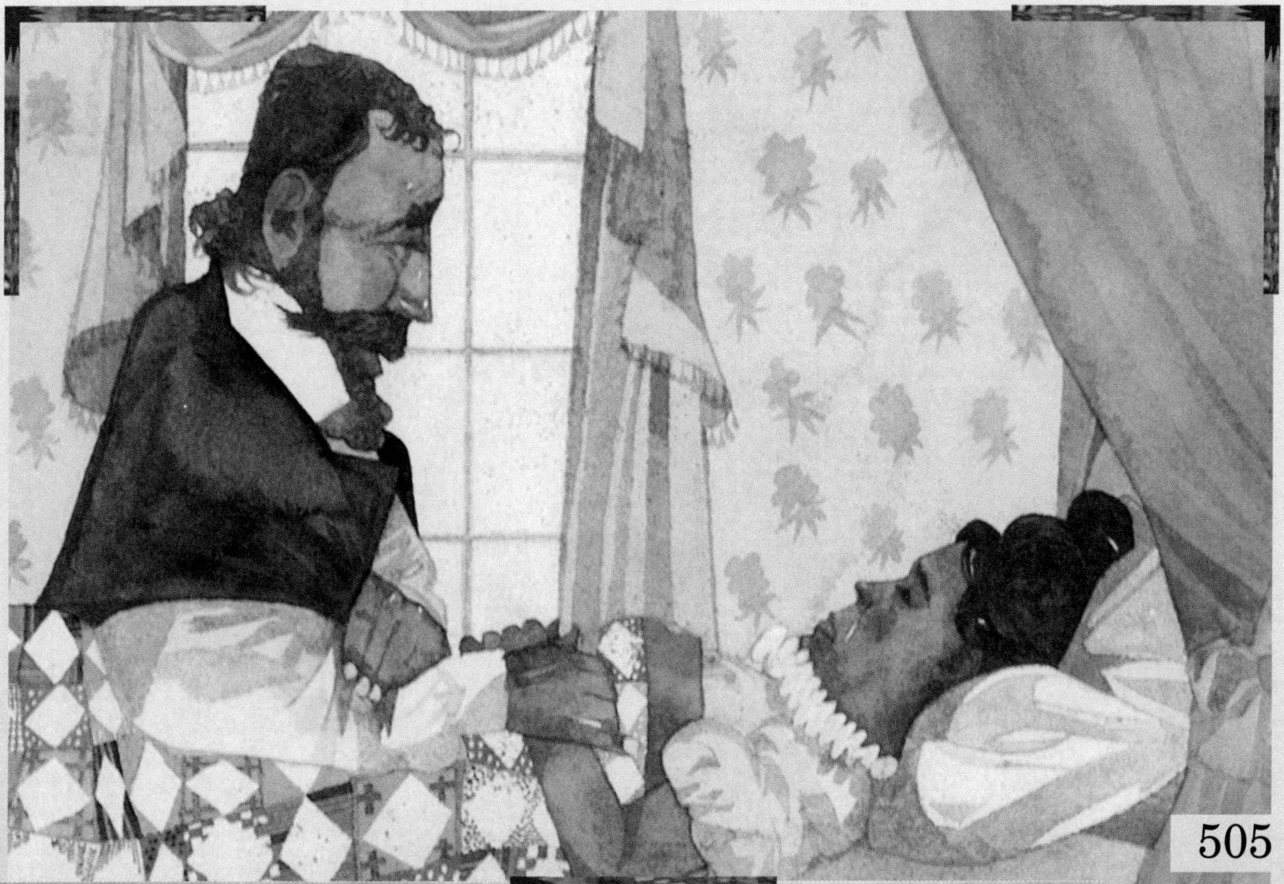

Pocahontas

from *The Virginia Colony*

Concept Connections

Linking the Selection

Think about the following questions, and then record your responses in the Response Journal section of your Writer's Notebook.

- Why was Matoaka nicknamed Pocahontas, which means "The Playful One"?
- How did Pocahontas show her fondness for Captain Smith?

Exploring Concept Vocabulary

The concept word for this lesson is ***conflict.*** If you don't know what this word means, look it up in a dictionary. Answer these questions.

- What did Captain Smith do during the ***conflict*** with Pocahontas's people in 1608?
- In this selection, we read that Pocahontas's people and the colonists argued. What have you read that might explain the cause of the ***conflicts?***

Write a sentence that includes the word ***conflict*** as well as one of the selection vocabulary words.

Expanding the Concept

Consider how her involvement with colonists had both positive and negative consequences for Pocahontas. How might her life have been different if she hadn't befriended the colonists? Try to use the word ***conflict*** in your discussion of Pocahontas. Add new ideas about the theme A Changing America to the Concept/Question Board.

Meet the Author

Dennis Fradin taught elementary school students before he became an author. Now he has written almost 150 books. He is a man who loves his work. He says, *"I have the time of my life as a children's book author. Each day I take about five steps from my bedroom into my office, where I spend my time reading, writing, rewriting, and phoning people for information. Often I travel to do in-person research."*

Mr. Fradin researches his books very carefully and sometimes rewrites them five or six times. He says, *"I also check over all my facts line by line to make sure everything is accurate. So all that keeps me pretty busy. I try not to let a day of the year go by without working."*

Meet the Illustrator

Robert Roth grew up on Long Island, New York, and studied art at the Rhode Island School of Design.

Mr. Roth has been drawing since he could pick up and hold a pencil. Almost everywhere he goes he carries a sketchbook. He likes to draw from real life outside the studio to keep his eye alert and his work fresh.

Focus Questions Were all the colonists in favor of the Revolution? Could the colonies have broken from England without a war?

Martha Helps the Rebel

A Play by Carole Charles

illustrated by Charles Shaw and Dennis Hockerman

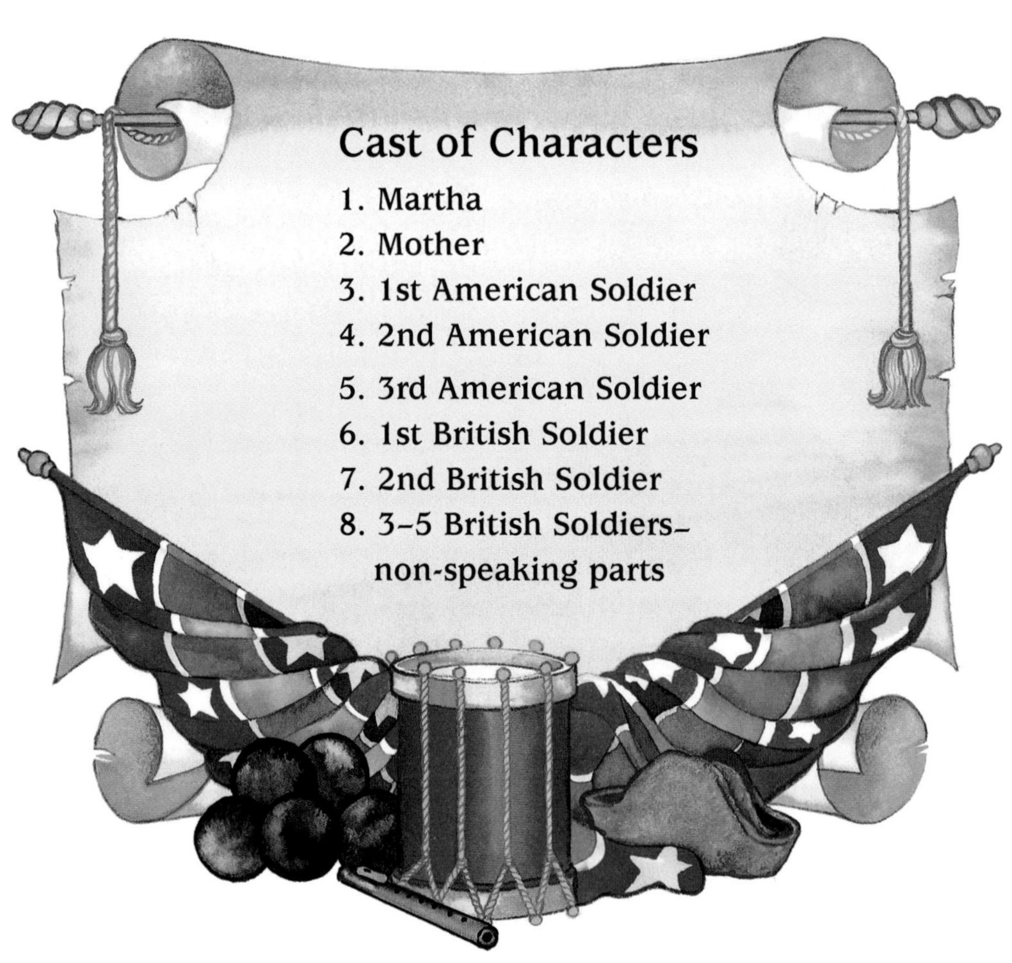

Cast of Characters

1. Martha
2. Mother
3. 1st American Soldier
4. 2nd American Soldier
5. 3rd American Soldier
6. 1st British Soldier
7. 2nd British Soldier
8. 3–5 British Soldiers–non-speaking parts

(Setting: South Carolina, 1780. From the back of their farmhouse, a mother and her ten-year-old daughter, Martha, watch three American soldiers walk through the nearby woods.)

Martha: Look at the soldiers, ma!

Mother: I see them, Martha. They must be coming from Charleston.

Martha: Are they American soldiers?

Mother: Yes.

Martha: I wish I were big enough to be a soldier like pa. I'd chase all the British soldiers right back to England! Would you like to be a soldier, ma?

Mother: *(musing)* Sometimes I would. But you and I need to take care of the farm until your pa comes home.

(Three American soldiers walking through the woods. British soldiers in hiding nearby.)

1st Am. Soldier: *(sings)* "Come all you brave soldiers, Both valiant and free, It's for independence, We all now agree."

2nd Am. Soldier: Hey, quiet down! Everyone in South Carolina can hear you.

1st Am. Soldier: Good! Then all the British soldiers in the colony will run at the sound of my voice. *(Sings the song again, just as loudly.)*

3rd Am. Soldier: Come on, quiet down. If any British soldiers have landed this far south, I'd like to hear them before they hear us.

1st Am. Soldier: Ah, there aren't any British around here.

3rd Am. Soldier: Maybe not. That's what we're supposed to find out.

(Woods. 1st Am. soldier whistling the tune from previous scene.)

2nd Am. Soldier: When we get back to Charleston, I'd like to . . .

(Interrupted by a musket shot, Whistling stops abruptly. 2nd Am. soldier yells and falls dead.)

3rd. Am. Soldier: British! Stay down!

(Shots fired from both sides.)

1st Am. Soldier: ***(whispering)*** Let's run for it. We'll never be able to hold them off here.

3rd Am. Soldier: All right . . . now!

(Musket shot strikes 3rd Am. soldier, who yells and falls.)

1st Am. Soldier: Oh, no! *(Fiercely, to himself)* I have to get out of here!

(Soldier exits, running, crouched. Sound of feet running, crashing through low brush. Muskets fire several more times.)

(Woods. American soldier enters, running through low brush. About eight British soldiers pursue. American soldier exits on other side.)

1st Br. Soldier: Let's get him!

2nd Br. Soldier: *(panting heavily)* I can hardly run with this heavy pack.

3rd Br. Soldier: *(also panting)* Hey, just a minute. Slow down. Listen, he can outrun us easily. We're wearing winter uniforms and carrying packs. All the American has to carry is a musket.

1st Br. Soldier: But we have to stop him before he reaches Charleston. The American army must not know our position or strength.

3rd Br. Soldier: *(still breathing heavily)* I know. So let's outsmart that American soldier. Hide the packs somewhere in the bushes. Then spread out and we'll search the ways to Charleston. He'll have to stop for food and water, perhaps for rest. If we move quickly, we'll find him.

(Martha grooms a riding horse. Mother enters. Mother and Martha see the American soldier running through the woods as if pursued.)

Martha: Ma, look!

Mother: I see. Martha, ride old Jonathan as fast as you can to that soldier. Bring him back by the stream bed so no one will see him. I'll wait in the kitchen.

Martha: What if there are British soldiers right behind him?

Mother: You said you wanted to fight. This is your chance. Hurry, before it's too late.

(Martha and horse exit. Sound of hoofbeats.)

(Kitchen. Mother is lowering a quilting frame from the ceiling. Frame has a nearly completed quilt attached. Soldier and Martha enter from side. Soldier appears haggard, exhausted.)

Mother: Martha, go back outside and ride old Jonathan hard around the pasture, as though you were exercising him. If anyone comes, I don't want a panting horse tied to my front porch.

Martha: Yes, ma. *(Exits.)*

Soldier: Ma'am, I . . .

Mother: *(interrupting)* We can talk later. Right now I want you up on those rafters, right over the spot where the quilting frame will be.

Soldier: Up there? But . . .

Mother: *(interrupting)* Soldier, if you want to live, you'd better get up on those rafters, and fast!

(American soldier balanced on the rafters. Mother raising the quilting frame. British soldiers can be seen through a window, approaching the house from the woods.)

Am. Soldier: Ma'am, you don't know how much I appreciate your help.

Mother: *(speaking as she raises the frame)* It's all right. My husband is a soldier with the Continental Army too. Maybe someone will help him one day.

Am. Soldier: I'm very grateful for . . .

Mother: *(interrupting)* Hush! *(whispering)* Soldiers coming! Don't make a sound!

(Loud knocks on the door.)

Br. Soldier: *(from outside)* Open up! *(More loud knocks.)* Open up, I say!

(Kitchen. American soldier completely hidden from view by quilt and frame. Mother has lifted hot skillet off fireplace in pretense of busyness. Loud knocks continue.)

Mother: Just a minute!

(More loud knocks. British soldiers push open the door and enter the kitchen.)

Br. Soldier: Sorry, ma'am. We're looking for someone.

Mother: *(indignant)* You might have waited until I opened the door!

(Soldiers begin searching the house.)

Mother: What are you doing!

Br. Soldier: Looking for someone, like I said. Arnold, you keep watch outside. Two of you search the barn and grounds. The rest of you search every inch of this house.

Mother: You have no right to search my house!

Br. Soldier: You have nothing to be afraid of, ma'am, *(threateningly)* unless we find an American soldier here.

(Kitchen. Mother seated. British soldiers still searching. Martha comes running in.)

Martha: Ma! What are they doing?

Mother: They're just looking for someone, Martha.

Br. Soldier: Where have you been, little girl?

Martha: *(defiant)* My name is Martha, not "little girl"! I've been out riding my horse.

Br. Soldier: *(quiet but threatening)* You wouldn't have been hiding an American soldier somewhere, would you?

Martha: *(still defiant)* I told you, I was riding my horse.

Mother: Martha, come sit down with me. They'll be leaving soon.

Martha: *(through clenched teeth)* I hope so!

(Kitchen. American soldier climbing down from rafters. Twilight.)

Mother: It's safe now. The British have gone.

Soldier: Thank you. I'm very grateful. *(Thoughtful)* Do you know if there are many British around?

Mother: We haven't seen British soldiers for several months, until today.

Martha: *(excited)* I'll bet there are thousands of British just over the hill, ready to attack Charleston!

Soldier: *(laughing gently)* Well, perhaps. But we rather expect an attack from the sea. That's how they attacked at the beginning of the war.

Martha: Maybe they're trying to trick you! You should go look for yourself. I'll bet there are thousands of British over there, just polishing their muskets and laughing.

Soldier: *(slowly)* That is possible. Perhaps I should take a look as soon as it's dark.

(Early morning, outside the farmhouse. Mother milking a cow. Martha enters, carrying a basket of eggs. Soldier rushes on stage.)

Soldier: You were right, Martha! The British are landing along the coast. It looks as though they are preparing to march on Charleston.

Mother: *(very nervous)* Keep your voice down! The British came back again last night. They're still looking for you, and for any other American soldiers. All the roads are guarded.

Soldier: And I know why! Most of our troops in Charleston are guarding the coast. If the British attack from the south, they will meet almost no resistance.

Martha: You'll have to tell them! You'll have to get through!

Mother: But how? It would be easier for . . . for this cow to pass the British. An American soldier couldn't make it!

Martha: I have an idea!

(Martha, mother, and soldier taking clothes out of a chest. Soldier half dressed as an old farmer.)

Mother: Pa won't mind our giving these clothes to you. They just might help you get past the British.

Martha: You really look like a farmer! *(Laughs with delight.)*

Soldier: Martha, you had a good idea. And making me look so old is the best part of the disguise.

(Dirt road. British soldiers standing guard, blocking road. American soldier disguised as old farmer enters, accompanied by Martha, who leads a milk cow.)

"Farmer": Afternoon, gentlemen.

1st Br. Soldier: Hold on, old man. Where are you taking the cow?

"Farmer": Yonder, to the next town. The little girl has a cousin who wants to buy her milk cow.

1st Br. Soldier: She looks old enough to take an old gentle cow to the next town by herself. Why are you going, mister?

Martha: I'll tell you why. Because I'm afraid to go by myself, that's why. I've never seen so many soldiers around here. I . . . I'm just afraid.

2nd Br. Soldier: Ah, let them go. You're scaring the little girl. The old man is harmless.

"Farmer": *(moving on)* Afternoon, gentlemen.

(American soldier disguised as farmer and Martha walk off with cow. British soldiers still stand guard. British troops approach in formation from south.)

1st Br. Soldier: I wish we knew what happened to that American soldier. If he makes it to Charleston, he'll tell them all about us.

"Farmer", offstage: *(sung in cracked old man's voice)* "Come all you brave soldiers, Both valiant and free, It's for independence, We all now agree."

Martha Helps the Rebel

Concept Connections

Linking the Selection

Think about the following questions, and then record your responses in the Response Journal section of your Writer's Notebook.

- Why did the British soldiers want to catch the American soldier?
- Why did Martha's mother help the American soldier?

Exploring Concept Vocabulary

The concept word for this lesson is ***revolution.*** If you don't know what this word means, look it up in a dictionary. Answer these questions.

- How does Martha's family support the ***revolution?***
- What does the American soldier hope the ***revolution*** will bring?

Write a sentence that includes the word ***revolution*** as well as one of the selection vocabulary words.

Expanding the Concept

Compare Martha with Pocahontas. Consider how their actions affected an individual as well as an entire population. Try to use the word ***revolution*** in your discussion. Add new ideas about the theme A Changing America to the Concept/Question Board.

Meet the Illustrator

Charles Shaw once served in the Army National Guard. He loves to illustrate the Texas frontier, children, and jazz musicians. His work can be found in a number of Texas museums and historical societies. Mr. Shaw is so well-known for his illustrations of Texas frontier life that the University of Texas asked him to create illustrations for a book called *Texas*, written by the famous novelist James Michener. Mr. Shaw has also contributed his illustrations to many other books and magazines.

Meet the Illustrator

Dennis Hockerman has been a designer and illustrator for 23 years. Besides illustrating children's books, he has worked for the greeting card, gift wrap, and toy industries. In his spare time, Mr. Hockerman enjoys working at his printing press creating hand-colored etchings. He works out of his home in Wisconsin, where he lives with his wife, three children, and pets.

Focus Questions What were the people who built our country like?
What does the past mean to me?

Prophecy in Flame

by Frances Minturn Howard
illustrated by Antonio Castro

Grandfather wrote from Valley Forge,
"My dear, I miss you; times are harder;
The cheeses sent from home received,
A fine addition to our larder."

Grandfather wrote, "The volunteers
Are leaving—going home for haying;
We lose militia day by day;
But still a few of us are staying."

Grandfather wrote, "Last night I gave
My blanket to a soldier who
Was wrapped in rags; Phoebe, my dear,
The nights are cold. I dream of you."

Grandfather wrote, “That grand old man
Who bears us up seems not to tire;
I speak of General Washington,
Who last night shared with us his fire.”

Grandfather dipped his quill and wrote,
Sanded and sealed his letter; sent it
Off with a splash of sealing wax,
Thinking of her for whom he meant it,

Nor dreamed that soldiers hungering here
Would feed a nation’s new desire,
And men unborn would warm themselves
At that same small, fierce-flickering fire.

Focus Questions What would the United States be like if there were no pioneers? What is it like to travel across the country in a wagon?

GOING WEST

from *Children of the Wild West*
by Russell Freedman

It was a typical wagon train of the 1840s. The swaying wagons, plodding animals, and walking people stretched out along the trail for almost a mile.

Near the end of the train, a boy holding a hickory stick moved slowly through the dust. He used the stick to poke and prod the cows that trudged beside him, mooing and complaining.

"Get along!" he shouted. "Hey! Hey! Get along!"

Dust floated in the air. It clogged the boy's nose, parched his throat, and coated his face. His cheeks were smeared where he had brushed away the big mosquitoes that buzzed about everywhere.

Up ahead, his family's wagon bounced down the trail. He could hear the *crack* of his father's whip above the heads of the oxen that pulled the wagon. The animals coughed and snorted. The chains on their yokes rattled with every step they took.

His mother sat in the front seat of the wagon, holding the baby on her lap. His sisters had gone off with some other girls to hunt for wild herbs along the road.

The family was traveling west along the Oregon Trail in what someday would be the state of Wyoming. They followed the sandy banks of the North Platte River past rocky hills dotted with sagebrush and greasewood. This was Indian country, the land of the Oglala Sioux.

Back in Missouri, their wagon had been a brand-new prairie schooner with red wheels, a blue body, and a fresh white canvas top. Now the top was stained and patched, the paint faded and crusted with mud. The wagon creaked and groaned, but it was still sturdy. On this hot July afternoon, the canvas cover had been rolled back and bunched so that any breezes could blow through the wagon.

The wagon was crammed with the family's possessions—with food, clothing, and furniture; with tools, bedding, kitchenware, and tent supplies. Tied to its side were a plow and a hoe. Hanging from a rope was a sealed pail of milk that bounced steadily as the wagon jolted along. By evening, the milk would be churned into butter.

There were forty wagons in the party, and nearly two hundred men, women, and children. A few of the pioneers rode saddle horses, but most of them walked. The only ones riding inside the wagons were little children with their mothers, and people who were sick or injured. Following the wagons were herds of milk cows and beef cattle, along with extra oxen, mules, and horses.

The pioneers had been up since four that morning, when the sentries started the day by firing their rifles. Hurrying about in the darkness, they had kindled fires, put on kettles of water, milked cows, pulled down tents, loaded wagons, and fixed breakfast. By seven, they were ready to roll. The train captain gave the signal to move out. Slowly the lead wagons rolled forward, and the others fell into line.

At noon they stopped for an hour's rest. The teams of oxen and mules were turned loose from the wagons but were not unyoked. Blankets and buffalo robes were spread out beside the trail. The pioneers ate a cold lunch, relaxed a bit, then rolled down the trail again.

As they moved along, they passed the splintered wreck of an abandoned wagon. Every two or three miles, they saw wooden grave markers where pioneers had been laid to rest beside the trail. As the day wore on, children began to climb aboard the wagons, finding nooks and corners where they could curl up and nap.

Late that afternoon, near a grove of willows, the train captain gave the signal to stop for the night. One after another, the wagons pulled off the trail and began to form a large circle, or corral. The wagons were locked together, front to rear, with chains; the front tongue of one wagon reached under the rear wheels of the next. A gateway was left open to admit the livestock. Then the last wagon was rolled into place, sealing the corral.

Safely inside, the pioneers tended their cattle, pitched tents, and started campfires for the evening meal. Families sat together eating beans, dried buffalo meat, and camp-baked bread from tin plates.

By 8 P.M., sentries had taken their posts around the corral. Children ran past playing tag. Some girls sat in a circle, sharing secrets and laughing. A boy lay sprawled on his belly beside a campfire, studying a tattered copy of the *Emigrants Guide to Oregon and California*. Grown-ups stood in small groups, chatting and planning the day ahead.

Gradually the pioneers drifted off to their tents and wagons, where they huddled under blankets and fell asleep. Even in July, the night was chilly at this high altitude. They had traveled perhaps fifteen miles that day, nearly seven hundred miles since leaving Missouri in May. They still had more than twice that distance to go.

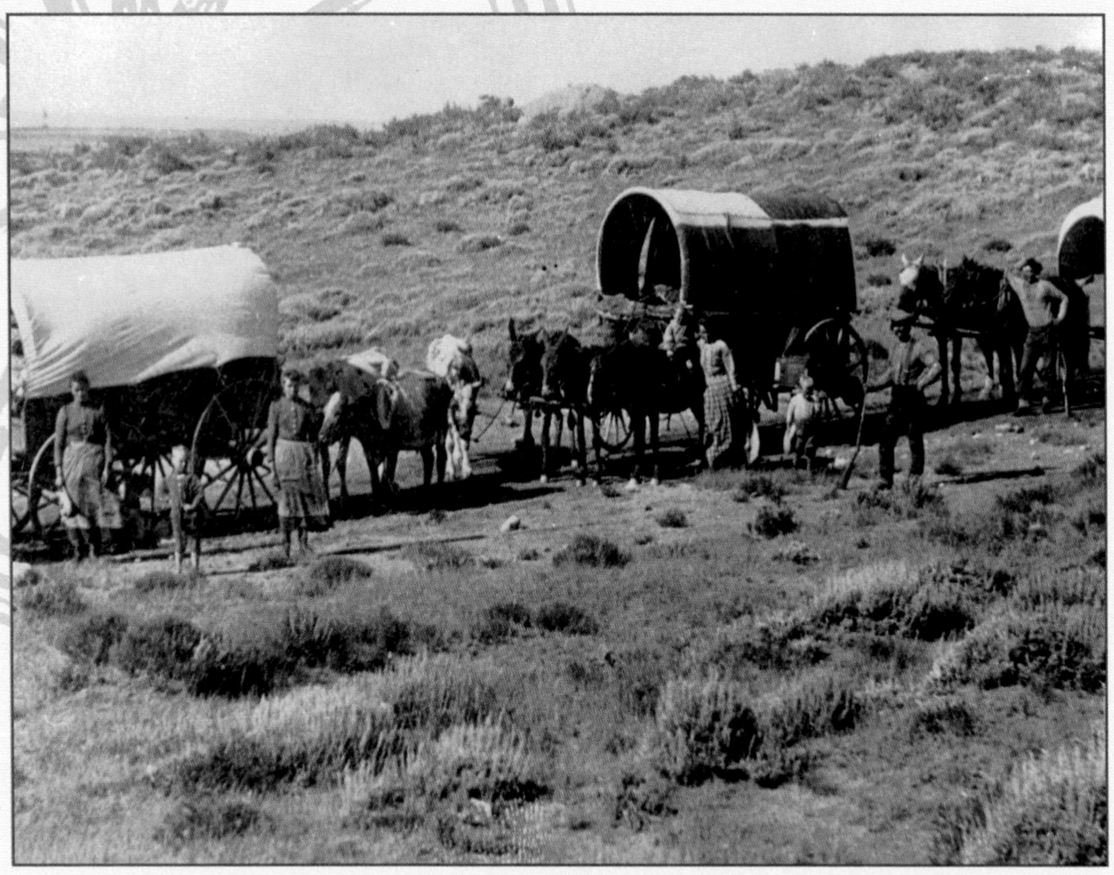

The first pioneers to travel west by wagon train had set out from Missouri in the spring of 1841. Each year after that, emigrants streamed westward in ever-increasing numbers. By 1869, when the first transcontinental railroad was completed, more than 350,000 pioneers had followed the ruts of the Oregon Trail across the continent.

At the beginning, most of them headed for the Pacific Coast. They went west to claim free land in the Oregon and California territories, to strike it rich by mining gold and silver, to settle in a new country where there was plenty of elbowroom and boundless opportunity.

They called themselves "emigrants" because, as they started their journey, they were actually leaving America. During the early 1840s, the United States ended at the banks of the Missouri River. The region that later would be Kansas and Nebraska had been set aside by the United States government as Indian territory. California was still a northern province of Mexico. The vast wilderness of the Oregon country was claimed jointly by the United States and Great Britain. Gradually these western territories would become part of the United States. But when the first emigrants set out, they were entering a foreign land.

GOING WEST

Concept Connections

Linking the Selection

Think about the following questions, and then record your responses in the Response Journal section of your Writer's Notebook.

- Why were animals an important part of the wagon train?
- What steps did pioneers take to protect themselves at night?

Exploring Concept Vocabulary

The concept word for this lesson is ***pioneer.*** If you don't know what this word means, look it up in a dictionary. Answer these questions.

- Why did ***pioneers*** travel West together in wagon trains?
- Why was the expansive territory of the West appealing to ***pioneers?***

Write a sentence that includes the word ***pioneer*** as well as one of the selection vocabulary words.

Expanding the Concept

Compare the pioneers' journey with the Pilgrims' voyage on the Mayflower. Discuss each group's expectations and the challenges they faced. Try to use the word ***pioneer*** in your discussion of the selections. Add new ideas about the theme A Changing America to the Concept/Question Board.

Meet the Author

Russell Freedman grew up in San Francisco. His parents were good friends with several authors. The authors would often come to the Freedman home to discuss the news of the day. These discussions helped Russell learn to develop his own thoughts. Later, as a reporter, Mr. Freedman came across a story about a sixteen-year-old boy who invented the braille typewriter. This story led to his first book, *Teenagers Who Made History*.

Mr. Freedman travels widely to do the research for his books. When he is not writing, he enjoys attending films, concerts, and plays.

Focus Questions How can one person's actions change a country's history? What makes people leave their homes to chase a dream?

The California Gold Rush

West With the Forty-Niners

by Elizabeth Van Steenwyk

It could be said that the story of the gold rush really began on the day in 1839 when John Augustus Sutter first arrived in California. He brought little with him from Switzerland except his dream of creating a farming empire in this sleepy possession of Mexico. Mexico had broken away from Spanish rule in 1821 and claimed California for itself. Millions of acres in California that once belonged to Spain were now owned by Mexican officials. Thousands of cattle grazed and grew fat on these huge land grants. They became California's leading, and only, product. The time and place seemed to be perfect for making Sutter's dream come true.

Sutter applied for Mexican citizenship. In 1840 he received a land grant of nearly 50,000 acres (20,235 hectares), in the Sacramento Valley. He built a fort made of adobe near the south bank of the American River. From this fort, he controlled the surrounding land, which he named New Helvetia. (Helvetia is another name for Switzerland.)

Meanwhile, overland emigrants from the United States began to arrive in the valley. They had followed trails established by fur trappers. After 1841, this route through the midsection of the country became known as the California Trail.

Settlers in this period before the gold rush also came by ship. More than 200 Mormons came ashore at Yerba Buena (soon to be called San Francisco). They had sailed around Cape Horn, the southernmost tip of South America, hoping to escape from the religious persecution they had experienced in the East. Many of them found work at Sutter's Fort.

By January 1848, Sutter's Fort was a lively place with a population of nearly 300. More settlers arrived every day, and a sawmill was urgently needed. Sutter appointed a carpenter named James Wilson Marshall to supervise construction of a sawmill about 45 miles (72.4 km) east of the fort. The location was at a bend in the south fork of the American River in the Coloma Valley.

On the afternoon of January 14, Marshall walked along a ditch that channeled water from the river to the sawmill. Earlier, he thought he had seen some shiny pebbles in the ditch and wanted to examine them more closely. He picked up a pebble about the size of a pea, and his heart began to race. It looked too yellow to be silver but didn't seem bright enough to be gold. He pounded it. It bent but didn't break. Could it be?

Marshall hurried back to some workmen, who were resting at the end of a long day. He announced that he had just found gold. At first, they were unimpressed. Only Henry Bigler, a Mormon from Virginia, thought it might be significant. In his diary, he wrote, "This day some kind of mettle [metal] was found in the tail race that looks like goald [gold]."

The next day, the workmen decided to have a better look at the shiny pebbles. Within minutes, they realized James Marshall knew what he was talking about. He really had discovered gold!

As news of James Marshall's gold discovery at the sawmill reached the Mormons at Sutter's mill, they, too, began to look for gold. They discovered enough to abandon their regular work and begin mining in earnest. This second site became known as Mormon Island.

After Marshall told Sutter of his discovery, Sutter tested the pebbles for himself and became convinced they were gold. He established legal claim to the land, buying it directly from the Indians. Then he asked his workers to say nothing of the discovery for six weeks.

But even Sutter himself could not keep quiet. He wrote to his friend, Mariano Vallejo, less than a week later, saying that he had discovered a "mina de oro."

By the second week of March, news of the discovery reached San Francisco. It traveled by word of mouth until the fifteenth, when the news appeared in print for the first time. However, the story appeared on the last page of the San Francisco *Californian* and was only one paragraph long. Even a second story in the other weekly newspaper, the *California Star*, did little to interest the local folks.

The owner of the *Star* was an enterprising man named Sam Brannan. He decided to put out a special edition and send it to the folks in the eastern United States. With this edition, he hoped to persuade people to move to San Francisco and buy the lots he owned. Then he would make a profit for himself.

San Francisco citizens remained skeptical about the gold discovery. But ranchers near Sutter's Fort began to believe it after they saw the results of the Mormon diggings at a flour mill site. They came and staked out claims for themselves.

Sam Brannan arrived next. After he saw that workers at Sutter's Fort were in a frenzy over the discovery, he bought up future store locations. Those who already had been prospecting displayed their pouches of gold dust as they prepared to dig for more. Sam Brannan realized that something important had happened here. He was determined to be a part of it.

On May 12, Brannan returned to San Francisco, displaying a bottle full of gold dust and shouting, "Gold! Gold! Gold from the American River." Excited people gathered around to ask questions and wonder. But they

didn't wonder long. On May 12, there were six hundred men in the city. Three days later, there were two hundred. The others had gone to the gold field. By the end of the month, the city had nearly closed down. Even the newspapers ceased operation—there was no one left to read them. Soon, men from all over California left other jobs and headed for the hills.

Two thousand copies of Sam Brannan's special edition *Star* reached Missouri by the end of July. Many newspapers reprinted stories from it, but most people dismissed the gold discovery idea. It was unimportant, they said, or too good to be true. So, they ignored it.

But the news wouldn't die. Stories continued to trickle back East in letters by private citizens and reports from government officials. Throughout the summer and fall, newspapers featured more stories about the great wealth to be found in the West. What most Americans needed, however, was official support for these tall tales. Finally, on December 5, 1848, President James K. Polk delivered a message to Congress. In it, he said that the news of California's gold discovery had been verified. Those tales weren't fiction; they were fact!

The gold rush was on!

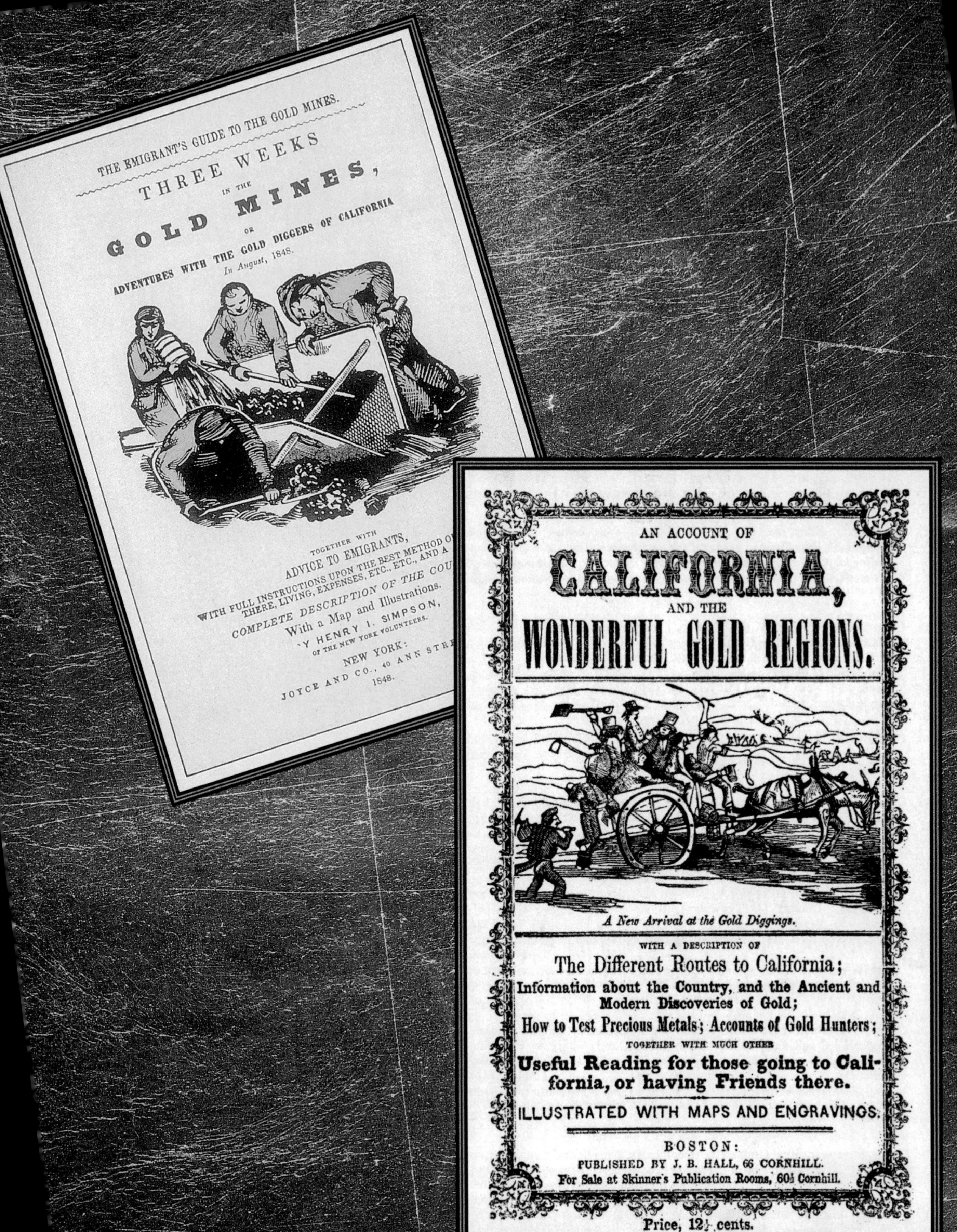
THE EMIGRANT'S GUIDE TO THE GOLD MINES.

THREE WEEKS IN THE GOLD MINES,

OR

ADVENTURES WITH THE GOLD DIGGERS OF CALIFORNIA

In August, 1848.

TOGETHER WITH

ADVICE TO EMIGRANTS,

WITH FULL INSTRUCTIONS UPON THE BEST METHOD O

THERE, LIVING, EXPENSES, ETC., ETC., AND A

COMPLETE DESCRIPTION OF THE COU

With a Map and Illustrations.

'Y HENRY I. SIMPSON,

OF THE NEW YORK VOLUNTEERS.

NEW YORK:

JOYCE AND CO., 40 ANN STRE

1848.

AN ACCOUNT OF

CALIFORNIA,

AND THE

WONDERFUL GOLD REGIONS.

A New Arrival at the Gold Diggings.

WITH A DESCRIPTION OF

The Different Routes to California;

Information about the Country, and the Ancient and Modern Discoveries of Gold;

How to Test Precious Metals; Accounts of Gold Hunters;

TOGETHER WITH MUCH OTHER

Useful Reading for those going to California, or having Friends there.

ILLUSTRATED WITH MAPS AND ENGRAVINGS.

BOSTON:

PUBLISHED BY J. B. HALL, 66 CORNHILL.

For Sale at Skinner's Publication Rooms, 60½ Cornhill.

Price, 12½ cents.

West With the Forty-Niners

Concept Connections

Linking the Selection

Writer's Notebook

Think about the following questions, and then record your responses in the Response Journal section of your Writer's Notebook.

- How did the discovery of gold help California grow?
- When did people in the East believe the news about gold in California?

Exploring Concept Vocabulary

The concept word for this lesson is ***gold rush.*** If you don't know what this word means, look it up in a dictionary. Answer these questions.

- What did Sam Brannan do to hasten the onset of the ***gold rush?***
- What was the first city affected by the ***gold rush?***

Write a sentence that includes the word ***gold rush*** as well as one of the selection vocabulary words.

Expanding the Concept

Discuss why the ***gold rush*** was so important to westward expansion. Add new ideas about the theme A Changing America to the Concept/Question Board.

Meet the Author

Elizabeth Van Steenwyk was born in 1928 in Galesburg, Illinois. She has written many books, both fiction and nonfiction, on such topics as figure skating, horses, American presidents, and California history. Her book *The Best Horse* was made into a motion picture. When asked why she writes for children, Elizabeth Van Steenwyk replies, *"I write for young children because there are so many more possibilities than limitations."*

Focus Questions Why was the railroad important in building America? Who were the people who built this country?

The GOLDEN SPIKE

by Dan Elish

illustrated by Alan Reingold

The one-street town of Promontory, Utah, was buzzing with activity on May 10, 1869. A crowd of one thousand people lined the streets. Reporters from nearly every paper in the country were on hand. A band from Salt Lake City raised its trombones and trumpets, ready to play. Top-level railroad executives milled about, waiting for the ceremony to begin—the ceremony that would mark the completion of the transcontinental railroad.

Work on this great project had begun a full eight years before. The Central Pacific line had started in San Francisco and built east, while the Union Pacific

Railroad had started in Omaha, Nebraska, and built west. Now these two great lines were to finally meet and for the first time in history connect the eastern and western United States.

And now, the crowd—mostly Irish and Chinese laborers who had borne the brunt of the work—pushed close.

"Gentlemen," said Leland Stanford, president of the Central Pacific, "with your assistance we will proceed to lay the last tie, the last rail, and drive the last spike."

With great pomp, Stanford picked up a silver-headed sledge hammer, lifted it over his head, aimed at a gold spike, and swung with all his might...only to miss!

The Irish and Chinese workers howled. Stanford was getting a taste of just how hard it was to build a railroad.

Now Thomas Durant, the vice president of the Union Pacific, took up the sledgehammer, and swung a mighty blow.

He missed as well.

As a worker was hastily summoned to pound in the final spike, a telegrapher sent the signal to the nation: "It's done!"

From New York to San Francisco the country cheered as one.

Back at Promontory, two great locomotives inched forward just close enough so that the two engineers could lean forward and shake hands with each other.

A San Francisco author, Bret Harte, wrote a poem to commemorate the event:

What was it the engines said,
Pilots touching, head to head,
Facing on a single track,
Half a world behind each back?

It was the joining of two worlds: East meets West. Before the railroad, Americans thought of the West as a wilderness populated mostly by Indians. On that day the fabric of American life changed forever. Farmers and ranchers had a new, more efficient way to send their goods to market. Settlers rushed west, and western cities grew up. America finally had the technological means to grow and thrive—and become the America that we know today. For the first time in history, a vast country was made one.

Concept Connections

Linking the Selection

Think about the following questions, and then record your responses in the Response Journal section of your Writer's Notebook.

- What job did the Golden Spike complete?
- Why was the Golden Spike event so important to the country?

Exploring Concept Vocabulary

The concept word for this lesson is ***unity.*** If you don't know what this word means, look it up in a dictionary. Answer these questions.

- How did completion of the railroad encourage a sense of ***unity*** among Americans?
- What part of the ceremony symbolized the new ***unity*** of the East and West?

Write a sentence that includes the word ***unity*** as well as one of the selection vocabulary words.

Expanding the Concept

The selections throughout this unit presented stories of America's growth and some of the people who made it happen. What conclusions can you draw about the changes America has undergone? Try to use the word ***unity*** in your discussion of the unit selections. Add new ideas about the theme A Changing America to the Concept/Question Board.

Meet the Author

Dan Elish When Dan Elish graduated from college, he thought he wanted to write music and lyrics. One day after rereading *Charlie and the Chocolate Factory,* he was surprised to see how much of the book's humor could be enjoyed by adults as well as children. *"This book prompted me to try one of my own,"* he said. He thought it would only take him a few months to write a book for children. Instead it took him a year and a half to write his first book, *The Worldwide Dessert Contest*!

Meet the Illustrator

Alan Reingold began his career as an illustrator after graduating from The Rhode Island School of Design. Since then, he has been commissioned to illustrate cover and interior art for domestic and international magazines. His realistic images can also be seen on movie posters, in national ad campaigns, and on book covers. Alan's first *Time* magazine cover hangs in the permanent collection of The National Portrait Gallery in Washington, D.C. Alan teaches illustration at Parsons School of Design.

Pronunciation Key

a as in **a**t

ā as in l**a**te

â as in c**a**re

ä as in f**a**ther

e as in s**e**t

ē as in m**e**

i as in **i**t

ī as in k**i**te

o as in **o**x

ō as in r**o**se

ô as in b**ou**ght and r**a**w

oi as in c**oi**n

o͝o as in b**oo**k

o͞o as in t**oo**

or as in f**or**m

ou as in **ou**t

u as in **u**p

ū as in **u**se

ûr as in t**ur**n, g**er**m, l**ear**n, f**ir**m, w**or**k

ə as in **a**bout, chick**e**n, penc**i**l, cann**o**n, circ**u**s

ch as in **ch**air

hw as in **wh**ich

ng as in ri**ng**

sh as in **sh**op

th as in **th**in

t̸h as in **th**ere

zh as in trea**s**ure

The mark (ˊ) is placed after a syllable with a heavy accent, as in **chicken** (chikˊ ən).

The mark (ˏ) after a syllable shows a lighter accent, as in **disappear** (disˏ ə pērˊ).

Glossary

A

abandon (ə ban´ dən) *v.* To give up something; to stop working on something.

abolitionist (ab´ ə lish´ ən ist) *n.* A person who wants to end slavery.

abreast (ə brest´) *adv.* Alongside of; next to.

accomplished (ə kom´ plisht) *adj.* Good at something because of practice.

accustomed (ə kus´ təmd) *adj.* Used to or familiar with something.

adjustable (ə jus´ tə bəl) *adj.* Able to be changed in size or position.

adobe (ə dō´ bē) *n.* A brick made out of clay.

advertise (ad´ vûr tīz´) *v.* To promote a product or service through print, radio, or television.

agate (ag´ it) *n.* A playing marble with swirls or stripes of several colors in it.

agent (ā´ jənt) *n.* Someone who represents or stands in for another person.

aggressive (ə gre´ siv) *adj.* Working hard with a lot of energy and drive to get something.

alarmingly (ə lär´ ming lē) *adv.* Filled with a sense of danger.

allotment (ə lot´ mənt) *n.* A share or part of something.

alloy (a´ loi) *n.* A mixture of metals.

ambitious (am bish´ əs) *adj.* Motivated to succeed.

amplify (am´ plə fī´) *v.* To make louder.

amputation (am´ pyōō tā´ shən) *n.* The act of cutting off a body part such as an arm or a leg.

analyze (a´ nəl īz´) *v.* To study something carefully.

anatomy (ə nat´ ə mē) *n.* The structure of the human body.

ancestor (an´ ses tər) *n.* A forefather; a parent, grandparent, great-grandparent, and so on.

anesthesia (an´ əs thē´ zhə) *n.* A loss of feeling brought about by drugs so that surgery can be performed.

Word History

Anesthesia comes from the Greek *an-*, which means "loss of" and *aisthesis*, which means "sensation," from the root *aisthe-*, meaning "to feel, to perceive." It was initially used in 1721 to describe a loss of feeling due to paralysis or nerve damage. The word was first used in its present meaning in 1848 to describe the state induced by new chemicals that medical science was developing for use in operations.

antibiotic (an´ ti bī ot´ ik) *n.* A chemical that kills disease germs.

antibody (an´ ti bo´ dē) *n.* Substance produced by the body that destroys or weakens germs.

antiseptic (an´ tə sep´ tik) *adj.* Free from germs; germ-killing.

appeal (ə pēl´) *v.* To make an earnest request.

appetizing (a´ pə tī´ zing) *adj.* Arousing the desire for food.

Pronunciation Key: **a**t; l**ā**te; c**â**re; f**ä**ther; s**e**t; m**ē**; **i**t; k**ī**te; **o**x; r**ō**se; **ô** in b**ou**ght; c**oi**n; b**o͝o**k; t**o͞o**; f**or**m; **ou**t; **u**p; **ū**se; t**û**rn; **ə** sound in **a**bout, chick**e**n, penc**i**l, cann**o**n, circ**u**s; **ch**air; **hw** in **wh**ich; ri**ng**; **sh**op; **th**in; **t̸h**ere; **zh** in trea**s**ure.

applicant (a´ pli kənt) *n.* A person who tries for a certain job or position.
appointment (ə point´ mənt) *n.* A job or office.
arctic (ärk´ tik) *adj.* Having to do with the region of the North Pole.
arrangement (ə rānj´ mənt) *n.* Plan or agreement.
artifact (är´ tə fakt´) *n.* A handmade object from an earlier time or culture.
artificial (är´ tə fish´ əl) *adj.* Made by humans rather than produced by nature.
asepsis (ā sep´ sis) *n.* The methods used to make sure there are no germs.
assert (ə sûrt´) *v.* To say firmly.

Word History

Assert is a French word that comes from the Latin word *asserere*. It can be traced back to the terms *ad-*, which means "toward," and *serere*, which means "to join."

asthma (az´ mə) *n.* A disease involving coughing and difficulty with breathing.
astronaut (as´ trə nôt´) *n.* A person who travels in space.
astronomer (ə stro´ nə mər) *n.* A person who studies objects outside Earth's atmosphere.
authoritative (ə thor´ i tā´ tiv) *adj.* Bossy; masterful.
awl (ôl) *n.* A tool with a sharp point used for making small holes in wood, leather, or tin.

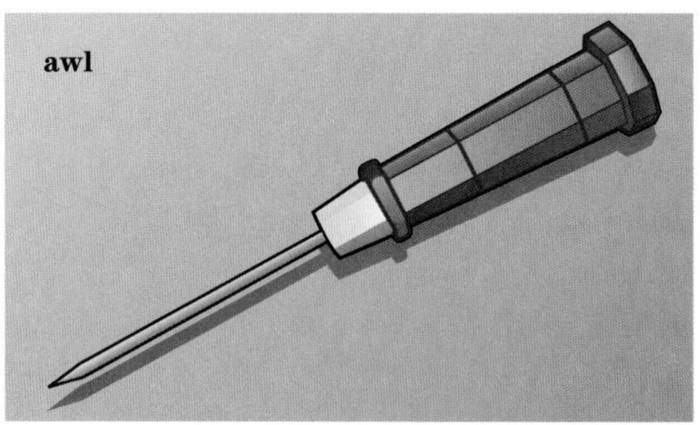

B

bacteria (bak tēr´ ē ə) *n. pl., sing.* **bacterium.** Disease germs; one-celled organisms that can be seen only with a microscope.
bank (bangk) *v.* To tilt an aircraft to one side while flying it.
bargaining (bär´ gə ning) *n.* Discussing terms; talking or arguing in order to agree upon something.
barge (bärj) *v.* To rudely push oneself into a place.
befall (bi fôl´) *v.* To happen to.
benefit (be´ nə fit´) *n.* Something given to workers in addition to pay, such as insurance, paid vacations, or sick days.
bioethics (bī´ ō e´ thiks) *n.* The study of ethics in biological research.
blood pressure (blud´ presh´ ər) *n.* The amount of force with which blood presses against the insides of the body's blood vessels.
blubber (blub´ ər) *n.* Whale fat.

bonito (bə nē′ tō) *n.* A fish similar to the tuna, found in the Atlantic Ocean.

boom (bo͞om) *v.* To grow suddenly and rapidly.

boundless (bound′ ləs) *adj.* Having no limits.

bow (bou) *n.* The curved front part of a boat.

brace (brās) *n.* A pair; a couple.

brainstorm (brān′ storm) *v.* To come up with many ideas quickly.

brandish (bran′ dish) *v.* To shake; to wave threateningly.

brazier (brā′ zhər) *n.* A metal frame for holding fire.

brush (brush) *n.* A growth of shrubs, small trees, and bushes.

brutality (bro͞o tal′ i tē) *n.* Cruelty; extremely harsh treatment.

buzz (buz) *v.* A low humming sound.

C

calculate (kal′ kyə lāt′) *v.* To measure; to figure out.

capacity (kə pas′ i tē) *n.* The ability.

capsize (kap′ sīz) *v.* To overturn in the water, as a boat.

captivity (kap ti′ və tē) *n.* Being held and confined.

card (kärd) *n.* An instrument used for combing cotton or wool fibers.

caribou (kar′ ə bo͞o′) *n.* A large deer, related to the reindeer.

cartilage (kär′ tl ij) *n.* Firm yet flexible tissue that is inside the human body.

catgut (kat′ gut) *n.* A strong thread made of dried animals' intestines, used in surgery to make stitches.

cell (sel) *n.* A small unit of organization.

Word Derivations

Below are some words derived from the word *cell.*

cellular	cellulose	celluloid
unicellular	cellulite	cell phone
fuel cell	single-celled	multicellular

century (sen′ chə rē) *n.* 100 years.

chafing (chā′ fing) *n.* A rubbing.

chartreuse (shär tro͞oz′) *n.* A yellowish-green color.

chattel (chat′ l) *n.* Anything movable that is owned by someone.

chemist (kem′ ist) *n.* A scientist who studies what substances are made of.

chorus (kōr′ əs) *n.* Part of a song that is repeated after each verse.

citizen (si′ tə zən) *n.* A person born in or made a member of a country.

Pronunciation Key: **a**t; l**ā**te; c**â**re; f**ä**ther; s**e**t; m**ē**; **i**t; k**ī**te; **o**x; r**ō**se; **ô** in b**ough**t; c**oi**n; b**o͝o**k; t**o͞o**; f**or**m; **ou**t; **u**p; **ū**se; t**û**rn; **ə** sound in **a**bout, chick**e**n, penc**i**l, cann**o**n, circ**u**s; **ch**air; **hw** in **wh**ich; ri**ng**; **sh**op; **th**in; **th**ere; **zh** in trea**s**ure.

civilization (siv′ ə lə zā′ shən) *n.* A culture, society, or group of human beings who have developed art, education, agriculture, trade, science, government, and so on.

claim (klām) *v.* A section of land declared as one's own.

clog (klôg) *v.* To block or fill up.

colleague (kol′ ēg) *n.* A member of the same profession as another person.

colonist (kol′ ə nist) *n.* A person who is a member of a settlement formed by people who have come to a new land.

colony (kol′ ə nē) *n.* A settlement formed by people who have come to a new land.

Word Derivations

Below are some words derived from the word *colony.*

colonial	colonies	colonize
colonially	colonist	colonized
colonialism	colonization	colonizing

comfortable (kəmpf′ tər bəl) *adj.* Providing physical ease and well-being.

commotion (kə mō′ shən) *n.* Noisy disturbance.

community (kə mū′ ni tē) *n.* All the people living in the same area; the area surrounding the place where you live.

complicated (kôm′ plə kā′ təd) *adj.* Hard to understand.

complication (kom′ pli kā′ shən) *n.* Another disease that makes a person's original disease get worse.

compound (kom′ pound) *n.* A closed-in area containing homes or other buildings.

compromise (kom′ prə mīz′) *n.* A settlement made by both sides giving up a little.

Word History

The French word **compromise** can be traced back to the Latin word *compromittere.* In Latin, *com-* means "with" or "together," while *promittere* means "to promise."

computer-generated (kəm pū′ tər je′ nə rā′ təd) *adj.* Made or drawn on a computer.

concentrated (kon′ sən trā′ tid) *adj.* Packed closely together.

concentration camp (kôn′ sən trā′ shən kamp) *n.* A fenced and guarded camp for keeping prisoners of war, refugees, and political prisoners.

conclusive (kən klo͞o′ siv) *adj.* Answering a question completely.

condemnation (kon′ dem nā′ shən) *n.* A judgment of guilty.

condominium (kôn′ də mi′ nē əm) *n.* An apartment building owned by the person or persons living in it.

confide (kən fīd′) *v.* To tell secrets to; to discuss private thoughts.

confidence (kon′ fi dəns) *n.* A belief in one's own ability.

confirm (kən fûrm′) *v.* To make sure.

connect (kə nekt′) *v.* To hook up with; to introduce someone to.

Word Derivations

Below are some words derived from the word *connect.*

connection	connective	connected
disconnect	reconnect	interconnect
connectable	connectability	connector

conscious (kon′ shəs) *adj.* Aware of; noticing the needs of.
consent (kən sent′) 1. *n.* Agreement; permission. 2. *v.* To agree.
console (kən sōl′) *v.* To comfort.
constellation (kon′ stə lā′ shən) *n.* A group of fixed stars having a name.

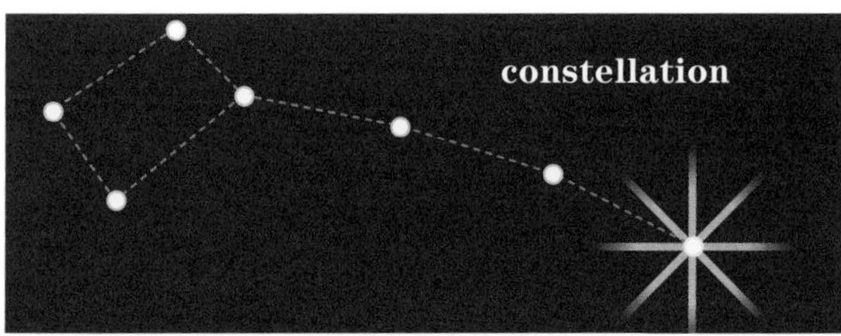

consternation (kon′ stər nā′ shən) *n.* Dismay; dread; anxiety.

Word History

Consternation came into usage in the English language around 1611. It comes from the Latin terms *consternare*, which means "to throw into confusion," and *-ation*, which means "act" or "process."

consult (kən sult′) *v.* To ask advice.
consumptive (kən sump′ tiv) *adj.* Sick with the disease tuberculosis, a lung infection.
contaminated (kən tam′ ə nā′ təd) *adj.* Unclean; mixed with something dirty.
Continental Army (kon′ tən en′ təl är′ mē) *n.* American Army that fought the British during the Revolutionary War.
continue (kən tin′ ū) *v.* To keep going; to last.
contract (kon′ trakt) *n.* A formal, written agreement.
controversial (kôn′ trə vûr′ shəl) *adj.* Subject to debate or disagreement.
conversation (kôn′ vər sā′ shən) *n.* Oral exchange of observations, opinions, or ideas.
conveyance (kən vā′ əns) *n.* The act of taking something from one place to another.
convince (kən vins′) *v.* To cause one to believe something.
coronary artery (kor′ ə ner ē är′ tə rē) *n.* An artery in the heart that supplies blood to the parts of the heart.
corps (kor) *n.* A group formed for a specific purpose.
county seat (koun′ tē sēt′) *n.* The town in which the government of a county is housed.
cradle (krā′ dl) *v.* To hold gently in one's arms.
crevasse (krə vas′) *n.* A deep crack in a glacier or in the Earth's surface.
crimson (krim′ zən) *adj.* Deep red in color.
crouch (krouch) *v.* To stoop or bend low, usually by bending the legs.
crude (kro͞od) *adj.* Rough; simple.
culturally (kul′ chər ə lē) *adv.* Having to do with the civilization of a given race or nation.
cunning (ku′ ning) *adj.* Tricky.
curandera (ko͞o′ rän de′ rä) *n.* A woman healer who uses folk medicine such as herbs and other plants to cure illness.

Pronunciation Key: **a**t; l**ā**te; c**â**re; f**ä**ther; s**e**t; m**ē**; **i**t; k**ī**te; **o**x; r**ō**se; **ô** in b**ou**ght; c**oi**n; b**o͝o**k; t**o͞o**; f**or**m; **ou**t; **u**p; **ū**se; t**û**rn; **ə** sound in **a**bout, chick**e**n, penc**i**l, cann**o**n, circ**u**s; **ch**air; **hw** in **wh**ich; ri**ng**; **sh**op; **th**in; **th**ere; **zh** in trea**s**ure.

customer (kus´ tə mûr) *n.* Person who buys something.

D

daub (dôb) *v.* To cover or coat by smearing something on.
defiant (di fī´ ənt) *adj.* Standing up against authority; resisting.
delectable (di lek´ tə bəl) *adj.* Very tasty.
demanding (di mand´ ing) *adj.* Requiring a lot of time or energy.
demonstrate (de´ mən strāt´) *v.* To show or prove.
deposit (di pôs´ ət) *n.* Money or valuable things in a bank or safe place.
desert (di zûrt´) *v.* To abandon.
design (di zīn´) *n.* A drawing or outline made to serve as a guide or pattern.
desolately (des´ ə lit lē) *adv.* In a hopeless or lonely way.
desperately (des´ pər it lē) *adv.* Hopelessly.
destination (des´ tə nā´ shən) *n.* The place where a journey ends.
determined (di tûr´ mənd) *adj.* Having a strong desire to complete something.
digestion (dī jes´ chən) *n.* The breakdown and absorption of food by the body.
din (din) *n.* A lot of noise; clamor; uproar; racket.
discard (dis kärd´) *v.* To throw away.
discourage (dis kûr´ ij) *v.* To keep from doing something.
disinfect (dis´ in fekt´) *v.* To cleanse of infection; to make free of germs.
dispel (di spel´) *v.* To drive away; to banish.

Word History

The word **dispel** comes from the Latin word *dispellare* and can be broken down into *dis-*, which means "apart," and *pellare*, which means "to drive." The prefix *dis-* can also mean "the opposite of," but not in this case.

display (di splā´) *v.* To show.
distinctly (di´ stin(k)t´ lē) *adv.* Very clearly.
distress (di stres´) *n.* Great pain, sorrow, or anxiety.
diverse (di vûrs´) *adj.* Different; varied.
document (do´ kyə ment´) *v.* To observe and record for future study.
don (don) *v.* To put on.
douse (dous) *v.* To splash.
dressing (dres´ ing) *n.* The cloth or other material used to cover a wound.
dubiously (do͞o´ bē əs lē) *adv.* Doubtfully; in an unsure way.
durable (do͝or´ ə bəl) *adj.* Able to last a long time; able to hold up to rough handling.

E

ear mite (ēr mīt) *n.* A small bug that lives in the ears of animals.

effective (i fek´ tiv) *adj.* Able to get results.

emigrant (e´ mi grənt) *n.* Someone who leaves his or her homeland to settle in a new one.

eminent (em´ ə nənt) *adj.* Celebrated; well-known; grand.

empire (em´ pīr) *n.* A group of countries, lands, or peoples under one government or ruler.

enchain (en chān´) *v.* To tie down or hold back.

encounter (in koun´ tər) *n.* Casual or unplanned meeting.

energetic (e´ nûr je´ tik) *adj.* Having energy; spirited.

enlightened (in lī´ tənd) *adj.* Free from ignorance.

entrepreneur (än´ trə prə nûr´) *n.* Someone who starts a business and then manages it.

enviously (en´ vē əs lē) *adv.* With jealousy.

epidemic (ep´ i dem´ ik) *n.* An outbreak of disease that spreads quickly to many people.

equipment (i kwip´ mənt) *n.* Instruments or tools.

erupt (i rupt´) *v.* To break out suddenly and with great force.

escort (i skort´) *v.* To go with and protect.

establish (i stab´ lish) *v.* To start, create, or found.

etch (ech) *v.* To make a pattern or design on a hard surface.

ethnically (eth´ nik lē) *adv.* Having to do with the national origins of a people.

excel (ik sel´) *v.* To do better than others.

executive (ig ze´ kū tiv) *n.* A person who directs or manages.

exhaust (ig zôst´) *v.* To tire out.

expectancy (ik spek´ tən sē) *n.* A state of waiting for something to happen. **life expectancy:** The number of years the average person will live.

expedition (ek´ spi dish´ ən) *n.* A journey made to accomplish something.

express (iks pres´) *n.* A rapid system of delivering goods or mail.

extent (ik stent´) *n.* The amount or limit.

external (ek stûr´ nl) *adj.* Outside; outward.

F

fabric (fab´ rik) *n.* An underlying structure or foundation.

facilities (fə sil´ i tēz) *n. pl.* Things designed to make a task easier or more convenient.

failure (fāl´ yər) *n.* Something that does not turn out well; something that is not a success.

faint (fānt) *adj.* Dim; weak; not clear.

falter (fôl´ tər) *v.* To be tongue-tied; to talk awkwardly.

Pronunciation Key: **a**t; l**ā**te; c**â**re; f**ä**ther; s**e**t; m**ē**; **i**t; k**ī**te; **o**x; r**ō**se; **ô** in b**ou**ght; c**oi**n; b**o͝o**k; t**o͞o**; f**or**m; **ou**t; **u**p; **ū**se; t**û**rn; **ə** sound in **a**bout, chick**e**n, penc**i**l, cann**o**n, circ**u**s; **ch**air; **hw** in **wh**ich; ri**ng**; **sh**op; **th**in; **th**ere; **zh** in trea**s**ure.

farmer's market (fär′ mərz mär′ kət) *n.* A place where people come to buy and sell fruits and vegetables for a short period of time.

fascinate (fa′ sən āt′) *v.* To completely and fully interest someone.

fatal (fāt′ l) *adj.* Deadly; causing death.

fee (fē) *n.* Money requested or paid for some service or right.

feebly (fē′ blē) *adv.* Weakly.

feisty (fī′ stē) *adj.* Full of energy.

ferry (fer′ ē) *v.* To carry across a river or a bay. —*n.* A boat that carries passengers, vehicles, or goods across a river or a bay; a ferryboat.

fiber (fī′ bər) *n.* Material or cloth.

Word Derivations

Below are some words derived from the word *fiber.*

fiberboard	fiberglass	fiber optics
fiberfill	fiberize	fibers
fibered	fiber-optic	fiberscope

fibrous (fī′ brəs) *adj.* Containing fibers, or long, narrow strips or cords.

fierce (fērs′) *adj.* Wild or threatening in appearance.

flank (flangk) *n.* The side.

forceps (for′ səps) *n.* Small pliers used in surgery.

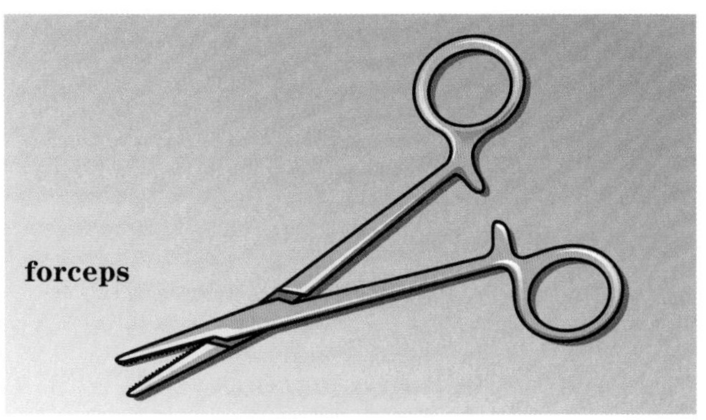
forceps

fortunate (for′ chə nət) *adj.* Lucky.

fowling piece (fou′ ling pēs′) *n.* A shotgun used for shooting wild birds.

fragrance (frā′ grəns) *n.* A sweet smell that is pleasing.

freight (frāt) *n.* Cargo; goods.

frenzy (fren′ zē) *n.* Wild excitement.

frustrate (frəs′ trāt) *v.* To make someone feel upset, helpless, or powerless in a situation.

fugitive (fū′ jə tiv) *n.* Person who runs away.

fund (fund) 1. *v.* To pay for. 2. *n.* Money collected and saved for a special purpose.

G

game (gām) *n.* Wild animals that are hunted.

game reserve (gām′ ri zûrv′) *n.* An area of land set aside for wild animals to live in without being hunted.

gaudy (gô′ dē) *adj.* Showy or flashy in a crude way.

generation (jen′ ə rā′ shən) *n.* 1. A group of people who are all about the same age. 2. The process of bringing into existence.

gesture (jes′ chər) *n.* A body movement that shows meaning.
gibbon (gi′ bən) *n.* A tailless ape from southeastern Asia.
glacier (glā′ shər) *n.* A large, slow-moving mass of ice.
glassy (glas′ ē) *n.* A glass marble with colored swirls.
gore (gor) *v.* To wound using a horn or tusk.
gorge (gorj) *n.* A steep, narrow opening between mountains; a small canyon.

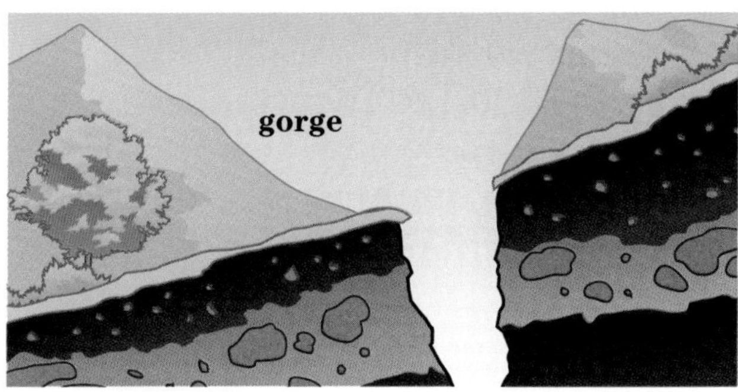

gossamer (gos′ ə mər) *adj.* Light; thin; flimsy.
greasewood (grēs′ wo͝od′) *n.* A shrub that grows in the western United States.
grindstone (grīnd′ stōn′) *n.* A round, flat stone used to sharpen tools.
grippe (grip) *n.* Influenza; the flu.
guild (gild) *n.* During the Middle Ages, a group of merchants or crafters.

H

haggard (hag′ ərd) *adj.* Having a worn look because of being very tired, afraid, or hungry.
hammer out (ham′ ər out) *v.* To discuss until an agreement is reached.
hardship (härd′ ship) *n.* Trouble; misfortune.
harness dressing (här′ nəs dres′ ing) *n.* A mixture used to polish leather.
harvest (här′ vist) 1. *n.* The act or process of gathering a crop. 2. *v.* To gather a crop.
haughty (hô′ tē) *adj.* Full of pride.

Word History

Haughty comes from the French word *haut*, which is derived from the Latin word *altus*. *Altus* means "high." **Haughty** came into the English language during the 15th century.

headland (hed′ lənd) *n.* A high piece of land that sticks out into a large body of water.
heap (hēp) *n.* A pile; a mound.
hearthstone (härth′ stōn) *n.* The stone floor of a fireplace.
heave (hēv) *n.* An upward movement.
hemorrhage (hem′ ər ij) *n.* Heavy bleeding.
herb medicine (ûrb′ me′ də sən) *n.* Plant with healing properties used to treat diseases or injuries.
heritage (hâr′ ə tij) *n.* Something handed down to a person from his or her ancestors.
hibernate (hī′ bər nāt′) *v.* To pass the winter in a long sleep.
highborn (hī′ born) *adj.* Born to the noble class.
highwayman (hī′ wā′ mən) *n.* A robber who steals from travelers on a road.
horizon (hə rī′ zən) *n.* The distant line where the ocean and the sky seem to meet.
hose (hōz) *n.* Stockings.

Pronunciation Key: **a**t; l**ā**te; c**â**re; f**ä**ther; s**e**t; m**ē**; **i**t; k**ī**te; **o**x; r**ō**se; **ô** in b**ou**ght; c**oi**n; b**o͝o**k; t**o͞o**; f**or**m; **ou**t; **u**p; **ū**se; t**û**rn; **ə** sound in **a**bout, chick**e**n, penc**i**l, cann**o**n, circ**u**s; **ch**air; **hw** in **wh**ich; ri**ng**; **sh**op; **th**in; **th**ere; **zh** in trea**s**ure.

house (houz) *v.* To provide shelter for.
hullabaloo (hə lə bə lo͞o´) *n.* An uproar.
hurtle (hûrtl) *v.* To move rapidly and with great force.
hygiene (hī´ jēn) *n.* Keeping oneself clean in order to stay healthy.

I

ice cap (īs´ kap) *n.* A thick layer of ice covering an area.
idly (īd´ lē) *adv.* Lazily.
imagine (i ma´ jən) *v.* To form a mental image of.
immaculate (i mak´ yə lit) *adj.* Extremely clean; spotless.
immune (i mūn´) *adj.* Free from; not able to get a certain disease.
impair (im pâr´) *v.* To weaken; to injure.
impracticable (im prak´ ti kə bəl) *adj.* Not possible with the methods or equipment available.
impression (im presh´ ən) *n.* An idea; a picture in the mind.
improvement (im proov´ mənt) *n.* Way of making something better.
improvise (im´ prə vīz´) *v.* To make changes in a song as it is being sung.
incision (in sizh´ ən) *n.* A cut made into the body during surgery.
indentured servant (in den´ chərd sûr vənt) *n.* A person who came to America under a contract to work for someone else for a period of time.
independence (in´ də pen´ dən(t)s) *n.* Freedom.
indescribably (in´ di skrī´ bə blē) *adv.* Unusually; extraordinarily.
indignantly (in dig´ nənt lē) *adv.* With anger; with an insulted feeling.
induct (in dukt´) *v.* To admit as a member.
in earnest (in ûr´ nəst) *adv.* Seriously.
ineffectively (in´ i fek´ tiv lē) *adv.* Uselessly; in vain.
infect (in fekt´) *v.* To introduce disease germs.

Word Derivations

Below are some words derived from the word *infect.*

disinfect	disinfectant	infected
infection	reinfect	infectious
disinfected	disinfection	infectiously

infirm (in fûrm´) *adj.* Weak; sickly.
infirmary (in fûr´ mə rē) *n.* A place where sick people are treated.
infomercial (in´ fō´ mər´ shəl) *n.* Extra-long television commercials.
infrasonic (in´ frə sô´ nik) *adj.* Having a sound of such low frequency that people cannot hear it.
inherit (in her´ it) *v.* To receive another's property after his or her death.
insulation (in´ sə lā´ shən) *n.* A material that keeps heat from being lost.
intern (in´ tûrn) *n.* A doctor who is being trained at a hospital.

internal (in tûr´ nl) *adj.* Inside; inner.
interracial (in´ tər rā´ shəl) *adj.* Including people of different races.
interrupt (in´ tə rupt´) *v.* To stop for a time; to break off.
intimidate (in tim´ i dāt´) *v.* To threaten; to frighten.
inundate (in´ ən dāt´) *v.* To swamp; to flood; to overwhelm.
investment (in vest´ mənt) *n.* The use of money to gain profit; The money spent to start or improve a business or savings program.
irrigate (ir´ i gāt) *v.* To wash with water or another liquid.

J

jolt (jōlt) *v.* To move in a sudden, rough way.

K

kidnap (kid´ nap) *v.* To seize and carry off a person.
kindle (kin´ dəl) *v.* To begin burning or cause to burn.
kindling (kind´ ling) *n.* Small pieces of wood or scraps used for starting a fire.

L

labor (lā´ bər) *n.* The beginning of the process of birth.
laborer (lā´ bər´ ər) *n.* One who works for pay.
land grant (land´ grant´) *n.* A gift of land from the government to a person.
lanyard (lan´ yərd) *n.* A woven friendship bracelet.
lapse (laps) *v.* To fall; to sink.

Word History

The word **lapse** came into English language usage around 1526. It comes from the Latin word *labi*, which means "to slip."

league (lēg) *n.* A distance of roughly three miles.
limited (li´ mə təd) *adj.* Having boundaries or limits.
listlessly (list´ ləs lē) *adv.* Without energy or interest.
livestock (līv´ stôk´) *n.* Farm animals, such as cattle, horses, or sheep.
lull (lul) 1. *v.* To put to sleep by soothing. 2. *n.* A short period of calm or quiet.
luxurious (lug´ zhoo̅r´ ē əs) *adj.* Giving much comfort and joy.

M

maintenance (mānt´ nəns) *n.* The work of keeping something in good condition.
mandolin (man´ də lin´) *n.* A stringed musical instrument.

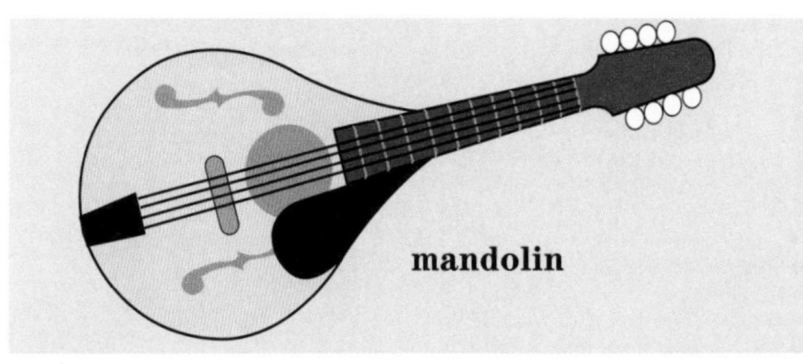

mandolin

maneuver (mə noo̅´ vər) *v.* To change the position of something; to move in a planned way.
manipulate (mə nip´ yə lāt´) *v.* To handle or control.

Pronunciation Key: **a**t; l**ā**te; c**â**re; f**ä**ther; s**e**t; m**ē**; **i**t; k**ī**te; **o**x; r**ō**se; **ô** in b**ou**ght; c**oi**n; b**o͝o**k; t**o͞o**; f**or**m; **ou**t; **u**p; **ū**se; t**û**rn; **ə** sound in **a**bout, chick**e**n, penc**i**l, cann**o**n, circ**u**s; **ch**air; **hw** in **wh**ich; ri**ng**; **sh**op; **th**in; **th**ere; **zh** in trea**s**ure.

manufacturing (man´ yə fak´ chə ring) *adj.* Making and selling products.

manuscript (man´ū skript) *n.* A handwritten document.

market (mär´ kit) *n.* A demand for something that is for sale.

Word Derivations

Below are some words derived from the word *market.*

market order	market share	marketer
market price	marketability	marketing
market research	marketable	marketplace
market researcher	marketed	unmarketable

marketing (mär´ ki ting) *n.* All the activities that lead to selling a product, including advertising, packaging, and selling.

mast (mast) *n.* A pole supporting a ship's sails.

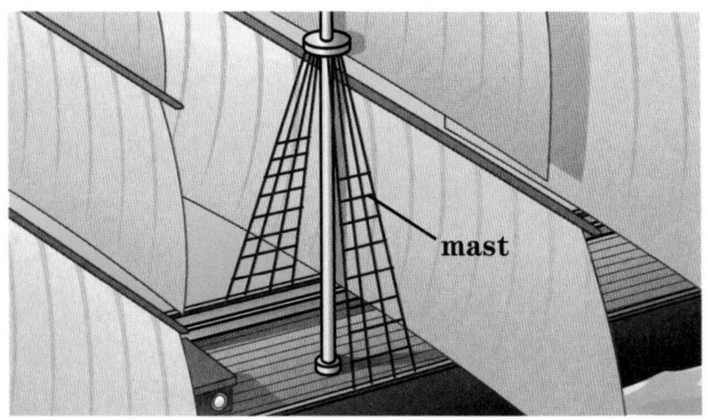

masterpiece (mas´ tər pēs´) *n.* A great work of art.

meditation (me´ də tā´ shən) *n.* A practice of quiet thinking.

melody (me´ lə dē) *n.* Series of musical tones; part of a song.

menacing (men´ is ing) *adj.* Dangerous; threatening.

merchandise (mûr´ chən dīz´) *n.* Things for sale; goods.

mesa (mā´ sə) *n.* High, flat land, like a plateau but smaller.

Word History

The Latin word *mensa*, meaning "table," passed into Spanish as the word **mesa.** In the 15th century, the word came to be used for the landform. This usage passed into English as the American desert Southwest was being explored and settled in the mid-19th century.

meticulously (mə tik´ yə ləs lē) *adv.* In an extremely careful and precise way.

microbe (mī´ krōb) *n.* An organism that is too small to be seen without a microscope.

middlings (mid´ lingz) *n.* A wheat by-product used in animal feed.

migrate (mī´ grāt´) *v.* To move from one place to another.

mild mannered (mī(ə)ld´ ma´ nûrd) *adj.* Gentle in nature.

milk wagon (milk´ wa´ gən) *n.* A horse-drawn wagon used to deliver milk very early in the morning.

mill (mil) *v.* To move around in a confused way.

misery (mi´ zə rē) *n.* Suffering.

mite (mīt) *adj.* A little bit.

mock (mok) *adj.* Fake.

Word Derivations

Below are some words derived from the word *mock.*

mock turtle soup	mockery	mockingbird
mocked	mock-heroic	mockingly
mocker	mocking	mock-up

monastery (mo′ nə stâr′ ē) *n.* A house for monks.
moneys (mun′ ēz) *n. pl.* Funds; a plural of *money.*
monk (mungk) *n.* A man who belongs to a religious order.
mural (myo͞or′ əl) *n.* A large painting, often on a wall.
musket (mus′ kit) *n.* An old-fashioned kind of gun, used before the modern rifle.
muslin (muz′ lin) *n.* A kind of cotton cloth.
muster (mus′ tər) *v.* To gather.
mystified (mis′ tə fīd′) *adj.* Bewildered; confused.

N

native (nā′ tiv) *adj.* Belonging to by birth.
nauseate (nô′ zē āt′) *v.* To make sick to the stomach.
net (net) *v.* To earn or get as a profit.
nomadic (nō mad′ ik) *adj.* Wandering from place to place.

O

obligation (ô′ blə gā′ shən) *n.* Responsibility; something a person is supposed to do.
obnoxious (əb nok′ shəs) *adj.* Annoying or offensive.

Word History

The word **obnoxious** comes from the Latin word *obnoxius* and can be broken down into the following parts: *ob-*, which means "in the way of" or "exposed to," and *noxa*, which means "harm." "Exposed to something harmful" is actually an archaic, or out-of-date, definition of **obnoxious.**

odds (odz) *n.* The chances that something will or will not happen.
omen (ō′ mən) *n.* A sign of a future event.
ominous (om′ ə nəs) *adj.* Unfavorable; threatening misfortune.
ongoing (on′ gō′ ing) *adj.* Continuing, steady.
organic (or gan′ ik) *adj.* Grown without chemicals; natural.
ornery (or′ nə rē) *adj.* Disagreeable.
overawed (ō′ vər ôd′) *adj.* Extremely respectful or fearful.
overlapping (ō′ vər la′ ping) *n.* Way of lying on top of something and partly extending over it.

P

P.S. Public School.
pachyderm (pak′ i dûrm′) *n.* Any large, thick-skinned, hoofed animal, such as the elephant.

Word History

Pachyderm comes from the combination of the Greek roots *pachys*, meaning "thick," and *derma*, meaning "skin." The first usages in English are in the early 19th century.

page (pāj) *v.* To call for someone over a loudspeaker.

Pronunciation Key: **a**t; l**ā**te; c**â**re; f**ä**ther; s**e**t; m**ē**; **i**t; k**ī**te; **o**x; r**ō**se; **ô** in b**ou**ght; c**oi**n; b**o͝o**k; t**o͞o**; f**or**m; **ou**t; **u**p; **ū**se; t**û**rn; **ə** sound in **a**bout, chick**e**n, penc**i**l, cann**o**n, circ**u**s; **ch**air; **hw** in **wh**ich; ri**ng**; **sh**op; **th**in; **th**ere; **zh** in trea**s**ure.

parch (pärch) *v.* To make hot and thirsty.

parchment (pärch′ mənt) *n.* Specially prepared animal skin, usually from sheep or goats, made into a tough translucent paper for writing.

passage (pas′ ij) *n.* A narrow corridor; a hallway.

pattern (pa′ tûrn) *n.* An arrangement of markings.

peculiar (pi kūl′ yər) *adj.* Strange; unusual.

pemmican (pem′ i kən) *n.* A mixture of powdered dried meat, dried berries, and fat.

perception (pər sep′ shən) *n.* The ability to experience things through one's senses.

persecution (pûr′ si kū′ shən) *n.* The mistreatment or harassment of a person or group of people.

persuade (pər swād′) *v.* To talk into believing.

pesky (pes′ kē) *adj.* Annoying.

physician (fə zi′ shən) *n.* Doctor.

physicist (fi′ zə sist) *n.* A person who studies matter and energy and how the two work together.

pilgrim (pil′ grim) *n.* 1. A person who travels to a holy place. 2. **Pilgrim:** A member of a religious group that came to America to find freedom of religion.

Word History

The combination of *per*, meaning "through" and *ager*, meaning "field," led to the Latin word *peregrinus*, meaning "one who is on a journey." The word passed into French as *pelegrin* and from there into English as *pelegrim*. With time the word transformed into the present-day **pilgrim.**

pitch (pich) *n.* A dark, sticky substance used to make things waterproof. —*v.* To lurch or fall suddenly.

plague (plāg) *n.* Any widespread disease; a disease that is spread in an epidemic.

plodding (plod′ ing) *adj.* Moving in a slow, heavy way.

plunge (plunj) *v.* To fall suddenly.

pneumonia (no͞o mōn′ yə) *n.* A disease of the lungs.

poacher (pō′ chər) *n.* A person who catches animals in a place where hunting is against the law.

pomp (pomp) *n.* A magnificent display or ceremony.

poppet (pop′ it) *n. British dialect.* A nickname showing affection, meaning "child."

popular (pop′ yə lər) *adj.* Well-liked by many.

porcelain (por′ sə lin) *n.* A fine, delicate china.

port (port) *n.* A place or town where ships come to load or unload.

portion (por′ shən) *v.* To share among; to distribute.

potential (pə ten′ shəl) *adj.* Possible.

poultice (pōl′ tis) *n.* A wad of something soft and moist, placed over a wound to heal it.

practitioner (prak ti´ shə nər) *n.* One who performs a professional service.
prairie schooner (prer´ ē sko͞o´ nər) *n.* A type of covered wagon used by pioneers.

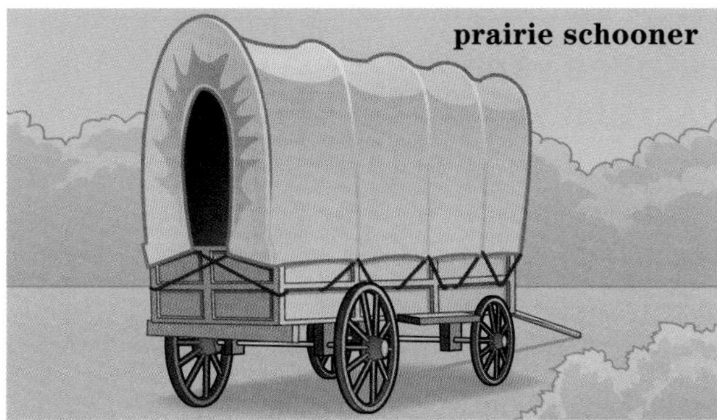

precision (pri sizh´ ən) *n.* Exactness; accuracy with details.
pretense (prē´ tens) *n.* A false show or appearance for the purpose of deceiving others.
prevailing (pri vā´ ling) *adj.* The most frequent; occurring most often.
privileged (priv´ lijd) *adj.* Enjoying luxuries and special treatment.
procession (prə se´ shən) *n.* A line of people moving forward in an orderly and ceremonial manner.
product (prô´ dukt´) *n.* Anything that is made or created.

Word Derivations

Below are some words derived from the word *product.*

production	productivity	counterproductive
reproduction	by-product	mass production
productive	productively	production line

profitable (prô´ fə tə bəl) *adj.* Able to make money.
profusely (prə fūs´ lē) *adv.* In abundance; in large amounts.
prominently (prô´ mə nənt lē) *adv.* Noticeably.
promote (prə mōt´) *v.* To advance in rank, position, or grade.
prospect (prô´ spekt) 1. *n.* A future possible event; something that could happen. 2. *v.* To search or explore for gold or other mining products.
prostration (pros trā´ shən) *n.* Exhaustion; extreme tiredness.
provide (prə vīd´) *v.* To supply what is needed.
provisions (prə vizh´ ənz) *n.* Things that are supplied for a special task, especially food and the necessary tools.
pulse (puls) *n.* The regular beating of the heart.
pursue (pər so͞o´) *v.* To chase.

Q

qualified (kwä´ lə fīd´) *adj.* Having the skills or education needed for a certain job or position; capable.
quarters (kwor´ tərz) *n.* Living accommodations; a place to live.
queer (kwēr) *adv.* Strange.
quill (kwil) *n.* A hollow wing or tail feather used for writing.

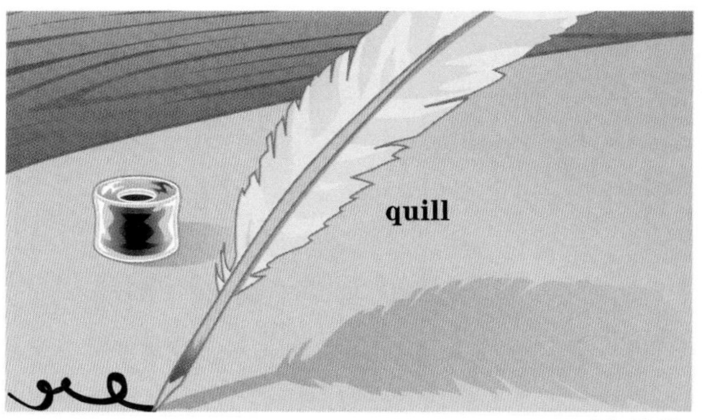

Pronunciation Key: **a**t; l**ā**te; c**â**re; f**ä**ther; s**e**t; m**ē**; **i**t; k**ī**te; **o**x; r**ō**se; **ô** in b**o**ught; c**oi**n; b**o͝o**k; t**o͞o**; f**or**m; **ou**t; **u**p; **ū**se; t**û**rn; **ə** sound in **a**bout, chick**e**n, penc**i**l, cann**o**n, circ**u**s; **ch**air; **hw** in **wh**ich; ri**ng**; **sh**op; **th**in; **t̸h**ere; **zh** in trea**s**ure.

R

racket (rak´ ət) *n.* Noise indicating confusion.

rafter (raf´ tər) *n.* Any of the long, heavy pieces of wood or metal that support a roof.

raised print (razd´ print´) *n.* A type of print for blind people in which letters of the alphabet are raised from the page so that they can be felt.

rambunctious (ram bungk´ shəs) *adj.* Active and noisy in a violent way.

ransom (ran´ səm) *n.* A large amount of money paid to free something or someone from captivity.

ration (rash´ ən) *n.* A fixed allowance of something; a limited share.

reasonable (rēz´ nə bəl) *adj.* Possessing sound judgment.

reception (ri sep´ shən) *n.* A party held to welcome someone.

reconsider (rē´ kən si´ dər) *v.* To think about again.

recruit (ri kro͞ot´) 1. *v.* To gain fresh people for a task. 2. *n.* A new member of a group or organization.

reflect (ri flekt´) *v.* To represent; to show.

Word Derivations

Below are some words derived from the word *reflect.*

reflected	reflection	reflector
reflecting	reflective	reflects

refugee camp (re´ fyo͞o jē kamp) *n.* A place where people who are forced to leave their homes live temporarily.

register (re´ jə stər) *v.* To show or record, as on a scale or meter.

related (ri lā´ təd) *adj.* Having some connection.

relations (ri lā´ shənz) *n.* The connections between people; people's associations with each other; the dealings people have with each other.

relay (rē´ lā´) 1. *n.* The passing along of something (like a message). (rē´ lā´) 2. *v.* To send along; to pass from one person to another.

relieved (ri lēvd´) *adv.* Comforted.

rendezvous (ron´ di vo͞o´) *v.* To meet or get together at a certain place.

renew (ri no͞o´) *v.* To repair; to restore.

resentment (ri zent´ mənt) *n.* A feeling of being insulted.

reservation (rez´ ər vā´ shən) *n.* The land set aside for Native Americans to live on.

restaurateur (res´ tə rə tûr´) *n.* Someone who owns or runs a restaurant.

restore (ri stor´) *v.* To bring something back to its original condition.

resume (ri zo͞om′) *v.* To start up again; to continue.

Word History

The word **resume** came into English usage in the 15th century. It comes from the Latin word *resumere. Resumere* can be broken down into the word parts *re-*, which means "again," and *sumere*, which means "to take up."

retire (ri tīr′) *v.* To go away to a private place.

rugged (ru′ gəd) *adj.* Sturdy and strong.

S

S.S. or **Schutzstaffel** (sho͞ots′ stä′ fəl) *German.* A special Nazi police force.

sac (sak) *n.* An inner body structure that is like a bag.

sandspit (sand′ spit) *n.* A bar of raised sand that juts out from an island.

satchel (sach′ əl) *n.* A small bag; a school bag.

Word History

Satchel comes from an older English word, *sachel. Sachel* is derived from the Latin word *saccus*, which means "bag." This word came into the English language during the 14th century.

scalpel (skal′ pəl) *n.* A small, straight, light knife used by surgeons.

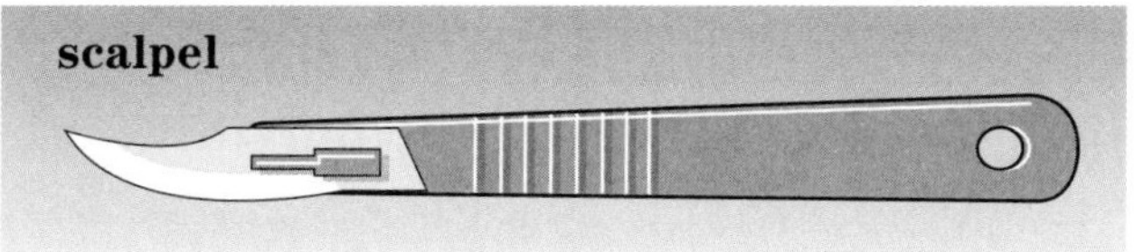
scalpel

scholarship (sko′ lər ship′) *n.* Money given to a student, often to help pay for college.

scribe (skrīb) *n.* A person who copies manuscripts by hand.

scullery (skul′ ə rē) *n.* A small room off the kitchen where dishes are washed, vegetables are prepared, and other chores are done.

scythe (sīth) *n.* A tool with a blade and a long handle used for cutting or mowing grass or crops.

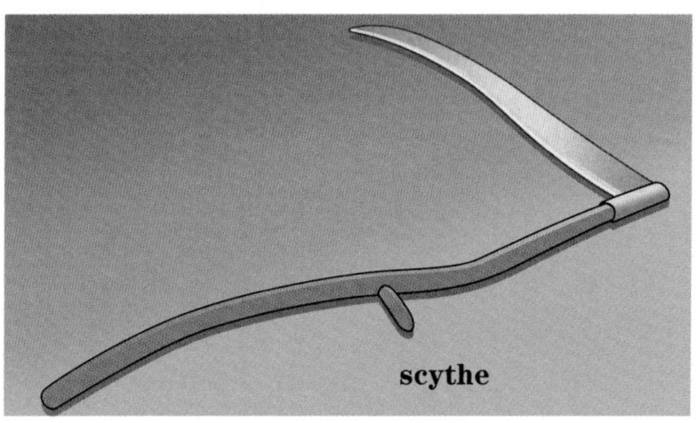
scythe

seep (sēp) *v.* To flow a little at a time.

sentries (sen′ trēz) *n.* People stationed to keep watch; a guard.

serpent (sûr′ pənt) *n.* A snake.

serum (sēr′ əm) *n.* The liquid part of blood.

service (sûr′ vəs) *adj.* Providing useful work rather than products.

settlement (set′ l mənt) *n.* A colony; a new community in a new land.

shan't (shant) Contraction of **shall not:** Will not.

sheepfold (shēp′ fōld′) *n.* A pen or shelter for sheep.

ship (ship) *v.* To send by boat, train, truck, airplane, or other mode of transportation.

Pronunciation Key: **a**t; l**ā**te; c**â**re; f**ä**ther; s**e**t; m**ē**; **i**t; k**ī**te; **o**x; r**ō**se; **ô** in b**ou**ght; c**oi**n; b**o͝o**k; t**o͞o**; f**or**m; **ou**t; **u**p; **ū**se; t**û**rn; **ə** sound in **a**bout, chick**e**n, penc**i**l, cann**o**n, circ**u**s; **ch**air; **hw** in **wh**ich; ri**ng**; **sh**op; **th**in; **th**ere; **zh** in trea**s**ure.

shock (shok) 1. *n.* A thick, bushy mass. 2. A dangerous condition in which a person's blood circulation becomes extremely slow.
siege (sēj) *n.* A group of illnesses, one after the other.
sign (sīn) *v.* For the hearing impaired, to make hand motions that mean something.
significant (sig ni′ fi kənt) *adj.* Important.
silkworm gut (silk′ wûrm gut′) *n.* Silk thread used in surgery.
simulate (sim′yə lāt) *v.* To make something seem like something else; to imitate.
sinew (sin′ū) *n.* A tough substance that joins muscle to bone; a tendon.
site (sīt) *n.* The ground occupied by a building.
situation (si′ chə wā′ shən) *n.* A position or state of affairs.
skeptic (skep′ tik) *n.* One who is doubtful.
skirt (skûrt) *v.* To move around the edge of.
sledge (slej) *n.* A sled or sleigh.
slop (slop) *n.* Food waste, usually garbage, fed to animals.
snare (snâr) *n.* A trap.
sole (sōl) *adj.* Single; one and only.
solution (sə lo͞o′ shən) *n.* A liquid that has something dissolved in it.
sorrowfully (sär′ ō f(ə) lē) *adv.* Full of grief or sadness.

sound (sound) *adj.* Secure; safe; sensible.
specialize (spe′ shə līz′) *v.* To concentrate on one activity or subject.
specific (spi si′ fik) *adj.* Exact; particular.
spout (spout) *v.* To come out through a narrow opening with great force.

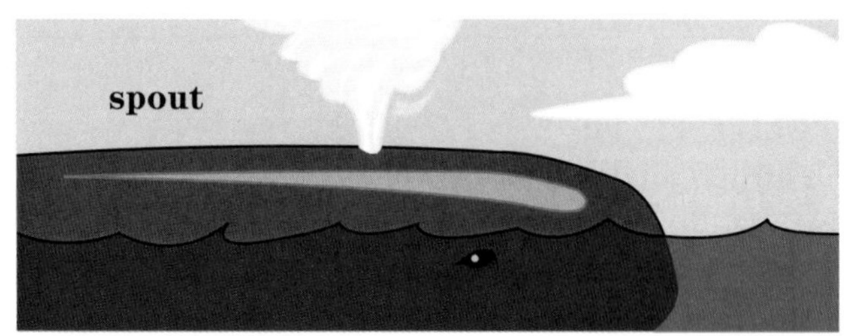

startling (stärt′ ling) *adj.* Surprising; astonishing.
stave (stāv) *n.* One of the thin, curved wood strips used to make a barrel.
steadily (sted′ ə lē) *adv.* In a regular or methodical way.
sterilize (ster′ ə līz′) *v.* To make free from germs.
sternum (stûr′ nəm) *n.* The breastbone; the flat, narrow, bony area to which the ribs are attached.
stethoscope (steth′ ə skōp′) *n.* An instrument for listening to sounds within the body.

Word History

Stethoscope comes from the French word *stéthoscope. Stéthoscope* is derived from the Greek word *stethos*, which means "chest," and *-scope*, which means "instrument." The word came to mean an instrument for listening to the chest.

stifled (stī′ fəld) *adj.* Suffocated or smothered.
stock (stok) *n.* All of the animals on a farm; livestock.

strain (strān) *v.* To overwork; to work to the utmost.

Word Derivations

Below are some words derived from the word *strain.*

restrain	restrains	straining
restrained	strained	strains
restraining	strainer	unrestrained

studious (sto͞o′ dē əs) *adj.* Dedicated to study and learning.
sturdy (stûr′ dē) *adj.* Strong.
stylus (stī′ ləs) *n.* A pointed writing instrument.

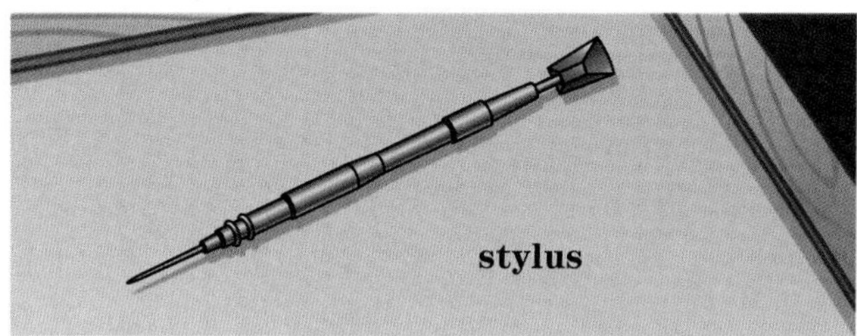

suburb (su′ bərb) *n.* A community at the edge of, but outside of, a large city.
summon (sum′ ən) *v.* To send for; to call someone to come.
superstition (so͞o′ pər stish′ ən) *n.* A belief in magic; a belief that is not based on reason.
supervise (soo′ pûr vīz′) *v.* To watch over or direct.
suture (so͞o′ chər) *v.* To stitch together; to sew up.
swallow (swä′ lō′) *n.* A type of bird.
sympathy (sim′ pə thē) *n.* A feeling of understanding for another's sadness or hurt.
symptom (simp′ təm) *n.* A sign that indicates what kind of illness someone has.

T

taut (tôt) *adj.* Stretched tight; tense.
technique (tek nēk′) *n.* Way of handling something.
thatched (thacht) *adj.* Covered with straw.
thrash (thrash) *v.* To thresh; to beat the grain from stalks; to beat.
threshold (thresh′ ōld) *n.* The bottom part of a doorway; the sill.

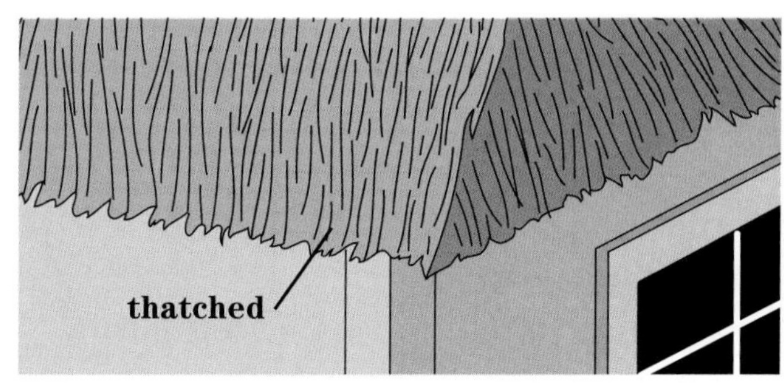

thrive (thrīv) *v.* To progress, grow, or prosper well.
throes (thrōz) *n.* Any violent spasm or struggle.
tidal (tīd′ l) *adj.* Having to do with the rise and fall of the sea.
tide (tīd) *n.* A current or flowing water.

Word Derivations

Below are some words derived from the word *tide.*

ebb tide	tidal wave	tidemark
high tide	tide table	tides
low tide	tideland	tidewater
tidal	tideless	tideway

timid (ti′ məd) *adj.* Shy; feeling or showing a lack of courage.
tinker (ting′ kər) *v.* To experiment with something.
toll (tōl) *n.* Damage; destruction.
toll-gate (tōl′ gāt) *n.* A gate where people must pay in order to use a road.

Pronunciation Key: at; lāte; câre; fäther; set; mē; it; kīte; ox; rōse; ô in bought; coin; bo͝ok; to͞o; form; out; up; tûrn; Ə sound in about, chicken, pencil, cannon, circus; chair; hw in which; ring; shop; thin; there; zh in treasure.

tongue (tung) *n.* A piece of board that fits into the groove of another board.
tottery (tot′ ə rē) *adj.* Unsteady; shaky.
trace (trās) *n.* One of the two straps or chains that connect an animal to a load being pulled.
tradition (trə dish′ ən) *n.* A custom that has been handed down or preserved through many generations.
traffic (tra′ fik) *n.* The people being serviced by a business.
transcontinental (trans′ kon tə nen′ təl) *adj.* Stretching across a continent.
transfusion (trans fū′ zhən) *n.* A transfer of blood into a person.

Word History

Transfusion came into English usage in the 16th century. It can be traced back to the Latin word *transfundere. Trans-* means "across" or "beyond," and *fundere* means "to pour." The suffix *-ion,* a Latin term, means "act" or "process." In this case, the word came to mean the act or process of pouring blood beyond one person to another.

treacherous (tre′ chə rəs) *adj.* Not safe because of hidden dangers.
trek (trek) *n.* A difficult journey or trip.
tribute (trib′ūt) *n.* Praise given in recognition of worth or value.
trickle (trik′ əl) *v.* To flow.
trifling (trī′ fling) *adj.* Not important.
trot (trot) 1. *n.* A slow run. 2. *v.* To run slowly.
troublesome (trə′ bəl səm) *adj.* Causing problems or difficulties.
trough (trôf) *n.* A container holding the drinking water or food for animals.

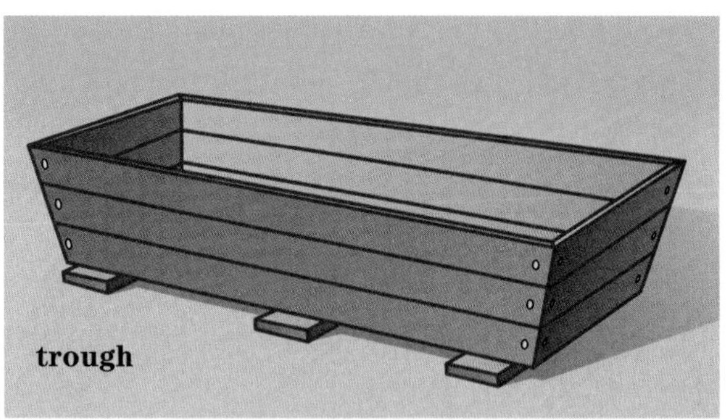
trough

U

uncharted (un chär′ tid) *adj.* Not shown on a map; not explored; not known.
unconscious (ən kon′ shəs) *adj.* Without physical or mental awareness; senseless.
unfortunate (ən forch′ nət) *adj.* Unlucky.
unsupervised (ən so͞o′ pər vīzd) 1. *adj.* Without being watched over by someone. (from **supervise** 2. *v.* To watch over, oversee.)
usher (ush′ ər) *v.* To escort or take someone someplace.

V

vaccine (vak sēn´) *n.* A preparation, usually liquid, given to prevent a disease.

valiant (val´ yənt) *adj.* Courageous or brave.

vanish (va´ nish) *v.* To disappear suddenly.

vendor (ven´ dər) *n.* A person or company that sells a product.

venture (ven´ chər) *n.* An uncertain undertaking; a new situation with a doubtful outcome.

veranda (və ran´ də) *n.* A covered balcony; a porch.

verge (vûrj) *n.* The place where something begins; the brink.

verify (vâr´ ə fī) *v.* To declare something real, authentic, or true.

via (vī´ ə) *adv.* By way of; passing through.

vibration (vī brā´ shən) *n.* Slight, rapid movements of an object.

vinyl (vī´ nl) *n.* A plastic-like fabric made by humans.

vital (vīt´ l) *adj.* Necessary for life.

Word History

The French word **vital** can be traced back to the Latin word *vita*, which means "life." The word came into the English language during the 14th century.

vouch (vouch) *v.* To bear witness; to confirm.

W

W.C. Water closet: A bathroom.

warden (wor´ dn) *n.* An officer in charge; a supervisor.

weed-infested (wēd´ in fes´ td) *adj.* Filled with unwanted or undesirable plants.

wick (wik) *n.* A braided or twisted string of a soft substance that soaks up the fuel in a candle or lamp and holds the flame.

wreckage (rek´ ij) *n.* The remains of something that has been wrecked or destroyed.

Y

yearn (yûrn) *v.* To long for.

yoke (yōk) *n.* A wooden frame used to join together two work animals.

Z

zephyr (zef´ ər) *n.* The west wind.

Acknowledgments

All rights reserved. Reprinted by permission of Children's Press an imprint of Scholastic Library Publishing, Inc.

From Carole Charles' "Martha Helps the Rebel" © 1975 by The Child's World, Chanhassen, MN. Reprinted with permission of copyright holder.

"Prophecy in Flame" from ALL KEYS ARE GLASS by Frances Minturn Howard, Boston, Massachusetts, copyright © 1950. Used by permission of the estate.

"Going West" from CHILDREN OF THE WILD WEST by Russell Freedman. Copyright © 1983 by Russell Freedman. Reprinted by permission of Clarion Books/Houghton Mifflin Company. All rights reserved.

From THE CALIFORNIA GOLD RUSH: WEST WITH THE FORTY-NINERS by Elizabeth Van Steenwyk, copyright © 1991 by Franklin Watts. All rights reserved. Reprinted by permission of Franklin Watts, an imprint of Scholastic Library Publishing, Inc.

"The Golden Spike" from THE TRANSCONTINENTAL RAILROAD, text copyright © 1993 by Dan Elish. Reprinted with permission of the author. All rights reserved.

Photo Credits

7, NASA; **8 (t),** Wells Fargo Bank, **(c)** ©Neil Johnson, **(bl)** ©1994 Jim McHugh/Outline Press Syndicate, Inc.; **11 (t),** ©Brian Payne/Black Star, **(b)** Courtesy Archives & Special Collections on Women in Medicine, Allegheny University of the Health Sciences; **12,** ©Library of Congress/PHOTRI; **14,** ©Tui De Roy/Minden Pictures; **15,** ©Ron Cohn/The Gorilla Foundation; **16,** ©North Wind Picture Archive; **17 (t),** ©Western History/Genealogy Department, Denver Public Library, **(b)** ©Bettmann/Corbis; **18-19,** NASA; **30, 46,** file photo; **64,** ©Paul Abdoo; **82-85,** NASA; **86,** ©Stanford News Services; **87,** ©Jim Ruymen/UPI/Corbis-Bettmann; **88 (l),** ©Walt Frerck/UPI/Corbis-Bettmann, **(r)** NASA; **89-93,** NASA; **94 (t),** NASA, **(b)** ©AP/Wide World Photos; **95,** ©AP/Wide World Photos; **96,** Gail Sakurai; **97,** NASA; **98,** The Art Institute of Chicago, Gift of Mrs. Richard E. Danielson and Mrs. Chauncey McCormick. Photograph ©2000, The Art Institute of Chicago, All Rights Reserved; **99 (t),** The Metropolitan Museum of Art, Rogers Fund, 1936. (JP 2581) Photograph ©1991 The Metropolitan Museum of Art, **(b)** Estate of Margaret Bourke-White Estate, courtesy Life Magazine ©Time Inc.; **112,** Doris Ettlinger; **126,** file photo; **126-130,** ©Aaron Haupt; **127 (l),** ©David Young-Wolff/PhotoEdit, **(b)** ©Aaron Haupt; **128 (t),** ©Aaron Haupt, **(b)** ©Myrleen Ferguson/PhotoEdit; **131,** Aaron Haupt; **132-134,** Wells Fargo Bank; **136,** ©Bettmann/Corbis; **139,** Wells Fargo Bank; **140,** ©Bettmann/Corbis; **141,** ©Bettmann/Corbis; **143,** Wells Fargo Bank; **146-153,** ©Neil Johnson; **154 (t),** Charlotte A. Watson Fund, 1942, Albright-Knox Art Gallery, Buffalo, New York, **(b)** Scala/Art Resource, NY; **155 (t),** The Brooklyn Museum, Brooklyn, New York. John B. and Ella C. Woodward Memorial Funds, **(b)** SuperStock; **157,** ©1994 Alan Levenson; **159, 160,** ©1994 Jim McHugh/Outline Press Syndicate, Inc.; **163,** ©1997 David McNew; **164-166, 169,** ©1994 Jim McHugh/Outline Press Syndicate, Inc.; **170 (t),** Marlene Targ Brill; **186,** Diane Paterson; **200,** file photo; **204 (t),** ©Archive Photos; **217, 219,** Bettmann/Corbis; **221,** ©AP Wide World Photo; **222 (t),** file photo, **(b)** Jim Roldan; **238,** file photo; **254 (t),** Carol Saller, **(b)** Gerald Talifero; **256 (t),** ©Erich Lessing/Art Resource, NY, **(b)** Nicolo Orsi Battaglini/Art Resource, NY; **257 (t, b),** Scala/Art Resource, NY; **258** ©Brian Payne/Black Star; **286 (t),** Paula G. Paul, **(b)** Robert Collier-Morales; **288,** Courtesy Archives & Special Collections on Women in Medicine, Allegheny University of the Health Sciences; **306 (t),** Marion Marsh Brown, **(b)** Diane Magnuson; **318 (t),** Maia Wojciechowska, **(b)** Ramon Gonzalez Vicente; **332,** Scott O'Dell; **335,** ©Robert E. Peary/National Geographic Image Collection; **339,** ©Library of Congress/PHOTRI; **340,** ©Dartmouth College Library; **343, 344,** ©Corbis; **347,** Courtesy of The Peary-MacMillan Arctic Museum, Bowdoin College; **350-351, 353,** ©Dartmouth College Library; **355, 357,** ©Bettmann/Corbis; **359,** Library of Congress/PHOTRI; **374,** file photo; **388 (t),** ©Archive Photos, **(b)** Yoriko Ito; **392,** ©UPI/Corbis-Bettmann; **402 (t),**©UPI/Corbis-Bettmann, **(b)** Susan Keeter; **404 (t),** Robert Schaap Collection, Vincent van Gogh Museum, Rijsmuseum, Amsterdam, **(b)** Museum purchase, The Philbrook Museum of Art, Tulsa, Oklahoma; **405 (t),** Margaret Bourke-White, Life Magazine ©Time Inc., **(b)** Abby Aldrich Rockefeller Folk Art Center. Photo:©Colonial Williamsburg Foundation; **412,** file photo; **417,** ©Tui De Roy/Minden Pictures; **418,** ©Charles Nicklin/Al Giddings Images, Inc.; **419,** ©Michael Durham/Oregon Zoo; **420-421,** ©Hal Beral/Corbis; **425,** ©Daniel J. Cox/Natural Selection; **432 (t),** courtesy Shelagh Wallace; **442,** ©Richard Sobol; **444,** The National Museum of Women in the Arts, Washington, D.C. Gift of Wallace and Wilhelmina Holladay; **445 (t, b),** SuperStock; **447-459,** ©Ron Cohn/The Gorilla Foundation; **472,** Bob Dorsey; **480,** ©Agence France Presse/Archive Photos; **484,** ©Werner Forman Archive/Field Museum of Natural History, Chicago/Art Resource, NY; **485,** ©St. Agustine Foundation at Flagler College; **486,** ©Stock Montage, Inc.; **487, 489,** ©North Wind Picture Archive; **490,** ©Werner Forman Archive/Field Museum of Natural History,Chicago/Art Resource, NY; **498,** James Watling; **500,** The Metropolitan Museum of Art, Rogers Fund, 1913. Photograph ©The Metropolitan Museum of Art; **501 (t),** Fine Arts Museum of San Francisco, Gift of Mr. and Mrs. John D. Rockefeller 3rd, 1979.7.3, **(b)** Quilled Buckskin Robe, National Museum of the American Indian, Smithsonian Institution; **502,** ©National Portrait Gallery, Washington DC. Photo: Art Resource, NY; **506,** Dennis B. Fradin; **518,** Charles Shaw; **529,** ©Corbis; **533,** ©North Wind Picture Archive; **534, 537,** Stock Montage, Inc.; **538 (l),** Stock Montage, Inc., **(r)** ©Bettmann/Corbis; **539,** ©Bettmann/Corbis.

Unit Opener Acknowledgments

Unit 1 photo by NASA; **Unit 2** illustrated by Robert Byrd; **Unit 3** illustrated by Rusty Fletcher; **Unit 4** illustrated by Mary Beth Schwark and Bob Kuester; **Unit 5** illustrated by Ruth Flanigan; **Unit 6** illustrated by Jan Adkins.

About the author

Angelica Zander Rudenstine was educated at Oxford University in England. She was a member of the curatorial staff of the Museum of Fine Arts, Boston, from 1961 to 1968 and Research Curator at the Solomon R. Guggenheim Museum until 1981. She is presently working as an independent art-historian and curator.

Her two-volume catalogue *The Guggenheim Museum Collection: Paintings 1880-1945* was published in 1976. She was co-author and general editor of Abrams' *Russian Avant-Garde Art: The George Costakis Collection,* co-organizer of the Costakis Collection exhibition, which traveled throughout the United States and Europe from 1981 to 1984, and co-author of its catalogue.

She has served on the Board of Directors of the College Art Association of America, the Editorial Board of the *Art Bulletin*, the Millard Meiss Publications Committee, Selection Panels in Art History for the National Endowment for the Humanities, and the Museum Panel of the National Endowment for the Arts. She is a Trustee of the American Academy in Rome and Chairman of its Fine Arts Committee.

In 1983 she was awarded a John Simon Guggenheim Memorial Foundation Fellowship.

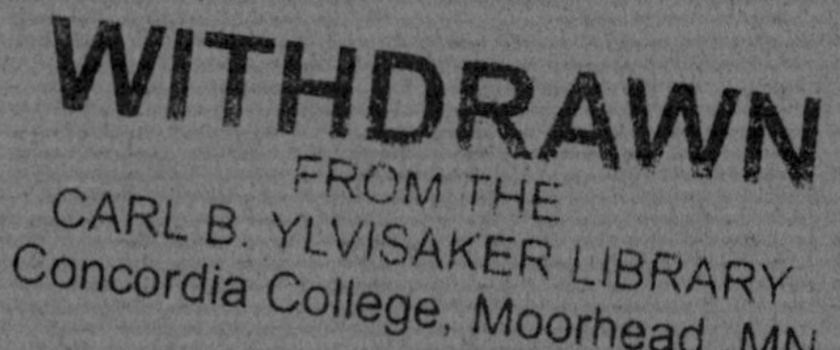

PEGGY GUGGENHEIM COLLECTION, VENICE

PEGGY GUGGENHEIM COLLECTION, VENICE

THE SOLOMON R. GUGGENHEIM FOUNDATION

by Angelica Zander Rudenstine

Harry N. Abrams, Inc., Publishers, New York

The Solomon R. Guggenheim Foundation, New York

Jacket front: Picasso, *La Baignade,* 1937.
Jacket back: Giacometti, *Femme égorgée,* 1932.

Library of Congress Cataloging in Publication Data

Peggy Guggenheim Collection.
Peggy Guggenheim Collection, Venice, The Solomon R. Guggenheim Foundation.
Includes index.
1. Peggy Guggenheim Collection—Catalogs. 2. Art, Modern—20th century—Catalogs. I. Rudenstine, Angelica Zander. II. Title.
N6488.5.G83P43 1985
709′.04′00740531 85-1307
ISBN 0-8109-0989-8

Published in 1985 by Harry N. Abrams, Incorporated, New York in collaboration with The Solomon R. Guggenheim Foundation, New York.

Printed and bound in Japan

This publication is supported by grants from the National Endowment for the Arts and the National Endowment for the Humanities. Additional funds have been provided by the Samuel H. Kress Foundation.

CONTENTS

Peggy Guggenheim seated in the garden of Palazzo Venier dei Leoni, 1975. (Dress by Fortuny.)

FOREWORD

Although I remember hearing about my second cousin Peggy Guggenheim as a boy from my mother in the 1940s, it was not until she showed her collection at the Solomon R. Guggenheim Museum in New York in 1969 that I met her for the first time. Over the next ten years, until her death in 1979, my wife, Dede, and I enjoyed a very warm relationship with her from a familial standpoint, during which time I believe I succeeded in erasing whatever doubts she might have had about her decision to entrust her Palazzo and her priceless collection to our stewardship. My predecessor, Harry Guggenheim, and Tom Messer, the Museum's trusted and capable Director, were directly instrumental in Peggy's decision to merge her collection with that of The Solomon R. Guggenheim Foundation (even though it was to remain in Venice), as I shall explain below.

Peggy, as everyone knows, was a free spirit. Her book *Out of This Century* (which my more conservative branch of the family referred to years ago as *Out of My Mind*) describes in considerable detail her colorful life during those years when she busily acquired works in heroic fashion. Perhaps Peggy inherited some of her independence from her father, Benjamin Guggenheim, one of the seven brothers who became wealthy in the mining business in the early 1900s. Like Peggy, Benjamin broke away from the family in order to be on his own, and lived life to the hilt. He went down on the Titantic after, as tradition has it, gallantly giving his life preserver to a lady friend and donning his tuxedo so that he could "die like a gentleman." Contrary to general belief, Peggy inherited virtually nothing from her father whose private business did not prosper after he left the family partnership. So Peggy's uncles set up a number of small trusts for her benefit and she later inherited a modest sum from her mother, Florette, a Seligman. Peggy's accomplishment as a collector was therefore all the more incredible and confirms the view that she was enormously shrewd as she tried to keep to her resolve to "buy a picture a day" in the early 1940s.

While she was acquiring works of art, her uncle (my grandfather), Solomon Guggenheim, was also assembling his collection under the direction of his confidante, Baroness Hilla Rebay, whom I knew well until Grandpa died in 1949. Hilla Rebay, a dogmatic, mercurial lady, had definite ideas about what works should be acquired by Peggy's uncle and on balance was enormously successful in assembling the works that formed the nucleus of the Guggenheim Museum's collection in New York. Although I am not aware of any rivalry between uncle and niece over the acquisitions that took place, it is a matter of public record now, reliably documented in extant correspondence, that no love was lost between Peggy and the Baroness, much as they both may have been devoted to their respective collections.

Although Harry Guggenheim, Solomon's nephew, was undoubtedly chagrined by his cousin Peggy's bohemian behavior when they were relatively young, he certainly respected her brilliant success as a collector in later years. I remember Harry's delight when Peggy agreed to exhibit her collection at the Guggenheim in New York in 1969 and when she subsequently decided to deed the collection in 1970 to the custody of The Solomon R. Guggenheim Foundation over which he presided as Chairman. Important as the amalgamation of these two collections was, I know that Harry was particularly elated about the family reconciliation. I recall a letter he wrote to her that included the sentence: "Come home — all is forgiven."

The dream, however, of joining the two collections was neither Harry's nor mine, but Tom Messer's, who envisioned, early on, the historic importance of such a combination. The impetus, too, came from Tom, who journeyed to Venice innumerable times and finally succeeded in allaying Peggy's doubts, which were partially fueled by other institutions also seeking her collection. This was no small task since Peggy could be suspicious of one's motivation — perhaps an understandable trait in the Guggenheim family.

And then, once she agreed in principle to entrust the Palazzo dei Leoni and her entire collection to us, the negotiations were conducted by Tom almost exclusively. Bernard Reis, a friend of Peggy's, was actively involved in this process, as was Chauncey Newlin as counsel for The Solomon R. Guggenheim Foundation, but Peggy herself had a firm idea from the beginning of what she would ultimately agree to. There was never any doubt about her desire to maintain the Collection in Venice. In fact, in her letter of 1969 to Harry Guggenheim outlining her terms for an arrangement between her Foundation and ours, she added the following postscript in longhand: "If Venice sinks, the Collection should be preserved somewhere in the vicinity of Venice."

The agreement therefore stated that the works of art would remain with Peggy in the Palazzo dei Leoni during her lifetime, even after her Foundation was dissolved. At her death, The Solomon R. Guggenheim Foundation would assume effective control of and responsibility for the Palazzo and its contents. Further basic conditions stipulated that the Collection be kept in Venice and be known as the Peggy Guggenheim Collection. And, finally, that it remain on view during the spring, summer, and fall season each year.

Accordingly, Peggy continued to live in her Palazzo and we commenced to bring her works of art to New York to do conservation work. The relationship with her was warm and cordial. Problems arose, however, when, for example, early in 1972, Peggy was robbed and appealed to me in my capacity as President of the Foundation to install a burglar-alarm system. Since the Collection was not yet legally ours, we resolved the issue by having Peggy present us with a painting in return for which we would pay for the alarm system. Although she readily agreed to my suggestion and we paid for the installation, I do not recall her ever giving us a painting as part of this bargain.

A more serious problem developed in late 1974 when the Collection became endangered by dampness resulting from the Palazzo's poor physical condition. Once again we were walking a tightrope because we were awaiting the necessary Italian approval of her gift to us of the Palazzo and as a tax-exempt public foundation we could not legally spend substantial sums of money for repairs to the building until ownership was finally resolved by the Italian authorities. However, though the legal transfer of the Collection and Palazzo did not take place until 1976, we did continue to assist Peggy financially in maintaining her treasure.

I think it is fair to state that during this protracted period Tom Messer and I, with the help of the staff members then involved — Orrin Riley in Conservation, Robin M. Green in Public Affairs, and Angelica Zander Rudenstine, who worked closely with Peggy for years in documenting her works of art — conducted ourselves in a manner that impressed her with the sincerity of our resolve to justify her faith in our future stewardship.

My affection for Peggy grew over the years and in 1977 she wrote me that she was "quite overcome" by my offer to "hold her hand" if she would only go to Texas for an operation she was contemplating at the time. But she went to Vienna where a specialist gave her "injections, exercises and medicines instead." One of the most endearing memories I have of Peggy involves a letter she sent me seeking assurance that we would never disturb the area in the garden where her beloved dogs were buried. Naturally, I assured her in this regard, and her own ashes now rest in a location contiguous to that spot.

Peggy died just before Christmas in 1979, so that it became necessary for Tom Messer to take charge of the situation there on December 26 in a frantic, yet systematic, effort to open the Palazzo and the Collection to the public on Easter Sunday, 1980, under our new arrangements. Our Director arrived in Venice simultaneously with one of the highest *aqua alta* floods in recent memory. Fortunately, Peggy's son, Sindbad Vail, and Philip Rylands, who was later to become the Peggy Guggenheim Collection's Administrator, had heroically retrieved those of Peggy's priceless works located in the dark and flooded basement of the Palazzo. Even so, Tom Messer was compelled to take emergency measures to secure the building together with its precious treasures against theft or possible damage due to flooding. He contacted the appropriate Italian authorities, held a press conference, appointed Philip Rylands, an English art historian resident in Venice, Administrator, and named Giosetta Capriati Development Officer. Over the next three months, the newly appointed staff, under the direction of Tom Messer and Henry Berg, then his Deputy Director, made preparations for the first public opening under the Foundation's auspices.

Having written Peggy five years earlier: "I pledge to you that one of my primary goals in my remaining years will be to see to it that your wishes are carried out faithfully and flawlessly," it was a very emotional moment for me when I addressed her friends and relatives, and other guests in the Palazzo garden at the opening on Easter Sunday and reiterated that pledge to provide the resources of The Solomon R. Guggenheim Foundation to fulfill her wishes. Peggy's home has now been converted into one of the finest modern art museums on the European Continent, and I can think of no greater monument to "L'ultima Dogaressa" than the present installation of her works in a reconstructed and safeguarded Palazzo. This would not have been possible without the Italian people, government officials, business leaders, and influential art-lovers who all cooperated in helping us to make a success of the transition. The Advisory Committee of the Peggy Guggenheim Collection, under the Chairmanship of Mme Claude Pompidou, has been indispensible to Tom Messer and Philip Rylands in the past four critical years of our administration. The distinguished Board of Trustees of The Solomon R. Guggenheim Foundation, too, deserves much gratitude for its unfailing support of the lengthy endeavor to assume the stewardship of Peggy's priceless collection.

PETER LAWSON-JOHNSTON, *President*
The Solomon R. Guggenheim Foundation

PREFACE

The systematic documentation of the collections of The Solomon R. Guggenheim Foundation began in the late 1960s and will no doubt continue indefinitely. But in terms of forseeable new catalogues, *Peggy Guggenheim Collection: The Solomon R. Guggenheim Foundation* assumes a position at approximately midpoint in relation to volumes already published and those clearly envisaged. *The Guggenheim Museum Collection: Paintings 1880-1945* and *The Guggenheim Museum: Justin K. Thannhauser Collection* have appeared within the past decade; *The Guggenheim Museum Collection: Sculpture and Works on Paper 1880-1945* and *The Guggenheim Museum Collection: Postwar Works* should, together with the current volume, complete the survey of the Foundation's collections and thereby afford to students as well as to general museum visitors a full and authoritative insight into that part of our holdings we consider permanent and most important.

The Peggy Guggenheim Collection, although now firmly established within this Foundation's framework, nevertheless constitutes an autonomous entity: this is due in part to its location in Peggy Guggenheim's former Venetian home, but also results from the fact that, like the Thannhauser Collection but unlike the remainder of the Solomon R. Guggenheim Museum collection, it was formed by a single personality and transferred in its entirety to the Guggenheim Foundation. The Peggy Guggenheim Collection consists in toto of over three hundred objects—a figure that includes examples of tribal art and decorative glass objects as well as modern works of varying degrees of importance. Under the terms of Peggy Guggenheim's will, none of these may be disposed of, but neither is there any obligation to exhibit or document any but the most representative works. Such documentation is offered here through my selection of ninety-five paintings, fifty sculptures, and thirty-two works on paper by ninety-two twentieth-century artists.

The Peggy Guggenheim Collection as presented here may be viewed from two separate perspectives. From the first, it can be seen as the self-sufficient achievement of its creator, representing an aspect of modern art in which Cubism, abstraction, and Surrealism, supplemented by early postwar painting from America and Europe, emerge as the dominant directions. From the second perspective it can be seen in relation to the collection of the Solomon R. Guggenheim Museum. In the latter case, it provides dimensions—such as Surrealism—that are barely represented in the New York institution; it strengthens tendencies—such as Cubism — that are already present; and relates to certain chapters of art history — such as Post-Impressionism and Expressionism — that are included among the New York holdings but remained outside the scope of Peggy Guggenheim's collection. The separate identity of the Peggy Guggenheim Collection is maintained through the seasonal installation at the Palazzo Venier dei Leoni in Venice, where it comes into its own annually from April to October. Its relation to the holdings in New York on the other hand was visibly established when a sizable selection of pictures from Venice occupied the permanent collection galleries of the Solomon R. Guggenheim Museum during the winter of 1982-83, as well as through the highly successful presentations of works drawn from both Foundation branches that have so far taken place — in Rome in 1982 and Sydney in 1983.

While exhibitions of the combined New York and Venice collections provide an intensity of qualitative concentration that very few modern art museums in the world can match, the Peggy Guggenheim Collection also has autonomous strength that is far from negligible. The works documented in this catalogue and displayed beside the Grand Canal, each through its own specific gravity and through the sequence they establish among themselves, have no equals in twentieth-century collections in Italy; the Peggy Guggenheim Collection thus fulfills a role as Italy's museum of modern art held in trust by an American foundation.

As already stated in the President's foreword to this catalogue, The Foundation took effective charge of the collection immediately upon Peggy Guggenheim's death in December 1979. The most urgent requirement at the time was the physical safeguarding of a collection that until then had not benefited from sustained conservation. Restoration of endangered works and immediate attention to architectural and environmental improvements that would secure Peggy Guggenheim's treasure for future generations, therefore, commanded the highest priority in the years immediately following the founder's death. At the time of this writing, the critical restoration phase is behind us, although some of the damage sustained in past decades must be considered irreversible, as the condition reports in the current publication indicate.

Installation of the collection and its elementary documentation in handbooks oriented to a broad public were next on the agenda and may now also be considered completed. The rational and didactic presentation of Peggy Guggenheim's masterpieces benefited from a division of the collection into two parts, of which one was reserved for permanent public display while the second was made available to students and others upon special request. Since the simultaneous redisposition of quarters within the Palazzo resulted in the freeing of large areas previously restricted to Peggy's private use, visitors now see a quantitatively reduced and qualitatively enhanced collection displayed in much more ample spaces than were available in the collector's lifetime. In addition, sculpture was relocated in spaces created by transforming the former garden into a sculpture court. The two- and three-dimensional works of art thus housed in the Palazzo and its garden in essence constitute the contents of the current catalogue.

The task of compiling this publication was, from the outset, placed in the hands of Angelica Zander Rudenstine, who had already completed her work on the first Guggenheim collection catalogue, which was devoted to those of our paintings of the pre-1945 period not included in the Thannhauser Collection. Study of individual works and extensive interviews with Peggy Guggenheim herself therefore preoccupied Mrs. Rudenstine, then Research Curator at the Solomon R. Guggenheim Museum, a position she had held since the mid-1970s. Concentrated research and writing relative to Peggy Guggenheim's holdings only began, however, two years after the collector's death, and the manuscript for this book was not completed until 1983, by which time the author made her contributions in a free-lance capacity. As expected, the result was eminently worth waiting for; Mrs. Rudenstine delivered a work exemplary in every respect, for which The Solomon R. Guggenheim Foundation and beyond it the world of art-historical scholarship remain greatly in her debt.

A publication as ambitious as the present book demands financial commitments impossible to undertake without generous assistance. We therefore express our very real gratitude to the National Endowment for the Arts, the National Endowment for the Humanities and the Samuel H. Kress Foundation for their essential support of this project.

Peggy Guggenheim Collection: The Solomon R. Guggenheim Foundation thus takes its place within a larger scheme of documentation, designed to complement, through exacting and consistent scholarship, the process of collecting upon which the Foundation's raison d'être is based.

THOMAS M. MESSER, *Director*
The Solomon R. Guggenheim Foundation

INTRODUCTION AND ACKNOWLEDGMENTS

This catalogue is intended not only for students and scholars but also for more general readers interested in a detailed discussion of individual works in the Peggy Guggenheim Collection. Like its predecessor, *The Guggenheim Museum Collection: Paintings 1800-1945*, the current study focuses primarily on questions and issues that can be addressed objectively or factually. Thus, a particular entry may contain a discussion of dating, of iconography, or of preparatory studies and their relationship to the final work. Or it may concentrate on the artist's medium, on his or her expressed attitude toward materials, on the nature of the work's surface, or on the physical changes that have been wrought by time or by human intervention.

The condition statements in each entry (some of which incorporate notes on process and technique) are directly linked to the art-historical analyses that follow them, since the information they contain may well affect the resolution of other questions. For example, a Giacometti sculpture may depend upon a minutely calculated set of interrelationships among its various parts for the definition of its aesthetic as well as its iconographic meaning. If these interrelationships have been altered, however minimally, the way in which the piece is read, evaluated, and understood will also be changed. In oil painting, a matte, unvarnished surface may constitute a critical ingredient in the artist's mode of expression, sometimes comparable in importance to the very composition itself: for artists as diverse as Braque, Picasso, Hartigan, and Vedova (to name only a few), this concern has been significant, and the preservation, or loss, of such surfaces must be taken into account in any reading or interpretation of the pictures involved. In the case of bronze sculpture, a variety of issues is raised by the material, the technical execution, and the finish of a piece: Brancusi, Moore, Richier, and Pomodoro, for example, have paid meticulous attention to questions of color (chemical composition) and of patina; Ernst, by contrast, has attached little importance to these matters in his sculpture, although the complexity and subtlety of surface textures in his paintings and collages bear witness to an entirely different set of priorities in those media. In the casting process, the role which the artist chooses to play can vary considerably; but posthumous casting, often executed without instructions from the artist regarding matters as fundamental as scale or materials, raises a set of aesthetic and other issues that must necessarily be addressed in any critical study of a sculptor's oeuvre.

When questions concerning the physical aspects of a work of art are at stake, specific technical and other objective evidence can be brought to bear on identified problems. In the case of iconography, however, the relationship between objective evidence and interpretation is clearly more complex. Peggy Guggenheim's collection is especially rich in works by artists of the Surrealist group. The "subject matter" of their art frequently involves references to literary texts, to political or social events and conditions, to biographical or autobiographical situations, or to significant intellectual movements or theories. An elucidation of the subject matter of particular paintings may require the identification and explication of such references. In addressing this material, I have attempted to adhere as strictly as possible to a given artist's own statements about his or her work, or to what the artist is known to have read, seen, or experienced. However, even data or evidence that seem to derive their authority from the artist's own testimony (broadly conceived) must be treated with caution. Iconographic elements tend to be intrinsically ambiguous or obscure (especially when Surrealist works are in question), and any effort to address them must involve hypotheses that are tentative rather than demonstrative in nature. Nonetheless, by respecting as much as possible the boundaries of the artist's statements or experiences, a core of fundamental information—relevant to a variety of modes of scholarship and criticism — can be compiled, and such information is presented here wherever possible. (See, for example, the discussions of Dalí's *La Naissance des désirs liquides,* cat. no. 41; Ernst's *La toilette de la mariée,* cat. no. 59, and *The Antipope,* cat. no. 60; or Masson's *L'Armure,* cat. no. 110.)

In abstract and nonobjective art, the nature of content or subject matter is further complicated by the issues of title or source. Titles may be intended to serve as elements in the structure of content, or may perform an entirely neutral function. The 1943 Motherwell collage in the Peggy Guggenheim Collection (cat. no. 128) originally carried a title (long forgotten, but now reinstated), which may offer clues toward a reading of the work's imagery; the titles of Still's pre-1947 paintings (later rejected by him, but originally his own) may imply the presence of a "mythic" or other subject matter; Pollock's titles, like his imagery, have become a focal point of a controversy concerning the presence or absence of an identifiable Jungian content.

Like the title, the source from which a composition has been abstracted may be of negligible or of paramount importance. The identification of specific sources in nature for Mondrian's paintings in 1914-15 or van Doesburg's in 1919 provides critical information in illuminating their progress toward an art without recognizable referent; but these sources may be largely incidental to the achieved content of the final work. In other cases, the very identification of the sources is a subject of dispute. The 1944 paintings of Gorky, for example, have been variously read as rooted in a figurative, narrative source and importantly illuminated by their titles, or as entirely free of decipherable imagery and therefore susceptible of neither literal nor metaphorical interpretation.

In examining such issues, I have attempted to establish in the first instance what is known by virtue of the artist's own testimony or through other documentary evidence. In those cases where an artist supplied a title, I have sought to reconstruct the context for it in order to clarify the title's apparent purpose, and to establish, as far as possible, whether it was intended to function descriptively, metaphorically, or merely neutrally (as a numerical title might). Similarly, in offering information regarding possible sources for an artist's imagery, I have focused mainly on those issues that were identified or raised in some important form by the artist himself, attempting thereby to present the evidence for an evaluation of content in its broadest sense.

By concentrating on factual art-historical problems posed by individual works, I have inevitably imposed certain constraints upon the format of this book. Stylistic analysis, comments of a more general or critical nature, and attempts to place a given work within the overall context of an artist's oeuvre are discussed only insofar as they can help to shed light upon specific art-historical questions. Consequently, the individual entries vary considerably in length, and the variations do not necessarily reflect the relative importance of the works in question. Thus the absence of any textual discussion of Braque's 1926 *Le compotier de raisin*—a work that Peggy Guggenheim regarded as one of the most outstanding acquisitions she ever made — results from the fact that the picture poses no significant art-historical problems.

As in all such undertakings, many questions remain unresolved. The principle objective has been — as in my earlier volumes — to explore fundamental problems and to present evidence in such a way as to distinguish (in Sir John Pope-Hennessy's words) "between what is possible, what is probable, and what is fact."

It has not seemed appropriate, within the context of this catalogue, to include a biographical study of Peggy Guggenheim herself, nor to attempt a full narrative history of her two galleries, Guggenheim Jeune (in London) and Art of This Century (in New York). Nonetheless, in view of the considerable historical importance of her activities, and of the demonstrable links between her role as a gallery owner and the growth of her collection, it has seemed important to provide the reader with some documentation concerning these particular aspects of her career. Thus in the Appendix (pp. 746-801) a schematic history of Guggenheim Jeune (1938-39) and Art of This Century (1942-47) is presented. The exhibition invitations, announcements, checklists, and catalogues of the two galleries are reproduced in their entirety. Also included are selected reviews of exhibitions and installations, occasional press reports of controversial events provoked by the activities of the galleries, and some evaluations (published and unpublished) of the nature and extent of Peggy Guggenheim's achievement. Frederick Kiesler's historic design for the interior of Art of This Century and installation of the collection is presented in brief, and several of his original drawings for the project are reproduced, together with Berenice Abbott's 1942 photographs of the completed installation.

Finally, incorporated into the brief commentary is a selection of information provided by Peggy Guggenheim herself (or by others in her circle) concerning the formation of her collection, the advice she received from various friends, the planning for her two galleries (and for various exhibitions held in them), the ideas for a museum in London and subsequently in Paris (both aborted by World War II), and the realization of the museum-gallery concept in New York.

The abbreviated history that emerges from such a presentation of documents and commentaries is — of necessity — fragmentary and indeed arbitrary, since it lacks the depth and much fuller articulation of light and shadow that a substantial historical study would provide. Such a comprehensive study, describing and evaluating the entire range of Peggy Guggenheim's achievement, must be recounted in another context. Within the present volume, it has been possible only to provide a very preliminary outline of selected events, deriving essentially from the primary source — the collector herself.

In the course of preparing this catalogue, I have been helped by many individuals and institutions.

First and foremost, Peggy Guggenheim, in the four years before her death on December 24, 1979, received me hospitably in Venice on many occasions. During those years she was always generous with her time, her knowledge, her reminiscences, and her insights. She was vital to the entire undertaking and had hoped to see the catalogue in published form.

After her death, I resumed work on the project in January 1982. Philip Rylands, Administrator of the Peggy Guggenheim Collection since that time, has been unfailingly generous in his support, fulfilling innumerable requests for aid and information, and sparing no effort to achieve results.

Photographic documentation was, in the early stages, the responsibility solely of Mirko Lion, for many years Peggy Guggenheim's regular photographer in Venice. He supplied a complete set of study photographs for research purposes and was generously responsive to all requests for new material. The photography for the publication itself was executed by Carmelo Guadagno and David Heald of the Guggenheim Museum in New York. Their dedication, sensitivity, and skill combined to produce photographs of outstanding quality. My thanks are also owed to their coordinator, Holly Fullam.

The task of editing the catalogue was carried out with diligence by Brenda Gilchrist, who made unusual efforts to introduce consistency into the manuscript. Malcolm Grear Designers demonstrated extraordinary patience, flexibility, and imagination in arriving at solutions for the most intractable problems in the layout of the book; collaboration with them has proved most rewarding. I have worked closely with a number of conservators; the results of our deliberations are described and acknowledged below (pp. 22-23).

Research was carried out in many different libraries. My thanks are due to Wladimiro Dorigo of La Biennale di Venezia, to members of the staff of the Frick Art Reference Library, The New York Public Library, the Thomas J. Watson Library of The Metropolitan Museum of Art, and the library of The Tate Gallery. I am also indebted to Mary Joan Hall, formerly of the Solomon R. Guggenheim Museum Library, and to Sonja Bay and Marion Wolf of the present staff, for many kindnesses. Mary Schmidt, Anne McArthur, and other members of the staff of The Princeton University Library generously provided me with congenial working space, made the exceptional resources of the Marquand Library available and helped in innumerable other ways. Clive Phillpot of The

Museum of Modern Art Library, together with Janis Ekdahl, Daniel Starr, and Daniel Pearl of his staff, provided assistance, space, and goodwill for me and for my assistants throughout the period of the book's preparation. At a time when the Museum of Modern Art's new building was under construction and their own facilities were far from ideal, they continued to offer the highest quality of professional service; the catalogue could not have been produced without them.

Many scholars, experts, and colleagues have shared their specialized knowledge with me, facilitated access to documentary materials, or assisted in other ways. I am indebted to Dawn Ades, Ronald Alley, Troels Andersen, Max Bill, Alan Bowness, Nicolas Calas, William A. Camfield, Giovanni Carandente, Ester Coën, the late Douglas Cooper, Pierre Daix, Eric Estorick, Maurizio Fagiolo dell'Arco, Sidney Geist, Jürgen Glaesemer, Clement Greenberg, Viviane Grimminger, Renilde Hammacher van den Brande, Jane H. Hancock, Anne d'Harnoncourt, Lynda Roscoe Hartigan, Dagmar Hnikova, Maurice Jardot, Joop M. Joosten, Lillian Kiesler, James Lord, Lydia Winston Malbin, Carmen Martinez, Pierre Matisse, Katherine J. Michaelson, David Mitchinson, Richard Morphet, Andrei B. Nakov, Peter Nisbet, Francis V. O'Connor, the late Sir Roland Penrose, the late Lee Krasner Pollock, Margaret Potter, John Richardson, Michèle Richet, Daniel Robbins, Merle Schipper, Athena Tacha Spear, Giuseppe Sprovieri, Evert van Straaten, Greta Ströh, James Johnson Sweeney, the late Joshua C. Taylor, Gary Tinterow, Peg Weiss, Sarah Whitfield, and Judith Zilczer.

For generous and careful readings of certain entries, as well as for other important assistance, I am especially grateful to Yve-Alain Bois, Marianne Martin, Piero Pacini, David Sylvester, and Nancy J. Troy.

I have been privileged to work with a group of outstanding research assistants. From 1975-78 Susan D. Ferleger Brades was my chief assistant, joined in some initial undertakings by Linda Shearer. During the years 1978-79, Susan Ferleger continued to help on a part-time basis while Dorothy Kosinski assumed the duties of chief assistant. Finally, in 1982-83 — the second phase of work on the catalogue — Lucy Flint, joined for one year by Ann Dumas, worked with me to bring the catalogue to a conclusion. After she left the museum in November 1983, Lucy Flint also read the entire book in manuscript and offered many suggestions for its improvement. These five colleagues made significant substantive contributions, in innumerable ways, to all aspects of this undertaking. My debt to them, both personal and professional, is immeasurable.

Cynthia Goodman was employed as research assistant for a shorter period of time and contributed in very important measure; and among the many museum interns who worked under my supervision, I am especially grateful to Elizabeth C. Childs, Sabine Dylla, Joan Friedman, Alison Greene, Margaret Sullivan, Eugenie Tsai, and Brian Wallis.

I also wish to thank Thomas M. Messer and the Trustees of the Guggenheim Museum for the strong support they provided from the project's inception.

Finally, I am much indebted to the artists and relatives of artists whose generous cooperation has contributed extensively to my knowledge and understanding of works in Peggy Guggenheim's collection. They are Pierre Alechinsky, Karel Appel, Marguerite Arp-Hagenbach, Francis Bacon, Elica and Luce Balla, Ethel Baziotes, César, Pietro Consagra, Alan Davie, the late Sonia Delaunay, Paul Delvaux, Piero Dorazio, Jean Dubuffet, Teeny Duchamp, Rae Ferren, Diego Giacometti, the late Juliette Gleizes, Françoise Guiter, David Hare, Grace Hartigan, Jacqueline and Jean Hélion, Hundertwasser, Madeleine Kemeny, Ibram Lassaw, Claude and Denise Laurens, Yulla Lipchitz, Heinz Mack, Marina Marini, André Masson, the late Joan Miró, Henry Moore, Robert Motherwell, Hanno Mott, the late Ben Nicholson, Eduardo Paolozzi, Virginie Pevsner, Arnaldo Pomodoro, Giuseppe Santomaso, John Tunnard, Günther Uecker, Victor Vasarely, and Emilio Vedova.

ANGELICA ZANDER RUDENSTINE
Princeton, New Jersey

EXPLANATORY NOTES

Biographical Data:

Since monographic studies exist on every artist included, biographical data has been limited to the date and place of an artist's birth and death, or, in the case of a living artist, to the date and place of birth and the present residence.

Titles:

The artist's title, where known, is given first in the original language. Following in parentheses are an English translation (where relevant) and other titles by which the work has been known.

Medium:

In the case of bronzes, the casting method is given. Wherever possible, the size of the edition, the whereabouts of other casts, and the name of the foundry is indicated. The date given for a bronze is that of the plaster original; where known, the date of the actual cast, especially important in the case of posthumous casts, follows in parentheses.

In the case of works on canvas, the presence of varnish applied by the artist is implied unless otherwise indicated.

In the case of works on paper, the nature of the paper is specified wherever possible; the presence of water marks is recorded.

Measurements:

In order to conform to other SRGM publications, measurements are given in inches followed by centimeters. Height precedes width; in the case of sculpture, at least one additional dimension is provided. If a painting or drawing is of irregular dimensions, the measurements have been taken at the widest point.

Right and left:

Unless otherwise stated these terms indicate the spectator's right and left.

Inscriptions:

The artist's inscriptions and signatures, whether on the recto or the verso of the work, are recorded in the entry; in the case of sculpture, foundry marks, cast numbers, incised signatures and inscriptions are similarly recorded. When clearly legible, all such inscriptions are also reproduced.

Provenance:

Information regarding provenance was, unless otherwise indicated, supplied to the author by Peggy Guggenheim herself. Although she had by 1976 preserved little in the way of physical documentation concerning acquisitions, her memory was remarkable, and her recollections were almost without exception borne out by subsequent research.

Condition:

Although it has not been possible to achieve a comprehensive account of the condition and conservation history of each work, an attempt has been made to assemble the important facts. If a painting has been cleaned, lined, or placed on a new stretcher; a work on paper cleaned, lined, or remounted; a sculpture cleaned, treated, or remounted, these facts are noted. Areas of damage, deterioration, and repair are indicated, with dates and methods of treatment included where known.

During the lifetime of Peggy Guggenheim, conservation measures were periodically undertaken at her request, either by artist friends or by professional conservators, the latter often staff members of a museum to which the collection had been lent. In response to questions from the author, Peggy Guggenheim was frequently able to recall that a given work had been restored, although specific information or records regarding the nature of the intervention no longer survived. Where relevant, these recollections are noted.

A condition report on the collection, prepared in 1964-65 by the Keeper of Conservation at The Tate Gallery, London, provides invaluable information regarding the condition of the collection at that date (see Abbreviations, p. 29, Tate Report). With the permission of the Director of The Tate Gallery, as well as that of the present Keeper of Conservation, this report is frequently cited in the catalogue entries.

Howard Hussey of New York, a long-time friend and assistant of Joseph Cornell, cleaned and restored the Cornells in Venice at Peggy Guggenheim's request in September 1976; he kindly shared the records of his work with the author and granted permission for citation from them (see cat. nos. 35-39).

Additional information regarding condition has been derived from reports on individual works prepared at various times by Orrin Riley and Lucy Belloli, former members of the Conservation Department at the Guggenheim Museum in New York; José Orraca, Suzanne Schnitzer, Margaret Watherston, Martina Yamin, all of New York; Merrit Safford, Helen Otis, and Marjorie Shelley of the Department of Paper Conservation, The Metropolitan Museum of Art; and Kasha Szeleysnki, The Tate Gallery, London.

The author consulted with all of the above restorers before, during, and/or after their work on the collection and benefited from their insights and observations.

Following the death of Peggy Guggenheim, Paul Schwarzbaum was appointed conservation consultant by the Director of The Solomon R. Guggenheim Foundation. In this capacity, he was charged with overall responsibility for the conservation of the Peggy Guggenheim Collection. He has made much information available to the author. Conservators appointed by him in the fields of painting, sculpture, and paper have worked closely with the author throughout the preparation of the catalogue. Especially fruitful collaborations were established with Marjorie Shelley, paper conservator, and Sergio Angelucci, sculpture conservator. Their knowledge and expertise have elucidated many questions, and they have contributed extensively to the catalogue as published.

Conservation of the collection is, naturally, a continuous process. The statements of condition and records of treatment included here are dated, thus providing the reader with a specific terminus ante quem. In some cases, treatment that is here described as "envisaged" or "projected" will have taken place by the date of publication of this volume.

Exhibitions:

An attempt has been made to provide complete exhibition histories. Exhibitions of Peggy Guggenheim's entire collection are included, starting with the installation at Art of This Century in New York in October 1942. Although the latter was clearly intended as a museum installation rather than a temporary exhibition (see Appendix, p. 771), its relatively short timespan (five years), and the impact of its presentation in New York, offer justification for its designation as an exhibition.

The comparative infrequency with which individual works from the collection have appeared in one-man or group exhibitions requires some explanation. After Peggy Guggenheim moved to Venice in 1947 and established her museum at the Palazzo Venier dei Leoni, the house was open to the public several hours each week during the Venetian season (Easter to November). Understandably, she wished the collection to be visible there. During the winter months, when the palazzo was closed, she preferred to lend the collection as a whole to another museum, thereby simultaneously maintaining its identity as a unit, making it available to a new public, and providing it with the security and protection of a professionally staffed institution. Under these general principles the collection was shown over the years in Florence, Milan, Amsterdam, Zurich, Brussels, London, Stockholm, Louisiana, New York, Paris, and Torino. Meanwhile, although individual loans for important retrospectives or group shows were frequently requested, they were granted only in exceptional cases.

References:

The references are selective rather than comprehensive. In general the entries include only early publications, catalogues raisonnés, and sources, including exhibition catalogues, that contribute something new to the understanding of the work of art. At least one color reproduction of the work is listed where possible. If the reader's attention is being drawn to a reproduction, the reference is given as: repr. p. 115. If the reader's attention is being drawn to the text, which may include a reproduction, the reference is given as: p. 115, repr.

Illustrations:

Every work in the catalogue is illustrated in black and white together with its entry; sculptures are shown in at least two views. Eighty-four works are also illustrated in color on plates gathered into five groups scattered throughout the book. The presence of a color plate and the page number on which it appears are indicated immediately following the title in the catalogue entry. Similarly the caption to each color plate includes the page number on which the text of the relevant entry begins.

ABBREVIATIONS

AAA:	Archives of American Art, Smithsonian Institution, Washington, D.C.
Alley, 1964:	R. Alley, *The Peggy Guggenheim Collection*, London, The Arts Council of Great Britain, 1964.
[Alley], *Peggy Guggenheim Foundation*, 1968:	*The Peggy Guggenheim Foundation, Venice*, Torino, 1968 (first edition). A handbook to the collection reprinted several times, the last edition 1979. The text was reprinted almost entirely from Ronald Alley's catalogue of the exhibition held at The Tate Gallery, 1964-65. References are to the first edition unless otherwise indicated.
Alley, *Tate Collection*, 1981:	R. Alley, *The Tate Gallery's Collection of Modern Art, Other than Works by British Artists*, London, The Tate Gallery, 1981.
Amsterdam, *P.G.*, 1951:	Amsterdam, Stedelijk Museum, *Surrealisme + Abstractie*, January 19-February 26, 1951; traveled to Brussels, Palais des Beaux-Arts, March 3-28, 1951.
A.Z.R. *Guggenheim*, 1976, Vol. I, Vol. II:	Angelica Zander Rudenstine, *The Guggenheim Museum Collection: Paintings 1880-1945*, New York, The Solomon R. Guggenheim Museum, 1976.
Calas, 1966:	N. Calas and E. Calas, *The Peggy Guggenheim Collection of Modern Art*, New York, 1966.
L. Flint, *Handbook*, 1983:	L. Flint, *Handbook: The Peggy Guggenheim Collection*, New York, The Solomon R. Guggenheim Foundation, 1983.
Florence, *P.G.*, 1949:	Florence, Palazzo Strozzi, *La Collezione Guggenheim*, February 19-March 10, 1949; traveled to Milan, Palazzo Reale, June 1949.

P. Guggenheim, *Art of This Century*, 1942: (re. REFERENCES) P. Guggenheim, ed., *Art of This Century; Objects—Drawings—Photographs—Paintings—Sculpture—Collages, 1910-1942*, New York, 1942.

P. Guggenheim, *Out of This Century:* 1946: P. Guggenheim, *Out of This Century: The Informal Memoirs of Peggy Guggenheim*, New York, 1946. Reprinted (revised) in *Out of This Century: Confessions of an Art Addict*, New York, 1979. References are to the 1946 edition unless otherwise indicated.

P. Guggenheim, *Confessions*, 1960: P. Guggenheim, *Confessions of an Art Addict*, London, 1960. Reprinted (revised) in *Out of This Century: Confessions of an Art Addict*, New York, 1979. References are to the 1960 edition unless otherwise indicated.

Lefranc retouching varnish: A commercial picture varnish based on methacrylate resin, with minor addition of microcrystalline wax.

Langhorne, 1977: E. L. Langhorne, "A Jungian Interpretation of Jackson Pollock's Art Through 1946," unpublished Ph.D. dissertation, University of Pennsylvania, 1977.

London, *P. G.*, 1964-65: London, The Arts Council of Great Britain, The Tate Gallery, *The Peggy Guggenheim Collection*, December 31, 1964-March 7, 1965.

Lucite 44: Poly (n-butyl methacrylate). Dupont.

Lucite 46: 50:50 copolymer of Lucite 44 and Lucite 45 (isobutyl methacrylate). Dupont.

Maimeri varnish colors: Powdered pigment ground in dammar (natural resin).

MNAM:	Musée National d'Art Moderne, Centre Georges Pompidou, Paris.
MoMA:	The Museum of Modern Art, New York.
New York, MoMA, *Cubism and Abstract Art*, 1936:	*Cubism and Abstract Art*, New York, The Museum of Modern Art, March 2-April 19, 1936; traveled to San Francisco Museum of Art, July 27-August 24, 1936; Cincinnati Art Museum, October 19-November 16, 1936; The Minneapolis Institute of Arts, November 29-December 27, 1936; Cleveland Museum of Art, January 1-February 7, 1937; The Baltimore Museum of Art, February 17-March 17, 1937; Rhode Island School of Design, March 24-April 21, 1937; Grand Rapids Art Gallery, April 29-May 26, 1937.
New York, MoMA, *Fantastic Art, Dada, Surrealism*, 1936-37:	*Fantastic Art, Dada, Surrealism*, New York, The Museum of Modern Art, December 7, 1936-January 17, 1937; traveled to Philadelphia, The Pennsylvania Museum of Art, January 30-March 1, 1937; Boston Institute of Modern Art, Inc., March 6-April 3, 1937; Springfield, Mass., Museum of Fine Arts, April 12-May 10, 1937; Milwaukee Art Institute, May 19-June 16, 1937; Minneapolis, University Gallery, University of Minnesota, June 26-July 24, 1937; San Francisco Museum of Art, August 6-September 3, 1937.
New York, Art of This Century, 1942-47:	(re. EXHIBITIONS) Permanent installation, designed by Frederick Kiesler, of Peggy Guggenheim's collection at Art of This Century. The installation opened on October 21, 1942, and closed in June 1947.
New York, *P. G.*, 1969:	New York, Solomon R. Guggenheim Museum, *Works from the Peggy Guggenheim Foundation*, January 16-March 23, 1969.

New York, *P. G.*, 1982-83:	New York, Solomon R. Guggenheim Museum, *60 Works: The Peggy Guggenheim Collection*, November 18, 1982-March 13, 1983.
O'Connor, 1967:	F. V. O'Connor, *Jackson Pollock*, exhibition catalogue, The Museum of Modern Art, New York, 1967.
O'Connor and Thaw:	F. V. O'Connor and E. V. Thaw, eds., *Jackson Pollock*, 4 vols., New Haven and London, 1978. References to this publication, unless otherwise indicated, are to vol. 1.
Paraloid B-72:	A methacrylate copolymer (Rohm and Haas, Acryloid B-72). The normal solvents for this resin are xylene and toluene.
Paris, *P. G.*, 1974-75:	Paris, Orangerie des Tuileries, *Art du XXe Siècle: Fondation Peggy Guggenheim, Venise*, November 30, 1974-March 3, 1975.
P. G.:	Peggy Guggenheim. This abbreviation is used to designate exhibitions and publications of the collection.
Rome, *Guggenheim: Venezia-New York*, 1982:	Rome, Campidoglio Pinacoteca Capitolina, *Guggenheim: Venezia-New York. Sessanta Opere 1900-1950*, January 23-March 28, 1982.
SRGM:	Solomon R. Guggenheim Museum, New York.
Stockholm, *P. G.*, 1966-67:	Stockholm, Moderna Museet, *Peggy Guggenheim's Samling från Venedig*, November 26, 1966-January 8, 1967; traveled to Louisiana, Humlebaek, January 19-March 5, 1967.

Tate Report: A condition report on the collection, prepared by The Tate Gallery's Keeper of Conservation, Stefan Slabczynski, with the assistance of Viscount Dunluce, before and during The Arts Council of Great Britain exhibition held at The Tate Gallery in 1964-65.

Torino, *P. G.*, 1975-76: Torino, Galleria Civica d'Arte Moderna, *Arte del XX Secolo, La Collezione Peggy Guggenheim, Venezia*, December 3, 1975-February 29, 1976.

Venice, Giardino, 1949: Venice, Giardino del Palazzo Venier dei Leoni, *Mostra di scultura contemporanea*, September, 1949.

Venice, Museo Correr, *Jackson Pollock*, 1950: Venice, Ala Napoleonica, Museo Correr, *Jackson Pollock*, July 22-August 12, 1950. Two catalogues were published, the second of which gives August 15 as the closing date. The exhibition traveled to Milan, Galleria d'Arte del Naviglio, October-November 1950, but no catalogue or checklist of the Milan portion of the exhibition (which may not have included all works) has been located.

Venice, *P. G.*, 1948 (Biennale): Venice, *XXIV Biennale di Venezia, La Collezione Peggy Guggenheim*, May 29-September 30, 1948.

Zurich, *P. G.*, 1951: Zurich, Kunsthaus, *Moderne Kunst aus der Sammlung Peggy Guggenheim*, April 15-May 14, 1951.

COLOR PLATES

Cat. no. 49, p. 259.
Duchamp, *Nu (esquisse), Jeune homme triste dans un train*, 1911-12.

Cat. no. 137, p. 611.
Picasso, *Le poète*, August 1911.

Cat. no. 19, p. 127.
Braque, *La clarinette*, summer-fall 1912.

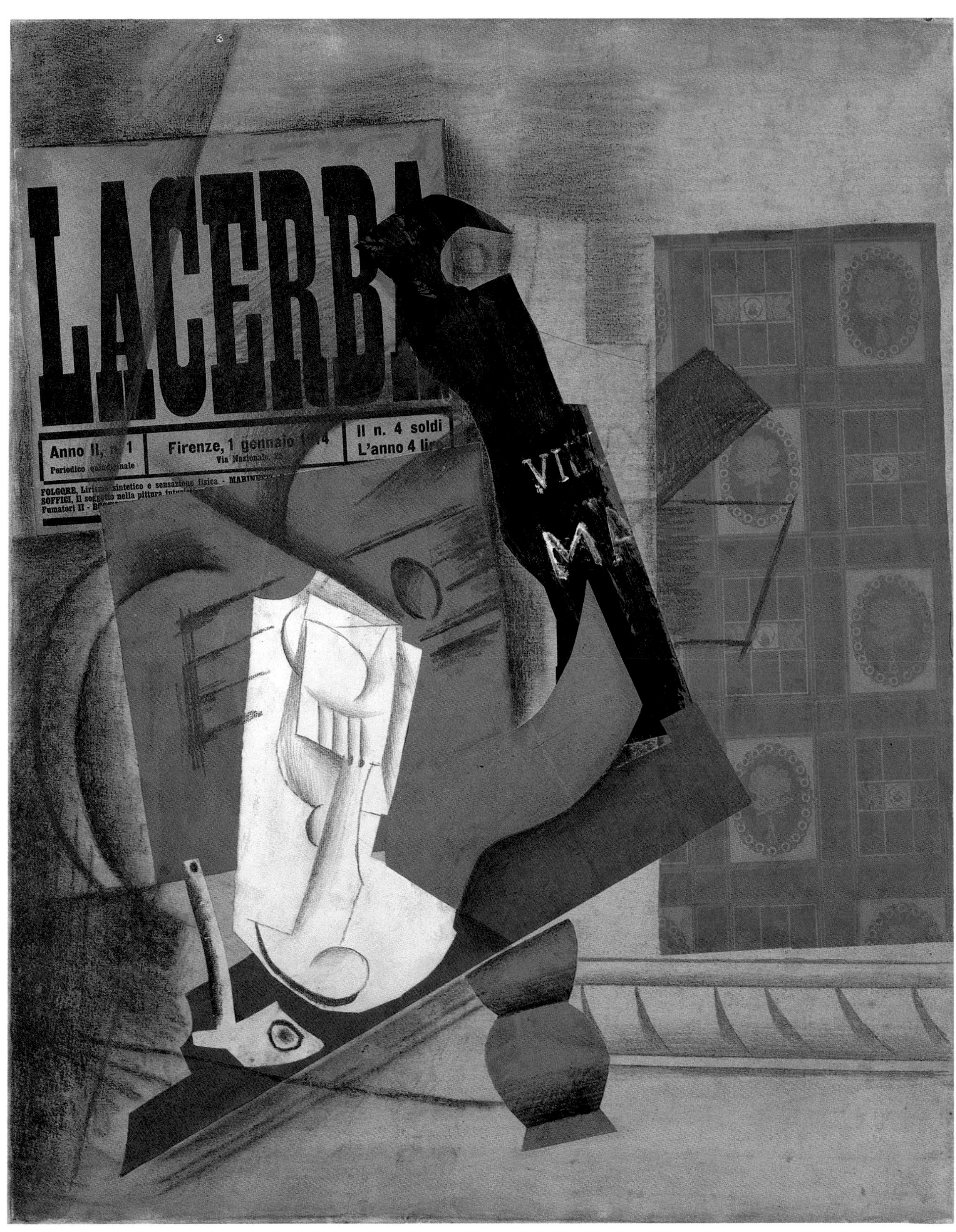

Cat. no. 138, p. 613.
Picasso, *Pipe, verre, bouteille de Vieux Marc*, spring 1914.

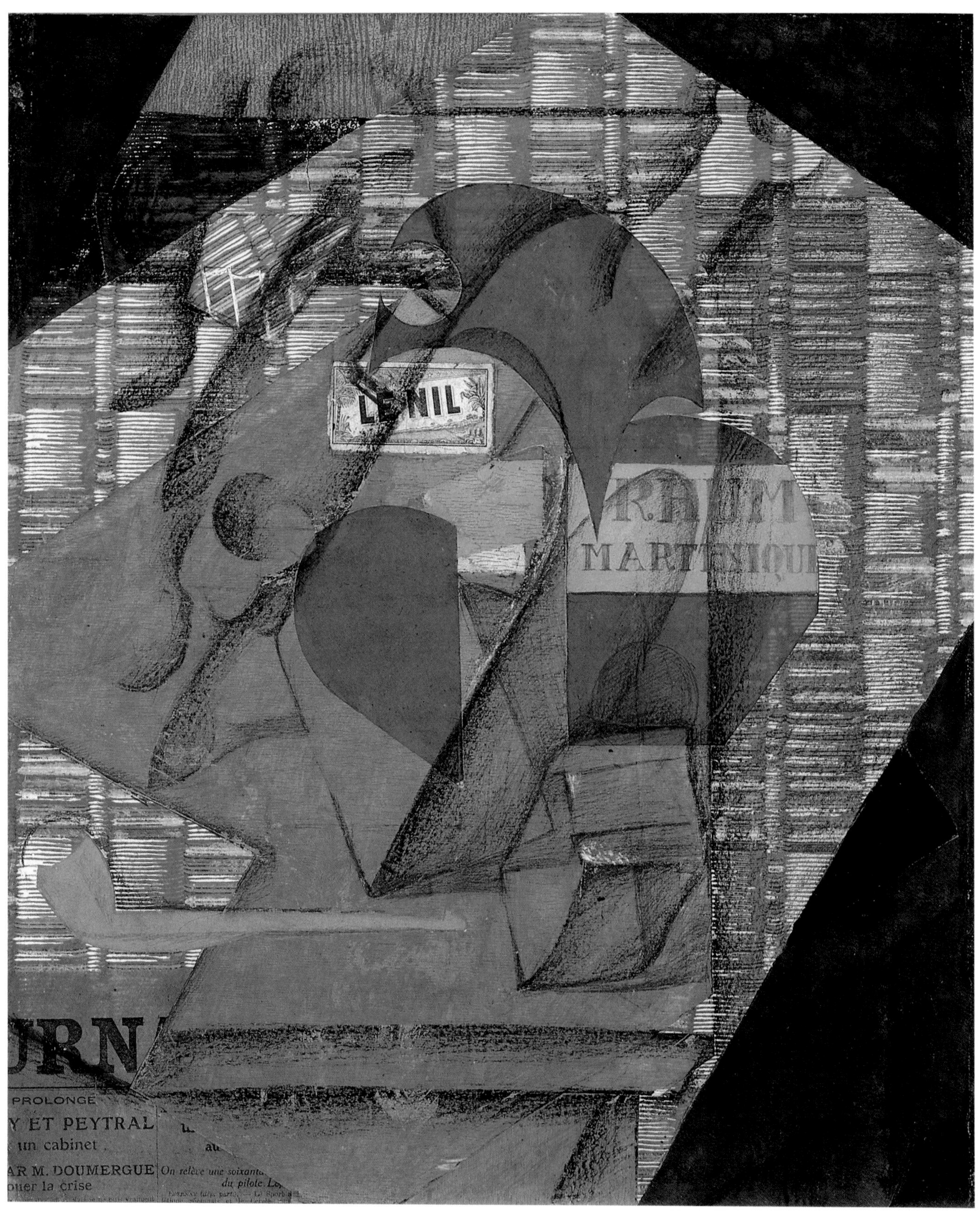

Cat. no. 74, p. 376.
Gris, *Bouteille de rhum et journal*, June 1914.

Cat. no. 108, p. 512.
Marcoussis, *L'Habitué*, 1920.

Cat. no. 71, p. 358.
Gleizes, *La dame aux bêtes (Madame Raymond Duchamp-Villon)*, completed by February 1914.

Cat. no. 177, p. 739.
Villon, *Espaces*, 1920.

Cat. no. 115, p. 532.
Metzinger, *Au Vélodrome*, ca. 1914 (?).

. no. 43, p. 208.
aunay, *Fenêtres ouvertes simultanément Ière partie 3e motif*, 1912.

Cat. no. 92, p. 439.
Kupka, Study for *Localisations de mobiles graphiques I*, ca. 1911-12.

Cat. no. 93, p. 442.
Kupka, *Autour d'un point*, ca. 1920-25.

Cat. no. 91, p. 434.
Kupka, Study for *Amorpha, Chromatique chaude* and for *Fugue à deux couleurs*, ca. 1910-11.

Cat. no. 82, p. 412.
Kandinsky, *Landschaft mit roten Flecken*, No. 2, 1913.

Cat. no. 13, p. 87.
Balla, *Velocità astratta + rumore*, 1913-14.

Cat. no. 162, p. 700.
Severini, *Mare = Ballerina*, January 1914.

Cat. no. 29, p. 152.
Chagall, *La pluie*, 1911.

CATALOGUE

Pierre Alechinsky

Born October 1927, Brussels.
Lives in Bougival.

1 Peignoir. 1972.
(*Dressing Gown*).

Color plate p. 507.

76.2553 PG 176a

Acrylic on wood-pulp paper mounted (with acrylic glue) on canvas, 38 3/16 x 60 7/16 (99.5 x 153.5).[1]

Signed l.l.: *Alechinsky*. Not dated.

PROVENANCE:

Purchased from the artist, Biennale, Venice, October 1972.

CONDITION:

The work has received no treatment. During the course of mounting the work on a prepared canvas, the artist repaired and retouched certain small tears and losses at the edges. All edges were secured with brown paper tape and the surface sprayed with acrylic varnish. There are some bubbles in the paint film. The condition is stable. (New York, Dec. 1982.)

The artist has stated (in conversation with the author, Apr. 1983) that the paper support is expected to serve only an intermediate, temporary purpose in the life of the work of art. His intention is that the poor quality paper will gradually disintegrate through the action of the acrylic emulsion. As the paper disappears, the image is intended, gradually and naturally, to transfer to the canvas secondary support. The varnish functions to protect the surface.

Alechinsky's first experiments with acrylics were made in 1965 in the New York studio of Walasse Ting. He abandoned oil painting shortly afterward and then habitually worked — as in this instance — with acrylic paints and loose sheets of paper spread on the floor. The freedom and mobility afforded by the unattached support functioned as elements in his technique.

In the case of *Peignoir*, the artist has described his compositional procedure as follows: The imagery evolved gradually from an initial linear *écriture* which covered the entire field. The application of color followed, and only during this second stage did he make the critical compositional choices and decisions. In deciding which parts of the *écriture* should remain and which should be suppressed through the addition of color, he forced the composition to emerge. With the application of the blue pigment on the right, "the major risk was taken," and this became for him the subject of the picture. Since the risk taken was a total risk, the picture could only totally fail or totally succeed in its application, with the blue *peignoir* becoming the very image that he sought in the work as a whole.[2] The title of the work thus rose directly out of the process of composition and serves as a reflection of its imagery.

EXHIBITIONS:

Venice, XXXVI Biennale, June 11-Oct. 1, 1972, no. 48 (*Vestaglia*); Paris, *P.G.*, 1974-75, no. 147; Torino, *P.G.*, 1975-76, no. 166; New York, *P.G.*, 1982-83, no. 49.

REFERENCES:

G. Soavi, XXXVI Biennale, Belgian Pavilion, *Alechinsky*, no. 23, repr. color; *Pierre Alechinsky: Paintings and Writings*, Paris, 1977, p. 229.

1. Alechinsky uses standard-sized sheets of tailors' pattern paper. The support, which is thin and flexible, stretches in the process of being glued to the canvas.
2. This description paraphrases the artist's own more poetic evocation of his process (in conversation with the author, Apr. 1983).

Karel Appel

Born April 1921, Amsterdam.
Lives in Paris and New York.

2 The Crying Crocodile Tries to Catch the Sun. 1956.
(*Crocodile*).

Color plate p. 505.

76.2553 PG 174

Oil on canvas, 57¼ x 44½ (145.5 x 113.1).

Signed and dated l.r.: *K. appel '56*.

PROVENANCE:

Purchased from the artist, Paris, March 6, 1957.

CONDITION:

The high level of oil content in the medium has resulted in poor drying, some areas remaining moist. Variations in temperature and humidity apparently induced liquifying and running of certain pigments after the work entered Peggy Guggenheim's collection. Uneven gradual drying of the thickly applied pigment has caused extensive pigment cracks, especially in the impasto areas.

Some mold on the surface was noted in 1968 (New York). Fungus was successfully removed from the surface (with ammonia, 10%, in water), Venice, 1981. The condition is stable. (Venice, Oct. 1982.)

Appel recalls that the original title of this work was *The Crocodile.*[1] Two or three months after the picture entered Peggy Guggenheim's collection, Appel visited her and found that the interior core of the black pigment in the crocodile's eyes had liquified and run, thus suggesting the new title, *The Crying Crocodile Tries to Catch the Sun*. Both he and Peggy Guggenheim agreed upon the revision, which she later abbreviated once again, with his permission, to *Crocodile*. He prefers the revised title, however, since it more nearly evokes his sense of the image.

Appel's technique, which depends on the use of thick, oily pigments often squeezed directly from the tube and then manipulated with palette knife or brush, is inherently subject to drying problems. While the outer skin of a paint high in oil content characteristically dries fast, the soft inner core dries slowly and indeed may never dry completely. The work is thus rendered especially vulnerable to changes in climatic conditions. Appel's understanding and acceptance of this problem led to the incorporation of certain risks into his underlying aesthetic. The unpremeditated changes in composition that occur, as they did in the present case, would be absorbed into what he perceived as the vitality of the image. The subject matter and imagery of the works themselves would be susceptible to comparable evolution and change, defining themselves only during the process of paint application, as the canvas was repeatedly shifted from a horizontal to a vertical position and back again.

In the present painting, initially the central form emerged as that of a human figure and the canvas was a horizontal (the present lower right corner being at the lower left). As the canvas was turned to the vertical position, the figure emerged as a crocodile with the sun on the right, and only then, with this unpremeditated development, did the composition crystallize for Appel.

EXHIBITIONS:

London, *P.G.*, 1964-65, no. 145, repr.; Stockholm, *P.G.*, 1966-67, no. 141, repr.; New York, *P.G.*, 1969, p. 166, repr.; Paris, *P.G.*, 1974-75, no. 146, repr.; Torino, *P.G.*, 1975-76, no. 163; New York, *P.G.*, 1982-83, no. 48, repr. color.

REFERENCES:

Calas, 1966, repr. p. 243; L. Flint, *Handbook*, 1983, no. 77, repr. color.

1. In an interview with Cynthia Goodman, New York, March-April, 1983.

Alexander Archipenko

Born May 1887, Kiev, Ukraine, Russia.
Died February 1964, New York.

3 La Boxe.[1] 1935.
(Boxing; Struggle; La Lutte).

76.2553 PG 26

Terra cotta. Height: 30⅛ (76.6).

Incised on reverse: „*LA BOXE" / C'est la musique / monumental* [sic] */ des volumes d'éspace* [sic] */ et de la matière / Archipenko / Paris 1913.*

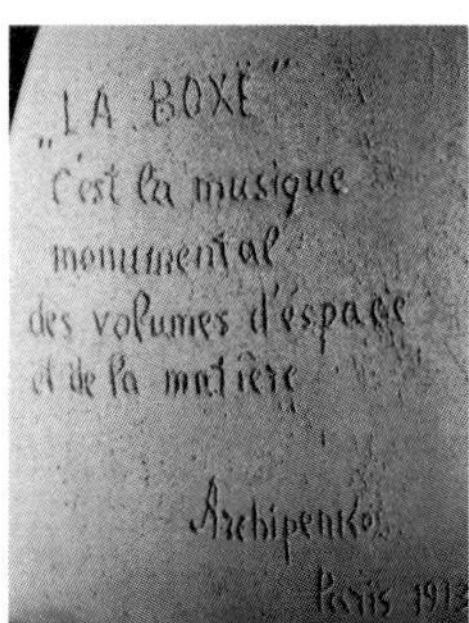

PROVENANCE:

Purchased from the artist, New York, ca. 1941.

CONDITION:

The work has received no treatment. A perpendicular crack in the lower front portion of the sculpture dating from the casting of the piece (7 in., 17.8 cm., in length) has not altered over time. A small break in the terra cotta at the lower edge (¾ in., 2 cm.) is a later damage. Apart from some water stains and darkening of the upper portions, the condition is stable. (Venice, Nov. 1982.)

1. The title, variously recorded as *La Boxe* and *La Lutte*, was given in all of the early sources, as well as on the early plasters, as *La Boxe*. Though this has been translated as *Boxing Match* and *Boxers*, and also as *Struggle*, the most exact translation would seem to be *Boxing*, implying both a literal and a metaphorical meaning.

Archipenko's original version of *La Boxe* was made of plaster, painted black and then polished. Two such plasters of identical size (height 23¾ in., 64 cm.), bearing the incised inscription *A. Archipenko / Paris 1914*, were cast from the same mold and exhibited during the first half of 1914.[2] By June 1914 the painter Alberto Magnelli had acquired one of the two casts and transported it, together with Archipenko's *Carrousel Pierrot* and *Medrano II*, to his home in Florence.[3] The second black plaster of *La Boxe* remained with Archipenko until 1921, when he departed for Germany and thence, in 1923, for the United States, leaving it and other works in the custody of Jean Verdier, who stored them on his property in Cannes. Archipenko was unable to retrieve these sculptures until after 1960.[4] During the intervening decades, while Archipenko was living in the United States, he made a number of copies and variants of his own earlier work (Michaelsen, 1976, p. 91). Peggy Guggenheim's terra cotta was such a variant, and since neither of the original plasters was available to him in 1935, he had to work in this case (as in others) from photographs and from memory, modeling the piece in clay, making a plaster mold, and casting the terra cotta from it. The specific impetus for the recreation of this sculpture was almost certainly a request from Barr to include *La Boxe* in his exhibition *Cubism and Abstract Art*. Barr was unaware at the time that both original plasters were in Europe and that Archipenko had therefore recreated the image in a new medium. In reproducing the 1935 terra cotta in his catalogue, Barr thus dated the work 1913 and made no textual allusion to the fact of a second version, nor to the difference in medium, scale, or date of execution.[5]

Archipenko's decision to make this second version 7⅜ in., 18.8 cm., taller than the original may have been a conscious one, though it could also be attributable to the fact that he had no precise information about the earlier dimension. The choice of terra cotta, however, arose out of his stated conviction that this was the most durable material available to him in the United States, where good marble or stone were unobtainable. Whether he would have pre-

2. Paris, *Société des Artistes Indépendants*, Mar. 1-Apr. 30, 1914, no. 85 ("*Boxe*"); Brussels, Galerie Georges Giroux, *Salon des Artistes Indépendants*, May 16-June 7, 1914, no. 4 ("*Boxe*"); Amsterdam, *De Onafhankelijken*, May-June, 1914, no. 11 ("*Boxe*, 1914"). Since the Brussels and Amsterdam exhibitions took place simultaneously, Archipenko would have been able to send 1 of the 2 plaster casts to each city. See also fn. 3, below.

3. By the time Apollinaire published the sculpture in *Les Soirées de Paris*, it was in Magnelli's collection. The Guggenheim Museum in New York, under James Johnson Sweeney's direction, acquired these 3 Archipenko sculptures from the Magnelli collection between 1955 and 1957.

4. AAA, correspondence between Jean Verdier and Archipenko, Aug. 5, 1952-Aug. 1, 1960. In a letter of July 29, 1960, Verdier mentions *La Boxe* as among the plasters still in storage in Cannes. The plaster was later shipped with others to the United States. In November 1966, at the request of Alfred H. Barr, Jr., the 2 original black plasters (the Magnelli cast by then in the collection of the SRGM and the Verdier cast in the collection of the artist's widow) were examined side by side. Calliper measurements were taken of all dimensions, and since all readings matched, Barr and Louise A. Svendsen concluded that both plasters had been cast from the same mold (MoMA files).

5. Barr did not learn of the terra cotta's 1935 date until 1944.

ferred to cast the sculpture in bronze had he been able to afford it at this time is not clear, but his specific interest in terra cotta and his mastery of it as a medium suggest that he may have seen it as inherently suited to his aesthetic needs.[6] It is interesting to note that apparently he did not himself comment on the striking differences between the original black painted plaster of *La Boxe*, the warm red terra cotta of 1935, and the chemically patinated blue and black bronzes of the 1960s. These questions of medium (as well as of scale) have also gone unnoted by subsequent commentators, and the various versions have generally been published interchangeably (see below REFERENCES). While the nature of the inventive image and the innovative formal vocabulary of *La Boxe* have been the focus of comment or discussion in almost all histories of early twentieth-century sculpture—as well as in all monographs on Archipenko—the material or facture have been ignored. In view of Archipenko's 1935 inscription on the terra-cotta sculpture (*"C'est la musique monumental des volumes d'éspace et de la matière")* it seems clear that his own sense of the material substance played an important part in his conception. This sensitivity to the expressive potential of materials and their surfaces is revealed in his meticulous painting and polishing of the original black plasters. The rich reflective tone produced led many of the early commentators to mistake the medium for artificial stone or for wood (see below REFERENCES). Archipenko clearly intended the painting and polishing to achieve the effect of bronze or stone, costly materials that were not available to him at the time. But the fact that he used color explicitly to disguise the material substance of his work was an aesthetic decision that also characterized his working methods much later in life, when costs were a less critical issue.[7]

While the matter of material and surface has not in the case of this sculpture been discussed in the literature, the powerful originality of the composition has led to some dispute about the date of the original conception.

Variously dated 1913 or 1914 by Archipenko himself, as well as by subsequent historians and commentators (see below EXHIBITIONS, REFERENCES, footnotes), the problem has been directly addressed only by Donald Karshan (1974) and Katherine Michaelsen (1976, 1977). Karshan argues in favor of a 1913 date for all Archipenko's 1914 *Salon* entries. He refers to a document that he claims establishes Archipenko's residence in Nice by February 9, 1914, and suggests the sculptor must therefore have completed these ambitious sculptures well

6. Letter of Mar. 1, 1935, addressed to Theodore Zarembsky, Detroit: "There is no good marble or stone in this country. Every hard stone or marble here is very breakable, on account of a to [sic] dry consistency, or it is to [sic] soft like plaster" (AAA). It was not until 25 years later that the sculpture was cast in bronze. Eight numbered casts, plus an artist's cast ("A"), were produced by the Sheidow Foundry between ca. 1960 and 1967, the Verdier plaster being used as the model. The latter plaster was subsequently given by the artist's widow to the Saarland Museum, Saarbrücken.

7. As late as 1955, in a letter to R. Wheelwright, Archipenko suggests various ways of treating the surface of a terra cotta: oil paint, for example, thinned with turpentine will penetrate the pores; a second coat can be used "to imitate different materials such as bronze..." (AAA).

before that date. At issue for Karshan is the case for Archipenko's originality, the priority of his experimental constructions, and the influence of his 1910-13 output on the sculpture of Picasso, Tatlin, Boccioni, Duchamp-Villon, Gabo, Lipchitz, and Laurens. He argues further that the 1914 date often ascribed to *La Boxe* by Archipenko himself (including its incision on both original plasters) may have been intended by the artist to document the work's earliest exhibition rather than the date of its inception or completion. This latter point is difficult to sustain, in view of the fact that the artist would have had to incise the date in the plaster while it was still wet; plausible arguments for such methodical postdating by Archipenko have not been offered and are, indeed, hard to imagine. Moreover, Karshan himself dated the work 1914 in his two earlier publications (1968, 1969).

Michaelsen rejects Karshan's interpretation of the Nice residence document, which she convincingly reads as dated November 1914 (1976, pp. 92, 93 fn. 7). Her analysis of Archipenko's development lends strong support to the 1914 completion date for the two black plasters.

Characterizing the Magnelli-Guggenheim plaster as Archipenko's most abstract sculpture (as Barr had done in 1936), she points out that though he was "capable of thinking in abstract terms," this was not his ultimate goal (1977, p. 145). Further, in discussing his relationship to the work of Boccioni and Duchamp-Villon, she suggests that whereas *La Boxe* did in fact predate Duchamp-Villon's *Horse* by several months and was unlikely to have been specifically influenced by Boccioni's sculpture, it is less important to establish priority than to grasp the nature of the "fruitful exchange of ideas" between these artists during the intensely creative months of 1913 and 1914 (1977, pp. 107-9).

Regarding the specific date of the black plasters, it seems most likely that Archipenko worked on the development of the conception during the final months of 1913 and the beginning of 1914, completing it by late February, when *La Boxe* would have been installed in the *Salon*. Archipenko's incised date of 1914 on the plaster and the subsequently often repeated date of 1913 would thus constitute a plausible combination of inception and completion dates. On the other hand, the 1913 date incised on the 1935 terra cotta and on the later bronzes reflects the principle, problematic in its implications, which he later articulated in his 1960 text, that the date of origin of an aesthetic idea constituted for him the correct date of the various later versions of a sculpted form. "Sometimes I sculpt a new version of the same statue after considerable time has elapsed. Of course, in modeling the same problem the forms are not as mathematically exact as if they were cast from the same mold. However, on all versions I prefer to keep the date of the first, since I want to conserve the chronology of the idea. The particular stylistic and creative approach I use equally in all versions unless changes are purposely made" (pl. 141). The problem of repetition, as opposed to original creation, is ignored here, and must be taken into account in any study of Archipenko's long career, where repetition of earlier forms constituted a clear pattern. A detailed study of his approach to media, color, and finish, and to the minute variations in composition among the various later versions of his early sculptures, is yet to be undertaken. Since the composition *La Boxe* remains one of his most striking achievements, and since the versions date from the early, middle, and final phases of his career, a comparative study of these issues could yield important data.[8]

EXHIBITIONS (1935 version only):

New York, MoMA, *Cubism and Abstract Art*, 1936, no. 3, repr. fig. 94 ("Boxing. 1913"); Syracuse, New York, Syracuse Museum of Fine Arts, *The Seventh National Ceramic Exhibition*, Oct. 27-Nov. 20, 1938, no. 32 (n.d.); New York, Art of This Century, 1942-47, p. 72, repr.; Venice, *P.G.*, 1948 (Biennale), no. 2; Florence, *P.G.*, 1949, no. 2; Amsterdam, *P.G.*, 1951, no. 4; Zurich, *P.G.*, 1951, no. 4; London, *P.G.*, 1964-65, no. 19, repr. p. 25; Stockholm, *P.G.*, 1966-67, no. 19, repr. p. 19; Torino, *P.G.*, 1975-76, no. 25, repr. color pl. 30.

REFERENCES:[9]

Les Soirées de Paris, Sommaire du N° 25, June 15, 1914, repr. opp. p. 336 ("*Boxe*, 1913, collection Magnelli, Florence"); H. Hildebrandt, *Alexander Archipenko*, Berlin, 1923, p. 11, repr. pl. 11 ("*Combat de Boxe*, 1913, 45 h., Sammlung Magnelli, Florence"; in his 1929 edition, Hildebrandt gives the medium as "artificial stone");[10] R. Schacht, *Alexander Archipenko, Sturm Bilderbücher 11*, Berlin, 1923, p. 10, repr. p. 24 ("*Boxkampf*, 1913"); E. Wiese, *Alexander Archipenko, Junge Kunst*, vol. 40, Leipzig, 1923, p. 7, repr. pl. VI ("1913, Holz,[10] Sammlung Magnelli, Florence"); R. Schacht, "Archipenko, Belling, Westheim," *Der Sturm*, Jahrg. 14, Heft 5, May 1923, p. 78, repr. [p. 69] ("*Boxe*, 1913"); C. Einstein, *Die Kunst des 20. Jahrhunderts*, Berlin, 1926, repr. pl. 541 ("*Der Boxkampf*. Holz.[10] 1913. Florenz, Slg. Magneli [sic]"); A. H. Barr, Jr., *Cubism and Abstract Art*, MoMA, New York, 1936, p. 104 (misprint date of 1917), repr. fig. 94 (1935 terra cotta as "*Boxing*, 1913"; in the catalogue entry, Barr gives the correct dimensions of the terra cotta); C. Giedion-Welcker, *Modern Plastic Art*, Zurich, 1937, repr. p. 39 ("*Boxing Match*, 1913, Florence. Coll. Magnelli," medium not mentioned; in her 1955 edition, New York, p. 45, the same photo is used, but this time she attributes the work, "in synthetic stone,"[10] to the Peggy Guggenheim Collection, still dating it 1913, and giving the dimensions of the plaster); P. Guggenheim, *Art of This Century*, 1942, repr. p. 72 (1935 terra cotta dated 1913); L. Zahn, *Eine Geschichte der Modernen Kunst*, Berlin, 1958, repr. opp. p. 156 (1935 terra cotta, dated "1913" and described as "Kunststein,[10] 61 cms."); A. Archipenko, *Archipenko: Fifty Creative Years 1908-1958*, New York, 1960, p. 49, repr. pl. 137 ("1935, terra cotta, second version"); R. Rosenblum, *Cubism and Twentieth-Century Art*, New York, 1960, p. 263, repr. pl. 192 (1935 terra cotta dated "1913-14"); H. Read, *A Concise History of Modern Sculpture*, New York, 1964, pp. 134, 227, repr. pl. 124 (1935 terra cotta, dated "1913"); Calas, 1966, pp. 87, 89, repr. p. 94 (1935 terra cotta); D. Karshan, "Archipenko," *Arts Magazine*, vol. 42, no. 6, Apr. 1968, pp. 37-38 (bronze, dated 1914); idem, *Content and Continuity*, Chicago, Kovler Gallery, 1968, p. 47 (dated 1914); idem, *Archipenko: International Visionary*, Washington, National Collection of Fine Arts, 1969, p. 49, repr. p. 48 (bronze, dated 1914); idem, *Archipenko: The Sculpture and Graphic Art*, Tübingen, 1974, pp. 11, 15, 18, 26, 34, repr. p. 25 (1966 bronze cast, dated 1913); K. J. Michaelsen, "The Chronology of Archipenko's Paris Years," *Arts Magazine*, vol. 51, no. 3, Nov. 1976, pp. 91-93 (plaster dated 1914); idem, *Archipenko: A Study of the Early Works, 1908-1920*, New York, Garland, 1977, pp. 106-11, 145, 178 (plaster dated 1914).

8. Karshan has commented on the subtlety of Archipenko's aims and achievements in the technical and aesthetic domain of bronze patination (1974, p. 41). He has also drawn attention to the need for a careful study of the changes introduced by the artist into the later variations of some of his early works. Such a study has not, however, hitherto been published.
9. Though the present version dates from 1935, these citations include some references to the original concept of 1913-14. The impact of the early image is thereby recorded, as is the fact that most authors have regarded the early and late versions as interchangeable and the differences in medium and scale insignificant.
10. There are no recorded wood or artificial stone versions and it seems certain that Hildebrandt, Wiese, Einstein, Giedion-Welcker, and Zahn were erroneously describing the early version in painted plaster.

Jean Arp (Hans Arp)

Born September 1886, Strasbourg.
Died June 1966, Basel.

4

4 Grand collage.

1955 reconstruction of an original made in Zurich, ca. 1918.
(*Large collage*; *Composition*).

76.2553 PG 52

Papier collé, watercolor wash, metallic paint on pavatex (masonite) painted with gray oil. Dimensions of entire support: 38⅜ x 30⅝ (97.6 x 77.8); dims. of image: 31½ x 23⁹⁄₁₆ (80 x 59.9).

Signed three times on reverse: *Arp*. Not dated.

PROVENANCE:

Original work purchased from the artist, Paris, 1940; returned to Arp for repair, ca. 1954; new version completed in Basel, 1955; delivered to Peggy Guggenheim, Venice, November 1956.[1]

CONDITION:

The original composition (figs. a and b) suffered extensive damage through overexposure to light. In creating the new collage, Arp apparently reused some of the original papers, though no part of the present work can with certainty be attributed to the earlier date.[2]

The procedure used in the 1955 work appears to have been as follows: watercolor wash, now partially absorbed, was applied over the black papers; gold paint was applied to the mottled paper after it was adhered to the support. The beige-chalky areas were painted with oil. The gray oil border, which was added to the new version, was painted after the collage was complete. The condition is stable. (New York, Feb. 1983.)

1. Peggy Guggenheim's recollections of this transaction coincide with those of Marguerite Arp-Hagenbach (in conversation with the author, Mar. 31, 1982), and with the evidence of correspondence of 1955-56 between Peggy Guggenheim, Arp, and Marguerite Arp-Hagenbach (preserved in the Fondation Arp in Clamart). Greta Ströh and Gabriele Mahn drew these letters to the author's attention, and the Fondation and Madame Arp granted permission to quote from them. On April 14, 1955, Arp wrote to Peggy Guggenheim as follows: "*Depuis très, très longtemps je voulais vous écrire que le collage est depuis très longtemps terminé.... J'espère que je pourrai bientôt revenir en Italie et vous apporter le collage qui me semble très réussi. Je vous conseille de protéger les papiers collés par un verre, mais j'espère que nous nous reverrons et que nous pourrons discuter cette question ensemble.*" On August 31, 1956, he wrote again: "*Permettez-moi de vous envoyer en signe de notre vieille amitié un collage que j'ai composé en partie avec les vieux papiers d'un collage se trouvant dans votre collection et dont le fond était absolument brûlé par le soleil. J'espère que cette composition vous plaira et que mon cadeau trouvera une bonne place dans votre admirable collection. J'ai fait emballer le tableau par la Kunsthalle de Bâle et l'expédition se fera par maison Bronner S.-A. de cette ville. J'aurais désiré vous l'apporter personnellement lors de ma prochaine visite à Venise, mais le colis serait trop encombrant pour être emmené comme bagage à main.*" On September 4, 1956, Marguerite Arp-Hagenbach wrote: "*Arp a collé les vieux papiers sur du pavatex qu'il a peint à l'huile.... Arp a signé le collage au dos.... le collage est très beau et Arp espère que vous serez contente de la restauration.*" On November 30, 1956, Peggy Guggenheim wrote: "*Cher Arp Quand je suis revenu de mon voyage en Yugoslavie j'ai trouvé le collage. J'étai ravie car il est si beau. Aussi le cadre me plait énormément. Je suis en train de préparer une petite gallerie dada où le mettre. Merci mille fois.*"
2. Marguerite Arp-Hagenbach and Peggy Guggenheim both recalled that the work had been completely remade in 1955, and this is borne out by the visual evidence, though not entirely by the letters. (The wording of these may, however, have been somewhat influenced by customs considerations.) Madame Arp recalled that Arp did try to remove the old papers from the extremely brittle and darkened support, but that they disintegrated in the process, thus forcing him to use new papers throughout.

fig. a.
Arp, *Grand collage*, original version, ca. 1918.
Photograph courtesy Fondation Arp, Clamart.

fig. b.
Installation photograph, Biennale, Venice, 1948, showing the original *Grand collage*. The work was exhibited with this orientation in the 1936 *Cubism and Abstract Art* exhibition, and in subsequent exhibitions until 1964.

The chronology of Arp's geometric collages, almost none of which were dated at the time of execution, poses considerable problems. Variously dated between 1915 and 1919 in the literature, these works are difficult to document on the basis of early exhibitions or publications. In attempting to arrive at a plausible date for the original version of *Grand collage*, a number of factors must be taken into account.

A major exhibition of Arp's work took place at Galerie Tanner in Zurich, November 14-30, 1915. Exhibiting jointly with Otto van Rees and Adya van Rees-Dutilh, Arp showed a group of eighteen works, including three textiles (executed by Adya from his designs), five charcoal drawings, and ten ink drawings, all entitled simply *Gestaltung (Configuration)*. (See H. Henkels, *Otto en Adya Van Rees. Leven en Werk tot 1934*, Utrecht, 1975, p. 40; A. Grieve, "Arp in Zurich," *Dada Spectrum: The Dialectics Of Revolt*, Iowa City, 1979, p. 177.)

Alastair Grieve and others have identified several of the works involved. They are characterized by the use of a spatially complex organization of overlapping and interlocking rectangles, wedge-shapes, arcs, curving and diagonal planes, segments of circles, and triangles. They must have been similar in many respects to the fresco murals Arp executed in the fall of 1915 with the van Reeses for the Pestalozzi school of Han Coray. (For a discussion of this commission and illustrations of the rediscovered frescoes, see H. Henkels, "Fresko's von Van Rees en Arp in Zürich," *Museumjournaal*, serie 23, nr. 1, feb. 1978, pp. 11-15.)

A review of the Galerie Tanner exhibition in a Zurich newspaper described Arp's contributions as largely Cubist in inspiration,[3] and it is clear that no geometric abstractions, such as the *Grand collage*, were shown on this occasion.

In February 1916, Hugo Ball opened the Cabaret Voltaire. Arp helped him to find works to exhibit there, and evidently also showed his own work. A collage reproduced in the June 1916 publication *Cabaret Voltaire* was probably typical of the work produced by him in the immediately preceding months (repr. Grieve, loc. cit., pl. 4; for a discussion of the Cabaret Voltaire, see also J. H. Hancock, "Form and Content in the Early Work of Jean Arp, 1903-1930," unpublished Ph.D. dissertation, Harvard University, 1980, pp. 123ff.). Arp himself later described a series of collages made in 1915: "I did collages in paper and cloth composed on a diagonal line. They were animated, and compositionally they were oriented more towards futurism than cubism" (Arp, "Conversation at Meudon," *Arp on Arp, Poems, Essays, Memories*, New York, 1972, p. 337). In an article on collage, he wrote of these same works: "I used printed paper, printed cloth, paper and cloth of all colors, that chance ... brought my way, and this material of manifold appearances was arranged in turbulent diagonals that announced the booming of the great whimsical drum of dadaism."[4]

As Grieve, Herbert Henkels, and Jane Hancock have all suggested, these collages probably date from the winter of 1915-16. Obviously influenced by Synthetic Cubism, they differ from the French examples in being entirely nonfigurative. That is to say, the patterns, colors, and textures are used entirely for their own pictorial values, not as allusions to real objects.

In November 1915 Arp met Sophie Taeuber. They soon began to work together, and Arp in later years repeatedly spoke of her influence on his work: "The clear tranquility emanating from Sophie Taeuber's vertical and horizontal compositions influenced the baroque, dynamic diagonals of my abstract 'configurations.' A profound and serene silence filled her constructions of colors and planes. Her extreme simplifications, her exclusive use of rectangular planes placed horizontally and vertically in the pictures which she made at the time, exercised a decisive influence on my work" (*Unsern Täglichen Traum*, Zurich, 1955, p. 11, quoted by Grieve, loc. cit., p. 188, and Hancock, op. cit., p. 119).

Though Sophie Taeuber's fabric designs in an all-over rectilinear geometric style probably date from as early as 1915 (Hancock, op. cit., p. 114), the emergence of her initial influence upon Arp cannot be documented earlier than the autumn of 1917. In November of that year, at the Kunstsalon Wolfsberg in Zurich, Arp for the first time showed a collage in which diagonals and curves were eliminated. The image was made up of roughly rectangular forms, though,

3. Dawn Ades supplied this information. The review appeared in the *Neue Zürcher Zeitung*, November 19, 1915, and mentions "Arp's geometrical fantasies."

4. Arp, "Collages," *Arp on Arp*, p. 328. For an illuminating discussion of these collages and of the development toward abstraction in Arp's oeuvre as a whole, see J. H. Hancock, op. cit., pp. 94ff.

as Grieve and Hancock have pointed out, they were far from precisely geometric, and their arrangement was entirely haphazard rather than based upon a grid (Grieve, loc. cit., p. 188, repr. p. 189; Hancock, op. cit., p. 116). Reproduced in *Dada* 2, December 1917, this collage bore the title *Tableau en papier*, though Arp later published it as *Rectangles arranged according to the laws of chance* (Kunstmuseum, Basel).

With the creation of the first *duo-collages*, a series of about half a dozen works the two artists produced together during part of the following year, Arp began actually to adopt Sophie Taeuber's conception of a composition made up of identical rectangular units arranged on a regular horizontal and vertical axis (fig. c). Each of the *duo-collages* measures approximately 31½ x 23¾ in. (80 x 60 cm.) and consists of thirty rectangles extending to the edges of the field on all four sides. Though some of the rectangles are further subdivided, the clarity and rigorousness of the composition in each case is uncompromising.[5] The colors predominantly used are gray, black, and white with occasional additions of blue, silver, or gold. Arp later wrote of these works: "No spot, no rip, no fiber, no inaccuracy was to perturb the clarity of our work. For our paper pictures we even discarded scissors, which we had originally used but which all too readily betrayed the life of the hand. We used a paper cutter instead. In our joint work ... we humbly tried to approach the pure radiance of reality. I would like to call these works the art of silence" ("And So the Circle Closed," *Arp on Arp*, p. 245).

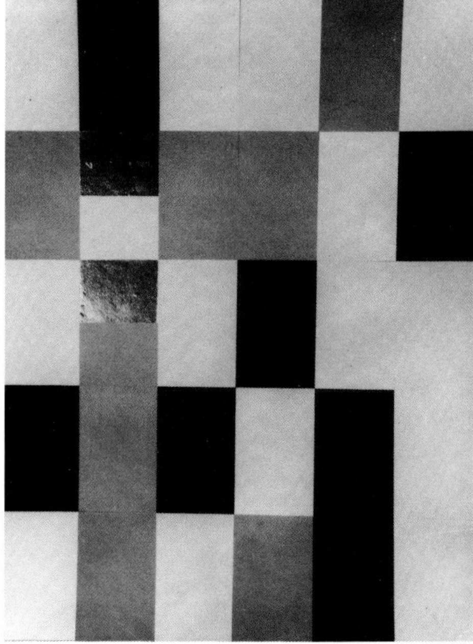

fig. c.
Arp and Sophie Taeuber, *Duo-collage*, 1918, white, black, blue, silver, and gray paper on cardboard, 32¼ x 23⅝ in., 82 x 60 cm., present whereabouts unknown. Photograph courtesy Fondation Arp, Clamart.

5. It is interesting to note that the Peggy Guggenheim collage, without its gray border, corresponds in size to the *duo-collages*. In its original form, it probably measured approximately 80 x 60 cm. the size of the present image. The Fondation Arp at Clamart records at least 6 extant *duo-collages*.

The source of Arp's original *Grand collage* (fig. a) clearly lies in the stylistic example of the *duo-collages*, and it must derive from approximately the same time. In only two respects does it differ markedly from the collaborative compositions: first, in contrast to the regular all-over structure of the latter, Arp has reintroduced a figure-ground relationship; second, he has incorporated subtle irregularities in the subdivisions within the major rectangular units.

Grieve has pointed out a striking compositional relationship between the *duo-collages* and Sophie Taeuber's backdrop for the puppet-play *Le Roi Cerf* (*König Hirsch*), which was performed at the Swiss Werkbund exhibition from May 1 to August 31, 1918.[6] In view of this relationship, the first *duo-collages* (hitherto not dated with any precision) seem most likely to date from no earlier than the winter of 1917-18. By 1919, Arp had abandoned geometric regularity in favor of a less restrictive mode, and the entire group of geometric collages, including *Grand collage*, was thus probably produced within the period from late 1917 to early 1919.

Some uncertainty exists concerning the way in which Arp intended *Grand collage* to be hung. The work was reproduced for the first time in Arp's and Lissitzky's 1925 publication *Kunstismen*, where the image plainly accords with its present orientation here (fig. d). Between 1925 and 1955, however, all illustrations and exhibitions (including some apparently approved — at least tacitly — by Arp himself) presented the work inverted, or "upside down." Whether Arp explicitly indicated the latter orientation by a signature or other markings

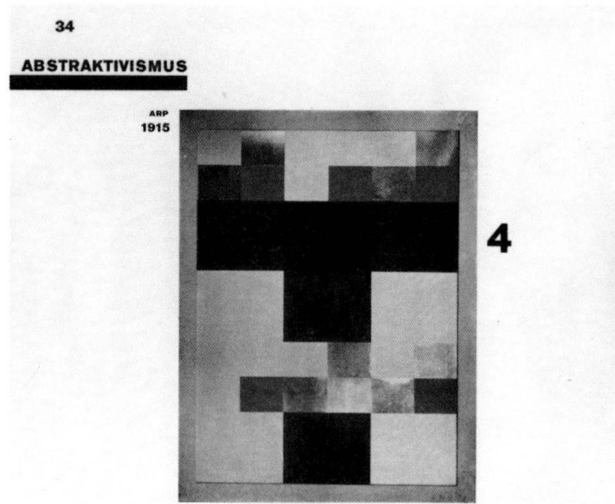

fig. d.
Arp, *Grand collage*, original version, as reproduced in El Lissitzky and H. Arp, *Die Kunstismen*, Zurich, Munich, Leipzig, 1925, p. 34.

6. The backdrop is reproduced in M. Hurlimann, "Zürcher Musik- und Theaterleben im ersten Weltkrieg," *Du Atlantis*, vol. 26, Sept. 1966, p. 728.

on the reverse of the work is not ascertainable. When the original was "restored" (indeed replaced) by Arp in 1955, Peggy Guggenheim found that the piece was signed on the verso in such a way as to call for a reinversion of the collage. She changed the orientation and, in effect, unwittingly reinstated the 1925 mode of presentation in all later publications and exhibitions.

It is evident that in various phases of his work, Arp deliberately introduced flexibility in the orientation and presentation of individual pieces (see, for example, cat. nos. 5 and 10). In the present case, it seems likely that when he embarked in 1955 upon the restoration (and ultimately the remaking) of the *Grand collage*, he used the 1925 photograph as his guide and, in the process, adopted the orientation, indicating his preference by the placement of his signature on the reverse. Given his tendency to experiment in such matters, however, one should allow for the possibility that he continued to regard both orientations as satisfactory.

EXHIBITIONS:

New York, MoMA, *Cubism and Abstract Art*, 1936, repr. p. 72 (the original collage which appears in exhibitions until London, 1964); New York, Art of This Century, 1942-47, p. 101 ("*Great Composition*. 1915, 27 x 34 in."); New York, Art of This Century, *Arp*, Feb. 1944, no. 1; Venice, *P.G.*, 1948 (Biennale), no. 3 (see fig. b); Florence, *P.G.*, 1949, no. 3 (dims. 69 x 88 cm.); Amsterdam, *P.G.*, 1951, no. 3; Zurich, *P.G.*, 1951, no. 5; London, *P.G.*, 1964-65, no. 45 (*Composition*; the new work); Stockholm, *P.G.*, 1966-67, no. 43, repr.; Paris, *P.G.*, 1974-75, no. 49; Torino, *P.G.*, 1975-76, no. 50; New York, *P.G.*, 1982-83, no. 32, repr.

REFERENCES:

El Lissitzky and H. Arp, *Die Kunstismen, Les Ismes de l'Art, The Isms of Art*, Munich, Leipzig, Zurich, 1925, no. 4, repr. p. 34 (dated 1915); J. J. Sweeney, *Plastic Redirections in Twentieth Century Paintings*, Chicago, 1934, p. 40, repr. p. 41 (described as a canvas); A. H. Barr, Jr., *Cubism and Abstract Art*, MoMA, New York, 1936, pp. 68, 74, 204, repr. p. 72; P. Guggenheim, *Art of This Century*, 1942, p. 101; J. Arp, *On my Way*, New York, 1948, pp. 39-40; Calas, 1966, repr. p. 52 (new work); L. Flint, *Handbook*, 1983, repr. color p. 109.

5 Soulier bleu renversé à deux talons, sous une voûte noire. Ca. 1925.
(Overturned Blue Shoe With Two Heels Under a Black Vault; Blauer, auf dem Kopf stehender Schuh mit zwei Absätzen unter einer schwarzen Wölbung).

Color plate p. 393.

76.2553 PG 53

Wood, painted, 31 1/4 x 41 1/8 (79.3 x 104.6). Depth of mount: 1 (2.5); depth of relief elements: 1 (2.5).

Not signed or dated.

PROVENANCE:

Purchased from the artist, Paris, winter 1940.

CONDITION:

In 1975 while the work was on loan to the Orangerie, Paris, it was noted by the artist's widow that the entire surface had at some previous time (date unknown) been repainted in acrylics, the colors and finish bearing little relation to Arp's original. André Mounier, the artist's assistant, working with Peggy Guggenheim's and Marguerite Arp-Hagenbach's approval, removed the acrylic, revealing traces of each of the original colors beneath. After unscrewing the blue and black forms, he repainted them and the white ground with Dutch oil pigments approximating as closely as possible Arp's original materials (Tollens Elastomat, Enamel Mat Satin; 18.01 AO Black/AO White; 11.15 AO Blue). He then reattached the forms to the ground with 4 screws.

In October 1982 (Venice) the work was superficially cleaned with ammonium hydroxide (2% in water) and 3% commercial lacquer thinner (ca. 70% toluene).

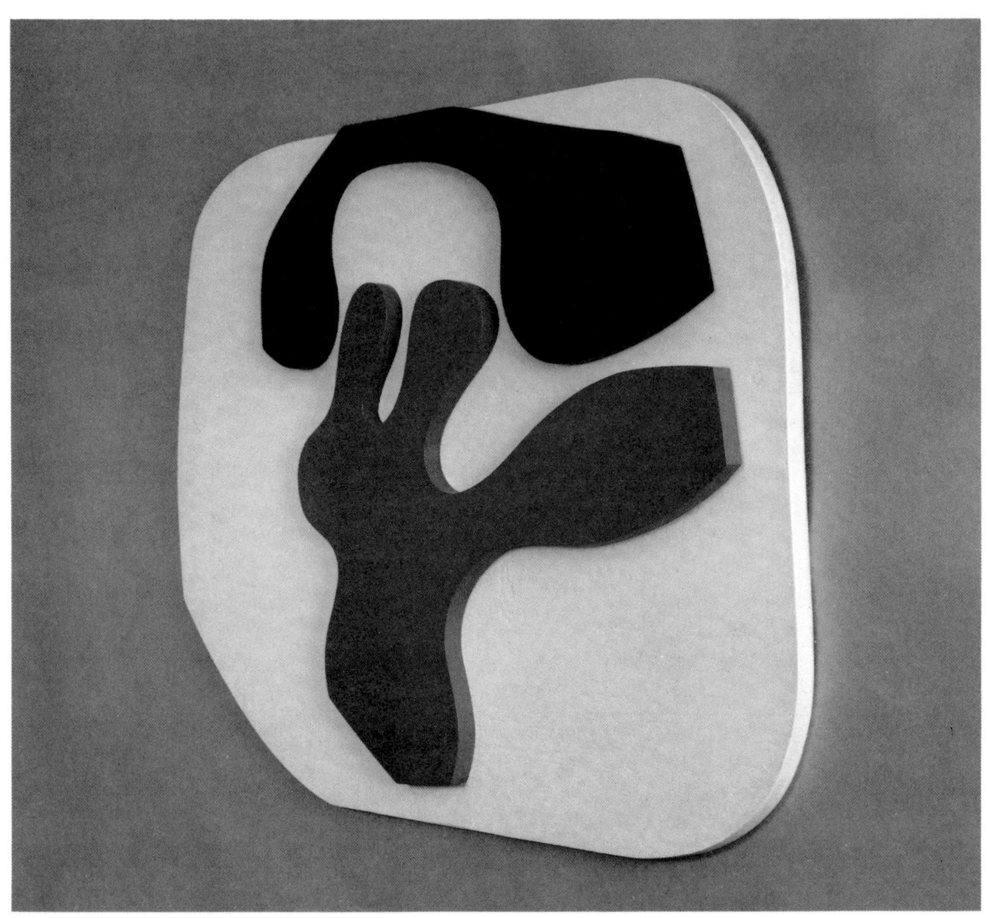

The title, date, and orientation of *Soulier bleu*... raise certain issues about Arp's work in wood relief during the 1920s.

Arp's "Object Language," developed in the years following 1918, was based upon an iconography of identifiable but schematically represented forms.[1] Having abandoned abstraction by the 1920s, he produced within that decade a group of approximately 160 wood and cardboard reliefs characterized by the use of images that were diverse yet always (in spite of apparent obscurities) legible. (See, for example, *Assiette, fourchettes et nombril*, wood relief, 23¼ x 24 in., 59 x 61 cm., B. Rau, 1981, no. 49, repr.; or *Cravates et tête,* wood relief, 20½ x 22$\frac{1}{16}$ in., 52 x 56 cm., B. Rau, 1981, no. 71, repr.)

In the disposition of individual forms on a flat support, Arp developed what he (and others) described as a kind of pictographic or ideographic language (see T. Tzara, "Arp," *Les feuilles libres*, vol. 9, no. 47, Dec. 1927-Jan. 1928, pp. 57-58; C. Zervos, "Hans Arp, Galerie Goemans," *Cahiers d'Art,* vol. 4, nos. 8-9, 1929, p. 420, both cited by Hancock, op. cit., p. 307, fn. 15). The objects, such as the blue shoe here, or the torsos, moustaches, plates, forks, bottles, lips, heads elsewhere, were always based on items from the real world, and the titles often identified these objects; yet they were juxtaposed in ways that discouraged simple representational readings, creating ambiguous and essentially poetic meanings.

As Jane Hancock has pointed out (op. cit., pp. 217ff.), Arp's efforts to combine everyday objects in surprising and irrational ways was analogous to the verbal puns and plays on words that characterized his own contemporary poetry, and many of the same images appear in both contexts:

mein tisch fällt auf den rücken und streckt
die vier beine von sich
unter meinem bett schaut einer meiner schuhe hervor.
"Vier Knöpfe zwei Löcher vier Besen."

In this respect, Arp found himself in sympathy with the Surrealist poets, who encouraged him to probe the imagery of his own works in an effort to interpret its underlying meanings. The titles which he then gave the works became clues to their interpretation, and often—in their turn—inspired new poems (see Arp, "Looking," in *Arp*, ed. J. T. Soby, New York, 1958, p. 14). The pictorial language of these reliefs was, thus, fundamentally representational, but it depended partly on the titles to become fully legible.

The present smooth, unmodulated, brushless oil surface of *Soulier bleu* ..., though not applied by the artist himself (see CONDITION), accurately reflects Arp's strong commitment to an entirely impersonal mode of execution. Although

1. The term "Object-Language" was used by Arp himself in "Conversation at Meudon," *Arp on Arp, Poems, Essays, Memories*, New York, 1972, p. 339. For a detailed and illuminating discussion of this phase in Arp's work, see J. Hancock, "Form and Content in the Early Work of Jean Arp, 1903-1930," unpublished Ph.D. dissertation, Harvard University, 1980, pp. 198ff.

in his lifetime he usually painted the reliefs himself, he took great pains to achieve the effect of something approaching a mechanical process.

In a conversation with Roger Bordier, Arp described his procedure in the wood reliefs as follows: "*D'abord, je dessine peu. Il m'arrive seulement de jeter quelques idées de formes sur le papier. Puis ces formes, je les découpe dans des cartons, les assemble, le découpage et l'assemblage se poursuivant jusqu'à ce que j'aie mis au point une maquette qui me paraisse satisfaisante. Enfin je ponce les bords de mes cartons pour faire disparaître les coups de ciseaux*" ("Arp, les reliefs et le plâtre," *Art d'aujourd'hui*, 5th ser., nos. 4-5, May-June 1954, pp. 44-45).

He then had the pieces cut in wood, "*dans des planches de trois centimètres d'épaisseur. J'utilise assez couramment le tilleul ou le sapin, mais aussi le chêne, le bouleau du Canada ... enfin je choisis le bois qui me paraît le mieux servir l'expérience en cours.*"

Rather than gluing the elements to the support, Arp then screwed them in place: "*Mes reliefs sont tous visés par derrière, ce qui me permet de les modifier imperceptiblement.*"

It was apparently not unusual for Arp, at subsequent times, to change the positions of the elements, to substitute others, or even to alter the orientation of the entire work. The rather improvisational nature of the original compositional process was in effect continued as Arp proceeded to make further adjustment over time.[2]

A strict chronology of the 1920s wood reliefs has not been established, and very little evidence exists to support chronologies that have thus far been published. None of the works were dated at their time of execution, and Arp produced an extensive series of closely related examples between 1924 and 1930. Though it has always been dated 1925, *Soulier bleu* ... may, in fact, have been made at almost any point in the period under discussion.

EXHIBITIONS:

New York, Art of This Century, 1942-47, p. 102, repr. p. 101 (on its side); New York, Art of This Century, *Arp*, Feb. 1944, no. 8 (dated 1928); Venice, *P.G.*, 1948 (Biennale), no. 4; Florence, *P.G.*, 1949, no. 4, repr.; Amsterdam, *P.G.*, 1951, no. 4, repr. n.p. (on its side); Zurich, *P.G.*, 1951, no. 6; London, *P.G.*, 1964-65, no. 46, repr. p. 39; Stockholm, *P.G.*, 1966-67, no. 44, repr.; New York, *P.G.*, 1969, p. 67, repr.; Paris, *P.G.*, 1974-75, no. 50, repr. (*Soulier Bleu*); Torino, *P.G.*, 1975-76, no. 51; Rome, *Guggenheim: Venezia-New York*, 1982, no. 38, repr. color; New York, *P.G.*, 1982-83, no. 33, repr.

REFERENCES:

P. Guggenheim, *Art of This Century*, 1942, p. 101, repr. p. 102 (on its side); R. Gaffé, *Peinture à travers dada et le surréalisme*, Brussels, 1952, repr. bet. pp. 40 and 41 (on its side with title *Soulier bleu renversé à deux talons)*; Calas, 1966, p. 91, repr. p. 102; B. Rau, *Jean Arp: The Reliefs. Catalogue of Complete Works*, New York, 1981, no. 73, repr.

2. Peggy Guggenheim's and R. Gaffé's publication of the work "on its side" (see REFERENCES and EXHIBITIONS) may well have been based on Arp's explicit encouragement to experiment with various orientations.

6 Tête et coquille. Ca. 1933.
(Head and shell).

76.2553 PG 54

Polished brass cast in two pieces (lost wax).
Height: 7¾ (19.7); length: 8⅞ (22.5).

Edition of five, plus artist's cast.[1]

Foundry: Bronzart (or possibly Brottal) in Mendrisio, the Ticino (first four casts). 1930s.
: Susse (fifth). 1974.
: Georges Rudier (artist's cast). 1983.

Not signed or dated. No foundry mark.[2]

PROVENANCE:
Purchased from the artist, 1938.[3]

CONDITION:
The lower surface is scratched from contact with a rough support. There are minor indentations and scratches on the surfaces where the two sections meet.

In March 1984 (Venice) the surface was degreased with trichloroethylene, washed with distilled water, and then with distilled water and neutral detergent; it was rinsed with distilled water and dried with alcohol and acetone. A protective coating of Paraloid B-72 was applied (to inhibit tarnishing). The overall condition is stable.

Tête et coquille has been consistently dated 1933 in the literature, and the plaster probably dates from that year. It has not been possible to establish precisely when the first four casts were made in Mendrisio, but they were probably all cast in the 1930s.

During the years 1929 to 1934, Arp worked almost exclusively in wood and plaster. Some of the plasters were later cast in bronze or carved in marble, but a large number of them were not. Conceived specifically with the characteristics of plaster in mind—a medium that Arp found especially congenial—the works were exhibited and reproduced early in this form. In the case of *Tête et coquille* (as in others), Arp apparently continued to express his preference for the plaster original even after the image had been later cast in bronze, since he often selected the plaster for reproduction and exhibition (see below EXHIBITIONS and REFERENCES).

1. Peggy Guggenheim's was the first; the second and third are in Swiss private collections, the fourth in the museum in Basel; the fifth, cast in 1974, was sold in 1975 to a collection in Japan. The 0/5, cast in 1983, is in the collection of the Fondation Arp. This and the casting information were supplied by Greta Ströh of the Fondation Arp.
2. Arp gave explicit instructions to his foundries that no signatures, dates, foundry marks, or numbers were to mar the exterior surfaces of his works. Marks, therefore, appear on the interior, when possible, or not at all. (Pierre Dintillac, Susse Fondeur, in correspondence with the author, Apr. 1983.)
3. Peggy Guggenheim recalled in print that she bought this piece after a visit to the foundry with Arp (*Confessions*). She later said, however, that she bought it from him in London in 1938 (conversations with the author, 1977 and 1978). It has hitherto not been possible to resolve this discrepancy. Since the early casts were made at a foundry in the Ticino, it seems more likely that the piece was bought in London.

6

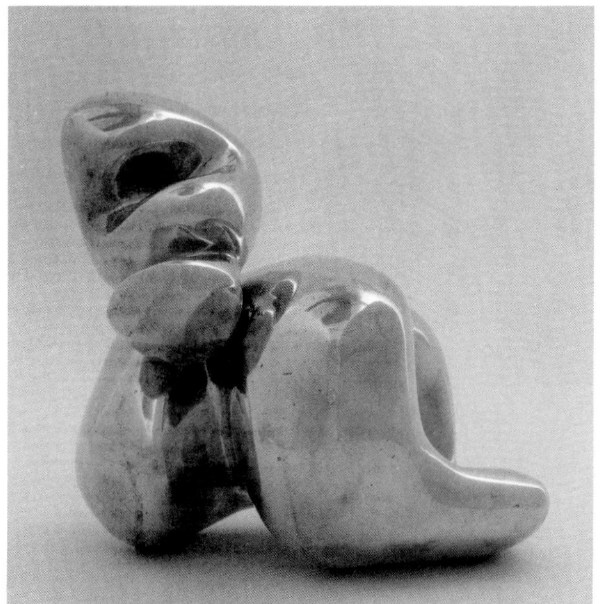

Stephanie Poley has suggested that the use of plaster in these inventions can to some extent be understood as an expression of Arp's "dada-surrealist" aesthetic at that time.[4] The works in question often consisted of multiple small elements, which were loosely arranged on a larger surface; they invited the participation of the viewer, who could pick up the individual pieces, hold them, examine them, and — most importantly — rearrange them. The physical involvement of the spectator was not merely tolerated — it was a necessary ingredient in the potential impact of the sculpture. This entire dimension was essentially lost, however, when these pieces were later cast in bronze: since the bronze surfaces were highly polished and slippery, the smaller pieces could not hold their positions; Arp was forced to fix them into place, thereby precluding any future rearrangements. In *Tête et coquille,* however, Arp arrived at a solution to the problem of creating a single sculpture out of multiple and movable parts, while ensuring the continuing separability of the elements. Both the plaster and bronze versions are constructed in such a way that one part rests securely on the other but can be removed easily. Although Arp clearly conceived of the sculpture as a single, organic, and unified whole, he may have also intended each of the individual parts to be experienced separately and to be capable of standing alone. In naming the piece *Tête et coquille* (rather than *Tête-coquille*), he seems to have wanted to draw attention to their status as individual objects, as well as to their role as parts of an integrated whole.

4. Pp. 47-49. Poley compares the nature of the spectator-involvement in these works with that of Giacometti's *Boule suspendue* (p. 37). Certainly it is true that Arp shared the Surrealists' contempt for the restrictive conventions of high art: "I exhibited along with the surrealists because their rebellious attitude toward 'art' and their direct attitude toward life were as wise as dada" ("dear monsieur brzekowski," *Arp on Arp, Poems, Essays, Memories*, New York, 1972, p. 35).

EXHIBITIONS:

Lucerne, Kunstmuseum, *Thèse, antithèse, synthèse*, Feb. 24-Mar. 31, 1935, no. 2 (plaster, dated 1934); London, Guggenheim Jeune, *Contemporary Sculpture*, Apr. 8-May 2, 1938, no. 2 (bronze); London, Guggenheim Jeune, *Contemporary Painting and Sculpture*, June 21-July 2, 1938, no. 1; New York, Art of This Century, 1942-47; New York, Art of This Century, *Arp*, Feb. 1944, no. 20; Venice, *P.G.*, 1948 (Biennale), no. 5; Florence, *P.G.*, 1949, no. 5; Venice, Giardino, 1949, no. 1; Amsterdam, *P.G.*, 1951, no. 5, repr. (with a brass base, subsequently lost); Zurich, *P.G.*, 1951, no. 7; London, *P.G.*, 1964-65, no. 47; Stockholm, *P.G.*, 1966-67, no. 45; New York, *P.G.*, 1969, pp. 68-69, repr.; Paris, *P.G.*, 1974-75, no. 51, repr.; Torino, *P.G.*, 1975-76, no. 52, repr. pl. 34.

REFERENCES:

P. Guggenheim, *Art of This Century*, 1942, p. 101, repr. p. 8; H. Arp, *On my Way, Poetry and Essays, 1912-1947*, New York, 1948, repr. p. 60 (plaster); M. Hagenbach, "Catalogue of Sculptures," in C. Giedion-Welcker, *Jean Arp*, New York, 1957, p. 108, cat. no. 15; P. Guggenheim, *Confessions*, 1960, p. 52; S. Poley, *Hans Arp: Die Formensprache im plastischen Werk*, Stuttgart, 1978, pp. 38, 42, 48, 174, 176, 218, repr. p. 48 (plaster).

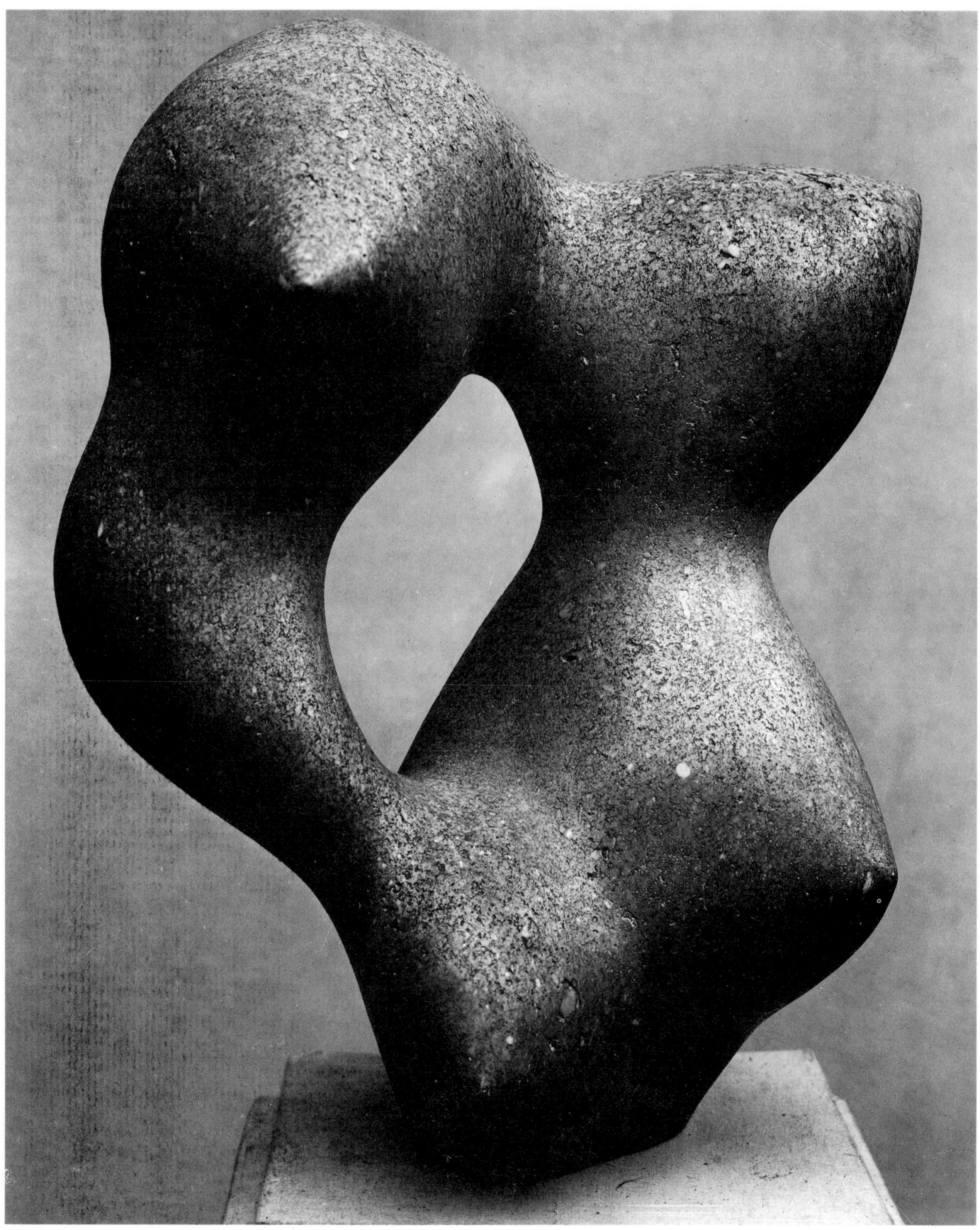

Cat. no. 7, as exhibited in the 1948 Biennale, Venice, before addition of the cylindrical base. Photograph by Ferruzzi, Venice, courtesy Archivio Storico delle Arti Contemporanee della Biennale di Venezia.

7 Couronne de bourgeons I. 1936.

(Crown of buds I; Le vase de seins; Corona di seni).

76.2553 PG 56

Pink limestone (*pierre calcaire*).[1] Height: 19⅜ (49.1); width: 14¾ (37.5); height of base (not original): 6 1/16 (15.4).

Not signed or dated.

PROVENANCE:

Purchased from the artist, New York, ca. 1943.

CONDITION:

One of the 2 upper points was broken off in a fall sustained by the piece sometime in the 1950s.[2] The second upper point was broken off at an unknown date and repaired with cement. One of the 2 lower points was slightly chipped in a subsequent fall (date unknown, but before 1977, when the author first recorded it). The fourth point remains intact. In 3 other places, cement fillings are visible (fig. a).

Owing to the porous nature of the limestone, the surface has deteriorated to some extent, resulting in a loss of smoothness. During February 1982 (Venice) a greenish algae, which had developed over the entire surface, was removed with a solution of 10% Vancide in water. After 2 cleanings, the surface was coated with Paraloid B-72.

The warm pink tone of the limestone is preserved only in the lower (protected) areas. The color has elsewhere been lost through long exposure to the atmosphere and is now largely pale gray. (Nov. 1982.)

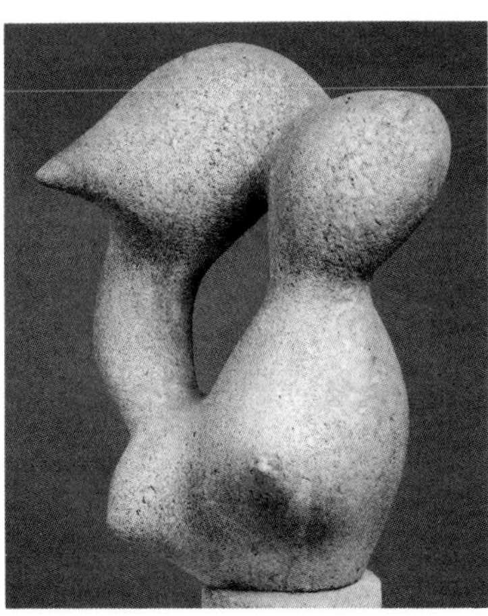

fig. a.
Cat. no. 7, with breaks and repairs visible.

1. According to Marguerite Arp-Hagenbach (in conversation with the author, Mar. 1982), Arp ordered this "*pierre calcaire*" from the Rhone Valley and carved only this single piece from it, working in his Meudon studio. He may have been assisted by the Italian stone carver Santelli, in whose Paris workshop he often carved.

   For a discussion of "rosa Kalkstein," see Poley, 1978, pp. 38, 203 fn. 59. However, Stephanie Poley is, clearly, discussing another type of limestone. She describes it as "*Kalkstein aus der Gegend von Lyon mit grossem, ungleichmässig gelblich und bräunlich gesprenkeltem Korn, von warmer Gesamttönung,*" and cites as the earliest example *Coquille formée par une main humaine* of 1935. The unmistakably pink color (now largely lost but still clearly visible in places) of Peggy Guggenheim's piece is not characteristic of the other pieces mentioned by Poley or those listed by Marguerite Arp-Hagenbach in her catalogue of works from the period (nos. 27, 50, 54).

2. Peggy Guggenheim (in conversation with the author, 1978). Marguerite Arp-Hagenbach recalled (in conversation with the author, Mar. 1982) that Arp had seen the broken *bourgeon* on a visit to Venice during the 1950s and had told Peggy Guggenheim that it could not be successfully repaired. He was not especially disturbed by the damage, however, recalling that "the sculptures of the Greeks also suffered such damage and were better left unrestored."

The pink limestone *Couronne de bourgeons I* was carved by the artist in 1936 and, according to his widow, was the only sculpture he ever produced in this particular stone. As with all of Arp's stone sculpture, it was preceded by a modeled plaster. A bronze edition followed in 1947,[3] and a cement cast was made at an unrecorded date (formerly Collection Schwarzman, Basel; sold Christies, May 17, 1984, Sale No. 5560, Lot 385).

In 1936 Arp also produced the variant *Couronne de bourgeons II* (fig. b). In this case the creation of the light gray cement cast soon after the plaster can be documented, since it was acquired by the writer Georges Hugnet by 1937.[4] It is interesting to note that when loaned by Hugnet to the 1938 Paris exhibition, it bore the appropriately evocative title *Le vase de seins*. Whether the title was added by Hugnet, or was Arp's own, has not yet been established.

This second version of the *Couronne* image was later cast in an edition of five bronzes, and at an unrecorded date, Arp carved it in marble (acquired by Edouard Loeb).

In both the initial conception and its variant, Arp's emphasis was clearly upon the four "breasts," reflecting his primary concern with issues of mass and volume rather than those of space and void. The particular nature of the relationship between volume and space in these two pieces is characteristic of Arp's later work, but unique in the 1930s. (For a discussion of this point see Poley, 1978, pp. 95-96.) In creating the variant form, Arp merely extended the lower section of the otherwise unaltered sculpture. But the result of this procedure was not simply an increase in height. The breast forms were forced outward, the central void acquired additional prominence, and an impression of centrifugal motion was introduced.

The critical balance in each version between the four breast elements and the void derives to a considerable extent from the fact that the sculptures were designed by the artist to stand directly on a larger, formally neutral surface. The addition of the small cylindrical base to the Peggy Guggenheim piece has affected this balance of relationships, changing the formal and aesthetic impact of the

3. The plaster (Von der Heydt Museum, Wuppertal) was used in the casting of the initial edition in 1947 of 3 bronzes (foundry unknown). One of the 3 appeared with the 1947 date in the Arp exhibition organized by Curt Valentin (Buchholz Gallery, New York) in 1949 (cat. no. 25). A fourth, artist's cast (0/3) was made by Godard in 1973. Greta Ströh, Fondation Arp, Clamart, supplied the information about the various casts of both versions of this sculpture. For an extensive discussion of Arp's method of working in plaster, and his attitude to materials, see Poley, 1978, pp. 24-30.

4. This was the first instance in Arp's career of the use of pale gray cast cement (Poley, 1978, p. 38). The archive at the Fondation Arp records Hugnet's ownership of the cement cast and his loan of it to the *Exposition Internationale du Surréalisme*, Jan.-Feb. 1938, no. 10. Marguerite Arp-Hagenbach's catalogue of 1957 records only this cement cast (no. 31), indicating that neither the bronzes nor the marble had been made by that date.

fig. b.
Arp, *Couronne de bourgeons II*, early photograph of 1936 cement in the collection of Georges Hugnet. Photograph by Robert David, courtesy Fondation Arp, Clamart.

fig. c.
Cat. no. 7, with cylindrical base added by Peggy Guggenheim at an unknown date.

whole (fig. c). In view of Arp's intense preoccupation in 1936 with the nature of the *Couronne de bourgeons* theme, a preoccupation which extended to the variety of new materials he used in their creation, it is clearly important to take note of any alteration in their structural presentation.[5]

EXHIBITIONS:

Venice, *P.G.*, 1948 (Biennale), no. 4 ("*Corona di seni*, 1945, Marmo"; medium and date similarly described in all subsequent *P.G.* publications until London, *P.G.*, 1964-65); Florence, *P.G.*, 1949, no. 7a; Venice, Giardino, 1949, no. 2, repr. (without base); Amsterdam, *P.G.*, 1951, no. 8; Zurich, *P.G.*, 1951, no. 10, repr. (without base); London, *P.G.*, 1964-65, no. 49, repr. (with base); Stockholm, *P.G.*, 1966-67, no. 47, repr.; New York, *P.G.*, 1969, p. 70, repr.; Paris, *P.G.*, 1974-75, no. 53, repr.; Torino, *P.G.*, 1975-76, no. 54.

REFERENCES:

M. Hagenbach, "Catalogue of Sculptures," in C. Giedion-Welcker, *Jean Arp*, New York, 1957, no. 30, p. 109, repr. p. 95 (without base); Alley, 1964, no. 49, repr. p. 40; Calas, 1966, p. 91, repr. p. 104; S. Poley, *Hans Arp: Die Formensprache im plastischen Werk*, Stuttgart, 1978, pp. 26, 30, 39, 85, 95, 96, 103, repr. p. 30 (without base).

5. The cylindrical base was added at an unrecorded date between 1951 and 1964 (see EXHIBITIONS). The method used to cement the sculpture to the base makes separation of the 2 elements, without damage to the soft limestone, extremely problematic. Alternative methods of display, in which the cylindrical base would be sunk into a pedestal, are under consideration (1983).

8 Mutilé et apatride. 1936.
(Maimed and stateless).

76.2553 PG 55

Newspaper, papier-mâché. Height (dimensions of piece placed on flat surface): $6\frac{3}{4}$ (17.1); width: $7\frac{3}{16}$ (18.3); depth: $9\frac{13}{16}$ (25). Dimensions of wood box (not original): $16\frac{1}{16}$ x 14 x $6\frac{5}{16}$ (40.8 x 35.5 x 16.0).

Not signed or dated.

PROVENANCE:

Purchased from the artist, Paris, 1940.

CONDITION:

The wood-pulp paper is highly and uniformly discolored due to acidity of materials and overexposure to light. There is soil and grime overall, and extensive scattered glue stains. Nails, which have been used to attach the work to the wood backboard, are rusted.

The following conservation and art-historical measures are envisioned: removal of the work from the box in which it was mounted after acquisition (fig. a); consolidation of the central projecting member; removal of all iron nails and filling of resulting holes with cellulose pulp and methyl cellulose; surface cleaning with alcohol and dilute ammonium hydroxide solutions; fumigation in thymol; mounting of the piece in its original orientation (main photograph), surrounded on all sides by a UF 3 Plexiglas display case. The condition is extremely fragile. (Venice, Nov. 1982.)

Cat. no. 8, as photographed in 1936. Photographer unknown.

According to Marguerite Arp-Hagenbach (in conversation with the author, Mar. 1982), this is the only surviving example of a series of "informal" papier-mâché objects made by Arp in the 1930s but later lost or inadvertently destroyed.[1]

Mutilé et apatride, a phrase taken from the newspaper text, was the title Arp himself used for the piece, though it has not been possible to establish whether the title inspired the suggestively symbolic image or was adopted in retrospect.

1. Ruth Tillard Arp, the artist's niece, believes that the papier-mâché objects all predated 1920, but agrees that this is the only surviving example (conversation with the author, Mar. 1982).

The informality and spontaneity of the medium argued for a disposition of the piece as freestanding sculptural object, and it was in this way that Arp published and exhibited the work in the years 1936-38. Peggy Guggenheim's addition of a wooden box with glass front, which necessarily conveys the impression of being integral to the object (fig. a), inadvertently introduced a new meaning. The change in orientation combined with the tangible quality of the enclosing, confining environment convey a perspective that is different from the original, on a literal, aesthetic, and metaphorical level.[2]

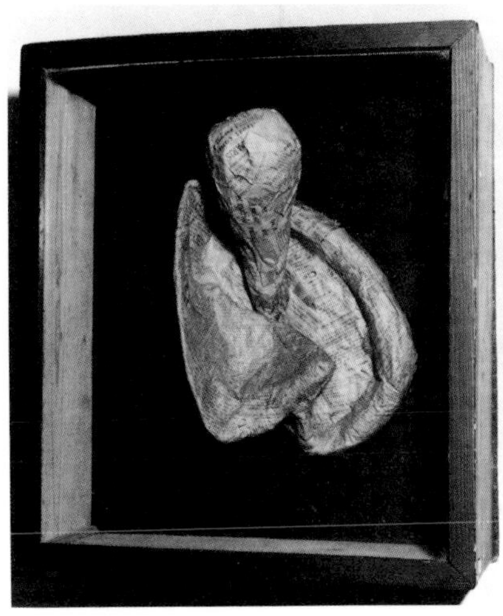

fig. a.
Cat. no. 8, as mounted and encased by Peggy Guggenheim sometime prior to 1944.

EXHIBITIONS:

Paris, Galerie Charles Ratton, *Exposition surréaliste d'objets*, May 1936, n. p. (*objets surréalistes*, "*Mutilé et apatride*, 1936"); London, New Burlington Galleries, *The International Surrealist Exhibition*, June 11-July 4, 1936, no. 15 ("*Object in Newspaper*, 1936"); Tokyo, Nippon Salon, *Exposition Internationale du Surréalisme*, June 9-14, 1937, no. 6, repr. ("*Objet* 1936"); Paris, Galerie Beaux-Arts, *Exposition Internationale du Surréalisme*, Jan. 17-Feb. 1938, no. 7 ("*mutilé et apatride*, 1936"); Amsterdam, Galerie Robert, *Exposition Internationale du Surréalisme*, spring 1938, no. 3 ("*Mutilé et apatride*, 1936"); New York, Art of This Century, 1942-47, p. 148; New York, Art of This Century, *Arp*, Feb. 1944, no. 21 ("*Mutilated and Stateless*, modeled newspapers"); Florence, *P.G.*, 1949, no. 6 (35 x 40 cm., indicating piece was mounted in box); Amsterdam, *P.G.*, 1951, no. 6; Zurich, *P.G.*, 1951, no. 8; London, *P.G.*, 1964-65, no. 48, repr.; Stockholm, *P.G.*, 1966-67, no. 46, repr.; Torino, Galleria Civica d'Arte Moderna, *Le Muse Inquietanti*, Nov. 1967-Jan. 1968, no. 107; Paris, *P.G.*, 1974-75, no. 52, repr.; Torino, *P.G.*, 1975-76, no. 53.

REFERENCES:

E. Tériade, "La peinture surréaliste," *Minotaure*, no. 8, 1936, repr. p. 8 ("*mutilé et apatride*, 1936"); H. Read, *Surrealism*, London [1936], repr. pl. 6 (*Mutilé et apatride*, 1936); P. Guggenheim, *Art of This Century*, 1942, p. 148; M. Hagenbach, "Catalogue of Sculptures" in C. Giedion-Welcker, *Jean Arp*, New York, 1957, p. 108 (mentioned in introductory note, but not included in catalogue); Calas, 1966, repr. p. 103; H. Read, *Arp*, London, 1968, p. 118, no. 138, p. 208, repr. p. 114; W. Rubin, *Dada and Surrealist Art*, London, 1969, repr. p. 272; J. Russell, "Der surrealistische Gegenstand," *Metamorphose des Dinges*, Brussels, 1971, p. 103; S. Poley, *Hans Arp: Die Formensprache im plastischen Werk*, Stuttgart, 1978, p. 176, repr. p. 213, fn. 453.

2. It has not been possible to establish when Peggy Guggenheim had the object mounted in its box. It must, however, have been prior to 1944, when it was reproduced in a review of Arp's New York exhibition.

9 Untitled. 1940.

76.2553 PG 57

Pencil on thin wove paper (watermark: VIDALON), 10½ x 8³⁄₁₆ (26.7 x 20.8).

Signed in pencil l.r.: *ARP*.

Not dated.

PROVENANCE:

Gift of the artist, summer 1940.[1]

CONDITION:

In 1978 (New York) the work was removed from the acidic mount to which it had been glued along the upper edge. Discoloration of the support (through overexposure to light) and scattered foxing were successfully treated with water, alkaline deacidification bath, weak bleach solution, rinsing. Tiny damages at edges were repaired with wheat starch paste and oriental fibers. The condition is stable. (Venice, Nov. 1982.)

Drawings by Arp in this style are rarely dated, though they have generally been attributed to the years 1942-46 (see, for example, *Hans Arp*, exh. cat., Galerie Der Spiegel, Cologne, 1976, nos. 22, 28). Peggy Guggenheim's acquisition of the present drawing in the summer of 1940, and her presumption that Arp had recently completed it, provide a *terminus ante quem* for a group of works that has hitherto eluded any clear chronological framework. Further study of the drawings of the 1940s will be necessary in order to arrive at a more definitive sense of their evolution and sequence.

EXHIBITIONS:

New York, Art of This Century, 1942-47, p. 148; New York, Art of This Century, *Arp*, Feb. 1944, no. 26; Florence, *P.G.*, 1949, no. 7; Amsterdam, *P.G.*, 1951, no. 7; Zurich, *P.G.*, 1951, no. 9; London, *P.G.*, 1964-65, no. 50; Stockholm, *P.G.*, 1966-67, no. 48; Paris, *P.G.*, 1974-75, no. 54, repr.; Torino, *P.G.*, 1975-76, no. 55.

REFERENCE:

P. Guggenheim, *Art of This Century*, 1942, p. 148.

1. Peggy Guggenheim recalled clearly (in conversation with the author) that Arp gave her the drawing when he came to stay with her at Le Veyrier on the Lac d'Annecy during the first summer of World War II. See also *Confessions*, 1960, p. 76.

10 Fruit-amphore. 1946? (cast 1951). (*Amphora fruit*).

76.2553 PG 58

Bronze (sand cast). Height: 29⅜ (74.5); length (measured from tip to tip): 38 15/16 (99); length (measured horizontally at ground plane): 29¾ (75.6).

Edition of one.[1]

Foundry: Unknown.

Not signed or dated. No foundry mark or cast number.

PROVENANCE:

Purchased from the Venice Biennale, July 1954.

CONDITION:

There are streaks of green corrosion on the vertical surfaces, and an overall green patina, affecting the appearance and condition of the bronze.

In March 1984 (Venice) the piece was cleaned. The surface was degreased with trichloroethylene, and washed with distilled water, then with distilled water and neutral detergent; it was rinsed with distilled water, and dried with alcohol and acetone. The surface was treated for 30 minutes with a 3% solution of benzotriazole in pure alcohol. A protective coating of Incralac (acrylic resin containing benzotriazole) was applied for outdoor exhibition.

According to Arp's assistant André Mounier, the sculptor's usual practice with large-scale bronzes was to allow the foundry to create the first patina. Arp would then work on a second patina himself, rubbing oil or wax into the surface and allowing the piece to weather in his garden. Instead of a highly polished surface, the bronze would thus acquire the opaque, deep, dark brown patina he sought. The outdoor exhibition over several years of the present piece has turned the patina to a greenish color, which does not correspond to Mounier's description and would not have occurred had the piece remained indoors.

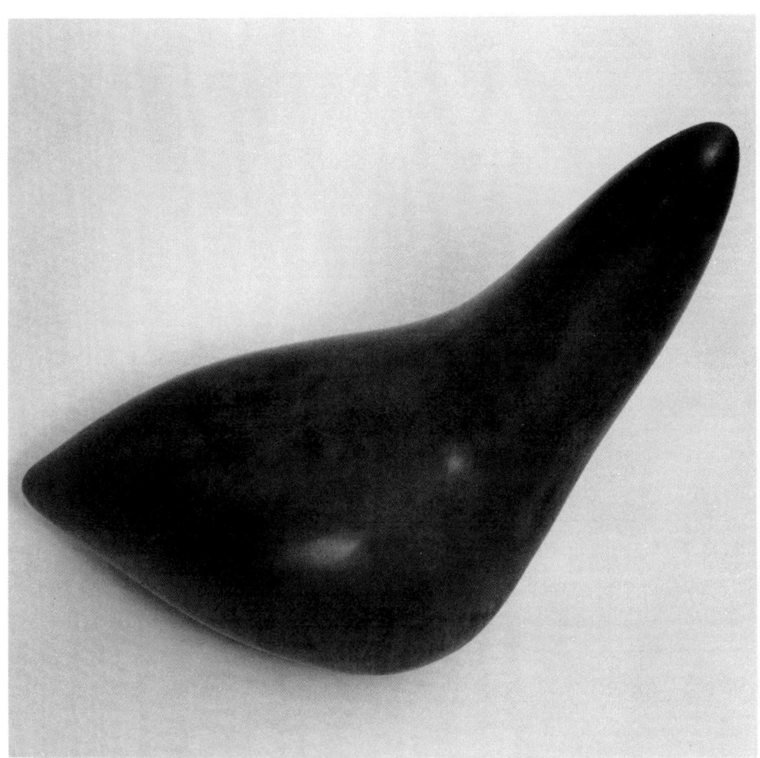

1. Though Giedion-Welcker refers to an edition of 3 bronzes, and such an edition was planned, the other 2 were never cast (information supplied by Greta Ströh, Fondation Arp, Clamart, Mar. 1982).

The origins and history of the form used by Arp in *Fruit-amphore* pose certain problems and afford some important insights into his working methods. His earliest use of a similar motif, though in a smaller, flatter, and more constricted format, was the 1939 *Feuille de pyramide* (9½ in., 24.1 cm., repr. Poley, 1978, p. 147). A subsequently enlarged and elongated version, *Amphore*, created in plaster by 1946, apparently survives only in the form of a reproduction in the artist's 1948 publication *On My Way* (fig. a). This plaster is generally thought to have been destroyed shortly afterward and never cast in bronze.[2]

A reexamination of the evidence, however, suggests that instead of destroying the plaster, Arp reused it, probably more than once, and eventually transformed it in the process of creating *Colonne de muse* in 1965.

In the first instance, the plaster appears to have served as the model from which the Guggenheim *Fruit-amphore* was cast.[3] In its elevated position on the slanting base (as reproduced fig. a), the 1946 plaster apparently measured 39¼ in. (100 cm.) in height, that is, from tip to tip. Peggy Guggenheim's bronze, when measured in the same way, is of almost exactly these dimensions (38$^{15}/_{16}$ in., 99 cm.) and, when observed from the same vantage point, seems to possess the same proportions. Although any comparison between a photograph and an actual sculpture is inherently problematic, there is reason to believe that the 1946 plaster was used to cast the 1951 bronze.

Further analysis suggests, moreover, that Arp reused the same plaster in the creation of two subsequent works. The 1957 *Bourgeon* (fig. c), though clearly representing a dramatic change in orientation and position (the piece is inverted and stands poised on one tip), is of precisely the same scale and form as *Fruit-amphore* (38$^{15}/_{16}$ in., 99 cm.). At a still later date, in 1965, Arp developed a wholly new conception: in *Colonne de muse* (fig. d) he split the form longitudinally, attaching the flat side of each half to a background plane almost twice the size of the figure. The dimensions along one side of the split form are precisely those of the 1951 *Fruit-amphore* (29⅜ in., 74.5 cm.). In short, given the close

2. Poley, 1978, p. 178, no. 28. Stephanie Poley describes the plaster *Amphore* as inspired by *Feuille de pyramide*. She states further that Arp destroyed the plaster when he became conscious of its close relationship to Brancusi's 1936 *Le miracle* (fig. b), but that the form continued to interest him. He thus returned to it in 1951, creating a new sculpture, *Fruit-amphore*, in which he isolated the "body" of the earlier piece from its association with a base, and placed its thickest lower part directly on the ground. Poley then cites *Bourgeon*, 1957, *Colonne de muse*, 1965, and *Bourgeon d'éclair*, 1965, as subsequent variations on the same theme. For an illuminating discussion of Arp's reductive method of using an individual sculpture as the point of departure for others, see Poley, 1978, pp. 33-34.

3. Poley makes the important point, based on conversations with Arp's assistant André Mounier and his widow, Marguerite Arp-Hagenbach, that the artist often made 2 identical plasters of a single image before casting in bronze, partly in order to be able to use parts of the image in the creation of new sculptures. Whether he did this in the case of *Amphore* has not been established. However, whether 1 or 2 identical plasters of *Amphore* existed, the hypothesis offered here is not substantively affected.

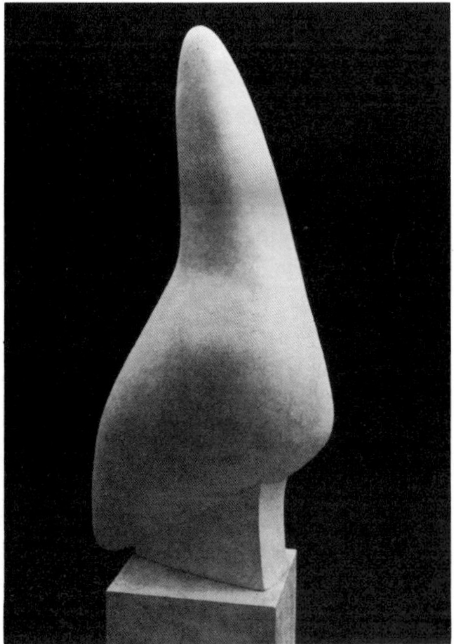

fig. a.
Arp, *Amphore*, plaster, probably destroyed. Photograph courtesy Rudolph Burckhardt from J. Arp, *On My Way*, New York, 1948, p. 116 (height given as 100 cm.; date, 1946).

fig. b.
Brancusi, *Le miracle*, 1936, marble, height: 42¾ in., 108.6 cm., SRGM, New York.

fig. c.
Arp, *Bourgeon*, 1957, bronze, height (tip to tip): ca. 38¹⁵⁄₁₆ in., 99 cm.

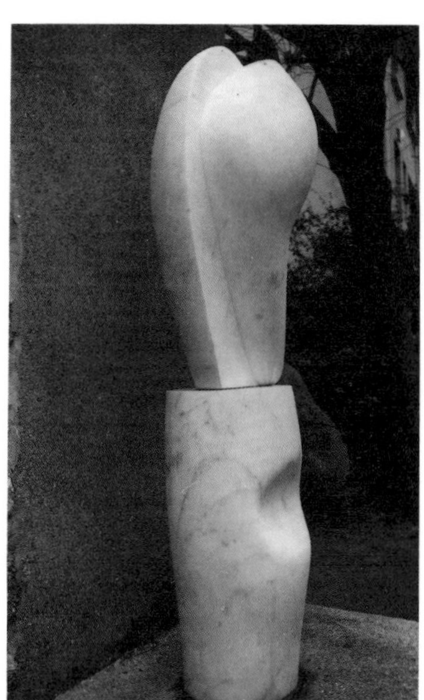

fig. d.
Arp, *Colonne de muse*, 1965, marble, length of "amphore" element, measured horizontally: ca. 29½ in., 75 cm.; total height of piece: 73⅝ in., 187 cm., Fondation Arp, Clamart.

correlation in dimensions and form among all of the works in the sequence from *Amphore* to *Colonne de muse*, it seems likely that Arp continued to work with a single plaster model throughout this period, achieving the variations through changes in position or presentation rather than through the creation of entirely new structures.[4]

The development of Arp's variations on the *Amphore* theme is also probably attributable in part to his complex relationship to Brancusi. Poley argues convincingly that the art of Brancusi posed considerable problems for Arp (1978, pp. 143, 147-48). The latter instinctively felt the danger implicit in the similarity between his work and Brancusi's, and he apparently declined an offer to work in the Rumanian's studio for precisely this reason. According to Arp's widow (in a 1970 interview with Poley), Arp at some point "became dissatisfied" with the original form of *Amphore* because of its resemblance to Brancusi's *Le miracle* (fig. b; see above, footnote 2). Whether this concern actually prompted him to destroy the plaster *Amphore* in the late 1940s is, however, far from clear. It seems more plausible that Arp did not fully confront the problem posed by *Le miracle* until after the 1951 casting of *Fruit-amphore*. Even then he seems to have responded not by destroying the plaster but by attempting more radical transformations of the image, first by inverting it (*Bourgeon*, 1957), later by splitting it (*Colonne de muse*, 1965), and only in this second instance definitively setting it apart from Brancusi's example.[5]

EXHIBITIONS:

Venice, XXVII Biennale, *Jean Arp*, June-Oct., 1954, no. 19; London, *P.G.*, 1964-65, no. 51; Stockholm, *P.G.*, 1966-67, no. 49; New York, *P.G.*, 1969, p. 71, repr.; Paris, *P.G.*, 1974-75, no. 55; Torino, *P.G.*, 1975-76, no. 56.

REFERENCES:

C. Giedion-Welcker, *Jean Arp*, New York, 1957, no. 115, p. 111; S. Poley, *Hans Arp: Die Formensprache im plastischen Werk*, Stuttgart, 1978, pp. 106, 178, no. 28, repr. p. 201, no. 9.

4. In March 1982, on a visit to Clamart, the author saw and measured 2 plasters of *Colonne de muse* in the artist's studio. A thorough search of all areas established that the original plaster or plasters of *Fruit-amphore* and of *Bourgeon* no longer existed. In discussions of the problem with Ströh, Mounier, and Marguerite Arp-Hagenbach, it emerged that a plausible argument can be made for Arp's use of *Amphore* as the model for casting both *Fruit-amphore* and *Bourgeon*, and that he subsequently split the same plaster in half to make the 2 plasters of the *Colonne de muse*.

5. It is interesting to note that Giedion-Welcker, in her 1957 publication of *Fruit-amphore*, specifically states that the original plaster was at that date still intact in the artist's studio.

   It is also conceivable, though compelling evidence on this point is lacking, that *Amphore* was used in yet a further guise: lying on its side on a 3-tiered base (see a photograph of Arp's garden taken by E. Scheidegger in 1953, repr. Poley, p. 179, no. 29). The title, medium, dimensions, and whereabouts of that piece are not known, but it cannot be ruled out that it represents yet another use of the original 1946 plaster, antedating the 1957 *Bourgeon* and the 1965 transformation into *Colonne de muse*.

Edmondo Bacci

Born July 1913, Venice.
Died October 1978, Venice.

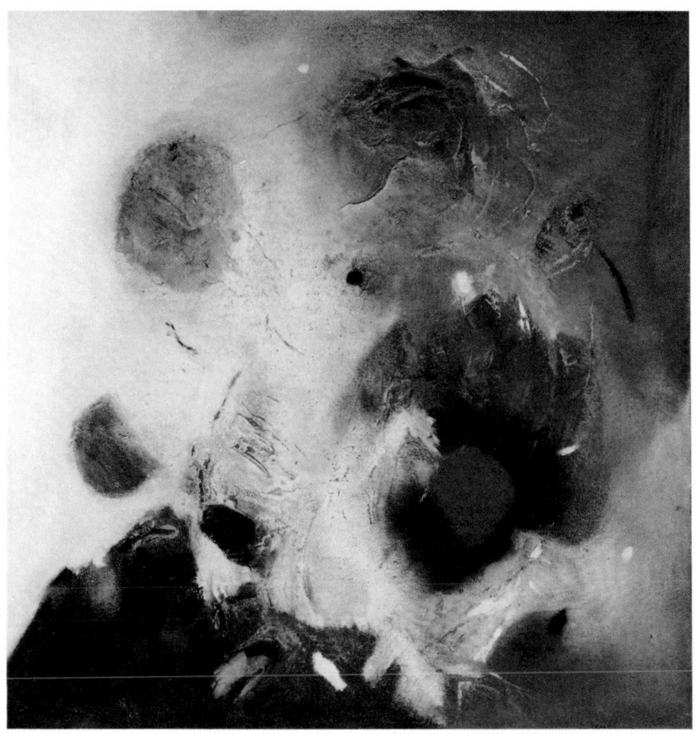

11 Avvenimento #247. 1956.
(*Event #247*).

76.2553 PG 164

Oil with sand on canvas, 55 3/16 x 55 1/8 (140.2 x 140).

Signed l.r.: *Bacci*; on reverse: *EDMONDO BACCI / Avvenimento #247.*[1] Not dated.

PROVENANCE:

Purchased from the artist, 1958.

CONDITION:

In 1983 (Venice) general consolidation of flaking impasto was carried out with Rhoplex AC 33 (methacrylate emulsion, Rohm and Haas), stock solution diluted 15% in water. The condition is fairly stable, though fragile. (Venice, June 1983.)

EXHIBITIONS:

New York, *P.G.*, 1969, p. 160, repr. ("*Event* 286, 1958"); Torino, 1975-76, no. 155 ("*Avvenimento* 286, 1958").

REFERENCES:

T. Toniato, *Bacci*, Venice, 1958 (repr. on its side, dated 1956); [Alley], *Peggy Guggenheim Foundation*, 1968, no. 164, repr. ("*Event* 286, 1958"); L. Flint, *Handbook*, 1983, no. 95, repr. color ("*Event* #247, 1958").

1. In spite of this inscription, the work has traditionally been published as #286 (see EXHIBITIONS and REFERENCES). The 1958 date usually assigned to the work resulted from this erroneous title.

Francis Bacon

Born October 1909, Dublin.
Lives in London.

12 Study for Chimpanzee. March 1957.

Color plate p. 508.

76.2553 PG 172

Oil and pastel on canvas (unvarnished), 60 x 46 1/16 (152.4 x 117).

Not signed or dated.

PROVENANCE:

Purchased from The Hanover Gallery, March 30, 1957.

CONDITION:

Bacon's practice during the 1950s was to work on the nap side of a commercially primed canvas and to apply no varnishes.

The unified background color of the 1950s pictures was applied either in pastel, as in the present case, or in oil thinned with turpentine to a consistency approaching a wash.

The magenta pastel background has suffered water damage in several places. The oil impasto (mixed in some places with sand) is poorly bonded to the support and shows some evidence of incipient cleavage and loss. Owing to the nature of the artist's technique, conservation measures pose considerable problems. The condition is fragile. (Venice, Nov. 1982.)

According to Ronald Alley, the work preceded Bacon's 1957 series of seven portraits of van Gogh. Five of these brilliantly colored canvases were shown in The Hanover Gallery exhibition, three painted in advance of the opening and two others added, with the paint still wet, during its course (Alley, *Bacon*, 1964, nos. 129-33).

Bacon recalls, however, that while the exhibition was still in an advanced stage of preparation, Erica Brausen, the director of the gallery, suggested that there was an insufficient number of works and requested that he produce one more. Specifically in response to this request, Bacon painted *Study for Chimpanzee*, a work he feels was never fully resolved.[1] The fact that the painting probably interrupted Bacon's intense involvement with the series of van Gogh portraits (described by Alley, *Bacon*, 1964, p. 110, as "a frenzy of work") must be taken into account in any evaluation of its "unresolved" quality and of its position within the artist's development.

A preoccupation with the expression of the animal through the human was already an important issue for Bacon in the 1950s and has continued as a leitmotif throughout his subsequent career. Statements by the artist on this issue are frequently cited, as are elucidations by others. (See, for example, his own statement: "animal movement and human movement are continually linked in my imagery of human movement," in D. Sylvester, *Interviews with Francis Bacon*, London, 1975, p. 116; and M. Leiris on Bacon's conception of human form: "*les hommes bizarrement ensauvagés que sont pour nous les singes*," in "Ce que m'ont dit les peintures de Francis Bacon," *Derrière le Miroir*, no. 162, Nov. 1966, p. 5.)

The strikingly simian qualities of the persona of *Van Gogh II* (Alley, *Bacon*, 1964, no. 129), and of the head and face of *Van Gogh III* (Alley, *Bacon*, 1964, no. 130), might thus throw light on the genesis of *Study for Chimpanzee*. Produced at short notice immediately after the two *Van Goghs*, when Bacon's energies were presumably fully engaged with that theme, *Study for Chimpanzee* may have functioned as part of the process of resolving critical issues within the *Van Gogh* series as much as it was a fully independent work in its own right.[2]

EXHIBITIONS:

London, The Hanover Gallery, *Francis Bacon*, Mar. 21-Apr. 26, 1957, no. 15; London, *P.G.*, 1964-65, no. 143, repr.; Stockholm, *P.G.*, 1966-67, no. 140; New York, *P.G.*, 1969, p. 143, repr. color; Paris, *P.G.*, 1974-75, no. 141, repr.; Torino, *P.G.*, 1975-76, no. 161, repr. pl. 67.

REFERENCES:

P. Guggenheim, *Confessions*, 1960, p. 158; R. Alley and J. Rothenstein, *Francis Bacon*, London, 1964, p. 110, no. 128, repr. n.p.; Calas, 1966, p. 227, repr. color p. 239; [Alley], *Peggy Guggenheim Foundation*, 1968, no. 172, repr.

1. In conversation with the author, March 1978, and with David Sylvester, December 1982 and February 1983, Bacon has expressed disapproval of the work. He also recalled telling Peggy Guggenheim at the time of her purchase: "If you wanted to buy one, why did you have to choose the worst?"

2. The question of whether the chimpanzee was based on a photograph or on another source has been raised with the artist, but not resolved. Lawrence Alloway first suggested that Amedée Ozenfant's photographs of monkeys might have provided Bacon with a source for some of his chimpanzees and baboons, though he does not refer specifically to the painting in Peggy Guggenheim's collection. See *Francis Bacon*, exh. cat. SRGM, New York, 1963, p. 25, fn. 7.

Giacomo Balla

Born July 1871, Torino.
Died March 1958, Rome.

13 Velocità astratta + rumore. 1913-14.
(*Abstract speed + sound*; *Automobile: Noise + Speed*; *Rumorautomobile + paesaggio*).

Color plate p. 46.

76.2553 PG 31

Oil on millboard (unvarnished) with wood frame made and painted by the artist. Dimensions of board: 20 1/16 x 28 5/8 (50.5 x 72.8); outer dims. of frame: 21 1/2 x 30 1/8 (54.5 x 76.5).

Signed l.l.: *BALLA FUTURISTA*. Not dated.

Reverse of cat. no. 13. In addition to Balla's sketch in colored pencils, the following inscriptions: *[VI]ALE PARIOLI 13. Van Petro VAN DOESBURG / Avenue Schneider / Clamart / Paris* (van Doesburg's studio from February 1924 to late in 1927).

PROVENANCE:

Remained with the artist until the mid-1920s;[1] gift of the artist to Theo van Doesburg by 1927;[2] purchased from Nelly van Doesburg, Paris, 1940.

CONDITION:

In 1964 (Tate Report) some cracks in the paint film, with possible incipient cleavage, were noted at the left and along the top edge. There were many small losses and abrasions in the foreground, and the support was buckled. The cleavage was secured, the surface lightly cleaned, and the losses inpainted.

In 1982 (Venice) further cleavage in one small area was noted; an oil resin varnish and some oil inpainting had been applied at an unknown date between 1964 and 1982. The varnish and inpainting were removed with n-Butylamine at 30% in water. The cleavage was set down with Gelvatol (polyvinyl alcohol at 15% in water and alcohol 1:1). Losses were filled with gesso and animal glue and inpainted with watercolor and Maimeri varnish colors. The surface was sprayed with Lefranc retouching varnish. The chalk sketch on the reverse was consolidated with Paraloid B-72 in trichloroethane at 3%. The condition is stable. (New York, Jan. 1983.)

1. On the reverse (see illustration) are traces of the address "[Vi] *ale Parioli 13*." According to the 2 daughters of the artist, Signorine Luce and Elica Balla (in conversation with the author, Nov. 1982), Balla stayed at that address for a few months during 1925 or 1926 as the guest of Aldo Ambron. It seems likely that the inscription dates from that sojourn and that the work still belonged to the artist at that time.

2. It has been impossible to establish the exact date of the gift, which is widely reported in the literature to have taken place before 1915. But van Doesburg had not developed an interest in Futurism by that time, and it is unlikely that the painting would have entered his collection until later. In fact the 2 artists seem not to have met until the mid-1920s. The van Doesburg address on the reverse (Avenue Schneider in Clamart, see illustration) provides further evidence: van Doesburg occupied a studio at that address between February 1924 and the end of 1927 (E. van Straaten, *Theo van Doesburg: 1883-1931*, The Hague, 1983, p. 183). On the basis of this evidence, and that cited in fn. 1, the gift would probably have been made sometime during the years 1925-27.

Balla's intense productivity in the years 1912 to 1914 arose almost entirely from an overriding concern to give pictorial expression to the concept and the visual experience of motion. His earliest explorations and achievements were clearly indebted to the chronophotographic research of Jules Étienne Marey in particular. (See, for example, *Dinamismo di un cane al güinzaglio* of May 1912, Albright-Knox Art Gallery, Buffalo, or *Ritmi dell'archetto* of autumn 1912, Collection Eric Estorick, London.) But by the end of 1912, the influence of the "photodynamics" of the Bragaglia brothers, whose work Balla first saw at that time, became even more decisive. (For a convincing discussion of this point, and of the parallel influences of Frank Bunker Gilbreth and Ernst Mach, see G. Lista, *Giacomo Balla*, Modena, 1982, pp. 43-49. On Balla's response to the work of Anton Giulio Bragaglia, see also S. B. Robinson, *Giacomo Balla Divisionism and Futurism, 1871-1912*, Ann Arbor, Michigan, 1981, pp. 90-95.)

Balla returned to Rome from a two-month stay in Dusseldorf in late December 1912. While in Germany he had been fully occupied with commissions for the Löwenstein house, and with the *Compenetrazioni iridescenti*. It seems probable that he did not begin his most intense activity on the theme of speeding automobiles until after his return to Rome.[3] It was precisely at that point that Boccioni noted a significant change in Balla's style. In a letter to Severini of January 1, 1913, Boccioni wrote that he had seen Balla the previous week, and that "*si è messo sulla via di una completa trasformazione. Ripudia tutte le sue opere e i suoi metodi. Ha comminciato quattro quadri di movimento (veristi ancora) ma incredibilmente avanzati e stranissimi a paragone di un anno fa*" (U. Boccioni, *Gli scritti editi e inediti.*, ed. Z. Birolli, Milan, 1971, pp. 363-64). Although it is not possible to be certain of the pictures Boccioni saw at that moment, it seems highly probable that Balla was in the process of developing his dynamic method of depicting speed, and especially the speed of the automobile. The subject in itself would have appealed to Boccioni far more strongly than Balla's earlier subjects such as the hand of the violinist or the figure of his daughter running on the balcony.[4]

According to the testimony of his two daughters (in conversation with the author, Nov. 1982, and Lista, op. cit., p. 49), Balla followed his usual practice — as he embarked on his new theme — of working from direct observation.

3. A small sketchbook (5⅛ x 3⅛ in., 13 x 8 cm.), published in full by Maurizio Fagiolo dell'Arco, contains an entire series of sketches on this theme and indicates some aspects of Balla's progression (*Analisi e sintesi. Un Taccuino di Balla*, Torino, Galleria Martano, 1974). Fagiolo dates the sketchbook 1912-14. Giovanni Lista, on the other hand, who published some of the individual pages from the sketchbook, dates the earliest of them 1910 (op. cit., nos. 209-14). The visual evidence of the notebook, which contains several sketches directly related to the more complex problems addressed by Balla in 1913, would tend to argue for the somewhat later dating of ca. 1912-14.

4. Only 1 painting depicting the subject of the speed of the "automobile + light" seems to have been dated 1912 by Balla (Lista, op. cit., no. 301). This work may have been inadvertently antedated at a later time. It is difficult to accept a date as early as 1912 for a resolved composition on this theme.

Standing on the corner of the Via Veneto, he spent several hours every day studying the visual effects created by passing automobiles and filled innumerable sketchbook pages with the results of his perceptions.

As he made his initial "translations" into pictorial form of the moving wheels, chassis, shadows, and surrounding "*ambiente*" of the passing vehicles, Balla also carried out parallel studies of the effects of light. From the outset, as in the 1912 *Compenetrazione iridescente,* the observation and depiction of the interpenetrating effects of light and motion continued to be important issues for him.

The earliest finished "automobile" paintings—showing dynamic or abstract speed combined with the effects of light—are difficult to date precisely. Two examples, however, were exhibited for the first time at the *Esposizione di pittura Futurista di "Lacerba,"* opening at the Galleria Gonnelli in Florence in November 1913 (*Plasticità di luci per velocità* and *Disgregamento d'auto in corsa*). It seems likely that during the previous ten months Balla had been fully occupied with the production of a large number of studies (in all media) on his new theme, and that he had also completed a sizable group of paintings in oil and gouache. (See, for example, Lista, op. cit., nos. 293-307, 311, 315-19, 321-22, 328-36, 362, 364-66, 369, 370.)

The Peggy Guggenheim painting is—like many of the other works in the new series—not dated. Moreover, the establishment of a chronology for Balla's development during this intense period presents unusually complex problems, since he clearly worked on several closely related issues simultaneously. It seems probable, however, that this introduction of the concept of *rumore* (noise) represented a stage beyond that which focused primarily upon light and speed. The crisscross and zigzag lines in the Peggy Guggenheim painting, representing the roar of the car as it speeds by, occur in relatively few works, and these are almost certainly datable toward the end of the series—either very late in 1913 or perhaps not before 1914.

A pastel drawing (fig. a) that includes many of the basic compositional elements of Peggy Guggenheim's painting but lacks the crisscross of the *rumore*

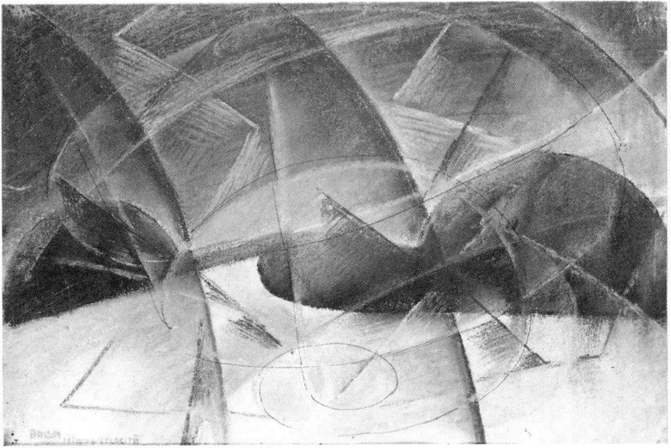

fig. a.
Balla, *Ritmo + velocità*, ca. 1913, pastel on paper, 10 13/16 x 16 3/4 in., 27.5 x 42.5 cm. Photograph courtesy Luce Balla, Rome.

probably served as one of a number of related preliminary studies. A pencil drawing (fig. b) that is far more detailed and that does include the *rumore* element was possibly also preparatory, although its highly finished, somewhat more articulated style suggests that it may have served as an intermediary between the Guggenheim painting and a second portrayal of the same motif (fig. c). In the latter painting, the degree of stylization and of concentrated linear emphasis on the central notion of *rumore* indicate a still later phase.[5]

The earliest occasion upon which a work containing the effect of *rumore* was exhibited was the *Esposizione di pittura futurista* at the Galleria Sprovieri, in February 1914. Of the twelve works shown by Balla, all of which were depictions of speed and motion, only one — *Plasticità rumore + velocità* — included the additional concept of "sound," a fact that lends further weight to the idea that this particular development was in fact a recent one. Consequently, a date of late 1913 or more likely 1914 seems appropriate for the Peggy Guggenheim picture.[6]

fig. b.
Balla, *Ritmo + rumore + velocità d'automobile*, not dated, pencil on paper, dimensions and present whereabouts unknown. Photograph courtesy M. Fagiolo dell' Arco.

5. The painting, in a private collection, Naples (fig. c), was dated 1914-15 in the catalogue of the Balla exhibition held at the Galleria Nazionale d'Arte Moderna in Rome in 1971-72, and then at the Musée d'Art Moderne de la Ville de Paris, 1972, cat. no. 13. Lista, op. cit., no. 323, dates the Naples painting 1913-14, and although he did not include the Peggy Guggenheim work in his publication, he placed it (in conversation with the author, 1982) toward the very end of the series, in 1914. M. Fagiolo, 1970, dates the Peggy Guggenheim picture 1913.
6. The presence on the reverse of cat. no. 13 of a chalk drawing possibly related to the 1914 exploration of the theme of vortices may also lend some further support to the notion of a 1914 date for the work itself (see illustration).

fig. c.
Balla, *Ritmo + rumore + velocità d'automobile*, ca. 1914, oil on paper mounted on canvas, $26\frac{3}{8}$ x $29\frac{1}{2}$ in., 67 x 75 cm., Private Collection, Naples.

The relationship of Peggy Guggenheim's painting to two others in the series remains to be examined. In a publication of 1970, Virginia Dortch Dorazio suggested that Balla had intended the Peggy Guggenheim painting to serve as the central panel in a triptych (fig. d). All three works were at some point photographed in frames specifically made for them by the artist; in each case, the actual painted composition extended (as in the Peggy Guggenheim picture) onto the frames themselves.[7]

Dorazio stated in her text that the works were intended by the artist to be hung together, portraying "three different moments of a speeding car penetrating the atmosphere. On the right is his visual perception of a car speeding on a highway within a green landscape. In the center the same 'abstract speed lines' of the car are seen with the addition of zigzag lines indicating the noise produced by the roaring car. On the left the speeding car and noise have passed and the highway remains in an empty landscape."

7. This photograph (or 3 individual photographs) has since been lost, and its origin is not entirely clear. Dorazio was unable to recall when the photograph(s) had been taken, or what had become of the print(s) (conversations with the author, 1982). The daughters of the artist were no longer in possession of the photograph by the winter of 1982 (conversation with the author). Both of the flanking works have since lost their original frames. They are reproduced in color (without frames) in Lista, op. cit., nos. 312, 314. A highly finished red pencil and graphite drawing, which may be a preparatory study for the right-hand work, is in a private collection in Rome (repr., Lista, op. cit., no. 332). A further undated oil version (repr. color, Lista, op. cit., no. 313) and a pastel dated 1914 (ibid., no. 379), both in private collections, are closest in composition to the right-hand work.

fig. d.
Balla, "Triptych" as presented by V. Dortch Dorazio. Right to left: *Velocità + paesaggio*, 1913, oil on cardboard, 19¾ x 25¾ in., 50 x 72 cm., Private Collection, Rome; cat. no. 13; *Velocità astratta—l'auto è passata*, 1913, oil on canvas, 19½ x 25¾ in., 50 x 65.5 cm., The Tate Gallery, London.

The artist's daughter Luce Balla recalled that the three pictures hung together both in their home and in an early exhibition or exhibitions (correspondence with R. Alley, Feb. 8 and 28, 1972; see Alley, *Tate Collection*, 1980, p. 30). The *III Biennale Romana*, held at the Palazzo delle Esposizione March 1-June 30, 1925, included three works by Balla collectively entitled *Paesaggio in velocità* (nos. 6-8). Although these works have not yet been identified, and no installation photographs have come to light, it does seem possible that the "triptych" under discussion was shown in this context.

The concept of the triptych has been accepted by Maurizio Fagiolo (1970), although not apparently by Lista. All three works are listed in the *Archivi del Futurismo* (nos. 62, 64a, 118a), but no suggestion of a serial relationship among them is indicated there. All three works remained in the artist's collection until about 1925, when he parted with the central piece, retaining the others until 1950.

The three pictures are clearly similar in scale, and they are obviously related in composition. The curved lines of the blue sky, reaching from top to bottom, the central horizontal of the green landscape, the white road, the sweeping red curves representing the speed of the car, and the pink vortex of accelerated motion are important elements of continuity in all three works; and there is no doubt that the set can be arranged to form an intelligible sequence. But at the same time, they derive from a larger group of works, several of which are similar in scale, subject matter, composition, and medium, and the notion of a triptych may well have actually presented itself to Balla after completing all, or most, of the various individual works in the series. The Peggy Guggenheim picture—with its introduction of *rumore*—probably postdates the others by at least some months, and the triptych would thus have been assembled post hoc.

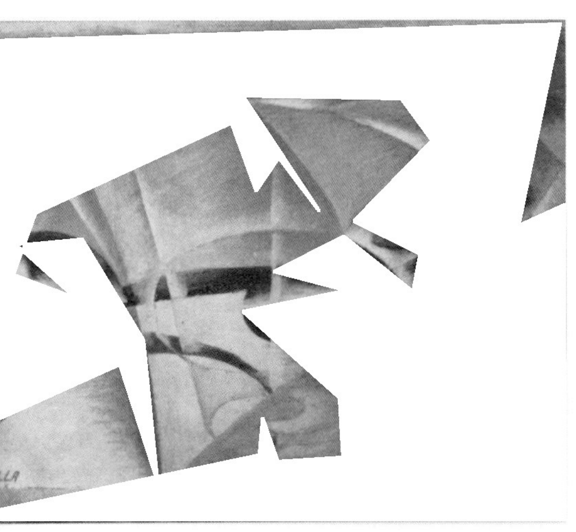

EXHIBITIONS:

New York, Art of This Century, 1942-47, p. 80, repr.; Venice, *P.G.*, 1948 (Biennale), no. 7 ("*Automobile e rumore*, 1912," the title and date by which the work has been known in all *P.G.* publications); Florence, *P.G.*, 1949, no. 8; Venice, XXV Biennale, *I firmatori del primo manifesto futurista*, June 8-Oct. 15, 1950, no. 1; Amsterdam, *P.G.*, 1951, no. 9; Zurich, *P.G.*, 1951, no. 11; London, *P.G.*, 1964-65, no. 23; Stockholm, *P.G.*, 1966-67, no. 23; New York, *P.G.*, 1969, p. 18, repr. color p. 19; Paris, *P.G.*, 1974-75, no. 22, repr. (*Automobile: bruit + vitesse*); Torino, *P.G.*, 1975-76, no. 30, repr. pl. 16; Rome, *Guggenheim: Venezia-New York*, 1982, no. 13, repr. color; New York, *P.G.* 1982-83, no. 9, repr.

REFERENCES:

F. Sapori, "L'Arte del maestro Giacomo Balla," *Il Futurismo*, II, no. 31, April 9, 1933, p. 3 (*Rumorautomobile + paesaggio*);[8] P. Guggenheim, *Art of This Century*, 1942, p. 80. repr. ("*Automobile and Noise*, 1912"); M. Drudi Gambillo and T. Fiori, *Archivi del Futurismo*, Rome, 1962, no. 118a; R. Alley, 1964, no. 23 ("*Car and Noise*, 1912"); M. Fagiolo dell'Arco, *Futur Balla*, Rome, 1970, p. 27 (dated 1913); V. Dortch Dorazio, *G. Balla*, New York, 1970, n.p. repr. fig. 3 (as central element of a triptych, all dated 1913); Alley, *Tate Collection*, 1981, p. 30 (1912); L. Flint, *Handbook*, 1983, p. 46, repr. color p. 47 (ca. 1913).

8. The right-hand panel from Dorazio's "triptych" (fig. d) is also reproduced in Sapori's article; its caption reads "*Paesaggio + linee di velocità automobile* (1912)." It does not appear adjacent to the Peggy Guggenheim painting and no direct connection between the 2 works is implied. Both are reproduced without their frames.

William Baziotes

Born June 1912, Pittsburgh.
Died June 1963, New York.

14 Untitled. 1943.

76.2553 PG 157

Gouache on black-wove construction paper, glued to wood-pulp cardboard, $9\frac{1}{16}$ x 12 (23 x 30.5).

Signed l.r.: *Baziotes*. Not dated.

PROVENANCE:

Purchased from the artist before the exhibition at Art of This Century, October 1944.

CONDITION:

There are small tears at the upper edge toward the left corner and center, and the left edge center. Traces of gray mold growth are in the black areas (not active). The acidity of the secondary support is probably causing deterioration of the primary support; removal is envisaged. The overall condition appears stable. (Venice, Nov. 1982.)

fig. a.
Cat. no. 14, verso composition, date unknown.

On the verso, Baziotes made a preliminary sketch for another composition (fig. a). It has thus far not proved possible to establish any relationship between this study (hitherto unpublished) and a completed work by the artist.

EXHIBITIONS:

New York, Art of This Century, *Paintings and Drawings by William Baziotes*, Oct. 3-21, 1944, no. 97; Venice, *P.G.*, 1948 (Biennale), no. 10 (dated 1945, the date ascribed to it until 1974); Florence, *P.G.*, 1949, no. 11; Amsterdam, *P.G.*, 1951, no. 12; Zurich, *P.G.*, 1951, no. 14; Bordighera, *II^A Mostra Internazionale Pittura Americana*, Mar. 1-31, 1953, no. 26; Paris, *P.G.*, 1974-75, no. 135; Torino, *P.G.*, 1975-76, no. 149.

15 The Room. 1945.

Color plate p. 678.

76.2553 PG 156

Gouache on pressboard, 17 15/16 x 24 (45.6 x 61.0).

Signed l.r.: *Baziotes*; on reverse in ink: "*The Room*" / *William Baziotes*. Not dated.

PROVENANCE:

Purchased from the artist, 1945.[1]

CONDITION:

In 1983 (New York) the delaminating and crumbling edges of the support were consolidated with methyl cellulose (400 cps Dow). Flaking and cleavage of pigment was consolidated with a mixture of methyl cellulose and rice paste. Damages and losses at the edges and corners were repaired, filled with tenjugo tissue, and inpainted with Windsor and Newton watercolor. A fine crackle evident in most areas is presently stable. The matte surface of the gouache has been preserved intact and no fixative or varnish has been applied. (New York, Feb. 1983.)

1. Peggy Guggenheim recalled purchasing the work from Baziotes in his New York studio not long after his one-man show at Art of This Century, October 1944. Baziotes apparently later gave the same title to a second work. It has been impossible to establish which of the 2 was exhibited at Samuel Kootz's gallery in 1946 and 1947, though it seems more likely to have been the second version, which has hitherto not been traced. (Such a painting, apparently measuring 10½ x 13½ in. was shown in a traveling exhibition of *Advancing American Art*, organized in 1946 by J. Le Roy Davidson under the auspices of the Office of International Information and Cultural Affairs of the U.S. State Department.)

In a 1947 statement about painting, William Baziotes wrote:

There is no particular system I follow when I begin a painting. Each painting has its own way of evolving. One may start with a few color areas on the canvas; another with a myriad of lines; and perhaps another with a profusion of colors.

Each beginning suggests something. Once I sense the suggestion, I begin to paint intuitively. The suggestion then becomes a phantom that must be caught and made real. As I work, or when the painting is finished, the subject reveals itself.

As for the subject matter in my painting, when I am observing something that may be the theme for a painting, it is often an incidental thing in the background, elusive and unclear, that really stirred me, rather than the thing before me (Possibilities, Winter 1947/8, p. 2).

This analysis by Baziotes directly confirms what Lawrence Alloway has described as the artist's "absorbing interest in automatism" in the early 1940s (*Baziotes*, exh. cat., SRGM, New York, 1965, p. 12). But it also throws additional light on the particular notion of subject matter that characterized Baziotes' work during this period. Baziotes himself stated that titles should be associative;[2] consequently they tend to offer only the most elliptical clues to the meaning of his work. Though he was, according to his widow, Ethel Baziotes, obsessed with the idea of rooms,[3] the title in the Peggy Guggenheim painting — as in other instances — serves essentially as a means of identifying the work rather than as a description of its "literal" content. The room, which is the picture's ostensible subject, has clearly been represented in the highly intuitive, elusive manner that Baziotes himself defined as his working method.

EXHIBITIONS:

New York, Kootz Gallery, *William Baziotes: Paintings, Watercolors*, Feb. 12-Mar. 2, 1946, no. 7? (*The Room*);[1] New York, Kootz Gallery, *Baziotes*, Apr. 7-26, 1947, no. 17? (*The Room*);[1] Venice, *P.G.*, 1948 (Biennale), no. 9; Florence, *P.G.*, 1949, no. 10; Amsterdam, *P.G.*, 1951, no. 11; Zurich, *P.G.*, 1951, no. 13; Bordighera, *II^A Mostra Internazionale Pittura Americana*, Mar. 1-31, 1953, no. 25; London, *P.G.*, 1964-65, no. 131; Stockholm, *P.G.*, 1966-67, no. 127; New York, *P.G.*, 1969, p. 144, repr.; Paris, *P.G.*, 1974-75, no. 134, repr.; Torino, *P.G.*, 1975-76, no. 148; New York, *P.G.*, 1982-83, no. 56, repr. color.

REFERENCES:

Calas, 1966, repr. p. 179; L. Flint, *Handbook*, 1983, p. 186, repr. color p. 187.

2. *Perspective*, No. 2 (Hunter College), 1956-57, pp. 27, 29-30. For a discussion of these issues, see also M. B. Hadler, "The Art of William Baziotes," unpublished Ph.D. dissertation, Columbia University, 1977, pp. 162-65.

3. In discussion with Cynthia Goodman, New York, June 4, 1983. Other works of the 1940s that reflect this "obsession" are: *The Grey Room*, present whereabouts unknown, exhibited at Art of This Century, 1944; *The School Room*, 1944, Kresge Art Center, Michigan State University; *The Waiting Room*, 1944, Menil Foundation, Houston, Texas.

Umberto Boccioni

Born October 1882, Reggio Calabria.
Died August 1916, Sorte (Verona).

Cat. no. 16, as restored by 1950; iron pedestal and base added in 1957.

16 Dinamismo di un cavallo in corsa + case. 1914-15.
(Dynamism of a speeding horse + houses; Cavallo + case costruzione dinamica di un galoppo; Cavallo + case—Dinamismo plastico).

76.2553 PG 30

Gouache and oil on wood, paper collage with gouache on wood, cardboard, copper sheet (*lastra di rame*); iron sheet coated with tin or zinc (*lastra di latta*). Height (including vertical iron support, which is not original): 44 1/2 (112.9); height (including original projecting wood strut, but excluding iron support): 38 3/16 (97); width: 45 1/4 (115).

Not signed or dated.

Reverse of cat. no. 16. All visible cardboard elements date from restoration executed before 1950.

PROVENANCE:

Filippo Tommaso Marinetti, possibly by 1917, certainly by 1923;[1] purchased from Benedetta Marinetti, 1958.

CONDITION:

The condition of cat. no. 16 is discussed in some detail below, where various problems raised by its previous restoration are addressed. Owing to the disproportionate weight of the cardboard used in this earlier restoration, the present structural balance of the entire work is seriously compromised. The overall condition of the cardboard (both original and restoration elements) is extremely brittle and fragile. The original cardboard has also darkened through exposure to light, thus altering the tonal balance between the painted and unpainted areas. The paper collage elements and the gouache (and oil) have considerably deteriorated.

Various approaches to the aesthetic, historical, and conservation questions posed by the piece are currently under study. (Venice, Nov. 1982-Mar. 1984.)

In his important article published in *Critica d'Arte* in 1977 (see REFERENCES), Piero Pacini was the first to point out that the construction *Dinamismo di un cavallo ...*, as originally conceived by Boccioni, had undergone several alterations since 1916. Although it is not entirely certain that Boccioni ever regarded the piece as finished (see below), the earliest record of the condition in which he is presumed to have left it is the photograph published contemporaneously in 1923 by Marinetti and Vincenzo Paladini (fig. a). Soon afterward, this photograph reached the Japanese critic Ţai Kambara, who reproduced it, with a brief commentary, in his text on Futurism published in Tokyo in 1925 (see below). Further evidence regarding the original arrangement of the construction's multidimensional parts is provided by a recently discovered photograph

1. After Boccioni's death in 1916, the works that remained in his studio came into the care of Marinetti, although it is not clear whether this occurred immediately or sometime later.

that probably dates from late 1914 or early 1915 (fig. b).[2] In this view of the unfinished construction, photographed in Boccioni's studio with his mother posing in front of it, certain elements that were less clear in the 1923 photograph can be discerned. Moreover, in two later photographs (figs. c and d), taken when the construction had long been in the Marinetti collection, some additional details emerge.[3]

When preparing his article, Pacini had little opportunity to study the actual object thoroughly, or under ideal circumstances; he nonetheless arrived at a series of hypotheses regarding its condition that have to a considerable extent been substantiated by an exhaustive recent study.[4]

In attempting to arrive at a clear understanding of the restorations, and of the relationships between these alterations and Boccioni's original intentions, certain established facts and some hypotheses must be taken into account. (References to the various elements, unless otherwise indicated, are to the numbered diagram, fig. e.)

The first fact to take into account concerns the cardboard elements representing most of the "houses" (*case*) of Boccioni's title (fig. e, sections 1-3). The originals were, at an unknown date, replaced with new cardboard in such a way that their basic form was significantly altered. It is more than likely that by the time this restoration was undertaken Boccioni's original elements had already been lost or damaged beyond repair, thus making it almost impossible to achieve an entirely intelligible or faithful reconstruction.[5]

Hitherto all the scholars who have worked on the problem have assumed that the early restoration took place at the time of the 1957-58 exhibition (see below EXHIBITIONS)—specifically under the supervision of Giovanni Carandente—but this was not the case: the construction had actually been fully restored by the time it was reproduced in a 1950 article in *Cahiers d'Art* (fig. f). In only one detail does this photograph depart from the current disposition of the object: the tip of the triangular "pitched roof" behind the horse's head has since broken

2. The author is indebted to Ester Coën for drawing this photograph to her attention and for conversations regarding the chronology of Boccioni's 1914 oeuvre. Dr. Angelo Calmarini in Milan, who owns the photograph, kindly granted permission for its publication.

3. The author is indebted to Marianne Martin for drawing her attention to the photograph reproduced in fig. d.

4. The following analysis is based on a lengthy examination of the piece carried out in Venice, Nov. 1982, by the author with Piero Pacini and Sergio Angelucci. This examination followed preliminary ones carried out by the author in 1977 (arising out of hypotheses comparable to those of Pacini, but based upon less secure documentary evidence). Correspondence between the author and Pacini (following his compelling publication) established clear agreement on the various aspects of the problem posed by the present condition of the object. The conclusions reached by the author are much indebted to his and Angelucci's collaboration.

5. An interview with one of Marinetti's daughters, Ala, published in *La Repubblica*, Rome, Nov. 11, 1982, quotes her recollection that when she and her sisters were children they used the object as a kind of hobbyhorse, riding it around the house. If accurate, this would certainly establish that the houses were no longer in place at the time.

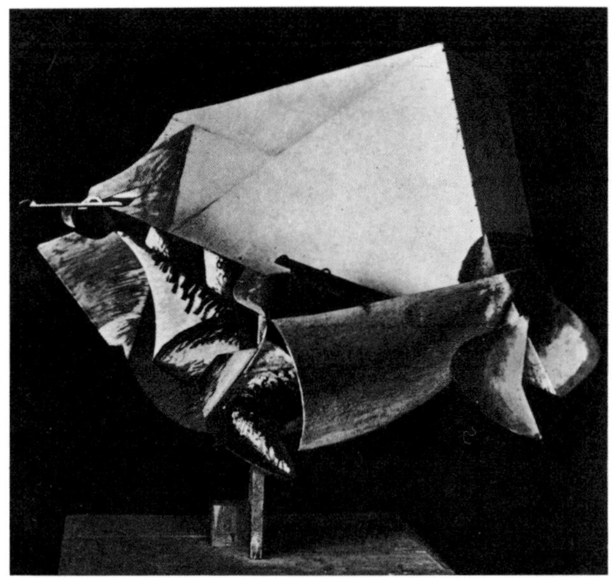

fig. a.
Cat. no. 16, as reproduced in *Noi*, ser. 11, anno 1, April 1923, p. 8; this photograph also appeared in V. Paladini, 1923, and T. Kambara, 1925.

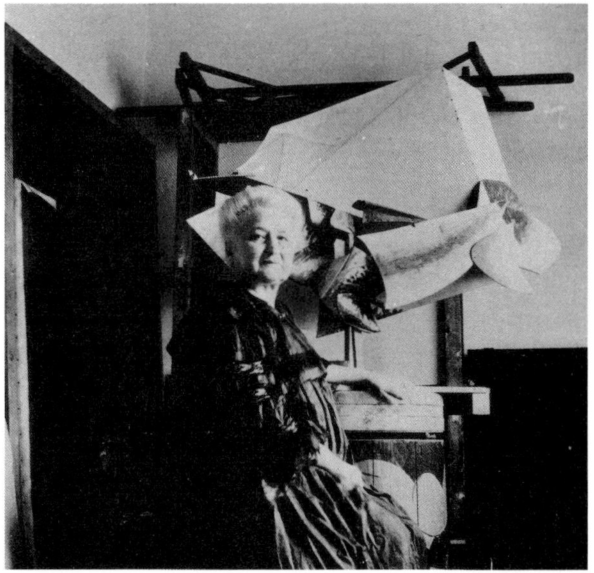

fig. b.
Cat. no. 16, unfinished, in Boccioni's studio; his mother is seated in front of the sculpture, ca. 1914-15. Photograph courtesy Dr. Angelo Calmarini, Milan.

fig. c.
Cat. no. 16, suspended from the ceiling in the residence of the Marinetti family, Piazza Adriana, 30, Rome, ca. 1934. Reproduced in *La Lettura*, vol. 12, no. 3, March 1934, p. 198.

fig. d.
Cat. no. 16, partially visible suspended from ceiling in Marinetti's residence, ca. 1934, with Marinetti himself standing at lower right. Photograph courtesy Marinetti Archive, Beinecke Rare Book and Manuscript Library, Yale University, New Haven, Connecticut.

KEY:
1. Houses, cardboard(?), now lost, replaced by restoration.
2. Houses, painted wood(?), now lost, replaced by restoration.
3. Houses, painted cardboard(?), now lost, replaced by restoration.
4. Houses, hypothetical top plane of unknown material, now lost.
5. Horse's body, painted cardboard (original intact).
6. Horse's body, painted wood (original intact).
7. Horse's neck and head, painted wood (original intact).
8. Horse's haunches, painted wood (original possibly intact).
9. Horse's haunches, painted wood (original possibly intact).
10. Horse's haunches, painted collage on wood (original largely intact, with restored section along lower edge).
11. Horse's body, painted collage on wood (original intact).
12. Horse's body, painted wood (original intact).
13. Central support, wood (original intact).
14. Horse's thigh, single piece of painted wood (original intact).
15. Horse's back, painted wood (original intact).
16. Horse's back-neck, painted collage on wood, nailed to central support (13) (original intact).
17. Horse's arched upper back, partially painted copper sheeting, screwed to wood section (15) (original intact, but bent out of position).
18. Hole cut through cardboard (5) to reveal painted crossbar behind (see fig. h).
19. Horse's nostrils, eye, and ears, iron sheeting coated with tin or zinc (original intact, but bent out of position).

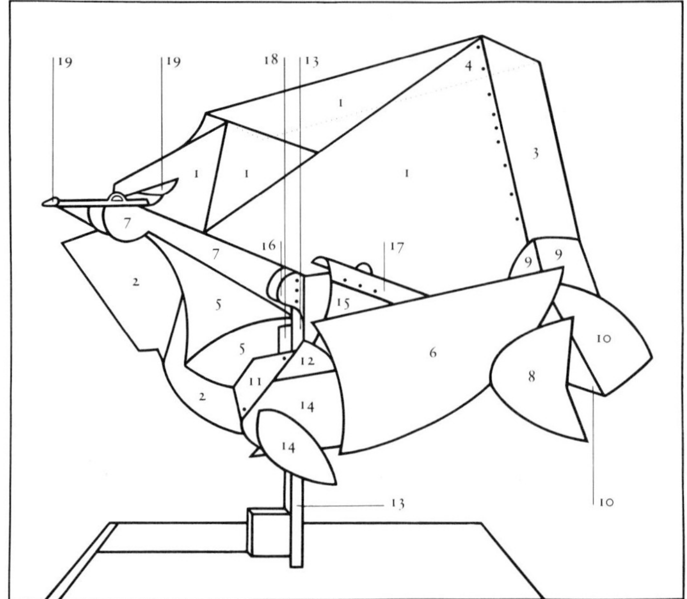

fig. e.
Diagram of cat. no. 16 based upon fig. a.

off. Even this detail was still in place, however, when Peggy Guggenheim bought the sculpture, and when Calas published it eight years later (see below REFERENCES). Thus, the early (and most fundamental) replacement of about one-half of Boccioni's original construction had taken place before 1950.[6]

When Carandente first saw the piece (in 1957) in the Marinetti house, it was leaning against a wall. It lacked any kind of "stand" to hold it upright for display purposes, and he decided to mount the existing wooden strut (an original element that projected downward from the body) to an iron pedestal support.[7]

Examination of the construction in its present state, and comparison with all available early documentation, has led to the following additional conclusions concerning both its current condition and its original state (fig. e):

A. One piece of Boccioni's original cardboard survives (5). This was originally brightly painted in such a way as to suggest two distinct planes, conveying a sense of the horse's body in motion. The wood-pulp cardboard, which was (and remains) nailed to the flat rear side of the horse's wooden neck, is in

6. Since commercial interest in Futurism was nonexistent in the 1940s, it would probably not have been in connection with a potential sale that the piece was restored. But because this construction was regarded by the Futurists themselves as extremely important, it is perfectly plausible to think that Marinetti prior to his death in 1944, or his widow afterward, might have decided with a member of their circle to repair the object . It has been suggested that Enrico Prampolini (who was close to the Marinetti household) undertook this project, but this remains to be definitively established.

poor condition; its multi-ply sections are separating in several places, and there are also some tears evident. The gouache used to paint its surface has substantially faded. Both the front and the back of this cardboard are painted, the front in black, red, and white, the back in black and red.

B. The long neck and head of the horse (7) were constructed out of wood, brightly painted in oil. Two rounded elements were added as schematic jowls. The wood is well preserved, the paint somewhat faded. It cannot be ruled out that some portions of this section have been retouched. The ears and nostrils of the animal were cut out of a thin sheet of iron coated with tin or zinc (19). (Careful examination of the 1923 photograph suggests that an eye may have been painted in.) This element was attached (with two nails) along the flat top edge of the wooden head; it has since been bent out of shape. (Compare its original position in fig. a.) Moreover, the "nostrils" were at some stage actually broken off and reattached with tin solder.[8]

C. A rounded piece of copper sheeting (17) was screwed (with three screws) to the horse's wood body (15). Clearly, this piece of wood had been painted black before use. It is probable that Boccioni used the wood of an old black table as the material for sections of his construction. Red oil paint, still present on the body, originally extended onto the copper, probably obscuring the join between the two. (See fig. a, where indeed the two elements appear continuous.) The copper element, suggestive of the horse's arching back, with a small loop on its upper surface (now lost), has been bent out of position. The loop was used in the Marinetti household (fig. c) to suspend the sculpture from a rope attached to the ceiling. It is possible that this was in fact Boccioni's original conception for displaying the piece (see footnote 7).

D. Several of the surviving wood sections (10, 11, 16) were covered with paper collage before being painted with red, black, and white gouache (or oil). The wood-pulp paper is in poor condition and has disintegrated in places; the paint has almost entirely faded.

E. The surviving wood elements (6-16) have suffered some minimal damage and distortion in position (see, for example, fig. i), but on the whole they remain in a reasonably good state of preservation. Doubt exists regarding the original nature of elements 8 and 9. Minor apparent discrepancies between their present contours and those revealed in the early photographs figs. a and b give rise to this doubt, which is thus far unresolved.

7. Giovanni Carandente, in correspondence and conversations with the author, August-November 1982. Oddo Verdinelli of the Istituto Centrale del Restauro constructed the pedestal, which is still in place. No other restoration of the piece was carried out or, indeed, thought to be necessary at the time. The wooden element is part of Boccioni's original construction. Whether the pedestal arrangement in the 1923 photograph (fig. a), in which the wooden element is attached to a small side block probably screwed into the wooden base, corresponded with Boccioni's original intention is, of course, impossible to say. No reliable evidence survives to indicate how the work was intended to be shown.

8. In the interview cited in fn. 5, Marinetti's daughter mentioned that the nose had broken during one of their games. Hiding it from their father, she and her sisters had managed somehow to reattach it. It must later have been repaired by a more professional hand.

F. The vertical element (13) projects below the construction and is now secured to the 1957 iron support; it also extends up through the center. The small slanting section to the left (16) is nailed to the upper edge of 13 (see three dots in diagram, fig. e, indicating location of the surviving original nails).

G. Regarding the houses, now entirely lost, it is possible to reconstruct at least three distinct planes that were part of the original composition; a fourth plane (and even additional planes) may have existed, but this cannot be established with certainty.

Element 1 was probably made of cardboard and formed the front plane. The material may have been comparable to that used in element 5. The spatial, or three-dimensional, elements of this plane (the pitched roofs at the left) were probably (although not certainly) created through the use of illusionistic drawing, shading, and painting, rather than through cutting and reassembling of separate parts. Some doubt remains on this point, but the evidence of the surviving photographs tends to support such a conclusion (see figs. a and b).

Element 3 (the lateral plane) may have been made of wood or of cardboard, although the visual continuity between planes 1 and 3, as demonstrated in fig. b, suggests that the material would have been the same in both. In the two photographs (figs. a and b) a line of nails is visible running down the join between the two planes. This establishes that they were constructed as separate pieces and that a wooden bar must have been inserted behind and between them at the join. The strut would have served as a means of connecting the two planes and of maintaining their stability within the structure as a whole.

The apparent right-angle construction of the flat wooden elements 9 and 10 may have been created purely through the illusionistic application of paint. The cardboard plane 3 would have been parallel to the wood element 9, which *appeared* to rest upon it. Examination of the side view of the work (fig. g) reveals the intricate method of construction Boccioni used to achieve this effect: by joining element 10 (left) to element 9 (right) with a crossbar of precisely the right length, he would have been able to set the two pieces of wood at an angle to one another that — when combined with their illusionistically painted surfaces — would suggest that the horse's limbs were literally wrapped around the wall of the house.

The width of lateral plane 3 must have been greater than that of element 9, in order to create this illusion of precise juxtaposition when the construction was seen — as it was clearly intended to be — from the front.

The height of plane 3 must have been the same as that of plane 1. The degree of its inclination (toward the back of the construction) has not, however, been fully established. Similarly, it is not clear, although it seems likely, that there was originally a horizontal top plane (here hypothetically introduced as element 4). None of the early photographs is taken from a sufficiently high angle to allow for a view of the top. It is thus impossible to ascertain whether Boccioni intended such a "closing" element to exist.

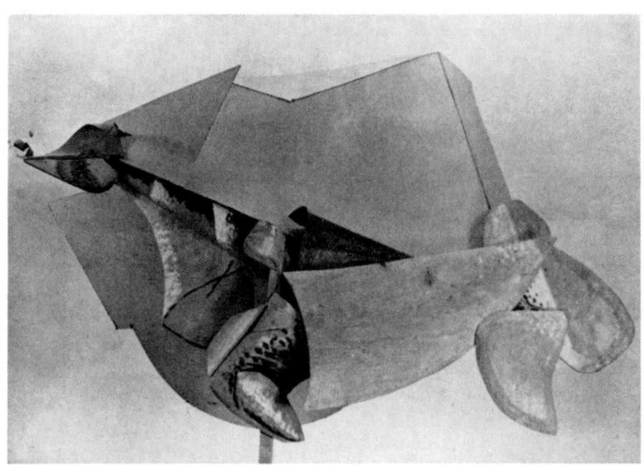

fig f.
Cat. no. 16 after restoration, reproduced in *Cahiers d'Art*, vol. 25, 1950, p. 51.

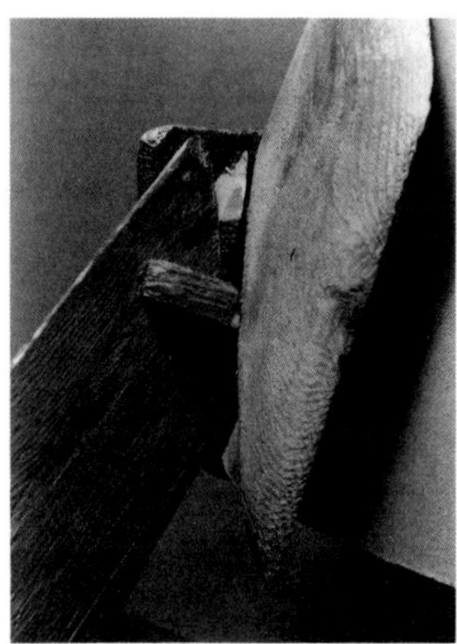

fig. g.
Detail of cat. no. 16; side view (right) showing original wood construction and loosening of crossbar (elements 10 [left] and 9 [right]).

fig. h.
Detail of cat. no. 16; side view (left) showing original construction and its juxtaposition with restoration. Original cardboard element 5 (right) is painted front and back. Crossbar joins it to 1940s restoration (left). Triangular wood form, nailed to crossbar, is partially painted in red gouache; crossbar is painted red and black; reverses of these elements are unpainted.

Finally, plane 2, which served to define two additional aspects of the houses, was probably made of wood, not cardboard. Its apparent thickness at the left edge (see fig. a), and the presence of what seems to be a wood-grain surface in addition to the paint, lends support to this notion. As in the case of the cardboard (5), the illusion of two distinct planar surfaces would have been created through the application of paint. In the photograph fig. b (where the vantage point is slightly lower than that of fig. a), the extension of this wood surface across almost the entire width of the construction is clearly discernible. Although at that stage not yet fully painted, the straight edge, slanting slightly upward, extends to the end of the horse's body. In fig. d, where one critical element (8) is temporarily missing, it is possible to see that plane 2 actually ended in a right angle just short of element 10. Even in the rather illegible photograph published in *La Lettura*, 1934 (fig. c), element 8 is missing and this detail also emerges.

The position of plane 2 at a slight angle to the main neck-head of the horse, rather than parallel to it, has also been tentatively established. A side view of the construction from the left (fig. h) reveals an original crossbar, which was attached at its right edge perpendicular to the horse's neck. The nail holding it in position is now somewhat loose, probably owing to the presence of the cardboard immediately above it, which was erroneously positioned during the 1940s restoration; its strictly perpendicular position

fig. i.
Detail of cat. no. 16; rear view of horse's "haunches"; top to bottom: elements 9, 10, 8. Element 10 is split, the lower portion having been added, probably during the 1940s restoration. Painted collage on this side of element 10 ends abruptly at the split. The lower edge of the restoration element is rounded at corner; in the original (see figs. a and b) the edge was straight.

> at the right edge has therefore been modified. The left edge of this crossbar is cut obliquely. Thus when the original plane 2 was nailed to the oblique edge, it would have been on a slant — closer to the horse at the tail than at the head. The roughly triangular piece of wood nailed to the crossbar would have served to reinforce the positions of the planes to its right and left. (Traces of red paint are still clearly visible on this triangular piece; the cross-bar is painted in red and black. The reverse sides of these pieces are not painted, suggesting that the sculpture was closed on the right side.)

As becomes clear from such examination of the original photographs in combination with the evidence offered by the piece itself, Boccioni's construction was extraordinarily complex, both in its use of materials and in its technical execution. Wood was used in several different thicknesses; some parts were brightly painted, others barely tinted, to suggest the varying effects of light on the speeding body of the horse and the houses. To intensify these effects, the ears and distended nostrils were made of tin (bright and silvery in tone), and the back was a shining copper. The pitched roofs of the houses — partly white, partly painted; part wood, part board; part in brilliant sunlight, part in shadow — were illusionistically colored and shaded in such a way that they appeared to be interwoven with the complex planar surfaces of the horse.

Only by examining Boccioni's earlier drawings and watercolors on this theme, many of which were 1913-14 studies for paintings, can one fully grasp his aims and intentions (see, for example, figs. j-n). His primary effort throughout was to establish an integration of the horse with its environment. As early as 1913, in his catalogue introduction for the exhibition of Futurist sculpture at La Boëtie in Paris, Boccioni had written that "*si une forme sphérique (équivalent plastique d'une tête) est traversée par la façade d'un palais situé plus loin, le demi-cercle interrompu et la façade carrée qui l'interrompt formeront une nouvelle unité, composée de l'ambience + objet.... La conception de l'objet sculptural devenant le résultat plastique de l'objet et de l'ambience, produit naturellement l'abolition de la distance qui existe par exemple entre une figure et une maison située deux cent mètres plus loin. Cette conception produit le prolongement d'un corps dans*

fig. j.
Boccioni, Study of horse and houses, 1913-14, ink on paper, 4 1/8 x 6 3/16 in., 10.4 x 15.7 cm., Civico Gabinetto dei Disegni del Castello Sforzesco, Milan.

fig. k.
Boccioni, Study of horse and houses, 1913-14, ink on paper, 4 1/16 x 6 3/16 in., 10.3 x 15.7 cm., Civico Gabinetto dei Disegni del Castello Sforzesco, Milan.

fig. l.
Boccioni, Study of horse and houses, 1913-14, ink and wash on paper, 8 x 12 in., 20.3 x 30.4 cm., Civico Gabinetto dei Disegni del Castello Sforzesco, Milan.

fig. m.
Boccioni, Study of horse and houses, 1913-14, watercolor on paper, 14 9/16 x 21 11/16 in., 37 x 55 cm., Private Collection.

le rayon de lumière qui le frappe, la pénétration d'un vide *dans le* plan *qui passe devant*."

Although the actual sculptures for this 1913 Paris exhibition were of a totally different order from the *Dinamismo di un cavallo* ... (they included *Tête + maisons + lumière, fusion d'une tête et d'une croisée, Développement d'une bouteille dans l'espace*, etc.), the problems Boccioni articulated in his catalogue remained important as he worked on the theme of his later major construction. He sought "not pure form but pure plastic rhythm, not the construction of bodies, but the construction of the action of bodies." Above all, he aimed to achieve "a complete fusion of environment and object, by means of the interpenetration of planes." (R. L. Herbert, trans., *Modern Artists on Art*, Englewood Cliffs, N.J., 1964, pp. 47-49.)

fig. n.
Boccioni, Study for cat. no. 16, 1913-14, ink on paper, 12⅞ x 16⅝ in., 32.7 x 42.2 cm., inscribed l.r.: *DINAMISMO PLASTICO / CAVALLO + CASE*, Collection Mr. and Mrs. Eric Estorick.

As he developed the concept for his mixed media construction *cavallo + case*, Boccioni had already completed two paintings on the subject: *Forme plastiche di un cavallo*, 1913-14 (Collection Sprovieri, Rome), and the much more closely related *Dinamismo plastico: cavallo + caseggiato*, 1913-14 (Civica Galleria d'Arte Moderna, Milan). In the latter work, and in various studies for the construction (such as fig. m and, especially, fig. n), many of the forms ultimately used in the construction occur: these include the body of the horse, its roughly triangular haunches, its head with ears laid back flat and nostrils distended, its long neck, and the four legs tucked up under the body as the animal races forward. Most clearly of all, in the drawing (fig. n), the triangular downward thrust of the houses seems literally to cut through the form of the horse, splintering its body and forming a new unity "*composée de l'ambience + objet.*"

Tai Kambara, writing in 1925 about the unusual power of the construction, conveys the degree to which he felt Boccioni actually succeeded in achieving an entirely new concept of forms: "In this sculpture the notion of a recognizable recreation of a house or horse has been abandoned, and instead each element of the sculpture becomes a spirit commanding space through the powerful lines inherent within the sculpture itself. This 'spirit' is not a conceptual bridge linking the artist and viewer, but is instead a direct expression of the life inherent in the object itself."[9]

Giuseppe Sprovieri (in conversation with the author, Nov. 3, 1982) cast interesting light on Boccioni's struggle to achieve such effects, and, significantly, indicated that the outcome never fully satisfied the artist. Beginning with a

9. The author is indebted to Janet Eimon of the department of East Asian Studies, Princeton University, for this translation of the Japanese text, kindly supplied by Professor Haga Tōru of the University of Tokyo.

pictorial solution that successfully integrated the horse, its speed, and the surrounding *"ambiente"* of houses, Boccioni set out to create a multimedia construction that would produce a similar effect. (Sprovieri distinctly remembered conversations with Boccioni in which he spoke of wanting to *"realizzare il quadro in tre dimensioni; ma non mi pare che esprima la cosa che voglio."*) Sprovieri felt that this enterprise consumed Boccioni's attention on the eve of World War I, that it represented for him a profound attempt to compromise between *"l'oggetività e l'astrazione."* Boccioni's struggle toward a three-dimensional conception unfolded in the lengthy series of drawings (such as figs. m-n). The Estorick example (fig. n) came closest to what Boccioni ultimately achieved in the construction itself — combining *"l'essenziale del cavallo con il suo ambiente."*

In other respects, too, Sprovieri's recollections provide interesting and important insights into the chronology and dating of Boccioni's work. Sprovieri recalled unequivocally, for example, that the construction was still in progress when Boccioni went to war. The arduous and complex task of executing the piece in a multimedia form occupied him into 1915. Indeed, Sprovieri suggested, the piece may well have remained unresolved (from Boccioni's point of view) even at the time of the artist's death.

Sprovieri's incisive recollections, although obviously to be treated with some caution in view of the time lapse involved, are consistent with the stylistic evidence. It is difficult to imagine, for instance, that Boccioni began work on the construction before he had completed the 1914 painting *Dinamismo plastico: cavallo + caseggiato* (Civica Galleria d'Arte Moderna, Milan). On the basis of presently available evidence, a precise date for the construction cannot be established. It seems unlikely, however, that Boccioni started work on it until late 1914; moreover the work appears to have remained unfinished. The manner in which Boccioni expected to exhibit it—on a pedestal or suspended in the manner of Fortunato Depero's dynamic constructions of 1915 — is thus far also unresolved.[10]

10. Giovanni Lista has indicated, in correspondence with the author, October-November, 1982, and in a round-table discussion about Boccioni held at Montalto Uffugo (Cosenza), October 30, 1982, that he has documentory evidence proving that *Dinamismo di un cavallo in corsa + case* was executed entirely in April 1915. He has also claimed evidence that this was Boccioni's original title for the work. Lista has not thus far published this material or made it available to other scholars.

In his book *Giacomo Balla* (Modena, 1982, pp. 60-61), dating the construction 1914, Lista suggested that the work was actually intended to have (or had?) moving parts: *"La scultura era articolata giacché permetteva una modificazione meccanica della sua struttura.... Per Boccioni la scultura era da considerarsi 'aperta,' cioè disponibile ad una nuova attualizzazione delle sue forme che avrebbe implicato la partecipazione attiva del fruitore dell'opera."* The evidence for this interesting interpretation is not offered by the construction itself and documentary proof has not yet been published. In his 1982 booklet *Futurisme* (see below REFERENCES), Lista suggested on the other hand that the form and fundamental aesthetic behind Boccioni's construction were indebted to the ideas expressed in Balla's and Depero's theoretical manifesto *Ricostruzione futurista dell'Universo*, published in 1915; he implied that Boccioni could not have begun the construction before this appeared in print.

EXHIBITIONS:

Milan, Galleria Centrale d'Arte, *Grande Esposizione Boccioni*, Dec. 28, 1916-Jan. 14,1917, no. 6 *("Costruzione dinamica d'un galoppo*, legno, latta, rame, cartone");[11] Milan, La Bottega di Poesia, *Umberto Boccioni*, Mar. 10-21, 1924, no. 45 *("Costruzione dinamica di un cavallo*, prop. Marinetti"); Rome, Galleria "la bussola," *Sculture Italiane, 1911-1957*, Dec. 20, 1957-Jan. 10, 1958, repr. cover (dated 1911-12); Torino, *P.G.*, 1975-76, no. 29, repr. pl. 15.

REFERENCES:

F. T. Marinetti, "I diritti artistici propugnati dai futuristi italiani, Manifesto al governo fascista," *Noi. Rivista d'Arte futurista*, ser. II, anno 1, no. 1, Apr. 1923, repr. p. 8 ("*Cavallo + case—Dinamismo plastico*, 1915"); V. Paladini, *Arte d'avanguardia e futurismo*, Rome, 1923, repr. n.p.; T. Kambara, *T25: A Study of the Futurist Movement*, Tokyo, 1925, pp. 321-22, repr. p. 320; A. Panzini, "Ottocento, novecento, futurismo, razionalismo," *La Lettura*, vol. 12, no. 3, Mar. 1934, repr. p. 198; *Cahiers d'Art*, vol. 25, Part I, 1950, repr. p. 51 ("*Cheval + maisons*, construction en bois et carton, coll. Mme. B. Marinetti, Rome"); G. M. Argan and M. Calvesi, *Boccioni*, Rome, 1953, p. 29 ("*Cavallo + case* [legno e cartone], coll. Marinetti"); M. Calvesi, "Il futurismo di Boccioni: formazione e tempi," *Arte Antica e Moderna*, Apr.-June, 1958, p. 169, fn. 26 (dated 1914); M. D. Gambillo and T. Fiori, *Archivi del Futurismo*, Rome, 1962, no. 342; G. Ballo, *Boccioni*, Milan, 1964, no. 573 ("*Cavallo + Cavaliere + Case*, 1914"); Calas, 1966, p. 89, repr. p. 92; M. Martin, *Futurist Art and Theory, 1909-1915*, Oxford, 1968, p. 195, repr. pl. 202; G. Bruno, *L'Opera completa di Boccioni*, Milan, 1969, no. 177a ("*Cavallo + cavaliere + case [costruzione dinamica di un galoppo]*, 1914"); P. Pacini, "Un Inedito e un 'Restauro' di Boccioni," *Critica d'Arte*, fasc. 154-56, July-Dec. 1977, pp. 152-64; G. Lista, *Futurisme, Abstraction et Modernité*, Paris, 1982, pp. 27-28; E. Coën and M. Calvesi, *Boccioni: L'Opera Completa*, Milan, 1983, pp. 110, 502, repr. p. 503.[12]

11. Marinetti, who prepared the memorial exhibition, correctly described the medium of the construction. It is interesting to note that neither on this nor on any subsequent occasion did he assign a date to it.

12. The Coën-Calvesi text is closely based on Pacini's 1977 article; it differs in certain details from the conclusions proposed here.

Constantin Brancusi

Born February 1876, Hobitza, Rumania.
Died March 1957, Paris.

7

17 Maiastra. 1912 (?).

76.2553 PG 50

Polished brass[1] (lost wax). Height (top of head to top of base): 24¼ (61.6); maximum circumference: 24⅞ (63.2); height of legs 8 5/16 (21.2).[2] Original height of stone saw-tooth base: ca. 6⅜ (16.2); present height of saw-tooth base (partially sunk into wooden pedestal): 4½ (11.5.).

Edition of one.

Foundry: Valsuani(?).

Signature and date not visible, but possibly beneath footing.[3]

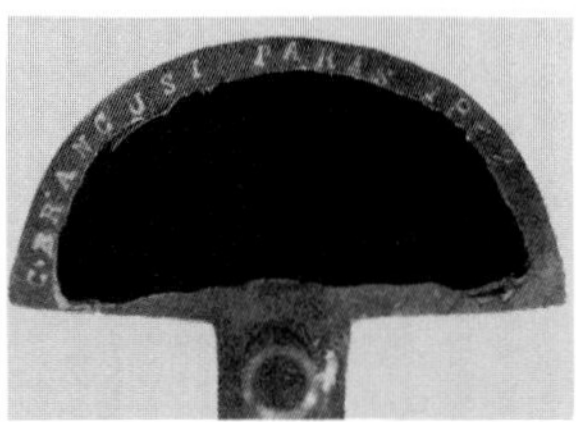

fig. a.
Underside of footing of *Maiastra*, 1912, Des Moines Art Center.

1. The precise alloys used by Brancusi in *Maiastra* and *Bird in Space* (cat. no. 18) have not been established. A nondestructive surface fluorescence x-radioisotope analysis (without sample) would provide the necessary data. Without such an analysis, it is impossible to make comparisons between the differentiations in colors Brancusi intended in these two and the other bronze Birds. For example, if the proportions of the alloy are those of brass (approximately 70% copper and 30% zinc and tin), the color would have a predominantly yellowish gold tone. It is known that Brancusi requested a "yellow" alloy in the case of the Steichen *Maiastra* (Spear, 1969, p. 25). Bronze proportions (of higher copper content) create a warmer reddish and ultimately darker tonality. Many of these tonalities have been altered since the pieces left the artist's studio—through the application of polishes, cleaning substances, or protective coatings. In view of Brancusi's obsession with the issue of surface, color, degree of polish, and nature of patina, it would be desirable to arrive at a fuller understanding than presently exists of the compositions of the metals he used.

   On the subject of Brancusi's method of finishing and polishing his own bronzes, see Spear, 1969, pp. 23-27. Because the highly reflective surfaces were of great importance to him, Brancusi was opposed to the use of any permanent or long-term preservative coatings such as lacquer or synthetic resin. He often gave instructions to purchasers of his bronzes on how they should be cleaned. (See, for example, a letter to John Quinn dated June 5, 1918: "To keep [the bronze] brilliant, you must have it wiped fairly often with a chamois skin—2 or 3 times a week.... If later on the patina... looks badly, kindly advise me and I will attend to it." And on Dec. 7, 1920, he wrote "clean [the bronze bird] as you would copper" [Quinn Collection, New York Public Library].)

2. The dimensions given by Sidney Geist (in inches only) are as follows: height, 24⅜; maximum circumference, 25⅜ (1968), 24⅝ (1970). Those of Athena Tacha Spear (in inches only): height, 24; maximum circumference, 25⅛; height of legs, 8⅛.

   The dimensions of all Brancusi's Birds (height overall, height of legs or footing, maximum circumference, minimum circumference) are extremely difficult to establish accurately. Spear and Geist—who have both written on the problem—record measurements that differ from one another in almost every instance. In the case of the Peggy Guggenheim Birds, neither scholar has published measurements that entirely coincide with those taken by the present author on 3 separate occasions in Venice. Spear generally used a cloth tape measure (as did the present author for circumference, although a steel tape, plumb line, and rod were used to measure the heights of both Birds). Geist used a steel tape for both dimensions, at least in some cases. (See Geist, 1970, pp. 74-75; Spear, 1971, p. 10.)

   Owing to the difficulty of arriving at a conclusive set of measurements for these works, attempts to characterize the development of the theme on the basis of varying proportions should be treated with some caution.

3. The signature and date would have been placed on the underside, in the same way as on the Des Moines *Maiastra* (fig. a). Because the Peggy Guggenheim example is cemented to its base, it has not been possible to establish the presence of such an inscription, though the probability of its existence is considerable.

PROVENANCE:

Purchased from the artist by Paul Poiret and his wife, Denise Boulet-Poiret, ca. 1912 (10,000 fr.);[4] purchased from Denise Boulet (ex-Poiret) through Nicole Groult (Poiret's sister), Paris, 1940.

CONDITION:

When the piece entered Peggy Guggenheim's collection, there was a gap of approximately ¼ in., 0.5 cm., between the Bird and the top of the base, the metal rod joining the 2 being plainly visible (fig. b). (For a discussion of the issues raised by this gap, see below.) During the 1960s, the gap was clumsily filled with cement, resulting in an unsatisfactory join between the 2 elements.[5]

Several tiny dents on the top of the Bird's head and elsewhere are visible.

At an unknown date, the artist's original sawtooth base was broken into 2 pieces and cemented together, with a loss in height of approximately 1 ¼ in., 3 cm. The scale and proportions of this base have been further altered in a recent mounting that sunk the lower edge into a newly constructed wood pedestal (see illustrations), resulting in an additional loss in height of ca. 11/16 in., 1.7 cm. For a view of the full height and original structure of the sawtooth base, see fig. b.

In March 1984 (Venice), the sawtooth base, which had been painted several times in different tones, was cleaned. The previous gesso repairs were removed, and streaks of green corrosion, deriving from the bronze, were removed as far as possible. The breaks and missing corner were repaired with mortar. The entire surface of the base was then coated with a layer of watercolor.

The cement filling around the edges of the lower footing of the Bird was removed, revealing the entire extent of the bronze edge. The interior of the eyes (which was not entirely smooth), the interior of the mouth, and the entire external surface were cleaned with extremely fine buffing liquid. The surface was degreased with trichloroethylene, and washed with distilled water, then with distilled water and neutral detergent; it was rinsed with distilled water and dried with alcohol and acetone. A protective coating of Paraloid B-72 was applied (to inhibit tarnishing).

The Rumanian word *maïastra*—translatable as "master bird" or "magical bird"—evokes multiple meanings within the context of Rumanian folklore.[6]

Recorded comments by Brancusi on the supernatural, magical, or mythological background of his *Maiastra* image are few; but expressions of his lifelong preoccupation with the problem of expressing in marble or bronze the essential qualities of the bird as a species and of flight were relatively frequent: "*Je n'ai cherché pendant toute ma vie que l'essence du vol. Le vol, quel bonheur!*" (1934, in conversation with C. Giedion-Welcker, 1959, p. 199). Or:

4. Spear, 1969, no. 4; confirmed by Peggy Guggenheim, in conversation with the author.

5. The Art of This Century photograph (fig. b), taken before the cementing of the base, was used in all publications up to 1963, when Ionel Jianou published photographs of the Bird in its pre- and postcemented condition. Subsequent publications have sometimes used one, sometimes the other. Jianou offered no explanation, and it has proved impossible to establish when or where the cementing took place; Peggy Guggenheim thought it would have been in the early 1960s in Venice.

6. For information on some of the myths and their literary sources see Spear, 1969, pp. 3-8; B. Brezianu, *Brancusi*, Bucharest, 1976, p. 232, fn. 2; Grigorescu, 1977, pp. 32-42. Spear has also drawn attention to the possible significance, as a source of inspiration for Brancusi, of Diaghilev's Paris production in June 1910 of Stravinsky's *L'oiseau du feu*, based on the Russian folk tale *Zhar-ptitsa*.

Although no visual sources for Brancusi's iconography of the bird have been cited, it seems probable there were precedents. These remain, however, to a large extent unexplored.

"*Comme enfant, j'ai toujours rêvé que je volais dans les arbres et dans le ciel. J'ai gardé la nostalgie de ce rêve et depuis 45 ans, je fais des oiseaux. Ce n'est pas l'oiseau que je veux exprimer mais le don, l'envol, l'élan*" (C. G. Guilbert, "Propos de Brancusi," *Prisme des arts*, no. 12, 1957, p. 7). Most striking of all, in their implied scope and ambition, were the words Brancusi dictated to Henri-Pierre Roché in spring 1936 on the subject of his entire series of Birds: "*Mes oiseaux sont une série d'objets différents sur une recherche centrale qui reste la même. L'idéal de la réalisation de cet objet devait être un agrandissement pour remplir la voûte du ciel*" (cited by Spear, 1969, p. 116).

Brancusi made a total of seven distinct versions of the *Maiastra*: three in marble and four in bronze. It is generally agreed that the earliest in the series was a marble, followed by the four bronzes — each somewhat different from the other — and concluding with the remaining two marbles. Details regarding the precise sequence and dating of the bronze versions remain a matter of some dispute, but insofar as these issues have some bearing on the nature of the artist's stylistic and aesthetic development, they must be taken into account.

In approaching the problem of sequence within the entire series of Birds, it should be noted that Brancusi himself compiled a handwritten list, probably in 1936 at the request of the Maharajah of Indore. Spear (1969, pp. 115-16) published a transcription — not a facsimile — of the list, with several additions and annotations of her own.[7] Under the heading "Maiastra," Brancusi listed only five examples instead of seven, omitting the first and last marbles; under "L'Oiseau d'or" he included three; and under "L'Oiseau dans l'espace," fifteen. The list entirely omits dates and, in a few cases, medium. It is difficult to know whether Brancusi regarded the list as a chronological record of his actual development of the Bird theme or — as seems more likely — a somewhat approximate compilation of the various types and the number of examples within each category. In the absence of a facsimile (which might have served to clarify the nature of the groupings, the placement of items on the page, the discrepancies in inks suggesting later additions), it is impossible to resolve this question. Thus, while Brancusi's sequence should be considered, it should be viewed with some caution.

Brancusi probably began work in 1910 on the earliest of the seven examples of the *Maiastra* (now in the collection of MoMA, New York). Carved in white

7. Spear argued, for example, that Brancusi may have added certain items to the list subsequent to its compilation because 3 of the bronze *Birds in Space* were, according to her deductions, probably not cast by 1936, when the list was presumably made. See also her discussion of the list, pp. 45-47.

Spear adopted the list as the framework for her chronology and explicitly departed from its sequence in only one instance — the placement of the Peggy Guggenheim and the Katharine Graham *Maiastras* (see below). Geist (who did not have the list at his disposal when he prepared his 1968 monograph and his 1969 exhibition catalogue) presented a chronology that differs in several respects from that of Spear, and in his 1970 review of her monograph (pp. 74-75) he indicated that he did not accept the chronology of the newly published list as infallible. Moreover, he suggested that Spear's adherence to it had serious consequences for her understanding of the series as a whole and of Brancusi's stylistic development.

marble and mounted on a three-part base, 70 in., 177.8 cm., high, it is the only version known as *Pasarea* ("majestic") *Maiastra*. Sidney Geist demonstrated (1969, p. 50, and 1970, p. 77) that the piece was reworked by Brancusi sometime between its original completion and 1914. In its first state, a square marble plate (convincingly interpreted by Geist as a stylized rendition or reminiscence of the bird's feet) had been placed between the columnar section of the bird's legs and the rectangular marble block on which the sculpture stood. Brancusi subsequently reworked the lower edge of the piece: by the time John Quinn purchased it in 1914, the marble plate had been removed and the undersurfaces of the legs and tail leveled; the *Maiastra* was resting directly on the marble rectangular block.[8]

Brancusi's decision to remove the marble plate and seek another way of defining the relationship between the sculpture and the base represented an important shift toward a simplication of form in the *Maiastra* series. It was a shift, however, that he did not resolve immediately, since he included the plate in the first of the bronzes and, possibly, even in a subsequent example (the Peggy Guggenheim bronze).

The first bronze *Maiastra* is generally accepted as the example sold to Edward Steichen (now in the collection of The Tate Gallery).[9] Appearing as the first entry on Brancusi's list, this bronze (probably of ca. 1911) has—like the 1910-12 state of the MoMA marble—a square plate beneath the footing. Its height (21⅞ in., 55.6 cm.) and maximum circumference (23½ in., 59.7. cm.) are virtually identical to those of the marble (height, 22 in., 55.9 cm.; circumference, 23¾, 60.4), and the minor discrepancies between the two are attributable to the shrinkage sustained by the metal during the cooling process. A plaster version (now lost) would have served—in this instance, as in all the others in the series—as the intermediate stage between the marble and the bronze.

8. See Geist, *Artforum*, vol. 7, no. 8, Apr. 1969, p. 16; Spear, 1969, pp. 45-46; and Geist, 1970, pp. 75-76, 77. The MoMA *Maiastra* was reproduced, with its marble plate in position, resting on a cracked marble rectangular base, in the catalogue of the Brancusi exhibition held at the Brummer Gallery in 1926. The reproduction, however, was obviously made from an old photograph, probably taken in 1912. An unpublished photograph of works in the Quinn collection, taken—according to Geist—in 1922, apparently shows the marble without its plate and resting on a solid (rather than cracked) base (Geist, 1970, pp. 75-76). Geist called attention to the fact that Brancusi did not visit New York until 1926 and would have been unable to make the changes in the piece between 1914 and 1922. It seems very probable, therefore, that he removed the plate, refinished the footing, and mounted the *Maiastra* on a new block between 1912 and 1914. The first state must thus have been completed between 1910 and 1912, the second state between 1912 and 1914.

9. Steichen was unable to recall which year (prior to 1913) he saw the *Maiastra* in a Paris *Salon*. Spear placed it (hors catalogue) in the 1911 *Salon des Indépendants* (1969, p. 45). The work is dated 1911 by Spear. Geist dated it 1912(?) in his 1968 monograph; 1910 (?) in his 1969 *Artforum* note; 1911(?) in his 1969 exhibition catalogue and 1975 monograph. He has since established that it was shown in the 1913 *Salon des Indépendants* and sold to Steichen in that year (see his essay in *Rodin Rediscovered*, exh. cat., The National Gallery of Art, Washington, D.C., 1981, p. 272).

The bronze *Maiastra* closest in scale to the Steichen-Tate example (which therefore almost certainly followed it) is the version purchased by Mrs. Eugene Meyer in 1911 or 1912 (now in the collection of her daughter, Katharine Graham).[10] Since the measurements and internal proportions of the Graham piece are so close to those of the Tate bronze, it seems likely that the same plaster (only slightly modified) was used as the basis for both. There is no trace of a plate in the Graham version, suggesting it was derived from the second state of the MoMA marble rather than the first. However, because the lower edge of the bronze has been described by Spear as uneven, it cannot be ruled out (as Geist suggested, 1970, p. 76) that a plate may originally have formed part of the footing.

Following the completion of the Graham *Maiastra*, Brancusi apparently decided to extend the height of the Bird by approximately 2 in., 5 cm. Spear convincingly argued that he again used the same plaster, merely adding a section to the lower portion (1969, p. 46; see her reproduction of the lost plaster involved, pl. 6; the lower portion differs in color from the rest of the plaster). Brancusi then made two further bronzes, one of which is now in the Peggy Guggenheim Collection, one in the Des Moines Art Center. These two bronzes are of virtually identical dimensions and proportions; the measurable differences

17

fig. b.
1942 photograph of cat. no. 17 before cementing of footing.

10. Geist, 1968, no. 70B; Spear, 1969, no. 3. The height of the Graham bronze according to both Geist and Spear is 22 in., 55.9 cm.; its circumference is $23\frac{1}{2}$ in., 59.7 cm. (Spear) or $23\frac{7}{8}$ in., 60.7 cm. (Geist).

between them are extremely slight.[11] The Des Moines bronze is dated 1912 (fig. a); the Peggy Guggenheim example was purchased by Poiret apparently in 1912 (see PROVENANCE). Both are consistently dated 1912 in the Brancusi literature.[12]

Owing to the close correspondence in date, scale, and proportions between these two bronzes, it is difficult to establish a chronological relationship between them. Geist (1968 and 1969), however, suggested — on stylistic grounds — that the Des Moines example preceded that of Peggy Guggenheim. He indicated an increase of ⅜ in., 1 cm., in both height and circumference from the Des Moines to the Peggy Guggenheim versions; and since the series as a whole is marked— according to Geist's analysis — by a progressive elongation of the Bird's form, and the Guggenheim example is the tallest and fullest of the four, he placed it last. Spear reversed the positions of these two examples, but did not discuss her reasons.[13] There seems almost no way on the basis of available evidence (and without placing the two bronzes side by side), to arrive at a judgment regarding their relationship. In one respect only might there be an argument for placing the Peggy Guggenheim bronze before that of Des Moines.

The earliest photographs of the Peggy Guggenheim sculpture located to date (1942) show a clear gap, or airspace, between the lower edge of the Bird's legs and the top of the base (see fig. b and CONDITION). The vertical metal rod (which in all the Birds connects the sculpture to the base) is plainly exposed in this 1942 photograph — a peculiarity occurring in no other piece from the series. In the absence of further documentation it is impossible to know what Brancusi's original intentions were, but given the consistently meticulous nature of his craftsmanship, he would surely not have regarded the footing of the piece as resolved or acceptable in this form. Thus it seems certain that at some point before Peggy Guggenheim acquired it, the *Maiastra* suffered damage or loss of some kind. In view of the precedent offered by the MoMA marble (first state), the Steichen-Tate bronze, and even — as suggested above — possibly the Graham bronze, the original existence in the Peggy Guggenheim case of a small plate beneath the columnar element of the legs must be considered a distinct possibility.

11. The Des Moines piece, formerly owned by Charles Cowles, is Geist, 1968, no. 71; 1975, no. 82; Spear, 1969, no. 5. In this case, as in others (see fn. 2), the problem of arriving at a reliable set of measurements renders the argument over millimeters somewhat academic. The following points can, however, be made. The legs and tail in both the Des Moines and the Peggy Guggenheim examples are approximately 2 in., 5.4 cm., longer than those of the other 3 versions. In the latter cases the height of the legs is 6¼ in., 15.8 cm.; in the former: 8⅛ in., 20.7 cm. (Des Moines); and 8 5/16 in., 21.2 cm. (Peggy Guggenheim). The circumferences of the Des Moines and the Peggy Guggenheim *Maiastras* are approximately 1 in., 2.5 cm., greater than those of the earlier versions. Thus the increased overall scale in these two *Maiastras* is concentrated in the maximum circumference and the elongation of the lower portion.

12. Only Alley (1964) dated the Peggy Guggenheim bronze 1915 (see REFERENCES).

13. Brancusi's list brackets the 4 bronzes together in the sequence "Steichen" (Tate), "Poiret" (Guggenheim), "Meyer" (Graham), "Brancusi" (Des Moines). As already noted above, the Graham bronze must have followed the Steichen, and Spear rejects Brancusi's sequence in this instance although she follows it in all others (see 1969, p. 45). It seems entirely possible, on the other hand, that Brancusi was listing the 4 bronzes merely in the order in which he sold them.

Peggy Guggenheim remembered (in conversation with the author on three separate occasions, 1976, 1978, and 1979) that Brancusi had been "furious" with her about the condition of the work and had promised to "repair" or "rebuild" it. She was unable to recall the exact cause of the artist's anger, except that it had had something to do with the footing or the base. She also could not recall the precise date of their exchange, remembering only that it had taken place after World War II in Paris. The conversation had presumably been provoked by Brancusi's encounter with a photograph of the piece — perhaps the illustration from the Art of This Century catalogue — since he never visited Peggy Guggenheim in Venice; he died before he was able to remedy the situation.

Because the tail of the Bird in the early photograph rests flush on the smooth, undamaged surface of the stone base, the approximately 3/16 in., 0.4 cm., gap between the legs and the stone cannot be attributed either to breakage or loss of the stone base, or to a simple loosening of the metal dowel. Rather the gap may have been originally filled by a plate similar in type to that now visible in the Tate example (which is, in fact, precisely 3/16 in., 0.4 cm., high).

Geist determined (1970, p. 77) that aspects of the Bird's image (and the difficulty of conceptualizing them) preoccupied Brancusi continuously throughout his career; the effort to arrive at a satisfactory rendering of the "feet" seems to have posed particularly difficult problems for him. In addition to the stylized solution of the plate, it is known, for example, that Brancusi at one stage experimented with a sawtooth footing.[14] And even with the far more abstracted *Birds in Space,* the footings—and their relationship to the increasingly elongated and simplified forms of the bodies — gave rise to a number of experimental solutions (see below, cat. no. 18, fn. 7).

If Brancusi actually used a plate to complete the footing of the Peggy Guggenheim bronze, this fact — as mentioned above — would lend support to the placement of the Des Moines example as the last of the bronzes. In discarding the plate in this last bronze, and in softly rounding the edges of the legs and tail, it may be said that Brancusi stripped the lower section of the form of all extraneous elements, allowing it to rise smoothly and directly out of the stone base. The way was thereby prepared for the final two marble *Maiastras,* but also for the *Oiseau d'or* series — Brancusi's first Birds "in flight." With this transition from a static form to a form that was apparently reaching upward, Brancusi encountered entirely new aesthetic and formal problems: "*J'ai voulu que* la Maïastra *dresse sa tête sans que ce mouvement exprime la fierté, l'orgueil ou la provocation. Ce fut le problème le plus difficile et ce n'est qu'après un long effort que je suis parvenu rendre ce mouvement intégré au jaillissement du vol*" (Jianou, 1963, p. 46).

14. See the gray marble in the collection of the MNAM, Paris, Spear, 1969, no. 7; this solution was also probably used in an early version of the Philadelphia Museum of Art marble (Spear, no. 6), although it survives only as a photographic record of the lost plaster cast (repr. Spear, pl. 6, right).

fig. c.
Cat. no. 17 installed in the Paris apartment of Paul Poiret; the model is Madame Poiret. Her arm masks the footing of the *Maiastra*; the proportions of the original stone base are, however, fully visible. Photograph by Delphi, date unknown, 8⅞ x 6⅝ in., 22.6 x 16 cm., Collection Athena Tacha Spear.

EXHIBITIONS:

New York, Art of This Century, 1942-47, p. 35, repr. p. 34; Venice, *P.G.*, 1948 (Biennale), no. 12; Florence, *P.G.* 1949, no. 13; Amsterdam, *P.G.*, 1951, no. 16, repr.; Zurich, *P.G.*, 1951, no. 15; London, *P.G.*, 1964-65, no. 43, repr. (dated 1915, the date attributed to it in subsequent *P.G.* publications until 1974); Stockholm, *P.G.*, 1966-67, no. 41, repr.; New York, *P.G.*, 1969, p. 30, repr. p. 31; Paris, *P.G.*, 1974-75, no. 43, repr.; Torino, *P.G.*, 1975-76, no. 48, repr. pl. 26 (dated 1915); Rome, *Guggenheim: Venezia-New York*, 1982, no. 30, repr. color.

REFERENCES:

P. Guggenheim, *Art of This Century*, 1942, repr. p. 34; C. Giedion-Welcker, *Plastik des XX. Jahrhunderts, Volumen und Raumgestaltung*, Stuttgart, 1955, repr. p. 126; C. Zervos, "Constantin Brancusi: sculptures, peintures, fresques, dessins," *Cahiers d'Art*, vol. 30, 1955, repr. p. 181; C. Giedion-Welcker, *Constantin Brancusi*, Neuchâtel, 1959, p. 30, repr. pl. 58; E. Ionesco, "Temoignages sur Brancusi," *Cahiers du musée de poche*, no. 3, 1959, p. 34; I. Jianou, *Constantin Brancusi*, Paris, 1963, pp. 45-46, repr. pls. 43, 44; R. Alley, 1964, no. 43 (dated 1915, the date attributed to it in subsequent *P.G.* publications until 1974); C. Giedion-Welcker, "Le message de Brancusi," *XXe Siècle*, xxvi, Dec. 1964, repr. p. 16; Calas, 1966, p. 90; S. Geist, "Brancusi," *Artforum*, vol. 5, no. 7, Mar. 1967, pp. 19-25; idem, *Brancusi: A Study of the Sculpture*, New York, 1968, cat. no. 72, pp. 43-44, 127-28, 200-1; idem, *Constantin Brancusi*, exh. cat., SRGM, New York, 1969, p. 53, repr. (not exhibited); A. T. Spear, *Brancusi's Birds*, New York, 1969, pp. 9-15, 17, 29, 45, 46, cat. no. 4, repr. pl. 7; S. Geist, "The Birds: A critique of the catalogue of a recent Brancusi monograph," *Artforum*, vol. 9, no. 3, Nov. 1970, pp. 74, 75, 76; A. T. Spear, Letters to the Editor, *Artforum*, vol. 9, no. 6, Feb. 1971, p. 10; S. Geist, *Brancusi: The Sculpture and Drawings*, New York, 1975, repr. no. 83; D. Grigorescu, *Brancusi*, Bucharest, 1977, pp. 32-37; Alley, *Tate Collection*, 1981, p. 72.

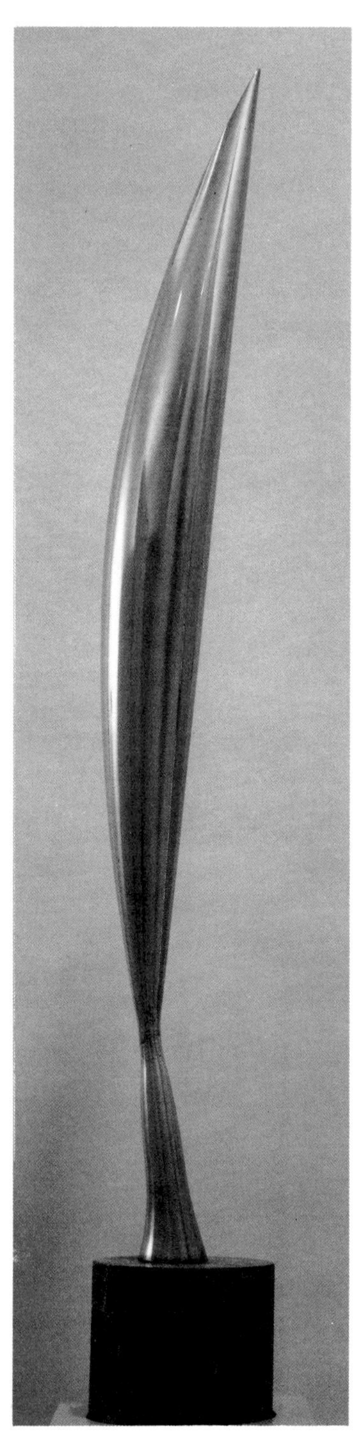

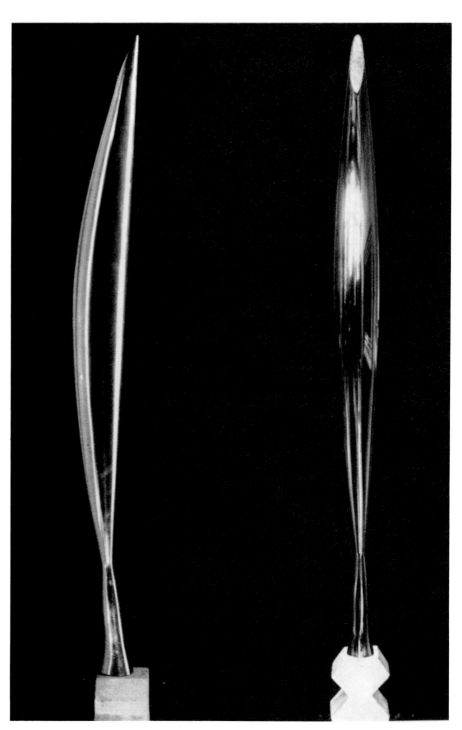

fig. c.
1942 photograph of cat. no. 18.

18 L'Oiseau dans l'espace. 1932-40.
(Bird in Space).

76.2553 PG 51

Polished brass[1] (lost wax). Height (plumbline measurement from tip to top of cement base): 53 (134.7);[2] maximum circumference: 13 15/16 (35.4); minimum circumference: 3 1/16 (7.8); height of footing: 9 (22.9);[3] height of cylindrical stone base: 6 11/16 (17).[4]

Edition of one.

Foundry: Unknown.

Not signed or dated.

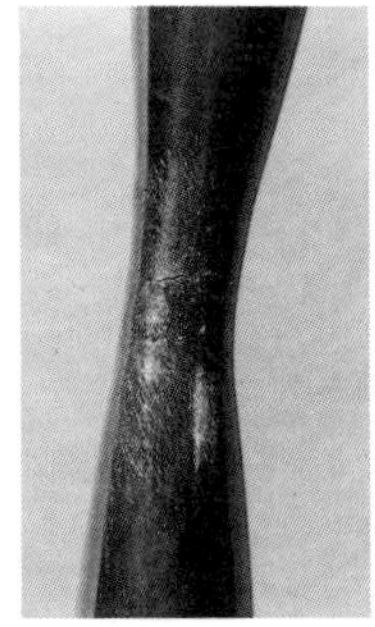

fig. a.
Photograph of break in cat. no. 18 before restoration.

fig. b.
Photograph of dent in cat. no. 18 before restoration.

PROVENANCE:

Purchased from the artist, Paris, winter 1940.

CONDITION:

In 1969 (New York) the piece suffered a fall and 2 damages occurred: a break at the narrowest point, across approximately 1/3 of the circumference (fig. a); and a dent with severe abrasion on the upper portion (fig. b). In both areas, evidence of repair is visible. There are dark marks and stains on the surface, and some green-white corrosion in the crevices of the repair.

The delicate balance and positioning of Brancusi's *Birds in Space,* each of which has a subtly different relationship between the curve and the straight edge, and between the "footing" and the inclination of the body, are inevitably affected by any change in the structure. The break and repair at the narrowest point have significantly altered the inclination of this piece and thus the nature of these relationships. (Compare the present profile with that in the 1942 photograph, fig. c.)

In 1984 an X-ray was taken to establish the extent of the internal damage (Rome, Ente Nazionale Energie Alternative, Laboratorio della Casaccia). The internal rod remains entirely intact, and the overall stability of the piece is thus unimpaired. The inclination of the upper body of the bird and its relationship to the footing have, however, clearly been altered by the fall.

The surface was degreased with trichloroethylene, and washed with distilled water, then with distilled water and neutral detergent; it was rinsed with distilled water and dried with alcohol and acetone. A protective coating of Paraloid B-72 was applied (to inhibit tarnishing).

1. See above, cat. no. 17, fn. 1.
2. As indicated by S. Geist (1968, pp. 95-97, 127-29) and A. T. Spear (1969, pp. 20-21), an important point of comparison among the various versions of the *Bird in Space* is the changing degree of inclination of the back of the body, requiring corresponding changes in the inclination of the footing. In the case of the Peggy Guggenheim *Bird,* the plumbline vertical from the uppermost tip of the bird to its base falls 2 3/4 in., 7 cm., behind the footing. This measurement, taken by the present author in 1979 and again in 1982, differs considerably from the 1 in., 2.5 cm., recorded by Spear in the early 1960s. Spear's measurements were taken prior to the damage and repair sustained by the piece in 1969, which undoubtedly explains the discrepancy (see CONDITION).
3. The dimensions given by Geist (in inches only) are as follows: height, 51 1/8; maximum circumference, 14 1/2 (1968), 13 7/8 (1970); height of foot, 8 1/2. Those of Spear (in inches only): height, 52 3/4; maximum circumference, 14 1/4; waist, 3; height of footing, 9.
4. It has not been possible to establish whether this base was supplied (or designed) by the artist, although it corresponds in proportions and style with others he made for the *Birds in Space.* Indeed, Spear stated that in all instances in which Brancusi sold a *Bird in Space* with a base, the section immediately beneath the Bird was a cylinder, 6-7 in., 15-18 cm., in diameter and height (1969, p. 35). Photographs of the contents of Brancusi's studio, and of exhibition installations

Following the final two marble *Maiastras* (see above, cat. no. 17), Brancusi produced a group of four Birds in which the rectilinear legs and curved tail were fully absorbed into an elongated, continuous curving form.[5] Dating from ca. 1919-20, these Birds (two marbles and two bronzes deriving from them) are approximately 10 in., 25 cm., taller than the preceding Birds. The lower part of the body is extremely tapered as it joins a triple sawtooth base; in addition, the Bird's back — which sweeps directly into the neck and upturned head — is considerably straighter than that of the *Maiastra*. Although the compression and abstraction of the form are increased, some descriptive elements (such as the open beak) are retained.

The earliest *Bird in Space*, carved in white marble, was completed by December 1923 when it was sold to John Quinn.[6] As noted by Geist (1968, pp. 85-86) and Spear (1969, p. 18), this conception was new in a number of respects. No longer standing, or even stretching, the Bird appeared to "propel itself upward" (Geist). It was over forty percent taller than its immediate predecessors, the descriptive open beak was replaced by a small, slanting oval plane, and the back was straight, seeming to support the rounded body like a spine. A distinct footing was added to the tapered lower edge: conical in shape, it was carved from a separate piece of marble and joined to the body by an internal rod.[7]

Over a period of approximately eighteen years, Brancusi completed a series of sixteen *Birds in Space*: seven in marble, nine in polished bronze. In some of these, he continued to incorporate a separate footing; in others (such as the

(4. cont.)
with which he was associated, generally show *Birds in Space* mounted on marble or stone cylindrical bases of approximately these proportions. (Exceptions do exist, such as the yellow marble *Bird* exhibited at the Wildenstein Galleries in New York in 1926, which was placed directly upon a stone cruciform base. See Geist, 1970, p. 78, who reproduced an installation photograph showing Brancusi standing next to the yellow marble *Bird*.)

Peggy Guggenheim's *Bird* was first published soon after her acquisition of it (fig. c). In these 2 views it stands, in 1 case, on a small rectangular block, and in the other, on a sawtooth base. These 2 photographs were frequently republished in the ensuing 2 decades, most recently (without comment on the base) by Geist (1968) and Spear (1969). It is clear that neither of these solutions could have originated with the artist. Peggy Guggenheim recalled that, as in the case of the *Maiastra* (cat. no. 17, see above p. 118), Brancusi expressed anger about the footing and/or base of the *Bird in Space* when they met in Paris after World War II. He again promised to remedy the situation. But while he was unable to fulfill this commitment to the *Maiastra*, he did perhaps provide instructions regarding the cylindrical base for the *Bird in Space*.

5. Geist, 1968, nos. 116, 117, 118, 133; Spear, 1969, nos. 8-11; also Brancusi's own list (described in cat. no. 17 above) under the heading "L'Oiseau d'or."

6. Marx-Schoenborn Collection, Geist, 1968, no. 146; Spear, 1969, no. 12. Height: 50⅝ in., 128.5 cm.; circumference: 18¾ in., 47.6 cm.

7. As Brancusi developed the *Bird in Space*, this part of the form posed serious (and continuing) problems for him and he apparently worked for almost 2 years on the initial resolution. In a letter to John Quinn, dated December 18, 1923, Brancusi explained the delay in delivery of the sculpture by referring to these difficulties with the lower portion (cited by Geist, 1969, p. 114). For discussions of the various solutions to the problem of the footings, the ratio of footing to body, and the structural balance of the *Birds in Space*, see Geist (1968, pp. 91, 95-97, 128-30), who places these issues within the context of their aesthetic implications. In this connection, see also Spear, 1969, pp. 18-21, and Geist, 1970, pp. 78-79, nos. 12-13.

18

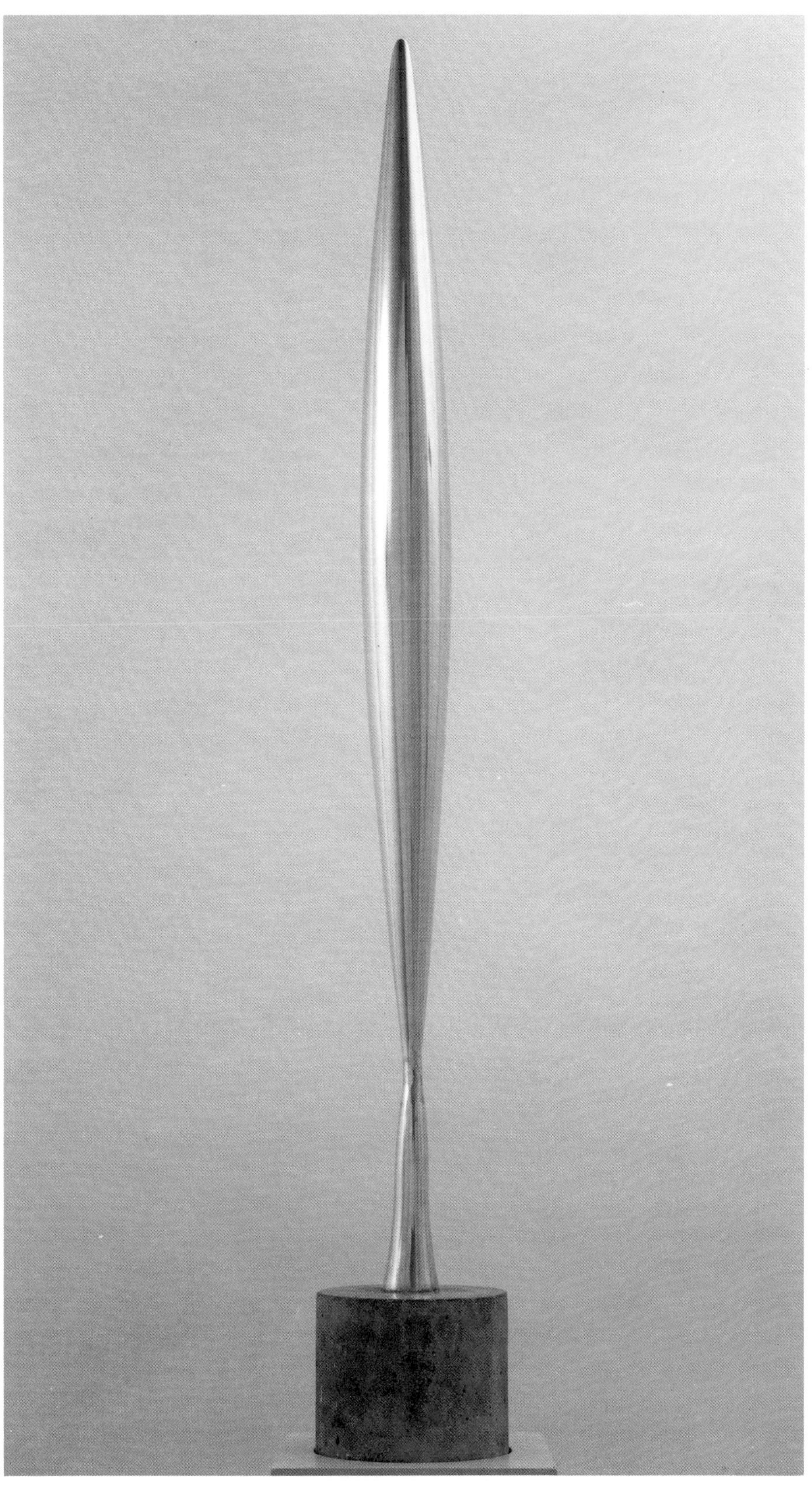

present example), he organically integrated the lower, undulating section in a continuous curve with the rising crescent shape of the body.

Whether every bronze was based on a marble version (as seems probable) is a matter of some dispute.[8] Evidently the Peggy Guggenheim bronze was derived from the gray marble in the collection of the Kunsthaus, Zurich, which is virtually identical to it in actual dimensions (height, circumference) and in relative proportions.[9]

The question of the dates of these two works and their chronological position within the sequence of the *Birds in Space* is difficult to determine with certainty. The Zurich marble has a *terminus ante quem* of January 19, 1932, when it was shown to Henri-Pierre Roché (Spear, 1969, no. 22). The Peggy Guggenheim bronze was completed sometime prior to June 1940, when Peggy Guggenheim purchased it. Spear—presumably depending to some extent on Brancusi's own list—placed the marble (which she dated 1931) and the bronze (dated 1930s) rather late in her sequence. According to her chronology, both examples followed two white marbles (nos. 17 and 21) and two polished bronzes (nos. 19 and 20) of substantially larger scale: these latter works are, respectively, ca. 18 in., 46 cm., and 21 in., 53 cm., taller than the Zurich/Peggy Guggenheim examples.

Geist, on the other hand, argued convincingly that, on technical and stylistic grounds, it is difficult to imagine Brancusi returning to the scale of his smaller versions (ca. 53⅛ in., 135 cm.) after having solved the formidable technical problems involved in carving—in a single marble piece—a version that measured approximately 70⅞ in., 180 cm. Geist suggested that Brancusi's stylistic

8. Spear originally stated that Brancusi "usually carved an original in marble (or wood) from which he cast several bronzes; and each time he conceived a new variation of the work, he first carved it, and from the new carved original he cast a new set of bronzes. Sometimes he worked on an intermediate plaster and then cast the bronzes, in which case the bronzes differ somewhat from the marble original. But bronzes after the same marble or plaster differ very little from one another" ("The Literature of Art," *Burlington Magazine*, vol. 111, no. 792, Mar. 1969, p. 154). Spear apparently subsequently concluded that at least some of the bronzes (nos. 15, 16, 18, 19, 20) were conceived independently of carved marble versions and built directly in plaster before being cast (1969, p. 47). Geist disputed her conclusion and asserted that every change in the size and design of the Birds took place in marble before being translated into bronze (1970, p. 80).

9. Geist, 1968, no. 162; Spear, 1969, no. 22; also probably Brancusi's own list, published by Spear, p. 116. For a note on Brancusi's list and some indication of the problems presented by its chronology, see cat. no. 17, p. 114.

The footing of the Zurich marble (height, 8⅝ in., 21.9 cm.) was carved as a separate piece. The height of the entire Bird is 53 in., 134.7 cm.; the maximum circumference, 13 15/16 in., 35.5 cm.

The plaster that almost certainly served as the intermediate step between the Zurich marble and the Peggy Guggenheim bronze is in the collection of the MNAM, Paris (Spear, 1969, H22 / 23).

See Spear, 1971, pp. 238-40 for additional arguments against Geist's suggestion that the Zurich marble served as the model for the Steichen and Baron Philippe de Rothschild bronzes. As noted above, cat. no. 17, p. 114, the absence of a published facsimile of Brancusi's list makes it difficult to judge whether the list was written in its entirety on a single occasion or—as Spear suggested—additions were made at later dates. Spear implied that the Peggy Guggenheim bronze may have been among those not cast by 1936, and therefore added.

development was consistent in nature and revealed (almost without exception) a steady progression from the smaller-scale to the taller and slenderer Birds.

In placing the Zurich marble and the Peggy Guggenheim bronze earlier than the much larger marbles and bronzes, Geist also proposed that the Zurich marble — in an early, and slightly thicker, state — must have served as the model for three other bronzes which Spear placed far earlier in her sequence and for which she posits no marble model. (The bronzes involved are her nos. 15, 16, 18, in the Steichen, de Rothschild, and MoMA collections, respectively. See fn. 8.) In proposing this solution, Geist arrived at a coherent grouping of the Zurich marble and the four bronzes deriving from it, all similar in proportions though manifesting refinements and differentiations (in the footings and the circumferences) consistent with the overall progression toward an increasingly attenuated form.

Regarding the dates of these works, Geist proposed a span of 1925-31 for the first and second states of the Zurich marble. In its revised form, this work had the reduced circumference and flattened curve in the lower part of the body that also characterize the Peggy Guggenheim bronze. The latter (which is the slenderest of all the versions approximately 53⅛ in., 135 cm., in height) might well have been cast in the early 1930s, soon after the completion of the marble, and received its finishing touches toward the end of the decade. If this is true, the probable presence of the work on Brancusi's 1936 list could be explained as something other than a later addition.

Peggy Guggenheim always maintained that when she purchased the *Bird* in 1940, Brancusi had several weeks of work to do in order to complete it. Since she was explicitly referring to the meticulous polishing by hand that all the bronzes required, this would not rule out the possibility that the piece was cast much earlier — that is to say at any time after January 1932.

EXHIBITIONS:

New York, Art of This Century, 1942-47, p. 35, repr. p. 37; Venice, *P.G.*, 1948 (Biennale), no. 13; Florence, *P.G.*, 1949, no. 14; Venice, Giardino, 1949, no. 3, repr.; Amsterdam, *P.G.*, 1951, no. 17; Zurich, *P.G.*, 1951, no. 16, repr.; London, *P.G.*, 1964-65, no. 44, repr.; Stockholm, *P.G.*, 1966-67, no. 42, repr.; New York, *P.G.*, 1969, p. 33, repr. p. 32; Paris, *P.G.*, 1974-75, no. 44, repr.; Torino, *P.G.*, 1975-76, no. 49, repr. pl. 25.

REFERENCES:

P. Guggenheim, *Art of This Century*, 1942, repr. p. 37 (2 views: 1 on small cement cube, 1 on double sawtooth base); C. Giedion-Welcker, *Plastik des XX. Jahrhunderts, Volumen und Raumgestaltung*, Stuttgart, 1955, p. 127; C. Zervos, *Constantin Brancusi: sculptures, peintures, fresques, dessins*, Paris, 1957 (first published in *Cahiers d'Art*, vol. 30, 1955), p. 85; P. Guéguen, "Brancusi: méditation sur l'œuvre brancusien," *Aujourd'hui*, no. 12, 1957, p. 9; C. Giedion-Welcker, *Constantin Brancusi*, Neuchâtel, 1959, p. 200, no. 8, repr. pls. 62, 63; I. Jianou, *Constantin Brancusi*, Paris, 1963, repr. pls. 49, 50; C. Giedion-Welcker, "Le message de Brancusi," *XXe Siècle*, xxvi, Dec. 1964, repr. p. 16; Calas, 1966, pp. 90-91, repr. color; S. Geist, *Brancusi: A Study of the Sculpture*, New York, 1968, cat. no. 196, pp. 127-28, 200-1; idem, *Constantin Brancusi*, exh. cat., SRGM, New York, 1969, p. 133, repr. (not exhibited); A. T. Spear, *Brancusi's Birds*, New York, 1969, pp. 47, 48, no. 23, repr. pl. 29; S. Geist, "The Birds: A critique of the catalogue of a recent Brancusi monograph," *Artforum*, vol. 9, no. 3, Nov. 1970, pp. 80, 82; A. T. Spear, Letters to the Editor, *Artforum*, vol. 9, no. 6, Feb. 1971, p. 10; idem, "Exhibition Review," *The Art Quarterly*, vol. 34, no. 2, 1971, p. 239.

Georges Braque

Born May 1882, Argenteuil.
Died August 1963, Paris.

19 La clarinette.

Sorgues, summer-fall 1912.
(*The clarinet*; *Clarinette et partition*; *Die Partitur*; *Still Life [The Waltz]*; *Nature morte*).

Color plate p. 35.

76.2553 PG 7

Oil with sand on fine linen canvas (unvarnished), 36 x 25⅜ (91.4 x 64.5).

Signed on reverse: *Braque*. Not dated.

PROVENANCE:

D.-H. Kahnweiler, 1912-14;[1] sequestered Kahnweiler stock, 1914-23; 4e Vente Kahnweiler, May 7-8, 1923, no. 134 (purchased by Léonce Rosenberg, 260 fr.,[2] photo no. 14.N.547, Rosenberg Archive, Paris); Marie Cuttoli and Henri Laugier by 1933 (Basel exhibition);[3] purchased from Marie Cuttoli, 1940, Paris.

CONDITION:

A 1912 photograph of the work in the Kahnweiler archives (fig. a) reveals lettering which had almost vanished by 1942 (see *Art of This Century*, p. 63). The *LUCK* of *GLUCK* and the strong *ET* above it (possibly indicating [CLARIN] *ET* [TE]?) were probably stenciled in charcoal on the unprepared canvas, a not uncommon practice for Braque at this date. With the passage of time, the charcoal disappeared.

In 1964 (Tate Report) the canvas was described as fragile; minute abrasions of impasto, some rippling of the canvas at the upper left edge, and a split in the canvas at the upper right edge were noted. The artist's omission of varnish was also noted, and the surface left untouched.

In 1979 (Venice), 2 losses about 2½ in., 6 cm., from the right edge were noted, as were some scattered minor flaking and abrasion elsewhere. A pattern of mottled dark brownish stain in 2 or 3 places suggests traces of an earlier mold, though this is not active. In 1982 some light inpainting of losses with watercolor was undertaken. The canvas tension was tightened and a light coat of Paraloid B-72 was sprayed over the surface.[4]

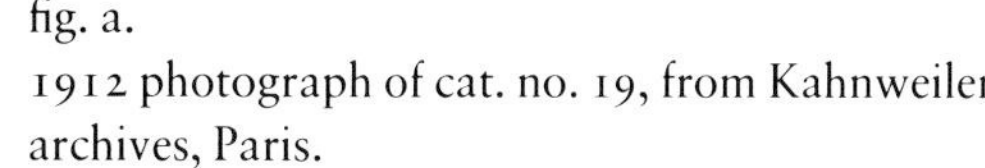

fig. a.
1912 photograph of cat. no. 19, from Kahnweiler archives, Paris.

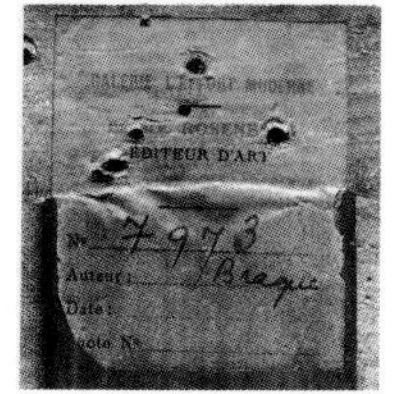

1. The Kahnweiler stock no. 1117; photo no. 1085.
2. Price supplied by G. Tinterow, Paris, 1982. A Galerie L'Effort Moderne label on the stretcher (see illustration) carries the number *7.913* (or *7.973*?).
3. Madame Cuttoli ran the Galerie Myrbor from 1929 to 1935 and probably purchased the work directly from Léonce Rosenberg.
4. Braque's intentionally matte, dry, frescolike unvarnished surface had been maintained intact until this time. His (and Picasso's) strong aesthetic conviction on this point has been almost universally overlooked in recent decades. Braque is known to have spoken throughout his career about his antipathy to any use of varnish, though in Picasso's case the position was most strongly held in connection with his Cubist oils.

During the summer of 1912 in Sorgues-sur-l'Ouvèze, Braque achieved two critically important innovations that had implications for Picasso's immediate development as well as his own.

The first innovation—and by far the more significant—was the "invention" (or "*révélation*" as he later called it) of *papier collé*. Picasso had already been at Sorgues since late June when Braque arrived there at the end of July. During the short period that elapsed between September 3 and September 12, after Picasso had left for Paris, Braque made his famous purchase of a roll of *faux-bois* printed paper and created his first (or perhaps first few) *papier collé*.[5]

Meanwhile, during the course of that same summer, although less precisely datable, Braque also began to mix sand with his pigments. As he wrote to Kahnweiler at the end of September: "*Le calme complet: je tâche d'en profiter le plus possible. Je travaille beaucoup. Depuis mon arrivée je travaille à une assez grande toile (1,60m), une femme où j'ai innové la peinture au sable. J'ai fait aussi un violon et une autre femme au violon, des petites natures mortes et commencé quelques autres.... enfin je suis très content d'être ici*" (quoted by I. Monod-Fontaine in *Georges Braque: Les papiers collés*, p. 41). Braque's initiation of both of these techniques (*papier collé* and the mixture of pigment with sand) during the Sorgues summer was further established in a letter written to him by Picasso, after the latter's return to Paris in early October: "*je emploie tes derniers procédés paperistiques et pusiereux*" (op. cit.). Picasso obviously attached significance to both innovations.

Isabelle Monod-Fontaine has pointed out that the two paintings which are perhaps the closest chronologically to the September *papiers collés* are *Le compotier* (oil with sand on canvas, 16⅛ x 13 in., 41 x 33 cm., Private Collection, Paris, repr. op. cit., p. 66) and *Compotier, bouteille et verre* (oil with sand on canvas, 23⅝ x 28¾ in., 60 x 73 cm., Private Collection, Paris, repr. op. cit., p. 66). The subject matter of these two paintings is clearly similar to that of the first *papiers collés*; in addition, their particular use of imitation wood-graining, their optical differentiations of hue (introduced through the use of sand), and their treatment of space, all point to important relationships between the canvases and the works on paper. The methods and media of each clearly contributed to the development of the other.

As Braque stated in his letter to Kahnweiler, however, he was also occupied during the summer with a sizable group of other works. The first painting in which he used sand was a portrait of a woman;[6] he mentioned in addition two pictures involving violins (one of them a portrait), some small still-lifes, and several other paintings. It seem likely, on stylistic grounds, that Peggy Guggenheim's *La clarinette* was among the works that emerged from this intensely productive period.

5. See D. Cooper in I. Monod-Fontaine, ed., *Georges Braque: Les papiers collés*, Paris, 1982, pp. 9-10; ibid., p. 41.

6. Monod-Fontaine does not identify this work or the others mentioned by Braque in his letter, and it is difficult to establish which they are.

As Douglas Cooper suggested, both Picasso and Braque spent a good part of the summer at Sorgues "experimenting with various technical means ... to make it easier for the eye to interpret objects or figures represented in their pictures."[7] The means they employed — "variations of texture, imitation wood-graining, self-explanatory details, and lettering, for example" — are characteristic of a number of paintings, including *La clarinette.*

Thus, even though both artists "set out to create and establish a strictly new pictorial reality, distinct from the reality we know, a reality which would exist on its own terms," they were also equally concerned to make certain that the imagery of their pictures remained legible — that their "objects" remained identifiable. "What Braque, as much as Picasso, sought to avoid was that through paying too much attention to ... spatial relationships and details of structure, their pictures might appear ... to be simply figurative abstractions." (Cooper, loc. cit.)

La clarinette reveals some of the ways in which Braque succeeded — as he had in the first *papiers collés* — in avoiding "figurative abstraction." Through the introduction of painted imitation wood-graining, he established the location of the table in the foreground and the paneled wall behind. The pegs and head of a guitar (upper left) and its rounded end (lower right) situated the instrument firmly behind the clarinet, which is diagonally — and prominently — placed at the center of the canvas. A bottle of *Marc Fin* and glasses stand on the table. The lettering of the printed sheet music (the *VALSE* by *GLUCK*)[8] completes the painting's clearly legible iconography while simultaneously alluding to an alternative mode of art — that of *collage.*

Braque avoided, therefore, the danger of figurative abstraction, but he also succeeded in creating a new form of pictorial reality — a " '*tableau objet*' existing as a thing in itself" (Cooper, loc. cit.). His use of subtle variations in texture and tone, within a limited chromatic scale, creates a remarkable range of pictorial and spatial effects: sand in certain areas instantly differentiates them optically from adjacent areas of a similar hue; painted letters juxtaposed with those executed in charcoal (the latter now unfortunately lost) offer softly modulated contrasts; the warm tones of the painted wood-grain and exploitation of the unpainted fine linen support (used — among other things — to form the body of the clarinet) emphasize and articulate additional textural values. The differentiations in tone, substance, and *facture* that Braque sought and achieved in this and other paintings of the summer and autumn of 1912 have, as one significant effect, their transformation into material objects. Made of paint, sand, cloth, charcoal, and other materials, they have a tangible presence and

7. E. A. Carmean, ed., *Georges Braque: The Papiers Collés*, Washington, 1982, p. 18. Cooper's original French text is to be found in the Paris catalogue, loc. cit., pp. 7-11.

8. Braque's inclusion of sheet music and composers' names is frequent during the Cubist years. Gluck's name appears in only this instance (although Bach, for example, occurs at least 5 times). Clarinettes and guitars both occur with considerable frequency.

reality of their own, even while representing familiar objects (bottles, glasses, etc.) from the real world. It is in this respect, among others suggested earlier, that Braque's paintings and *papiers collés* from this period are closely related to one another. Whether *La clarinette* actually preceded or followed the first *papiers collés* is difficult to establish; it seems evident, however, that the picture derived from the same set of creative impulses and discoveries which produced works in both modes — painting and *papier collé* — at essentially the same moment.[9]

EXHIBITIONS:

Basel, Kunsthalle, *Georges Braque*, Apr. 9-May 14, 1933, no. 59 (*Die Partitur*);[10] The Hague, Gemeentemuseum, *Hedendaagsche Fransche Kunst*, Feb. 15-Mar. 15, 1936, no. 11, repr. ("*Stilléven*, ‚Valse', 1912 [lent by] Dr. Laugier"); New York, Art of This Century, 1942-47, p. 62, repr. p. 63 (*The Waltz*); New York, Art of This Century, *15 Early, 15 Late Paintings*, Mar. 13-Apr. 10, 1943, no. 201; Venice, *P.G.*, 1948 (Biennale), no. 14 (*Il valzer*); Florence, *P.G.*, 1949, no. 15; Venice, XXV Biennale, June 8-Oct. 15, 1950, *I Quattro maestri del cubismo*, no. 9; Amsterdam, *P.G.*, 1951, no. 18, repr.; Zurich, *P.G.*, 1951, no. 17, repr.; London, *P.G.*, 1964-65, no. 7, repr. ("*Still Life* [also known as The Waltz]"); Stockholm, *P.G.*, 1966-67, no. 7, repr.; New York, *P.G.*, 1969, p. 54, repr.; Paris, *P.G.*, 1974-75, no. 6, repr. p. 41; Torino, *P.G.*, 1975-76, no. 7, repr. color pl. 6; Rome, *Guggenheim: Venezia-New York*, 1982, no. 2, repr. color.

REFERENCES:

Bulletin de L'Effort Moderne, no. 6, 1924, repr. betw. pp. 8 and 9 (*Nature morte*); G. Isarlov, *Georges Braque*, Paris, 1932, no. 145 (*La clarinette*); André Lhote, "Georges Braque," *Cahiers d'Art*, vol. 8, nos. 1-2, 1933, repr. p. 44 (dated 1913); P. Guggenheim, *Art of This Century*, 1942, p. 62, repr. p. 63; Calas, 1966, p. 21, repr. color p. 30; N. Worms de Romilly and J. Laude, *Braque: Cubism 1907-1914*, Maeght, 1982, no. 157 (dated 1912-13).

9. Remarkably few oils are identified in the recently published catalogue of Braque's Cubist oeuvre as having sand in the medium. (See N. Worms de Romilly, 1982, nos. 144, 147, 148, 157 [Peggy Guggenheim's], 183.) Braque certainly made much more frequent use of the device, but this has often gone unnoticed or unrecorded.

10. One label, formerly on the reverse, reads "Dr. Laugier. Bâle 1933 / 107"; another: "Kunsthalle Basel." The exhibition customs list in the Kunsthalle archive contains as the entry for 107: "Nature morte à la musique" lent by Dr. Laugier.

20 Le compotier de raisin. 1926.
(The bowl of grapes; Guéridon, compotier; le compotier et le pichet blanc; Pichet et raisins).

Color plate p. 396.

76.2553 PG 8

Oil with pebbles and sand on fine linen canvas (unvarnished), 39⅜ x 31¼ (100 x 80.8).

Signed and dated l.l.: *G Braque / 26.*

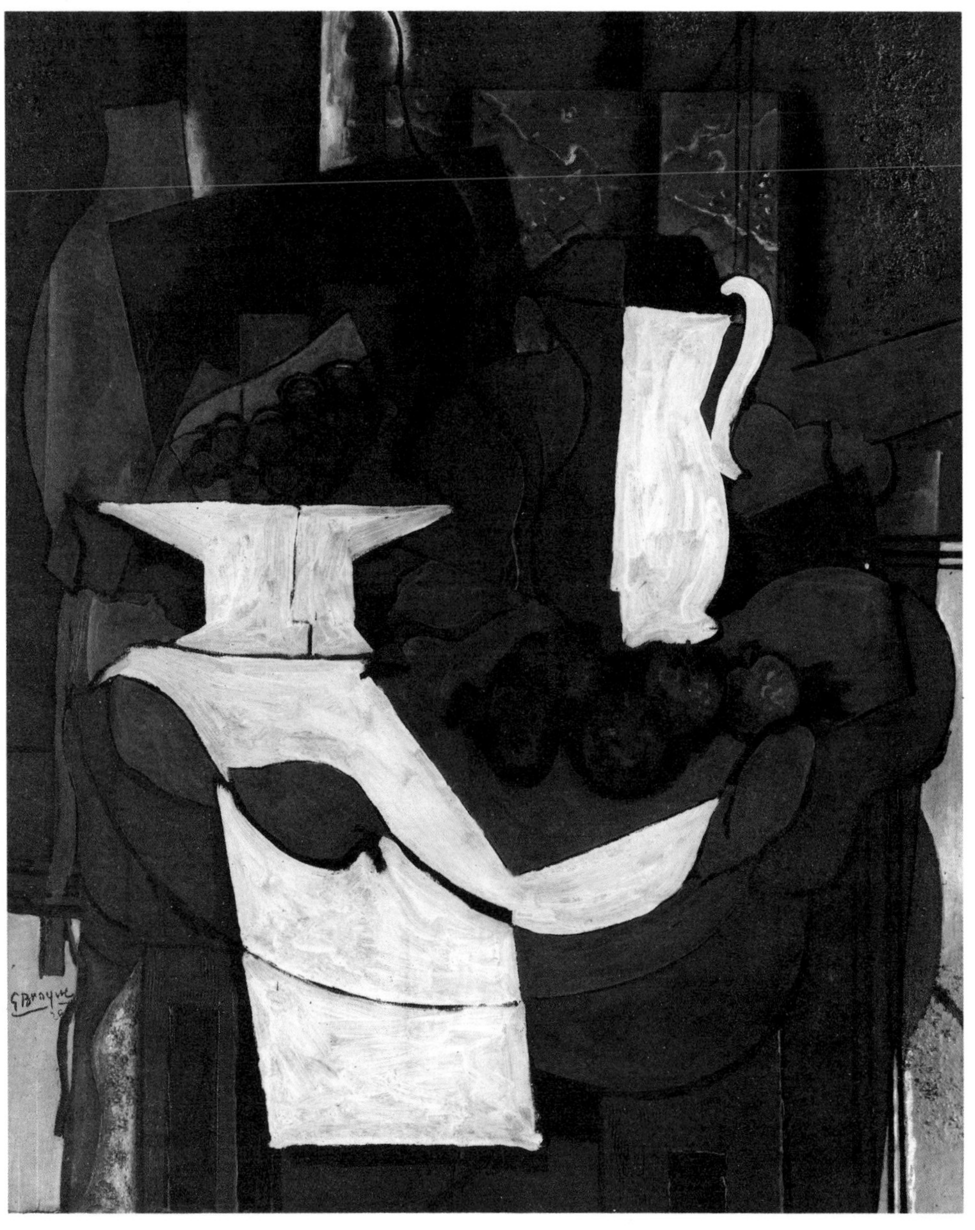

20 PROVENANCE:

Paul Rosenberg, Paris, 1926 (photo no. 1356)—at least 1936 (Brussels exhibition); Howard Putzel, New York; sold to Kenneth McPherson, New York;[1] purchased from Kenneth McPherson, New York, 1945.

CONDITION:

The work was painted directly on a fine linen canvas. The reverse is partially stained by penetration of black paint. The paint film, which was generally applied very dry, is well preserved, with almost no crackle or losses. The edges show some wear; there is a small hole at the upper right hand corner (4⅞ in., 12.5 cm., from right and top) and a puncture in the lower section of the white jug.

In November 1981 (Venice) some areas of incipient cleavage were consolidated with Paraloid B-72 at 10%. The losses were inpainted. The previously unvarnished surface was sprayed with a light coat of Lefranc retouching varnish.[2] The condition is stable though fragile. (New York, Feb. 1983.)

EXHIBITIONS:

Brussels, Palais des Beaux-Arts, *Braque*, Nov. 21-Dec. 13, 1936, no. 30 (*Pichet et raisins*, lent by Paul Rosenberg);[3] Venice, *P.G.*, 1948 (Biennale), no. 15; Florence, *P.G.*, 1949, no. 15a; Amsterdam, *P.G.*, 1951, no. 19; Zurich, *P.G.*, 1951, no. 18; London, *P.G.*, 1964-65, no. 8, repr.; Stockholm, *P.G.*, 1966-67, no. 8, repr.; New York, *P.G.*, 1969, p. 55, repr.; Paris, *P.G.*, 1974-75, no. 7, repr.; Torino, *P.G.*, 1975-76, no. 8; New York, *P.G.*, 1982-83, no. 4, repr. color.

REFERENCES:

Bulletin de l'Effort Moderne, no. 29, Nov. 1926, repr. p. 4 *(Le compotier de raisin); Cahiers d'Art*, vol. 2, no. 1, 1927, repr. p. 9; G. Isarlov, *Georges Braque*, Paris, 1932, no. 431 ("*Guéridon, compotier*, Paul Rosenberg photo no. 1356"); *Cahiers d'Art*, vol. 8, nos. 1-2, 1933, [repr. betw. pp. 50-51]; Calas, 1966, repr. color p. 46; N. Mangin, ed., *Catalogue de l'Œuvre de Georges Braque*, Maeght, 1968, repr. p. 77 ("*Guéridon [cruche, compotier et fruits]*").

1. Peggy Guggenheim remembered that McPherson bought the work from Putzel, but did not know when Putzel acquired it, nor from whom. It is likely that he purchased it directly from Paul Rosenberg.
2. See above, cat. no. 19, fn. 4.
3. A torn label on the stretcher carries the imprint of the Palais des Beaux-Arts, the handwritten title "*le compotier et le pichet blanc*," and the name of Paul Rosenberg. This information corresponds closely with the information in the catalogue entry cited above. Cat. no. 37 in the Brussels exhibition was "*Le compotier et le pichet blanc*," but was not listed as a loan by Paul Rosenberg.

Victor Brauner

Born June 1903, Piatra Neamt, Rumania.
Died March 1966, Paris.

21 Le Surréaliste. January 1947.
(*The Surrealist*).

Color plate p. 502.

76.2553 PG 111

Oil on canvas, 23⅝ x 17¾ (60 x 45).

Signed and dated l.r.: *VICTOR BRAUNER / I. 1947*; inscribed on reverse (see illustration): *PASSÉ / PRESENT / AVENIR* (left, bottom to top); *NECESSITÉ / DESTIN / MAGIE / VOLONTE / LIBERTÉ / SURRÉALITÉ* (right, bottom to top); *TITRE DU TABLEAU: / LE SURREALISTE* (center); *LE SURRÉALISME / .NATURE. LIBRE. NATURANTE.* (lower center); *VICTOR BRAUNER / I 1947* (lower right obscured by stretcher).

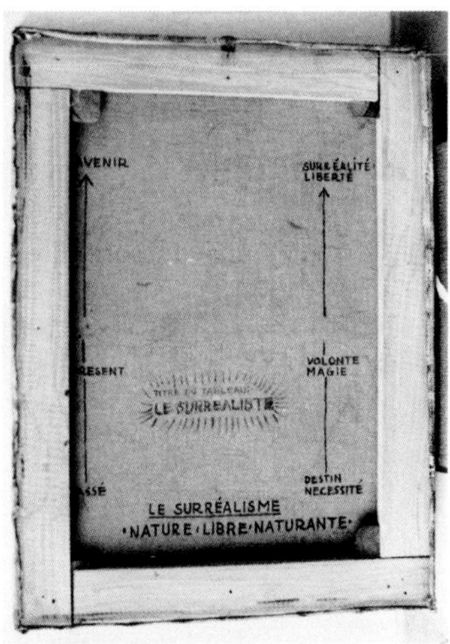

PROVENANCE:

Purchased from the artist, Paris, winter 1948-49.

CONDITION:

In 1968 (New York) the surface was partially cleaned with distilled water, areas soluble in water being cleaned with petroleum benzine (Fisher Scientific B-264). The entire lower ⅛ in., 0.5 cm., of the painting was consolidated with Lucite 46.

In 1982 (Venice) a thick, discolored coat of varnish with extensive bloom was removed. Some inpainting, especially in the hat, was removed at the same time. Minor losses along the edges, in the water, and in the sky were inpainted with watercolor. Some surface crackle and scattered ground cracks are visible, but these and the overall condition are stable. (New York, Feb. 1983.)

At several points in his career, Brauner explicitly indicated that the content of his pictures was intended to be explicable and open to interpretation: "*Ma peinture est autobiographique. J'y raconte ma vie.... Ma peinture est aussi symbolique et elle est chaque fois un message, pas un message métaphysique, mais un message direct et poétique.... Chaque chose est personnifiée par une forme, chaque forme est personnifiée par une chose...*" (text of 1962 quoted by D. Bozo, *Victor Brauner*, exh. cat., MNAM, Paris, 1972, p. 84). Or in 1963: "[Surrealism] is more concerned with subject-matter, expecting the latter to reveal the artist's subconscious or allow us to rediscover forgotten archetypes" (interview by E. Roditi, *Art Voices*, Sept. 1963, n.p.). Or on another occasion: "What matters to me is that there should be a little story in every picture, in all of them. There must be a little story" (E. Tadini, *Victor Brauner*, exh. cat., Galleria Schwarz, Milan, 1966, n.p.).

21

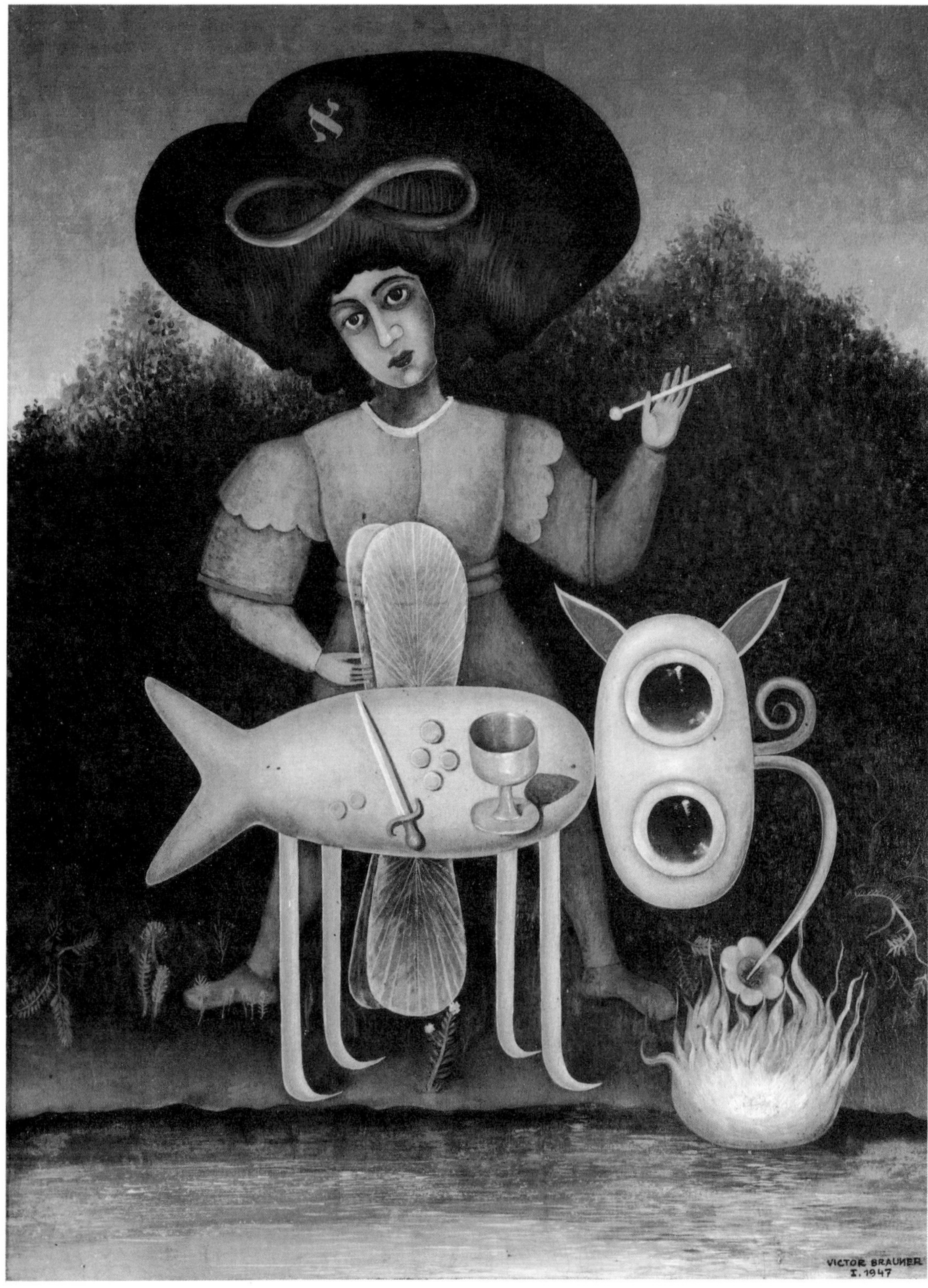

According to the compelling interpretation of *Le Surréaliste* offered by Nicolas Calas (who knew the artist well and wrote perceptively about his art as early as 1945), the picture represents an idealized portrait of Brauner as a young man. The artist portrays himself in the role of the Juggler — the archetype of the Surrealist poet. As Calas points out, Oswald Wirth's detailed explication of the symbolism of the Tarot Juggler throws important light on Brauner's depiction. To Wirth the Juggler denotes the capacity of the poetic self to create its own personality. The individual in pursuit of self-realization plays with his destiny as a juggler plays with his baton. (O. Wirth, *Le Tarot des Imagiers du Moyen Âge*, Paris, 1927, pp. 101-4.)

There are, of course, many versions of the tarot pack and its origins are still obscure. The basic format, however, consists of seventy-eight cards. Fifty-six are divided among four suits — wands, cups, swords, pentacles (metal discs inscribed with five-pointed stars) — known as the Minor Arcana. The remaining cards are known as the Major Arcana. These cards "depict symbolic figures, elements in nature, the experience of Man in his spiritual journey, his hopes and fears, his joys and sorrows."[1] The Juggler is the first card in the Major Arcana.

Though Calas did not identify the sources from which Brauner took his image, it seems most likely that two main prototypes of the tarot deck contributed to Brauner's conception of the Juggler: the Marseille tarot and the Waite tarot. In the Marseille tarot (fig. a), the Juggler wears a costume similar to that of Brauner's figure, with belted waist, scalloped sleeves, and the same large hat; like the

fig. a.
The Juggler from the Marseille Tarot. Photograph courtesy Rare Book Division, The New York Public Library, Astor, Lenox and Tilden Foundations.

1. E. Gray, *A Complete Guide to the Tarot*, New York, 1972, pp. 1-2. For other aspects of the tarot discussed here, see also K. Seligmann, *Magic, Supernaturalism, and Religion*, New York, 1968, pp. 428-34; P. Marteau, *Le Tarot de Marseille*, Paris, 1949, pp. 9-12; A. E. Waite, *Pictorial Guide to the Tarot*, 1st ed., London, 1910, edition cited here, New York, 1982.

Surréaliste, he also has his left hand raised bearing the wand, while his right hand is bent at the elbow. In both works, too, the objects laid out before the Juggler include a knife (or sword), a goblet, and coins.

In the Waite tarot, the first card in the Major Arcana is called the Magician rather than the Juggler. The Waite image, like the *Surréaliste*, bears above his head the sign of infinity, the horizontal figure *8*, which, according to Waite's text, "is also the mysterious sign of the Holy Spirit, the sign of life, like an endless cord, forming the figure *8* in a horizontal position" (1910, p. 72). On the table in front of the Magician are the cup, sword, wand, and a pentacle representing money, acquisition of fortune, or trade (Gray, 1972, p. 65). According to Waite's description, the pentacle in the magician card carries the same significance as the coins in the Marseille Juggler.

Thus, the attributes of the Juggler/Magician and of *Le Surréaliste* signify the four suits of the Minor Arcana: wands (fire), cups (water), swords (air), and pentacles (earth). As defined by Waite these are the "symbols of the four tarot suits signifying the elements of natural life, which lie like counters before the adept and he adapts them as he wills" (1910, p. 75).

Although the aleph on the hat of the *Surréaliste* is present in neither the Marseille nor the Waite tarot, it is a common element in several other versions. As the first letter of the Hebrew alphabet, it was appropriate for the first card of the Major Arcana. Each of the other twenty-one cards are labeled with one of the other twenty-two letters in the Hebrew alphabet, a factor which has given rise to various interpretations. Kurt Seligmann, for example, cites the Cabala "in which the Aleph expresses the spirit of the living God" who, as master spirit of the universe, tosses all things of creation about as if they were juggler's objects (op. cit. in fn.1, p. 428).

The "table" where the juggler's objects are traditionally displayed is transformed in Brauner's painting into a large insect (or demon) in front of a body of water upon which floats a ball of fire. Calas suggested that in his departure from the traditional tarot representation, Brauner has incorporated a covert reference to the tarot devil, a card which suggests that "no human goal can be reached without the help of the devil." Thus, "the devil is represented as serving the Surrealist-Juggler and illustrating Wirth's claim that the artist alone makes use of the devil without binding himself by contract."[2]

The evidence for Calas's reading of the painting as a form of self-portrait is persuasive. As Alain Jouffroy noted, Brauner began (in 1946) a series of "*métamorphoses imaginaires qui va lui permettre de peindre, comme il le dit lui-même, 'diverses autobiographies de substitution'* " (*Brauner*, Paris, 1959, p. 51). At about this time Brauner also began signing his works with the infinity sign; Gordon Onslow-Ford recalled in conversation that Brauner identified himself

2. Calas sees the flaming ball as a reference to the crayfish from card xviii representing the house of Cancer. It may, on the other hand, represent the flaming torch carried by the devil in the Waite tarot, or simply the fire of the suit of wands.

with this sign.[3] Thus, though Sarane Alexandrian has rightly pointed out the difficulty of identifying specific works as autobiographical in the narrow sense,[4] it seems clear that the imagery of *Le Surréaliste* accords not only with the identity of the Surrealist poet as Brauner saw it in 1947, but with the conception of himself as artist-creator.

EXHIBITIONS:

Florence, *P.G.*, 1949, no. 21; Amsterdam, *P.G.*, 1951, no. 22; London, *P.G.*, 1964-65, no. 101, repr. p. 64; Stockholm, *P.G.*, 1966-67, no. 96, repr.; Torino, Galleria Civica d'Arte Moderna, *Le Muse Inquietanti*, Nov. 1967-Jan. 1968, no. 174, repr. p. 131; New York, *P.G.*, 1969, p. 126, repr.; Paris, *P.G.*, 1974-75, no. 95, repr. p. 81; Torino, *P.G.*, 1975-76, no. 109; New York, *P.G.*, 1982-83, no. 45, repr.

REFERENCES:

Calas, 1966, pp. 123-24, repr. color p. 158; D. Bozo, *Victor Brauner*, exh. cat., MNAM, Paris, 1972, introduction n.p. and cat. no. 80.

3. In conversation with C. Goodman, Feb. 18, 1983, Onslow-Ford also suggested that there was some physical resemblance between Brauner and *Le Surréaliste*. Works signed with the infinity sign include *Tableau autobiographique*, 1948 (Collection Hersaint, Paris) and *Victor Victorach rentre en lui-même pour y trouver la tranquillité*, 1949 (repr. *Victor Brauner*, exh. cat., Alexander Iolas, Paris, 1971, n.p.). The infinity sign also carries the symbolism of the alchemical uoroborus, in that instance as a snake devouring its own tail. Brauner's interest in alchemy is well documented in various contexts. See, for example, his *La Pierre Philosophale* of 1939-40.
4. *Victor Brauner L'Illuminateur*, Paris, 1954, p. 20.

22 Téléventré. 1948.

Color plate p. 503.

76.2553 PG 112

Wax encaustic on millboard, 28½ x 23⅝ (72.5 x 60).

Not signed or dated. Inscribed on reverse: *NAISSANCE SYMBOLIQUE DU DOCTEUR FAUSTROLL.*

PROVENANCE:

Acquired from the artist by Pegeen Vail (as an exchange), 1949; purchased from the estate of Pegeen Vail, 1971.

CONDITION:

The support is badly warped out of plane and there is some crackle with possible cleavage. The composition was incised into the wax, color being applied afterward. In general the surface is rather fragile. (Venice, June 1983.)

The inscription on the reverse identifies *Téléventré* as a homage to Alfred Jarry's *Gestes et opinions du Docteur Faustroll Pataphysicien — Roman neo-scientifique-suivi de speculations*, published in Paris in 1911, a text that achieved great popularity with the Surrealists.

The nature of 'Pataphysics, and of its possible relationship to the world of Brauner's iconography, is difficult to establish. According to Jarry's definition, 'Pataphysics is the "purest" of sciences, reaching as it does beyond both physics and metaphysics. Its purity lies in its dedication not to the laws and generalizations of conventional science, but to the discovery that every event is in fact unique and constitutes an exception to any possible scientific law. Conventional scientific explanations are, therefore, viewed as imaginary: no better than (indeed more constricting than) other explanations. 'Pataphysics offers a way out of such constriction by describing "a universe which can be — and perhaps should be — envisaged in place of the traditional one."[1]

For those individuals who achieve a 'Pataphysical view of the universe, experience can take on a wholly new aspect and events can be viewed "in the manner of a child looking through a kaleidoscope or an astronomer studying the galaxy" (Shattuck, loc. cit. p. 29). One constructs one's own vision of the universe and its operations, creating one's "self" and one's own world view. "Like the sorcerer's apprentice, we have become victims of our own knowledge — principally of our scientific and technological knowledge. In 'Pataphysics resides our only defense against ourselves.... 'Pataphysics allows a few individuals, beneath their imperturbability, to live up to their particular selves.... 'Pataphysics, then, is an inner attitude, a discipline, a science, and an art, which allows each man to live his life as an exception, proving no law but his own" (Shattuck, loc. cit., pp. 29-30).

Brauner's own idiosyncratic view of the world, and his confidence in the capacity of each poet and artist to discover new manifestations of the self, provide echoes of the major themes to be found in Jarry's text. As Sarane Alexandrian noted, *"il s'agit pour Brauner, par le moyen de la peinture, de faire l'experience de ce qui dépasse la compréhension"* ("La symbolique de Brauner," *Cahiers d'Art*, vol. 24, 1949, p. 321).

In addition, the specific imagery of *Téléventré* (perhaps itself a 'Pataphysical concept implying paranormal communion with the womb), may allude more directly to the birth of Dr. Faustroll, as described in chapter VIII of Jarry's novel: *"Le docteur Faustroll naquit en Circassie, en 1898 (le xxe siecle avait [-2] ans), et à l'âge de soixante-trois ans. A cet âge-là, lequel il conserva toute sa vie, le docteur Faustroll était un homme de taille moyenne ...; de peau jaune d'or, au visage glabre.... "*

1. R. Shattuck, translations from Dr. Faustroll, *Evergreen Review*, vol. 4, no. 13, May-June 1960, p. 131. Shattuck's exposition of 'Pataphysics forms the basis of the summary offered here.

Faustroll was born a fully grown man, and hence deprived of his childhood, a fact that may have powerfully impressed Brauner. In an interview published in 1952, Brauner spoke of the deep sense of deprivation he had felt as a baby when he was weaned too early from his mother's breast:

> *Un fait a pris une importance considérable dans ma vie: J'ai été sevré trop tot. Depuis, je portais sans cesse le regret de cette enfance manquée. Il est possible d'expliquer autrement cet attrait de l'enfance qui me paraît assez général. Vous connaissez le mot de Brancusi: "Le jour où je ne serai plus enfant, je serai mort." Poussée à ces limites, l'idée devient inquiétante. Comme tout le monde croit son existence prénatale, son traumatisme unique et différent de celui du voisin, personne n'a confiance dans les ressources du langage commun pour l'exprimer.*[2]

Whether a symbolic connection between Brauner's own "lost infancy" and Faustroll's was made by the artist as he conceived *Téléventré* cannot be established, but such a connection would have been entirely consistent with Brauner's approach to his art.

The iconography of the painting itself is characteristic of Brauner's work of the period. Alexandrian cogently demonstrated as early as 1949 that the artist was obsessed with prenatal nostalgia and that many of his most important works touch upon this theme.[3] The prenatal state, according to Alexandrian, represented for Brauner a condition of unconscious unity of self and contentment—very different from the actualities of life after birth. In the case of *Téléventré*, the newborn male seems to emerge from the womb in two parts: on the left, the head and torso are lifted from the mouth of a serpent by the large bird (merged with the mother-figure); on the right, the lower half is held firmly in the mouth of a corresponding serpent.[4] The depiction (possibly alluding simultaneously to Faustroll and to the artist himself) carries overtones of curtailed infancy as well as of a powerful sense of identification between masculinity and dependence on the maternal provider. In this case, as in others, the painting serves as an illustration of Brauner's sense of his art as a process of self-discovery and self-relevation: "*Chaque tableau que je fait est projeté des sources les plus profondes de mon angoisse, car c'est bien* [de] *cela qu'il s'agit,* [et] *est une histoire où j'essaie de perfectionner un champ radiant protecteur fondamental*" (1950, quoted by D. Bozo, *Victor Brauner*, exh. cat., MNAM. Paris, 1972, p. 86).

EXHIBITIONS:

Paris, *P.G.*, 1974-75, no. 96; Torino, *P.G.*, 1975-76, no. 110.

REFERENCE:

[Alley], *Peggy Guggenheim Foundation*, 1973, no. 112.

2. M. Clarac-Serou, "Victor Brauner," *Arte e Letteratura*, 3rd ser., no. 3, Dec. 1952, p. 8.
3. "La symbolique de Brauner," *Cahiers d'Art*, vol. 24, 1949, pp. 324-29; idem, *Victor Brauner L'Illuminateur*, Paris, 1954, pp. 68-70.
4. "*On sait que chez Brauner le serpent est un symbole agonistique très profond....*" See Alexandrian, 1949, p. 325.

23 Consciousness of Shock. April 1951.

76.2553 PG 113

Wax encaustic on hardboard, 25¼ x 31½ (64 x 80).

Signed and dated l.l.: *VICTOR BRAUNER / IV. 1951.*

PROVENANCE:

Purchased from the Galleria del Cavallino, Venice, September 30, 1955.

CONDITION:

Consolidation of flaking areas was attempted in Venice in the 1950s (by Bacci). In 1964, at the time of the Tate exhibition, the fragility of the work was noted, and some further consolidation took place. In 1968 (New York) the cleavage in the whites was noted again, but no restoration was attempted. The present condition continues to be fragile, especially in the whites. (Venice, 1982.)

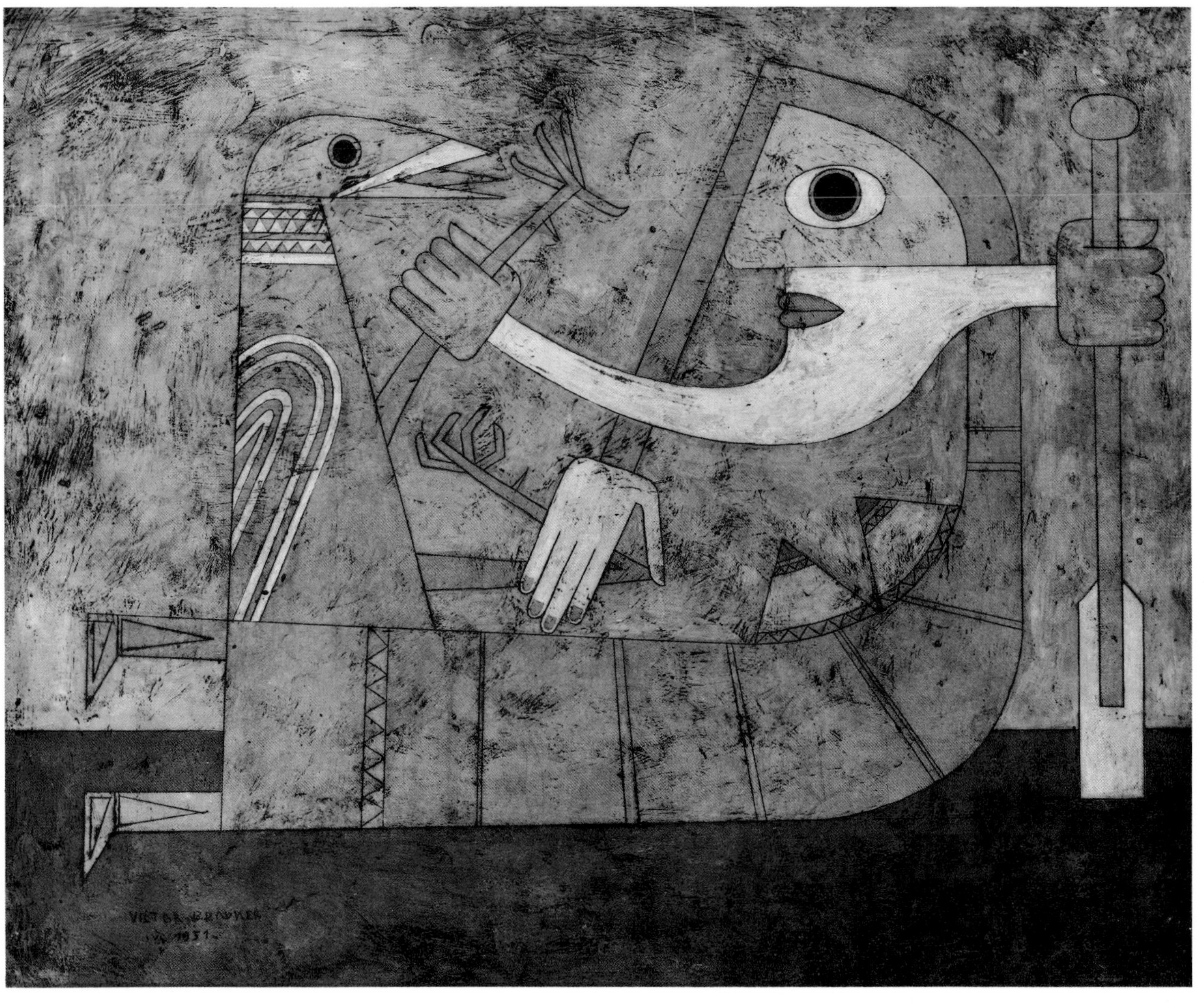

Nicolas Calas interprets *Consciousness of Shock* as an adaptation of two Egyptian themes, the "Sun Barge" and the "Heavenly Vault." According to this reading, Brauner combines two humans and a bird into a single being: "a female body most prominently forms the vessel. The two yellow fists belong to the third figure symbolic of the mind steering the barge. Man and woman have apparently joined forces here to restrain the aggressive bird" (Calas, 1966).

Though Brauner's imagery and style here and elsewhere betray a generalized Egyptian influence, it is difficult to establish any direct connection between the individual images and Egyptian prototypes. The Egyptian Sun God Re was indeed part bird, part man, but Brauner's own free use of the concept of bird-humans seems more plausibly attributable to his invention of an idiosyncratic personal iconography than to any consistent reference to Egyptian themes and meanings. *("Je suis, dans mon désordre apparent, organisé selon des lois de l'imagination.")*

In discussing the autobiographical nature of many of Brauner's animal-human or bird-human forms, Sarane Alexandrian particularly drew attention to the artist's tendency to fantasize. Rather than creating an alter ego (such as Ernst's Loplop, the bird), Brauner depicted himself in the guise of every form of beast or object ("*C'est moi, sous une autre apparence et dans une autre condition*"), aiming thereby to achieve a new form of "metaphysical" portrait (*Victor Brauner L'Illuminateur*, Paris, 1954, p. 20). In this respect his imaginative identification with a multitude of animal and bird forms differs markedly from the more directly autobiographical nature of a painting such as *Le Surréaliste*, in which the iconography is more explicit in its symbolism and hence more accessible to particular interpretation.

EXHIBITIONS:

London, *P.G.*, 1964-65, no. 102; New York, *P.G.*, 1969, repr. color p. 127; Paris, *P.G.*, 1974-75, no. 97, repr. p. 82; Torino, *P.G.*, 1975-76, no. 111.

REFERENCE:

Calas, 1966, pp. 124-25, repr. color p. 159.

Alexander Calder

Born July 1898, Lawnton, Pennsylvania.
Died November 1976, New York.

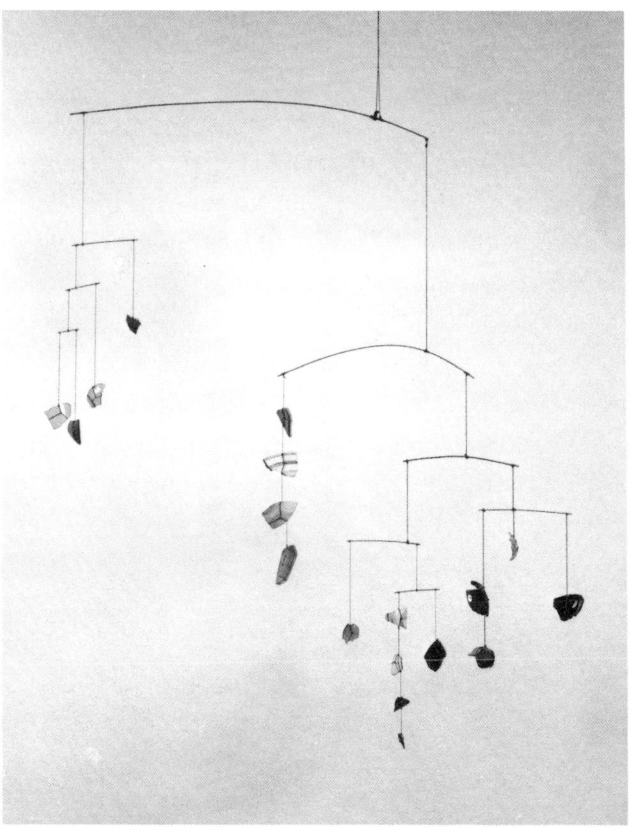

24 Mobile. Ca. 1934.

76.2553 PG 139

Glass and china fragments, each of which is tied with wire; six iron wire suspension elements painted red; knotted red nylon thread (not original). Height: ca. 65¾ (167); width: ca. 46$^{1}/_{16}$ (117).

Not signed or dated.

PROVENANCE:

Purchased from the artist, Paris, 1950.[1]

CONDITION:

In 1969 (New York) some of the threads apparently wore through and pieces of the mobile fell and broke (the original material of the threads is not recorded). The threads were at that time all replaced with nylon, the knots saturated with Elmer's glue and painted red. The broken pottery and amber glass were repaired with epoxy, missing fragments filled with spackle. The damaged glaze on 2 pieces of pottery ([a] green, yellow, violet; [b] light blue, white, pink, green) was replaced with dry pigment in Lucite 46. Two other pieces were inpainted with Windsor and Newton watercolor and sprayed with Grumbacher Tuffilm spray.

Venice, June 1983, the amber glass broke again, the glue having softened and disintegrated. This was repaired.

It is impossible to say whether the disposition of the mobile elements corresponds precisely with Calder's original composition, since no photographs of the work in its earlier state exist. The present condition is stable. (Venice, Nov. 1982.)

1. Peggy Guggenheim was in Venice and Calder in Paris when she bought the work sight unseen —one of the two such instances documented in her collecting career (see cat. no. 34). Nelly van Doesburg transported it to Venice for her.

The date of this work poses considerable problems that remain unresolved. Peggy Guggenheim always assumed that the mobile was made at about the time she purchased it, and it appears with the date 1950 in all her publications. There is, however, no evidence to substantiate the point. No bill or other document of acquisition survives, communication with Calder having apparently been purely verbal.

Mobiles of this type (wire or wooden bars arranged in tiers on a roughly horizontal/vertical axis, suspended with string from which fragments of broken glass and china dangle) seem to date from the years 1934-35. It was during those years that Calder made his initial efforts in the medium, and the simplicity of the concept reflects some of the experimental quality of that early phase.

Occasional late examples of this type may have been made, and in an interview with Katharine Kuh conducted in the late fifties, Calder seemed to refer to such a possibility when he spoke of his use of glass: "I haven't used it much lately. A few years ago I took all sorts of colored glass I'd collected and smashed it against the stone wall of the barn. There's still a mass of glass buried there. In my early mobiles I often used it" (*The Artist's Voice*, New York, 1960, p. 44). But even here, the implication of his final remark is that he had not made such mobiles in the 1940s or 1950s.

Related to the dating question is that of the title. As H. H. Arnason has pointed out, Calder in the 1930s tended to entitle these works merely "Mobile." In the later stages he tended on the other hand to use more evocative and usually poetic titles. The lack of a title for the Peggy Guggenheim work, though not decisive, adds possible weight to the hypothesis that the mobile dates from the 1930s.

EXHIBITIONS:

Amsterdam, *P.G.*, 1951, no. 26; New York, *P.G.*, 1969, p. 111 (a glass sculpture by Egidio Costantini was erroneously reproduced here and the illustration of cat. no. 24 was omitted).

25 Mobile. 1941.
(*Arc of petals*).

76.2553 PG 137

Sheet aluminum, iron suspension wire, copper rivets; thirteen upper aluminum leaves painted black, one unpainted; thirteen lower leaves unpainted. Height: ca. 84¼ (214).

Not signed or dated.

PROVENANCE:

Purchased from the artist, New York, 1941.

CONDITION:

In several places, friction has caused the wire to wear thin at the circular joints, rendering the piece fragile. The black leaves have been repainted several times. In one instance, the single large unpainted aluminum leaf was mistakenly painted black; this was cleaned with solvent in 1981 and restored to its original color. The overall condition is fragile. (Venice, Nov. 1982.)

The technique used by Calder in this and other mobiles involves neither soldering nor welding of the iron wire and aluminum elements. The fourteen upper leaves are each secured to the iron suspension wire with an end rivet. The squarish "shoe-shaped" leaf, made of a piece of folded and hammered aluminum to give extra weight, is fastened with four such rivets (fig. a). The thirteen smaller leaves are each pierced with holes; the iron wire is threaded through the holes and its end bent back to secure it in place (fig. b). The circular joints in the iron arms were twisted into shape either manually, or with pliers (fig. c).

fig. a.
Detail of cat. no. 25, "shoe-shaped" leaf showing riveting.

fig. b.
Detail of cat. no. 25, showing system of wire threading.

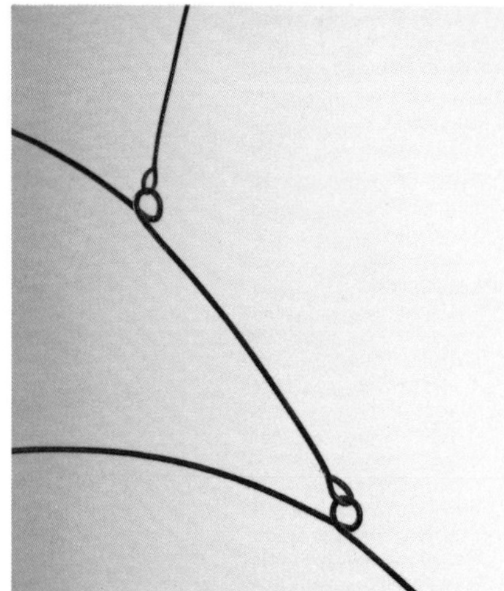

fig. c.
Detail of cat. no. 25, showing wire suspension.

Calder has explained the process of calculating the balance of weights and counterweights required in these particular mobiles. "I begin with the smallest and work up. Once I know the balance point for the first pair ... I anchor it by a hook to another arm, where it acts as one end of another pair of scales, and so on up. It's a kind of ascending scale of weights and counterweights (C. Curtis, "Calder Made Easy," *Horizon*, vol. 14, no. 1, p. 57). As he proceeded upward, one element might prove too light, or too heavy. By shortening the wire branch, or doubling the weight of a suspended element (as in the black "shoe" form in Peggy Guggenheim's work), Calder was able to reestablish the balance.

Joan M. Marter has pointed out that during the 1930s Calder was to some extent using his knowledge of engineering and physics as a background in calculating the critical issues of balance and motion in his work, rather than evolving his technique entirely intuitively ("Alexander Calder; Cosmic Imagery and the Use of Scientific Instruments," *Arts Magazine*, vol. 53, Oct. 1978, pp. 108-13). In the preparatory drawing for his mobile *Steel Fish* of 1934, he carefully plotted and measured all the elements to be included and precisely determined the fulcrum for the principal objects to be balanced (Marter, loc. cit., pp. 112-13, fig. 27).

Whether he continued to use such technical knowledge for his work in the 1940s has not been established, but drawings similar to the one published by Marter have not been discovered.

The title *Arc of petals* was used in all of Peggy Guggenheim's 1943 Calder exhibition correspondence with MoMA and in James Johnson Sweeney's catalogue of the show. It is not certain if the title was Calder's own or was invented by Sweeney or Peggy Guggenheim. Calder was closely involved in the preparations for the exhibition, and it seems plausible that the title may have been at least tacitly accepted by him.

EXHIBITIONS:

New York, Art of This Century, 1942-47, p. 96, repr. p. 97; New York, MoMA, *Alexander Calder*, Sept. 29-Nov. 28, 1943, no. 69 (*Arc of Petals*); Venice, *P.G.*, 1948 (Biennale), no. 19; Florence, *P.G.*, 1949, no. 19; Venice, Giardino, 1949, no. 4; Amsterdam, *P.G.*, 1951, no. 24, repr.; Zurich, *P.G.*, 1951, no. 23; London, *P.G.*, 1964-65, no. 115; Stockholm, *P.G.*, 1966-67, no. 110; New York, *P.G.*, 1969, p. 110, repr.; Paris, *P.G.*, 1974-75, no. 117; Torino, *P.G.*, 1975-76, no. 130; Rome, *Guggenheim: Venezia-New York*, 1982, no. 52, repr. color.

REFERENCE:

P. Guggenheim, *Art of This Century*, 1942, p. 96, repr. p. 97 (*Mobile*).

26 Silver Bed Head. Winter 1945-46.

76.2553 PG 138

Silver. Height: 63 (160); width: 51⁹⁄₁₆ (131).

Not signed or dated.

PROVENANCE:

Commissioned from the artist, and made in New York, winter 1945-46.

CONDITION:

The hammered bars of silver have been bent and attached with silver threads and joins. One of the joins is broken and the elements bent out of shape at that juncture. Repairs of this break, realignment of the parts, overall cleaning, and the application of a protective coating are envisaged. (Venice, Nov. 1982.)

Peggy Guggenheim commissioned this headboard from Calder in the winter of 1945. It took several months to complete. When she moved to Venice, it was installed on the wall behind her bed and remained there until her death.[1] Unique among Calder's creations in silver, its individual elements are clearly reminiscent of many of his works as a jeweler — his earrings, pendants, or necklaces. Its imagery is also closely related to his book illustrations of the same period. (See, for example, a set of drawings he made in 1946 for *Selected Fables* of Jean de La Fontaine, trans. Eunice Clark, New York, 1948.)

Only three of the elements are movable: two fishes and an insect.[2] The remaining elements in the large composition are cut, hammered, intricately assembled, twisted into spirals, and interlocked in such a way as to suggest mobility without allowing it.

EXHIBITIONS:

Florence, *P.G.*, 1949, no. 20; Amsterdam, *P.G.*, 1951, no. 25 (dated 1944); Zurich, *P.G.*, 1951, no. 24.

REFERENCE:

P. Guggenheim, *Confessions*, p. 111, repr. opp. p. 49.

1. Though still in its original location, the headboard has since been partially covered with a Plexiglas sheet screwed into the wall.

2. In her Memoirs (see REFERENCE), Peggy Guggenheim referred to 2 movable elements: a fish and a butterfly. There are in fact 2 fishes, both of which hang at the lower left. The insect (which resembles a bee with wings spread or a dragonfly rather than a butterfly) is presently suspended at the left center (see illustration). More frequently it has been hung right of center, its chain looped to the upper right of the arch (see repr. *Confessions*). The insect itself dangled freely, and with some mobility, in the open space between the large spiral tendril and the leaves below. The 2 fishes, although technically removable from their hooks, are not mobile while suspended.

Massimo Campigli

Born July 1895, Florence.
Died May 1971, St. Tropez.

27 Il Gioco a Palla. 1946.
(*The Ball Game*).

76.2553 PG 160

Tempera with gesso on canvas, 26¼ x 23 7/16 (66.5 x 59.5).

Signed and dated l.l.: *Campigli* 46; on reverse: *No. 33*.

PROVENANCE:

Purchased from the artist, through Galleria d'Arte del Cavallino, Venice, 1948.

CONDITION:

In 1964 (Tate Report) elevated cracks in the paint layer with some incipient cleavage were noted in 3 areas near the lower edge. These were consolidated.

There is crackle in the paint layer over a large part of the surface with some pigment cleavage and some minor losses. The condition is fragile. (Venice, June 1983.)

EXHIBITIONS:

Venice, Giardini di Castello, *Premio di Pittura di "La Colomba,"* July 1-31, 1946, no. 13, repr.; Venice, *P.G.*, 1948 (Biennale), no. 20; Florence, *P.G.*, 1949, no. 21; Amsterdam, *P.G.*, 1951, no. 27; London, *P.G.*, 1964-65, no. 134, repr.; Stockholm, *P.G.*, 1966-67, no. 131, repr.; Torino, *P.G.*, 1975-76, no. 152, repr. pl. 152.

César (Baldaccini)

Born Marseille, January 1921.
Lives in Paris.

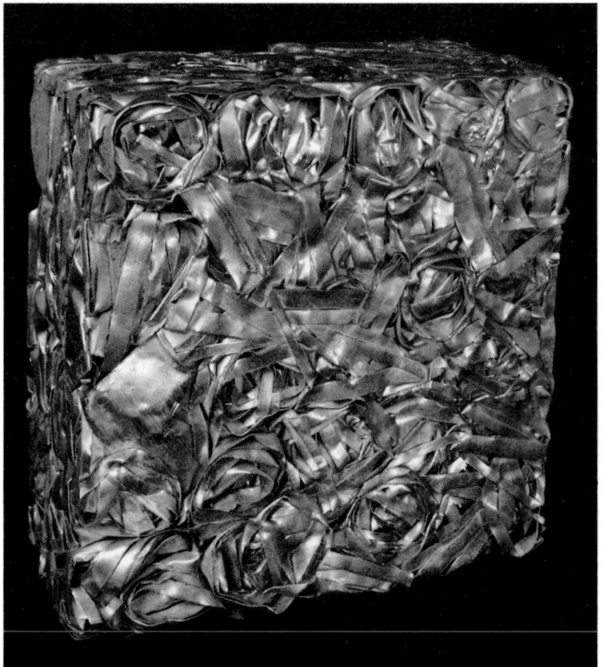

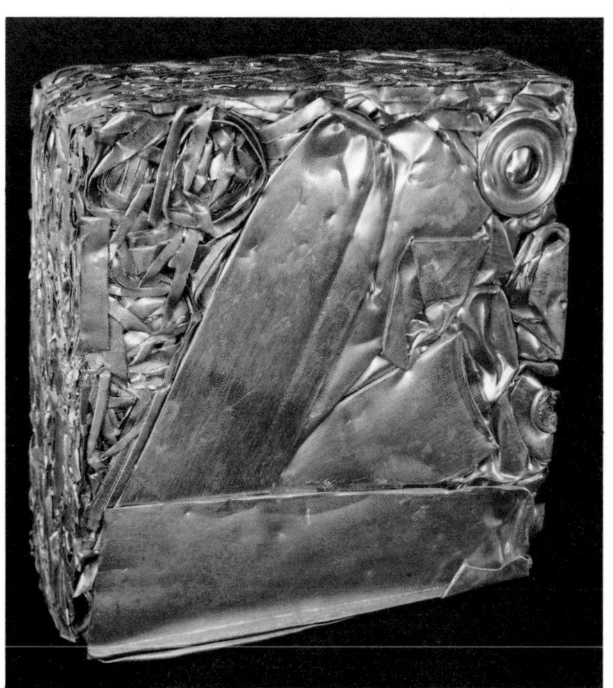

28 Compression. 1969.

76.2553 PG 207

Aluminum. Height: $13\frac{15}{16}$ (35.4); varying width of narrow edges: $4\frac{7}{8}$-$5\frac{1}{2}$ (12.5-14); width of front and back: $14\frac{3}{16}$ (36).

Signed u.l. on narrow edge (scratched into aluminum): *César*. Not dated.

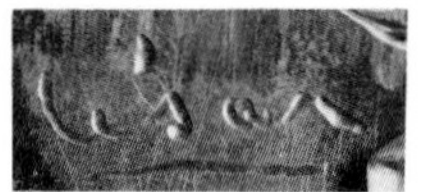

PROVENANCE:

Purchased from Il Capricorno, Venice, June 28, 1971.

CONDITION:

Brown spots of glue are visible in certain places. Three circular pieces ($2\frac{3}{8}$-$2\frac{15}{16}$ in., 6-7.5 cm., in diameter) became detached from the block and were readhered, Venice, March 1984. The condition is stable.

The work is made from aluminum bottles, either whole or sliced with a sharp cutting device, compressed into a rectangular block. Though the piece is held in place largely through pressure, some glue was apparently used to secure individual elements.

EXHIBITION:

Torino, *P.G.*, 1975-76, 194bis.

Marc Chagall

Born July 1887, Vitebsk.
Lives in St. Paul de Vence, France.

29 La pluie. 1911.
(*Rain*; *Farm reminiscence*).

Color plate p. 48.

76.2553 PG 63

Oil (and possibly some charcoal) on canvas (unvarnished), 34⅛ x 42½ (86.7 x 108).

Signed and dated l.l.: *Chagall / 911*.

PROVENANCE:

Early history unknown;[1] purchased from J. B. Neumann or Karl Nierendorf, New York, 1941.[2]

CONDITION:

The unprimed but sized canvas was on the whole thinly painted and no varnish was used. Drying cracks and flaking are present only in the clouds and the roof, revealing crimson underneath and suggesting *pentimenti* in these areas. Apart from an area approximately 12 in., 30.5 cm., long at the top right edge, another ca. 2 in., 5 cm., long at the bottom left, where extensive retouching has taken place, and some scattered pinpoint losses, the condition is stable. (New York, Feb. 1983.)

1. It has not been possible to establish whether Chagall left this (with other works) in Paris or in Berlin with Herwarth Walden when he went back to Russia at the outbreak of the war in 1914. He was subsequently unable to retrieve these groups of pictures when he returned to western Europe in 1922, and he does not recall whether this work was among them or to whom he otherwise sold it.
2. Peggy Guggenheim recalled buying it from one or the other.

Chagall moved to Paris from Russia in 1910. In the immediately ensuing years, his reminiscences of his rural upbringing in Vitebsk provided the most persistent imagery for his compositions. Franz Meyer has described Chagall's successive elaboration of single motifs in the Rain group as characteristic of his method at this time. Demonstrated by the studies reproduced here (figs. a and b), the process involved spontaneous sketches, which were gradually intensified, with a growing emphasis on structure and pattern. Meyer convincingly attributes this process to the influence of Cubism, and, specifically, to Chagall's personal response to the structural coherence of Cubist composition. Chagall himself has consistently acknowledged his debt to Cubist "architecture" (see, for example, J. J. Sweeney, "An Interview with Marc Chagall," *Partisan Review*, vol. 11, no. 1, winter 1944, pp. 89-90). He has also insisted that the imagery of his paintings ("cows, milkmaids, roosters and provincial Russian architecture") is to be read not as a vocabulary of anecdotal subject matter but as "elements in a composition... with different values of plasticity, but not different poetic values" (ibid.). The perceptible tightening of the structure thus corresponds directly to his rejection of "illustrational logic" in favor of the "visual effectiveness of the painted composition."

fig. a.
Chagall, Study for cat. no. 29, ca. 1911, watercolor on paper, dimensions and present whereabouts unknown.

fig. b.
Chagall, Study for cat. no. 29, ca. 1911, gouache on cardboard, 8⅞ x 11 13/16 in., 22.5 x 30 cm., signed u.r.: *Marc Chagall*, Tretiakov Gallery, Moscow, Gift of George Costakis.

EXHIBITIONS:

New York, Art of This Century, 1942-47, p. 46, repr. (*Farm reminiscence*, the title by which the work was known in all *P.G.* publications until R. Alley, 1964.); Venice, *P.G.*, 1948 (Biennale), no. 21; Florence, *P.G.*, 1949, no. 22; Amsterdam, *P.G.*, 1951, no. 28; Zurich, *P.G.*, 1951, no. 26; London, *P.G.*, 1964-65, no. 56 *(Rain);* Stockholm, *P.G.*, 1966-67, no. 54, repr.; New York, *P.G.*, 1969, p. 80, repr. p. 81; Paris, *P.G.*, 1974-75, no. 56; Torino, *P.G.*, 1975-76, no. 61, repr. color, pl. 28; Rome, *Guggenheim: Venezia-New York*, 1982, no. 25, repr. color; New York, *P.G.*, 1982-83, no. 22, repr. color.

REFERENCES:

P. Guggenheim, *Art of This Century* , 1942, p. 46, repr.; F. Meyer, *Marc Chagall: Life and Work*, New York, 1963, pp. 149-50, repr. cl. cat. no. 102 (*Rain*; Meyer's title was presumably based on the artist's own title); Calas, 1966, p. 75, repr. color p. 79.

Giorgio de Chirico

Born July 1888, Vólos, Greece.
Died November 1978, Rome.

fig. a.
De Chirico, drawing (possibly preparatory) for cat. no. 30, not signed or dated, ink on paper, $4\frac{7}{16}$ x $6\frac{1}{8}$ in., 11.3 x 15.5 cm., Private Collection, Rome. Photograph courtesy M. Fagiolo dell'Arco.

30 La tour rouge. 1913.

(*The red tower*; *The rose tower*).

Color plate p. 242.

76.2553 PG 64

Oil on canvas, 28 15/16 x 39 5/8 (73.5. x 100.5).

Signed and dated l.l.: *G. de Chirico / 1913*.

PROVENANCE:

Purchased from the artist by Olivier Senn, Le Havre, during the 1913 *Salon d'Automne*;[1] Galerie Bonaparte (Van Leer), Paris, by 1936; purchased by Pierre Matisse, June 17, 1936; sold by Matisse to R. Sturgis Ingersoll, Philadelphia, October 1936 (information supplied by Pierre Matisse, correspondence with the author); Bignou Gallery, New York, by 1941;[2] purchased from Bignou, 1941.[3]

CONDITION:

In 1964 (Tate Report) there were some minor abrasions near the upper edge (right) and very small areas of darkened inpainting near the upper right and lower right corners. There was some uncertainty about the presence of varnish.

In 1978 (New York) an uneven spotty condition existed, attributed to long exposure to moist atmosphere and resulting in deterioration of the media. The paint film was described as extremely thin and showing a loss of opacity in certain areas.

The canvas was flattened at 130°, lined on Mylar 1400 with BEVA, strip-lined with Lucite 44-treated linen strips attached with Plus-Ten contact cement. It was stapled to the original stretcher. Eight applications of Lucite 44 were sprayed on the surface. The solvents required for removal of this varnish may affect the adhesion between liner and original canvas.

The loss of opacity noted above reveals 2 statues, in the left foreground, painted out by the artist but now partially visible (see below). The sarcophagus, the edges of the support, and other scattered small areas show signs of retouching. The overall condition is stable. (New York, Mar. 1983.)

1. Since this was the first sale of de Chirico's career it represented a significant event, described in detail in his autobiography: "*Lo stesso anno esposi al* Salon d'Automne *per la seconda volta e vendei un quadro; era la prima volta nella mia vita che vendevo un quadro.... L'acquirente era un signore di Le Havre; era un uomo anziano e che si chiamava Olivier Senn. Come prezzo credo che avessi dichiarato alla segreteria dell' esposizione quattrocento franchi. Una mattina, mentre stavo in casa, venne la domestica a dirmi che un signore di nome Senn desiderava parlarmi; risposi che entrasse e cosí conobbi il primo acquirente di mie pitture. Egli però non mi disse subito che voleva acquistare un mio quadro; mi disse che veniva due volte l'anno a Parigi per visitare le gallerie e le esposizioni, che s'interessava molto alla pittura e che era un grande amico del pittore Othon Frietz* [sic]; *mi chiese se volevo andare a far colazione con lui ed io acquicettai; durante il pasto cominciò a parlare del* Salon d'Automne, *disse che aveva notato i miei quadri e che aveva pure notato la loro originalità, e finalmente mi espresse il desiderio di acquistare quello della torre rossa, però trovava che il prezzo di quattrocento franchi era superiore alle sue disponibilità e mi chiese di lasciargli il quadro per 250 franchi. Era la prima volta che qualcuno mi offriva del denaro in cambio d'una mia pittura; ero molto emozionato e lusingato...*" (*Memorie*, pp. 101-2).
2. The intervening history of the picture remains unknown. De Chirico stated that he had heard of the picture's appearance for sale in a gallery on the rue la Boëtie in about 1926 (*Memorie*, p. 102). James Thrall Soby in 1941 attributed the picture to the collection of Wright S. Ludington, Santa Barbara, an error that was subsequently widely published in the literature. Ludington, however, owned only 1 de Chirico, which he purchased from Pierre Matisse in the 1940s; he never owned *The red tower* (correspondence with the author, June 1982). It has so far not been possible to identify other owners of the work.
3. The English collector Arthur Jeffress mentioned to Peggy Guggenheim that the picture was for sale at Bignou and she instantly went to buy it, fearing that Jeffress might otherwise acquire it himself.

fig. b.
Infra-red reflectogram of cat. no. 30, showing *pentimenti*. Reclining and standing figures were probably statues. Photograph by Studio Art System, Venice, 1983.

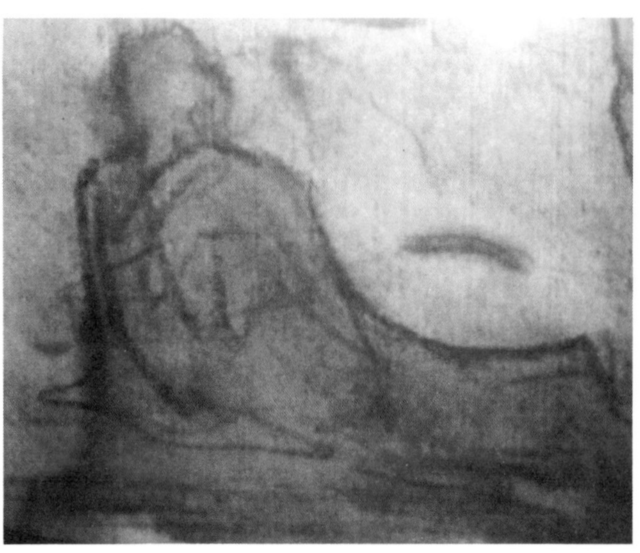

fig. c.
Infra-red reflectogram of cat. no. 30, showing reclining figure. Photograph by Studio Art System, Venice, 1983.

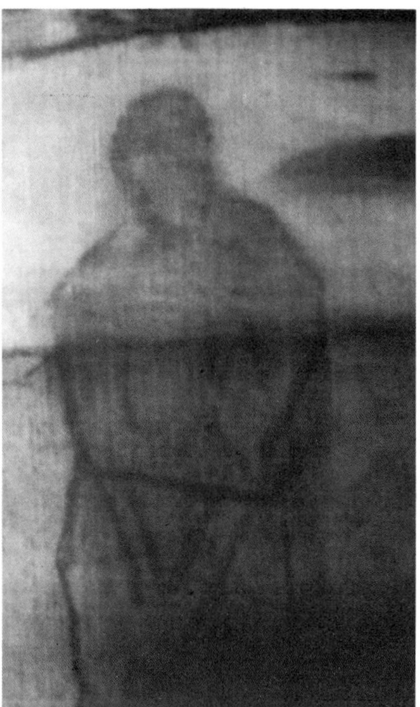

fig. d.
Infra-red reflectogram of cat. no. 30, showing standing figure. Photograph by Studio Art System, Venice, 1983.

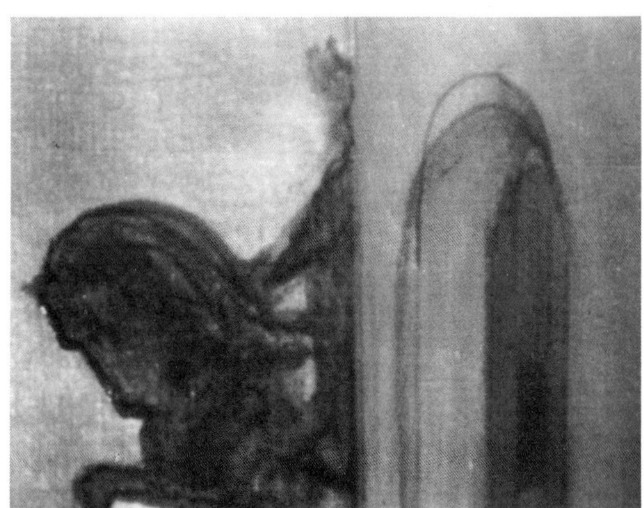

fig. e.
Infra-red reflectogram of cat. no. 30, showing *pentimenti* in head of statue and right arcade. Photograph by Studio Art System, Venice, 1983.

fig. f.
Infra-red reflectogram of cat. no. 30, showing *pentimenti* in left arcade. Photograph by Studio Art System, Venice, 1983.

fig. g.
Infra-red reflectogram of cat. no. 30, showing *pentimenti* in tower; the doorway, originally placed on the left side, is faintly visible as a *pentimento* with the naked eye. Photograph by Studio Art System, Venice, 1983.

De Chirico's original plans for the composition of *La tour rouge* involved two alternatives that differed radically from the finished work. Long recognized as a *pentimento,* the shadowy forms on the left have recently become more clearly identifiable through the use of infra-red reflectography (figs. b-g).[4]

De Chirico had first introduced in the left foreground a tall, draped, standing female figure, facing the spectator with her head slightly inclined (figs. b, d). This figure — possibly a statue but more likely an actual personnage — was drawn onto the canvas (probably in charcoal). The figure is clearly reminiscent, both in position and in style, of the foreground figure in *La mélancolie d'une belle journée*, which was painted in late 1912 or early 1913 (Private Collection, Brussels, oil on canvas, 36 1/16 x 41 1/8 in., 89 x 104.5 cm.). In the latter instance (as in other approximately contemporary works), however, the figure (whose head is also bowed) stands with its back to the spectator.

Following this — and probably as a substitute rather than an addition — de Chirico introduced a reclining statue (also apparently drawn in charcoal, but more summarily executed; see figs. b, c). In this case, too, a relationship with *La mélancolie d'une belle journée* exists. In the latter work the central focus of the composition (at the center right) is the large Ariadne statue, which rests upon a monumental pedestal.

4. Studio Art System, Venice, collaborated with the author in studying the underdrawing of *La tour rouge* and supplied the equipment from which the photographic prints were made. The equipment used by Studio Art System (Vidicon, filters, lenses, monitor) is custom made and does not, therefore, carry any of the normal manufacturer's identification marks or specifications.

Other aspects of de Chirico's underdrawing reveal less significant but nonetheless interesting *pentimenti*: the head and hat of the mounted statue (at the upper right) originally projected further into the composition, and the arcades on both sides were slightly different in their proportions (figs. e, f); the entrance to the tower was originally on the left rather than the right (fig. g); and an illegible signature (not illustrated) was placed, but then scratched out, in the lower right corner.[5]

It is difficult to place de Chirico's early ideas for this composition within the chronology of his work during late 1912 and early 1913. It seems possible, for example, that the experimental placement of the figures may have preceded *La mélancolie d'une belle journée*, but that the ultimate resolution of the composition may have followed it. Both *La tour rouge* and *La mélancolie d'une belle journée* were shown in the 1913 *Salon d'Automne*, the latter having previously been given to N. D. Calvocoressi. As Maurizio Fagiolo dell'Arco has pointed out (1981, p. 116), de Chirico's concentration during these years on the philosophical implications of individual works resulted in a deliberate and rather slow working method; the precise transitions from one painting to another are therefore difficult to trace.

In the lengthy reference to *La tour rouge* in his autobiography, *Memorie della mia Vita* (1945, p. 101), de Chirico drew attention to the equestrian statue partially visible in the right background: "*In fondo, dietro un muro appariva un monumento equestre simile a quei monumenti dedicati a militari ed eroi del Risorgimento che si vedono in tante città italiane e specialmente a Torino.*" The statue has been frequently identified as Carlo Marochetti's monument to Carlo Alberto (repr. *Fantasmi di Bronzo: Guida ai monumenti di Torino, 1808-1937*, Torino, 1978, p. 71). This statue had been erected in 1861 in the Piazza Carlo Alberto, Torino, and de Chirico would certainly have seen it during his brief 1911 stay in the city (on his way to Paris).

Although the forelegs of de Chirico's horse correspond precisely to those of Marochetti's monument, the placement of the rider and the form of his scarcely visible hat do not. It seems most likely — as Fagiolo proposed (1982, p. 33) — that de Chirico deliberately chose not to refer to a specific identifiable statue, intending rather to evoke in a more general way the imagery of the Risorgimento and a heroic historical past. Thus, while he often used images that were based on generally recognizable typologies, his aim was to create an iconography that was more universal — even symbolic — in its resonance and meaning.

Torino itself undoubtedly carried powerful associations for de Chirico, which nourished his own developing language—both verbal and pictorial—of mystery and solitude. He wrote, for example, of Nietzsche's "*strana e profonda poesia,*

5. It is unfortunately not even possible to discern how many letters were involved—e.g., whether the artist used "Georgio de Chirico," a signature he abandoned after 1912, or the "G. de Chirico" of his subsequent years.

infinitamente misteriosa e solitaria, che si basa... sulla Stimmung *del pomeriggio d'autunno, quando il tempo è chiaro e le ombre sono piú lunghe che d'estate, poiché il sole commincia ad essere piú basso... ma la città italiana per eccellenza ove appare questo straordinario fenomeno è Torino*" (*Memorie*, 1945, p. 81). But here again, the specific locus of Torino is significant only as a source of more general inspiration — as an evocative image rather than an actual, recognizable place that de Chirico wished to depict. Similarly, the general notion of the Italian "*piazza con dei portici ai lati*" (which de Chirico mentioned in his autobiographical reference to *La tour rouge*) carried for him enigmatic and melancholy associations — all essentially evocative rather than literal — with antiquity. In a manuscript of June 15, 1913 — approximately the time when *La tour rouge* was painted — he wrote:

> *le nostre menti sono perseguitate da visioni. Essi poggiano su fondamenta immortali. Sulle pubbliche piazze le ombre distendono i loro enigmi matematici. Sulle mura si ergono torri senza senso ricoperte di piccole bandiere multi-colori; dovunque è infinito, e dovunque è mistero. Una sola cosa rimane immutabile come se le sue radici fossero congelate nelle viscere dell' eternità: la nostra volontà di artisti-creatori....*

And of the arcades:

> *Non esiste niente di simile all'enigma dell'*arcata *inventata dai romani. Una strada, un arco: il sole sembra diverso quando sommerge di luce un muro romano. In tutto ciò c'è qualcosa di più misteriosamente triste che nell'architettura francese.*
>
> *E anche di meno crudele. L'arcata romana è una fatalità. La sua voce parla per mezzo di enigmi intrisi di una poesia stranamente romana; le ombre su antiche mura e una strana musica, profondamente turchina, simile in qualcosa ad un pomeriggio sulla riva del mare, come questi versi de Orazio:*
>
> *Ibis Liburnis inter navium*
> *Amica propugnacula....*

(Ms. published by Fagiolo, 1981, p. 105. The original text, in French, is in the collection of the Musée Picasso, Paris.)

Many of the qualities and associations mentioned by de Chirico were those which struck Apollinaire. In his review of the 1913 *Salon d'Automne*, he drew particular attention to the atmosphere of de Chirico's piazzas and their surrounding arcades: "*de curieux paysages plein d'intentions nouvelles, d'une forte architecture et d'une grande sensibilité*" (*L'Intransigeant*, Nov. 16, 1913).

Marianne Martin has drawn attention to the possibility of one other significant ingredient in the formation of de Chirico's iconography of this period: that of contemporary stage conventions, and in particular the work of the *La Voce* group and of the English actor-artist-scenographer Gordon Craig ("Reflections on De Chirico and *Arte Metafisica*," *Art Bulletin*, vol. 60, June 1978, pp. 342-53). As Martin pointed out, much of de Chirico's art of this metaphysical period is "inescapably scenographic" and his interest in opera and theater is extensively and fully documented. Moreover, he shared Craig's interest in a drama without plots or players, and hence without words: "inaudible dramas denying the verbalization of uncodifiable experience" (Martin, loc. cit.). In response to a critic who mentioned (as early as 1914) the scenographic qualities to be found in these paintings, de Chirico responded vigorously — in an oft-quoted statement — "*que mes peintures n'ont rien à voir avec des décors ce qui d'ailleurs est suffisamment prouvé par leurs titres*" (Letter to the Editor, *Paris-Midi*, Mar. 16, 1914, p. 2). In a restricted sense, de Chirico was, of course, correct. The works are clearly not intended to be seen as "scenery," nor do they have that effect. Nonetheless, de Chirico was fully aware of the latest developments in the scenographic field. He himself used theatrical metaphors to express his sense of aesthetic achievement. It seemed to him that Greek architecture, for example, was "guided by a philosophic aesthetic; porticoes, shadowed walks and terraces were erected like theatre seats in front of the great spectacles of nature (Homer, Aeschylus): the tragedy of serenity" (M. Carra, ed., *Metaphysical Art*, trans. of Italian texts, New York, 1971, p. 90, cited by Martin, p. 346). In addition — as Martin points out — de Chirico saw in Max Klinger's *Crucifixion* "a theatrical aspect [which] is *desired* and *conscious* because only the metaphysical side has been used... augmenting the spiritual power of the work" (ibid., p. 134). It is clearly within contexts such as this that a relationship between de Chirico's 1913 piazza compositions and the contemporary theater might be seen.

EXHIBITIONS:

Paris, Grand Palais, *Salon d'Automne*, Nov. 15, 1913-Jan. 5, 1914, no. 410 (*La tour rouge*); New York, Art of This Century, 1942-47, p. 51 (*The rose tower*, the title by which the work was known in most publications until 1982); New York, Art of This Century, *Masterworks of Early de Chirico*, Oct. 5-Nov. 6, 1943, no. 5; Venice, *P.G.*, 1948 (Biennale), no. 22; Florence, *P.G.*, 1949, no. 23, repr.; Amsterdam, *P.G.*, 1951, no. 29, repr.; Zurich, *P.G.*, 1951, no. 27; London, *P.G.*, 1964-65, no. 57, repr.; Stockholm, *P.G.*, 1966-67, no. 55, repr.; Torino, Galleria Civica d'Arte Moderna, *Le Muse Inquietanti*, Nov. 1967-Jan. 1968, no. 48, repr.; New York, *P.G.*, 1969, p. 76, repr. p. 77; Paris, *P.G.*, 1974-75, no. 57, repr. color opp. p. 27; Torino, *P.G.*, 1975-76, no. 62, repr. color pl. 36; Rome, Galleria Nazionale d'Arte Moderna, *Giorgio de Chirico*, Nov. 11, 1981-Jan. 3, 1982, vol. 1, p. 60, no. 6, repr.; New York, *P.G.*, 1982-83, no. 23, repr. color.

REFERENCES:

J. T. Soby, *The Early Chirico*, New York, 1941, p. 34, repr. n.p. (erroneously attributed p. viii to Collection Wright S. Ludington, Santa Barbara); P. Guggenheim, *Art of This Century*, 1942, p. 51, repr.; G. de Chirico, *Memorie della mia Vita*, Rome, 1945, pp. 101-3; I. Faldi, *Il Primo de Chirico*, Venice, 1949, p. 16, repr. pl. vii; J. T. Soby, *Giorgio de Chirico*, New York, 1955, pp. 44, 48, 49-50, 71, repr. p. 170; J. C. Sloane, "Giorgio de Chirico and Italy," *Art Quarterly*, vol. 21, spring 1958, p. 10, repr. fig. 6; C. Bruni (with G. de Chirico and I. Far), *Catalogo generale Giorgio de Chirico*, Venice, 1971, vol. III, repr. no. 164; I. Far de Chirico, D. Porzio, A. Jouffroy, W. Schmied, and M. Fagliolo dell'Arco, *Giorgio de Chirico: La vita e l'opere della pittura metafisica*, Milan, 1979, p. 19, repr. pp. 19 and 285; E. Coën, *La metafisica, Museo Documentario*, Ferrara, 1981, p. 167, repr. p. 228; M. Fagiolo dell'Arco, *Giorgio de Chirico, Il Tempo di Apollinaire, Paris, 1911-15*, Rome, 1981, pp. 89, 128, repr.; idem, "De Chirico in Paris, 1911-1915," in *De Chirico*, exh. cat., MoMA, New York, 1982, pp. 18, 19, 33, repr. pl. 13.

31 La nostalgie du poète. 1914.
(*The nostalgia of the poet*; *The Dream of the Poet*).

Color plate p. 243.

76.2553 PG 65

Oil and charcoal on canvas, 35 5/16 x 16 (89.7 x 40.7).

Signed l.l.: *G. de Chirico*. Not dated. Titled on stretcher, in the hand of Paul Guillaume: *La nostalgie du poète*.

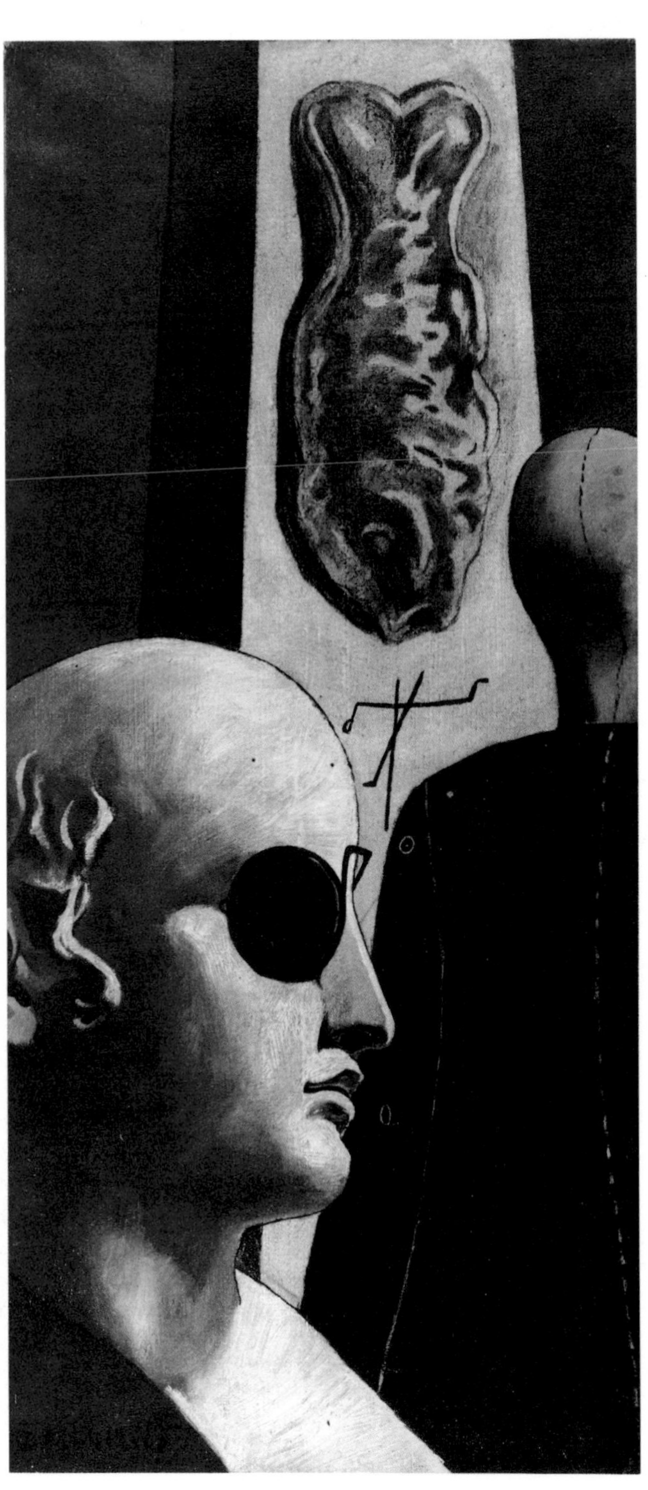

PROVENANCE:

Paul Guillaume, Paris;[1] Nancy Cunard, Vernon and Paris, probably purchased from Guillaume in the 1920s;[2] purchased from Nancy Cunard, Paris, 1940.

CONDITION:

In 1964 (Tate Report) 2 pinpoint holes in the forehead of the statue, a ca. ¼ in., 0.6 cm., puncture above the eyebrow, 2 further punctures near the bottom edge (center), and 3 other tiny losses were noted. It is not clear whether these damages were repaired at the Tate or subsequently.

Apart from inpainting in the areas noted above, the surface, including the delicate areas applied entirely in charcoal (the fish-mold and its surrounding shadow), is in excellent condition. The natural resin varnish was probably applied by the artist partly in order to protect this obviously vulnerable area. (New York, Nov. 1982.)

De Chirico's *Nostalgie du poète* must be considered in connection with the closely related *Portrait de Guillaume Apollinaire*, which was probably completed slightly earlier in the same year (fig. a). The identification of the black profile silhouette against a bright green ground in the Paris painting as Apollinaire is virtually undisputed.[3] Apparently given to the poet as a gift from the

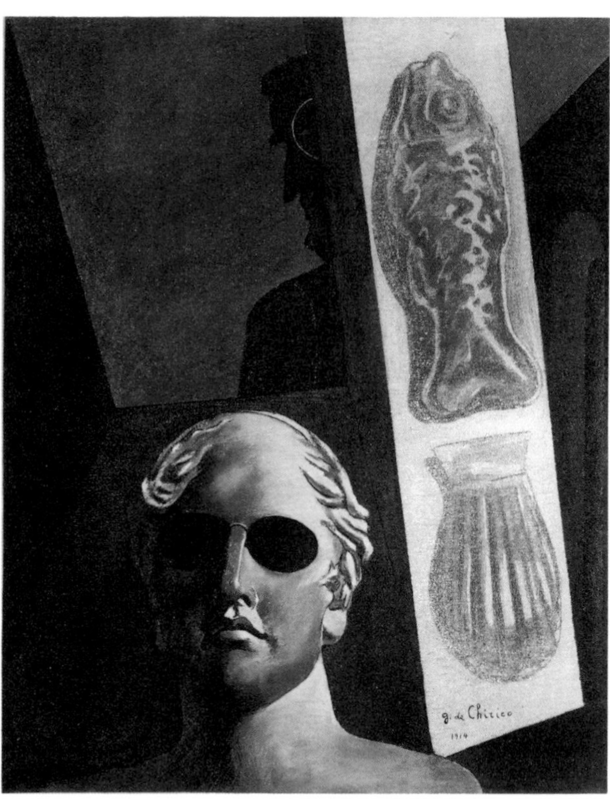

fig. a.
De Chirico, *Portrait d'Apollinaire*, 1914, oil on canvas, 32⅛ x 25⁹⁄₁₆ in., 81.5 x 65 cm., Musée National d'Art Moderne, Centre Georges Pompidou, Paris.

1. When de Chirico left Paris for Italy in 1915, he entrusted all his Paris work to his dealer, Paul Guillaume; the present picture would have been included, unless he had already given it to Guillaume earlier under the terms of his contract. (Regarding the contract, see M. Fagiolo dell' Arco, 1981, p. 47.) The handwriting on the stretcher, of the title *La nostalgie du poète*, is definitely Guillaume's, who still had the picture at the time of his 1922 exhibition.
2. On the stretcher in ink is Nancy Cunard's address: *Puits carré, Chapelle Réanville, Vernon-Eure*. She was collecting by the 1920s and may well have purchased the picture at that time. Peggy Guggenheim recalled that when she purchased the work, Nancy Cunard had owned it for a long time.
3. Only W. Bohn, 1981, p. 112, claims that the silhouette bears no resemblance to Apollinaire.

artist, the painting was not immediately delivered by the dealer, Paul Guillaume. In two letters to Guillaume on the subject, Apollinaire referred to the work as a portrait of himself. In the first of these (dated May 6, 1915), he called the work — prophetically — "*mon portrait en homme-cible*," fully ten months before he was actually wounded in the war by a bullet in the head. In the second letter (dated May 16, 1915), he was even more explicit in identifying the work as a picture of himself: "*J'aurais préféré que l'homme cible fût chez moi où ma mère aurait pu le regarder quand cela lui aurait plu, puisque, outre que c'est une œuvre singulière et profonde, c'est encore un portrait ressemblant, une ombre ou plutôt une silhouette comme on en faisait au commencement du xixe siècle.*" (Both letters published in *Les Arts à Paris*, Jan. 7, 1923.)

In de Chirico's haunting obituary of Apollinaire, published at the end of 1918 in *Ars Nova*, he refers twice to the portrait, and to the brilliant Veronese green of its background "screen:"

> *When his numismatic profile, which I stamped on the Veronese sky of one of my metaphysical paintings, appears in my memory, I think of the grave melancholy of the Roman centurion intent on crossing the pontoon bridges thrown out along the conquered lands, far from the consoling warmth of hearth and the acreage of his plowed soil....*
>
> *I see again, as one sees in dreams, a six-story apartment house, gray-coated, and at the top two rooms under the roof.*
>
> *The curtain opens and a picture of marvellous tenderness forms in silence by itself: between the tragic innocence of the varnished canvases of the Douanier-Painter and the metaphysical architectures of the undersigned, I see the glow of an oil lamp, cheap pipes, yellow nicotine stains, long bookshelves of plain lumber bulging with volumes, silent friends seated in the shadow; ... and there, as though under the luminous ray of a magic lantern, the fatal rectangle of a Veronese sky is traced on the wall, and on that sky the profile of the sad centurion curves once again.... It is Apollinaire, the returning Apollinaire; it is the poet and friend who defended me on earth and whom I will never see again*" (quoted in English in Fagiolo, 1982, pp. 24-25).

The "antique" bust in the foreground of both the *Portrait de Guillaume Apollinaire* and *La nostalgie du poète* has been variously interpreted as an idealized portrait of Apollinaire or Apollo. More frequently (and more convincingly), however, these busts, with their eyes covered, have been seen as a symbolic commentary on the aesthetic vision, on the capacity of the true artist (in any medium) to penetrate hidden meanings and to give them expression. Willard Bohn, for example (1975, p. 165), views the darkened eyes of the ancient busts as a "metaphysical emblem." On one level they are a metaphor for literal blindness; on another, for the archetypal image of the visionary poet — "evoked with the blindness of a Homer or Milton and the clairvoyance of a Blake or Rimbaud" (p. 158). The glasses are seen as concealing "a penetrating gaze to divine our innermost thoughts." The apparently blind artist is able to transcend physical limitations and see more deeply and more imaginatively than those with ordinary vision.

Similarly Alain Jouffroy (1979, pp. 97-98) reads these figures as symbols of clairvoyance. He associates their power with that of the dead, and suggests that de Chirico was expressing a yearning to exist in the worlds of both the living and the dead, allowing him thus to penetrate the hidden meanings of life.

Fagiolo (1982, p. 28) sees the dark glasses as "an expedient for visualizing the blinding quality of poetic light." Like Bohn, he attributes to the image the prophetic powers of the seer (the blind Homer) or the soothsayer (Tiresias). He draws attention to de Chirico's own emphasis upon "inner gaze" or inner vision: "*Ce que j'écoute ne vaut rien: il n'y a que ce que mes yeux voient ouverts et plus encore fermés*" ("Le mystère et la création," 1913, published by A. Breton in *Le Surréalisme et la Peinture*, Paris, 1928, p. 38).

As was first pointed out by Raffaele Carrieri (*Giorgio de Chirico*, Milan, 1942, pp. 4-5), the emergence of the mannequin figure in de Chirico's 1914 paintings may have been inspired by his brother Alberto Savinio's play *Les chants de la mi-mort*, published in Apollinaire's magazine *Les soirées de Paris*, July-August 1914. The protagonist of Savinio's play is a musician without voice, eyes, or face, and Savinio himself (in conversation with James Thrall Soby, Milan, 1948) apparently confirmed Carrieri's hypothesis (Soby, 1955, pp. 97-98).

Bohn (1975, pp. 158-59) concurs with Carrieri's general hypothesis, but pursues the source one step beyond Savinio to Apollinaire's pantomime *Le musicien de Saint-Merry* of 1913 (published February 1914). Here the chief protagonist — again with no eyes, ears, or nose, and dark "with a strawberry tint to his cheeks" — is conceived as the persona of Apollinaire himself. Moreover, Bohn suggests that the specific form of de Chirico's early mannequins (the tailor's "dummy" with dotted-line seams) may well have sprung directly from a sketch by Savinio, intended to depict (as an illustration for his own play) the character in Apollinaire's poem. The image of the mannequin is thus seen as deriving originally from Apollinaire, but also as constituting an actual allusion or reference to him.

In Fagiolo's account of *La nostalgie du poète*, the mannequin is viewed as a form which, in its own context, parallels and "replaces" the silhouette of the Paris *Portrait*. He attributes no specific symbolic meaning to the mannequin in this painting, but alludes to the significance that the image will acquire in later works.[4]

4. Soby and Bohn both point out that the mannequin actually appears for the very first time in *I'll be There... The Glass Dog*, also of 1914, but probably a slightly earlier work. For an illuminating brief discussion of the mannequin as Ka (the soul as double), the possible reading of the black silhouette as an evocation of Fantômas, and the relationship of this image to the contemporary shadow theater, see M. Martin, 1982, pp. 88-92. Marianne Martin also suggests that although Apollinaire's protagonist in "Le Musicien de Saint-Merry" probably lay behind de Chirico's mannequins there were a number of other sources incorporated at the same time: "the sculpture of Boccioni, Brancusi, knights in armor, Marinetti's hero Mafarka, Diaghilev's dancers, dressmakers' dummies, and possibly Kandinsky's mute figures."

Fagiolo alone, however, proposes a complex iconographic scheme for the *Portrait de Guillaume Apollinaire*, and he suggests that the proposed interpretation also applies in most of its details to *La nostalgie du poète*. According to his analysis — which is in some respects highly speculative, though always suggestive — the busts do not represent purely symbolic figures (such as "the clairvoyant artist"), nor are they specific representations of the Greek god Apollo. Rather, they are images of Orpheus.[5] The fish molds in the two paintings allude to the actual fish that were transformed into musicians by Orpheus, in Apollinaire's poem *Le Bestiaire ou Le Cortège d'Orphée*. A woodcut by Raoul Dufy, made specifically for the 1911 Apollinaire publication, does indeed show Orpheus surrounded by fish, which are identified in the poem with the figure of Christ. The hieroglyphic sign in *La nostalgie* is interpreted as a cryptic allusion to the theological Greek *ichthys*, while the "shell" in the *Portrait de Guillaume Apollinaire* is viewed as a reference to Orpheus's lyre (which "derives precisely from the shell").

Fagiolo sees Orpheus/Apollinaire embodying the reign of a new religion — a metaphor for the new art movement Orphism, of which Apollinaire was the champion. Finally, and more universally, Fagiolo reads the entire image — a triumph of Orpheus — as the metaphorical triumph of painting itself.

EXHIBITIONS:

Geneva, *Exposition Internationale d'Art Moderne*, Dec. 26, 1920-Jan. 25, 1921, no. 41 (*La nostalgie du poète*); Paris, Galerie Paul Guillaume, *de Chirico*, Mar. 21-Apr. 1, 1922, no. 37 (*La nostalgie du poète*); Paris, Galerie Surréaliste, *Œuvres Anciennes de Georges de Chirico*, Feb. 15-Mar. 1, 1928, no. 12, repr. (*La nostalgie du poète*); New York, Art of This Century, 1942-47, p. 51 (*The Dream of the Poet*, 1915);[6] New York, Art of This Century, *Masterworks of Early de Chirico*, Oct. 5-Nov. 6, 1943, no. 15; Venice, *P.G.*, 1948 (Biennale), no. 23; Florence, *P.G.*, 1949, no. 24, repr.; Amsterdam, *P.G.*, 1951, no. 30; Zurich, *P.G.*, 1951, no. 28; London, *P.G.*, 1964-65, no. 58, repr. (dated 1914); Stockholm, *P.G.*, 1966-67, no. 56, repr.; Torino, Galleria Civica d'Arte Moderna, *Le Muse Inquietanti*, Nov. 1967-Jan. 1968, no. 50; New York, *P.G.*, 1969, p. 78, repr. color; Paris, *P.G.*, 1974-75, no. 58, repr.; Torino, *P.G.*, 1975-76, no. 63, repr. pl. 35; Rome, *Guggenheim: Venezia-New York*, 1982, no. 28, repr. color; New York, MoMA, *Giorgio de Chirico*, Apr. 3-June 29, 1982, repr. color pl. 40.

REFERENCES:

R. Queneau, "À propos de l'Exposition de Chirico à la Galerie Surréaliste, 15 fevrier-1 mars, 1928," *La Révolution Surréaliste*, no. 11, Mar. 15, 1928, p. 42 (*La nostalgie du poète*);[7] P. Gug-

5. Fagiolo presents an intricate argument regarding the origin of the Orpheus image, which was created—he argues—from that of the Venus de Milo, since no ancient prototype for the Orpheus figure exists.
6. This is the earliest appearance of the title *The Dream of the Poet*, which subsequently persisted in the literature. Whether a free translation by Peggy Guggenheim or by one of her circle of *La nostalgie du poète*, it carries a meaning that is distinctly different from the original. The 1915 date ascribed to the work here was published in all succeeding *P.G.* publications until Alley, 1964.
7. Queneau's comment about the work is characteristically Surrealist: "*Du haut d'une tour, un parachutiste se lance, et grâce à certains effets de perspective, on voit la tour grandir à mesure que l'homme descend; il ne touchera plus terre.*"

genheim, *Art of This Century*, 1942, p. 51, repr. p. 53 ("*The Dream of the Poet*, 1915"); R. Carrieri, *Iconografia Italiana di Apollinaire*, Milan, 1942, n.p., repr. pl. 13; A. Breton, "Genèse et perspective artistiques du surréalisme," *Labyrinthe*, no. 5, Feb. 15, 1945, repr. p. 11 ("*Le songe du poète*, 1915"); R. Gaffé, *Giorgio de Chirico le Voyant...*, Brussels, 1946, repr. no. 9 ("*La nostalgie du poète*, 1914"); I. Faldi, *Il Primo de Chirico*, Venice, 1949 ("*Ritratto di un poeta*, 1913"); J. T. Soby, *Giorgio de Chirico*, New York, 1955, pp. 80, 97, 98, 101-2, repr. p. 200 (dated 1914); J. C. Sloane, "Giorgio de Chirico and Italy," *The Art Quarterly*, vol. 21, no. 1, spring 1958, pp. 15-16; C. Bruni (with G. de Chirico and I. Far), *Catalogo generale Giorgio de Chirico*, Venice, 1971, vol. 3, no. 167, repr.; W. Bohn, "Apollinaire and de Chirico: The Making of Mannequins," *Comparative Literature*, vol. 25, no. 2, spring 1975, p. 161; I. Far, de Chirico, D. Porzio, A. Jouffroy, W. Schmied, and M. Fagiolo dell'Arco, *Giorgio de Chirico: La vita e l'opere della pittura metafisica*, Milan, 1979, pp. 97-98, repr. pp. 20, 286; E. Coën, *La Metafisica, Museo Documentario*, Ferrara, 1981, no. 52, repr. p. 249 (*La nostalgia del poeta*); M. Fagiolo dell'Arco, *Giorgio de Chirico, Il Tempo di Apollinaire, Paris 1911-1915*, Rome, 1981, pp. 13, 134, repr.; A.-M. del Monte, *Giorgio de Chirico*, exh. cat., Galleria Nazionale d'Arte Moderna, Rome, 1981, vol. 1, p. 66, repr.; W. Bohn, "Metaphysics and Meaning: Apollinaire's Criticism of Giorgio de Chirico," *Arts Magazine*, vol. 55, Mar. 1981, p. 112, repr.; M. Fagiolo dell'Arco, "De Chirico in Paris, 1911-1915," in *De Chirico*, exh. cat., MoMA, New York, 1982, p. 28, repr. color pl. 40; M. Martin, "On De Chirico's Theater," ibid., p. 98.

---

32 Le doux après-midi. Before July 1916.
(*The gentle afternoon*; *Bel après midi*; *Pomeriggio soave*; *Il Pomeriggio gentile*).

Color plate p. 244.

76.2553 PG 66

Oil on canvas, 25 11/16 x 22 15/16 (65.3 x 58.3).

Signed and dated l.r.: *G. de Chirico 1916*.

PROVENANCE:

Paul Guillaume, Paris, 1916-1934;[1] Madame Paul Guillaume, 1934-37; purchased from Madame Guillaume, Paris, by Pierre Matisse, summer 1937; purchased from Pierre Matisse, New York, November 15, 1941.

CONDITION:

By 1964 (Tate Report) the painting had been lined, apparently in order to repair a sizable damage near the center of the canvas (covering half of the upper left biscuit, part of the lower left one, and the area between). Extensive retouching in that area was noted, as well as smaller areas of loss and inpainting elsewhere. Cleavage and blistering paint along a vertical line in the upper left quadrant (the white form) were consolidated with wax resin and inpainted. There was some doubt about the presence of varnish.

In 1972 in Venice the painting suffered severe water damage during a burglary (fig. a). It was extensively restored on all four sides and along the left third of the composition. Retouching of the area above the candycane probably dates from prior to 1964.

In 1982 (Venice) some minimal inpainting of tiny losses was carried out. In 1983 (Venice) the picture was cleaned again. Areas of discolored earlier retouching were removed; gesso buildup of the surface was necessary in some areas of extensive loss (the green at upper edge). Inpainting with Windsor and Newton watercolor was followed by a light coat of Paraloid B-72.

The surface has been extensively abraded and retouched; the condition is stable. (Venice, 1983.)

1. Though de Chirico returned to Italy in the summer of 1915, he continued to send paintings to his dealer, Paul Guillaume, in Paris. See above, cat. no. 31, PROVENANCE, and fn. 1.

fig. a.
Cat. no. 32 in 1972 before restoration.

De Chirico joined the Italian army's Twenty-seventh Infantry regiment in 1915 and was posted to Ferrara in June; he remained there until late in 1918 when he moved to Rome.

In his 1945 autobiography he recorded something of his response to the beauties of Ferrara. In particular, he recalled the aspects of the city that provided direct inspiration for the metaphysical qualities characteristic of his work during that period: "*L'aspetto di Ferrara, una delle città piú belle d'Italia, me aveva colpito; ma quello che mi colpí soprattutto e m'ispirò nel lato metafisico nel quale lavoravo allora, erano certi aspetti d'interni ferraresi, certe vetrine, certe botteghe, certe abitazioni, certi quartieri, come l'antico ghetto ove si trovavano dei dolci e dei biscotti dalle forme oltremodo metafisiche e strane*" (G. de Chirico, *Memorie della mia Vita*, Rome, 1945, pp. 122-23).

The reference to the old ghetto, with its "metaphysical" cakes and biscuits, suggests the extent of de Chirico's fascination with the Jewish religion — a religion that was essentially new to him. His brother, Alberto Savinio (who was a fellow-soldier with him in Ferrara), articulated in even greater detail the degree to which these pastries were regarded by the brothers as "mysterious" — evocative of a forbidden or secret universe, of rites of immortality, even of connections with the powers of darkness. These allusions, moreover, became associated in the mind of Savinio (and presumably of de Chirico) with the "simplicity and passionate dryness of the Semitic character":

> *Nelle vetrine dei pasticcieri s'ergono in immense piramidi i dolci neri bizzarrissimi che mai nessun vivente mangiò né mangerà.*
>
> *Tagliati, essi presentano la complicata anatomia mineralogica delle loro interiora. Sono spezzati di schisti....*
>
> *Quei dolci metallici, compatti piú dei libri di Balzac, non sono destinati ai mortali. Accompagnano le libazioni offerte alle divinità infernali della regione. Il rito mortuario vuole che, morendo un ferrarese, vengano posti a fianco del cadavere un* pan pepato *e un* pan di cedro, *che faciliteran l'ingresso del morto nei regni sotterranei. Colui che morde in quei dolci fatalissimi, assapora l'eternità. Han riscontro, quei* pan massí, *con la semplicità e l'aridezza del carattere semitico* (*Hermaphrodito*, 1918, Einaudi edition, Torino, 1974, pp. 50-51).

As Maurizio Fagiolo dell'Arco has pointed out, de Chirico's contact with the Jewish quarter in Ferrara made him aware for the first time of the rich religious history and symbolism of Judaism. The contact also created in de Chirico a sense of the sacrificial meaning and value of ordinary objects. This last point was to some extent reinforced by Filippo de Pisis in his 1918 article on de Chirico and Carlo Carrà. De Pisis argued for an understanding and acceptance of the contemporary artist's striving to combine fantasy and careful observation in new ways and to evoke the mystery contained in even the most mundane and insignificant objects, whose very "insignificance" may appeal to his particular sensibility: "*La sua fantasia ... non segue più determinati indirizzi; egli ha bisogno di esternare verginalmente la sua anima d'uomo moderno estremamente completa e fantasmagorica, ma pure ingenua e impressionabilissima. Sente il bisogno di fissare alcuni lucidi momenti di doloroso sconforto e di visione diretta del mistero, racchiuso negli oggetti più comuni ed insulsi; anche la sconclusionatezza di essi lo attira*" (*Gazzetta Ferrarese*, Feb. 12, 1918, reprinted in *La pittura metafisica*, exh. cat., Palazzo Grassi, Venice, 1979, pp. 125-26).

De Chirico himself also drew attention to the powerful emotive and lyrical effects that could be achieved through a lucid yet also evocative depiction of commonplace objects: "*La furberia più terribile che ritorna di là dagli orizzonti inesplorati per fissare nella metafisica esterna, nella terribile solitudine d'un inspiegabile lirismo: un biscotto, l'angolo formato da due pareti, un disegno evocante un chè della natura del mondo scimunito e insensato che ci accompagna in questa vita tenebrosa. L'evocazione spettrale di quegli oggetti che l'imbecillità universale rilega tra le inutilità*" (Feb. 15, 1919, *Noi metafisici*, reprinted in *La pittura metafisica*, 1979, p. 146).

Le doux après-midi clearly derives from the context of de Chirico's Ferrarese sojourn — a sojourn that apparently awakened in him a new responsiveness to the mystery latent in ordinary objects. The precise illusionistic depiction of the biscuits in works such as this contrasts with the picture's intended spatial and contextual ambiguities — the lack of a defined "setting" and absence of chiaroscuro definition. Moreover, de Chirico introduced further levels of incongruity, and hence of potential meaning: the literal objects from the real world that are physically present — the sweets, biscuits, cakes of Ferrara — are painted not only illusionistically with cast shadows but with a physically expressive *facture*. Because of the very thickness of the pigment, these objects seem to be detached from the surface. Yet they are framed (as if in a picture within a picture): their relationship to "reality" is thus explicitly undermined, the more so since it is within *this* picture that de Chirico placed his signature.

Meanwhile the "architectural" structures from another world are thinly painted, perhaps to suggest that they are not directly present but exist as a metaphysical extension. In effect, they inhabit a realm with its own nonrational laws of perspective and light — a realm that carries a disconcerting sense of mystery.

EXHIBITIONS:

Paris, Salon d'Antin [Galerie Barbazanges], *L'Art Moderne en France*, July 1916 ("*Le Doux Après midi [nature morte, œuvre d'Italie]*");[2] Paris, Galerie Paul Guillaume, *G. de Chirico*, Mar. 21-Apr. 1, 1922, no. 26; Paris, Galerie Paul Guillaume, *Chirico*, June 4-12, 1926, no. 7; New

2. Information supplied by M. Fagiolo dell 'Arco, correspondence with the author, June 1984. Although no printed catalogue of this exhibition has come to light, a complete typed catalogue has been located in the Severini Archive. In Severini's hand at the top of the first page is written: "*Organisé p. Salmon,*" a fact that corresponds with the description of this exhibition in Severini's own memoirs: "*Dopo l'esposizione di madame Bongard, André Salmon ne organizzò un'altra, molto piú importante in una galleria detta galleria Barbazange, nell'avenue d'Antin 26. Anzi, si chiamava a quel momento: Salon d'Antin.... A questa esposizione presero*

York, Pierre Matisse Gallery, *Giorgio de Chirico*, Nov. 19-Dec. 21, 1935, no. 16; New York, Pierre Matisse Gallery, *Early Paintings by French Moderns*, Jan. 3-31, 1939, no. 4 (dated "about 1917"); New York, Pierre Matisse Gallery, *Giorgio de Chirico*, Oct. 22-Nov. 23, 1940, no. 12; New York, Art of This Century, 1942-47, p. 51; New York, Art of This Century, *Masterworks of Early De Chirico*, Oct. 5-Nov. 6, 1943, no. 16; Venice, *P.G.*, 1948 (Biennale), no. 24; Florence, *P.G.*, 1949, no. 25; Amsterdam, *P.G.*, 1951, no. 31; Zurich, *P.G.*, 1951, no. 29; London, *P.G.*, 1964-65, no. 59; Stockholm, *P.G.*, 1966-67, no. 57; Torino, Galleria Civica d'Arte Moderna, *Le Muse Inquietanti*, Nov. 1967-Jan. 1968, no. 55, repr.; New York, *P.G.*, 1969, p. 79, repr.; Paris, *P.G.*, 1974-75, no. 59, repr.; Torino, *P.G.*, 1975-76, no. 64; Rome, Galleria Nazionale d'Arte Moderna, *Giorgio de Chirico*, Nov. 11, 1981-Jan. 3, 1982, vol. 1, no. 13, repr.; New York, *P.G.*, 1982-83, no. 24, repr.

REFERENCES:

J. T. Soby, *The Early Chirico*,New York, 1941, pp. 25, 68, repr. pl. 58; P. Guggenheim, *Art of This Century*, New York, 1942, p. 51; I Faldi, *Il Primo de Chirico*, Venice, 1949, pp. 20-21, repr. pl. 20; J. T. Soby, *Giorgio de Chirico*, New York, 1955, p. 114, repr. p. 229; G. Marchiori, *Arte e Artisti d'avanguardia in Italia*, Milan, 1960, pp. 94-95; I. Far, *Giorgio de Chirico*, Milan, 1968, repr. color pl. 4; C. Bruni (with G. de Chirico and I. Far), *Catalogo Generale Giorgio de Chirico*, Venice, 1971, vol. III, repr. no. 175; I. Far, D. Porzio, A. Jouffroy, W. Schmied, and M. Fagiolo dell'Arco, *Giorgio de Chirico: La vita e l'opere della pittura metafisica*, Milan, 1979, repr. p. 268; E. Coën, *La Metafisica, Museo Documentario*, Ferrara, 1981, no. 91, repr.

(2. cont.)
parte veramente quasi tutti i pittori d'avanguardia di un certo valore. Picasso vi mandò il suo grande quadro Les Demoiselles d'Avignon..." (G. Severini, *Tutta la vita di un pittore, Roma —Parigi*, 1946, pp. 249-50).

Severini's carefully typed catalogue of 120 works (complete with artists' full names and nationalities) provides important new information of various kinds. For example, it records the earliest public exhibition of *Les Demoiselles d'Avignon* (21 years before its otherwise first recorded appearance at the Petit Palais in June of 1937). The catalogue also offers clear evidence that Paul Guillaume exhibited de Chirico's paintings immediately after he received them. Specific opening and closing dates for the exhibition are not recorded; however, the announcement at the bottom of the typed list of 2 musical and 2 literary gatherings taking place during July suggests that the exhibition was open during that month. *Le doux après-midi* must, therefore, have been completed and sent to Paris by July 1916.

Pietro Consagra

Born October 1920, Mazara del Vallo, Sicily.
Lives in Rome.

33

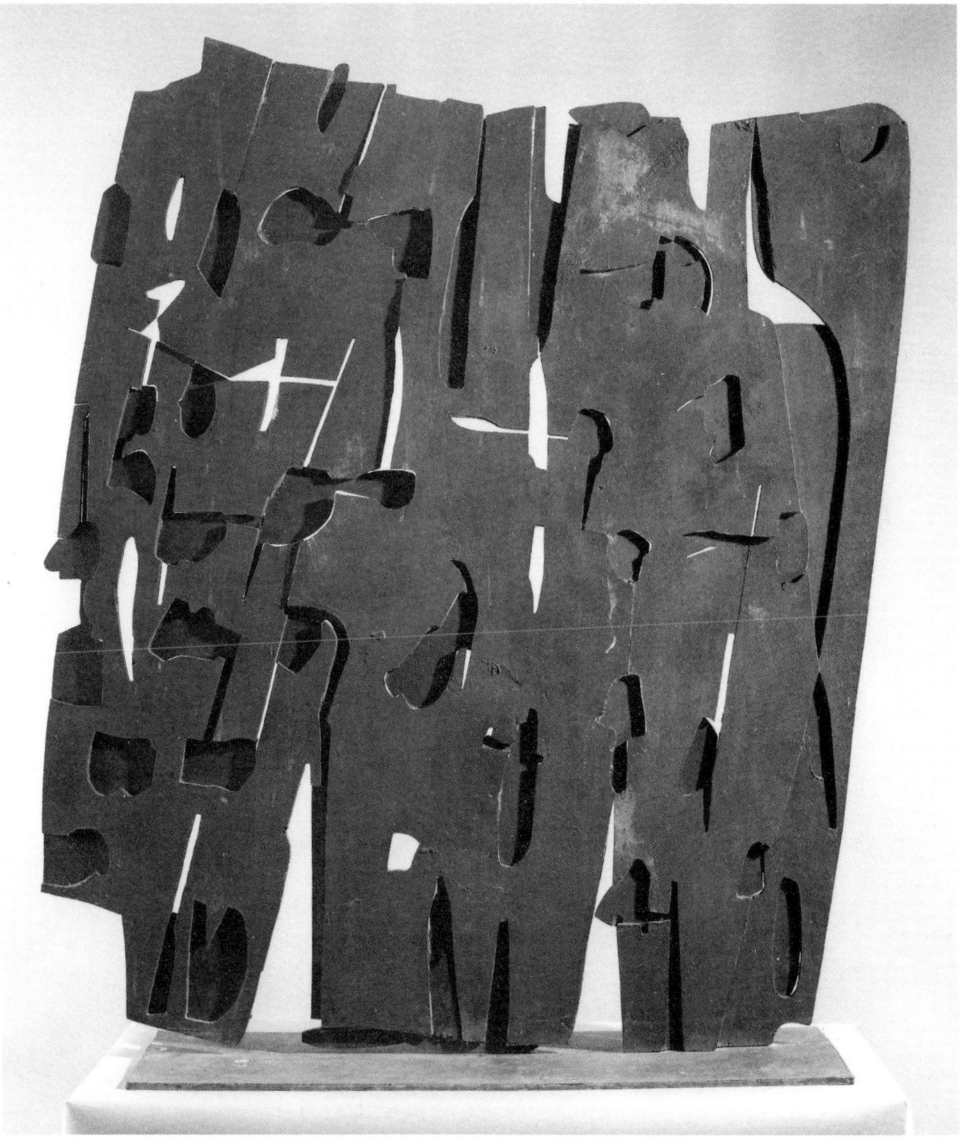

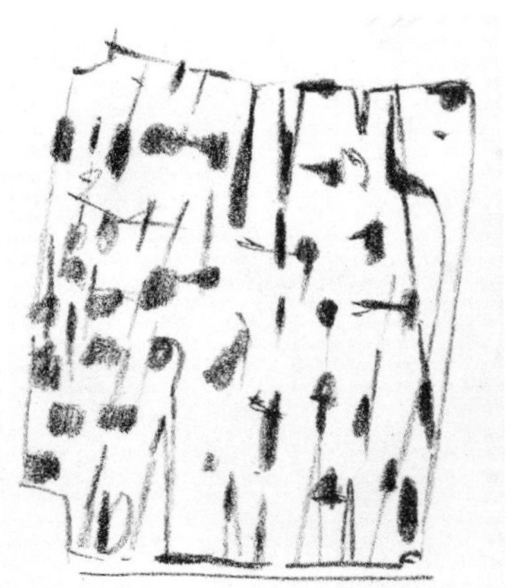

fig. a.
Consagra, preparatory drawing for cat. no. 33, 1958, pencil on paper, $5\frac{1}{8} \times 3\frac{9}{16}$ in., 13×9 cm., Collection the artist, Rome.

33 Colloquio Mitico. 1959.
(Mythical Conversation).

76.2553 PG 204a

Bronze (sandcast and soldered), $33\frac{11}{16}$ x 28 (85.5 x 71).

Edition of two.

Foundry: Olmeda, Rome.

Signed, dated, and numbered: *Consagra 59* 2 / 2.

PROVENANCE:

Purchased from the artist, Rome, 1973.

CONDITION:

Through the effects of the atmosphere, streaks of green corrosion are visible, especially on the back and the base. The artist's intended difference in patina between the foreground (light) and background (dark) has been lost in the general darkening of the entire piece. The following conservation steps are envisaged: repatination by the artist himself, to retrieve the 2 contrasting colors of the bronze; thorough cleaning; anticorrosive treatment, and the application of a protective coating. (Venice, Nov. 1982.)

Reverse side of cat. no. 33.

Before casting the two bronzes of the present edition, Consagra made three numbered bronze casts the size of the original maquette (14 9/16 x 12 3/8 in., 37 x 31.5 cm.). One cast of a larger size followed (72 13/16 x 61 in., 185 x 155 cm.). The entire group was completed during the year 1959.[1]

The sculptor stressed (in conversation with the author, November 1982) that in each case the light patina of the foreground plane and the dark of the background plane are critical elements in the composition. In insisting upon this fact, Consagra was elaborating on one aspect of his continued preoccupation with the concept of frontality, a notion that has been at the center of all of his mature work: "*l'aspetto dominante del mio lavoro, che coincide da un lato con la mia particolare sensibilità di scultore e dall'altro con una scelta diciamo cosciente, ideologica delle possibilità della scultura, è la frontalità. Il costruttivismo avrebbe potuto portarmi a fare delle sculture tridimensionali,... invece io ho scartato questa tridimensionalità dalla scultura perché la frontalità, e quindi il carattere bidimensionale, mi è subito apparso come il piú ricco di aperture. La frontalità è nata dentro di me come alternativa al totem, cioè alla scultura che doveva sorgere al centro di uno spazio ideale*" (Interview with Carla Lonzi, in *Pietro Consagra*, exh. cat., Galleria del'Ariete, Milan, June 1967).

The moderate, human scale of the 1950s *Colloqui* (literally, "Conversations") was intended to force a direct confrontation or dialogue with the spectator but without the sculpture assuming a monolithic or overpowering role. The subtle interplay of surface texture, articulation, and color constitute essential ingredients in the artist's conception of this dialogue.

EXHIBITIONS:

Palermo, Palazzo dei Normanni, *Mostra di Pietro Consagra, Sculture*, Feb. 24-Apr. 24, 1973, no. 30, repr.; Paris, *P.G.*, 1974-75, no. 170 (as *Circonférence mystique*); Torino, *P.G.*, 1975-76, no. 192.

1. The large cast has not yet been mounted and remains in the artist's collection.

Guillaume Corneille

Born July 1922, Liège, Belgium.
Lives in Paris.

34 La grande symphonie solaire. 1964.
(*The great solar symphony*).

76.2553 PG 176

Oil on canvas, 51 1/16 x 63 13/16 (129.6 x 162).

Signed and dated u.r.: *Corneille* '64; on reverse: "*la grande symphonie / solaire*" / *Corneille* '64.

PROVENANCE:
Purchased form the artist, August 1964.

CONDITION:
The work has received no treatment. The condition is stable. (Venice, Nov. 1982.)

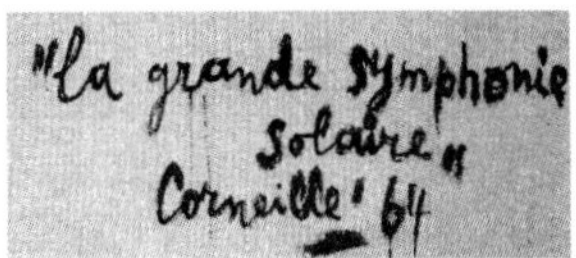

Comme convenu je vous fait parvenir la photo couleur d'une de mes toiles récente.
C'est une œuvre fortement rythmée et aussi très forte en couleurs. Je crois que c'est une toile très représentative de mon art.

haut
Sens de la toile.
bas
1m 30 hauteur
1m 60 largeur
LA GRANDE SYMPHONIE SOLAIRE

Ecrivez-moi ce que vous en pensez. Elle restera dans mon atelier jusqu'à ce que j'aie reçu de vous une réponse.

fig. a.
Excerpt from Corneille's letter to Peggy Guggenheim, July 1964.

Peggy Guggenheim purchased the picture on the basis of a color photograph sent to her by Corneille from Paris in July 1964.[1] The photo was accompanied by a small sketch (fig. a) in which he indicated top and bottom, size, and the major elements in the composition, describing it thus: "*Une œuvre fortement rhythmée et aussi très forte en couleurs. Je crois que c'est une toile très représentative de mon art.*"

The works produced by Corneille during his five successive summers in Cadaquès (1962-66) are consistently characterized by luxuriant color. Though clearly nonrepresentational, they nonetheless convey—either through their imagery or their titles — recurring references to cosmic themes. It is in this sense, as well as from a purely formal point of view, that the artist considered the work representative.

EXHIBITIONS:
London, *P.G.*, 1964-65, no. 147; Torino, *P.G.*, 1975-76, no. 165.

1. This was one of 2 instances documented to date when Peggy Guggenheim bought a work sight unseen (see cat. no. 24, PROVENANCE).

Joseph Cornell

Born December 1903, Nyack, New York.
Died December 1972, Flushing, New York.

35 Fortune Telling Parrot. Ca. 1937-38.[1]
(Parrot Music Box).

Color plate p. 500.

76.2553 PG 126

Box construction. Height: 16 1/16 (40.8); width: 8 3/4 (22.2); depth: 6 11/16 (17).

Not signed or dated.

PROVENANCE:

Purchased from the artist, New York, March 1942.[1]

CONDITION:

In 1976 (Venice) the following conservation measures were carried out: the outside of the box was waxed and cleaned; the glass and the blue chenille rope edging of the foreground "wall" were cleaned. Two of the 4 circular mirrors (upper left and lower right), which had become loose, were reattached. Paper collage elements on the cylinder that had become loose or detached were reattached (glue residue indicating precise positions of detached elements).

The condition of all elements is stable. (Venice, Nov. 1982.)

DESCRIPTION:

Cabinet construction of dark polished wood. Two brass handles, 1 on each side of exterior. The 1 in., 2.5 cm., section at front of top edge is hinged for opening, to remove glass in slotted position. Interior of glass front painted with blue edge. Hole at top for penetration of wood handle (now lost, replaced by pencil) to turn cylinder; hole on lower right side with crank to turn now nonfunctioning music box, hidden at lower right. The cylinder is attached by a thin blue metal rod to the music box, and is intended to revolve, as in a hurdy-gurdy, while the music plays. Behind the glass facing, filling approximately the lower third of the field, is a cardboard panel covered with pale blue paper; curved top edged with blue chenille rope.

Four circular apertures in panel have mirrors glued to them from reverse; 7 varnished leaves glued to face of panel. Far left, blue paper cutout "Little Bear" (Ursa Minor) with gold stars glued to face of panel. Gray stuffed parrot with red tail, white around eye, white above feet, black beak, yellow eye, perched on curved wood branch, which is cantilevered from rear wall and attached to floor of box; white string loop over beak secured to hook screwed into interior top of box. Bright blue string is also attached to bird's upper thigh, secured to nail on rear wall.

Revolving "fortune-telling" cylinder; collage decoration of cylinder's surface includes paper cutouts of: Algerian (?) fortune-teller gypsy; stars; checkerboard patterns; figure of man; letters; $; polka dots; King of Hearts; Jack of Clubs; numbers 1-9, plus 0; rooster (black/white); roosters' feathers (ditto); male dancer (Nijinsky ?); 2 hands playing cat's cradle; palm of hand; reptiles; butterfly (colored); lizard (black/white); cheetah's or cat's head (black/white); printed word: *SEE*; 3 sepia photos of young girls, possibly the same 1 at 3 different ages (ca. 3 years old, ca. 15 years old, ca. 20 years old).

Rear left and right interior walls of box lined with pale blue paper. Right interior wall: 5 circular apertures with mirrors glued to them from reverse, alternating with varnished leaves. Interior top and left edges: 3 mirror-backed circular apertures, alternating with varnished leaves. Floor of box has 2 pieces of mirror, covering two-thirds of area.

1. In a letter of March 12, 1942, to Peggy Guggenheim, then the wife of Max Ernst, Cornell wrote: "Dear Mrs. Ernst, The check for the thimbles is acceptable, but no more so than your kind and sincere appreciation of the objects. I am glad that you like them well enough to keep a couple of them in your home.... I am sorry that I can only remember the approximate dates you ask as follows: Fortune telling Parrot, ca. 1937-38..." (AAA, Peggy Guggenheim Papers, reel ITVE 1, frame 149).

Cornell's designation of the box as "Fortune Telling Parrot" provides the only known documentation for this title; it is possible that he was using the phrase merely descriptively and that the alternative *Parrot Music Box* (by which the box has hitherto been known) was acceptable to him. In a diary entry for October 31, 1952, Cornell referred to 2 additional boxes on this theme: "This morning had put large Fortune Telling Parrot on celler [sic] table for dismantling —the lattice of one has been already—the music box parrot still wrapped up in garage" (AAA,

Cornell's use of parrots, cockatoos, and other exotic birds has been linked to a romantic nostalgia for travel and to the sailor's literal *souvenirs de voyage* upon return from distant and exotic places.

Cornell himself, in a diary note of February 28, 1960, indicated a possible source for the parrot boxes in a statement entitled "Parrots Pasta and Pergolesi," writing that "magic windows of yesterday ... pet shop windows splashed with white and tropical plumage the kind of revelation symptomatic of city wanderings in another era.... The 'context' 'atmosphere' or whatever the mot juste in which these feathered friends came into being is a warm and rich one ... scintillating songs of Rossini and Bellini and the whole golden age of the bel canto ... indelible childhood memory of an old German woman a neighbor's pet parrot may have added to the obsession of these ... feathered friends" (AAA, Joseph Cornell Papers, reel 1060, cited by Ades, loc. cit.). The multiple associations here of the bel canto singer Giuditta Negri Pasta (1798-1865), the composer Giovanni Battista Pergolesi (1710-1736), and Cornell's own early childhood recollection of a neighbor's exotic pet are characteristic of his use of multiple sources and of his tendency to create a wide range of allusions. Moreover, the possible biographical implications of the *Fortune Telling Parrot* are underscored by Cornell's own passing comment to Nicolas Calas in 1966 that this was the most "autobiographical" of all his boxes (letter from Calas to Cornell, January 3, 1966, AAA, Joseph Cornell Papers, reel 1056). Years later (in conversation with the author, April 1983), Calas recalled that Cornell had not elaborated upon this elliptical comment.

There are at least eighteen boxes in which parrots, parakeets, or cockatoos appear. Peggy Guggenheim's piece was the earliest in the series; the others all date from the 1940s and 1950s. *Fortune Telling Parrot* is unique in its juxtaposition of parrot and fortune-telling wheel, as well as in the hurdy-gurdy aspect of the musical device.

EXHIBITIONS:

New York, Art of This Century, *Objects by Joseph Cornell; Marcel Duchamp: Box Valise; Laurence Vail: Bottles*, Dec. 1942 (no cat.);[2] Amsterdam, *P.G.*, 1951, no. 32.

REFERENCES:

Calas, 1966, pp. 122-23, repr. p. 156 ("*Parrot Music Box*, 1945"); D. Waldman, *Joseph Cornell*, New York, 1977, p. 21, repr. pl. 70 (dated 1945); D. Ades, "The Transcendental Surrealism of Joseph Cornell," in K. McShine, ed., *Joseph Cornell*, exh. cat., MoMA, New York, 1980, p. 37, repr. pl. 131 (dated ca. 1945).

(1. cont.)
Joseph Cornell Papers, reel 1059, frame 603). It has not been possible to identify these 2 later works, both of which may have been dismantled and never reassembled. Their possible iconographical relationship to Peggy Guggenheim's box cannot, therefore, be established. However, the presence in Cornell's note of both designations suggests that he attached specific significance to each and lends support to the notion that "Fortune Telling Parrot" was his intended title for the Peggy Guggenheim box.

2. Since Peggy Guggenheim purchased the box in March 1942 she would certainly have included it in the exhibition.

36 Swiss Shoot-the-Chutes. 1941.
(*Hôtel de l'Ange*).

76.2553 PG 127

Box construction. Height: 21 3/16 (53.8); width: 13 13/16 (35.2); depth: 4 1/8 (10.5).

Signed, titled, and dated on reverse (typed, except signature in ink): *Swiss Shoot-the-Chutes / Object 1941 / Joseph Cornell / Joseph Cornell.*

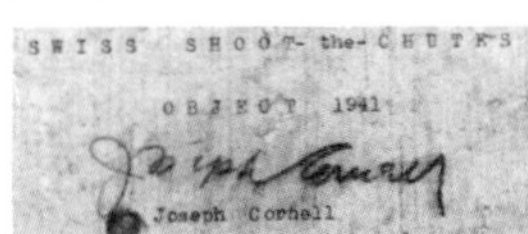

PROVENANCE:

Purchased from the artist, New York, ca. 1943.[1]

CONDITION:

In 1976 (Venice) the following conservation measures were carried out: the glass facing was removed and cleaned. The map had been lifting off its cardboard support in several places and was readhered with cabinetmaker's glue. Several of the collage elements within the apertures were also consolidated with glue. The box was nailed down top and bottom. The ball, which had been lost, was replaced with a grayish-yellow wood ball.

The cream-colored paint on the wood box is soiled and abraded, with some losses of both wood and paint. Three of the upholstery nails that frame the front of the box are missing. The paper elements are in stable condition. (Venice, Nov. 1982.)

DESCRIPTION:

Painted wood box construction with top edge hinged at rear to open (for removal of glass, etc.). Two hinged openings at right edge, upper with wood knob, lower with metal latch (now fastened shut with 2 wire threads, not by artist). Front edge of box surrounded by simulated black upholstery nails. (These are wood, glued in strips to the surface. The strips have been broken off in 4 places, leaving gaps.) Behind glass front is cardboard panel covered with 2 collaged portions of map of Switzerland. Top half is right way up; join across center with bottom half upside down. Visible identifying locations (top half): *S..HW.IZ*; (lower half): *GRAUBÜNDEN; ZURI[CH]; GLARUS*. Thirty-four circular or semicircular openings cut into cardboard. Sixteen openings are filled or partially filled with pasted fragments of photographs or printed pictures: cows (4; 3 black and white, 1 sepia): ballet dancer (1);[2] skiers (2: 1 blue, 1 brown); Red-Riding Hood with wolf (1, partially filling hole); blue-and-white snow-capped mountains (4); black-and-white peasant girl in costume (1); paper cutout collage of label, "Hôtel de l'Ange"; brownish mountains (1); grassy wooded slope (1). Twelve bells distributed along runways: 2 at top, 4 on second, 4 on third, 2 on bottom. Top section of box has mirror attached to entire rear wall. String of 8 colored wood beads (white, red, blue) hanging vertically within one hole, in front of a cutout black-and-white reproduction of a head from a painting (unidentified) attached to rear wall. This head is visible full front through 1 hole, from 3/4 right through another. Openings in lower left corner have fragments of straw glued to greenish painted rear wall. Colored print of blue sky and clouds visible through 2 center holes. Small wooden ball, dropped into opening on upper right side, passes through interior along a series of 4 slanted runways, ringing bells; it exits through hinged door on the lower right side.

1. Peggy Guggenheim purchased 2 boxes and 1 object from Cornell before the opening of her gallery (letter from Cornell, Mar. 12, 1942, AAA, Peggy Guggenheim Papers, Reel ITVE I, frame 149), and a number directly after the December 1942 exhibition; she also purchased many in the subsequent few years. She sold and gave away most of these before closing the gallery, retaining only the 5 now in the collection. She was unable to recall precisely when she acquired the present box, but thought that this, *Setting for a Fairy Tale* (cat. no. 37), and *Soap Bubble Set,* (cat. no. 39) were purchased soon after the 1942 exhibition, in which she believed they appeared.
2. Identified by Sandra L. Starr as Fanny Elssler (1810-1884). Starr offers an elaborate interpretation of *Swiss Shoot-the- Chutes,* based upon events in Elssler's life and political events of the 1940s (see REFERENCES).

36

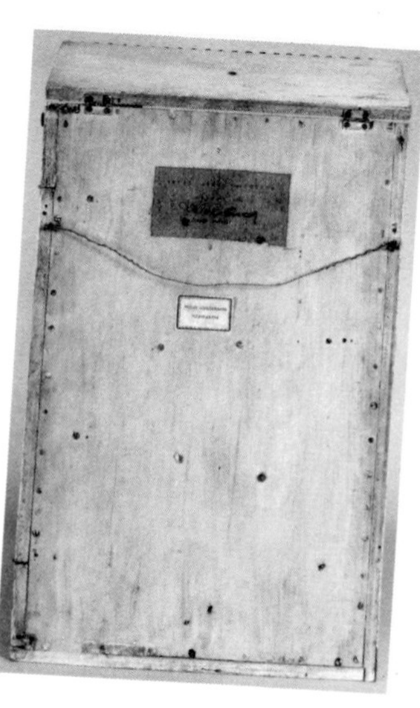

Swiss Shoot-the-Chutes was Cornell's first game box and was followed by several others in which balls are used, as they were in the slot machines of the old penny arcades. On childhood visits to Coney Island, Cornell would play these machines: insertion of a penny would release a ball, which then traveled through slides and trapdoors, hitting various targets and ultimately rewarding the fortunate player with prizes and souvenirs to take home.

Years later, Cornell wrote of his own boxes, or so-called toys: "perhaps a definition of a box could be as a kind of 'forgotten game,' a philosophical toy of the Victorian era, with poetic or magical 'moving parts,' achieving even a slight measure of this poetry or magic... that golden age of the toy alone should justify the box's existence" (Mar. 1960 diary entry, AAA, Joseph Cornell Papers, reel 1060).

Surely illustrative of these fragmentary thoughts is Cornell's own ca. 1949 *Forgotten Game* (Collection Mr. and Mrs. E. A. Bergman, Chicago), which is closely related to *Swiss Shoot-the-Chutes* in its use of a ball that travels down a series of slides and is glimpsed through circular apertures as it descends, emerging finally to ring a bell at the bottom.

Dawn Ades has seen in this and other boxes of the same type a "nostalgia for the lost games of childhood, but also for the golden age of the Victorian toy in which scientific invention was blended with pure imagination... pedagogical function with entertainment" ("The Transcendental Surrealism of Joseph Cornell," in *Joseph Cornell*, exh. cat., MoMA, New York, 1980, p. 29).

In addition to its identity as a game box, *Swiss Shoot-the-Chutes* must also be understood as an early expression of Cornell's romantic notions about travel, his fascination with exotic details about foreign countries and cities. Though he never left the United States, his quest for information about distant parts of the globe led him to collect guide books, maps, prints, illustrated travel texts, as well as shipping and train schedules. His library contained guide books to Switzerland (clearly used in this instance) and many other countries. The sign for "Hôtel de l'Ange" (the title by which this box has hitherto been known) itself evokes the notion of a voyage that is more dream than reality, as do the titles of many of the other hotel (or travel) boxes: *Hôtel de l'Etoile, Grand Hôtel de l'Univers, Hôtel de la Mer,* and *Grand Hôtel de l'Observatoire.*

EXHIBITIONS:

New York, Art of This Century, *Objects by Joseph Cornell; Marcel Duchamp: Box Valise; Laurence Vail: Bottles*, Dec. 1942 (no cat.);[1] Amsterdam, *P.G.*, 1951, no. 32.

REFERENCES:

Calas, 1966, pp. 122-23, repr. p. 155 ("*Hotel de l'Ange*, 1944"); D. Waldman, *Joseph Cornell*, New York, 1977, repr. pl. 67 ("*Hotel de l'Ange*, 1944"); L. Flint, *Handbook*, 1983, p. 170, repr. color p. 171; S.L. Starr, *Joseph Cornell and the Ballet*, Pasadena, 1983, pp. 50-52.

PEGGY GUGGENHEIM
FOUNDATION

37 Setting for a Fairy Tale. 1942.

76.2553 PG 125

Box construction. Height: 11 9/16 (29.4); width: 14 3/8 (36.6); depth: 3 7/8 (9.9).

Titled, signed, and dated on reverse (typed, except signature in ink): *Object 1942 / Joseph Cornell / Joseph Cornell / Setting for a Fairy / Tale.*

PROVENANCE:

Purchased from the artist, New York, ca. 1943.[1]

CONDITION:

In 1976 (Venice) the following conservation measures were carried out: the facing glass was cleaned; the broken mirror at rear of box was replaced; several broken twigs were glued back into place. Some loose pieces of mica at edges were reattached. The condition is stable. (Venice, Nov. 1982.)

DESCRIPTION:

Natural wood handmade box with glass front. Interior of glass front painted with black edge. Lower interior edge of box painted blue, spotted with white paint, and dotted with white mica chips inserted into painted surface. Paper facade palace cutout with figures in foreground is glued to rectangular mirror, which provides mirrored glass for each window; facade then glued to ca. 1/4 in., 0.5 cm., wood backing carved to shape of palace. Twigs, partially painted white, positioned behind palace, some attached with wire to lower half of rear wall of box, which is painted blue. Upper half of same wall lined with mirror.

Upper gray paper label visible on reverse apparently covering a hole(?); lower label carries inscription by artist of title, signature, and date.

fig. a.
Jacques Androuet du Cerceau, "Le Chasteau de Boulongne, dit Madrit," engraving, 10 1/4 x 19 1/16 in., 26 x 48.5 cm., from *Le Premier Volume des plus excellents Bastiments de France*, Paris, 1607. Photograph by Michael J. Pirrocco. The identical engraving appears in the 1576 edition, as well as in 19th-century editions.

1. See above, cat. no. 36, fn. 1.

Cornell made at least thirteen palaces between 1942 and the mid-1950s; Peggy Guggenheim's was the first.[2] Although this example (and at least two others) present white palaces, the series is generically known in the literature as "the pink castles" or "the pink palaces"—a description that occurs in Cornell's own diary notes for the first time on July 8, 1947. The palaces are unusually consistent in their use of imagery and materials. The particular engraving Cornell used for his mis-en-scène is *Le Chasteau de Boulongne, dit Madrit* from *Le premier volume des plus excellents Bastiments de France*, by Jacques Androuet du Cerceau, Paris, 1576 (fig. a). In his "Palace" dossier (preserved in the Joseph Cornell Study Center at the Smithsonian Institution) Cornell preserved engravings, reproductions, cutouts, and notes on various European palaces and imaginary castles, some of which are identified. Several photostatic copies of the du Cerceau engraving survive, but the identifying caption is in each case missing.[3]

Working with photostats that could be enlarged (or reduced) at will, and with boxes of different sizes, Cornell was able to vary the scale of his otherwise identical image. In certain cases (such as the Peggy Guggenheim version and at least five others), the palace fills the entire "proscenium" space; in four others, the palace occupies a proportionately smaller area, and the surrounding "forest" of twigs is considerably expanded. (See, for example, *Untitled* [Pink Palace], 10 x 16 7/16 in., 25.4 x 41.8 cm., ca. 1946-48, Private Collection, New York, repr. color, *Joseph Cornell*, exh. cat., MoMA, New York, 1980, pl. 7.) In at least nine instances, Cornell used precisely the same engraving as in the Peggy Guggenheim example. In most, he tinted the palace in varying shades of pink; in a few—as in cat. no. 37—he left the photostat of the black-and-white engraving untouched. The proscenium device, which creates an interior frame, is usually blue and often decorated with spattered white paint or mica chips. In some cases (for example, cat. no. 37), it is merely painted dark blue or black.

In two instances engravings of entirely different palaces were used: *The Palace* of 1943, titled and dated by Cornell (present whereabouts unknown, 10 1/2 x 20 1/4 in., 26.7 x 51.4 cm., repr. MoMA catalogue, p. 36); and *Castle* of 1944, also titled and dated by the artist (formerly Collection Dorothea Tanning, 10 7/8 x 20 7/8 in., 27.7 x 53.1 cm.). These two were probably second and third in the sequence, although this has not been established with certainty. Cornell would, in that case, have first produced three distinct white palaces; only after these would he have embarked upon the extensive variations based on the original (Peggy Guggenheim) engraving. These variations were then in most cases tinted pink.

2. Lynda Roscoe Hartigan, Curator, Joseph Cornell Study Center, National Museum of American Art, who is preparing a catalogue raisonné of Cornell's work, has kindly supplied information on several of the palaces.

3. This source, hitherto unidentified, was located by Elizabeth C. Childs, New York, 1984. Cornell might have used the original 16th-century edition, or 1 of several later printings. In trimming the title and other legends from the top of the engraving, he cut off the spires of the 2 tallest roofs.

The title of the first of this series of palaces—*Setting for a Fairy Tale*—places the image with unusual explicitness at the center of one of Cornell's major preoccupations: that of childhood fantasy, invention, and imagination, and the realm of the fairy tale. All his shadow boxes are to some extent theaters in which imagined dramas take place. But in this instance, by clearly designating the image a "stage set," he perhaps came closer than at any other time to making his medium demonstrably literal. Nonetheless, by creating the setting, and leaving the tale untold, he retained his customary distance — evoking the "fairy-tale" world, but leaving the text open to imaginative speculation.

As has been pointed out by Sandra L. Starr, it is conceivable that Cornell's initial inspiration for the palace theme might have been the tale of "The Sleeping Beauty"—specifically in its balletic form (*Joseph Cornell: Art and Metaphysics*, exh. cat., Castelli-Feigen-Corcoran Gallery, New York, 1982, pp. 65-66). The ballet was an especially successful vehicle for several of Cornell's favorite dancers. Pavlova (1881-1931) danced the role of Princess Aurora in New York in 1916. Cornell is known to have seen Irina Baronova (b. 1919) perform it in 1941; and — most significant of all — Tamara Toumanova (b. 1919), whom Cornell had met in the winter of 1940 and with whom he developed a warm friendship, was renowned for her interpretation of the part.

If the initial inspiration of the enchanted castle was in part Toumanova and "The Sleeping Beauty," the impulse to undertake a later version of the palace series may even have been stimulated by an historical event. June 2, 1953 was the Coronation Day of Queen Elizabeth II of England; Cornell recorded in his diary for that day a set of associations linking the Coronation to his renewed engagement with the palace theme: "Coronation Day... taking box from garage shelves (left unfinished from Zizi period) — reshaping same day and making adjustment on cluttered shelves. White mirrored palace... sudden realization of pink palace, trees and snow covered steps mount morning without box" (AAA, Joseph Cornell Papers, reel 1059).

The identification of specific "sources" for Cornell's imagery does not, however, imply a restrictive approach, which would run counter to Cornell's own elliptical mode of expression. Theatrical, fictional, or historical events regularly provided the artist with thematic inspiration, which he then transformed to suit his own imaginative purposes.

EXHIBITIONS:

New York, Art of This Century, *Objects by Joseph Cornell; Marcel Duchamp: Box Valise; Laurence Vail: Bottles*, Dec. 1942 (no cat.);[4] Amsterdam, *P.G.*, 1951, no. 32.

REFERENCE:

[Alley], *Peggy Guggenheim Foundation*, 1968, no. 125, repr. n. p.

4. See above, cat. no. 36, fn. 1.

38 Untitled (Pharmacy). Ca. 1942.

Color plate p. 501.

76.2553 PG 128

Box construction. Height: 14 (35.5); width: 12 1/16 (30.6); depth: 4 3/8 (11.1).

Not signed or dated.

PROVENANCE:

Purchased from the artist, New York, March 6, 1945?.[1]

CONDITION:

In 1976 (Venice) the following conservation measures were carried out: back mirror wall, front glass, and exterior of all bottles were cleaned. Some abrasions and damages in lining paper were patched with excess paper folded under at bottom edge, and inpainted with gouache and watercolor. Box was cleaned and waxed with Venetian furniture wax.

The printed patterned lining paper, originally green on white, has discolored (along the right, front, and lower edges) to brownish green through overexposure to light. The condition is stable. (Venice, Nov. 1982.)

DESCRIPTION:

Cabinet construction of polished wood, latched on both sides, but without hinged front to which latches could be hooked. Nails fastening top to sides are counter sunk, the top refinished, so that no joins are visible. Interior side walls and floor and front edges lined with green-and-white patterned printed paper. Back wall lined with mirror. Interior divided by 3 glass shelves into 4 equal horizontal spaces containing total of 22 sealed apothecary jars. Contents of each jar (top to bottom, left to right): (1) blue powder with touches of red; (2) white and beige tinted rocks; (3) fragments of bird's nest, thread, straw, with white marbles; (4) fragments of architectural engraving from German text; (5) black rocks, red powder; (6) white chalk surrounded by engraving of Italian(?) city view; (7) transparent marbles in transparent liquid (partially evaporated); (8) shell with red and pink powder; (9) small cogs and wheels; (10) blue powder plus fragment of Spanish(?) street map (legible words: "*Pal' de la Diputacion / Luchana de Urg / C. de Bertendona / Castarloa*"); (11) glittering purple rocks (quartz?); (12) 3 yellow wood beads: 1 square on pale purple chord, 1 rectangular with rounded edges on stick, 1 circular loose; (13) shiny, fluffy white feathers and brown seeds; (14) dried leaves; (15) green powder, strips of white paper surrounding rolled-up map fragment; (16) gold-coated interior; (17) red-brown fine wire and 3 wheels/cogs from clock mechanism; (18) pale blue shells, blue liquid (evaporated, but leaving waterline); (19) dried leaves and seed pods; (20) yellow, red, black-with-blue markings feathers; (21) white feathers; (22) black beetle with brown powdery cubes.

Five indentations in upper and lower interior edges indicate that glass dividers originally structured the space into 6 vertical sections.

The box is almost certainly unfinished, or else incomplete. In the four other boxes of this type, vertical glass dividers compartmentalize the bottles, which are equal in number on every shelf, and a wooden hinged front completes the cabinet (see, for example: *Untitled [Grand Hotel Pharmacy]*, ca. 1947, Collection Mr. and Mrs. Billy Wilder, Los Angeles; *Untitled [Pharmacy]*, 1943, Collection Mrs. Marcel Duchamp, Paris; *Untitled [Pharmacy]*, 1950, Menil Foundation, Houston, Texas; *Untitled [Pharmacy]*, 1952-53, Collection Muriel

1. In the Joseph Cornell Papers (AAA, reel 1058) an entry for March 6, 1945, reads "Peggy is taking large cabinet of bottles." Whether this comment refers to the present construction, or even whether Peggy Guggenheim is the subject of the reference, has not been firmly established. The date of acquisition remains uncertain, though it certainly precedes the closing of Art of This Century in 1947.

Kallis Newman, Chicago). The incomplete latching device on the exterior of the Peggy Guggenheim box suggests that the front piece is missing or was possibly never supplied; meanwhile the slat indentations on the interior upper and lower edges were clearly intended to hold the vertical glass dividers in place.

Whether these elements were originally present and have since been lost is unclear, but it seems unlikely that Cornell would have parted with the box in its present state. This hypothesis is further supported by an entry in the Joseph Cornell Papers dated August 27, 1968: "'Pharmacy' in disaray [sic] Venice" (AAA, reel 1063c).[2]

Cornell created approximately a half a dozen Pharmacy boxes of this type,[3] which are clearly related to one another beyond the fact that the ready-made glass bottles and the mirrored boxes that house them are virtually identical. No two boxes contain precisely the same ingredients, and the juxtaposition of images, colors, and evocative details varies from work to work. Nonetheless, certain elements recur, creating a thread of continuity from one box to another.

For example, the engraving of an Italian(?) city view, feathers, sand, shells, colored marbles, dried leaves, seeds, and transparent liquids — all of which appear in the Peggy Guggenheim box — are also present in several other boxes, although the marble may be red and the powder orange (Menil Foundation box), or the marble blue and the shells pink (Duchamp Collection box). Common to other boxes are allusions to exotic foreign parts — whether in the form of hotel names ("Hôtel de la Mer," "Grand Hôtel de l'Univers"), fragmentary street maps of unidentified cities, or ground plans and elevations of Renaissance palaces. Perhaps of even greater significance, in at least two other instances, is the glowing presence of a bottle with a gilded interior, creating a possible "alchemical" dimension for the box as a whole (see the Menil Foundation and Duchamp Collection boxes).

Carter Ratcliffe has written persuasively about the critical connections between the work of Duchamp and that of Cornell (*Joseph Cornell*, exh. cat., MoMA, New York, 1980, pp. 63-65). Apart from the obvious notion of the ready-made, "Duchamp is crucial to Cornell because he is the first of the Parisians to make effective use of glass. For Duchamp, glass is the substance of irony, the means by which detachment can be symbolized and effected all at once. Cornell learned from this how to make voyeurism — the despotism of 'the bodily eye' — presentable. Even more crucially, he learned from Duchamp how to give aesthetic weight to mechanically replicated images." In describing Cor-

2. Howard Hussey, in conversation with Lucy Flint, February 9, 1983, and Lindsay F. Noble, in conversation with the author, February 10, 1983, concurred that the box gave an unfinished impression.

3. Cornell also made some Pharmacy boxes of a casket type (with hinged and clasped lid). In these the bottles were set into holes in a tray lined with patterned paper. A detailed study of the contents of all 5 of the related Pharmacy boxes has not been completed. Lynda Roscoe Hartigan (see above, cat. no. 37, fn. 2) kindly supplied descriptions of the Mr. and Mrs. Billy Wilder Collection and Menil Foundation boxes. In addition to the 5 boxes of this type recorded here, at least 1 unfinished example is known (Estate of Joseph Cornell).

nell's repetitious use of photostatic reproductions and mirrors—"those simplest duplicating machines of all" — Ratcliffe points out that Cornell was to some extent exploiting the notion that "to duplicate an image endlessly is often to make its spell all the more binding."

In the Pharmacy boxes, Cornell uses the simple device of an apparently ready-made pharmaceutical cabinet to create a work that, from one point of view, consists of ordinary (even manufactured) objects. At the same time, the arrangement of the various objects and ingredients—the unexpected juxtapositions of the mundane and the exotic — produces original and strange effects. Indeed, the possibility exists that an alchemical metaphor is intrinsic to the meaning of these particular boxes. The practice of pharmacy, which uses ordinary chemicals to produce new compounds, functions here as an analogue for a more mysterious mode of transformation: alchemy signifies the power by which art achieves its own transmutations.

EXHIBITIONS:

New York, Art of This Century, *Objects by Joseph Cornell; Marcel Duchamp: Box Valise; Laurence Vail: Bottles*, Dec. 1942 (no cat.);[4] Amsterdam, *P.G.*, 1951, no. 32.

REFERENCES:

Calas, 1966, p. 122, repr. p. 154; F. Licht, *Sculpture: 19th and 20th Centuries*, Greenwich, 1967, p. 338, repr. no. 264; D. Waldman, *Joseph Cornell*, New York, 1977, p. 24, repr. pl. 66; L. Flint, *Handbook*, 1983, p. 172, repr. color p. 173.

4. The work's appearance in this exhibition remains to be definitely established. See above, cat. no. 36, fn. 1.

fig. a.
Detail of cat. no. 39, showing the artist's title, date, and signature.

39 Soap Bubble Set. 1942.

76.2553 PG 129

Box construction. Height: 15¾ (40); width: 18⅜ (46.7); depth: 2⅝ (6.7).

Titled, signed, and dated along left interior edge (typed, except signature in ink): *Soap Bubble Set joseph cornell 1942 Joseph Cornell* (fig. a).

PROVENANCE:

Purchased from the artist, New York, ca. 1942.[1]

CONDITION:

In 1947, during the shipment of the entire collection to Venice, the central section of the construction fell apart. Peggy Guggenheim attempted to reassemble or reconstitute it according to her memory, but did not succeed. When Cornell subsequently visited her in Venice (1968), he was greatly distressed by the appearance of the piece and told her that he could no longer accept it as a work by his hand.[2]

Some further light is thrown on the problem by Nicolas Calas in a letter to Cornell dated January 3, 1966: "Both Lolya (my wife) and I have been puzzled and bothered by the problem posed by the candlestick in the 'Soap-Bubble Box'—this is the title given to us. We hope we are not bothering you too much in our turn by sending you the plate and asking you to be kind enough to comment on the object between the two wine glasses. You said over the phone you never used candlesticks in your boxes. Could the candlestick have been added since the box left your hands? It now occurs to me that if the object is in fact a candlestick it may be a replacement for the original object which may have broken—needed to keep the cord taut and the little glass circular platform aloft (the one above the candlestick)..." (Joseph Cornell Papers, AAA, reel 1056).

Cornell never responded to this letter, and Calas was unable to make further progress in resolving this issue (conversation with the author, New York, Apr. 1983). Other Cornell boxes containing such objects have not thus far come to light, however, and the Calas hypothesis remains a plausible one.

Beyond the anomaly of the "candlestick," the twisted, knotted cord and its awkward relationship to the centrally suspended, but slightly off-balance, glass disc and ball are also uncharacteristic of Cornell's structurally coherent and visually refined style, lending further support to the notion that the arrangement at the center of the box is inconsistent with his intentions. Until an early photograph of the piece, or other documentary record is found, it is impossible either to rectify the situation or to evaluate the degree to which it departs from the original conception.

In 1976 (Venice) the following conservation measures were carried out: cleaning of all glass elements; cleaning of the enameled blue / black wooden balls; cleaning of the exterior of the wood box and waxing with Venetian furniture wax; cleaning and polishing of the ornamental studs holding the glasses in place; cleaning of the brown velvet at inner bottom and sides of box.

The lunar map pasted to the rear wall of the box has seriously photo-oxidized and discolored: the green-yellows of the moonscape and vivid pale blue of the sky still visible in the 1966 Calas reproduction have faded to brownish and grayish tones. (Venice, June 1983.)

DESCRIPTION:

Cabinet construction of polished wood with removable glass front, but top nailed closed now. Rear wall lined with colored 19th-century German map of the moon from which heading, *DIE SICHTBARE SEITE DER MONDOBERFLÄCHE*, has been cropped

1. See above, cat. no. 36, fn. 1.

2. Peggy Guggenheim's description of these events was detailed and clear. She was, however, unable to recall how the box originally looked and what precisely had transpired regarding the center of the construction. Howard Hussey, in conversation with Lucy Flint, February 9, 1983, confirmed the story, having heard it at the time from Cornell.

(or hidden by upper shelf).[3] Horizontal wood divider in 3 sections along top creates shelf; 9 wood balls painted blue, with touches of gold highlighting, are suspended from hooks and eyes screwed into upper surface of this compartment (fig. b). Wood and glass compartments at left and right side each contain a white clay pipe held in place with fine cord (fig. c). Brown velvet lining rear wall of upper compartment behind balls, and lower interior edge of box including ca. 1 15/16 in., 5 cm., up each side. Left, right, and upper interior sides of box lined with collaged sections of printed lunar tables (see fig. c).[4] Two cordial glasses standing left and right of center on brown velvet are secured in place with 3 pins. Each contains a blue, painted wood ball suspended from green cord. Ball on right not touching interior of glass; ball on left rests on bottom. Green suspension cord, threaded through holes in the balls, is also threaded through holes in wood shelf at top of compartment and knotted above. Two loose balls lying on velvet at base of box (possibly misplaced). Glass circular plate suspended with cord at center, certainly misplaced. Wooden ball resting on glass plate, threaded with cord which is knotted above hole in upper shelf and descends across front of shelf to wrap several times around yellow, turned wood "candlestick" shape at lower center (certainly misplaced and probably not original [see CONDITION]). Glass plate with hole drilled through center rests over top of this yellow wood object. Six extra holes drilled in upper shelf may indicate original positions of some of the cords.

fig. b.
Detail of cat. no. 39.

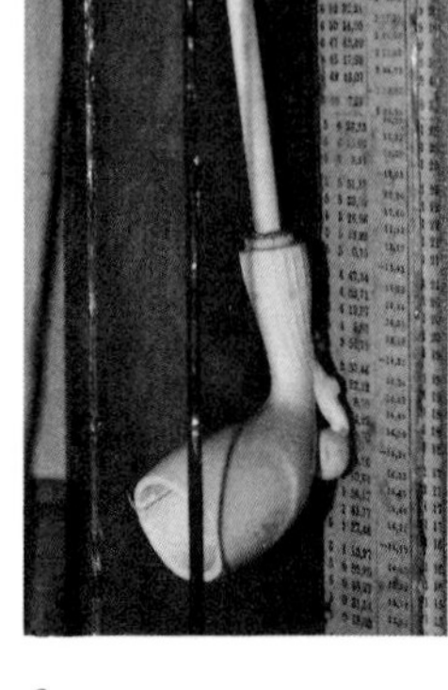

fig. c.
Detail of cat. no. 39.

Cornell's earliest Soap Bubble Set (Wadsworth Atheneum, Hartford) dates from 1936 and was encased in the first of Cornell's handmade wood boxes.

The clay pipes, of which he had dozens, were purchased at the New York World's Fair in 1939. He used them in a series of at least eighteen related boxes constructed during the following two decades, Peggy Guggenheim's being the third. Dawn Ades has suggested that in Cornell's Soap Bubble Sets, "where the clay pipe becomes a bubble-blowing pipe, the bubbles themselves become heavenly bodies" ("The Transcendental Surrealism of Joseph Cornell," in *Joseph Cornell*, exh. cat., MoMA, New York, 1980, p. 31).

In Peggy Guggenheim's and the 1936 sets, the heavenly body in question is the moon; in others, it is the sun with attendant constellations (ibid., pl. 81). Ades has convincingly argued that "Cornell sees the exercise of the imagination

3. The map, which appears in several other Cornell boxes, is by J. H. Mädler and belongs to a series of maps prepared by him in 1837 in connection with the publication of his book (co-authored with W. Beer), *Der Mond*, Berlin, 1837. A closely related map by Mädler showing an overall view is also dated 1837: *General-Karte der sichtbaren Seite der Mondoberfläche zugleich als Überseits-Blatt*, 19½ x 16⅛ in., 49.5 x 41 cm., Department of Astronomy, Princeton University. Peter Cziffra, Astronomy Librarian, and Martin Schwarzschild, Eugene Higgins Professor of Astronomy, Emeritus, Princeton University, helped the author to identify this source.

4. These lunar tables show declinations in degrees and minutes, and right ascension in hours and minutes. They have been cut into sections in such a way as to render them to some extent indecipherable.

in playing as something like the first flexing of the creative powers of the human mind whether in science or in art.... The transformation of the soap bubble into a world is not just a visual pun, but a significant comment on the human imagination" (ibid., pp. 31-32).

Cornell's deep and lifelong interest in cosmology, sky charts and maps, constellations, and the progress of astronomy is well documented. He subscribed to periodicals in the field, and his library contained a good many books on the subject, including C. Flammarion, *The Wonders of the Heavens* (1871), three editions of H. Elijah Burritt, *The Geography of the Heavens and Class Book of Astronomy* (1838, 1852, 1873), and O. M. Mitchell, *The Planetary and Stellar Worlds* (1859). His use of Mädler's maps has not hitherto been noted. It is likely that he had several loose copies of the individually printed maps like the one reproduced here (fig. d). In other instances he used even earlier maps, some of which he photostated in various sizes. The iconography of the Soap Bubble Sets is closely linked with that of the large series of Navigation and Celestial Navigation boxes, may of which also contain maps and charts, pipes and glasses. The presence here of the lunar tables seems to bring the object into close association with the Navigation series. (See Ades, loc. cit., pp. 32-34 for a discussion of the idea of the voyage in Cornell's work.)

fig. d.
J. H. Mädler, *General-karte der sichtbaren Seite der Mondoberfläche zugleich als Übersichts-Blatt zur grössern Mondkarte von Wilh. Beer und Joh. Heinr. Mädler*, Berlin, 1837, 27 15/16 x 23 7/16 in., 71 x 59.5 cm., Firestone Library, Princeton University. Photograph by Michael J. Pirrocco.

EXHIBITIONS:

New York, Art of This Century, *Objects by Joseph Cornell; Marcel Duchamp: Box Valise; Laurence Vail: Bottles*, Dec. 1942 (no cat.);[5] Amsterdam, *P.G.*, 1951, no. 32.

REFERENCES:

Calas, 1966, p. 123, repr. color p. 157; D. Waldman, *Joseph Cornell*, New York, 1977, repr. pl. 73.

5. See above, cat. no. 36, fn. 1.

Salvador Dalí

(Salvador Felipe Jacinto Dalí y Domenech).

Born May 1904, Figueras, Spain.
Lives in Port Lligat.

40 Untitled. 1931.
(*Woman sleeping in a landscape*).

Color plate p. 494.

76.2553 PG 99

Oil on canvas, 10 11/16 x 13 3/4 (27.2 x 35).

Signed and dated l.r.: *à Gala Salvador Dalí 1931*.

PROVENANCE:
Purchased from Henriette Gomès, Paris, 1940.[1]

1. Madame Gomès was unable to recall where and when she acquired the work, but thought it most likely she got it from Dalí (conversation with the author, Paris, Oct. 1982).

   It is conceivable that the work belonged in the early 1930s to a member of the Zodiaque group, which consisted of 11 collectors who agreed to purchase works by Dalí on a monthly basis starting in January 1933. In that event, Madame Gomès would have acquired it from one of them. (For the list of the Zodiaque group, see *Salvador Dalí*, exh. cat., MNAM, Paris, 1979, vol. 2, p. 32.)

   In her memoirs, Peggy Guggenheim speaks of insisting on the work being signed before she purchased it. The work was duly taken to Dalí in Arcachon, signed, and returned to Madame Gomès, from whom it was then purchased (*Out of This Century*, 1946, p. 247).

CONDITION:

In 1964 (Tate Report) the condition was described as poor. Extensive and pronounced elevated crackle over most of the surface layer and some small losses and abrasions were noted. The apertures in the crackle allowed daylight to penetrate. A thin, evenly applied varnish covered the surface.

The surface dirt was removed. Elevated crackle was consolidated with wax-resin adhesive; the canvas was impregnated with wax resin, and further elevated crackle in areas lacking impasto was pressed down from the reverse. The painting was lined on a hot table, the new canvas having been washed, stretched, and impregnated with wax-resin mixture. It was then attached to a new stretcher. Losses were filled with Paraloid B-72 and whiting and inpainted with Paraloid B-72 as medium.

In November 1982 (Venice) surface dirt was removed with ammonium hydroxide (3% in water). The upper edge was retouched with Maimeri varnish colors. A coat of Lefranc retouching varnish was applied to the entire surface.

Examination reveals extensive inpainting of the edges and of the heavy impasto beneath the head and wrist of the figure and along the shadow. Scattered inpainting elsewhere corresponds to the losses visible in the 1964 conservation photos. Though the surface has suffered considerable damage, the condition is stable. (New York, Mar. 1983.)

After its acquisition, the work was entitled *Woman sleeping in a landscape*, a blandly descriptive title bearing no relationship to Dalí's evocative approach to the titling of such works and almost certainly an invention of Peggy Guggenheim. Characteristic titles such as *Symbiose de la tête aux coquillages*, 1931, and *L'Echo anthropomorphe*, 1931, were given by Dalí to comparable works of this period and undoubtedly the present painting originally carried such a designation. It has not proved possible to establish this with certainty, but titles of two as yet unlocated works shown in the 1932 *Dalí* exhibition at the Galerie Pierre Colle might be regarded as possible candidates: no. 7, *Effet Surréaliste*, and no. 8, *Hallucination affective*.

Peggy Guggenheim's painting belongs to a group of works that are closely related in theme as well as in format. A wide desolate beach provides the setting, probably based on Dalí's native Cadaquès. Occasional jagged rocks appear, sometimes — as in the present case — with a mysterious male figure emerging from their shadows. A single youthful female usually occupies the open space; in several instances the head and shoulders of the nude (or diaphanously draped) female form are partially studded with — or transformed into — shells.[2] The experience of solitude and the process of metamorphosis are among the major themes of these works. Whether these themes can be more specifically correlated — according to Dalí's own "*principe de metamorphose paranoïaque*" — with

2. Among the related oils are the following (all reproduced in the exhibition catalogue, *Salvador Dalí*, MNAM, Paris, 1980): *Solitude*, 1931, repr. color no. 88; *Symbiose de la tête aux coquillages*, 1931, repr. color no. 89; *Ombre du grand piano approchant*, 1931, repr. no. 91. For a related oil depicting a man with shells placed in a hollow of his shaved head, see *Le Bureaucrate moyen*, 1930, repr. A. M. Reynolds, *Salvador Dalí*, Cleveland, 1974, p. 54.

events in the artist's own life or to interpretable subject matter of a more hallucinatory nature is not clear.[3] However, some connections in imagery and in pictorial method may be relevant.

In his autobiography, for example, Dalí recounts the traumatic experience of being banished from his household by his father; the news of his expulsion arrived in the form of a letter: "*Quand je reçus cette lettre, ma première réaction fut de me faire couper les cheveux. En fait je fis mieux: je me rasai la tête, puis j'enterrai ma chevelure sacrifiée avec les coquilles vides des oursins mangés à midi. Cela fait, je montai sur une des collines de Cadaquès, d'où l'on dominait tout le village et passai là deux longues heures à contempler le panorama de mon enfance, de mon adolescence et de ma maturité*" (*La Vie Secrète de Salvador Dalí*, Paris, 1952, p. 196).

Precise parallels are difficult to sustain, but there are nonetheless some obvious associative connections between the imagery of the early 1930s paintings (such as cat. no. 40) and the main details of the passage cited: the setting of the beach; the predicament of isolation and solitude; the occurrence of significant sexual encounters or transformations, represented by objects of desire in the paintings or by the act of self-emasculation (the shaving of the head) in the narrative; the way in which human and nonhuman forms are merged or identified with one another.

An alternative (or additional) set of related images and mode of associative depiction is suggested by the 1927 film scenario for *La Coquille et le Clergyman*, by Antonin Artaud, which has descriptions such as "*ses seins sont remplacés par une carapace de coquillages:... mais entre les doigts de ses mains des ciels, des paysages phosphorescents.*" In the scenario, and in Artaud's preface to it, themes of metamorphosis, including the fusion of unexpected visual images, are offered as examples of a pictorial or cinematic language that is entirely distinct from the verbal. According to Artaud's theory of film, images act directly and intuitively on the mind, evoking "*la vérité sombre de l'esprit, en des images issues uniquement d'elles-mêmes, et qui ne tirent pas leurs sens de la situation où elles se développent mais d'une sorte de nécessité intérieure et puissante qui les projette dans la lumière d'une évidence sans secours.... Les images naissent, se déduisant les unes des autres en tant qu'images, imposent une synthèse objective plus pénétrante que n'importe quelle abstraction*" (Paris, 1927). Artaud's exposition clearly contains ideas to which Dalí responded, and his scenario — as well as his theory — may have contributed to certain aspects of Dalí's developing iconography.

Nicolas Calas (1966) suggested yet another set of associations between Dalí's work and photographic prototypes. He argued that a direct relationship could be traced between Dalí's painting and Man Ray's photograph *Primat de la ma-*

3. For some notes on the nature of Dalí's theory on the consistently autobiographical and psychoanalytic content of his work, see below, cat. no. 41.

tière sur la pensée of 1931: "It should be recalled that Dalí often said he wanted to produce 'handmade photographs.' While Man Ray's photograph suggests dematerialization of the forms of a woman who seems to be melting and spreading, Dalí's suggests despiritualization through materialization.... Dalí is intent on shattering illusions. This is not the dreamlike vision of a lovely naked girl lying fast asleep on a coastal plain. Her nudity is no longer protected by the darkness of night, but the light that is falling upon her is not that of dawn—it is a photographer's spotlight."

A specific connection between Dalí's 1931 image and Man Ray's *Primat de la matière sur la pensée* cannot be established with certainty. (The photograph was published in the December 1931 issue of *Le Surréalisme au Service de la Révolution.*) But in drawing the analogy between Dalí's work and the aesthetics of photography, Calas focused on a set of relationships about which Dalí himself wrote extensively in the 1920s, and which undoubtedly played an important role in the development of his particular representational style (see especially Dalí's essay "La Fotografia, pura creacio de l'esperit," *L'Amic de les Arts*, Sept. 31, 1927). By basing his own illustrational mode on an extremely precise—almost academic—depiction of form, Dalí sought to simulate, as closely as possible, the intensity of objective vision available to the photographer.

The precision and polish of the photographic image was further enhanced in Dalí's mind by the camera's speed, flexibility, and capacity to fuse and superimpose details that otherwise lacked logical interconnections. In a film scenario of ca. 1930-31, he expressed this sense of the way in which the assemblage and juxtaposition of inherently banal fragments of reality could achieve effects of extraordinary profundity: "*Par la magie des collages les images sont transformées profondément selon les exigences de la pensée subconsciente. Une simple substitution, déplacement ou omission couvre d'énigme et de trouble poétique la plus quotidienne et banale des images.*"[4]

In this sense, as Calas suggested, the Peggy Guggenheim picture and related works of approximately the same date reflect Dalí's attempt to establish a "photographic" aesthetic within the medium of painting.

EXHIBITIONS:

New York, Art of This Century, 1942-47, p. 122 (*Woman sleeping in a landscape*, the title by which the work is known in all subsequent publications); Venice, *P.G.*, 1948 (Biennale), no. 25; Florence, *P.G.*, 1949, no. 26; Amsterdam, *P.G.*, 1951, no. 34; Zurich, *P.G.*, 1951, no. 30; London, *P.G.*, 1964-65, no. 89; Stockholm, *P.G.*, 1966-67, no. 86; New York, *P.G.*, 1969, p. 130, repr.; Paris, *P.G.*, 1974-75, no. 86; Torino, *P.G.*, 1975-76, no. 97; New York, *P.G.*, 1982-83, no. 42, repr.

REFERENCES:

P. Guggenheim, *Art of This Century*, 1942, p. 122; P. Guggenheim, *Out of This Century*, 1946, p. 247; Calas, 1966, p. 115, repr. color p. 141.

4. The scenario was first published, and convincingly dated, by D. Ades, in *Studio International*, vol. 195, nos. 993-94, 1982, pp. 5-10.

41 La Naissance des désirs liquides.
1931-32.
(*Birth of liquid desires*).

Color plate p. 493.

76.2553 PG 100

Oil and collage on canvas (unvarnished),[1]
$37\frac{7}{8}$ x $44\frac{1}{4}$ (96.1 x 112.3).

Signed and dated, l.c.: *Gala Salvador Dalí 1932*; inscribed on reverse (probably not by the artist): *plaisirs liquides*.

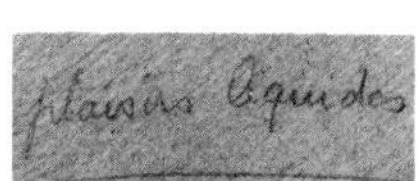

PROVENANCE:
Purchased from Gala Dalí, Paris, 1940.

CONDITION:

In 1964 (Tate Report) the painting showed some minimal evidence of crackle, small blisters in a few areas, and a few minute areas of retouching. The overall condition was described as good.

The collage element on the pedestal is cracked at all corners with several losses. The canvas, which was lined at an unknown date, is buckled out of plane, and retouching in several areas is visible. It has not been possible to establish when these restorations took place. The condition is fragile (Venice, Nov. 1982.)

La Naissance des désirs liquides, dated — and almost certainly painted — in 1932, apparently was conceived the previous year. A study for a work of this title appeared in Dalí's one-man exhibition at the Galerie Pierre Colle (June 3-15, 1931) as "No. 10. *Etude* (Naissance des désirs liquides) (Coll. Comte E. de Beaumont)." No photograph of this *Etude* was published at the time, and its identity has thus far not been established.[2] The 1931-32 date proposed here encompasses the initial conception of the theme and its ultimate execution in the Peggy Guggenheim painting. Dalí's rather rapid working method would suggest that he completed the painting itself in a relatively short period of time in 1932.

1. Suzanne Bernard has drawn attention to Dalí's experimental use, during the late 1920s and early 1930s, of lacquers, resins, and retouching varnishes mixed with pigment (*Salvador Dalí*, exh. cat., MNAM, Paris, 1980, p. 410, n. 29). Lacquer is said to be present, for example, in the medium of *L'Âne pourri*, 1928. Dalí's own comments regarding his technique during the period in question are illuminating: "*Je travaillais alors avec des vernis à retoucher, ce qui est absolument absurde parce qu'il faut aller très vite sans s'arrêter puisqu'ils sèchent rapidement comme une laque; ils ressemblent à un émail très fin qu'on ne peut ni blaireauter, ni reprendre.... Je fais un morceau: sec! Un autre morceau: sec! Comme de l'aquarelle. C'était à prendre ou à laisser! Evidemment, si je faisais une petite partie, je finissais le maximum puisque je ne pouvais pas revenir dessus*" (*50 Secrets Magiques* [written in 1947], Lausanne, 1974, p. 156).

   It has not been possible to conduct a pigment analysis of *La naissance des désirs liquides*, but the smooth, brushless surface and "miniaturist" technique are similar to certain areas of *L'Âne pourri*. The brillant enameled or crystalline surfaces of areas such as the central male's head in the Peggy Guggenheim painting suggest the presence of a resin in the medium, and the thinness of the paint application, with the absence of *pentimenti*, accords with Dalí's description of his working method at the time. Thus, whereas Dalí did not varnish the surface of the completed painting, he may have selectively mixed a resin with some of the oil medium.
2. Drawings with some of the same subject matter, although bearing different titles, do exist; however, some of these (such as *Guillaume Tell, Gradiva et bureaucrate moyen*) are ruled out by their provenance. A preparatory drawing for *La Mémoire de la femme enfant* (Collection François Petit, Paris, repr. *Salvador Dalí*, exh. cat., MNAM, Paris, 1980, p. 186) should be borne in mind as a possibility; its provenance has not been fully established, but the work could have passed through the hands of de Beaumont.

According to Dalí's own testimony, the content of his art throughout the particularly productive years 1929-33 was deeply indebted to Freud and to psychoanalytic theory. The nature (as well as the limits) of this debt has been extensively discussed in much of the literature.[3]

During the course of 1929, Dalí's paintings were dominated by obsessive images of eroticism and autosexuality, some of which were derived from childhood memories, others from contemporary literary texts. By his own account, his state of mind often verged upon madness.[4] By 1930 he had fallen in love with Gala, but this new relationship brought to the surface anxieties concerning impotence and even castration. In particular, the threatening nature of his relationship with his father became a central preoccupation of his art. He adopted the legend of William Tell as a metaphor or castration-myth in which the father was portrayed as a menacing presence, aggressively willing to sacrifice (or mutilate) his son.[5] As René Crevel wrote at the time: "*Comme Freud ressuscita Œdipe, il a ressuscité Guillaume Tell*" (*Dalí ou l'Anti-obscurantisme*, Paris, 1931, p. 29).

During the years 1930-32, Dalí painted several works on the William Tell theme: *Guillaume Tell, La Jeunesse de Guillaume Tell, La Vieillesse de Guillaume Tell, Figures d'Après Guillaume Tell*, and — in 1933 — *L'Enigme de Guillaume Tell.* These paintings, and the large-scale drawing *Guillaume Tell, Gradiva et bureaucrate moyen* (as well as several other studies), share with *La Naissance* certain distinguishing iconographic elements, which have not been specifically discussed in the literature.

The central couple in *La Naissance* is identifiable (especially by analogy with *Guillaume Tell, Gradiva et bureaucrate moyen*) as William Tell/the father, locked in an erotic embrace with a "Gradiva" figure. Gradiva served as a complex symbol for Dalí, as she did for other Surrealists. She was an object of desire, a stimulus of erotic longing. She was also quite literally (in the original tale by

3. See, for example, S. Dalí, "L'Âne pourri," *Le Surréalisme au Service de la Révolution*, 1930, no. 1, pp. 9-12. This was the first text in which Dalí expounded his developing aesthetic theory, eventually more fully defined as the *méthode paranoïaque-critique*, and involving a highly self-conscious manipulation of so-called hallucinatory experience. By inducing a simulated paranoia and using the pictorial imagery that emerged from it, Dalí expected to involve the viewer in his most personal obsessions. See also his 1935 lecture delivered at MoMA: *Surrealist Paintings, Paranoiac Images.*

   For illuminating discussions of his use of Freud and psychoanalytic theory, see W. Rubin, *Dada and Surrealist Art*, New York, 1969, p. 216; D. Ades, 1982, pp. 65, 70-78. For Georges Bataille's important Freudian analysis of *Le Jeu Lugubre* of 1929, see *Documents*, no. 7, Dec. 1929.

4. *The Secret Life of Salvador Dalí*, trans. H. M. Chevalier, New York, 1942, pp. 222-24.

5. For Dalí's own account of the crisis in his relations with his father, which led to his expulsion from his parent's house, see above cat. no. 40; also S. Dalí, *The Secret Life of Salvador Dalí*, 1942, pp. 251, 253-54, and idem, *The Unspeakable Confessions of Salvador Dalí*, London, 1976, p. 99. For Dalí's elucidation of parts of the William Tell iconography, see ibid., p. 30; idem, "L'Enigme de Salvador Dalí," *XXe Siècle*, no. 43, Dec. 1974, p. 93; also D. Ades, 1982, p. 89.

William Jensen that became the subject of Freud's analysis) a statue, a work of art, and consequently a "muse" symbolic of the powers of dream and imagination. Finally, she was the mediator between subjective desire and its realization in the objective world—the active agent whose intercession facilitated the release of repressed erotic emotion.[6]

Dalí identified Gradiva with his wife, Gala, and he drew an explicit analogy between the cure that Gradiva/Zoe effected upon the hero of Jensen's tale and Gala's alleviation of his own madness. The Gradiva figure in *La Naissance* is, however, forcefully possessed, not by the son but by the threatening (and hermaphroditic[7]) father figure, William Tell — an image evoking the themes of sexual aggression, father-son rivalry, and castration anxiety that characterize several of the Tell paintings.[8]

Other iconographic elements in *La Naissance*, while they carry the resonance of various symbols in Dalí's repertoire, elude a limited or precise analysis. As in other works of this period, they have multiple connotations. The youth at the left, for example, bears some relation to the young man in *Guillaume Tell, Gradiva et bureaucrate moyen*: the two figures, otherwise nude, wear a gartered stocking on one leg, suggesting perhaps that they are prisoners of a conventional, rational, and repressed society. (Tell himself, always the emblem for Dalí of repressive authority, wears a similar stocking in *L'Enigme de Guillaume Tell.*) The gesture of the young man, turning away and retreating into the recesses of the encircling, womblike rock formation, implies defeat at the hands of the victorious father and a possible lapse into autoeroticism. In these respects, *La Naissance* may in part portray the eclipse of the hero/son — the repression of his virility. Yet the presence of Gradiva suggests the beginning of another process: as in Jensen's original tale, repression is ultimately transformed into fulfilled

6. For a discussion of the myth as interpreted by Freud in 1907 and used by Dalí, Masson, Eluard, and others, see W. Chadwick, "Masson's *Gradiva*: The Metamorphosis of a Surrealist Myth," *Art Bulletin*, vol. 52, Dec. 1970, pp. 415-22. For Dalí's own reference to the identification of Gala with Gradiva, see *The Secret Life of Salvador Dalí*, p. 248.

   The raised foot of the figure in *La Naissance* explicitly evokes the "girl splendid in walking" of the original classical Greek relief, as well as the obsessional delusions she inspired. Dalí produced several other drawings and paintings of Gradiva during the period following 1930. In *Guillaume Tell, Gradiva et le bureaucrate moyen* (Private Collection, Paris) the image of the central couple is similarly conceived.

7. The female breasts, like those in many of Dalí's Tell images ("*ce Guillaume Tell ressuscité dans des tableaux et des poèmes... une poitrine de femme ballottant sur un torse contourné*," René Crevel, op. cit., 1931, pp. 29-30) suggest an association with Apollinaire's 1917 play *Les Mamelles de Tirésias* (which recounts the life of a man who is able to give birth). Apollinaire's "surrealism" or "fantasy" in the play relies explicitly on the capacity of man to create the unnatural, which is, however, by analogy, natural. The aesthetic intention is thus antirealistic and illogical, yet at the same time retains a clear relationship to the most banal reality. In this sense, Apollinaire's approach is closely allied to Dalí's, and *Les Mamelles de Tirésias*, with its multiple "birth" implications, would have offered an appropriate associative source for Dalí's image.

8. See especially *Guillaume Tell*, 1930, Private Collection.

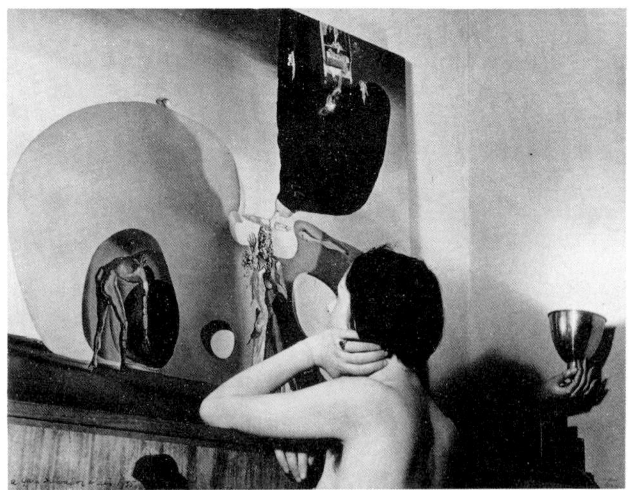

fig. a.
Man Ray, *Gala Dalí and "Birth of Liquid Desires,"* 1935, photograph, 11 3/8 x 15 7/16 in., 29 x 39.2 cm., Museum of Fine Arts, Boston.

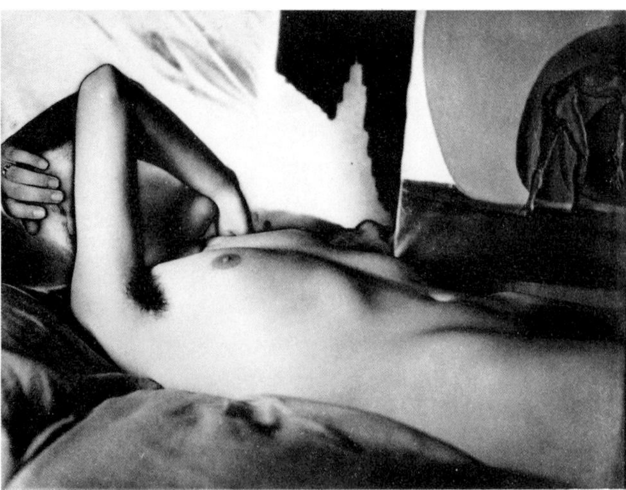

fig. b.
Man Ray, photograph, 1934, Collection Lucien Treillard, Paris.

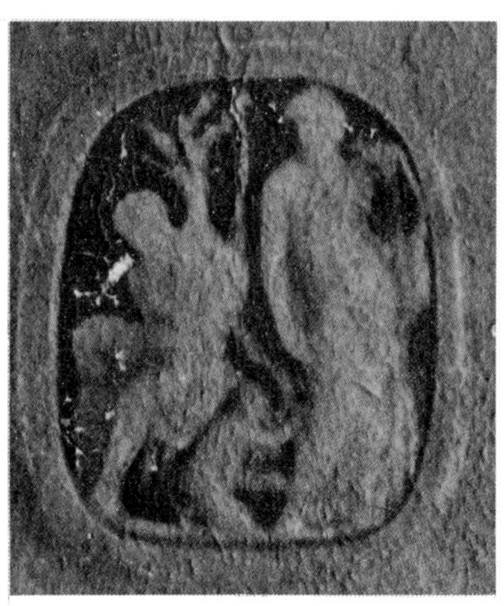

fig. c.
Detail of cat. no. 41, collage chromolithograph depicting a gem with scene of "The Flaying of Marsyas," location of original gem unknown.

desire. In this sense, the youth is perhaps at the start (*naissance*) of a curative journey. Two photographs by Man Ray, pointedly juxtaposing a Gradiva/Gala figure with the youth of Dalí's canvas, seem to reinforce such an interpretation (figs. a and b).

The small marble "relief" at the lower center of the composition (fig. c), a chromolithographic reproduction of a gem with a scene of Apollo and Marsyas, collaged to the surface of the canvas, functions, in effect, as a commentary on the main action.[9] William Tell/the father kneels on — and hence dominates — the pedestal (a pose that precisely echoes his stance in the painting *Guillaume Tell*). The subject of the relief — "The Flaying of Marsyas" — may be read in two ways: as the cruel Apollonian conquest and repression of erotic impulses epitomized by the satyr-rival; or as the eventual triumph of released imagination and art in the person of Apollo and — by extension — of the muse Gradiva. In its complexity, the scene holds in tension the various themes and meanings intrinsic not only to *La Naissance* but to much of Dalí's work of this period:

the preoccupation with conflict between rivals; the threat of physical mutilation or emasculation in defeat; and the power of art — including the possibility of intercession by "Olympian" mediators.

Other images in *La Naissance* carry similarly evocative, complex, and, in certain cases, contradictory associations. The loaf of bread on Tell's head may be read as a transposed reference to the apple in the original Tell legend. Within Dalí's personal iconography, it also carries allusions to the destructive "cannibalism" (sexual and psychological) of the father-figure. On other levels Dalí apparently implies an assault on the dual nature of bread itself: its symbolic status as sacred substance and its more literal and basic nutritional function. (Elsewhere Dalí actually used the loaf of bread as the focus of an antiutilitarian, antireligious, and anti-Communist polemic.[10])

A small "soft" watch resting (almost invisibly) in one of the niches of the large yellow rock is set at 6:55; although many of Dalí's clocks and watches are set at this hour, its significance is not clear. The primary associations of the soft watch itself are with sexual impotence as well as with Dalí's expressed interest in relativity and "the collapse of a fixed cosmic order."[11]

In the upper right of the painting, the open chest of drawers evokes associations with Dalí's 1932 film scenario *Babaouo*, in which "*une armoire de taille moyenne, aux portes et aux tiroirs ouverts, laissant voir du linge débordant dans un tumultueux désordre*," seems to serve as a metaphor for sexual violence and despoilment.[12] The cypress trees to the left of the *armoire* carry various associations for Dalí. In particular, there is a close connection with his 1931 text *Rêverie*, which records the details of an elaborate erotic and onanistic fantasy.

9. The specific gem used by Dalí has not been traced, but the iconographic type is characteristic of the Marsyas and Apollo theme. See, for example, a late 15th-century example formerly in the Medici collection (repr. A. Furtwängler, *Die Antiken Gemmen*, Berlin, Leipzig, 1900, vol. I, pl. XLII, no. 28). Apollo stands to the right with his lyre; Marsyas — his hands tied behind his back to a tree — is seated facing left; between them the child Olympos kneels with both arms raised toward Apollo.

   L. Aragon was the first to draw attention to Dalí's use of collage within the context of his paintings at this time, when he wrote that "*les parties de chromo collées passent pour peintes alors que les parties peintes passent pour collées. Veut-il par là dérouter l'œil, et se réjouit-il d'une erreur provoquée?*" (*La peinture au défi*, Paris, 1930, p. 27).

   For further discussion of Dalí's use of collage, see W. Rubin, *Dada, Surrealism, and Their Heritage*, New York, exh. cat., 1968, p. 111; D. Ades, 1982, p. 83.

10. For a discussion of this point, and of Dalí's obsession with the image of objects (edible or inedible) balanced on the heads of figures in his work, see Ades, 1982, pp. 158-61. See also Dalí's own discussions in *La Vie Secrète de Salvador Dalí*, Paris, 1952, pp. 239-42, 249-50, 252-57.

11. S. Dalí, unpublished notes for the interpretation of the painting *The Persistence of Memory*, MoMA, New York, 1931; idem, *The Secret Life of Salvador Dalí*, 1942, pp. 317-18; see also, *Dictionnaire abrégé du Surréalisme*, Paris, 1938, p. 17.

12. *Babaouo: scénario inédit précédé d'un abrégé d'une histoire critique du cinéma et suivi de Guillaume Tell, ballet portugais*, Paris, 1932, p. 36. The image recurs frequently in Dalí's paintings of the 1930s.

The setting for his *Rêverie* includes a "*groupe de cyprès*," a "*fontaine aux cyprès*" (in the painting displaced to the chest of drawers), and "*l'aspect désolé ruiné des alentours de la fontaine, agravé par le tas de pierres calciné du mur*."[13] Moreover, a miniscule inscription within one of the crevices of the dark wall of rock — *Consigne: gâcher l'ardoise totale(?)* — although elliptical and almost impenetrable on a literal or metaphorical level, makes the connection with *Rêverie* even more explicit. The same phrase is the inscribed title of a drawing which portrays the various women of *Rêverie*, lasciviously entwined with one another, each carefully labeled in Dalí's characteristically tiny hand: Dulita, Matilde, Gala (Gallo in the text), and Elena (missing from the text).[14] The enigmatic "motto" seems to urge the destruction of whatever exists. It may also, on the other hand, express a radical Surrealist impulse to break through the barriers of conventional reality, or, alternatively, indicate a more pointed desire to transform the repressive and menacing overtones implicit in *La Naissance* itself.

The title of the painting and its imagery are perhaps most evocative of Georges Bataille's *L'Histoire de L'Oeil*. Published in 1928, the story had a powerful impact upon Dalí and remained a critical text in the development of his own ideas, including the nature of his method and — in certain instances — the specific details of his iconography. The imagery of the novel is highly subjective and associative: the fetishistic obsession with the eye, which lies at the heart of the text, is transferred by Bataille to related ovoid objects (especially eggs and testicles). These in turn continuously suggest liquid equivalents: milk, water, the liquid substances of the egg and of the prenatal womb, blood, all bodily secretions (urine, semen, etc.). Sexuality, within the context of extreme violence and mutilation, as well as of procreation and birth, is the central theme of Bataille's story and provides the framework for all the otherwise disconnected images and experiences described.[15]

In *La Naissance*, two barely visible fried eggs, deposited in a crevice of the yellow rock, provide one inevitable link to *L'Histoire de L'Oeil*, while also carrying the connotation of the concept of birth explicit in Dalí's title. Variations of the ovoid egg form recur, moreover, throughout the painting, perhaps nowhere more obviously than in the left side of the giant yellow "rock," which functions as a womblike enclosure for the retreating youth. In a related painting of the same year, *La Naissance des angoisses liquides* (fig. d), Bataille's associative iconographic system, so closely echoed in the imagery at the upper right of *La Naissance des désirs liquides*, is used again in the single "standing" cypress,

13. "Rêverie," Oct. 17,1931, published in *Le Surréalisme au Service de la Révolution*, no. 4, Dec. 1931, pp. 33-34.

14. The drawing is in the collection of François Petit, Paris, repr. *Salvador Dalí*, exh. cat., MNAM, Paris, 1980, p. 168. The 1933 date on the sheet was, according to Petit (in conversation with the author, Sept. 1982), added much later; a date of 1931 seems more plausible. A literal translation of the inscription might be "Command [or password or task]: to ruin [or spoil] the total slate(?)" Calas's translation: "Password: keep the slate clean," was based on a misreading of the original: *garder* instead of *gâcher*.

fig. d.
Dalí, *La naissance des angoisses liquides*, 1932, oil on canvas, 21⅝ x 18⅛ in., 55 x 46 cm., Collection Davlyn Gallery, New York.

partly "clothed" or draped, and the fountain waters, suggestive of birth and fructification but also of autoeroticism and excretion.[16]

In these works of both Bataille and Dalí, an identifiable set of related images and associative methods exerted a powerful fascination; Bataille's example clearly provided the material for many of Dalí's major paintings of the period. In the case of *La Naissance des désirs liquides*, which remains in many of its details open to multiple readings and interpretations, the governing metaphors are those of liquids and their associations with different forms of desire (whether autosexuality, eroticism, the violence of rape or despoilment, or the mutilation of rivals). Meanwhile, a parallel preoccupation with the process of creativity and birth inevitably evokes associations with metamorphosis and regeneration.

EXHIBITIONS:

Paris, Galerie Pierre Colle, *Dalí*, June 19-29, 1933, no. 13 (*Naissance des désirs liquides*); Barcelona, Galerie d'Art Catalonia, *Salvador Dalí*, Dec. 8-21, 1933, no. 2 ("*Naixement dels desigs liquids*, 1932"); Paris, Galerie des Beaux-Arts, *Exposition internationale du Surréalisme*, Jan. 17-Feb. 1938, no. 45 ("*Naissance des désirs liquides*, 1933"); New York, Art of This Century, 1942-47, p. 122, repr.; New York, Art of This Century, *15 Early, 15 Late Paintings*, Mar. 13-Apr. 10, 1943, no. 205; Venice, *P.G.*, 1948 (Biennale), no. 26; Florence, *P.G.*, 1949, no. 26 repr.; Amsterdam, *P.G.*, 1951, no. 33, repr.; Zurich, *P.G.*, 1951, no. 31; London, *P.G.*, 1964-65, no. 90, repr.; Stockholm, *P.G.*, 1966-67, no. 87, repr. (as "Liquid desires"); Torino, Galleria Civica d'Arte Moderna, *Le Muse Inquietanti*, Nov. 1967-Jan. 1968, no. 223, repr.; New York, *P.G.*, 1969, p. 131, repr.; Paris, *P.G.*, 1974-75, no. 87; Torino, *P.G.*, 1975-76, no. 98, repr. color pl. 44; London, The Arts Council of Great Britain, Hayward Gallery, *Dada and Surrealism Reviewed*, Jan. 11-Mar. 27, 1978, p. 267, no. 11.7, repr.; Paris, MNAM, *Salvador Dalí: Retrospective 1920-1980*, Dec. 18, 1979-Apr. 21, 1980, no. 122, repr. color p. 187 (not exhibited); Rome, *Guggenheim: Venezia-New York*, 1982, no. 45, repr. color.

REFERENCES:

H. Read; *Art Now*, London, 1933, p. 129, repr. pl. 114 ("*Composition*, 1933, photo Man Ray"); D. L. Torres, "Lo real y lo superreal en la pintura de Salvador Dalí," *Gaceta de Arte*, Tenerife, July 1934, vol. viii, no. 28, repr. p. 3; P. Guggenheim, *Art of This Century*, 1942, repr. p. 122; Calas, 1966, pp. 116-17, repr. color; R. Lebel, "Il Surrealismo: Tanguy, Dalí, Brauner, Dominguez e Altri," *L'Arte Moderna*, no. 61, vol. vii, 1967, p. 258, repr. color p. 260; S. Wilson, in *Salvador Dalí*, exh. cat., The Tate Gallery, London, 1980, p. 16; D. Ades, *Dalí*, London, 1982, p. 93, repr. color fig. 75; L. Flint, *Handbook*, 1983, p. 140, repr. color p. 141.

15. Roland Barthes, in a detailed analysis of the eye-egg-testicle motif, determined that the images in Bataille's text are not used as metaphors (carrying symbolic meaning in the conventional sense) but as figures of substitution and contiguity. Bataille's eroticism is seen therefore as essentially metonymical—confusing the identity and function of associated objects rather than using them symbolically. ("La métaphore de l'œil," *Critique*, nos. 195-96, Aug.-Sept. 1963, pp. 770-77.) Dalí's approach seems to be at least in part comparable, although in his work metaphorical dimensions are also often implied.

16. In both the title and the content of this image—the combination of anguish and pleasure—the text of *Rêverie* (and its importance for an understanding of *La Naissance des désirs liquides*) is evoked once more: "*Je pense, soudain, avec une étrange émotion, mélange d'angoisse et de plaisir, que la disparition du mur permettra, vers la fin de l'après-midi, aux ombres des cyprès de se répandre lentement*" (loc. cit., p. 34).

Alan Davie

Born September 1920, Grangemouth, Scotland.
Lives in Hertfordshire and St. Lucia, West Indies.

42 Peggy's Guessing Box. 1950.
(*Untitled*).

76.2553 PG 169

Collage and oil on masonite, $47^{15}/_{16}$ x $59^{15}/_{16}$ (121.7 x 152.2).

Signed and dated l.r.: *Alan Davie 51*.[1]

PROVENANCE:
Purchased from the artist on a visit to his Barnet studio, 1950; sent to Venice, February 1951.[1]

CONDITION:
In 1964 (Tate Report) some minimal lifting of paper collage elements was noted, but the condition was otherwise described as good. The thinly painted surface remains in stable condition. (Venice, Nov. 1982.)

For approximately a year between 1949 and 1951, Davie used collage as an ingredient in his oil painting. He glued fragments of papers torn from magazines and newspapers to the surface before applying the paint, which he mixed himself from permanent powder pigments, oil, and turpentine. As in this example, the collage elements were often used with economy, making only a minimal visual impact on the compositionally dense surface.

Although the work was listed in Davie's catalogue raisonné as both *Peggy's Guessing Box* and *Untitled*, the former title was assigned to it by Davie at the time of the sale to Peggy Guggenheim.

In commenting on the relationship of title to work in this and other instances, Davie said: "My titles are not meant to be taken literally. They really are poetic interpretations of the work after the event.... The first reason for a title is that it is a form of identification ... the second is that it can become a two or three word poem which is complementary to the visual image.... I am a poet as well as a painter and the actual poetry is independently important to me" (interview with Susan D. Ferleger, Aug. 1979).

Davie's intention in the selection of his title was not to find a descriptive formula, or an interpretative or literary expression for a metaphorical content. The words were carefully chosen to coexist with the painting rather than to illuminate it.

EXHIBITIONS:

London, *P.G.*, 1964-65, no. 141 (*Untitled*); Stockholm, *P.G.*, 1966-67, no. 138; Paris, *P.G.*, 1974-75, no. 148, repr. p. 103; Torino, *P.G.*, 1975-76, no. 160.

REFERENCES:

Calas, 1966, repr. p. 236 (*Untitled*); A. Bowness, *Alan Davie*, London, 1967, no. 33, repr. pl. 9 ("*Peggy's guessing box*, 1950, postdated 1951"); [Alley], *Peggy Guggenheim Foundation*, 1968, no. 168 (*Untitled*).

1. Davie's personal catalogue raisonné records that the work (Opus number 474) was completed in 1950. The artist and his wife both recalled (in an interview with S. D. Ferleger, Aug. 1979) that Peggy Guggenheim visited them shortly afterward and purchased the picture, which was not, however, shipped to Venice until February of 1951. Davie believed that the work was actually completed in 1950, the signature and date being added just before shipping in 1951. He did not entirely rule out the possibility that he had made some minor revisions in the painting at that time.

Peggy Guggenheim's first encounter with Davie's work in December 1948 led to immediate response, enthusiasm, and support on her part. She purchased several works by him during the next few years.

Robert Delaunay

Born April 1885, Paris.
Died October 1941, Montpellier.

43 Fenêtres ouvertes simultanément Ière partie 3e motif. 1912.
(Windows open simultaneously 1st part, 3rd motif; Fenêtres).

Color plate p. 42.

76.2553 PG 36

Oil on canvas, oval, 22⅜ x 48⅜ (57 x 123).

Originally signed and dated l.r.: *r.D.12* (fig. a; this signature was lost and replaced ca. 1948 by *DELAUNAY*, not in the artist's hand. See below CONDITION).

PROVENANCE:

Purchased from the artist by Léonce Rosenberg, May 28, 1923 (document from the Delaunay Archives, Paris); purchased from Rosenberg, Paris, 1940.

CONDITION:

The picture was extensively restored in Venice in 1948 (Peggy Guggenheim, in conversation with the author, 1977). No record of this restoration survives, but it seems evident that at this time extensive losses at all edges (some extending 2¾ in., 7 cm., into the composition) were built up with gesso and then repainted, the original signature and surrounding area being lost in the process (fig. a). This earlier signature was replaced with the *DELAUNAY* now present. The entire surface was coated with natural resin varnish. It is not clear whether it had been varnished previously.

In 1964 (Tate Report) the condition of the work was described as poor and the extensive restoration noted. General crackle, abrasion of impasto, and considerable losses were also noted.

In 1982 (Venice) the previous varnish (much discolored) was removed with lacquer thinner (commercial preparation, principally toluene). The excessive buildup of gesso and overpainting, which had resulted in some avoidable blurring of the artist's original compositional lines, was removed with n-Butylamine at 30% in water. Owing to its problematic condition, however, the replacement signature of 1948 was left intact. Extensive flaking of the pigment layer indicated the need for consolidation of the surface with Rhoplex AC33 (methacrylate emulsion, Rohm and Haas), 5% in water. Due to the poor condition of the canvas, the painting was lined; the adhesive used was glue paste. Extensive losses, especially at the edges, were filled with gesso and rabbit skin glue (fig. b). Certain aspects of the original composition (especially in the pale blue area extending ca. 3 in., 7-8 cm., from the left edge) were retrieved during the cleaning and were inpainted with watercolor. The surface was coated with Le Franc retouching varnish. The overall condition is relatively stable. (New York, Feb. 1983.)

fig. a.
Photograph of cat. no. 43, taken ca. 1942. The artist's original signature and date are visible lower right.

fig. b.
Cat. no. 43 after cleaning and application of gesso repairs, before inpainting.

Delaunay's work on the series of twenty-two versions of *Les Fenêtres* began in April of 1912 and occupied the remainder of that year.[1] During this same period, he wrote two important essays in which his new aesthetic preoccupations and developing theories were presented. Slightly earlier, in a letter to Kandinsky, probably written in late March or early April, he spoke of his new concerns: "*J'attends encore un assouplissement des lois que j'ai trouvées basées sur des recherches de transparence de couleur, comparables aux notes musicales, ce qui m'a forcé de trouver le* mouvement de la couleur. *Ces choses, que je crois inconnues de tout le monde, sont pour moi encore dans l'œuf*" (*Du Cubisme à l'art abstrait*, p. 178).

By the time he had finished the two essays — "La Lumière"[2] and "Réalité, peinture pure"[3] — later that year, certain other critical influences had been brought to bear upon his thinking and had significantly affected the development of the style of the entire *Fenêtres* series.

1. See Langner, 1962; A.Z.R. *Guggenheim*, 1976, vol. 1, pp. 109-12; and Spate, 1979, pp. 375-76, for some of the basic facts about the series.
2. Trans. by Paul Klee and published as "Über das Licht," in *Der Sturm*, 3, nos. 144-45, Jan. 1913. Original text published in *Du Cubisme à l'art abstrait*, pp. 146-50.
3. First published by Apollinaire in *Soirées de Paris*, December 1912. Delaunay's original text, which differs slightly from that in *Soirées de Paris*, is published in *Du Cubisme à l'art abstrait*, pp. 158-60.

As Virginia Spate first pointed out, the writings of Leonardo were probably the most important single influence.[4] Delaunay himself explicitly acknowledged the debt in a 1924 text in which he outlined his own perceptions concerning the originality of the *Fenêtres* (their "*sensibilité et nouveauté plastique et poétique*"): "*La première fois que j'ai relevé une trace de cette pensée, c'est dans les notes de Léonard de Vinci qui écrit sur la différentiation des arts de peindre [et de] la littérature, mais cette appréciation ne touche que le côté fonction de l'œil. Il cherche à prouver la supériorité intellectuelle donnée par la simultanéité, par nos yeux,* fenêtres de l'âme, *sur la fonction auditive et successive de l'ouie.*

"*Il [ne] s'agissait comme vous le voyez, dans le tableau des* Fenêtres *que de la* couleur *pour la* couleur" (*Du Cubisme à l'art abstrait*, p. 171).

The passages that Delaunay transcribed from Péladan's translations of the writings of Leonardo (*Textes choisis*, Paris, 1907, and *Traité de la peinture*, Paris, 1910) are in some cases incorporated almost verbatim into the texts written during 1912. In other cases Delaunay absorbed the concepts and adjusted them slightly to his own purposes. Thus, for example, he copied Leonardo's notes on the capacity of the eye to illuminate the "soul." Immediately following these, he copied the notes on the limitations inherent in literary (as compared to pictorial) description. For Leonardo, even the most accurate or evocative verbal descriptions were incapable of achieving an effect of total harmony because they proceed sequentially rather than simultaneously. The pertinent passages from Leonardo — as transcribed by Delaunay — are the following:

358. *L'œil, qu'on appelle fenêtre de l'âme, est la principale voie par où le sens commun peut considérer, largement et dans leur splendeur, les œuvres infinies de la nature,...parce que la poésie parle à l'imagination avec les lettres*, tandis que la peinture donne réellement devant l'œil une image dont il aperçoit (le poète) la ressemblance comme si les choses étaient naturelles. *La poésie ne donne pas cette ressemblance et n'agit pas sur la sensibilité par la voie de la puissance visuelle comme fait la peinture.*

360. *L'œil, par qui la beauté de l'univers est révélée à notre contemplation, est d'une telle excellence que quiconque se résignerait à sa perte se priverait de connaître toutes les œuvres de la nature dont la vue fait demeurer l'âme contente dans la prison du corps, grâce aux yeux, qui lui représentent l'infinie variété de la création: qui les perd abandonne cette âme dans une obscure prison, où cesse toute espérance de revoir le soleil, lumière de l'Univers.*

4. Spate, 1979, pp. 187-91. Spate had already mentioned this issue in her 1970 Ph.D. dissertation (Bryn Mawr College), pp. 151-53, and Pierre Francastel had earlier recognized the importance of the notes when he came across them among Delaunay's papers. He briefly drew attention to the fact in his 1957 publication (p. 167), noting that Leonardo's concepts clearly influenced Delaunay's concept of "*Simultanisme*."

365. ... *Il arrive dans la beauté de n'importe quelle chose fictive du poète, que le fait de donner ses parties séparément en des temps successifs empêche la mémoire d'en percevoir l'harmonie (Du Cubisme à l'art abstrait,* p. 175).

If these transcriptions are compared with passages from Delaunay's own "La Lumière" and "Réalité, peinture pure," the influence of Leonardo is immediately apparent:[5]

La vision humaine est douée de la plus grande Réalité puis-qu'elle nous vient directement de la contemplation de l'Univers. L'œil *est notre sens le plus élevé, celui qui communique le plus étroitement avec notre* cerveau, la conscience. *L'idée du mouvement vital du* monde *et* son mouvement est simultanéité. *Notre compréhension est* corrélative *à notre* perception....

La perception auditive ne suffit pas pour notre connaissance de l'Univers elle n'a pas de profondeur. *Son mouvement est* successif, *c'est une sorte de mécanisme, sa loi est* le temps *des horloges* mécaniques *qui, comme elle, n'a aucune relation avec notre perception du* mouvement visuel dans l'Univers....

La perception auditive ne suffit pas pour notre connaissance de l'Univers puisqu'elle ne reste pas dans la durée. Sa successivité commande fatalement la parité ("La Lumière," *Du Cubisme à l'art abstrait*, pp. 146-47).

Nos Yeux sont les fenêtres de notre nature et de notre âme. C'est dans nos yeux que se passe le présent, la "science mathématique" et par conséquent notre sensibilité. Nous ne pouvons rien sans la sensibilité, donc sans lumière. Par conséquent notre âme tient sa vie dans l'harmonie et l'harmonie ne s'engendre que de la simultanéité où les mesures et les proportions de la lumière arrivent à l'âme par nos yeux, sens suprême[6] ("Note sur la construction de la réalité de la peinture pure," ibid., p. 159).

Spate has cogently argued that Leonardo's ideas influenced Delaunay in his search to provide a rationale for an art that was to be concerned purely with the representation of color and light: "Delaunay believed that, since light is composed of prismatic colour, pure colour painting could be a 'representative harmony,' a microcosm of the large harmony of being; following Leonardo, he called this 'representative harmony' the 'eternal subject.' He thus claimed a very profound meaning for non-figurative painting as an embodiment of the relationship between the individual and the whole" (Spate, 1979, p. 190).

Virtually all the *Fenêtres* paintings lack any trace of the representational perspective and "focus" of Delaunay's immediately preceding works. In developing

5. Spate (1979, pp. 188-89) quotes parts of the Leonardo and the corresponding Delaunay passages in an excellent translation (into English) and discusses their impact. For some further discussion of this point, as well as of the influence of the theories of Chevreul and Rood, see Buckberrough, 1982, pp. 119ff.

6. Spate has convincingly suggested an additional source in Leonardo's writings for this concept, though it does not appear among Delaunay's extant notes: "*Ne sais-tu pas que notre âme est faite d'harmonie, et l'harmonie ne s'engendre que de la simultanéité où la proportion des objets se fait voir, et entendre*" (*Traité de la Peinture*, 41:86).

his new approach to pictorial space, Delaunay created a continuum of color planes (some dark, some light, some opaque, some transparent). This "surface" pattern, however, does not eliminate the illusion of depth per se: because of the precise way in which the colors are juxtaposed, certain planes appear to project forward toward the viewer, others appear to angle as if they were sides of a cube, and still others carry a kind of transparency — as if they were indeed "panes" of Delaunay's "*fenêtres*."

Although there is an illusion of depth, Delaunay's pictorial space is organized in such a way that it has no single focal point: the eye is forced to move continuously over the entire surface of the canvas; each of the color planes is equally dependent on the others — "no color can be perceived in isolation and [each] can only be seen 'simultaneously' with all the others" (Spate, 1979, pp. 194-97). The relationship of the pictorial solution to the theoretical formulations of Leonardo, and those of Delaunay himself, is striking.

No entirely satisfactory chronology for the *Fenêtres* has been established. Since Delaunay was experimenting throughout the series with different ways of depicting light, movement, and space, the paintings do not reveal any clearly definable chronological order.

In attempting to place the Peggy Guggenheim painting within the series, the problematic condition of the work must also be borne in mind: its original balance of colors, and the opacity and transparency of individual planes, have clearly been altered by the passage of time. Nonetheless, on the basis of various pieces of evidence (see, for example, Spate, 1979, pp. 375-76; Buckberrough, 1982, pp. 112ff.), it seems likely that this unique oval composition was painted rather late in the *Fenêtres* series, probably in the autumn of 1912.

Supporting arguments for a late 1912 date are provided by Sherry Buckberrough, who gives a full summary of the dating problems and proposes a plausible set of chronological guidelines.[7] In so doing, she suggests that there is a close relationship between the curved forms present in the various stages of the *Fenêtres*, and the circular forms that tend to dominate Delaunay's work during 1913 and 1914. The Peggy Guggenheim painting plays a significant role within the context of Buckberrough's argument. On the right side of the composition, for example, the curving forms begin to combine in ways that suggest incipient "color wheels." These wheels, in turn, create an apparent rotational movement through the surface of the composition—a circular movement that is reinforced by the oval format of the canvas itself. The separate color segments of the wheels provide a means of opening up the space, and, in effect, of "opening" the window. The curving or circular imagery of the Peggy Guggenheim picture, like that of other examples late in the *Fenêtres* series, links it directly with the *Formes circulaires* of 1913. This context would suggest a date of late 1912 for the Guggenheim work, a tentative placement that is consistent with available evidence.

7. 1982, pp. 111-18, 133ff. Buckberrough's argument, which is intricate and illuminating, encompasses the work of 1913-14, and its full scope therefore lies beyond the confines of the present, necessarily limited, commentary.

EXHIBITIONS:

Belin, Der Sturm, *R. Delaunay, Julie Baum, Ardengo Soffici*, Jan. 27-Feb. 20, 1913, no. 6 ("*Fenêtres ouvertes Simultanément / Ière Partie 3e Motif*, M3000")?;[8] New York, MoMA, *Cubism and Abstract Art*, 1936, no. 45, repr. (Coll. Léonce Rosenberg); New York, Art of This Century, 1942-47, p. 66 (dated 1913); Venice, *P.G.*, 1948 (Biennale), no. 28 (dated 1913); Florence, *P.G.*, 1949, no. 28 (dated 1913); Amsterdam, *P.G.*, 1951, no. 36; Zurich, *P.G.*, 1951, no. 32; London, *P.G.*, 1964-65, no. 29; Stockholm, *P.G.*, 1966-67, no. 28; New York, *P.G.*, 1969, p. 62, repr.; Paris, *P.G.*, 1974-75, no. 37; Torino, *P.G.*, 1975-76, no. 36, repr.; New York, *P.G.*, 1982-83, no. 11, repr. color.

REFERENCES:

R. Delaunay, Album (containing first edition of G. Apollinaire's poem *Les Fenêtres*), Paris [1912, published by André Marty in connection with the Berlin exhibition of Jan. 1913], no. 6 (*Fenêtres ouvertes simultanément Ire Partie 3e motif*)?;[9] R. Delaunay, ca. 1918-19, *Du Cubisme à l'art abstrait*, ed. P. Francastel, Paris, 1957, p. 108, no. 7;[10] idem, "Fenêtres sur la ville 1911 et 1912," ca. 1924, ibid., p. 63; idem, "Notes historiques sur la peinture," 1924, ibid., pp. 170-72;[11] idem, letter to André Lhote, 1933, ibid., pp. 97-98 (erroneously identified as a 1924 letter to Sam Halpert; see G. Vriesen and M. Imdahl, *Robert Delaunay: Light and Color*, trans. from German by G. Pelikan, New York, 1969, p. 69, fn. 29); A. H. Barr, Jr., *Cubism and Abstract Art*, New York, 1936, no. 45, repr. fig. 58; R. Delaunay, notes written on *Les Fenêtres*, ca. 1938-39, *Du Cubisme à l'art abstrait*, p. 87; idem, lecture delivered Feb. 16, 1939, ibid., pp. 229-30; idem, "Notes sur le développement de la peinture de R. D.," ca. 1939-40, ibid., pp. 66-67; M. Seuphor, *L'Art Abstrait*, Paris, 1949, p. 210; G. Habasque, *Catalogue de l'œuvre de Robert Delaunay* in *Du Cubisme à l'art abstrait*, ed. P. Francastel, Paris, 1957, p. 266, no. 111; J. Langner, "Zu den Fenster-Bildern von Robert Delaunay," *Jahrbuch der Hamburger Kunstsammlungen*, Band 7, 1962, pp. 76ff.; J. Golding, *Cubism: A History and Analysis, 1907-1914*, rev. ed., Boston, 1968, pp. 172-76; G. Vriesen and M. Imdahl, op. cit., pp. 42ff.; A.Z.R. *Guggenheim*, 1976, vol. 1, pp. 109-12; M. Hoog, *Robert Delaunay*, trans. from French by Alice Sachs, New York, 1976, repr. color p. 33; V. Spate, *Orphism: The Evolution of Non-figurative Painting in Paris,* 1910-1914, Oxford, 1979, pp. 193, 375-76, repr. color pl. 1; S. A. Buckberrough, *Robert Delaunay: The Discovery of Simultaneity*, Ann Arbor, 1982, pp. 117, 135, 143, 145, 151, 159, 160, 181, repr. pl. 50.

8. A Der Sturm label on the stretcher, partially torn, carries the fragmentary title: "*Fenêtres ouvertes Sim . . . /Motif.*" Of the 21 works exhibited at Der Sturm, 10 of which were paintings of *Fenêtres* and 2 studies, only no. 6 includes the word "*ouvertes*" in the title. The matter is further complicated, however, by the presence on the reverse of another example, of the identical title (Tate Gallery, London, Alley, *Tate Collection*, 1981, cat. no. T. 920). It is not certain that the Tate inscription was contemporary with the painting's completion (since Delaunay frequently added such inscriptions years later). It is unclear whether it was the Tate's picture or Peggy Guggenheim's that was exhibited at Der Sturm and listed (though not reproduced) in the 1912 Album. The presence of the Der Sturm label on the reverse of the Peggy Guggenheim picture, however, lends some weight to the presumption that the exhibited picture was hers.
9. See above, fn. 8.
10. This text can be dated 1918-19 on the grounds that it refers to the 1917 exhibition held in Stockholm and to an exhibition in Barcelona that must have taken place while the Delaunays were staying there during the war.
11. This passage is dated 1928-30 by Francastel. Spate, however, has pointed out (1979, p. 356, fn. 30) that part of it was published in *Nouvelles littéraires*, Oct. 25, 1924.

Paul Delvaux

Born September 1897, Antheit, Belgium.
Lives in Brussels.

44 L'Aurore. July 1937.
(The break of day; La naissance du jour; l'Aube; Die Baumfrauen).

Color plate p. 251.

76.2553 PG 103

Oil on canvas (unvarnished), 47¼ x 59¼ (120 x 150.5).

Signed and dated l.r.: *P. DELVAUX. / 7.37.*

PROVENANCE:

Purchased from E.L.T. Mesens, London, June 1938.[1]

CONDITION:

In 1964 (Tate Report) small holes pierced from the rear were observed in the arm and breast of the second figure from the left. There were signs of a horizontal branched crackle in the sky, some retouching along the top of the sky and over damages in the center. Apart from some surface dirt, the condition was described as fairly good. The work had not been varnished at that point.

According to Peggy Guggenheim the picture was at various times damaged by rain. Mitigation of water stains and some inpainting had been attempted on at least one occasion by the Venetian artist Edmondo Bacci.

In 1978 (New York) a bloom or whitish film over much of the surface was noted (possibly due to salt deposits). The paint film was extremely dry, thinly applied, and in parts abraded through cleaning. There were traction cracks in some places, with flaking apparent at both top and bottom margins. Retouching of certain areas was clearly visible under UV.

Soil and staining of the surface proved extremely difficult to remove except in the sky area, which was cleaned with 5% Soilax solution and rinsed with distilled water. Flaking areas at top and bottom were consolidated with several applications of dilute Lucite 44. A brush coat of Lucite 44 was applied to certain parts of the womens' bodies. The work was removed from its stretcher and flattened. It was then lined on Mylar 1400 with BEVA, strip-lined with Lucite 44-treated linen strips using Plus-Ten contact cement, and stapled to a new stretcher.

The surface is abraded, but the condition stable. The presence of Lucite 44 is evident under UV. (New York, Mar. 1983.)

Images of "metamorphoses," and their explication, recur again and again in the literature on Delvaux. (See, for example, J. Clair, "Un rêve autobiographique," *Delvaux: Catalogue de l'œuvre peint*, 1975, p. 89: "*Contre le monde de la science, elle* [la femme] *affirme son appartenance au monde de la nature: femme-fleur, femme-lierre, femme-arbre, elle ressuscite les mythes de Daphné et d'Hélène-Dentritis. Elle est la source des métamorphoses et elle commande aux éléments.*")

L'Aurore is the earliest instance in Delvaux's oeuvre of such an image, and it is unique in its use of the *femme-arbre* motif. By the artist's own recent testimony, however, its relationship to the very concept of metamorphosis is also unique in other respects: "L'Aurore *n'est pas seulement le premier, mais aussi l'unique tableau dans lequel j'ai employé la métamorphose des arbres en femmes. Dans mes autres tableaux dans lesquels j'ai employé des formes végétales (fleurs,*

1. In addition to *L'Aurore*, E.L.T. Mesens bought several important works by Delvaux from 1934 onward. As Vovelle (1972, p. 210) has pointed out, it was primarily through the support and intervention of Mesens that Delvaux was brought to the attention of the Surrealists, shown in their exhibitions, and published in their magazines.

feuilles) je ne l'ai pas vu, ni employé comme une métamorphose, mais plutôt comme un ornement imaginatif, pas comme une transformation de l'être féminin."[2]

In the artist's mind, as he looks back on these images of nude females, their flowing tresses adorned with or transformed into leaves and flowers, they convey neither a literal evocation of an Ovidian Daphne (*Metamorphoses* 1. 548-67) nor a more suggestive metaphor for the relationship between woman and nature. These vegetal forms represent for him essentially a lyrical mode of "*ornement imaginatif.*"

Although the notion of metamorphosis, as depicted in *L'Aurore*, may appear to evoke Ovidian themes (in this instance the story of Phaeton's mourning sisters transformed into poplar trees from *Metamorphoses* 2. 340-66), the connection is at best fortuitous. Moreover, it is important to note that Delvaux has described the metamorphosis as one of tree into woman, and not the reverse. Delvaux read Ovid in his youth and may well have retained a memory of the Phaeton tale, but the nature of his sensibility would argue against any direct connection between a text and a picture. His aim in the paintings is to evoke a certain mood — "*un sentiment poétique*" — and he explicitly rejects even a subconscious association with classical sources: "*Dans mon tableau* (L'Aurore) *je n'ai pas voulu employer des reminiscences à l'antiquité, ni à Ovide, ni à d'autres. Pour moi ces femmes-arbres étaient l'interprétation d'une idée et d'une pratique surréaliste à laquelle j'étais sensible à ce moment. C'était une trouvaille de mon imagination.*"

In this respect his recent memories coincide with his earlier formulation in the 1971 *7 Dialogues*, where he had suggested that the image of a *femme-arbre* represented a Surrealist paradox: "*Je tente une approche de la Nature en dehors même de toute représentation naturaliste ... le réalisme crée ainsi: l'impression de non-réalisme*" (J. Meuris, *7 Dialogues avec Paul Delvaux accompagnés de 7 lettres imaginaires*, Paris, 1971, pp. 97-98).

Delvaux's explanation of the presence of the small bowler-hatted figure in the rear background reinforces this interpretation of the picture's suspension between two levels of reality. Often described as a self-portrait (see below REFERENCES), Delvaux on the contrary conceived the figure functioning merely as a foil to the "unreality" of the *femmes-arbres*: "*J'ai crée ce petit bonhomme bourgeois et conventionnel pour avoir un contraste insolite avec mes femmes nues, avec mes créatures de rêve. Une réalité banale parmi une realité poétique.*"

This concept of the real and the unreal, the physical and the imaginary, the banal and the poetic that permeates the picture is crystallized for Delvaux above all in the centrally placed mirror, in which a woman's breast and part of a torso

2. This and the following quotations are taken from an interview with Delvaux conducted at the author's request in Brussels, January 1983, by Renilde Hammacher van den Brande. The author is much indebted to her for conveying the questions to the artist and to him for graciously addressing them.

are reflected, but they are the breast and torso of an invisible presence mysteriously evoked but not explained: "*Le miroir pour moi n'est pas un ornement, c'est un objet magique—réel et irréel. Il est là comme un personnage mystérieux, non seulement un reflet, mais aussi une autre presence. Je l'ai représenté parfois comme le reflet d'une femme qui n'existe pas, ou même parfois seulement un cadre, qui suggère un miroir dans lequel l'être réel est représenté. Le miroir par sa magie est un élément très important dans mes imaginations.*"

It is interesting to note that Duchamp, in creating his homage *In the Manner of Delvaux* (fig. a), appears to have been responding specifically to these "magical" connotations carried by the mirrors in the Belgian's work.[3]

fig. a.
Duchamp, *In the Manner of Delvaux*, 1942, collage, 13⅜ x 13⅜ in., 34 x 34 cm., Collection Vera and Arturo Schwarz, Milan.

EXHIBITIONS:

Brussels, Palais des Beaux-Arts, *Paul Delvaux*, Mar. 5-16, 1938, no. 6 ("*La Naissance du jour*"); London, The London Gallery, *Paul Delvaux*, June 1938, no. 14 (checklist in *London Bulletin*, no. 3, June 1938, p. 3); New York, *Art of This Century*, 1942-47, p. 131, repr.; Venice, *P.G.*, 1948 (Biennale), no. 29; Florence, *P.G.*, 1949, no. 29, repr.; Amsterdam, *P.G.*, 1951, no. 37, repr.; Zurich, *P.G.*, 1951, no. 33; London, *P.G.*, 1964-65, no. 93, repr.; Stockholm, *P.G.*, 1966-67, no. 88, repr.; Torino, Galleria Civica d'Arte Moderna, *Le Muse Inquietanti*, Nov. 1967-Jan. 1968, no. 215, repr.; New York, *P.G.*, 1969, p. 109, repr. color p. 108; Paris, *P.G.*, 1974-75, no. 102, repr.; Torino, *P.G.*, 1975-76, no. 101, repr. pl. 49; New York, *P.G.*, 1982-83, no. 43, repr. color.

REFERENCES:

J. Scutenaire, "Paul Delvaux," *London Bulletin*, no. 3, 1938, repr. p. 9; L. and P. Haesaerts, "Paul Delvaux, le noctambule," *Les Beaux-Arts*, no. 281, June 17, 1938; *The Studio*, vol. 116, Aug. 1938, repr. p. 121; P. Guggenheim, *Art of This Century*, 1942, repr. p. 131 (the small bowler-hatted figure is identified here, and in subsequent *P.G.* publications, as a self-portrait of the artist); P. Waldberg, *Le Surréalisme*, Geneva, 1962, repr. color p. 110; Calas, 1966, p. 120, repr. color p. 152; P. A. De Bock, *Paul Delvaux*, Brussels, 1967, p. 289, repr. pl. 28; X. Gauthier, *Surréalisme et sexualité*, Paris, 1971, p. 123; J. Vovelle, *Le Surréalisme en Belgique*, Brussels, 1972, p. 180, repr. p. 210; M. Butor, J. Clair, and S. Houbart-Wilkin, *Delvaux: Catalogue de l'œuvre peint*, Brussels, 1975, pp. 138, 291, no. 85, repr. color p. 292; G. Picon, *Journal du Surréalisme 1919-1939*, Geneva, 1976, repr. color p. 163; S. Houbart-Wilkin, "La femme et le miroir," in *Hommage à Paul Delvaux*, exh. cat., Brussels, 1977, n.p.

3. Delvaux, who knows Duchamp's work and has always admired it, never met him, and was unaware of the existence of Duchamp's "homage" until it was brought to his attention in the interview.

Theo van Doesburg

(pseud. of Christian E. M. Küpper).

Born August 1883, Utrecht.
Died March 1931, Davos, Switzerland.

45 Composition in gray (Rag-time). 1919.
(Composition, motif Ragtime; Komposition in Grau [Rag-Time]; Composition en gris; Composition).

Color plate p. 387.

76.2553 PG 40

Oil on canvas (unvarnished), 38 x 23¼ (96.5 x 59.1).

Signed and dated with monogram l.c.: *1918 VD*; with monogram on reverse: *1918 VD* (photographed before relining, 1965).

PROVENANCE:

Purchased from Nelly van Doesburg, London, 1939.[1]

CONDITION:

In 1964 (Tate Report) the unvarnished surface was described as very dirty. Certain areas of the canvas showed extensive crackle with advanced cleavage. The danger of losses in these sections was considered sufficient to render the painting unsafe for travel. Some preliminary consolidation was apparently executed before the work was shipped to London. The off-white ground showed extensive crackle and cleavage, as did the hard, brittle paint film, the cleavage being especially severe at the divisions of the rectangles. There were small losses and some retouching of losses at the lower right. The canvas was impregnated with wax resin adhesive and lined (14 pts. beeswax; 4 pts. dammar; 1 pt. gum elemi). The stretcher (which was not the original, but ¼ in., 0.5 cm., smaller on all 4 sides, causing stress to the support) was replaced with a stretcher of the original dimensions. The surface was cleaned and cleaving pigment secured. There is no record of retouching at this point.

A diagonal tear in the support (lower center) and a second diagonal damage (lower left) were clearly repaired at some point, and retouching in those areas is apparent; the edges also show evidence of retouching.

Some much earlier reworking of the composition by the artist is evident in areas that have now discolored to greenish gray and to some extent lost their opacity. Some of the black lines were strengthened, the horizontal at the bottom of the canvas the most obvious example. The monogram and date on the front and back may have been added during 1 of these stages of reworking by the artist. Since the picture was in his hands until his death, he could have revised the details at any point between 1919 and 1931.

The overall condition is stable. (New York, Mar. 1983.)

Composition in gray (Rag-time) of 1919, traditionally known as *Composition* or *Composition in gray*, 1918, was first unmistakably identified in print with the music/dance theme in Jean Hélion's 1931 obituary of van Doesburg (see below REFERENCES). The painting was reproduced by Hélion with a caption ("*rag-time*, 1919") providing the correct date. These two facts correspond with those recorded in the catalogue of the 1920 Geneva exhibition where the painting was first shown. But the absence of an illustration in that catalogue, and the subsequent designation of the picture in all published sources as *Composition* or *Composition en gris*, 1918 (the date inscribed on both the front and the back

1. Peggy Guggenheim recalled buying this work considerably earlier than cat. no. 46. Though she could not precisely recall whether it was included in her exhibition *Abstract and Concrete Art* of May 1939 (where it would have been hors catalogue), she felt reasonably certain that 1939 was the date of acquisition.

of the canvas), have, until recently, obscured the correct identity of the work, as well as its original title, date, and source of inspiration. Recent research, however, has demonstrated conclusively that a painting by this title appears in van Doesburg's own personal lists, and that — by process of elimination — it must be the Peggy Guggenheim work.[2]

In the Van Doesburg Archive, a typed list of the works exhibited by the artist in Weimar in 1923 includes as No. 23, "*Komposition in Grau (Rag-time)*, 1918," offered for sale at "400 G.M. netto." The installation photographs (see fig. e) show the Peggy Guggenheim picture; through a careful study of the list and the installation photographs, it has been possible to establish that "No. 23" and the Guggenheim work are one and the same. In a further list of van Doesburg's own works (preserved in the same archives), probably compiled in 1926-27 as a preparatory outline toward an oeuvre catalogue of the De Stijl years, the Guggenheim painting appears as "*Compositie XX... 1918 (in grijs, Rag-time)*."[3]

Although the title of the work is definitively established by these various documents, conflicting evidence regarding the date remains. In the Van Doesburg Archive, however, are two important letters that bear on this issue; they were written to his close friend Antony Kok. In the first letter, dated April 2, 1919, van Doesburg writes:

> *... I am also busy working on a special thing which is inspired by a Rag-time. This is an extremely difficult undertaking, and I am battling with it every day. I want to render it [the painting] completely according to the spirit [of the Rag-time] and I see it clearly before me. I have already made a large number of studies on paper, and just this evening I have found a few sections that please me. It's striking that in my work I always maintain two "stages" simultaneously: [on the one hand] the pure composition of well-balanced inter-relationships between color and plane, between one color and the next, and between one plane and the next; [on the other hand] "individual representations" in which I do not start out from the general, but rather from a specific individual idea, such as, for example, the dance, or the bull in motion, etc. If you think about the works of mine that you have seen, you will also be struck by this.*[4]

2. Joop Joosten and Evert van Straaten generously shared the results of their research on these points prior to the 1983 publication (see REFERENCES). Several of the newly established facts about the painting's history derive from the Van Doesburg Archive now in the collection of the Dienst Verspreide Rijkskollekties, The Hague. See also C. Blotkamp, 1982, who published some of the archival information in his essay.

3. This list is published, with an explanatory note by van Straaten, 1983, pp. 185-86. Although the roman numerals used here by van Doesburg have not yet been fully explained, it seems likely that they designate the sequence of the works produced during the De Stijl and immediately preceding era, rather than serving as a new set of titles for the works involved.

4. "... *Ook ben ik nog bezig aan een bizonder ding, geinspireerd door een Rag-time. Dit is een ontzettend moeilijk geval, waarmee ik dagelijks een complete veldslag voer. Ik wil het geheel volgens den geest hebben en heb het duidelijk voor mij. Ik maakte reeds een groot aantal*

Six weeks later, on May 18, 1919, he wrote to Kok: "*I am now busy completing my Rag-time (dance V).*"[5]

In describing the work as "dance V," van Doesburg explicitly suggests that he saw his "dance" pictures as constituting an independent series, or at least as thematically interrelated in a more than superficial sense. The preceding four works were probably: *Dance I* and *II* of 1916 (a diptych now in the collection of the Dienst Verspreide Rijkskollekties, The Hague, repr. Troy, 1982, fig. 2); two stained glass windows of 1917 based on the dance theme (in the same collection, repr. Troy, 1982, fig. 4); *Tarantella* of 1918 (now lost, repr. van Straaten, 1983, p. 86); and *Rhythm of a Russian Dance*, also of 1918 (MoMA, New York). It is of course important to consider the Peggy Guggenheim picture within the context of these earlier explorations, as well as in relation to van Doesburg's continuing preoccupation with the problem of rendering movement and rhythm (whether of dance or of music) in pure pictorial form.

As Nancy Troy has demonstrated (1982), van Doesburg's interest in dance motifs can be traced to at least 1916. During that year he executed the two paintings entitled *Dance I* and *Dance II* depicting entirely legible, representational images of a single dancer seen first from the front, then from the back. The body is rendered in a sequence of flat, decorative, geometric sections, combined as if in a cutout collage. The double composition conveys the movement of the dance merely through the rhythmic juxtapositions and arrangements of triangular and semicircular segments. In two stained glass windows of the following year, the same forms were further schematized and abstracted, and the figure of the dancer inverted. In August 1918, J.J.P. Oud was probably describing these windows when he wrote: "The idea is represented by means of the abstract figure and counter-figure, striving for movement and counter-movement, in other words for rest in motion" ("Glas-in-lood van Theo van Doesburg," *Bouwkundig Weekblad*, 39, 1918, p. 202, cited and translated by Troy, 1982).

Troy convincingly argues that in these much more abstract renditions of the dance, van Doesburg began to exploit the compositional potential of the window leading that supports the glass; through this process the grid structure of the lead began to alter his entire mode of composition.[6]

studies op papier en vond juist vanavond enkele gedeelten die mij bevallen. 't Is eigenaardig dat ik altijd twee momenten in mijn werk houdt: zuivere kompositie van evenwichtige verhouding van kleur tot vlak, van kleur tot kleur en vlak tot vlak en 'einzelbildungen' waarbij ik niets van de algemeene, maar van 'n individueele idee uitga bv. dans, stier in beweging e.d. Als je de dingen, die je van mij gezien hebt nog voor den geest kunt halen zal je dit ook opvallen" (Van Doesburg Archive, Dienst Verspreide Rijkskollekties, The Hague).

5. "*Ben nu aan het uitvoeren van mijn Rag-time (dans V)*" (ibid.).

6. This idea had been briefly mentioned in passing by Welsh, 1976, p. 87. Blotkamp, 1982, pp. 25-28, elaborated upon the point, and on some issues he reached conclusions that are different from Troy's. Troy's fundamental observations regarding the importance of the stained glass windows in the development of van Doesburg's abstract idiom remain undisputed.

Meanwhile, in a July 1917 letter to Kok, possibly sent while he was working on the windows, van Doesburg wrote: "I feel that dance is the most dynamic expression of life and it is therefore the most important subject for a pure plastic art."[7]

In all four of the "dance" works that preceded *Rag-time*, van Doesburg's method of composition involved a gradual process of abstraction from a figural source. (See, for example, the series of sketches of Indonesian dancers from which *Dance I* and *II* were derived, Troy, 1982, fig. 3; or the series of seven preparatory studies for *Rhythm of a Russian Dance* — all owned by MoMA; or the sketches for *Tarantella* published by van Straaten, 1983, p. 86.) In the case of *Rag-time*, van Doesburg must have followed a similar course, although the long series of studies — mentioned in his April 2, 1919 letter to Kok — have not so far come to light.

Two drawings do exist, however, that seem to illuminate van Doesburg's method of proceeding in this work. The first of these (fig. a) shows, in extremely stark, dry, stylized form, a dancing couple, and has hitherto been known in the literature as *Tango*. Robert Welsh suggested a possible connection between this drawing and the Venice painting, although he was far from certain about the relationship (1976, p. 88). The style of the drawing is stilted and awkward; it conveys, in some respects, the impression of having been executed after the painting, as a kind of pedagogical exercise — an attempt to illustrate post hoc the figural source for an existing abstract composition. On the other hand, in the light of the procedure followed by van Doesburg in other works of the previous year, it seems more likely that this large-scale drawing actually served as a preparatory study for the painting.

Van Straaten recently published a group of otherwise unknown drawings that were apparently made with a similar thick brush and black paint (1983, pp. 85-86). In these examples, as van Straaten's photographs demonstrate, van Doesburg started from an extremely realistic gouache landscape of considerable size; over this work he placed tracing paper, and with a series of thick black brush-strokes he picked out only the straight lines of the composition (whether vertical, horizontal, or diagonal). Some curves remained in the initial traced efforts to

7. "*Ik voel den dans als de meest dynamische uitdrukking van het leven en daarom voor zuiver beeldende kunst als het belangrijkste onderwerp*," letter of July 14, 1917, cited by C. Blotkamp, 1982 p. 27.

The complex interrelationship of van Doesburg's various projects in applied art and painting during this critical period, and the impact on his thinking of the work of Bart van der Leck and Mondrian, have been discussed by Welsh, Troy, Joosten, and Blotkamp in the publications cited here, as well as in others. The particular place of the Peggy Guggenheim painting within van Doesburg's use of dance — and of music motifs — has not, however, been explored. The important ideas about the picture's genesis contained in the April 1919 letter to Kok (especially his statement "*Ik wil het geheel volgens den geest hebben*") and the relationship of these ideas to the probably contemporary essay he published in the November 1919 issue of *De Stijl* ("Aanteekeningen over de nieuwe muziek") throw some new light on the ways in which van Doesburg was using the stimulus of music and dance in his effort to arrive at "pure plastic form."

fig. a.
Van Doesburg, Study for cat. no. 45, signed in monogram and dated 1918, gouache on tracing paper on cardboard, 37 7/8 x 21 3/4 in., 96.3 x 55.3 cm., Dienst Verspreide Rijkscollecties, The Hague.

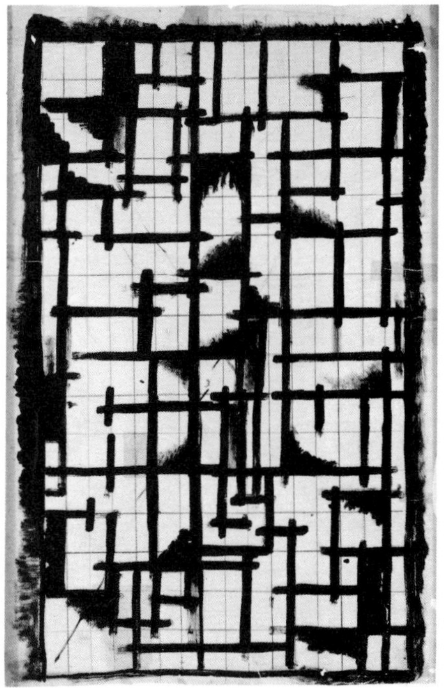

fig. b.
Van Doesburg, *Untitled*, not signed or dated, gouache on paper, 25 9/16 x 16 15/16 in., 65 x 43 cm., Museum des XX. Jahrhunderts, Vienna.

"abstract" the linear quality of the landscape, but these were suppressed in subsequent drawings. The composition was ultimately executed as a work in stained glass, and its final form was that of a rectilinear grid. (Van Straaten also published a similar preparatory tracing taken from a realistic landscape that led eventually to the abstract, linear *Composition XII* of 1918, now in the collection of the Oeffentliche Kunstsammlung, Basel, repr. S. Polano, 1979, pl. 81.)

The second drawing that may be related to the compositional evolution of *Rag-time* is a gouache in the collection of the Museum des XX. Jahrhunderts, Vienna (fig. b; this has until now been published as a horizontal: see, for example, Polano, 1979, pl. 73). Although it is not possible to trace a definite connection between the arrangement of lines and planes in this sketch and that of the Peggy Guggenheim painting, the nature of the scalloping and shading (which is unusual although not unique in works of this period) and the general proportions of the composition do suggest a possible relationship. It also seems clear that in the gouache and in *Rag-time* van Doesburg was engaged in a similar process of abstraction from a figural source, while simultaneously accommodating the composition to the demands of a grid. (It should, in addition, be noted that the Vienna gouache also bears some resemblance to a few sections of the preparatory drawings for *Tarantella*, where some similar shading of rectangular planes occurs as the figure is abstracted into a planar form. To this

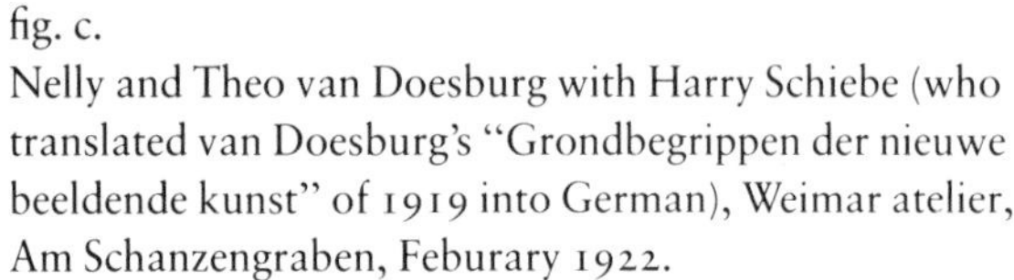

fig. c.
Nelly and Theo van Doesburg with Harry Schiebe (who translated van Doesburg's "Grondbegrippen der nieuwe beeldende kunst" of 1919 into German), Weimar atelier, Am Schanzengraben, Feburary 1922.

fig. d.
Installation photograph, van Doesburg exhibition held at Landesmuseum, Weimar, 1923-24.

extent the Vienna drawing — although obviously not a study for *Tarantella* — provides evidence for a comparable methodology.)

Finally, it seems important to discuss the anomalous presence on Peggy Guggenheim's painting (recto and verso) of the date 1918. It is evident from the Kok letters that van Doesburg was working intensely on the picture during the spring of 1919. ("This is an extremely difficult undertaking, and I am battling with it every day.") Even if his original figural sketches (such as those of Indonesian dancers used for *Dance I* and *II*, or that for the *Tarantella*, repr. van Straaten, 1983, p. 86) were completed before 1919, or indeed before 1918, the actual process of working out the pictorial solution, through an arduous process of gradual abstraction, was taking place in the spring of 1919. In addition, as was noted above, the picture was also dated 1919 on the occasion of its first exhibition (in December 1920). When van Doesburg moved to Weimar in 1922, and began to teach and work at the Bauhaus, he brought the picture with him, and it hung — with very little else — in his Weimar studio (fig. c). It was also exhibited (together with the large drawing of almost the same dimensions) in van Doesburg's important Weimar exhibition of 1923-24 (see installation photos, figs. d and e). The picture, therefore, was almost certainly used by van Doesburg as an important didactic image in his pedagogical program at the Bauhaus. It seems not unlikely that within this challenging context (when he is known to have been anxious about his role as a pioneer and leader of the avant-garde), van Doesburg may have antedated both the drawing and the painting in order to reinforce the image that he wished to project.[8]

8. The final "8" of the 1918 on the reverse of the painting, as well as that at the lower left of the large drawing, do, when examined carefully under magnification, show signs of having been altered, although it is impossible to state with certainty that a "9" was initially there instead.

fig. e.
Installation photograph, van Doesburg exhibition held at Landesmuseum, Weimar, 1923-24.

The fact that *Rag-time* can be definitively ascribed to the spring of 1919 raises some important questions concerning the chronology of all of van Doesburg's work during the years 1918-19. In view of the spatial ambiguities created by the planar shading in the Guggenheim work, and "the radical asymmetry of its internal divisions," Welsh (1976, p. 88) and Joosten (1982, p. 60) convincingly placed the picture chronologically before *Composition XVI: In Dissonances* (Oeffentliche Kunstsammlung, Basel, repr. Polano, 1979, pl. 99) and *Composition XVII* (Gemeentemuseum, The Hague, repr. ibid., pl. 101). Both of these latter works, usually dated 1918, or — in the case of *Composition XVII* — sometimes 1918-19, demonstrate a far more regular division of the field according to an overall grid structure, and in neither of them do the lines stop short of the edge of the canvas. Indeed in The Hague picture, the work is constructed as a perfect square divided on the principle of ten modules in each direction. It now seems clear (in the light of the evidence regarding the execution of *Rag-time*) that these two paintings cannot have been painted — or at least fully resolved — until after May 1919. (Joosten does in fact date both the Basel and The Hague paintings 1919.)

The original source of Peggy Guggenheim's picture can perhaps be established with greater precision than the rather general notion of "rag-time dance music." In her unpublished memoirs, Nelly van Doesburg describes her first encounter with van Doesburg on the occasion of a lecture he was giving at the Haagsche Kunstkring (1920). She was deeply impressed by him and could not rest until she was introduced, which occured at a dinner party not long afterward. There was intense conversation about art, and van Doesburg was apparently delighted to learn that she was a pianist. He immediately asked if she could play Stravinsky, Schönberg, and Satie: "He was especially mad about Satie. I had not even heard the name, but I dared not confess it.... I just mumbled that modern music was extremely hard to play. The next day he sent me a package of music by Erik

Satie, with — among other things — 'Ragtime' and 'Pièce en forme de poires' etc.... "[9] On the basis of this incident, it seems plausible to assume that the "Ragtime" by Erik Satie was the particular music to which the dance of van Doesburg's *Composition in gray (Rag-time)* owes its origin.

Finally, it is interesting to note that whereas Mondrian's interest in American dance music and jazz is well-known, van Doesburg's has been hitherto entirely unrecorded.

EXHIBITIONS:

Geneva, Palais Électoral, *Exposition Internationale d'Art Moderne*, Dec. 26, 1920-Jan. 25, 1921, no. 29 ("*Composition, motif Ragtime*, 1919"); Weimar, Landesmuseum, *Ontwikkelingstentoonstelling van T. van Doesburg*, Dec. 1923-Jan. 1924, no. 23 (typed checklist, "*Komposition in Grau (Rag-Time)* 1918");[10] Barcelona, Galerie Dalmau, *Exposición de arte moderno nacional y extranjero*, Oct. 31-Nov. 15, 1929, no. 14 ("*Composition en gris*, 1918"); Paris, Parc des Expositions, 2e *Exposition de l'Association artistique* "*1940*," Jan. 15-Feb. 1, 1932, no. 40 ("*Composition en gris*, 1918");[11] Amsterdam, Stedelijk Museum, *Theo van Doesburg*, May 2-31, 1936, no.

fig. f.
Van Doesburg retrospective in the Parc des Expositions, Paris, January 15-February 1, 1932; the retrospective formed part of the second exhibition of "*1940*."

9. Original Dutch manuscript published by Wies van Moorsel, in *Theo van Doesburg 1883-1931*, ed. E. van Straaten, The Hague, 1983, pp. 17, 19: "*Op een zaterdagmiddag werd in de Haagsche Kunstkring, ter gelegenheid van de tentoonstelling La Section d'Or (1920)... door Theo van Doesburg een lezing over moderne kunst gehouden. Al snel... had ik mijn ogen alleen nog maar gericht op de man, die op het podium zonder in zijn papieren te kijken... met grote gebaren op en neer lopend zonder ophouden sprak... Vooral was ik getroffen door zijn buitengewoon warme en innemende stem. Ik denk dat men dat coup de foudre noemt. In ieder geval rustte ik niet, voordat ik aan hem voorgesteld werd. Het werd een fantastische avond, waarin alleen maar over kunst gesproken werd. Theo van Doesburg vond het geweldig dat ik pianiste was en vroeg me of ik ook muziek speelde van Strawinsky, Schönberg en Satie. Hij was vooral dol op Satie. Ik kende zelfs de naam niet... maar durfde dat niet te zeggen... en mompelde maar dat moderne muziek moeilijk te spelen was. De volgende dag... stuurde hij me een pak muziek van Eric Satie, met o.a. 'Ragtime' en 'Pièce en forme de poires'* etc."

10. See installation photo, fig. e. The author is indebted for this information and a copy of the checklist to E. van Straaten.

11. See installation photo, fig. f. The exhibition included a retrospective of 59 works by van Doesburg, who had died the previous year.

39 ("*Compositie in grauw*, 1918");[12] Basel, Kunsthalle, *Konstruktivisten*, June 16-Feb. 14, 1937, no. 1 or 2?;[13] London, Guggenheim Jeune, *Abstract and Concrete Art*, May 1939 (hors catalogue?);[14] New York, Art of This Century, 1942-47, p. 86, repr. p. 87;[15] New York, Art of This Century, *Theo van Doesburg*, Apr. 29-May 31, 1947, no. 24; Venice, *P.G.*, 1948 (Biennale), no. 30; Florence, *P.G.*, 1949, no. 30; Amsterdam, *P.G.*, 1951, no. 38, repr.; Zurich, *P.G.*, 1951, no. 34; London, *P.G.*, 1964-65, no. 33, repr.; Stockholm, *P.G.*, 1966-67, no. 34, repr.; Eindhoven, Stedelijk van Abbemuseum, *Theo van Doesburg*, Dec. 13, 1968-Jan. 26, 1969, p. 80, A22, repr., traveled to The Hague, Feb. 7-Mar. 23, 1969, Basel, Kunsthalle, June-July 1969 (German ed. of catalogue); Paris, *P.G.*, 1974-75, no. 30, repr.; Torino, *P.G.*, 1975-76, no. 40, repr. pl. 22; Rome, *Guggenheim: Venezia-New York*, 1982, no. 33, repr. color; New York, *P.G.*, 1982-83, no. 18, repr.

REFERENCES:

J. Hélion, "theo van doesburg ist tot," *a bis z*, 2 folge, Cologne, 1931, repr. p. 58 ("*rag-time 1919*"); *Theo van Doesburg*, exh. cat., Stedelijk van Abbemuseum, Eindhoven, 1968, A22, repr. p. 80; R. P. Welsh, "Theo van Doesburg and Geometric Abstraction," in *Nijhoff Van Ostaijen, "De Stijl": Modernism in the Netherlands and Belgium in the First Quarter of the 20th Century*, The Hague, 1976, pp. 87-88, repr. pl. 15; S. Polano, ed., *Theo van Doesburg: Scritti di arte e architettura*, Rome, 1979, p. 529, no. 137, repr. pl. 87; N. Troy, "Theo van Doesburg: From Music into Space," *Arts Magazine*, vol. 56, no. 6, Feb. 1982, p. 101, fn. 6; J. Joosten, "De beginjaren van De Stijl—rondom Van Doesburg," *Tableau*, vol. 5, no. 1, Sept.-Oct., 1982, pp. 58, 60, repr.; C. Blotkamp, *De Beginjaren van de Stijl, 1917-1922*, Utrecht, 1982, pp. 36, 37, 39; R. P. Welsh, "De Stijl: A Reintroduction," in *De Stijl: 1917-1931: Visions of Utopia*, New York, 1982, p. 31, fn. 28; E. van Straaten, *Theo van Doesburg*, The Hague, 1983, pp. 92, 186.

12. The picture, which appears in an installation photograph owned by Joop Joosten, was listed in the catalogue as being for sale.
13. Both entries are "*Composition 1918*" and no installation photo or other substantiating evidence has yet been found.
14. The work is not included in the catalogue, but see fn. 1 above.
15. From 1942 onward, the picture was consistently titled *Composition* and dated 1918.

46 Contra-Compositie XIII. 1925-26.
(*Counter-Composition XIII*).

Color plate p. 388.

76.2553 PG 41

Oil on canvas (unvarnished), 19⅝ x 19⅝ (49.9 x 50.0).

Signed and dated l.c.: *Théo V.D. 1926*; on reverse of canvas (photographed before relining): *DOESBURG*; on stretcher (photographed before replacement): *CONTRE-COMP: / XIII / 1926*.

PROVENANCE:

François Arp, Strasbourg;[1] Dr. Roth, Strasbourg;[1] Nelly van Doesburg;[2] purchased from Nelly van Doesburg, Paris, 1940.

CONDITION:

In 1964 (Tate Report) some small scratches and minimum losses near the top edge (left corner and center) were noted. The unvarnished paint film was described as in good condition.

In 1969 (New York) the painting was wax-lined and mounted on a honeycomb panel. Pressure from the original stretcher had caused ridges to form on the surface, the paint layer had cracked, and there was extensive cleavage between the paint layer and canvas. The varnish (applied at an unspecified time) was discolored. A portion of the lower edge of the composition had been hidden by the previous stretching and/or frame. After cleaning and mounting, this area was restored to view, and some inpainting was required to compensate for the previous losses. (Compare the lower edge of the composition in fig. c where the tip of the black triangle touches the bottom edge of frame.) The final digit of the date 1926 was slightly obliterated during this process. Scattered inpainting was also necessary in the pale blue triangle (lower center) and the yellow triangle. The cracks in the paint layer were successfully laid down in the lining process. The surface was sprayed with a synthetic varnish (unspecified). The condition is stable. (New York, Dec. 1982.)

Van Doesburg's *Counter-Compositions*, of which there are eleven, date from the years 1924-27. In the list of his own works, compiled in about 1926-27 as a preparatory outline toward an oeuvre catalogue of the De Stijl years, van Doesburg included the eleven works under the heading "Architectuur-periode." The Peggy Guggenheim painting appears as no. VIII on the list and is dated 1926.[3]

1. Van Doesburg's sketch for the work (see fig. a) includes the notations "Collectie Dr. Roth, Strasbourg" and "F. Arp, Strasbourg." The typed list of his works (preserved in the Van Doesburg Archive, Dienst Verspreide Rijkskollekties, The Hague, see below, fn. 3) also includes "Strasbourg: Dr. Roth." Evert van Straaten suggested (in correspondence with the author, Dec. 1982) that the picture would have belonged first to Jean Arp's brother, François, and then Dr. Roth, a collector whom van Doesburg apparently greatly admired and who may have acquired the painting while van Doesburg was in Strasbourg working on the Café Aubette in 1926-28.
2. Nelly van Doesburg repurchased many of van Doesburg's works after his death, although it has not been possible to establish precisely when this transpired in the case of *Counter-Composition XIII*.
3. As mentioned above, cat. no. 45, fn. 3, the roman numerals on this typed list seem intended to establish a sequence rather than to serve as new titles. The entry for the Peggy Guggenheim work is: "*C.C.... 1926 VIII (genummerd als XIII) Strasbourg.* [in pencil]: *Dr. Roth.*" The *XIII* is clearly a reference to yet another system of numbering that van Doesburg used on the works themselves and in the notebook containing sketches for the *Counter-Compositions* (see below, fn. 4).

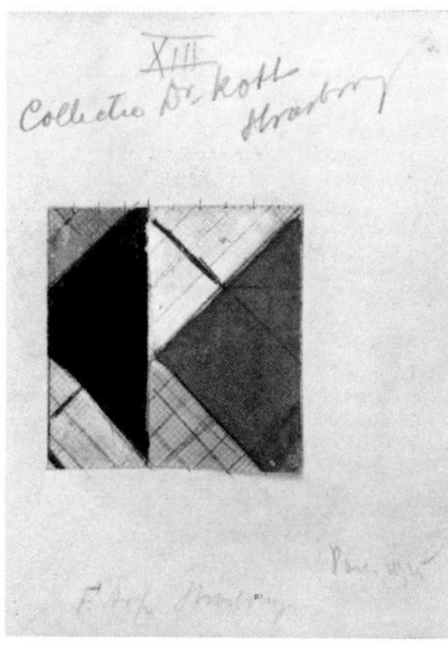

fig. a.
Van Doesburg, Study for cat. no. 46, page from a sketchbook, ink, pencil, gouache, and watercolor on graph paper mounted on cardboard, 4⅝ x 4⅝ in., 11.7 x 11.7 cm., Dienst Verspreide Rijkscollecties, The Hague.

A further document of importance concerning the evolution of the *Counter-Compositions* is a hand-bound notebook containing small colored sketches on graph paper. These probably served as preliminary ideas and studies for the *Counter-Composition* series, although not all the sketches were ultimately used. Those which he did carry out — or intended to carry out — as paintings, van Doesburg later mounted on cardboard and bound together into a small notebook. It is difficult to say with certainty when he assembled this notebook, although it was certainly in existence by the time he compiled the list mentioned above.[4]

The pencil, ink, gouache, and watercolor sketch for the Peggy Guggenheim painting (fig. a) appears as no. XIII in the notebook. It is divided across its upper edge into ten equal modules (as are several of the other examples in the notebook). In certain readily visible compositional details, as well as in color, the sketch differs from the completed picture: the white triangle in the upper left corner of the painting is blue in the sketch; the gray triangle at the upper right, white. In the lower left corner, which is equally divided in the painting between yellow and white, the sketch is white with a faintly tinted reddish wash. The

4. Nancy J. Troy and Yve-Alain Bois first drew the existence of these documents to the author's attention in 1982. Both have provided invaluable help in solving various questions regarding this work and cat. no. 45. Evert van Straaten, who is preparing a facsimile edition of the notebook, and Joop Joosten have also supplied information on the documents and helped to clarify a number of issues (in correspondence with the author, 1982-83).

major triangular forms remain identical in proportions, position, and color in the sketch and the completed work. The discrepancies — comparable in nature to the ones demonstrated by other sketches in the notebook in relationship to the paintings that derived from them — support the notion that the notebook drawings served as preliminary studies rather than as records of the completed pictures. Van Straaten plausibly concluded (in correspondence with the author, Dec. 1982) that the book in which these studies were subsequently mounted became a kind of *liber veritatis* into which van Doesburg added notes concerning exhibitions, sales, etc.

The dating of the Peggy Guggenheim picture presents a problem that is relatively easy to resolve. The sketch (fig. a) is dated 1925. Van Doesburg must have begun work on the painting in 1925 because he expected to show it in the December exhibition *L'Art d'aujourd'hui*, submitting its title (with those of *Counter-Compositions VI, XI*, and *XII*) for publication in the catalogue. But apparently neither *XII* nor *XIII* were ready in time; van Doesburg sent *XIV* and *XV* in their place (see below, fn. 11). He then probably completed *Counter-Composition XIII* during the early months of 1926.[5]

It is not entirely clear whether the establishment of a definite sequence of inception (or completion) of these individual paintings was important to van Doesburg at the time. However, not only did he send nos. *XIV* and *XV* to the exhibition in December (when *XII* and *XIII* were not yet ready), but he also carefully corrected the numbers in his own personal copy of the already-printed catalogue; this fact suggests that, for his own purposes at least, he did wish to retain a record of the order in which the works were begun. Otherwise he might simply have renumbered *Compositions XIV* and *XV* to make them accord with the catalogue designations (*XII* and *XIII*).

The use of the diagonal, line which is characteristic of most of the *Counter-Compositions*, marks an important change in van Doesburg's entire aesthetic position. The notion of the diagonal emerges first within the context of his architectural projects; but soon afterward — sometime in 1924 — it became a central element in the paintings he called *counter-compositions*.

The earliest reference to a "dynamic diagonal rhythm," which van Doesburg suggested might be achieved within an essentially horizontal/vertical scheme, probably occurred in his 1921 correspondence with J.J.P. Oud.[6] But it was in

5. The date and monogram on the face of the Peggy Guggenheim painting had not been added by the time the work was photographed for reproduction in the 1926-27 issue of *De Stijl* (see REFERENCES). It is not known when the picture was signed on the face or when the information was stenciled onto the reverse of the canvas and the stretcher.

6. In a letter to Oud concerning color schemes he had been asked to provide for housing blocks in Rotterdam, he spoke of the need to start with the working out of contrasts, largely through the balance of horizontals and verticals; but he demonstrated further that the correlation of the verticals and horizontals would in fact produce a "dynamic diagonal rhythm" (see fn. 7, and Troy, loc. cit., Feb. 1982, p. 96).

his 1923 collaboration with Cornelis van Eesteren that his ideas were significantly transformed.[7]

The precise nature of the interchange of ideas between van Eesteren and van Doesburg is a matter of considerable dispute and uncertainty. It is generally acknowledged, however, that, at the very least, the younger man taught van Doesburg some basic architectural techniques. They worked together on a number of projects during 1923, none of which were commissioned buildings but many of which were shown as models in the exhibition *Les Architectes du Groupe "de Stijl" (Hollande)*, which took place at Léonce Rosenberg's Galerie L'Effort Moderne, Paris, October 15-November 15, 1923.

As Troy has pointed out, the collaboration provided van Doesburg with the opportunity of "working out an abstract architectural credo concomitant with that which he had already established in painting and abstract design" (loc. cit., Feb. 1982, p. 98). Moreover, in the course of their preparations for the exhibition, van Eesteren exposed van Doesburg to the technique of axonometric projection. This was to have a critical impact on his approach to design and, consequently, on his related development in painting.[8] As they worked on the preparations for the Paris exhibition, van Eesteren provided the axonometric line drawings for the houses they were designing. Van Doesburg selectively traced certain sections of these drawings, using a system not unlike the one he had established in 1918-19 for the process of abstraction from a figural source (see above, cat. no. 45). In the process, he altered the architectural character of the drawings and introduced a much more pictorial conception. That is to say, his renditions of the original axonometrics, while conveying a sense of three-dimensional projection, actually consist of a group of "colored planes suspended in space and they bear little resemblance to the architectural structure from which they were derived" (Troy, loc. cit., 1982, p. 99).

These so-called *counter-constructions*, made largely for the *Maison particulière* of 1923, were in one sense abstract proposals for a coloristic architecture. They were conceived initially in linear form, and then — after being colored— in planar form; but they remained fundamentally pictorial, not architectural (see those illustrated in van Straaten, 1983, p. 132). This essential pictorial quality is revealed with particular force in a close-up tracing van Doesburg made

7. For the earliest of these, a set of decorations for the University of Amsterdam, see N. J. Troy, "The Abstract Environment of De Stijl," in *De Stijl: 1917-1931: Visions of Utopia*, New York, 1982, repr. color, pp. 186-87. For discussions of the complex set of interrelationships between van Doesburg's architectural projects of the mid-1920s and his paintings, as well as the relationship of his work to that of Mondrian, see Troy's entire essay; also S. Polano, "De Stijl/Architecture = Nieuwe Beelding," ibid., pp. 90-93; N. Troy, "Mondrian's Designs for the *Salon de Madame B . . . , à Dresden*," *Art Bulletin*, vol. 62, Dec. 1980, pp. 645-47; idem, "Theo van Doesburg, From Music into Space," *Arts Magazine*, vol. 56, no. 6, Feb. 1982, pp. 95-101; C. Blotkamp, "Mondrian↔architectuur," *Wonen—TABK*, 1982, nos. 4-5, pp. 15-51.

8. According to this system, an architectural plan can be rendered simultaneously in section and in elevation while also allowing for the measurement of scale relationships in 3 dimensions.

from one of van Eesteren's axonometric plans (ibid., p. 131). The arbitrarily selected planes seem to float in midair, although they are presented in a three-dimensional perspective. In this drawing, with its diagonal thrust and strong planar elements, the impending transition from the *counter-constructions* to the *counter-compositions* is already implicit.[9]

During the years 1924-26, van Doesburg revised his definition of Neoplasticism to include "Elementarism." He thus provided a theoretical basis for the *counter-composition.* The horizontal/vertical axis, which had been so fundamental a principle of Mondrian's Neoplasticism—as well as of van Doesburg's (and Mondrian's) paintings since 1917—was now sacrificed. Instead, van Doesburg began to paint pictures in which rectangular forms were placed at a 45° angle to the edge of the canvas (see Troy, loc. cit., Feb. 1982, p. 99). In several essays published during the succeeding years, van Doesburg explained the principles that governed the structure of these *counter-compositions*, based as they were upon his newly developed conviction that "the modern spirit" demanded the addition of an oblique dimension to the more limited orthogonal formulations of Neoplasticism (*De Stijl*, VII, nos. 73-74, pp. 17-28; nos. 75-76, pp. 35-43; no. 78, pp. 82-87).

As 1924 drew to a close, relations between Mondrian and van Doesburg cooled noticeably, and a more or less complete break occurred between them by the middle of 1925.[10] Although this break is often attributed in the literature simply to van Doesburg's introduction of the diagonal, the issues were obviously much more complex. Carel Blotkamp has convincingly argued that even in the early 1920s the two artists began to develop divergent views regarding the ways in which the fourth dimension could be expressed in architecture. Van Doesburg saw the issue in terms of time and space; Mondrian saw it in more static terms. Although Mondrian felt that the inclusion of the fourth dimension in architecture was a desirable aim, he was also persuaded that it could not be achieved successfully (see Blotkamp, loc. cit., 1982, p. 43). The growing differences between the two artists on the subject of architectural theory were thus probably just as important as those concerning the diagonal in easel painting.

9. Van Doesburg's designs for the interior of a "flower-room" for the Vicomte de Noailles at Hyères, probably executed in 1924, may have been—in some sense—van Doesburg's earliest experiments in the *counter-composition* mode. Although the designs were for an interior "architectural" space, their conception, arrangement, and use of color suggest the direction van Doesburg took in the Peggy Guggenheim *Counter-Composition* and others (see the drawing in the collection of the Stedelijk van Abbemuseum, Eindhoven, repr. color, *De Stijl: 1917-1931: Visions of Utopia*, pl. 154).

10. On June 5, 1925, van Doesburg wrote to his friend A. Kok, "A complete break with Mondrian was inevitable" ("*Met Mondrian is 't tot 'n absolute breuk moeten komen*"), van Straaten, 1983, p. 136. On December 4 Mondrian wrote a cold, polite letter to van Doesburg stating that he could see no possibility for collaboration between them, and indeed regretted that he had not been able to prevent the publication in a recent issue of *De Stijl* of articles and photographs that were his own.

As Mondrian later said in an interview with James Johnson Sweeney, the lozenge (or diamond) shape of the canvas itself also played a part in the dispute between the two artists: "Doesburg, in his late work, tried to destroy static expression by a diagonal arrangement of the lines of his compositions. But through such an emphasis the feeling of physical equilibrium which is necessary for the enjoyment of the work of art is lost. The relationship with architecture and its vertical and horizontal dominants is broken. If a square picture, however, is hung diagonally, as I have frequently planned my pictures to be hung, this effect does not result. Only the borders of the canvas are on 45° angles, not the picture" ("Eleven Europeans in America," *The Museum of Modern Art Bulletin*, vol. 13, nos. 4-5, 1946, p. 35). Van Doesburg's own use of Mondrian's preferred solution (the diamond) was originally exemplified by *Counter-Composition V*, 1924 (Stedelijk Museum, Amsterdam), which appears as a lozenge in the small book of sketches and was apparently originally intended to be displayed as such (see above p. 229 and fn. 4). A further example is van Doesburg's *Counter-Composition VIII*, also of 1924 (The Art Institute of Chicago); when this work and Peggy Guggenheim's were directly juxtaposed in the posthumous exhibition at the 1939 *Salon des Réalités Nouvelles*, the essence of the problem was clearly demonstrated (fig. b).

In view of the fundamental break that occurred between the two artists during the time when van Doesburg's primary preoccupation was the *counter-composition*, the photograph of Mondrian taken by Fritz Glarner in 1942 (fig. c) is

fig. b.
Installation photograph, *Salon des Réalités Nouvelles*, Galerie Charpentier, Paris, 1939. Photograph courtesy Dienst Verspreide Rijkscollecties, The Hague.

fig. c.
Piet Mondrian standing in front of cat. no. 46 in the exhibition *Masters of Abstract Art*, 1942. Photograph by Fritz Glarner, courtesy the Glarner Archive, Kunsthaus, Zurich.

especially expressive: it shows Mondrian absorbed by those aspects of van Doesburg's pictorial achievement that had been most responsibile — two decades earlier — for the rupture between them.

EXHIBITIONS:

Paris, *L'Art d 'aujourd'hui*, no. 57, Dec. 1925 (*Contre-composition XIII*);[11] Paris, Galerie Charpentier, *Salon des Réalités Nouvelles*, June 30-July 15, 1939 (no cat.);[12] New York, Helena Rubinstein's New Art Center, *Masters of Abstract Art*, Apr. 1942, no. 15 ("*Counter Composition*, 1928, lent by Art of This Century");[13] New York, Art of This Century, 1942-47, p. 86 (dated 1928); New York, Art of This Century, *Theo van Doesburg*, Apr. 29-May 31, 1947, no. 29; Venice, *P.G.*, 1948 (Biennale), no. 31 (dated 1920); Florence, *P.G.*, 1949, no. 31 (dated 1928); Amsterdam, *P.G.*, 1951, no. 39; Zurich, *P.G.*, 1951, no. 35; London, *P.G.*, 1964-65, no. 34; Stockholm, *P.G.*, 1966-67, no. 35; Paris, *P.G.*, 1974-75, no. 31; Torino, *P.G.*, 1975-76, no. 41; New York, *P.G.*, 1982-83, no. 25, repr. color.

REFERENCES:

De Stijl, 7e Jaar, Serie XIII, VII, no. 78, 1926-27, repr. p. 95 ("*Contra-compositie* [1926]"; the work had not been signed or dated when the photograph was taken); S. Polano, ed., *Theo van Doesburg: Scritti di arte e di architettura*, Rome, 1979, p. 535, cat. no. 177, repr. pl. 219 (dated 1926); E. van Straaten, *Theo van Doesburg*, The Hague, 1983, p. 186.

11. Though included in the catalogue, the picture was apparently not exhibited. A copy of the catalogue in the Van Doesburg Archive, annotated in ink by the artist, shows no. 57 *Contre-composition XIII* deleted and *XIV* substituted. To this entry, and to the entry for no. 56 (*Contre-composition XII*, which has been deleted and replaced by *XIV*), the date 1925 has been added, also in ink. Thus, though both *Contre-composition XIV* and *XV* were apparently completed by December 1925, *XIII* was apparently not yet ready for exhibition at that point. The author is indebted to Yve-Alain Bois for drawing this annotated catalogue to her attention.

12. See installation photo, fig. b. The frame that was on the picture in this installation is still in place. Although it was probably not made during van Doesburg's lifetime, it closely resembles frames he made starting in about 1927 (information supplied by Joop Joosten), and probably belongs to a group of frames Nelly van Doesburg had copied for the 1932 retrospective (see installation photo, cat. no. 45, fig. f). In further support of the notion that the present frame is closely modeled on a van Doesburg concept is a photograph (Van Doesburg Archive, Dienst Verspreide Rijkskollekties, The Hague) showing Nelly van Doesburg posing in 1929 in front of *Composition Simultané* (now Yale University Art Gallery). In that photograph the frame (which was definitely designed by the artist) is virtually identical in type to that of the Peggy Guggenheim picture. In both instances, the thin white strip of wood that surrounds the painting projects slightly forward from the canvas surface, and the width of the black frame is approximately the same.

    Van Doesburg's views on framing, always strongly held, changed at various times of his life. In the earlier 1920s, he designed frames that projected the picture forward, as Mondrian had done as early as 1916 (see below, cat. no. 121). In this connection he wrote a strongly worded letter to Evert and Thijs Rinsema, expressing the need for such frames on certain pictures (June 24, 1923, published by K. Schippers, *Holland Dada*, Amsterdam, 1974, pp. 179-81). See also van Doesburg's position ca. 1920 on the aesthetics of the frame, expressed in his essay "Lijsten-aesthetiek," published in 1920 in *De Stijl*, III, no. 11, pp. 92-95.

13. Though the work is erroneously dated 1928 in the catalogue, the installation photo, fig. c, clearly identifies the work. The author is indebted to Yve-Alain Bois and Dagmar Hnikova for drawing this photograph to her attention, and to Nancy Troy for identifying the exhibition in which it was taken.

Piero Dorazio

Born Piero D'Orazio June 1927, Rome.
Lives in Todi.

47 Unitas. 1965.

76.2553 PG 168

Oil on canvas, 18 1/16 x 30 1/4 (45.8 x 76.5).

Signed, dated, and titled on reverse: *Piero Dorazio 1965 / "Unitas."*

PIERO DORAZIO 1965
" UNITAS "

PROVENANCE:

Purchased from Galleria Paolo Barozzi, Venice, acting for Marlborough Gallery, Rome, May 8, 1966.

CONDITION:

The work has received no treatment. Apart from some minimal surface soil, the condition is stable. (Venice, Nov. 1982.)

Writing in 1966 about Dorazio's recent work, Nello Ponente placed the artist within the general "trend of European painting which draws its ideological premises from the masters of the so-called 'geometrical-abstract' movement, not only Mondrian and De Stijl, but also Moholy Nagy, Max Bill, Albers, Magnelli and Kandinsky in his final period. Yet Dorazio's strict sense of order produces results that are fundamentally different in the language of their expression.... His spaces are open and his color runs through them ... producing variety and modulation to a sustained rhythm" (*Piero Dorazio*, exh. cat., Marlborough, London, Jan. 1966, n. p.).

Ponente and Dorazio himself both emphasize the process by which the artist attempts to fuse conscious objective experimentation—exploring different color combinations and the range of visual stimuli they produce — with a more intuitive or poetic approach to the creation of visual images. "My research is grounded on the one hand in what I know would result from applying an acquired method (therefore to be avoided) and what I would like to know or see through the strictly intuitive experience of sensations and their inter-relationship in the final unity of an image.... I do not paint 'to express myself,' or 'to represent something.' ... Rather I try to exploit the potential offered by the visual stimuli of color, form, space, surface, movement, and light, and through these to arrive at a statement which constitutes in itself an independent visual fact" (correspondence with the author, Oct. 1983).

EXHIBITIONS:

London, Marlborough New London Gallery, *Dorazio*, Jan. 1966, no. 43; Paris, *P.G.*, 1974-75, no. 154; Torino, *P.G.*, 1975-76, no. 159.

REFERENCES:

E. B. Henning, "On Piero Dorazio," *Art International*, vol. 11, nos. 9-10, Dec. 20, 1965, repr. p. 20; M. Volpi Orlandini, J. Lassaigne, and G. Crisafi, *Dorazio*, Venice, 1977, no. 817, repr.; L. Flint, *Handbook*, 1983, p. 202, repr. color p. 203.

Jean Dubuffet

Born July 1901, Le Havre.
Lives in Paris.

48 Chataine aux Hautes Chairs. August 1951.
(*Fleshy face with Chestnut Hair*; *Head of a Woman*).

Color plate p. 682.

76.2553 PG 121

Oil-based mixed media on board (Isorel), 25$\frac{9}{16}$ x 21$\frac{1}{4}$ (64.9 x 54).

Signed, titled, and dated on reverse: *Chataine aux / hautes chairs / J. Dubuffet / août 51.*

PROVENANCE:

Frua de Angeli, Paris, 1960;[1] Galerie L. Bourdon, Paris, 1960-62;[2] purchased by Galerie Europe, Paris, June 1962; returned to Galerie Bourdon; purchased from Galerie Bourdon, February 25, 1964.

CONDITION:

As was the artist's intention (see below), certain elements in the medium remain soft and hence changeable. In 1982 (Venice) 2 small losses at the left edge and the lower right corner were filled with wax and inpainted. Apart from the vulnerability inherent in the medium, the condition is stable. (New York, 1983.)

The medium used and the technique followed by Dubuffet in this work are described in his *cahier de travail:*[3]

> *Tableau fait en une seule opération, dans le temps d'une heure ou deux. (Sur un ancien tableau présentant des reliefs.)*
>
> *Travail avec — selon les endroits: pâte bl.z. + C.O. + téréb. — et pierrolin assoupli avec diluant. Empreintes.*
>
> *Colorer avec jus (huile — beaucoup d'huile — avec une pointe d'essence).*
>
> *Le fond a été fait comme suit: peint d'abord avec jus épais ton rougeâtre (rouge hélio moyen avec toute petite pointe de noir et un peu de blanc, jus fait d'huile + téréb. + un peu de colle d'or) et aussitôt par-dessus, légèrement, du plat du pinceau pour ne frotter que les parties en relief, un ton rose clair (fait du même ton avec beaucoup de blanc, avec le même jus).*
>
> *Le lendemain, 31 âout, le tableau a été très transformé, et est une grande tête.*
>
> *1. essuyé la figure avec chiffon mouillé d'essence;*
>
> *2. teinté avec jus jaune;*
>
> *3. passé un ton clair épais avec le plat du pinceau sur les reliefs;*
>
> *4. passé un jus léger brunâtre pour teinter, gratter — repasser ton très clair du plat du pinceau sur les reliefs, tamponner avec chiffon — gratter à nouveau — tamponner à nouveau, etc.*
>
> *Le fond a été transformé: d'abord passé en bleu violâtre foncé. Puis ton sombre.*[4]

Dubuffet has frequently attested that the unpredictable nature of these experimental media plays an important part in the literal vitality of his work. Max Loreau, in a cogent analysis of the function of *matière* in Dubuffet's anticultural

1. It has not been possible to establish when the collector Frua de Angeli acquired the work, nor whether it came directly from Dubuffet.
2. The records of the Secrétariat de Jean Dubuffet indicate that the work was purchased by Galerie Europe in June 1962. Since Peggy Guggenheim bought the work from the Galerie Bourdon, it must have been reacquired by that gallery during the intervening period.
3. The description quoted here is of the closely related *Haute tête en pomme de terre*, August 31, 1951. In correspondence with Madame Armande de Trentinian of the Secrétariat, and through examination of the *Chataine*, it has become clear that the technique used in the 2 works was almost identical.
4. The abbreviated media mentioned are: zinc white (*bl.z.*), glue (*c.o., colle d'or*), turpentine (*téréb.*), diluted varnish (*pierrolin assoupli avec diluant*). The various layers were applied, scraped, gouged, and incised with putty and palette knives.

aesthetic, argued that the physical properties of the medium stand as a literal, as well as a metaphorical, assault upon any conventional notion of form. (For a full and illuminating discussion of this phase in Dubuffet's development, see M. Loreau, *Jean Dubuffet: Délits, Déportements, Lieux de haut jeu*, Lausanne, 1971, pp. 139-54.) Thus, the fact that the actual substance of which the work is made fluctuates, moves, alters, and liquifies is a significant factor in its effectiveness: "For a long time, [during] this year [1951], I used a paste which I made myself at the time I used it (it dries very quickly); I mixed zinc oxide with a lean but viscous varnish, rich in gum, very much like the one sold in New York under the name of dammar varnish. This paste, while still fresh, repels the oil, and the glazes one applies on top of it organize themselves into enigmatic branchings. Gradually, as it dries, its resistance to the [rich, oily] colored sauces weakens, and it assembles them differently. Its behavior changes every fifteen minutes" (P. Selz and J. Dubuffet, *The Work of Jean Dubuffet*, exh. cat., MoMA, New York, 1962, p. 63). Though the *matière* of *Chataine* no longer fluctuates in this extreme sense, its surfaces and degrees of stability are sufficiently diverse to carry the artist's original intention.

The work belongs to the series *Tables paysagées, paysages du mental, pierres philosophiques* (1950-52), which are characterized by especially heavy relief and textural complexity.

EXHIBITIONS:

Stockholm, *P.G.*, 1966-67, no. 100; New York, *P.G.*, 1969, p. 120, repr. color; Paris, *P.G.*, 1974-75, no. 138, repr. p. 99; Torino, *P.G.*, 1975-76, no. 119; New York, *P.G.*, 1982-83, no. 47, repr. color.

REFERENCES:

M. Loreau, *Catalogue des travaux de Jean Dubuffet*, Paris, 1967, Fasc. VII, fig. 75; L. Flint, *Handbook*, 1983, p. 158, repr. color p. 159.

COLOR PLATES

Cat. no. 136, p. 605.
Picabia, *Très rare tableau sur la terre*, 1915.

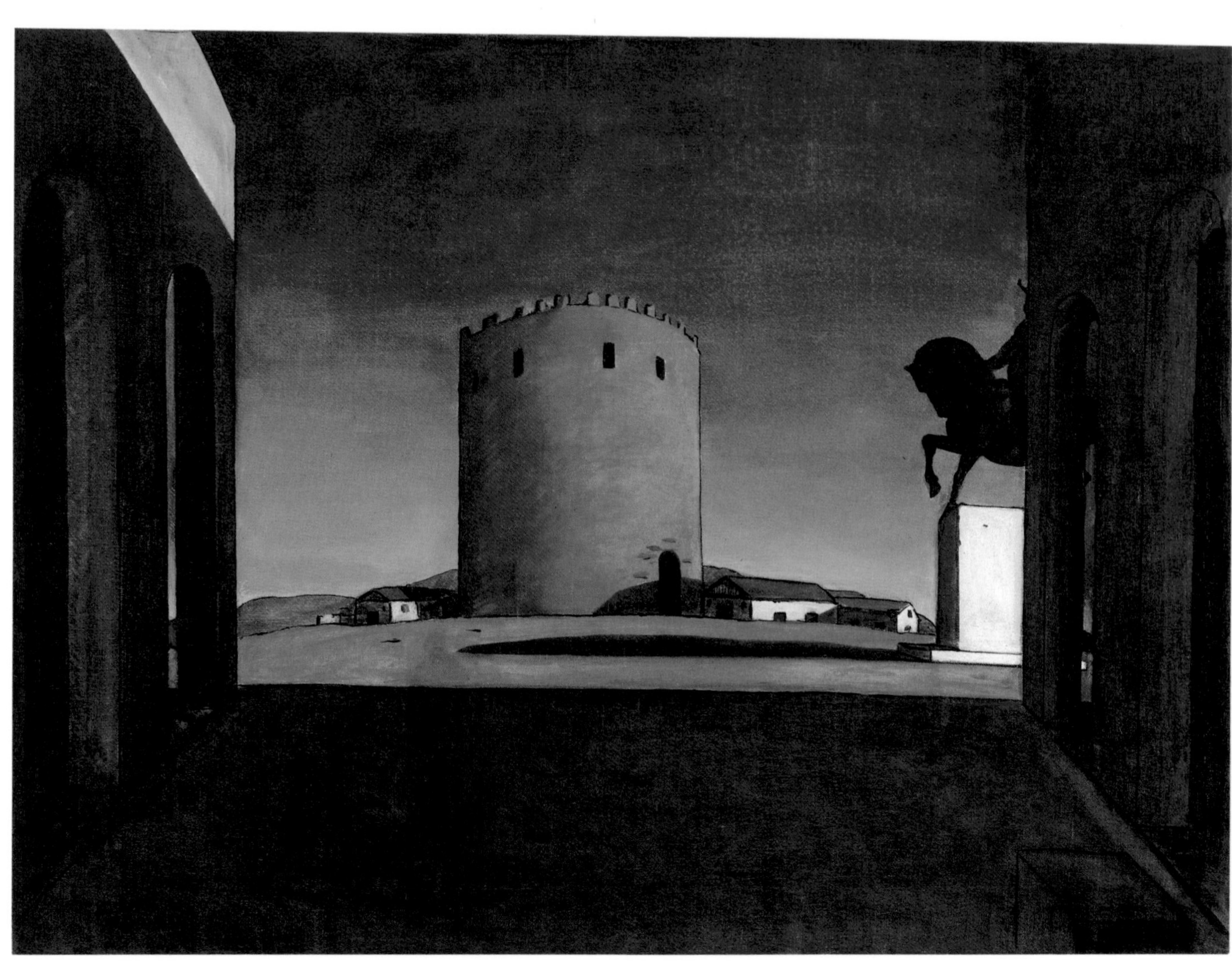

Cat. no. 30, p. 155.
De Chirico, *La tour rouge*, 1913.

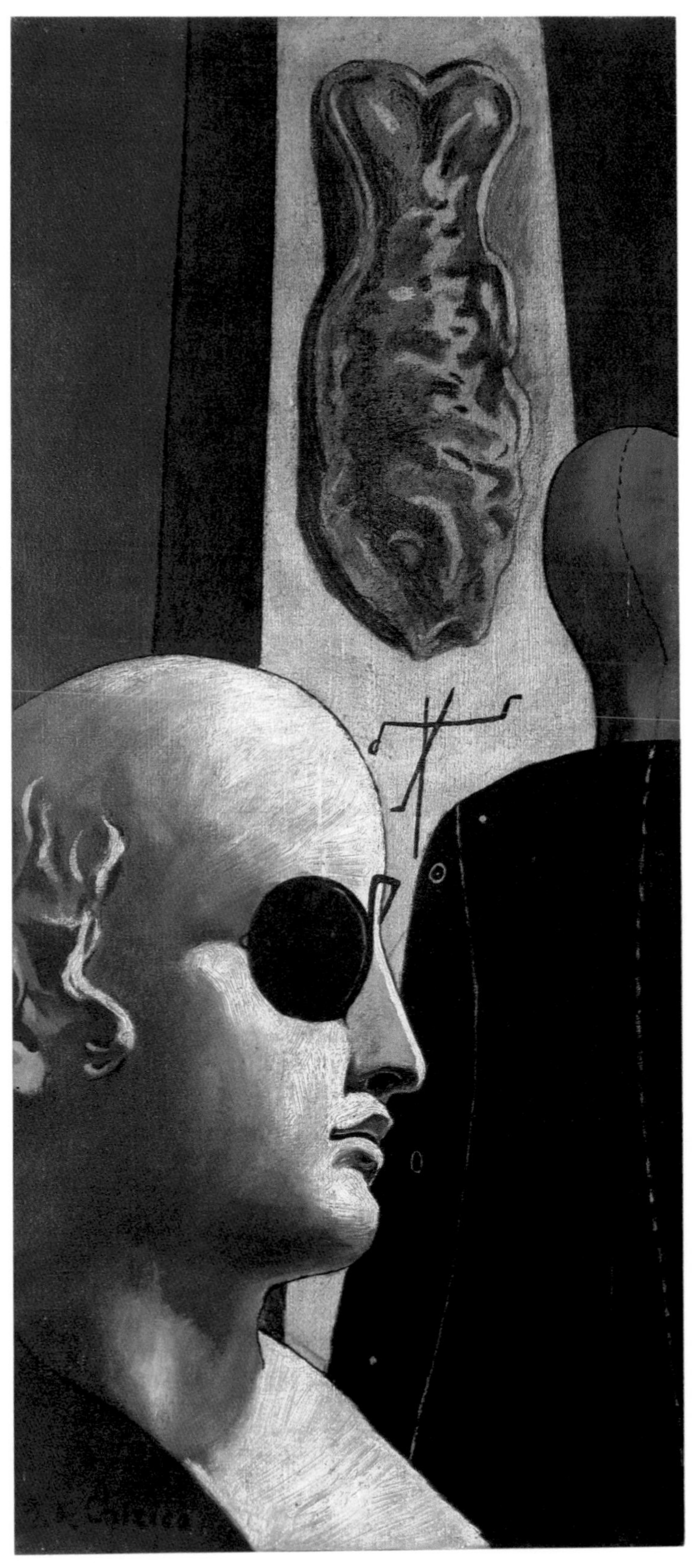

Cat. no. 31, p. 161.
De Chirico, *La nostalgie du poète*, 1914.

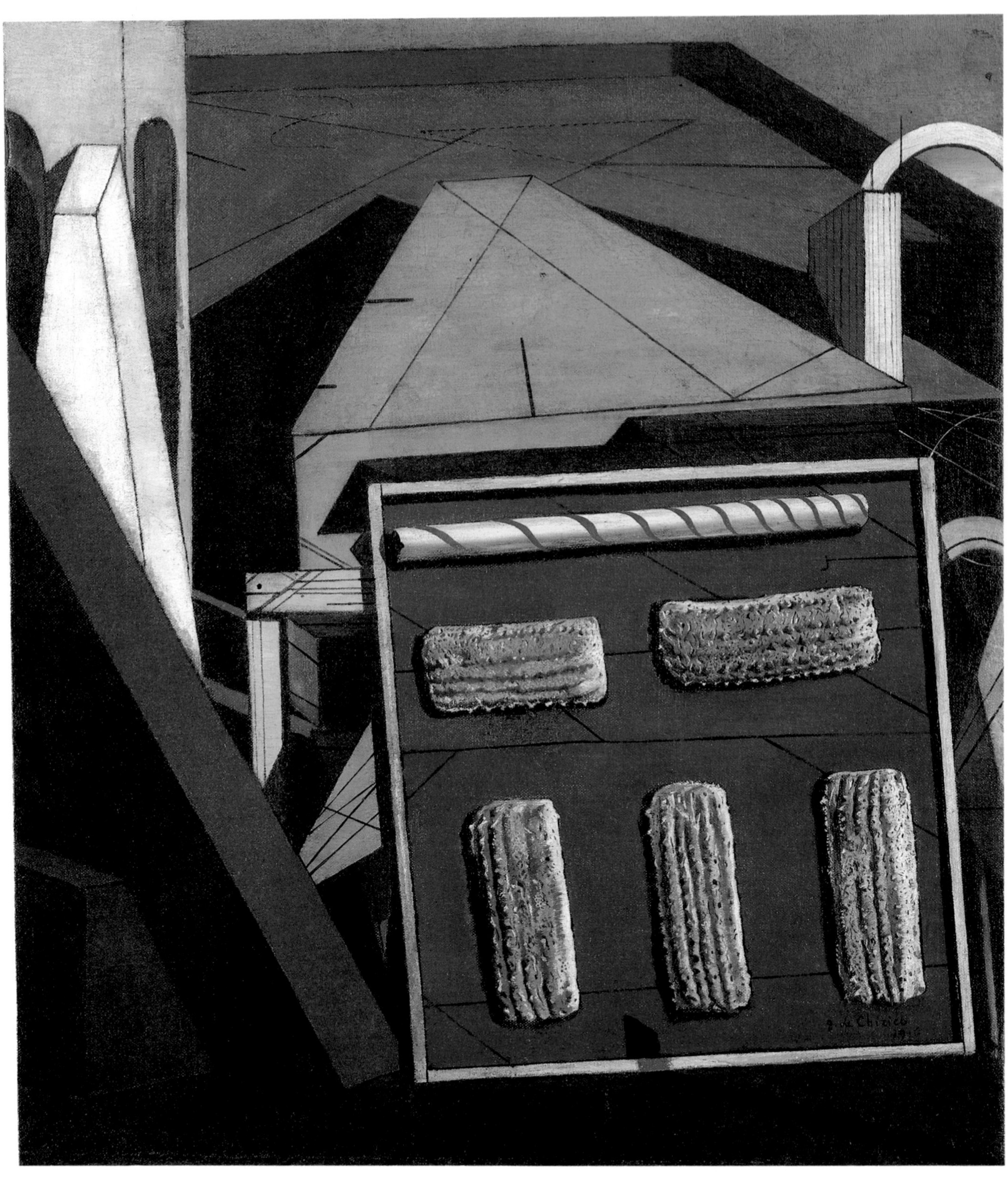

Cat. no. 32, p. 166.
De Chirico, *Le doux après-midi*, before July 1916.

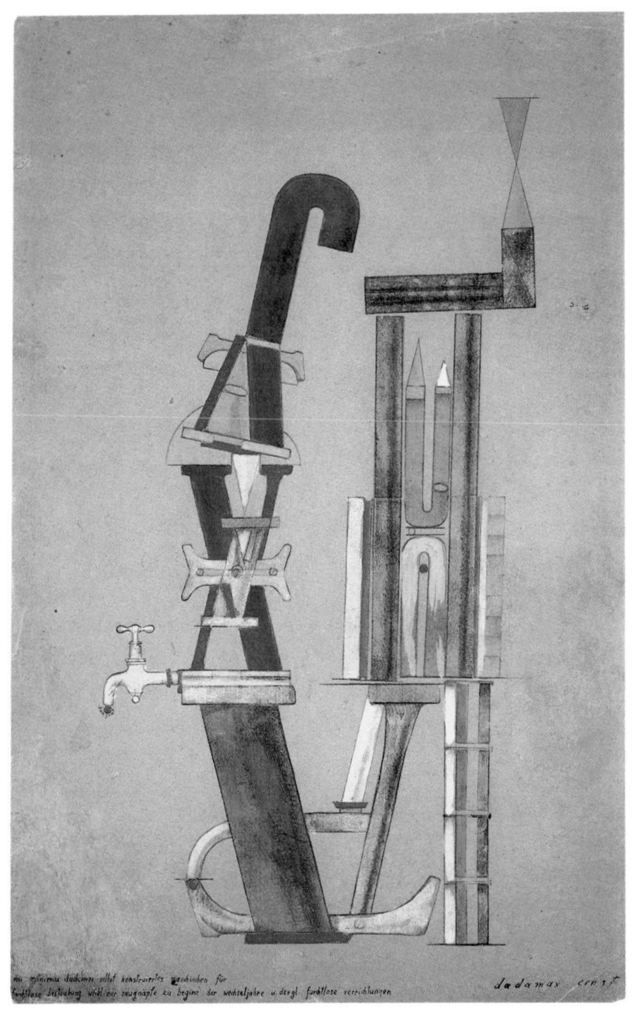

Cat. no. 51, p. 282.
Ernst, *Von minimax dadamax selbst konstruiertes maschinchen*, 1919-20.

Cat. no. 55, p. 292.
Ernst, *Le Facteur Cheval*, 1932.

Cat. no. 56, p. 298.
Ernst, *Couple zoomorphe*, 1933.

Cat. no. 52, p. 285.
Ernst, *Le Baiser*, 1927.

Cat. no. 59, p. 306.
Ernst, *La toilette de la mariée*, 1940.

Cat. no. 61, p. 312.
Ernst, *The Antipope*, December 1941-March 1942.

Cat. no. 53, p.287.
Ernst, *La Forêt*, 1927-28.

Cat. no. 44, p. 215.
Delvaux, *L'Aurore*, July 1937.

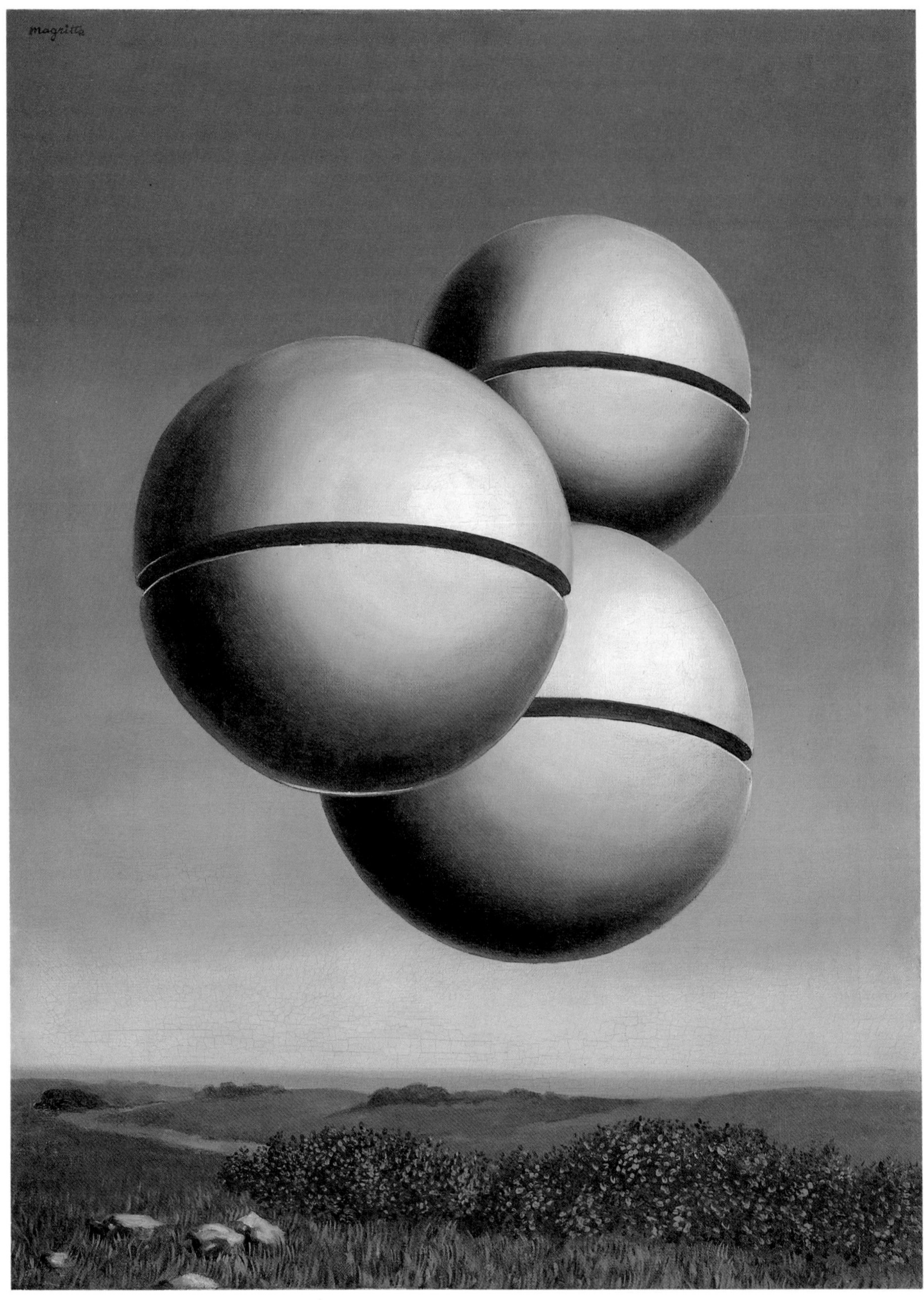

Cat. no. 102, p. 467.
Magritte, *La voix des airs*, 1931.

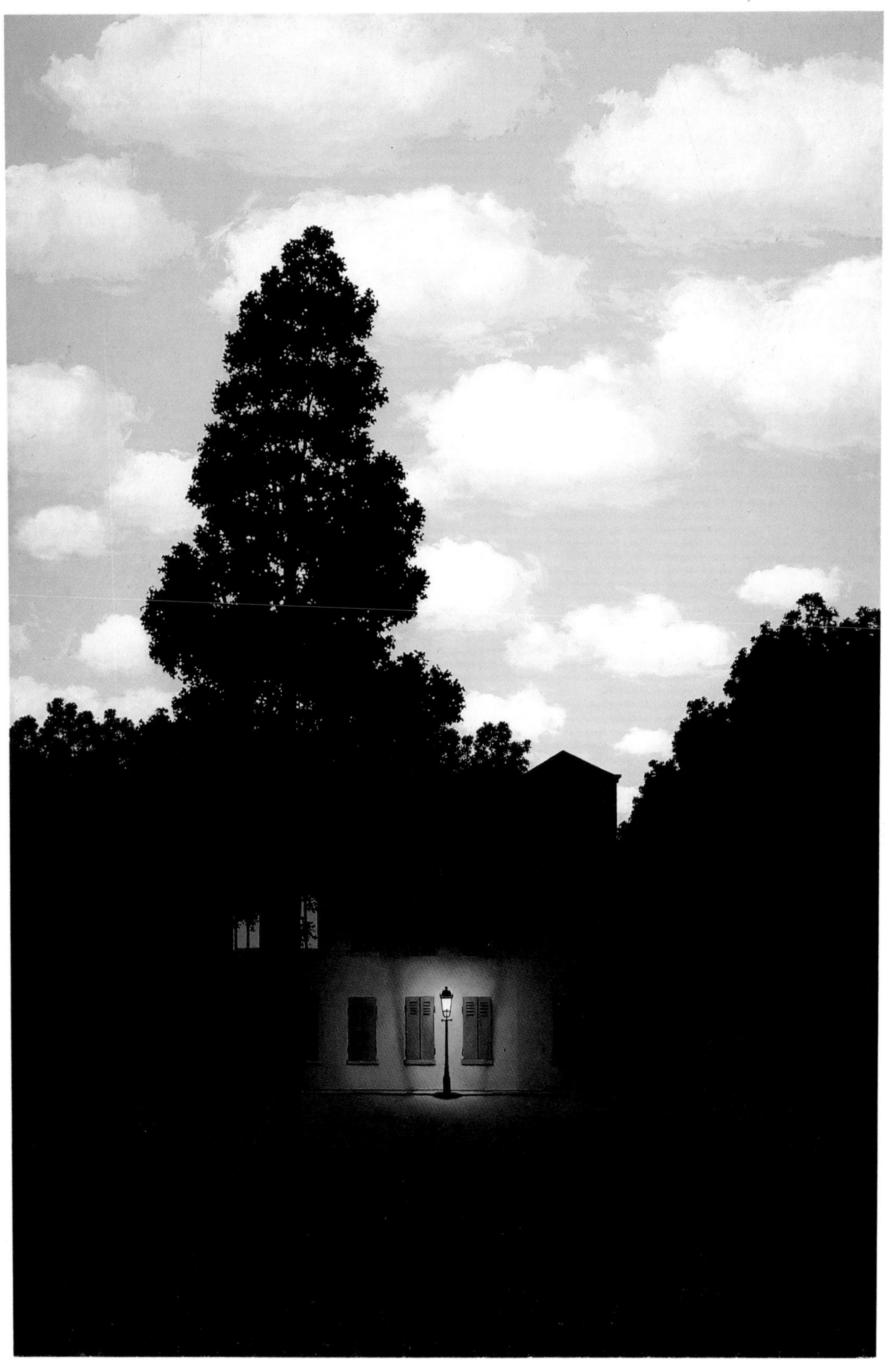

Cat. no. 103, p. 471.
Magritte, *L'Empire des lumières*, 1953-54.

Cat. no. 116, p. 535.
Miró, *Peinture*, 1925.

Cat. no. 117, p. 540.
Miró, *Intérieur hollandais*, summer 1928.

Cat. no. 110, p. 520.
Masson, *L'Armure*, ca. January-April 1925.

Henri-Robert-Marcel Duchamp

Born July 1887, Blainville.
Died October 1968, Neuilly-sur-Seine.

49 Nu (esquisse), Jeune homme triste dans un train. 1911-12.
(Nude [study], Sad young man on a train).

Color plate p. 33.

76.2553 PG 9

Oil on textured cardboard (¼ in., 0.7 cm., thick), nailed to masonite. Brown paper tape surrounding all edges covers join between cardboard and masonite and serves as ⅜ in., 2 cm., surround to painting itself. (This is now covered by the frame.) Dimensions of cardboard support: 39⅜ x 28¾ (100 x 73); visible painted surface within taped edges: 38 9/16 x 27 15/16 (98 x 71).

Signed and dated l.r.: *Marcel Duchamp / 12*; on reverse (in the artist's hand): *Marcel Duchamp / nu (esquisse) / Jeune homme triste dans un train / marcel Duchamp / W. Pach / N.Y.C.* Also on reverse (in the artist's hand): *return to W. Pach / 148 W. 72nd St. N.Y.*[1]

PROVENANCE:

Purchased from the artist (Chicago Armory Show), by Manierre Dawson, April 7, 1913 ($162);[2] purchased from Dawson before 1937 by Walter Pach (lender to The Arts Club of Chicago exhibition);[3] purchased from Pach, 1942.[4]

CONDITION:

There are very few pinpoint losses, and the condition of the paint layer is stable. There has apparently been no restoration. The cardboard support is fragile and has become extremely brittle in places, showing signs of disintegration (fig. a).

The cardboard was nailed to the masonite before the work was begun. After completing the picture, Duchamp applied the brown paper tape, which has now become worn, brittle, and torn in many places, partly owing to the presence of the frame. At several points along the taped edges, "nail heads," which do not correspond to actual nails beneath, seem to have been painted onto the surface (fig. b). These appear at irregular intervals and cannot be fully explained as trompe l'oeil elements. Nonetheless, it cannot be ruled out that these "painted" nails were added by Duchamp to introduce confusion regarding the "true" nature of the support. A trace of black paint at the inner edge of the paper tape indicates that Duchamp partially reinforced the black border to the right of the figure after he applied the tape.

Peggy Guggenheim recalled that Duchamp varnished the painting in New York not long before the opening of Art of This Century in October 1942. She was not certain whether he made any other alterations or restorations at that time. She was also unable to recall precisely when the work was placed in its present black frame.

The presence of a typed exhibition "label" on the lower right edge of the work (fig. c) indicates that Duchamp at some stage displayed the work unframed and that the brown paper tape thus served as an intentional framing device. The number corresponds to the catalogue entry of the 1948 Biennale; installation photographs reveal that the picture *was* exhibited there unframed, with the paper tape in place.

fig. a.
Upper right edge of cardboard support of cat. no. 49, showing disintegration. Fragments of surviving brown paper tape are visible above and below the nail hole, as well as along the right edge of the masonite subsupport.

fig. b.
Lower left corner of cat. no. 49, showing painted simulated nail heads, one of which partially corresponds to an actual nail beneath.

fig. c.
Lower right corner of cat. no. 49, showing exhibition label ("33") and the nature of the paper tape.

Various art-historical questions are raised by Duchamp's *Nu (esquisse), Jeune homme triste dans un train.* They concern the title of the work and its subject matter; its relationship to Futurism and to chronophotography; its date and precise place within the sequence of works produced by the artist during late 1911 and early 1912; and, finally, the possible connection of its subject with literary sources and events in the artist's own life.

When the painting was first publicly exhibited at the Armory Show of 1913, it was listed in the New York catalogue as *Nu (sketch)* and in the Chicago and Boston catalogues as *Sketch of a Nude.* The question of the picture's relationship to the two versions of the *Nu descendant un escalier (Nude descending a Staircase)* was thus raised, if only implicitly, from the very beginning.[5] The artist's inscription on the reverse (see above), which almost certainly dates from the time of the exhibition, expands upon the simple description of the figure as a sketch for (or of) a nude, by also designating it — as if with a subtitle — *Jeune homme triste dans un train.*

Several scholars have posited a direct relationship (such as that of a study to a completed work) between *Jeune homme triste* and *Nu descendant.* Robert Lebel, for example (1967, p. 20), in an interview with Duchamp, referred to the

1. The same black ink (or paint?) is used for all parts of the inscription. Madame Teeny Duchamp (in conversation with the author, Paris, Sept. 1982) confirmed that the entire inscription was in the artist's hand. The instructions to return the work to Pach's New York address would have been plausible in 1913, since Pach was one of the organizers of the Armory Show.
2. Dawson's purchase of *Sketch of a Nude* from the Chicago Armory Show (cat. no. 108) has been traditionally (and convincingly) identified with this work (Lebel, 1959, p. 28; Brown, 1963, p. 240; Tompkins, 1966, p. 56; d'Harnoncourt and McShine, 1973, p. 256; Cabanne, 1976, p. 108, etc.). (In a 1963 "re-creation" of the New York Armory Show at the Henry Street Settlement in New York, *Nu[sketch],* cat. no. 242, was represented by a watercolor from the collection of the Philadelphia Museum of Art rather than by *Jeune homme.*)
3. It has not been possible to establish precisely when Pach bought the painting. Cabanne (1976, p. 108) indicates that it was soon after the Armory Show. Pach himself, however, stated (1938, p. 160): "After Mr. Dawson had lived for years with the picture... he wrote me, 'It looks like a Rembrandt.'..." It seems more likely that Pach's recollection was correct.
4. Duchamp's 1941 *Boîte-en-valise* (Peggy Guggenheim Collection) contains a reproduction of *Jeune homme* with Pach noted as the owner. Peggy Guggenheim probably acquired the painting early the following year.
5. The second version of the *Nu descendant un escalier* also appeared in the Armory Show. Both versions are in the collection of the Philadelphia Musuem of Art, The Louise and Walter Arensberg Collection: *Nu descendant un escalier* (No. 1), oil on cardboard, 38 1/16 x 23 13/16 in., 96.7 x 60.5 cm., signed and dated l.l.: *Marcel Duchamp / 11 / Nu descendant un escalier. Nu descendant un escalier* (No. 2), oil on canvas, 57 1/2 x 35 1/16 in., 146 x 89 cm., signed and dated l.c.: *Marcel Duchamp 12*; titled l.l.: *Nu descendant un escalier*; signed and dated on verso (transcribed but not photographed before lining in 1957): *Marcel Duchamp 12.*

painting as "*une esquisse du* Nu descendant," a point that Duchamp apparently did not at the time contradict.[6] Arturo Schwarz (1970, p. 16) described *Jeune homme triste* and *Nu* (No. 1) as "two versions of the same picture notwithstanding the different titles," and further described *Jeune homme triste* as an "unfinished preliminary study leading to the two versions of *Nude Descending a Staircase*, the first of which was painted during the same December."

William Rubin, on the other hand, suggested a less direct relationship between the two works (1968, p. 23). He saw *Jeune homme triste* as the first attempt on Duchamp's part to deal with the issue or theme of motion. In this particular sense, the picture served to prepare the way for *Nu descendant*, even though it was a fully independent work rather than a study for the other.

Although the precise chronological relationship between these works has not been definitely established (and will be discussed below), Rubin's clarification of the issue of subject matter is persuasive. Both paintings represent "studies" or "explorations" of the problem of depicting motion, although they do so in distinctly different ways.

In 1964 Duchamp himself offered confirmation on this point: "Very much attracted by the problem of motion in painting, I made several sketches on that theme.... [Nu (No. 1)] is the first study for the *Nude descending a staircase*. You can see a number of anatomical parts of the nude which are repeated in several static positions of the moving body compared with the final version.... This is only a rough sketch in my search for a technique to treat the subject of motion" (Marcel Duchamp, notes for an unpublished lecture, St. Louis, Nov. 24, 1964, quoted in A. d'Harnoncourt and K. McShine, 1973, p. 256).

In this passage, Duchamp clearly used the term "sketch" to describe both the *Nu* (No. 1)—which he regarded as only a *rough* sketch—and the "final version." He saw both as "explorations" of the general subject of motion in painting. Understood in this way, the titling of *Jeune homme* as *Nu (esquisse)* also becomes clear. Like the *Nu descendant un escalier*, it represented for Duchamp another in a series of "studies" on the subject of depicting motion.

The difference in approach to the problem of movement in the two paintings was described by Richard Hamilton as follows: "The sad young man is stationary in a mobile ambience — the painting attempts to render the experience of standing still in a moving vehicle. On the other hand, the descending nude is itself moving in a stationary ambience" (1966, p. 36).

Hamilton's distinction — clearly accurate — raises a number of issues. Among these is the relationship of *Jeune homme* and *Nu descendant* to the theory and practice of Futurism on the one hand, and to developments in chronophotog-

6. Lebel implies a similar connection in his 1957 text, p. 30. For a possible further reinforcement of Lebel's point, see W. Seitz, 1963, where Duchamp seems to refer to *Jeune homme triste* as "the 1911 sketch for 'The Nude' "; however, this seems more likely to have been a question of a direct confusion with *Nu* (No. 1), rather than a specific designation of *Jeune homme triste*. That is to say, Duchamp may have momentarily forgotten which of the two works he sold at the Armory Show.

raphy on the other. In a 1946 interview with James Johnson Sweeney, Duchamp made his own first (published) statements concerning these questions:

I do not feel there was any connection between the Nude Descending a Staircase *and futurism. The futurists held their exhibition at the Galerie Bernheim Jeune in January 1912. I was painting the* Nude *at the same time. The oil sketch for it, however, had already been done in 1911. It is true I knew Severini. But I was not a café frequenter. Chronophotography was at the time in vogue. Studies of horses in movement and of fencers in different positions as in Muybridge's albums were well known to me. But my interest in painting the* Nude *was closer to the cubists' interest in decomposing forms than to the futurists' interest in suggesting movement, or even to Delaunay's Simultaneist suggestions of it. My aim was a static representation of movement — a static composition of indications of various positions taken by a form in movement — with no attempt to give cinema effects through painting....*

Futurism was an impressionism of the mechanical world. It was strictly a continuation of the Impressionist movement. I was not interested in that. I wanted to get away from the physical aspect of painting" ("Eleven Europeans in America," *The Museum of Modern Art Bulletin*, vol. 13, nos. 4-5, 1946, pp. 19-20).[7]

Guy Habasque (1959, pp. 128, 132) elaborated on one aspect of this important statement, writing that "the successive profile views of the *Sad Young Man* ... do not convey the young man's movement, but imply, by way of static postures of the traveler jolted by the train, the movement of the train itself.... he does not try to materialize movement, but to suggest it by an abstract representation of its consequences." In suggesting this "abstract representation of its consequences," Duchamp was in effect distancing himself from the more "physical aspect of painting" in order to render a more cerebral version of his chosen

7. There are several points of minor confusion in Duchamp's recollection as cited here (although the central facts of a photographic — rather than a Futurist — influence, and a basic relationship to Cubism, remain clear).

The Futurist exhibition did not actually open until February 5, 1912. *Nu descendant* must have been completed by the end of February or early in March (in time to be submitted to the *Salon des Indépendants* which opened on March 20, 1912). It is unlikely that Duchamp could have completed such a complex work very fast, and it seems probable that he began it some time in January and completed it in February — perhaps after the Futurist exhibition opened.

He further complicated the chronology of these events on subsequent occasions by repeatedly referring to the impression made on him at the Futurist exhibition by Balla's *Dinamismo di un cane al guinzaglio* (Albright-Knox Art Gallery, Buffalo): the Balla did not in fact appear in the show and was not even painted until May.

"Muybridge," meanwhile, was probably being used by Duchamp here in an almost generic sense to cover his recollection of the field of chronophotography as a whole. Muybridge was in fact less important to Duchamp's own development than Marey (see below). Thus, Duchamp's recollections, while generally indicative of the situation, are not entirely accurate in their individual details. In view of the 30-year time-lapse between the events and the interview, this is hardly surprising.

subject. Although, as Anne d'Harnoncourt has suggested (1980, p. 22), Duchamp's relationship to Futurist theory and to the ambience of Futurist principles remains to some extent unclear, his main concerns were not fundamentally those of the Futurists; his more general affinities were with the Cubists, and his specific visual analysis of motion seems almost certainly to have been indebted not to the Futurists, but to early studies in the field of chronophotography.[8] Richard Hamilton points out (1964, p. 23) that it was the French photographer Etienne-Jules Marey (1830-1903) rather than the American Eadweard Muybridge (1830-1904) who provided Duchamp with his most useful models. Although Duchamp had undoubtedly seen the work of both men (which was widely available at the time), their techniques were quite distinct. Muybridge "developed a technique of serial photography by which a rapid sequence of still shots made it possible to examine motion as a chain of changing relationships. His photographs are presented as strips of separate frames showing a breakdown of stages of the total image of the event, man jumping, etc.... Marey's approach was to superimpose separate stages of movement by multiple exposure on the same plate. To reduce the resultant complexity into terms that made strict analysis possible he devised means to simplify the forms. He covered his figures with black cloth and drew lines in white along the axes of the limbs—he used lights to indicate paths of travel. Marey's concern was less with changes in anatomical structure than with changes in relationship between parts of the organism."

Duchamp's schematic approach (especially as it is manifested in the final version of the *Nu descendant*) clearly owed a debt to Marey—a debt that is reflected in Duchamp's own description of his procedures: "The reduction of a head in movement to a bare line seemed to me defensible. A form passing through space would traverse a line; and as the form moved, the line it traversed would be replaced with another line—and another and another. Therefore I felt justified in reducing a figure in movement to a line rather than to a skeleton" (interview with J. J. Sweeney, loc. cit., p. 20).

In the 1967 *Entretiens* with Pierre Cabanne (pp. 46-47), Duchamp remained entirely consistent on these points, and added a further description of his particular aims (and techniques) in the *Jeune homme triste*:

> *Il y a d'abord l'idée du mouvement du train et puis celle du jeune homme triste qui est dans un couloir et qui se déplace; il y avait donc deux mouvements parallèles correspondant l'un à l'autre. Ensuite, il y a la déformation du bonhomme que j'avais appelée le parallélisme élémentaire. C'était une décomposition formelle, c'est à dire en lamelles linéaires qui se suivent comme des parallèles et déforment l'objet. L'objet est complètement étendu, comme élastisé. Les lignes se suivent parallèlement en changeant doucement pour former le mouvement ou la forme en question. J'ai également employé ce procédé dans le "Nu descendant un escalier."*

8. Various critics and historians, including Janneau (1929), Soby (1945), and Marcel Jean (1960) have argued that Futurist influence *is* present to a significant degree in *Jeune homme triste* and *Nu descendant*.

In other words, Duchamp's conception involved an analytical discontinuity — one static image following upon another — rather than a synthesized continuity of fused images such as Balla (and others) strove to achieve. "I discarded completely the naturalistic appearance of a nude, keeping only the abstract lines of some twenty different static positions in the successive action of descending." (Notes for an unpublished lecture, 1964, loc. cit., p. 256. For an important discussion of Marey's influence on Duchamp, see J. Clair, *Duchamp et la photographie*, 1977, pp. 30-38.)

The precise dates of the Peggy Guggenheim painting and the two related Arensberg nudes, as well as their sequence, remain unresolved. Dated 1912 on its surface,[9] and in the earliest literary reference (Apollinaire), *Jeune homme triste* was first dated 1911 by Janneau (1929) and in sources thereafter until 1937 when Pach reinstated 1912 (Chicago exhibition catalogue). This date was consistently assigned to the work until 1957 when Lebel for the first time used the specific month "December 1911" — the date that (in most instances) has been subsequently accepted.

Nu descendant (No. 1) has been consistently dated late in 1911. In 1964, Duchamp himself identified it as "the first study for *Nude descending a staircase*" and stated that it was done in the last months of 1911 "at the same time when I was painting the cubist chess players ..." (notes for an unpublished lecture, loc. cit., p. 256).

Nu descendant (No. 2) is dated 1912 on its surface, and it must have been completed in time to be submitted to the March *Salon des Indépendants* (i.e., by early March), a firm *terminus ante quem*.

A close analysis of certain aspects of the works themselves helps to illuminate the problems of sequence and date. For example, *Nu* (No. 1) shares with *Jeune homme* the black side border (which in the case of *Jeune homme* also extends across the top edge). While the two paintings (and at least two earlier works) are linked in this way, *Nu* (No. 1) is substantially less sophisticated in its handling of pigment, form, structure, light and shade than either *Jeune homme* or *Nu* (No. 2). Indeed, the differences are so striking that it is difficult to imagine that *Nu* (No. 1) followed *Jeune homme* (although such a sequence has been frequently implied in the literature). It seems much more likely that both *Jeune homme* and *Nu* (No. 2) followed *Nu* (No. 1).

The chronological relationship between the two later works, however, presents more difficult problems. Duchamp achieved in *Nu* (No. 2) a compositional integration of figure and environment — an articulation and fluency — which seems more assured and advanced than that of *Jeune homme*. Moreoever, some of the forms in the second *Nu* (especially the hips) bear an obvious relationship to the machinelike vocabulary of the immediately following *King and Queen Surrounded by Swift Nudes* and *The Passage from the Virgin to the Bride*. These

9. Since Duchamp varnished the picture in 1942 (see CONDITION), it is impossible to know whether he added the signature and date (which *are* under the varnish) at that time, or at the time of completing the work.

particular indications seem to suggest (and it is a point generally accepted in the literature) that the *Nu* (No. 2) was painted at a slightly later date than the *Jeune homme*. At the same time, the distinction in aims represented by the *Nu* and the *Jeune homme* must be borne in mind in assessing whether there is in fact an actual "progression" from one to the other. In *Jeune homme triste*, for example, the delicate faceting of the body, and the subtly diffused shading introduced at the left and the right of the figure, allowed Duchamp to convey precisely the kind of motion he sought (and which Hamilton perceived): the motion of the train, as opposed to that of the figure. The latter emerges from the shadows and is directly confronted for a fleeting moment, then disappears into the darkness again as the train races by. The rhythmic delicacy and the dematerialized quality of the surface texture, which Duchamp employed so effectively to achieve this result, are necessarily different in nature from the means he used to define the more assertive and dynamic action of the figure in *Nu descendant*. Thus, much of the stylistic evidence suggests that *Nu* (No. 2) was the final work of the three, yet it is possible that the differences in style were essentially the result of differences in purpose, and that the last two paintings were produced more or less contemporaneously.

Finally, it is important to examine the question of a possible literary source for *Jeune homme triste*, and its probable autobiographical content. Duchamp himself described *Jeune homme* as an image of himself—and of an actual event: "*C'était autobiographique: un voyage que j'avais fait de Paris à Rouen seul dans le compartement. Il y avait le pipe pour indiquer mon identité*" (Cabanne, 1967, p. 55). Duchamp stated, in addition, that the alliteration in the title played an important role in conveying the wit that formed part of the meaning: "*Le* 'Jeune homme ...' *montrait déjà mon intention d'introduire l'humour dans le tableau ou, en tout cas, l'humour de jeux de mots: triste, train. Je crois qu'Apollinaire l'a appelé 'Mélancolie dans un train.' Le jeune homme est triste parce qu'il y a le train qui vient après. 'Tr' est très important*" (ibid., p. 47).[10] Duchamp suggests here that the choice of the word *triste* — rather than *mélancolie*, for example — was inevitable because it was governed (prospectively) by *train*, with which it was linked through the "*tr*" sound. Although the alliteration is important in itself, Duchamp seems to imply that there is also significance and humor in the juxtaposition of meanings. *Triste* suggests romantic sentiment and a possible romantic setting. *Train* strikes a note of incongruity: it is both more mundane and more self-consciously modern than anticipated. At a deeper level, however,

10. For interpretations of the painting as a sign of "mourning," see Schwarz, Lebel, Dorival. The black border around 3 sides of the work (see above) has been cited as further evidence for such an interpretation. The "sadness" of the Duchamp figure is, moreover, seen by some as directly attributable to the "loss" of his sister, who had married a Rouen pharmacist on August 24, 1911—an event that is said to have deeply shaken Duchamp. Duchamp denied any implication of mourning in the black edges, claiming for them merely a pictorial function—"*la bordure noire...m'a surtout servi à cadrer le tableau pour le mettre à son échelle*" (Lebel, 1967, p. 20; see also Schwarz, 1960, p. 121 fn. 26).

train represents a complex choice: journeys by train can indeed be evocative, and the interaction of *train* with *triste* consequently calls into play a set of serious feelings and associations that are obviously of central importance to the painting as a whole. In other words, the *jeux de mots* in Duchamp's title work to qualify interpretations that are too simply subjective or romantic in nature, but also serve to reinforce and enrich the painting's dominant tone of sadness.

Thus, although *Jeune homme* is a haunting work that conveys a strong sense of "sadness," the wit of its title and the analytic style of the painting itself — the fact that it is a calculated "study" in the visual effects of motion — must also be taken into account in arriving at a full interpretation of the work.

A reading of the painting that takes into account both the serious tone of *tristesse* and the playfulness Duchamp himself insisted upon is consistent with the picture's primary literary connections. Michel Sanouillet (among others) has pointed to the relationship between Duchamp's work of this period and his early interest in the poetry of Jules Laforgue (in *Marcel Duchamp*, 1973, p. 50). Duchamp is known to have executed at least three sketches to illustrate Laforgue's *Complaintes*, and one of these sketches (*Encore à cet astre*) is considered by most scholars to be the earliest study for *Nu descendant un escalier*. Sanouillet suggests, in addition, that Laforgue's poem *Complainte du Pauvre Jeune Homme* may have inspired Duchamp's *Jeune homme triste dans un train*, and that an illustration for the poem — since lost — may also have been made.[11]

Laforgue's poetry was, of course, a complex blend of postromantic sentiment transmuted by wit and irony. It may well be that some of these qualities had an oblique effect on the tone of the *Jeune homme triste*, although direct substantive connections between the painting and the content of any particular poem (such as the *Complainte du Pauvre Jeune Homme*) are very difficult to sustain. Duchamp himself implied — in a statement to Sweeney (loc. cit., 1946, p. 19) — that he was probably more interested in Laforgue's titles than in his actual poetry. In short, there does seem to be a strong case for viewing at least the title of the *Jeune homme triste* as deriving (in altered form) from Laforgue; beyond that, some traces of Laforgue's self-consciousness and wit, as well as his sentiment, may have had some effect on Duchamp's painting.

Several critics have argued for more explicitly sexual interpretations of the *Jeune homme triste*; there have also been suggestions that the figure in the painting is explicitly androgynous in nature. In discussing this set of issues as they bear upon the *Nu*, Rubin suggested (1968, p. 24) that "whereas such [sexual] readings follow automatically from the situations and plastic elements of [Duchamp's] later painting ... there is nothing in the *Nude* to prompt, not to say compel, notions of 'subjectivism' or sex." These comments apply with equal

11. Sanouillet actually refers to Laforgue's poem as *Pauvre Jeune Homme M* and states that this was the original title of Duchamp's painting. Evidence for this is not cited, and has not been found by the present author. For a discussion of Laforgue and the relationship of his poetry to Duchamp's work of this time, see also Johnson, 1976.

aptness to the *Jeune homme triste.* The figure is clearly identified in the latter title (and by Duchamp's testimony) as a male (and as an "autobiographical" image), but the painting itself does not suggest that special emphasis should be placed on the specific sexual identity (whether masculine or androgynous) of the principal figure. The *Nu*, meanwhile, seems fundamentally lacking in sexual identity: it is not explicitly legible as either male or female. In both cases Duchamp's expressed intention to deal with the subject of motion in pictorial terms takes precedence over all other concerns. As Duchamp himself said of the *Nu*: "The movement is an abstraction, a conclusion contained in the picture and there is no need to know whether or not a real person is descending an equally real staircase. Basically the movement is in the eye of the spectator, who incorporates it into the picture."[12]

EXHIBITIONS:

Paris, Galerie La Boétie, *Salon de "La Section d'Or,"* Oct. 10-30, 1912, no. 20? (*Peinture*);[13] New York, Association of American Painters and Sculptors, Inc., 69th Infantry Armory, *International Exhibition of Modern Art*, Feb. 15 (17?)-Mar. 15, no. 242 (*Nu [sketch]*), traveled to The Art Institute of Chicago, Mar. 24-Apr. 16, no. 108 (*Sketch of a Nude*); Boston, Copley Hall, Apr. 28-May 19, no. 40 (*Sketch of a Nude*); The Arts Club of Chicago, *Exhibition of Paintings by Marcel Duchamp*, Feb. 5-27, 1937, no. 8 (dated 1912; lent by Pach); New York, MoMA, *Art in Our Time*, May 10-Sept. 30, 1939, no. 176, repr. n.p. (dated 1912); New York, Art of This Century, 1942-47, p. 56, repr. p. 57 (dated 1912); Venice, *P.G.*, 1948 (Biennale), no. 33 (dated 1912); Florence, *P.G.*, 1949, no. 33 (dated 1912); Amsterdam, *P.G.*, 1951, no. 41, repr. (dated 1911); Zurich, *P.G.*, 1951, no. 37 (dated 1912); London, *P.G.*, 1964-65, no. 9, repr. (dated 1911, the date attributed to it in all subsequent exhibition catalogues); Stockholm, *P.G.*, 1966-67, no. 9, repr.; New York, *P.G.*, 1969, p. 73, repr.; New York, MoMA, *Marcel Duchamp*, Dec. 3, 1973-Feb. 10, 1974, no. 70, repr. p. 256; Paris, *P.G.*, 1974-75, no. 15, repr. color, n.p.; Torino, *P.G.*, 1975-76, no. 9, repr. color; Paris, MNAM, *Marcel Duchamp*, Jan. 31-May 2, 1977, no. 62; Rome, Galleria Nazionale d'Arte Moderna e Contemporanea, *Apollinaire e l'Avanguardia*, Nov. 30, 1980-Jan. 4, 1981, no. 78, repr. color; Rome, *Guggenheim: Venezia-New York*, 1982, no. 9, repr. color; New York, *P.G.*, 1982-83, no. 8, repr. color.

REFERENCES:

G. Apollinaire, *Les Peintres Cubistes*, Paris, 1913, [p. 73, repr. n.p.], ("*jeune homme mélancolique dans un train*, 1912"); G. Janneau, *L'art cubiste*, Paris, 1929, p. 24 ("*Jeune homme*, 1911"); G. Hugnet, "L'Esprit Dada dans la peinture," *Cahiers d'Art*, vol. 7, nos. 1-2, 1932, p. 64 ("*Jeune homme triste dans un train*, 1911");[14] A. Breton, "Phare de la Mariée," *Minotaure*, vol. 2, no. 6, winter 1935, p. 46 (parts appeared also in *London Bulletin*, nos. 4-5, July, 1938, p. 17; entire article appeared in *Le Surréalisme et la peinture*, 1945, p. 112; 1965 Fr. ed., p. 38; *Surrealism and Painting*, 1972, p. 90, repr. p. 88); R. Huyghe, *Histoire de l'art contemporain: La peinture*, Paris,

12. P. Cabanne, *The Brothers Duchamp*, Boston, 1976, p. 68. Cabanne does not give a context for the quotation or a date; it is therefore difficult to know whether it might be applied with equal validity to the *Jeune homme triste*, though this does seem likely.
13. According to W. Camfield, Duchamp was unable to recall which of his works was shown under the entry *Peinture*, but he thought that it could have been *Jeune homme triste* ("La Section d'Or," unpublished master's thesis, Yale University, 1961, p. 71 fn. 108).
14. The title and date as cited are included hereafter only in those REFERENCES that depart from "*Jeune homme triste dans un train*, 1911."

1935, p. 339; W. Pach, *Queer Thing, Painting: Forty Years in the World of Art*, New York and London, 1938, pp. 157-58, 160, repr. betw. pp. 164 and 165 (dated 1912); A. Breton, *Anthologie de l'humour noir*, Paris, 1940, p. 222; M. Duchamp, *From or by Marcel Duchamp or Rrose Sélavy [Boîte-en-Valise]*, repr. no. 24 ("Neuilly, Dec. 1911, Coll. Pach"); P. Guggenheim, *Art of This Century*, 1942, repr. p. 57 (dated 1912); J. T. Soby, "Marcel Duchamp in the Arensberg Collection," *View*, 5th ser., no. 1, 1945 (spec. Duchamp issue), p. 12 ("*Young Man in a Train*, 1912"); G. Buffet-Picabia, *Aires Abstraites*, Geneva, 1957, p. 156; G. Hugnet, *L'Aventure Dada (1916-1922)*, Paris, 1957, pp. 34, 36; R. Lebel, "Marcel Duchamp: Liens et ruptures: Premiers essais: Le Cubisme: le nu descendant un escalier," *Le Surréalisme même*, 3, autumn 1957, pp. 30, 31 (dated Dec. 1911); G. Habasque, *Cubism*, trans. S. Gilbert, Geneva, 1959, pp. 128-29, 132, repr. color p. 130; R. Lebel, *Sur Marcel Duchamp*, Paris, 1959, pp. 8, 9, 13-14, 28, [37], 90, repr. pl. 48, cat. no. 86 on p. 162 (Eng. trans. by G. H. Hamilton, N.Y., 1959); M. Jean, *The History of Surrealist Painting*, trans. S. W. Taylor, New York, 1960, p. 32 (dated Dec. 1911); W. Rubin, "Reflexions on Marcel Duchamp," *Art International*, vol. 4, no. 9, Dec. 1, 1960, pp. 49, 50; L. D. Steefel, Jr., "The Position of 'La Mariée mise à nu par ses célibataires, même' (1915-1923) in the Stylistic and Iconographic Development of the Art of Marcel Duchamp," unpublished Ph.D. dissertation, Princeton University, 1960, pp. 28, 44, 46, 49, 107, 109, 111, 127-28, 319, 372, 374 fn. 53, repr. pl. 15 (dated 1911-12); M. W. Brown, *The Story of the Armory Show*, [New York], 1963, pp. 182, 240 [cat. no. 242], (dated 1912); W. Seitz, "What's Happpened to Art? An Interview with Marcel Duchamp on Present Consequences of New York's 1913 Armory Show," *Vogue*, Feb. 15, 1963, p. 110; R. Hamilton, "Duchamp," *Art International*, vol. 7, no. 10, Jan. 16, 1964, p. 23; R. Hamilton, *The Almost Complete Works of Marcel Duchamp*, exh. cat., The Tate Gallery, London, 1966, 2nd ed., p. 36, repr. (cat. no. L86 [not exhibited], dated Dec. 1911); C. Tomkins, *The World of Marcel Duchamp*, New York, 1966, pp. 14, 15, 26, 85, repr. color p. 26; P. Cabanne, *Entretiens avec Marcel Duchamp*, Paris, 1967, pp. 47-48, 55, 58, 76, 175; idem, "Marcel Duchamp: le voyage au bout du scandale," *Galerie des Arts*, no. 45, June 1967, p. 5 (dated 1912); B. Dorival and J. Cassou, *Raymond Duchamp-Jacques Villon-Marcel Duchamp*, exh. cat., MNAM, Paris, 1967, pp. 28, 35; R. Lebel, "Marcel Duchamp maintenant et ici, dialogue avec Robert Lebel, *L'Œil*, no. 149, May 1967, pp. 20, 77, repr. p. 19; W. Rubin, *Dada and Surrealist Art*, New York, 1968, pp. 22, 23-24, repr. p. 25 (fig. 3); A. Schwarz, *The Complete Works of Marcel Duchamp*, rev. ed., New York, 1970, pp. 16, 49, 50, 107, 108, 110-11, 121 fns. 25-26, 512, repr. p. 432, cat. no. 179, repr. color pl. 56 (p. 252); J. Burnham, "Unveiling the Consort: Part I," *Artforum*, vol. 10, no. 7, Mar. 1971, p. 59; J. Golding, *Duchamp: The Bride Stripped Bare by Her Bachelors, Even*, New York, 1973, pp. 25, 60; A. d'Harnoncourt and K. McShine, eds., *Marcel Duchamp*, exh. cat., MoMA and Philadelphia Museum of Art, New York, 1973, cat. no. 70, repr. p. 256; also pp. 13, 50, 70 fn. 2, 72 fn. 13, 79, 130; S. Dalí, *Comment on devient Dalí*, Paris, 1973, p. 239; J. Chalupecký, "Nothing but an Artist," *Studio International*, vol. 189, no. 973, Jan.-Feb. 1975, p. 32; J. Masheck, ed. and intro., *Marcel Duchamp in Perspective*, Englewood Cliffs, N.J., 1975, pp. 5-8; M. Rowell, "Kupka, Duchamp and Marey," *Studio International*, vol. 189, no. 973, Jan.-Feb. 1975, p. 50; P. Cabanne, *The Brothers Duchamp: Jacques Villon, Raymond Duchamp-Villon, Marcel Duchamp*, trans. H. and D. Harrison, Boston, 1976 (first pub. in Switzerland, 1975), pp. 67-68, 108, repr. color p. 69; R. Johnson, "Poetic Pathways to Dada: Marcel Duchamp and Jules Laforgue," *Arts Magazine*, vol. 50, no. 9, May 1976, pp. 86, 87-88, 89, repr. p. 87; L. D. Steefel, Jr., "Marcel Duchamp's 'Encore à cet Astre': A New Look," *The Art Journal*, vol. 36, no. 1, fall 1976, pp. 23-30; *Duchamp: Tradition de la rupture ou rupture de la tradition?* (Colloque de Cerisy), Paris, 1977, pp. 57 (J. Suquet), 58, 133 (J. Clair), 172 (R. Micha), 362 (J. Dee); J. Clair, ed., *Marcel Duchamp: Catalogue raisonné, L'Œuvre de Marcel Duchamp*, vol. II, exh. cat., MNAM, Paris, 1977, pp. 50, 168, repr. color p. 48 (pl. 12), cat. no. 62; J. Clair, *Duchamp et la photographie*, Paris, 1977, p. 30, 34, repr. p. 32; T. Reff, "Duchamp & Leonardo: L.H.O.O.Q.-Alikes," *Art in America*, vol. 65, no. 1, Jan.-Feb. 1977, pp. 89-90, 91; A. d'Harnoncourt, "Futurism and the International Avant-Garde," *Futurism and the International Avant-Garde*, exh. cat., Philadelphia, 1981, p. 22, repr. fig. 17; A. G. Marquis, *Marcel Duchamp: Eros, c'est la vie*, Troy, New York, 1981, pp. 72-73, 74, 84, 94, 113.

Raymond Duchamp-Villon

(Pierre-Maurice-Raymond Duchamp Villon).

Born November 1876, Damville, near Rouen.
Died October 1918, Cannes.

50 Le Cheval. 1914 (cast ca. 1930).
(*The Horse*).

76.2553 PG 24

Bronze (sand cast) with black-green patina with large areas of pale green. Height: 17 3/16 (43.6); depth: 16 1/8 (41).

Edition: size unknown.

Foundry: unknown.

Inscribed on base (incised into original plaster): *R. Duchamp-Villon / 1914*.

PROVENANCE:

Purchased from Marcel Duchamp, Paris, 1940.

CONDITION:

Extensive green corrosion of the surface was caused by outdoor exhibition of the sculpture over a period of many years.

In February 1984 (Venice) the piece was cleaned. The streaks of corrosion (which interfered with the legibility) were successfully removed from the rear slanting plane with a Fiberglas brush. This area was then treated with ammonium sulphide and silver nitrate to reintegrate its patina with the brownish black of the adjacent surfaces. The entire surface of the piece was degreased with trichloroethylene, and washed with distilled water, then with distilled water and neutral detergent; it was rinsed with distilled water and dried with alcohol and acetone. The surface was treated for 30 minutes with a 3% solution of benzotriazole in pure alcohol. A protective coating of Incralac (acrylic resin containing benzotriazole) was applied (for outdoor exhibition). The condition is stable. (Venice, Mar. 1984.)

When Duchamp-Villon died in 1918, he left what can be regarded as a definitive conception in plaster of *Le Cheval.* The work had preoccupied him almost continuously during the years 1914-18, and there is considerable evidence to support the notion that his earliest work on the subject dated from 1913, or even possibly 1912.[1] According to the testimony of his brothers, Marcel Du-

1. According to Walter Pach (New York, 1924, p. 112), Duchamp-Villon was at work on the sculpture for approximately 1 year before World War I broke out in 1914. William Agee (1967, p. 103, fn. 5) argued that—in view of the other projects that occupied the artist in 1913-14—he was unlikely to have started the sculpture before 1914. Albert Elsen, in his review of Agee's text (1969, p. 523), suggested that at least the small "chess-size" studies for the horse (which Agee had apparently not seen) must have been made in 1913. Judith Zilczer pointed out that within a ca. 1912 sketch for *La maison cubiste*, a sketch for an equestrian monument contained the basic idea later developed into *Cheval* (1980, p. 15, repr. p. 16, fig. 21). Both of the artist's brothers had also indicated a 1912-13 origin for the ideas, if not the execution of any models. (See Marcel Duchamp, "Raymond Duchamp-Villon," Société Anonyme Archive, Yale University; Jacques Villon, letter to Alfred H. Barr, Jr., Aug. 30, 1938, cited below. The latter document contains information regarding the completion of *Cheval* before World War I, a suggestion that conflicts with evidence provided elsewhere by Villon; for clarification of this point, see below, fn. 6.)

champ and Jacques Villon, and of his close friend and biographer, Walter Pach, Duchamp-Villon planned to have the work cast in an enlarged size (in steel). He apparently did create an armature for projected use in the enlargement and casting of the piece (fig. a), but died before full preparations had been completed. It thus fell to his brothers to attempt to carry out his plans.

Although it is possible to establish a number of facts regarding the existing plaster casts and their bronze versions, a great many questions remain unresolved.[2]

The earliest bronze cast appears to have been made in 1921-22. John Quinn purchased the plaster maquette from Madame Duchamp-Villon in May 1921; at the time, he expressed his intention to have the plaster, which he believed to be unique, cast in bronze.[3] This was duly accomplished, almost certainly at Roman Bronze Works in Corona, Queens, sometime between May 1921 and March 1922.[4] As far as can be established, the casting seems to have been carried out without the supervision or advice of Marcel Duchamp or Jacques Villon; it is possible, however that Pach (who was also a close friend of Quinn) may have been involved. Probably only one bronze would have been cast, although this is not certain (see fn. 4). The current location of the Quinn plaster is unknown, its last documented appearance having been the 1927 John Quinn Sale where it appeared as no. 700.[5]

The second casting of the 17 in., 44 cm., *Le Cheval* seems to have taken place about 1930 in France. An important question related to this casting — and subsequent ones — is whether Duchamp-Villon himself had originally created a series of identical plasters (rather than merely the "unique" example, which Quinn assumed), or whether one or more additional plasters were later created without the participation of the artist. No documentary evidence survives to establish the existence of such additional plasters by Duchamp-Villon; the existing documents, in fact, tend to point toward the opposite conclusion. For

2. Marie-Noëlle Pradel, who is apparently preparing a major study of the sculpture of Duchamp-Villon, may have solved a number of the questions posed here. It has unfortunately not proved possible to discuss these questions with her.

3. "...I am going to have them [*The Horse* and *Portrait of Dr. Gossett*] cast in bronze.... I assume that the plaster of the Horse which you sent me is the one on which your husband actually worked and is the only one in existence" (letter from Quinn to Mme. Duchamp-Villon, May 14, 1921, John Quinn Memorial Collection, New York Public Library, Astor, Lenox, and Tilden Foundations). No response to this letter has been located among the Quinn papers.

4. John Quinn dealt extensively with Roman Bronze between 1918 and the early 1920s and his ledgers indicate that several bronzes were cast there. Although research in the Roman Bronze Archives has been undertaken at the request of the author, it has so far not been demonstrated precisely when the cast was made. At this point it is only possible to state with certainty that 1 bronze cast was made for Quinn sometime between May 1921 and March 1922, the date when it was exhibited at the Sculptors' Gallery. This cast is now in the collection of Edgar Kaufmann, jr.

5. It has not been possible to establish whether the plaster shown in the 1929 exhibitions at the Brummer Gallery and at The Arts Club of Chicago was the one formerly owned by Quinn, although this seems likely.

fig. a.
Armature for the projected enlargement of cat. no. 50 apparently built by Duchamp-Villon himself; dimensions and location unknown.

example, an important letter from Villon to Barr (dated August 30, 1938) indicates that only one final maquette was made:

> *Vers 1913, le parallelisme entre le mouvement machine et le mouvement animal, s'imposant à son esprit, il conçut le cheval, qu'il mit au point après maintes recherches, au commencement de l'été 1914, dans une maquette de 0.45 m. x 0.44 cm. x 0.23 cm.... Aussitôt cette maquette terminée il commença, suivant le plan qu'il s'était tracé, à l'agrandir — donnait à la plus grande dimension 1 mètre.*
>
> *Je joins à ma lettre deux photos de ce travail d'agrandissement, au point où'il était la jour de la déclaration de la guerre — point où il devait rester.*[6]
>
> *Sachant son désir de voir terminée cette œuvre qu'il considérait comme capitale, j'ai, lorsque j'ai pu, fait terminer l'agrandissement sous ma surveillance et en tenant compte de ce que désirait Duchamp-Villon et cela d'après la maquette qui lui servait à lui même. La seule chose que je n'ai pu faire, ce fut de faire fondre en* "ACIER" *(POLI) le cheval agrandi. J'ai du contenter d'un* "bronze," *devant les difficultés rencontrées pour la réalisation "acier" que mon frère eut préférée* (Archives of the Department of Painting and Sculpture, MoMA).

6. One of these photographs is the armature, fig. a. The other has not been identified. Villon's statement that the maquette was actually completed by the summer of 1914 seems to have been a lapse of memory. Pach, for example, reports that much earlier Villon wrote to him about the continuation, and improvement, of the concept, which took place while Duchamp-Villon was attached, as a doctor, to a cavalry regiment: "*Pendant la guerre, ayant mieux connu le cheval... il n'avait cessé de songer à son œuvre commencée, et c'est par douzaines que l'on a retrouvé des croquis modifiant sa maquette première*" (Pach, Paris, 1924, p. 15). This point is made again by Villon in the memoir he wrote about his brother (Francastel, 1954, p. 307).

fig. b.
Plaster maquette for *Le Cheval*, height: 17½ in., 44 cm., Private Collection, on loan to the Philadelphia Museum of Art.

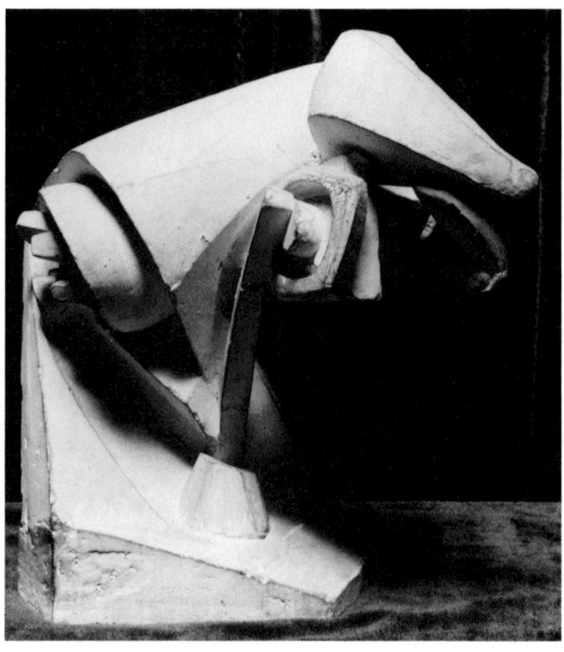

fig. c.
Plaster maquette for *Le Cheval*, height: 17½ in., 44 cm., Musée de Grenoble.

Twice in this letter, Villon speaks of only a single final plaster maquette made by Duchamp-Villon himself. Since one such plaster was sold to Quinn in 1921, three years after Duchamp-Villon's death, it is possible that the two brothers decided to have additional plaster casts made from this maquette before the 1921 sale was consummated, preserving in France a model from which they could ultimately make bronzes, and which could also serve as the basis for the projected enlargement. Again, it is theoretically possible that Duchamp-Villon himself made such replicas before his death, but no proof of this has been located.[7]

Evidence regarding the precise date of the ca. 1930 bronze casting of the 44 cm. *Le Cheval*, of its smaller sketch models, and of the 100 cm. enlargement, remains thus far circumstantial. The 1929 Brummer Gallery exhibition of works by Duchamp-Villon contained only plasters and one can probably assume therefore that no bronzes had yet been cast. The 1931 exhibition at the Galerie Pierre, on the other hand, contained several bronzes (see below EXHIBITIONS and fn.

7. At least 2 virtually identical plasters of the final maquette (44 cm.) are presently known: 1 is on loan from a private collection to the Philadelphia Museum of Art (fig. b). This is almost certainly the example formerly in the collection of Mme. Duvernoy (Duchamp-Villon's widow). It may also correspond to an example once recorded in the collection of Suzanne Duchamp Crotti, although the latter may be additional. The second known identical plaster is in the Musée de Grenoble, received as a gift from the family of the artist in 1930 (fig. c). As was noted above, the Quinn plaster is apparently lost; if found, this would probably be a third.

12). Although Pach told Barr (in December 1948) that "the bronze casts of *The Horse* were made by Jacques Villon and [the sculptor] Albert Pommier" (note in the Archives of the Department of Painting and Sculpture, MoMA), he did not specify either the date, the sizes, or the numbers in each category. It was at the 1931 Galerie Pierre exhibition, however, that Barr apparently first saw the 100 cm. bronze (at that time "unique" as he later noted); it seems likely, therefore, that in preparation for that exhibition, Duchamp-Villon's brothers had a number of the surviving plasters of various sculptures cast in bronze, and that they took this same opportunity to execute their brother's planned enlargement of *Le Cheval*.

It has not been possible to determine which foundry was used, or how large an edition of each sculpture was cast at the time. It does seem possible, however, that two casts of the 44 cm. *Le Cheval* were made on this occasion, one of which became the property of Duchamp, the other, of Villon. These would then have been acquired respectively by Peggy Guggenheim (in 1940) and Willem Sandberg for the Stedelijk Museum, Amsterdam (in 1948). Whether additional casts were made at the same time (or indeed whether these two were in fact made then) remains a matter of speculation.

The 100 cm. enlargement, which figured prominently at the center of the Galerie Pierre installation and was then acquired by MoMA, was based on the armature (fig. a) that was built by Duchamp-Villon himself and remained in his studio after his death. The considerably greater enlargement known as *Le Cheval Majeur*, authorized by Duchamp in 1966 (1.5 m.), was carried out under the auspices of Louis Carré and cast by Georges Rudier.[8]

Several complex issues are raised by the fact that the artist himself did not participate in the execution of the multiple posthumous castings — in various sizes — of his 1914 plaster sculpture. There seems no doubt that Duchamp-Villon envisaged an enlargement of the piece from its 44 cm. size and that he created an armature for that purpose, but little more is known about his full intentions. Villon (in the 1938 letter to Barr cited above) and Pach (in a May 18, 1921, note to Quinn) indicate only that Duchamp-Villon explicitly wanted the work cast in steel, a material he is known to have admired because it embodied for him the vibrant quality of the machine age.[9] The very fact that the enlarged piece was ultimately executed in bronze (and later in lead) appears to be at odds with the artist's own wishes. Even if a bronze had been originally

8. Editions in both lead and bronze (of the 44 cm. size) were also carried out by Louis Carré during the 1950s. Examples from the bronze edition (all unnumbered) are in the collections of the MNAM, Paris, The Washington University Art Gallery, St. Louis, and the Hirshhorn Museum and Sculpture Garden, Washington, D.C. A 1955 edition of 6 examples (of the 100 cm. size) was cast by Susse; all of these are now in museums (see Alley, *Tate Collection*, 1981, p. 193, for locations).

9. Agee, 1967, p. 89, quotes Duchamp-Villon's reaction to a dynamo exhibited at the Galeries des Machines at the 1900 Exposition Universelle: "a work filled with power and audacity, proclaiming in a fantastic hall, the glory of steel."

intended, it is obviously impossible to know what decisions Duchamp-Villon would have made concerning the exact composition of the material (and hence its color), the patina, and the all-important issue of scale.[10]

Duchamp-Villon's own uncompromising struggle to perfect the image of the horse in its plaster form, and his gradual refinement of its lines and surfaces, are clearly reflected in the innumerable preparatory studies that preceded the final plaster maquette. Further light is cast on his principles by the incomplete manuscript cited in footnote 10. In discussing the arduous process of executing a sculpture, Duchamp-Villon described the constant alterations and adjustments the artist is forced to make in his effort to articulate the image that exists in his imagination; the chance transitions that occur, even when the piece seems finished; and the accidents that can lead to final resolution. Even at the last, "*toutes les possibilités de l'œuvre lui apparaissent, et il en voit tant qu'elle ne lui suffit plus*" (quoted in Pach, Paris, 1924, p. 30).

The evolution of the image of the horse can to a very large extent be traced in the sketches, clay models, and plasters that exist in the artist's estate and in various collections. Elsen (1967 and 1969) and Agee (1967) have provided extensive analyses of the sculptor's progress from the original realistic studies of a horse plus rider. Elsen has written: "Having first made the form of the horse compact with the rider, he then went on to discard the rider, symmetry and considerable equine references as he contracted his shapes into a few strong competing gestures. He reworked his earlier stylized treatment of chest, flanks and legs — the areas of the animal's locomotion — until they assumed spring, gear, and piston rod-like shapes" (1967, p. 23).

Several of the drawings reveal the sculptor's effort to include the idea of movement in his piece. In the series of studies on a single sheet (fig. d), his verbal notations indicate that he was continuously concerned about the interrelated issues of proportion, energy, and motion. In several studies that probably followed (figs. e-g), he focused on details that gave clearer expression to the circular rhythm or motion that he was attempting to achieve. The squaring of many of the drawings, meanwhile, apparently aided him in his struggle with problems of proportion. Efforts to abstract the figure—creating a series of sweeping curves

10. Duchamp-Villon's sensitivity to the materials with which he worked is borne out in a number of different ways—most clearly in the work he completed himself. In the unfinished manuscript found among his papers after his death, he drew attention to at least 1 of the respects in which the sculptor's attitude to his material was critical: "*La nécessité de ne point perdre pied entraîne un goût des qualités physiques de la matière. Les idées de volumes, de cohérence, de dureté, de poids, et même de durée accompagnent les idées les plus constructives d'espaces et de rapport d'espaces—car la spéculation pure voit les volumes prendre une vie spéciale et leur fait perdre toute consistance, d'où le peu d'importance donnée, au début de la conception, à la matière qui sera choisie...*" (complete text in Pach, Paris, 1924, pp. 27-34).

In his 1968 review of the Knoedler exhibition, Daniel Robbins raised a number of important questions regarding the posthumous casts, as did Elsen in his 1969 review of the Hamilton-Agee book. Sylvia Hochfield (1974) quoted the opinion of Sidney Geist on all of the posthumous castings and enlargements, none of which, in his opinion, reflected the artist's own sensibility.

fig. d.
Studies for cat. no. 50, not signed or dated, ink and pencil on paper, 12⅛ x 7⅞ in., 30.9 x 20 cm., inscribed in pencil, upper left: *trop immobile / mal proportionné*; upper right, with directional arrows indicating circular movement: *mouvement / en 2 parties / à etudier;* upper center, right: *immobile—arrière-main / bonnes proportions*; center (possibly referring to sketch in left corner): *manque un peu / d'energie*; lower left corner: *mouvement esquissé / tête et cou mal / placés*, Estate of the artist, Paris.

fig. e.
Duchamp-Villon, Study for cat. no. 50, not signed or dated, pencil on dark brown paper, 7¼ x 10⅝ in., 18.5 x 27 cm., Estate of the artist, Paris.

fig. f.
Duchamp-Villon, Studies for cat. no. 50, not signed or dated, pencil on purple paper, 5⅞ x 9 in., 14.9 x 23 cm., Estate of the artist, Paris.

fig. g.
Duchamp-Villon, Studies for cat. no. 50, not signed or dated, pencil on paper, 8¼ x 12 in., 21 x 30.6 cm., Estate of the artist, Paris.

fig. h.
Duchamp-Villon, Study for cat. no. 50, not signed or dated, red india ink on gray paper, 5 1/8 x 6 5/8 in., 13 x 17 cm., Estate of the artist, Paris.

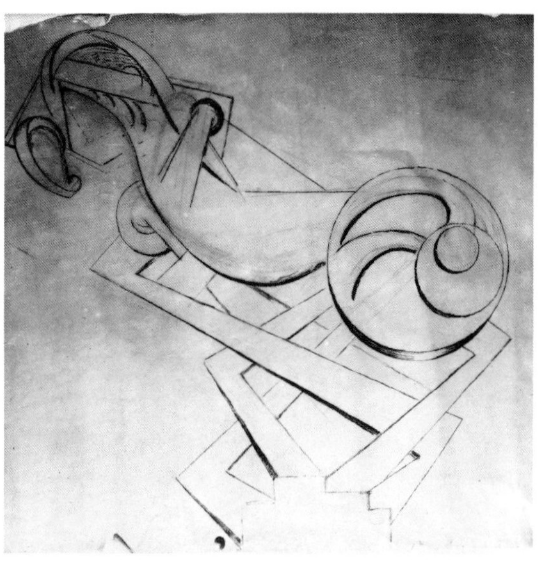

fig. i.
Duchamp-Villon, Study for cat. no. 50, not signed or dated, ink and pencil(?) on paper, dimensions and location unknown.

fig. j.
Duchamp-Villon, Studies for cat. no. 50, not signed or dated, purple ink on paper, 10 x 7 7/8 in., 25.5 x 20 cm., Estate of the artist, Paris.

and planes — and to introduce the "machine" elements, emerged in drawings such as figs. h and i. Finally, the precisely rendered drawings of fig. j reveal in elaborate detail how Duchamp-Villon gradually transformed the leg of the horse until he arrived at the highly compressed "piston" that constituted his ultimate resolution.

The clay models, which the artist probably produced contemporaneously with many of the later drawings, suggest his efforts to shorten the extended horizontal

fig. k.
Duchamp-Villon, plaster sketch model for cat. no. 50, height: 14½ in., 36.8 cm., Philadelphia Museum of Art, Gift of the Family of the Artist (View I).

fig. l.
Duchamp-Villon, plaster sketch model for cat. no. 50, height: 14½ in., 36.8 cm., Philadelphia Museum of Art, Gift of the Family of the Artist (View II).

of the galloping horse and thus increase the tautness of the image. In the process, much of the clarity and articulation of detail, and the differentiation of surfaces, lines, and planes, were temporarily sacrificed (see, for example, Zilczer, 1980, figs. 24 and 25). The impression of movement — so critical in many of the drawings — was also significantly reduced as the work became more compact.

In the penultimate plaster (figs. k and l) the image became much more fully articulated and many of the elements of the sculpture as eventually realized were now present, if only in rough and blocklike form. At the same time, the figure of the horse was now turned in on itself and appeared more inert; the precision, grace, and finely wrought surfaces of the final stage were still lacking. (Indeed, pencil lines visible on the plaster itself indicate the areas Duchamp-Villon intended to pare down, as he worked to create the proportions he sought.)

In a 1924 essay about Duchamp-Villon, Pach described both the process and the artist's intentions in this final work of his career: "The work began, as all of Duchamp-Villon's later productions did, with naturalistic studies, the planes and directions of line and mass which seemed essential to the idea and the design gradually taking precedence over the details which partook more of the accidental. Simultaneously the work became an expression of Duchamp-Villon's idea that the world of today translates its thought in terms of the machine, which, with its power and speed, the dominant interests of the period, penetrates our whole conception of life" (New York, 1924, p. 112). In a 1913 letter to Pach, Duchamp-Villon had written: "The power of the machine imposes itself upon us and we can scarcely conceive living bodies without it; we are strangely moved by the swift brushing by of beings and of objects, and we accustom ourselves, without knowing it, to perceive the forces of the former group in terms of the forces they dominate in the latter one." By the time he had completed his metaphor for the fusion of a "being" and the machine, Duchamp-Villon had abandoned many aspects of his initial conception, with its strong emphasis on literal movement. Instead, in the opposing thrusts of the machinelike parts and the curving, arching shapes suggestive of the horse's head and neck, he created an image endowed with the latent power and energy of a coiled spring. The image of Duchamp-Villon's horse derives its particular dynamism from the very containment and control of movement within a highly compressed form.

EXHIBITIONS:[11]

New York, The Sculptors' Gallery, *Exhibition of Contemporary French Art*, Mar. 24-Apr. 10, 1922, no. 34 (bronze, erroneously dated 1919, Coll. John Quinn); Paris, Galerie Vavin-Raspail, *Exposition de la Section d'Or, 1912-1925*, Jan. 12-31, 1925, no. 13 ("*Le Cheval*, 1914"; probably plaster); Paris, *Salon des Indépendants, Trente Ans d'Art Indépendant*, Feb. 20-Mar. 21, 1926, no. 2933 ("*Cheval*, 1914"; probably plaster; see Agee, 1967, p. 139); New York, Brummer Gallery, *Memorial Exhibition of the Works of Raymond Duchamp-Villon*, Jan. 5-Feb. 9, 1929, no. 9 ("*Horse*, plaster"; presumably ex Quinn collection); Chicago, The Arts Club of Chicago, *Sculpture by Raymond Duchamp-Villon*, Mar. 28-Apr. 12, 1929, no. 6 ("*Horse*, plaster"; presumably ex Quinn collection); Paris, Galerie Pierre, *Sculptures de Duchamp-Villon 1876-1918*, June 8-27, 1931, no. 26? ("*Etude de cheval*. Bronze, 1914");[12] London, Guggenheim Jeune, *Contemporary Sculpture*, Apr. 8-May 2, 1938, no. 13 ("*Cheval*, bronze");[13] New York, Art of This Century, 1942-47, p. 65, repr.; Venice, *P.G.*, 1948 (Biennale), no. 35; Florence, *P.G.*, 1949, no. 35; Amsterdam, *P.G.*, 1951, no. 43, repr.; Zurich, *P.G.*, 1951, no. 39; London, *P.G.*, 1964-65, no. 18, repr. p. 25; Stockholm, *P.G.*, 1966-67, no. 18, repr. pl. 19; New York, *P.G.*, 1969, p. 34, repr. p. 35; Paris, *P.G.*, 1974-75, no. 18; Torino, *P.G.*, 1975-76, no. 24, repr. pl. 14.

REFERENCES:[14]

A. Gleizes, *Du Cubisme et des moyens de le comprendre*, Paris, 1920, repr. n.p. (plaster); W. Pach, *Raymond Duchamp-Villon Sculpture, 1876-1918*, Paris, 1924, pp. 12, 14, 15, repr. pp. 75, 77, 79 (probably Quinn plaster);[15] W. Pach, *Masters of Modern Art*, New York, 1924, pp. 86, 111-12, repr. pl. 29; *The John Quinn Collection*, American Art Association, Inc., sale catalogue, 1927, p. 236, no. 700 (plaster); C. Zervos, "Raymond Duchamp-Villon," *Cahiers d'Art*, vol. 6, 1931, p. 227, repr. (plaster; review of Galerie Pierre exh.); C. Giedion-Welcker, "New Roads in Modern Sculpture," *Transition*, no. 23, July 1935, p. 199, repr. opp. p. 203 (Grenoble plaster); idem, *Moderne Plastik*, Zurich, 1937, p. 52 repr. (Grenoble plaster, erroneously captioned "bronze"); W. Pach, *Queer Thing, Painting: Forty Years in the World of Art*, New York, 1938, pp. 144-46; P. Guggenheim, *Art of This Century*, 1942, p. 65, repr. (bronze); W. P. Valentiner, *Origins of Modern Sculpture*, New York, 1946, p. 132, repr. p. 120; A. C. Ritchie, *Sculpture of the Twentieth Century*, New York, 1952, pp. 27-28; J. Villon, "Raymond Duchamp-Villon," in P. Francastel, ed., *Les Sculpteurs célèbres*, Paris, 1954, p. 307; J. Golding, *Cubism: A History and an Analysis*, Boston, 1959, p. 170; C. Giedion-Welcker, "Verankerung und Vorstoss bei Raymond Duchamp-Villon," *Werk*, Apr. 1964, pp. 147, 151-52; R. V. Gindertael, "L'Œuvre majeure de Duchamp-Villon," *XXe Siècle*, no. 23, May 1964, p. 44; Alley, 1964, p. 25; Calas, 1966, p. 87, repr. p. 93; A. Elsen, "The Sculpture of Duchamp-Villon," *Artforum*, vol. 6, no. 2, Sept. 1967, pp. 19, 22, 23; G. H. Hamilton and W. C. Agee, *Raymond Duchamp-Villon, 1876-1918*, New York, exh. cat., 1967, pp. 22-23, 86-103; D. Robbins, "Duchamp-Villon at Knoedler's," *Burlington Magazine*, vol. 110, Jan. 1968, p. 41; A. Elsen, review of G. H. Hamilton and W. C. Agee, "Raymond Duchamp-Villon," *Burlington Magazine*, vol. 111, July 1969, pp. 523-24; S. Hochfield, "The Problem of Sculptural Reproduction," *Art News*, vol. 73, Nov. 1974, p. 24; P. Cabanne, *The Brothers Duchamp*, Boston, 1976, pp. 110, 136, repr. pp. 128-29; J. Zilczer, "Raymond Duchamp-Villon: Pioneer of Modern Sculpture," *Philadelphia Museum of Art Bulletin*, vol. 76, no. 330, fall 1980, pp. 15-17.

11. Though the Peggy Guggenheim bronze cast is probably of ca. 1930, the exhibitions listed here include pre-1930 exhibitions of the original plaster and of the first bronze cast in this size (1921, Quinn collection, later Edgar Kaufmann, jr.). Exhibitions after 1931 are limited to those in which the Guggenheim bronze appeared, or might have appeared.
12. The catalogue of the 1931 Galerie Pierre exhibition gives no dimensions. It seems clear, as Agee was the first to suggest, that no. 23, listed in capital letters, was the then newly cast enlargement of the sculpture (100 cm.), which is visible at the center of the installation. Whether the Peggy Guggenheim bronze—also probably recently cast—was included in the exhibition is not clear. The installation photo does not include it, but the photo does not show the entire exhibition. Visible on the sideboard are 2 tiny bronzes of *Le Cheval*, presumably cat. nos. 29 and 30 ("*Petit cheval*, bronze" and "*Autre petit cheval*, bronze").
13. Peggy Guggenheim was not certain that this was the cast she subsequently purchased in Paris, but she suspected that it was.
14. Though the present version was probably cast in 1930, some of the citations refer to the original 44 cm. plaster of 1914 and some to other 44 cm. bronze casts. The impact of the early image is thus recorded, as well as the curious fact that most authors have regarded the plaster and bronze versions as interchangeable and the differences in medium and scale as insignificant.
15. Neither material nor cast number is specified in this reference, or in many of those that follow.

Max Ernst

Born April 1891, near Cologne.
Died April 1976, Paris.

51 Von minimax dadamax selbst konstruiertes maschinchen. 1919-20.
(*Little machine constructed by minimax dadamax in person; petite machine construite par minimax dadamax en personne*).

Color plate p. 245.

76.2553 PG 70

Handprinting(?), pencil and ink frottage, watercolor and gouache on heavy brown pulp paper, 19½ x 12⅜ (49.4 x 31.5).

Signed l.r.: *dadamax ernst*. Not dated.

Inscribed l.l.: *von minimax dadamax selbst konstruiertes maschinchen für / furchtlose bestäubung weiblicher saugnäpfe zu beginn der wechseljahre u. dergl. furchtlose verrichtungen*; around spout of tap: *bonjour*.

PROVENANCE:

Purchased from the artist, New York, 1941.

CONDITION:

In 1978 (New York) a substantial tear in the lower left corner, which had previously been repaired (date unknown) with glue and tape, was properly repaired. Two other losses at the left edge were repaired. General surface dirt was removed; extensive surface glue and moisture stains were mitigated and losses were inpainted with watercolor where necessary.

The overall condition is stable. (Mar. 1983, New York.)

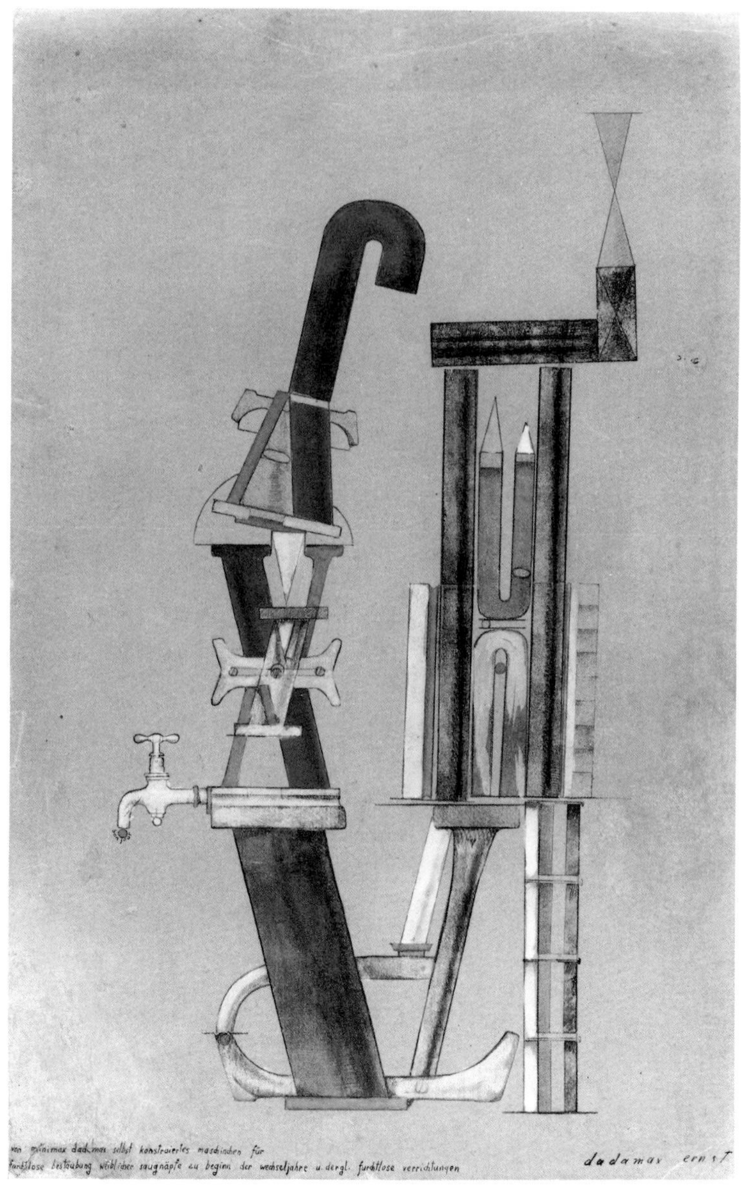

Ernst's earliest Dada collages date from 1919. They are clearly indebted in style and mode of expression to Picabia's machine works of 1915 onward. Ernst would have seen these in the *Anthologie dada* of 1918, in the issue of "*391*" published in Zurich in February 1919, and in several other Dada publications. The inventiveness and subtle symbolism of Picabia's example stimulated Ernst to develop a fertile machine language of his own, which dominated his work over the course of the next two years.

At exactly the same moment, Ernst produced a group of works on paper that convey some of the effects of collage, but without its techniques. He created visual collages of dissociated, disconnected elements, without the use of either scissors or paste. *Von minimax dadamax*... belongs to this latter group, which includes a number of other works similar in scale and subject matter: for example, *Femme* BELLE *et femme* DEBOUT (Private Collection, Switzerland, Spies, 1975, no. 317); *Erectio sine qua non* (Private Collection, Torino, ibid., no. 322); *La grande roue orthochromatique qui fait l'amour sur mesure* (Collection Michel Leiris, Paris, ibid., no. 324); and *Selbstkonstruiertes Maschinchen* (Collection E. A. Bergman, Chicago, ibid., no. 318). All these works, of approximately the same date and size, share with the Peggy Guggenheim piece sharp wit, obvious sexual overtones, and complex verbal-visual puns.

In each case, the technical procedures are very similar. The main compositional elements derive partly from the use of printer's plates. The latter were probably intaglio plates used for the printing of technical or engineering manuals, though it has not been possible to identify the precise sources. The images from the plates were transferred to the heavy paper support partly by means of handprinting on the surface, partly by frottage.[1] Certain of the contours were then outlined with graphite and ink. Pencil and ink shading, as well as gouache and watercolor, were applied over the printed or frottaged forms. Actual pencil drawing was limited to a few negligible details.

In an autobiographical note, "Comment on force l'inspiration," Ernst explained how the detached contemplation of scientific diagrams, removed from their normal context, had initially provoked a visionary response in him. They gave rise to multiple hallucinatory images, and out of these images Ernst developed his own new language:

> *A l'époque où nous étions particulièrement passionnés par les recherches et les premières découvertes dans le domaine du collage, il arriva que, tombant par hasard ou comme par hasard sur (par exemple) les pages d'un catalogue où figuraient des objets pour la démonstration anatomique ou physique, nous y trouvâmes réunis des éléments de figuration tellement distants que l'absurdité même de cet assemblage provoqua en nous la succession hallucinante d'images contradictoires, se superposant les unes aux autres avec la persistance et la rapidité qui sont le propre des souvenirs amoureux. Ces images appelaient elles-mêmes un plan nouveau, pour leurs rencontres dans un inconnu nouveau (le plan de non-convenance).* (*Le Surréalisme au Service de la Révolution*, nos. 5-6, 1933, p. 44.)[2]

1. For a discussion of Ernst's frottage technique, see *La Forêt*, cat. no. 53. According to L. Lippard, 1962, pp. 23, 25, Ernst's first experiments with such plates occurred as he sat in a printer's shop waiting for some proofs of a Dada magazine. He found some rough discarded plates and promptly put them to use.
2. The text was written, and partially published in English, in 1932. Excerpts were subsequently published as "Inspiration to Order." For full bibliographical information, see below, cat. no. 53, fn. 1, and cat. no. 56, fn. 3.

Ernst went on to explain how, by modifying the diagrams only slightly with pen or pencil, he was able to transform relatively mundane images into expressions of his most intense visions and desires: "*Il suffisait alors d'ajouter en peignant ou en dessinant, et pour cela en ne faisant que reproduire docilement* ce qui se voit en nous, *une couleur, un griffonnage, un paysage étranger aux objets représentés, le désert, le ciel, une coupe géologique, un plancher, une seule ligne droite signifiant l'horizon, pour obtenir une image fidèle et fixe de notre hallucination et transformer en un drame révélant nos plus secrets désirs....*" The text cited here provides the context for an understanding of Ernst's conception of collage during these years. It was a medium in which "*ce n'est pas la colle qui fait le collage*" (*Max Ernst Œuvres de 1919 à 1936*, Paris, 1937, p. 31). The essence of the works of this period consisted in such incongruous juxtapositions, resulting in "two distant realities on a plane foreign to them both." At the same time, Ernst created subtle and imaginative transitions — through drawing or painting — between each newly introduced image and its surrounding environment. As Aragon wrote in 1930: "*Là où il faudrait saisir la pensée de Max Ernst, c'est à l'endroit où avec un peu de couleur, un crayonnage, il tente d'acclimater le fantôme qu'il vient de précipiter dans un paysage étranger* ("La Peinture au Défi," in *L'Exposition de Collages*, exh. cat., Galerie Goemans, Paris, 1930, p. 23). The startling impact of the images lies precisely in the apparent naturalness and pictorial harmony with which Ernst presents the dislocated and disjunctive forms.

EXHIBITIONS:

New York, MoMA, *Fantastic Art, Dada, Surrealism*, 1936-37, no. 329 ("Self-Constructed little machine ca. 1919"); New York, Art of This Century, 1942-47, p. 149; Paris, Galerie Denise René, *Max Ernst*, June 1945, no. 1 ("Dada Max, 1919"); Venice, *P.G.*, 1948 (Biennale), no. 36 ("Dadamax, 1919"; the work appears with this title and date in all subsequent *P.G.* catalogues until London, 1964-65); Florence, *P.G.*, 1949, no. 36; Amsterdam, *P.G.*, 1951, no. 44; Zurich, *P.G.*, 1951, no. 40; London, *P.G.*, 1964-65, no. 63, repr. (*Little Machine constructed by Minimax Dadamax in person*); Stockholm, *P.G.*, 1966-67, no. 61, repr.; New York, *P.G.*, 1969, pp. 184-85, repr.; Paris, *P.G.*, 1974-75, no. 71, repr.; Torino, *P.G.*, 1975-76, no. 68; New York, *P.G.*, 1982-83, no. 26, repr.

REFERENCES:

M. Ernst, "Au delà de la peinture," *Cahiers d'Art*, vol. 11, nos. 6-7, 1936, repr. p. 150 (essay reprinted in *Max Ernst Œuvres de 1919 à 1936*, Paris, 1937, pp. 13-46, repr. p. 14); L. Lippard, "The Technical Innovations of Max Ernst," unpublished master's thesis, New York University, 1962, p. 61, repr.; Alley, 1964, no. 63, repr.; R. Penrose, *Max Ernst's Celebes*, 52nd Charlton Lecture, University of Newcastle upon Tyne, 1972, p. 8, repr. p. 9; W. Spies, *Max Ernst Collagen: Inventar und Widerspruch*, Cologne, 1974, pp. 46, 48, 64, 190, 195, repr. no. 80; idem and S. and G. Metken, *Max Ernst: Oeuvre Katalog Werke 1906-1925*, vol. 2, Houston and Cologne, 1975, no. 321, repr.; C. F. Stuckey, "Duchamp's acephalic symbolism," *Art in America*, vol. 65, Jan. 1977, p. 97, repr.; L. Flint, *Handbook*, 1983, p. 98, repr. color p. 99.

52 Le Baiser. 1927.
(The Kiss).

Color plate p. 247.

76.2553 PG 71

Oil on canvas (unvarnished), 50¾ x 63½ (129 x 161.2).

Signed l.l.: *max ernst*; signed and dated on reverse (very faint): *max ernst 1927*.

PROVENANCE:

Galerie Van Leer, Paris, 1927[1] -1940; purchased from Van Leer, 1940.[2]

CONDITION:

In 1964 (Tate Report) considerable crackle with some incipient cleavage and some flaking and losses in the sky were noted. The flaking pigment was consolidated with wax resin adhesive. The surface was cleaned and the minor damages retouched. The painting had not been varnished and no varnish was applied.

In 1982 (Venice) the somewhat discolored areas of inpainting in the sky were retouched with Maimeri varnish colors. The surface had apparently been varnished in the intervening years. Some black transfer from rabbet of previous frame was removed. The condition is stable. (New York, Mar. 1983.)

1. The picture belonged to Van Leer by the time of its October 1927 publication in *La Révolution Surréaliste*, but it was not shown in the gallery's March-April Ernst one-man exhibition, suggesting that it was not painted until the summer.
2. Peggy Guggenheim recalled buying *Le Baiser, La Forêt,* and *Vision* (1931, Spies, 1976, no. 1797, present whereabouts unknown) all on the same day from A. D. Mouradien, who was a partner of Van Leer at the time.

Lucy Lippard has characterized *Le Baiser* as the central work in a group that marked important technical innovations in Ernst's development. In 1925 he began to use the technique of frottage that became critical to his achievement in the late 1920s (see *La Forêt*, cat. no. 53). In the Horde series of winter 1926-27, he introduced a new variation, placing the wet, painted canvas over long pieces of heavy string that had been dropped, or arranged, in intricate coils and tangles. He then rubbed the canvas, producing a complex surface texture that carried much of the linear definition of the string beneath. Only then did he "compose" the picture with the brush, spontaneously transforming the arbitrarily derived shapes into specific jagged, often monstrous, figures and landscape. The element of the unpredictable, of the automatic, was inherent in his process.

With the *Le Baiser* group, he took a new step, dipping the string in paint and dripping or arranging it on the surface of the canvas. The smooth sinuous quality of line in these pictures of later 1927 may be seen as perhaps their dominant characteristic.

In *Le Baiser* itself, a frottage base was probably applied over the entire surface of the canvas. Its residual appearance as the black shadow to the left of the central figure and in certain areas of the ochre-orange suggests the use of either wood or other heavy material to produce this texture. The linear structure of the central group clearly was created through the use on the frottaged surface of the paint-soaked string, though the lines were then partially painted over with a brush, creating a system of stronger and weaker linear elements. Further brushing of the orange-brown areas followed, and the blue was applied only after the rest of the composition had completely dried.

Breton and other writers on Ernst, and, more recently, scholars such as Lippard, have written cogently about the importance of automatism as a determining factor in Ernst's working method during this period. However, traces of a pencil grid on this and other canvases raises questions concerning Ernst's actual reliance upon automatism. The possibility that he may—at this and other stages—have developed his compositions in preparatory drawings rather than entirely on the canvas, combining a more deliberate and calculated method with his automatic freedom, must be taken into account in an analysis of his intention and of the results. (On this point, see also cat. no. 59, fn. 4.)

EXHIBITIONS:

Paris, Galerie Georges Bernheim, *Max Ernst*, Dec. 1-15, 1928, no. 32; Berlin, Galerie Alfred Flechtheim, *Max Ernst*, Mar. 2-Easter 1929, no. 27; Cologne, Im Staatenhaus, *Deutscher Künstlerbund*, May-Sept., 1929, no. 70; New York, Art of This Century, 1942-47, p. 103; Venice, *P.G.*, 1948 (Biennale), no. 37; Florence, *P.G.*, 1949, no. 37; Amsterdam, *P.G.*, 1951, no. 45; Zurich, *P.G.*, 1951, no. 41; London, *P.G.*, 1964-65, no. 64, repr. color p. 5; Stockholm, *P.G.*, 1966-67, no. 62; Torino, Galleria Civica d'Arte Moderna, *Le Muse Inquietanti*, Nov. 1967-Jan. 1968, no. 121, repr. p. 89; New York, *P.G.*, 1969, p. 86, repr.; Paris, *P.G.*, 1974-75, no. 72; Torino, *P.G*, 1975-76, no. 69, repr. pl. 42; Rome, *Guggenheim: Venezia-New York*, 1982, no. 40, repr. color; New York, *P.G.*, 1982-83, no. 27, repr. color p. 33.

REFERENCES:

La Révolution Surréaliste, nos. 9-10, Oct. 1, 1927, repr. n.p., as an advertisement for the Galerie Van Leer (captioned "*Nuit d'Amour*"); J. de Bosschère, "Max Ernst," *Cahiers d'Art*, vol. 3, no. 2, 1928, repr. p. 69; J. Viot, "Max Ernst," *Cahiers d'Art*, vol. 8, nos. 5-6, 1933, repr. p. 219; P. Guggenheim, *Art of This Century*, 1942, p. 103; A. Cirici-Pellicer, *El Surrealismo*, Barcelona, 1957, p. 31, repr. no. 23; P. Guggenheim, *Confessions*, 1960, p. 70; L. Lippard, "The Technical Innovations of Max Ernst," unpublished master's thesis, New York University, 1962, p. 70; Calas, 1966, pp. 112-13, repr. color p. 131; W. Spies and S. and G. Metken, *Max Ernst: Oeuvre Katalog Werke 1925-1929*, vol. 3, Houston and Cologne, 1976, no. 1135, repr.

---

53 La Forêt. 1927-28.
(*The Forest*).

Color plate p. 250.

76.2553 PG 72

Oil on canvas (unvarnished), 37⅞ x 51 (96.3 x 129.5).

Signed l.r.: *max ernst*. Not dated.

PROVENANCE:

Purchased from A. D. Mouradien, Paris, 1940.

CONDITION:

In 1964 (Tate Report) a whitish residue over the dark areas was noted, as were scattered areas of crackle with cleavage, retouching, and flaking in the more heavily painted sky. The cleavage was secured and losses retouched. No varnish was applied to the matte surface.

In 1978 (New York) the following conditions were noted: a bloom over certain portions of the canvas (probably due to moisture), some ripples and distortions of the support, and scattered flaking of the paint film, especially near the lower edge. The very thin canvas was flattened and lined on Mylar 1400 using BEVA and strip-lined with Lucite 44-treated linen strips; the work was mounted on a new stretcher. Superficial cleaning followed by watercolor inpainting of losses along all four edges was carried out, and the surface was varnished with a light coat of Lucite 44 (spray). Some minimal cleavage and loss have occurred since the above treatment. The condition is fragile. (Mar. 1983, New York.)

Ernst's development of the frottage technique, discovered (by his own testimony) in 1925 (but possibly used somewhat earlier), reached its fullest expression in the late twenties.[1] The system he initially employed involved placing pieces of paper on randomly selected parts of a wood floor or other surface and rubbing them with a pencil, producing a succession of images, patterns, and textures that could be combined into a more subjective vision or used as the inspiration to create one. The technique and the materials used are readily discernible in

1. The self-consciously ritualistic description Ernst offers of his "discovery" was first published in an English translation, "Inspiration to Order," *This Quarter*, Paris, vol. 5, no. 1, Sept. 1932, pp. 79-85. It first appeared in French as "Comment on force l'inspiration," *Le Surréalisme au Service de la Révolution*, nos. 5-6, 1933, pp. 43-45. For important discussions of frottage, see M. Ernst, "Au delà de la peinture," *Cahiers d'Art*, vol. 11, nos. 6-7, 1936, pp. 152-56; L. Lippard, "The Technical Innovations of Max Ernst," unpublished master's thesis, New York University, 1962, chapter IV; W. Rubin, *Dada, Surrealism, and Their Heritage*, New York, 1968, p. 82; W. Spies, *Max Ernst*, New York, 1968, pp. v-ix.

53

fig. a.
Ernst, *La forêt petrifiée*, 1929, charcoal frottage on paper, 29 1/8 x 38 9/16 in., 74 x 98 cm., Musée National d'Art Moderne, Centre Georges Pompidou, Paris.

these initial drawings, many of which served as preparatory studies for subsequent paintings (Lippard, p. 64; see, for example, fig. a). Lippard has cogently demonstrated, however, that as the possibilities implicit in the technique were extended into oil (grattage), by scraping a thickly painted canvas over a textured surface, Ernst's experimentation with a vast range of materials and procedures became so complex as to obscure the specific technical methods followed.[2]

2. Grattage apears to have been used for the first time in the winter of 1926-27.

In the present work, for example, the entire surface seems to have been first covered with an oil grattage, though the subsequent reworking has rendered it impossible to establish what constituted the textured base. The surface was then rubbed, scraped, and scumbled, some thin layers of black, green, red, and yellow being applied on top of the rubbed areas with a spatula or a palette knife. The actual form of the "forest" composition and the bird were articulated with the white linear "drawing," some of which is scratched or incised into the surface but most applied on top of it. As the final stage Ernst brushed in the entire gray sky, giving the composition its actual definition and thereby fully reversing the notion of a conventional figure-ground relationship. The circular sun was incised into the final layer of paint; its effect of apparent hovering between foreground and background was created through the application of gradations of pigment over the incised lines.

In this and other works of the late twenties, the frottage and grattage techniques, with their inherently accidental and even, in some sense, automatic qualities, undoubtedly acted as a creative stimulant to Ernst. But there was no question of "psychic automatism" in Breton's sense of that term. Ernst's technique here as elsewhere combined a carefully controlled, complex manipulation of structure and media (which included, in some cases, a squaring of the canvas),[3] and a considerable freedom to respond to accidental effects. As Spies has stated, Ernst "subordinated the 'fluency' of his line and movements of his hand to a broader pictorial continuum.... His [apparently automatic] techniques always remained secondary to a complex and premeditated pictorial unity..." (*Max Ernst Loplop: The Artist in the Third Person*, New York, 1983, p. 72).

The images that emerged from these grattage compositions possessed a hypnotic and even obsessive character. Ernst himself explained: "*J'insiste sur le fait que les dessins ainsi obtenus perdent de plus en plus, à travers une série de suggestions et de transmutations qui s'offrent spontanément, — à la manière de ce qui se passe pour les visions hypnagogiques, — le caractère de la matière interrogée (le bois) pour prendre l'aspect d'images d'une précision inespérée, de nature probablement à déceler la cause première de l'obsession*" ("Comment on force l'inspiration," *Le Súrrealisme au Service de la Révolution*, nos. 5-6, 1933, p. 45).

In this context, the "enchantment" and "terror" actually experienced by Ernst at age three when his father took him into a forest is, as he himself later acknowledged, continually evoked in the images of the forest compositions of the late 1920s and beyond ("Some Data on the Youth of M.E.," *Beyond Painting*, New York, 1948, p. 27).

Ernst's repeated description of the forest as oppressive on the one hand and liberating on the other is obviously important for any interpretation of these paintings. For example, "The wonderful joy of breathing freely in an open space,

3. For this problem see cat. no. 52, and cat. no. 59, fn. 4.

yet at the same time the distress at being hemmed in on all sides by hostile trees. Inside and outside, free and captive, at one and the same time." (Lippard, "The World of Dadamax Ernst," *Art News*, vol. 74, Apr. 1975, p. 27; the source and date of this quotation are not given.)

The precise dating of Ernst's forest paintings of the late 1920s, a period of intense experimentation and of continual reworking of certain ideas, poses specific problems. A detailed study of the stylistic development remains to be undertaken. Though usually dated 1928, the present painting was dated 1927 by Spies; in the absence of compelling stylistic or other evidence, the painting is here more provisionally dated 1927-28.

EXHIBITIONS:

New York, Art of This Century, 1942-47, p. 103; Venice, *P.G.*, 1948 (Biennale), no. 38; Florence, *P.G.*, 1949, no. 38; Amsterdam, *P.G.*, 1951, no. 46; Zurich, *P.G.*, 1951, no. 42; London, *P.G.*, 1964-65, no. 65, repr.; Stockholm, *P.G.*, 1966-67, no. 63, repr.; New York, *P.G.*, 1969, p. 87, repr.; Paris, *P.G.*, 1974-75, no. 73; Torino, *P.G.*, 1975-76, no. 70; New York, *P.G.*, 1982-83, no. 28, repr.

REFERENCES:

Calas, 1966, p. 113, repr. color p. 132; W. Spies and S. and G. Metken, *Max Ernst: Oeuvre Katalog Werke 1925-1929*, vol. 3, Houston and Cologne, 1976, no. 1192, repr.

---

54 La mer le soleil le tremblement de terre. 1931.
(Sea, sun, earthquake).

76.2553 PG 73

Oil, gouache, and collage on canvas (unvarnished), 17⅞ x 14⅞ (45.4 x 37.8).

Signed l.r.: *max ernst*; on reverse (photographed before lining): *la mer le soleil le tremblement de terre / made in France.*
Not dated.

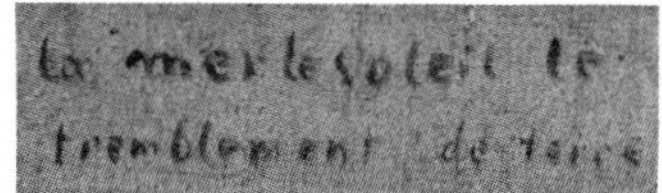

PROVENANCE:

Purchased from the artist, New York, 1941.

CONDITION:

In 1964 (Tate Report) some abrasion of the collage was noted, but the unvarnished oil surface was described as in good condition, and no treatment was necessary.

Extensive oil inpainting in the sky areas was carried out at an unrecorded date and place. These areas were severely discolored by 1978, when the work was treated in New York. It was concluded that removal of the inpainting would adversely affect the original paint film. The discoloration was therefore to some extent mitigated with further watercolor inpainting, though this was not completed. Owing to the unstable condition of the paint film, it was judged necessary to first flatten the support and then line it on Mylar 1400 with BEVA. Strip-lining of the edges with Lucite 44-treated linen strips was followed by mounting on a new stretcher and varnishing with Lucite 44 (spray).

The wallpaper collage strips (woodblock printing on lightly flocked paper) have suffered some abrasion and losses. There has been scattered retouching in these areas (date unknown), and some new flaking of these retouched areas. The overall condition is fragile. (Venice, Nov. 1982.)

The imagery and technique employed in this work occur in a series of similar compositions dating from the early 1930s, though Ernst had used wallpaper as a collage element as early as 1920 (see Spies, vol. 2, nos. 353-55). The application of a coat of thick dry pigment into which parallel lines are incised with a sharp instrument was also used, for example, in an almost identical work of the same title, dated 1931, now in a private collection in Paris (Spies, no. 1799; other closely related compositions are published by Spies, nos. 1802-5). In the Paris example, as in Peggy Guggenheim's, the wallpaper was subsequently applied in strips, the joins being painted over with gouache.

Although represented here in emblematic, simplified form, the sea and sun are clearly legible. The elliptical reference to the "earthquake" remains visually elusive but recalls two passages in Ernst's autobiographical notes "Au delà de la Peinture." An earthquake is included in the list of hallucinatory experiences arising out of his 1925 discovery of frottage: "*J'ai vu une* feuille de lierre flotter sur l'océan *et j'ai ressenti un tremblement de terre fort doux*" (*Cahiers d'Art*, vol. 11, nos. 6-7, 1936, p. 158). Later in the same text, he uses "*un tremblement de terre fort doux*" as a metaphor for the paradoxical nature ("*la violence calme*") that is the driving force behind his own thinking. In both cases plausible connections with the metaphorical imagery and mood of the present work can be made.

EXHIBITIONS:

New York, Art of This Century, 1942-47, p. 103 (dated 1930, the date assigned to it in all subsequent *P.G.* publications until London, 1964-65); Venice, *P.G.*, 1948 (Biennale), no. 39; Florence, *P.G.*, 1949, no. 39; Amsterdam, *P.G.*, 1951, no. 47; Zurich, *P.G.*, 1951, no. 43; London, *P.G.*, 1964-65, no. 66 (dated 1931); Stockholm, *P.G.*, 1966-67, no. 64; New York, *P.G.*, 1969, p. 88, repr.; Paris, *P.G.*, 1974-75, no. 74, repr.; Torino, *P.G.*, 1975-76, no. 71.

REFERENCES:

P. Guggenheim, *Art of This Century*, 1942, p. 103 (dated 1930); Alley, 1964, no. 66 (Alley convincingly dated the work 1931 on the basis of its relationship to Spies, no. 1799); P. Schamoni, *Max Ernst: Maximiliana (The Illegal Practice of Astronomy)*, Boston, 1974, repr. color p. 50; W. Spies and S. and G. Metken, *Max Ernst: Oeuvre Katalog Werke 1929-1938*, vol. 4, Houston and Cologne, 1979, no. 1801, repr.

---

55 Le Facteur Cheval. 1932.
(*The Postman Cheval*).

Color plate p. 245.

76.2553 PG 74

Paper and fabric collage with pencil, ink, and gouache on manila paper, 25⅜ x 19¼ (64.3 x 48.9).

Signed and dated l.r.: *max ernst 1932*; inscribed l.l.: *le facteur cheval*. Post mark on envelope: *18*[30] */ 17 V / 1932 / PARIS RUE DES HALLES.*

PROVENANCE:

Purchased from the artist, New York, 1941.

CONDITION:

In 1978 (New York) glue and paper tape were removed from all verso edges and a paper patch from the recto (lower right corner). The recto and verso—both heavily soiled and foxed—were cleaned. Loose collage elements were readhered. Overexposure to light has caused some fading, especially of the photograph of reclining nudes, now barely visible through the window of the business envelope. There is some darkening of the paper support. The condition in general is stable. (New York, Feb. 1983.)

Le Facteur Cheval belongs to a suite of large format collages (ca. 26 x 20 in., 65 x 50 cm.) made between 1930 and 1933. The series is known generically as *Loplop présente*, and the bird Loplop, *le Supérieur des Oiseaux*, Ernst's alter ego, appears in innumerable guises.[1]

1. The Loplop collages have recently been published in a comprehensively detailed and illuminating monograph by Werner Spies (1983). Lucy Lippard's earlier discussion of this group ("The Technical Innovations of Max Ernst," unpublished master's thesis, New York University, 1962, pp. 47-53) made many of the critical observations that have formed the basis of all subsequent commentaries.

   The inital work from which the series derives its generic name was probably the 1930 composite collage-construction (Private Collection, Paris, Spies, 1983, pl. 44) in which a bird-man literally presents to the viewer a "picture" in a frame, composed, in its turn, of a collection of disconnected individual elements painted, glued, nailed, or attached with strings onto the surface.

Ernst's earliest references to the bird Loplop occur in the captions to his 1929 collage novel *La Femme 100 Têtes*. Definitions of the bird as his alter ego, his "private phantom," occur in the catalogue of a one-man exhibition held in 1930 at Galerie Vignon, in the 1936 publication of "Au delà de la Peinture,"[2] and in the *Dictionnaire abrégé du Surréalisme*, published in Paris in 1938, p. 11.

The group of collages under discussion are, as Lippard first pointed out, usually based upon one or two clearly dominating forms: a large emblematic rectangle (the artist as easel) with square "pointed-off" feet at the base and either a circular head or a bird's head above. Loplop is seen, as it were, presenting a work of art—a picture within a picture. Some of these collages are, however, less explicit: they may contain merely a rectangular form and a hand (*Jeune homme debout*, 1931, repr. Spies, 1983, pl. 61) or a group of birds and a piece of coral, each placed within a rectangular "picture" format but without the presenting artist (*Colombes et corail*, 1922, repr. ibid., pl. 33).

2. "*En 1930, après avoir composé avec acharnement et méthode mon roman* La Femme 100 Têtes, *j'ai eu la visite presque journalière du* Supérieur des oiseaux, *nommé* Loplop, *fantôme particulier d'une fidélité modèle, attaché à ma personne*" ("Au delà de la Peinture," *Cahiers d'Art*, vol. 11, nos. 6-7, 1936, p. 160). On this point, see Spies, 1983, pp. 9-10.

The critical stylistic departure represented by these works lies in their unequivocal identity as collages per se. Ernst's earlier "pseudocollages" of 1919-20 (see above, cat. no. 51) and the collages of the novels, such as *La Femme 100 Têtes*, had been characterized by a homogeneity of surface, an effect Ernst himself described as a form of "visual alchemy." In the collage novels he had managed — through ingenious and meticulous cutting, joining, pasting, and photographic reproduction—to unify the picture plane and create disconnecting irrational compositions that nonetheless conveyed the impression of pictorial continuity.[3]

In the Loplop collages, on the other hand, his aim was to create complex tactile surfaces, calling attention to the diversity of materials and textures used and indeed to the very process itself.

In the case of *Le Facteur Cheval*, this diversity and complexity are especially striking. For example, one type of printed marbleized paper (blue/white) is used for Loplop's head and body; these forms in turn are joined by a penciled neck at the base of which is an appliqué embroidered silk "bow tie." Loplop's characteristic legs and feet are added in pencil. Glossy embossed chromolithographic postcard fragments of a smiling female face, together with details of her clothing and hair, are revealed through four cutout "peep holes." A photograph of a demure, though provocative group of young ladies is partially removed from (incongruously) a business envelope; through the shadowy cellophane window of the envelope's center, a group of reclining female nudes (a reference to the hidden, or "enclosed," aspect of the ladies above?) is barely visible.

The second large rectangle (left) is of a darker marbleized printed paper (blue/black), and the cutout bird (Loplop in another guise) has a thick dry gouache surface, applied with palette knife and grattage. The cutout coral (or organic plant?) underneath was painted with brown wash and the details articulated with minutely applied ink lines. At the lower left, the horizontal and crisscross bands of color on the rectangular-shaped field have also — as in the case of the bird—been applied with grattage. This area is interrupted by a peephole cutout, and by a simple band of directly applied red gouache. A strong horizontal pencil line here, and the penciled shading elsewhere on the white paper, serve to create further spatial illusion, define contours, and provide distinctive transitions between collage elements and the contrasting support, introducing additional levels of complexity into the work as a whole.

The postman Ferdinand Cheval (1836-1924), to whom the collage is dedicated, was something of a legendary figure in the late 1920s and 1930s. As Nicolas Calas noted, the Surrealists were among the first to recognize and acclaim the achievement of his "fantastic edifice, the Palais idéal" (figs. a and b). The Surrealist writer and filmmaker Jacques Brunius came from the vicinity of

3. William Seitz drew attention to some of these qualities in *The Art of Assemblage*, exh. cat., MoMA, New York, 1961, p. 41: "in [Ernst's] collage novels, the physical identity and discreteness of the original segments—the interval—is intentionally lost in a new synthetic representation." See also Lippard, op. cit., and Spies, 1983, pp. 31-32.

fig. a.
Detail of Palais Idéal, Hauterives, built by Ferdinand Cheval.

fig. b.
Detail of Palais Idéal, Hauterives, built by Ferdinand Cheval.

Hauterives (Drôme), where the palace still stands, and it was he who first brought the monument and the story of its creation to the attention of Breton, although it is not clear whether this was before or after the death of Cheval in 1924.[4] By 1929 the Palais had become a place of pilgrimage for the entire Surrealist group.

Cheval was a simple postman (though in many ways clearly a sophisticated man). The striking story of his achievement is contained in a number of letters and documents, but especially in the pages of his own extensive diary, from which Brunius quoted:

4. Information supplied by Ann Cottance, the daughter of Brunius, in conversation with the author, Paris, Nov. 1982. Her father had collected extensive material on the postman and his Palais Idéal and had assembled an album on the subject. This has since been lost. Notes by Brunius and photographs of the Palais, which were among the Brunius papers acquired by the English book collector John Lyle, were later destroyed in a fire (correspondence with J. Lyle, Mar. 1978). For Brunius's articles on the Facteur Cheval see *Variétés* (Brussels), June 15, 1929, pp. 93-98; *Architectural Review*, no. 80, Oct. 1936, pp. 147-50; "Un palais idéal," *La Revue des sports et du monde* (Paris), 1936, pp. 31-33. For a full description of the entire undertaking, with many of the Facteur's own letters and diary entries, and an extensive photographic record of the structure itself, see J. P. Jouve, Cl. Prevost, and C. Prevost, *Le Palais Idéal du facteur Cheval: Quand le Songe devient la réalité*, Paris, 1981.

A country postman, like my 27,000 comrades, I tramped each day from Hauterives to Tersanne.... What could one do whilst walking eternally against the same background, unless one dreamed.... I used to construct in a dream a fairy palace; one that would surpass all imagination as completely as the genius of an ordinary man could achieve (with gardens, grottoes, towers, castles, museums and sculptures), seeking to create again all the ancient architecture of primitive times.... Then, just at the time when this dream of mine was fading ... an incident suddenly revived it: my foot knocked against a stone which nearly made me fall.... It was of a shape so bizarre that I picked it up and carried it away. The next day, I returned to the same spot and there found more stones more beautiful still.... It was thus that I said: "Seeing that nature produces the sculpture I myself will be the architect and the mason!" (Architectural Review, 1936, pp. 147-48).

From 1879 until at least 1912, Cheval collected stones, rocks, and other materials on his daily thirty-two-kilometer postal round. In the evenings he worked on the construction of his imaginary palace, often rising in the middle of the night to complete by candlelight a portion inspired by a vision or dream.

The completed "building" was a complex structure of extraordinary fantasy and imagination "*où le songe devient la réalité*" (Cheval's diary). Something of the Surrealists' reaction to Cheval's grandiose scheme is captured in Brunius's words: "At the meeting place of primitive art and of the art of madmen and of children Cheval established a monstrous system of imagined memories.... This many-sided palace, luxuriant and at the same time secret, contradictory, and inconsistent in its themes, with walls strewn with pathetic inscriptions, ... this plaything of an inspired child, this rock vibrant with strangeness and ingenuousness, is without doubt the frankest and most telling structure that has ever been raised quite simply as a monument to the imagination" (loc. cit., 1936, p. 150). Breton, meanwhile, in a 1933 article on "*le message automatique*," described Cheval as "the uncontested master of mediumistic architecture and sculpture" (*Minotaure*, nos. 3-4, Dec. 1933).[5]

That Ernst should wish to honor the aspirations and achievements of Cheval is not surprising. Like Breton, Ernst would have found echoes of his own aesthetic ambitions and ideas in the postman's tenacious commitment to the dictates of dreams and visions, and in his determination to create an inspired, original art form.

In *Le Facteur Cheval*, Loplop is seen in his characteristic role of "presenting" a work of art: the open envelope with its photographs at the lower right. The allusion is both to Cheval and to his extraordinary enterprise. On the literal level the envelope and its somewhat commonplace emerging photograph are fragments from the postman's prosaic métier. The reclining nudes, however,

5. Roland Penrose, in correspondence and conversation with the author, spoke of the "Facteur Cheval" as having dominated the thoughts of the Surrealists for a long time.

veiled by the cellophane, point to an elusive world of dreams and imagination, to subterranean visions of desire and beauty which stand as metaphors for the postman's own creative inspiration.[6]

In the very choice of collage as his medium, Ernst seems to pay special homage to Cheval's own art form. For although the Palais Idéal was a bizarre, multi-dimensional "architectural" construction, it was obsessively additive in its structural principles, with innumerable individual and disparate elements grafted side by side onto each of its many surfaces. In this sense, the creation may well have struck Ernst as an imaginative reinvention of the very art of collage.

EXHIBITIONS:

Tenerife, Areneo de Santa Cruz, *Exposición Surrealista*, May 11-21, 1935, no. 35 ("*El cartero*"); New York, MoMA, *Fantastic Art, Dada, Surrealism*, 1936-37, no. 366, repr.; Paris, Galerie des Beaux-Arts, *Exposition Internationale du Surréalisme*, Jan.-Feb. 1938, no. 82 (dated 1931); New York, *Art of This Century*, Oct. 1942-47, p. 149 (dated 1931); Venice, *P.G.*, 1948 (Biennale), no. 40; Florence, *P.G.*, 1949, no. 40 (dated 1931); Amsterdam, *P.G.*, 1951, no. 48 (dated 1931); Zurich, *P.G.*, 1951, no. 44 (dated 1931); London, *P.G.*, 1964-65, no. 67 ("*The Postman Horse*"); Stockholm, *P.G.*, 1966-67, no. 65; Torino, Galleria Civica d'Arte Moderna, *Le Muse Inquietanti*, Nov. 1967-Jan. 1968, no, 125; New York, *P.G.*, 1969, p. 88, repr.; [not exhibited, erroneously recorded in catalogue *Die Fotomontage*, Ingolstadt, Ausstellungsräume Stadttheater, Jan. 11-Feb. 5, 1969, no. 56, as "Fotomontage, 1931"]; Paris, *P.G.*, 1974-75, no. 75, repr.; Torino, *P.G.*, 1975-76, no. 72, repr. pl. 43; New York, *P.G.*, 1982-83, no. 29, repr.

REFERENCES:

M. Ernst, *Max Ernst Œuvres de 1919 à 1936*, Paris, 1937, repr. p. 73; A. H. Barr, Jr., *Fantastic Art, Dada, Surrealism*, p. 224; Calas, 1966, no. 75, repr. color p. 134; U. M. Schneede, *Max Ernst*, Stuttgart, 1972, p. 125, repr. p. 124 (dated 1929/30); S. Metken, "Facteur Chevals Posttasche, die Bildpostkarte in der Kunst," *Kunstwerk*, vol. 27, Jan. 1974, p. 5; W. Spies, *Max Ernst Collagen: Inventar und Widerspruch*, Cologne, 1974, p. 210, repr. color no. 36 (dated 1929/30); idem, *Max Ernst: Oeuvre Katalog Werke 1929-1938*, vol. 4, Houston and Cologne, 1979, no. 1854 (dated 1932); idem, *Max Ernst Loplop: The Artist in the Third Person*, New York, 1983, pp. 31-32, repr. color pl. 17.

fig. c.
Valentine Hugo, *Portrait du Facteur Cheval* (detail), not dated, oil on canvas, 27 9/16 x 35 7/16 in., 70 x 90 cm., Collection Selma and Nesuhi Ertegun.

6. It is interesting to note in this connection that a portrait-homage to Cheval by the Surrealist painter Valentine Hugo (fig. c) depicts the postman as if in a trance. The 2 reclining nudes behind him appear as images of desire deriving from a world of vision or imagination, but also (since they are literally fused with the surrounding rocks which form the basis of Cheval's enterprise) as metaphors, in Surrealist terms, for the critical inspirational function of dreams and visions.

56 Couple zoomorphe. 1933.

(Zoomorphic couple; couple zoomorphe en gestation).

Color plate p. 246.

76.2553 PG 75

Oil on canvas (unvarnished), 36¼ x 28⅞ (91.9 x 73.3).

Signed l.r.: *max ernst*; signed, titled, and dated on reverse: *couple zoomorphe / 1933 / max ernst.*

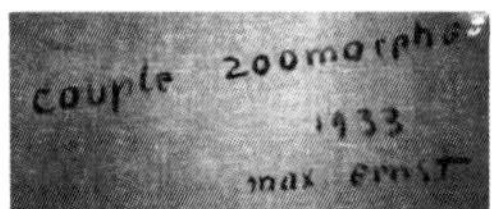

PROVENANCE:

Jeanne Bucher, Paris by 1938;[1] purchased from a dealer while traveling with Ernst in the American West in 1941.[2]

CONDITION:

Sometime prior to 1964 (Tate Report) certain losses in the paint layer had been inpainted, the most extensive being an area ca. 2½ in., 6 cm., in diameter at the upper left. This is now discolored and clearly visible to the naked eye (pink). Three other minor flaws in the background are evident, and some deep pigment cracks show signs of recent losses. Though minimal incipient cleavage of pigment was noted in 1964, the overall condition was described as good and no treatment was apparently undertaken.

In 1982 (Venice) a Fieux contact lining was applied. A layer of soil was removed from the surface with ammonium hydroxide (2.5% in water); earlier retouches were not removed. Some small new losses were inpainted with watercolors and varnish colors. The painting was mounted on an ICA spring stretcher (untensioned), and the surface was sprayed with a light coat of Lefranc retouching varnish.

Three substantial areas of matte surface in the lower third of the composition show some evidence of earlier retouching. The drier pigment composition in those areas as well as the apparent interruption of certain lines of the composition may indicate later reworking by the artist. It has hitherto not been possible to examine the painting under circumstances that would allow for a more definitive analysis of the condition in these areas. The overall condition is stable. (New York, Mar. 1983.)

Ernst's technique in this work, as in others of this period, is extremely complex. The following hypothetical reconstruction of the procedure he followed is based on examination with the naked eye. Laboratory examination at some future date may well lead to some modification of these conclusions.

Sprayed and sponged pigment (black) was first applied over a heavily prepared canvas, which had been coated with pale blues, reds, and pinkish tones. The outlines of two gigantic paws or feet, barely visible in the lower right corner of the canvas, suggest an early compositional idea (reminiscent of some of the massive extremities in painted versions of Loplop), which Ernst then abandoned and covered with ensuing layers of paint. Thinned skeins of glossy paint were poured in controlled lines down portions of the surface, sometimes diagonally, sometimes from top to bottom. Several pieces of heavy string or rope, lightly

1. The picture was lent by Bucher to the *Exposition Internationale du Surréalisme* and to Pittsburgh. When it appeared in the Mexican exhibition of 1940, no lender was listed. Though it was shown at the Mayor Gallery in 1933, there is no record that the gallery ever owned it.

2. Peggy Guggenheim, in conversation with the author, recalled that she and Ernst had found the picture while traveling in the West and that he had persuaded her to buy it. She was unable to remember exactly where they had found it, though she recalled that it had been with a well-known female dealer.

coated with paint, were then laid down on the surface; further spraying over the rope resulted in a denser overall sprayed effect, but left the rope "drawing" as a lighter contrast—apparently in relief, but actually beneath the sprayed and sponged layer. These linear markings were then partially highlighted with carefully brushed lines. Further drips of the thinned glossy paint were then poured extensively, and sprayed pigment was applied yet again in limited areas. The final phase of the composition was the application of the cream background which, as in the case of *La Forêt* (cat. no. 53), provided the outer contours and definition of the figures. Touches of fine brushwork were used to define details of contour, but in almost every case it was the application of the cream ground that articulated compositional form.

The multiple zoomorphic image—apparently combining bird and octopus, male and female—seems almost literally illustrative of a passage in Ernst's text "Comment on force l'inspiration," written in 1932, the year before the picture was painted.[3] In this text Ernst described the creative process as an experience in which one form continually suggests another, and indeed actually becomes another as the artist consciously forces himself to "see into" each successive form. Ernst characterized this experience as "a hallucinating succession of contradictory images superimposed one upon another with the persistence and rapidity proper to amorous recollections." He went on the suggest that any image, no matter how prosaic, if approached with sufficiently intense concentration, could in this way be imaginatively transformed into other images. As a specific example he cited a Second Empire decorative floral pattern that might become a "chimera which had about it something of bird and octopus and man and woman." Although the specific reference here was apparently to an actual illustration from a Second Empire pattern book, which Ernst converted with minimal alteration into a wittily elegant bird figure for a Loplop collage,[4] it seems likely that in the *Couple zoomorphe* — finished the following year — he effectively achieved a full realization of the fantasized hybrid figure he had described in "Comment on force l'inspiration."

In *Couple zoomorphe*, sinuous tentacles of an octopus (one of the totems of Surrealism) encircle the two figures. In fact, the octopus-like creature (at the lower right) flows into and unites the couple, whose main forms also interpenetrate and merge with one another. The total effect is that of a single chimera. The head of the left hand figure is featureless, except for its single "eye"; its vaguely female form contrasts with the apparently male bird form at the right. The gestures are at once embracing and threatening.

In this sense the painting expresses Ernst's continuing preoccupation with some of the central images and themes of Surrealism: the octopus, the androgyne,[5] the fantastic bestiaries of the unconscious, and the bird — his own emblematic alter ego.

The text, of course, provides no interpretative structure for an understanding of the image and all such texts must be approached with caution. Ernst himself was at pains throughout his life to avoid such simple connections, wishing to maintain the ambiguity inherent in his imagery and to thwart simplistic solutions. The nature of his art demanded precisely that the incomprehensible and the mysterious remain elements of paramount importance. But the insights he offers into the sources of his process, whether technical or "inspirational," inevitably illuminate the texture as well as the content of his art and must therefore be taken into account.

3. The text was first partially published in English in *This Quarter*, Paris, vol. 5, no. 1, Sept. 1932, pp. 79-85; subsequently in French in *Le Surréalisme au Service de la Révolution*, nos. 5-6, 1933; excerpts, again in English, in *Max Ernst Œuvres de 1919 à 1936*, Paris, 1937, pp. 71-74.

4. W. Spies, *Max Ernst Loplop: The Artist in the Third Person*, New York, 1983, p. 90.

5. For a discussion of the significance of the androgyne in Surrealist painting and literature see, for example, A. Béguin, "L'Androgyne," *Minotaure*, no. 11, May 1938, pp. 10-13; X. Gauthier, *Surréalisme et Sexualité*, Paris, 1971, pp. 72, 77, 79, 84, 85, 87, 88, 90, 91, 93, 96; R. Knott, "The Myth of the Androgyne," *Artforum*, vol. 14, no. 3, Nov. 1975, pp. 38ff.

EXHIBITIONS:

London, The Mayor Gallery, *Max Ernst*, June-July, 1933, no. 19 ("*couple zoomorphique en gestation*, 1933");[6] Philadelphia, Gimbel Galleries, *Max Ernst Surrealist Exhibition*, Jan. 25-Feb. 13, 1937, no. 10; Paris, Galerie des Beaux-Arts, *Exposition Internationale du Surréalisme*, Jan.-Feb. 1938, no. 73 (Collection Jeanne Bucher); Pittsburgh, Carnegie Institute, *The 1938 International Exhibition of Paintings*, Oct. 13-Dec. 4, 1938, no. 307 ("*Zoomorphous Couple*, lent by Bucher"); London, The London Gallery, *Max Ernst*, Dec. 1938-Jan. 1939, no. 41? ("*Le couple* 1933 oil...40 gns.");[7] Mexico, Galeria de Arte Mexicano, *Exposición Internacional del Surrealismo*, Jan.-Feb. 1940, no. 34 ("Pareja zoomorfa. 1933"); New York, Art of This Century, 1942-47, p. 103; Venice, *P.G.*, 1948 (Biennale), no. 41; Florence, *P.G.*, 1949, no. 41; Amsterdam, *P.G.*, 1951, no. 49 ("*couple animal*"); Zurich, *P.G.*, 1951, no. 45 ("Tierpaar"); London, *P.G.*, 1964-65, no. 68, repr.; Stockholm, *P.G.*, 1966-67, no. 66, repr.; Torino, Galleria Civica d'Arte Moderna, *Le Muse Inquietanti*, Nov. 1967-Jan. 1968, no. 122, repr. p. 90; New York, *P.G.*, 1969, p. 89, repr.; Paris, *P.G.*, 1974-75, no. 76 repr.; Torino, *P.G.*, 1975-76, no. 73; Rome, *Guggenheim: Venezia-New York*, 1982, no. 41, repr. color; New York, *P.G.*, 1982-83, no. 30 repr.

REFERENCES:

H. Read, *Art Now*, London, 1933, repr. no. 98 ("*Couple zoomorphe en gestation*"); P. Guggenheim, *Art of This Century*, 1942, p. 103; Calas, 1966, p. 114, repr. color p. 135; W. S. Rubin, *Dada and Surrealist Art*, New York, 1968, p. 326, repr. p. 319; W. Spies and S. and G. Metken, *Max Ernst: Oeuvre Katalog Werke 1929-1938*, vol. 4, Houston and Cologne, 1979, no. 2127 ("*Couple zoomorphe en gestation*").

6. This title, though presumably at the time supplied by Ernst, was apparently discarded by him subsequently (Peggy Guggenheim in conversation with the author).
7. It has not been possible to establish with certainty whether the entry refers to the Peggy Guggenheim picture, though no other 1933 oil carries a comparable title.

---

57 Jardin gobe-avions. 1935-36.
(*Garden Airplane-Trap*).

76.2553 PG 76

Oil on canvas (unvarnished), 21¼ x 25½ (54 x 64.7).

Signed and dated l.r.: *max ernst 35-36*.

PROVENANCE:

Purchased from the artist, New York, 1941.

CONDITION:

The work has had no extensive treatment and the unvarnished surface is well preserved. There is some abrasion and scattered flaking of the paint film in a few limited areas, indicating general fragility. (Venice, Nov. 1982.)

During the years 1934-35, Ernst painted about fifteen works on the theme of the *Jardin gobe-avions*. In each example ribbonlike wing, or propeller, forms and lush foliage are scattered across the boxlike structures of a desolate landscape.

Calas (1966) drew an analogy with the piled-up slabs of ice in Caspar David Friedrich's *The Wreck of the "Hope,"* a comparison suggestive both visually and metaphorically, since Ernst deeply admired Friedrich, and was himself giving expression to cosmic themes typical of Northern Romantic painting.

57

In his 1936 autobiographical notes, "Au delà de la peinture," Ernst offered his own clues to the predatory theme of this large series of paintings, which he had recently completed: he described a visionary experience of "*des jardins voraces dévorés par une végétation de debris d'avions.*"

In the light of Ernst's evocative description, John Russell (1967) has provided the most compelling interpretation of the imagery in these paintings (an interpretation subsequently taken up by Günter Metken and others). Russell sees the composition as a metaphor for the games of power and victimization played out in human sexual relationships: "These are obsessional images, set in a landscape which owes something to the trays in which an etymologist keeps his specimens and something to the lofty mountain country of the Incas." In Russell's reading, the airplane is seen as a "ponderous derivative of the bird"; thus Ernst's lifelong interest in birds (and, in this instance, in the trapping of birds) takes on a new significance:

> *The trapper was trapped in his turn and the airplane, once brought to earth, proved to be even more dangerous than its captor....*
>
> *...Those flowered sprays look like the trophies of victory; but they may, equally well, be wreaths laid upon the grave of some passionate impulse. Inert, cut off to all appearances from their roots, seemingly no more than ornamental, they may yet prove to have a demonic power. Everything about them looks innocent: even their scent is proverbial. But somewhere within those sweet-smelling entrances, the trap has been laid...*

Russell points out the double theme implicit in the *Garden Airplane-Traps*: "On the one hand, the vulnerability not merely of the bird, with whom Ernst had so often identified himself, but of that mechanized and seemingly all-powerful bird, the airplane. On the other, the capacity for deceit and destruction which lies hidden within what is traditionally a zone of exalted pleasure."

In these and other canvases of the mid-1930s, the nature of landscape is characterized as unequivocally hostile and predatory, though the inevitable paradox (suggested by the flowers) remains.

EXHIBITIONS:

Tokyo, Nippon Salon, *Exposition Internationale du Surréalisme*, June 9-14, 1937, no. 41, repr.; Paris, Galerie Beaux-Arts, *Exposition Internationale du Surréalisme*, Jan.-Feb. 1938, no. 76; New York, Art of This Century, 1942-47, p. 103 (dated 1936, the date assigned to it in all subsequent *P.G.* exhibitions until London, 1964-65); Venice, *P.G.*, 1948 (Biennale), no. 42; Florence, *P.G.*, 1949, no. 42; Amsterdam, *P.G.*, 1951, no. 50; Zurich, *P.G.*, 1951, no. 46; London, *P.G.*, 1964-65, no. 69, repr. (dated 1935-36); Stockholm, *P.G.*, 1966-67, no. 67, repr.; Torino, Galleria Civica d'Arte Moderna, *Le Muse Inquietanti*, Nov. 1967-Jan. 1968, no. 128, repr. (dated 1935); New York, *P.G.*, 1969, p. 90, repr.; Paris, *P.G.*, 1974-75, no. 77, repr.; Torino, *P.G.*, 1975-76, no. 74.

REFERENCES:

M. Ernst, *Max Ernst: Œuvres de 1919 à 1936*, Paris, 1937, repr. p. 97; M. Jean, *The History of Surrealist Painting*, New York, 1960, pp. 243-44, repr. (dated 1936); W. Rubin, "Max Ernst," *Art International*, vol. 5, no. 4, May 1961, p. 35; Alley, 1964, no. 69; Calas, 1966, pp. 114-15, repr. color; J. Russell, *Max Ernst: Life and Work*, New York [1967], pp. 114, 116, 124, repr. color p. 342 (dated 1934, credited to Private Collection, Paris); U. M. Schneede, *Max Ernst*, Stuttgart, 1972, repr. pl. 305 (dated 1935, credited to Private Collection, Paris); G. Metken, "Blumen des Bösen," *Die Weltkunst*, no. 4, Dec. 1972, pp. 1603-4, repr.; W. Spies and S. and G. Metken, *Max Ernst: Oeuvre Katalog Werke 1929-1938*, vol. 4, Houston and Cologne, 1979, no. 2191, repr.

---

58 La ville entière. 1936-37.
(The entire city; La cité éternelle; City Absolute).

76.2553 PG 77

Oil on canvas, 38 x 63 1/8 (96.5 x 160.4).

Not signed or dated. (Since unsigned works by Ernst are extremely rare, it is probable that a signature, and perhaps a date, on the reverse were concealed in the lining process.)

PROVENANCE:

Gift of the artist, 1941, New York.

CONDITION:

According to Tate Gallery records of 1967 the work had been wax-lined prior to its arrival in London for restoration in that year. The records do not indicate whether it had been varnished, but do note that it had apparently been overcleaned resulting in damage to the paint film. The records note further that since the above lining had proved ineffective, the decision was made to remove it and to reline the work afresh. By this time, the painting already showed considerable wear, including abrasion and widespread traction cracks with extensive cleavage; there was considerable discolored inpainting, especially in the sky.

The 1967 restoration included removal of the earlier lining; cleaning of the surface; removal of old inpainting; consolidation of cleaving areas with wax-resin lining mixture (14 pts. beeswax; 4 pts. dammar; 1 pt. gum elemi); impregnation of the canvas with wax-resin lining mixture and adhesion on the hot table to a similarly prepared lining canvas; mounting on a new stretcher. Losses were filled with a putty and inpainted; some of the earlier oil retouching was toned down.

In 1978 (New York) some new areas of cleavage were consolidated with heat and wax-resin. The surface was varnished with Lucite 44 (spray).

The artist's complex textures of surface, differentiation in brushwork and other techniques, as well as much of the detail of the actual design have been lost. (Venice, Nov. 1982.)

58

La ville entière is one of a group of thirteen canvases, probably all painted during the years 1935-37, in which similar scenes are depicted (Spies, 1979, nos. 2210-20, 2260-61). In most examples, as Lippard has pointed out, Ernst used decorated relief blocks (for textile printing) to create the sequential patterns of the city walls, though it has not been possible to establish whether he used the frottage surface from the blocks as a point of departure—the pattern suggesting the subject matter—or whether he chose the blocks specifically to illustrate and develop a preconceived subject matter.

In several other examples the surface texture and design of both city walls and foreground foliage are built up from layers of thick paint, frottage, scraping, rubbing, printing on the surface, and minute detailing with a fine brush (see, for example, those in the Kunsthaus, Zurich, Spies, no. 2220, and The Tate

Gallery, London, Spies, cat. no. 2218). The abrasion and flattening of the surface in the Peggy Guggenheim picture, however, have tended to obliterate both design and texture, and the rich effects of contrasting technical processes have been largely lost. It is still possible to detect faint areas of repetitive patterning in the city walls, but whether these were achieved by frottage or actual printing on the surface is difficult to say.

Of the thirteen works in the series, only one is dated by the artist (Collection Dominique de Menil, Spies, no. 2214, 1935). Werner Spies dates eleven out of the group in 1935 and only two in 1936-37. Lucy Lippard gives a general date of 1934-36 for the series. Though Ernst apparently recalled painting one example at Sir Roland Penrose's Château le Pouy (Gers) in the south of France in 1934 (Alley, *Tate Collection*, 1981, p. 210), it seems unlikely on stylistic grounds that he started the series before 1935. (Penrose, in correspondence with the author, Nov. 1982, felt sure that the theme of *La ville entière* originated later than 1934, after the Penroses had left le Pouy. He suggested 1936-37 as a more plausible date.) Until further evidence emerges, a date of 1936-37 for the present work and a general date of 1935-37 for the series seem the most plausible.

In the series *La ville entière,* the combination of deserted, crumbling mountain citadels and grotesque, apparently destructive foliage is reminiscent of the almost contemporary series *Jardin gobe-avions* (cat. no. 57). Both series have often been described as elegiac commentaries on the ruin of civilization, brought about by the ravages of man or of nature.

Werner Hofmann, by contrast, has suggested that Ernst's stance in such works is that of a dispassionate observer of the "arbitrarily creative-destructive" continuum of "natural history." He writes: "Out of the skepticism of Nietzsche (in his refusal to acknowledge the human 'perception of the world' as the only valid one) comes the Surrealist doubt about the institutions, conventions and systems conceived by man, about the hierarchies of values and structures of belief, about scientific measurements and the alleged rules and norms of art."[1]

According to Hofmann's interpretation, therefore, Ernst's "arid continents" and cities—overgrown with weeds—are neither symbols of a tragic breakdown in civilization nor echoes of a Romantic Vanitas theme (such as was embodied in Caspar David Friedrich's depiction of the cathedral of Meissen in ruins, or Hubert Robert's portrayal of the disintegration of the Grande Galerie of the Louvre). They are visions presented by an "uncommitted onlooker" of "vanished and forgotten phases of the earth's history, and presentiments of what is to come."[2]

1. "Max Ernst and Tradition," *Inside the Sight*, exh. cat., Rice University, Houston, 1973, pp. 15-16. See also W. Spies, *Max Ernst Loplop: The Artist in the Third Person*, New York, 1983, pp. 96-97, who compares the imagery of the *Ville entière* paintings with Breton's metaphor for man's ultimate feeling of estrangement (or "dépaysement"), as expressed in the Surrealist text *Le château étoilé*.
2. Hofmann's brief analysis is contained within a broader discussion that is especially illuminating of Ernst's relationship to Leonardo's *Trattato* and the dissociation in perception.

EXHIBITIONS:

New York, Valentine Gallery, *Max Ernst*, Mar. 23-Apr. 11, 1942, no. 1 ("*The endless town*, 1937"; the work has been consistently so dated in all subsequent *P.G.* publications); Venice, *P.G.*, 1948 (Biennale), no. 43 (*Città eterna*); Florence, *P.G.*, 1949, no. 43; Amsterdam, *P.G.*, 1951, no. 51 (*la cité éternelle*); Zurich, *P.G.*, 1951, no. 47 (*Die ewige Stadt*); New York, *P.G.*, 1969, p. 91, repr.; Paris, *P.G.*, 1974-75, no. 78 (*Cité entière*); Torino, *P.G.*, 1975-76, no. 75 (*La città intera*).

REFERENCES:

P. Guggenheim, *Art of This Century*, 1942, p. 103 ("Endless Town, 1937"); L. Lippard, "The Technical Innovations of Max Ernst," unpublished master's thesis, New York University, 1962, pp. 76-77 (speaking of the series and its techniques; Lippard uses the title *City Absolute*); J. Russell, *Max Ernst: Life and Work*, New York, 1967, p. 118; W. Spies, *Max Ernst*, New York, 1968, pp. XIV, XVII; W. Spies and S. and G. Metken, *Max Ernst: Oeuvre Katalog Werke 1929-1938*, vol. 4, Houston and Cologne, 1979, no. 2260, repr. (dated 1936/37).

---

59 La toilette de la mariée. 1940.
(*Attirement of the bride*).

Color plate p. 248.

76.2553 PG 78

Oil on canvas, 51 x 37⅞ (129.6 x 96.3).

Signed and dated l.r.: *max ernst 1940*; on reverse (recorded but not photographed before lining): *max ernst*.

PROVENANCE:

Gift of the artist, 1942.[1]

CONDITION:

In 1964 (Tate Report) some extremely minor losses were noted, as was retouching along the bottom edge. There was some doubt about the presence of varnish; however, a grayish residue resembling disintegrated varnish but soluble in water was observed. Sometime between 1964 and 1969 (New York, SRGM exhibition), the painting was wax-lined.

In 1982 (Venice) a much discolored natural resin varnish (applied at an unspecified time and place) was removed with commercial lacquer thinner (of unspecified constituents); considerable soil and extensive retouching at the edges were removed. Small scattered losses were inpainted with watercolor, and a light coat of LeFranc retouching varnish was applied (spray). The condition is stable. (New York, Mar. 1983.)

The technique of decalcomania as practiced in the 1930s was first described in print in 1936 by Breton, the discovery being attributed to Oscar Dominguez: "*Etendez au moyen d'un gros pinceau de la gouache noire, plus ou moins diluée par places, sur une feuille de papier blanc satiné que vous recouvrez aussitôt d'une feuille semblable sur laquelle vous exercez du revers de la main une pression moyenne. Soulevez sans hâte par son bord supérieur cette seconde feuille.*"

1. At the time of the Valentine Gallery exhibition the picture still belonged to Ernst; he gave it to Peggy Guggenheim afterward. It is interesting to note that in the Valentine catalogue the title of the picture, contrary to all the others except one, is given in French, as it is in the 1942 *View*. There is some cause to believe, therefore, that Ernst objected to its translation into English.

("D'une décalcomanie sans objet préconçu [décalcomanie du désir]," *Minotaure*, no. 8, 1936, p. 18; examples by Dominguez, Breton, Jacqueline Breton, Tanguy, and Marcel Duchamp were reproduced. The definition was republished in abbreviated form in the *Dictionnaire Abrégé du Surréalisme*, Paris, 1938, p. 9.)

Lucy Lippard has pointed out that decalcomania was not an entirely original invention at this date, since Alexander Cozens had used it in the eighteenth century, and Victor Hugo in the nineteenth in his wash drawings.[2] But the

2. "The Technical Innovations of Max Ernst," unpublished master's thesis, New York University, 1962, p. 82, fn.1.

rediscovery of the technique in the mid-1930s was to have an important impact on Ernst's stylistic development.[3]

Breton wrote in 1942 that the "texture" derived from the technique "has the greatest plasticity, since it can render the entire complex atmosphere of that region of miracles *par excellence*, the grotto, as well as the iridescence of foliage, coral and feathers (otherwise so difficult to obtain) brilliantly displayed by Max Ernst in his canvases of 1940-41" (Introduction, *Art of This Century*, New York, 1942, pp. 26-27).

In the case of *La toilette de la mariée*, the most visible use of decalcomania is in the picture-within-a-picture at the upper left. This rectangular surface was initially treated with decalcomania and, after it had dried, the sky and the nude female body were brushed in, the contrasting, smooth unified color creating the spatial illusion of the figure-ground relationship. Decalcomania was also used to create the marbleized right edge of the main composition, the headdress of the otherwise nude female (right), and the feathered cloak of the central figure. In these instances, however, Ernst also used a combination of scumbling, highlighting, and articulated minute brushstrokes to create the veils of color that, to varying degrees, obscure the decalcomania base. The nude bodies, the tiled floor and background, the green bird with a spear (left), and all other elements of the composition were brushed in afterward, the outermost contours of the feathered forms being retouched last of all. It has not yet been possible to establish whether in this instance the entire surface of the canvas was first covered with a decalcomania base, though it seems likely.[4]

This picture has not been extensively discussed in the literature, although a few explications of the theme and iconography have been proposed.

Nicolas Calas (1966) identified the bird-man as Ernst himself—Loplop, the totemic alter ego of the artist—tempting Furia. He suggested a connection with

3. Lippard's penetrating discussion of the technique (Chapter V) is by far the most extensive in the Ernst literature, though some minor questions remain unresolved. Ernst credits Dominguez with the "discovery" in 1936, while Lippard, on the other hand, gives a date of 1935; in neither case is evidence cited. A further issue that remains unclear concerns the origins of the use of decalcomania with oil. Lippard states that Dominguez began applying the process to oils within a year of his first experiments in gouache and ink, and that Ernst thus adopted an already developed methodology, putting it to more elaborate and complex uses. Other scholars, on the other hand, have specifically attributed to Ernst the extension of the technique into oil, suggesting that it was precisely this new exploitation of the medium that constituted a major aspect of his contribution (see, for example, J. Richardson, "Max Ernst: Artist or Painter," *Art News*, vol. 59, Apr. 1961, p. 54; J. Russell, *Max Ernst: Life and Work*, New York, 1967, p. 126; W. S. Rubin, *Dada, Surrealism, and Their Heritage*, New York, 1968, p. 139). Though it seems likely that Dominguez experimented to some extent with the oil medium, it was, as all commentators agree, Ernst's more imaginative use of the technique that allowed "the poetic possibilities of decalcomania [to be] realized as significant art" (Rubin, op. cit.).

4. Barely visible traces of a penciled grid near the lower edge of the composition raise interesting further questions about Ernst's procedures, most specifically about the degree to which he allowed automatic principles to dominate his compositional thinking. Infra-red reflectography might be helpful in achieving a greater understanding of these questions (see also *Le Baiser*, cat. no. 52).

Duchamp's *The Bride Stripped Bare by Her Bachelors, Even*, the broken weapon standing as an echo of the broken glass. Evan Maurer (1974) read the painting as representing the third stage in the alchemical process. The "royal marriage" between a king and queen, which results in the birth of the Philosopher's stone, is taken here as the basic source for Ernst's iconography; individual details of the composition (owl, pelican, arrow, peacock feathers, toad, etc.) are identified as important symbolic objects and figures in a number of alchemical texts.

Like other paintings by Ernst, this is essentially a visionary work, evocative and powerful in the dramatic action it represents, yet enigmatic and intentionally ambiguous in its meaning. Any single interpretation is bound to result in oversimplification. Nonetheless certain sources — including statements from Ernst's own writings — seem relevant to the picture's iconography.

In his 1936 autobiographical essay, "Au delà de la peinture," Ernst described (and dated very precisely) a number of his own visionary experiences. In one of these, dated December 24, 1933, Ernst mentioned the title (*avant la lettre*) of *La toilette* ... : "*j'ai eu la visite d'une jeune* chimère en robe de soir. *Huit jours plus tard j'ai rencontré un* nageur aveugle. *Un peu de patience (une quinzaine de jours d'attente) et j'assisterai* à la toilette de la mariée. La mariée du vent *m'embrassera en passant au grand galop (simple effet d'attouchement)*" (*Cahiers d'Art*, vol. 11, nos. 6-7, 1936, p. 160).

In 1938, Ernst published a preface entitled "Loplop présente la mariée du vent" to Leonora Carrington's "La maison de la peur."[5] His text includes references to his alter ego: "*Est-ce l'homme qu'on appelle Loplop, le supérieur des oiseaux, à cause de son caractère doux et féroce? Sur son énorme chapeau blanc, il a arrêté dans son vol un extraordinaire oiseau au plumage émeraude, au bec crochu, à l'œil dur.*" Loplop and his emblematic counterpart — the bird with emerald plumage and hooked beak — are followed by dwarfs ("*un millier de nains*") and a lover-companion: "*la mariée du vent.*" The context within which the preface appears tends to identify "*la mariée*" as Leonora Carrington.

Thus in a 1936 memoir describing visionary experiences, Ernst refers in turn to a painting already completed (*Nageur aveugle*, 1924), a preface yet to be published, and a picture yet to be painted (*La toilette de la mariée*). By inference and proximity, *La toilette de la mariée* becomes closely associated with *La mariée du vent*: both works are in turn associated with Loplop (or Ernst himself) and Carrington.

In 1940 — the date of *La toilette de la mariée* — Carrington painted a portrait of Ernst as The Bird Superior, dressed in a flowing robe of feathers. Carrington wrote the text to accompany the portrait, in which the feathered Bird Superior is presented as a metaphor for Ernst's creativity: "The Bird Superior with all his feathers painting different images at once, moves slowly around the room

5. For details concerning the relationship between Leonora Carrington and Ernst during the late 1930s and early forties, see below, cat. no. 61.

evoking trees and plants out of the furniture."[6] This text also includes the character of Fear (in the form of a horse), a clear allusion to Carrington's own 1938 story, "La maison de la peur" (for which Ernst had written the Loplop preface), and her identification with its central character.

In 1942 Carrington published a sadistic tale, "The Sisters," in which a tyrannical heroine awaits the arrival of her lover (and potential husband), an enigmatic king-figure. A younger sister, imprisoned in the household, escapes and is then revealed to be a vampire: "Its body, white and bare, was adorned with feathers which grew from the shoulders and around the breasts."

The precise composition date of "The Sisters" is not known. When Carrington published the tale in 1942, however, she used a reproduction of *La toilette de la mariée* to illustrate it.[7]

A precise chronological sequence including all the various elements described above is difficult to establish. Suffice it to say that between 1936 and 1940/42, various pictorial and literary allusions in the work of both Carrington and Ernst suggest important and continuing iconographical and thematic interconnections.

Given this context, it seems plausible, at one level of meaning, that such connections emerge in *La toilette de la mariée*. The man-bird at the left of the painting can be viewed as an image of Loplop ("*un extraordinaire oiseau au plumage émeraude, au bec crochu, à l'œil dur*"). This figure ("*j'assisterai à la toilette de la mariée*") seems cast partly in the role of "presenter" of the bride; he holds a spear — with obvious sexual connotations — and he seems to evoke both the seductive and the destructive aspects of desire ("*son caractère doux et féroce*"). The artist here, as in Carrington's description of him, seems to play multiple roles: he is the primary creative force, and appears to control and present much of the action; he is simultaneously associated with images of desire as well as with those of power and fear.

Efforts to trace close iconographic links between "The Sisters" and *La toilette de la mariée* are unlikely to prove fruitful. Yet the moods of the two works are certainly related: both are characterized by themes of anticipation or expectant union, an atmosphere of mingled apprehension and desire, the tyrannical and threatening character of a central female, and the presence of a younger figure — perhaps a potential rival — who presses forward but is held at bay.

Neither the pictures nor the texts should be read as mere commentaries on the relationship between Carrington and Ernst, or even as explicit references to it; nevertheless they do seem in various ways to embody the combination of ambivalent feelings and attitudes associated with the experience of human love (fear, cruelty, desire, power, and destructiveness) expressed repeatedly in the work of Ernst and Carrington during these years.

6. The date of the text is not known. It was first published in *View*, 2nd ser., no. 1, Apr. 1942, p. 13.

7. The publication was in *View*, vol. 1, nos. 11-12, Feb.-Mar. 1942.

EXHIBITIONS:

New York, Valentine Gallery, *Max Ernst*, Mar. 23-Apr. 11, 1942, no. 18; New York, Art of This Century, 1942-47, p. 103, repr. p. 105; Venice, *P.G.*, 1948 (Biennale), no. 44; Florence, *P.G.*, 1949, no. 44; Amsterdam, *P.G.*, 1951, no. 52, repr.; Zurich, *P.G.*, 1951, no. 48, repr.; London, *P.G.*, 1964-65, no. 70; Stockholm, *P.G.*, 1966-67, no. 68; Torino, Galleria Civica d'Arte Moderna, *Le Muse Inquietanti*, Nov. 1967-Jan. 1968, no. 131, repr.; New York, *P.G.*, 1969, pp. 92-93, repr.; Paris, *P.G.*, 1974-75, no. 79, repr.; Torino, *P.G.*, 1975-76, no. 76; New York, *P.G.*, 1982-83, no. 31.

REFERENCES:

L. Carrington, "The Sisters," *View*, vol. 1, nos. 11-12, Feb.-Mar. 1942, repr. p. 7; Calas, 1966, p. 115, repr. color p. 137; U. M. Schneede, *Surrealism*, New York, 1973, p. 72, repr. color p. 73 (dated 1939); E. Maurer, "In Quest of the Myth: An Investigation of the Relationships Between Surrealism and Primitivism," unpublished Ph.D. dissertation, University of Pennsylvania, 1974, pp. 283-87; J. Leymarie, *Art du XXe Siècle: Fondation Peggy Guggenheim Venise*, Paris, 1974, cat. no. 79; H.-A. Baatsch, "La Légende Rhénane de Max Ernst," *XXe Siècle*, no. 48, June 1977, p. 70, repr. (dated 1939).

---

60 'The Antipope.'[1] Ca. 1941.

76.2553 PG 79

Oil on thin cardboard mounted on cardboard, 12¾ x 10⅜ (32.5 x 26.5).

Not signed or dated.

PROVENANCE:

Gift of the artist, late 1942, New York.

CONDITION:

There are no restoration records for this work. However, areas of repair and inpainting, especially in the sky and around the head of the central figure, are clearly visible. There are some areas of traction cracks (see, for example, the stomach of the left-hand figure) and some abrasion and wear, especially at the edges. The primary support has in certain places become slightly detached from the secondary support. The overall condition is stable. (Venice, Nov. 1983.)

The technique employed by Ernst here is decalcomania (for a description see above, cat. no. 59, *La toilette de la mariée*). The entire surface was first covered with a decalcomania base. A sponge technique of dabbing paint onto the surface was used in the arm and back of the central figure (see above, cat. no. 56, *Couple zoomorphe*, for more extensive use of this technique). Leaf imprints were added to the red garments of the figures at the far left and second from the right. Traditional brushwork was used only in the spears, in scattered small details, and in the blue sky (painted last, to define the outer contours of figures).

1. According to Peggy Guggenheim's memoirs (1960), the painting appears to have had no title when Ernst gave it to her: "Because my hand was placed where it was, and because it was between two spears, I named the painting 'Mystic Marriage.' " Only after he painted the large version, cat. no. 61, did she give this smaller one the same title: *The Antipope*. For a discussion of the iconographical issues involved, see below, cat. no. 61.

60 

EXHIBITIONS:

Florence, *P.G.*, 1949, no. 45 (erroneously dated 1942); Ostende, Palais des Thermes, *Gloires de la Peinture moderne—Hommage à James Ensor*, 1949, no. 77, repr. (with incorrect dimensions); Amsterdam, *P.G.*, 1951, no. 54 (*le petit antipape*); Zurich, *P.G.*, 1951, no. 49; London, *P.G.*, 1964-65, no. 71, repr.; Stockholm, *P.G.*, 1966-67, no. 69, repr.; New York, *P.G.*, 1969, p. 94, repr. color; Paris, *P.G.*, 1974-75, no. 80; Torino, *P.G.*, 1975-76, no. 77.

REFERENCES:

P. Guggenheim, *Confessions*, 1960, pp. 93-94; idem, *Out of This Century*, New York, 1979, pp. 261-62.

The Antipope.

December 1941-March 1942.

61

Color plate p. 249.

76.2553 PG 80

Oil on canvas, 63¼ x 50 (160.8 x 127.1).

Signed and dated l.r.: *max ernst 41-42*; on reverse: *The Antipope / max ernst / dec. 1941-march 1942.*

PROVENANCE:

Purchased from the artist, New York, late in 1942.

CONDITION:

There are extensive pigment and ground cracks in the green background. Some minimal scattered flaking reveals the light green ground layer (see area between horse far right and blond female). The condition is otherwise stable. (Venice, Nov. 1982.)

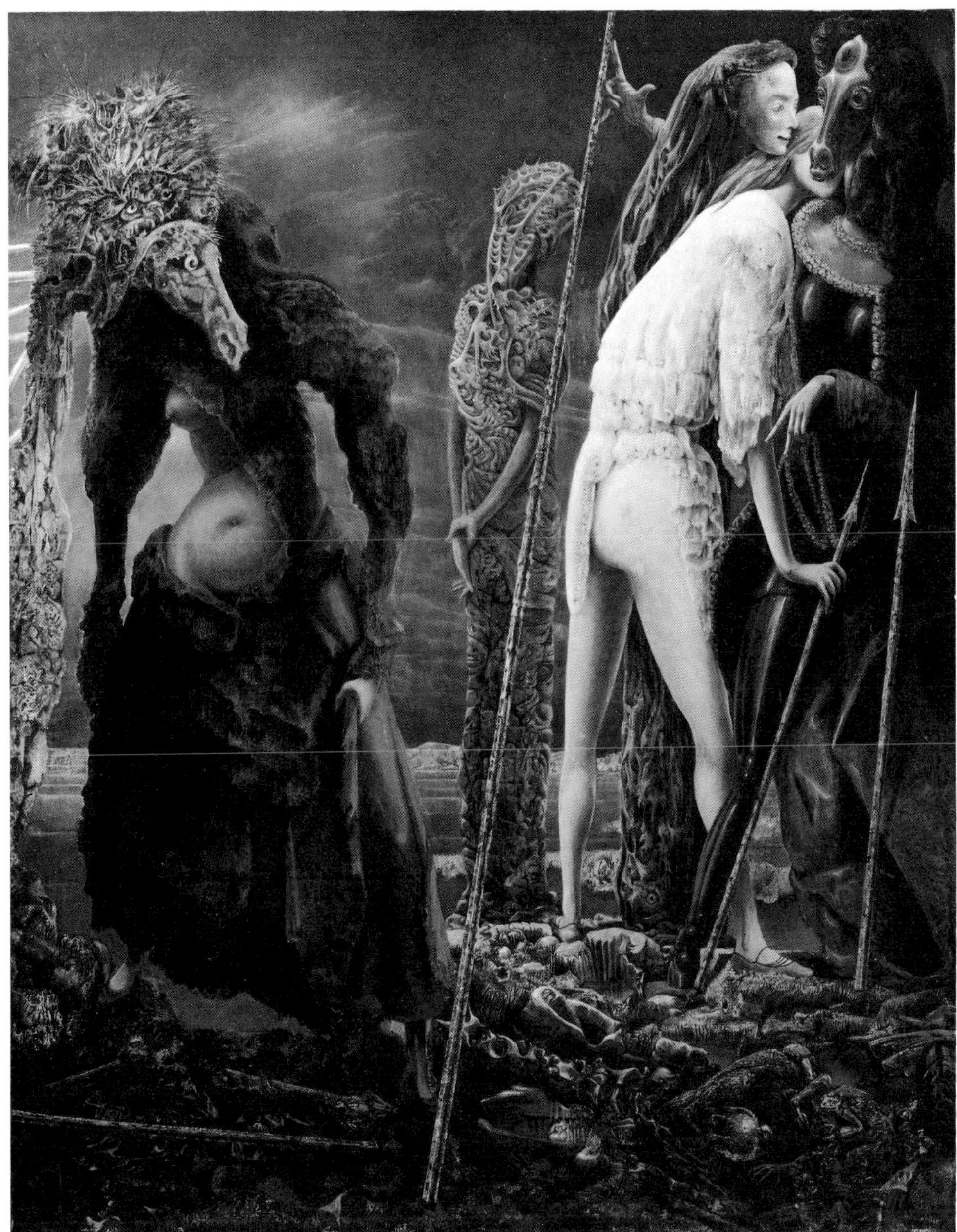

Unlike the first version of the composition, in which decalcomania is the dominant technique (cat. no. 60), this second version is executed in a combination of decalcomania, sponging, extensive traditional brushwork, and the printing of leaves into wet paint. The entire lower landscape is built on a decalcomania base that has been painstakingly transformed with fine brushwork into an intricate web of birds, frogs, fossil-like vegetation, encrusted rocks, shells, and mosses. The red robe and horse-owl head of the figure at the left, the body and hair of the skeletal figure at the center (seen from the rear), and the trunklike base of the female figure to her right are the result of similar technical combinations. To an even greater degree than in the case of *La toilette de la mariée* (cat. no. 59), the multiple techniques are combined in such a way as to obscure their origin and sequence.

The imagery of the two versions of *The Antipope* was explicitly interpreted by Peggy Guggenheim in her memoirs:

> *One day when I went into his studio I had a great shock. There on his easel was a little painting I had never seen before. In it was portrayed a strange figure with the head of a horse. It was Max's own head, with the body of a man dressed in shining armour. Facing this strange creature, and with her hand between his legs, was a portrait of me, but not of me as Max had ever seen me. It was my face at the age of eight. I have photographs of myself at this age and the likeness is unquestionable. I burst into tears and told Max he had at last painted my portrait. He was rather surprised as he had never seen the photos. Because my hand was placed where it was, and because it was between two spears, I named the painting "Mystic Marriage." At my request Max gave me this painting. Later he painted an enormous canvas of this same subject, slightly changing it, and my lovely little innocent child's head turned into that of a terrible monster. He called the big painting "Anti-Pope". I own both of them and they now bear the same title* (*Confessions*, 1960, pp. 93-94).

When this episode was published in the 1946 edition of the memoirs, it was considerably longer:

> *I asked for it as a present, telling Max that now he need never marry me, as this sufficed. I have still to describe the rest of the painting, as this was only one-third of it. In the center was a figure which Max admitted to be [Pegeen's][1] back, and on the left hand side was a terrifying sort of monster. It portrayed a woman in a red dress with her stomach exposed. This was undoubtedly my stomach, but the figure had two heads and resembled nobody. They were animal heads and one looked like a skeleton. Sidney Janis claimed I was this monster, which he considered very strong, but that was later when Max took this for a theme and made an enormous canvas of it. In this new painting my beautiful girl's head disappeared completely and gave way to a portrait of a strange unknown person accompanied by [Pegeen]. The original [Pegeen] in this painting gave way to a totem pole with a head made of a substance resembling brains. Much later I showed these photos to Alfred Barr because I wanted him to corroborate my theory, and he was much impressed by the resemblance* (*Out of This Century*, 1946, pp. 303-04).

Several things are important to note in these passages. First, Peggy Guggenheim clearly read both pictures biographically, and she observed some significant changes between them: in the first painting she saw herself as an innocent, youthful creature placed next to Ernst who was portrayed partly in the guise of a horse, partly a man in shining armor. (It is not clear that Ernst shared this reading.) In the second canvas she found herself at least partially embodied in the monstrous figure on the far left, with the crimson robe and exposed torso ("this was undoubtedly my stomach"). In addition, Pegeen, whom she had seen

1. In the 1946 edition, Pegeen appears under the pseudonym Deirdre; only in the 1979 revised edition is she correctly identified.

as a central figure in the small picture (an identification that Ernst apparently allowed), was, in the larger canvas, identified as the partially nude female resting her head on "Ernst's" shoulder; behind and closely intertwined with her was a striking if somewhat spectral figure with a mane of long dark hair, whom Peggy Guggenheim described as "a terrible monster" (1960); in the earlier text (1946), she described her more neutrally as "a strange unknown person accompanied by [Pegeen]."

In short, the second, larger canvas was viewed by Peggy Guggenheim to have transposed some of the key figure relationships of the earlier picture, and also some of its major values. Peggy Guggenheim saw herself as having undergone a substantial metamorphosis from a youthful and affectionate girl to at least a partial identification with the later menacing monstrous figure. Meanwhile a new and complex set of erotic relationships had been introduced by the close intertwining of the three figures at the right.

Granted that biographical readings are invariably problematic (particularly in the case of Surrealist pictures), Peggy Guggenheim's own testimony—as well as some additional known biographical facts about the artist—do suggest that the two canvases may be concerned not only with important recurring themes and preoccupations of Ernst's work as a whole but with quite specific situations and relationships.

Lucy Flint (1983), for example, has suggested an interpretation based on the complex personal relationship that existed between Ernst and Leonora Carrington. According to this reading, Carrington's long-standing involvement with Ernst (initially her teacher), her obsession with horses, and the competitive tension between her and Peggy Guggenheim all become elements in the iconography of the paintings under discussion. For instance, the gothic tale "La dame ovale" by Carrington, published in Paris in 1939 with seven collage illustrations by Ernst, was dense with verbal and visual references to horses. In the introduction to the Spanish edition of the tale by Agusti Bartra, Carrington is said to identify the horse as the highest of beings and — by extension — as her own alter ego. Moreover, in an earlier tale by Carrington, "La maison de la peur," published in Paris in 1938, the preface by Ernst ("Loplop présente la mariée du vent") alludes to "*des chevaux à toutes les fenêtres.*" Once again metamorphoses of horses into women, and vice-versa, abound in the text and illustrations. And like "La dame ovale," the tale creates an eerie twilight world filled with animal/human violence.[2]

During the winter of 1940-41, when Peggy Guggenheim first came to know Ernst well, he was (according to her memoirs) deeply involved with Carrington and shared a house with her in the Ardèche. In Marseilles, amidst the confusion

2. Horses also appear in most of Carrington's paintings of the late 1930s. When Peggy Guggenheim first visited Max Ernst in the winter of 1938-39 hoping to buy a painting of his, she found Carrington there and managed only to purchase a work of hers. It was called *The Horses of Lord Candlestick* (*Confessions*, 1960, p. 71). See also Carrington's *Self-Portrait* of 1937, which portrays her as a young beauty with long hair, accompanied by 2 horses.

of the early months of the German occupation, they were separated, but when he found a temporary haven in Lisbon awaiting passage to America, he and Carrington were reunited. According to Peggy Guggenheim, "after two months of dreadful complications and miseries on all sides Leonora married a Mexican friend and went to New York with him" (*Confessions*, p. 86). Ernst meanwhile left with Peggy Guggenheim and her family, arriving in New York on July 14, 1941. They lived together for some time, deciding shortly after the bombing of Pearl Harbor that they should be married. The relationship was far from uncomplicated, however, and on the eve of their marriage, Pegeen — who had long opposed the union — tried once more to intervene and prevent it (*Out of This Century*, 1979, pp. 257, 264). Ernst, it seems, continued to yearn for Leonora, and he apparently painted a series of landscapes in which her portrait appeared again and again (*Confessions*, p. 93). Peggy Guggenheim acknowledged her jealousy, which — she wrote — "was a cause of great unhappiness."

It is against this background of intense and entangled relationships that Ernst produced both versions of *Antipope* in 1941-42. Although the small version cannot be precisely dated, the large canvas was begun shortly after his marriage to Peggy Guggenheim in December 1941 and was finished in March. Ernst was seeing Leonora constantly during this period and as 1942 progressed he "was so insane about [her] that he really could not hide it" (*Out of This Century*, 1979, pp. 264-66).

In April 1942, just after the large canvas was completed, an issue of *View* appeared dedicated to Ernst. It contained a short poetic essay on him written by Carrington ("The Bird Superior, Max Ernst"); it also reproduced a portrait she had painted of Ernst in 1940. The essay opened with the words: "Fear, in the form of a horse and dressed in the furs of a hundred different animals.... " The portrait, meanwhile, depicted Ernst in a flowing fur robe, with a white horse (reminiscent of Carrington as the "snow horse" in "La dame ovale") in the background silhouetted against the landscape. In addition the first issue of *VVV*, published in June of 1942 with Ernst as editorial advisor, reproduced a collage of fragments by Ernst. Among these fragments, significantly, there is a detail from *The Antipope* focusing on the powerful juxtaposition of the heads of the key figures — the spectral woman and the armored horse (fig. a).

In light of the accumulated evidence, the question arises whether the trio of closely linked figures at the right, set in opposition to the single figure at the left, allude — on one level — to the complex of relationships involving Ernst, Carrington, Peggy Guggenheim, and Pegeen Vail. Within this context, Ernst would be symbolically identified with the slightly androgynous, but unmistakably powerful, controlling aristocratic "hero" in armor, Carrington with the figure gazing intently at him, and Pegeen with the figure between them, drawn into the orbit of the hero in an apparently supportive role. Yet she is alluring in her own right, effectively separating "Carrington" from the hero — and in this respect is perhaps portrayed as an inevitable extension of Peggy Guggenheim. The singular, threatening, but physically provocative "anti-hero" at the left may evoke the ambiguous role played by Peggy Guggenheim herself.[3]

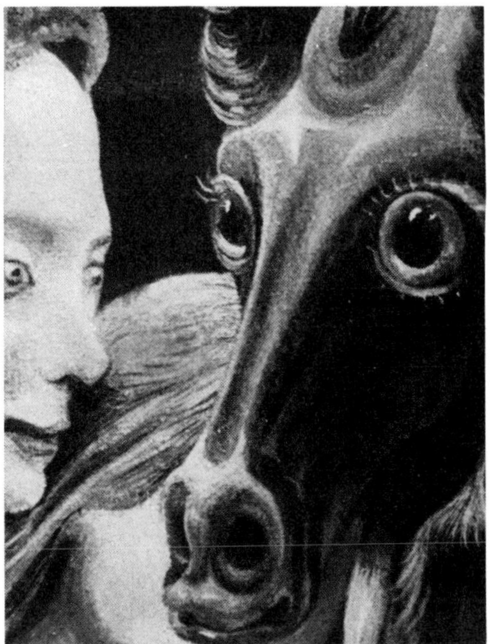

fig. a.
Detail of cat. no. 61, reproduced without caption or other identifying text in *VVV*, no. 1., June 1942, p. 58.

fig. b.
Papstesel from Johann Wolf, *Lectiones memorabiles*, Lauingen, 1608; reproduced in A. Warburg, "Heidnisch-antike Weissagung in Wort und Bild zu Luthers Zeiten" (1920), *Gesammelte Schriften*, vol. 2, Leipzig, 1932, pl. LXXXII, fig. 145a. Photograph by Michael J. Pirrocco.

In its totality, the painting may be seen as dramatizing a climactic moment in which the chivalric hero banishes or exposes his female antagonist. The drama is essentially an erotic one, but its additional symbolic overtones (the armor of the chivalric knight, the transcendent "spiritual" gaze of the hero and "Carrington") may provide a context for the religious metaphor of the painting's title: the hero's apparent victory is a triumph over destructive powers invoked by the concept of "antipope." Indeed, Ernst's iconographical conception of the antipope figure almost certainly derives from a tradition of satiric religious images dating from the time of the Reformation. (See, for example, fig. b.)[4]

3. A possible thematic relationship between this painting and *La Toilette de la mariée*, cat. no. 59, should be borne in mind. In technique, composition, and in specific imagery there are significant connections between the 2 works, and they both seem to allude—however obliquely—to aspects of the Ernst / Carrington relationship.

4. Philipp Melanchthon's anti-papal pamphlet on the so-called *Papstesel* (or "popish ass") appeared in 1523 and was widely disseminated by the end of the century, English and French translations being available by at least 1579. Johann Wolf's exhaustive *Lectiones memorabiles*, from which the particular image of fig. b is taken, was first published in 1600. It has thus far not been possible to establish a definite link between Ernst's image and the 16th-17th century prototypes, but the visual evidence is compelling.

It is interesting to note that in the smaller version of *The Antipope* (cat. no. 60) the long ass's

It is important to stress that even if the specifically biographical elements outlined above to some extent inspired the composition of *The Antipope*, they remain only secondary aspects of Ernst's more fundamental concern with the universal issues of power, manipulation, and potential destructiveness in sexual relations. The sinister metamorphoses of the figures, and the intricate tangle of frogs, beetles, dead birds, and scorpions lurking within the vegetation, recall — as Suzi Gablik has suggested — Lautréamont's "Les chants de Maldoror."[5] In this critical nineteenth-century text, rediscovered and much used by the Surrealist group, Ernst found constant echoes of his own conception of nature as the metaphor for destructiveness in human relations. In this and other respects his pictorial references were consistently general rather than narrowly autobiographical in their connotations.

Henry Miller understood the broadly universal ramifications of Ernst's often personal iconography when he wrote in the "Ernst" issue of *View*:

> *In the figures and landscapes ... we see the vestigial traces of a suprasensual world which, like our own sorry world, appears to be on the brink of collapse ... the unearthly vegetation, the symbolic episodes, the haunting passages which lead ... from the fabulous to the invisible and frightening realities ... are not dream images.... They are the product of an inventive mind endeavoring to translate in worldly language experiences which belong to another dimension. If they are horror-laden ... it is not in the familiar nightmarish sense which we are accustomed to ascribe to the functional processes of the night mind. They are compact with wonder and mystery, awesomely real* (*View*, 2nd ser., no. 1, Apr. 1942, p. 17).

EXHIBITIONS:

New York, Valentine Gallery, *Max Ernst*, Mar. 23-Apr. 11, 1942, no. 31; New York, Art of This Century, 1942-47 (not listed in catalogue, but see REFERENCES); Venice, *P.G.*, 1948 (Biennale), no. 45, repr.; Florence, *P.G.*, 1949, no. 46 (erroneously dated 1941); Amsterdam, *P.G.*, 1951, no. 53; Zurich, *P.G.*, 1951, no. 50; London, *P.G.*, 1964-65, no. 72, repr.; Stockholm, *P.G.*, 1966-67, no. 70, repr.; Torino, Galleria Civica d'Arte Moderna, *Le Muse Inquietanti*, Nov. 1967-Jan. 1968, no. 132, repr. (dated 1941); New York, *P.G.*, 1969, p. 95, repr.; Paris, *P.G.*, 1974-75, no. 81; Torino, *P.G.*, 1975-76, no. 78; Rome, *Guggenheim: Venezia-New York*, 1982, no. 42, repr. color.

REFERENCES:

[Unsigned], review of Valentine Gallery Ernst exhibition, *Art Digest*, vol. 16, no. 13, Apr. 1942, p. 18, repr.; [Unsigned], review of opening exhibition, "*Art of This Century*," ibid., vol. 17, Nov. 1, 1942, p. 8, repr.; P. Guggenheim, *Confessions*, 1960, pp. 93-94; U. M. Schneede, *The Essential Max Ernst*, London, 1972, repr. color p. 171, no. 335; P. Guggenheim, *Out of This Century*, New York, 1979, pp. 261-62; L. Flint, *Handbook*, 1983, no. 49, repr. color.

(4. cont.)
ears, the scaley stomach, and clawlike hand bring Ernst's figure into even closer relationship with the *Papstesel* source.

The author is indebted to Gert Schiff for drawing her attention to Warburg's 1920 essay.

5. "The Snake Paradise: Evolutionism in the Language of Max Ernst," *Art in America*, vol. 63, no. 3, May-June 1975, pp. 35-36.

62 Jeune femme en forme de fleur.

Great River. 1944 (cast 1957).
(*Young woman in the form of a flower*).

76.2553 PG 81

Bronze (lost wax). Cast in three parts and soldered.

Height at back: 12 13/16 (32.6); at front: 13 3/4 (35); width: 14 (35.6); depth: 8 7/16 (21.5).

Edition of nine, all unnumbered and unsigned.[1]

Foundry: Roman Bronze Works, Inc., Corona, New York.

PROVENANCE:

Purchased from Alexander Iolas, early 1960s.[2]

CONDITION:

The soldering joins of the 3 pieces are readily visible. The awkward sections in which the work was cast are attributable to Ernst's technique of assemblage (see below). The surface shows no sign of having been worked by the artist after casting and the nature of the original patina is unusually dull and opaque. The condition is stable. (Venice, June 1983.)

1. There is no foundry mark on the piece, and it is not recorded at Roman Bronze Works, which has incomplete information on those years. However, Philip Schiavo of Roman Bronze recognized the casting technique as definitely theirs (correspondence and conversations with the author, Apr.-June 1983). Alexander Iolas has no record of when or where the piece was cast or of the size of the edition. Members of Ernst's family who have kindly attempted to supply information conclude that there is no clear documentation about these questions. It seems likely that the casting was done at the request of Iolas, who borrowed the plaster original from Mr. and Mrs. Jimmy Ernst. Though the plaster appeared in the Ernst exhibition at The Jewish Museum in 1966 (cat. no. 99, collection Brooks Jackson, New York), it has apparently since disappeared (information supplied by Brooks Jackson, Nov. 1982).

   Ernst himself was apparently not involved in the casting of *Jeune femme en forme de fleur*.
2. Iolas apparently has no records of the transaction and was unable to recall the date. Peggy Guggenheim recalled only that it was sometime in the early 1960s. It is possible that this piece and the following were purchased after the 1961 exhibition at Le Point Cardinal.

Jeune femme en forme de fleur was one of approximately twelve sculptures Ernst made in plaster the summer of 1944 while he was visiting Julien Levy in Great River, Long Island. About ten years had elapsed since the summer he had spent making sculpture with Giacometti in Maloja, Switzerland, and he had not worked in this medium during the intervening time. None of the 1944 plasters were cast in bronze until the mid-1950s when Alexander Iolas undertook to have a number produced for a forthcoming exhibition; several of the plasters meanwhile had apparently been destroyed.

For most of the Great River sculptures, Ernst used molds readily available in the house or garden (flower pots, milk cartons, egg boxes, even automobile parts, etc.) to cast individual shapes in plaster. He then assembled a selection of cast objects into sculptural "constructions." His approach closely approximated that of assemblage rather than of more traditional forms of modeled sculpture. What clearly interested him at this time was the possibility of building in three dimensions many of the images and forms that preoccupied him in his paintings and collages. This produced results that from a strictly technical point of view were often idiosyncratic. The construction of *Jeune femme en forme de fleur*, for example, an assemblage of three pieces, seems to derive from the impetus to create a three-dimensional analogue for certain pictorial forms, not from any intrinsic sculptural logic of its own.

It has not been possible to identify the precise, preexisting receptacles Ernst might have used in the plaster casting of this work, but when the piece's three individual parts were eventually cast into bronze (1957) — probably without Ernst's participation — the soldering joins of the rather summarily worked plaster assemblage were necessarily somewhat curious in placement. The surface linear patterning and patina also remained rather primitive in execution. In this respect, it is interesting to compare the handling of some of Ernst's sculptural surfaces with the extraordinary linear precision, textural complexity, and pictorial subtlety of his paintings and collages.

EXHIBITIONS:

New York, Alexander Iolas Gallery, *Max Ernst*, spring 1957 (no catalogue available);[3] Paris, Le Point Cardinal, *Max Ernst: L'Œuvre Sculpté*, Nov. 15-Dec. 31, 1961, no. 20, repr.; London, *P.G.*, 1964-65, no. 73; Stockholm, *P.G.*, 1966-67, no. 71; Paris, *P.G.*, 1974-75, no. 82, repr.; Torino, *P.G.*, 1975-76, no. 79.

REFERENCES:

[J. Hugues], A. Bosquet, *Max Ernst: L'Œuvre sculpté, 1913-1961*, exh. cat., Le Point Cardinal, Paris, 1961, n.p., no. 20 repr. (edition of 9 bronzes listed); A. Ferrier, "Max Ernst sculpteur," *L'Œil*, no. 84, Dec. 1961, p. 68 (edition of 9 bronzes listed); M. Ragon, "Max Ernst: La sculpture c'est mes vacances," *Arts, Lettres, Spectacles, Musique*, no. 844, 1961, n.p.; Calas, 1966, p. 186, repr. p. 196; L. R. Lippard, "The Sculpture," *Max Ernst: Sculpture and Recent Painting*, exh. cat., The Jewish Museum, New York, 1966, p. 41; idem, "Max Ernst and a Sculpture of Fantasy," *Art International*, vol. 11, no. 2, Feb. 20, 1967, p. 42; idem, "The World of Dadamax Ernst," *Art News*, vol. 74, Apr. 1975, p. 29.

3. According to Brooks Jackson, this and other Ernst sculptures were cast on Iolas's initiative specifically for inclusion in this exhibition. No further documentation has been found to date.

63 Dans les rues d'Athènes.
Huismes. 1960 (cast January 1961).
(*In the streets of Athens*).

76.2553 PG 82

Bronze (sand cast) with dark black-green patina.

Height (including base): 38¾ (98.4); width (widest point): 19⁹⁄₁₆ (49.7); depth of base: 7³⁄₁₆ (18.3).

Edition of eight (?).[1]

Foundry: Georges Rudier.

Inscription on base (in wax): *I / III MAX ERNET* [sic] / *Georges Rudier / Fondeur Paris.*[2] Not dated.

PROVENANCE:

Purchased from Alexander Iolas, early 1960s (see above, cat. no. 62, fn. 2).

CONDITION:

There are some areas of pitting corrosion and green streaking corrosion on the base and the back.

In March 1984 (Venice) the piece was cleaned. The surface was degreased with trichloroethylene, and washed with distilled water, then with distilled water and neutral detergent; it was rinsed with distilled water and dried with alcohol and acetone. The surface was treated for 30 minutes with a 3% solution of benzotriazole in pure alcohol. A protective coating of Incralac (acrylic resin containing benzotriazole) was applied (for outdoor exhibition).

The plaster original of *Dans les rues d'Athènes* was made in Ernst's studio at Huismes in 1960 and was cast in bronze by January of 1961. During the years 1955-61 Ernst produced a group of a dozen sculptures, many of which are closely related in their use of mask-forms to the Peggy Guggenheim piece. He also designed a group of more than two dozen actual masks, which were carved in gold and silver by the master silversmith François Hugo in Aix-en-Provence (see [Hugues], 1961, nos. 46-71).

The explicit frontality and schematic simplification of form characteristic of these sculptures — indeed characteristic of Ernst's entire oeuvre in the medium — has often been attributed to the influences of Giacometti and of American Indian art.

1. It is not known exactly how large the edition was, though the existence of 8 casts seems probable. Peggy Guggenheim's cast was the first in a projected initial edition of 4 (I / III, II / III, III / III and O / III). I / III was cast by Georges Rudier, the other 3 apparently by Valsuani, although this latter fact has not been definitively established. (Information supplied by Dorothea Tanning, May 1983. Georges Rudier has confirmed, in correspondence with the author, Aug.-Oct. 1983, that only a single sand cast of the piece was made by his foundry.) In 1974, at Ernst's request, 4 casts were made by Susse (E.A. 1/3, E.A. 2/3, E.A. 3/3, and II / III; information supplied by P. Dintillac, Fonderie Susse, Apr.-May 1983). Two casts bearing the number II / III may thus exist. The locations of the other casts and of the original plaster have not been established. The Rudier cast (Peggy Guggenheim's) weighs 29.5 kilograms, the Susse casts, 45 kilograms.
2. The incorrect spelling of Ernst's name suggests that the mold may have been broken during some part of the casting and the name then incised afresh by a foundry employee who did not know the correct spelling. It is not clear whether the artist was present at any stage in the casting of the piece. The surface dryness indicates that no working of the bronze (to create a patina) took place after the casting. Regarding Ernst's apparent attitude to the surface of his sculptures, see above cat. no. 62.

fig. a.
Giacometti, *Femme*, 1928, plaster, height: 15¾ in., 40 cm., The Museum of Modern Art, New York.

Ernst's earliest extensive work in sculpture was under the guidance of Giacometti, when they spent the summer of 1934 together in Maloja, Switzerland. There is no doubt that Giacometti's plaque sculptures (themselves indebted to cycladic examples), his 1928 *Femme* (fig. a) or 1926 *Couple* (repr. *Alberto Giacometti*, exh. cat., SRGM, New York, 1974, p. 50), or even his monumental commission for the Vicomte de Noailles at Hyères (repr. R. Hohl, "Odysseus und Kalypso...," *Arnold Böcklin*, exh. cat., Kunstmuseum, Basel, 1977, p. 117) were known to Ernst. The austere economy of means in these works, as well as their strict frontality, would certainly have been in accord with Ernst's own natural mode of expression in sculpture. In addition—as has been frequently pointed out—Ernst developed an early and intense interest in American Indian culture, drawing inspiration from the Kachina dolls of Arizona and New Mexico, the masks of the ancient Eskimos and of the Hopi, Zuni, and Apache tribes, and the totem poles of the Pacific Northwest coast.[3] Patrick Waldberg has convincingly described the clear similarities between Ernst's conception of form and that of the Indians:

> *Max Ernst's art, like that of the Hopi, Navaho and Apache Indians who were his neighbors for more than ten years, is neither realistic nor abstract, but emblematic. With few exceptions, he never tried to capture the appearance of the human being (nor, for that matter, of things). Throughout his work, man is represented by some substitute, either an imaginary form or a mask, usually by a bird, but often, too, by a schematized figure whose head may be a rectangle, a triangle or a disk. In a similar manner, the Indians use simple geometric forms in their paintings, figurines and masks. Here the head may be a circle, there a square, elsewhere a triangle.... Thus forms do not represent appearances, but ideas* (loc. cit., 1971, p. 57).

In his response to Indian art, Ernst would select details and generalized concepts from a variety of different sources and a wide range of cultural contexts. His absorption of the essentially emblematic character of these images into his own formal language suggested the nature of his response. As Robert Goldwater described it, this was a characteristic shared by most sculptors of his generation: "[He] pays homage to the primitive, but he does so without evoking any particular image. The immense variety of specific styles fuse into the generalized vision of a three-dimensional object, non-naturalistic, rough, simplified, and

3. See P. Waldberg, *Max Ernst*, Paris, 1958, pp. 348-49; idem, in *Homage to Max Ernst* (*XXe Siècle*), New York, 1971. P. Guggenheim, in *Confessions*, 1960, pp. 90-92, also bore witness to Ernst's interest in American Indian artifacts. She first observed his passion for Kachina dolls and Indian masks on their journey to Arizona and New Mexico in 1941. She also described his frequent visits to the Museum of the American Indian (to which Breton had introduced them) and the steady growth in the early 1940s of Ernst's collection of Indian artifacts. Ernst had, of course, also been exposed to a great deal of Pacific Islands and other primitive art in Paris in the 1930s, in exhibitions as well as in the collections of Charles Ratton and André Breton.
For further discussion of the issue of Ernst's response to primitive art, see E. M. Maurer, "In Quest of the Myth: An Investigation of the Relationship between Surrealism and Primitivism," unpublished Ph.D. dissertation, University of Pennsylvania, 1974, pp. 240-44.

magically evocative, an object with pervasive overtones of ritual use and sexual symbolism [which] ... deliberately effaces the precision and detail, the limited ceremonial function and iconography of most primitive works."[4]

Ernst acknowledged and consistently made use of his familiarity with primitive and other art; indeed, he argued explicitly that the concept of an artist who can create *ex nihilo*, without imaginatively exploiting the "inexhaustible store of buried images" available to him, is a myth to be dispelled.[5] While drawing upon earlier art, Ernst's sculptural language is also dependent on his own previous work. The linear pattern on the front surface of the 1944 *Femme en forme de fleur* is a quotation from the imagery of the 1934 *Nageur aveugle* (J. Russell, *Max Ernst: Life and Work*, London, 1967, Chronological Survey, no. 63). The schematic masklike frontality of *Tête-oiseau* (1934-35, ibid., pl. 137) and the double mask of *Un ami empressé* (1944, [Hugues], 1961, no. 26) are echoed in the images and construction of *Dans les rues d'Athènes*. While the Loplop bird perched on the upper right "shoulder" of the figure in the latter recalls the masks of the relief murals at Sedona (1949, repr. P. Waldberg, loc. cit., 1971, [p. 55]), the composite masked mermaid and centaur(?) at the lower left are emblematic quotations from the monumental 1946 *Capricorn* (ibid., [pp. 53, 56]) and the still earlier cement sculptures made at St. Martin d'Ardèche.

As both Lucy Lippard and Werner Spies have argued in different ways, Ernst's sculptural oeuvre constitutes an unusually complex whole, the number of iconographic and formal links between the individual works requiring that they be studied in their totality. Particular forms recur again and again in different contexts; the entire repertoire of images is endlessly self-referential. Individual pieces, as a consequence, take on significance as part of a larger and extremely intricate fabric.[6]

EXHIBITIONS:

Paris, Le Point Cardinal, *Max Ernst: L'Œuvre Sculpté*, Nov. 15-Dec. 31, 1961, no. 40, repr.; London, *P.G.*, 1964-65, no. 74, repr.; Stockholm, *P.G.*, 1966-67, no. 72, repr.; New York, *P.G.*, 1969, p. 96, repr. p. 97; Paris, *P.G.*, 1974-75, no. 82 bis, repr.; Torino, *P.G.*, 1975-76, no. 80.

REFERENCES:

[J. Hugues], A. Bosquet, *Max Ernst: L'Œuvre sculpté, 1913-1961*, exh. cat., Le Point Cardinal, Paris, 1961, n.p., no. 40 repr. (edition of 3 bronzes listed); A. Ferrier, "Max Ernst sculpteur," *L'Œil*, no. 84, Dec. 1961, p. 68 (edition of 6 bronzes listed), repr. p. 64 (plaster); Calas, 1966, p. 186, repr. p. 197.

4. R. Goldwater, "Truth to What?" *Arts Yearbook*, no. 8, 1965, p. 67, cited by L. Lippard in her seminal essay "Max Ernst and a Sculpture of Fantasy," *Art International*, vol. 11, no. 2, Feb. 20, 1967, p. 44.
5. "Was ist Surrealismus?" preface to exhibition catalogue, Kunsthaus, Zurich, Oct. 11-Nov. 4, 1934. For an illuminating discussion of the issue of "quotation" and the "system of references," see W. Hofmann, "Max Ernst and Tradition," in *Max Ernst: Inside the Sight*, Houston, 1973, pp. 7-18.
6. On the subject of Ernst's sculpture in general, see W. Spies in *Max Ernst: Inside the Sight*, Houston, 1973, pp. 27-31; idem, *The Return of La Belle Jardinière*, New York, 1972, pp. 74-78.

John Ferren

Born October 1905, Pendeleton, Oregon.
Died July 1970, East Hampton, New York.

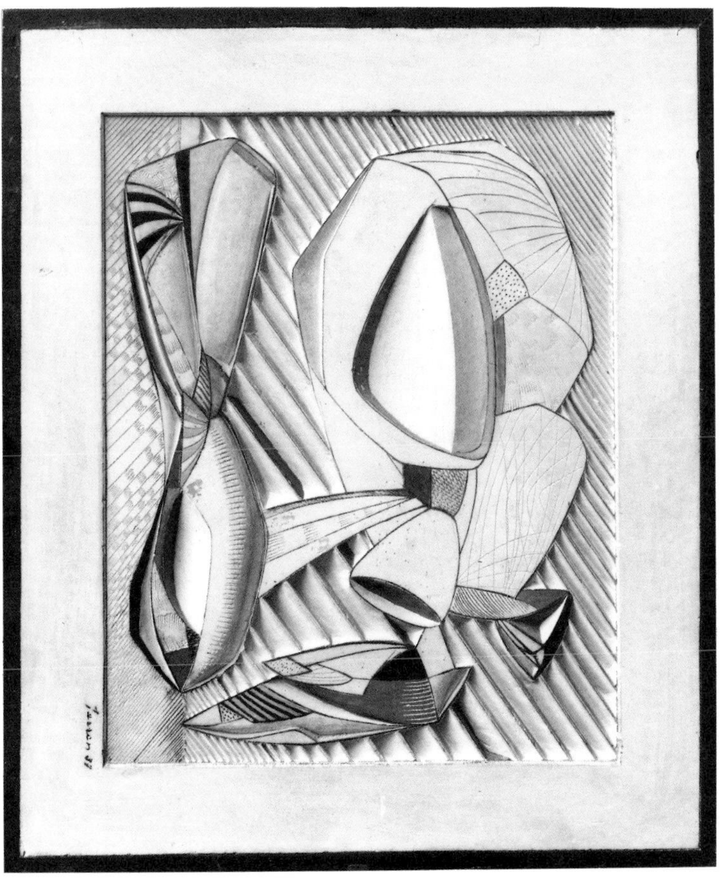

64 Tempora. 1937.

76.2553 PG 49

Plaster print, carved and tinted with ink and tempera. Dimensions of plaster: 15 x $12\frac{5}{8}$ (38.1 x 32.1); dims. of image: $11\frac{13}{16}$ x $9\frac{7}{16}$ (30 x 24); outer dims. of artist's frame: $18\frac{9}{16}$ x $16\frac{3}{16}$ (47.1 x 41.1).

Signed and dated along left edge of image: *Ferren 37*;[1] on reverse: *Top / Ferren / 1937 / JF 48*.[2]

PROVENANCE:

Purchased from the artist, New York, October 11, 1941.

CONDITION:

There has been some minimal flaking of the painted areas. The surface of the plaster is abraded in a few places, with some scattered chips and losses. The condition in general is stable. (Venice, 1980.)

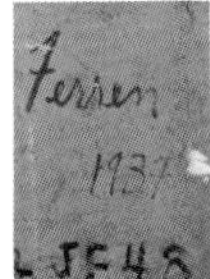

1. Since its acquisition by Peggy Guggenheim, the work has usually been published and exhibited as a horizontal composition, with the signature at the lower right. The artist's instructions on the reverse, however, indicate the correct orientation as vertical.
2. Ferren's record book lists 55 plaster reliefs, of which this is number 48. The author is indebted to Rae Ferren, the artist's widow, for this and other information.

During 1935 Ferren worked at Stanley William Hayter's Atelier 17 in Paris. Hayter had in 1931 revived a nineteenth-century technique of plaster-relief printing first described by Maxime Lalane (1827-1886). Ferren adapted the technique for his own use, creating fifty-five such reliefs between 1935 and 1938. The technique (which, according to Ferren, "demanded terrific concentration and a very steady hand") was as follows: a copper plate was etched or engraved, inked, and placed face upward on a sheet of glass or other smooth surface. A frame was placed over it allowing several inches on all sides for a margin. Plaster mixed with water was poured over the plate in the frame. Once the plaster was dry, the plate was heated slightly and removed; the etched lines of the plate stood out in relief on the plaster and provided guidelines for subsequent carving, inking, and painting. (See U. E. Johnson, "New Expressions in Fine Printmaking," *The Brooklyn Museum Bulletin*, vol. 14, no. 1, fall 1952, pp. 25-26; cited by C. Bailey, *Ferren*, exh. cat., The Graduate Center of the City University of New York, May 1979, pp. 10-11.) In his use of hatched and scored lines, of small fragments of mosaic that were occasionally imbedded in the plaster while it was still damp, and of the application of black ink and color, Ferren achieved effects of some textural complexity.

In an interview conducted by Dorothy Seckler in June 1965,[3] Ferren explained that he had originally conceived the plasters as three-dimensional studies for paintings. However, Pierre Matisse was impressed with them and gave him a contract to produce more during 1936 and 1937. After this intense period of activity in the medium, Ferren felt he had exhausted its possibilities and never returned to it.

EXHIBITIONS:

New York, Art of This Century, 1942-47, p. 149; Venice, *P.G.*, 1948 (Biennale), no. 46; Florence, *P.G.*, 1949, no. 48; Amsterdam, *P.G.*, 1951, no. 56; Zurich, *P.G.*, 1951, no. 52; London, *P.G.*, 1964-65, no. 42.

REFERENCES:

P. Guggenheim, *Art of This Century*, 1942, p. 149; Calas, 1966, repr. p. 231; [Alley], *Peggy Guggenheim Foundation*, 1968, no. 49.

3. Ferren Papers, AAA.

Sam Francis

Born June 1923, San Mateo, California.
Lives in Santa Monica, California.

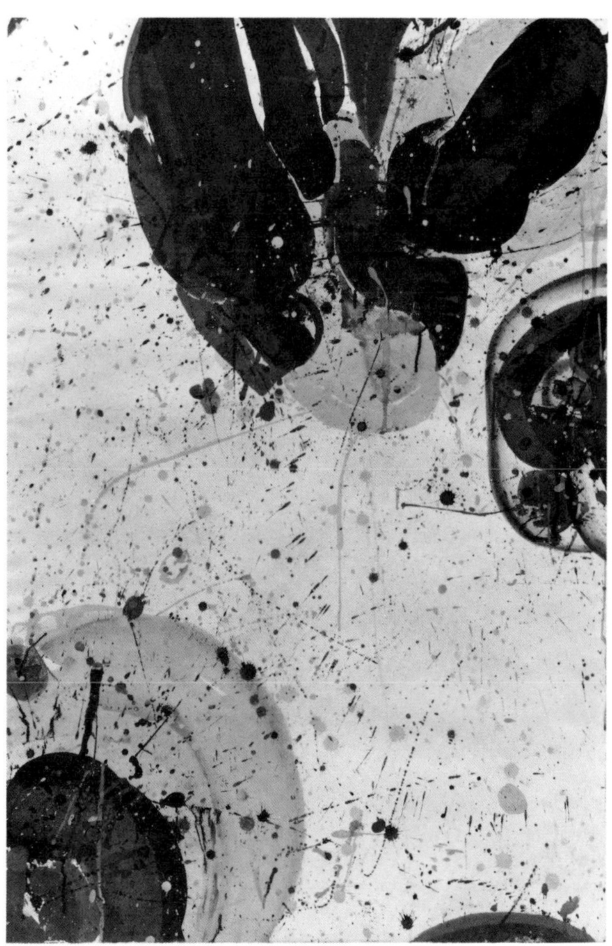

65 Untitled. March 1964.[1]
(*Blue, Yellow, Green; Tobago*).

76.2553 PG 185

Acrylic[2] on wove paper mounted on masonite, 40⅞ x 27⅜ (103.7 x 69.5).

Signed on stretcher: *SAM FRANCIS / TOP*. Not dated.

PROVENANCE:
Purchased from Kornfeld und Klipstein, Bern, October 1966.[3]

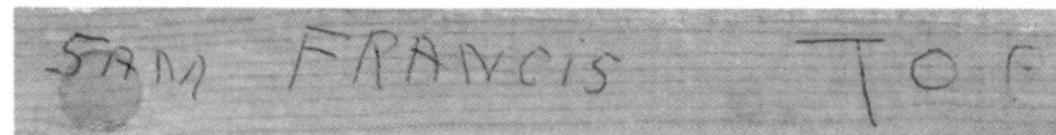

1. According to Tooth and Sons, this precise date would have been supplied by Francis himself (correspondence with the author, June-July 1978). Of the 24 works on paper in their exhibition, 19 were done in Tokyo.
2. Though consistently published since its acquisition as gouache, the medium is acrylic; Francis used acrylics for the entire series of "colored drawings" on his Tokyo journey, as well as for other works during the years 1962-68. Thus, the works in the Tooth and Sons 1965 exhibition, although described as gouaches, were probably all acrylics.
3. Kornfeld and Klipstein had the work on consignment from Francis for an exhibition of his work.

CONDITION:

Owing to the uneven density and application of the medium and the attachment of the support with spots of glue to the masonite backboard, there is some cockling throughout.

In November 1982 (Venice), as an interim measure, the paper was detached from the masonite support and a layer of Sekeishu tissue inserted behind it.

The support has darkened to some extent at the edges, but in spite of its direct contact with acidic backboard and glass, its condition is stable. (Venice, June 1983.)

Francis made his first journey to Japan in 1957, and returned frequently in subsequent years, especially during the 1960s. As has been stated in the literature, it was largely under the influence of oriental art that Francis's previously tight compositional density opened up, and the white field became a centrally important factor in his style. (See, for example, W. Schmied, *Sam Francis*, exh. cat., Albright-Knox Art Gallery, Sept. 1972, p. 11: "The complete use of the white plane as an essential part of the whole composition of the painting is a result of the artist's encounter with oriental art, with a mental attitude which leaves space as a principle of style." See also R. T. Buck, Jr., ibid., pp. 20-23.)

Painted in Tokyo during an extended visit in 1964, the present work belongs to a sizable group of acrylics on paper that mark the final stage of Francis's concentration on a white field articulated by a tracking and spattering of high-keyed color over its entire surface. In the immediately following works, as Robert Buck has pointed out, the organic shapes and spattered pigment were replaced by a tighter pictorial structure. The colors remained intense in this next phase but they were restricted to the edges, the pure white field standing in stark contrast at the center.

Francis apparently preferred not to title the works on paper dating from 1964-68 (correspondence with E. W. Kornfeld, Aug. 1975). Identifying titles, deriving from Francis's use of color, were assigned to the group of works exhibited by Tooth and Sons in 1965, the present work being listed as *Blue, Yellow, Green*. The title *Tobago*, used by Peggy Guggenheim, represents an inadvertent misreading by her of the word "Tokyo."

EXHIBITIONS:

London, Arthur Tooth and Sons, Ltd., *Sam Francis gouaches*, June 29-July 17, 1965, no. 2, repr. ("*Blue, Yellow, Green*, Tokyo, March 1964"); Bern, Kornfeld und Klipstein, *Sam Francis: Ausstellung von Ölbildern und Farbigen Zeichnungen von 1962 bis 1966 geschaffen in Tokyo und Los Angeles*, Sept.-Oct. 1966, no. 48, repr. (*Untitled*); Stockholm, *P.G.*, 1966-67, no. 130 ("*Tobago*, gouache," the title and medium under which it was published from its acquisition by Peggy Guggenheim until 1982); New York, *P.G.*, 1969, p. 167, repr.; Paris, *P.G.*, 1974-75, no. 243, repr.; Torino, *P.G.*, 1975-76, no. 175.

REFERENCE:

[Alley], *Peggy Guggenheim Foundation*, 1968, no. 184.

Alberto Giacometti

Born October 1901, Borgonovo, Switzerland.
Died January 1966, Chur, Switzerland.

66 Projet pour une place. 1931-32.
(Model for a square; Model for a garden).

76.2553 PG 130

Wood. Height without base: 6¾ (17.1); height of base: ⅞ (2.3); dims. of base: 12⅜ x 8⅞ (31.4 x 22.5).

Not signed or dated. Stamped on bottom of base: *Made in France.*

PROVENANCE:
Purchased from the artist, Paris, 1940.

CONDITION:
The zigzag (snake) form was broken at an unknown date and repaired with glue. It was then somewhat clumsily nailed back onto the base. There are cracks in the base, some of which penetrate across the surface to the edges. Water stains are visible in certain areas, as well as some abrasions and scratches around the base of the tallest ("stele") element. The general condition of the wood is good. (Venice, Nov. 1982.)

For a discussion of the various changes that the piece has undergone, see below.

The unique wood version of *Projet pour une place* was made by Ipústegui (a Basque cabinetmaker living in Paris), who executed most of the sculptor's wood pieces during this period. He always worked directly from the plaster model supplied by Giacometti.[1] Several aspects of Ipústegui's original construction and Giacometti's intended composition have, however, been lost. Ipústegui originally carved the pieces in such a way that some of them would rest on pegs that protruded from the base. The cone shape still survives in this original form, and

1. Diego Giacometti, in conversation with the author, Paris, April 2, 1982. In an oft-cited 1948 letter to Pierre Matisse, Giacometti refers to this "menusier" though not by name (Giacometti, exh. cat., Pierre Matisse Gallery, New York, 1948, p. 21). He is identified here for the first time.

fig. a.
Giacometti, *Projet pour une place*, plaster, present whereabouts unknown, 10¼ x 6$\frac{5}{16}$ x 7$\frac{1}{16}$ in., 26 x 16 x 18 cm. Photograph by Marc Vaux, Paris.

fig. b.
Photograph of cat. no. 66 by Man Ray, present whereabouts unknown. Originally reproduced in *Cahiers d'Art*, vol. 7, nos. 1-2, 1932, p. 341, with caption: "*Projet pour une place (en pierre), 1930-31*." The photograph represents the wood piece now in Peggy Guggenheim's collection, the wood elements in their original positions.

can be removed from the peg on which it rests. The central "stele" and the hollowed-out hemisphere, which are now firmly fixed, must have also been originally attached with pegs and dowel-holes. The snake form may, on the other hand, have been fixed in place (with glue?) as was the curved low form at the "rear."

When Peggy Guggenheim published this piece for the first time in her 1942 *Art of This Century* catalogue, it appeared with the "stele" and hemisphere in reverse positions; in addition, the stele was placed in such a way as to "face" out of the composition (fig. c). After 1942, the piece was again published in this form on at least two occasions (see REFERENCES). Not until sometime after Peggy Guggenheim's return to Europe in 1947 did she reverse the positions of the two critical parts; she also had them firmly fixed in place with screws (or nails?) and glue.[2]

Reversing the position of these two elements, however, only partially restored the composition as originally conceived by Giacometti.[3] The photograph of the actual plaster from which Ipústegui worked (fig. a) shows that the central stele originally stood "facing" right — almost directly confronting the open side of the hollowed-out hemisphere. Moreover, when Ipústegui's wood piece was itself first photographed by Man Ray and published in the 1932 *Cahiers d'Art* (fig. b), all the carefully established relationships among the different elements in

2. The bottom of the base is partially coated with shellac applied to hide the new holes. It has not been possible to establish when this was carried out.

3. It is probable that the repair of the zigzag shape (see CONDITION) took place at the same time, both repairs possibly following upon a fall in which the various pieces became detached and in part broken. The earliest publication of the present organization of the pieces is in Alley, 1964.

fig. c.
Photograph of cat. no. 66 as reproduced by Art of This Century, 1942-45. The wood elements are not in their original positions.

Giacometti's plaster model had been faithfully executed by the cabinetmaker. (László Gloser pointed out that Man Ray took pains to photograph the piece in an appropriately surrealist "light." *Picasso und der Surrealismus*, Cologne, 1974, p. 56.)

The evidence clearly indicates that the present orientations of the hemisphere (slightly altered) and of the stele (completely reversed) are considerably at variance with Giacometti's original composition.[4]

Projet pour une place must have been executed in plaster (fig. a) by 1931, since the completed wood version was reproduced in *Cahiers d'Art* in 1932. In addition, Giacometti's well-known drawing *Objets mobiles et muets*, which includes a sketch of *Projet pour une place*, was published by December 1931 (see REFERENCES).

Giacometti attached great importance to the *Projet*. He intended it to be executed as a larger-than-life outdoor sculpture in stone.[5] People were to be able to walk through it, sit on parts of it, and respond at first hand to its individual elements. As he later wrote to Pierre Matisse: "*Je voulais qu'on puisse marcher sur la sculpture s'y assayer* [sic] *et s'y appuyer*" (1948, p. 40).

4. When confronted in 1982 with a photograph of the wood piece in its present disposition, Diego Giacometti responded at a single glance: "*Mais c'est complètement faux. Il faut que ce soit remplacé... comme ça... il faut le tourner*," gesturing with his hands as if to turn the stele around and also to adjust the position of the "complementary" hemisphere. When the photo of the original plaster (fig. a) was produced for comparison, he said: "*Oui, c'est ça; c'est juste comme ça. Mais l'autre, ce n'est pas juste du tout. C'est impossible.*" (Conversation with the author, Apr. 1982.) Diego Giacometti's instantaneous and emphatic response to an image he had not seen for approximately 4 decades reveals the extraordinary sensitivity he has always had to every detail of his brother's work, and reinforces the notion, so obviously inherent in all aspects of Alberto Giacometti's oeuvre, that the subtle interrelationships that exist between 1 form and another are crucial ingredients in his tautly economical, expressive language. (For a discussion of further examples of this issue, see below, cat. no. 70.)

5. The caption under Man Ray's 1932 photograph (fig. b), which describes the piece "*en pierre*," refers specifically to this ambition, rather than to any existing sculpture.

fig. d.
Giacometti, *Progetti per cose grandi all' aperto*, ca. 1931, ink on paper, 4 3/4 x 4 1/16 in., 12 x 10.4 cm., signed l.r.: *Alberto Giacometti*, not dated, Collection Eberhard Kornfeld, Bern.

fig. e.
Brassaï, Interior of Giacometti's studio in 1932, showing the over life-size plaster pieces for *Projet pour une place* and the plaster of *Femme égorgée*. Photograph courtesy Brassaï.

A drawing probably executed in about 1931 (fig. d) testifies to Giacometti's ambitions for the piece. Labeled "*progetti per cose grandi all'aperto*," it contains sketches for several projects, among which is the *Projet pour une place* presented as if it were already executed in stone ("pietra"), with a human figure added in order to indicate the scale.

Giacometti was, according to his brother's testimony, sufficiently anxious to find a patron for this undertaking that he decided (with Diego Giacometti's help) to execute the individual parts full size in plaster. This was in fact accomplished, and the large cumbersome objects — the tallest of which was about two meters high — stood in the small, cramped studio for many months until they were finally discarded (fig. e).[6]

The precise location of this project within Giacometti's oeuvre remains to some extent unresolved. It has been suggested that its origin must be associated with a commission Giacometti received from the Vicomte de Noailles for a large garden sculpture. Evidence on this particular point is, however, lacking, and it seems more likely that the *Projet* was conceived quite independently.

6. Diego Giacometti, in conversation with the author, spoke of the intense feeling Alberto had for this project, and how disappointed he was that it was never brought to realization. He also said that the giant plaster pieces took up so much room in the studio that they eventually had to be destroyed.

It was early in 1930, as Michael F. Brenson first demonstrated, that the Vicomte de Noailles commissioned Giacometti to execute a sculpture for the garden of his château at St. Bernard, Hyères.[7] This piece, *Figure dans un jardin*, was completed in August 1933. The sculpture was the third monumental piece commissioned for the garden, preceded by Lipchitz's *Joie de Vivre* (1927) — a tall cylindrical bronze, which was placed on a high pedestal in the garden, and a marble sculpture by Laurens (1928), which was placed on the roof of the château. The Vicomte de Noailles and Giacometti decided that his piece should be very different: "*Il était question de silhouette étrange et mystérieuse, une ou plusieurs qui seraient placées dans le jardin*" (letter from the Vicomte to M. F. Brenson. Feb. 14, 1972).

The commission was, according to material in the de Noailles archives, received by Giacometti in January or February of 1930. Brenson has proposed that the over life-size figures in plaster for *Projet pour une place* (visible in the 1932 photograph of the studio, fig. e) were made in explicit response to the de Noailles commission, as the first step toward its realization. He also suggested that only after building these large-size plaster pieces was Giacometti able to evolve the distinctive group of three standing plaster silhouettes, *Trois personnages dans un pré*, which served as the basis for the piece that was installed at the château (see footnote 7).

Brenson has shown that in September 1930, Giacometti—who had previously depended on descriptions of the de Noailles estate and the site for his sculpture there — visited Hyères for the first time. Giacometti showed the Vicomte photographs of the plaster *Trois personnages dans un pré*, which were clearly well received. In a letter to Giacometti of September 27, de Noailles refers to "*les personnages mystérieux d'Hyères.*" By the end of November, however, Giacometti had decided to reduce the number of figures from three to one. Early in 1931 he ordered the stone from a quarry in Burgundy, where Diego went to work on the initial cutting of the figure.[8] When the stone had been cut to approximately the right size for the intended piece, it was transported to Hyères and installed in the garden (April 1931). The two brothers worked on it *in situ* during parts of the spring of 1931 and the spring of 1932. When they returned

7. For a photograph of the single abstract figure of the completed de Noailles commission (ca. 8 ft., 2.5 m. high), see R. Hohl, "Odysseus und Kalypso..." *Arnold Böcklin*, exh. cat., Kunstmuseum, Basel, 1977, p. 117. For a photograph of the initial conception, showing 3 tall stele-like figures standing in a landscape (the so-called *Trois personnages dans un pré*), see C. Giedion-Welcker, "Ein Gespräch in Maloja," *Du*, Feb. 1962, p. 28, where the caption erroneously dates the figures 1927. These plaster figures were actually made full scale in 1930 by Alberto and Diego and placed in a field in Maloja. The 2 brothers then photographed the figures and left them there, where they eventually disintegrated. The chronological facts relating to the Hyères commission, as presented here, are largely dependent on Brenson's extremely illuminating research and presentation (1974, pp. 94ff.).

8. For a description of the nature of Diego's collaboration with Alberto on this piece, see Brenson, p. 97. Alberto drew the outlines onto the stone, but Diego did most of the carving.

to Paris in June 1932, the work was almost finished. In August 1933, Alberto returned to Hyères once more to make the final adjustments.

To summarize: The commission was received in January or February of 1930. The only documented first conception is *Les trois personnages dans un pré*, which the Vicomte approved in late September of that year. Giacometti then decided to reduce the three figures to one. By the spring of 1931 some work had been done by Diego on cutting the Burgundy stone down to size; during the springs of 1931 and 1932 both brothers periodically worked at the piece, and on a short visit in August 1933 Alberto completed it.

Although Brenson's research has made it possible to trace the chronology for the evolution of this commission in detail, the relationship between the *Projet pour une place* and the *Figure dans un jardin* remains to be established. As already suggested, there is no concrete evidence for the hypothesis that the *Projet* constituted Giacometti's first idea for the Hyères commission. An analysis of the château site, moreover, raises serious doubts as to whether Giacometti would have intended so complex and large a group as the *Projet* (perhaps as much as three meters across, according to the proportions in the drawing, fig. d) for so restricted an area. (The piece was to be placed at the corner of a terrace not far from the entrance to the château; see Brenson, 1974, p. 95.)

It seems more likely that, after completing *Trois personnages dans un pré* late in 1930, Giacometti continued to concern himself with the general concept of "*progetti per cose grandi all'aperto*." Since he had one large commission in progress—and had long stretches of time when he could not work on the project —he might well have begun sketches and plans for a new piece in the hope of acquiring a second commission. The publication of Man Ray's photograph in the 1932 *Cahiers d'Art* (fig. b), suggesting that this was a project "to be executed in stone," may even have been intended to serve as an incentive to patronage.[9]

Diego Giacometti has confirmed (in conversations with the author, Apr. and Nov. 1982) that, insofar as he can recall, the *Projet pour une place* bore no relation to the Hyères commission. He felt certain that the small plaster version of *Projet pour une plâce* came first and was followed by the wood, and that only as a third stage—specifically in the hope of attracting a commission—did the brothers make the large pieces in plaster (fig. e). The desired commission never materialized and this second project had to be abandoned, while the first —that for Hyères—was completed soon thereafter. It would seem likely that the approximate date for the various versions of the *Projet pour une place* (small

9. Further evidence to support the notion that *Projet pour une place* was a separate idea following upon the Noailles *Figure* is provided by Giacometti's provisional catalogue of early works (Pierre Matisse, 1948, handwritten facsimile, p. 4). Though the drawing of *Projet* immediately precedes that of *Figure*, the former is dated by Giacometti "1932?," the latter "1931-32." Thus, although he was unable to recall with precision the actual years involved, Giacometti did apparently think of the *Projet* as something that followed (rather than preceded) the development of the single *Figure*. His *artistic* memory—involving chronological relationships, as opposed to literal dates—is liable to have been accurate.

plaster model, wood version, and large individual plaster pieces) would be early 1931 to early 1932, although it is possible that all three versions were completed by the end of 1931.[10]

Brenson and Reinhold Hohl have each offered interpretations of the iconography of *Projet pour une place*. According to Brenson's account, "The forms can be understood as the disassociated or disassembled parts of a man and a woman. The tallest form has the concavity and the contraction of so many of Giacometti's women.... The zigzag resembles the neck of the female in the 1929 *Homme et Femme*." He sees the smooth hollowed "crater" as possibly a female head, the concave hemisphere as possibly a male head, the cone as a phallus. The entire female is thus represented by the central vertical, the zigzag, the slab, and the "crater"; the male by the concave hemisphere and the cone (p. 67). From a different point of view, Brenson suggests that the work may be understood as a series of images identified with memories of childhood (p. 68).

Hohl, on the other hand, sees the Surrealist sculpture of Giacometti as profoundly metaphorical. He proposes an interpretation essentially dealing with the gulf between the sexes and compares the metaphor of *Projet pour une place* with that of Böcklin's *Odysseus and Calypso* (1974, pp. 29-30; 1977, p. 117). According to his reading, the cone represents "woman," the stele "tree." The hollow hemisphere is "head" (knowledge, reflection—that which hinders man's integration into nature and comes between man and woman). The zigzag form is a serpent, and the composition as a whole is seen as an Expulsion from Paradise.

EXHIBITIONS:

New York, Art of This Century, 1942-47, p. 120, repr. (as *Model for a Garden*, the title attributed to it in all *P.G.* publications); New York, Art of This Century, *A. Giacometti*, Feb. 10-Mar. 10 [16], 1945, no. 7; Venice, *P.G.*, 1948 (Biennale), no. 49; Florence, *P.G.*, 1949, no. 53; Amsterdam, *P.G*, 1951, no. 61; London, *P.G.*, 1964-65, no. 109, repr.; Stockholm, *P.G.*, 1966-67, no. 54, repr.; New York, *P.G.*, 1969, p. 121, repr.; Paris, *P.G.*, 1974-75, no. 112, repr.; Torino, *P.G.*, 1975-76, no. 124.

REFERENCES:

A. Giacometti, "Objets mobiles et muets," *Le Surréalisme au Service de la Révolution*, no. 3, Paris, Dec. 1931, p. 18; C. Zervos, "Quelques notes sur les sculptures de Giacometti," *Cahiers d'Art*, vol. 7, nos. 8-10, 1932, repr. p. 341 (see fig. b here); P. Guggenheim, *Art of This Century*, New York, 1942, p. 120, repr. (see fig. c here, which records the condition of the piece as shown at Art of This Century); *View*, 4th ser., no. 4, Dec. 1944, repr. p. 112 (an advertisement for Giacometti exhibition at Art of This Century); *Giacometti*, exh. cat., Art of This Century, New York, 1945, repr. back cover (as above); A. Giacometti, letter to Pierre Matisse, *Giacometti*, exh. cat., Pierre Matisse Gallery, New York, 1948, p. 41; J. Dupin, *A. Giacometti*, Paris, 1963, repr. p. 207 (the plaster, dated 1931); F. Meyer, *Giacometti*, Stuttgart, 1968, pp. 76-78 (dated 1931); R.

10. In addition to being the subject of Brassaï's 1932 photograph (fig. e), the large-scale plasters are also visible in Giacometti's 1932 drawings of his studio (see below, cat. no. 68, figs. c and d). The small *Projet* is also seen in these drawings, though whether it is the plaster or the wood version is not clear.

Hohl, "Alberto Giacometti's Atelier im Jahr 1932," *Du*, May 1971, pp. 361-62; idem, *A. Giacometti*, London, 1972, pp. 79, 298, fn. 17, repr. p. 58 (plaster); C. Huber, "Alberto Giacometti: Palais à Quatre heures du matin, 1932," *Jahresbericht der öffentlichen Kunstsammlung Basel*, 1967-73, pp. 181-82; R. Hohl, *Giacometti*, exh. cat., SRGM, New York, 1974, pp. 22, 29, 30, repr. p. 16 (plaster); M. F. Brenson, "The Early Work of Giacometti: 1925-35," unpublished Ph.D. dissertation, Johns Hopkins University, 1974, pp. 65-66, 68-69, 78-79, 94, 96, 187; R. Hohl, "Odysseus und Kalypso: Der Mythus der existentiellen Impotenz bei Arnold Böcklin und Alberto Giacometti," *Arnold Böcklin*, exh. cat., Kunstmuseum, Basel, 1977, p. 117; D. Hall, *Alberto Giacometti's Woman with Her Throat Cut*, The Scottish National Gallery of Modern Art, 1980, p. 12.

---

67 Femme qui marche. 1932.
(*Woman walking*).

76.2553 PG 132

Plaster, iron wire armature. Height without base: 54¾ (139); height of base along left (viewer's) side: 3¾ (9.5); height along right side: 4⁵⁄₁₆ (11.0); depth of base: 14⁹⁄₁₆ (37); width of base: 9⁷⁄₁₆ (24); width across shoulders: 10¹¹⁄₁₆ (27.2).

Signed and dated on top of base (incised into the plaster): *Alberto Giacometti / 1932-36.*[1]

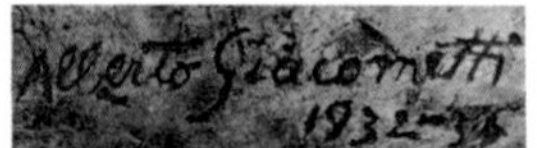

PROVENANCE:

Purchased from the artist, Paris, by Pierre Matisse, October 1936;[2] purchased from Pierre Matisse, New York, October 15, 1941.[3]

CONDITION:

At an unspecified date, the bottom of the base was built up with gesso on 2 sides and a portion of a third to compensate for losses in those areas and to reestablish the correct slope of the base and resulting perpendicular position of the figure.

There are severe cracks in the lower legs and ankles and some losses. The surface is abraded, darkened, stained, and worn; the piece is inherently fragile. (Venice, June 1983.)

Femme qui marche exists in two versions, both of which have been cast in bronze.[4] The other *Femme*, which is almost identical in size to the Peggy Guggenheim piece, has a small triangular indentation below the breasts on the central axis of the body (repr. R. Hohl, 1971, p. 70). This is almost certainly—as suggested by Ronald Alley—the work that is visible in Giacometti's 1932 drawing of his studio (see below, cat. no. 68, fig. c).[5]

1. According to Diego Giacometti (in conversation with the author, Apr. 2, 1982) the piece had been complete since long before 1936, a fact that is borne out by the Brassaï photographs made in 1932 and so dated in the latter's record book (figs. c and d). When Pierre Matisse came to purchase the work in October 1936 it had been standing in Giacometti's studio for 4 years and was slightly damaged. Giacometti apparently restored it and added the date at that time.
2. A letter from Giacometti to his mother dated October 21, 1936, speaks of the sale with delight. Information supplied by James Lord, Paris.
3. Pierre Matisse supplied the precise date of sale.

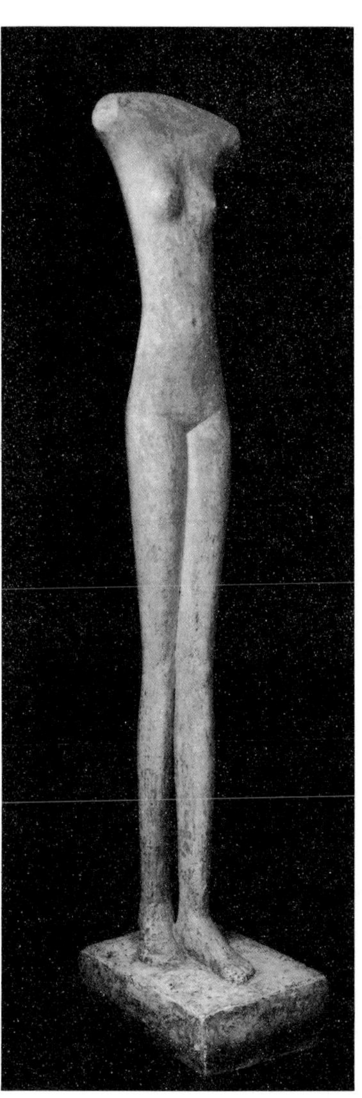

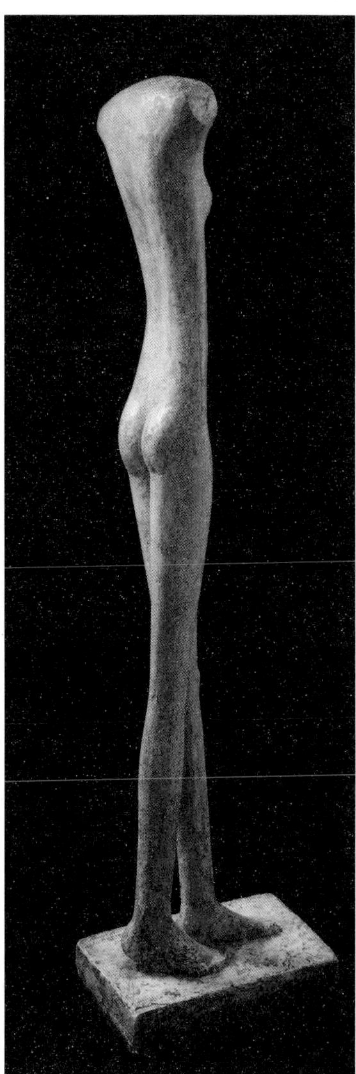

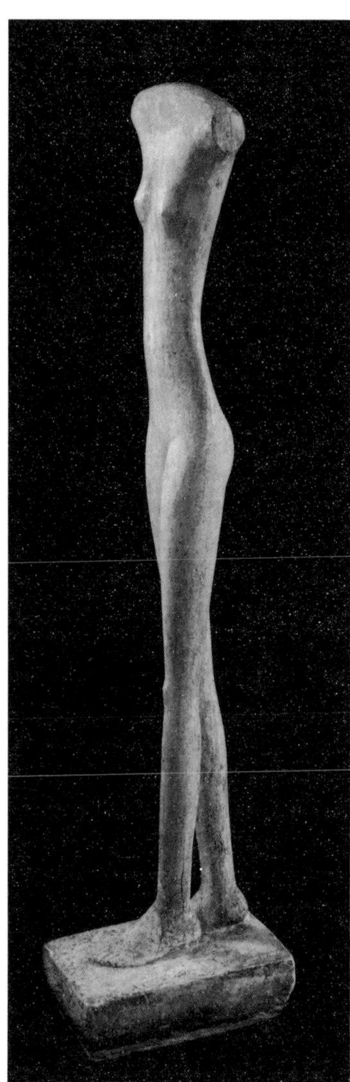

4. Giacometti authorized Peggy Guggenheim to cast an edition of 6 bronzes from her plaster and to sell them. The edition was completed in 1961 at the Fonderia Artistica Ferruccio Bianchi, Venice; the sixth cast was given by Peggy Guggenheim to the artist, who later gave it away. In 1969, 3 years after the artist's death, Peggy Guggenheim had an additional (unauthorized) cast made from the original plaster at the foundry of Stefan Costi, Treviso. Of these 7 authentic casts from Giacometti's original plaster, 1 is in the Peggy Guggenheim Collection, 1 in the collection of the SRGM, New York. The locations of the other 5 casts have not been firmly established by the author, although 4 of them are probably in private collections. The identification of the casts from this edition (which carry no foundry marks and several of which seem to be unnumbered) has become additionally complicated in recent years: a number of *surmoulages*, made without Peggy Guggenheim's knowledge, have begun to appear on the market in Europe and the United States.

   A cast of the version with indentation is in the collection of The Tate Gallery, London (Alley, 1981, pp. 276-77, repr.), and the original plaster, formerly in the collection of Erica Brausen, London, is in a private collection in Paris. Reinhold Hohl and Michael Brenson have each suggested that there were additional *Femme qui marche:* at least 1 (Hohl) and maybe 2 (Brenson). It seems more probable, as proposed here, that there were in fact only 2 altogether, 1 of which was first altered in 1933 and then again in 1936 (see below).

5. Brenson suggests tentatively that this is yet another version, 1974, p. 194, fn. 13.

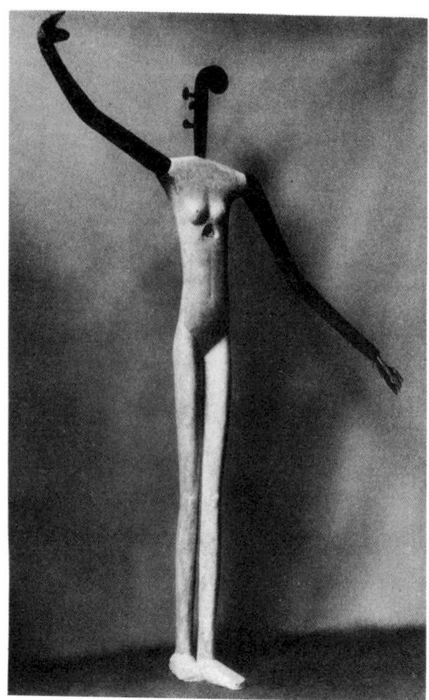

fig. a.
Giacometti, *Mannequin*. The original plaster of the *Femme qui marche* (with indentation), height: ca. 67 in., 170 cm. The plaster arms and head, painted black, were added on the occasion of the 1933 Pierre Colle exhibition. Photograph by Marc Vaux.

fig. b.
Giacometti's *Mannequin* with head and arms painted white, probably as installed in *The International Surrealist Exhibition*, London, 1936, although some of the works shown are not listed in the catalogue.

In the following year, Giacometti changed this second piece radically (fig. a), adding plaster arms and a head, all painted black. The head consisted of the neck, scroll, and pegs of a cello (reminiscent of Magritte's 1926 *L'homme du large*); a claw was attached to the end of the figure's left arm, a bunch of feathers to the right. The occasion for these additions was — as Alley suggested — the June 1933 Surrealist exhibition at the Galerie Pierre Colle where the sculpture appeared as *Mannequin*.

Diego Giacometti recalled (in conversation with the author, Apr. 1982) that these elements were added to the existing *Femme qui marche* (with indentation) "*à la romaine*" — i.e., in such a way that they might be easily removed. Diego himself made the arms and head, with projecting square elements that could be slipped in and out of square cavities carved into the plaster.

Giacometti later decided to send the same sculpture to London for the June 11-July 4, 1936 *International Surrealist Exhibition*; it was probably at this time that he painted the arms and head white (fig. b). Soon after the exhibition opened, however, and for reasons that are not entirely clear, the arms and head were removed. Indeed, as Alley pointed out (1981, p. 277), a London newspaper report on the show commented (three days after the opening) that the sculpture had been temporarily withdrawn from exhibition.[6] The withdrawal was clearly arranged in order to permit removal of the arms (and head) of the piece. According to the testimony of Diego Giacometti, James Lord, and David Sylvester, Alberto did not visit London before 1955, and hence could not have performed this task.[7]

Nonetheless, had the arms become too loose to sustain their position, it would have been perfectly plausible for one of the organizers of the exhibition to contact Giacometti and ask for his advice. He could then have suggested that the head and arms be slipped out and the cavities simply plastered over. This is presumably what occurred.

To summarize: Giacometti made only two versions of the *Femme qui marche*. One (Peggy Guggenheim's) remained in Giacometti's studio without interruption from its creation in 1932 until Pierre Matisse bought it in 1936. The other was changed into *Mannequin* in 1933 through the addition of black appendages. These were painted white by 1936. By about the middle of June 1936, the *Femme* was returned to its original state—the head and arms removed and the cavities plastered over.

It was in this condition that Sir Roland Penrose purchased the piece—during the London exhibition; shortly thereafter he sold it to Valerie Cooper; in 1955 it was acquired by Erica Brausen and a bronze edition was cast.

The precise dates of the two versions are difficult to establish with certainty. Alley has concluded that the version with an indentation was produced first, and he cites Diego Giacometti as the source for this information. Brenson (1974, pp. 166-67) places the Peggy Guggenheim plaster first, and he persuasively identifies a number of important differences between what he calls the "first" and the "second" conceptions, although he does not define those differences in terms of a stylistic progression.

Diego Giacometti (in conversation with the author, April and November 1982) stated that the Peggy Guggenheim plaster must have preceded the other, because of its greater simplicity; the version with the identation would have been conceived afterward, as a variation and an elaboration on the initial theme.

Interpretations of the *Femme qui marche* have been offered by Hohl and Brenson. Hohl, in comparing the indentation below the breasts with a similar "cavity" in *1 + 1 = 3* (1934), suggests that both hollows represent "the invisible

6. *The Sunday Referee*, June 14, 1936, p. 16, apparently reproducing the sculpture with arms but not a head, suggesting that the additions were not all removed at the same time. Though the installation view in fig. b has not hitherto been identified with the London exhibition, the presence of other objects exhibited there—but not in Paris—argues for this identification.

7. Sir Roland Penrose purchased the sculpture out of the exhibition. He recalled (in conversation with Alley) that the sculpture arrived in London with white arms, though not—he thought—with a head. He thought also that Alberto had been in London and had removed the arms soon after the exhibition opened. Sir Roland's recollections were clearly for the most part correct, e.g., the fact that there *were* white additions, and that they were removed soon after the exhibition opened. The discrepancy between the installation photo (fig. b) and that in the *Sunday Referee* does suggest that there was a time lapse of a few days between the one removal and the other.

fig. c.
Cat. no. 67 in Giacometti's studio, 1932.
Photograph courtesy Brassaï.

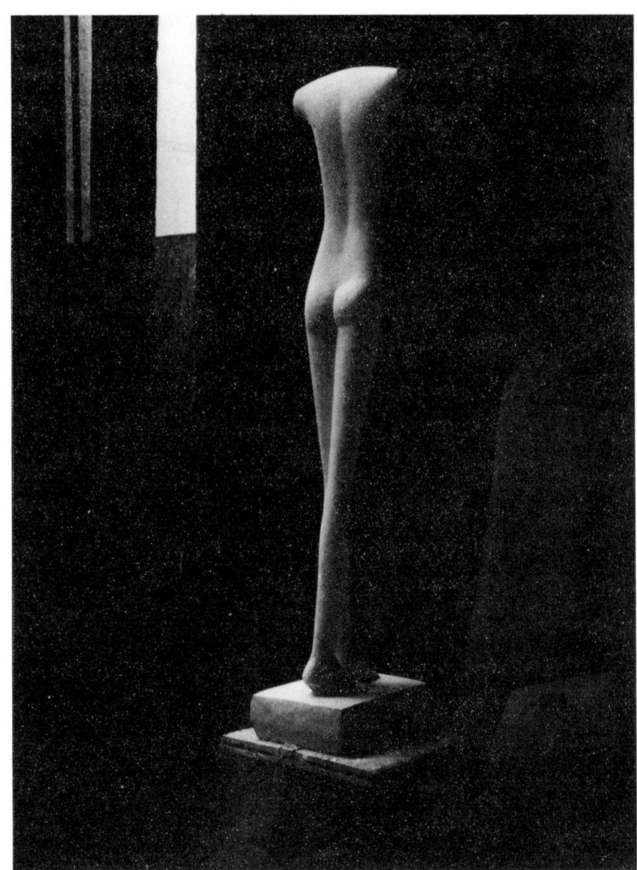

fig. d.
Cat. no. 67 in Giacometti's studio, 1932.
Photograph courtesy Brassaï.

object" or, rather, the spaces left for it. Treating *1 + 1 = 3*, *The Invisible Object*, and the versions of the *Femme qui marche* as a group, Hohl observes that they embrace a similar theme concerning the continuity of life, a counterpoint to the theme of death he perceives in *No More Play*. "Taken as a whole, the series shows that Giacometti was not merely making Surrealist objects during these years, but was trying to actualize a comprehensive compositional idea" (1971, p. 104).

Brenson sees different sets of implications in the two *Femme qui marche* versions. In the first (Peggy Guggenheim's), he sees a "haunting and elusive presence," on the one hand "fluid" and "tactile," on the other "physically and psychologically inaccessible." In the second version, he reads the combination of breasts and indentation as a face. The impression created by the piece is ambiguous: the "face" expresses fear, while the figure in its entirety represents a mixture of oppression and vulnerability (1974, pp. 166-168).

Giacometti's own comment about *1 + 1 = 3*, revealing in its very restraint, may also have some relevance to *Femme qui marche*: he saw it as the last figure in a series in which he had tried to combine the natural human forms that fascinated him with the nonobjective forms he thought were inappropriate for sculpture (cited by Hohl, 1971, p. 104).

EXHIBITIONS:

New York, Art of This Century, 1942-47, p. 120 (dated 1934, the date ascribed to it in all *P.G.* publications until 1974); New York, Art of This Century, *Giacometti*, Feb. 10-Mar. 10 [16], 1945, no. 8; Venice, *P.G.*, 1948 (Biennale), no. 50; Florence, *P.G.*, 1949, no. 54; Venice, Giardino, 1949, no. 8; Amsterdam, *P.G.*, 1951. no. 62; Zurich, *P.G.*, 1951, no. 58; Paris, *P.G.*, 1974-75, no. 114, repr. (dated 1932-36).

REFERENCES:

P. Guggenheim, *Art of This Century*, 1942, p. 120; A. Giacometti, handwritten "Tentative catalogue of early works," published in *Alberto Giacometti*, exh. cat., Pierre Matisse Gallery, New York, 1948, between pp. 24 and 25 (a sketch labeled "femme qui marche, plâtre 1933. P. Matisse"); P. Guggenheim, *Confessions*, 1960, pp. 131-32; C. Giedion-Welcker, Alberto Giacometti," *Kunstwerk*, nos. 1-2, 1966, repr. p. 7 (dated 1934); J. Dupin, *A. Giacometti*, Paris, 1963, pp. 217-18 (dated 1932-34, erroneously described as bronze); R. Hohl, *Alberto Giacometti: Sculpture, Painting, Drawing*, London, 1971, pp. 103-4, 300, fn. 33, repr. p. 70 (the other version, with and without arms, in plaster, dated 1932); M. F. Brenson, "The Early Work of Giacometti: 1925-1935," unpublished Ph.D. dissertation, Johns Hopkins University, 1974, pp. 166-71; Alley, *Tate Collection*, 1981, pp. 276-77.

---

68 Femme égorgée. 1932 (cast 1940).
(*Woman with her throat cut*).

76.2553 PG 131

Bronze solid cast (sand cast) with dark brown-black patina. Width (at greatest diagonal extent): 35 1/16 (89); height: 9 1/8 (23.2).

Edition of six.[1]

Foundry: Alexis Rudier, Paris.[1]

Not signed, dated, or numbered. No foundry mark.

PROVENANCE:

Purchased from the aritst, Paris, 1940.

CONDITION:

In March 1984 (Venice) the piece was cleaned. The surface was degreased with trichloroethylene, and washed with distilled water, then with distilled water and neutral detergent; it was rinsed with distilled water, and dried with alcohol and acetone. The surface was treated for 30 minutes with a 3% solution of benzotriazole in pure alcohol. A protective coating of microcrystalline wax was applied.

Some slight abrasion of the movable element has occurred. The condition is otherwise stable. (Venice, Mar. 1984.)

1. Peggy Guggenheim's bronze was the first cast, and bears no marks of any kind. Pierre Matisse's was the second cast, and bears the number 2/5 (Pierre Matisse, in conversation with the author, Mar. 8, 1982). The rest of the casts were made by Rudier under Giacometti's supervision in 1949 from Pierre Matisse's bronze, which was sent to Paris for this purpose. The original plaster was no longer available at that time. Diego Giacometti (in conversation with the author, Apr. 1982) explained that the complexity of the piece, which had to be molded in several pieces, necessitated breakage of the plaster original by the time the casting process was finished. The locations of these 3 additional casts, all of which are numbered, and dated 1932, are: Kunsthaus Zurich, Alberto Giacometti Stiftung, 3/5; MoMA, New York, 4/5; Scottish National Gallery of Art, 5/5, formerly Nelson Rockefeller Collection.

The evolution of Giacometti's *Femme égorgée* can be traced with some precision from its earliest inception in 1930 until its completion in 1932.[2]

Sometime in 1930, Giacometti was commissioned by Pierre David-Weill to make two "firedog" andirons and a "wall-relief." He received this commission through the intervention of Masson, who was executing works for David-Weill at the time. The relief sculpture Giacometti produced, entitled *Femme en forme d'araignée* (repr. R. Hohl, 1971, p. 361), was cast in bronze in approximately 1930 and remained in the David-Weill collection until World War II, when it

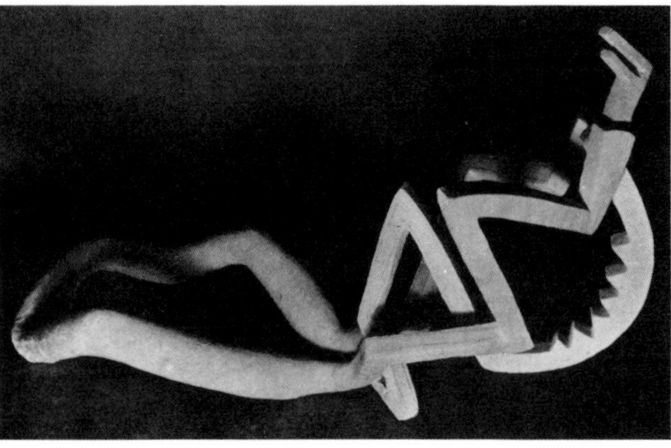

fig. a.
Giacometti, *Femme angoissé dans une chambre la nuit*, 1931-32, plaster, destroyed, ca. 39⅜ in., 100 cm., repr. *Cahiers d'Art*, vol. 7, nos. 1-2, 1932, p. 339. Photograph by Man Ray (present whereabouts unknown), 1932.

was lost; it has never been recovered.[3] A drawing exists, however, of *Femme en forme d'araignée* suspended from a string, directly above the bed in one of two extremely detailed depictions Giacometti made of his own studio in 1932 (fig. c). By that time, the sculpture was apparently complete since its appearance in the drawing closely approximates the work as executed.

Not long afterward, Giacometti produced a large plaster figure entitled *Femme angoissée dans une chambre la nuit* (fig. a). This plaster was photographed by Man Ray and published in an article by Christian Zervos in *Cahiers d'Art*, where Zervos wrote:

> *L'attachement de Giacometti à la technique de la sculpture, se manifeste tout particulièrement dans la figure de femme qu'il fut amené par le hasard des circonstances à réaliser ces temps derniers. Cette figure singulière opère un charme magique sur le spectateur. Il s'en dégage quelque chose de satanique qui exerce une violente prise sur l'imagination et produit sur les nerfs une sensation presque douloureuse. Par son expression, cette figure n'aurait pas manqué d'arracher l'attention des spectateurs et de procurer à l'artiste des éloges ou des critiques violentes. Seulement Giacometti n'est pas satisfait de tout ce qui peut donner à son œuvre un air d'artifice. Il a donc préféré reprendre cette figure entièrement pour en poursuivre l'accomplissement plastique dans les formes les plus harmonieuses. Il travaille sans répit à clarifier cette figure à en rendre les formes les plus parfaites possibles, tout en faisant sortir de préférence son caractère d'énigme. C'est l'image vraie des choses vivantes; une surface simple et des dessous mystérieux* (*Cahiers d'Art*, vol. 7, nos. 8-10, 1932, p. 342).

Although he continued to struggle with *Femme angoissée*, Giacometti was apparently never able to resolve its difficulties, at least to his own satisfaction.

2. Much of the information contributing to an understanding of the evolution of this piece has been assembled by Reinhold Hohl in his comprehensive article of 1971 (*Du*). For a further illuminating analysis, see Hall, 1980.
3. Information supplied by Michel David-Weill (son of Pierre), New York, March 1982. Pierre David-Weill apparently referred to Giacometti's sculpture as "Dragon-bronze" (see R. Hohl, *Alberto Giacometti*, exh. cat., Duisburg, 1977, p. 119). Hohl places *Femme en forme d'araignée* later in the sequence of related pieces than does the present author.

fig. c.
Giacometti, *Dessin de mon atelier*, 1932, pencil on paper, 12½ x 17¾ in., 31.8 x 45 cm., Kunstmuseum, Basel, Kupferstichkabinett, Inv. No. 1972.12.

fig. d.
Giacometti, *Dessin de mon atelier*, 1932, pencil on paper, 12⅞ x 19⅜ in., 32.7 x 49.3 cm., Kunstmuseum, Basel, Kupferstichkabinett, Inv. No. 1971.416.

According to Diego Giacometti (in conversation with the author), the piece—which was almost two meters long and hence occupied a considerable amount of space—remained in the studio for some time, but was eventually discarded.[4]

During the second half of 1932, Giacometti also finished the two meticulous drawings of his studio mentioned above (figs. c and d). The drawings contain what is in effect an informal inventory of Giacometti's sculptures produced by that time, some still in process but many complete. In the foreground of fig. d, there is a reclining figure closely resembling *Femme angoissée* in its curvilinear contour, the handling of the legs, and the upward thrust of the head and neck, though it is slightly more naturalistic in its overall rendering.

According to Diego Giacometti, this piece never advanced beyond the sketch stage and was not executed in plaster. Nonetheless, it represents a stage in Giacometti's continuing efforts to experiment with various possible solutions for *Femme angoissée*. It is possible, although external evidence for a precise chronology is lacking, that this sketched figure—in its tentativeness, simplicity, and greater naturalism—may have preceded the plaster *Femme angoissée*.

Two other related drawings (on one sheet; fig. b) are also difficult to place within the chronology, though the lower one probably represents an intermediate phase between *Femme angoissée* and *Femme égorgée*. The figure in this

fig. b.
Giacometti, Studies for cat. no. 68, 1932, pencil on paper, 13⅛ x 8⅝ in., 33.4 x 22 cm., Musée National d'Art Moderne, Centre Georges Pompidou, Paris.

4. Peggy Guggenheim recounted in her 1946 memoirs the now oft-quoted story that she had found a Giacometti plaster in a Paris gallery, brought it to Giacometti for repair, and been persuaded by him to take *Femme égorgée* instead. J. Leymarie, in his catalogue for Peggy Guggenheim's Paris exhibition (Paris, *P.G.*, 1974-75, p. 92), identified the statue in question as *Femme angoissée*. It is possible that it survived until 1940 and somehow found its way into the hands of a gallery owner. Diego Giacometti, however, suspects that the *Femme angoissée* "perished" much earlier (conversation with the author, Apr. 1982).

fig. e.
Giacometti, *Femme égorgée*, original plaster, present whereabouts unknown.
Photograph courtesy Brassaï.

sketch, with its elongated torso and limbs disposed in ways related to those of *Femme angoissée*, nonetheless has a prominent long neck (with circular "rings") that brings it into immediate relationship with *Femme égorgée*. The ultimate conception of *Femme égorgée*—with its open spiked body flat on the ground—has not yet been achieved, but certain important elements are already present.

The upper sketch is in many respects far closer to *Femme égorgée*; the figure lies fully on its back, its neck sharply bent and "cut" (though lacking the encircling rings). The highly stylized character of the drawing suggests, however, that it may indeed postdate *Femme égorgée* and be related to yet another project.[5]

The plaster version of *Femme égorgée* was completed by the fall of 1932 when Brassaï photographed it (fig. e). Brassaï's photograph presents the object precisely as Giacometti intended it to be viewed: the pod (or phallus) form rested in the hand (or claw), as Giacometti himself always placed it, and the piece was to be shown directly on the floor without a base.[6]

By eliminating the base altogether, Giacometti achieved a striking resolution (anticipated in some of his own earlier work) of a persistent dilemma in modern sculpture. *Femme égorgée*—given its particular form and its clearly horizontal

5. This drawing and a third even more highly stylized version (Graphische Sammlung, Staatsgalerie, Stuttgart, inv. no. C79/2916) may have been produced in connection with Giacometti's 1933 drawing for *Minotaure*, nos. 3-4, Dec. 12, 1933, p. 78. That issue of the journal contained Jacques Lacan's article on a gruesome double murder by the Papin sisters. Meanwhile, during the same year, Violette Nozières's murder of her parents had absorbed the attention of many of the Surrealists, including, probably, Giacometti. His preoccupation with murder and violence would thus have been sustained in various ways.

6. Diego Giacometti was explicit on this point, though he made no attempt to characterize the form.

disposition — would have posed unusually difficult problems with respect to the notion of a base. William Rubin has suggested that Giacometti "saw the issue through to one of its logical conclusions" by simply placing his sculptured figure on the floor: "The elements of its vaguely crustacean female anatomy — and hence the reading of its sexually violent iconography — can be apprehended only from above." (*Dada, Surrealism, and Their Heritage*, exh. cat., MoMA, 1968, p. 116. For a discussion of the issue of horizontality in Giacometti's work of the early 1930s, see R. Krauss, "Giacometti," in W. Rubin, ed., *"Primitivism" in 20th Century Art: Affinity of the Tribal and the Modern*, New York, 1984, pp. 502-33.)

Reinhold Hohl (1971) has offered a detailed explanation of the genesis of the two studio drawings (figs. c and d), and in the process has offered an interpretation of *Femme égorgée*. According to Hohl, Giacometti met the Italian noblewoman Donna Madina Arrivabene Valenti Gonzaga (later the Contessa Visconti) at a Paris soirée in the early spring of 1932. She made several visits to Giacometti's studio, where he sketched portraits of her in pencil. Hohl proposes that it was within the context of this relationship that Giacometti produced the two meticulous drawings of his studio, one of which was almost certainly dedicated to Donna Medina and bears the inscription: "*dessin de mon atelier que vous m'avez fait la grande joie de ne pas le* [sic] *trouver détestable*."

Hohl also suggests (though without specifying the evidence) that Giacometti once warned the Contessa that her unusually long and beautiful neck was in effect fatally tempting — almost inviting strangulation or throat-cutting. It was precisely such a vision of beauty as evocative of danger — as an actual incitement to violence — that shaped part of the conception underlying *Femme angoissée*.

Hohl views *Femme égorgée* in its totality as a work combining the images of the David-Weill sculpture with that of *Femme angoissée*. The threatening female-spider figure of the earlier work and the more passive suffering figure of *Femme angoissée* are imaginatively fused to produce a new creature that is both menacing and victimized. In Hohl's view, this new image gives expression to Giacometti's ambivalent feelings regarding the dual nature of women as well as alluding to the tantalizing figure of the Contessa.

Michael Brenson (1974) sees evidence of ambivalence and duality not only in *Femme égorgée* but in *Femme angoissée*. Both works suggest the open, vulnerable, accessible nature of women associated with procreation and life; both also communicate a sense of danger, menace, and even revulsion. Brenson points out that this fusion of conflicting qualities recalls works by Picasso (especially the women of 1929-32); it also recalls the image of a male straddling a female, whose throat he is about to cut, in one of Masson's 1931 drawings for the *Massacres*.[7]

7. Brenson also draws attention to Michel Leiris's nightmare recollection, published in his autobiography, of having had his throat cut in a childhood operation. Giacometti's close friendship with Leiris would certainly have involved knowledge of this experience.

Femme égorgée emerges as a piece complex in its range of associations and allusions, and powerfully original in its form. Brenson captures something of this unique and self-transforming capacity in his detailed analysis of the piece, though his analogies may be more literal than Giacometti's elusive and suggestive imagery allows (pp. 128-29).

Giacometti himself, with characteristic reticence, spoke in a more general way of the tensions and ambiguities inherent in his work of this period in a revealing 1947 letter to Pierre Matisse:

> *Il ne s'agissait plus de présenter une figure extérieurement ressemblante, mais de vivre et de ne réaliser que ce qui m'avait affecté, ou que je désirais. Mais tout ceci alternait, se contredisait et continuait par contraste. Désir aussi de trouver une solution entre les choses pleines et calmes et aiguës et violentes. Ce qui donna pendant ces années là (1932-34 à peu près) des objets allants dans des directions assez différentes une de l'autre ...* [une] *femme égorgée la carotyde tranchée ...* (*Alberto Giacometti*, exh. cat., Pierre Matisse Gallery, New York, 1948, pp. 39-40).

EXHIBITIONS:

New York, Art of This Century, 1942-47, p. 120, repr. p. 121; New York, Art of This Century, *Giacometti*, Feb. 10-Mar. 10 [16], 1945, no. 6 (dated 1931, the date ascribed to it in *P.G.* publications until Alley, 1964); Venice, *P.G.*, 1948 (Biennale), no. 48; Florence, *P.G.*, 1949, no. 52, repr.; Venice, Giardino, 1949, no. 7; Amsterdam, *P.G.*, 1951, no. 60, repr.; Zurich, *P.G.*, 1951, no. 57; London, *P.G.*, 1964-65, no. 110, repr. (dated 1932-33, the date ascribed to it in all subsequent *P.G.* publications); Stockholm, *P.G.*, 1966-67, no. 105, repr.; Torino, Galleria Civica d'Arte Moderna, *Le Muse Inquietanti*, Nov. 1967-Jan. 1968, no. 184; New York, *P.G.*, 1969, p. 122, repr. color; Paris, *P.G.*, 1974-75, no. 113, repr.; Torino, *P.G.*, 1975-76, no. 125; Rome, *Guggenheim: Venezia-New York*, 1982, no. 50, repr. color.

REFERENCES:

M. Raynal, "Dieu-table-cuvette. Les Ateliers de Brancusi, Despiau, Giacometti," *Minotaure*, nos. 3-4, Dec. 1933, repr. pp. 46-47 (the plaster); P. Guggenheim, *Art of This Century*, 1942, p. 120, repr. p. 121 (dated 1931, the date ascribed to it in all *P.G.* publications until Alley, 1964); idem, *Out of This Century*, 1946, p. 248; A. Giacometti, letter to Pierre Matisse, *Giacometti*, exh. cat., Pierre Matisse Gallery, New York, 1948, p. 41; R. de Solier, "Giacometti," *Les Cahiers de la Pléiade*, no. 12, Paris, 1951, p. 44; J. T. Soby, *Modern Art and the New Past*, Oklahoma City, 1957, pp. 123-24; P. Guggenheim, *Confessions*, 1960, p. 74; P. Bucarelli, "La Sculpture d'Alberto Giacometti," *Cimaise*, Jahrg. 9, no. 61, Sept.-Oct. 1962, p. 70; J. Dupin, *A. Giacometti*, Paris, 1962, n.p.; D. Sylvester, *Alberto Giacometti*, exh. cat., The Arts Council of Great Britain, London, 1965, no. 15a, repr. pl. 5; F. Meyer, *Giacometti*, Stuttgart, 1968, p. 82; W. S. Rubin, *Dada and Surrealist Art*, New York, 1968, p. 252, repr. pl. 222; A. Elsen, *The Partial Figure of Modern Sculpture*, exh. cat., The Baltimore Museum of Art, 1969, p. 61, repr.; G. Metken, "Alberto Giacometti," *Das Kunstwerk*, Jahrg. xxiii, No. 5/6, Feb.-Mar. 1970, p. 46; C. Huber, *Alberto Giacometti*, Lausanne, 1970, pp. 3ff., 47ff., repr. p. 3; D. Hnikova and B. von Meyerburg-Campell, *Die Sammlung der Alberto Giacometti-Stiftung*, Zurich, 1971, p. 100; R. Hohl, "Alberto Giacometti's Atelier im Jahr 1932," *Du*, May 1971, pp. 361-62; idem, *Giacometti*, exh. cat., SRGM, New York, 1974, p. 22; M. F. Brenson, "The Early Work of Giacometti, 1925-35," unpublished Ph.D. dissertation, Johns Hopkins University, 1974, pp. 121-29, 165; D. Hall, *Alberto Giacometti's Woman with Her Throat Cut*, The Scottish National Gallery of Modern Art, 1980, pp. 3-30; A. G. Wilkinson, *From Gauguin to Moore*, exh. cat., Art Gallery of Ontario, 1981, pp. 234-37, repr.

69 **Femme debout ("Leoni").**
1947 (cast November 1957).
(Standing Woman ["Leoni"]; Lion woman).

76.2553 PG 134

Bronze (sand cast). Height (top of head to ankle): 54 5/16 (138); average height (at back) of sloping base: 5 15/16 (15); at front: 2 5/8 (6.7); depth of base: 13 5/8 (34.6); width of base at front: 5 1/4 (13.3); width of base at back: 5 15/16 (13.9).

Edition of six, plus two.[1]

Foundry: Susse, Paris.

Signed along side of base (in the wax): *Alberto Giacometti*; foundry mark on back of base: *Susse Fondeur Paris*. Not dated.

PROVENANCE:

Purchased from the artist, Paris, 1957.

CONDITION:

There are some traces of yellowish green corrosion.

In February 1984 (Venice) the piece was cleaned. The surface was degreased with trichloroethylene, and washed with distilled water, then with distilled water and neutral detergent; it was rinsed with distilled water, and dried with alcohol and acetone. The surface was treated for 30 minutes with a 3% solution of benzotriazole in pure alcohol. A protective coating of Incralac (acrylic resin containing benzotriazole) was applied (for outdoor exhibition). The condition is stable. (Venice, Mar. 1984.)

In the years immediately following World War II, Giacometti made a series of works that determined the course of his postwar art. In his 1947 letter to Pierre Matisse, he described the arduous process by which he had first attempted (during the years 1935-40) to achieve the "likeness" of a model. Working directly from such models, and concentrating at that stage only on the head (the entire figure presenting insurmountable difficulties), Giacometti found that the "likeness" he sought constantly eluded him, and the subject became rather "*un objet totalement inconnu et sans dimensions.... Enfin, pour tâcher de les réaliser un peu, je recommençais à travailler de mémoire, mais ceci surtout pour savoir ce qui me restait de tout ce travail.... Mais voulant faire de mémoire ce que j'avais vu, à ma terreur, les sculptures devenaient de plus en plus petites, elles n'étaient ressemblantes que petites, et pourtant ces dimensions me révoltaient et, inlassablement, je recommençais pour aboutir, après quelques mois, au même point*" (*Alberto Giacometti*, exh. cat., Pierre Matisse Gallery, New York, 1948, pp. 43, 45).

As he struggled, large figures struck Giacometti as "untrue," and small ones — the inch-high pared down figures he had been producing — "intolerable." Eventually, however, he found that by using drawing as an intermediary he could begin to create entire figures. To his surprise, these achieved the "likeness" he sought, but only when they were "*longues et minces*."

The "*longues et minces*" figures (many of them standing women), which were produced in the following years, vary in their proportions, and Peggy Guggenheim's "*Leoni*" is unusual in the uncompromising flatness of its form. It embodies, nonetheless, critical elements of Giacometti's postwar aesthetic. As described by Jean-Paul Sartre in his essay written in 1947 on Giacometti,[2] the

1. On a visit to Paris in the autumn of 1957, Peggy Guggenheim saw the plaster original at Giacometti's studio and decided to commission a cast in bronze. Giacometti named it "*Leoni*," in reference to the Palazzo Venier dei Leoni.

   Susse made 8 casts between November 1957 and 1965. Peggy Guggenheim's is not numbered but was the first of 2 casts made in November. Other casts, some of which are numbered, have been traced to the following present or former locations: 2/6, ex-Janis, Private Collection, Florida; 3/6, formerly Collection Lady Hulten; 4/6, Marlborough Gallery, London, 1973; 6/6, Private Collection, Switzerland; Fondation Maeght cast, so marked.

2. "La recherche de l'absolu," *Les Temps Modernes*, Jan. 1948, pp. 1153-63; trans. into English in *Alberto Giacometti*, exh cat., Pierre Matisse Gallery, N.Y., 1948, pp. 2-22. The essay was closely based on conversations with Giacometti and is expressive of the artist's own views of his work rather than of independent subjective insights brought to bear on the work by Sartre alone (information supplied by D. Sylvester).

process of creating the figures involved repeated building and destruction of each individual piece as he sought to mold a figure in stone without "petrifying" it: "*Il brise tout et recommence encore.... Ce qui le gêne, c'est que ces esquisses mouvantes, toujours à mi-chemin entre le néant et l'être, toujours modifiées, améliorées, détruites et recommencées, se mettent à exister seules et pour de bon, entreprennent loin de lui une carrière sociale...*" (loc. cit., pp. 1155-56). Giacometti was reluctant to let these figures take on such permanence, such independence, hence the continual destruction, the search for more perfect solutions. Working in plaster because of its weightless character ("*une matière sans poids, la plus ductile, la plus périssable, la plus spirituelle*"), Giacometti was able to create ephemeral (and destructible) figures. The medium of plaster afforded him control and the continuous possibility of refinement of form, as he sought to create women that were still more slender, still longer, and still lighter. As Sartre observed, "*ses personnages, pour avoir été destinés à périr dans la nuit même où il sont nés, sont seuls à garder, entre toutes les sculptures que je connais, la grâce inouïe de sembler périssables. Jamais la matière ne fut moins éternelle, plus fragile, plus près d'être humaine*" (loc. cit., p. 1156).

The morphology of the "*longues et minces*" figures (such as "*Leoni*") depends in important respects on the particular conception of distance—between viewer and sculpture—that Giacometti incorporated as an integral part of these works:

> *A dix pas, je me fais* [d'une] *femme nue une certaine image; si je m'approche et si je la regarde de tout près je ne la reconnais plus: ces cratères, ces galeries, ces gerçures, ces herbes noires et rèches, ces luisances graisseuses, toute cette orographie lunaire, il ne se peut pas que ce soit la peau lisse et fraîche que j'admirais de loin.... Ainsi la statue ne ressemblera vraiment ni à ce qu'*est *le modèle, ni à ce que* voit *le sculpteur; on la construira selon certaines conventions assez contradictoires, en figurant certains détails qui ne sont pas visibles de si loin, sous le prétexte qui'ils existent, et négligeant certains autres, qui existent tout autant, sous le prétexte qu'on ne les voit pas. Qu'est-ce à dire sinon qu'on s'en remet à l'œil du spectateur pour recomposer une figure acceptable?...si je suis proche, je découvrirai des détails que, de loin, j'ignorais. Et nous voilà conduits à ce paradoxe que j'ai des rapports* réels *avec une illusion...*(loc. cit., pp. 1158-59).

Sartre characterized Giacometti's resolution of the paradox as follows:

> *En acceptant d'emblée la relativité, il a trouvé l'absolu. C'est qu'il s'est avisé le premier de sculpter l'homme tel qu'on le voit, c'est-à-dire à distance. A ses personnages de plâtre il confère une* distance absolue ... *ces statues ne se laissent voir qu'à distance respectueuse. Pourtant tout est là: la blancheur, la rondeur, l'affaissement élastique d'une belle poitrine mûre. Tout sauf la matière.... Nous savons maintenant de quel pressoir Giacometti s'est servi pour comprimer l'espace: il n'en est qu'un seul, la distance; il met la distance à portée de la main, il pousse sous nos yeux une femme lointaine—et qui reste lointaine quand même nous la touchons du bout des doigts* (loc. cit., pp. 1159-60).

David Sylvester, in characterizing the "peculiar tendency" of Giacometti's vision, has pointed out that unlike normal vision (in which the mind corrects the retinal image so that distant objects are not perceived as small but as life-size and distant), Giacometti was reacting in these postwar figures to what is strictly visible.[3] The resulting intense and narrow focus "upon a compact form out there in space, this attentiveness to apparent size at a given distance, [produced] the hallucinatory sense of nearness and farness which is probably the most characteristic feature of Giacometti's work. Getting this sense of distance into a painting is a matter of controlling the notional space which painting creates automatically; getting it into a sculpture is another matter. The sculptor has to win a notional space within and around his forms, win it in the face of the fact that they inhabit the same real space as himself."

In the single standing figures (for example, "*Leoni*"), Giacometti was, as Sylvester argued, concerned to create a notional distance between the sculpture as a whole and the eye of the beholder. The figure remains "beyond reach," whatever the physical distance between it and the viewer. The strict frontality of "*Leoni*"—like that of the other standing women—also serves to introduce the notion of a forced confrontation between viewer and sculpture. And, indeed—as Sylvester suggested—Giacometti's very preoccupation with the issue of distance in these figures may have been specifically inspired by its relevance to the notion of confrontation. It is important to note that the single female figures created by Giacometti during these years are without exception stationary; the men, on the other hand, are usually in motion. In its immobility, "*Leoni*" (for which Isabel Lambert served as model)[4] epitomizes both the self-containment of the standing women and the aesthetic of confrontation. In the *Piazza* of 1947-48 (cat. no. 70), Giacometti for the first time combined the single motionless frontal woman with the walking men; in so doing, he forced the issue of interrelationships betwen the figures themselves, thereby reducing that between viewer and sculpture.

EXHIBITIONS:

London, *P.G.*, 1964-65, no. 112, repr. (*Lion Woman*, 1946-47, the title and date by which the work was known in all *P.G.* publications until 1974); Stockholm, *P.G.*, 1966-67, no. 107, repr.; Torino, Galleria Civica d'Arte Moderna, *Le Muse Inquietanti*, Nov. 1967-Jan. 1968, no. 185, repr. p. 138; New York, *P.G.*, 1969, no. 122, repr. p. 123; Paris, *P.G.*, 1974-75, no. 115, repr. (*Femme debout*); Torino, *P.G.*, 1975-76, no. 127; Rome, *Guggenheim: Venezia-New York*, 1982, no. 51, repr. color.

REFERENCE:

L. Flint, *Handbook*, 1983, cat. no. 61, repr. color p. 131.

3. "The residue of a vision," *Alberto Giacometti*, exh. cat., The Arts Council of Great Britain, 1965, n.p.
4. Information supplied by D. Sylvester.

70 **Piazza.** 1947-48 (cast 1948-49).[1]

75.2553 PG 135

Bronze (sand cast), with original dark brown-black patina on base. Wood fills the entire interior of the base, which has an edge of 3/16 (.4). Height of base: 1 3/4 (4.5); length of base: 24 5/8 (62.5); width of base: 16 7/8 (42.8). Height of figures: Figure 1: 5 3/4 (14.6); Figure 2: 5 11/16 (15); Figure 3: 5 5/16 (13.6); Figure 4: 6 1/2 (16.5); Figure 5: 6 1/8 (15.5).

Edition of six.[2]

Foundry: Alexis Rudier, Paris.

Signed on top of base (in wax): *A. Giacometti*; signed and numbered on side of base: *A. Giacometti. 3/6*. Not dated. No foundry mark.

PROVENANCE:

Purchased from the artist, Paris, summer 1949.[3]

CONDITION:

In 1979 the author noted that the figures were seriously distorted out of position. In each case the bodies and limbs had been bent, and the stance of the figures, the degree of inclination, and the relationships among arms, torso, and legs altered to such an extent that the original configurations and composition were clearly compromised.

In November 1982, Diego Giacometti, who had participated in the original creation of the sculpture, agreed to undertake an extensive restoration.[4] He noted that restoration had taken place at an unknown time and that several of the legs had been soldered into incorrect positions. He also indicated that the dryness and brittleness of the patina of the figures, which was uncharacteristic and differed from that of the base, was attributable to the application of heat during this earlier restoration. Each of the figures required realignment, and the previous repairs (which had been executed by someone who had technical competence but did not have access to reliable information about the positions of the figures) had to be revised.

The figures were repositioned by Diego Giacometti according to the artist's original conception; the figures (but not the base) were then repatinated.

The extreme fineness and delicacy of the figures renders the sculpture fragile, but the condition is stable. (Venice, Nov. 1982.)

1. It has not been possible to establish exactly when the casts were made, although it was probably in 1949.
2. The other 5 casts, all but 1 of which carry Rudier's foundry mark, are in the following locations: 1/6, MoMA; 2/6, the Colin Collection, New York; 4/6, Collection Mr. and Mrs. Morton G. Neumann, Chicago; 5/6, Wadsworth Atheneum, Hartford; 6/6, Kunstmuseum, Basel, Emanuel Hoffman Stiftung.
3. Peggy Guggenheim's daughter, Pegeen Vail, transported the piece to Venice just in time for the September 1949 opening of the Giardino del Palazzo Venier exhibition.

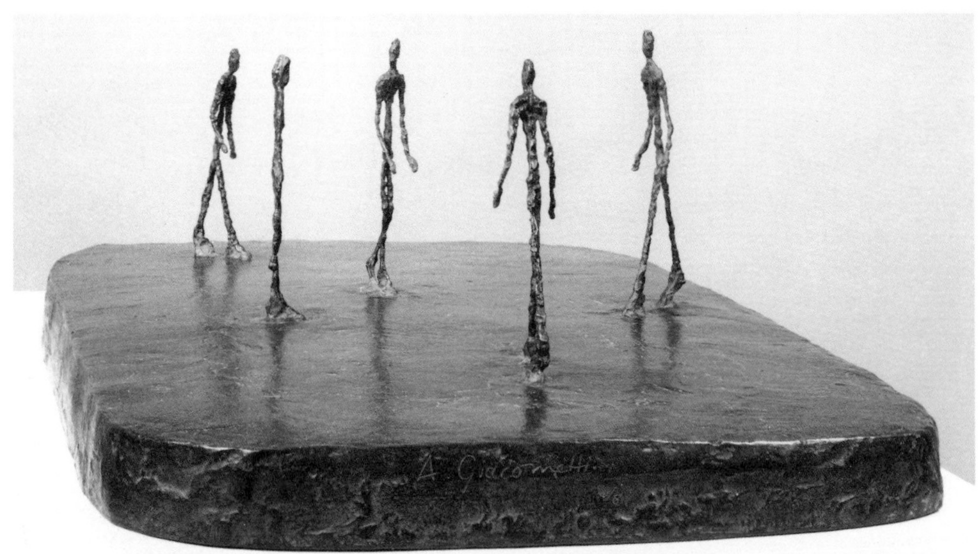

4. James Lord, who also noted the poor condition of the piece, suggested that Diego Giacometti might be willing to undertake the restoration and initially approached him on behalf of the SRGM.

fig. a.
View of cat. no. 70, showing relative positions of the figures.

fig. b.
View of *Piazza* (larger version), showing relative positions of figures, National Gallery of Art, Washington, D.C. Gift of Enid A. Haupt, 1977.

A slightly larger version of *Piazza* was made soon after the original and was also cast by Rudier in an edition of six. The figures in this version are a little taller, varying in height from 6 13/16 in., 17.3 cm., to 7 13/16 in., 19.8 cm.[5] The relative positions of the figures in the two versions are not identical (figs. a and b).

In *Piazza*, five figures occupy an intimate space, as if about to encounter one another. Only the woman stands motionless, erect, and frontal. The men, appearing to move toward one another, are set upon paths that in fact preclude an actual meeting. The general disposition of the figures (though not their relative positions) is identical in both the first and second versions of the sculpture (figs. a and b). But there is one important difference: In the latter, one of the men walks directly toward the woman and thus significantly alters the focus of

5. The dimensions of the base in the large version are 25 1/16 x 17 5/16 in., 63.6 x 44.0 cm. Diego Giacometti, recalling from memory almost precisely the difference in dimensions between the two pieces, remembered that the larger one was made second. Though the present locations of the 6 casts of this series are not fully established, the following is known: 1/6, Collection Mr. and Mrs. Albert List; 2/6, formerly Collection Nelson Rockefeller; 3/6, formerly Collection Lady Hulten; 4/6, The National Gallery of Art, Washington, D.C., Gift of Mrs. Enid Haupt; 5/6, formerly Collection Alex Maguy, destroyed in a fire; 6/6, Collection Virginia Lust Gallery.

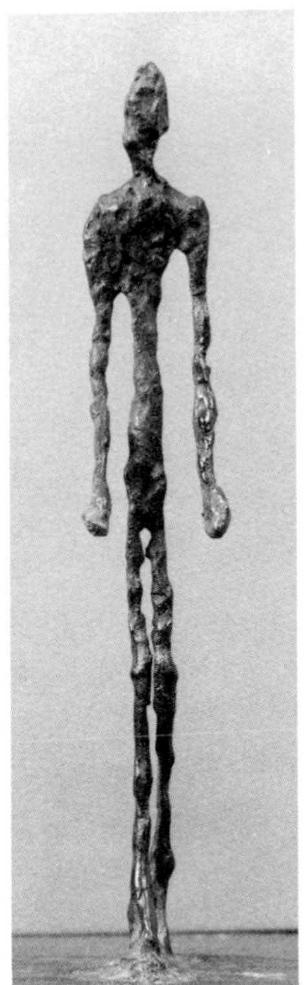

fig. c.
Detail of cat. no. 70, showing Figure numbered 2 in fig. a.

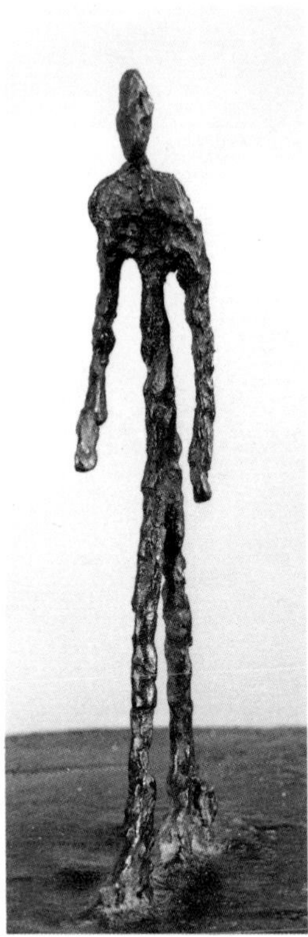

fig. d.
Detail of cat. no. 70, showing Figure numbered 3 in fig. a.

fig. e.
Detail of cat. no. 70, showing Figure numbered 5 in fig. a.

the piece. Here the two central "facing" figures become the primary actors in the tableau; the remaining three take on a different role—that of unconcerned passersby. In the smaller, original version, by contrast, compositional tension is created by the clear absence of any possible contact.

In both works, the carefully calibrated positions of the individual figures, the insistent straightness of their backs and legs, the slight parallel curves in certain arms, and the perpendicular relationship of each figure to the base—all combine to create the distinctive geometry and uncompromising austerity of the entire composition. Even minimal alterations in these interrelationships (an arm, hand, or leg bent out of line, a torso twisted into contrapposto, or a back slightly arched) constitute major distortions that immediately impinge upon the clarity and precision of the iconography. (See above CONDITION.)

Carlo Huber drew attention to the additional power of the piece if viewed at eye level (figs. c-e): the figures acquire monumentality, and, instead of appearing to be participants in a remote drama, seem—at least to some extent—to enter the viewer's immediate world. Even from this perspective, however, the sense of an established relationship is strictly limited, and the viewer "remains separated by the conceptual distance in which the artist has deliberately chosen to isolate [the figures]" (J. Lord, *Alberto Giacometti Drawings*, London, 1972, p. 24).

fig. f.
Giacometti, *Figures on a City Street*, 1947, pencil on paper, 7⅞ x 5½ in., 20 x 14 cm., Collection Louis Clayeux, Paris. Photograph courtesy James Lord, Paris.

fig. g.
Giacometti, *Figures on a City Square*, 1947, pencil on paper, 12⅞ x 20 in., 32.7 x 41.7 cm., Collection Gene R. Summers, Chicago. Photograph courtesy James Lord, Paris.

Several drawings of 1947 exist suggesting early conceptions for *Piazza* (see, for example, figs. f-h). But as Lord has convincingly argued, they cannot be regarded as preparatory studies in the conventional sense: "Giacometti never made formal preparatory studies for his sculptures. His very idea of the purpose of sculpture and his means of trying to realize that purpose precluded any such methodical or schematic techniques.... the real relation of his drawings to his sculpture is seen at its most profound in those drawings that embody as drawings the same unique and momentous aesthetic innovation that the sculptures embody as sculptures" (*Alberto Giacometti Drawings*, London, 1971, p. 23).

Piazza has often been interpreted as a work intended to express the loneliness and isolation — indeed the alienation — of man in contemporary society (see, for example, F. Meyer, 1968). Lord, however, has argued convincingly that works such as *Piazza* are not fundamentally "expressionist" in nature; rather, the artist deliberately wanted "to exclude ... intimate feelings or human convictions, for he knew that that kind of self-expression may all too easily lead to bombast and triviality" (op. cit., p. 24). In this sense, *Piazza* reveals itself as a rigorously objective and, in effect, analytic work whose power is essentially iconic in nature. While Giacometti may well be preoccupied with the "distance" between his figures, or their lack of contact, or the emptiness of the space they are compelled to traverse, his approach to these themes is extraordinarily complex. As Sartre has suggested: " ... *chez lui la distance n'est pas un isolement volontaire, pas même un recul: elle est exigence, cérémonie, sens des difficultés.*

fig. h.
Giacometti, *Standing Woman*, 1947, pencil on paper, 18½ x 10⅝ in., 47 x 27 cm., Collection Lord Weidenfeld, London. Photograph courtesy David Sylvester, London.

C'est le produit—il l'a dit lui-même—des puissances d'attraction et des forces répulsives.... Il a sculpté des hommes qui traversent une place sans se voir; ils se croisent, irrémédiablement seuls et pourtant il sont ensemble.... *Entre les choses, entre les hommes, les ponts sont rompus; le vide se glisse partout, chaque créature secrète son propre vide*" (*Derrière le Miroir*, no. 65, May 1954, n.p.).

EXHIBITIONS:

Venice, Giardino, 1949, no. 9, repr. (dated 1948); Amsterdam, *P.G.*, 1951, no. 64 (dated 1948); London, *P.G.*, 1964-65, no. 113, repr. (dated 1948-49, the date ascribed to it in all subsequent *P.G.* publications); Stockholm, *P.G.*, 1966-67, no. 108, repr.; Paris, *P.G.*, 1974-75, no. 116; Torino, *P.G.*, 1975-76, no. 128.

REFERENCES:

F. Ponge, "Réfléxions sur les statuettes, figures et peintures d'Alberto Giacometti," *Cahiers d'Art*, vol. 26, 1951, repr. p. 78; J. Lanes, "Alberto Giacometti," *Arts Yearbook*, no. 3, 1959, pp. 153-54, repr. p. 155; C. Giedion-Welcker, "Alberto Giacometti's Vision der Realität," *Werk*, vol. 46, no. 6, June 1959, p. 210, repr.; F. Meyer, *A. Giacometti*, Stuttgart, 1968, pp. 156-58, repr. pl. 19; J. Dupin, *Giacometti*, Paris, 1963, repr. p. 243; C. Huber, *Alberto Giacometti*, Lausanne, 1970, pp. 72, 75, repr.

Albert Gleizes

Born December 1881, Paris.
Died June 1953, Avignon.

71 La dame aux bêtes (Madame Raymond Duchamp-Villon).
Completed by February 1914.
(*Woman with animals [Madame Raymond Duchamp-Villon]*).

Color plate p. 39.

75.2553 PG 17

Oil on canvas, 77⁵⁄₁₆ x 45¹⁵⁄₁₆ (196.4 x 114.1).

Signed and dated l.r.: *Alb Gleizes / 1914.*

PROVENANCE:

Purchased from the sitter, Madame Raymond Duchamp-Villon, through Marcel Duchamp, Paris, 1940.

CONDITION:

According to Peggy Guggenheim's recollections, the work was damaged when she bought it; Jacques Villon (brother-in-law of the sitter) restored some portions of it. Shortly thereafter, in the fall of 1940, Delaunay apparently restored some other parts.[1]

By 1964 (Tate Report) the canvas had been glue-paste lined with somewhat coarse canvas, apparently in order to secure several tears or cuts and 1 puncture in the original canvas. A large area at the lower right, including the section below the foot and around the signature, and an area of small losses in the orange and black to the left of the ringed hand had been extensively retouched. These reworkings may well have been the work of Villon and Delaunay. There were considerable surface soil and dark streaks of discolored varnish down most of the left side of the picture. Several cracks and losses were observed but not retouched. A tear in the canvas (along the line of the nose), which had presumably been secured in the lining process, had become detached and was curling up; this was reattached.

In 1982-83 (Venice) considerable cleavage of the paint layer was noted, especially in the blues and yellows. The discolored varnish, observed in 1964, had in some areas oxidized the pigment.

Areas of cleavage were set down with Gelvatol (polyvinyl alcohol at 15% in water and alcohol, 1:1). Dirt was removed from the surface with ammonium hydroxide (3% in water). The varnish, which contained oil, was removed with dimethylformamide (1 pt.) and acetone (2 pts.). The extensive previous retouches (which had not discolored) were left intact.

Apart from 2 small areas (readhered with a solution of polyvinyl acetate emulsion, 50% in water), the previous lining was in good condition; it was, however, reinforced with a Fieux contact lining to give additional support.

The painting was mounted on an ICA spring stretcher and given a light spray of Lefranc retouching varnish. Windsor and Newton watercolors and glazes of Maimeri varnish colors were used to reintegrate the surface. The condition is stable. (Venice, Mar. 1984.)

During the years 1913-15, Gleizes showed an intense interest in portraiture. The genre served as an important vehicle in his attempt to develop an increasingly nonfigurative style. Depending upon lengthy sittings and many preparatory drawings, Gleizes attempted in these portraits to retain something of the essential "likeness" of the sitter, while introducing an increasingly complex analytical fragmentation of surface.

1. In *Out of This Century*, 1946, p. 260, reference is made to this episode. In conversation with the author, 1978, Peggy Guggenheim recalled that the Delaunays visited her in Grenoble in the early fall of 1940 and that Delaunay retouched some of the damaged areas.

The portrait of the publisher *Eugene Figuière*, for example (Musée des Beaux-Arts, Lyon, oil on canvas, 56¼ x 40⅛ in., 143 x 102 cm.), a work which was shown in the 1913 Salon d'Automne and attracted a good deal of attention there, shares many of the characteristics of *La dame aux bêtes*, as well as of the 1913 *L'Homme au hamac* (Albright-Knox Art Gallery, Buffalo, oil on canvas, 51¼ x 61¼ in., 130 x 155.5 cm.), first exhibited in Prague in 1914. In these large and ambitious works, facial characteristics and "attributes" are presented directly and representationally. Figuière's role as an avant-garde publisher is evoked through the use of printed titles, floating in space, of the recently published works of Apollinaire, Jacques Nayral, and Paul Fort, and of Gleizes's and Metzinger's own *Du Cubisme*, which Figuière had published in 1912.

In Peggy Guggenheim's picture, the cats and the dog, the sitter's face, with its prominent nose, her hand, and her hat (as well as her shoe) are depicted with the most literal (if also mildly witty) specificity. In both these works — and in the Buffalo painting — Gleizes imposed upon the literal elements the planes, rectangles, and wedges that dissect the entire surrounding space and dominate the pictorial structure.

Little biographical information has hitherto been located about the sitter, Yvonne Duchamp-Villon. It is known that her brother, the painter Jean Bon, was a close friend of Duchamp-Villon, and that she married Duchamp-Villon in 1903. Marcel Duchamp, her brother-in-law, painted a half-length seated portrait of her in 1906-7 (repr. R. Lebel, *Marcel Duchamp*, New York, 1959, pl. 12, formerly Collection Mme. H. P. Roché). Madame Duchamp-Villon was recognized as a woman of considerable character; she was also devoted to animals, and for this reason—among others—was a particular favorite of Gleizes's wife, Juliette.[2] After the death of her husband, Madame Duchamp-Villon remarried and became Madame Lignières.

As was his practice, Gleizes must surely have made an extensive series of preparatory studies for a work of this scale and ambition (see, for example, the eight studies that preceded his *Portrait d'un médecin militaire*, 1914-1915, SRGM, repr. A.Z.R., *Guggenheim*, 1976, vol. I, pp. 146-47). No trace of these studies has been found, and it cannot be ruled out that they were destroyed during World War I.[3] The portrait itself was first presented at the 1914 Salon, where Apollinaire described it as one of the most interesting pictures exhibited. It then disappeared from view — into the household of the Duchamp-Villons. World War I broke out not long afterward and the painting remained largely unknown until its purchase by Peggy Guggenheim in 1940. A study of its important place within the development of Gleizes's 1913-14 style remains to be undertaken.

EXHIBITIONS:

Paris, *XXXe Salon des Indépendants*, Mar. 1–Apr. 30, 1914, no. 1392 (*La dame aux bêtes, portrait de Mme D.V.*); New York, Art of This Century, 1942-47, p. 73, repr. p. 74; Venice, *P.G.*, 1948 (Biennale), no. 51; Florence, *P.G.*, 1949, no. 55; Amsterdam, *P.G.*, 1951, no. 65, repr.; Zurich, *P.G.*, 1951, p. 59; London, *P.G.*, 1964-65, no. 11, repr.; Stockholm, *P.G.*, 1966-67, no. 11, repr.; New York, *P.G.*, 1969, p. 44, repr. p. 45; Paris, *P.G.*, 1974-75, no. 12, repr.; Torino, *P.G.*, 1975-76, no. 16, repr. pl. 5.

REFERENCES:

G. Apollinaire, "Le Salon des Indépendants, Avant-vernissage," *L'Intransigeant*, Feb. 28, 1914; idem, ibid., Mar. 2, 1914; A. Salmon, "Le Salon," *Montjoie*, 2e année, no. 3, Mar. 1914, p. 26;[4] P. Guggenheim, *Art of This Century*, 1942, p. 73, repr. p. 74; idem, *Out of This Century*, 1946, p. 260; G. Habasque, *Le Cubisme*, Geneva, 1959, p. 100, repr. color p. 98; P. Cabanne, *L'Epopée du Cubisme*, Paris, 1963, p. 272; M. Sérullaz, *Le Cubisme*, Paris, 1963, p. 84; Alley, 1964, p. 11; L. Flint, *Handbook*, 1983, p. 30, repr. color p. 31.

2. Daniel Robbins, in conversation with the author, June 1983. For a discussion of Gleizes's style during the years 1913-15, see D. Robbins, "The Formation and Maturity of Albert Gleizes: A Biographical and Critical Study, 1881-1920," Ph.D. dissertation, New York University, 1975, pp. 165ff.

3. In his March 2 review of the Salon, Apollinaire referred to one of these studies, which was apparently included in the show though not listed in the catalogue: "*Le portrait de femme de Gleizes est varié et plein de fougue. Il est accompagné d'une étude d'une grande sensibilité.*"

4. Of Gleizes's 3 entries in the Salon, Salmon wrote: "*Au portrait féminin de M. Albert Gleizes je préfère, et pense n'être pas seul à les préférer, les deux paysages si fortement équilibrés.*"

Julio González

Born September 1876, Barcelona.
Died March 1942, Arceuil.

72 "Monsieur" Cactus.
Iron original completed August 24, 1939, Arceuil[1] (cast 1953-54).
(*L'Homme Cactus I*).

76.2553 PG 136

Bronze with black patina and some greenish areas (lost wax). Height (without wood base, which is not part of the work): 23 5/16 (64.3); width: 9 13/16 (25); depth: 6 11/16 (17).

Edition of eight.[2]

Foundry: Valsuani.

Not signed or dated; stamped and incised into wax before casting (on lowest projecting element): *cire / Valsuani / perdue / © by R. Gonzalez / 3/3*.

PROVENANCE:

Purchased from Roberta González, the artist's daughter, by Pegeen Vail on Peggy Guggenheim's behalf, Paris, 1956 (date confirmed by Carmen Martinez, June 1983).

CONDITION:

In 1969 (New York) the piece fell and broke at the neck. There was evidence of a previous repair in this area. Brass rod and flux were used to resolder the 2 sections; this repair was filed down, but the wall proved too thin to support the joint. Some of the nails became detached during the repair. The neck was filled with plastic filler and the nails reattached with epoxy.

There are traces of pitting corrosion. In the areas where resin was used there are corrosion marks that pose problems for the stability of the material. Comparison between the Peggy Guggenheim piece and the iron original (fig. a) indicates that considerable breakage, loss, and distortion of the projecting nail elements have occurred. Eight nails are missing. The composition and structure have suffered considerable damage. (Venice, Nov. 1982.)

1. Three postcards written by González from Arceuil to his young daughter include comments on the progress of the piece. The first is dated August 21, 1939: "*Il sera fini demain, Mr. Cactus?*" The second is undated: "*Demain Mr. Cactus fini (Gracias a Deu).*" The third dated August 24, 1939: "*Mr. Cactus est terminé. C'est une bonne nouvelle.*" All 3 are preserved among the papers in the artist's estate (information supplied by Margit Rowell). On the basis of this evidence, Rowell retitled the work—previously known as *L'Homme Cactus I*—"*Monsieur Cactus.*" She argued further (1983, p. 195) that although documentary evidence has not yet been located, the companion piece (*L'Homme Cactus II*), with its more feminine silhouette, was likely to have been conceived as "*Madame Cactus.*" Jörn Merkert, who has recently completed the catalogue raisonné of González's sculpture, has accepted both designations (conversation with the author, June 1983).
2. Three casts are numbered: 1/3-3/3. Five are marked: O, OO, E.A., H.C., M.A.M. Barcelone. The locations of the casts are as follows: 1/3, Hans Hartung, Paris, Antibes; 2/3, Gemeentemuseum, The Hague; O, Museum of Fine Arts, Montreal; OO, González Estate, Paris; E.A., Private Collection, Lugano; H.C., Donation González, MNAM, Paris; M.A.M. Barcelone, Donation González, MAB Barcelona. All casts were mady by Valsuani. The author is indebted to Jörn Merket for helping to establish this sequence and some of the locations.

72

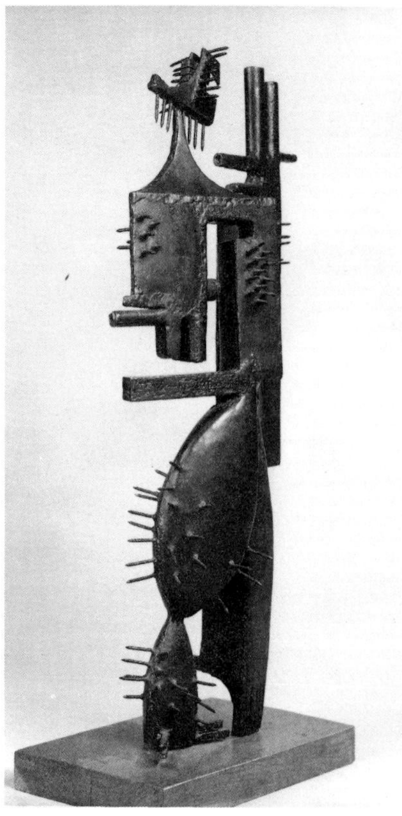

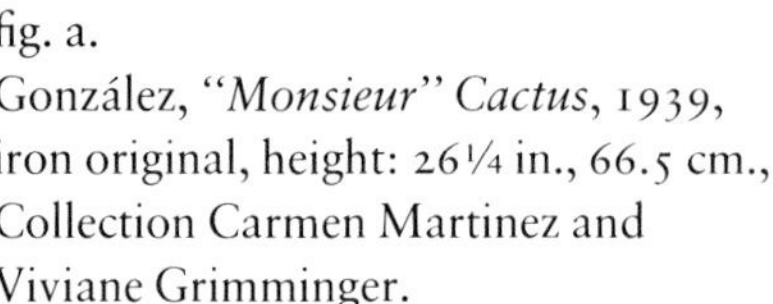

fig. a.
González, *"Monsieur" Cactus*, 1939, iron original, height: 26¼ in., 66.5 cm., Collection Carmen Martinez and Viviane Grimminger.

fig. b.
González, *"Monsieur" Cactus*, 1939, iron original.

González was a prolific draftsman, and many of his mature sculptures are extensively documented in preparatory studies.[3] Perhaps his largest single series of drawings was produced in connection with two Cactus figures of 1938-39 (figs. a-c). Well over four dozen preparatory or related studies are known, and additional sketches on the theme exist that postdate the completion of both iron pieces.[4]

González apparently began to develop his ideas for the theme sometime early in 1938. A small group of highly expressive drawings dating from that year represents an instantly recognizable response to Picasso's January 1937 *Sueño y Mentira de Franco* (fig. d). The two Spaniards — close friends since the beginning of the century, and collaborators since the years 1928-29—undoubtedly

3. Rowell (1983, p. 29) has argued that González did not use "sequential drawings" in his mature phase: "once he found his personal style, he could not make precise preparatory drawings, because each sculpture's syntax was formulated in the act of making. His was an additive process involving disparate materials.... Consequently he could not *see* a sculpture until it was formed." She described the particular use of drawing in the case of the Cactus figures as "variations on a theme... in order to find the most expressive postures and relationships among components. But many of these drawings were visual exercises having little to do with the sculptures that followed, because from this time González was thinking in terms of the expressive constructed equivalent of an idea."

fig. c.
González, *"Madame" Cactus*, 1939, iron original, height: 30¾ in., 78 cm., Staatliche Kunsthalle, Karlsruhe, West Germany.

fig. d.
Picasso, *Sueño y Mentira de Franco (Dream and Lie of Franco)*, detail of plate 2, etching and aquatint, January 8, 1937, 15¾ x 23½ in., 40 x 59.7 cm. (entire sheet), Peggy Guggenheim Collection.

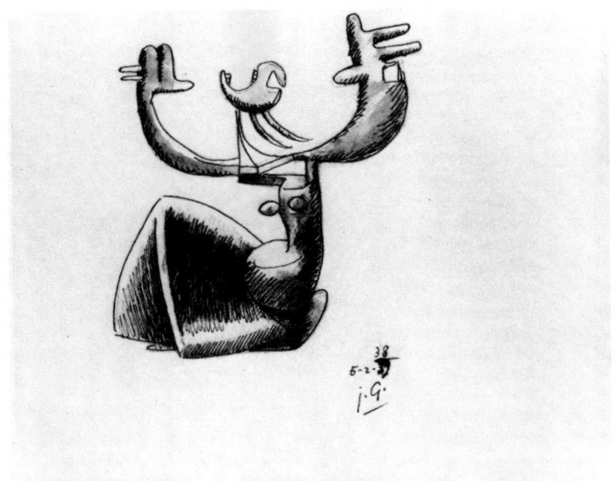

fig. e.
González, ink and wash on paper, 9½ x 12¼ in., 24 x 21 cm., Collection Michael and Juliet Rubenstein, New York.

4. Many of the drawings are reproduced in J. Gibert, *Projets pour sculptures: personnages*, Paris, 1975, pp. 65, 66, 67 bottom, 68, 69, 75 bottom, 76 bottom, 77-94 (hereafter Gibert); see also Rowell, 1983, cat. nos. 217-21, 227-32; R. Krauss, *J. Gonzalez; Sculpture and Drawings*, exh. cat., The Pace Gallery, New York, 1981, n.p.

   Carmen Martinez and Viviane Grimminger generously offered the author access to their entire collection of drawings on this theme, many of which are unpublished.

   It seems likely that some drawings identified by Gibert as studies on the Cactus man theme (see, for example, pp. 60 top and 61 top) were made in connection with other subjects.

shared a deep revulsion toward the Franco regime. As Josephine Withers has pointed out, González's work in the years following the bombing of Guernica (April 26, 1937) shows a new expressive content that seems to have arisen directly from his reaction to the Spanish situation. (For a discussion of this point, see Withers, 1978, pp. 87-98.) During the early months of 1939, the period of González's most intense preparatory work for the Cactus figures, his native city of Barcelona, one of the principal centers of resistance, fell to the Fascists, and the Civil War came to a close.

Although no documentary evidence has been found concerning González's political views, the visual evidence strongly suggests (as Withers has argued) that the emotions embodied in the Cactus figures (and their studies) express González's response to contemporary political events.

As Withers, Rosalind Krauss, Rowell, and others have pointed out, González's achievement as a sculptor was deeply affected by the work of Picasso. At this late stage in his career, however — the Cactus figures were among his very last sculptures — Picasso's influence was in most respects implicit rather than explicit. Rowell, for example, has described how González, by the mid-1930s, tended to absorb and fully transform his sources: "borrowed or recognizable morphological components nourished his idiom and provoked permutations with his personal style.... he never hesitated to look to other artists for a primary formulation of motifs. Yet, transformed, decontextualized and integrated into his own constructive process, this basic vocabulary was of secondary importance" (1983, pp. 27-28).

No period of González's career is more characteristic of this process than the final five years, although in the case of the Cactus drawings, the original source in Picasso's imagery (the upturned head of the screaming woman) remains a central and fully recognizable element, insistently preserved throughout the series. Only in the last stages, as González approached the final sculptural resolution, did the literalness of violent emotion give way to much more abstract, but still powerful, expressive forms (fig. i).

The early drawings (figs. e, g, h) reveal the extent of González's initial debt to Picasso. The central image of the woman with arms raised, upturned head, mouth open in an anguished scream, long hair streaming, are direct quotations from the 1937 Picasso etching (fig. d). But already in these drawings González has in some respects set out upon a different path: the fingers on each hand have lost some of Picasso's dynamic contortion and are rendered more schematically; they have taken almost precisely the form (though not the positions) of the hands of the finished male Cactus sculpture. Similarly, the violently expressive nostrils and eyes in the Picasso print have been altered in the early González drawings: the nose is indicated "negatively" by an abstract indentation, and the eyes are pushed to the outermost right edge of the head.

These particular solutions were sustained throughout many of the studies that followed, as well as in the finished sculptures. At the same time, the large group of drawings presents an unusually complicated pattern of development, and the precise relationship of any one drawing (or set of drawings) to the evolution of

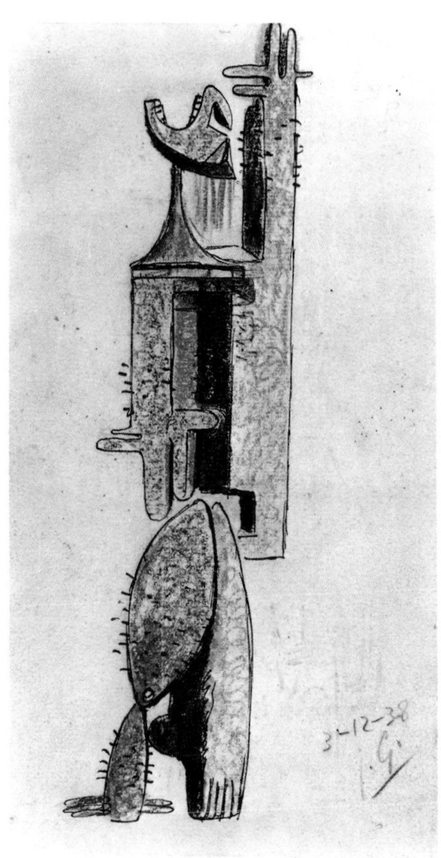

fig. f.
González, crayon and ink on paper, 12 x $6\frac{3}{4}$ in., 30 x 16 cm. Photograph courtesy Carmen Martinez and Viviane Grimminger.

fig. g.
González, crayon on paper, $9\frac{5}{8}$ x $12\frac{1}{2}$ in., 24.5 x 31.8 cm. Photograph courtesy Carmen Martinez and Viviane Grimminger.

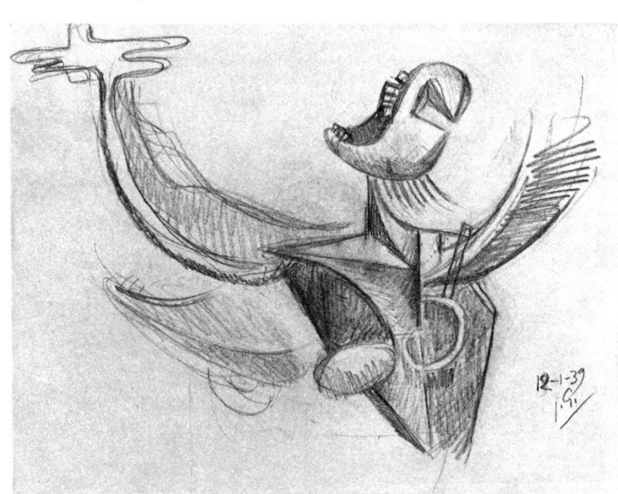

fig. h.
González, crayon on paper, $9\frac{15}{16}$ x $12\frac{13}{16}$ in., 25.2 x 32.6 cm. Photograph courtesy Carmen Martinez and Viviane Grimminger.

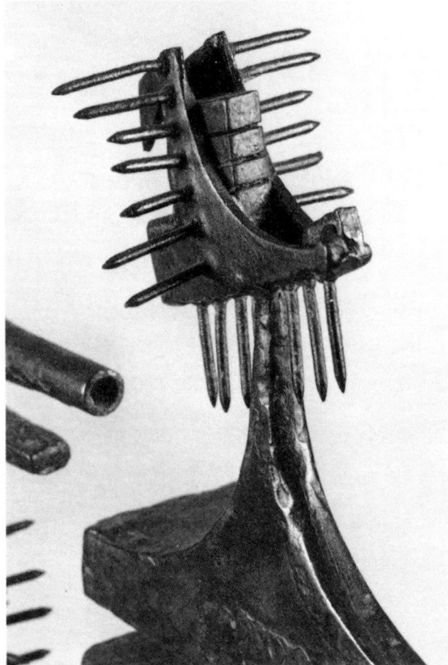

fig. i.
González, iron original of cat. no. 72 (detail).

the sculptures is difficult to trace. An analysis of the available material suggests, however, that González began his work on the theme in about January or February 1938 with only a female figure in mind. By December 1938 a masculine form began to appear in a small group of related drawings. At a critical juncture, in March 1939, González undertook an intensive study of both a male and a female image, although complex variations and cross-references continued to characterize the evolutionary process. By April, and even more evidently by June, the major characteristics of the male and the female figures had been essentially delineated; the final resolutions, however, were achieved only during the welding of the iron pieces themselves.

In many of the later drawings, the gender of the figures is difficult to establish; some of the details that ultimately characterized the female figure were first introduced in the more masculine figural type, and vice versa. No single, visibly defined line of development is revealed. A pattern is discernible, but many important questions remain unanswered. A brief survey of some of these issues does, however, shed light on González's creative process.

The drawings made between January or February and December 1938 are consistently of a female figure (figs. e and g; see also several drawings reproduced in Gibert, op. cit., pp. 65-69, and the rather different though not entirely unrelated "Marguerite" drawings of November 1938, ibid., pp. 75-79). Throughout these studies, González experimented with different approaches to the image of the anguished woman originally borrowed from Picasso.

Between December 1938 and February 1939, however, the pattern becomes more complex. The artist continued to explore variations on the theme of a female figure (figs. h, j, k): the head remains constant, but the seated woman becomes a standing one, and various new conceptions of legs, arms, and torso emerge. In December 1938 González also made his earliest studies for a very different figure; blocklike and rectilinear, these forms represent the initial ideas for the male statue (fig. f and Gibert, p. 79 bottom, p. 80 top and bottom).

Even in the December 1938 drawings, however, the sexual identity is not always clear. Some drawings (such as Gibert, p. 79 bottom) are obvious fusions of "Marguerite" characteristics with the new (and increasingly important) rectilinear body structure; others (such as fig. f) retain the "Picasso" head, with long hair, while simultaneously displaying an anatomical structure closely related to the finished iron sculpture *"Monsieur" Cactus.*

The next stage of intense — and decisive — development occurred in late March and in April 1939. In a series of densely covered sheets dated March 16-24 (figs. l-p), González concentrated on developing the masculine image that had first appeared in December. The form at the left of fig. l, for example, derives directly from that of fig. f; the hair is now shorter and an obviously bristling beard has been added — a feature explored in greater detail in fig. p where the stylized parallel lines begin to resemble the iron-nail beard of the completed sculpture. By the end of March the main components of the male sculpture were established: the rectangular, heavy torso, the strong arms (one of which points upward, one downward), the upturned head with bristling hair and beard, and

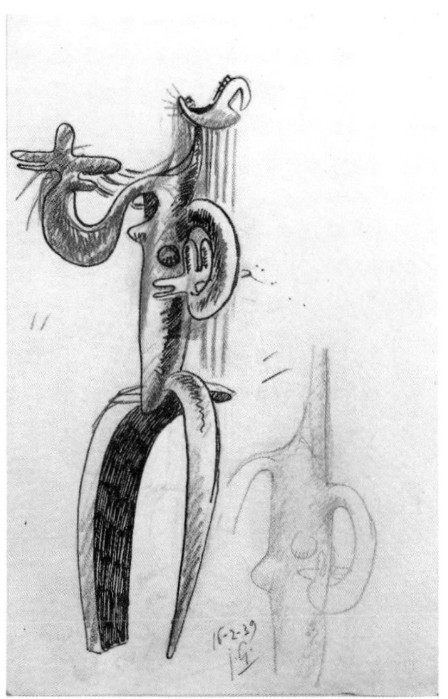

fig. j.
González, ink and pencil on paper, 12⅜ x 7⅞ in., 31 x 20 cm. Photograph courtesy Carmen Martinez and Viviane Grimminger.

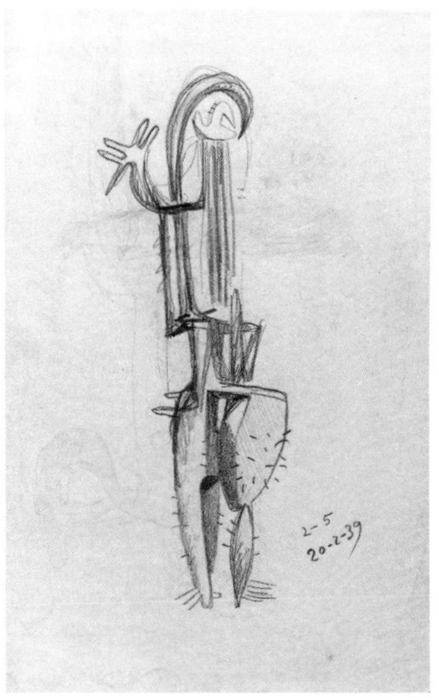

fig. k.
González, verso of fig. j., pencil on paper. Photograph courtesy Carmen Martinez and Viviane Grimminger.

fig. l.
González, verso of fig. m., ink and colored pencil on paper, 9¾ x 12¾ in., 24.8 x 32.4 cm. Photograph courtesy Carmen Martinez and Viviane Grimminger.

fig. m.
González, recto of fig. l. Photograph courtesy Carmen Martinez and Viviane Grimminger.

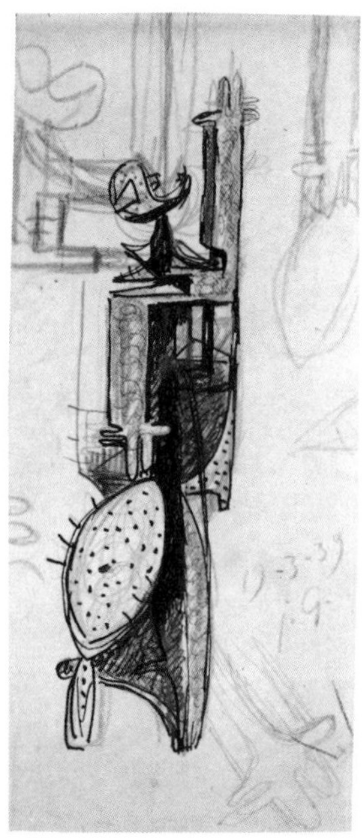

fig. n.
González, ink and crayon on paper, $9\frac{7}{16}$ x $4\frac{5}{16}$ in., 24 x 11 cm. Photograph courtesy Carmen Martinez and Viviane Grimminger.

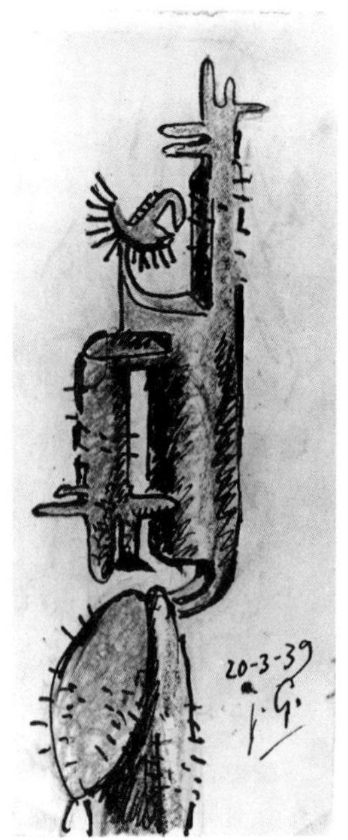

fig. o.
González, pencil, ink, and crayon on paper, $8\frac{9}{16}$ x $3\frac{5}{8}$ in., 22.2 x 9.2 cm. Photograph courtesy The David and Alfred Smart Gallery, The University of Chicago, The Joel Starrels, Jr. Memorial Collection.

fig. p.
González, pen and crayon on paper, $12\frac{3}{8}$ x $7\frac{7}{8}$ in., 31 x 20 cm. Photograph courtesy Carmen Martinez and Viviane Grimminger.

the open "screaming" mouth. The only major element missing is the horizontal bar that protrudes (in the final sculpture) from the center of the figure — in all probability a phallus.

Although the complex steps that led to the formulation of the companion piece, *"Madame" Cactus*, lie outside the scope of this study, a brief outline is necessary in view of the fact that the development of González's ideas for the two sculptures were closely intertwined. The turning point of resolution for the female figure also appears to have occurred in March-April; this can be traced in a group of important drawings, three of which are shown here (figs. q-s). The upper portion of fig. q is clearly reminiscent of González's earliest ideas (figs. e and h). It is also related to a group of "dancing" — probably male — figures dating from February and March (Gibert, pp. 89-91). Whether these figures (perhaps suggesting a "dance of death"?) are male or female is less important than the relationship of their kinetic, curving torsos, particularly their thrusting legs, to analogous forms González began to use as he worked on new drawings for *"Madame" Cactus*. Compare, for example, the legs in fig. q with those in fig. s (and even with the upper legs in fig. r). In addition, the elegant sweep and curving body line of the finished sculpture (fig. c) can be traced back through fig. s specifically to fig. r (and then more obliquely to fig. q).

fig. q.
González, pencil on paper, 12⅜ x 7⅞ in., 31 x 21 cm. Photograph courtesy Carmen Martinez and Viviane Grimminger.

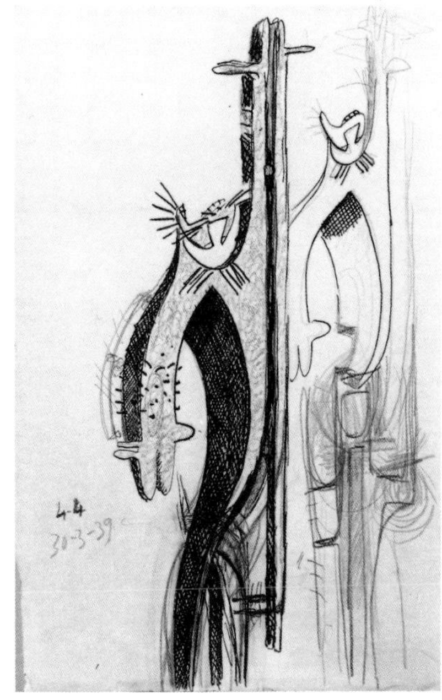

fig. r.
González, ink and colored pencil on paper, 12¼ x 9½ in., 31.1 x 24.1 cm. Photograph courtesy Carmen Martinez and Viviane Grimminger.

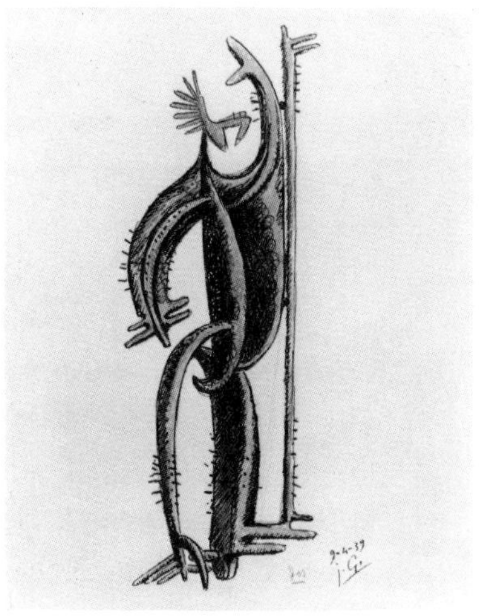

fig. s.
González, ink and oil pastel on paper, 12¾ x 9⅞ in., 32.4 x 25.1 cm., Collection Hans Hartung, Antibes.

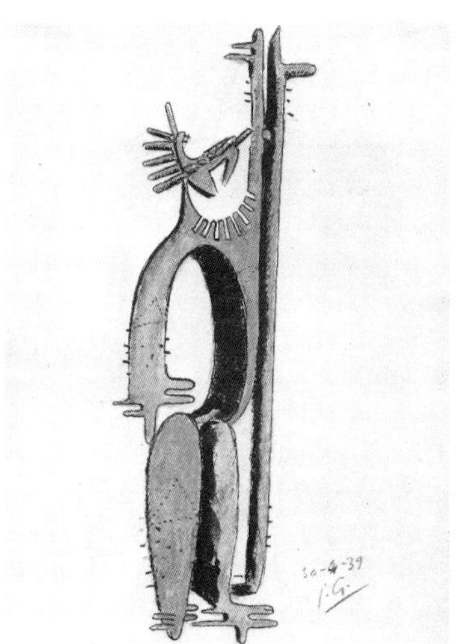

fig. t.
González, ink, watercolor, wash, and crayon on paper, 13 x 9$^{15}/_{16}$ in., 33 x 25.2 cm. Photograph courtesy Carmen Martinez and Viviane Grimminger.

It was at this point in the process that González incorporated into his thinking some elements from the 1933 *Prophet* by Pablo Gargallo (repr. Withers, 1978, p. 27 and Rowell, 1983, p. 189). As Rowell has noted, Gargallo's work appears to have influenced the stance of the male in fig. s, the open treatment of the torso, and the introduction of the long stave held by a raised arm. It is interesting to note, however, that even though Gargallo's *Prophet* was obviously male (as

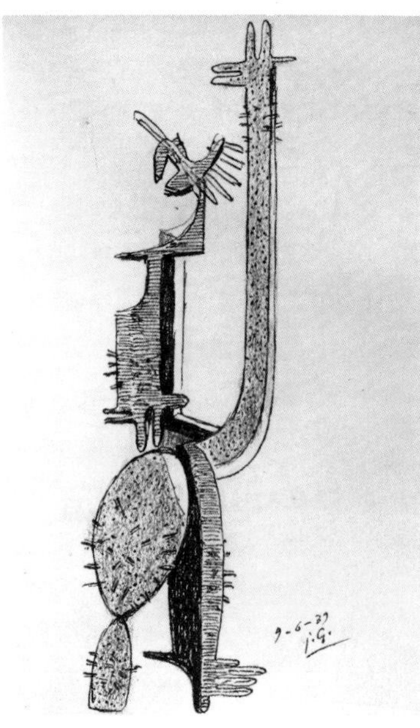

fig. u.
González, ink and crayon on paper, 10¼ x 6¹¹⁄₁₆ in., 26 x 17 cm. Photograph courtesy Carmen Martinez and Viviane Grimminger.

were González's initial variations on it), it had a more direct influence on González's female Cactus piece than on the male (see figs. r, t, u): the long thin right arm (which was in the end deprived of its supporting stave), the graceful crescent curve that leads from the arm toward the head, and the "fringe like" depiction of the hair — including its negative imprint — all played a critical role in the final sculptural resolution of *"Madame" Cactus.*

In short, many of the key differentiating components of the female figure were settled by late April 1939. Additional revisions and modifications continued to absorb González in June (see, for example, fig. u) and even July. But the basic form of the piece did not radically alter during those months.

The exact completion date for *"Madame" Cactus* is not known, although it was probably finished by late summer. González's intense relief at having completed *"Monsieur" Cactus* was vividly expressed in the correspondence with his daughter (see footnote 1). The extent of the struggle involved becomes evident from a study of the drawings.

EXHIBITIONS:

London, *P.G.*, 1964-65, no. 114, repr. (dated 1939-40, the date ascribed to it in all publications until M. Rowell, 1983); Stockholm, *P.G.*, 1966-67, no. 109, repr.; New York, *P.G.*, 1969, p. 36, repr. p. 37; Paris, *P.G.*, 1974-75, no. 111, repr.; Torino, *P.G.*, 1975-76, no. 129, repr.

REFERENCES:

E. A. Carmean, "Cactus Man Number Two," *The Museum of Fine Arts, Houston: Bulletin*, N.S., vol. 4, no. 3, fall 1973, p. 43; J. Withers, *Julio González: Sculpture in Iron*, New York, 1978, pp. 87-91, 97-98, 168, repr. p. 88; M. Rowell, *Julio González*, exh. cat., SRGM, New York, 1983, pp. 26, 28, 29, 189, repr. color p. 188 (iron); L. Flint, *Handbook*, 1983, p. 124, repr. color p. 125.

Arshile Gorky

(Vosdanik Adoian).

Born April 1904, Khorkom, province of Van, Armenia.
Died July 1948, Sherman, Connecticut.

73 Untitled. Summer 1944.

Color plate p. 669.

76.2553 PG 152

Oil on canvas (unvarnished), 65 3/4 x 70 3/16 (167 x 178.2).

Signed and dated l.r.: *A. Gorky / 44.*

PROVENANCE:

Purchased from the artist, New York, 1945.[1]

CONDITION:

In 1964 (Tate Report) some small abrasions at the edges were noted, but the condition of the unvarnished surface and white ground was described as otherwise excellent.

Stretcher impressions are visible, especially along the lower edge. There are some minor abrasions and losses, some soil, and handling marks. Owing to the artist's use of media (thin turpentine washes and stains, with minimum oil medium, on a zinc white ground), cleaning poses problems that are difficult to solve. No treatment has so far been attempted.

The condition is generally stable, though the surface is clearly vulnerable. (New York, Feb. 1983.)

During 1943-44, the first year of his fully mature, independent style, Gorky spent nine months at Crooked Run Farm in Hamilton, Virginia, his wife's family home. He made large numbers of drawings after nature, outdoors, "*sur le motif* ";

1. André Breton took Peggy Guggenheim to Gorky's studio in New York and urged her to buy a painting. She chose this work from several available canvases. Since Breton and Gorky met for the first time at a dinner given in Breton's honor by Margaret La Forge Osborn in 1944, the purchase must have postdated that occasion. The work was recorded among her possessions for the first time in 1945.

he then worked for months in the studio developing them into full-scale canvases. The present painting, according to the testimony of his widow, Mrs. Alexander Fielding, was completed in the Virginia barn studio; Jim Jordan places it first in the series of paintings executed there after the summer drawings of 1944 (1982, p. 85).

As Ethel Schwabacher first pointed out, many of these paintings were closely modeled on the drawings: "often he squared off a drawing and transferred it to canvas, neither adding to nor subtracting from the original conception. It was a matter of concretizing ideas rather than creating them..." (*Arshile Gorky*, New York, 1957, p. 98). In other instances Gorky apparently struggled to base the paintings directly on the inspiration of nature, but found that he could not: "When he painted from his drawings it was different from drawing from nature because he was editing his own emotion and adding and using all his conscious knowledge of his art.... he sometimes said he wished he could eliminate that art and make the paintings as direct on the canvas as the emotion was within him in front of nature.... he would like to eliminate the artistic and conscious selection" (letter from Agnes Gorky to Ethel Schwabacher, Gorky Archive, Whitney Museum of American Art).

In few cases, if any, is the compositional relationship between drawing and painting as close as it is in the Peggy Guggenheim example. The study (fig. a, color plate p. 669) includes not only every important aspect of the linear structure but the precise colors of the final painting. For the first time, Gorky retained the white background of his preparatory drawing as a critical element in his composition, a factor that affected the draftsmanlike impact of the painting.[2] But whereas the linear correspondences between drawing and painting are remarkably exact, the nature of the media used to introduce color in the two works creates strikingly different effects. In the drawing the hues are conveyed in the unmodulated glossy medium of wax crayon; in the painting, the very same hues appear in the form of matte veils of largely transparent, flowing washes of oil pigment diluted with turpentine.[3] Thus, although the imagery is virtually identical in the two works, the pictorial realization is not.

Harry Rand has pointed out that "when [Gorky's] confidence as an artist was confirmed by achievement of a personal style, the very titles as well as the content and references in his work became an issue in his painting" (*Arshile Gorky: The Implications of Symbols*, Montclair and London, 1981, p. 87). The absence

2. Gorky's widow has stated that this was the first painting with a white background (Alley, 1964, p. 76). It is interesting to note that, according to Harold Rosenberg, de Kooning introduced Gorky to the fine "liner" brush, which allowed him to transfer the linear essence of his drawings to canvas: "One day... de Kooning found [Gorky] cursing his inability to paint a long thin line. He was trying to do it with his 'fat Rubens brushes,' and de Kooning was amazed to learn that Gorky had never heard of the signpainter's liner brush. Having bought one, de Kooning remembers, Gorky sat around all day in an ecstasy painting long beautiful lines" (*Arshile Gorky: The Man, the Time, the Idea*, New York, 1962, p. 68).

3. According to Julien Levy, Gorky's technique was heavily influenced in this respect by Matta's example (*Arshile Gorky*, New York, 1966, p. 24).

of a title for cat. no. 73, unusual though not unique during this period, has been explained in various ways. Ronald Alley first suggested that the picture was sold before Gorky had time to give it a title. Jordan, who found this a plausible explanation, also raised the question of Gorky's possible anxiety regarding his "poetic" titles on the grounds that they would be either misinterpreted or thought "excessively romantic" (1982, p. 86). The issue remains unresolved, as does the related question of the imagery in the painting and its legibility as subject matter.

During the years 1943-44, Gorky's work grew more abstract in appearance: its imagery became less decipherable, and the relationship between the pictures and their sources of inspiration more difficult to trace.

As early as the spring of 1944, James Johnson Sweeney characterized the nature drawings as a fundamental turning point in Gorky's development: "The product was a series of monumentally drawn details of what one might see in the heavy August grass, rendered without thought of his fellow-artist's ambitions or theories of what a picture should be. And the result of this free response to nature was a freshness and personalization of idiom which Gorky had never previously approached, and a new vocabulary of forms on which he is at present drawing for a group of large oil paintings" (*Harper's Bazaar*, vol. 78, Apr. 1944, pp. 122, 124).

William Seitz, discussing a drawing shown in the (1952) Gorky exhibition at the Julien Levy Gallery, wrote: "Like the other drawings in the exhibition, the study can hardly be called 'abstract.' A careful observer can discover the petals, stamens, and pistils of flowers, the characteristic structures of insects, and the inner and outer forms of the human body. Yet they cannot be analyzed and labeled individually. Each 'hybrid' detail retains, to the end, the hypnotic ambiguity at which Gorky aimed. His subject matter will not yield its poetry to either botany or physiology" (*The Daily Princetonian*, Oct. 14, 1952, p. 2). Ten years later, Seitz was to comment that "no two spectators will decode Gorky's allusions in the same way" (*Arshile Gorky*, exh. cat., MoMA, New York, 1962, p. 33).

Schwabacher also suggested that the minutiae of natural form and structure inspired Gorky in the 1943-44 works to create a new and intensely personal vocabulary: "Sitting before nature, Gorky dissected root, stem, insect, leaf and flower, studying genesis and process; out of these studies he created an alphabet of forms.... The plants and grasses seemed to grow beneath his eyes..." (*Arshile Gorky*, New York, 1957, p. 97).

On a 1974 visit to Virginia, Jordan made an effort to locate some of the actual landscape views from which Gorky might have worked, but concluded that the artist had been less interested in recording a specific environment than in observing the "perishable flesh" of landscape — "ephemera [such as] seed pods, twists of weed fronds, succulent grasses and vines" ("Arshile Gorky at Crooked Run Farm," *Arts Magazine*, vol. 50, no. 7. Mar. 1976, pp. 99-103).

Richard Reiff, in drawing attention to the similarity between *The Fireplace in Virgina* series and the landscape series, asserts that they "illustrate a homogeneity of intent and effect which suggests only that Gorky had no real interest in the landscape of Virginia nor in fireplaces *per se*, and that it hardly mattered what he used as point of departure, either an interior or a landscape.... The source, since it is only incidental, becomes lost beyond recovery" (*A Stylistic Analysis of Arshile Gorky's Art from 1943-1948*, New York, London, 1977, p. 33).

The underlying opinion in these readings of the "drawings after nature" and their translation into full-scale paintings is the sense that Gorky was able to transpose actual observations into a new pictorial language, but that his purpose was not a depiction of nature as such. The process of working outdoors liberated his capacity to create compositions that were to some extent free of literal subject matter and of direct references to earlier art, but the imagery which arose from this freedom was essentially indecipherable.

Rand by contrast argues for a close correlation, on the one hand, between the imagery and its sources and, on the other, between that imagery and its potential as sign or metaphor to elucidate the meaning of the artist's work as a whole. Although he has not specifically discussed the imagery of Peggy Guggenheim's painting, he has offered detailed readings and interpretations of other works from this period. He argues for a clearly traceable relationship between images and their sources in nature (even in works that appear to be nonobjective), and explicates a set of meanings arising out of that imagery (see, for example, his discussion of *Waterfall*, 1943, op. cit., pp. 84-89, and *Housatonic Falls*, 1943, pp. 89-92). While acknowledging that Gorky took pains "to assure that the specific contents of his work would not be open to speculation," and that the real "meaning" of his paintings would be available to him alone, Rand nonetheless claims that the iconography of even the most elliptical landscapes of this and the subsequent period is indeed both retrievable and susceptible of interpretation.

EXHIBITIONS:

Venice, *P.G.*, 1948 (Biennale), no. 52 (dated 1934); Florence, *P.G.*, 1949, no. 56 (dated 1943); Amsterdam, *P.G.*, 1951, no. 66; Zurich, *P.G.*, 1951, no. 60; Bordighera, *11ᴬ Mostra Internazionale Pittura Americana*, Mar. 1-31, 1953, no. 14; London, *P.G.*, 1964-65, no. 127, repr.; Stockholm, *P.G.*, 1966-67, no. 123, repr.; Torino, Galleria Civica d'Arte Moderna, *Le Muse Inquietanti*, Nov. 1967-Jan. 1968, no. 262, repr.; New York, *P.G.*, 1969, p. 140, repr.; Paris, *P.G.*, 1974-75, no. 130, repr.; Torino, *P.G.*, 1975-76, no. 144, repr. pl. 65; London, The Arts Council of Great Britain, *Dada and Surrealism Reviewed*, Jan. 10-Mar. 27, 1978, no. 15.16, repr.; New York, SRGM, *Arshile Gorky*, Apr. 24-July 19, 1981, no. 182, repr. color; New York, *P.G.*, 1982-83, no. 50, repr. color.

REFERENCES:

Alley, 1964, p. 76; Calas, 1966, p. 163, repr. p. 167; J. Jordan, *Gorky Drawings*, exh. cat., M. Knoedler & Co., Inc., New York, 1969, p. 58; D. Waldman, *Arshile Gorky*, exh. cat., SRGM, New York, 1981, p. 57, repr. color, no. 182; J. M. Jordan and R. Goldwater, *The Paintings of Arshile Gorky: A Critical Catalogue*, New York and London, 1982, pp. 85-86, cat. no. 285, repr.; L. Flint, *Handbook*, 1983, p. 174, repr. color p. 175.

Juan Gris

(pseud. of José Victoriano González).

Born March 1887, Madrid.
Died May 1927, Paris.

74

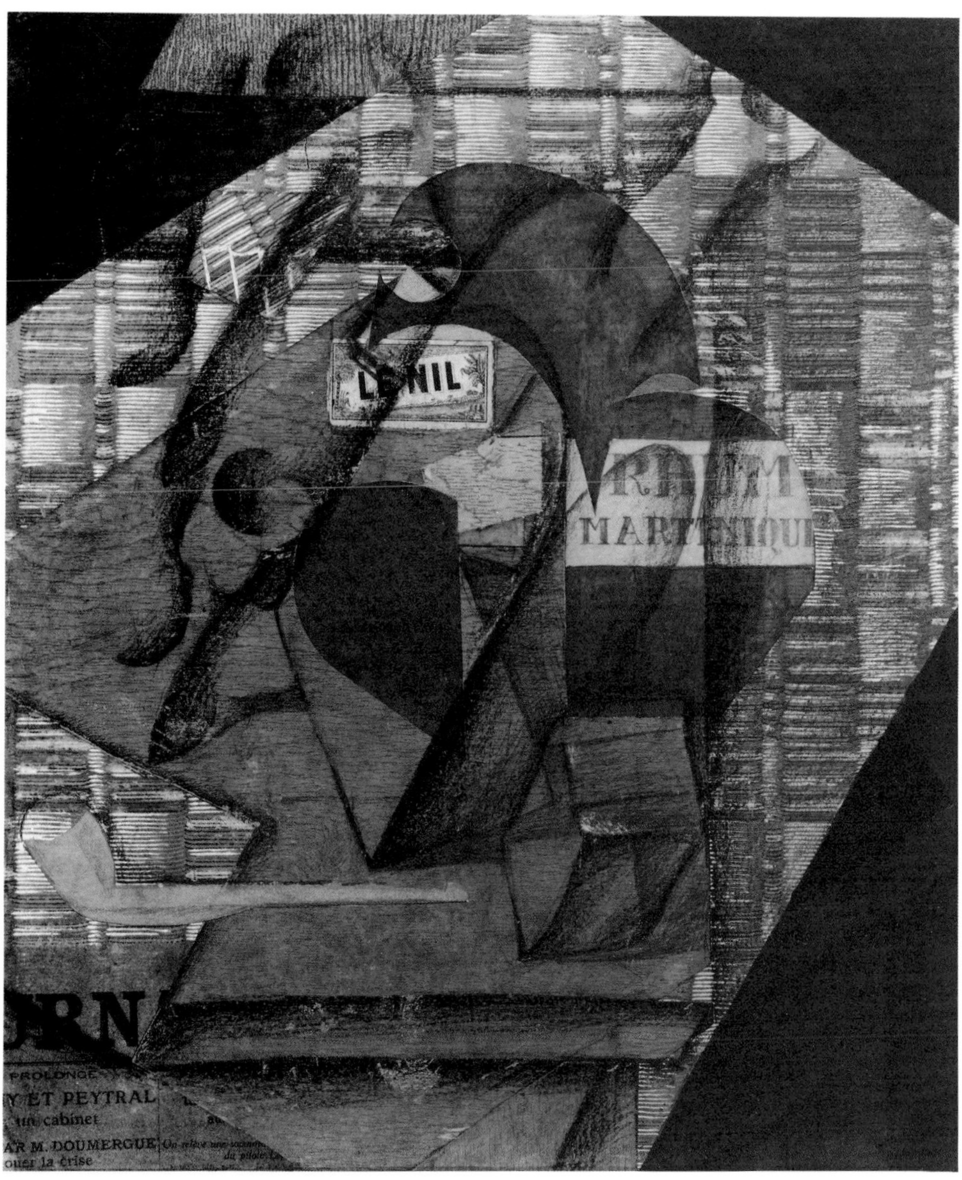

74 Bouteille de rhum et journal.
June 1914.
(*Bottle of rum and newspaper*; *The Bottle of Martinique Rum*).

Color plate p. 37.

76.2553 PG 11

Faux-bois paper, patterned wallpaper, white-wove paper, brown paper, printed tobacco and matchbox covers, gouache, conté crayon, pencil, and varnish on newspaper glued to canvas, 21⅝ x 18¼ (54.8 x 46.2).

Signed on reverse: *Juan Gris*. Not dated.

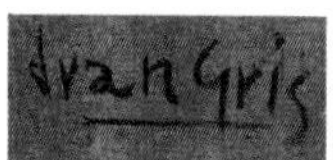

PROVENANCE:

Sold to D.-H. Kahnweiler, 1914 (stockbook no. 2212); Sequestered Kahnweiler stock 1914-23; 4ᵉ *Vente Kahnweiler*, Hôtel Drouot, Paris, May 7-8, 1923, no. 281 (purchased with lots 283 and 285 for total of 110 fr., buyer unknown);[1] Paris, Hôtel Drouot, cat. no.76, *Estampes modernes, tableaux...*, Nov. 7, 1934, no.93 (*Nature morte: objets de fumeurs*, neither seller nor buyer recorded in Drouot archives); Bernard Poissonnier, Paris;[2] purchased from Poissonnier by Galerie Simon, Paris, July 1938 (stockbook no. 12640); purchased from Galerie Simon by Guggenheim Jeune (Peggy Guggenheim), London, April 1939.

CONDITION:

A tear through paper and canvas (5¾ in., 14.5 cm., from left, 2 in., 5 cm., from top) was already present and repaired by 1964 (Tate Report). At that time, cleavage of the *papier-collé* elements at the edges was secured and some losses inpainted with watercolor.

The surface is abraded in places and there has been some flaking with losses in the green gouache areas. One piece of collage (printed matchbox cover *ALLUMETTES FRANÇAISES*), attached just below the collage label *LE NIL* until at least 1942 (fig. a), had been lost by 1964.

The various papers have considerably darkened through overexposure to light, and the wood-graining of the *faux-bois* has in some instances almost entirely faded. In the process, the relative values of parts of the composition and the contrasts between varnished darks and unvarnished lights have to a large extent been lost and the legibility of individual forms blurred. The 1942 photograph of the work (fig. a) reveals the original structure and clarity of the composition. Apart from this severe photo-oxidation, the general condition is stable. (Venice, Nov. 1982.)

Gris's complicated process of composition in this collage was followed in a number of other approximately contemporary works. In *Guitare et Verres*, for example (MoMA, New York, formerly Nelson A. Rockefeller Collection, Cooper, 1977, no. 91, 36 x 25½ in., 91.5 x 64.7 cm.), he made use of the same media and the same sequence of techniques.[3] In each case a sheet of newspaper was first glued down over the entire surface of the canvas. Though this was probably intended to act purely as a receptive surface for collage elements and to be fully covered by the ensuing stages of composition, it is now discernible (in both works) through the growing transparency of the dark green gouache.[4]

1. Price supplied by Gary Tinterow, Oct. 1982.
2. Poissonnier offered the picture for sale to Douglas Cooper in 1934-35 (correspondence with the author).
3. The author is indebted to Jean Volkmer, formerly Chief Conservator of Paintings at MoMA, and to Terrence Mahon of her staff, for collaborating on an examination of the Rockefeller picture in the MoMA laboratory.

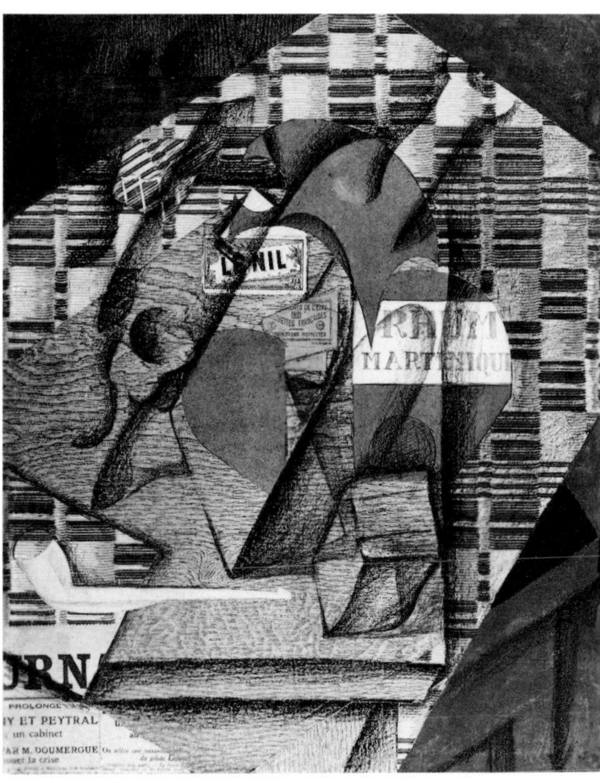

fig. a.
Ca. 1942 photograph of cat. no. 74.

In both compositions, Gris used the same two distinct colors of *faux-bois* (wood-grain) paper, and in each case he selectively, and with miniaturist precision, applied a natural resin varnish to certain, but not all, areas of the "wood" surfaces. Drawing and shading of forms was accomplished with a combination of pencil and conté (or lithographic) crayon with touches of white gouache. Stenciled pencil lettering was used in both works, as were fragments of newsprint or other printed material. While the painted checked tablecloth in the Rockefeller picture is contrasted with the "wallpaper," or *papier-peint*, collage surface of the Peggy Guggenheim central field, touches such as the literal collage pipe of the latter work may be described as analogous to the depiction of the guitar's curving body at the lower left of the former.

Although the discoloration of the papers has obscured much of the original transparency, contrasts, and subtlety of trompe-l'œil effects in the Peggy Guggenheim work, the intricate compositional structure is still legible. In several instances, objects that were pasted on last (closest to the picture plane) act visually as background elements, and vice versa.

The sequence of steps taken by Gris was approximately as follows: first, a piece of newspaper was glued down to cover the entire canvas. The patterned wallpaper of the central field was glued down on its diagonal axis; the varnished *faux-boix* of the table area was glued down over it. (It is not possible to say

4. This phenomenon is characteristic of at least 4 other 1914 *papiers collés* by Juan Gris known to the author. The precise reasons for Gris's use of newspaper in these works as an intermediate support—rather than as an aesthetic ingredient in the composition—require further study.

whether Gris varnished these before or after incorporating them into the composition.) The three corner areas were painted with dark green gouache. Initial drawing of the bottle, glass, and table was added in conté crayon. A cutout shape of white paper, the upper and lower portions painted a matte light brown, a broad strip of white left untouched between them, was pasted down to the right of the center; the stenciled lettering *RHUM MARTINIQUE* was added in pencil on the unpainted area. Printed collage elements — *LE JOURNAL* (lower left), *LE NIL*, and *ALLUMETTES FRANÇAISES* (center) — and the cutout paper pipe (lower left) were pasted down. Two additional sections of painted brown matte paper were added to give definition to the bottle (its shoulder and its inner base). Four tiny additional sections of this painted brown matte paper were added to differentiate shadows within the bottle. Extensive drawing with conté crayon followed: in the lower right the literally rendered table was completed with a black gouache top edge; in the center of the composition the forms of bottles, table edge, and glass were subtly shaded and delineated in such a way as to create the concrete foreground elements and the transparent background of the still-life and the table on which it rests.

Although closely related in significant ways to the contemporary *papiers collés* of Picasso and Braque, Gris's works of this moment are characterized by a complexity, density, and intricacy of conception that was foreign to both Picasso and Braque. As John Golding has pointed out, Gris, by covering the entire field of the canvas, used the medium virtually as a new technique: "Sometimes the scraps of paper are cut out to correspond exactly to the shapes or contours of the objects which they represent, and each is subsequently carefully modelled or made completely representational by the addition of over-drawn or over-painted detail.... The *papier collé* is thus assimilated into works that have the appearance of being immensely elaborate and complex paintings, and what distinguishes Gris's original approach to *papier collé* from that of Braque and Picasso is that he used it to give his work a sense of definition and certainty, a precision and exactitude that he could not achieve by any other means" (*Cubism: A History and an Analysis, 1907-1914*, Boston, 1959, p. 111; see also pp. 105-10 for an illuminating discussion of collage and *papier collé* as practiced by Picasso and Braque).

EXHIBITIONS:

New York, Art of This Century, 1942-47, p. 70, repr. p. 71; New York, Art of This Century, *15 Early, 15 Late Paintings*, Mar. 13-Apr. 10, 1943, no. 213; Venice, *P.G.*, 1948 (Biennale), no. 53; Florence, *P.G.*, 1949, no. 57, repr.; Venice, XXV Biennale, June 8-Oct. 15, 1950, *Quattro maestri del cubismo*, no. 17; Amsterdam, *P.G.*, 1951, no. 67, repr.; Zurich, *P.G.*, 1951, no. 61; London, *P.G.*, 1964-65, no. 10, repr.; Stockholm, *P.G.*, 1966-67, no. 10, repr.; New York, *P.G.*, 1969, p. 74, repr.; Paris, *P.G.*, 1974-75, no. 8, repr.; Torino, *P.G.*, 1975-76, no. 10, repr. pl. 4.

REFERENCES:

P. Guggenheim, *Art of This Century*, 1942, p. 70, repr. p. 71; Calas, 1966, p. 23, repr. p. 39; D. Cooper and M. Potter, *Juan Gris*, Paris, 1977, vol. I, no. 108, repr.

David Hare

Born March 1917, New York.
Lives in New York.

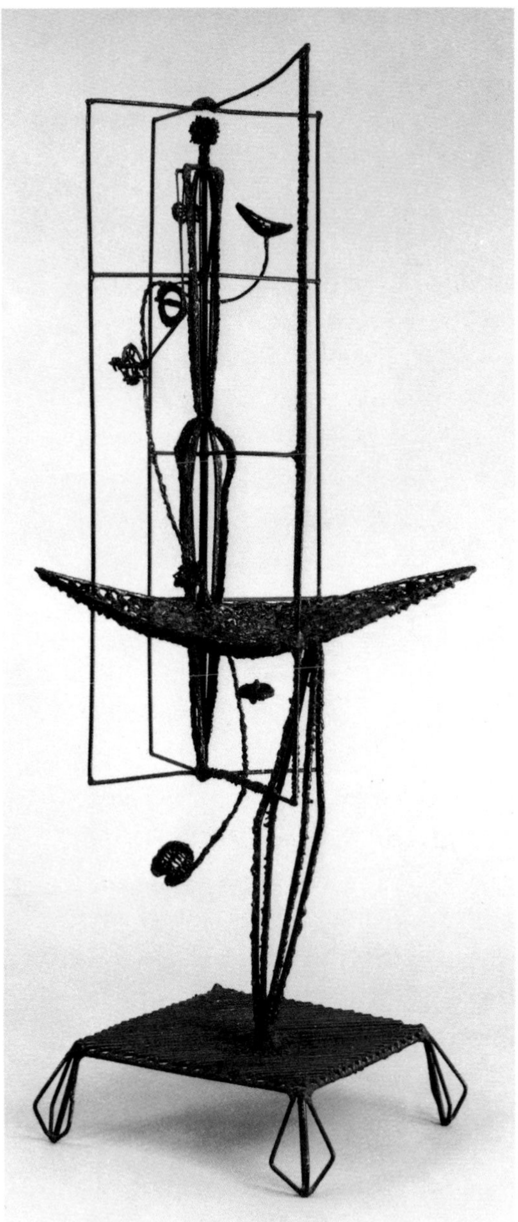

75 Moon Cage. 1955.

76.2553 PG 201

Welded steel, brass spray. Height: 30⅛ (76.5).

Signed on base: *HARE*. Not dated.

PROVENANCE:

Purchased from the artist on a visit to his New York studio, ca. 1955.[1]

1. Peggy Guggenheim and David Hare both recalled that she bought the work on a visit to the studio, but neither could remember the precise year.

CONDITION:

The steel has oxidized, resulting in an overall brownish tone. The differentiation of color intended by the artist (black in the case of the steel, bright golden in the case of the brass) has thus been partly obscured, though initial cleaning in June 1983 reestablished some contrast. Whitish residue from the flux used by the artist in the welding process is visible in places. A break near the base of the long, curving slender element, which runs vertically through the sculpture, was at an unrecorded date soldered into an erroneous position. This was repositioned according to the original design in June 1983, resoldered with a brazing alloy based on silver, patinated with ammonium sulphide and retouched with watercolor. The condition is fragile. Further cleaning and anticorrosive treatment is envisaged. (Venice, June 1983.)

The piece is constructed from steel rods welded together with an oxyacetylene torch.[2] The rods in this and related sculptures were precoated with copper to facilitate welding. The copper necessarily melts during the process and the steel subsequently acquires the anticipated black patina. Brass spray was in this instance applied in specific places (the lower moon form, the long curving element running through the center of the sculpture, and the upper small moon form) to provide tonal and coloristic contrast with the blackened steel. (See CONDITION.)

Hare regards his work as neither abstract nor representational. Hence he sees it as resistant to interpretation. "The piece is not figurative literally. A combination of images is more interesting to me. Ambiguity is important; a confusion of images makes you more conscious of the image you are interested in." Although nonrepresentational as a total entity, the sculpture does present an elliptical configuration that can be read as "window, person, and moon which together make a fourth object: the sculpture." The ambiguity remains the essential ingredient, the "images" being susceptible to a variety of readings on different levels.

Hare suggests, for example, that one possible implication of the spatial ambiguity may be that "you are in a house and would like to get out, or you are out and would like to be in." In offering these alternative readings, however, he emphasizes the importance of maintaining the range of potential interpretations, both of the formal configuration and of its implications.

REFERENCE:

Calas, 1966, repr. p. 203.

2. Information on the technique and imagery of the sculpture published here derives from a conversation between David Hare and the author June 3, 1977.

Grace Hartigan

Born March 1922, Newark, New Jersey.
Lives in Baltimore, Maryland.

76

76 Ireland. 1958.

76.2553 PG 182

Oil on canvas (unvarnished), 78¾ x 106¾ (200 x 271).

Signed and dated l.r.: *Hartigan '58.*

PROVENANCE:

Purchased from Tibor De Nagy Gallery, New York, April 30, 1959.[1]

CONDITION:

Apart from some tears in the tacking edge, a few extremely small pigment losses, and a small blister caused by a puncture from the reverse (19¹¹⁄₁₆ in., 50 cm., from the bottom edge, 36¼ in., 92 cm., from the left), the surface and support are in stable condition. One area of drying cracks (near the top of the canvas, 27⁹⁄₁₆ in., 70 cm., from the left edge) occurs in a section of brown applied over white. The artist's intended contrasts between matte areas and areas heavier in oil content have been maintained, and no varnish has been applied.[2] (Venice, Mar. 1984.)

In 1958 Grace Hartigan, an artist of Irish descent, visited Europe for the first time, and traveled extensively in Ireland. On her return to the United States she painted a series of pictures with Irish titles (*Dublin*, *Bray*, *Dun Laoghaire*, and *Guinness*), of which the present work was the largest. Though in no sense landscapes, or pictures with any literal subject matter, they constitute for the artist abstract evocations of "place," and in that sense are deeply rooted in her experience of Ireland.[3]

EXHIBITIONS:

New York, Tibor de Nagy, *Grace Hartigan*, Apr. 28-May 30, 1959, no. 5, repr.; London, *P.G.*, 1964-65, no. 152, repr.

1. The work was purchased on a visit to the artist's studio before the exhibition at Tibor de Nagy (Grace Hartigan, correspondence with the author, June 1983).
2. Hartigan has never varnished her oils, feeling that varnish of any kind destroys the surface subtleties of a painting (conversation with the author, June 1983).
3. Conversation with the author, June 1983.

COLOR PLATES

Cat. no. 104, p. 476.
Malevich, *Untitled*, ca. 1916.

Cat. no. 100, p. 460.
Lissitzky, *Untitled*, ca. 1919-20.

Cat. no. 45, p. 219.
Van Doesburg, *Composition in gray (Rag-time)*, 1919.

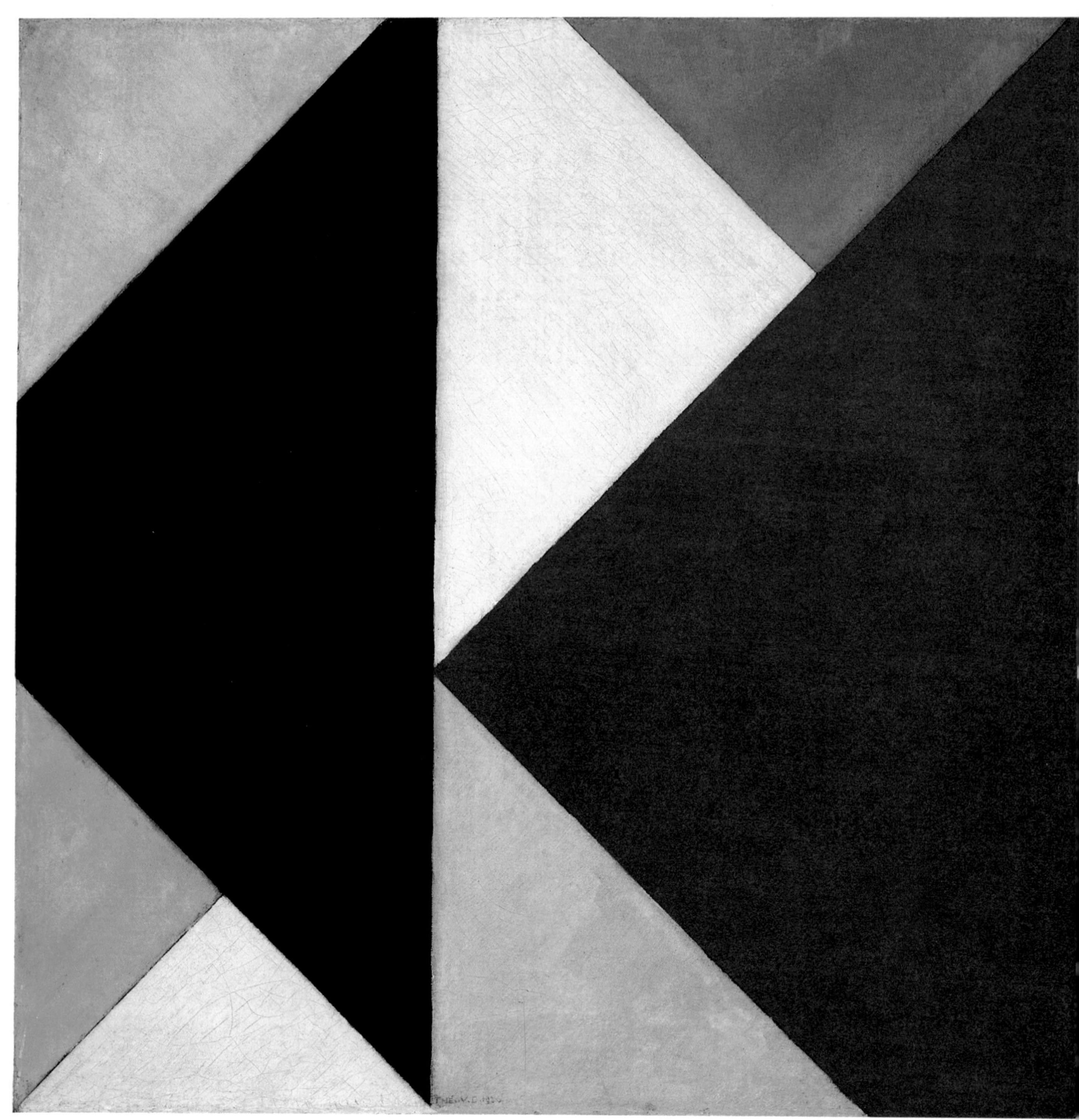

Cat. no. 46, p. 228.
Van Doesburg, *Contra-Compositie XIII*, 1925-26.

Cat. no. 121, p. 560.
Mondrian, *Composition*, 1938-39.

Cat. no. 97, p. 452.
Léger, *Les hommes dans la ville*, 1919.

Cat. no. 77, p. 403.
Hélion, *Equilibre*, 1933-34.

Cat. no. 78, p. 405.
Hélion, *Composition*, August 16, 1935-December 2, 1935.

Cat. no. 5, p. 66.
Arp, *Soulier bleu renversé à deux talons, sous une voûte noir*, ca. 1925.

Cat. no. 131, p. 590.
Ozenfant, *Guitare et bouteilles*, 1920.

Cat. no. 129, p. 587.
Nicholson, *February 1956 (menhir)*, 1956.

Cat. no. 20, p. 131.
Braque, *Le compotier de raisin*, 1926.

Cat. no. 139, p. 617.
Picasso, *L'Atelier*, 1928.

Cat. no. 140, p. 623.
Picasso, *La Baignade*, February 12, 1937.

Cat. no. 118, p. 546.
Miró, *Femme assise II*, February 27, 1939.

Cat. no. 83, p. 418.
Kandinsky, *Weisses Kreuz*, January-June 1922.

Jean Hélion

Born April 1904, Couterne (Orne), France.
Lives in Paris and Châteauneuf-en-Thymerais.

77 Equilibre. 1933-34.[1]
(*Equilibrium*).

Color plate p. 391.

76.2553 PG 44

Oil on canvas (unvarnished), 38⅜ x 51⅝ (97.4 x 131.2).

Signed, dated, and inscribed on reverse: *Hélion / 33 (Paris) 34 / (p. 6)*[2] *Hélion.*

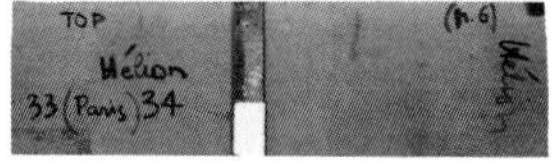

PROVENANCE:

Purchased from the artist, New York, 1943, after the exhibition at Art of This Century.

CONDITION:

In 1964 (Tate Report) areas of cleavage in the yellow rectangle were laid down and retouched. Apart from a small area of crackle with incipient cleavage near the left margin, the condition was described as fairly good. The work had not been varnished.

The large black central form was reworked at an unknown date, possibly by the artist. (See below, the entry in his working diary.) The yellow rectangular form (right) shows signs of some breakdown in the paint film and some blotching. This area is fragile. The condition is otherwise fairly stable. (Venice, June 1983.)

1. These precise dates were supplied by the artist, whose working diary contains detailed information on the sequence of his works, exhibitions in which the pictures appeared, and collections to which they were sold. There are also comments on aesthetic intention, compositional problems, etc. Hélion kindly provided the author with the entries on both the Peggy Guggenheim works, as well as information on several related works.
2. "*P. 6*" is the page reference in the working diary.

Hélion's working diary contains the following observations:

Tableau fond blanc général et un 2ème fond partiel accroché dans les structures. Masse simple à droite; masse plurielle à gauche. Dualisme systématique. Les axes s'inclinent et passent par différentes échelles. Petits éléments et gros éléments. Peint sur une toile difficile, sinon impossible à tendre parce que hygrophile.... [3]

D'abord un essai de tableau selon un dessin figurant dans le catalogue de Gallery of Living Art que j'ai donné à Jean Blair.[4] *Raté. Gratté.*

Puis nombreuses études sur l'assemblage de différents dessins. Je veux passer du singulier au pluriel. Concevoir des éléments. Après deux mois le tableau sort, et c'est mon premier pas vers la grande composition.

Bien peint; sauf le dégradé noir a commencé à craquer au milieu; la 2ème couche a été mise trop tôt sur le noir mal sec. Je devrai le repeindre?

Hélion's series of variations on a theme of equilibrium date from the years 1932-35. Commenting on the earliest of these (Collection Mr. and Mrs. Roy Friedman, Chicago), a sparse centralized composition in which two slightly curved but rectangular planes are held in balance, as if on a scale, by two slightly curved lines, Hélion wrote in his journal that "*en cherchant la réaction de l'espace et du mouvement sur les éléments, c'est à dire en construisant l'œuvre en mouvement, ou plutôt en équilibre sur le mouvement, mes images sont devenus plus souples.... Pour établir des relations entre des surfaces aussi complexes que celles qui sont définies par des courbes, il faut disposer des nuances.*"

The extreme economy of form in the Friedman oil was elaborated in subsequent variations by the introduction of increasingly complex interrelationships, although the essential structural issues outlined above continued to govern Hélion's thinking. In the present work, as suggested by the diary notes, Hélion's concern is with the balance between a simple, primarily rectilinear planar structure on the right and an intricately balanced composition of curving planes, bars, and lines on the left. The issue of creating the tension and equilibrium between the two halves of the composition, and the suspension of parts within each half, posed especially complex new problems. The extensive series of preparatory drawings and studies mentioned in the diary notes (thus far not located) reflected Hélion's characteristic working method. Only through a process of exhaustive research and gradual refinement of interrelationships did he arrive at the resolution of the problems each phase presented. The process included small-scale oil studies, and, in most instances, resulted in a group, or series, of closely related full-scale oils. The small composition in the collection of MoMA (fig. a), which almost certainly postdates Peggy Guggenheim's picture, may well represent a stage in the development of such a series arising out of the present work, though other full-scale oils of this particular composition have not come to light.

3. The absorbent nature of the canvas might have been due to glycerine used in the original glue sizing to add suppleness (Hélion, in correspondence with the author, Nov. 1976).

4. Jean Blair was the artist's wife at the time.

fig. a.
Hélion, *Equilibre*, 1934, oil on canvas, 10¾ x 13¾ in., 27.3 x 35 cm., The Museum of Modern Art, New York, Acquired through the Lillie P. Bliss Bequest.

Hélion's judgment that the Peggy Guggenheim *Equilibre* represented a turning point in his search for "la grande composition" is borne out by an examination of its place within his development during the years 1933-35.

EXHIBITIONS:

Paris, Galerie des "Cahiers d'Art," *Hans Arp-Ghika, Jean Hélion, S. H. Taeuber-Arp*, July 3-Aug. 2, 1934 (no cat.);[5] Hollywood, Calif., Putzel Gallery, *Jean Hélion*, 1936 (no cat.);[6] New York, Art of This Century, *Jean Hélion*, Feb. 8-Mar. 6, 1943, no. 28; Venice, *P.G.*, 1948 (Biennale), no. 59 (dated 1934, the date attributed to it in all *P.G.* publications until 1964); Florence, *P.G.*, 1949, no. 65; Amsterdam, *P.G.*, 1951, no. 75; Zurich, *P.G.*, 1951, no. 68; Venice, Sala dei Specchi, Palazzo Giustiniani, *Hélion: Pitture dal 1928 al 1951*, Aug.-Sept., 1951, no. 10, repr.; London, *P.G.*, 1964-65, no. 37, repr. (dated 1933-34); Stockholm, *P.G.*, 1966-67, no. 38, repr.; Paris, Centre National d'Art Contemporain, *Hélion, 100 tableaux, 1928-1970*, Dec. 11, 1970-Feb. 1, 1971, p. 24, repr.; Paris, *P.G.*, 1974-75, no. 41, repr.; Torino, *P.G.*, 1975-76, no. 44.

REFERENCE:

Calas, 1966, p. 24, repr. p. 45.

5. The picture's appearance in this exhibition is documented in the artist's working diary.
6. The picture's appearance in this exhibition is documented in the artist's working diary. A review of the show appeared in the *Los Angeles Times*, Feb. 21, 1937, but the precise dates of the exhibition have not been established. Putzel opened his gallery in Hollywood in August 1936, though he had already been managing the Stanley Rose Gallery since the autumn of 1935, and before that the Paul Elder Gallery in San Francisco.

---

78 Composition.

August 16, 1935-December 2, 1935.[1]

Color plate p. 392.

76.2553 PG 45

Oil on canvas (unvarnished), $57\frac{1}{8}$ x $78\frac{13}{16}$ (145 x 200.2).

Signed and dated on reverse: *Hélion 35*.

PROVENANCE:

Acquired from the artist, by exchange, Venice, 1951.[2]

CONDITION:

In 1964 (Tate Report) a large rectangular area of elevated crackle in the center of the work was noted, but the general condition was described as good. The work had not been varnished.

The mottled discoloration of the blue is apparently the result of water damage. There is scattered crackle of the pigment layer, especially in the white central rectangle; there are some signs of incipient cleavage. The condition is somewhat fragile. (Venice, June 1983.)

78

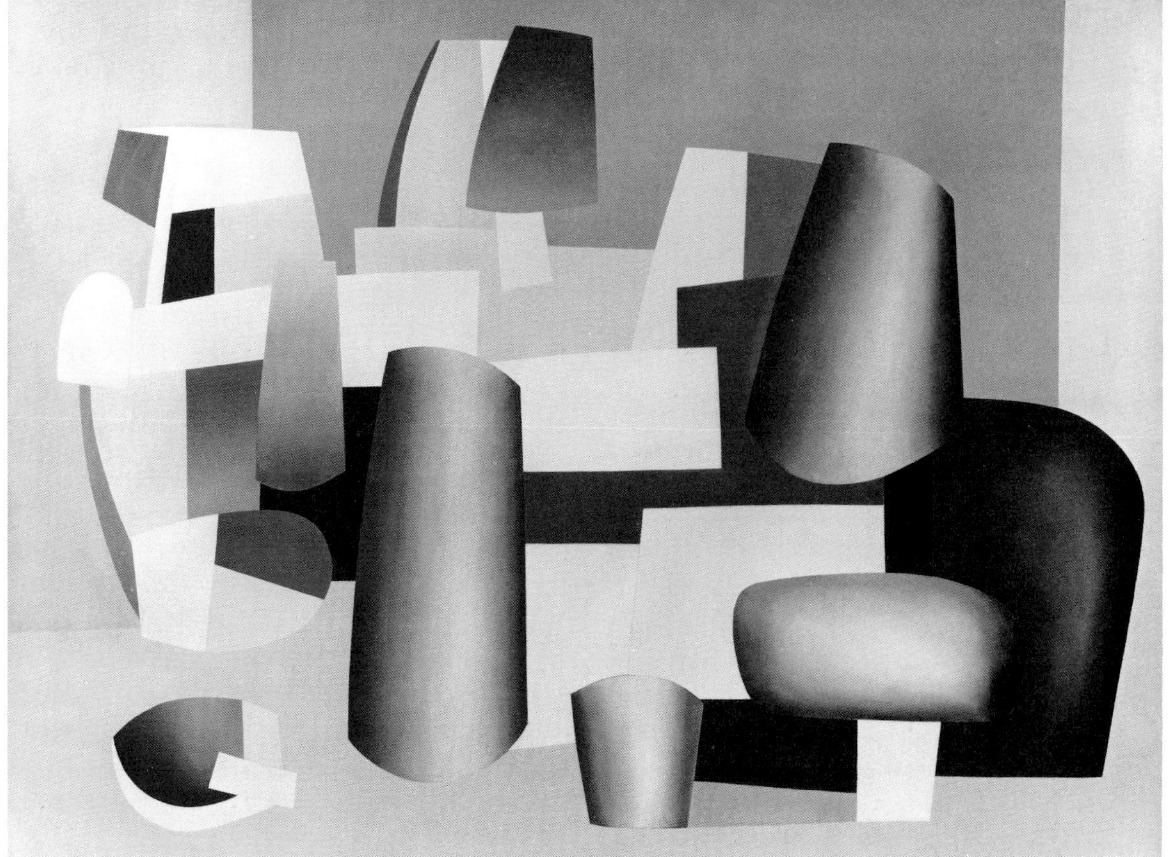

Hélion's diary notes contain the following observations: "*Dessin de la série du tableau coll. Chrysler. Mais en couleurs, ordre, rythmes très différents. Couleurs déshonorées — de bonbons, savons, poudre de riz, dont j'espère pourtant faire quelque chose de fort par un ajustement des oppositions.*" And: "*Vient bien, lentement, 3 sept. 35, — conduit provisoirement 19 rue Daguerre en novembre 35. terminé 51 Bd. Saint-Jacques. Tableau délicat, rapports rares. Très féminin, malgré mes efforts. 16-12-35. Excellent tout de même.*"

The present work is the third in a series of closely related compositions that are comparable in scale but (as Hélion's diary entry suggests) not in color. The

1. Information from Hélion's working diary, 1933-38, p. 62. See above, cat. no. 77, fn. 1.

2. At the close of the 1951 Venice exhibition, which Peggy Guggenheim organized, she asked Hélion to give her this work in exchange for *The Chimney Sweep*, 1936, which she had owned since ca. 1941 (*Art of This Century*, 1942, repr. p. 95). The latter subsequently entered the collection of the Rhode Island School of Design.

first (formerly Chrysler Collection, now Private Collection, New York) and the second, *Ile de France* (Tate Gallery, London; Alley, *Tate Collection*, 1981, pp. 359-60), also date from 1935, and Hélion always hoped and intended that the three be exhibited together; this has so far not been achieved.

As noted elsewhere by this author (A.Z.R. *Guggenheim*, 1976, Vol. I, p. 197), Hélion's large compositions of 1934-35 constitute his most fully developed expression of the notion of equilibrium. The three 1935 compositions discussed here are characterized, as were works of 1934, by an all-over design of interlocking elements. But the clear emphasis on modeled cylindrical forms is new here, and leads directly into Hélion's *Figures* of 1936. He himself has written of a compositional progression from "simple to complex, from elementary to complete, from flat to shaded, from shaded to '*modelé*.' " But at every stage he retained elements from the previous stages. (Letter to Michael Compton, Oct. 29, 1965, cited by Alley, op. cit.) In this same text, Hélion describes the way in which the left-hand side of the composition in *Ile de France* (and the point applies similarly to the present work) "comprises an upright abstract figure" deriving from paintings of 1934. This "figure" in turn is set in opposition to and integrated with the broader compositional structure dominated by "*gros volumes*." In their critical emphasis on the modeled forms of the "*gros volumes*," these three works, which are among Hélion's most successful abstract compositions, nonetheless contain the elements for his eventual transition back into an increasingly figurative mode. (For a more detailed discussion of the developments within this phase of Hélion's work, see M. S. Schipper, "Jean Hélion: The Abstract Years, 1929-1939," unpublished Ph.D. dissertation, University of California at Los Angeles, 1974, pp. 115-24.)

EXHIBITIONS:

Paris, Galerie des "Cahiers d'Art," *Hélion*, Feb. 25-Mar. 14, 1936 (no cat.);[3] Chicago, The Arts Club of Chicago, *Jean Hélion*, Feb. 4-18, 1938;[4] Venice, Sala dei Specchi, Palazzo Giustiniani, *Hélion: Pitture dal 1928 al 1951*, Aug.-Sept., 1951, no. 9; London, *P.G.*, 1964-65, no. 38, repr. (*Large Volumes*, the title by which it was known in all *P.G.* publications until 1983); Stockholm, *P.G.*, 1966-67, no. 39, repr.; New York, *P.G.*, 1969, p. 133, repr. color; Paris, *P.G.*, 1974-75, no. 42; Torino, *P.G.*, 1975-76, no. 45.

REFERENCES:

H. Wescher, "New York in Paris," *Axis*, no. 6, summer 1936, repr. p. 29 (installation photo, "Cahiers d'Art" exhibition); C. Zervos, "Position actuelle de Jean Hélion," *Cahiers d'Art*, vol. 26, 1951, repr. p. 174 (as "*Les gros volumes*," the title by which it has been known in all *P.G.* publications until 1983); Calas, 1966, repr. p. 44; L. Flint, *Handbook*, 1983, repr. color p. 83.

3. The installation photo published in *Axis*, no. 6, summer 1936, p. 29, includes the picture. Its appearance in the exhibition is corroborated by the entry in Hélion's working diary.
4. Hélion's working diary contains the information "*Envoyé chez Valentine, N.Y. mi mars* [1936] / *Exp. à Chicago Arts Club.*" According to the catalogue, the 19 works in the 1938 Chicago exhibition, all untitled, were lent by the Valentine Gallery, New York, which presumably had them on consignment since exhibiting a group in April 1936. The present work was subsequently returned to Hélion; he then lent it, together with others, to his friend the writer Raymond Queneau, who kept it until Hélion returned to Paris from the U.S. in 1946.

Morris Hirshfield

Born April 1872, Poland.
Died July 1946, New York.

79 Two Women in Front of a Mirror.
1943.

76.2553 PG 122

Oil[1] on canvas, 52 3/8 x 59 7/8 (133 x 152).

Signed and dated lower right: *M. Hirshfield / 1943.*

PROVENANCE:

Sidney Janis, New York; purchased from Janis (partial exchange for *Girl Looking Through a Doorway*), March 1947.

CONDITION:

In 1964 (Tate Report) extensive ground and pigment crackle with cleavage over the entire surface was noted. In February 1965, the crackle was laid down and the picture wax-lined on linen canvas (14 pts. beeswax, 4 pts. dammar, 1 pt. gum elemi) under pressure. The surface was cleaned. The canvas was placed on a new stretcher. Two punctures (in the "*derrière*" of the left-hand nude) were filled and inpainted.

The general condition is stable. (Venice, Nov. 1982.)

EXHIBITIONS:

Venice, *P.G.*, 1948 (Biennale), no. 62; Florence, *P.G.*, 1949, no. 68; Amsterdam, *P.G.*, 1951, no. 78; Zurich, *P.G.*, 1951, no. 73; London, *P.G.*, 1964-65, no. 105, repr.; Stockholm, *P.G.*, 1966-67, no. 101, repr.; New York, *P.G.*, 1969, p. 22, repr. p. 23; Paris, *P.G.*, 1974-75, no. 110, repr.; Torino, *P.G.*, 1975-76, no. 120.

REFERENCES:

P. Guggenheim, *Confessions*, 1960, p. 112; M. Jean, *The History of Surrealist Painting*, London, 1960, repr. p. 304; Calas, 1966, pp. 121-22, repr. color p. 153.

1. The medium was described in the Tate Report as "decorator's oil paint" and was found to be not soluble in either water or benzine.

Hundertwasser

(pseud. of Friedrich von Stowasser).

Born December 1928, Vienna.
Lives in Venice, Vienna, and New Zealand.

80 Casa Che Protegge — Die Schutzhütte.
May 1960.[1]
(*Shelter*; *Protecting House*; *Composition 1*).

76.2553 PG 186

Watercolor on wood-pulp, wove wrapping paper, with chalk and polyvinyl ground, 25 3/16 x 19 3/8 (64 x 49.2).

Signed and dated u.l.: *Hundertwasser 1960*.

PROVENANCE:

Purchased from Galleria d'Arte il Canale, Venice, July 9, 1960.

CONDITION:

The support has been glued to a wood-pulp board, which is foxed. The primary support, which was folded into quarters, is cockled throughout. Creases are visible in the lower left corner; running from the left edge horizontally across almost the entire design; in the upper right quadrant from top edge running vertically through the white. There is a tear at the right end of the horizontal fold. Paint losses are visible along the major horizontal and vertical folds. Some light spots due to mold (inactive) are visible in the blacks. The condition is stable. (Venice, Nov. 1982.)

EXHIBITIONS:

Venice, Galleria d'Arte il Canale, *Anti-Procès*, June 18-July 8, 1960 (pamphlet; the work's appearance in this exhibition is recorded in the artist's oeuvre catalogue; it was purchased by Peggy Guggenheim on this occasion); Paris, Galerie Raymond Cordier et Cie, *Retrospective Hundertwasser 1950-1960*, Oct. 4-Nov. 4, 1960 (pamphlet with reproduction); London, *P.G.*, 1964-65, no. 155 (*Composition No. 1*, reproduced as a horizontal, as it is frequently in subsequent publications); Stockholm, *P.G.*, 1966-67, no. 143; New York, *P.G.*, 1969, p. 175, repr. (*Protecting House*); Paris, *P.G.*, 1974-75, no. 149, repr.; Torino, *P.G.*, 1975-76, no. 176.

REFERENCES:

L'Œil, no. 74, Feb. 1961, repr. p. 11 (advertisement for Galerie Raymond Cordier et Cie); Calas, 1966, p. 228, repr. color p. 247 ("*Composition No. 1* [*Protecting House*]," as a vertical).

1. The work is recorded in the artist's handwritten oeuvre catalogue, no. 435. It was begun in Vienna; he completed the painting after moving to Paris in May.

Asger Jorn

Born March 1914, Vejrum, Jutland, Denmark.
Died May 1973, Aarhus, Denmark.

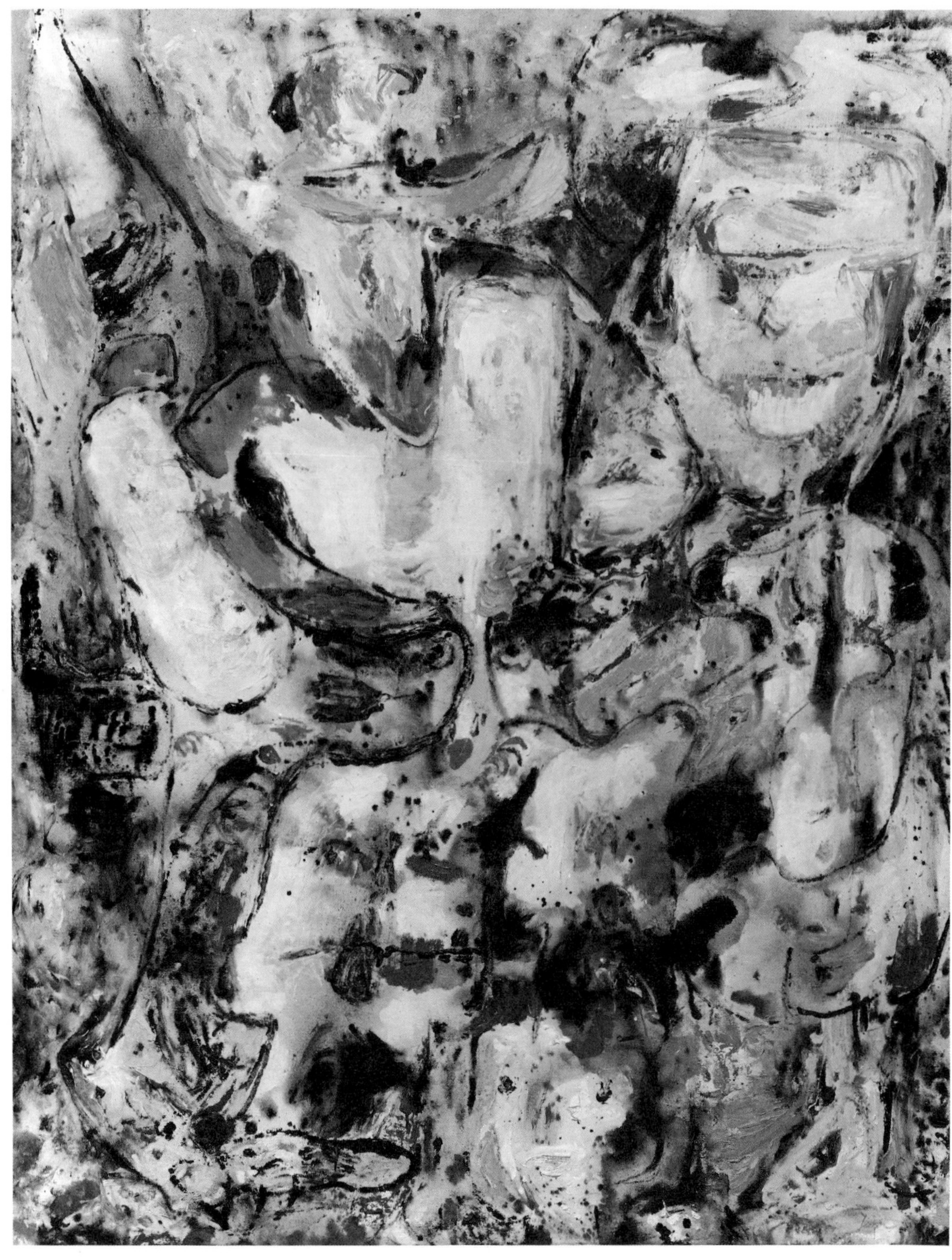

81 Untitled. 1956-57.
(*Figures*).[1]

Color plate p. 506.

76.2553 PG 175

Oil on canvas (unvarnished), 55 1/2 x 43 3/8 (141 x 110.1).

Signed l.r.: *Jorn*. Not dated.

PROVENANCE:

Purchased from Galleria d'Arte del Cavallino, Venice, July 31, 1957.[2]

CONDITION:

The work has received no treatment. Very thinly painted, and unvarnished, the work has scattered minor areas of crackle, but in general is in stable condition. (Venice, Nov. 1982.)

The work has been dated both 1956 and 1957 without evidence being cited for either case. Atkins's date of 1956-57 is based on stylistic grounds rather than external evidence or information from the artist (correspondence with the author, July 23, 1983).

Though Jorn generally titled his paintings of the mature years 1954-64, some of them, including the present work, remained untitled. The artist's own explanation of the problem throws light on his attitude toward the nature of content in his work at this time: "For me the aim is to find a title that cannot be confused with that of any other work, and which at the same time is the least deceptive, the least meaningful, the most neutral, the most abstract, the furthest removed from any resemblance to what I myself had visualized, so that the title obliterates, as far as possible, my own intentions in relation to the work.... I maintain that the value of an image lies in its adaptability to several interpretations.... I'm careful not to be too specific, and not to give too precise and unequivocal a name to a picture, so that the title shall always contain an ambiguity that allows the spectator to read his own interpretation into the image, without feeling restricted by a title that forces him in this or that direction" (Atkins, 1972, p. 143).

EXHIBITIONS:

London, *P.G.*, 1964-65, no. 146 ("*Figures*, 1957"); Stockholm, *P.G.*, 1966-67, no. 142; New York, *P.G.*, 1969, p. 162, repr. color ("*Figures*, 1957"); Paris, *P.G.*, 1974-75, no. 145, repr.; Torino, *P.G.*, 1975-76, no. 164.

REFERENCES;

G. Atkins, with the help of T. Andersen, *Asger Jorn: The Crucial Years, 1954-64*, New York, 1977, no. 1042, repr.; L. Flint, *Handbook*, 1983, no. 76, p. 160, repr. color.

1. The title *Figure* or *Figures* was given to the work by the dealer from whom Peggy Guggenheim bought it, a common practice among dealers with Jorn's untitled works.
2. Jorn was in Italy with Guy Atkins at the time and expressed "annoyance" that Peggy Guggenheim had not been offered a more important example of his work (Atkins, in correspondence with the author, July 23, 1982).

Vasily[1] Kandinsky

Born December 1866, Moscow.
Died December 1944, Paris.

82 Landschaft mit roten Flecken, No. 2.
1913.
(*Landscape with red spots No. 2; Landscape with Church II [with Red Spot]*).

Color plate p. 45.

76.2553 PG 33

HL II[2] (Russian): 1913, 169: *Пейзаж (с церковью 2)* [*с красным пятном* inserted above after *пейзаж*] / *Продан Eddy / в Чикаго (400) Herbstsalon i3 / Wolfskehl (эскиз).* (See fig. a.)[3]

HL III (German): 1913, 169: *Landschaft mit roten Flecken (No. 2) / (Nach Studie „mit Kirche" 1910) / Herbstsalon 1913. / Verkauft an Eddy / 400 m.* (See fig. b.)

Oil on canvas (unvarnished), 46¼ x 55⅛ (117.5 x 140).

Not signed or dated.

PROVENANCE:

Purchased from the artist by Arthur Jerome Eddy (1859-1920), Chicago (400 marks); Mrs. Jerome Eddy, 1920-32; Jerome O. Eddy (died 1951), 1932-41; Karl Nierendorf, New York, by 1941; purchased from Karl Nierendorf, New York, 1941.

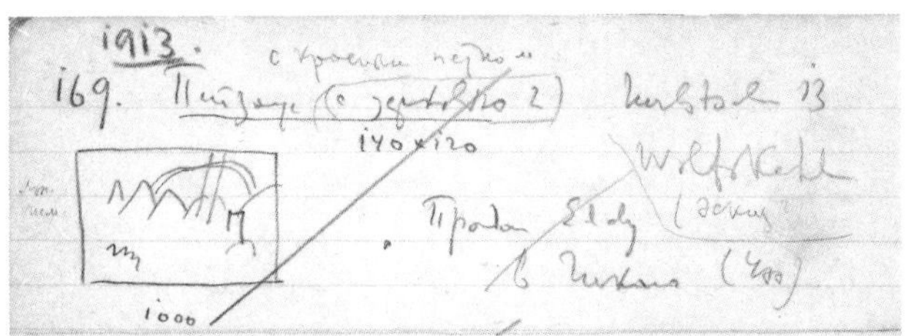

fig. a.
Entry from Kandinsky Handlist II.

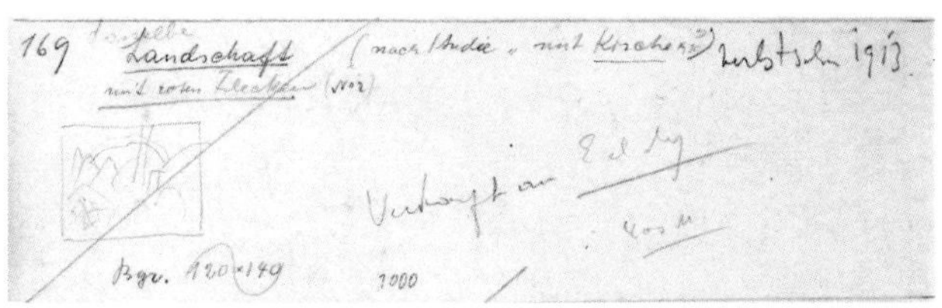

fig. b.
Entry from Kandinsky Handlist III.

1. Throughout his years in Germany and France, Kandinsky himself consistently used the German spelling "Wassily" for his first name. The Guggenheim Museum has adopted instead an Americanized transliteration from the Russian.
2. Kandinsky kept handwritten lists of his own works in a "*Hauskatalog*," here translated as Handlist (HL). For a full and detailed description of these Handlists and their contents, see H. K. Roethel and J. Benjamin, 1982, pp. 16-20. Handlist II lists the paintings, 1909, no. 62, through 1922, 243, in Russian. From 1922, no. 244, through 1926, no. 370, the entries are in German. HL III contains a list in German, in Gabriele Münter's hand, of Kandinsky's paintings from 1909, no. 62, through 1916, no. 204.

   Hans Konrad Roethel and Jean Benjamin offer the argument that the Russian list (HL II) in Kandinsky's hand, usually thought to predate the German version in Münter's hand (HL III), actually postdates it: that is, they suggest that Kandinsky copied and revised Münter's "masterlist," translating it into Russian, while they were together in Stockholm in 1916. The original titles would thus have been the German ones. Though this argument is in many respects compelling, the transcribed entries in the original languages from HL II and HL III are supplied here with photographs, since certain information emerges from the juxtaposition of the 2 versions and from the way in which the data is recorded in each.
3. The painting has been published with several different titles. In HL II (fig. a) Kandinsky initially recorded the title as *Landscape (with Church 2)*; he then squeezed in the words *with red spot* (in the singular) above, as an afterthought. In the German version (fig. b) Münter recorded the work as *Landscape with red spots (No. 2)*, adding the parenthetical note: *(after Study "with Church" 1910)*.

   In a letter to Galka Scheyer, dated March 23, 1936, Kandinsky discussed the Stendahl Galleries exhibition and several questions he had regarding the checklist, which Scheyer had apparently sent to him together with some press clippings (including a review from the *Herald Express*). Kandinsky wrote as follows: "*Jedenfalls ist in meinem Hauskatalog zermerkt Eddy hätte die „Landschaft mit rotem Fleck" 1913 gekauft. (Allerdings im Katalog [meinem] heisst das Bild Landschaft mit Kirche 2). Nach der Abbildung im Herald Express ('Landscape' betitelt) muss es doch dasselbe sein das Eddy hatte. Ich würde Ihnen für diese Angaben (rückseite der Bilder) sehr dankbar sein, damit ich sie in m. Katalog vermerken kann.*"

   Kandinsky appears to be using the Russian HL as the primary source for his information since it is here that the picture is recorded with the title he claims as his own: *Landscape with Church 2*. (In citing "*Landschaft mit rotem Fleck*" he quotes directly from the Stendahl Galleries checklist, which he has before him, so that Scheyer will know to which work he is referring.) He is, moreover, persuaded that the full accurate title would have been recorded on the reverse of the picture together with the appropriate HL number (as was his usual practice). He thus asks Scheyer to check the verso, just to be certain that the picture was the same one, presumably wondering if it might be *Landschaft mit Kirche I*, the whereabouts of which he apparently did not know. In a later letter to Scheyer (September 28, 1936) he again refers to the

CONDITION:

In 1964 (Tate Report) the surface was described as in good condition, and the artist's characteristically matte unvarnished surface was intact.[4] A crack in the paint layer just above the lower edge (probably from stretcher pressure) was visible along the length of the canvas. Some crackle just left of center was noted.

In October 1982 (Venice) discolored natural resin varnish (applied by a restorer at an unknown date) was removed. The work was cleaned and a Fieux contact lining was applied; scattered minor losses, especially on the lower edge toward the right corner, upper left corner, and top edge, were filled and inpainted with watercolors. The surface was lightly coated with Lefranc retouching varnish (spray). Stretcher marks are visible on all 4 sides. The condition is stable. (New York, Feb. 1983.)

A companion piece to the Guggenheim painting—*Landschaft mit roten Flecken, No. 1* (Museum Folkwang, Essen)—was painted in January 1913, apparently "for an auction for the benefit of Else Lasker-Schuler, and was bought by [Kandinsky's friend Karl] Wolfskehl" (Roethel and Benjamin, 1982, no. 459).

The compositions and colors of the two oils (in Essen and the Peggy Guggenheim Collection) are virtually identical, and both are thinly painted. Kandinsky almost certainly completed the second version before the first had left the studio, perhaps because the latter was destined for immediate sale. In spatial conception and pictorial resolution, however, the two works differ considerably. In the Essen picture, the environment surrounding the church and the Bavarian mountains is very densely composed: barely an inch of canvas lacks the application of Kandinsky's vibrant color. In the Peggy Guggenheim version, by contrast, the artist left the outer edges of the field almost entirely unpainted; only the thinnest ground application covers the primed canvas in these areas, and the central image seems to float in an indeterminate space. The outlines of the forms are less delineated in the Peggy Guggenheim picture, and the effect is therefore more suggestive and elusive. The process of "veiling" the imagery—characteristic of Kandinsky during the years 1911-13—is manifestly evident.[5]

In neither the Essen nor the Peggy Guggenheim painting did Kandinsky work *sur le motif*. Rather, as frequently happened during this period, he took as a

(3. cont.)
picture as "*die Landschaft mit rotem Fleck*." It is not clear whether he does so because he is referring once again to the Stendahl Galleries checklist, or because he regards the title as appropriate. Nowhere in the 1936 correspondence with Scheyer does he seem to express a strong feeling about the title, or a preference for one or the other titles. He appears concerned only that the records on each of his works, meticulously updated as frequently as possible, should continue to contain accurate information on the locations of the paintings.

Peg Weiss, who is preparing an edition of Galka Scheyer's correspondence with The Blue Four, drew these letters to the author's attention and encouraged publication of the information contained in them.

4. Kandinsky did not apply varnish to any of the works now preserved in the Städtische Galerie in Munich, the largest extant collection of pre-World War I canvases from his hand. These works remain in an unvarnished condition. Though no statement by Kandinsky on the subject has come to light, it seems clear on the basis of this evidence alone that he did not wish the surfaces of at least the pre-World War I paintings to be varnished. Data on the later works is much more difficult to gather, since no single large collection of unrestored works is extant. Further study of this issue vis-à-vis his post-1914 oeuvre is required.

fig. c.
Kandinsky, Study for *Landschaft mit roten Flecken*, 1913, black chalk, 10¾ x 14$^{15}/_{16}$ in., 27.4 x 37.9 cm., signed l.l.: [monogram]; inscribed by the artist on reverse: *Zu Landschaft mit roten Flecken*. Not dated. Städtische Galerie, Munich, GMS 442.

point of departure an earlier work of his own. The HL entries for the first and second 1913 paintings (figs. a and b) state that the compositions were directly based on a *Studie "mit Kirche"* of 1910. Roethel and Benjamin convincingly identified this source as the *Studie für Murnau mit Kirche II* [6] (not Kandinsky's title), which Sixten Ringbom had earlier also cited as the origin for the composition (1970, p. 145). Ringbom, in an illuminating and persuasive stylistic analysis, traces the gradual evolution of Kandinsky's conception from the rather literally delineated church, surrounding buildings, and mountains into a far more abstract, although still legible, landscape. Ringbom identifies the drawing in the Städtische Galerie (fig. c) as the vital intermediary step,[7] in which Kandinsky begins to "dissolve the landscape of 1910.... The village houses have been stripped of all material volume leaving only irregularly triangular and square traces of their outlines.... The roof on the right of the tower has fused with the churchyard, and the dots of the roof now merge with the 'gravestones' into one uniform pattern" (1970, p. 146).

In the two 1913 oils that follow (*Landschaft mit roten Flecken, No. 1* and *No. 2*), Ringbom rightly detects the still unmistakable topography of the Mur-

5. The large areas of unpainted canvas, combined with the lack of signature, date, or verso inscription (very unusual for Kandinsky—see fn. 3), raise the question of whether the artist at first perhaps regarded the work as unfinished. Although the exhibition and publication of it by the end of 1913 argue that he ultimately felt entirely satisfied with it, the possibility that he initially had some doubts regarding the total resolution of the composition cannot be ruled out. The question should also be considered within the context of the great difficulties Kandinsky experienced in spring 1913 resolving the problems of the edges in *Bild mit weissem Rand* (see Kandinsky, "Das Bild mit weissem Rand," *Kandinsky 1901-1913*, Berlin, 1913, pp. xxxix-xxxxi).

6. Roethel and Benjamin, no. 347. Some question remains about precisely which *Studie* Kandinsky is referring to. In the Russian HL entry for Peggy Guggenheim's painting (fig. a), Kandinsky notes on the right-hand side that Wolfskehl owned the sketch, obviously not referring to the first large oil of the subject, which Wolfskehl also owned. Presumably on this basis Roethel and Benjamin give a tentative provenance for no. 347 as Collection Wolfskehl, but it seems that this has not been definitively established. It would be of some interest to know that Karl Woflskehl had the two paintings hanging side by side.

7. Erica Hanfstaengel (1974, p. 90) convincingly dates this drawing 1913, accepting Kandinsky's verso description of it as a study for the 1913 oils. Roethel and Benjamin (1982, p. 452) suggest that the drawing may date from 1910.

nau landscape, as well as the church spire even though it has now "grown out of the picture field." But within the "skeletal structure" of these legible forms, color functions in an entirely different manner. In his exactly contemporary text "Rückblicke" (*Kandinsky 1901-1913*, Berlin, 1913, p. xxxiv), Kandinsky stated that one of the essential characteristics of the new style was "*das Überfliessen der Farbe über die Grenze der Form.*" As the material objects became "emptied of descriptive color," the colors acquired an independent role, "hovering" or "floating" in a manner characteristic of the 1913 pictures.

Ringbom describes Kandinsky's progression here as one in which the dissolving of figurative elements to the point at which they "lose their coherence and meaning" is combined with the introduction of "blots of color or linear motifs" that have no representational justification (1970, p. 142). The red spot (or spots), which clearly played descriptive roles in the 1910 study and in the painting that followed, are retained by Kandinsky as purely pictorial accents in the 1913 versions. Though sufficiently important to him, from a tonal standpoint, to be incorporated into the titles, they had entirely lost any descriptive role.

Ringbom extends his discussion of the evolution of form in these landscapes beyond the Peggy Guggenheim picture to *Helles Bild* (SRGM). According to his argument, this later painting of 1913 represents the ultimate disintegration of the legible landscape imagery through the emancipation of color; but it also reflects a "spiritualization" of forms he attributes directly to the influence of Rudolf Steiner's Theosophical texts. (For a discussion of this argument within the context of Kandinsky's explicit claim that *Helles Bild* was among the first works to be painted entirely without any "referent," see A.Z.R. *Guggenheim*, 1976, Vol. I, pp. 273-76.) Efforts to link Steiner's texts and Kandinsky's stylistic development in 1913 pose considerable problems. At best the Steiner theories —which Kandinsky certainly knew and absorbed—constituted one among a number of influences on Kandinsky as he worked on the issue of "veiling" and abstraction. Apart from the question of Steiner's possible influence, however, Ringbom's cogent stylistic analysis casts important light on the particular way in which Kandinsky exploited his own earlier work (rather than sources in nature) as a primary stimulus toward the creation of an increasingly nonobjective art.[8]

Within the context of this evolution, it is interesting to note that in his September 28, 1936, letter to Galka Scheyer, Kandinsky cited "*Landschaft mit roten Flecken 2*" as an excellent example of "*Entstellung der Wirklichkeit.*" He mentioned to Scheyer that Alfred Barr was planning an exhibition on the subject of "*Phantastik in der Kunst, oder Phantastische Wiedergabe der Wirklichkeit in der Malerei und Plastik.* [or] ... *Phantastische Entstellung der Wirklichkeit.*" (The show, which apparently gave rise to many rumors in Paris, was *Fantastic*

8. See P. Weiss, 1982, p. 81, for an interesting comment upon the possible relationship between *Landschaft mit roten Flecken I* and the preparatory drawings for *Schwarze Linien* of late 1913. She convincingly points out that the same residual landscape elements are present, although by that point almost fully absorbed into a lyrical abstraction.

Art, Dada, Surrealism.) In the letter Kandinsky expressed doubt that he would be invited to participate in such a show, but he urged Scheyer to bring Alexei Jawlensky to Barr's attention, since he would be an artist highly appropriate for inclusion. As a postscript to this letter, which dealt with a number of other, unrelated issues, he added: "*Ich denke eben nochmals an die N.Y. geplante Phantasie-Ausstellung. Vielleicht wäre es ganz gut, Barr meine Landschaft vorzuschlagen die bei Ihnen ist, d.h. die 'Landschaft mit rotem Fleck,' oder wie sie wohl jetzt heisst. Das wäre ein gutes Beispiel für die Entstellung. Was meinen Sie? In meiner Erinnerung ist diese Landschaft ein grosses und gutes Bild*" (see above, p. 413, fn. 3).

The precise meaning Kandinsky was attributing to the word *Entstellung* (distortion, misrepresentation, transformation, or even possibly manipulation of reality) was obviously colored to some extent by what he understood of Barr's plans for the exhibition. However, his choice of this particular painting as a suitable example raises interesting questions regarding his sense of its essential content and meaning. His use of the term *Entstellung* requires further study, but may suggest that such works were exemplary of a process by which the imagination affects significant transformations of images derived ultimately from nature.

EXHIBITIONS:

Berlin, Der Sturm, *Erster Deutscher Herbstsalon*, Sept.-Nov. 1913, no. 184 (*Landschaft mit roten Flecken*); Chicago, The Art Institute of Chicago, *Exhibition of Paintings from the Collection of the Late Arthur Jerome Eddy*, Sept. 19-Oct. 22, 1922, no. 38 (*Landscape with red notes*);[9] Los Angeles, Stendahl Galleries, *Kandinsky, 1903-1933*, opened Feb. 24, 1936, no. 10 (*Landschaft mit roten* [sic] *Fleck*); New York, Nierendorf Gallery, *Kandinsky*, Mar. 1941, no. 4 ("*Landscape with Red Spots*, 1912"); New York, Art of This Century, 1942-47, p. 42, repr. p. 43 (*Landscape with red spot*); Venice, *P.G.*, 1948 (Biennale), no. 65; Florence, *P.G.*, 1949, no. 71, repr.; Amsterdam, *P.G.*, 1951, no. 83, repr.; Zurich, *P.G.*, 1951, no. 79, repr.; London, *P.G.*, 1964-65, no. 26, repr.; Stockholm, *P.G.*, 1966-67, no. 25, repr.; New York, *P.G.*, 1969, p. 14, repr. p. 15; Paris, *P.G.*, 1974-75, no. 24, repr. color; Torino, *P.G.*, 1975-76, no. 33, repr. color, pl. 19; Rome, *Guggenheim: Venezia-New York*, 1982, no. 19, repr. color; New York, *P.G.*, 1982-83, no. 14, repr. color.

REFERENCES:

W. Kandinsky, *Kandinsky 1901-1913*, Berlin [1913], repr. p. 9 (*Landschaft mit roten Flecken 2*); P. Guggenheim, *Art of This Century*, 1942, p. 42, repr. p. 43; W. Grohmann, *Wassily Kandinsky: Life and Work*, trans. from German by N. Guterman, London, 1959 (first published in English, New York, 1958, and in German, Cologne, 1958), pp. 106, 332, no. 169, repr. p. 356, fig. 86 (*Landscape with Church II [with Red Spot]*); Calas, 1966, p. 27, repr. color p. 55; S. Ringbom, *The Sounding Cosmos: A Study of the Spiritualism and the Genesis of Abstraction*, Abo, 1970, pp. 146-49, 156, repr. pl. 49; E. Hanfstaengl, *Wassily Kandinsky: Zeichnungen und Aquarelle im Lenbachhaus München*, Munich, 1974, no. 222; P. Weiss, *Kandinsky in Munich*, exh. cat., SRGM, New York, 1982, pp. 80-81 (the Essen version); idem, *Kandinsky und München*, exh. cat., Städtische Galerie, Munich, 1982, pp. 81-82; H. K. Roethel and J. Benjamin, *Kandinsky: Catalogue Raisonné of the Oil Paintings*, Vol. I, *1900-1915*, New York, 1982, no. 460, repr; L. Flint, *Handbook*, 1983, p. 56, repr. color p. 57.

9. Courtney Donnell, The Art Institute of Chicago, supplied information regarding the Eddy exhibition.

83 **Weisses Kreuz.** January-June 1922.
(*White Cross*).

Color plate p. 400.

76.2553 PG 34

HL II (Russian and German entry): 1922, 243: белый крест / *Verkauft an Herrn Nierendorf / Köln / im Atelier / 80 T.m. netto* / (in Nina Kandinsky's hand): *Peggy Guggenheim?*

Oil on canvas (unvarnished), $39\frac{9}{16} \times 43\frac{9}{16}$ (100.5 x 110.6).

Signed and dated on reverse: *K / 1922 / No. 243.*

PROVENANCE:

Purchased from the artist by Karl Nierendorf, Cologne and New York, by 1937; purchased from Karl Nierendorf, New York, 1941.

CONDITION:

In 1964 (Tate Report) there was some branched crackle with cleavage in the lower left corner and a small area in the lower right corner. Apart from a vertical craquelure in the white trapezoid and a very few small losses and abrasions, the condition was described as good. The painting had a very matte finish and some exposed ground areas.

In 1968 (New York) an allover pattern of surface cracks and small scattered paint losses were noted. The light priming, where visible, had become brown through exposure to dirt, which was general over the entire surface. The painting was treated with solvents on a vacuum table to minimize cracks. The canvas was lined with wax-resin adhesive on Fiberglas lining fabric and mounted with further wax resin on a honeycomb panel. New losses were retouched with dry pigment in polyvinyl acetate (AYAB) and the surface lightly sprayed with synthetic resin varnish.

Retouching is visible in the lower left half of the white trapezoid and along most of the left top and right edges. The surface of this work has clearly suffered considerable damage, and the differentiation in brushstroke, density of paint application, and even some value relationships have been lost. The condition is, however, stable. (New York, Feb. 1983.)

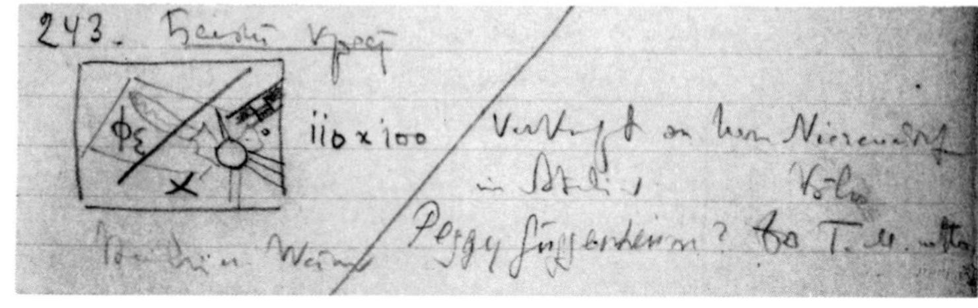

fig. a.
Entry from Kandinsky's Handlist II.

Kandinsky's Handlist entry, which is the second for 1922, indicating that the picture was begun early in the year, also contains the notation "*Berlin u. Weimar.*" Kandinsky left Soviet Russia for Berlin in December 1921; he moved from Berlin to Weimar in June 1922. Thus he apparently worked on *Weisses Kreuz* over a period of several months between January and June. The period in question was one during which Kandinsky's recent experiences in Russia — and in particular the assimilated influences of the work of Malevich, Rodchenko, and Popova, among others — were beginning to find direct expression in his work. The nature of these complex influences, especially that of Rodchenko, undoubtedly played a major role in the establishment of Kandinsky's post-1921 style. A detailed study of works such as *Weisses Kreuz*, within the context of these Russian developments, remains to be undertaken.

EXHIBITIONS:

New York, Nierendorf Gallery, *Kandinsky—A Retrospective View* (College Art Association Exhibition), Mar. 12-28, 1937, no. 19 ("*Composition 243*, $600"), traveled to Cleveland Museum of Art, and Germanic Museum, Harvard University; New York, Nierendorf Gallery, *Kandinsky*, Dec. 1942-Feb. 1943, no. 7; New York, Art of This Century, 1942-47, p. 42, repr. p. 45 (*Composition*, the title by which the picture was known in *P.G.* publications until Alley, 1964); Venice, *P.G.*, 1948 (Biennale), no. 66; Florence, *P.G.*, 1949, no. 72, repr.; Amsterdam, *P.G.*, 1951, no. 84; Zurich, *P.G.*, 1951, no. 81; London, *P.G.*, 1964-65, no. 27, repr. (*White Cross*); Stockholm, *P.G.*, 1966-67, no. 26, repr.; New York, *P.G.*, 1969, p. 16, repr.; Paris, *P.G.*, 1974-75, no. 25; Torino, *P.G.*, 1975-76, no. 34; Rome, *Guggenheim: Venezia-New York*, 1982, no. 20, repr. color; New York, *P.G.*, 1982-83, no. 15, repr.; New York, SRGM, *Kandinsky: Russian and Bauhaus Years, 1915-1933*, Dec. 9, 1983-Feb. 12, 1984, cat. no. 81, repr., traveled to Atlanta, Ga., The High Museum, Mar. 15-Apr. 29, 1984, Zurich, Kunsthaus, May 29-July 15, 1984, Berlin, Bauhaus Archiv, Aug. 10-Sept. 23, 1984.

REFERENCES:

New York, *Art of This Century*, 1942, p. 42, repr. p. 45 (as *Composition*); W. Grohmann, *Wassily Kandinsky: Life and Work*, trans. from German by N. Guterman, London, 1959, no. 243, p. 334, repr. p. 360, fig. 134; Calas, 1966, p. 28, repr. p. 56; L. Flint, *Handbook*, 1983, p. 58, repr. color p. 59; H. K. Roethel and J. Benjamin, *Kandinsky: Catalogue Raisonné of the Oil Paintings*, Vol. II, *1916-1944*, New York, 1983, no. 684, repr.; C. Poling, *Kandinsky: Russian and Bauhaus Years*, exh. cat., SRGM, New York, 1983, pp. 37-38.

84 **Empor.** October 1929.
(*Upward; En haut*).

76.2553 PG 35

HL III (German): 1929, 470: *Los Angeles II 36*. (In Nina Kandinsky's hand): *Peggy Guggenheim. Venezia / b. Nierendorf / America(?) b. Emmy.*[1]

Oil on cardboard (unvarnished), 27½ x 19¼ (70 x 49).

Signed and dated l.l.: *K / 29*; on reverse (possibly in another hand): *No. 470 / i929—„Empor" /* 49 x 70.

PROVENANCE:
Valentine Dudensing, by 1932-January 1935; on consignment to Galka Scheyer, Pasadena, California, January 1935-39; on consignment to Karl Nierendorf, New York, by September 6, 1939 to 1941 (see fn. 1); purchased from Karl Nierendorf, New York, 1941.

CONDITION:
In 1964 (Tate Report) the unvarnished oil surface was described as in good condition apart from some very minor scattered losses at the edges.

In 1981 (Venice) some minor losses in the support were filled. Previous restorations at the edges (discolored and of unknown date) were removed and retouched.

In 1984 (New York) the work, which had been tacked to a stretcher with thin nails, was removed. Losses in the top layer of cardboard and in the paint layer at the lower left corner were restored through implantation of acid-free ragboard adhered with Jade (polyvinyl acetate emulsion); retouching was executed with acrylic colors. An interleaf of thin Japanese paper was adhered to the entire reverse with wheat starch paste. The support was then adhered with BEVA to a 2-ply acid-free ragboard, which was glued with Jade to a honeycomb panel faced with Fiberglas. The condition is stable. (New York, Feb. 1984.)

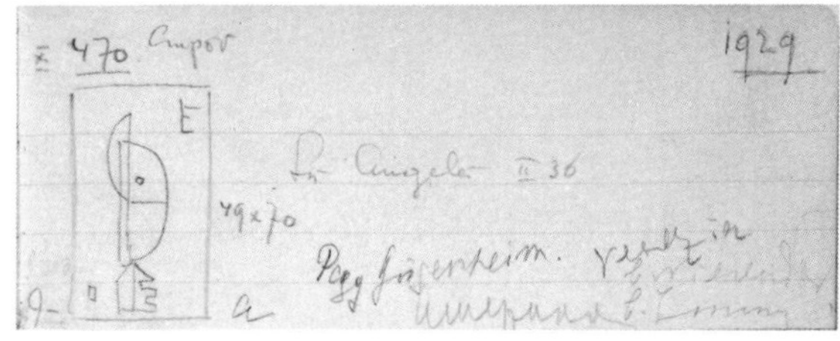

fig. a.
Entry from Kandinsky's Handlist III.

Clark Poling has pointed out (1983, p. 77) that in *Empor*, as in other works of this period, Kandinsky demonstrates an affinity for the *Abstrakte Köpfe* of Alexei Jawlensky, sixteen of which were exhibited at the Galerie Ferdinand

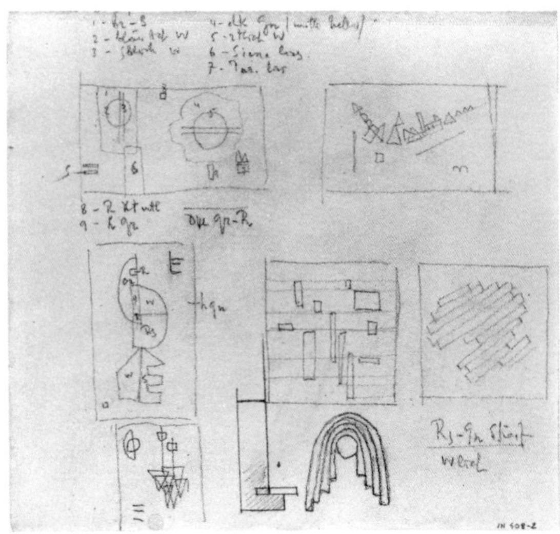

fig. b.
Kandinsky, sheet of sketches including preparatory study (with color notes) for cat. no. 84, pencil on paper, 7⅛ x 7¾ in., 17.9 x 19.7 cm., Musée National d'Art Moderne, Centre Georges Pompidou, Paris, Nina Kandinsky Bequest.

Möller in Berlin, and many of which Kandinsky would have known well before that date. In its physiognomic imagery based upon quasi-geometrical elements, Kandinsky's composition is, however, (as Poling notes) even closer to the contemporary work of Paul Klee.

EXHIBITIONS:

New York, Valentine Gallery, *Kandinsky*, Nov. 1932, no. 13; Los Angeles, Stendhal Galleries, *Kandinsky 1903-1933*, opened Feb. 24, 1936, no. 25; New York, Nierendorf Gallery, *Kandinsky*, Mar. 1941, no. 10 (*Rising*); New York, Art of This Century, 1942-47, p. 42; Venice, *P.G.*, 1948 (Biennale), no. 67; Florence, *P.G.*, 1949, no. 73; Amsterdam, *P.G.*, 1951, no. 85; Zurich, *P.G.*, 1951, no. 80; London, *P.G.*, 1964-65, no. 28; Stockholm, *P.G.*, 1966-67, no. 27; New York, *P.G.*, 1969, p. 17, repr. color; Paris, *P.G.*, 1974-75, no. 26, repr.; Torino, *P.G.*, 1975-76, no. 35, repr. pl. 18; New York, SRGM, *Kandinsky: Russian and Bauhaus Years, 1915-1933*, Dec. 9, 1983-Feb. 12, 1984, cat. no. 286, repr., traveled to Atlanta, Ga., The High Museum, Mar. 15-Apr. 29, 1984, Zurich, Kunsthaus, May 29-July 15, 1984, Berlin, Bauhaus Archiv, Aug. 10-Sept. 23, 1984.

REFERENCES:

P. Guggenheim, *Art of This Century*, 1942, p. 42; W. Grohmann, *Wassily Kandinsky: Life and Work*, trans. from German by N. Guterman, London, 1959, no. 470, repr. p. 376, fig. 323; Calas, 1966, p. 28, repr. p. 57; H. K. Roethel and J. Benjamin, *Kandinsky: Catalogue Raisonné of the Oil Paintings*, Vol. II, *1916-1944*, New York, 1983, no. 914, repr.; C. Poling, *Kandinsky: Russian and Bauhaus Years*, exh. cat., SRGM, New York, 1983, pp. 77-78.

1. "Emmy" (Galka) Scheyer was the organizer of The Blue Four. According to correspondence in the Galka Scheyer Archives, Norton Simon Museum, Pasadena, Valentine Dudensing (who had the work by at least 1932 when he exhibited it) sent the picture on consignment to Scheyer in January 1935. Further correspondence establishes that it was consigned by her to Karl Nierendorf by September 6, 1939 (information supplied by Peg Weiss). A Nierendorf label removed from the reverse in 1984 carries the number 129, probably a Nierendorf inventory reference.

Zoltan Kemeny

Born March 1907, Banica, Transylvania (Hungary).
Died June 1965, Zurich.

85 Mouvement partagé. 1957.
(*Divided movement*).

76.2553 PG 208

Prefabricated copper elements with copper and iron filings soldered to copper sheet nailed to wood. Copper sheet: 30¾ x 19⅞ (78.5 x 50.7); wood mount: 31⅛ x 20⅛ x 1 (79 x 51 x 2.5).

Signed and numbered on reverse: *KEMENY / N23*. Not dated.

PROVENANCE:

Purchased from the artist by Paul Facchetti, 1957; purchased from Paul Facchetti, Paris, January 1964.[1]

1. Kemeny won the International Prize for Sculpture at the Venice Biennale later that year.

CONDITION:

In 1964 (Tate Report) 9 of the prefabricated copper elements became detached from the copper sheet. They were reattached with epoxy resin (Araldite).

By 1982 (Venice), 1 other element had become detached. Active green and a white corrosion is present, probably deriving from substances used in the soldering process, which was as follows: the copper sheet was covered with a soldering paste; the pieces were placed in position and the sheet inserted in an oven, where the elements were baked onto the surface. Owing to presence of corrosion, the condition is fragile. (Venice, June 1983.)

Kemeny's experiments in a variety of media and techniques constituted a critical element in his aesthetic. In dealing with prefabricated industrial metal, which he ordered from catalogues, and avoiding all traditional sculptural techniques, he identified himself with advanced modern science and anticipated far more extensive collaboration with scientific colleagues in the future. His reliefs, the earliest dating from 1954, defined themselves in pictorial rather than sculptural terms ("*Mon problème numéro un: libérer mon tableau du mur*," quoted by M. Ragon, *Kemeny*, exh. cat., Fondation Maeght, Mar. 23-May 31, 1974, n.p.). The critical issue within the pictorial framework was to create a kinetic effect, conceived in terms of the movement of color (see, for example, Kemeny's statement accompanying his 1958 exhibition at Gallery One in London). The demands of the medium required a painstaking, deliberate process of conception, composition, construction. Small detailed preparatory drawings (such as fig. a) were followed by a large, exact-scale technical "cartoon" of the projected relief. Each element was then often worked on individually with tools prior to its soldering to the copper sheet. Since the heat applied during the soldering process frequently altered the natural colors of the metal, Kemeny used acids to introduce chemical changes until the colors met his expectations. Though the overall design was fully calculated in advance, certain improvisational decisions could be made as the soldering took place.

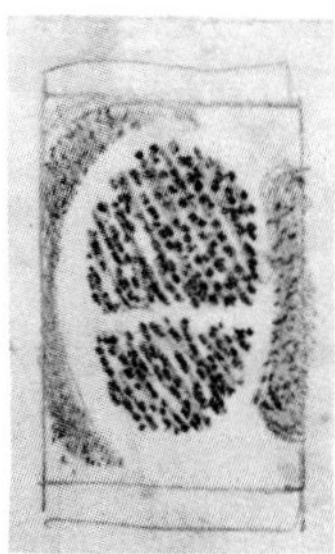

fig. a.
Kemeny, detail from sheet of sketches, ca. 1957, pencil on tracing paper, dimensions of entire sheet: 7⅝ x 6¾ in., 19.4 x 17.1 cm., SRGM, New York, Gift of Madeleine Kemeny.

EXHIBITIONS:

Zurich, Kunsthaus, *Zoltan Kemeny*, Apr. 8-May 18, 1959, no. 24; New York, Sidney Janis Gallery, *Kemeny*, May 23-June 11, 1960, no. 1; Dusseldorf, Kunsthalle, *Zoltan Kemeny*, Nov. 9-Dec. 9, 1962, no. 1; Hannover, Kestner Gesellschaft, *Zoltan Kemeny*, Feb. 12-Mar. 24, 1963, no. 1; Otterlo, Rijksmuseum Kröller-Müller, *Zoltan Kemeny*, June 8-July 21, 1963, no. 2; London, *P.G.*, 1964-65, no. 173; New York, *P.G.*, 1969, p. 141, repr.

REFERENCES:

M. Ragon, *Zoltan Kemeny*, Neuchâtel, 1960, no. 23, repr. (erroneously as a horizontal composition); [Alley], *Peggy Guggenheim Foundation*, 1968, no. 208, repr.; G. Picon and E. Rathke, *Kemeny: Reliefs en métal*, Switzerland, 1973, p. 207, no. 35, repr. p. 53.

Paul Klee

Born December 1879, Münchenbuchsee, Bern.
Died June 1940, Muralto-Locarno.

NOTE: Klee kept a detailed record of his work in an Oeuvre Catalogue (hereafter OC), which he began in the spring of 1911 and continued until his death. It is not totally complete, and omissions are especially frequent in the pre-1911 years. The document is preserved in the Klee Stiftung, Bern. It covers the years 1883-1940 and records 733 paintings, 3,159 so-called colored sheets, 51 glass paintings, 15 sculptures, and 1 collage; the numbers inscribed on the works themselves coincide in almost all cases with the numbers in the OC, although there are exceptions.

The entries in the OC include date, number, title, and description of medium; the latter category is not always complete nor in every case entirely accurate, and an effort has been made, therefore, to analyze the medium and technique independently of, as well as in relationship to, the OC entry. The entries in the present catalogue include Klee's OC entry verbatim; any discrepancy between this and the actual medium of the work is noted.

86 Bildnis der Frau P. im Süden. 1924.

(Portrait of Frau P. in the South).

OC *1924, 243, Bildnis der Frau P. im Süden Aquarell und Olf. Zeichg Whattman Aquarell / blockpapier.*

Color plate p. 498.

76.2553 PG 89

Watercolor and oil transfer drawing on heavy wove (Whatman) paper mounted by artist on pulpboard, painted with gray gouache borders. Primary support: 14¾ x 10¾ (37.6 x 27.4); secondary support: 16¾ x 12¼ (42.5 x 31).

Signed l.c.: *Klee*; inscribed on l.c. of mount: *1924 243 Bildnis der Frau P. im Süden*; in left corner on mount: *VII*.

PROVENANCE:

Early history unknown; Karl Nierendorf, New York, by 1941; Gift of Karl Nierendorf, 1941.

CONDITION:

In 1964 (Tate Report) the top right corner of the secondary support was repaired and inpainted.

In 1983 (New York) this repair, which had darkened, was removed and the corner reattached with purified rice paste and Sekeishu tissue. The front of the tear was cleaned and filled with cellulose pulp and methyl cellulose. The perimeter of the secondary support surface was cleaned. The secondary support was hinged on all sides to 100% ragboard and the composition flattened. The condition is excellent. (New York, Mar. 1983.)

Klee's oil transfer technique, first used in 1919, has been analyzed and documented by Jürgen Glaesemer (*Paul Klee: Handzeichnungen I*, Bern, 1973, pp. 258-60).[1] The artist first brushed Japan paper with black oil color or printer's ink to create a kind of carbon paper; when it was almost dry, he placed it face down on a clean sheet of paper or cloth and laid a preparatory drawing (face up) on top of it. He then traced over the drawing with a stylus, thus transfering its outlines in soft black to the lower sheet. Drawings that have been used for oil transfer are easily identified by the stylus marks clearly visible on them.

The preparatory drawing used to transfer the composition to the present painting has not been located.

Klee made a journey to Sicily in 1924. Whether the work is a reminiscence of this voyage, either literally or metaphorically, is difficult to say, and "Frau P." remains for the present unidentified.

EXHIBITIONS:

New York, Art of This Century, 1942-47, p. 47; Venice, *P.G.*, 1948 (Biennale), no. 68; Florence, *P.G.*, 1949, no. 74, repr.; Amsterdam, *P.G.*, 1951, no. 86; Zurich, *P.G.*, 1951, no. 82; London, *P.G.*, 1964-65, no. 79, repr.; Stockholm, *P.G.*, 1966-67, no. 76, repr.; New York, *P.G.*, 1969, p. 40, repr.; Paris, *P.G.*, 1974-75, no. 60, repr. color, n.p.; Torino, *P.G.*, 1975-76, no. 87, repr. pl. 40; New York, *P.G.*, 1982-83, no. 21, repr. color.

REFERENCE:

P. Guggenheim, *Art of This Century*, 1942, p. 47.

1. For some illuminating recent observations on the role of the oil transfer process in Klee's work, see J. Jordan, "Klee's prints and oil transfer works: Some further reflections," *The Graphic Legacy of Paul Klee*, exh. cat., Bard College, Annandale on Hudson, New York, 1983, pp. 96-102.

87 Zaubergarten. March 1926.
(Magic Garden).

OC *1926 141 (E1) Zaubergarten Ölfarben, Gipsplatte mit Holzrahmen verankert, Originalleisten.*

Color plate p. 499

76.2553 PG 90

Oil on gypsum plaster-filled wire mesh mounted in wood frame. Plaster: 20½ x 16⅝ (50.2 x 42.1); exterior of artist's wood frame: 20⅞ x 17¾ (52.9 x 44.9).

Signed and dated u.r.: *Klee 1926 E1.*

PROVENANCE:

Purchased from the artist by D.-H. Kahnweiler, Galerie Simon, 1938 (stock book no. 01153); purchased from D.-H. Kahnweiler, 1940.

CONDITION:

Klee's construction of the support included gluing a layer of newspaper to the back of the plaster-filled wire mesh, which was then mounted with long nails onto the frame (fig. a).

In 1964 (Tate Report) the nails were treated for rust, and losses in the plaster between them were restored. In 1978 (New York) considerable cracks and losses at the edges were consolidated with polyvinyl acetate emulsion (PVAE, Union Carbide Corp.), filled with gesso and inpainted with watercolors. Hairline cracks and small losses elsewhere were noted. Although remarkably preserved, the surface is vulnerable and the condition in general fragile. (Venice, Nov. 1982.)

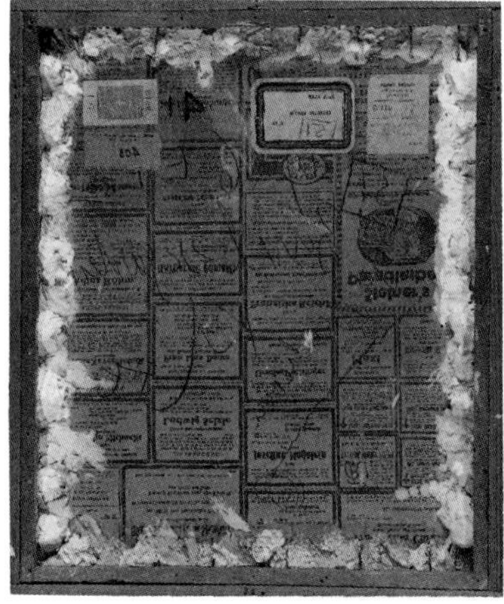

fig. a.
Reverse of cat. no. 87, showing Klee's construction of the support and frame.

In his diary, Klee made two comments that establish the date of this work as March 1926. On March 14 he noted cryptically that he had prepared some wooden frames with wire mesh and gypsum plaster grounds: "*Gipsgründe in Holzrahmen über Drahtgaze gestrichen.*" On March 18 (the next entry) he noted that he had completed the underpainting in oil of *Gartenbild: "Gartenbild in Öl — weisse Struktur — untermalt."*

It seems clear from the March 14 entry that Klee was experimenting with this particular structure for the first time. Although he had worked frequently with plaster in the past, the format used in the Peggy Guggenheim work was new: a wooden stretcher, wire mesh, and gypsum plaster were combined in such a way as to create something closer to an "object" than a painting.

87

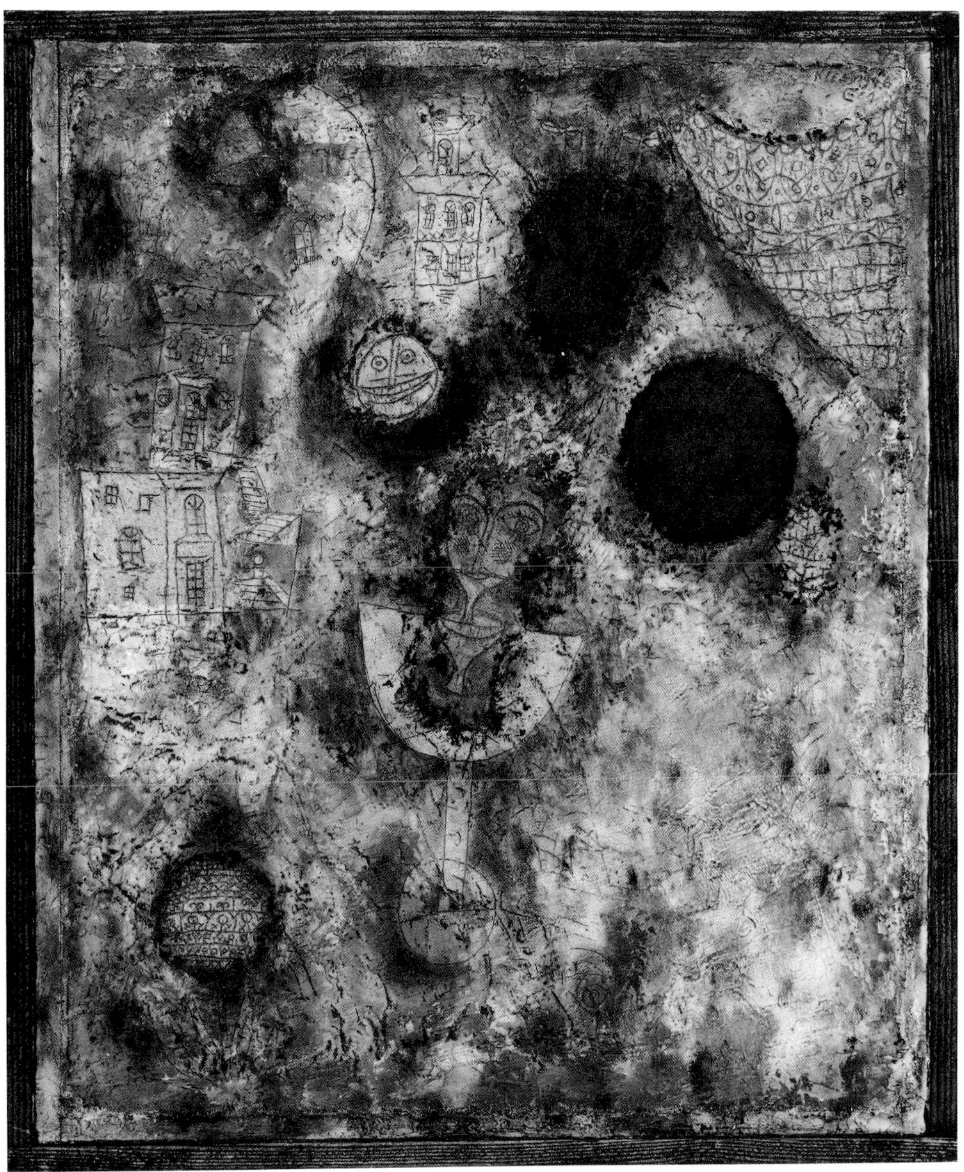

As Christian Geelhaar and Jürgen Glaesemer have both suggested, Klee's experimental approach to the issue of media, his sensitivity to materials, and his interest in inventing original means of expression have yet to be fully studied. (For a discussion of these issues see C. Geelhaar, *Paul Klee und das Bauhaus*, Cologne, 1972, pp. 74ff.; and J. Glaesemer, "Die Plastiken von Paul Klee," in *Paul Klee: Das graphische und plastische Werk*, exh. cat., Wilhelm-Lehmbruck-Museum, Duisburg, 1975.)

The imagery of the *Zaubergarten* is suggestive of Klee's interest in the theater, specifically, the world of puppetry. As early as 1916 he built a puppet theater (Kasperltheater) for the entertainment of his son, Felix. The puppet's heads were made of vividly painted plaster and papier-mâché, the bodies of cloth. Between

1919 and 1925 Klee apparently made annual additions to the theater's cast of characters, which ultimately reached a full complement of fifty players (see Glaesemer, loc. cit.; and F. Klee, *Paul Klee: His Life and Work*, New York, 1962, p. 49). Backdrops for the stage were also created by Klee.

In addition (as has often been noted), Klee, Oskar Schlemmer, and others at the Bauhaus shared an interest in the tales of E.T.A. Hoffmann, whose complex world of fantasy, with its imaginative, yet grotesque characters and its exploration of psychological truths, is reflected in much of Klee's work of this period.

In the *Zaubergarten* the images are drawn in a childlike manner. They inhabit a space that is unreal — the fluid and nonrational space of dream or fantasy, in which disembodied heads and other objects float as naturally as does the crescent moon. The faces are masklike, and — in construction and physiognomic type — the central character bears a certain resemblance to the puppets of the Klee Kasperltheater. A partly drawn curtain at the upper right adds to the "theatrical" implications of the scene, which combine to evoke the fantastic and magical world of Hoffmann, the inventiveness of puppetry, and the theatrical visions and imaginative dreams of childhood. (For a discussion of some other aspects of Klee's interest in the theater and its influence on his imagery and style, see *The Theater of the Bauhaus*, ed. W. Gropius, Middletown, Connecticut, 1961; *Paul Klee: Puppets, Sculptures, Reliefs, Masks, Theatre,* intr. by F. Klee, Neuchâtel, 1979.)

EXHIBITIONS:

New York, Art of This Century, 1942-47, p. 47, repr. p. 49; Venice, *P.G.*, 1948 (Biennale), no. 69; Florence, *P.G.*, 1949, no. 75, repr.; Amsterdam, *P.G.*, 1951, no. 87, repr.; Zurich, *P.G.*, 1951, no. 83; London, *P.G.*, 1964-65, no. 8; Stockholm, *P.G.*, 1966-67, no. 77; New York, *P.G.*, 1969, p. 41, repr. color; Paris, *P.G.*, 1974-75, no. 61, repr.; Torino, *P.G.*, 1975-76, no. 88, repr. pl. 39.

REFERENCES:

P. Guggenheim, *Art of This Century*, 1942, p. 47, repr. p. 49; Calas, 1966, p. 77, repr. color p. 84; *Paul Klee: Briefe an die Familie, 1893-1940*, Band 2 (1907-1940), ed., F. Klee, Cologne, 1979, p. 1019.

Willem de Kooning

Born April 1904, Rotterdam.
Lives in The Springs, East Hampton, Long Island.

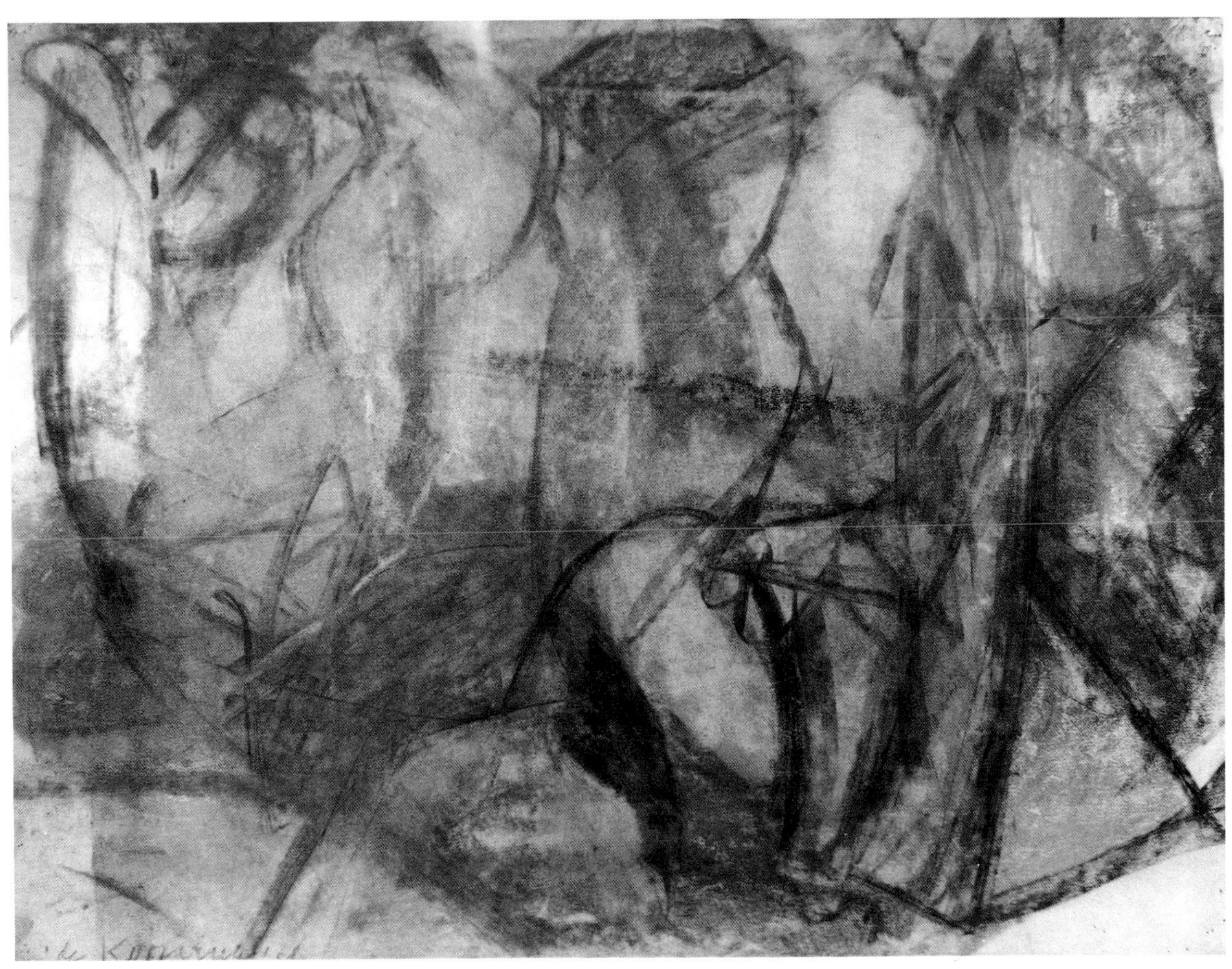

88 Untitled. 1958.

Color plate p. 677.

76.2553 PG 159

Pastel and charcoal (fixed) on heavy wove paper, 22 7/16 x 30 1/2 (57 x 77.5).

Signed and dated l.l.: *de Kooning '58*.

PROVENANCE:

Purchased from the artist in his New York studio, ca. 1960.

CONDITION:

The work was matted with a thin acidic board and has thus discolored along the entire perimeter. There are a slash along half of the left edge, a small cut at the center of the left edge, and some scratches across the surface at the right side (vertical), along the upper edges (horizontal), and in the lower right quadrant. The gloss (visible in raking light) is due to fixative. The overall condition is stable. (Venice, Nov. 1982.)

This work is one of a sizable group of pastel and charcoal drawings of the late 1950s. De Kooning's working method in such drawings has been vividly described by Thomas B. Hess: His "line — the essence of drawing — is always under attack. It is smeared across the paper, pushed into widening shapes, kept away from the expression of an edge. But then, on top of the erasures will come more lines. The edge will be reaffirmed, underlined, modeled. And then the wiping, erasing action resumes — until the drawing stops...."[1]

In Peggy Guggenheim's example, de Kooning has used pastel in such a way that the boundaries between zones of color are continually blurred; yet this tendency exists simultaneously with a strong impulse to give linear and plastic definition to specific forms through the process of rapid drawing in charcoal. The result is a combination of the figural and the abstract that characterizes many of de Kooning's drawings of this period. Although the actual forms in the Peggy Guggenheim pastel retain a relationship to the Woman drawings and paintings of the previous years (*Warehouse Manikins* of 1949, Collection Mr. and Mrs. Bagley Wright, Seattle, or *Untitled [Woman, Wind and Window]* 1950, formerly Collection Alfonso A. Ossorio), they are much less definitive. The inclination in such work is toward a greater openness and abstraction, but the engagement with the human form — however tenuous — remains apparent and furnishes important links with de Kooning's immediately preceding (as well as later) work. Clement Greenberg's comments about the pre-1953 works are equally illuminating in relation to many of the later examples: "The supple line that does most of the work in de Kooning's pictures, whether these are representational or not, is never a completely abstract element but harks back to the contour, particularly that of the human form.... it is a disembodied contour, seldom closing back upon itself to suggest a solid object.... He wants in the end to recover a distinct image of the human figure, yet without sacrificing anything of abstract painting's decorative or physical force."[2]

EXHIBITIONS:

London, *P.G.*, 1964-65, no. 133; Stockholm, *P.G.*, 1966-67, no. 129; New York, *P.G.*, 1969, p. 135, repr.; Paris, *P.G.*, 1974-75, no. 137, repr. (with caption for cat. no. 89,); Torino, *P.G.*, 1975-76, no. 151.

1. T. B. Hess, *Willem de Kooning Drawings*, Greenwich, 1972, pp. 16-17.
2. Foreword to the catalogue of the de Kooning exhibition, Workshop Art Center Gallery, Washington, D.C., 1953, cited by T. B. Hess, *Willem de Kooning*, exh. cat., MoMA, New York, 1968, pp. 138-39, fn. 11.

89 Untitled. 1958.

Color plate p. 677.

76.2553 PG 158

Oil on wove paper (Favor-Bristol blind stamp), mounted on masonite mounted on plywood, 23 x 29⅛ (58.5 x 74.0).

Signed and dated l.r.: *de Kooning '58*.

PROVENANCE:

Purchased from the artist in his New York studio, ca. 1960.

CONDITION:

In 1983 (New York) the support was detached mechanically from the masonite mount, which had caused discoloration of the paper support. Tape and adhesive residue on verso were removed with water, reagent alcohol and steam, and the surface cleaned to remove dust and dirt. Impasto areas, which had suffered some breaks and substantial losses, were consolidated with methyl cellulose (400 cps, 2%, Dow). Abrasions caused by previous frame were inpainted with Windsor and Newton cadmium yellow. Four thumbtack holes at corners (clearly the artist's) were left untouched. The work was hinged around the entire perimeter with Okawara tissue to 100% ragboard support. Owing to the hygroscopic nature of the paper and the heavy impasto of the paint layer, the composition cannot lie flat. The condition is stable, but the paint layer, especially the heavy impasto, is fragile. (New York, Mar. 1983.)

Although it is difficult to place this picture within de Kooning's oeuvre, *Untitled* probably belongs to the series from the late 1950s that were inspired by the landscape of highways.

In his often quoted December 1960 interview with David Sylvester, de Kooning spoke of his response to such subjects; he was not painting landscape in a literal sense, but "sensations of that, outside the city — with the feeling of going to the city or coming from it."[1]

According to Thomas B. Hess, de Kooning "saw the highway as an enormous connection, with an environment of its own. It moves through the 'left-over' spaces of the city: the dumps and flats, industrial marshes, bitumized plains."[2] De Kooning acknowledged the general source of inspiration for these pictures, but also suggested that the point of reference for a particular work would often arise from — rather than precede — the painting in question. For example, in the picture *Merritt Parkway* (Private Collection, Detroit), de Kooning did not set out to paint an image of the parkway; the "connection" emerged as the work progressed, until the artist unexpectedly recognized a reminiscence or evocation of the parkway experience. The subject of this and other "abstractions" of the late 1950s is, inevitably, ambiguous. As de Kooning has said, his paintings offer as subject matter only a "glimpse of something, an encounter like a flash."[3]

The scale of the small oils on paper varied greatly, and, whether mounted or not, they functioned neither as studies for larger paintings nor as entirely independent works. They should be viewed as "aspects of a unified process" that de Kooning carried on at many levels simultaneously.[4] The Peggy Guggenheim oil, though clearly related in style, and even in palette, to a large canvas such as *Suburb in Havana* (Collection Mr. and Mrs. Lee V. Eastman, New York), functions essentially as a parallel exploration of a similar theme rather than as a preparatory stage in a more ambitious undertaking.

EXHIBITIONS:

London, *P.G.*, 1964-65, no. 132, repr.; Stockholm, *P.G.*, 1966-67, no. 128, repr.; New York, *P.G.*, 1969, p. 134, repr.; Paris, *P.G.*, 1974-75, no. 136, not repr.; Torino, *P.G.*, 1975-76, no. 150; New York, *P.G.*, 1982-83, no. 51, repr.

REFERENCES:

Calas, 1966, repr. p. 181; L. Flint, *Handbook*, 1983, p. 176, repr. color p. 177.

1. "Content is a glimpse," excerpts from BBC interview, December 30, 1960, published in *Location*, vol. 1, no. 1, spring 1963, p. 47.
2. T. B. Hess, *Willem de Kooning*, exh. cat., MoMA, New York, 1968, p. 103.
3. De Kooning, 1960 interview, loc. cit.
4. Hess, op. cit., p. 13.

František Kupka

Born September 1871, Opŏcno, Bohemia.
Died June 1957, Puteaux.

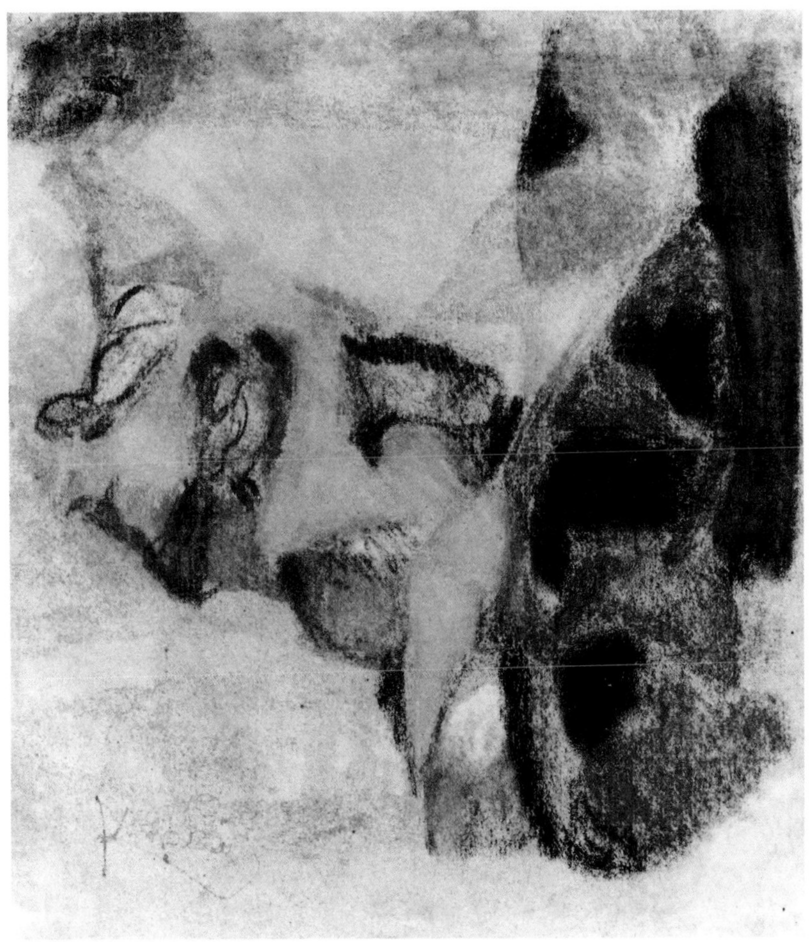

90 Untitled. ca. 1910?
(*Etude chromatique*).

76.2553 PG 12

Pastel on wove paper, 9¼ x 8 3/16 (23.5 x 20.8).

Signed l.l. in ink: *Kupka*; on reverse: purple ink stamp: *Frank Kupka / 7 rue Lemaître / Puteaux (Seine)*; red ink stamp: *Kupka*. Not dated.

PROVENANCE:

Eugénie Kupka, Paris, 1957-64; Karl Flinker, Paris, 1964; sold to Gimpel Fils, London, 1964; purchased from Gimpel Fils, March 1965.

CONDITION:

In 1978 (New York) the work was detached from a wood mount to which it had been adhered along the upper edge with glue and glassine tapes, elsewhere with 8 Scotch-tape hinges. Adhesive residue on the reverse and heavy stains on the obverse of the support (caused by the Scotch tape) were removed as far as possible with solvent. Small tears at the edges were repaired with Japanese tissue. The support, which was originally blue (lower left corner retains trace of this), has faded to buff due to photo-oxidation (overexposure to light). Uneven discoloration and staining of the support have altered all tonal relationships within the work. Though there is no evidence of fixative, the pigment remains intact; the condition is stable. (Venice, Nov. 1982.)

It has so far proved impossible to locate comparable works that might throw light on the subject or date of this work. The condition, which makes it difficult to assess the relative color values, necessarily complicates the problem. The work bears some resemblance to charcoal studies of ca. 1910 (see, for example, Rowell, *František Kupka 1871-1957: A Retrospective*, New York, 1975, cat. no. 54). Until further evidence emerges, it is difficult to place this work with any certainty.

EXHIBITIONS:

London, Gimpel Fils, *Kupka Gouaches 1904-1945*, Sept.-Oct., 1964, no. 2 ("*Etude chromatique*, 1910 / 11"); Paris, *P.G.*, 1974-75, no. 32; Torino, *P.G.*, 1975-76, no. 11.

REFERENCE:

Calas, 1966, repr. p. 33.

---

91 Study for *Amorpha, Chromatique chaude* and for *Fugue à deux couleurs*. Ca. 1910-11.
(Study for *Amorpha, Warm Chromatic* and for *Fugue in two colors*; Study for *The Fugue*).

Color plate p. 44.

76.2553 PG 13

Pastel on machine-made laid-line paper, 18 15/16 x 19 (46.8 x 48.3).

Signed in ink l.r.: *Kupka*. Not dated.

PROVENANCE:

Eugénie Kupka, Paris, 1957-64;[1] Karl Flinker, Paris, 1964-66; purchased from Karl Flinker, Paris, February 1966.

CONDITION:

The support, which was originally blue, has discolored to brown due to photo-oxidation (overexposure to light). A loss at the upper right corner was replaced (at an unknown date). There is staining at the lower center from tape on the verso. Moderate abrasions throughout the pastel surface are attributable to the work's previous framing in direct contact with the glass. The serious disruption of the artist's original color relationships (caused by the darkening of the support) must be taken into account in any evaluation of this work's place in Kupka's development of the Fugue theme. The condition is otherwise stable. (Venice, Nov. 1982.)

Kupka's controversial entries in the 1912 *Salon d'Automne* were *Amorpha, Chromatique chaude* (fig. d) and *Amorpha, Fugue à deux couleurs* (fig. e), the latter the first purely nonfigurative composition ever to be shown in Paris.

Lillian Lonngren was the first to point out that the curvilinear abstract structures of these two paintings derive originally from a highly conventional ca. 1908-9 portrait of Kupka's stepdaughter, Andrée, posing with a ball in the garden of their Puteaux house (*Art News*, vol. 56, Nov. 1957, pp. 44-46, 54-56).[2]

1. Information from Karl Flinker.

In the more than fifty studies that followed this portrait, culminating in the two paintings exhibited at the *Salon*, Kupka attempted on the one hand to depict the motions of the ball, of the curving gestures of the girl's arm and the gyrations of her body in space, and on the other to destroy the conventional relationships between figure and ground, between light and shade. As he confronted the problem of distilling into pictorial form the trajectories of the various elements crossing and overlapping one another and penetrating the deep space, Kupka developed a formal language that would express sequential movement on a single plane and rotational movement through space within the two-dimensional picture plane.[3]

2. Subsequent writers on Kupka have in general repeated this interpretation. See, for example, D. Fédit, *L'Œuvre de Kupka*, Inventaire des collections publiques françaises, no. 13, MNAM, Paris, 1966, pp. 75-77; L. Vachtová, *Kupka*, London, 1968, pp. 75ff.; M. Rowell, *Kupka*, exh. cat., SRGM, New York, 1975, pp. 60-67, 70-74, cat. nos. 30-32, 61-63, 71-75, 83-92; V. Spate, *Orphism: The Evolution of Non-figurative Painting in Paris, 1910-14*, Oxford, 1979, pp. 125ff. It is important to note that Kupka himself added an inscription to one of the *Jeune fille au ballon* drawings: *Genèse des disques et de la „Fugue.*" Though it is not known when he added this inscription it is significant that he identified these works as a continuous series.

3. For a discussion of Kupka's multiple aims in these and a group of contemporary paintings, see Rowell, op. cit., especially pp. 60-62, 72-75.

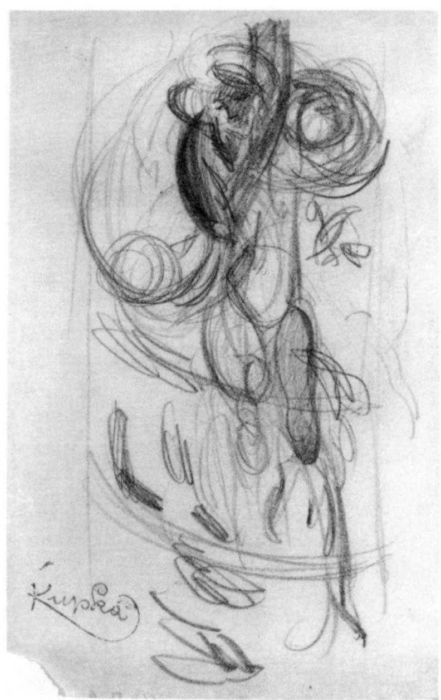

fig. a.
Kupka, Study after *La petite fille au ballon,* 1908-9, pencil on paper, 8⅛ x 5¼ in., 20.6 x 13.3 cm., stamped l.l.: *Kupka,* The Museum of Modern Art, New York, Gift of Mr. and Mrs. František Kupka.

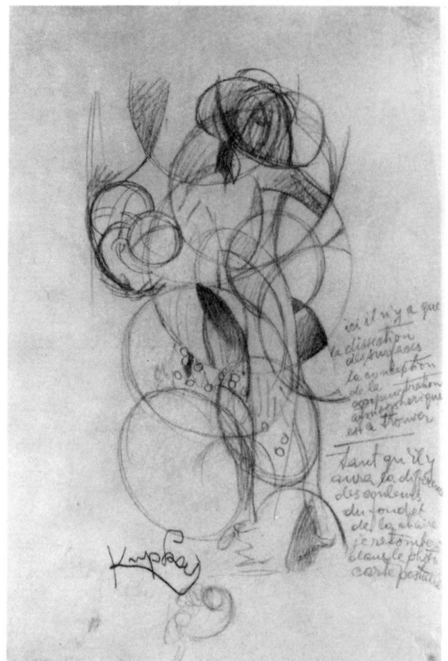

fig. b.
Kupka, Study after *La petite fille au ballon,* 1908-9, pencil on paper, 10¾ x 7⅜ in., 27.3 x 18.7 cm., inscribed r. margin: *ici il n'y a que / la dissection / des surfaces / la conception / de la conpénétration* [sic] / *atmosphérique / est à trouver / tant qu'il y / aura la différence / des couleurs / du fond et / de la chaire* [sic] / *je retomberai / dans le* [sic] *photo / carte postale,* The Museum of Modern Art, New York, Gift of Mr. and Mrs. František Kupka.

In a note written on one of the earlier drawings of the series (fig. b), Kupka expressed a central part of his dilemma: *"ici il n'y a que la dissection des surfaces. La conception de la conpénétration atmosphérique est à trouver. Tant qu'il y aura la différence des couleurs du fond et de la chaire je retomberai dans le photo carte postale."* What Kupka was at pains to suppress here was any residual reference to his naturalistic source as well as to the conventional pictorial structure of figure and ground. He wished instead to create an intelligible structure in which the concept of motion and space could be conveyed through a uniformly lighted composition of color and rhythm alone.

Peggy Guggenheim's pastel, hitherto not associated with this group of studies, represents an early stage in Kupka's struggle with these issues. The rotational trajectory of the ball (in blue) is traced in the foreground plane; at the upper left it passes momentarily behind, but in general it moves directly in front of, the curving arm or body (in brown), which in turn gyrates in front of the light tonal substructure of the green background plane. "*Conpénétration atmosphérique*" eludes Kupka here as it does in the pencil drawing (fig. b).[4] Although the motion of the ball and the contrary motion of the twisting body are to some

fig. c.
Kupka, Study for *Amorpha, Fugue à deux couleurs*, 1911-12, gouache and ink, 4⅞ x 5⅛ in., 12.4 x 13 cm., The Museum of Modern Art, New York, Gift of Mr. and Mrs. František Kupka.

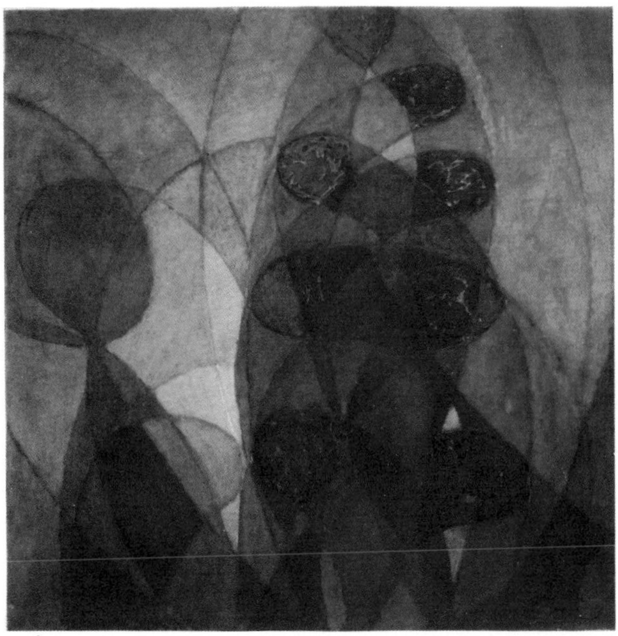

fig. d.
Kupka, *Amorpha, Chromatique chaude*, 1911-12, oil on canvas, 42½ x 42½ in., 108 x 108 cm., Private Collection.

degree successfully abstracted here from their original sources, the critical problem Kupka set for himself has remained unresolved, as it has in the coloristically related *Amorpha, Chromatique chaude* (fig. d). In this latter work, as Virginia Spate has convincingly argued (op. cit., pp. 128-29), the progress toward an abstract language is clearly marked, but the relation of form to space remains strongly rooted in traditional concepts.

In subsequent, or possibly parallel, stages (such as fig. c), the arabesque expressing the ball's motion in space is retained; but the palette is radically altered to the stark red, blue, black, white of *Amorpha, Fugue à deux couleurs*. In a large group of studies and in the final work, the colors are for the first time used without the introduction of illusionistic light, allowing Kupka to achieve his primary aim.

4. A contemporary oil *Conpénétrations* (Private Collection; Rowell, op. cit., cat. no. 68), in which the arabesque of the ball in motion weaves in and out of an allover field of narrow vertical planes, is part of yet another thematic sequence of works arising out of *La petite fille au ballon*.

fig. e.
Kupka, *Amorpha, Fugue à deux couleurs*, 1912, oil on canvas, 83⅛ x 86⅝ in., 211 x 220 cm., Národní Galerie, Prague.

EXHIBITIONS:

Paris, Galerie Karl Flinker, *Kupka: Pastels et Gouaches, 1906-1945*, June 1964, no. 1 ("Etude pour *La Fugue* (I), 1911-12"); Paris, *P.G.*, 1974-75, no. 33.

REFERENCES:

J. Cassou and D. Fédit, *Kupka*, Paris, 1964, repr. color p. 23 ("*La Fugue*, 1911-12"); ibid., New York, 1965 ("Study for *The Fugue*, 1911-12"); M. Rowell, *František Kupka 1871-1957: A Retrospective*, New York, 1975, p. 160 ("study for *Amorpha, Fugue à deux couleurs* of 1912").

91A Study for *Femme cueillant des fleurs*.

ca. 1910?
(Study for *Woman picking flowers*).

76.2553 PG 13a (reverse of cat. no. 91).

Pastel on paper, 18 7/16 x 19 1/16 (46.8 x 48.3).

Stamped signature u.r. (added after the artist's death): *Kupka*; stamp in center of composition: *Frank Kupka / 7 rue Lemaître, Puteaux (Seine)* (the address to which Kupka moved in 1906). Not dated.

PROVENANCE:

See above, cat. no. 91.

CONDITION:

Since this work has been pressed down against a secondary support, the pastel surface is severely abraded with extensive staining. The image is discernible, but in poor condition. (Venice, Nov. 1982.)

91A

Published here for the first time, this study may represent an early exploration of the theme *Femme cueillant des fleurs*. In spite of its abraded condition, certain aspects of its technique and palette bring it into close proximity with the pastels in that series, of which many are apparently lost but seven are known. (For discussion of the theme, see cat. no. 91, fn. 2; Fédit, op. cit., pp. 56-61, who dates the series 1910 "at the latest"; Rowell, op. cit., pp. 60-61, 136-41, who dates it 1909-10; Spate, op. cit., pp. 138-39, who dates it 1910-11.)

---

92 Study for *Localisations de mobiles graphiques I*. Ca. 1911-12.
(Study for *Organization of graphic motifs I*; *Dynamique*[1]).

Color plate p. 43.

76.2553 PG 15

Pastel on wove paper (watermark: CANSON), 12 15/16 x 12 7/16 (32.9 x 31.6).

Signed l.l. in black ink: *Kupka*. Not dated.

PROVENANCE:

Eugénie Kupka, Paris, 1957-64;[2] Karl Flinker, Paris, 1964-66; purchased from Karl Flinker, Paris, February 1966.

CONDITION:

There are some scattered brown spots (possibly foxing) at the upper right, and a few at the center top edge (foxing but not active). The condition is stable. (Venice, Nov. 1982.)

1. This title was assigned by Karl Flinker, Denise Fédit, or Andrée Martinel-Kupka at the time of the 1964 exhibition.
2. Information supplied by Flinker.

92

This drawing is one of an extensive group of pencil, ink, pastel, and gouache studies for *Localisations de mobiles graphiques I* (fig. a). The latter painting and its closely related sequel *Localisations de mobiles graphiques II* (Private Collection) were exhibited at the October 1913 *Salon d'Automne* (nos. 1149 and 1150) and would thus have been completed by some time in September of that year. Kupka may have begun work on parts of the theme as early as 1910 (as suggested by M. Mladek in M. Rowell, *František Kupka 1871-1957: A Retrospective*, exh. cat., SRGM, New York, 1975, pp. 44-45). The majority of the sketches for the two ambitious oils probably date from 1911-12, though some may have been done as late as 1913.

Margit Rowell has indicated that the concept "*localisations de mobiles graphiques*" is defined and developed in two stages in Kupka's writings (ibid., pp. 198-99). The terms "*mobile*" and "*mobile graphique*" occur for the first time in a manuscript of 1910-11 containing Kupka's preliminary notes in French for his book *Tvoření v Umění Výtvarném (La création dans les arts plastiques)*, which he finished in 1913 and published in 1923. According to Rowell, the terms are defined in the text as "the outer expression of the artist's inner motivations (or motives) and identified as '*motifs-mobiles*' (motive-motifs) as opposed to '*motifs-sujets*' (subject-motifs) or the motif derived from a subject in the perceived world" (manuscript of 1910-11, pp. 30-31, Private Collection).

In the same text, Kupka apparently also offers a definition of the phrase "*localisations de motifs-mobiles graphiques*"; but he develops the concept more fully in a handwritten draft dating from 1912-13 of Chapter V of the same book.[3] Rowell summarizes Kupka's elucidation of the phrase in the following

fig. a.
Kupka, *Localisations de mobiles graphiques I*, 1912-13, oil on canvas, 78¾ x 76⅜ in., 200 x 194 cm., Collection Thyssen-Bornemisza, Lugano.

way: "In our inner visions, fragments of images float before our eyes. In order to capture these fragments, we unconsciously trace lines between them and by thus setting up a network of relationships, we arrive at a coherent whole. These lines drawn to organize our visions are like 'stereoscopic bridges' between fragments in space.... The lines of this network define points in space and directions. They provide the scaffolding of the image; they capture the rhythmic relationships between impressions. And this is the real subject of the painter in the lyrical or tragic schema of nature poeticized or dramatized. Details, forms, figures, objects may subsequently be added to articulate the image further" (manuscript of ca. 1912-13, Collection Karl Flinker, Paris).

The nature of the compositional process in Kupka's studies for *Localisations de mobiles graphiques* reflects these principles. In the Peggy Guggenheim work, the ground lines receding right to left toward two separate vanishing points and the accumulation of detail ("forms, figures, objects") in the foreground suggest that this was a relatively early conception for the work. The interrelationships are sketched out, but the clarity of later stages is lacking. In subsequent studies the recession is from left to right toward a common vanishing point, and the foreground detail is more coherently defined, bringing these later stages into a closer relationship with the finished painting. In all these studies, and many others, the elaborate superstructure of converging diagonals ("drawn to organize our visions") functions increasingly as the " 'stereoscopic bridges' between fragments in space." As Kupka envisaged, these bridges provide on one level a

3. The present author has not studied the Kupka manuscripts cited here.

structural coherence defining "points in space and directions.... the scaffolding of the image." On another more suggestive level they operate to "capture the rhythmic relationships between impressions." *Localisations de mobiles graphiques I* retains a focus on the superstructure, and on a ground-level linear thrust into depth, which is a critical element in the entire group of preparatory studies, including Peggy Guggenheim's. In *Localisations de mobiles graphiques II*, however, the upper structural framework converges with the lower linear perspective to create a unified circular movement into vertiginous space. In this respect, Kupka moves his conception closer to cosmic themes such as *Création* of 1911-20 (Národní Galerie, Prague) and even prepares the way for the 1919-20 series of *Conte de pistils et d'étamines* (D. Fédit, *L'Œuvre de Kupka*, MNAM, Paris, 1966, no. 72; Národní Galerie, Prague, repr. L. Vachtová, *Kupka*, London, 1968, pp. 161-62; Collection Wilhelm Hack, Cologne, repr. M. Rowell, *Kupka*, exh. cat., SRGM, New York, 1975, p. 217).

EXHIBITIONS:

Paris, Galerie Karl Flinker, *Kupka: Pastels et Gouaches, 1906-1945*, June 1964, no. 13; Paris, *P.G.*, 1974-75, no. 35; Torino, *P.G.*, 1975-76, no. 14.

REFERENCE:

D. Fédit, "Les gouaches de Kupka," *Quadrum*, vol. 16, 1964, repr. color p. 5, pl. 3 (dated 1912-13).

---

93 Autour d'un point. Ca. 1920-25.
(Around a point).

Color plate p. 43.

76.2553 PG 16

Watercolor, gouache, and graphite on wood-pulp wove paper, $7^{15}/_{16}$ x $9^{3}/_{8}$ (20.1 x 23.8).

Stamped signature l.l. (added after the artist's death): *Kupka*; on reverse, purple ink stamp: *Frank Kupka / 7 rue Lemaître / Puteaux (Seine)*. Not dated.

PROVENANCE:

Eugénie Kupka, Paris, 1957-64;[1] Karl Flinker, Paris, 1964-66; purchased from Karl Flinker, February 1966.

CONDITION:

In 1983 (New York) the work was mechanically removed from a wood-pulp paper secondary support that had been deeply stained by acid migration. Brown paper tape, which had been used on the verso to adhere the primary to the secondary support, was removed with alcohol and water. Repeated spray deacidification of the verso (calcium hydroxide), with drying between applications, achieved pH 8.2. Tears at the upper edge and right edge, and loss at the upper left edge, were repaired. Traces of animal glue at the lower right were removed with water. The condition is stable. (New York, Jan. 1983.)

1. Information supplied by Karl Flinker.

The present watercolor belongs to a large group of closely related studies that culminated in a single highly abstract oil, *Autour d'un point* (fig. b). Although the earliest ideas for the image apparently date from 1911 (clarifying Kupka's 1911-30 date on the final oil), the majority of the dozens of sketches were executed between 1920 and 1930 (see D. Fédit, *L'Œuvre de Kupka*, Inventaire des collections publiques françaises, no. 13, MNAM, Paris, 1966, pp. 119-22; for additional studies see M. Rowell, *Kupka*, exh. cat., SRGM, New York, 1975, cat. nos. 152-59). The sketches for *Autour d'un point* thus follow Kupka's return to biological and botanical themes in the 1919-20 series *Conte de pistils et d'étamines*, and demonstrate his continued preoccupation with cosmic themes.

No satisfactory chronology for this group has been established, and the repetition of motifs with very little variation makes the dating of individual examples extremely problematic. Nonetheless, a plausible framework situates the more explicitly floral examples, including the present work, in the early twenties. Kupka's subsequent development of the motif into a less fluid and organic and more geometric composition coincides with his parallel reworking in a similar stylistic direction of *Lignes animées* (MNAM), which was originally completed by 1920 but reworked ca. 1924-33 (see Fédit, op. cit., no. 75).

The Peggy Guggenheim study is almost certainly unfinished. The rapidly painted scumbled brownish area in the lower right, which, in its singular lack of articulation contrasts with Kupka's careful treatment of this detail in other examples (see fig. a), may suggest that he abandoned the study before it was entirely resolved.

fig. a.
Kupka, *Autour d'un point*, not dated, gouache and watercolor on paper, 12½ x 12½ in., 31.7 x 31.7 cm., Collection Mr. and Mrs. M. A. Gribin.

fig. b.
Kupka, *Autour d'un point*, ca. 1925-30, reworked ca. 1934, oil on canvas, 76⅜ x 78¾ in., 194 x 200 cm., Musée National d'Art Moderne, Centre Georges Pompidou, Paris.

EXHIBITIONS:

Paris, Galerie Karl Flinker, *Kupka: Pastels et Gouaches, 1906-1945*, June 1964, no. 46 (dated "*vers 1920*"); Milan, Galleria del Levante, *Kupka*, Apr. 1965, traveled to Rome, Galleria del Levante, May 1965, cat. no. 9, repr. (dated 1913/14); New York, *P.G.*, 1969, p. 21, repr. (c. 1914); Paris, *P.G.*, 1974-75, no. 36 (c. 1914); Torino, *P.G.*, 1975-76, no. 15 (c. 1914); New York, *P.G.*, 1982-83, no. 13 (n.d.).

REFERENCES:

J. Cassou and D. Fédit, *Kupka: Gouaches and Pastels*, Paris, 1964, repr. color p. 33; idem, New York, 1965, repr. color p. 33.

Ibram Lassaw

Born May 1913, Alexandria, Egypt.
Lives in East Hampton, Long Island.

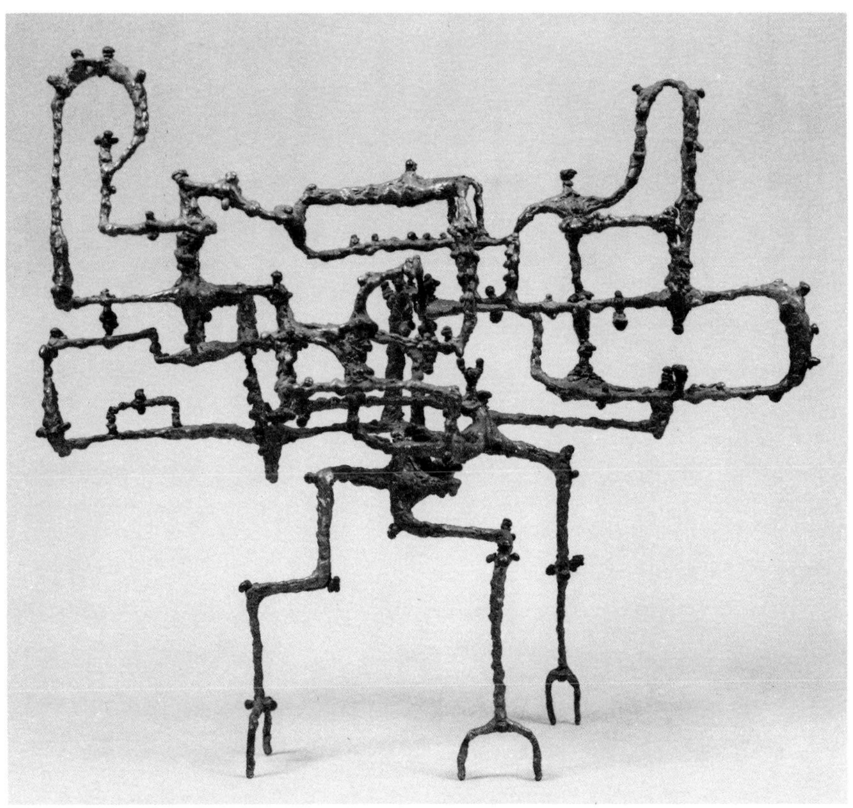

94 Corax. December 1953.

76.2553 PG 202

Chromium bronze with additional metals. Height: 19½ (49.5); width: 23 (58.8); depth: 10 (25.5).

Signed and dated on horizontal member: *LASSAW 53*.

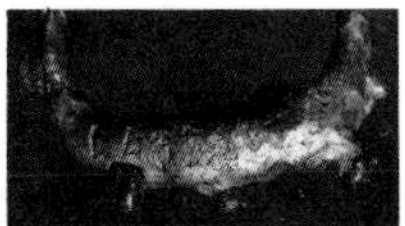

PROVENANCE:

Purchased from the artist through Samuel Kootz Gallery, New York, April 30, 1959.

CONDITION:

The presence of corrosion and welding residue in some places poses problems for the stability of the metal. The artist's original intention was to achieve a differentiation in color among the various materials of the sculpture: the overall surface was in different tones of golden yellow but the "knoblike" copper areas were blue-green, created through the application of acid. These differentiations have been obscured through weathering. Cleaning and anticorrosive treatment are envisaged, which may reintroduce some differentiation in color. (Venice, Nov. 1982.)

Lassaw's technical procedure in this and other sculpture of the 1950s was as follows:[1] the construction of the armature, in thin galvanized iron wire, was executed without preparatory drawings. The image or composition, which was at this stage in his career always nonrepresentational and without figurative subject matter, emerged as the artist worked and was not the result of a pre-

1. Lassaw discussed his technique in an interview with Lucy Flint, November 1982.

94

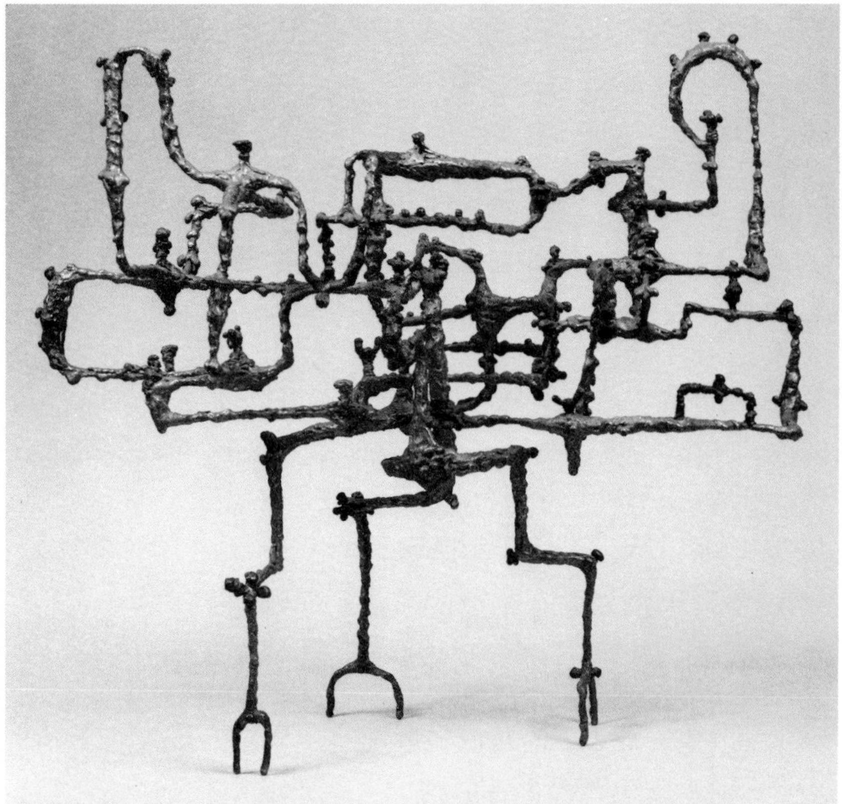

conceived design. Once the armature was built, the artist began the process of "painting in metals," using an oxyacetelene torch and various alloys of bronze to produce different coloristic and textural effects. First the bronze wire was dipped into flux, a commercial product made essentially of borax which prevents the hot metal from oxidizing and allows it to flow more easily. The process of building upon the armature with molten bronze often took weeks of laborious work. Nickel silver or zinc was then often combined with brass, silicon bronze, or phospher bronze, the molten metals being applied and worked in various thicknesses to coat the armature and give it tactile substance and articulation.

The pieces were conceived in the round, every side and angle playing a role in the overall compositional effect.

The title, always assigned by Lassaw after the completion of the work, served to identify the piece but not to elucidate a meaning. Though a title might have suggestive associations for Lassaw himself (*corax*, the Greek word for raven, bearing certain connotations for him), it is intended to add no illustrative dimension to the piece itself.

EXHIBITIONS:

New York, Riverside Museum, *Eighteenth Annual: American Abstract Artists 1954*, Mar. 7-28, 1954, no. 60; New York, Samuel Kootz Gallery, *Lassaw: New Sculpture*, Oct. 23-Nov. 13, 1954, no. 5; London, *P.G.*, 1964-65, no. 169; New York, *P.G.*, 1969, p. 161, repr.; Paris, *P.G.*, 1974-75, no. 165; Torino, *P.G.*, 1975-76, no. 190.

REFERENCE:

Calas, 1966, repr. p. 217.

Henri Laurens

Born February 1885, Paris.
Died May 1954, Paris.

5

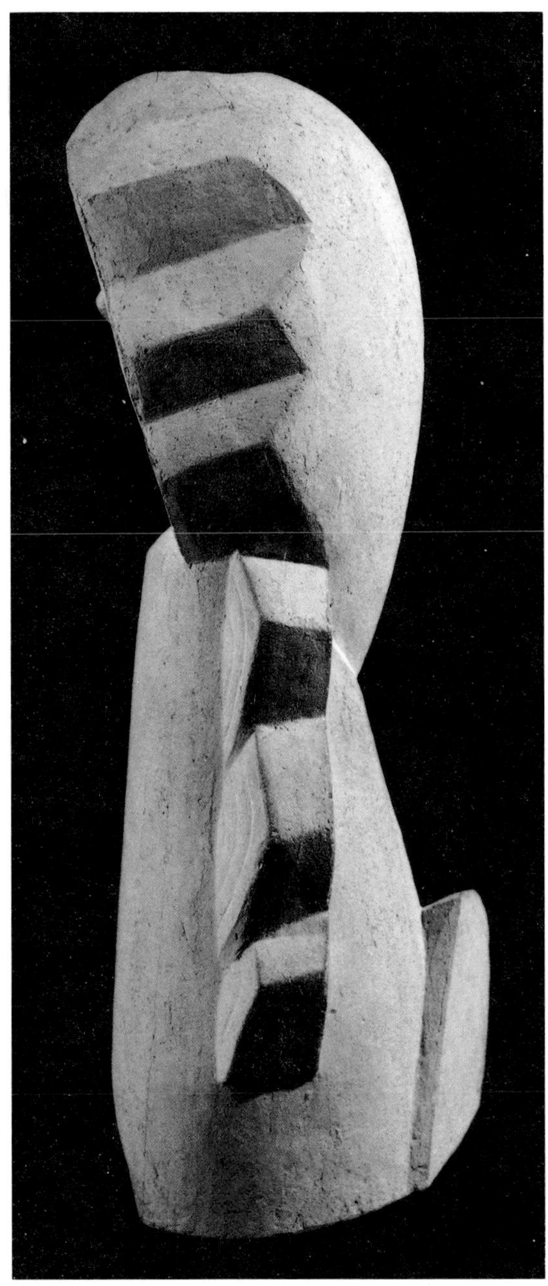

95 Tête de jeune fillette. 1920 (cast 1959).
(Head of a young girl).

76.2553 PG 27

Terra-cotta cast. Height: 13½ (34.2); width: 6½ (16.5).

Incised into the terra-cotta interior: *VI*. Not signed or dated.

Edition of six, plus "O."

All casts by Jean van Dongen.[1]

PROVENANCE:

Purchased from Galerie Louise Leiris, Paris (stockbook no. 6243), February 23, 1962.

CONDITION:

A small repair is visible near the right bottom edge. A vertical surface crack, (4½ in., 11.5 cm., long), starts at the base, but does not penetrate through the terra cotta to the hollow interior. It probably occurred during the firing of the piece. The condition is otherwise stable. (Nov. 1982.)

Although Laurens worked extensively on the theme of the young girl during the years 1920-21, no stylistic or chronological sequence for the various versions has been established.

Before Laurens cast the six terra cottas of the present piece, he first made a stone version with a base (fig. a). The stone version's crisp sharpness of edge and line, the tight compactness of composition, gave way in the terra cotta to a softer modeling of form.

A comparison between the original stone version (fig. a) and the almost exactly contemporary stone *Guitar* of the same year (M. Laurens, 1955, p. 87) contributes to the establishment of a plausible chronology for the series of variations on the theme of the young girl, and an understanding of the role they played in developing Laurens's mature independent sculptural style.

Although the spare, contained, lucid but elliptical structure of the *Guitar* is mirrored to some extent in the *Tête de jeune fillette*, the latter is more anecdotal and decorative in its detail. In the wood and stone variations that followed the present *Tête* (see, for example, M. Laurens, 1955, pp. 89-91, 94, 99), Laurens elaborated further on the decorative, graceful, and inherently two-dimensional qualities of the image. Only in 1922, with works such as *Femme accroupie* (ibid., p. 102), did he implicitly acknowledge the limitations of this course by beginning to explore the structural potential inherent in the *Guitar*. Thus the series of increasingly elegant, attenuated, and decorative variations on the *Tête de jeune fillette* theme surrendered to the weighty, almost archaic, but expressively sculptural forms that were to characterize his production in the late 1920s. It is

1. D.-H. Kahnweiler purchased the original clay model, and the rights to cast it, in late 1920 or early 1921. Three casts were commissioned in 1921 from Jean van Dongen, who made 3 more in 1959, the present example being the last, no. VI (information supplied by Monsieur and Madame Claude Laurens and by Galerie Louise Leiris, Mar. 1982). The "O" cast was also made in 1959 and subsequently given by Kahnweiler to the MNAM. An unnumbered and undated cast, signed HL and presumably from the 1921 edition, was acquired by the Kunstmuseum Hannover in 1955. The whereabouts of the other 4 casts, as well as of the stone and wood versions, has not been established.

fig. a.
Laurens, *Tête de jeune fillette*, ca. 1920, stone version, height: 15⁹⁄₁₆ in., 39.5 cm., present whereabouts unknown. Photograph courtesy Galerie Louise Leiris.

precisely in their inelegance and oppressively massive presence that sculptures such as *Femme au bras levé* (1929) or *Petit Caryatide* (1929) demonstrate Laurens's departure from the gracile, delicate forms of 1920-21. In this sense, *Tête de jeune fillette* stands at a pivotal point, representing for Laurens perhaps the final possible articulation of the vocabulary he had derived from Cubism.

EXHIBITIONS:[2]

London, *P.G.*, 1964-65, no. 20. repr.; Stockholm, *P.G.*, 1966-67, no. 20, repr.; Paris, *P.G.*, 1974-75, no. 19, repr.; Torino, *P.G.*, 1975-76, no. 26, repr. pl. 9.

REFERENCES:

M. Laurens, *Henri Laurens sculpteur*, Paris, 1955, repr. p. 86 (stone version, height given as ca. 50 cm.); C. Goldschneider, *Laurens*, New York, 1959, repr. n.p. no. 6 (stone version); P. G. Brugière, "Pierres sculptées, d'Henri Laurens," *Cahiers d'Art*, vols. 33-35, 1960, repr. p. 135 (stone version, height given as 39.5 cm.); Calas, 1966, repr. p. 55 (Peggy Guggenheim cast).

2. Early exhibitions of the stone or terra-cotta version have not yet been traced. The earliest appearance of the stone sculpture may have been at Yverdon, Hôtel de la Ville, *Sept Pionniers de la Sculpture Moderne*, July 18-September 28, 1954, no. 7, repr. The wood version appeared in the MNAM exhibition, *Henri Laurens*, May 9-June 17, 1951, no. 13. The terra-cotta version appeared at the Stedelijk Museum, Amsterdam, March-April 1962, no. 8.

Fernand Léger

Born February 1881, Argentan (Orne).
Died August 1955, Gif-sur-Yvette.

96 Study of a nude. Paris, winter 1912-13.

76.2553 PG 19

Oil on wood-pulp paper, 25 x 19 1/16 (63.6 x 48.5).

Signed in pencil u.l. (upside down, possibly by another hand): *FL*. Not dated.

PROVENANCE:

Purchased from the artist by Galerie Kahnweiler (stockbook no. 1513), 1913; probably sequestered Kahnweiler stock, 1914-23, and sold in an unidentified lot at one of the Kahnweiler sales, 1921-23; whereabouts unknown 1923-45; purchased from a New York dealer, 1945.[1]

1. Peggy Guggenheim recalled going with André Breton to a dealer in New York to purchase this work, but was unable to be more specific than this. She had not acquired it by the time her gallery opened in 1942; it is recorded among her possessions for the first time in 1945.

CONDITION:

Until 1983, the highly acidic wood-pulp paper had been glued to an off-white paper and acidic millboard. The support had thus become extremely brittle, degraded, and discolored to dark yellow-ocher (see L. Flint, *Handbook*, 1983, color repr. p. 23). Brown stains in the lower left and some elsewhere were possibly due to moisture.

In March 1983 (London) the paper was successfully removed from its mount. It was then washed, deacidified with magnesium bicarbonate, and bleached (hydrogen peroxide and magnesium bicarbonate in a 1:2 solution). After successive treatments, washing, and further deacidification, the work was lined with Japanese paper. The support has regained flexibility and strength, much of its original color has been retrieved, and the condition is stable. (London, July 1983.)

The identification of the medium used by Léger in this and several related works poses interesting issues. Described in the Kahnweiler stock book as *dessin rehaussé*, the medium has been described since the 1940s as gouache, charcoal and wash, or gouache and watercolor. During and after examination and restoration in London 1983 (see CONDITION), it was concluded that the medium was oil. Léger had applied the paint in varying thicknesses, but in most areas it was almost completely drained of oil and in some places greatly diluted to a washlike consistency. The tubed paint would have been squeezed onto newspaper or another highly absorbent surface. When most of the oil had been absorbed, the dry pigment was applied with a bristle brush. A 1913 "gouache" in the Rosengart collection, Lucerne (A.Z.R. *Guggenheim*, 1976, Vol. II, p. 463), also examined in London, was similarly painted in oil and on a comparable paper. The entire issue of Léger's 1912-13 work in gouache, watercolor, or oil on paper, and his exploitation of the flexible potential of these media, clearly requires further study.[2]

During the winter of 1912-13, Léger was fully occupied with work on *Le modèle nu dans l'atelier* completed in March 1913. (See A.Z.R. *Guggenheim*, 1976, Vol. II, pp. 456-60 for a discussion of this work and reproductions of several related studies.) While exploring this theme, and possibly in the immediate wake of the painting's completion, Léger produced studies that went considerably further in their abstraction of form than the painting itself. In the present example the seated figure on the left remains marginally legible (especially in light of the painting and its preparatory studies), but the curves of her body are integrated with the surrounding environment, and the rectilinear and planar elements now overlap with the figure in the shallow pictorial space, as if to deprive the composition of its subject, substituting a new order of formal coherence. While reminiscent to this extent of some elements of *La femme en bleu* completed during the previous autumn, this drawing and some related works on paper also look forward to the nonobjective *Contrastes de formes* of 1913.

2. The author is indebted to Kasha Szeleynski of The Tate Gallery Conservation Department for insights into this question, and for the initial identification of the medium as oil. In treating the work, Kasha Szeleynski found slight traces of oil on the reverse of the paper, and also found, as cleaning proceeded, that the medium behaved like oil rather than gouache. Though a chemical analysis was not conducted, the case for the oil medium is a compelling one.

EXHIBITIONS:

Venice, *P.G.*, 1948 (Biennale), no. 71; Florence, *P.G.*, 1949, no. 77; Amsterdam, *P.G.*, 1951, no. 89; Zurich, *P.G.*, 1951, no. 85; London, *P.G.*, 1964-65, no. 13; Stockholm, *P.G.*, 1966-67, no. 13; Paris, *P.G.*, 1974-75, no. 9; Torino, *P.G.*, 1975-76, no. 18; London, The Tate Gallery, *The Essential Cubism, 1907-1920*, Apr. 27-July 10, 1983, no. 107, repr.

REFERENCE:

Calas, 1966, repr. p. 41 (upside down; owing to the placement of the signature, the work was also exhibited upside down in Peggy Guggenheim's house).

---

97 Les hommes dans la ville. 1919.
(*Men in the city*).

Color plate p. 390.

76.2553 PG 21

Oil on canvas (unvarnished), 57⅜ x 44¹¹⁄₁₆ (145.7 x 113.5).

Signed l.r.: *F. LEGER / 19*; on reverse: *LES Hommes dans la VILLE / ETAT DEFINITIF / F. LEGER / 19.*

PROVENANCE:

Purchased from the artist, Paris, April 9, 1940.[1]

CONDITION:

In 1964 (Tate Report) the unvarnished painting was described as in good condition with the exception of many minute losses in the upper center red square; a craquelure near the center top edge and above the signature at the lower right was elevated in places but without imminent danger of cleavage.

The work shows extensive drying cracks that were, at an unknown date, consolidated with adhesive. There are some scattered areas of incipient cleavage, but the condition in general is fairly stable. The discoloration of pigment in several areas is due to extensive reworking by the artist. (New York, Feb. 1983.)

1. "The day Hitler walked into Norway I walked into Léger's studio and bought a wonderful 1919 painting from him" (*Out of This Century*, 1946, p. 252). Peggy Guggenheim recalled that Léger had bought the picture back from someone, but she was not sure when or from whom. Since E. Tériade, 1928, records the work as belonging to "Galerie Léonce Rosenberg," and since it was still for sale at the time of the 1933 Zurich exhibition, it seems likely that Rosenberg had it as part of his contract with Léger but later returned it to the artist unsold.

At some point between the arrival of the work in the gallery of Léonce Rosenberg and its acquisition by Peggy Guggenheim, Léger made some minor changes in the composition. (The photographs published by Raynal, 1920; Tériade, 1928; Cooper, 1949; and Zervos, 1952, record the work prior to changes; however, since the changes certainly predate 1940, Cooper, Zervos, and, possibly, Tériade were using old photographs.) While making these changes, Léger also probably reworked other parts of the surface (see CONDITION).

Léger frequently reworked and altered his compositions, or added small details (see, for example, *Le modèle nu dans l'atelier*, A.Z.R. *Guggenheim*, Vol. II, 1976, p. 456). In this example, the changes are largely of a decorative nature.

They include the vertical and horizontal lines within the arches at the left margin; the seven small vertical lines to the right of the main figure's head; the two dotted x's in the lower center; the thirteen dots and six x's in the checkerboard shape at the right. In addition, two areas that are now light in value (above the figure's left elbow and below his forearm) were formerly equal in value to the darkest portions of the composition.

An earlier and significantly smaller version of the composition (fig. a), also of 1919, is closely related in its use of color to the final state, though its compositional structure is less intricate and less resolved.

fig. a.
Léger, *Les hommes dans la ville*, 1919, oil on canvas, 25⅝ x 21⅜ in., 65 x 54.3 cm., present whereabouts unknown.

EXHIBITIONS:

Zurich, Kunsthaus, *Fernand Léger*, Apr. 30-May 25, 1933, no. 75 ("*Les hommes dans la ville*, 115 x 146, 1919, verkäuflich"); New York, Art of This Century, 1942-47, p. 68, repr. p. 69; Venice, *P.G.*, 1948 (Biennale), no. 70; Florence, *P.G.*, 1949, no. 76, repr.; Amsterdam, *P.G.*, 1951, no. 88, repr.; Zurich, *P.G.*, 1951, no. 84, repr.; London, *P.G.*, 1964-65, no. 14, repr.; Stockholm, *P.G.*, 1966-67, no. 14, repr.; New York, *P.G.*, 1969, p. 46, repr. color p. 47; Paris, *P.G.*, 1974-75, no. 11, repr. color; Torino, *P.G.*, 1975-76, no. 20, repr. pl. 12; Rome, *Guggenheim: Venezia-New York*, 1982, no. 7, repr. color; New York, *P.G.*, 1982-83, no. 5, repr. color.

REFERENCES:

M. Raynal, *Fernand Léger*, Paris, 1920, pl. 17; E. Tériade, *Léger*, Paris, 1928, repr. p. 31 (Galerie Léonce Rosenberg); P. Guggenheim, *Art of This Century*, 1942, p. 68, repr. p. 69; J. J. Sweeney, "Léger and the Search for Order," *View*, 4th ser., no. 2, summer 1944, p. 86; D. Cooper, *Fernand Léger et le nouvel espace*, Geneva, 1949, p. 73, repr. p. 81; C. Zervos, *F. Léger: Œuvres de 1909 à 1952*, Paris, 1952, repr. p. 41; P. Guggenheim, *Confessions*, 1960, p. 74; L. Flint, *Handbook*, 1983, repr. color p. 25.

Jacques Lipchitz

(Chaim Jacob Lipschitz).

Born August 1891, Druskienicki, Lithuania.
Died May 1973, Capri.

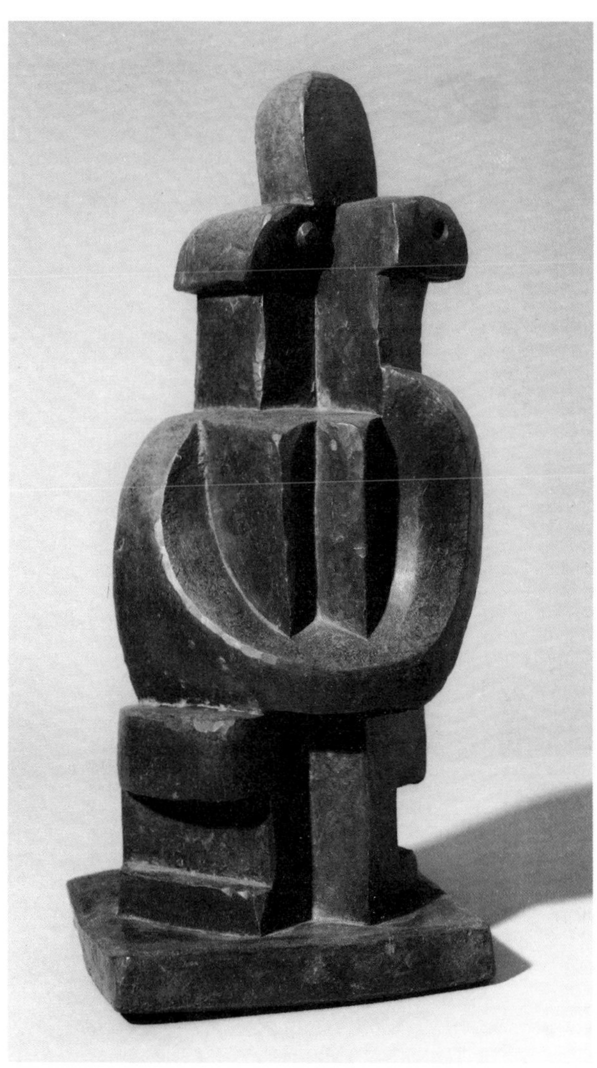

98 Pierrot assis. Paris, 1922.
(*Seated Pierrot*).

76.2553 PG 28

Lead. Height (including base): 13 5/16 (33.5).

Edition of seven.

Foundry: Unknown.

Signed, dated, and numbered on reverse of base: *J.L.* 22 4 / 7.

PROVENANCE:

Purchased in London, 1938.[1]

CONDITION:

The surface was partially worked by the artist after casting. Because of the softness of the medium, the piece is inherently vulnerable. The base has become seriously warped, owing to the weight and malleability of the lead. The overall surface has become opaque, a condition that is remediable through rubbing with a soft cloth. The condition is otherwise stable. (Venice, Nov. 1982.)

Sometime in the course of 1922, Lipchitz, who had been working in conditions of extreme financial difficulty, was visited by the American art collector Albert C. Barnes who purchased eight of his works and commissioned several others. The precise month of Barnes's visit is not known, but *Pierrot assis*—which was cast in lead because Lipchitz was unable to afford any other material — had evidently been completed by that time. It was only after this visit, but still in 1922, that Lipchitz modeled *Homme assis*, a somewhat different (and larger) conception, which he was able to cast in an edition of seven bronzes.[2] This revised version (fig. a) reveals a distinctive change in style.

fig. a.
Lipchitz, *Homme assis*, 1922, plaster, height: 20 9/16 in., 52.3 cm., Musée National d'Art Moderne, Centre Georges Pompidou, Paris, Don de la Fondation Jacques et Yulla Lipchitz.

1. Peggy Guggenheim recalled that she purchased the piece from an unidentified English woman who was raising money to support the Republican cause in Spain.
2. The size of the bronze edition is recorded in the exhibition catalogue published by Marlborough-Gerson, New York, March-April 1968, *Lipchitz: The Cubist Period 1913-1930*. It has not been possible to establish which foundry cast the bronze edition of *Homme assis*. The plaster original (height 20 9/16 in., 52.3 cm.) is in the collection of the MNAM, Paris, Don de la Fondation Jacques et Yulla Lipchitz, AM 1976-834.

   The *Homme assis* also exists in a version carved from Brittany granite, apparently in the same year (Museum of Fine Arts, Richmond, height 20½ in., 50.8 cm.). The granite version may have been the first to be publicly exhibited (Paris, *Cent sculptures par Jacques Lipchitz*, exhibition organized by Jeanne Bucher, June 13-28, 1930). Lipchitz later rejected direct carving as a medium in favor of modeling. In a 1945 interview with James Johnson Sweeney, he described direct carving as inhibiting his creativity: "Ideas come with unimaginable rapidity; they are capricious; the artist must catch them and fix them as quickly as possible and the technique best suited for this is modelling" ("An Interview with Jacques Lipchitz," *Partisan Review*, winter 1945).

The fluid, softly modeled curvilinear structure of *Pierrot assis* is replaced in *Homme assis* by a hard-edged rectilinear, blocklike form, which is also more literal in its use of representational details (such as the fingers and eyes). In describing this transition (though without actually referring to *Pierrot assis*), Lipchitz himself later said:

During 1922, despite the personal difficulties that continued much of the year, some of my new sculptural ideas began to come clearly into focus. The Seated Man *is a major departure for me, composed as it is from simplified rectangular masses. In its effect it does have a relationship to the frontalized* Seated Man with Guitar *of 1918 and, even more, with the 1920* Man with Guitar. *But now the entire form is solidly cubic in a literal sense rather than traditionally cubist, with the figure frontalized diagonally on the square base, the vertical masses pulled together by the curving, enclosing arms. The figure is squat, compressed, with a great sense of sheer weight. It shows a deliberate restriction of means, which adds to the total tension. This was the time when the mad fantasy of the surrealists was beginning to sweep Paris, and it is conceivable that in my own way I was reacting by carrying my sculpture to an opposite extreme of clarity and compression (*My Life in Sculpture, by J. Lipchitz with H. H. Arnason, London, 1972, p. 70).

Maurice Raynal, in a 1947 essay, perceptively attributed the sharply angular nature of works such as *l'Homme assis* to a struggle—not yet fully resolved by Lipchitz—to accommodate both architectonic and more lyrical elements within his mode of expression: "*La conception architectonique la plus lyriquement calculée évoque une poésie soumise à des prosodies qui font de ces compositions des mouvements de sûreté audacieuse empreinte d'un classicisme qui en garantit déjà la durée. La priorité le plus souvent donnée aux jeux sévères des lignes droites et des angles, les exigences du néophyte en faveur d'une rigidité souvent sévère, l'attachement à un dépouillement indispensable fléchissent devant les séduisantes sollicitations de la courbe*" (M. Raynal, *Jacques Lipchitz*, Paris, 1947, p. 14).

In the immediately ensuing works such as *Homme assis avec guitare*, Lipchitz reintegrated the curvilinear and organic vocabulary that had characterized *Pierrot assis* but had been almost totally suppressed in *l'Homme assis*.

EXHIBITIONS:

Zurich, Kunsthaus, *Ausstellung Abstrakte und Surrealistische Malerei und Plastik*, Oct. 6-Nov. 3, 1929, no. 64 ("*Pierrot assis*, blei, 1922, 700 Fr."); New York, Art of This Century, 1942-47, p. 77, repr.; Venice, *P.G.*, 1948 (Biennale), no. 73; Florence, *P.G.*, 1949, no. 79; Amsterdam, *P.G.*, 1951, no. 91, repr.; Zurich, *P.G.*, 1951, no. 87; London, *P.G.*, 1964-65, no. 21; Stockholm, *P.G.*, 1966-67, no. 21; New York, *P.G.*, 1969, p. 98, repr.; Paris, *P.G.*, 1974-75, no. 20, repr.; Torino, *P.G.*, 1975-76, no. 27, repr. pl. 10.

REFERENCES:

L'Esprit Nouveau, vol. 18, [1923?], repr. n.p.; P. Guggenheim, *Art of This Century*, 1942, p. 77, repr. (erroneously dated 1921, the date ascribed to it in all *P.G.* publications until 1983); Calas, 1966, repr. p. 96 (erroneously dated 1921); L. Flint, *Handbook*, 1983, p. 38, repr. color p. 39.

99 Aurelia. New York, 1946.

76.2553 PG 29

Bronze (lost wax, solid cast). Height (without base): 25 3/8 (64.5).

Signed near base (scratched into the wax model): *J Lipchitz*. No date or foundry mark.

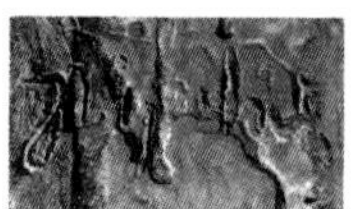

Foundry: Unknown.

Edition of one.

PROVENANCE:

Purchased from Curt Valentin, New York, 1946.

CONDITION:

There are a few light pit marks of possible corrosion. The piece is screwed with a brass screw into the wood base, which, owing to outdoor exhibition, is seriously cracked and warped but which is almost certainly not original.

In February 1984 (Venice) the bronze was removed from the wood base and cleaned. The surface was degreased with trichloroethylene, and washed with distilled water, then with distilled water and neutral detergent; it was rinsed with distilled water and dried with alcohol and acetone. The surface was treated for 30 minutes with a 3% solution of benzotriazole in pure alcohol. A protective coating of Paraloid B-72 (acrylic resin) was applied. The condition of the bronze is stable.

The piece was modeled in wax, the artist developing the form largely with his hands and using visible finger prints to achieve certain tactile effects. The surface suggests extensive working of the wax model, but almost no subsequent working of the bronze. Without the usual intermediary step of a plaster cast, the mold was baked directly onto the exterior of the wax. The bronze was then poured into the mold, creating the solid bronze (and thus necessarily unique) piece. The projecting undulating "string" forms may have been made from wax foundry "bars," heated, shaped, and integrated into the figure as the artist worked on the wax model.

The title, which has been described by the artist's widow and her son as strangely uncharacteristic of Lipchitz, may possibly have been invented by Peggy Guggenheim or Curt Valentin, though evidence on this has thus far not been found.[1]

EXHIBITIONS:

Venice, *P.G.*, 1948 (Biennale), no. 74; Florence, *P.G.*, 1949, no. 80; Venice, Giardino, 1949, no. 11; Amsterdam, *P.G.*, 1951, no. 92; Zurich, *P.G.*, 1951, no. 88; London, *P.G.*, 1964-65, no. 22, repr.; Stockholm, *P.G.*, 1966-67, no. 22, repr.; New York, *P.G.*, 1969, p. 99, repr.; Paris, *P.G.*, 1974-75, no. 21; Torino, *P.G.*, 1975-76, no. 28, repr. pl. 53.

REFERENCE:

Calas, 1966, repr. p. 194.

1. Yulla Lipchitz and her son, Hanno Mott, in conversations with Lucy Flint, November 8 and November 11, 1982, respectively, concurred with the description of the casting technique and the fact that this was a unique cast. They were unable to throw any light on the possible inspiration for the image.

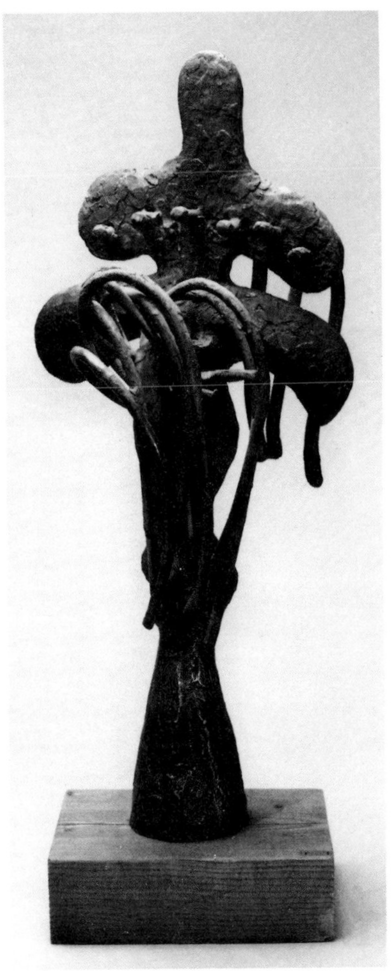

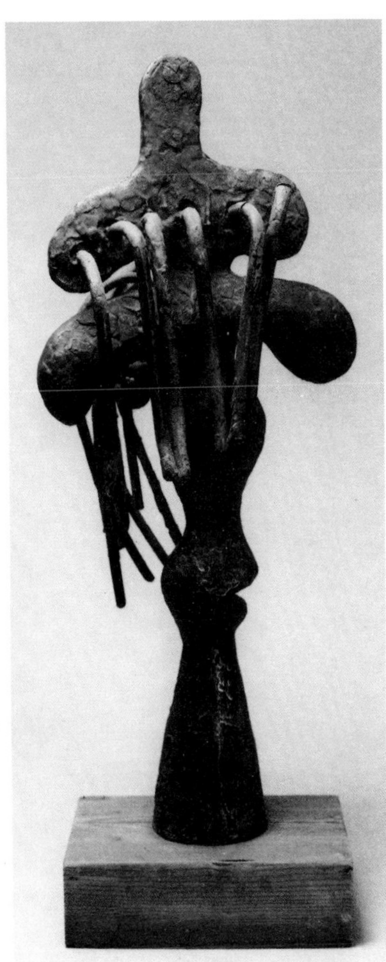

El Lissitzky

(Lazar Markovich Lisitskii).

Born November 1890, Pochinok, Smolensk.
Died December 1941, Moscow.

100 Untitled. Ca. 1919-20.

Color plate p. 386.

76.2553 PG 43

Oil on canvas (unvarnished), 31 5/16 x 19 1/2 (79.6 x 49.6).

Inscribed on reverse, extremely faintly visible through heavy layer of wax, not in the artist's hand: *El Lissitzky*. Not dated.

PROVENANCE:

Theo van Doesburg, probably as a gift from the artist;[1] Nelly van Doesburg, 1931-40; purchased from Nelly van Doesburg, Paris, 1940.

CONDITION:

Peggy Guggenheim recalled that the work was restored and probably lined in New York while she was living with Max Ernst in the early 1940s, but she did not have details.

In 1964 (Tate Report) the canvas was described as having been lined with wax. A branched crackle covered almost the entire oval background area, though the edges were not dangerously elevated. Some losses were noted, including a diagonal line of crackle with loss running from the left edge near the top, and numerous small losses of paint in the dark red area. The canvas was described as "originally not varnished, but now has a shiny surface, probably due to wax relining." Wax was also visible along the lower edge.

In 1976 (Venice) some consolidation of the surface was carried out, though records of this do not survive.

In September 1983 (Venice) the canvas had a heavy coat of wax on the reverse, though no actual lining, and was slack on the stretcher, which was not original. Wax had penetrated the surface in several places, and the canvas was dry and brittle. A gray film lay over the entire surface; some discolored inpainting and widespread crackle, especially in the whites, were also noted. The wax on the reverse was mechanically removed and a Fieux contact lining applied. The canvas was then mounted on an ICA spring stretcher. The surface was cleaned with a solution of dimethylformamide, acetone, n-Butylamine in equal proportions with 2 pts. water. Losses were filled with gesso and rabbit skin glue and inpainted with Windsor and Newton watercolors. A light coat of Paraloid B-72 (at 2% in acetone) was sprayed over the entire surface. The condition is stable. (Venice, Sept. 1983.)

Examination of the rather thinly painted surface reveals that Lissitzky, after applying the gray ground, drew the entire composition onto the canvas in graphite. Many of his original outlines are still visible, and he seems to have made no changes in the composition, or adjustments to the edges of the forms, after his initial execution in pencil. This was characteristic of Lissitzky's procedure and can be observed in other examples of his work. Whether he worked directly from a rough preparatory sketch, such as fig. a,[2] or whether some more precise *modello* intervened before the drawing on the canvas, is not clear. The meticulous precision and premeditation of his *alla prima* execution are typical of Lissitzky, and offer an interesting contrast with the more intuitive and exploratory approach of Malevich.

1. Lissitzky arrived in Berlin late in 1921. He and van Doesburg met for the first time in 1922 and their association became a close one. They were joint signatories of the important declaration prepared by the International Faction of Constructivists at the Congress of International Progressive Artists held in Dusseldorf in May 1922. The influence of Lissitzky on the subsequent issues of *De Stijl*, and the impact of his 1923 *Prounenraum* on van Doesburg's development in the mid- to late twenties were critical. He almost certainly gave the painting to van Doesburg during the period of their close collaboration and friendship in Germany, which would probably have been by late 1923.
2. Peter Nisbet brought the photograph in the Stedelijk Van Abbemuseum to the author's attention.

   The drawings reproduced in fig. a are part of a larger group (including at least 6 others) that entered the Tretiakov Gallery in about 1962 (information supplied by A. B. Nakov). The drawings are all undated. It is conceivable that some of them predated Lissitzky's move to Vitebsk and arose out of his initial response to Malevich's work. On the other hand they may date from the Vitebsk period or even postdate it, thus constituting a *ricordo* of earlier compositions.

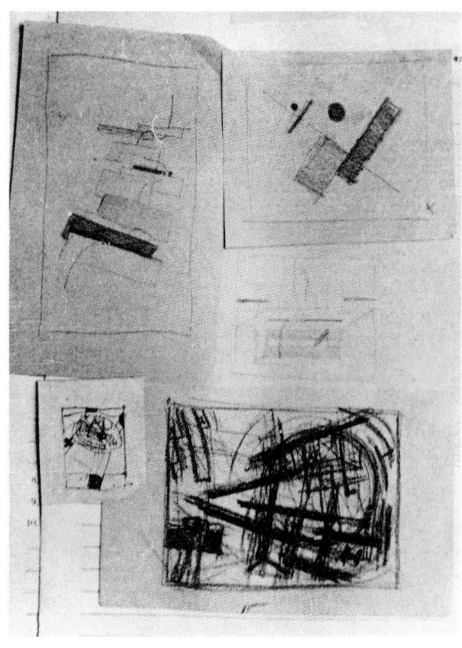

fig. a.
A photograph, currently in the archives of the Stedelijk van Abbemuseum, Eindhoven, recording sketches by Lissitzky preserved in the Tretiakov Gallery, Moscow. The date of the photograph is not known. Visible at the upper left is a study for cat. no. 100. The haphazard arrangement of the sketches would indicate that they were grouped specifically to be photographed and were not actually mounted in this way.

Peggy Guggenheim's painting, with its assertively two-dimensional planar structure, is closely related in many respects to Malevich's paintings of 1915-18 (see, for example, cat. no. 104 in the present volume, ca. 1915-16; *Untitled*, ca. 1917, MoMA, New York, repr. T. Andersen, *Malevich*, Amsterdam, 1970, p. 97, no. 61; or *Suprematism*, 1915-16, Wilhelm Hack Museum, repr. color, A. B. Nakov, *Kasimir S. Malevic: Scritti*, Milan, 1977, betw. pp. 335 and 337). The flatness of the composition (interrupted only minimally by the curving lines that interpenetrate the planes) is not entirely typical of Lissitzky's mature nonobjective oeuvre. The dating of the painting, its placement within Lissitzky's conceptual development, and its relationship to the drawing (fig. a) thus pose complex problems.

The earliest development of Lissitzky's nonobjective production, and the origins and precise date of his first response to Malevich's revolutionary ideas, remain to a large extent uncharted. But it is widely accepted in the literature that his first nonobjective lithographs and paintings date from the winter of 1919-20, after he came into direct personal contact with Malevich in Vitebsk. These "earliest" nonobjective works demonstrate a remarkable command of Suprematist theory and practice; they are especially indebted — as Andrei B. Nakov has noted (*The Suprematist Straight Line*, London, 1977, pp. 21-23) — to Malevich's didactic "interplanetary" Suprematism. But they are on the whole characterized by an excavation of space and a multidimensional complexity that betray Lissitzky's deeply ingrained architectural sensibility, and which result in a distinctly personal statement. (See, for example, the six sizable paintings displayed behind Lissitzky in the oft-reproduced photograph of his Vitebsk studio;[3] also, for a series of the Proun lithographs usually dated 1919, but more likely of 1920-21, see A. Z. Rudenstine, ed.,*The Russian Avant-Garde: The George Costakis Collection*, New York, 1981, pls. 453, 455-62, 466-67). It is difficult to imagine that Lissitzky could have achieved this level of stylistic resolution in an entirely new pictorial idiom without some intermediate stage. Yet in the absence of a corpus of such experimental work, his development does appear to have involved a remarkably sudden transformation from the earlier representational paintings to the assured Prouns of ca. 1920-21.

A brief summary of his activities in the years immediately preceding his move to Vitebsk in July 1919 provides the context for examining this phase of his development.

Having studied architecture at the Technische Hochschule in Darmstadt, Lissitzky returned to Russia when World War I broke out in 1914. By 1916 he had acquired a diploma in architecture and engineering from Riga's technical institute, which was moved to Moscow during the war years. Thereafter he began the practice of architecture and worked for a time in the Moscow atelier of Boris Velikovsky. He also spent a considerable part of the time in Kiev, although almost certainly visiting Moscow periodically.

During these years, his pictorial production seems to have been largely limited to the illustration of Jewish books. He had also assembled a considerable collection of Jewish folk art. He did, by his own testimony (in an autobiography written in 1941), participate in the "*Bubnovyi valet*" exhibitions of 1916 and 1917 in Moscow, although there is no record of either the titles or the styles of the works he showed. Also participating in these exhibitions were the Supremus group (newly constituted in 1916), and—significantly—Malevich himself, who showed a large group of recent Suprematist works in 1917 (see Andersen, op. cit., p. 163; and Nakov, op. cit., pp. 383-84). This exhibition was followed in the winter of 1918-19 by the *Tenth State Exhibition: Non-Objective Creation and Suprematism*, which, according to recent research conducted by Vasilii Rakitin, Lissitzky definitely saw, and which had a profound influence on him (see V. Rakitin in *El Lissitzky*, exh. cat., Staatliche Galerie Moritzburg, Halle, 1982, p. 18).[4]

Published sources, including Lissitzky's own 1941 autobiographical notes, have stated that he was personally invited by Chagall in 1919 to become professor of architecture and graphics in Vitebsk. Rakitin has established, however, that the invitation actually came from the head of the Vitebsk art workshop, Vera Ermolaeva, and that Lissitzky took up his position by July 16, 1919 (loc. cit.). Rakitin convincingly suggests, moreover, that Lissitzky was already by this time to some extent responsive to Suprematism, and that, although Chagall had agreed to the appointment, the Lissitzky who arrived in Vitebsk was not the

3. The photograph (repr. S. Lissitzky-Kuppers, *El Lissitzky*, London, 1968, p. 28) is always dated 1919, but it seems unlikely that is was taken before 1920 or even 1921. Among the works visible on the easel or the wall are early versions of *Proun 1c, Proun 23 No. 6, Proun 1A Bridge 1, Proun 1D*. The dates of all of these works pose problems that remain unresolved, although a date of ca. 1920-21 seems most likely.

4. Rakitin places this exhibition in the winter of 1918-19, although it has usually been dated simply 1919. This earlier date for it is, thus, of considerable importance. Rakitin cites no evidence for the fact that Lissitzky saw the exhibition and began his Suprematist experiments at that time. Presumably his conclusions are based on material deposited in Soviet archives.

same artist — from a conceptual or aesthetic point of view — as the one Chagall had known and admired earlier. By late August 1919 — that is to say, before Malevich's arrival — Lissitzky had apparently submitted several works in a Suprematist vein to a propaganda competition.

Rakitin's research appears to establish for the first time that Lissitzky may have been actively engaged in the execution of works in a Suprematist style before he came under Malevich's personal influence in the fall of 1919. Some of his more demonstrably planar works — such as the Peggy Guggenheim picture, or its preparatory drawing (fig. a) — may therefore represent an early stage in Lissitzky's assimilation of the new style. Even if such works postdated the first (apparently overwhelming) personal encounter between the two men, they become more plausible if seen within the context of Lissitzky's more gradual preparation during the previous year. During 1920 Lissitzky produced works of extraordinary spatial complexity, and the theoretical writings that accompanied them constituted in some sense an actual critique of "two-dimensional" Suprematist easel painting. It seems unlikely that Lissitzky would have returned, after such accomplishments, to the compositional problems of the Peggy Guggenheim work. It does seem likely, however, that this example belongs to the early stage of a dialogue with Malevich, a dialogue that continued to preoccupy him into the mid-1920s.

EXHIBITIONS:

New York, Art of This Century, 1942-47, p. 84, repr. p. 85 ("*Composition*, 1921," the title and date assigned to it in *P.G.* publications until 1983); Venice, *P.G.*, 1948 (Biennale), no. 75; Florence, *P.G.*, 1949, no. 81 (dated 1911); Amsterdam, *P.G.*, 1951, no. 93, repr.; Zurich, *P.G.*, 1951, no. 89; London, *P.G.*, 1964-65, no. 36, repr.; Stockholm, *P.G.*, 1966-67, no. 37, repr.; New York, *P.G.*, 1969, p. 83, repr.; Paris, *P.G.*, 1974-75, no. 39, repr.; Torino, *P.G.*, 1975-76, no. 43, repr. pl. 24.

REFERENCES:

P. Guggenheim, *Art of This Century*, 1942, p. 84, repr. 85; Calas, 1966, p. 27, repr. p. 54; L. Flint, *Handbook*, 1983, p. 62, repr. color p. 63.

Heinz Mack

Born March 1931, Lollar/Hessen.
Lives in Mönchengladbach, Federal Republic of Germany.

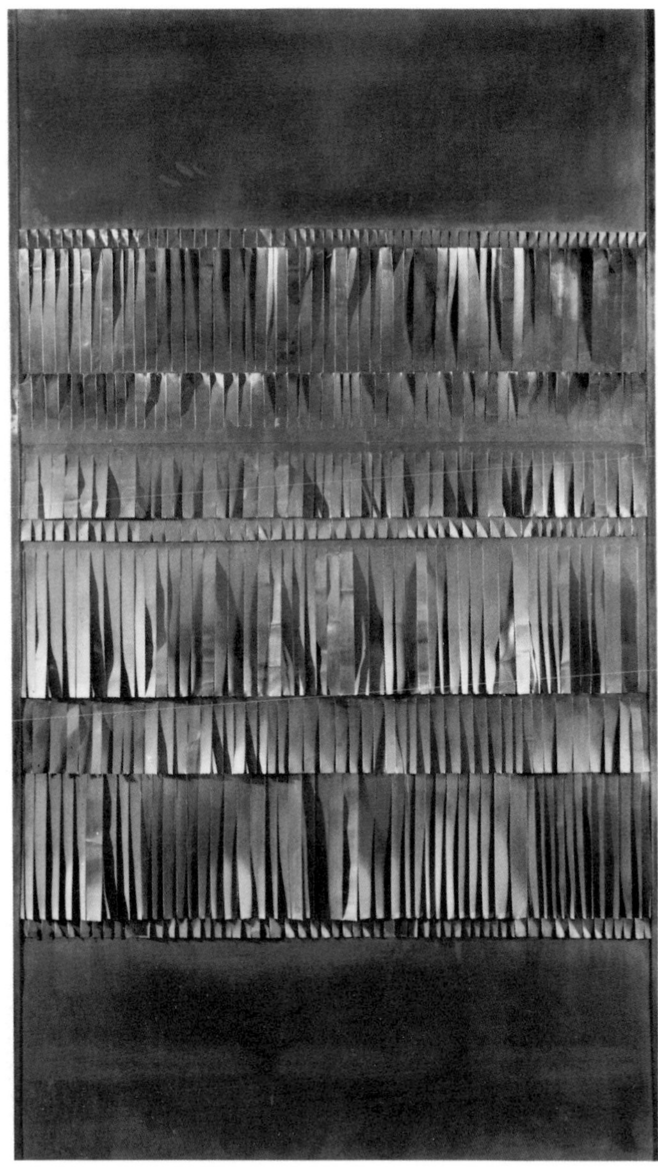

101 Cardiogram eines Engels. 1964.
(*Cardiogram of an Angel*).

76.2553 PG 228

Aluminum foil sheets nailed to masonite on wood; edges secured with plastic strips; 68 1/8 x 39 9/16 (173 x 100.5).

Signed and titled on reverse: „*Cardiogram eines Engels*" / „*Mack*". Not dated.

PROVENANCE:

Purchased from McRoberts and Tunnard, London, February, 1965.

CONDITION:

A few scattered spots of oxidation are visible. Some of the thin aluminum sheets, which were cut with a sharp instrument, have become slightly bent, but the condition in general is stable. (Venice, Nov. 1982.)

Mack's earliest light reliefs date from 1956-57. In that year, together with Otto Piene and Günther Uecker (see below, cat. no. 173), he formed the Dusseldorf Group Zero, which was based on a set of shared aesthetic goals. The three artists developed a pictorial language fundamentally dependent on the use of light. Through their manipulation of the implicit and explicit movement created by light (especially by its effects on vibrating surfaces), they sought and discovered new means of transforming and expanding the literal space of the picture plane.

Mack described his accidental discovery of the potential of aluminum as early as 1958:

> *Eine unerwartete Möglichkeit, ästhetische Bewegung sichtbar zu machen, ergab sich, als ich zufällig auf eine dünne Metallfolie trat, die auf einem Sisalteppig lag. Als ich die Folie aufhob, hatte das Licht Gelegenheit, zu vibrieren. Da der Teppich mechanisch hergestellt war, blieb natürlich auch der Abdruck mechanisch und dekorativ; die Bewegung des reflektierten Lichtes war völlig gleichgültig und langweilig. Meine Metallreliefs, die ich besser Lichtreliefs nennen möchte, und die allein durch den Druck der Finger geformt werden, benötigen anstelle der Farben das Licht, um zu leben. Spiegelblank poliert, genügt ein geringes Relief, um die Ruhe des Lichtes zu erschüttern und in Vibration zu bringen* ("Die Ruhe der Unruhe," *Zero* 2, Dusseldorf, 1958).

In the following year, Mack experimented extensively in his new medium, using aluminum sheets, or aluminum grids from the air and space industry, sometimes working entirely with his hands, sometimes (as in *Cardiogram eines Engels*) cutting designs into the sheets with a sharp tool, and then nailing and/or gluing the low relief constructions to the wood surface. In each phase his ultimate aim, as he describes it, is to achieve a dematerialization (*immaterielle Erscheinungsweise*) of apparently material objects.[1] In one sense, the effects of light and movement that are so integral to his work are finally only the means by which he seeks to achieve his larger purposes.

EXHIBITION:

London, McRoberts and Tunnard Gallery, *Group Zero: Mack, Piene, Uecker*, June 23-July 18, 1964, no. 5.

REFERENCES:

J. A. Thwaites, "The Story of Zero," *Studio International*, vol. 170, no. 867, July 1965, repr. p. 3 ("*Light Relief*, 1963"); [Alley], *Peggy Guggenheim Foundation*, 1968, no. 226; Calas, 1966, repr. p. 222 (as a horizontal).

1. See "Licht ist nicht Licht" (1966), in *"Mackazin": Die Jahre 1957-67*, Frankfurt, 1967, p. 97, and other texts published by Mack in this anthology. For an illuminating discussion see also M. Staber, *Heinz Mack*, Cologne, 1968.

René François Ghislain Magritte

Born November 1898, Lessines, Belgium.
Died August 1967, Brussels.

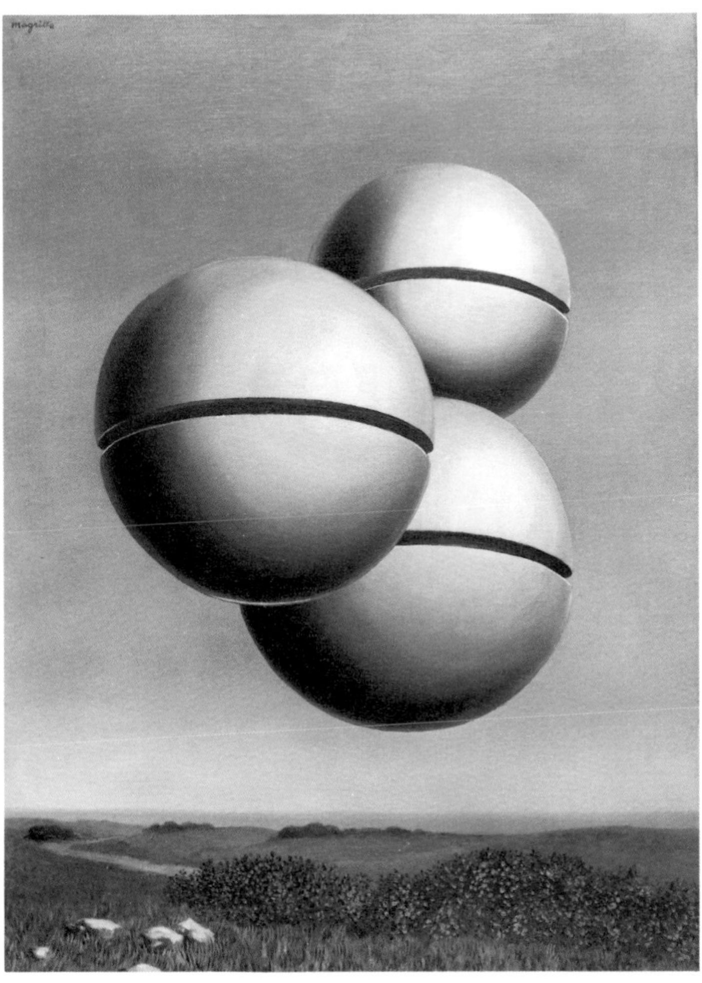

102 La voix des airs. 1931.

(*Voice of space*; *The Voice of the Winds*; *La voix des vents*).

Color plate p. 252.

76.2553 PG 101

Oil on canvas (unvarnished), 28⅝ x 21⅜ (72.7 x 54.2).

Signed u.l. in blue paint: *magritte*; on stretcher in blue pencil (very faint, almost certainly not in the artist's hand): *"LA VOIX DES AIRS"* / 1932 / *MAGRITTE.*

PROVENANCE:

Purchased from the artist by Claude Spaak, probably in January 1932; returned to Magritte by May 1940; purchased from Magritte before May 23, 1940.[1]

CONDITION:

In 1964 (Tate Report) several discolored retouchings in the sky were noted (above the bells left, just below the signature, and near the top right corner). An extensive, fine surface crackle between the lower edge of the bells and the landscape, where white had been applied over blue, was also present. The work had not been varnished.

In 1982 (Venice) the picture was given a surface cleaning with a solution of ammonium hydroxide (2.5% in water). Some scattered holes and discolored inpainting required retouching. A Fieux contact lining and a light coat of LeFranc retouching varnish (spray) were applied. Inpainting visible at the edges is of an unknown date. The condition is stable. (Venice, Mar. 1983.)

1. Information supplied by David Sylvester. Spaak told Sylvester that he remembered Magritte visiting him shortly before the Germans took Paris (June 14), and asking for the return of one of his pictures, specifically in order to sell it to Peggy Guggenheim who was rumored to be buying extensively. Magritte needed the money and, having nothing suitable to offer her, promised to give Spaak another work in exchange, to which the latter agreed. Magritte sold the picture to Peggy Guggenheim that day and departed immediately for Carcassonne; dated correspondence establishes his arrival there by May 23rd. After World War II had ended he gave Spaak the promised replacement.

   Peggy Guggenheim's own recollection of the transaction corroborated Spaak's: she was visiting Lefebvre-Foinet when Magritte appeared with a picture under his arm. Her impression was that the visit was accidental and bore no relation to her presence there. However, he offered to sell her the painting, and she accepted, paying him on the spot.

   Magritte's response to a questionnaire from MoMA, in which he confuses their picture with

In responding to the questionnaire submitted by Alfred H. Barr, Jr., concerning the MoMA version of *La voix des airs*, Magritte made a number of points about the origin of the title, the versions of the composition, and the theme. He stated that the title *La voix des airs* (as opposed to *La voie des airs*) was accurate; that there were four pictures bearing this same title, the invention of which he attributed to Paul Eluard; that the MoMA version, dating from 1928, was the second of the four; and that it was preceded by a much smaller version painted earlier in the same year.[2]

Magritte's recollection of these points appears to have been accurate in all but one detail: the earliest example of the composition, though considerably smaller than the MoMA picture, bears the title *Les fleurs de l'abîme (II)* (see below).

The four oil versions of the composition to which Magritte refers are:

1. *Les fleurs de l'abîme (II)*, 1928, 16⅜ x 10¾ (41.5 x 27.3), Private Collection, Brussels. Sylvester, catalogue raisonné, Vol. I, no. 233 (in press).
2. *La voix des airs*, 1928, 25⁹⁄₁₆ x 19¹¹⁄₁₆ (65 x 50), Albright-Knox Art Gallery, Buffalo, acquired by exchange and George B. and Jenny R. Mathew Fund, from MoMA. Sylvester, catalogue raisonné, Vol. I, no. 234.
3. *La voix des airs*, 1931, 28⅝ x 21⅜ (72.7 x 54.2), Peggy Guggenheim Collection. Sylvester, catalogue raisonné, Vol. II.
4. *La voix des airs*, 1935(?), 10 x 7 (25.4 x 17.8), Private Collection, Italy. Sylvester, catalogue raisonné, Vol. II.[3]

Sylvester has offered a convincing explanation for Magritte's memory that the four titles were identical. Having painted *Les fleurs de l'abîme (II)* (which took its image from the center of a more diffuse composition, *Les fleurs de l'abîme I*), Magritte inscribed its title on the reverse. The title *La voix des airs* was proposed by Eluard at some point after this (and perhaps not until he saw the second version). Magritte accepted this substitution, which he then gave to the second and subsequent versions, while also assigning it (retroactively) in his own mind to the original. Hence, the MoMA picture was indeed the second version of the image, though it was, strictly speaking, the first to carry the actual written title.

(1. cont.)
Peggy Guggenheim's on some points, confirms this provenance. He states that the picture was first exhibited at the Palais des Beaux-Arts, where it was purchased, and that it was later sold to Peggy Guggenheim *"lors de mon exode à Paris quelques heures avant l'occupation de Paris en 1940"* (letters of Nov. 16 and 28, 1947, collection records, MoMA, New York).

2. Though Magritte had confused the MoMA version with Peggy Guggenheim's on the question of provenance (see above, fn. 1), he clearly did not do so in these other respects.

3. The date of this small version has not been established. It is known to Sylvester only from photographs, and a precise dating will only be possible if the painting itself can be traced and examined. Sylvester inclines provisionally to connect it with a group of small replicas painted in 1935 for inclusion in the New York Julien Levy exhibition of 1936. It cannot be ruled out, however, that it preceded Peggy Guggenheim's, which would then become the fourth in the series. The present author has not seen either this small version or *Les fleurs de l'abîme (II)*.

In this connection, Magritte's stated views on the role of titles should be borne in mind: "*Le meilleur titre ... c'est un titre poétique, autrement dit un titre compatible avec l'émotion plus ou moins vive que nous éprouvons en regardant un tableau. Le titre poétique n'a rien à apprendre, mais il doit nous surprendre et nous enchanter*" (cited by J. Vovelle, 1972, p. 141). It is evident from this statement that Magritte was deeply concerned about titles, and it is known that he consulted extensively with his poet friends as he developed them. However, this statement also makes it clear that he saw titles primarily as a means of capturing the emotions or feelings generated by a work. It would be entirely consistent for him, therefore, to substitute a new title for a particular work should it seem more compatible with the emotion experienced than the original title.

In response to Barr's questionnaire concerning the meaning of the work, Magritte had written: "*Une des intentions*, consciente, *était de trouver un sentiment nouveau de l'espace.*" He described it as "*une peinture d'imagination obtenue avec les sujets: un paysage et des grelots de fer (que l'on place au cou des chevaux).*"

Magritte was repeatedly during the course of his life asked to elucidate the meanings of his works, but he consistently argued that attempts to understand his "iconography" only failed to grasp the nature of his pictorial aims: "*Ma conception de la peinture [exclue] l'intention de donner à la peinture une signification explicable.*" And elsewhere: "*Étant donné que ma peinture ne correspond pas — dans la mesure du possible — à des significations explicables, il ne convient pas de tenter de la faire "comprendre." Il s'agit* de poésie visible, *c'est à dire, de la description d'une pensée qui unit des figures apparaissant dans le monde, de telle sorte que soit évoqué le mystère du visible et de l'invisible. Il est nécessaire pour que cela soit possible d'avoir recours à l'imagination et de n'accorder aucune valeur à l'imaginaire.*"[4] By juxtaposing the precisely rendered, gigantic man-made "*grelots*" with the miniature "imaginary" natural landscape; by creating a startling inversion of scale; and by forcing the heavy metallic objects to hover and float, as if weightless, but also to move menacingly (if noiselessly) out from the picture plane, Magritte indeed invented a new sense of space.

In this sense Magritte's meanings are to be found not through the decoding of a complex iconography but through an apprehension of his "*poésie visible.*" Even though he used and reused particular images, they do not carry specific, fixed meanings, nor do they achieve the status of symbols. The "*grelot*" recurs in paintings throughout Magritte's career; in his lecture, "La ligne de vie," delivered at the Koninklijk Museum van Schoone Kunsten in Antwerp, he suggested how he conceived their function:

> *Je montrais dans mes tableaux des objets situés là où nous ne les rencontrons jamais. C'est la réalisation d'un désir réel, sinon conscient, pour la plupart des hommes....*

4. Collection records, MoMA, New York.

> *Étant donné ma volonté de faire hurler les objets les plus familiers, ceux-ci devaient être disposés dans un ordre nouveau, et acquérir un sens bouleversant: Les lézardes que nous voyons dans nos maisons et sur nos visages, je les trouvais plus éloquentes dans le ciel. Les pieds de table en bois tourné perdaient l'innocente existence qu'on leur prête s'ils apparaissaient soudain dominant une forêt.... Les grelots de fer, pendus au cou de nos admirables chevaux, je les fis pousser comme des plantes dangereuses au bord des gouffres....*
>
> *Les tableaux peints pendant les années qui suivirent, de 1926 à 1936, furent également le résultat de la recherche systématique d'un effet poétique bouleversant qui, obtenu par la mise en scène d'objets empruntés à la réalité, donnerait au monde réel, à qui ces objets étaient empruntés, un sens poétique bouleversant par échange tout naturel* (L. Scutenaire, *René Magritte*, Brussels, 1947, pp. 79-80).[5]

Though the "*grelot*" was used frequently, and always in unexpected contexts, in Magritte's work, it was — like other objects in the paintings — specifically devoid of any intrinsic or symbolic meaning.

Magritte's wife, Georgette, in responding to a direct question about the symbolic connotation of the "*grelot*," underlined this point once more: "*Jamais de symbole dans ses toiles.... Il disait qu'on ne pouvait représenter un sentiment, une notion, une idée ... René partait d'un objet, d'un personnage, d'une montagne ... Jamais d'une idée*" (R. Passeron, *Magritte*, Paris, 1970, n.p.).

EXHIBITIONS:

Brussels, Palais des Beaux-Arts, *Guiette, Magritte, Picard*, Dec. 19, 1931-Jan. 6, 1932, no. 51 ("*La voix des airs*, 1931");[6] New York, Art of This Century, 1942-47, p. 118 ("*Voice of the Winds*, 1930"); Venice, *P.G.*, 1948 (Biennale), no. 76 (dated 1930); Florence, *P.G.*, 1949, no. 82 (dated 1930); Amsterdam, *P.G.*, 1951, no. 94, repr. ("*La voix des vents*, 1932"; hereafter "*Voice of the Winds*, 1932" in all *P.G.* publications until 1982); Zurich, *P.G.*, 1951, no. 90 ("*Die Stimme der Winde*, 1932"); London, *P.G.*, 1964-65, no. 91; Stockholm, *P.G.*, 1966-67, no. 89; Torino, Galleria Civica d'Arte Moderna, *Le Muse Inquietanti*, Nov. 1967-Jan. 1968, no. 206, repr.; New York, *P.G.*, 1969, p. 112, repr. p. 113; Paris, *P.G.*, 1974-75, no. 100, repr. p. 83; Torino, *P.G.*, 1975-76, no. 99; New York, *P.G.*, 1982-83, no. 41, repr. color ("*Voice of Space*, 1932?").

REFERENCES:

P. Guggenheim, *Art of This Century*, 1942, p. 118 (dated 1930); E. Calas, "Magritte; Variations on the theme of the Bell," *Arts Magazine*, vol. 41, no. 7, May 1967, pp. 23-24, repr.; J. Vovelle, *Le Surréalisme en Belgique*, Brussels, 1972, p. 122; H. Torczyner, *Magritte*, New York, 1977, repr. color p. 93 (with erroneous caption).

5. Excerpts from Magritte's original lecture were published in the Brussels periodical *Combat* (vol. 3, no. 105, 1938), but the passage cited here was not included. Magritte sent the amended text of the lecture to Scutenaire for publication, probably in October 1938. It was prepared by Scutenaire during the Occupation but not published until 1947. (Information supplied by Sylvester, whose forthcoming catalogue raisonné contains an extensive discussion of this important text and its three different manuscript states.)
6. A fragment of a Palais des Beaux-Arts label is attached to the original stretcher (now replaced).

103 **L'Empire des lumières.** 1953-54.
(*Empire of light*; *Domain of Lights*;
Il domino della luce).

Color plate p. 253.

76.2553 PG 102

Oil on canvas (unvarnished), 76[15/16] x 51[5/8] (195.4 x 131.2).

Signed l.l.: *Magritte*; on reverse: „*L'EMPIRE DES / LUMIÈRES*" / *1953-54*.

PROVENANCE:

Purchased from the artist, October 19, 1954, after the Biennale.[1]

CONDITION:

In 1964 (Tate Report) the unvarnished surface was cleaned with distilled water, and the condition was described as excellent.

In July 1981 (Venice) white spots (microorganisms) in the dark areas and a bloom with extensive mold were removed from the surface (a fungicide inert to colors was used). A light coat of Lefranc retouching varnish was applied (by spray). The condition is stable. (Venice, Nov. 1982.)

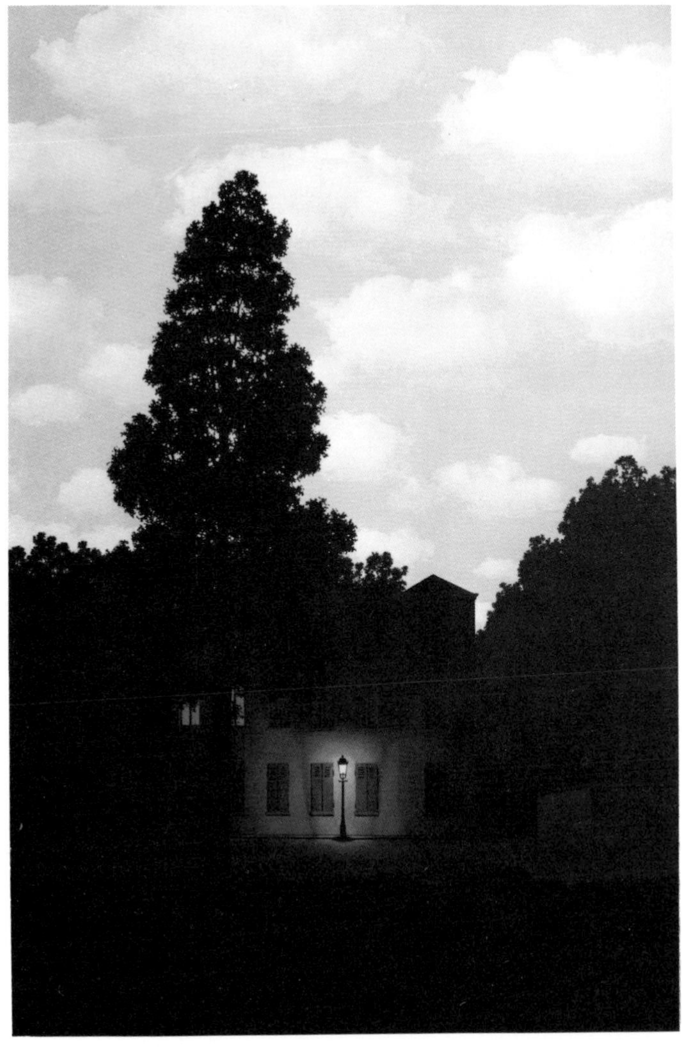

1. The author is indebted to David Sylvester for sharing information from the Magritte correspondence indicating that Alexander Iolas originally expected to buy this work from Magritte before the Biennale opened. In a letter of May 5, 1954, Magritte lists the painting among only

Magritte commented in several different contexts on the composition *L'Empire des lumières*, of which he painted at least eighteen oil versions between 1948 and 1964.

In response to a questionnaire sent to him by MoMA concerning the 1950 *L'Empire des lumières II*, he wrote:

Ce tableau a été imaginé et réalisé sans modèle—c'est une composition d'éléments familiers plus ou moins fidèlement reproduits.... Il existe L'Empire des Lumières (I) *peinture à l'huile, toile de 50 x 65cm., réalisé en 1948, dont le sujet est semblable à* L'Empire des Lumières (II). *Ces deux tableaux sont des variantes d'une même idée.... L'auteur comprend la signification du tableau ... comme une possibilité de donner plus de force à la vision du spectateur, et singulièrement à cause des idées de la nuit et du jour qui sont présentes dans ce tableau* (collection records, MoMA, New York).[2]

In a statement of late April 1956, Magritte cites *L'Empire des lumières* as a paradigm for his conception of pictorial language:

Pour moi, la conception d'un tableau, c'est une idée d'une chose ou de plusieurs choses, qui peuvent devenir visibles par ma peinture.

Il est entendu que toutes les idées ne sont pas des conceptions de tableaux. Il faut, bien entendu, qu'une idée soit suffisamment stimulante pour que je m'applique à peindre fidèlement la chose ou les choses dont j'ai eu l'idée.

La conception d'un tableau, c'est-à-dire l'idée, n'est pas visible dans le tableau: une idée ne saurait être vue par les yeux.

Ce qui est représenté dans un tableau, c'est ce qui est visible pour les yeux, c'est la chose ou les choses dont il a fallu avoir l'idée.

Ainsi, ce qui est représenté dans le tableau "L'Empire des Lumières," ce sont

(1. cont.)
3 for sale out of the 27 to be shown, the other 24 being already in private collections. The price was 80,000 Fr. to the public, 40,000 to Iolas. Iolas replied that he definitely wanted to buy the painting, sight unseen, and offered 30,000 Fr., but the sale was never consummated. Magritte somewhat impatiently offered it to Iolas for the last time in a letter of October 25, 1954, obviously not having yet learned of Peggy Guggenheim's purchase the previous week.

2. Magritte's letter is dated "29.1.50," but cannot in fact have been written before 1951, the year that MoMA wrote to him about it. The painting was purchased from the Hugo Gallery on December 20, 1950. It is not entirely clear which version of the composition is identified here as *L'Empire des lumières I*. According to information kindly supplied by Sylvester, 2 versions preceded the MoMA picture: *L'Empire des lumières*, 39⅜ x 31½ in., 100 x 80 cm., started though not finished in 1948, Private Collection, Brussels, repr. H. Torczyner, pl. 390; and *L'Empire des lumières*, 19 x 23 in., 48.3 x 58.5 cm., dated 1949, formerly in the collections of Charles Byron and then Nelson Rockefeller, which was the first version to be completed (repr. cover of *Retrospective Magritte*, exh. cat., Palais des Beaux-Arts, Brussels, 1972). It seems likely that Magritte is referring here to the latter work. Peggy Guggenheim's picture is, according to Sylvester's chronology, perhaps the eighth of the known versions. Magritte also produced at least 5 gouaches. It is interesting to note that Georgette Magritte commented to Sylvester that the Peggy Guggenheim version was the best of the series, a judgment Sylvester believes Magritte probably shared. For an illuminating discussion of Magritte's practice of painting replicas and slight variants of his best paintings, and the commercialism that this implies, see Sylvester, *Magritte*, New York, 1969, pp. 8-9.

les choses dont j'ai eu l'idée, c'est-à-dire, exactement, un paysage nocturne et un ciel tel que nous le voyons en plein jour. Le paysage évoque la nuit et le ciel évoque le jour.

Cette évocation de la nuit et du jour me semble douée du pouvoir de nous surprendre et de nous enchanter. J'appelle ce pouvoir: la poésie.

Si je crois que cette évocation a un tel pouvoir — poétique, c'est entre autres raisons, parce que j'ai toujours éprouvé le plus grand intérêt pour la nuit et pour le jour, sans jamais ressentir, cependant, de préférence pour l'un ou pour l'autre.

Ce grand intérêt personnel pour la nuit et pour le jour, est un sentiment d'admiration et d'étonnement. (The original manuscript, datable late April 1956, with corrections, is in the Archives de L'Art Contemporain, Brussels, published in facsimile in *Peintres belges de l'imaginaire*, exh. cat., Paris, 1972. The statement was originally delivered as part of a ten-minute television address by Magritte.)

In the notes for a 1961 exhibition catalogue, Magritte wrote: "*Inspiration gives the painter what he must paint:* likeness, which is a thought capable of becoming visible through painting: for instance, the thought might be a pipe with the inscription, 'This is not a pipe', or the thought might consist of a nocturnal landscape under a sunny sky. Such thoughts evoke mystery, '*de jure*', whereas, '*de facto*', mystery is evoked by a pipe resting on an ash-tray, or by a nocturnal landscape under a starlit sky." (*Magritte*, exh. cat., Obelisk Gallery, London, 1961; cited in a new translation, by D. Sylvester, *Magritte*, New York, 1969, p. 84.)

And in a June 4, 1965, letter to James Thrall Soby, he wrote:

La pensée inspirée qui ressemble à ce qui lui est offert de visible devient *ce qui lui est offert* et *en évoque le mystère. La pensée inspirée unit ce qui lui est offert dans* un ordre qui évoque le mystère. *Exemple: elle unit un paysage nocturne et un ciel étoilé (Mon tableau "L'Empire des Lumières"). (Une pensée n'ayant que des similitudes ne peut considérer qu'un ciel étoilé avec un paysage nocturne).*

La pensée inspirée qui évoque le mystère du visible peut-être décrite par la peinture: elle est en effet constituée uniquement *par du visible: ciels, arbres, personnes, solides, inscriptions, etc.* (collection records, MoMA, New York).

The "visible things," the familiar elements of a landscape, are, as Magritte insists again and again, carefully, logically, "faithfully" depicted. The "inspiration" consists in the surprising or unsettling juxtaposition.

The paradoxical image of *L'Empire des lumières* has been cited, not only by Magritte but by his commentators as a particularly poetic one:

Le viol des idées reçues et conventions, dès qu'on touche aux luminaires, est là [*dans* L'Empire des Lumières] *tel que, je le tiens de René Magritte, la plupart de ceux qui passent vite croient avoir aperçu les étoiles dans le ciel diurne* (André Breton, 1964).

Une muraille se dressait devant une forêt inquiétante de nuit dense, épaisse. On remarquait un bec de gaz, deux fenêtres évoquaient par leurs touches

> *discrètes de saumon l'intimité d'une lampe. Là-dessus le ciel était d'un bleu très pur de midi. Je pense à un vers de Paul Eluard: 'la nuit où l'homme fait le jour'. Magritte a réussi à me faire voir la nuit en plein jour. L'harmonie des syllabes chez Eluard, l'intelligence picturale chez Magritte opèrent ce qu'il faut bien appeler un miracle. Qu'importe vraiment l'étymologie réelle de 'poète'. Le poète invente un monde que nous reconnaissons comme nôtre* (Brindeau, 1956).[3]

For Brindeau, as for Magritte himself, the poetic achievement in *L'Empire des lumières* lies precisely in the particular coincidence of likeness and mystery: "It must be said that just any image which denies 'common sense' does not '*de jure*' evoke mystery if it is no more than an occasion for contrariness. Likeness is not concerned with agreeing with 'common sense', or with defying it, but only with spontaneously assembling shapes from the world of appearance in an order given by inspiration."[4]

EXHIBITIONS:

Brussels, Palais des Beaux-Arts, *René Magritte*, May 7-June 1, 1954, no. 92, repr. (*L'Empire des lumières VI*);[5] Venice, XXVII Biennale, June 19-Oct. 17, 1954, no. 52; London, *P.G.*, 1964-65, no. 92, repr.; Torino, Galleria Civica d'Arte Moderna, *Le Muse Inquietanti*, Nov. 1967-Jan. 1968, no. 211; Stockholm, *P.G.*, 1966-67, no. 90, repr.; New York, *P.G.*, 1969, p. 112, repr. color p. 113; Paris, *P.G.*, 1974-75, no. 101; Torino, *P.G.*, 1975-76, no. 100, repr. pl. 50; Rome, *Guggenheim: Venezia-New York*, 1982, no. 46, repr. color.

REFERENCES:

S. Brindeau, "lettre ouverte," *La Tour de Feu*, no. 51, 1956, p. 14; A. Breton, Introduction, *Magritte*, exh. cat., University of St. Thomas, Houston, 1964, n.p.; P. Waldberg, *René Magritte*, Brussels, 1965, pp. 104-6; J. T. Soby, *René Magritte*, exh. cat., MoMA, New York, 1965, p. 18; C. Finch, "The Alchemy of the Image," *Art and Artists*, vol. 1, no. 6, Sept. 1966, p. 8; S. Gablik, *Magritte*, London, 1970, pp. 121-23; J. Vovelle, *Le surréalisme en Belgique*, Brussels, 1972, pp. 77, 109, 119, 143 fn. 30, 147; H. Torczyner, *Magritte: Ideas and Images*, New York, 1977, pp. 177-81.

3. Vovelle, 1972, p. 147, cites Brindeau's text in his discussion of the close relationship between Magritte's and Paul Eluard's poetic style.

4. Magritte, as translated and quoted in D. Sylvester, op. cit., p. 84.

5. The number *VI* is used here erroneously. In a letter of April 4, 1954, from Magritte to E.L.T. Mesens, 9 pictures are listed in connection with this exhibition. The sixth work on the list is *L'Empire des lumières*, which Mesens then apparently assumed was the sixth version of this theme. Information supplied by Sylvester.

Kazimir Severinovich Malevich

Born February 1878, near Kiev.
Died May 1935, Leningrad.

104

104 Untitled. Ca. 1916.
(*Suprematist Composition*).

Color plate p. 385.

76.2553 PG 42

Oil on canvas, 20⅞ x 20⅞ (53 x 53).

Not signed or dated.

PROVENANCE:

Left by the artist in Berlin, 1927;[1] purchased by MoMA, New York, November 12, 1935; exchanged with Peggy Guggenheim, January 27, 1942, for Max Ernst, *Harmonious Breakfast*.[2]

CONDITION:

In 1964 (Tate Report) noted were: a branched crackle over much of the surface, 2 distinct sets of stretcher marks (indicating replaced stretcher) with cracks at the margins, some losses at the edges, 2 small areas of cleavage, 2 small pierced holes with losses, and general soil of the surface. Cleavage was consolidated with wax resin adhesive; holes on the front (apparently from an earlier tacking edge) were filled and inpainted.

In 1968 (New York) an all-over pattern of surface cracks was noted, with sharp ridges and cracks at the stretcher marks (see fig. a). The streaky gray quality of the green forms was attributed to spottily applied varnish. Extreme soil throughout, deeply ingrained in the brushwork, was also apparent. The painting was removed from the stretcher and treated on a vacuum table, lined on Fiberglas fabric and mounted on a honeycomb panel. The surface was cleaned and scattered abrasions retouched. A synthetic resin varnish was sprayed on the surface.

At an unknown location and date between 1969 and 1979, the work was removed from the panel and the lining; the edges of the canvas were cut, and a linen lining was applied with synthetic emulsion adhesive.

In 1982 (Venice) areas where the canvas had been cut were filled to level with gesso and animal glue; reintegration of the surface was carried out with watercolor and Maimeri varnish color glazes. Varnish was removed with commercial lacquer thinner. Some flaking paint in the horizontal cracks was consolidated and losses retouched with Maimeri varnish colors.

The support is now uneven and distorted in its topography, especially in the green, and is buckled in places. The paint film shows considerable evidence of flattening, especially in the whites; the overall condition of the work, which is stable, nonetheless poses some problems for an accurate evaluation of Malevich's original intentions. (New York, Mar. 1983.) For a discussion of some of these issues see below.

1. Before the closing of his 1927 one-man exhibition in Berlin, Malevich returned to Leningrad, leaving his works in the care of the architect Hugo Häring. A meticulously careful, detailed history of this exhibition and the subsequent intricacies of the dispersal of the works was published by Troels Andersen in 1970 (see REFERENCES). According to Andersen (pp. 57-58), most of the works were deposited with the forwarding agent, Gustav Knauer, in Berlin. Alexander Dorner, director of the Hannover Museum, later received from Knauer a box containing most of the Suprematist paintings and some other works. These remained in Hannover until late 1935, when Dorner was forced to leave Germany under Nazi pressure. Meanwhile Malevich had died in May 1935, convinced that the entire exhibition had been destroyed.

   While preparing his exhibition *Cubism and Abstract Art*, Alfred H. Barr, Jr., had visited Dorner. Dorner had shown him the large group of works by Malevich, and Barr arranged to buy 2 paintings and 2 drawings (for $200). He also arranged to borrow and buy a total of 21 items for the exhibition, and Dorner managed to ship them to him via Holland in the autumn of 1935, marked "technical drawings." Conditions in Germany for the holders of Malevich's works were, as Andersen has pointed out, extremely difficult. The "Entartete Kunst" auctions were not far off; abstract art was officially in total disrepute. Barr apparently managed to cross the border out of Germany with 2 of the paintings wrapped inside his umbrella.

   MoMA eventually received 9 paintings and gouaches from the group, 7 of which are still in the collection. Peggy Guggenheim's picture was certainly among those stored by Dorner and sold to Barr in 1935. Barr later told her that he had indeed carried the picture out, rolled up in an umbrella (Peggy Guggenheim, in conversation with the author, 1978).

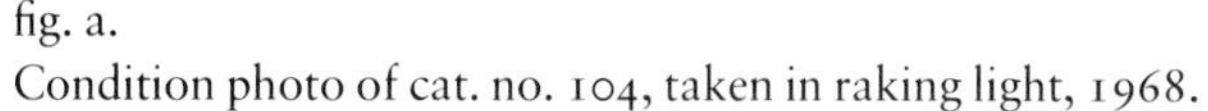

fig. a.
Condition photo of cat. no. 104, taken in raking light, 1968.

fig. b.
X-ray of cat. no. 104.

In view of the clear provenance of the Peggy Guggenheim Malevich and the considerable evidence regarding its complicated restoration history (see above), some facts can be established about the autograph nature of its present surface.

The composition itself, the disposition of the forms on the white field, and the relationship of the painting to its preparatory drawing, all lend support to the 1915-16 date proposed by Andersen.[3] The painting was not included in the exhibition *0.10* of December 1915-January 1916—the first public presentation of Malevich's recently developed Suprematist style. But the work clearly emerges from the early stages of his articulation of Suprematism and would probably have been painted sometime during the first year.

Although many aspects of the original execution remain visible, certain changes have taken place, some of them plausibly attributable to the artist's own hand.

Examination of the X-rays (fig. b) and the 1919 installation photographs (figs. d and e) throws light on Malevich's compositional process, the character of his brushwork, and the adjustments he made at various stages while working on the canvas itself. He first covered the entire field with a white background. The paint was applied in characteristic short, visibly differentiated, tactile brushstrokes, often moving in a circular pattern. The facture is extremely subtle and even, but far from unmodulated. Its surface rhythm is entirely consistent with its appearance in the X-ray, and only minimal disturbance of its original texture is visible, although the paint layer is now distorted.

2. Though initially accepted, this painting was not actually accessioned. On July 3, 1942, MoMA acquired instead Ernst's *Napoleon in the Wilderness*, 1941.

3. Andrei B. Nakov, who is preparing the catalogue raisonné of Malevich's oeuvre, concurs with this dating (in conversation with the author, 1983).

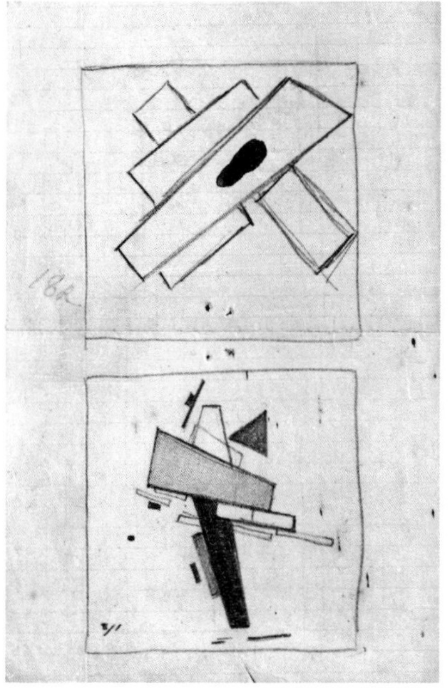

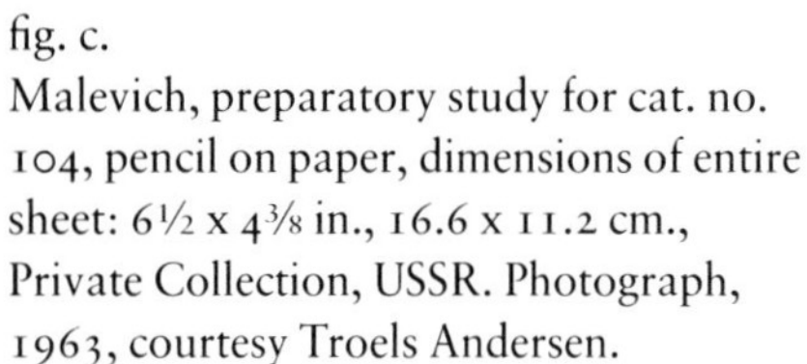

fig. c.
Malevich, preparatory study for cat. no. 104, pencil on paper, dimensions of entire sheet: $6\frac{1}{2}$ x $4\frac{3}{8}$ in., 16.6 x 11.2 cm., Private Collection, USSR. Photograph, 1963, courtesy Troels Andersen.

fig. d.
Detail of installation photograph, fig. e.

Malevich then proceeded to sketch in the outlines of the forms, probably—though not certainly—in charcoal or pencil.[4] In doing so, he followed the general plan of his preparatory sketch (fig. c), although he introduced some obvious changes—notably the placement off center of the blue form and the suppression of the secondary horizontal at its base. The black drawn outlines of some of these forms are plainly visible on the X-ray.

After preliminary painting of the composition, Malevich reworked it, introducing several important changes. The most obvious of these is the reduction in size (at the top and left edges) of the horizontally placed green form. The left edge of the blue form was also slightly modified at this point, as were other small details, revealing the essentially intuitive nature of Malevich's compositional process. Although the fundamental structure was established in advance, the execution inevitably demanded the exercise of a subtle flexibility. The painting was shown, with all of these *pentimenti* fully resolved, in the artist's 1919 one-man exhibition in Moscow (figs. d and e).

Marked differences in facture do, however, now characterize the surface of the painting, and the curiously mottled appearance of the green, together with the somewhat anomalous color combinations of some other areas, pose certain questions regarding the possibility of other subsequent alterations.

4. Examination with infra-red reflectography, which has not thus far been possible, would establish more definitively the character of Malevich's underdrawing.

fig. e.
Installation photograph, first one-man exhibition of Malevich's work, Moscow, winter 1919-20. Photograph© George Costakis, Athens, 1981.

First, it is clear from the X-ray — as well as from examination of the present surface with the naked eye — that the compositionally pivotal black form extending down from the center at some point suffered major losses. This black area has been extensively repainted with minutely applied vertical, parallel brushstrokes that are entirely different in nature from anything visible elsewhere on the surface and can only be explained as posthumous restoration. The place and date of this work have not been established.

Questions of greater complexity are raised by the uneven discoloration of the green horizontal form, and by the facture and colors of the brown-ocher-red, the yellow, and the gray bars. All these areas suggest reworking at a stage beyond 1919, although the nature of the handling indicates the hand of Malevich himself.[5]

The 1919 installation photograph (fig. d), although inherently problematic as a source of information, suggests that the facture of the green area in particular has changed somewhat, although the generally tactile quality of the brushwork was also characteristic of the initial execution. The evidence offered by the X-ray also suggests that this and the other cited areas have been reworked slightly. The extent of the revisions, and the apparent lack of either damage or losses in those areas, signify that they are attributable to the artist himself. The character of the workmanship, moreover, seems similar in certain respects to that of

5. The mottling in the green area was attributed (in 1968) to discolored varnish that was removed at the time (see CONDITION). The current nature of the surface is not, however, attributable to varnish.

Malevich's work of the late 1920s. The question arises whether the artist retouched the surface of this painting in 1927 before sending it to Warsaw for exhibition. It is difficult to establish the plausibility of this hypothesis with certainty. But in view of the evident authenticity of the work as a whole, and the anomalous nature of some portions of it, the explanation offered here provides potential clarification. Further study of the problem is, however, necessary.

The present orientation of the painting accords with that of the preparatory drawing and with the hanging of the work in the 1919-20 Moscow exhibition (fig. e). When the picture was shown in Warsaw, however, it hung in the reverse direction (see below EXHIBITIONS). Malevich abandoned the notion of a "top" or "bottom" for his canvases during his Vitebsk period (i.e., after 1919). He insisted to his students that such restrictive ideas should be eliminated from "suprematist discourse" since they had been overtaken by "the new logic of a non-referential space" (see A. B. Nakov, *The Suprematist Straight Line*, exh. cat., Annely Juda Fine Art, London, 1977, p. 24). It was on this premise (and, as Nakov pointed out, "as a purely didactic demonstration of a philosophical principle") that Malevich post hoc altered the orientation of many of his Suprematist paintings during the 1920s. The original orientation of the Peggy Guggenheim painting is reestablished here on the grounds that it reflects the process of conception and execution.

EXHIBITIONS:

Moscow, *Sixteenth State Exhibition, one-man exhibition, K. S. Malevich*, winter 1919-20 (no cat., installation photo, fig. e);[6] Warsaw, Hotel Polonia, one-man exhibition, Mar. 8-28, 1927 (no cat.; installation photo [showing the work hung in the reverse direction] published in *Malevich, Suprematismus. Die Gegendstandlose Welt*, trans. H. von Riesen, Cologne, 1962, opp. p. 33); Berlin, *Grosse Berliner Kunst-Ausstellung*, one-man exhibition, May 7-Sept. 30, 1927 (no cat., the Warsaw exhibition); New York, MoMA, *Cubism and Abstract Art*, 1936, no. 154, repr.; New York, MoMA, *Understanding Modern Art*, May 6-June 30, 1941 (no cat.); New York, Art of This Century, 1942-47, p. 82, repr. p. 83; Venice, *P.G.*, 1948 (Biennale), no. 77; Florence, *P.G.*, 1949, no. 83; Amsterdam, *P.G.*, 1951, no. 95, repr. n.p.; Zurich, *P.G.*, 1951, no. 91; London, *P.G.*, 1964-65, no. 35, repr.; Stockholm, *P.G.*, 1966-67, no. 36, repr.; New York, *P.G.*, 1969, p. 38, repr. color p. 39; Paris, *P.G.*, 1974-75, no. 38, repr.; Torino, *P.G.*, 1975-76, no. 42, repr. pl. 23; New York, *P.G.*, 1982-83, no. 16, repr. color p. 22.

REFERENCES:

A. H. Barr, Jr., *Cubism and Abstract Art*, New York, 1936, no. 154 ("*Suprematist Composition*, c. 1915"); P. Guggenheim, *Art of This Century*, 1942, p. 82, repr. p. 83 ("*Suprematist Composition*, 1915," the title and date subsequently attributed to it in all *P.G.* publications); P. Guggenheim, *Confessions*, 1960, p. 91; Calas, 1966, p. 26, repr. p. 53; T. Andersen, *Malevich*, Amsterdam, 1970, no. 58, repr. (dated 1915-16); L. Flint, *Handbook*, 1983, p. 60, repr. color p. 61.

6. This photo, which was first published in Angelica Zander Rudenstine, ed., *Russian Avant Garde Art: The George Costakis Collection*, New York, 1981, p. 491, provides the only current evidence that this work was shown in the Moscow exhibition.

Man Ray

Born August 1890, Philadelphia.
Died November 1976, Paris.

105 Silhouette. 1916.
(*Ballet Silhouette*).

76.2553 PG 68

India ink, charcoal underdrawing, and white gouache(?) on wood-pulp board (with machine-mold textured imprint), $20\frac{15}{16}$ x $25\frac{1}{4}$ (51.6 x 64.1).

Signed and dated l.r.: *Man Ray 1916*; titled l.l.: *Silhouette*.

PROVENANCE:
Purchased from the artist, Paris, April 10, 1940.

CONDITION:
In 1978 (New York) water stains at the lower right, center right, and lower left were treated and mitigated. Several abrasions and losses were inpainted with watercolors.

The acidic support has darkened and discolored unevenly (see color repr., L. Flint, 1983). The scratches, abrasions, and indentations are still visible, and there are some new minor losses of black ink, but the overall condition is stable. (Venice, Nov. 1982.)

Early in 1915, Man Ray—who had been painting in a derivative Cubist mode—began to work in a style that was entirely new for him: "I changed my style completely, reducing human figures to flat-patterned disarticulated forms. I painted some still-lifes also in flat subdued colors, carefully choosing subjects that in themselves had no aesthetic interest. All idea of composition as I had been concerned with it previously, through my earlier training, was abandoned, and replaced with an idea of cohesion, unity and a dynamic quality as in a growing plant (*Self-Portrait*, Boston, 1963, p. 55).

In the fall of that year, he had his first one-man exhibition at the Daniel Gallery in New York. In an obvious attempt to reflect his new interest in the expressive possibilities of a flat pictorial space, he entitled several of the works *Study in Two Dimensions.*[1] He installed them, without frames, as an intrinsic part of a carefully constructed false wall. This device gave the impression that the pictures had actually been painted directly onto the walls of the gallery — an additional means of emphasizing their intended flatness (*Self-Portrait*, p. 59).

During the course of the following year, Man Ray embarked upon his major painting, *The Rope Dancer Accompanies Herself with Her Shadows* (fig. a). Peggy Guggenheim's *Silhouette* served as a preparatory study for the painting; and Man Ray later told Arturo Schwarz that the dancer theme had been inspired by Degas' pastels of ballet dancers: "I made a drawing of the *Rope Dancer* in a mechanical way, which is now in the Peggy Guggenheim Collection. A very mechanical drawing with a violin scroll in the foreground like an old Degas, a pastel, you know.... So I started to make drawings of the Dancers with their short ballet skirts, into a mechanical composition, using mechanical instruments. Then I made a large scale project, the size of the canvas, on paper... " ("Interview with Man Ray," *New York Dada: Duchamp, Man Ray, Picabia*, Munich, 1974, pp. 88-89).

In his autobiography, Man Ray did not mention the Peggy Guggenheim drawing, but he elaborated considerably on the compositional procedure that resulted in the large painting:

I had started a large canvas which I rigged up with ropes and pullies, to be drawn up into the skylight when not being worked on. The subject was a rope dancer I had seen in a vaudeville show. I began by making sketches of various positions of the acrobatic forms, each on a different sheet of spectrum-colored paper, with the idea of suggesting movement not only in the drawing but by a transition from one color to another. I cut these out and arranged the forms into sequences before I began the final painting. After several changes in my composition I was less and less satisfied. It looked too decorative and might have served as a curtain for the theater. Then my eyes turned to the pieces of colored paper that had fallen to the floor. They made an abstract pattern that might have been the shadows of the dancer or an architectural subject, according to the trend of one's imagination if he were looking for a representative motive. I played with these, then saw the painting as it should be carried out. Scrapping the original forms of the dancer, I set to work on the canvas, laying in large areas of pure color in the form of the spaces that had been left outside the original drawings of the dancer. No attempt was made to establish a color harmony; it was red against blue, purple against

1. For an illuminating discussion of aspects of this stylistic development, see F. Naumann, 1982, who published in this context Man Ray's 1916 *Primer of the New Art of Two Dimensions*. In this treatise, as Naumann points out, Man Ray attempts "to establish a theoretical basis for all the arts by demonstrating that their modes of expression all possess the potential for reduction on a flat surface."

fig. a.
Man Ray, *The Rope Dancer Accompanies Herself with Her Shadows*, 1916, oil on canvas, 52 x 73⅜ in., 132.1 x 186.4 cm., The Museum of Modern Art, New York, Gift of G. David Thompson.

> *yellow, green versus orange, with an effect of maximum contrast. The color was laid on with precision, yet lavishly — in fact, the stock of colors was entirely depleted. When finished, I wrote the legend along the bottom of the canvas:* The Rope Dancer Accompanies Herself With Her Shadows (*Self-Portrait*, pp. 66-67).

Although this description leaves some ambiguities, Carl Belz learned some further clarifying details in a 1962 interview with Naomi Savage (the artist's niece).[2] Man Ray originally intended to use the actual forms of the conventionally clad ballet dancer — a figure probably not unlike the one depicted in the Peggy Guggenheim drawing. (Such a figure appears "in motion" and in the form of a transparent abstraction at the upper center of the completed large painting [fig. a]). Had this initial idea been followed, the painting would have been composed of a series of cutouts used as stencils on the canvas. These stencils would have been direct representations, in flat silhouette, of actual dancers, and the effect might have been similar to that of the Peggy Guggenheim drawing.

Man Ray undoubtedly found the figures too banal, "too mechanical," and he abandoned them. Only afterward did he perceive the possibilities offered by the jagged and irregular fragments of paper that were left over from the cutting-out process. He enlarged these and rearranged them to create his new composition. The shape of the original dancer, in a certain sense, thus determined the outlines of the "shadows," although — as Belz pointed out — Man Ray took advantage of the fact that shadows rarely replicate with any precision the out-

2. "Man Ray and New York Dada," *The Art Journal*, vol. 23, no. 3, spring 1964, pp. 212-13.

fig. b.
Man Ray, *The Rope Dancer Accompanies Herself with Her Shadows*, 1918, aerograph and tempera, $15\frac{5}{8}$ x $17\frac{1}{2}$ in., 39.7 x 44.5 cm., Collection The Morton G. Neumann Family. Photograph by Michael Tropea.

lines of their sources. In addition, Man Ray's introduction of the various brilliant colors for the shadow panels undermined their identity as "shadows."

In the Peggy Guggenheim drawing, the oval black shadows are intended as literal and "mechanical" projections of the dancers' swirling skirts; the only variation is in the size of the shadow, reflecting variations in the source of light.

In yet another variation — a 1918 aerograph of the *Rope Dancer* (fig. b) — Man Ray used a combination of airbrush and precisely articulated drafting technique to create a composition in which the flatness of the Peggy Guggenheim *Silhouette* is integrated with a complex play on the notion of light and depth. Placing cutout stencils of the dancers on the paper, Man Ray sprayed gouache over them until he had achieved the desired consistency. The linear elements were added when the gouache was dry.

EXHIBITIONS:

New York, Daniel Gallery, *Man Ray*, closed Jan. 16, 1917 (opening date unknown), no. 5, repr. (*Ballet-silhouette*); Paris, Librairie Six, *Exposition dada Man Ray*, Dec. 3-31, 1921, no. 14(?) ("*Silhouette 1919*");[3] New York, Art of This Century, 1942-47, p. 151 (*Drawing*); Florence, *P.G.*, 1949, no. 126a (with wrong dimensions); Amsterdam, *P.G.*, 1951, no. 152 (dated 1913); Zurich, *P.G.*, 1951, no. 136 ("*Silhouette*, 1916"); Bordighera, *II*^{A} *Mostra Internazionale Pittura Americana*, Mar. 1-31, 1953, no. 8; London, *P.G.*, 1964-65, no. 61, repr.; Stockholm, *P.G.*, 1966-67, no. 59; New York, *P.G.*, 1969, no. 63, repr.; Torino, *P.G.*, 1975-76, no. 66.

3. It has not been possible to verify whether the Peggy Guggenheim work was exhibited with the wrong date or whether a later (unidentified) version is involved. Francis Naumann, in correspondence with the author, September 1983, mentioned a work entitled *Silhouette: The Dancer Dances*, which was exhibited hors catalogue in Man Ray's last show at the Daniel Gallery (Nov.-Dec. 1919). The latter work is, however, also unidentified and its date unknown.

REFERENCES:

R. J. Cole, *New York Evening Sun*, Jan. 9, 1917, p. 18; P. Guggenheim, *Out of This Century*, 1946, p. 252; A. Schwarz, "Interview with Man Ray," *New York Dada: Duchamp, Man Ray, Picabia*, Munich, 1974, pp. 88-89; F. Naumann, "Man Ray: Early Paintings 1913-1916, Theory and Practice in the Art of Two Dimensions," *Artforum*, vol. 20, no. 9, May 1982, repr. p. 38; L. Flint, *Handbook*, 1983, repr. color p. 95.

---

106 Untitled. 1923.

76.2553 PG 69a

Rayograph, gelatin silver print, 11 3/8 x 9 1/4 (28.8 x 23.5).

Signed and dated in pencil on mount l.r.: *Man Ray 23*; stamped on reverse of Rayograph and mount: *Man Ray / 31bis Rue / Campagne / Première / Paris-14e*; in pencil on reverse of Rayograph: *Wystava fot. Modern / Kraków / Kwiecień 1931* and *Original à retourner.*[1]

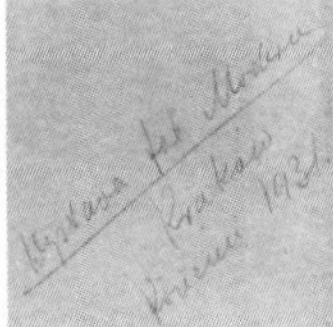

PROVENANCE:

Purchased from the artist, Paris, April 10, 1940.

CONDITION:

In 1978 the Rayograph was treated in the Department of Conservation, University of Delaware. Mold and a bluish tinge were present on the surface (the latter caused by the fact that the emulsion had not been fully fixed by the artist, and the silver sulphide had migrated). The primary mount was in good condition, but had been contaminated by an acidic mat and mount. Foxing and soil on the verso of the primary support were extensive.

The surfaces of the mount and photo were cleaned. Adhesive residue was removed, and the picture immersed in a weak alkali solution. It was rinsed in 4 baths to remove the alkali. A weak silver reducing solution was used to remove the dichroic fog, followed by 5 rinses. The mount was washed in alkali solution to remove soil. The work was attached to the original mount with Japanese starch paste. Losses at the edges were inpainted with watercolors, and the work hinged to 100% rag buffered board.

The condition is stable. (Venice, Nov. 1982.)

EXHIBITIONS:

Krakow, Apr. 1931(?);[1] New York, Art of This Century, 1942-47, p. 151 (*Five Rayograms*);[2] Venice, *P.G.*, 1948 (Biennale), no. 115 (*rayogram*);[3] Florence, *P.G.*, 1949, no. 126; Amsterdam, *P.G.*, 1951, no. 151; Zurich, *P.G.*, 1951, 1 of nos. 137-41; London, *P.G.*, 1964-65, no. 62a; Stockholm, *P.G.*, 1966-67, no. 60a; Paris, *P.G.*, 1974-75, no. 64a; Torino, *P.G.*, 1975-76, no. 67a; Paris, MNAM, *Man Ray*, Dec. 16, 1981-Apr. 13, 1982, traveled to Rotterdam, Museum Boymans-van Beuningen, May 8-July 4, 1982, Hannover, Kestner Gesellschaft, Sept.-Nov. 1982.

1. It has thus far proved impossible to substantiate the penciled inscription on the verso, referring to an exhibition of modern photography in Krakow, Poland in April 1931.
2. Of the 5 "Rayograms" listed, Peggy Guggenheim subsequently gave 3 to The Tel Aviv Museum.
3. It is impossible to say which of the 5 Rayographs was exhibited.

106

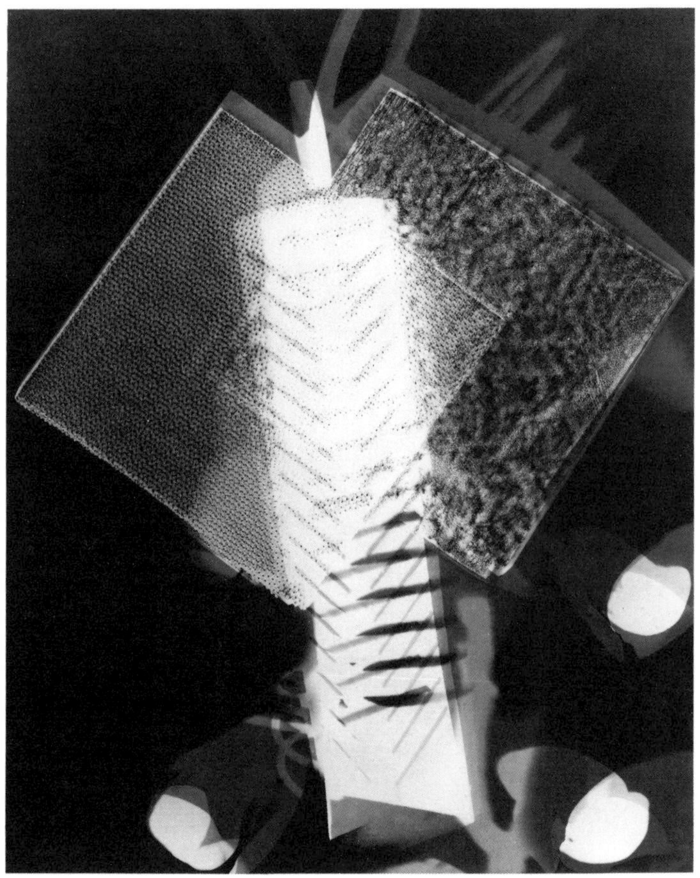

107 Untitled. 1927.

76.2553 PG 69b

Rayograph, gelatin silver print, 11 15/16 x 10 (30.4 x 25.4).

Signed and dated in pencil on Rayograph, l.r.: *Man Ray / 27*.

PROVENANCE:

Purchased from the artist, Paris, April 10, 1940.

CONDITION:

In 1982 the Rayograph, which had symptoms similar to those of cat. no. 106 above, was treated in New York. In addition to the conditions already described, advanced stages of active foxing (metal mold) in the center of the Rayograph (in the area of glass and hand) were present. The foxing had digested the image gelatin, leaving dull areas. There was a yellow stain upper left and image losses at the edges.

Paper and glue accretions were removed from the verso with moisture. The image was cleaned with 1% solution of ammonium hydroxide (28% sol.). The dichroic fog was removed, as in the earlier case. The Rayograph was immersed in a 2% solution of thiourea to remove sulphide remaining in the deeply textured paper. Foxing was further reduced with local application of .05% calcium hypochloride, followed by repeated washings to remove all chemical residues. A coating of methyl cellulose was applied. Image losses were inpainted with watercolor and the Rayograph hinged to an acid-free board.

Necessary local cleaning of the central areas of the composition (the glass) has resulted in some loss of subtle detail; some loss in the density of the blacks has also occurred. The condition is stable. (New York, Oct. 1982.)

107

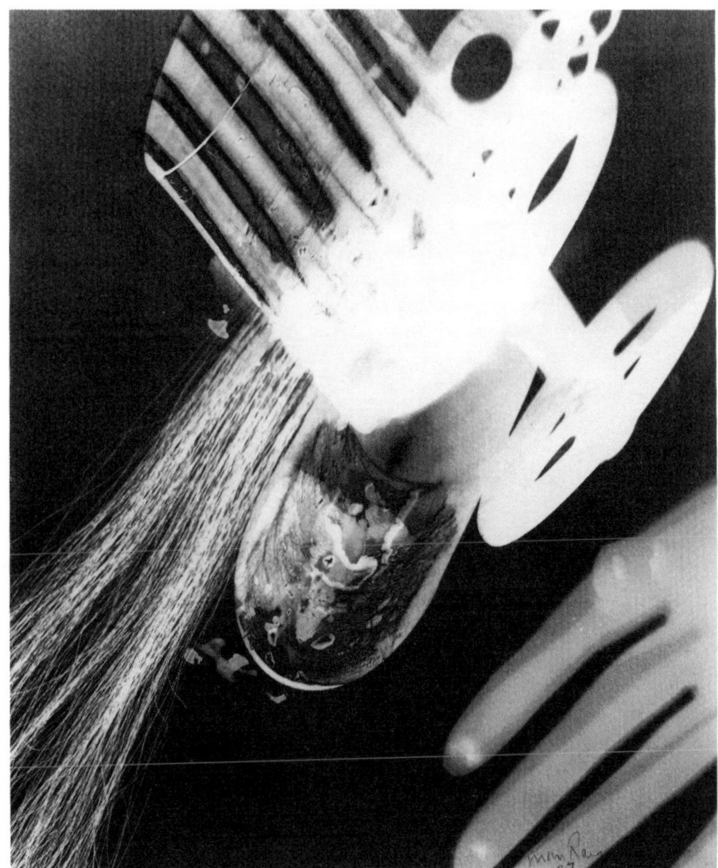

Man Ray's earliest Rayographs date from 1921. In his autobiography (published four decades later), he described his "discovery" of the process as entirely accidental:

> *It was while making these prints that I hit on my Rayograph process, or cameraless photographs. One sheet of photo paper got into the developing tray — a sheet unexposed that had been mixed with those already exposed under the negatives — I made my several exposures first, developing them together later — and as I waited in vain a couple of minutes for an image to appear, regretting the waste of paper, I mechanically placed a small glass funnel, the graduate and the thermometer in the tray on the wetted paper. I turned on the light; before my eyes an image began to form, not quite a simple silhouette of the objects as in a straight photograph, but distorted and refracted by the glass more or less in contact with the paper and standing out against a black background, the part directly exposed to the light.... In the morning I examined the results, pinning a couple of the Rayographs — as I decided to call them — on the wall. They looked startlingly new and mysterious.... [Tristan Tzara] spotted my prints on the wall at once, becoming very enthusiastic; they were pure Dada creations, he said, and far superior to similar attempts — simple flat textural prints in black and white — made a few years ago by Christian Schad, an early Dadaist.*

Tzara came to my room that night; we made some Rayographs together, he disposing matches on the paper, breaking up the match box itself for an object, and burning holes with a cigarette in a piece of paper, while I made cones and triangles and wire spirals, all of which produced astonishing results (*Self-Portrait*, Boston, 1963, pp. 128-29).[1]

From a technical point of view, the process was — as May Ray suggested — extremely simple: a piece of photographic paper was exposed to a bare light bulb, which cast onto the paper the shadows of any objects that intervened between the two. Those areas of the paper exposed longest to the light emerged blackest on the finished Rayograph; those areas shielded or blocked from the light emerged whitest. The achievements of Man Ray were instantly recognized by both Dada and Surrealist writers as of major importance in the development of new spheres of pictorial expression, comparable in their implications to the developments they saw in contemporary literature.

Tzara was, as Man Ray reported, his earliest supporter, and the following year they jointly published an album of twelve Rayographs, *Les Champs délicieux, rayographies* (Paris, 1922).[2] In his preface to the publication — "*La photographie à l'envers*" — Tzara made a case for the aesthetic opportunities he perceived in this new field of "photography," and suggested that the work of Man Ray posed a formidable challenge to conventional forms of visual expression:

Quand tout ce qu'on nomme art fut bien couvert de rhumatismes, le photographe alluma les milliers de bougies de sa lampe, et le papier sensible absorba par degrés le noir découpé dans quelques objets usuels. Il avait inventé

1. Whether the discovery was truly accidental or whether Man Ray was in fact stimulated by Christian Schad's experiments (the earliest of which date from 1918 in Zurich) has not been established. According to Van Deren Coke (*The Painter and the Photograph*, exh. cat., Art Gallery, University of New Mexico, 1964, p. 24), Tzara did show Man Ray some of Schad's examples during the course of 1921 (and 1 was published by Tzara in the 1920 issue of *Dadaphone*). Though definitive evidence on this point has apparently not been found, the possibility exists that he was stimulated by Schad's work.

   Contact between László Moholy-Nagy and the work of Man Ray is also difficult to trace with certainty. Moholy produced his first photograms in 1922, and whereas Tzara is said to have taken a copy of *Les Champs délicieux* to the Bauhaus to show Moholy (a fact supported by the testimony of Lissitzky), Moholy denied any prior knowledge of either Schad's or Man Ray's work when he began to experiment with the medium early in 1922. Only in the fall of that year (after he had written an article on the subject for *De Stijl*) did Moholy claim to have heard about Man Ray's work from Harold Loeb and Matthew Josephson. (On this point see A. Haus, *Moholy-Nagy Fotos und Fotogramme*, Munich, 1978, p. 79-80.)

   The technique itself was originally used by William Henry Fox Talbot (1800-1877) in his "Photogenic drawing" process of the 1830s. Talbot was concerned with making representational depictions of natural subject matter, but his pioneering work in all aspects of photography was well known on the Continent, and it is possible that his experiments provided the stimulus for Schad, Man Ray, or Moholy.

2. The title carried an allusion to André Breton's Surrealist novel *Les champs magnétiques* of 1919. Breton later described the novel as "le fruit des premières applications systématiques de l'écriture automatique" (*Entretiens*, Paris, 1952, p. 56).

la force d'un éclair tendre et frais, qui dépassait en importance toutes les constellations destinées à nos plaisirs visuels. La déformation mécanique, précise, unique et correcte est fixée, lisse et filtrée comme une chevelure à travers un peigne de lumière.

Est-ce une spirale d'eau ou la lueur tragique d'un revolver, un œuf, un arc étincelant ou une écluse de la raison, une oreille subtile avec un sifflet minéral ou une turbine de formules algébriques? Comme la glace rejette l'image sans effort, et l'écho la voix sans nous demander pourquoi, la beauté de la matière n'appartient à personne, car elle est désormais un produit physico-chimique.

The impact of the Rayographs on Surrealist writers was equally powerful. Breton saw in them a crucial undermining of photography's literal, "positive," or "pretentious" aspects.[3] Louis Aragon drew an analogy between the nature of Man Ray's imaginative invention of a new mode of expression with that of Max Ernst's "invention" of collage: "*C'est une opération philosophique de même caractère, au delà de la peinture, et sans rapport réel avec la photographie*" ("La peinture au défi," *Exposition de collages*, Galerie Goemans, Paris, 1930, p. 25).

Robert Desnos attributed to the Rayographs a quality of expressiveness and freedom comparable in significance to *l'écriture automatique:* "There does not yet exist a word for the designation of Man Ray's invention, these abstract photographs in which he makes the solar spectre participate in adventurous constructions.... [He] succeeded in creating landscapes which are foreign to our planet, revealing a chaos that is more stupefying than that foreseen by any Bible: here the miracle allows itself to be captured without resistance and something else, besides, leaves its anguishing thumbprint on the revelatory paper" (R. Desnos, "The Work of Man Ray," trans. M. McD. Jolas, *Transition*, no. 15, 1929, p. 265).

Like Desnos, Georges Ribemont-Dessaignes (in a 1924 essay) characterized the world depicted in the Rayograph as one of astonishing strangeness; but he drew particular attention to the nature of perception captured by the medium: it was, significantly, the same as that experienced in dreams. In this respect, Ribemont-Dessaignes saw the medium as expressive of one of the central preoccupations of Surrealist thought:

[Man Ray a] décloué le volet d'un étonnant univers. A en tenir les morceaux on s'étonne de les reconnaître comme ces êtres ou ces objets des rêves qui ont la faculté d'être en même temps ceci et cela, et de changer de personnalité au moment qu'on la croit saisir.... on interroge sa fantaisie qui mêla ces silhouettes mystérieuses dans un espace certainement échappé à quelque nouveau champ de gravitation....

...dans un espace où le son ne semble pas devoir se propager, il semble qu'on ait découvert de multiples manières de se mouvoir, et pour aller d'extraor-

3. *La Revolution Surréaliste*, nos. 9-10, Oct. 1, 1927, "*...il s'est appliqué d'emblée à lui ôter son caractère positif, à lui faire passer cet air arrogant qu'elle avait de se donner pour ce qu'elle n'est pas*," etc.

dinaires nuages flottants sur un ciel de haute altitude à un verre de cristal. On sent qu'on n'a plus les mêmes dimensions que celles qui président à son corps s'il se meut sous la forme du regard, le long d'un ressort en spirale émergé de silhouettes de rappel familier (*Man Ray*, Paris, 1924, pp. 5-6).

The place of the Rayograph within the general context of Surrealist aesthetics as defined by the writers of the time was a significant one. For Man Ray, the medium offered an aesthetic and technical freedom especially suited to his intentions and his sensibility. In a much later characterization of the nature of the Rayograph image, he captured something of the quintessential freedom of the process, the accidental ingredient in its successful application, and the tenuous nature of the result: "Like the undisturbed ashes of an object consumed by flames, these images are oxidized residues fixed by light and chemical elements of an experience, an adventure."[4]

EXHIBITIONS:

New York, Art of This Century, 1942-47, p. 151 (see above, cat. no. 106, fn. 1); Venice, *P.G.*, 1948 (Biennale), no. 115 (see above, cat. no. 106, fn. 3); Florence, *P.G.*, 1949, no. 126; Amsterdam, *P.G.*, 1951, no. 151; Zurich, *P.G.*, 1951, 1 of nos. 137-41; London, *P.G.*, 1964-65, no. 62b; Stockholm, *P.G.*, 1966-67, no. 60b; Paris, *P.G.*, 1974-75, no. 64b; Torino, *P.G.*, 1975-76, no. 67b; Paris, MNAM, *Man Ray*, Dec. 16, 1981-Apr. 13, 1982, did not travel to Rotterdam and Hannover.

REFERENCE:

"Man Ray: Eight Photographic Studies" (unsigned), *Transition*, no. 15, 1929, repr. foll. p. 26 (upside down).[5]

4. "Man Ray on Man Ray: The Rayograph 1920-1928," Paris, February 1963. Reprinted in *Man Ray*, exh. cat., Los Angeles County Museum, 1966, p. 26.

5. The Rayograph had not been signed by the time it was reproduced in *Transition*. Whether its orientation in this publication was given by Man Ray, who subsequently changed his mind, or whether it was a mistake on the publisher's part, has not been established.

COLOR PLATES

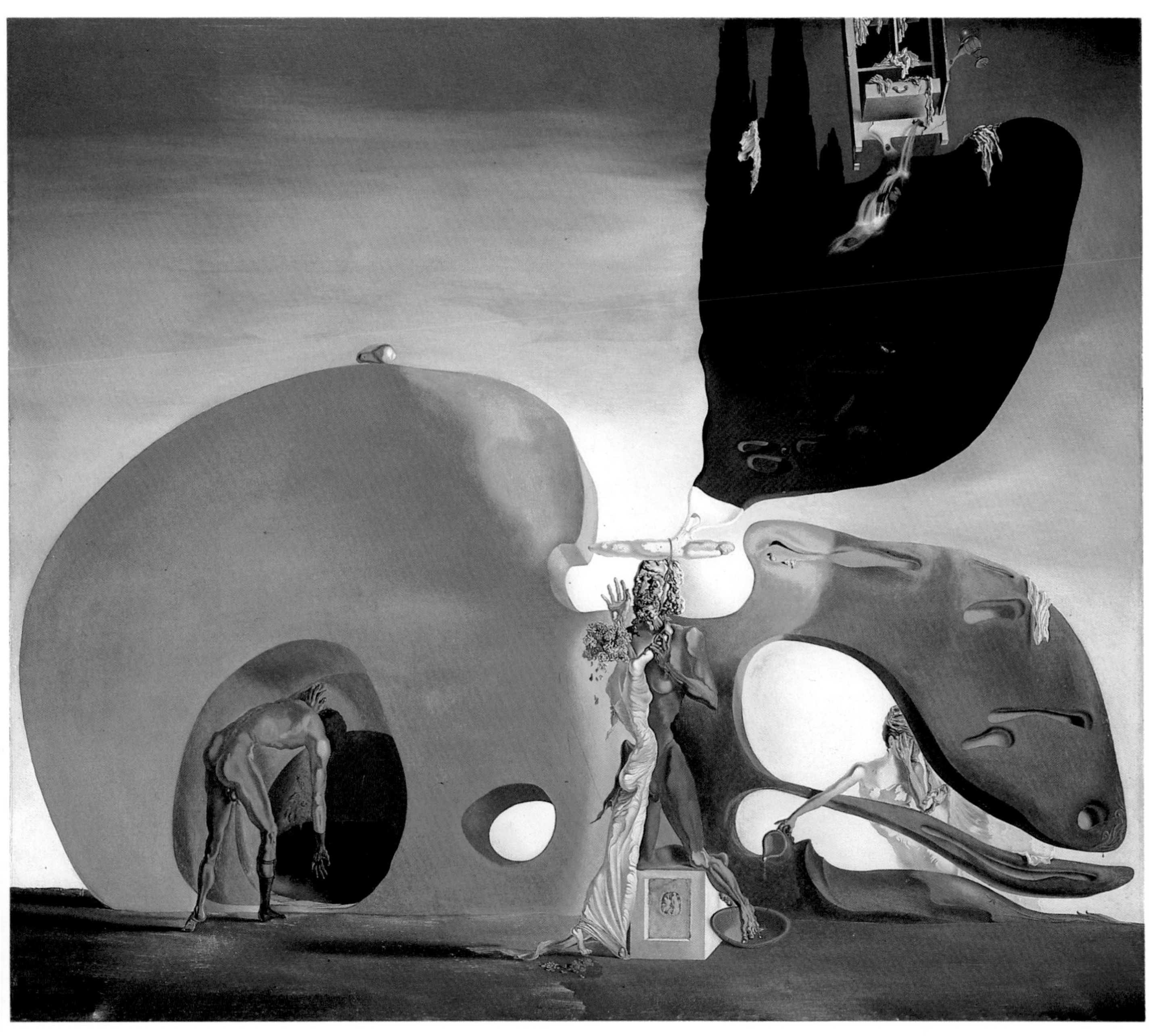

Cat. no. 41, p. 198.
Dalí, *La Naissance des désirs liquides*, 1931-32.

Cat. no. 40, p. 194.
Dalí, *Untitled*, 1931.

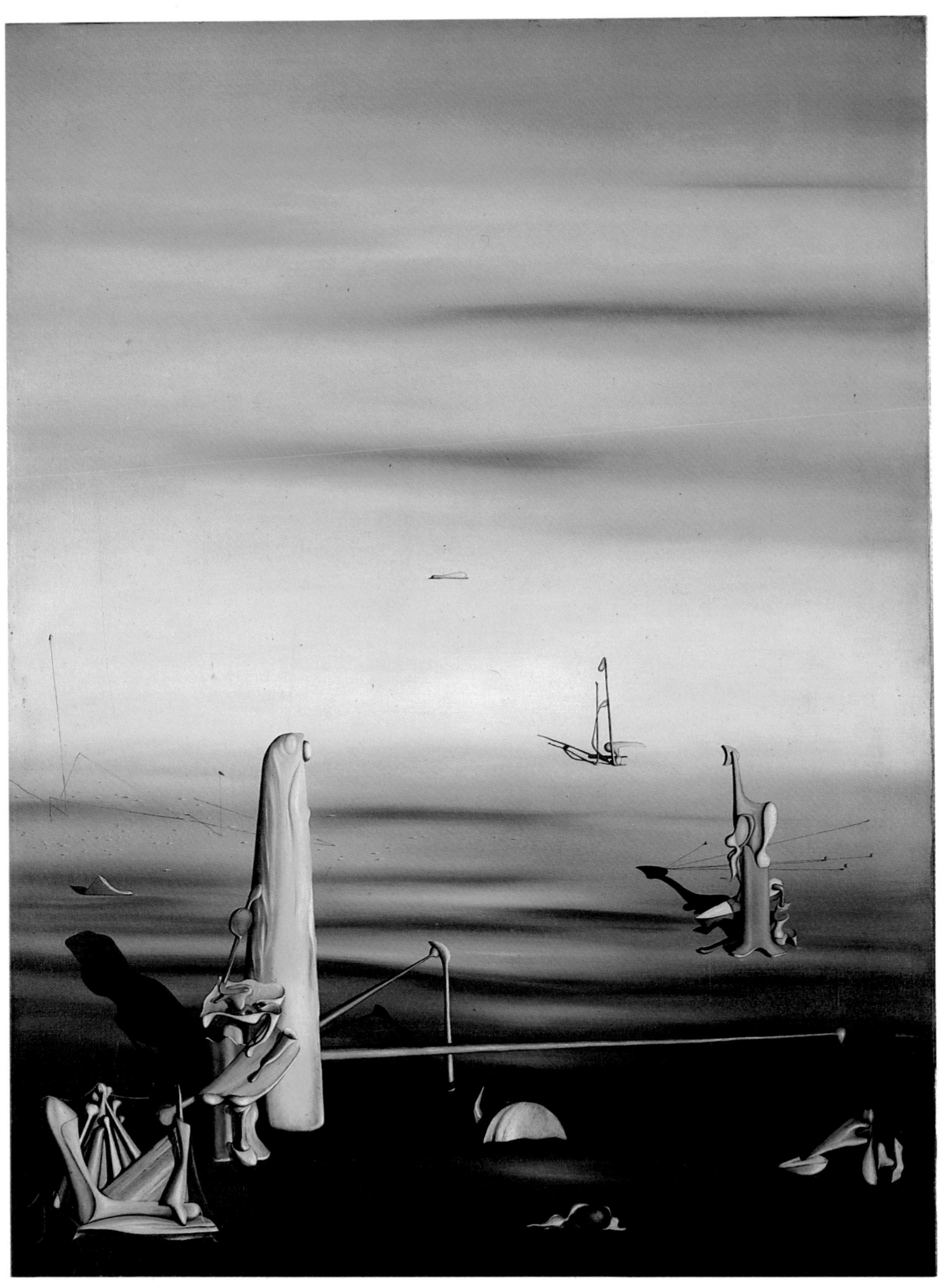

Cat. no. 167, p. 717.
Tanguy, *Le soleil dans son écrin*, 1937.

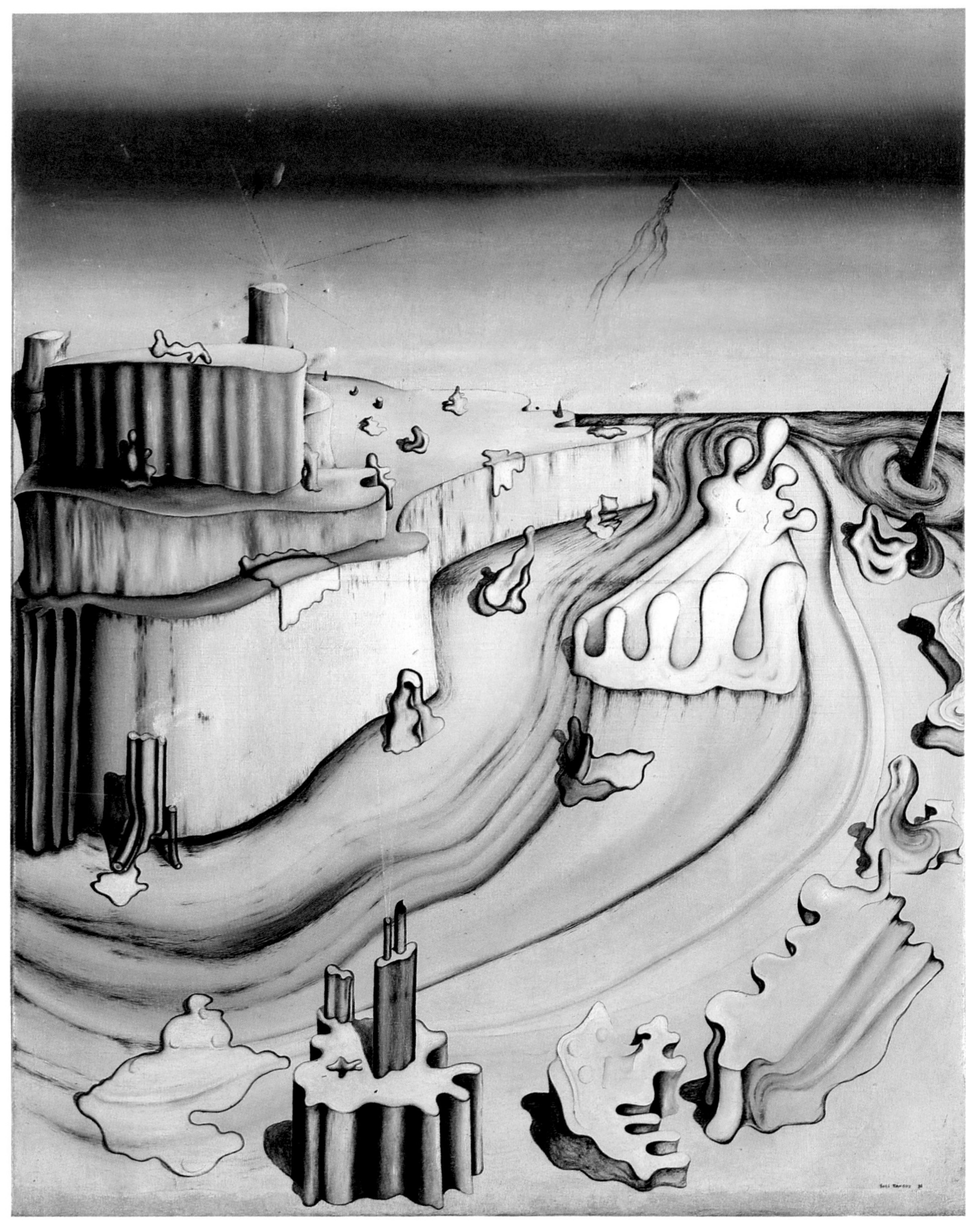

Cat. no. 166, p. 713.
Tanguy, *Palais promontoire*, 1931.

Cat. no. 169, p. 719.
Tanguy, *En lieu oblique*, March 1941.

Cat. no. 86, p. 425.
Klee, *Bildnis der Frau P. im Süden*, 1924.

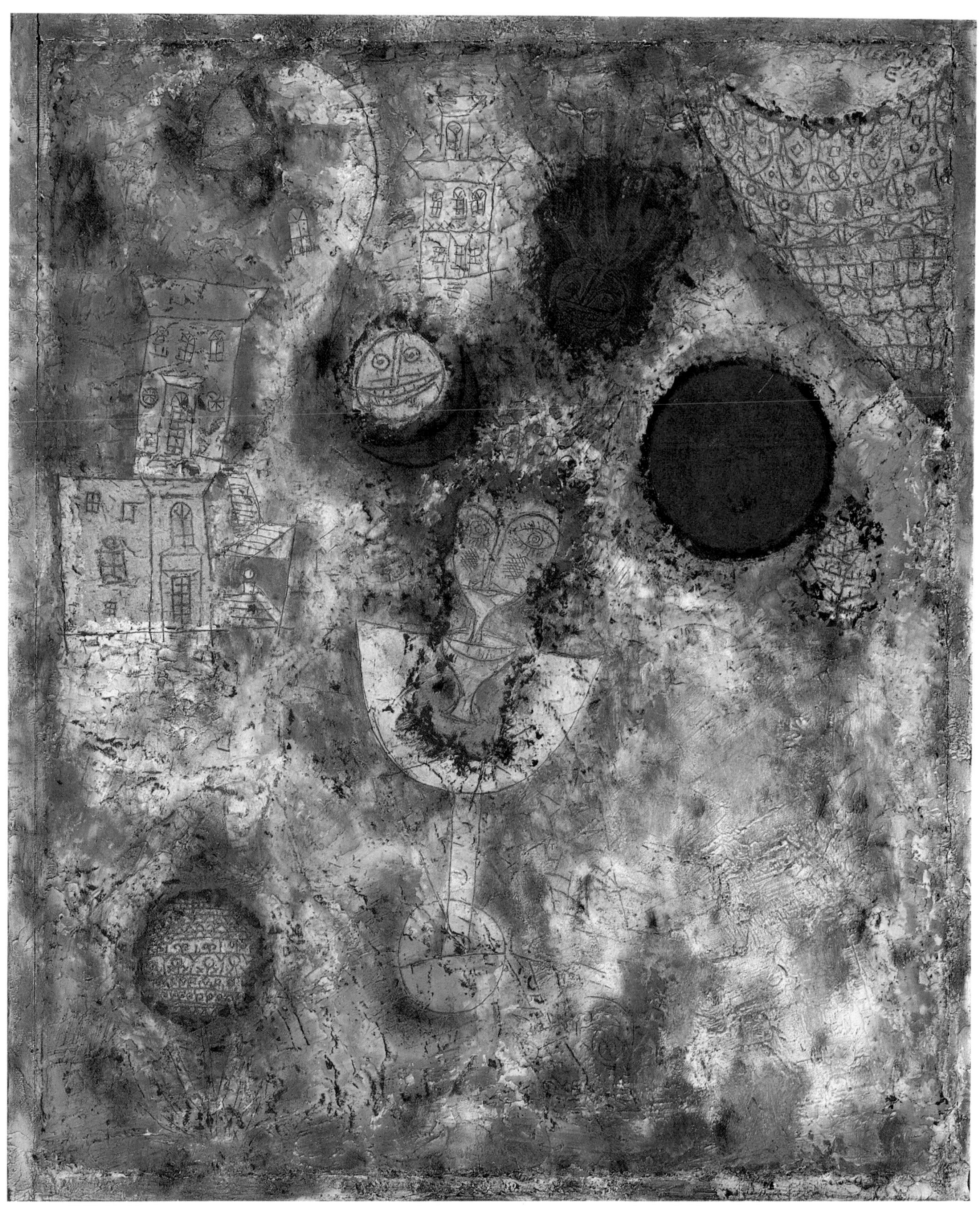

Cat. no. 87, p. 426.
Klee, *Zaubergarten*, March 1926.

Cat. no. 35, p. 177.
Cornell, *Fortune Telling Parrot*, ca. 1937-38.

Cat. no. 38, p. 187.
Cornell, *Untitled (Pharmacy)*, ca. 1942.

Cat. no. 21, p. 133.
Brauner, *Le Surréaliste*, January 1947.

Cat. no. 22, p. 138.
Brauner, *Téléventré*, 1948.

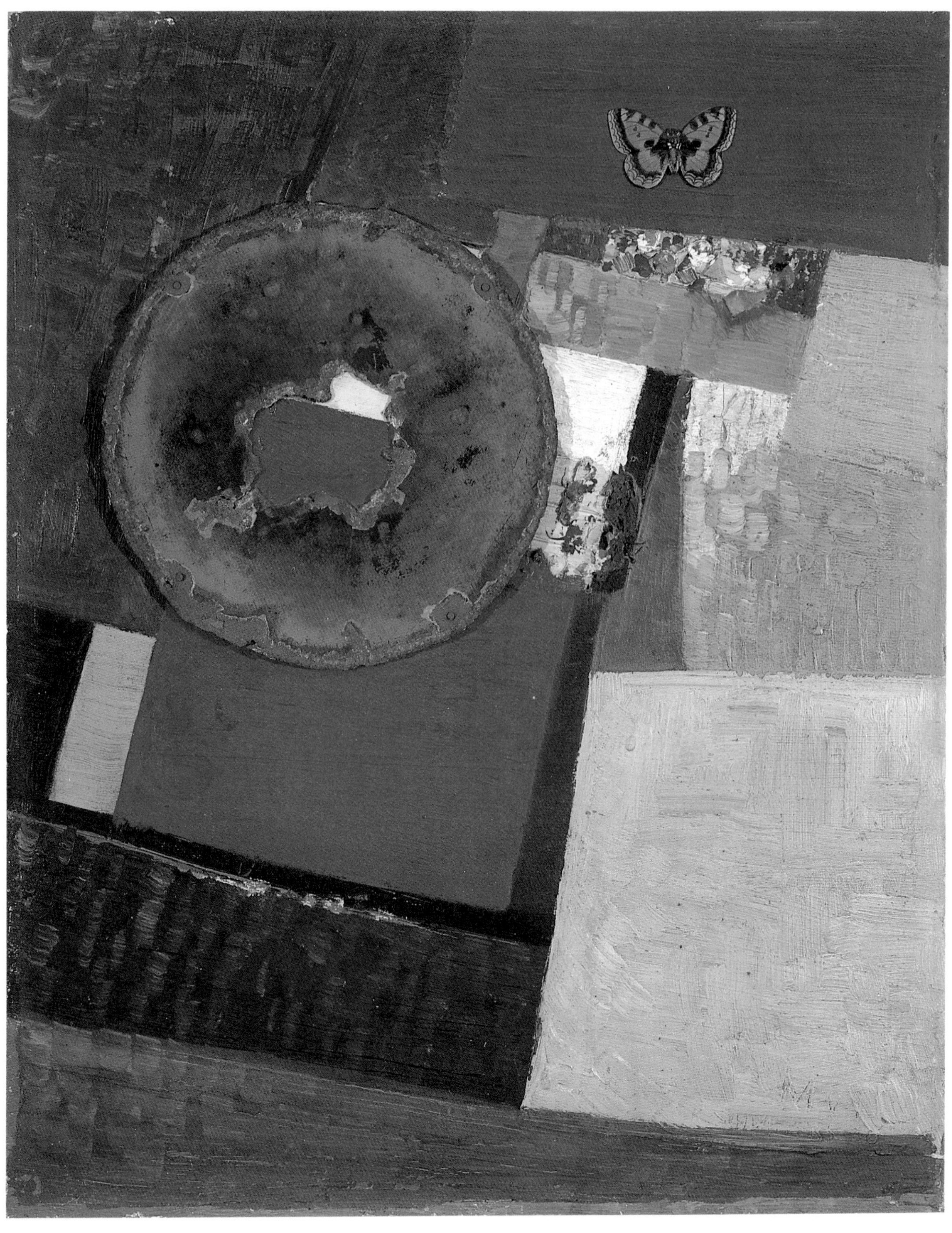

Cat. no. 161, p. 698.
Schwitters, *Maraak, Variation I*, 1930.

Cat. no. 2, p. 52.
Appel, *The Crying Crocodile Tries to Catch the Sun*, 1956.

Cat. no. 81, p. 411.
Jorn, *Untitled*, 1956-57.

Cat. no. 1, p. 51.
Alechinsky, *Peignoir*, 1972.

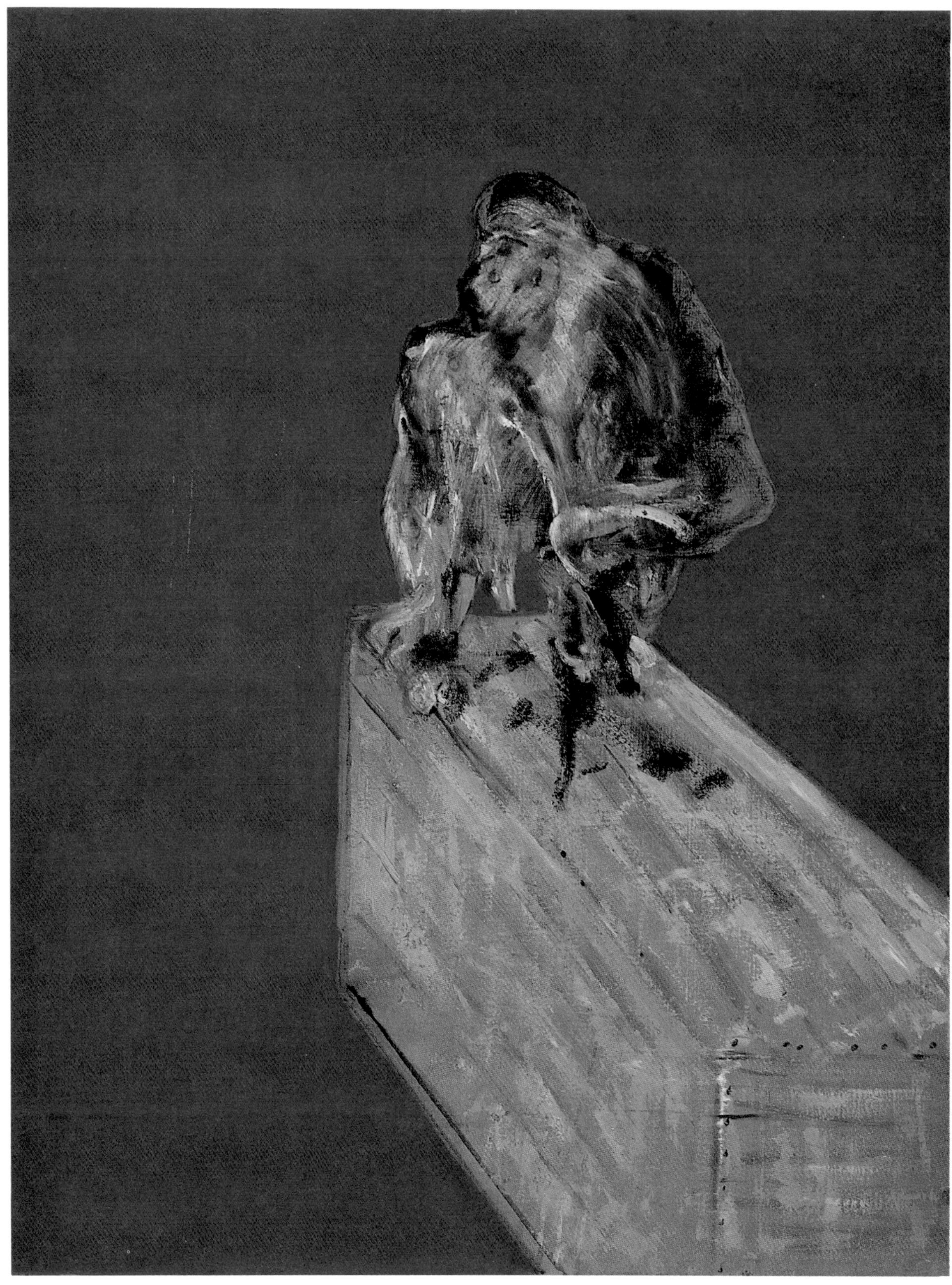

Cat. no. 12, p. 84.
Bacon, *Study for Chimpanzee*, March 1957.

Louis Marcoussis

(Ludwig Casimir Ladislas Markus).

Born November 1878, Warsaw.
Died October 1941, Cusset, near Vichy.

108

108 L'Habitué. 1920.
(*The Regular*).

Color plate p. 38.

76.2553 PG 22

Oil with sand and pebbles on canvas, 63¾ x 38³⁄₁₆ (161.9 x 97).

Signed and dated l.l.: *L. Marcoussis /1920.*

PROVENANCE:

Galerie Vignon (Galerie Myrbor), Paris, by 1929 to 1940;[1] purchased from Madame Marie Cuttoli, Paris, 1940.

CONDITION:

By 1964 (Tate Report) the painting had been glue-lined. Some losses, abrasions, and considerable surface dirt were noted. Retouching of losses in the areas of the figure's right (viewer's) hand and the upper left margin had apparently been carried out without filling.

In 1982 (Venice) an efflorescence in the blue areas was removed with compresses. Minor losses were inpainted with watercolor and the painting sprayed with a light coat of Lefranc retouching varnish. There are some drying cracks but the overall condition is fairly stable. (New York, Mar. 1982.)

EXHIBITIONS:

Berlin, Der Sturm, *Archipenko, Delaunay, Gleizes, Klee, Marcoussis* [53 works],... Oct. 1922, no. 25; Anvers, Art Contemporain, *Exposition d'Art Français Moderne*, May 15-June 20, 1926, no. 7; Brussels, Palais des Beaux-Arts, *L'Art Vivant en Europe*, Apr. 25-May 24, 1931, no. 496; Amsterdam, Stedelijk Museum, *Tentoonstelling van Fransche Schilderkunst uit de twintigste eeuw*, Apr. 9-May 2, 1932, no. 152 (no lender listed, but presumably lent or shipped by Galerie Vignon on behalf of the artist [see fn. 1]); New York, Art of This Century, 1942-47, p. 73, repr. p. 75; Venice, *P.G.*, 1948 (Biennale), no. 78; Florence, *P.G.*, 1949, no. 84; Amsterdam, *P.G.*, 1951, no. 96, repr.; Zurich, *P.G.*, 1951, no. 92; London, *P.G.*, 1964-65, no. 15, repr.; Stockholm, *P.G.*, 1966-67, no. 15, repr.; New York, *P.G.*, 1969, p. 57, repr. p. 56; Paris, *P.G.*, 1974-75, no. 14, repr.; Torino, *P.G.*, 1975-76, no. 21; New York, *P.G.*, 1982-83, no. 7, repr. color.

REFERENCES:

Sélection, Marcoussis issue, no. 7, 1929, p. 28 (Gal. Myrbor); E. Tériade, "Documentaire sur la jeune peinture III. Conséquences du cubisme," *Cahiers d'Art*, vol. 5, no. 1, 1930, p. 19; P. Guggenheim, *Art of This Century*, 1942, p. 73, repr. p. 75; H. Read, *A Concise History of Modern Painting*, New York, 1959, repr. p. 229; J. Lafranchis, *Marcoussis*, Paris, 1961, Peinture no. 35, p. 105, repr. pp. 106, 243; P. Daix, *Cubists and Cubism*, Geneva and New York, 1982, repr. color p. 143; L. Flint, *Handbook*, 1983, p. 32, repr. color p. 33.

1. Two undated labels for exhibitions in Amsterdam and Brussels on the reverse indicate the Galerie Vignon as owner or lender (see EXHIBITIONS). Marcoussis exhibited regularly at the Galerie Myrbor, rue Vignon, and it seems the Galerie Vignon was sometimes known by this name. Though the labels carry the name Vignon, the work was credited to the Myrbor in the 1929 *Sélection* (see REFERENCES). Marie Cuttoli, who ran the Galerie Myrbor from 1929 to 1935, sold this work to Peggy Guggenheim in 1940 and may have had it throughout this period.

Marino Marini

Born February 1901, Pistoia.
Died August 1980, Viareggio.

109 L'angelo della città. 1948 (cast 1950?).
(*The angel of the city*; *Cavaliere*; *L'angelo della cittadella*).

76.2553 PG 183

Bronze (cast in three pieces, lost wax). Height (to top of base): 65 15/16 (167.5); Dimensions of base: 31 5/8 x 20 9/16 x 1 3/4 (80.4 x 52.3 x 4.5); arm span of figure: 41 3/4 (106).

Signed on base: *M.M.* Not dated.

Edition of three.[1]

Foundry: Fonderia d'Arte M.A.F. Milan.

PROVENANCE:
Purchased from the artist, Milan, 1949.

CONDITION:
There is a deep crack on the right side (viewer's) of the bronze base, which probably occurred in the casting. There is some surface pollution, some streaks of green corrosion, and some small pitting corrosion.

In March 1984 (Venice) the sculpture was cleaned. The surface was degreased with trichloroethylene, and washed with distilled water, then with distilled water and neutral detergent; it was rinsed with distilled water, and dried with alcohol and acetone. The surface was treated for 30 minutes with a 3% solution of benzotriazole in pure alcohol. A protective coating of Incralac (acrylic resin containing benzotriazole) was applied (for outdoor exhibition). The condition is stable.

Peggy Guggenheim's memoirs indicate that she originally purchased the work when it existed only in plaster: "There was also a Marino Marini, which I bought from him in Milan. I went to borrow one for the sculpture show, but ended up buying the only thing available. It was a statue of a horse and rider, the latter with his arms spread way out in ecstasy, and to emphasize this, Marini had added a phallus in full erection. But when he had it cast in bronze for me he had the phallus made separately, so it could be screwed in and out at leisure. Marini placed the sculpture in my courtyard on the Grand Canal, opposite the Prefettura, and named it the *Angel of the Citadel*" (*Confessions*, 1960).

Several illustrations of the plaster have been published crediting it to the Guggenheim collection (see below EXHIBITIONS and REFERENCES), but whether Peggy Guggenheim initially purchased the plaster and only later decided to have it cast in bronze, or planned the casting from the beginning and simply borrowed the plaster in the interim, has not been established. The date of the casting and the present whereabouts of the plaster also remain unknown.

The plaster of the figure on horseback as originally published in 1948 had no arms (fig. b); at that time the genitals of the rider were rendered in a naturalistic

1. The foundry has no records of the casting, and the artist's widow was unable to recall what had become of the plaster. A cast formerly in the collection of Edgar Kaufmann, installed at the entrance to Frank Lloyd Wright's Fallingwater, was destroyed in a tornado in 1956 (information supplied by Edgar Kaufmann, jr., correspondence with the author, 1984). A third cast was, according to P. Waldberg, 1970, at one time in the collection of C. J. Engels, Curaçao.

109

109

manner with an erect, but not separate, phallus. By 1949 (fig. c) the work, still in plaster, apparently had entered Peggy Guggenheim's collection: arms had been added, the joins in the plaster being clearly visible in the reproduction, and the phallus had been removed, but the figure was otherwise only minimally reworked. The plaster statue, complete with arms, was published in this form, probably installed in the Palazzo Reale, Milan,[2] with paintings from the Peggy Guggenheim Collection hanging behind it (Carli, 1950). The piece was still at this stage entitled *Cavaliere*, but attributed in Carli's caption to the Peggy Guggenheim Collection. Subsequent reproductions of the plaster statue, in which the nature of the joins in the arms is the most decisive identifying feature, occur as late as 1978 mistakenly labeled "bronze," although the work had indeed been cast in bronze at least as early as 1953 when Umbro Apollonio published it for the first time.

An additional photograph of the plaster, standing in Marini's studio (fig. d), provides evidence of important changes: a thick band of plaster is added to the right (viewer's) side of the horse's head; the front part of the body carries deep striations. Both these elements were subsequently removed before the work was cast. The presence of the fully modeled phallus (which was cast as a separate, removable piece) lying between the horse's front legs suggests that this photograph records a stage of reworking by the artist after the exhibition of the plaster (fig. c), and not long before the casting of the bronze itself. It is interesting to note that Marini was clearly involved at every stage of the casting process, and worked extensively on the finished bronze (scratching linear elements into the cold surface).

It seems probable, on the basis of the evidence now available, that Peggy Guggenheim originally purchased the plaster. In about 1950 she apparently returned it to the artist to be cast in bronze, at which time he modeled the erect phallus, which was separately cast. Moreover, only after he had personally installed the bronze in the courtyard outside the palazzo, does he seem to have given it its present title.

A preparatory drawing for the statue (fig. a) supports the view that Marini conceived the figure with arms (although with the horse's head down) from the start.[3]

2. The plaster version of the sculpture, recently purchased by Peggy Guggenheim, may have been lent to the Milan showing of *La Collezione Guggenheim*, which opened in Florence in February. Since the work is not listed in the catalogue, this remains a matter of speculation, but the installation and its 1950 publication by Carli would be explicable in this way. Since Marini's studio would have been close to the Palazzo Reale, it is not improbable that he and Peggy Guggenheim decided, at the last moment, to include the work. Peggy Guggenheim would undoubtedly have been able to clarify this history, but she had died by the time the problem arose in the course of research for the present publication. Marini's widow, and others knowledgeable about his work, have been unable to throw any light on the issue.

3. Marini did a large number of drawings on this theme, several of which may have been specifically related to his development of the Peggy Guggenheim sculpture, but many of which were not. The drawing reproduced here has been identified as a preparatory study by Mario di Micheli and by Marina Marini, the artist's widow.

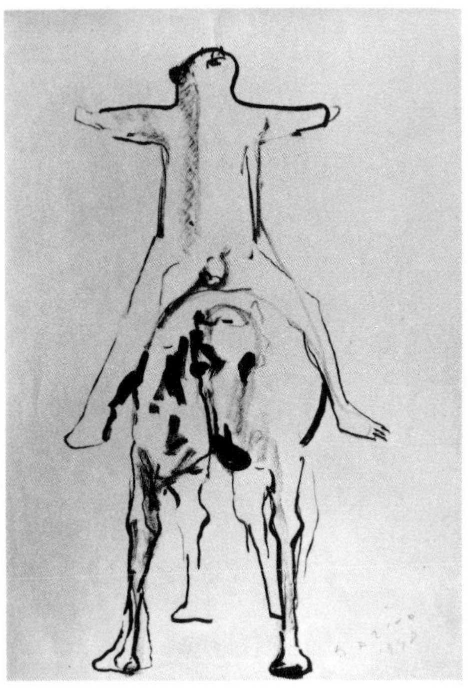

fig. a.
Marini, Study for *L'angelo della città*, ink on paper, $15\frac{3}{4}$ x $11\frac{13}{16}$ in., 40 x 30 cm., Private Collection, Milan.

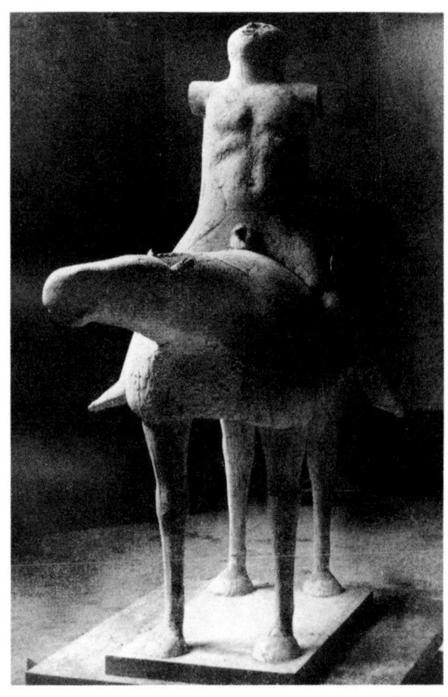

fig. b.
Marini, *L'angelo della città*, plaster original before addition of arms. Photograph courtesy Centro di Documentazione dell' Opera di Marino Marini, Pistoia.

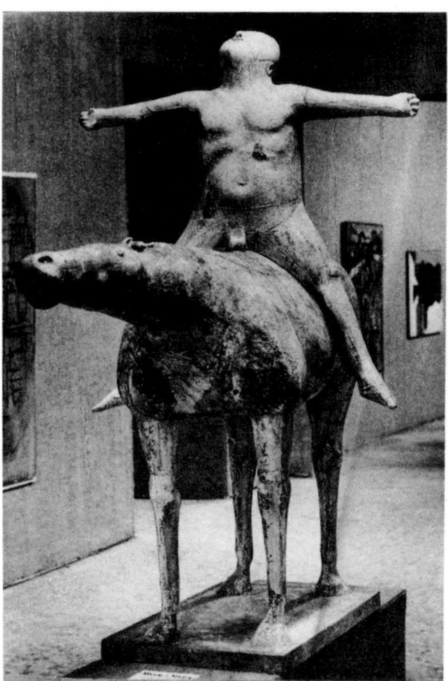

fig. c.
Marini, *L'angelo della città*, plaster original. Photograph courtesy Centro di Documentazione dell'Opera di Marino Marini, Pistoia.

fig. d.
Marini, *L'angelo della città*, plaster original. Photograph courtesy Centro di Documentazione dell'Opera di Marino Marini, Pistoia.

A polychrome wood version, apparently even larger than the Peggy Guggenheim bronze, was formerly in the Krayenbühl Collection, in Zurich, but its present whereabouts is unknown (P. Waldberg, 1970, repr. p. 209, height 70¾ in., 179.8 cm.).

The subject of horse and rider was a major preoccupation of Marini throughout his career. First introduced in 1936 (*Cavaliere*, bronze, Collection Emilio Jesi, Milan), the artist continued to explore the theme in many different contexts. As he explained to Joseph-Paul Hodin in 1952:

Per noi Italiani, che siamo una nazione politica, una figura equestre ha qualcosa di eroico, di romantico. È una sensazione indefinibile, ma che è sempre presente. Talora i cavalieri sono dolenti, oppure euforici, o anche tragici, soprattutto quando l'uomo si ritrova disarcionato. In questo evento sta la poetica dell'uomo e del cavallo. Tutto è calmo, placido. Poi, d'un tratto, scatta l'agitazione, tutto si oscura, si satura di angoscia. Siamo veramente alla tragedia. Ma queste varianti sono sempre debitrici dell'epoca a cui appartiene l'immagine del cavaliere. Quando questi vive in un contesto tranquillo, il cavallo è calmo; quando vive in un periodo inquieto, anche il cavallo è turbato. ("Il richiamo del Nord," *Omaggio a Marino Marini*, special issue of *XXᵉ Siècle*, Milan, 1974 [p. 33]).

The sources of inspiration may have been at some level located in his Italian origins (Etruscan statuettes, the Marcus Aurelius in Rome, Donatello's *Gattamelata*, Verrocchio's *Colleoni*); or possibly they were — as Marini himself claimed — more northern in spirit:

Io avevo sentito di andare verso il Nord; ho sempre inteso spostarmi a Nord che è il punto positivo per me in quanto, essendo io impregnato di Sud, essendo impregnato dei nostri valori italici, ho bisogno di un contrasto.

Viaggiando per l'Italia, a Venezia, a Padova, non mi ero mai impressionato alla vista di monumenti equestri, ma Bamberg, in Germania, mi fece una grande impressione, forse perché nasce in un mondo di fiaba, lontano da noi, in un angolo sperduto (Hodin, ibid., pp. 7-8).

But the critical element in these weighty and intentionally static figures was the degree to which they worked within an iconographic tradition to convey a subjective contemporary interpretation:

*Le mie statue equestri esprimono il tormento causato dagli avvenimenti di questo secolo. L'inquietudine del mio cavallo aumenta ad ogni nuova opera; il cavaliere è sempre più stremato, ha perduto il dominio sulla bestia e le catastrofi alle quali soccombe somigliano a quelle che distrussero Sodoma e Pompei. Aspiro dunque a rendere evidente l'ultimo stadio della dissoluzione di un mito, del mito dell'individuo eroico e vittorioso, dell'*uomo di virtù *degli umanisti* (Hodin, ibid., p. [11]).

L'angelo della città seems to express the "*mito dell'individuo eroico e vittorioso*" that Marini was later to destroy. According to K. Martin (1974), Marini initially entitled the work *Resurrezione*, describing it as "*quasi un simbolo della speranza e della gratitudine che mi hanno invaso poco dopo la guerra.*" When he later changed the title to *L'angelo della città*, he did so in order to convey a sense of invocation.

EXHIBITIONS:

Milan, Palazzo Reale, *La Collezione Guggenheim*, June 1949, hors catalogue?;[2] Venice, Giardino, 1949, no. 12, repr. (the plaster, without phallus, but as "bronzo, coll. P. Guggenheim").

REFERENCES:

R. Carrieri, *Marino Marini: Scultore*, Milan, 1948, repr. pl. 89 (plaster before addition of arms, "*Cavaliere*, 1948 [primo stato], gesso, proprietà dell'Autore"); E. Carli, *Marino Marini*, Milan, 1950, pp. 18-19, repr. pl. 36 (plaster, "*Cavaliere*, collezione Guggenheim"); *Marino Marini*, exh. cat., Kestner Gesellschaft, Hannover, 1951, repr. cover (a detail of the plaster, with arms; the piece was not exhibited); H. List, "Marino Marini," *Die Kunst und das schöne Heim*, 50 Jahrg. Heft 7, Apr. 1952, p. 254 (the artist in his studio working on the plaster); U. Apollonio, *Marino Marini: Sculptor*, rev. ed., Milan, 1953, n.p. (bronze); R. Carrieri, *Pittura e scultura d'avanguardia (1890-1955) in Italia*, Milan, [1955], pl. 220 (the plaster, with arms, in the studio of the artist: "*Il Cavaliere*, gesso, proprietà dell'Autore"); P. Guggenheim, *Confessions*, 1960, pp. 130-31; G. Carandente, *Mostra di Marino Marini*, exh. cat., Rome, 1966, pp. 17, 38, 39; A. M. Hammacher, *Marino Marini: Sculpture, Painting, Drawing*, New York, 1969, [p. 143] ("the artist in his Milan studio in the late 1940s"; the plaster of the complete statue without erect phallus is behind him); P. Waldberg and G. di San Lazzaro, *Marino Marini: Complete Works*, New York, [1970], pp. 13, 187, 359, no. 250a, repr. n.p.; W. Haftmann, "Tragédie de la forme," *Hommage à Marino Marini* (special issue of *XXe Siècle*), Paris, 1974, [p. 77]; P. Volboudt, "Sculptures dans la ville," ibid., repr. p. 58; K. Martin, "La fine di un mito," ibid. (Italian translation), Milan, 1974, [p. 66]; C. Pivorano, *Marino Marini: Scultore*, Milan, n.d., pp. 15, 84, repr. figs. 107, 110 in text, cat. no. 256b; [K. Azuma], *Marino Marini*, Tokyo, 1978, pl. 105 (the plaster in the artist's studio late 1940s, but as "*The Town's Guardian Angel*, bronze, 1949"); L. Flint, *Handbook*, 1983, p. 208, repr. color p. 209.

André Masson

Born January 1896, Balagny (Oise).
Lives in Paris.

110 L'Armure. Ca. January-April 1925.
(*The Armor*).

Color plate p. 256.

76.2553 PG 106

Oil on canvas (unvarnished), 31¾ x 21¼ (80.6 x 54).

Signed on reverse: *André Masson*. Not dated.

PROVENANCE:

Purchased from the artist by D.-H. Kahnweiler, May 1925 (stockbook no. 8929, photo no. 10618); purchased by André Breton, May 1925 (payment recorded in the stockbook); Georges Bataille, 1925-36;[1] Galerie Simon, 1936-40;[2] purchased from Galerie Simon, 1940.

CONDITION:

In 1964 (Tate Report) the unvarnished, dry, matte surface was described as in good condition. A small puncture from the back of the canvas near the right edge (center) had caused some cleavage and loss. Further areas of crackle with elevated pigment were noted near the left edge and the bottom.

The picture appears to have had no treatment. The surface is well preserved and fairly stable. (Venice, Nov. 1982.)

Masson's *L'Armure* was reproduced in the fourth number of *La Révolution Surréaliste* and was shown in the first Surrealist group exhibition of November 1925; before the end of the year, it had passed through the hands of André Breton into the collection of Georges Bataille.[3]

This early provenance suggests the emblematic status *L'Armure* instantly achieved: in its synthesis of the various emerging tendencies of the period, it was prized by the writers of Breton's circle as well as by those who were nearer to Bataille.

Masson himself and the Surrealist writers who were closest to him, as well as more recent commentators, have repeatedly emphasized that the imagery of these works was always symbolically charged. Michel Leiris, for example, has described the pomegranates, scrolls of paper, and other perpetually recurring iconographical details in these paintings as "an array of emblems brought together, as it were, by an alchemist." Leiris saw in Masson's conception of painting a means of "defining, both for himself and others, man's condition ... man's destiny. Mythology [a 'mythology of his own ... apart from any that is traditional'] is the essence of Masson's art, because what counts for him is awareness, emotional awareness: and so, emotionally charged images are the most dominant.... From the start [his] art was always full of symbolism" (*André Masson and His Universe*, trans. D. Cooper, Geneva/Paris/London, 1947, p. viii). Breton wrote in 1939 that "*L'érotisme, dans l'œuvre de Masson, doit être*

1. André Masson distinctly recalled that the first owner of the painting was Georges Bataille, who acquired it very soon after it was painted. Bataille's initial ownership of the work is also frequently cited in the literature. Masson remembered precisely where it hung on Bataille's wall, and he insisted that it never hung "chez Breton" (conversation with the author, Apr. 3, 1982). Since Breton is, however, recorded in the Kahnweiler stockbook as the purchaser, and also appears in the catalogue of the 1925 Galerie Pierre exhibition as the lender (see below, fn. 3), it seems likely that Bataille acquired the painting from Breton, or that Breton actually purchased it from Kahnweiler on behalf of Bataille.
2. According to Masson (conversation with the author, Apr. 1982), Bataille returned the picture to Kahnweiler in exchange for the large drawings Masson had completed in May-June 1936 for the review *Acéphale*, founded jointly by Masson and Bataille. Though Bataille was extremely reluctant to part with the painting, he urgently wanted to own the drawings. Unable to afford them, he acquired them by exchange.
3. Breton, like Bataille, saw the painting as profoundly expressive of an inner reality, a symbolic world. In addition, according to Masson, he was convinced of its revolutionary character and proudly displayed a reproduction of it to the leader of the gas workers' union, to which he belonged at the time, hoping thereby to help establish the political credentials of *La Révolution Surréaliste*. Not surprisingly, the leader's response was unequivocally hostile and contemptuous: "*Je regarde ça [L'Armure] et je dis que ce peintre là est malade, un fou sadique.*" The account of the episode was offered by Masson (in conversation with the author, Apr. 1982) as an example of Breton's political naïveté and to suggest the diverse effects produced by *L'Armure*: "*Cela m'amusait beaucoup, quand Breton venait au Cafe Cyrano me raconter l'histoire. C'était un scandale, mais c'était amusant.*" For a brief discussion of the evolution of Breton's political ideas in 1924-27 and the gradual rapprochement between Surrealism and Communism, see D. Ades, *Dada and Surrealism Reviewed*, London, 1978, pp. 195-203. Breton took over the direction of *La Révolution Surréaliste* with the fourth issue (in which *L'Armure* was reproduced); the second and third issues had been directed by Antonin Artaud.

tenu pour la clé de voûte" (*Minotaure*, May 1939, p. 13). Masson meanwhile has indicated that the "mythological," or symbolic, content so evident in these paintings has from the start been based ultimately on his own experience: "*Tout ce que je peins se rapporte à ce que j'ai vécu, à tout ce par quoi j'ai pris conscience. Si rien n'est purement plastique rien n'est purement imaginaire: mes allégories, mes thèmes mythologiques puisent leur substance dans l'évènement où je vis.*"[4]

In the case of *L'Armure*, Masson has offered some elliptical insights into aspects of the painting's imagery: "*Cette Armure féminine, elle a un aspect de cristal. La tête est remplacée par une flamme. Le cou coupé. Le sexe voisine avec une grenade ouverte: le seul fruit qui saigne. Un oiseau s'approche de l'aisselle (le nid). Le corps armé est environné de banderolles de papier mimant les courbes du corps feminin*" (cited by Clébert, 1971, p. 32).

Taken together, Masson's comments help to provide a framework for understanding the complex of images in *L'Armure* and to suggest the particular resonance carried by certain iconographic details.

During World War I, Masson fought for a long period at the front and was seriously wounded. On April 17, 1917, the second day of the offensive at the Chemin-des-Dames, he was shot in the chest. Otto Hahn reported that he remained on his feet, oblivious of pain, hovering between consciousness and hallucinatory unconsciousness. In this state, a vision appeared before him in the sky: a "torso of light" or — according to his perception — the "light-drenched torso of death." Convinced that he was in fact dead, he found himself irresistibly drawn toward the torso, which was suspended before him like the emblem of a new "posthumous" freedom (O. Hahn, *André Masson*, New York, 1965, pp. 6-7).

The torso of this vision, with its irresistible attraction and its evocation of death, points to the close association between eroticism and violence that became a fundamental element in the work of Masson, and which lies at the symbolic center of *L'Armure*.[5]

Breton and Robert Desnos, in their introduction to the catalogue for the November 1925 Surrealist exhibition at the Galerie Pierre, made elliptical ref-

4. "Je cherche la sérénité à travers la tragique," *Les Lettres françaises*, no. 1071, Mar. 11-17, 1965, p. 12. For an example of Masson's partial explication of his paintings of the mid-1920s within such a framework, see his comments on *Homme dans une tour*, A.Z.R. *Guggenheim*, 1976, Vol. II, pp. 506-8.

5. This frequently noted preoccupation with the relationship between eroticism and violence, which many Surrealist writers shared, was felt with particular intensity by Georges Bataille, who saw eroticism (as opposed to simple sexual activity) as a psychological quest that would result in the reestablishment of the "fundamental continuity of existence" (*Death and Sensuality*, New York, 1962, pp. 11, 20-21). Masson described this equation of eroticism with violence or death as perhaps the "most difficult and profound" ingredient in Bataille's philosophy (see A. Masson, "Some Notes on the Unusual Georges Bataille," *Art and Literature*, no. 3, autumn-winter, 1964, p. 105). Jean-Paul Clébert noted that the imagery and symbolism of *L'Armure* would thus have found an immediate response in Bataille: "*On voit bien ce qui peut séduire Bataille et les thèmes qui lui sont chers désormais, le cou coupé, le fruit saignant, la femme armée*" (*Les Lettres Nouvelles*, 1971, p. 58).

erence to the double meaning of the torso in the painting when they wrote of *L'Armure*: "*un homme ... est visité nuitamment par les miracles et mieux que d'une ombre il est suivie de l'*armure, *de l'armure de verre cause de ses insomnies.*" Masson's "*Armure*," with her "*aspect de cristal*," recalls, moreover, the woman "clothed in glass" or the "*torse de femme adorablement poli bien qu'il fut dépourvu de tête et de membres*" of Breton's *Poisson soluble*, published in mid-1924 with the first Surrealist *Manifesto*. Masson and Breton had met for the first time not long before.

Leiris's 1925 Surrealist glossary, *Glossaire: j'y serre mes gloses*, parts of which were published adjacent to *L'Armure* in the fourth number of *La Révolution Surréaliste* (see below REFERENCES), contains further evocative clues to the erotic and even tragic overtones of the painting's imagery: "*Armure — ramure de larmes pétrifiées; Epaules — pôles des ailes disparues; Flamme — fluide mâle; Flanc — blanc il s'élance comme une flamme; Incendie — le sang, les sens: indices de cendre; Torse — torche vive, une spire en sort sans traces.*"

In a 1926 article on Surrealism, the imagery of *L'Armure* (reproduced with the text) apparently inspired Desnos to write: "*Dans un port de l'extrême-Levant une foule étrange, où les femmes nues qui écrasent des grenades sur leurs seins coudoient des colporteurs décapités, se presse. Ils disent qu'ils attendent un homme que le ciel et l'amour inspirèrent* ("Surréalisme," *Cahiers d'Art*, vol. 1, no. 8, Oct. 1926, p. 210).

In each of these "texts," allusions to the elements of Masson's vocabulary throw light on (or echo) the implied content of *L'Armure* and other paintings by the artist. Desnos's figures are decapitated — as is the torso in *L'Armure*; this destruction of the head (the locus of reason) suggests the primacy of dreams and hallucinations in the Surrealist context. ("*La tête est remplacée par une flamme. Le cou coupé.*") The flame in turn consumes, burns, and destroys: "*comme une flamme apparaît dans presque tous mes tableaux de cette époque, je pense qu'il s'agit de la flamme brûlante et non éclairante*" (Masson, cited by Clébert, 1971, p. 26). While the flame does not illuminate the physical world, it carries positive connotations. It is a phallic symbol, evoking the idea of passion; it also alludes to the ideas of Heraclitus, for whom fire was the source of all inspiration and hence of all power.[6]

The open pomegranate — "*le seul fruit qui saigne*" — also carries erotic overtones. Carolyn Lanchner observed that the pomegranate is virtually ubiquitous in Masson's works of the 1920s and has remained perhaps "the single most important image in his work" (1976, p. 93). It serves as a symbol of life and death, fertility and mortality; like woman, it carries seeds, but its bleeding implies destruction. On one occasion at least, the physical violence of war — a head split open in battle — reminded Masson of the ripe pomegranate: "As an

6. Masson refers to his reading of Heraclitus in *Anatomy of My Universe*, New York, 1943, section III, n.p. For further discussion of Masson's interest in Heraclitus, see Beatty, 1981, p. 192. See also her discussion (pp. 241-42, 266) of the relationship between woman and flame in Masson's work and in the Surrealist writing of the 1920s.

adolescent, I have seen among the casualties of combat a shattered skull: a ripe pomegranate and blood on the snow design the scutcheon of war.... The secret world of Analogy, the magic of the Sign, the transcendence of Number were thus revealed to me" (*Anatomy of My Universe*, New York, 1943, section v, n.p.). Beatty has suggested (1981, p. 184) that Masson's use of the pomegranate in such contexts constitutes in part a metaphorical statement of the reality of pain as an intrinsic part of life: a reminder that man enters life through a wound.

The bird (which makes its nest in the armpit of the woman) also carries multiple meanings in Masson's work, and in 1925 became a central element in his iconography. In *L'Aile*, for example, the bird is interpreted as the flowering of Masson's own artistic freedom—the *anima* of the artist. Replacing the head (reason and logic) it links man with the cosmos (imagination).[7]

In this painting, as in other works of the period, diaphanous scrolls, which fade into and effectively fuse with their environment, reinforce the complex and even labyrinthine pattern of the imagery and help to create the dreamlike atmosphere. Masson called attention to these qualities in describing his pictorial (and symbolic) aims as "*faire fusionner les corps avec un environnement pour créer un espace où, autant que possible, suivant la définition hermétique, il n'y a plus ni haut ni bas; où ce qui est au dedans est aussi au dehors*" (cited by Clébert, 1971, p. 32). Masson seems to allude here to the significance he attached to Gerard de Nerval (a significance he discussed more explicitly in other contexts). Describing de Nerval as "*prophète et pratiquant du mariage du rêve et de la vie,*"[8] Masson saw him successfully fusing the contrasting realities of the internal—or psychological—experience and the external world.

Masson has often referred to the critical role poetry played in his development of a pictorial language. (See, for example, a letter written to Margit Rowell and Rosalind Krauss, April 19, 1972: " ... poetry was of capital importance. Our ambition [Miró's and his] was to be a painter-poet and in that we differed from our immediate predecessors, who while going around with the poets of their generation, were terrified of being labelled 'literary painters.' As painters purporting to work from poetic necessity we were taking a great risk ... " *Joan Miró: Magnetic Fields*, New York, 1972, p. 40). And while it is clear that the content of his work is heavily indebted to poetic and other literary texts, it is also the case that the multiplicity of meanings evoked by any one image argues against too literal or specific a reading of the iconography. Masson himself stressed the symbolic (and even literary) aspects of his art, but he also described the nature of his intentions as generalizing and evocative rather than restrictive,

7. For a discussion of the significance of the bird in Masson's work of 1924-25, see Beatty, 1981, pp. 219-20, 295-98; also Lanchner, 1976, p. 112.

8. "45 rue Blomet," Mar. 1968, reprinted in F. Will-Levaillant, ed., *André Masson, le rebelle du surréalisme, écrits*, Paris, 1976, p. 81. For a discussion of de Nerval and Novalis see Beatty, 1981, pp. 86, 88, 285-94. She discusses in particular the ways in which their works are haunted by death (often depicted as dream) and birth (containing seeds of death), and argues convincingly that the "texture" of these writings had a profound effect on Masson in the mid-1920s.

implying a resistance to simplistic readings, when he wrote that "*dès 1923, je me voyais d'opter pour une surnaturalisme, qui devait contenir la nature entière — cela ou abandonner la peinture* ("Mouvement et Metamorphose," *Plaisir de Peindre*, Nice, 1950, p. 194). Much of the imagery that occurs in *L'Armure* and throughout the paintings of the mid-1920s can also be found in the contemporary writings of Artaud, Leiris, Bataille, Louis Aragon, and Breton. In their work, as in Masson's, the fundamental effort was to discover a language that was rich in its multiple associations, so that any particular image or idea might lead naturally to the next, recreating (or rediscovering) a "lost continuity" of experience (G. Bataille, *Death and Sensuality*, p. 15).[9]

EXHIBITIONS:

Paris, Galerie Pierre, *La Peinture Surréaliste*, Nov. 14-25, 1925, no. 5 ("André Masson. [Appartient à M.A.B.]");[10] New York, Art of This Century, 1942-47, p. 110, repr. p. 111; New York, Art of This Century, *15 Early, 15 Late Paintings*, Mar. 13-Apr. 10, 1943, no. 221; Venice, *P.G.*, 1948 (Biennale), no. 79; Florence, *P.G.*, 1949, no. 85; Amsterdam, *P.G.*, 1951, no. 98; Zurich, *P.G.*, 1951, no. 93; London, *P.G.*, 1964-65, no. 96, repr.; Stockholm, *P.G.*, 1966-67, no. 91, repr.; Paris, *P.G.*, 1974-75, no. 88, repr.; Torino, *P.G.*, 1975-76, no. 104.

REFERENCES:

La Révolution Surréaliste, no. 4, July 15, 1925, repr. p. 22; R. Desnos, "Surréalisme," *Cahiers d'Art*, vol. 1, no. 8, Oct. 1926, repr. p. 210 (upside down); A. Masson, *Métamorphose de L'Artiste*, Geneva, 1956, vol. 1, p. 21; J. P. Clébert, *La Mythologie d'André Masson*, Geneva, 1971, p. 32; idem, "Georges Bataille et André Masson," *Les Lettres Nouvelles*, May 1971, pp. 57-58; C. Lanchner, in *André Masson*, exh. cat., MoMA, New York, 1976, pp. 112, 115, 117; F. L. Beatty, "A. Masson and the Imagery of Surrealism," unpublished Ph.D. dissertation, Columbia University, 1981, pp. 133, 288, 289, 290, 297.

9. See M. A. Caws, *The Poetry of Dada and Surrealism*, Princeton, New Jersey, 1970, pp. 30-35, 70-72, for a discussion of "linkage" in Surrealist literature. Surrealism is described here as a "search for the continuous," cited by Beatty, 1981, p. 352, fn. 728.

10. Though titles are not given in the catalogue list, the preface by Desnos and Breton contains clues to the works exhibited. Thus, regarding *L'Armure*: "[*Il*] *est visité nuitamment par les miracles et mieux que d'une ombre il est suivi de* l'armure[5]*, de l'armure de verre cause de ses insomnies.*"

111 Two Children. 1942.

76.2553 PG 107

Bronze (lost-wax solid cast), with original brown patina. Height: 6 (15.3); length: 4¼ (10.7).

Incised (into wax) on base: *VI*; signed with monogram (cursive): *AM*. Not dated.[1]

Foundry: unknown.

Edition of six.[2]

PROVENANCE:

Gift of Curt Valentin, New York, 1946.

CONDITION:

The original brown patina is well preserved and the overall condition stable. (Venice, Nov. 1982.)

1. According to the inventory of Curt Valentin's estate, this sculpture was made in 1942.
2. Doris Birmingham, who wrote her Ph.D. dissertation on "André Masson in America: The Artist's Achievement in Exile, 1941-45," University of Michigan , 1978, had this information among her research notes, but was uncertain of the source. Masson, in conversation with the author, April 3, 1982, recalled only that Curt Valentin took responsibility for locating the foundry and making arrangements for the casting, though he thought that he probably supervised the actual casting of the piece himself. He was unable to recall the size of the edition.

During his American sojourn (1941-45), Masson apparently had only two bronzes cast: the present work and *The Praying Mantis*, both in 1942.

In recalling his work on *Two Children*, Masson described the evolution of the figures as the entirely spontaneous result of manipulating a piece of clay: "*La scupture est venue comme ça, entre mes mains ... pas un portrait ... rien à faire avec des vrais enfants ... pas de dessins. Non, elle est venue comme ça ... je me rappelle très bien*" (conversation with the author, Paris, Apr. 3, 1982).

EXHIBITIONS:

Venice, *P.G.*, 1948 (Biennale), no. 80 (dated 1941, the date ascribed to it in *P.G.* publications until 1964); Florence, *P.G.*, 1949, no. 86; Amsterdam, *P.G.*, 1951, no. 100; Zurich, *P.G.*, 1951, no. 95; London, *P.G.*, 1964-65, no. 97 (dated 1942); Stockholm, *P.G.*, 1966-67, no. 92; Torino, *P.G.*, 1975-76, no. 105.

REFERENCE:

Calas, 1966, repr. p. 195.

---

112 Oiseau fasciné par un serpent. 1942.[1]
(Bird fascinated by a snake).

76.2553 PG 108

Tempera on watercolor paper, 22¼ x 29¾ (56.5 x 75.5).

Signed u.l.: *André Masson*. Not dated.

PROVENANCE:

Purchased from Curt Valentin, February 23, 1943 (information from the Curt Valentin inventory).

CONDITION:

Two tears (upper center and upper left edge) were repaired at an unknown date. A further tear in the lower right corner is also visible. The support is cockled throughout owing to its framing between glass and cardboard. With the exception of some scratches in the tempera (corresponding to the tear upper center and to small tears along upper edge), the condition is stable. (Venice, Nov. 1982.)

1. According to the Curt Valentin inventory, the work arrived at the gallery in September 1942 and was sold to Peggy Guggenheim February 23, 1943.

112

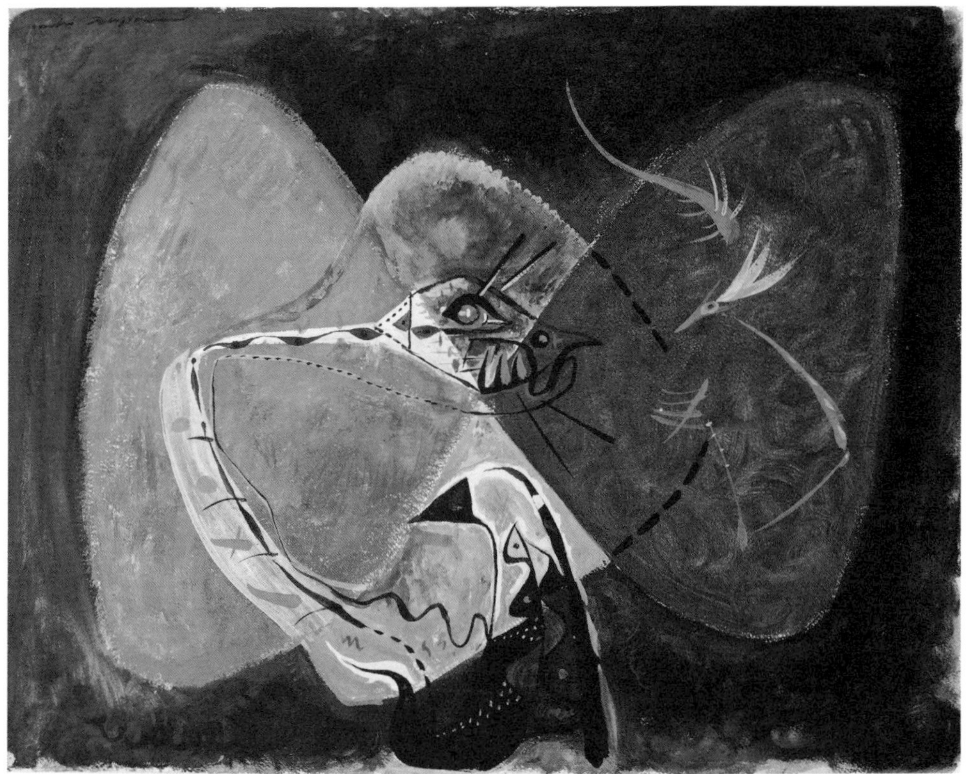

An almost identical composition, *Serpent et papillon* (oil with sand on wood panel, 10 x 14 in., 25.5 x 35.6 cm., Collection Mr. and Mrs. Dan R. Johnson, New York) represents Masson's elaboration of the theme of the Peggy Guggenheim tempera in a strongly textural idiom.

Confronted with black-and-white photographs of the two works, Masson recalled, on the one hand, the textural contrasts, and, on the other, the coloristic similarities between them: "*C'était une fantaisie en vert et gris — tous les deux ... presque les mêmes couleurs, mais tout à fait différent quand même*" (conversation with the author, Paris, Apr. 3, 1982). Though he was unable to recall the chronological relationship, he suspected that the oil followed the tempera.

EXHIBITIONS:

Venice, *P.G.*, 1948 (Biennale), no. 81; Florence, *P.G.*, 1949, no. 87 (dated 1943, as in all subsequent *P.G.* publications); Amsterdam, *P.G.*, 1951, no. 102; Zurich, *P.G.*, 1951, no. 96; London, *P.G.*, 1964-65, no. 98; Stockholm, *P.G.*, 1966-67, no. 93; Paris, *P.G.*, 1974-75, no. 89, repr.; Torino, *P.G.*, 1975-76, no. 106.

REFERENCES:

Calas, 1966, repr. p. 130; D. Birmingham, "André Masson in America: The Artist's Achievement in Exile, 1941-45," unpublished Ph.D. dissertation, University of Michigan, 1978, cat. no. 19, p. 188, repr. p. 291.

Matta

(Roberto Sebastian Antonio Matta Echaurren).

Born November 1911, Santiago, Chile.
Lives in Tarquinia and Paris.

113 The Dryads. New York, 1941.

76.2553 PG 109

Pencil and colored crayon on paper, $22\frac{15}{16}$ x $28\frac{15}{16}$ (58.2 x 73.4).

Signed, titled, and dated l.r.: *Matta. The Dryads 1941 NYC.*

PROVENANCE:

Purchased from the artist, New York, ca. 1943.

CONDITION:

In 1978 (New York) the work was removed from framing between acidic board and glass. Extensive foxing of verso and recto due to mold growth was treated; considerable discoloration of support was mitigated. Taping of edges and animal glue stains on verso were removed. A small tear at the lower edge center, ¾ in., 2 cm.; 3 smaller semicircular cuts; 2 slashes to left of tear at lower edge, 1–1⅜ in., 2.5–3.5 cm., were all repaired. The work was fumigated in a thymol cabinet and mounted on 4-ply 100% rag board. The condition is stable. (New York, Mar. 1983.)

EXHIBITIONS:

Venice, *P.G.*, 1948 (Biennale), no. 84 (*Drawing*, the title by which the work was known until 1982); Florence, *P.G.*, 1949, no. 90; Amsterdam, *P.G.*, 1951, no. 105; Zurich, *P.G.*, 1951, no. 99 (*Zwei Tänzerinnen*); London, *P.G.*, 1964-65, no. 99; Stockholm, *P.G.*, 1966-67, no. 94; Paris, *P.G.*, 1974-75, no. 103; Torino, *P.G.*, 1975-76, no. 107, repr. pl. 51; New York, *P.G.*, 1982-83, no. 46, repr.

REFERENCE:

L. Flint, *Handbook*, 1983, p. 146, repr. color p. 147.

114 Le Dénommeur renommé. 1952-53.
(The Un-nominator renominated).

Color plate p. 683.

76.2553 PG 110

Oil on canvas, 47⅜ x 68⅞ (120.4 x 175).

Not signed or dated.

PROVENANCE:

Purchased from the Galleria d'Arte del Cavallino, Venice, 1953.

CONDITION:

There are some scratches and abrasions of the paint film at the lower edge. The painting has received no treatment and the condition in general is stable. (Venice, Nov. 1982.)

EXHIBITIONS:

Venice, Sala Napoleonica (organized by Galleria del Cavallino), *Matta*, Aug. 1953, repr. color p. 13, exh. pamphlet; London, *P.G.*, 1964-65, no. 100, repr.; Stockholm, *P.G.*, 1966-67, no. 95, repr.; New York, *P.G.*, 1969, p. 145, repr.; Paris, *P.G.*, 1974-75, no. 104, repr.; Torino, *P.G.*, 1975-76, no. 108.

Jean Metzinger

Born June 1883, Nantes.
Died November 1956, Paris.

115

115 Au Vélodrome. Ca. 1914 (?).
(*At the cycle-race track*; *Le coureur cycliste*; *The Bicyclist*).

Color plate p. 41.

76.2553 PG 18

Oil and collage on canvas (unvarnished), 51⅜ x 38¼ (130.4 x 97.1).

Signed l.l.: *Metzinger*; on reverse in charcoal (photographed before lining): *Metzinger*. Not dated.

PROVENANCE:

Purchased from the artist by John Quinn through Carroll Galleries, New York, February 1916;[1] John Quinn estate 1924-27; purchased from the Quinn Collection Sale by J. B. Neumann, New York, 1927 (American Art Galleries, New York, *The Renowned Collection of Modern and Ultra-Modern Art formed by the late John Quinn*, Feb. 9-12, 1927, no. 266, "*Au Velodrome*" $70); J. B. Neumann, New York, 1927-42;[2] purchased from Neumann, 1945.

CONDITION:

In 1964 (Tate Report) 2 tears, previously repaired with glued patches and retouched, were noted (1 ca. 2 in., 5 cm., near center of left edge; 1 ca. ⅜ in., 2 cm., at lower center). Some crackle with cleavage and loss, especially in the blacks and in the collage area, and considerable surface dirt were noted. The lack of varnish was also recorded.

In 1982 (Venice) the work was cleaned with ammonium hydroxide (3% in water). The composition had penetrated the unprimed fine canvas and was entirely visible on the reverse (fig. a). A Fieux contact lining was applied: flaking paint in the handlebars was reattached with Gelvatol (polyvinyl alcohol at 15% in water and alcohol, 1:1). A light coat of Lefranc's retouching varnish (spray) was applied.

Scattered flaking and small losses in the blue painted wedge at the upper left reveal red underpainting. The granules of dry pigment, creating the effect of sand, are combined with the underpaint rather than the surface film. The brown-painted edge of the composition shows considerable evidence of retouching. The condition is fragile. (Feb. 1982.)

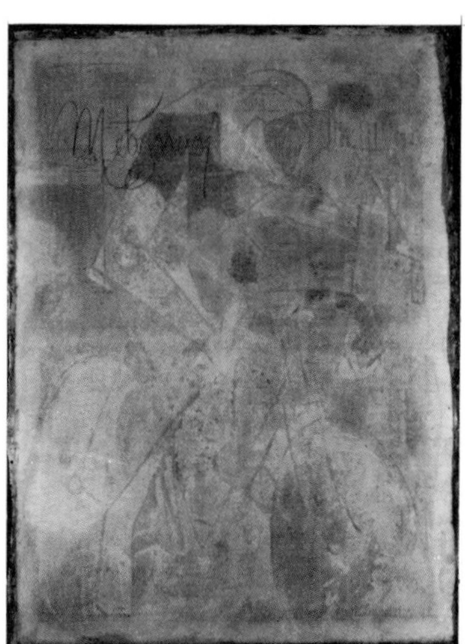

fig. a.
Reverse of cat. no. 115
before lining, 1982.

1. A recently discovered label, removed from the work in 1964, helped to establish the hitherto unknown Quinn ownership. Among the Quinn papers (New York Public Library) is a receipt for 4 pictures sent to Quinn on February 10, 1916. These were *At the Velodrome*, *A Cyclist*, *Head of a Young Girl*, and *Yellow Plume*. Each was priced at $100. All 4 had been shown in the Carroll Galleries' *Third Exhibition of Contemporary French Art*, March 8-April 3, 1915, where Quinn had seen them. Subsequent correspondence of March-August 1916 between Quinn and Harriet Bryant, of the Carroll Galleries, and Jean Metzinger (or his brother and agent, Maurice Metzinger) refers to Quinn's purchase of all 4 works, as does Quinn's own unpublished ledger, Vol. I.

fig. b.
Metzinger, pencil and black crayon on cream paper, 14¾ x 10¼ in., 37.5 x 26 cm., signed and dated l.r.: *Metzinger (1911)*, Musée National d'Art Moderne, Centre Georges Pompidou, Paris.

The dating of *Au Vélodrome* presents problems that are characteristic for Metzinger. Few of his works were dated at the time of execution, and a satisfactory chronology of his oeuvre remains to be undertaken. It has already been pointed out by the author that the task of tracing his stylistic development is especially difficult because of his persistently conservative and academic tendencies. (For a discussion of some of these issues, see A.Z.R. *Guggenheim*, Vol. II, pp. 510-14.)

Although the related drawing in the MNAM (fig. b) is dated 1911, the date and the signature appear to have been added at a later time, over an erased or scumbled area; moreover, the handwriting may not be Metzinger's. No dates for the work appear in the Quinn records, in his correspondence with Metzinger, or in published catalogues of his collection.

The organization of space and the relationship between foreground and background forms in *Au Vélodrome* suggest the influence of Juan Gris's 1913 style, although the treatment of form and structure lacks the pictorial rationale of the models. By retaining three-dimensional modeled forms and traditional perspective in parts of the composition while suppressing them in others, as he did in his landscapes of ca. 1913-14, Metzinger suggests the degree to which he continues to be drawn to traditional modes of representation. Nonetheless, *Au Vélodrome* achieves a level of individuality and resolution which is striking for the artist.

A date of 1914 for the work is the most plausible, though it is possible that the picture dates from late in 1913.

2. Included in the Neumann sale at Rains Galleries, New York, January 24, 1936, no. 64, but apparently bought in since the work continued to be exhibited after this date with Neumann as lender (see EXHIBITIONS).

EXHIBITIONS:[3]

New York, Carroll Galleries, *Third Exhibition of Contemporary French Art*, Mar. 8-Apr. 3, 1915, no. 33 (*At the Velodrome*); Toledo, Ohio, The Toledo Museum of Art, *Contemporary Movements in Painting*, Nov. 6-Dec. 11, 1938, no. 73 (*Bicyclist*), repr. n.p.;[4] New York, New Art Circle, *Documents of Modern Painting*, Sept. 23-Nov. 30, 1940 (checklist, *The Bicyclist*); Cincinnati Art Museum, *Expressionism*, Apr. 20-May 20, 1941, repr. p. 11 (*The Bicyclist*); Venice, *P.G.*, 1948 (Biennale), no. 85 ("*Velodromo*, 1944"); Florence, *P.G.*, 1949, no. 91 ("*Velodromo*, 1914"); Amsterdam, *P.G.*, 1951, no. 106; Zurich, *P.G.*, 1951, no. 100; London, *P.G.*, 1964-65, no. 12, repr.; Stockholm, *P.G.*, 1966-67, no. 12, repr.; New York, *P.G.*, 1969, p. 59, repr.; Paris, *P.G.*, 1974-75, no. 13, repr.; Torino, *P.G.*, 1975-76, no. 17, repr. pl. 7; New York, *P.G.*, 1982-83, no. 6, repr.

REFERENCES:

John Quinn: Collection of Paintings, Water Colors, Drawings and Sculpture, New York, 1926, p. 11 ("*Au Vélodrome*, 50½ x 38 in."); *Art News*, Jan. 18, 1936, repr. p. 20, announcement of the Rains sale (*Au Vélodrome*); New York, Rains Galleries, *modern paintings . . . watercolors and drawings from the collection of J. B. Neumann and from the studio of Hilaire Hiler*, Jan. 24, 1936, no. 64, repr. ("Au Vélodrome"); *Art Digest*, vol. 13, Dec. 1, 1938, repr. p. 12, review of Toledo exhibition (*Bicyclist*, lent by Neumann); Calas, 1966, p. 25, repr. p. 50 (*Cycle Racing Track*).

3. A one-man Metzinger exhibition opened at the Galerie Berthe Weil in Paris, May 27, 1914; no catalogue has been located. A fragment of an old French label on the stretcher of the present picture reads *N°1* "*Au Velodrome*" and may derive from this exhibition, but substantiating evidence remains to be found. The 1936 Neumann auction entry for the picture (see REFERENCES) includes the comment: "It was shown in many exhibitions." With the exception of the 1915 Carroll Galleries show, however, none have been traced. According to the catalogues of the *Salon des Indépendants* (1911-14) and the *Salon d'Automne* (1911-13), the picture was not shown in either.

4. Quinn purchased 2 paintings by Metzinger after the 1915 exhibition, *A Cyclist* and *At the Velodrome*; both appeared in the 1927 sale of his estate. *A Cyclist* was not reproduced in the catalogue of the sale but was described (no. 124) as representing a bicycle racer at the velodrome. It was purchased by Max J. Sulzberger for $65, but all trace of it has since been lost. Neumann occasionally referred to the companion piece (*Au Vélodrome*) as *The Bicyclist*, thereby introducing some confusion into the identification of the two works. The original title was restored by Peggy Guggenheim in 1948.

Joan Miró

Born April 1893, Barcelona.
Died December 1983, Palma, Majorca.

116 Peinture. 1925.
(*Painting; Two Personages and a flame*).

Color plate p. 254.

76.2553 PG 91

Oil on canvas (unvarnished), 45 1/8 x 57 3/8 (114.5 x 145.7).

Signed and dated l.r.: *Miró 1925*; on reverse (recorded, but not photographed before lining): *Joan Miró 1925*.

PROVENANCE:

Gift of Max Ernst, 1941.[1]

CONDITION:

In 1964 (Tate Report) the matte, unvarnished surface was described as in good condition. At an unknown date between 1964 and 1982, a vertical tear (ca. 3/4 in., 2 cm.) in the "flame" form, lower right, was repaired with a patch.

In 1982 (Venice) the patch was removed and the tear repaired with rice paper and Paraloid B-72 (at 20%) in acetone. A Fieux contact lining was applied; small losses were filled and inpainted with watercolors. A light coat of Paraloid B-72 (at 1% in acetone) was sprayed over the entire surface. The work was mounted on an ICA spring stretcher (untensioned).

Vertical and horizontal stretcher marks are clearly visible on the thinly painted surface, which is abraded in places. A graphite eye has been added to the "flame" form, certainly not by the artist. The edges of the lined canvas are somewhat distorted. Retouching is visible in the upper right corner and along the upper edge. The condition is stable. (New York, 1983.)

Toward the end of 1924 Miró's style changed markedly, and the works of 1925 represent a new departure in every sense. The immediately preceding paintings tended toward dense compositions of carefully delineated figurative detail. Even when elliptical (as in *The Family* or *The Hunter*), the imagery was clearly legible, the metaphors accessible. The subsequent development was of a different order. William Rubin has argued in connection with *The Birth of the World* (painted in the summer of 1925 and surely the masterpiece of the era) that the primary impetus for the change was undoubtedly Miró's contact with Masson and André Breton (*Miró in the Collection of The Museum of Modern Art*, New York, 1973, pp. 31-33). The ideas explored by Breton in his first Surrealist Manifesto of 1924, the "automatic" drawings Masson produced in the winter of 1923-24 and later, the notion of psychic automatism, and the efforts of the Surrealist poets to create forms that were more expressive in their freedom — all contributed in various ways to Miró's new style.

The most striking characteristic of his 1925 paintings was the loosely brushed, thinly applied background that covered the entire field of each canvas. By creating a monochromatic, but by no means unmodulated, surface, with no horizon line or other explicit spatial definition, Miró entirely suppressed all trace of traditional perspective for the first time in his work. But by handling the background in the works with extreme painterly subtlety — with infinite variations

1. Peggy Guggenheim presumed that Ernst had acquired the painting as a gift directly from Miró, although she was not certain.

116

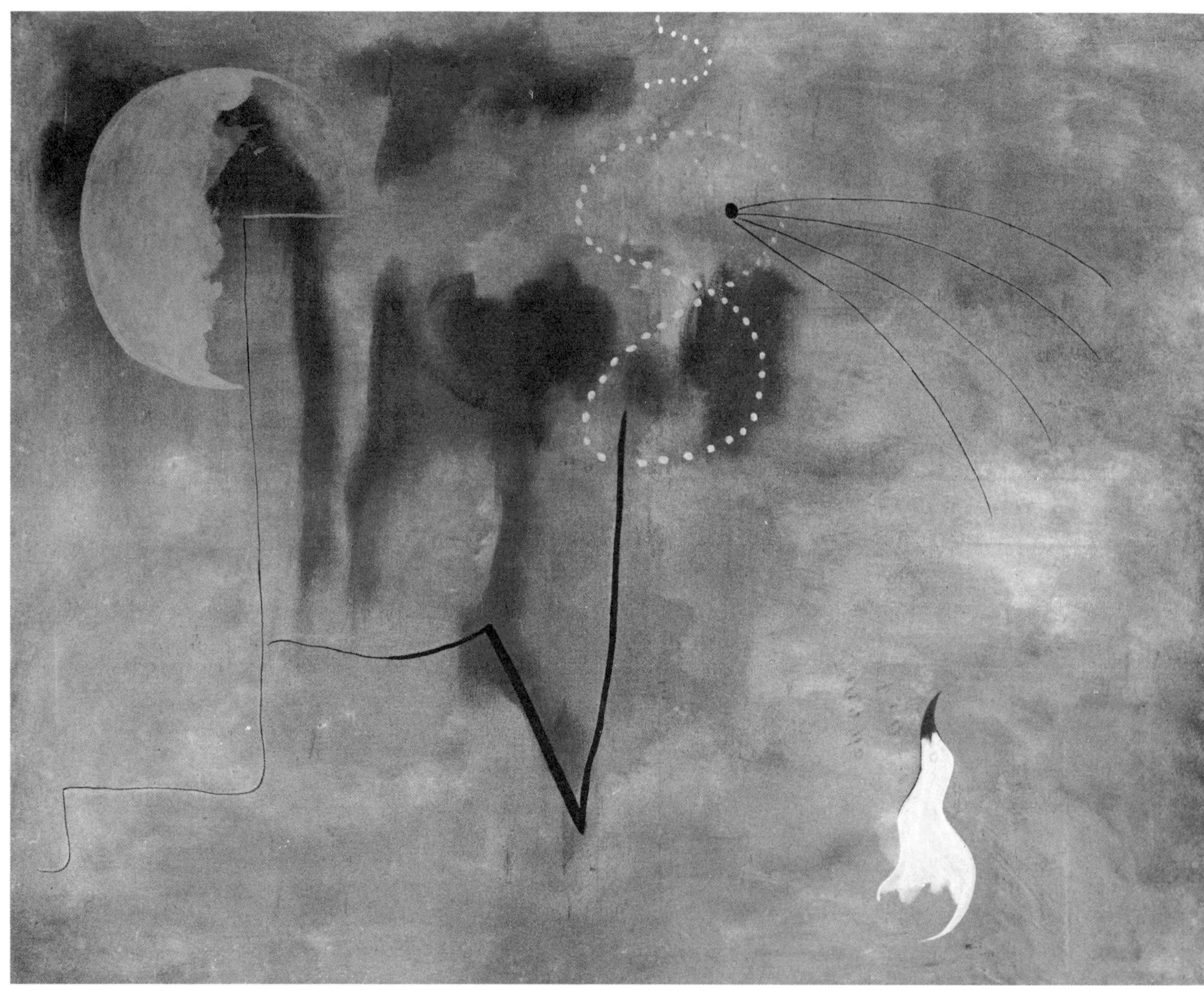

in texture, degrees of transparency, weight, and substance — he created what he himself called "an unlimited atmospheric space" (cited by Rubin, op. cit., p. 32). On this surface, he then "drew" his sparse and usually calligraphic compositions.

Although these paintings were described by Breton not long after their creation as "pure psychic automatism," it is clear — as Rubin, Rosalind Krauss, Margit Rowell, and others have pointed out — that Miró's procedure involved various stages of self-conscious deliberation. Whereas he undoubtedly allowed the process of free association to uncover motifs for him as he was "in the act of painting them" (Rubin, op. cit., p. 32), his own editing and shaping of the compositions as they developed were critical to the final result. In a conversation with James Johnson Sweeney several years later, Miró gave an eloquent description of this process: "rather than setting out to paint something, I begin painting and as I paint, the picture begins to assert itself, or suggest something under my brush. The form becomes a sign for a woman or a bird as I work.... The first stage is free, unconscious.... The second stage is carefully calculated" ("Joan Miró: Comment and Interview," *Partisan Review*, Feb. 15, 1948, p. 212).

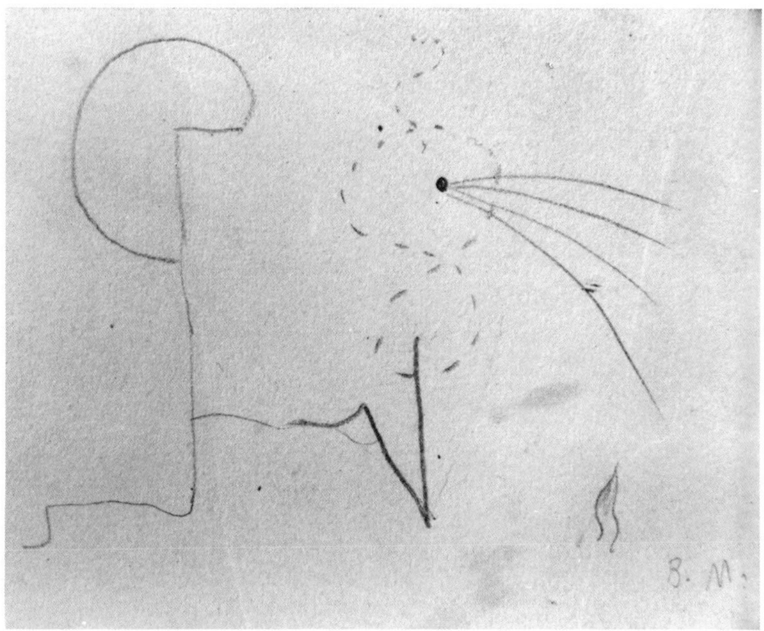

fig. a.
Study for *Peinture*, pencil on sketchbook page, 3 3/16 x 4 1/4 in., 8.2 x 10.8 cm., Collection Fundació Joan Miró, Barcelona.

Numerous preparatory drawings for paintings from different periods of Miró's life, which emerged relatively recently from his studio, have given additional substance to his statement (*Dessins de Miró*, exh. cat., MNAM, Paris, 1978). Some of these drawings show rather clear imagery from which a more indeterminate form has evolved; others—such as fig. a, a study for *Peinture*—closely approximate the imagery of the completed painting, and give no inkling of a possible earlier figural "source." It is not always easy to establish precisely the role such drawings played within the compositional process. But it seems most likely that they emerged while Miró was actually working on the painting and not in advance. In this sense, they represent some part of the "carefully calculated" second stage.

The technical procedure used by Miró in *Peinture* was in some respects similar to that of *The Birth of the World*, although the latter work is far more innovative technically and aesthetically. In *Peinture*, a glue sizing was first applied to the canvas in irregular densities. The paint was then brushed on in an extremely fluid form, very low in oil content, producing a matte, dry surface. In some areas the paint appears merely to stain the canvas with lighter or darker shades of sienna; in others, scumbled smudges and spots have been created by rubbing the paint (over slightly thicker sizing) with a cloth while it was still wet. This combination of thinly applied washes and slightly denser scumbled rubbings is characteristic of most of the 1925 paintings.

Rosalind Krauss has elucidated the function of line in these works: "It was as though part of Miró's thinking ... was focused on the problem of how to deprive line of its 'natural' weight. A line that was allowed to curve back on itself to close the contour of a figure would interrupt the liquidity of the color field, damming its flow by the suggestion of a corporeal presence.... Miró's line turns away from description in these paintings, and becomes something else. In places it is perforated, a dotted line marking an object's placement within the space of the picture, without however embodying the object.... At other places the line becomes pictograph, charging the field with Miró's own special meanings and associations" ("Magnetic Fields: The Structure," in *Magnetic Fields*, exh. cat., SRGM, New York, 1972, p. 14). In emphasizing the function of line, and the premeditation involved in its use, Krauss further clarifies the extent to which the paintings must be seen as much more than the product of psychic automatism or of dreams (even though Miró, according to his own testimony, sometimes incorporated hallucinatory images into the paintings — see Krauss, op. cit., p. 15).

The degree to which the images or "signs" (as Miró called them) are interpretable as a legible iconography varies a great deal in these paintings. Krauss and Rowell have demonstrated convincingly that the paintings of the years 1924-27 were deeply affected by the poetic environment in which Miró lived — an environment not only of poets but of *peinture-poésie*. In many instances, the rich vocabulary of "signs" he evolved presents clearly discernible allusions to actual poetic sources; in others it offers clues to a more elusive but nonetheless recognizable erotic or visionary subject matter. In some cases, however, perhaps especially in these 1925 paintings, the "signs" are as often purely pictorial as allusive.

Miró rarely titled the paintings of that year himself, and his strong objections to the misleading (and often vulgarizing) titles that have been attached to some of them since their creation were reported by Jacques Dupin (1962, pp. 166, 168). In the specific case of the Peggy Guggenheim painting, Miró categorically rejected the title (*Deux personnages et une flamme*) by which it has traditionally been known, and suggested that the picture had no title at all.[2] The absence of titles has the effect, of course, of concentrating attention on the significance of Miró's purely pictorial choices or decisions rather than on the "representational" or even symbolic meaning of particular figures and images. In describing his work on *The Birth of the World*, for example, Miró emphasized precisely this pictorial aspect of the creative process: "One large patch of black in the upper left seemed to need to become bigger. I enlarged it and went over it with opaque black paint. It became a triangle to which I added a tail. It might be a bird" (Rubin, op. cit., p. 33). The important issue here, obviously, is the pictorial role of the black, not its identity, or lack of identity, as a bird. Similarly, by preferring the title *Peinture* to *Deux personnages et une flamme*, Miró seemed to be giving priority to pictorial considerations and—at the very least—subordinating other forms of meaning. He may actually have wished to rule out the specific interpretation implied by that title, suggesting thereby that the "signs" he had placed

2. In response to questions from the author, conveyed by Rowell, January 1979.

on the canvas did not lend themselves to such a reading. From another point of view, however, he may simply have been insisting that his iconography was intentionally ambiguous and nonrestrictive in nature.[3]

EXHIBITIONS:

New York, Art of This Century, 1942-47, p. 112 ("*Two Personages and a Flame*," the title under which it has traditionally been published in subsequent *P.G.* publications); Venice, *P.G.*, 1948 (Biennale), no. 86; Florence, *P.G.*, 1949, no. 92; Amsterdam, *P.G.*, 1951, no. 107; Zurich, *P.G.*, 1951, no. 101; London, *P.G.*, 1964-65, no. 81 (*Painting*); Stockholm, *P.G.*, 1966-67, no. 78 (*Painting*); Torino, Galleria Civica d'Arte Moderna, *Le Muse Inquietanti*, Nov. 1967-Jan. 1968, no. 250, repr.; New York, *P.G.*, 1969, p. 101, repr.; Paris, *P.G.*, 1974-75, no. 83, repr. (*Painting*); Torino, *P.G.*, 1975-76, no. 89; New York, *P.G.*, 1982-83, no. 36, repr.

REFERENCES:

P. Guggenheim, *Art of This Century*, 1942, p. 112; J. Dupin, *Joan Miró: Life and Work*, New York, 1962, cat. no. 129, repr. (*Painting*); Calas, 1966, pp. 110-11, repr. p. 126; R. Penrose, *Miró*, New York, 1969, p. 48, repr. pl. 29.

3. For a note on the multiplicity of meanings conveyed by Miró's signs in relation to the SRGM's 1925 *Personnage*, see A.Z.R. *Guggenheim*, 1976, Vol. II, pp. 521-24.

Images such as the dot radiating spokes in *Peinture* have been convincingly interpreted in other contexts within Miró's oeuvre as representative of male genitals, or of an eye projecting lines of vision, or of a star. When formed out of colored dots, the same image has been seen to function as fireworks. The flame occurs with great frequency and has been read as the "element" of fire, or as expressive of sexual excitement or the female sex. Meanwhile, the dotting of lines was described by Miró—in conversation with Rubin—in purely pictorial terms, devoid of any symbolic significance. It was a means of changing the speed of the line "purely for the sake of equilibrium." In the case of the meandering dotted line behind the *Hunter*, for example, Miró suggested that it "might be construed as indicating the volume of the hunter's body, just as the dotted lines of the sardine allude to its volume, but the decision to introduce them was entirely based on compositional needs" (op. cit., p. 26). The images or "signs" in *Peinture* occur in other paintings and may carry analogous or related meanings. But Miró's continual modification of such motifs precludes a simple or mechanical interpretation. The ambiguities implicit in the iconography remain.

117 **Intérieur hollandais.**
Montroig, summer 1928.
(*Dutch Interior II*).

Color plate p. 255.

76.2553 PG 92

Oil on canvas (unvarnished), $36\frac{1}{4}$ x $28\frac{3}{4}$ (92.0 x 73.0).

Signed and dated on reverse: *Joan Miró / Intérieur hollandais / 1928*.

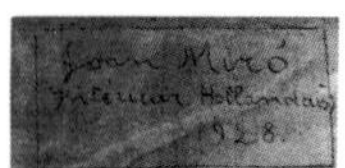

PROVENANCE:

Remained with the artist until at least 1937 (see EXHIBITIONS); acquired by Peggy Guggenheim, Paris, 1940.[1]

CONDITION:

In 1964 (Tate Report) the work was described as in extremely fragile condition and unsafe to travel. The matte unvarnished pigment showed signs of extensive crackle with blistering, cleavage, and losses, especially in the yellow area top right half (where the color was changing), and in the lower right third of the composition. Considerable retouching of the upper left corner, the right edge, and a large section in the lower left quadrant was observed. It is not clear whether conservation was attempted at this time.

Some conservation measures were apparently taken in Venice in 1974, but no written record survives.

In 1982 (Venice) the bonding of the yellow and white areas was found to be extremely poor, with extensive flaking. In these areas, and at the lower right (brown), discolored previous fixatives and retouching were also noted. The cleaving paint in the yellow area was consolidated with Paraloid B-72 in a 3% solution. The retouched areas lower right (brown) were cleaned with dimethylformamide. Inpainting of discolored areas and losses was carried out with Windsor and Newton watercolors and Maimeri varnish colors. The surface was lightly sprayed with Paraloid B-72 (at 2%). The condition is fragile. (Venice, Nov. 1982.)

In the spring of 1928, Miró made a two-week journey to Holland. He was deeply impressed by Dutch genre and still-life painting, and returned to Montroig for the summer with a collection of postcards purchased at the Rijksmuseum and elsewhere.[2] As he later explained to Dora Vallier: "*Autour de 1928, je faisais souvent des tableaux à partir d'une carte postale.... C'étaient des cartes postales très banales, tout à fait réalistes et elles me servaient comme point de départ. Avant d'aboutir au tableau je faisais beaucoup de dessins préparatoires, de plus en plus libres, de plus en plus détachés du sujet.... J'ai fait aussi des 'Intérieurs hollandais' en procédant de la même manière*" (*Cahiers d'Art*, vol. 33-35, 1960, p. 168). Though he described the postcards as "*banales*" he also indicated to Vallier precisely why the achievements of the Dutch painters struck him so forcibly: "*Lors de mon voyage en Hollande, ce qui m'a vraiment impressionné,*

1. Peggy Guggenheim was unable to recall where she purchased this work but thought that it came from D.-H. Kahnweiler. The work did not, however, pass through Kahnweiler's gallery. She subsequently suggested Pierre Loeb as the most likely alternative; it has thus far not proved possible to establish this provenance with certainty.

2. See Sweeney, 1949 and 1954; Gullón; W. Erben, *Joan Miró*, New York, 1959, pp. 125-27; also Vallier, Dupin, Lassaigne, Penrose, and Rubin, who all discuss Miró's transformation of his Dutch sources. Erben was the first to examine the original postcards and drawings with Miró, and to present the relationship in some detail. Rubin's numbered diagram of *Dutch Interior I* identifies every element in the Miró version in terms of Sorgh's original composition.

fig. a.
Jan Steen, *The Dancing Lesson*, not dated, oil on canvas, 27 x 23 1/4 in., 68.5 x 59 cm., Rijksmuseum, Amsterdam.

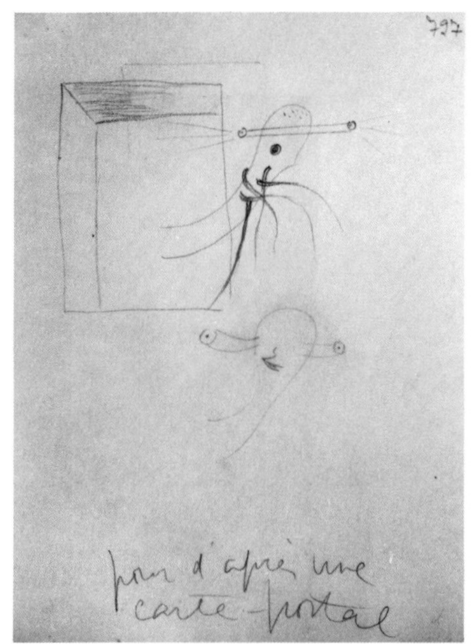

fig. b.
Miró, Study for cat. no. 117, 1928, pencil on paper, 5 5/16 x 4 3/4 in., 13.6 x 12 cm., Fundació Joan Miró, Barcelona.

c'était une nature morte dans laquelle on pouvait voire même les objets pas plus grands qu'une puce. J'ai été séduit par cette capacité des peintres hollandais de faire ressortir des points minuscules comme des grains de poussière et de concentrer l'attention sur une petite étincelle au milieu de l'obscurité. C'est là leur grand pouvoir de fascination" (ibid.).

Dutch Interior II is based on Jan Steen's *De Dansles* (*The Dancing Lesson*) (Rijksmuseum, Amsterdam; fig. a). It was the second of three such interiors, the first, *Dutch Interior I,* based on H. M. Sorgh's *The Lutanist* of 1661 (MoMA, Rubin, 1973, pp. 43-45). The source for the third in the series, *Dutch Interior III* (Private Collection, New York), has apparently not been identified.

From an examination of the surviving drawings (figs. b-g) and the original source (fig. a), it can be seen that Miró's transformation involved a complex process of borrowing, adaptation, and metamorphosis. In some cases he enlarged and flattened out his figures drastically, combining figural source with pictorial effect. In the case of the white balloonlike figure of the "man" at the left of *Dutch Interior II*, for example, Miró increased the relative scale of Steen's figure, but also endowed him with the striking accent of light carried by the white linen napkin on the far right of Steen's painting. Steen's hat plume in Miró's work becomes a vast encircling ribbon around the entire composition—expressive of the much more muted, but nonetheless palpable, circular rhythm of Steen's group. In other instances, Miró reduced Steen's figures to miniscule ciphers: Steen's dancing cat, which in fig. e has a momentary incarnation as a ballerina, becomes a tiny black "sign" of indeterminate species, his black frying pan (left), in Miró's imaginative metamorphosis, a combination object and fish-

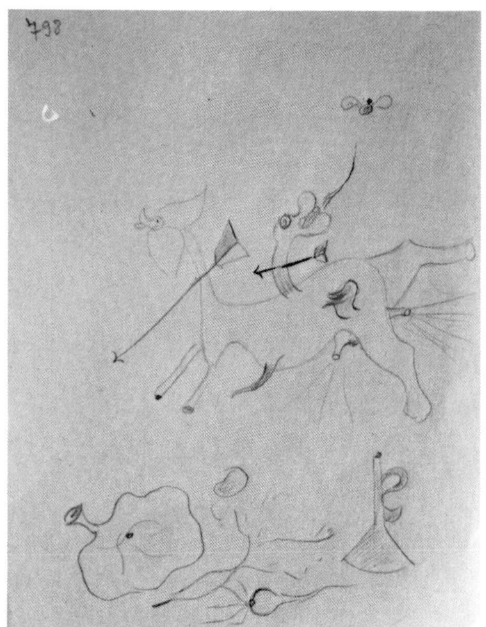

fig. c.
Miró, Study for cat no. 117, 1928, pencil on paper, 8⅝ x 6⅝ in., 21.9 x 16.8 cm., Fundació Joan Miró, Barcelona.

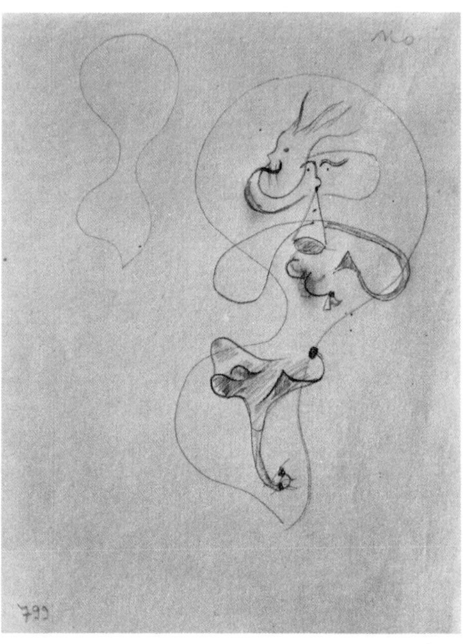

fig. d.
Miró, Study for female figure in cat. no. 117, 1928, pencil on paper, 8⅝ x 6⅝ in., 21.9 x 16.8 cm., Fundació Joan Miró, Barcelona.

fig. e.
Miró, Study for man with "dancer" in cat. no. 117, 1928, pencil on paper, 8⅝ x 6⅝ in., 21.9 x 16.8 cm., Fundació Joan Miró, Barcelona.

fig. f.
Miró, Studies for bird-fish with frying pan and chair (lower left corner), for man (upper left), for cups, pitchers (lower right), 1928, pencil on paper, 8⅝ x 6⅝ in., 21.9 x 16.8 cm., Fundació Joan Miró, Barcelona.

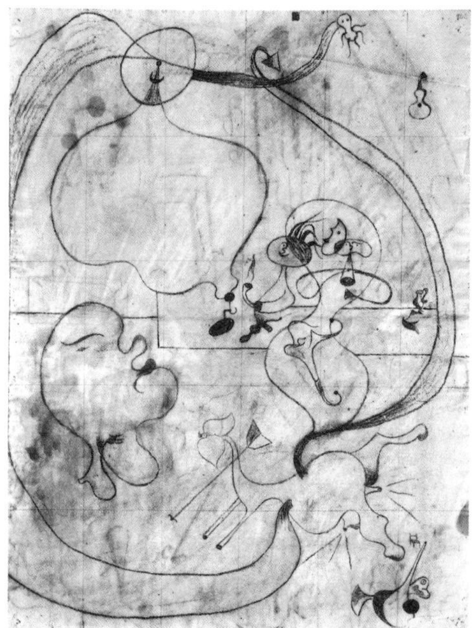

fig. g.
Miró, final preparatory drawing (squared) for cat. no. 117, 1928, charcoal on paper, 24¼ x 18¾ in., 61.5 x 47.5 cm., Fundació Joan Miró, Barcelona.

fig. h.
Miró, *Dutch Interior I*, 1928, oil on canvas, 36⅛ x 28¾ in., 92 x 73 cm., The Museum of Modern Art, New York.

bird (lower right). In the sketch designated as first in Miró's numbering of his sketchbook pages, he explored the idea of assigning the window and its peering "voyeur" a wittily prominent role in the drama (fig. b); but by the end of the process, the figure had been entirely suppressed and the window reduced to a miniature "sign."

Other characters hover between resemblance and total transformation. The young boy at the center of Steen's group survives in strikingly recognizable form in Miró's version — even his pipe, with realistically rendered smoke, remains intact.

The buxom musician retains something of her curvilinear shape — rendered schematically as a figure eight — in both the drawing (fig. d) and the final painting. Miró, with virtuoso draftsmanship, combines the essential swirls of her full, sweeping skirt into a single rippling apron form, which becomes somewhat flattened and decorative in the painting. The puckered brow and puffed up cheeks, the encircling arms and short stubby "horn" (replacing the longer variety in Steen's original), are taken through to the painting itself, although the breasts are abandoned at that stage. While the musician may lose some of her alluring femininity, the dog—the most recognizable quotation of all—acquires (in the drawings and the final painting) an erotic persona. Here Miró's emphasis proves characteristically perspicacious, however, for within Steen's "banal" scene, there are clear erotic implications.

Perhaps the most whimsical and evocative metamorphosis is that of the plump young child at the left of Steen's painting, converted by Miró into a biomorphic figure of potatolike proportions and mien.

Finally, in his reduction to miniature scale of the lute (guitar), chair, pitcher, and window, Miró seems to be paying homage to the Dutch artist's capacity *"de faire ressortir des points minuscules comme des grains de poussière et de concentrer l'attention sur une petite étincelle au milieu de l'obscurité."*

The elaborately precise final drawing, executed in charcoal, served as a cartoon, its squaring corresponding to that of the canvas itself.[3] Miró was, at this stage, prepared to leave nothing to chance. The balance between the elements and their intricate relationship to the Jan Steen source had been established in minute detail, and only in the (all-important) application of color did Miró apparently allow himself to proceed in a more characteristically intuitive fashion.

EXHIBITIONS:

New York, Valentine Gallery, *Joan Miró*, Oct. 20-Nov. 8, 1930, no. 8 or 9 (both "*Intérieur Hollandais*, 1928");[4] Chicago, The Arts Club of Chicago, *Exhibition of Paintings by Joan Miró*, Jan. 27-Feb. 17, 1931, no. 8 or 9 (both "*L'intérieur Hollandais*, 1928," repr. cover); Tokyo, Nippon Salon, *Exposition Internationale du Surréalisme*, June 9-14, 1937, no. 82 ("*Peinture*, 1925"; the works in this exhibition were selected and sent to Japan by the artists themselves); New York, Art of This Century, 1942-47, p. 112; Venice, *P.G.*, 1948 (Biennale), no. 87, repr.; Florence, *P.G.*, 1949, no. 93; Amsterdam, *P.G.*, 1951, no. 108, repr. p. 49; Zurich, *P.G.*, 1951, no. 102; London, *P.G.*, 1964-65, no. 82, repr.; Stockholm, *P.G.*, 1966-67, no. 79, repr. p. 44; Torino, Galleria Civica d'Arte Moderna, *Le Muse Inquietanti*, Nov. 1967-Jan. 1968, no. 255, repr.; New York, *P.G.*, 1969, p. 102, repr. p. 103; Paris, *P.G.*, 1974-75, no. 84, repr.; Torino, *P.G.*, 1975-76, no. 90, repr. pl. 47.

REFERENCES:

E. Tériade, "Documents sur la jeune peinture," *Cahiers d'Art*, vol. 4, nos. 8-9, 1929, repr. [p. 364]; J. G. Frey, "Miró and the Surrealists," *Parnassus*, Oct. 1936, p. 14; P. Guggenheim, *Art of This Century*, 1942, p. 112; J. J. Sweeney, "Miró," *Theatre Arts*, Mar. 1949, pp. 39-41, repr.; R. Gullón, "Juan Miró, por el camino de la poesia," *De Goya al arte abstracto*, Madrid, 1952, pp. 122-23, 132-33; J. J. Sweeney, "Miró," *Art News Annual*, XXIII, 1954, pp. 186-87, repr. p. 71; G. Ribemont-Dessaignes, *Joan Miró*, Paris, 1956, pp. 81-82; D. Vallier, "Avec Miró," *Cahiers d'Art*, vols. 33-35, 1960, p. 168, repr. p. 167; J. Dupin, *Joan Miró: Life and Work*, New York, 1962, pp. 170-71 (studies), 189-98, cat. no. 235, repr. pl. 25; J. Lassaigne, *Miró*, Geneva, 1963, pp. 54-55, 58-61, repr. color p. 57; Calas, 1966, p. 111, repr. color p. 127; R. Penrose, *Miró*, New York, 1969, pp. 62-63, 172; W. S. Rubin, *Miró in the Collection of The Museum of Modern Art*, New York, 1973, pp. 43-45, 119-20; L. Flint, *Handbook*, 1983, p. 120, repr. color p. 121.

3. The squaring is visible in several places where the paint has lost opacity or where actual losses have occurred. In this respect, as in many others, Miró's procedure in the Peggy Guggenheim painting closely approximates that of *Dutch Interior I*. Rubin's discussion of the latter illuminates many aspects of Miró's procedure in both pictures. A full study of *Dutch Interior III* remains to be undertaken. It shares some characteristics with the Peggy Guggenheim painting, especially the encircling ribbon (or serpent?) form, which surrounds the figure.

4. The entire Valentine Gallery exhibition traveled to Chicago, where Peggy Guggenheim's picture was reproduced on the cover of the catalogue. The pictures must have been sent to Valentine Dudensing on consignment; those unsold were then apparently returned to the artist after the 2 exhibitions.

118 Femme assise II. Paris, February 27, 1939. (*Seated Woman II*).

Color plate p. 399.

76.2553 PG 93

Oil on canvas (unvarnished), $63\frac{3}{4}$ x $51\frac{3}{16}$ (162 x 130).

Signed u.r.: *Miró*; on reverse: *JOAN MIRÓ / "Femme assise II" / 27 / II / 1939.*

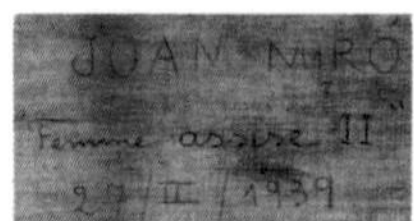

PROVENANCE:

Purchased from the artist by Pierre Matisse, summer 1939 (correspondence with the author, Jan. 10, 1978); purchased from Pierre Matisse, November 15, 1941.

CONDITION:

In 1964 (Tate Report) the matte unvarnished surface was described as in good condition. Some minor damage at the bottom edge was noted. The picture was surface cleaned.

In 1974 (Venice) the work was restored. Extensive retouching of the edges and of the ocher areas apparently dates from this time, though no written record of this restoration survives.

The open-weave support is brittle and weak; there are tears at the edges and at all corners. The paint layer is poorly bonded to the thin, granular ground and there are extensive linear cracks in the paint film, with scattered losses. Miró himself apparently added some retouches and dots in various locations after the work was dry: the lead white of these additions is clearly distinct from the whites used elsewhere and from that of the restoration. The overall condition is extremely fragile. (New York, July 1982.)

Femme assise II was painted in Miró's Paris studio, rue Blanqui, in February 1939; it followed by two months the entirely different *Femme assise I*, now in the collection of MoMA (fig. a).[1] Both paintings depict a woman with a long neck and arms raised. In each an oval sun (red in the first version, black in the

fig. a.
Miró, *Femme assise I*, oil on canvas, $64\frac{3}{8}$ x $51\frac{5}{8}$ in., 163.5 x 131.1 cm., signed and dated on reverse: *Joan Miro / Femme assise I / 24 / 12 / 1938*, The Museum of Modern Art, New York, Fractional Gift of Mr. and Mrs. William A. Weintraub.

1. Dupin, 1962, p. 345, confused the sequence and dates of the 2 works, placing Peggy Guggenheim's first, on December 4, 1938, the companion piece second, on December 7.

118

second) is juxtaposed with a rectangular window in the upper right; in each the sex of the woman is a central focus: in the case of *Femme assise I*, it is grotesquely, if whimsically, enlarged — a spider form within a fiery "solar" oval. William Rubin has pointed out that it is presented as a pictorial analogy to the similarly fiery sun and to the head, functioning thus as a dual symbol.[2] In the case of *Femme assise II*, the sex has become "a precious delicate pendant attached to a lurid 'baroque' necklace inside which a little threatening head of the same shape seems to be lusting for it" (Dupin, 1962, p. 512). The menacing nature

2. 1973, pp. 78 and 130. The frequent correspondence among heads, suns, and sexual identity in Miró's iconography has been elucidated by Rubin and, extensively, by R. E. Krauss and M. Rowell in *Magnetic Fields*, exh. cat., SRGM, New York, 1972.

of this image is suggestive of the marked contrast between the two works as a whole.

In *Femme assise I*, "the large, simply contoured, and almost relentlessly flat forms play host to pure colors of a saturation beyond anything posited in Miró's earlier work" (Rubin, 1973, p. 78). The black upper body and brilliant Prussian blue skirt are silhouetted against a pure yellow wall (above) and black floor (below). "The head floats like a red balloon attached to the neck by a linear string, and the breasts and hands are drolly miniscule in relation to the giant torso" (ibid.).

Femme assise II, by contrast, is a painting of violently expressive form and content. The wall behind the figure is a scumbled, rubbed, and viscous combination of white, bister, gray, and blue. The details of the head, with its open screaming mouth, are painted, as Dupin has suggested, with "as much minuteness as cruelty" (1962, p. 312). The woman's left hand, which "seems hideously mutilated," is similarly treated with frenzied but intricate brushstrokes, mirroring in color and form the green, black, white, red, and ocher minutiae of the grotesque head. As Penrose noted (1969, p. 94), the blackness of the entire figure (so unlike the vibrant colorful juxtapositions in *Femme assise I*) "belongs to the night"—a fact underlined by the black shadow over the sun at the upper right. The portrait is menacing both in its iconography and in its handling of paint.

When questioned in 1979 about the meaning of the image, Miró replied thoughtfully that it was a direct response to events in the Spanish Civil War, that it was "*très violent*" and "*tragique*."[3] The explication is especially telling in light of Miró's 1939 response to a questionnaire formulated by Georges Duthuit on the relationship between art and politics:

> *Le monde extérieur, les événements contemporains ne cessent d'influencer le peintre, cela va de soi. Le jeu des lignes et des couleurs, s'il ne met pas à nu le drame du créateur, n'est rien d'autre qu'un divertissement bourgeois. Les formes qu'exprime l'individu attaché à la société doivent déceler le mouvement d'une âme qui veut s'évader de la réalité présente, d'un caractère particulièrement ignoble aujourd'hui, puis s'approcher de réalités neuves, offrir enfin aux autres hommes une possibilité d'élévation.... Si nous ne tâchons pas de découvrir l'essence religieuse, le sens magique des choses, nous ne ferons qu'ajouter de nouvelles sources d'abrutissement à celles qui sont offertes aujourd'hui aux peuples, sans compter.*
>
> *L'horrible tragédie que nous traversons peut secouer quelques génies isolés et leur donner une vigueur accrue. Que les puissances de régression connues sous le nom de fascisme s'étendent encore cependant, qu'elles nous plongent un peu plus avant dans l'impasse de la cruauté et de l'incompréhension, et c'en est fini de toute dignité humaine....*
>
> *...Mais ce qui compte, dans une œuvre, ce n'est pas ce qu'y veulent découvrir trop d'intellectuels, c'est ce qu'elle entraine, dans son mouvement ascendant,*

3. In response to questions from the author, transmitted by M. Rowell, January 1979.

de faits vécus, de vérité humaine les trouvailles plastiques n'ayant en elles-mêmes aucune espèce d'importance. Il ne faut donc pas confondre les engagements proposés à l'artiste par les politiciens professionnels et autres spécialistes de l'agitation avec la nécessité profonde qui lui fait prendre part aux convulsions sociales, l'attache, lui et son œuvre, à la chair et au cœur du prochain et fait, du besoin de libération de tous, son propre besoin (Cahiers d'Art, vol. 14, nos. 1-4, 1939, p. 73).

Miró's insistence here on the artist's need to use his own form of expression to participate in the social upheavals of his day acts as a telling commentary on the image of *Femme assise II*: "What counts in a work of art is not what intellectuals seek to discover there, but what the work carries, in its ascendant movement, of living events, of human truth."

Miró's native city of Barcelona fell to the Nationalists in late January 1939. Whether the painting constituted a direct response to this event or a more general comment on the "powers of regression known as fascism" is not clear. Miró had painted an equally grotesque and violent *Tête de Femme* in 1938 (repr. Penrose, 1969, pl. 64). But the events of late January 1939, which struck especially intensely at the heart of his own past, might well have given rise to the tragic transformation of *Femme assise I* into *Femme assise II*. The first was completed on Christmas Eve 1938; the second in February 1939. In some sense, Miró may well have been giving expression in the "violent" and "tragic" second version to his sense of the artist's "need to participate in the universal search for liberation."[4]

EXHIBITIONS:

New York, Pierre Matisse Gallery, *Paintings—Gouaches—Joan Miró*, Apr. 10-May 6, 1939, no. 5 (*Woman seated II*, 1938); New York, Art of This Century, 1942-47, p. 112, repr. p. 114 (dated 1938-39); New York, Art of This Century, *15 Early, 15 Late Paintings*, Mar. 13-Apr. 10, 1943, no. 224 (dated 1938-39); Venice, *P.G.*, 1948 (Biennale), no. 88 (dated 1939, the date henceforth ascribed to it in *P.G.* publications); Florence, *P.G.*, 1949, no. 94, repr.; Amsterdam, *P.G.*, 1951, no. 109, repr. p. 48; Zurich, *P.G.*, 1951, no. 103, repr.; London, *P.G.*, 1964-65, no. 83, repr.; Stockholm, *P.G.*, 1966-67, no. 80, repr.; Torino, Galleria Civica d'Arte Moderna, *Le Muse Inquietanti*, Nov. 1967-Jan. 1968, no. 258, repr.; New York, *P.G.*, 1969, p. 104, repr. color p. 105; Paris, *P.G.*, 1974-75, p. 85, repr. color n.p.; Torino, *P.G.*, 1975-76, no. 91, repr. pl. 48; Rome, *Guggenheim: Venezia-New York*, 1982, no. 49, repr. color; Houston, Museum of Fine Arts, *Miró in America*, Apr. 21-June 27, 1982; New York, *P.G.*, 1982-83, no. 37, repr. color.

REFERENCES:

P. Guggenheim, *Art of This Century*, 1942, p. 112, repr. p. 114 (dated 1938-39); J. Dupin, *Joan Miró: Life and Work*, New York, 1962, no. 517, pp. 312, 345, repr. p. 335 ("*Seated Woman I*, Dec. 4, 1938"); Calas, 1966, p. 112, repr. color p. 128; W. S. Rubin, *Dada, Surrealism, and Their Heritage*, New York, 1968, pp. 132, 135, repr. ("*Seated Woman I*, 1938"); R. Penrose, *Miró*, New York, 1969, pp. 92-94, repr. p. 93 ("*Seated Woman I*, 1938"); W. S. Rubin, *Miró in the Collection of The Museum of Modern Art*, New York, 1973, pp. 78, 130, repr. p. 130 (*Seated Woman II*, 1939); J. Miró, *Carnets Catalans*, Tome II, Geneva, 1976, pp. 63, 147 (dated "4.12.38"); B. Rose, *Miró in America*, exh. cat., Houston, 1982, pp. 22-23.

4. For a discussion of a comparable possible relationship between González's "*Monsieur*" *Cactus* and the fall of Barcelona, see cat. no. 72.

Piet Mondrian

Born March 1872, Amersfoort.
Died February 1944, New York.

119 Untitled (Oval Composition).
Paris, 1914.
(*Scaffold*).

76.2553 PG 37

Charcoal on wood-pulp wove paper, glued to Homosote panel. Dimensions of paper: 60 x 39⅜ (152.5 x 100); dimensions of panel: 60 x 40½ x ½ (152.5 x 102.8 x 1.3).

Signed and dated l.r.: *PM 12.*

PROVENANCE:

Collection of the artist, 1914-42; purchased from Valentine Dudensing, New York, February 1942 (see below, cat. no. 120, fn. 1).

CONDITION:

See below, cat. no. 120. The conservation history and condition problems of the 2 works are comparable; in both cases the paper is extremely brittle and the work thus very fragile. (Venice, Nov. 1982.)

fig. a.
Mondrian, Paris facades, pencil on paper, 6½ x 4⅛ in., 17 x 10.5 cm., Marlborough Fine Art (London), Ltd. Loose sheet from Mondrian Sketchbook III.

fig. b.
Mondrian, *Composition in Oval (Tableau III)*, oil on canvas, 55⅛ x 39¾ in., 104 x 101 cm., Stedelijk Museum, Amsterdam.

As has been pointed out by Joop Joosten (1980, p. 66), this monumental charcoal drawing represents a stage in Mondrian's development of *Composition in Oval (Tableau III)* (fig. b).

Mondrian moved to Paris by May of 1912, but — as established by both Robert Welsh and Joosten — it was not until 1913 that he began to concentrate on facades of buildings. Some of the facades he chose were visible from the windows of his apartment at 26 rue du Départ; others were in the immediate vicinity of Montparnasse. (See R. P. Welsh, *Piet Mondrian*, exh. cat., The Art Gallery of Toronto, 1966, pp. 144-54; idem and J. M. Joosten, *Two Mondrian Sketchbooks: 1912-1914*, Amsterdam, 1969, especially pp. 72-82; J. M. Joosten, "Mondrian Between Cubism and Abstraction," in *Piet Mondrian: A Centennial Exhibition*, SRGM, New York, 1971, pp. 60-61.) During the winter of 1913-14, Mondrian made a considerable number of such sketches and, as Joosten has suggested, there was a strong correlation between the rectilinear character of the buildings he chose as his "models" and the increasingly strong emphasis on a horizontal-vertical structure in his compositions.

Included among the several drawings that probably preceded the Peggy Guggenheim example is undoubtedly a loose sketchbook page (fig. a) depicting rather realistically rendered corner facades. Joosten had identified this sheet as originating in Mondrian's Sketchbook III, dating from the 1913-14 Paris period in question.

The Peggy Guggenheim drawing retains numerous characteristics of the small sketch, including the three-dimensional definition of the projecting portion of the central building, the location of the windows, and the articulation of the wall surfaces. However, Mondrian obviously adapted the sketch to suit his evolving ideas, while proceeding to create a composition based on strong vertical and horizontal axes contained within an arbitrary pictorial oval. With this drawing he was, in effect, moving through the process of flattening and abstraction that led ultimately to the firmer, clearer, and more uncompromising resolution of the Stedelijk painting.[1]

The scale of the oval image in the Peggy Guggenheim drawing is almost exactly the same as that of the finished painting — although the actual sheet of the drawing is even larger than the Stedelijk canvas. It is thus clear that in some sense the Venice drawing served as a form of "cartoon," the term carrying a complex and somewhat unconventional meaning when applied to Mondrian, however: in certain cases, the final drawing is in fact comprehensive in its articulation of the details of a finished painting; in other instances — such as the Peggy Guggenheim work — the drawing serves a more preparatory purpose.

The Stedelijk painting (fig. b) represents a more advanced stage of abstraction than the Venice drawing. Nonetheless, it is unlikely that any further drawings intervened between the two: it would appear rather that Mondrian treated the Venice "scale" drawing as a basic *modello* and continued to a final resolution of the image in charcoal on the primed canvas itself. Extensive painted *pentimenti* and some underdrawing can be seen in the Amsterdam *Oval Composition* in those areas where the paint has lost its opacity, lending support to such a hypothesis, which is in any case entirely characteristic of Mondrian's practice in a great many other works (see, for example, *Composition 1916* in the SRGM collection, A.Z.R. *Guggenheim*, 1976, Vol. II, p. 575; and the discussion below, cat. no. 120). An examination of the surface of the Stedelijk painting (and of related works of 1914) with infra-red reflectography would serve to clarify Mondrian's actual process of composition and the extent to which he arrived at the final stages of this composition through a complex process of drawing on the canvas itself.[2]

It is interesting to note that the image in the cartoon, while generally defined by an oval format, is not entirely contained within the oval, except at the right and bottom edges. On the other two sides the oval is implied, but can only be completed conceptually beyond the confines of the rectangular paper support. In the painting (fig. b), the oval is interrupted on all four sides; the entire composition is thus forced into a tighter relationship with the outer limits of the support, and the flatness of the image is consequently strengthened.

1. For illuminating discussions of some of the issues raised by Mondrian's use of drawing, see R. Welsh, *Mondrian*, exh. cat., Staatsgalerie Stuttgart, 1980, pp. 35-57; J. Joosten, in ibid., pp. 63-72; Y.-A. Bois, "Mondrian, Draftsman," *Art in America*, vol. 69, no. 8, Oct. 1981, pp. 95-113; idem, "Du projet au procès," *L'Atelier de Mondrian*, Paris (Macula), 1982, pp. 26-34.

2. For a discussion of Mondrian's use of the large-scale drawings, see R. Welsh, op. cit., p. 46. He points out—convincingly—that the large-scale final drawing for *Composition in Oval: KUB* (Seuphor, 1956, cl. cat. 280 and 281) is worked out in extraordinary detail. In that instance the word "cartoon" can accurately be used.

In this and other respects, considerable light is shed on the Peggy Guggenheim drawing and its ultimate translation into painted form by a long letter written by Mondrian to H. P. Bremmer on January 29, 1914: "I construct line and color combinations upon a flat plane with the aim of giving form to *general* [principles of] *beauty* in the most conscious possible manner. Nature (or that which I see) inspires me and provides me, as it does every painter, with the emotional stimulation through which the creative drive occurs. However, I wish to approach truth as closely as is possible, and therefore I abstract everything until I arrive at the fundamental quality (albeit an external fundamental quality!) of objects.... I am of the opinion that, through the use of horizontal and vertical lines — constructed *consciously*, though not by *calculation*, and directed by higher intuition — which have achieved harmony and rhythm, such basic forms of beauty — whenever necessary complemented by other curved or diagonal lines — can produce a work of art which is as strong as it is true.... And *chance* must be avoided as much as *calculation*. Furthermore, it seems necessary to me to break off the horizontal and vertical lines; for, should these directions not be opposed by others, then they again would be expressing something 'determined,' which is to say mundane. And it is precisely this which I feel: that through art one must not seek to express something mundane [i.e. lit.: human].... Finally, I must add that I have been influenced by seeing the work of Picasso which I admire *greatly*. I am not embarrassed to speak of this influence.... And in spite of this debt, I know that I am quite different from Picasso, as is generally recognized" (cited in English translation in J. M. Joosten, loc. cit., 1971, p. 61; Dutch original in "documentatie over mondriaan(1)," *Museumjournaal*, serie 13, no. 4, 1968, p. 211).

The issues discussed by Mondrian in this letter are clearly illustrative of the compositional processes represented by *Untitled (Oval Composition)*, the sketch that preceded it (fig. a), and the painting that followed (fig. b). Here, as elsewhere in his writings, it is clear that the formal problem he set himself was at the center of his concerns, the specific "source," or referent, playing a subsidiary and, indeed, often an entirely accidental role.[3]

During the period when Mondrian was at work on the Stedelijk painting, he was also occupied with two related oval compositions: *Composition in Oval: KUB* (Gemeentemuseum, The Hague, repr. Seuphor, 1956, cl. cat. 281) and *Oval Composition with Light Color Planes* (MoMA, repr. Seuphor, 1956, cl. cat. 283). All three oval paintings were based on facade drawings and were characterized by similar processes of compositional abstraction. As Joosten has observed, work on all three was apparently still in process in May 1914 when Mondrian wrote again to Bremmer about an exhibition Bremmer was instrumental in organizing at the Galerie Walrecht in The Hague.[4] The exhibition was

3. See in this connection Mondrian's essay "L'expression plastique nouvelle dans la peinture," *Cahiers d'Art*, vol. 1, no. 7, 1926, p. 182; also C. Holty, "Mondrian in New York," *Arts*, vol. 31, no. 10, Sept. 1957, p. 18.

4. Joosten, loc. cit., 1971, pp. 61-62.

to take place in June and July, but on May 5 Mondrian wrote that, although he was sending some relatively recent work, he could not send the newest things because they were not yet entirely finished. He implied, moreover, that the latter group represented a stylistic departure and felt that their omission from the Walrecht show would allow for a desirable stylistic unity within the small group of works that could in fact be exhibited: *"de allerlaatste kan ik niet zenden, omdat ze niet gereed zijn. Mischeen is dit ook wel goed omdat de kleine expositie dan meer één geheel vormt* (J. M. Joosten "documentatie over mondriaan (1)," *Museumjournaal*, serie 13, no. 4, 1968, p. 213).

The three oval paintings (which undoubtedly did constitute a new departure) were not exhibited at the Galerie Walrecht and indeed were not shown at all in Holland during World War I. When Mondrian left Paris for what he anticipated would be a short visit to Holland in July 1914, he left these and other works behind; but war broke out soon afterward, and he was compelled to remain in Holland for the next four years. He was unable to retrieve the paintings until 1919. Although it is impossible to date these pieces precisely, the available evidence suggests that Mondrian worked on them very deliberately throughout the early months of 1914 and that they were not yet finished when he wrote to Bremmer in May, but that they were probably complete by the time he left for Holland in July. No clear sequence is discernible; in all likelihood, Mondrian moved back and forth among them, resolving their interrelated problems simultaneously. Within this general chronological framework, the Peggy Guggenheim drawing can plausibly be ascribed to the first few months of 1914.[5]

EXHIBITIONS:

New York, Valentine Gallery, *Mondrian*, Jan.-Feb. 1942, no. 26 ("*Scaffold*—1912," the title and date attributed to the work in all *P.G.* publications until 1982); New York, Art of This Century, 1942-47, p. 54; Venice, *P.G.*, 1948 (Biennale), no. 89; Florence, *P.G.*, 1949, no. 95; Amsterdam, *P.G.*, 1951, no. 110; Zurich, *P.G.*, 1951, no. 104; London, *P.G.*, 1964-65, no. 30, repr.; Stockholm, *P.G.*, 1966-67, no. 31, repr.; New York, *P.G.*, 1969, p. 24, repr. p. 25; Paris, *P.G.*, 1974-75, no. 27, repr.; Torino, *P.G.*, 1975-76, no. 37, repr. no. 21.

REFERENCES:

M. Seuphor, *Piet Mondrian: Life and Work*, New York, 1956, p. 381 (cl. cat. no. 277), p. 404; J. M. Joosten, "Mondrian's Lost Sketch-books from the Years 1911-1914," in *Mondrian*, exh. cat., Staatsgalerie Stuttgart, 1980, p. 66.

5. The date 1912 inscribed on the face of the drawing is explicable on the following grounds: *Oval Composition* is 1 of a group of works that remained undated by Mondrian until 1941, by which time he was living in New York. Indeed the works were probably mostly dated when he was specifically preparing for his 1942 exhibition at the Valentine Gallery. By that time—3 decades after the drawings had been made—he had inadvertently mistaken the date of his first journey to Paris, placing it in 1910 instead of in May 1912. As a result, the drawings are all dated approximately 2 years earlier than he intended. According to this principle, the Peggy Guggenheim drawing would properly have been dated 1914—the date corresponding to the stylistic and circumstantial evidence. See R. P. Welsh, *Piet Mondrian*, exh. cat., The Art Gallery of Toronto, 1966, pp. 7, 226; idem, in *Two Mondrian Sketchbooks: 1912-1914*, Amsterdam, 1969, [p. 11], fn. 20. Scholars all concur that this was a genuine error on Mondrian's part, and did not represent a conscious attempt to antedate his prewar oeuvre.

120 The Sea. Holland, 1914.

76.2553 PG 38

Charcoal and gouache on wood-pulp wove paper, glued to Homosote panel.

Dimensions of paper: 34½ x 47⅜ (87.6 x 120.3); dimensions of panel: 35½ x 48⅜ x ½ (90.2 x 123 x 1.3).

Signed and dated l.r.: *14 PM.*

PROVENANCE:

Collection of the artist, 1914-42; purchased from Valentine Dudensing, New York, February 1942.[1]

CONDITION:

In 1964 (Tate Report) the drawing (which had not been glazed) was described as very vulnerable; some losses and abrasions were noted and the paper had become detached from its support in 2 places. The paper was reattached, abrasions were retouched with watercolor, and the work reframed with acrylic sheeting (not UF).

In preparation for the January 1942 Valentine Gallery exhibition, Mondrian had worked with Carl Holty to mount the drawings onto Homosote panels.[2] The highly acidic secondary support combined with the heavy glue (probably acidic animal glue) have contributed to the deterioration of the wood-pulp paper of the primary support. Dark staining in various places is due to glue seeping out at the edges or through small tears and pinholes; apart from a tear of ca. 1⅝ in., 4 cm., lower center, these damages are small. Foxing is visible throughout, but damage to the charcoal drawing through abrasion is minimal. The wood-pulp paper is extremely brittle and the work thus very fragile. (Venice, Nov. 1982.)

The chronological problems related to Mondrian's drawings of the sea and the "pier-and-ocean" (as well as those of the Domburg church facade) have provoked considerable discussion. Peggy Guggenheim's large drawing *The Sea* belongs to an extensive group of such works, which represent an important turning point in Mondrian's development.

Robert Welsh first suggested in 1966 that although Mondrian began to paint views of the sea as early as 1908-9, it would have been unlikely that he conceived the drawings contained within an oval before he had seen and absorbed the oval compositions of Picasso and Braque (*Piet Mondrian*, exh. cat., The Art Gallery of Toronto, 1966, pp. 130, 156). Mondrian could not have seen these compo-

1. Peggy Guggenheim went to the Valentine Gallery exhibition with Alfred H. Barr, Jr. She recalls giving him "first choice," since she felt that the MoMA collection was more important than hers (conversation with the author, Venice, 1978). The MoMA purchase (*Pier and Ocean*, 1914, acc. no. 34.42) was a drawing of similarly large dimensions, also formerly mounted on a Homosote panel. See below, footnote 2.
2. See C. Holty, "Mondrian in New York," *Arts*, vol. 31, no. 10, Sept. 1957, p. 18: "When Piet came from England, he had brought with him some new canvases, some partly finished ones and a fat roll of large and smaller drawings that he had never exhibited. I suggested... that he show these drawings... I said I would mount [them] or see to it that they got mounted.... The paper... was heavy and terribly dry and had to be moistened on the reverse side before it could be pasted onto the 'Homasote' [sic] panels. It was like saddling a bronco to control those large sheets of billowing and flapping paper, and there were no heavy furniture pieces or other substantial objects to use as weights when we got to the pressing-down part."

   Conservation measures were undertaken in 1968 by MoMA on their comparably mounted work, and the drawing was successfully detached from the Homosote. The presently stable condition of the MoMA drawing indicates possible avenues for conservation of the other drawings mounted by Mondrian and Holty in this manner. The author is indebted to Antoinette King, Paper Conservator, for the opportunity to examine the MoMA drawing.

120

sitions prior to his arrival in Paris in 1912, and it is doubtful that he absorbed their impact immediately. Thus Welsh suggested a date of ca. 1912-13 (at the earliest) for the drawings within an oval format in Mondrian's important Sketchbook I. The large drawings (including Peggy Guggenheim's cat. no. 120) would have been made the following year, consistent with the 1914 date that is, in fact, inscribed upon most of them.

The fundamental structure of this chronology has not been seriously questioned, but the dating and provenance (from Paris or Holland) of the Sketchbook drawings have tended to vary considerably, as the complexities of Mondrian's stylistic and theoretical development have come under closer scrutiny.

Writing in 1969 (p. 12), Welsh inclined toward a slightly later date for the initial works on the pier-and-ocean theme. He called attention to the fact that with one exception—the drawing on page 57 of the Sketchbook, which seemed more advanced than the others—all the drawings anticipated rather closely the large charcoal and ink versions (including the Peggy Guggenheim work). Since these larger works seemed to derive mainly from 1914 (Seuphor, 1956, cl. cat. 226-30, 234-37), Welsh tentatively assigned the Sketchbook to Paris, 1913, and even held open the possibility that it too may have been done during the following year in Domburg, after Mondrian's return to Holland in July. (See above, cat. no. 119, for details concerning Mondrian's whereabouts in 1913-14.)

In his 1980 analysis of Mondrian as a draftsman (p. 48), Welsh did not specifically discuss the dating of the Sketchbook sheets. However, in placing the large drawings slightly later than previously ("late in 1914 or early in 1915"), he implied a rather more definite post-Paris origin (in second half of 1914) for Sketchbook I.

Joop Joosten (Stuttgart exh. cat., 1980, p. 68), after an extensive study of all the surviving sketches of the period (many of which are dispersed and derive from as many as eight different sketchbooks), concluded that most (if not all) of the drawings and texts in Sketchbook I date from the post-Paris period. Under this assumption, the drawings would have occupied Mondrian's attention during his late summer visit to Domburg in 1914. They would have been followed shortly afterward by the large drawings, and then by the far more abstract *Composition X (Pier and Ocean)*, which was completed by September 1915.[3] In 1982 Joosten suggested an even later dating for some of the large drawings associated with this theme, leading to an even tighter connection than had been previously proposed between Mondrian's progress on *Composition X*, *Composition 1916*, and *Composition with Line* of 1917 — the first work in which he may be said to have been totally free of any naturalistic motif.[4]

Ulrike Gauss, who prepared the catalogue entries for the 1980 Stuttgart exhibition, dated the Sketchbook I drawings 1913-14 (cat. nos. 60-63), apparently adhering to Welsh's earlier notion that they were completed in Paris. The single most "advanced" of these drawings (Sketchbook, p. 57) was placed by Gauss at a point immediately following Mondrian's return to Holland in July 1914; meanwhile, all the larger drawings (including Peggy Guggenheim's) were ascribed to that same calendar year — 1914.

The precise assignment of these various drawings to specific months is obviously less important than an understanding of their role within Mondrian's general development. Yve-Alain Bois has demonstrated (1981 and 1982) that the stylistic evolution of the series of drawings on the motifs of the sea and the pier-and-ocean (as well as the parallel development based on the Domburg church facade) is exceptionally complex. Although the basic progression is a logical one, it does not reveal, for example, a clear, unbroken pattern toward abstraction. Mondrian in these works did not use drawing in a purely instrumental way to bring about, invariably, a transition from an objective "source" to an abstracted image in which all allusions to naturalistic detail have been eliminated. The drawings, in short, cannot be regarded as if they were distillations of particular images from nature (or from architecture): "*pour Mondrian*

3. Collection Rijksmuseum Kröller-Müller, Otterloo, oil on canvas, 33 7/16 x 42 1/2 in., 85 x 108 cm. Purchased by H. P. Bremmer before October 4, 1915 (J. Joosten, "documentatie over mondriaan (2)," *Museumjournaal*, serie 13, no. 5, 1968, p. 268, letter 14).

4. In the Dutch checklist for the de Stijl exhibition (Stedelijk Museum, Amsterdam, Rijkmuseum Kröller-Müller Otterloo, 1982, no. 263), Joosten plausibly dated the MoMA drawing (Seuphor, 1956, cl. cat. 238) 1915. The more problematic circular drawing in the Janis collection (church facade, Seuphor, cl. cat. 259) he dated 1916(?), well after the completion of *Composition X*. In conversation and correspondence with the author 1982-1983 Joosten suggested that the Peggy Guggenheim drawing, as well as the MoMA one, would probably date from 1915. Like Yve-Alain Bois (see below), he proposed a complex integration within the oeuvre of late 1914-17 of a number of different concerns which are contemporaneous and stylistically interrelated.

il ne s'agissait plus d'opérer une stylisation de ce qu'il avait sous les yeux pour nous en livrer une quelconque essence" (1982, p. 30).

Mondrian's approach to drawing, as Bois has suggested, was much more complex, involving a dynamic and continuous interplay between images from nature and more purely formal conceptions. The process was genuinely dialectical; Mondrian sought to resolve the inevitable tensions between naturalistic motifs and abstract considerations of balance, or "equilibrium" (to use Mondrian's own term). Each successive solution in a particular sequence tended to create new dilemmas, which in turn required a fresh response — sometimes by the introduction of essentially naturalistic allusions, sometimes by more formalistic inflections. The result in the major drawings — and subsequently in the paintings — was a hard-won final "synthesis."

In both the sea and the pier-and-ocean drawings (including, Bois convincingly argues, all the drawings from Sketchbook I), Mondrian's method can be traced in precisely the terms described above (1982, p. 31). In some of the sea drawings, for example, Mondrian clearly achieved a solution to the specific problem of the horizon line (see the large drawings in the collections of the Staatsgalerie Stuttgart and the Moderna Museet, Stockholm, repr. Stuttgart catalogue, pls. 95, 96). The forceful curves and horizontals in the upper sections of these works function to resolve this dilemma in something approaching abstract terms. But as Bois pointed out, Mondrian was either dissatisfied with the solution or concluded that the problem itself was not posed in appropriate terms: the horizontal emphasis (suggested by the sea) constituted too powerful a residual image, and Mondrian therefore began the search for a counteracting force.

In several drawings that followed (in the collections of Sidney Janis; Mr. and Mrs. Burton Tremaine; the Gemeentemuseum, The Hague; Seuphor, 1956, cl. cat. 234, 235, 237), Mondrian reintroduced the legible element of the vertical pier, a move that might be interpreted as something of a retreat: "The introduction of this particular, delineated motif into what had previously been an overall composition based on the sea alone might be misinterpreted as the sign of a renewed dependence on a specific form visible in nature. It should, however, be seen as a direct application of the theories of equilibrium that appear in Mondrian's writings at about the same time. Thus, although it appears to be out of sequence, the vertical 'Pier and Ocean' [element in these] drawings represents a formal solution which will precipitate Mondrian's move toward a totally abstract art" (Bois, 1981, p. 111).

Implicit in this argument lies a fundamental conviction that the "equilibrium" between the vertical and the horizontal (of which Mondrian was also writing at this time) was being addressed simultaneously in all the artist's work — the drawings of the sea, the pier-and-ocean, and the Domburg church facade.[5] The horizontal thrust in the sea drawings (such as Peggy Guggenheim's) was at some level impeding Mondrian's progress toward the total equilibrium he sought, and he responded by introducing the vertical element of the pier. But as Bois persuasively argues, the exactly contemporary struggle with the Gothic arcades of the church facade presented an analogous problem with the vertical axis. Only by a process of gradual integration of the issues posed in both sequences was Mondrian able to arrive at a preliminary resolution in the 1915 *Composition X* and a far more complete one in the 1917 *Composition with Line.*

Placing the Peggy Guggenheim drawing within the framework just described is obviously complicated. The drawing has a powerful horizontal thrust and a rather weaker vertical axis descending from the top. In these respects, it is similar to—and roughly contemporaneous with—the facade in the collection of Sidney Janis (Seuphor, 1956, cl. cat. 272). Both works must have preceded other drawings in which a greater equilibrium of broken vertical and horizontal lines was achieved: see, for example, the pier-and-ocean drawings in the collections of the Gemeentemuseum (Seuphor, 1956, cl. cat. 237) and MoMA (Seuphor, 1956, cl. cat. 238). Finally, the 1915 painting *Composition X* would have been executed after all the drawings just mentioned. (Contrast its very assertive vertical, ascending from the bottom edge, with the much less pronounced vertical — descending from the top—in the Peggy Guggenheim piece.) In summary, the Peggy Guggenheim work seems ascribable to the second half of 1914, after Mondrian had returned to Holland but before the completion of several other key drawings (and of *Composition X*).

Mondrian's development during 1914-15 reveals his constant effort to discover satisfactory ways of reconciling images from nature with the increasing formal and abstract compositional demands he imposed upon his work. From one point of view, many of the works of these years can be regarded as interpretations or translations of particular natural images into an appropriate and even expressive abstract vocabulary. Joosten has pointed out that the single painting from this period — *Composition X* — calls to mind Mondrian's 1942 autobiographical statement: "Observing sea, sky, and stars, I sought to indicate

5. In Sketchbook I, for example, Mondrian wrote the following notes: "Since the male principle is the vertical line, a man shall recognize this element in the ascending trees of the forest; he sees his complement in the horizontal line of the sea. The woman, with the horizontal line as a characteristic element, recognizes herself in the recumbent lines of the sea and sees herself complemented in the vertical lines of the forest [which represent the male element]. Thus the impression differs. In art it is unified, because the artist is sexless. Since the artist accordingly represents the female and male principle, and not nature directly, a work of art transcends nature" (translated by R. Welsh, 1969, p. 22). Welsh argues for a reading of this and other texts that is rooted in a spiritualistic Theosophical framework. The works of 1914-15 (including especially the large drawings such as Peggy Guggenheim's cat. no. 120) are seen by him as implying "a dualist polarity between the spiritual and material essence of natural phenomena. Whereas the spiritual essence was identified with masculine verticality (trees, upright figures, church facades), matter was seen as feminine horizontality (undulating dunes, reclining figures and the horizon itself)." In Welsh's view, the sea drawings (with their horizontal emphasis) and the pier-and-ocean examples (with the vertical axis created by the row of piers) were conceived "as an abstracted image of cosmic union, a form of schematized intercourse between spirit and matter" (1980, p. 48). Other scholars, while taking Mondrian's association of the horizontal/vertical with the female/male into account, have attributed to it a far less explicitly religious or symbolic content (see, for example, Bois, 1982, p. 31). The Sketchbook I drawings, and their accompanying texts, represent a set of visual and intellectual concerns that are almost impossible to separate from Mondrian's complex pictorial evolution from autumn 1914 to spring or summer 1915, and their date in the post-Paris period thus seems compelling.

their plastic function through a multiplicity of crossing vertical and horizontals" (1973, p. 55). It also seems clear that, in the complex graphic developments of 1914-15, the specific motif behind any given work became less important as Mondrian worked simultaneously on solutions involving all three of his major themes (the sea, pier-and-ocean, and church facade). The process involved a continuous effort to free himself entirely from any dependence on motifs. As Bois suggested: "*Le problème formel est le premier, le référent n'est qu'accidental: c'est un auxiliare dont Mondrian n'aura bientôt plus besoin*" (1982, p. 30).

EXHIBITIONS:

New York, Valentine Gallery, *Mondrian*, Jan.-Feb. 1942, no. 25 ("*Ocean*-1914," the title and date attributed to the work in all *P.G.* publications); New York, Art of This Century, 1942-47, p. 54; Venice, *P.G.*, 1948 (Biennale), no. 90; Florence, *P.G.*, 1949, no. 96; Amsterdam, *P.G.*, 1951, no. 111; Zurich, *P.G.*, 1951, no. 105; London, *P.G.*, 1964-65, no. 31; Stockholm, *P.G.*, 1966-67, no. 32; New York, *P.G.*, 1969, p. 27, repr. p. 26; Paris, *P.G.*, 1974-75, no. 28, repr.; Torino, *P.G.*, 1975-76, no. 38.

REFERENCES:

M. Seuphor, *Piet Mondrian: Life and Work*, New York, 1956, p. 125 (cl. cat. no. 229); R. P. Welsh and J. M. Joosten, *Two Mondrian Sketchbooks: 1912-1914*, The Hague, 1969, p. 12; J. Joosten, "Abstraction and Compositional Innovation," *Artforum*, Apr. 1973, p. 55; R. Welsh, "Mondrian as a Draftsman," in *Piet Mondrian; Drawings, Watercolors, New York Paintings*, exh. cat., Stuttgart, 1980, p. 48; U. Gauss, ibid., pp. 86-87; Y.-A. Bois, "Mondrian, Draftsman," *Art in America*, vol. 69, no. 8, Oct. 1981, p. 111; idem, "Du projet au procès," *L'Atelier de Mondrian*, Paris (Macula), 1982, pp. 26-34.

---

121 Composition. 1938-39.

(*Composition with Red*).

Color plate p. 389.

76.2553 PG 39

Oil on canvas mounted on painted wood support. Dimensions of canvas: 41 7/16 x 40 5/16 (105.2 x 102.3); outer dimensions of wood support: 43 x 41 3/4 (109.1 x 106); depth of wood support: 1 (2.5).

Signed and dated l.r.: *PM 39*; faintly discernible, in the artist's hand, on the center stretcher member (preserved by restorer in constructing new stretcher): *PIET MONDRIAN composition*.

PROVENANCE:

Purchased from the artist, London, 1940.[1]

1. Peggy Guggenheim, who had moved to Paris, asked Herbert Read to choose a work from Mondrian's London studio and send it to her. He selected this and had it shipped to Paris.

CONDITION:

Mondrian himself apparently "cleaned" the picture in New York in the early 1940s (Peggy Guggenheim, in conversation with the author, Venice, 1978). For a discussion of this issue, see below.

In 1964 (Tate Report) the paint film was described as cracked over the entire surface, the edges of the cracks dangerously elevated and brittle with extensive incipient cleavage though almost no losses. A circular crack in the lower center was the direct result of a customs stamp on the reverse (see fig. a). The surface was cleaned and impregnated with wax resin from the reverse in an attempt to secure the areas of cleavage.

In 1968 (New York) the extensive pressure cracks in the white areas were noted again. The varnish (possibly containing oil in addition to synthetic resin) was much discolored and had partially crosslinked, rendering it practically insoluble. The painting was given water-chemical treatment on a vacuum table to minimize the pressure cracks in the whites; it was lined with wax-resin adhesive and Fiberglas and stapled to a honeycomb panel. The varnish then proved soluble in xylene (possibly owing to vacuum-table treatment). The surface was successfully cleaned, and a spray coat of synthetic resin varnish applied.

The present dimensions are probably not precisely the same as those of the work before restoration. The edges show extensive wear, loss, and inpainting. Some inpainted losses in the blacks and minor retouchings in the whites are visible under UV. The condition is stable. (Venice, Nov. 1982.)

fig. a.
Photograph of cat. no. 121 taken in raking light, 1964.
Circular crack in lower center was caused by customs stamp on reverse.

Mondrian's concern with the framing of his paintings is well known. As has been discussed by this author, his decision to mount a picture *upon*, rather than recessing it *within*, a frame dates from as early as 1916: "So far as I know, I was the first to bring the painting forward from the frame, rather than set it within the frame. I had noted that a picture without a frame works better than a framed one and that the framing causes sensations of three dimensions. It gives an illusion of depth, so I took a frame of plain wood and mounted my picture on it. In this way I brought it to a more real existence." (J. J. Sweeney, "Eleven Europeans in America," *The Museum of Modern Art Bulletin*, vol. 13, nos. 4-5, pp. 35-36. See also A.Z.R. *Guggenheim*, 1976, Vol. II, pp. 577-78.) In the ensuing years, Mondrian experimented with a number of framing solutions, but the critical issue for him apparently remained the projection of the work from its surrounding frame.

In the case of the Peggy Guggenheim *Composition* the stapling of the canvas onto the honeycomb panel (see CONDITION) represents a clear departure from Mondrian's practice; but the relationship of the canvas to the narrow wood frame corresponds to his principle. The canvas projects approximately 1 in., 2.5 cm., from the frame, as do works demonstrably framed by Mondrian himself (see, for example, *Composition*, 1929, A.Z.R. *Guggenheim*, 1976, Vol. II, cat. no. 206). But whereas the latter frame and the others known to have been made by the artist are constructed out of two longer slats (on the sides) and two shorter slats (top and bottom), Peggy Guggenheim's is constructed out of four pieces of almost equal length.[2] Moreover, Mondrian's practice in the years following 1936-37 tended toward the construction of a broader surround for the canvas, the edges being masked by strip framing or tape.[3] In spite of this, the critical detail of the painting's projection lends support to the possibility that the principles of the construction, at least, originated with Mondrian.

The question of the surface itself and Mondrian's possible reworking of it in New York in the early 1940s raises certain problems. It is widely known that Mondrian's working method during the Neoplastic period involved a complex process of compositional adjustment on the canvas itself. The placement of lines and the choice of colors (including the blacks) were matters of continual change and evolution. As Yve-Alain Bois has suggested, the relationship between the color and the linear structure was dialectical, changes in the one always necessitating adjustment in the other. (See "Du projet au procès," *L'Atelier de Mondrian*, Paris (Macula), 1982, p. 36.)

Peggy Guggenheim reported (in conversation with the author) that Mondrian "restored" the picture in New York shortly before the opening of her gallery at Art of This Century. She was unable to recall precisely what he did, but she remembered that it came back "much cleaner." In his 1943 article in *Pro Arte* (see below REFERENCES), Max Bill described the work in detail, although he did not have it before him at the time. He had seen the picture in Paris, before Mondrian's move to London in September 1938; it was at that stage quite unfinished; no color had been added, and the placement and number of black lines were, as he recalled, probably not identical to those of the completed composition. During the ensuing two years, while Mondrian remained in London, he

2. Margaret Watherston, who lined the picture in 1968, is certain that this wood mount was present when she received the picture. The Tate photographs of 1964 also show a mount of this kind, though it is not clear whether the mount is constructed in the same manner. Peggy Guggenheim recalled no restoration work beyond that described above.

3. Joosten, correspondence with the author, January 1983.

periodically sent Max Bill photographs of finished paintings. With precision and care, he specified the colors he had used directly on the reverse of the photographs. Bill's extremely specific description of the Peggy Guggenheim painting in the 1943 text was based upon such a photograph:[4] "*Die rechtwinklig sich schneidenden horizontalen und vertikalen Linien ergeben ständig sich schiebende und überdeckende Flächen, die in ausgewogenem, reichem Rhythmus zueinander stehen, in die man sich vertiefen kann wie in eine komplizierte Fuge. Die Beschränkung auf wenige Farben, reduziert auf weiss (Fläche), schwarz (Linien), grau (kleine Fläche links oben) und rot (kleine Fläche unten rechts), gibt dem Werk Mondrians die Kraft des entschiedenen, klaren Geistes.*"

The small gray plane at the upper left is, of course, no longer there, the palette of the work as it now stands being limited to white, black, and red. But on the photograph, preserved in Max Bill's archives, the small horizontal plane at the upper left corner is labeled in Mondrian's hand "grey"; the plane at the lower right, "red." Thus, one can only hypothesize that when Mondrian "restored" the work in New York, he readjusted the colors and suppressed the gray. He would, in all likelihood, have simultaneously repainted the other areas, especially the black lines with which he was in any event almost never satisfied.[5]

In a letter to Hilla Rebay of October 10, 1930 (already cited by the author, see A.Z.R. *Guggenheim*, Vol. II, p. 584), Mondrian drew attention to the thickness of his paint surface and its resultant resistance to damage. His habit of applying successive layers of paint, of reworking and readjusting the composition as he proceeded, required exceptional patience. Each layer had to dry completely before another could be applied, and he therefore worked simultaneously on a large number of paintings.[6] But contrary to his expectations, this method also resulted in the increased vulnerability to cracks of the pristine surfaces themselves. The 1964 condition of the paint layer of cat. no. 121 (fig. a) is not uncharacteristic of his Neoplastic pictures,[7] posing considerable problems for their long-range preservation.

4. Information kindly supplied by Max Bill, in conversations with the author, March 21 and 30, 1984.

5. Herbert Read related the experience of visiting Mondrian 2 or 3 times and finding him "always engaged in painting the black lines in the same picture, and I asked him whether it was a question of the exact width of the line. He answered No: it was a question of its intensity, which could only be achieved by repeated applications of paint" ("Reminiscences of Mondrian," *Studio International*, vol. 172, no. 884, Dec. 1966, p. 239).

6. An important addition to the evidence on this point was published by A. Roth ("Piet Mondrian," in *Begegnung mit Pionieren*, Basel and Stuttgart, 1973, p. 151). In a letter of December 29, 1929, to Roth, who had expressed the wish to buy a painting, Mondrian wrote that he greatly regretted not being able to send him one immediately but that he would do so as soon as possible. He was working on many at the same time—"*ça dure (avec le temps pour sêcher) toujours longtemps avant qu'elles soient finies.*"

7. A considerable number of these Neoplastic paintings have been extensively restored and in some cases entirely overpainted.

EXHIBITIONS:

London, *Living Art in England*, Jan. 18-Feb. 2, 1939, no. 29? ("*Composition No. 1*, 1938, 41" x 41" 80 gns.");[8] London, Guggenheim Jeune, *Abstract and Concrete Art*, May 1939, no. 32? ("*Composition of Red and White*, 1939"); New York, Art of This Century, 1942-47, p. 54, repr. p. 55; Venice, *P.G.*, 1948 (Biennale), no. 91; Florence, *P.G.*, 1949, no. 97; Amsterdam, *P.G.*, 1951, no. 112, repr. n.p.; Zurich, *P.G.*, 1951, no. 106, repr.; London, *P.G.*, 1951, no. 32, repr.; Stockholm, *P.G.*, 1966-67, no. 33, repr.; New York, *P.G.*, 1969, p. 28, repr. color; Paris, *P.G.*, 1974-75, no. 29, repr. color n.p.; Torino, *P.G.*, 1975-76, no. 39; Rome, *Guggenheim: Venezia-New York*, 1982, no. 35, repr. color; New York, *P.G.*, 1982-83, no. 17, repr. color.

REFERENCES:

The London Bulletin, no. 14, May 1, 1939, repr. p. 6; P. Guggenheim, *Art of This Century*, 1942, p. 54, repr. p. 55; M. Bill, "Von der abstrakten zur konkreten Malerei im XX. Jahrhundert," *Pro Arte et Libris* (Geneva), no. 2, 1943, p. 206, repr. (dated 1938); M. Seuphor, *Piet Mondrian: Life and Work*, New York, 1956, cl. cat. no. 606, p. 428, repr. p. 391, fig. 399; Calas, 1966, p. 36, repr. p. 58.

8. The catalogues for this and the following exhibition were published in *The London Bulletin*, no. 14, May 1, 1939. On p. 6 the Peggy Guggenheim painting is reproduced together with an article by Herbert Read entitled "An Art of Pure Form." It has not been possible to establish with certainty that the picture appeared in both exhibitions, though this seems likely. Joop Joosten has pointed out (in correspondence with the author) that below the lower right corner of *The London Bulletin* reproduction a "29" is visible, indicating that the photo may have actually been taken in the earlier exhibition. If this is the case, Mondrian would certainly have begun work on the canvas sometime the previous year. The tentative dating of the canvas in 1938-39 is based on this not yet fully established fact.

Henry Moore

Born July 1898, Castleford, Yorkshire.
Lives in Much Hadham, Hertfordshire.

122 Ideas for Sculpture. 1937.

76.2553 PG 190

Black and white chalk, brown crayon on wood-pulp wove paper, laid down on cardboard, 15 x 22 (38 x 56).

Signed and dated in india ink l.l.: *Moore 37.*

PROVENANCE:

Purchased from the artist, 1938, London?[1]

CONDITION:

The paper support has darkened considerably, partly due to acid migration from the cardboard secondary support and to photo-oxidation from overexposure to light. There are support losses in the lower right and lower left corners and a water stain at the lower left. Two thin vertical scratches are near the center. Foxing is visible near the center of the right edge and in the lower right quadrant. The support is brittle and fragile. Owing to its darkening, the value relationships between design and ground have altered significantly, but the overall condition of the design is stable. (Venice, Nov. 1982.)

1. Peggy Guggenheim (in conversation with the author) recalled that she either received this and the following drawing (cat. no. 123) from Moore during World War II, or purchased them at the time of the exhibition *Contemporary Sculpture* (see EXHIBITIONS). Moore was unable to clarify the circumstances of the acquisition, since he had no memory or record of it (in conversation with Susan D. Ferleger, at the request of the author, Feb. 1979).

Although Moore described this sheet and two closely related drawings (figs. a and b) as "Ideas for Sculpture," no specific complete sculptures evolved from them. Various details were used in subsequent pieces; in particular, Moore recalled (in a discussion with the author, June 1975) that the small vertical elements jutting up from the figure at the bottom center of the Peggy Guggenheim sheet became the basis for the string supports in some of the 1938 string sculptures. In general, however, the drawings of this period served as important points of departure, as general inspiration, rather than as specific sketches for actual pieces. In an often quoted interview of August 18, 1937, Moore spoke of his attitude to drawing at that time:

> *My drawings are done mainly as a help toward making sculpture — as a means of generating ideas for sculpture.... Experience, though, has taught me that the difference ... between drawing and sculpture should not be forgotten.... At one time whenever I made drawings for sculpture I tried to give them as much the illusion of real sculpture as I could.... But I now find that carrying a drawing so far that it becomes a substitute for sculpture, either weakens the desire to do the sculpture, or is likely to make the sculpture only a dead realisation of the drawing. I now leave a wider latitude in the interpretation of the drawings I make for sculpture* (*The Listener*, London, vol. 18, no. 449).

The drawings in Peggy Guggenheim's collection may be said to belong to a transitional stage in Moore's use of the medium. They illustrate his rejection of

fig. a.
Moore, *Ideas for Sculpture*, 1937, chalk, 15 x 22 in., 38.1 x 55.9 cm., Collection Bernard Meadows, England. Photograph courtesy Henry Moore (HMF 1306).

fig. b.
Moore, *Studies for Sculpture* , 1937, pencil and chalk on paper, 22 x 15 in., 56 x 38.1 cm., Private Collection. Photograph courtesy Henry Moore (HMF 1304).

the principle of illusionism in drawing — the use of cast shadows, the attempt to create fully three-dimensional form — but they still serve as "jumping off points," as stimulants toward sculptural ideas. As he later described the functions of such drawing, he recalled: "In those days I needed drawing to inspire me. I would make sheets and sheets like these and then as I looked back at them, certain things would jump out at me as suitable or exciting to develop into sculptural form" (discussion with the author, June 1975). Some years later, however, Moore explained, he began to realize that drawing itself, even with this limited aim, interfered with the possibility of a fully three-dimensional conception. As he created sculpture, he saw himself becoming trapped by the frontal view that any given drawing presented. That view inevitably determined the sculpture's development, even though he could infer other dimensions imaginatively without drawing them. "The other sides and views become secondary, no matter how hard one tries to make them otherwise. The drawing makes the form two-dimensional in emphasis." Thus he temporarily abandoned drawing as a basis for sculpture and turned to clay maquettes, making only forms that could be held in one hand. Because there was no dominant view, the freedom to create in three dimensions suddenly became infinite. "The release from drawing was like a divorce in a way. I had to wean myself from it totally and for a while I did no drawing at all." Later, when he had completely adapted to working with maquettes as preparations for sculpture, he began to draw again, focusing on scenery and natural forms; but he found that he never used the medium of drawing again in quite the same way. "While I must draw as a sculptor draws, I no longer draw as a preparation for sculpture." Thus the drawings of the late thirties represent for Moore a moment when ideas for sculpture grew naturally out of the process, and the restrictive nature of the medium had not yet become an impediment to freedom. (All above quotations from discussion with the author, June 1975.)

By the mid-1950s, as David Sylvester has cogently argued, Moore's creative process became quite different. Eliminating drawing almost totally, he improvised sketch-models or maquettes directly in clay, often using a found pebble or a bone fragment as a point of departure. At this stage, "Moore's unordered point of departure [was] to use his hands on something they [could] get hold of" (*Henry Moore*, exh. cat., The Tate Gallery, London, 1968, p. 55).

EXHIBITIONS:

London, Guggenheim Jeune, *Contemporary Sculpture*, Oct. 1938, no. 31 or 32? (*Drawing*);[2] New York, Art of This Century, 1942-47, p. 150; Venice, *P.G.*, 1948 (Biennale), no. 92; Florence, *P.G.*, 1949, no. 99; Amsterdam, *P.G.*, 1951, no. 114; Zurich, *P.G.*, 1951, no. 107; London, *P.G.*, 1964-65, no. 158; Stockholm, *P.G.*, 1966-67, no. 147; Paris, *P.G.*, 1974-75, no. 159, p. 104; Torino, *P.G.*, 1975-76, no. 180.

REFERENCE:

P. Guggenheim, *Art of This Century*, 1942, p. 150.

2. It has not been possible to establish with certainty that this or the following drawing (cat. no. 123) appeared in the exhibition, though it is likely. See also above, fn. 1.

123 Untitled. 1937.

76.2553 PG 189

Black chalk, pastel, colored crayon on wood-pulp wove paper glued down on wood-pulp board, 15 x 22 (38 x 56).

Signed and dated in graphite l.r.: *Moore / 37*.

PROVENANCE:

Purchased from the artist, 1938, London? (see above, cat. no. 122, fn. 1).

CONDITION:

The paper support has darkened to some extent, due to overexposure to light and to acid migration from the cardboard secondary support. Foxing is most pronounced in the lower left quadrant and slight elsewhere. The support is brittle and fragile, but the design is in stable condition. (Venice, Nov. 1982.)

fig. a.
Moore, *Figures with architecture*, 1938, watercolor, 15 x 22 in., 38.1 x 55.9 cm., Collection the artist (HMF 1377).

EXHIBITIONS:

London, Guggenheim Jeune, *Contemporary Sculpture*, Oct. 1938, no. 31 or 32? (*Drawing*; see above, cat. no. 122, fn. 2); New York, Art of This Century, 1942-47, p. 150; Venice, *P.G.*, 1948 (Biennale), no 93; Florence, *P.G.*, 1949, no. 100; Amsterdam, *P.G.*, 1951, no. 115; Zurich, *P.G.*, 1951, no. 108; London, *P.G.*, 1964-65, no. 157; Stockholm, *P.G.*, 1966-67, no. 146; Paris, *P.G.*, 1974-75, no. 158; Torino, *P.G.*, no. 179.

124 Stringed Object (Head). 1938 (cast 1956).
(*String Figure*).

76.2553 PG 191

Bronze with original black patina on concave surfaces, polished convex surfaces, and coarse string. Length: 2 15/16 (7.5); width: 2 1/16 (5.2).

Edition of nine, plus artist's cast, all unnumbered.[1]

Foundry: Fiorini.

Not signed or dated.

PROVENANCE:

Gift of the artist, on the occasion of the purchase of *Family Group* (cat. no. 126), June 21, 1956.

CONDITION:

A break in the single piece of cord was first noted by the author in 1978.

The black patina on the concave surfaces was created by the artist through the application of "liver of sulphide." At some later date, these areas were apparently varnished; the varnish layer is flaking in places, creating an uneven surface.

Projected conservation measures include the removal of the varnish, and the repair or replacement of the string. (Venice, Nov. 1982.)

1. The 9 bronzes of the edition were distributed, by gift or sale, between 1956 and 1963, the artist retaining one. Peggy Guggenheim's was the first to leave the studio. The artist's cast, still owned by him in 1983, remains unfinished; the holes have not been fully bored and the string has not been inserted.

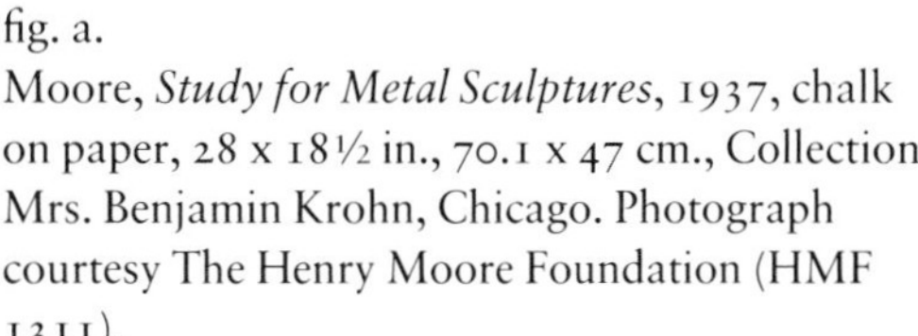

fig. a.
Moore, *Study for Metal Sculptures*, 1937, chalk on paper, 28 x 18½ in., 70.1 x 47 cm., Collection Mrs. Benjamin Krohn, Chicago. Photograph courtesy The Henry Moore Foundation (HMF 1311).

fig. b.
Moore, *Three Stringed Figures in a Setting*, 1938, 14½ x 14½ in., 36.8 x 36.8 cm. Photograph courtesy The Henry Moore Foundation (HMF 1370).

Moore's initial work with "stringed figures" dates from 1937. In published statements he has attributed their origin to mathematical models he saw in the Science Museum at South Kensington—"hyperbolic paraboloids and groins and so on, developed by Lagrange in Paris, that have geometric figures at the ends with colored threads from one to the other to show what the form between would be. I saw the sculptural possibilities of them and did some" (C. Lake, "Henry Moore's World," *Atlantic Monthly*, vol. 209, no. 1, Jan. 1962).

The "sculptural possibilities" Moore perceived involved "interpenetration of space, transparent space, and shape in space."[2] In the specific drawing that preceded Peggy Guggenheim's piece (fig. b), the spatial concerns posed internally by the relationship between taut string and dense curvilinear bronze were extended into the surrounding environment: by placing the objects in an architectural setting, Moore further emphasized and clarified their spatial complexities. Insofar as these pieces posed primarily spatial issues, Moore has described them as representing "the most abstract" phase in his development. But he has also stated that the very term "abstract" seems neither a useful nor a relevant term within the context of his work. "Everything has a relationship to nature," and the "ovoid form" of Peggy Guggenheim's sculpture, for example, is on the one

2. The comments published here regarding the stringed figures derive from Moore's conversations with the author, June 1975; with Susan D. Ferleger, February 1979, and with Lucy Havelock Allen, June 1979. For an illuminating analysis of the stringed figures as a genre, see D. Sylvester, *Henry Moore*, exh. cat., The Tate Gallery, London, 1968, p. 105.

hand reminiscent of "fruits, melons, nuts," and on the other "suggestive of a head." These associations with a source in nature, even at a considerable remove, are "unavoidable." Nonetheless, to the extent that the "stringed figures" tended increasingly to pose strictly formal problems, which depended largely on "ingenuity" for their solution, he found them limited and abandoned the form by 1939.

REFERENCES:

D. Sylvester, ed., *Henry Moore: Sculpture and Drawings 1921-1948*, 4th ed. rev., London, 1957, p. 12, no. 187, repr. p. 14 (*Stringed object*); Calas, 1966, no. 127, repr. p. 198 (*String Figure*).

---

125 Reclining Figure. 1938 (cast 1946).[1]

76.2553 PG 192

Polished bronze (lost wax). Height: 5 3/8 (13.6); length: 12 3/8 (31.5).

Edition of one(?).[2]

Original foundry unknown.

Foundry for present cast: Modern Art Foundry, New York.

Not signed or dated.

PROVENANCE:

The original cast was purchased from the artist, London, 1938.

CONDITION:

Stable. (Venice, Nov. 1982.)

The relationship between the small *Reclining Figure* and the large Green Hornton stone *Recumbant Figure* of the same year (55 in., 140 cm., The Tate Gallery, London) epitomizes some of Moore's major preoccupations of the late 1930s. In discussing this relationship (in conversation with the author, June 1975),

1. The original, unique bronze cast was stolen during *The National Arts and Antiques Exhibition* in 1945. Since MoMA owned a lead version, Peggy Guggenheim obtained permission from Moore and the museum to cast a second bronze from this lead. This was executed by Modern Art Foundry, Long Island City, April-May 1946, but without the supervision or instructions of the artist and thus without his characteristically meticulous work on the finish and patina. The extent to which the appearance of this piece corresponds with his original intention is therefore not clear.
2. In spite of the fact that several sources record 3 bronze casts (see, for example, Read, 1944), The Henry Moore Foundation has no records on this point. Moore's own resources in the late 1930s were insufficient to allow for extensive casting in bronze, and Bernard Meadows was unable to recall that any bronze casts were made during these years (conversation with the author, July 1983). It seems unlikely that Moore himself was able to commission 3 bronze casts of the *Reclining Figure*, though he clearly did have one made (P. Guggenheim, *Confessions,* 1960, pp. 55-56). Some months after the 1938 exhibition of sculpture at Guggenheim Jeune, he offered her a choice between a lead and a bronze; she chose the bronze. The existence of casts other than the original of 1938 (stolen, present wherabouts unknown), and Peggy Guggenheim's 1946 cast has not been established. The Henry Moore Foundation Archive does, however, include a photograph of a bronze cast attributed to the collection of Rudolph Mock, Tennessee. Efforts to trace this piece have been unsuccessful.

Moore characterized the issues as follows: "In the late twenties and early to mid-thirties, I was mainly doing direct carving in stone. My efforts were concentrated on making contact with the material, on experiencing the physical aspects of making sculpture, and on the struggle involved. But in the later thirties I was feeling the limitations imposed by stone."

Most striking among these limitations were the fact that thin, fragile forms eluded him, that the material could not be easily penetrated, that three-dimensional parts within the whole were precluded, and that experimentation was difficult to introduce spontaneously as he worked. In search of greater flexibility, he began to experiment with lead, since he was unable at that time to afford bronze. The low melting point of the metal was a great advantage. The work could be done on a kitchen or primus stove at home and no foundry was necessary. Moore described himself (and his assistant, Bernard Meadows) as inexperienced; the plaster molds were often imperfect and the technique somewhat primitive. "The lead did not always flow into every corner and crevice of the mold, and about one out of every four casts had to be discarded." But the critical issue of "freeing myself from the domination of direct carving and of stone" was successfully confronted in these small lead pieces. "The three-dimensional form was crucially important, together with the freedom lead offered, allowing me the new experience of creating thin, fragile forms, like the arms in this small *Reclining Figure*: they would have been impossible in stone. It was a period of opening-up of forms, and penetrating the material, together with a liberating of fantasy. One could follow up an inspired idea quickly, whereas with stone, or even wood, every part took so long to carry out that the fantasy was less free."

The reclining figure persisted as the dominant theme in Moore's repertoire of forms, but as lead, and then bronze, became more accessible media, the actual realization of the figure took on a wholly new character. The fragility of individual parts, the penetration of the form, and the introduction of holes and concave forms resulted in a new vocabulary.

David Sylvester has cogently analyzed and elucidated the development of Moore's conception of form and content during this critical period, placing the small (lead) *Reclining Figure* at a fundamental turning point (1948, pp. 160, 163). The growing apparent "abstraction" of 1936-38 had implied a no less forceful "communication of human emotions." On the contrary, as the forms became increasingly massive, inanimate, primeval, Moore's achievement was to continue to give expression to a single life force, in which man is "everywhere implied." But with the small *Reclining Figure*, the "process of evolution from the primeval back to the human was rendered visible."

In the small sculptures such as *Reclining Figure*, Moore exploits the properties of the new medium, giving the forms "so much open space and so little solid mass, that they are skeletons rather than bodies, scaffoldings rather than buildings." (Sylvester, 1948, p. 164; on the general subject of the reclining figure in Moore's work, see also Sylvester, *Henry Moore*, exh. cat., The Tate Gallery, London, 1968, pp. 5-7.)

fig. a.
Moore, *Reclining Figure*, 1933, pencil on paper, 4½ x 7 in., 11.4 x 17.8 cm., Collection the artist (HMF 1027).

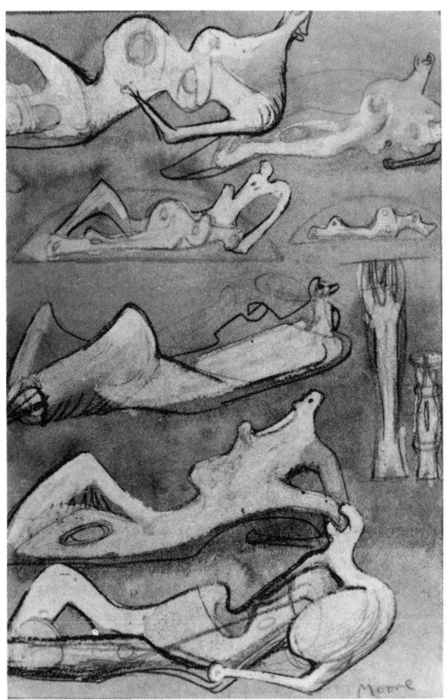

fig. b.
Moore, *Reclining Figures*, 1938, 11 x 7 in., 28 x 17.8 cm., medium and present whereabouts unknown. Photograph courtesy The Henry Moore Foundation (HMF 1395).

One of Moore's early ideas for the particular form of the 1938 *Reclining Figure* can be traced to a 1933 pencil sketch (fig. a) in which the main structural elements and the relationships between head, shoulders, arms, and upper body are already clearly indicated. In subsequent sketches of 1938 (for example, fig. b), further aspects of the subject are explored, although no single explicit preparatory study for the Peggy Guggenheim bronze appears. Given Moore's conception of the role of drawing at this stage in his career (see above, cat. no. 122), an indirect relationship between the drawings and the finished sculpture is precisely what one would expect.

The 1938 bronze originally owned by Peggy Guggenheim has invariably been considered identical to the 1946 cast now in her collection (see footnote 1). But a close comparison of the 1946 version with an early photograph (fig. c; the only presently known record of the original bronze), suggests the possibility of some important differences between the two pieces.

In the earlier photograph, the torso of the figure appears to be partly hollowed out: the indentation at its top end is somewhat deeper, and the entire torso seems to be twisted slightly upward and leftward, in contrapposto to the legs. All these apparent emphases are absent from the extant bronze and its source, the 1938 lead (fig. d).

Photographic evidence such as that provided by fig. c is inherently problematic, since accidents of lighting, vantage point, reflection, and shadow can substantially affect the appearance of any three-dimensional object. Nonethe-

fig. c.
Moore, *Reclining Figure*, 1938 cast, formerly Peggy Guggenheim Collection, present whereabouts unknown.

fig. d.
Moore, *Reclining Figure*, 1938, cast lead, 5¾ x 13 in., 14.6 x 33 cm., The Museum of Modern Art, New York. Photograph courtesy The Henry Moore Foundation.

less, the apparent differences between the early photo and the extant bronze are striking, and one cannot rule out the possibility that the 1938 bronze derived from a different lead cast than the 1946 version.[3]

EXHIBITIONS:

New York, Art of This Century, 1942-45, p. 150, repr.; New York, The Seventeenth Regiment Armory, *The National Arts and Antiques Exhibition*, Sept. 24-30, 1945 (catalogue in *Art News*, vol. 44, no. 12, Oct. 1-14, p. 23, repr.); Venice, *P.G.*, 1948 (Biennale), no. 94 (1946 cast exhibited here and hereafter); Florence, *P.G.*, 1949, no. 98, repr. p. xxxiii (1942 photograph of original piece); Venice, Giardino, 1949, no. 15, repr. (1942 photograph); Amsterdam, *P.G.*, 1951, no. 113, repr. (1942 photograph); Zurich, *P.G.*, 1951, no. 109; London, *P.G.*, 1964-65, no. 159, repr. p. 89; Stockholm, *P.G.*, 1966-67, no. 148, repr. p. 70; New York, *P.G.*, 1969, p. 106, repr.; Paris, *P.G.*, 1974-75, no. 160, repr.; Torino, *P.G.*, 1975-76, no. 181.

REFERENCES:

H. Read, "Three English Sculptors," *XXe Siècle*, IIe année, no. 1, 1939, repr. p. 23 (the lead version); P. Guggenheim, *Art of This Century*, 1942, p. 124, repr. (1938 cast); H. Read, *Henry Moore: Sculpture and Drawings*, London, 1944, pls. 101a, 101b (the lead version); D. Sylvester, ed., ibid., 4th ed. rev., 1957, no. 192, repr. p. 114 (lead); idem, "The Evolution of Henry Moore's Sculpture I," *Burlington Magazine*, 90, June 1948, p. 163, repr. fig. 6 (lead); P. Guggenheim, *Confessions*, 1960, pp. 55-56; W. Grohmann, *Moore*, Berlin, 1960, repr. no. 26.

3. The artist, in conversation with the author, July 11, 1983, expressed the view that the problem raised here could not be solved on the basis of photographs. He was unable to recall any details about the original casting, or whether there might have been 2 versions of the *Reclining Figure*, as suggested here.

126 Family Group. Ca. 1944 (cast 1956).

76.2553 PG 193

Bronze (lost wax) with original brown patina. Height at left, with base causing fluctuation of 1/8 in., 4 cm., left to right: 5 5/8 (14.2); at right: 5 3/8 (13.8). Dimensions of base: 2 15/16 x 4 3/16 x 5/16 (7.5 x 10.7 x 0.8).

Edition of nine, plus artist's cast, all unnumbered. Peggy Guggenheim's was the first sold.

Foundry: Fiorini.

Not signed or dated.

PROVENANCE:

Purchased from the artist, June 21, 1956.

CONDITION:

The bronze sculpture was, at an unknown date, cemented to a base which was not the artist's (see illustrations).

In February 1984 (Venice) the bronze was successfully removed from the base and cleaned. The surface was degreased with trichloroethylene, and washed with distilled water, then with distilled water and neutral detergent; it was rinsed with distilled water and dried with alcohol and acetone. The surface was treated for 30 minutes with a 3% solution of benzotriazole in pure alcohol. A protective coating of Paraloid B-72 (acrylic resin) was applied. The condition is stable. (Venice, Mar. 1984.)

This family group is one of an extensive series of ideas developed during 1944-46 in connection with a commission (ultimately not executed) from Impington Village, Cambridgeshire. (For Moore's description of the history of this commission, see P. James, ed., *Henry Moore on Sculpture*, London, 1966, pp. 224-29.)

David Sylvester has catalogued the various stages of the theme, listing seven models for a sculpture in stone, one for a sculpture in terra cotta, and six for a sculpture in bronze (1948, p. 193, fn. 51). Peggy Guggenheim's example belongs

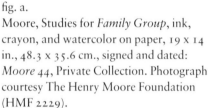

fig. a.
Moore, Studies for *Family Group*, ink, crayon, and watercolor on paper, 19 x 14 in., 48.3 x 35.6 cm., signed and dated: *Moore 44*, Private Collection. Photograph courtesy The Henry Moore Foundation (HMF 2229).

fig. b.
Early photograph by the artist of 3 terra-cotta *Family Group* maquettes; the maquette for cat. no. 126 is at right. Photograph courtesy The Henry Moore Foundation.

to the second group (II, h) — the sculpture conceived in terra cotta — which Sylvester dates 1945. In Moore's record book, however, the date 1945 has been corrected in the artist's hand to 1944. The existence of detailed 1944 drawings for the group lends support to this date for the first maquette (see, for example, fig. a). The original sketch model for this group survives only in a photograph of three such models (fig. b).

Following the small Peggy Guggenheim maquette (for which the terra-cotta original also survives), the sculpture was modeled on a somewhat larger, though not monumental, scale (17⅜ in., 45 cm., HMF no. 265, fig. c). This terra cotta was cast in bronze in 1946 (edition of five, according to the records of The Henry Moore Foundation).

Sylvester has drawn attention to a "painful inconsistency" between the styles of the parents and the children in the *Family Group*. The father's "stirrup-like torso" and the mother's "hollow gourd-like torso" demonstrate some characteristic elements of Moore's established style of the early to mid-1940s, but the children suffer from an "overgeneralised naturalism." The stylistic conflict, inherent and unresolved in this instance within a single sculptural group, is also —as Sylvester suggests—to be found in comparing various examples of Moore's work from the mid-1940s. It is important to note, however, that the issue of naturalism, so explicit in the terra cottas, where the specificity of facial characteristics is strongly marked, is suppressed in the more masklike bronze versions, where the details of eyes, nose, mouth, eyebrows have been omitted.

fig. c.
Moore, *Family Group*, 1945-46, terra cotta, height: 17⅝ in., 45 cm., Private Collection. Photograph courtesy The Henry Moore Foundation (HMF 265).

EXHIBITIONS:

London, *P.G.*, 1964-65, no. 160, repr. (dated 1946, the date ascribed to it in all *P.G.* publications); Stockholm, *P.G.*, 1966-67, no. 149; Paris, *P.G.*, 1974-75, no. 161; Torino, *P.G.*, 1975-76, no. 182.

REFERENCES:

D. Sylvester, "The Evolution of Henry Moore's Sculpture II," *Burlington Magazine*, 90, July 1948, pp. 193-94; idem, ed., *Henry Moore: Sculpture and Drawings 1921-1948*, 4th ed. rev., London, 1957, no. 235 (dated 1945).

---

127 Three Standing Figures. 1953.

76.2553 PG 194

Bronze (figures hollow cast, lost wax; base sand cast), black-green patina. Height of left figure: 28³⁄₁₆ (71.7); center figure: 28⅛ (72); right figure: 28¹⁄₁₆ (71.3). Height of base: ⁹⁄₁₆-¾ (1.5-2); width of base: 26¾ (68); depth of base: 11⅜ (29).

Edition of eight, plus artist's cast, all unnumbered. Peggy Guggenheim's was the sixth sold.

Foundry: Gaskin.

Not signed or dated.

PROVENANCE:

Purchased from the artist, January 24, 1956.[1]

1. Peggy Guggenheim's recollection of the purchase at Henry Moore's house is corroborated by Moore's diary entry for January 14, 1956, which notes a visit by her, followed by shipment of the work to her on January 24.

CONDITION:

The figures were screwed to the base with 2 bolts and washers for each figure; 1 screw was replaced at an unknown date, and its washer was missing. There is widespread green corrosion with small areas of pitting corrosion.

In February 1984 (Venice) the piece was cleaned. The surface was degreased with trichloroethylene, and washed with distilled water, then with distilled water and neutral detergent; it was rinsed with distilled water and dried with alcohol and acetone. The surface was treated for 30 minutes with a 3% solution of benzotriazole in pure alcohol. A protective coating of Incralac (acrylic resin) containing benzotriazole) was applied (for outdoor display). The screws (5/16 Whitworth screws), which had become worn, and the corroded iron washers were replaced with stainless-steel washers and screws.

Moore's work on this group began in 1951 when a number of preparatory drawings were made (figs. a-c). He recalled that these drawings were done prior to the sculpture "to generate ideas," and that he may have had the sheet of thirteen figures (fig. a) with him in the studio while he worked out the first maquette. The latter was cast in bronze in 1952 in an edition of eight (height 10 in., 25.4 cm., Bowness, 1965, no. 321, repr. pl. 48).

A note at the end of the record book entry for the maquette reads "(Enlarge by 2?)"; the artist later decided in favor of an enlargement by almost three when he recast the piece the following year. The present larger sculpture is identical in form, and in the interrelationships of figures, to the maquette; the latter does not, however, have a bronze base.

fig. a.
Moore, *Studies for Standing Figures*, 1951, pencil on paper, 11½ x 9½ in., 29.2 x 24.2 cm., present whereabouts unknown. Photograph courtesy The Henry Moore Foundation (HMF 2691).

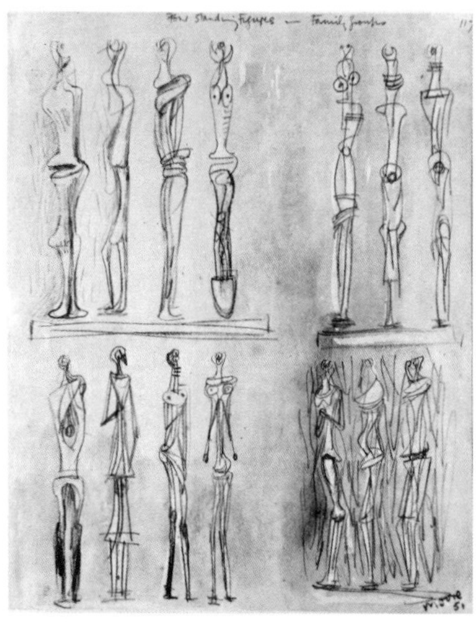

fig. b.
Moore, *Studies for Standing Figures*, 1951, pencil on paper, 11½ x 9½ in., 29.2 x 24.2 cm., Private Collection. Photograph courtesy The Henry Moore Foundation (HMF 2666).

fig. c.
Moore, *Three Standing Figures*, 1951, chalk, crayon, and watercolor on paper, 19½ x 15¼ in., 49.5 x 38.7 cm., The Art Institute of Chicago, Gift of Curt Valentin.

127

fig. d.
Moore, *Three Standing Figures*, unfinished plaster: the central figure lacks the 3 rings at its neck, and its arms remain unmodeled. Photograph courtesy The Henry Moore Foundation.

EXHIBITIONS:

London, *P.G.*, 1964-65, no. 161, repr.; Stockholm, *P.G.*, 1966-67, no. 150, repr.; New York, *P.G.*, 1969 p. 107, repr.; Paris, *P.G.*, 1974-75, no. 162, repr.; Torino, *P.G.*, 1975-76, no. 183, repr. pl. 54.

REFERENCES:

A. Bowness, ed., *Henry Moore: Sculpture and Drawings 1949-1954*, 2nd ed. rev., London, 1965, no. 322, repr. pl. 49; H. Read, *Henry Moore: A Study of His Life and Work*, New York, 1965, no. 157, repr. p. 177.

Robert Motherwell

Born January 1915, Aberdeen, Washington.
Lives in Greenwich, Connecticut.

128 Personage (Autoportrait).
December 9, 1943.
(*Surprise and Inspiration*).

Color plate p. 681.

76.2553 PG 155

Collage of Japanese and western papers, gouache and black ink on thick pulpboard, 40⅞ x 25¹⁵⁄₁₆ (103.8 x 65.9).

Signed and dated in pencil l.r.: *Robert Motherwell / 1943*; on reverse: *Robert Motherwell / 9 December 1943*.

PROVENANCE:

Purchased from the artist before the exhibition at Art of This Century, October 1944.[1]

CONDITION:

In 1983 (New York) the work was removed from its frame in which it had been in direct contact with glass and acid backboard. It was determined that the line scored along the entire left side of the composition, almost through the support to the verso, had been present when the work was made, since drips of blue gouache are visible inside the incision. This weakened scored area was stabilized and reinforced with Japanese tissue and rice starch paste. Some tears in the collage elements were repaired with cellulose fibers and rice paste; the edges and some areas of flaking gouache were consolidated. The work was fumigated with thymol. It was hinged to a 100% ragboard honeycomb panel conforming to the support.

There is some water staining in the upper left quadrant and along the left and lower edges, which may have occurred during the original drying of the medium.

Some fading of the colors through overexposure to light is clearly evident. The pale pink collage elements in particular have totally changed in value, originally having been brilliant magenta. (One fragment of collage, which has been folded over since the work was completed, retains the original hue.) These changes must be taken into account in any evaluation of the structure of the composition.

The crackle in the crimson gouache is stable, but fragile. (New York, Jan. 1983.)

Motherwell's earliest collages date from 1943, the year Peggy Guggenheim invited Baziotes, Motherwell, and Pollock to submit collages for an international collage exhibition she was planning to hold at her gallery in April-May. Neither Pollock nor Motherwell had made collages before, and they decided to experiment with the medium in Pollock's studio.[2] They both subsequently participated in the April-May exhibition.[3] The following winter, living on Eighth Street facing

1. In an interview with the author, Provincetown, Massachusetts, August 27, 1982, Motherwell recalled that Peggy Guggenheim initially preferred another collage he had made early that year: *Pancho Villa, Dead and Alive* [MoMA]. But "very honorably, knowing that the Modern was interested in that, she felt that the museum should get first choice, and she would take what was left. So she took this one which I happen to think was the best." *Pancho Villa* was acquired by MoMA in May 1944, shortly before the opening of the Spring Salon at Art of This Century (see Appendix, p. 779).
2. For a description of these and subsequent events, see Arnason, 1966, pp. 23-24 and Simon, 1967.
3. Motherwell's name is not on the list of artists represented (see Appendix, p. 774). Evidence for Motherwell's participation in the show exists, however, in the purchase of his *Joy of Living* on that occasion by Sadie A. May, who gave it to The Baltimore Museum of Art soon afterward. A receipt for payment received by Peggy Guggenheim is in the files of the Baltimore Museum, dated May 11 (information supplied by Brenda Richardson).

128

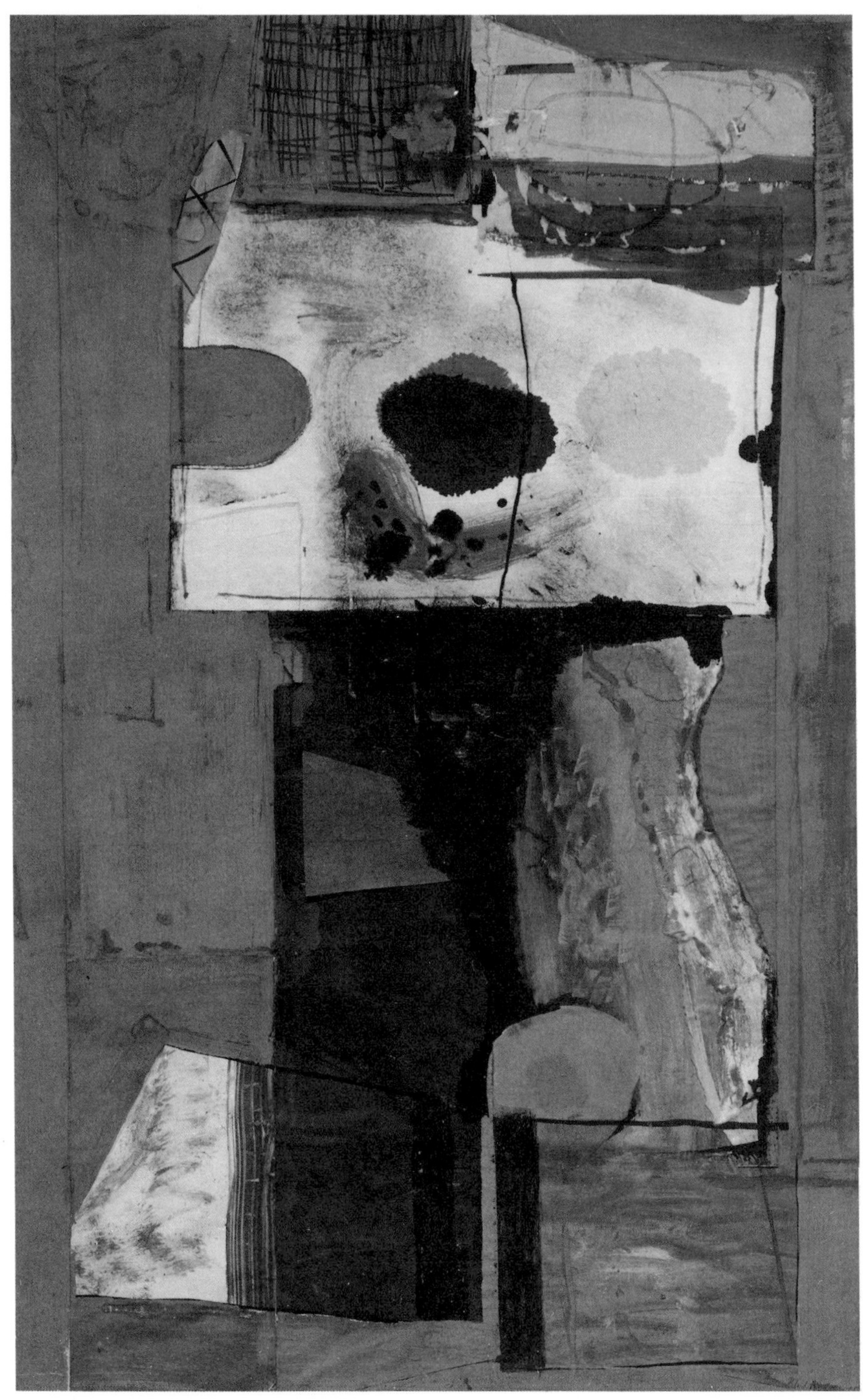

MacDougal, Motherwell recalls that he dedicated a major part of his creative energy to collage.[4] The works he had produced in Pollock's studio were relatively small (ca. 14 x 20 in., 35 x 50 cm.), the size of sketchbook sheets. He had shown these small works to Matta, who had encouraged him to increase the scale, and during the ensuing months Motherwell struggled with the problems of scale and of expressive means. When his first one-man show, consisting of eight paintings, thirty colored drawings, two etchings, two drawings, and six collages, opened at Art of This Century in October, the collages represented for Motherwell "the core" of the exhibition and had the greatest resonance for him as his work developed in the subsequent period (see Arnason, 1966, and Simon, 1967).

The question of the title of the present collage raises important issues regarding content and interpretation. Initially exhibited as *Personage (Autoportrait)*, the work inexplicably appeared in the 1946 exhibition *Fourteen Americans* as *Large Collage*. By 1948, when Peggy Guggenheim's collection had been transferred to Venice, the title had been changed to *Surprise and Inspiration*, apparently on her initiative.[5]

Motherwell himself, reminded in 1982 of the original title, found it convincingly evocative of certain memories and meanings. Though striving in the early forties for an elliptical pictorial language, which would destroy figuration in its literal sense, Motherwell was nonetheless concerned to arrive at titles that might evoke some aspect of the "content" of a work. Thus Robert C. Hobbs's 1976 comments about the artist's titling process seem to Motherwell to apply to the works of the 1940s as well: "In naming a work, he looks for metaphors that localize the experience without delimiting it, that provide a leverage in prying up the content so that the viewer can get beyond the abstractness of the work and realise exactly what has been emphasised" ("On Robert Motherwell's Elegies to the Spanish Republic," *Robert Motherwell*, exh. cat., Städtische Kunsthalle, Dusseldorf, 1976, p. 29).

Motherwell has rejected the spontaneous interpretive suggestion he himself made in 1976 that the "the true subject matter" of the present collage is "a wounded person."[6] He has recalled that the image carried an essentially nonfigurative content, but that it was nonetheless evocative of aspects of his own personality: "It would have struck me as a kind of contemplative, inactive, passive, lonely in many respects personage, which in my own being I am very much [in my relations with other people]. Or, it's almost a kind of shock of

4. "No one will ever know what went into those collages—that whole winter." Interview with the author, August 27, 1982. Unless otherwise indicted, the information cited in the present entry derives from the 1982 interview.

5. Motherwell has no explanation for the origins of this title, which he has always presumed she (or a member of her circle) invented.

6. The plates in Arnason's 1977 monograph are accompanied by comments, which Motherwell "reluctantly" agreed to supply for the book. They were dictated "off the top of my head... and are to be read in that light." In retrospect, Motherwell feels that these comments, most of which were made in response to the titles without the images in front of him, have no validity.

recognition, that *that's* the way I feel inside to myself. And with those three ovals in the center, that very well could be a masklike form."

These observations suggest a specifically anthropomorphic content, and Motherwell acknowledges such a presence. But the content suggested itself ex post facto and cannot be regarded as a source of inspiration for the composition. "Collage was an enormously liberating experience for me.... The way I [made] collages was flat, on the table. I could literally move everything around before gluing it down. This also helped counteract representation.... What makes representation, really, is the degree to which you make things sculpturally, or in deep three-dimensional space, and working flatly tends to negate that, just automatically.... I started manipulating materials with ... no idea about how they would come out, and I basically still work that way. There was a total freedom from literal subject matter."[7]

Only after the work was complete would the title suggest itself, arising out of the unpremeditated image of the finished product. Once selected, the title carries a certain metaphoric significance that cannot be ignored.

EXHIBITIONS:

New York, Art of This Century, *Robert Motherwell*, Oct. 24-Nov. 11, 1944, no. 13 ("*Personage [Autoportrait]*, 1944"); New York, MoMA, *Fourteen Americans*, Sept. 10-Dec. 8, 1946, no. 58, repr. p. 35 ("*Large Collage*, 1943"); Venice, *P.G.*, 1948 (Biennale), no. 95 ("*Sorpresa ed ispirazione*," the title by which the work has been known in all subsequent *P.G.* publications); Florence, *P.G.*, 1949, no. 101; Amsterdam, *P.G.*, 1951, no. 116; Zurich, *P.G.*, 1951, no. 110; Bordighera, *11ᴬ Mostra internazionale pittura americana*, Mar 1-31, 1953, no. 12; London, *P.G.*, 1964-65, no. 130, repr.; Stockholm, *P.G.*, 1966-67, no. 126, repr.; New York, *P.G.*, 1969, p. 163, repr.; Paris, *P.G.*, 1974-75, no. 133, repr.; Torino, *P.G.*, 1975-76, no. 147, repr. pl. 64; Rome, *Guggenheim: Venezia-New York*, 1982, no. 55, repr. color; New York, *P.G.*, 1982-83, no. 57, repr. color p. 63.

REFERENCES:

W. C. Seitz, "Abstract-Expressionist Painting in America," unpublished Ph.D. dissertation, Princeton University, May 1955, repr. fig. 142 (*Large Collage*); K. McShine, "Chronology," in *Robert Motherwell*, exh. cat., MoMA, New York, 1965, p. 74; H. H. Arnason, "On Robert Motherwell and His Early Work," *Art International*, vol. 10, no. 1, Jan. 20, 1966, p. 24; S. Simon, "Concerning the Beginnings of the New York School, 1939-1943: An Interview with Robert Motherwell," *Art International*, vol. 11, no. 6, summer 1967, p. 22; M. Pleynet, "La méthode de Robert Motherwell," in *Robert Motherwell: Choix de peintures et de collages 1941-1977*, exh. cat., MNAM, Paris, 1977, n.p.; H. H. Arnason, *Robert Motherwell*, New York, 1977, pp. 19-20, p. 104, repr. pl. 59.

7. Motherwell wrote about this working method as early as 1946. See "Beyond the Aesthetic," *Design*, vol. 47, no. 8, 1946.

Ben Nicholson

Born April 1894, Denham, Buckinghamshire.
Died February 1982, London.

129 February 1956 (menhir). 1956.

Color plate p. 395.

76.2553 PG 46

Oil with black ink(?) on carved board, $39\frac{1}{8}$ x $11\frac{13}{16}$ (99.4 x 30).

Signed, titled, and dated on reverse: *Ben Nicholson / Feb 56 / (menhir).*

PROVENANCE:

Purchased from Gimpel Gallery, London, March 19, 1957.

CONDITION:

The work has received no treatment. The frame, designed by the artist, is considerably soiled and abraded. The surface of the work itself is in stable condition. (Venice, Nov. 1982.)

Nicholson's technique here (and in other reliefs) has not been studied in detail, and since he preferred to maintain a certain secrecy about his methods they remain difficult to describe with precision.

The dry matte surface was achieved through the use of an oil paint thinned to such an extent that it created the effect of watercolor. It was applied in several layers, each layer allowed to dry before it was rubbed down to an even smoothness. A new coat was then applied, and the procedure repeated.

In describing his work on a 1935 white relief to a close friend, the artist Willie Barns Graham,[1] Nicholson spoke of having applied many more than four or five coats of paint: "There are numerous coats, put on and rubbed down when quite firm and dry and then rubbed down again and repeated again and again and again." He used a razor blade during certain stages of the scraping process, and also compared his experience of scrubbing the surface of the reliefs to that of his mother scrubbing the kitchen table. The two black vertical lines were applied with a fine brush on top of the final layer, their shiny surface contrasting with the "fresco" appearance of the relief ground.

In his determination to achieve an utterly smooth, resistant, matte surface, Nicholson probably experimented with numerous techniques at various points in his career. On the basis of examination of works of different dates, however, a generally consistent approach evidently continued at least into the 1950s; the above comments by the artist would thus probably apply to the technique used in the present work.

The construction of the frame, which in this instance, as in others, Nicholson designed himself, was always carefully calculated so that no one element would extend the entire length of the work, the joins being flush with the squared end of each wooden element and never beveled at the corners.

EXHIBITIONS:

London, *P.G.*, 1964-65, no. 39, repr.; Stockholm, *P.G.*, 1966-67, no. 40, repr.; Paris, *P.G.*, 1974-75, no. 40, repr. (with frame); Torino, *P.G.*, 1975-76, no. 46, repr. pl. 27 (with frame).

REFERENCES:

Calas, 1966, repr. p. 238 (with frame); J. Russell, *Ben Nicholson*, London, 1969, repr. pl. 264; L. Flint, *Handbook*, 1983, p. 148, repr. color p. 149.

1. Willie Barns Graham kindly responded to questions about Nicholson's technique, conveyed to her on behalf of the author by Alan Bowness.

Kenzo Okada

Born September 1902, Yokohama, Japan.
Died July 1982, Tokyo.

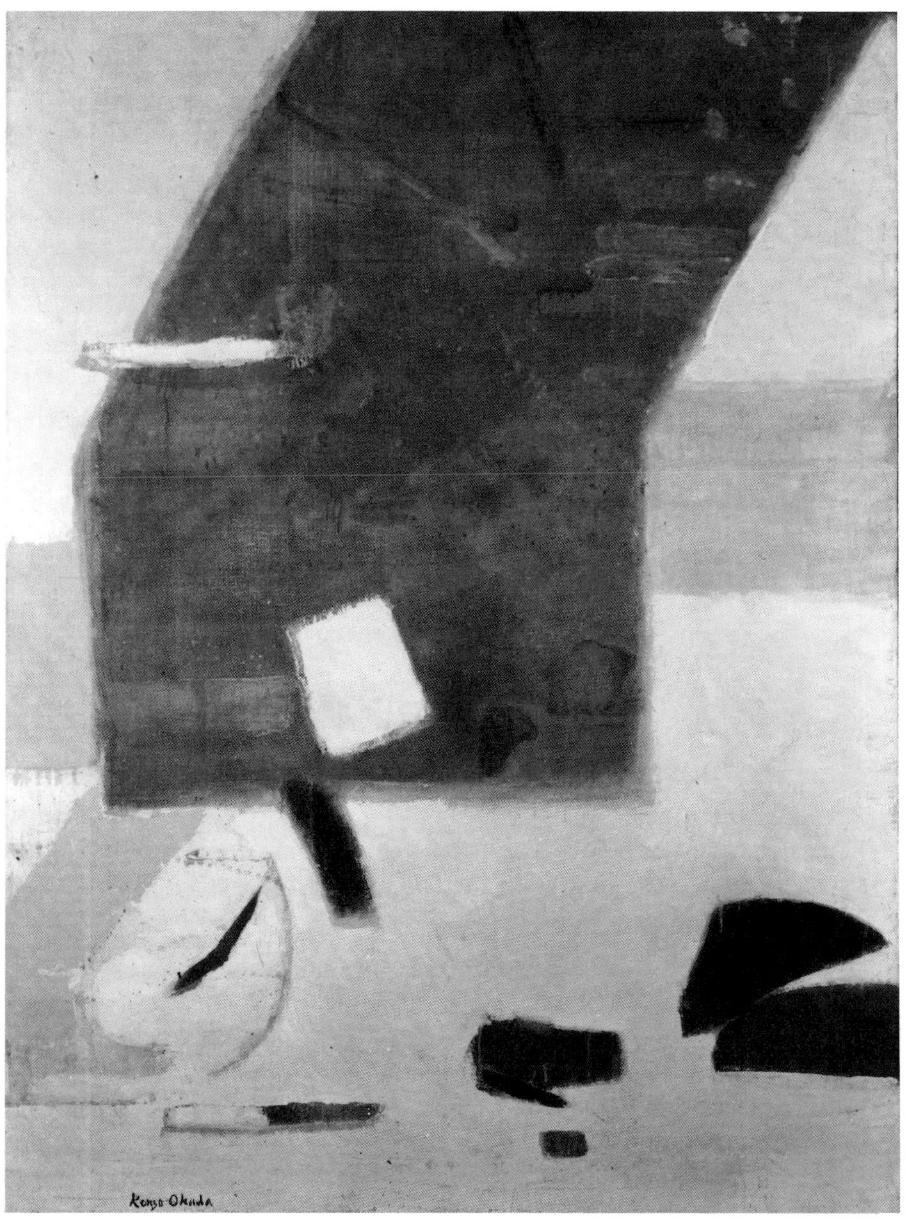

130 Above the White. 1960.

76.2553 PG 184

Oil on canvas, 50 1/8 x 38 1/16 (127.3 x 96.7).

Signed l.l.: *Kenzo Okada*. Not dated.

PROVENANCE:

Purchased from Betty Parsons Gallery, New York, March 2, 1961.

CONDITION:

The work has received no treatment and is in stable condition. (Venice, Nov. 1982.)

EXHIBITIONS:

London, *P.G.*, 1964-65, no. 153; Torino, *P.G.*, 1975-76, no. 173.

Amédée Ozenfant

Born April 1886, Saint-Quentin, Picardy.
Died May 1966, Cannes.

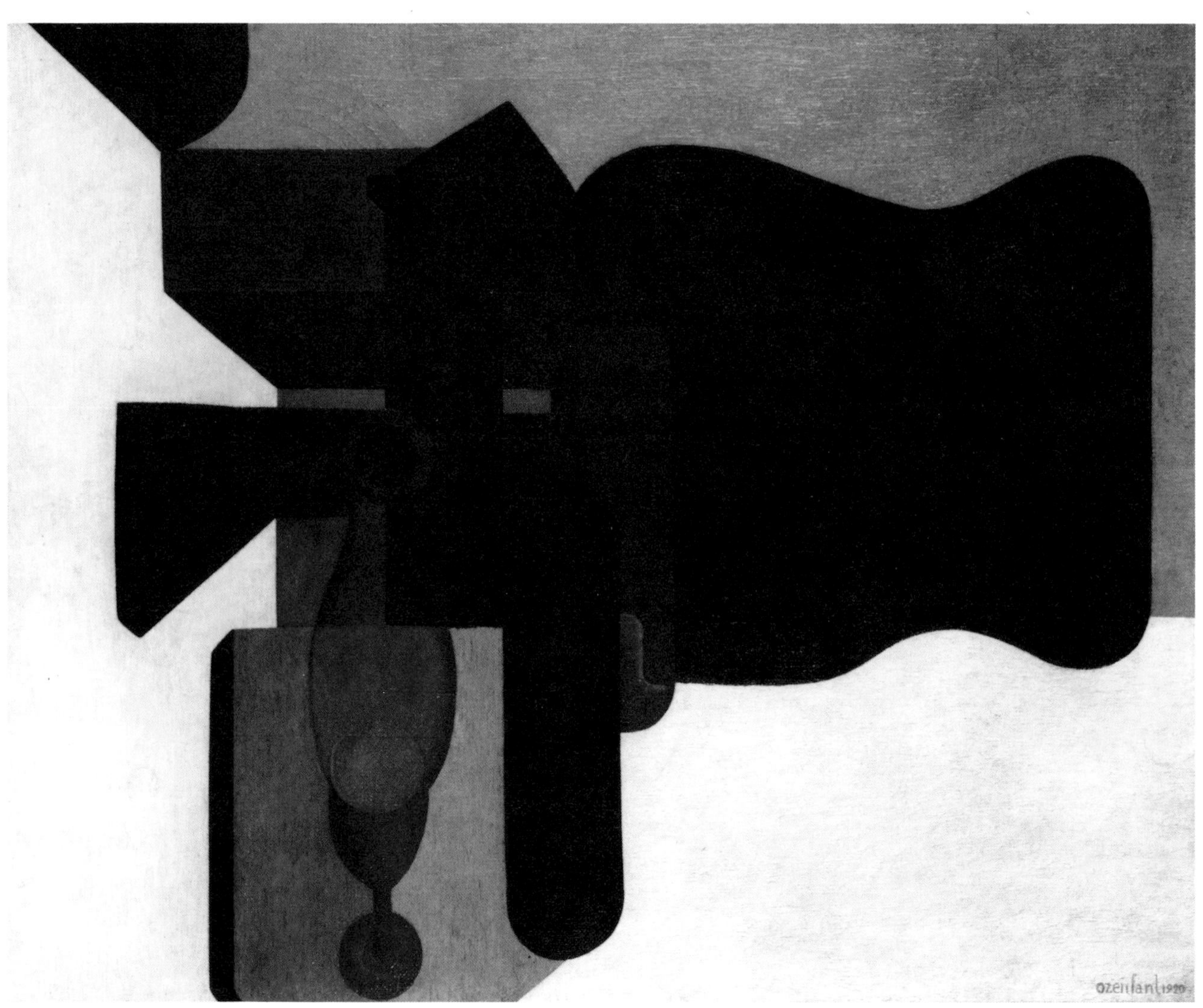

131 Guitare et bouteilles. 1920.
(*Guitar and bottles*; *Purist Still Life*; *Still Life*).

Color plate p. 394.

76.2553 PG 24

Oil on canvas, $31\frac{11}{16}$ x $39\frac{5}{16}$ (80.5 x 99.8).

Signed and dated l.r.: *ozenfant 1920*.

PROVENANCE:

Purchased from the artist, New York, ca. 1941.

CONDITION:

In 1964 (Tate Report) widespread elevated crackle with cleavage in scattered areas over the lower half of the composition, and some scratches with inpainting in the brown guitar right, were noted. The cleaving pigment in 2 areas was consolidated with wax resin adhesive.

In 1968 (New York) widespread cleavage of the paint layer through the central and lower portions was observed. In certain places, the artist had applied a gesso ground over the oil priming; this ground had become brittle, detaching from the canvas in places and causing flaking of the paint layer. Pressure cracks had developed in several places, especially in the upper areas. The browns had been thinly painted directly onto the primed canvas; poor bonding in these areas had resulted in substantial losses, which had been overpainted and in turn become discolored.

Gesso was applied from the reverse (after the application of a layer of Magna Medium color) to establish evenness of support. The painting was treated with chemicals and water on a vacuum table to minimize cracks, then lined with wax resin adhesive and Fiberglas and mounted on a honeycomb panel. The surface was cleaned and paint losses filled with gesso, inpainted, and sprayed with synthetic resin varnishes (unspecified).

The paint layer is stable. Present discoloration and streaking in the white areas may be due to varnish residue, or soil. (New York, Mar. 1983.)

This still-life, originally perhaps entitled *Esprit Nouveau* (see below EXHIBITIONS), belongs to a group of works by Ozenfant exemplifying the mature phase of Purism.

In their theoretical writings on the notion of *l'esprit nouveau*, Ozenfant and Jeanneret (Le Corbusier) advocated the development of a pictorial language that would directly respond to what they saw as the scientific or "constructive" nature of the times. The principal characteristics of such a pictorial language would be lucidity, a highly self-conscious technical precision, and a fundamentally representational form:

> *un esprit nouveau: c'est un esprit de construction et de synthèse guidé par une conception claire.... L'esprit de construction et de synthèse, d'ordre et de volonté consciente qui se manifeste de nouveau, n'est pas moins indispensable, qu'on le sache, aux arts et aux lettres, qu'aux sciences pures ou appliquées ou qu'à la philosophie....*
>
> *Nous voulons... affirmer avec force que l'esprit constructif est aussi nécessaire pour créer un tableau ou un poème que pour bâtir un pont (L'Esprit Nouveau,* vol. 1, 1920, p. 1).
>
> *La science ne progresse qu'à force de rigueur. L'esprit actuel c'est une tendance à la rigueur, à la précision, à la meilleure utilisation des forces et des matières, au moindre déchet, en somme une tendance à la pureté.*
>
> *C'est aussi la définition de l'Art.*
>
> *L'Art s'est donc occupé de récréer sa langue, à reprendre conscience de ses moyens....*
>
> *... Un tel but exclut nécessairement l'ancienne erreur des métaphysiciens d'autrefois, des romantiques créateurs d'arrangements hypothétiques sans contact suffisant avec la nature, des fantaisies personnelles arbitraires qui font nécessairement de l'œuvre une construction sans généralité et sans intérêt pour les hommes....*
>
> *L'art comme la science doit, on le voit, prendre d'abord connaissance de ces*

lois principales qui lui constitueront une langue dont il pourra se servir pour créer des constructions cohérentes avec la nature, intelligibles et satisfaisantes (L'Esprit Nouveau, vols. 11-12, 1921, pp. 1347-53).

In these and other texts, Ozenfant and Le Corbusier make careful distinctions between the goals and methods of science and of art. But the basic compatibility of the two fields (the "*communauté d'esprit*"), the shared need to create a universal language, brings them into necessary and constructive alignment with each other.

In his paintings of 1920-21, Ozenfant illustrates the nature of these theoretical principles. He often painted three or more subtly differentiated versions of a single composition, in which he explored the potential aesthetic impact of reversals of light and dark, or of new color combinations, within a fundamentally stable structure. The Peggy Guggenheim painting, for example, is related to two other virtually identical compositions, one of which is in the collection of the SRGM, New York (for a discussion of the relationship among these three canvases, see A.Z.R. *Guggenheim*, 1976, Vol. II, pp. 586-87).

Obviously influenced to a considerable extent by an architectural sense of pictorial language, derived from the work of Le Corbusier, Ozenfant's still lifes of the period typically combine side views of objects (or "elevations") with top views (or "plans"). He thus intended to preserve the integrity of the object's basic contour, conveying a maximum of information without resorting—as the Cubists did—to fragmentation of the image.

EXHIBITIONS:

Paris, Galerie Druet, *Ozenfant et Jeanneret*, Jan. 22-Feb. 5, 1921, possibly 1 of nos. 6-20? (all "Natures mortes 1919-20"); The Arts Club of Chicago, *Amédée Ozenfant*, Jan. 2-27, 1940, no. 15? ("*Still Life Esprit Nouveau*, 1920, 'for sale' "), traveled to San Francisco Museum of Art, Mar. 5-Apr. 9, St. Paul, Minn., Gallery and School of Art, Oct. 3-20, 1940;[1] New York, Art of This Century, 1942-47, p. 79, repr. (*Purist Still Life*, the title by which the work was known until 1964); Venice, *P.G.*, 1948 (Biennale), no. 97; Florence, *P.G.*, 1949, no. 103; Amsterdam, *P.G.*, 1951, no. 118, repr.; Zurich, *P.G.*, 1951, no. 114, repr.; London, *P.G.*, 1964-65, no. 17, repr. (*Guitar and Bottles*); Stockholm, *P.G.*, 1966-67, no. 17, repr.; New York, *P.G.*, 1969, p. 63, repr.; Paris, *P.G.*, 1974-75, no. 17; Torino, *P.G.*, 1975-76, no. 23; New York, *P.G.*, 1982-83, no. 20, repr.

REFERENCES:

Bulletin de "L'Effort Moderne," no. 35, 1927, repr. betw. pp. 8 and 9 (as "*Guitare et bouteilles*"); P. Guggenheim, *Art of This Century*, 1942, p. 79, repr.; Calas, 1966, p. 43; P. Guggenheim, *Out of This Century*, pp. 307-8; A.Z.R. *Guggenheim*, 1976, Vol. II, p. 587; L. Flint, *Handbook*, 1983, p. 80, repr. color p. 81.

1. Though there is no definite proof that the present work was shown in the Chicago exhibition, a second version of this composition appeared there as "no. 17, *Esprit Nouveau (2)*" (now SRGM, New York, A.Z.R. *Guggenheim*, 1976, Vol. II, cat. no. 208). The 2 works appeared on the San Francisco checklist as 32 x 39½ in., and the price for each was $1000. Given the close relationship between these 2 compositions, it cannot be ruled out that the Peggy Guggenheim version was at that moment given the title *Still Life Esprit Nouveau* and that the 2 works were shown together as *Still Life Esprit Nouveau* and *Esprit Nouveau* (2).

Eduardo Paolozzi

Born March 1924, Edinburgh.
Lives in London.

132 *Chinese Dog* 2. May 1958.

76.2553 PG 200

Bronze (lost wax). Height: 36⅜ (92.3); width: 25³⁄₁₆ (64).

Edition of one.

Foundry: Susse.

Signed (in wax): *Eduardo Paolozzi London*; on base: *62*; dated: *5 58*.

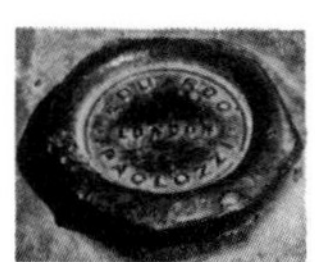

PROVENANCE:

Purchased from the Hanover Gallery, London, December 1958.

CONDITION:

There are some pitting corrosion and green streaks of corrosion.

In February 1984 (Venice) the piece was cleaned. The surface was degreased with trichloroethylene, and washed with distilled water, then with distilled water and neutral detergent; it was rinsed with distilled water, and dried with alcohol and acetone. The surface was treated for 30 minutes with a 3% solution of benzotriazole in pure alchohol. A protective coating (for outdoor display) of Incralac (acrylic resin containing benzotriazole) was applied. The condition is stable. (Venice, Mar. 1984.)

Chinese Dog 2, and its earlier version *Chinese Dog* of 1956,[1] were made at a small cottage in Thorpe-le-Soken, Essex, where Paolozzi lived for a number of years. The artist produced a large body of work in this mode, and has explained his procedure as follows: "I began with clay rolled out on a table. Into the clay I pressed pieces of metal, toys, etc. I also sometimes scored the clay. From there I proceeded in one of two ways. Either I would pour wax directly onto the clay to get a sheet, or I would pour plaster onto the clay. With the plaster I then had [both] a positive and a negative form on which to pour wax. The wax sheets were pressed around forms, cut up and added to forms, or turned into shapes on their own."[2]

The additive and improvisational processes just described have remained characteristic elements of Paolozzi's working method throughout his career. By pressing fragments of ready-made objects into the clay sheets (in this case wheels, pieces of metal, bottle tops, broken parts of mechanical toys pressed into a

1. Height: 23 in., 58 cm., present whereabouts unknown. Like the Peggy Guggenheim piece, this much smaller but closely related work was shown in the Hanover Gallery exhibition and is reproduced in the catalogue (no. 27).
2. Letter to the author, August 5, 1983.

fig. a.
Paolozzi, sections of wax mold similar to those used in the assemblage of *Chinese Dog 2*. Photograph courtesy the artist.

heavily worked — or scored — base), and by gradually building up the figure itself out of pieces of wax sheeting cut and pressed together around an armature, Paolozzi was essentially appropriating some of the techniques and effects of collage. It is to the inspiration of collage that he has consistently returned throughout the years, and his comments about that medium provide clues to the understanding of his own sculptural enterprise: "the search for invisible meanings is composed of new texts from old books and constructions from found materials ... paper on wood, paint on tin, string on card, shadow on wall ... improbable events can be frozen into peculiar assemblies by manipulation. ... Divine ambiguity is possible with collage — flesh marred by object or object masquerading as flesh.... The word 'collage' is inadequate as a description because the concept should include 'damage, erase, destroy, deface and transform.' "[3]

In order to create the *Chinese Dogs* (so named to convey their alien or foreign nature) Paolozzi, used "damaged" and "destroyed" elements, making wheels "masquerade" as eyes and metal as flesh. It was through these unexpected juxtapositions of materials and techniques that he formulated the particular vocabulary of his sculptures of the 1950s.

EXHIBITIONS:

London, Hanover Gallery, *Paolozzi: Sculpture*, Nov. 11-Dec. 31, 1958, no. 2, repr.; London, *P.G.*, 1964-65, no. 167, repr.; New York, *P.G.*, 1969, p. 169, repr.; Torino, *P.G.*, 1975-76, no. 188.

3. Artist's statement in *Eduardo Paolozzi: Work in Progress*, exh. cat., Kölnisches Kunstverein, 1979, p. 7.

Antoine Pevsner

Born January 1884, Orel, Russia.
Died April 1962, Paris.

133 La Croix Ancrée. 1933.
(*Anchored cross*).

76.2553 PG 60

Black marble (base), brass sheets painted black, crystal. Dimensions of marble base: 15 3/16 x 13 5/16 (38.6 x 33.8); overall length (diagonal): 33 5/16 (84.6); height of semicircular crystal sheets: 9 15/16 (25.2); height of triangular crystal sheets: 5 9/16 (14.2).

Signed and dated (incised into bronze): *A. PEVSNER 1933*.

A. PEVSNER 1933

PROVENANCE:

Purchased from the artist, Paris, 1940.

CONDITION:

The semicircular crystal sheets do not fit precisely into their slots, suggesting that they may be later replacements. There are some minor damages to the edges of the glass sheets; 2 of the original copper screws are missing; the condition is otherwise stable. (Venice, Nov. 1982.)

In a letter to Willem Sandberg dated January 1, 1951, Pevsner described the piece as follows: " *'La croix Ancrée' 1934 (construction). Bronze, Fond marbre noir et cristal. C'est un bas relief qui a été conçu pour être placé sur le mur (accrocher)*" (exhibition file, Stedelijk Museum, Amsterdam).

The fact that Pevsner dated the piece 1934 must be taken into account. However, the incised 1933, which would have been contemporary with the construction itself, argues for acceptance of the earlier date.[1]

EXHIBITIONS:

Amsterdam, *Tentoonstelling Abstrakte Kunst*, Apr. 2-24, 1938, no. 59 ("*Ruimtelijke constructie* 1933; *brons*");[2] New York, Art of This Century, 1946-47; Venice, *P.G.*, 1948 (Biennale), no. 100 (dated 1934, the date attributed to it in all *P.G.* publications until 1983); Florence, *P.G.*, 1949, no. 106; Amsterdam, *P.G.*, 1951, no. 122; Zurich, *P.G.*, 1951, no. 118; London, *P.G.*, 1964-65, no. 53; Stockholm, *P.G.*, 1966-67, no. 51; Paris, *P.G.*, 1974-75, no. 45, repr.; Torino, *P.G.*, 1975-76, no. 58, repr.

REFERENCES:

P. Guggenheim, *Art of This Century*, 1942, p. 89 ("*Relief Construction*, 1934"); R. Massat, *Pevsner et le constructivisme*, Paris, 1956, repr. n.p. (dated 1934); P. Peissi and C. Giedion-Welcker, *A. Pevsner*, Neuchâtel, 1961, p. 150, repr. pl. 75; L. Flint, *Handbook*, 1983, p. 64, repr. color p. 65 (dated 1933).

1. Virginie Pevsner confirmed that Pevsner usually signed and dated his constructions as he worked on them, sometimes adding more than 1 year if the work extended over a longer period (conversation with the author, Paris, Sept. 1979).
2. A fragment of a handwritten label on the reverse of the base reads: "*Exposition de Amsterdam 1938 / Monsieur Pevsner / Scupture N° 38*." The entry in the Stedelijk catalogue is not conclusive, but probably corresponds to this piece.

133

134 **Surface développable.** 1938-August 1939.[1]
(Developable surface).

76.2553 PG 61

Bronze and copper. Height (without base): 19⅞ (50.5); width along longest side: 12³⁄₁₆ (31); along shortest side: 11 (28). Copper-edged base, tin soldered: 11⁷⁄₁₆ x 11⁷⁄₁₆ (29 x 29); height of base: ⅝ (1.6). Construction screwed into base with eight copper screws (one of which is missing, one of which has been replaced).

Not signed or dated.

PROVENANCE:

Purchased from the artist, Paris, 1940.[2]

CONDITION:

The paint, which was almost certainly retouched (or totally reapplied) by someone other than Pevsner, is flaking in places, has lost opacity, and is generally soiled. Oxidization of the metal has caused further discoloration. Attempts to clean the sculpture were made in 1969 (New York), but these were unsuccessful. The surface was at that time sprayed with Lucite 46.

The condition of the construction itself is stable, though its appearance and finish have suffered considerable distortion. (Venice, Nov. 1982.)

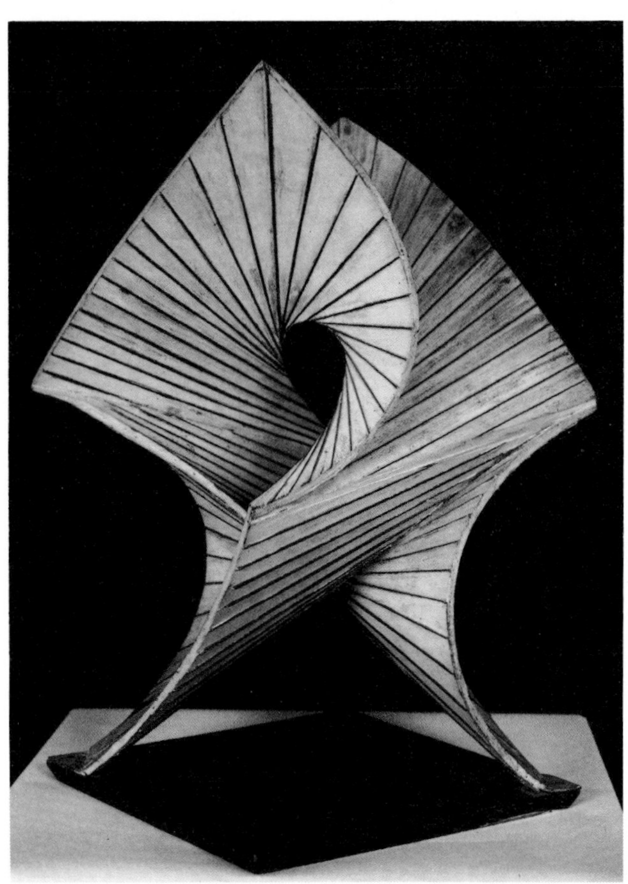

1. Virginie Pevsner, the artist's widow, recounted (Sept. 1979) that her brother left for a trip to the United States in August 1939 and was immediately recalled upon the outbreak of World War II. On the eve of his departure, Pevsner asked him to come to his studio to see the present piece, which was just finished. No one else had at that date been allowed to see it. Her brother, who was wounded in action, died in January 1940.
2. Peggy Guggenheim visited the Pevsners with Nelly van Doesburg in 1940. She bought the piece instantly upon seeing it.

134

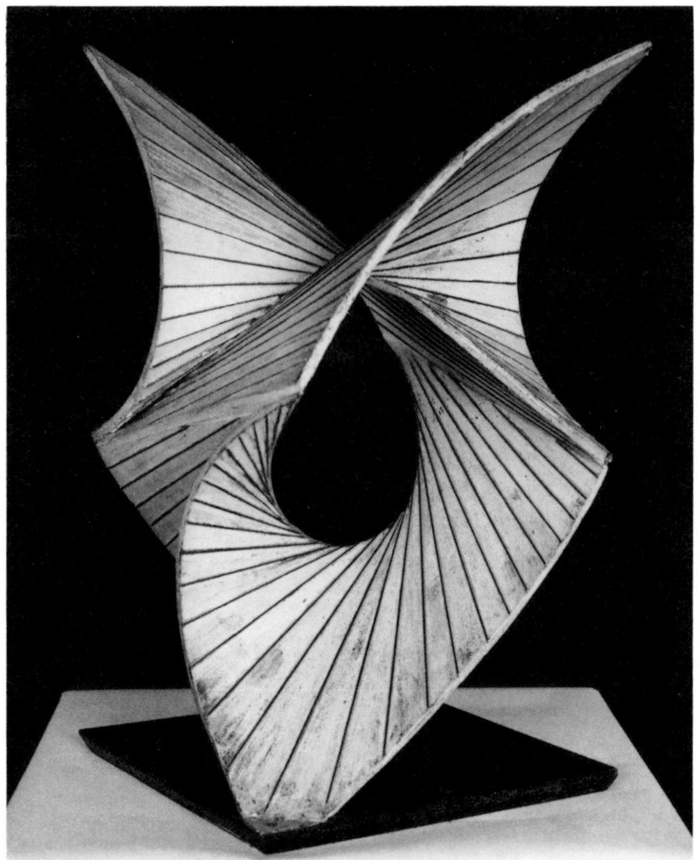

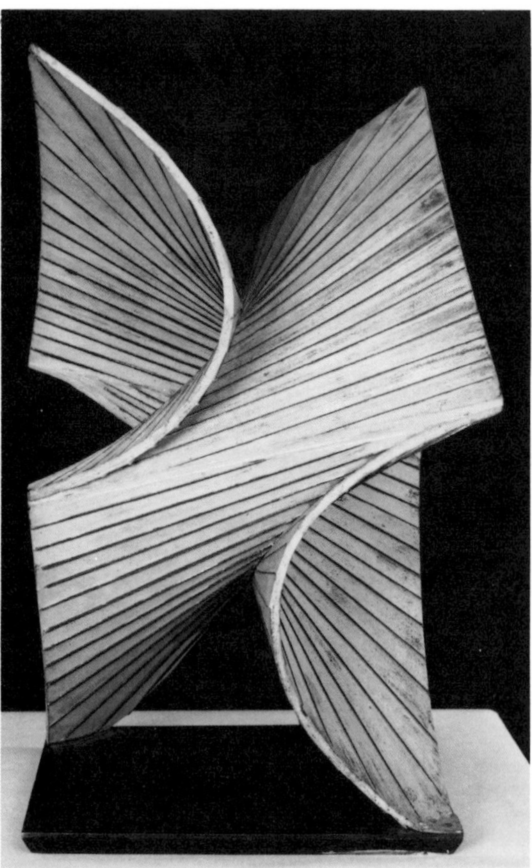

The medium and technique of this piece pose considerable problems for analysis and description. Though initially published as bronze and gesso, by 1949 the medium was given as oxidized copper. Pevsner himself, in a letter to Willem Sandberg of January 1, 1951, described the piece as follows: "*(Construction)* ... *Surface développable / (Bronze et tige dorée) 1939 / 1938*" (exhibition file, Stedelijk Museum, Amsterdam).

The actual process appears to have been as follows: three sheets of bronze were soldered together and then twisted into the present form. The highly polished (or gilded?) thin bronze strips ("*tige dorée*") were inserted after the subtly modeled piece took its final shape. Incisions to receive these bars would have been carved into the sheet bronze and the strips inserted after the metal was fully cold.

The artist's widow (in conversation with the author, September 1979) indicated that although neither she nor anyone else had ever been permitted to observe Pevsner at work, she felt confident in stating that he had never used paint or other applied color to create the effects he sought. The intrinsic qualities of the materials employed were an important ingredient in his aesthetic, and any differentiation in color, texture, weight, or transparency had to be achieved through the exploitation of the material's inherent potential rather than through a process of obscuring the substance.

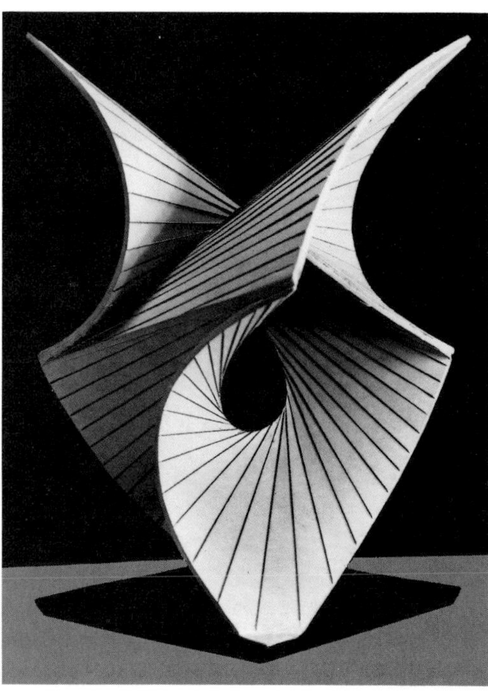

fig. a.
Ca. 1942 photograph of cat. no. 134.

It has not been possible to reconcile this principle with the visual evidence afforded by the construction in its present state, though it is impossible to say whether the materials applied by the artist are still intact or whether subsequent restoration is involved (see above CONDITION). The pristine white surface visible in the early photographs (fig. a) can only have been attained by the application of a substance such as paint, not by an oxidization process. It cannot totally be ruled out, though this is unlikely, that Pevsner had evolved a personal technique of treating the bronze in such a way that — at least for some period of time — it remained white. The present coat of paint seems, in either case, to have been applied later by another hand.

EXHIBITIONS:

New York, Art of This Century, 1942-47, p. 90, repr. ("*Surface Developing a Tangency with a Left Curve*, 1938-39"); Venice, *P.G.*, 1948 (Biennale), no. 101 ("costruzione in bronzo e gesso"); Florence, *P.G.*, 1949, no. 105 ("*Superficie che sviluppa una tangenza con una curva a sinistra*, costruzione in gesso e bronzo, 1938-39"); Amsterdam, *P.G.*, 1951, no. 121, repr.; Zurich, *P.G.*, 1951, no. 117 ("Metall"); London, *P.G.*, 1964-65, no. 54, repr. (as oxidized copper, the medium attributed to the piece until 1983); Stockholm, *P.G.*, 1966-67, no. 52; New York, *P.G.*, 1969, p. 64, repr.; Paris, *P.G.*, 1974-75, no. 46 (not repr.);[3] Torino, *P.G.*, 1975-76, p. 59 (not repr.).[3]

REFERENCES:

P. Guggenheim, *Art of This Century*, New York, 1942, p. 89 ("*Surface Developing a Tangency with a Left Curve*, 1938-39"); R. Massat, *Pevsner et le constructivisme*, Paris, 1956, repr. n.p. (upside down, "*Construction surface développable.* 1938, bronze"); P. Peissi and C. Giedion-Welcker, *A. Pevsner*, Neuchâtel, 1961, no. 150, repr. pl. 84.

3. There has been considerable confusion in the literature between cat. no. 134 and cat. no. 135. In the Paris and Torino catalogues, the reproduction is of cat. no. 135, though the caption indicates the present piece.

135 Surface développable. 1941.

(Developable surface).

76.2553 PG 62

Bronze and silver gilt. Height (including double base of bronze on slate): 21 5/8 (55); dimensions of base: 14 1/4 x 19 5/16 (36.3 x 49.1).

Signed and dated (incised into four corners of base): *A.P. 41*; *Pevsner*; *41*; *A.P.*

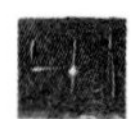

PROVENANCE:

Gift of the artist, ca. 1947.[1]

CONDITION:

In 1949 the piece was severely damaged in a fall, breaking into several pieces. Approached by Peggy Guggenheim, Pevsner agreed to attempt to restore the work, which she sent to him in Paris. After many months, the piece was returned to Peggy Guggenheim.[2]

According to the artist's widow, Virginie Pevsner, who did not witness the restoration, the system of soldering employed by her husband in such pieces involved working with 1 strand of bronze at a time, in 3-4 cm. sections, alternately cooling and heating the materials. Only by frequent and extensive cooling could the form be kept intact. She was not able to recall whether Pevsner had to replace large sections of the present piece or whether he was able to work with the original fragments.

The soldering process described by Virginie Pevsner coincides with the visual evidence. The individual bars are finely soldered together; a stronger solder is used at the edges, then filed down, and the ridges recreated with a file (fig. a). Some soft tin solder seems to have been used in the restoration.

New breaks in the structure have occurred, some of considerable length, and the piece is thus extremely fragile.

The entire surface was apparently originally coated with silver gilt. Early photographs (fig. b) reveal a glistening surface that corresponds with Pevsner's 1951 description of the piece as "*Bronze argenté.*"[3] The silver gilding may well have been carried out with mercury, which, in its original application, would have evaporated at a low temperature leaving the silver firmly adhered to the bronze support. The silver surface has now largely been lost, almost certainly owing to the high temperatures required for the soldering restoration described above.

The original slate base (visible in the early photograph, fig. b) was broken sometime after Peggy Guggenheim's death, but was repaired in March 1984.

In March 1984 (Venice) the piece was washed with distilled water. Breaks in the joins between the strands were repaired with epoxy resin (Araldit Ciba Geigy); the procedure was rendered reversible by the interposition of a layer of epoxy resin soluble in acetone (Araldit 488). A protective coating of Paraloid B-72 was applied. On this layer, retouching was carried out in order to reestablish the visual continuity in those areas where it had been clearly interrupted by the soldering stains of Pevsner's earlier restoration. This was accomplished with Maimeri restoring color and—in 1 case—with the application of silver leaf on Lukas Mixtion varnish. The condition is fragile.

fig. a.
Detail of cat. no. 135, showing soldering at edges.

1. Peggy Guggenheim and Virginie Pevsner both recalled that Pevsner sent this piece to New York after World War II. During the war years Peggy Guggenheim had arranged to send some financial support to Pevsner through Alec Ponizavsky, who lived in Monte Carlo. It is possible that the sculptor sent this gift in return for the support he had received, though this was never explained.
2. The information in this paragraph was supplied both by Peggy Guggenheim and by Virginie Pevsner.
3. Letter to Willem Sandberg, Stedelijk Museum, Amsterdam, January 1, 1951, exhibition archive, Stedelijk Museum.

fig. b.
Ca. 1942 photograph of cat. no. 135.

135

EXHIBITIONS:

Florence, *P.G.*, 1949, no. 107 ("*Superficie che sviluppa una tangenza con una curva a sinistra, N.* 2. Costruzione in bronzo argentato, 1941"); Venice, Giardino, 1949, no. 16, repr. (title and date as above); Amsterdam, *P.G.*, 1951, no. 123, repr.; Zurich, *P.G.*, 1951, no. 119 ("Metall"); London, *P.G.*, 1964-65, no. 55 (erroneously dated 1938-39; this error recurred in *P.G.* publications until 1975); Stockholm, *P.G.*, 1966-67, no. 53; New York, *P.G.*, 1969, p. 65, repr.; Paris, *P.G.*, 1974-75, no. 47, repr. (with the caption for 76. 2553 PG 61); Torino, *P.G.*, 1975-76, no. 60, repr. pl. 32 (with the caption for 76. 2553 PG 61).

REFERENCES:

P. Peissi and C. Giedion-Welcker, *A. Pevsner*, Neuchâtel, 1961, p. 150, repr. pl. 89; Calas, 1966, repr. p. 98 (erroneously dated 1938-39).

François Marie Martinez Picabia

Born January 1879, Paris.
Died November 1953, Paris.

136 Très rare tableau sur la terre. 1915.
(*Very rare picture on the earth*).

Color plate p. 241.

76.2553 PG 67

Oil and metallic paint on paper board; silver and gold leaf applied to plywood relief cylinders, which are screwed to support from reverse. Wood frame constructed by artist as integral part of the work. Inner dimensions of paper board support: 44 9/16 x 33 1/2 (113.2 x 85.2); inner edge of frame: 46 9/16 x 35 1/2 (118.2 x 90.2); outer dims. of frame: 49 1/2 x 38 1/2 (125.7 x 97.8).

Titled u.l.: *TREZ RARE TABLEAU SUR LA TERRE*; signed l.l.: *Picabia*.Not dated.

PROVENANCE:

Purchased from Gabrielle Buffet-Picabia, Paris, 1940.

CONDITION:

The paper board is bent at the left edge and creased at the lower left edge. Both the left and right edges show extensive breaks and losses indicating that the support was forced into the frame at some stage. The bronze paint used on 3 interior edges of the frame was applied after framing. There are scratches and losses in the rectangular gold and silver leaf sections, revealing white bole (clay) underneath. There are slight traces of (inactive) foxing in the lower third of the composition. The overall condition is stable. (New York, Feb. 1983.)

As William Camfield has convincingly argued, Picabia's earliest machine paintings date from the summer of 1915 (1979, pp. 77-82).[1] In an oft-quoted interview published in the New York *Herald Tribune* on October 24, 1915, Picabia spoke of the critical role the machine was beginning to play in his pictorial vocabulary and emphasized its potential as the only appropriate contemporary source for a symbolic language.

1. Several authors have argued that earlier manifestations of mechanomorphism began to emerge in Picabia's work of 1913, though all scholars agree that only from 1915 are Picabia's paintings consistently and exclusively machinist. For discussions of the earlier date, see, for example, P. Pearlstein, "The Symbolic Language of Francis Picabia," *Arts*, vol. 30, no. 4, Jan. 1956, pp. 40, 43, who sees analogies between machine and human forms in *Je revois en souvenir ma chère Udnie*, dated by him late 1913; M. Sanouillet, *Picabia*, Paris, 1964, pp. 24, 28, who describes *Catch as Catch Can*, 1913, as "*la première toile qu'on puisse qualifier de 'mécanique'* " though placing the "*vrai tableaux mécaniques*" in 1915; F. Will-Levaillant, 1969, pp. 74, 78, who sees a radical change in Picabia's work of 1913-15 as his Orphic style dissolves and the seeds of his machinist style are sown. Like Pearlstein, she describes *Je revois*... as "*sans doute la première toile de Picabia que l'on peut qualifier de 'mécanomorphe'*." She is tentative in her discussion of the chronology of the period, concluding that "*entre 1913 et 1915, sans avoir rompu avec ses recherches de composition abstraite colorée, Picabia s'intéressait aux possibilités offertes par l'imagerie 'mécanique'*." Camfield first argued his position on the importance of 1915 as the turning point, in his unpublished dissertation, Yale University, 1964, and in a 1966 article, "The Machinist Style of Francis Picabia," *Art Bulletin*, vol. 48, nos. 3-4, Sept.-Dec. 1966, pp. 309-22.

136

Almost immediately upon coming to America [June 1915] *it flashed upon me that the genius of the modern world is machinery, and that through machinery art ought to find a most vivid expression.*

I have been profoundly impressed by the vast mechanical development in America. The machine has become more than a mere adjunct of human life. It is really a part of human life — perhaps the very soul. In seeking forms through which to interpret ideas or by which to expose human characteristics I have come at length upon the form which appears most brilliantly plastic and fraught with symbolism. I have enlisted the machinery of the modern world, and introduced it into my studio.... of course, I have only begun to work out this newest stage of evolution. I don't know what possibilities may be in store. I mean to simply work on and on until I attain the pinnacle of mechanical symbolism.

It is apparent that Picabia's 1915-22 machinist paintings and drawings entirely justify the artist's early claim for a "mechanical symbolism." Moreoever, his actual machine sources—taken from contemporary magazines, technical handbooks, catalogues, advertisements, etc.—have in many instances been identified, and the symbolic content of the paintings has been considerably elucidated in the process. (See especially Camfield, loc. cit., pp. 313ff.; 1979, pp. 77-90; also Pearlstein, loc. cit., and W. I. Homer, "Picabia's *Jeune fille américaine dans l'état de nudité* and Her Friends," *Art Bulletin*, vol. 57, no. 1, Mar. 1975, pp. 110-15.)

In the case of *Très rare tableau sur la terre*, a specific source has not to date been found, although its probable derivation from the design for an actual piece of machinery was suggested as early as 1916. A reviewer of the Modern Gallery exhibition in which *Très rare tableau sur la terre* appeared, drew attention to such specific sources for Picabia's machinist vocabulary and referred in passing to the Peggy Guggenheim picture (mistaking the collage wood elements with their coating of gold and silver leaf for "pieces of real metal"): "There can be no uncertainty whatsoever in classifying Picabia in his latest phase. He is a machinist. His various philosophical observations, comments and strictures on humanity and life in general are expressed in the most literal concrete terms of machinery — valves, pistons, cogs, fly wheels, belting and boilers, sometimes actually built out in relief with pieces of real metal — and the laws that are assumed to govern their action are the laws of physics and chemistry" (*Christian Science Monitor*, 1916).

The major elements of the picture are two prominently placed cylinders with pistons, a shaft and flywheels, a number of curvilinear rods, and a "vaporous" (steam?) chamber below. The relative specificity of the elements suggests that Picabia may have based his design—in a highly simplified way—on a particular type of steam or internal combustion engine, such as a Stirling (fig. a), where

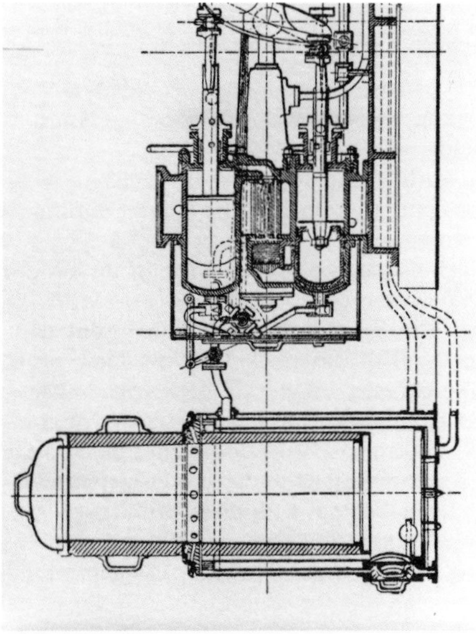

fig. a.
Diagram (detail) of a double-acting engine invented by Sir William Siemens in 1863.

many of the main components of Picabia's design are found in a roughly comparable configuration.[2]

The correspondence between the Stirling engine and Picabia's painting, however, is obviously not as close as in some analogous "machine" works, such as the artist's 1919 *L'Enfant Carburateur* (SRGM), which is based almost precisely on the diagram of a Racing Claudel Carburetor (see A.Z.R. *Guggenheim*, 1976, Vol. II, pp. 592-95). The lack of close correspondence between diagram and painting in *Très rare tableau sur la terre* may indicate that a more precise source exists that has simply not yet been discovered. On the other hand, this was perhaps the first — certainly among the first — of Picabia's machine paintings. The artist may well have undertaken his earliest experiments by making freer and somewhat more imaginative assemblages of mechanical parts, using technical diagrams mainly as a general point of departure. As Camfield has pointed out (1979), *Très rare tableau sur la terre* represented the first known example of collage in Picabia's oeuvre. The complex three-dimensional construction — with wooden cylinders and rod, an integrated wooden frame, and the multiple media used on the surface (including carefully applied sheets of gold and silver leaf) — represents in itself an effort to create an "imitation" machine. Moreover, the very complexity of the piece and its method of fabrication seem calculated to suggest various parallels between the intricacies of machine design and Picabia's new mode of artistic expression.[3]

EXHIBITIONS:

New York, Modern Gallery, *Picabia Exhibition*, Jan. 5-25, 1916, no. 5;[4] New York, The Society of Independent Artists, *Second Annual Exhibition*, Apr. 20-May 12, 1918, no. 586;[5] Paris, *Salon des Indépendants*, Jan. 28-Feb. 29, 1920, no. 3551; Paris, au Sans Pareil, *Exposition Dada: Francis Picabia*, Apr. 16-30, 1920, no. 3; Paris, Galerie Goemans, *Exposition de collages*, Mar. 1930, no. 26, repr.; Paris, Léonce Rosenberg, *Exposition Francis Picabia*, Dec. 9-31, 1930, no. 8;[5] New York, MoMA, *Cubism and Abstract Art*, 1936, no. 201, repr.; New York, Art of This Century, 1942-47, p. 60, repr. p. 61; Venice, *P.G.*, 1948 (Biennale), no. 102; Florence, *P.G.*, 1949, no. 108; Amsterdam, *P.G.*, 1951, no. 124, repr.; Zurich, *P.G.*, 1951, no. 120; London, *P.G.*, 1964-65, no. 60, repr. (with frame); Stockholm, *P.G.*, 1966-67, no. 58, repr. (with frame); New York, *P.G.*, 1969, p. 43, repr. p. 42; Paris, *P.G.*, 1974-75, no. 62, repr.; Torino, *P.G.*, 1975-76, no. 65, repr. pl. 31 (withdrawn early); [Paris, MNAM, *Francis Picabia*, Jan. 23-Mar. 29, 1976, no. 52, repr. color cover, not exhibited]; Rome, *Guggenheim: Venezia-New York*, 1982, no. 29, repr. color (with frame); New York, *P.G.*, 1982-83, no. 25, repr. color (with frame).

2. This particular engine may not have been available for Picabia to see. However, Irvin Glassman, Professor of Mechanical and Aerospace Engineering at Princeton University, who drew the diagram to the author's attention, suggests that engines of this type (generally described as "Stirling" engines even when designed by others) were quite distinctive. They were widely used in machines of various kinds from the late 19th century onward and may well have provided the inspiration for Picabia's design.
3. For an interesting and imaginative interpretation of the image as alchemical turbine, see Linde, 1976.
4. According to Sanouillet, the exhibition of 16 works traveled to the McClees Gallery, Philadelphia, in May 1916 (op. cit., p. 30). No catalogue of this exhibition has been located.
5. William Camfield provided details about this exhibition.

REFERENCES:

Anon., "Picabia's Puzzles," *Christian Science Monitor*, 29 Jan., 1916; Anon., "Current News of Art and the Exhibitions," *The Sun*, 16 Jan., 1916, section 3, p. 7; G. Kahn, *Mercure de France*, vol. 138, 1920, p. 506; L. Aragon, *La Peinture au défi*, exh. cat., Galerie Goemans, Paris, 1930, repr. pl. vii; A. Breton, "Genèse et perspective artistiques du surréalisme," *Labyrinthe*, no. 5, Feb. 15, 1945, repr. p. 11; idem, *Le Surréalisme et la peinture*, New York, 1945, repr. betw. pp. 48 and 49; G. Buffet-Picabia, "Some memories of Pre-Dada: Picabia and Duchamp" (1949), *The Dada Painters and Poets: An Anthology*, ed. R. Motherwell, New York, 1951, p. 261; idem, *Aires abstraites*, Geneva, 1957, pp. 35-36; M. Le Bot, *Francis Picabia et la crise des valeurs figuratives*, Paris, 1968, p. 127; W. Rubin, *Dada, Surrealism, and Their Heritage*, New York, 1968, pp. 56, 58, 146, repr. color p. 57; F. Will-Levaillant, "Picabia et la machine: symbole et abstraction," *Revue de l'Art*, no. 4, 1969, p. 74; G. Buffet-Picabia, *Picabia*, exh. cat., MNAM, Paris, 1976, p. 7; U. Linde, ibid., p. 24; J. H. Martin, "Locutions latines et étrangères extraites du Petit Larousse," ibid., p. 48; W. A. Camfield, *Picabia*, Princeton, 1979, p. 88, repr. pl. 119.

Pablo Ruiz Picasso

Born October 1881, Malaga.
Died April 1973, Mougins.

137 Le poète. Céret, August 1911.
(*The poet*).

Color plate p. 34.

76.2553 PG 1

Oil on fine linen canvas (unvarnished), 51 5/8 x 35 1/4 (131.2 x 89.5).

Signed and dated l.l.: *Picasso / 10*; inscribed by the artist on reverse (recorded but not photographed before lining): *Picasso / Ceret.* The signature and date on the face must have been added at a later date, probably in the 1920s or 1930s. (See M. Jardot, *Picasso*, exh. cat., Paris, 1955, p. 46, for a discussion of the fact that Picasso and Braque rarely signed their pictures on the obverse between the years 1907 and 1914.)

PROVENANCE:

Purchased from the artist by D.-H. Kahnweiler, 1911;[1] Wilhelm Uhde, Paris, by 1914?;[2] Paris, Hôtel Drouot, *Vente Wilhelm Uhde*, May 30, 1921, no. 48?;[2] Alfred Flechtheim, Berlin, by 1932 (Zurich exh. cat., possibly purchased at the Uhde sale, 1921?); George L. K. Morris, New York, by 1936 (MoMA exh. cat.); purchased from Morris, 1941.

CONDITION:

By 1964 (Tate Report) 3 tears had already been repaired with patches on the reverse (date unknown). The matte unvarnished surface intended by Picasso was still intact at that point;[3] the canvas was described as fragile, with some minute abrasions, a few small losses, and some signs of incipient cleavage. Undulations and wrinkles in the support, due to poor stretching, were also noted. At this time 1 paper patch and the paint beneath it—used as an adhesive—were removed. The edges of the L-shaped tear (ca. 1 1/2 x 3 in., 3.8 x 7.6 cm.) were realigned, and a linen patch applied with Vinamal b525. Some small blisters in the lower left were secured with wax resin adhesive. The area of the tear and other small losses were filled with Paraloid B-72.

In 1968 (New York) the canvas was flattened on the vacuum table. The reverse was treated with a light coating of Magna Medium color to create a barrier to the lining adhesive. The painting was lined with wax resin adhesive and Fiberglas; the surface was cleaned, and gesso fillings were used to fill losses, which were then retouched with dry color in polyvinyl acetate (AYAB). The surface was coated with synthetic resin varnish.

Comparison of the present surface with that of other works by the artist from this period indicates that it has been flattened; Picasso's subtly modulated variations in tone, texture, and brushwork have been considerably affected by the lining and by the application of the heavy coat of varnish. Possible approaches to the removal of the varnish are under study. (New York, Mar. 1983.)

Picasso began his summer sojourn at Céret in the Pyrenees on about July 10, 1911, and Braque joined him there approximately one month later (Daix, 1979, pp. 89, 266). During the ensuing weeks, they worked in extremely close collaboration. Basing his conclusions partially upon Pierre Descargues's discovery that Braque's *Le Portugais* was painted in Céret (*Braque de Draeger*, Paris and New

1. The Kahnweiler stockbook records the work as no. 788, *Le Poète*, purchased in 1911; a Galerie Kahnweiler label formerly on the stretcher (noted, but not photographed) confirms this provenance.
2. Daix and Rosselet (1979), who do not include the Kahnweiler provenance, suggest that the work probably belonged to Uhde and appeared in the 1921 Uhde sale as no. 48, "*Le Fumeur de Pipes*, 1,30 m x 0,37 m, signé au dos." No other *Pipe-smoker* of these dimensions has apparently been located. Moreover *Le poète* was published by Uhde in his 1928 book on Picasso, together with other works that had previously been in his collection.
3. See above, cat. no. 19, fn. 3 for a comment on the importance of the unvarnished surface of the Cubist oils to both Picasso and Braque.

York, 1971, p. 106), Pierre Daix has argued convincingly that five important figure paintings by the two artists were completed during the month of August: Braque's *Le Portugais* (Kunstmuseum, Basel, oil on canvas, 28¾ x 23 7/16 in., 73 x 59.5 cm.) and *L'Homme à la guitare* (MoMA, New York, oil on canvas, 45⅝ x 31⅞ in., 116 x 81 cm.); Picasso's *L'Homme à la pipe* (Kimbell Art Museum, Fort Worth, Texas, oil on oval canvas, 35¾ x 27⅞ in., 90.7 x 71.0 cm.), *Le poète*, and *l'Accordéoniste* (SRGM, New York, oil on canvas, 51¼ x 35¼ in., 130.2 x 89.5 cm., see A.Z.R. *Guggenheim*, Vol. II, pp. 599-601). As Daix has pointed out (p. 89), in each of the five works "the figure is constructed on an abstract armature, triangular in Braque's case, pyramidal in Picasso's. In Braque's pictures we find the curtain tieback that Picasso had included in his still-lifes of spring 1911. The armchair, on the other hand, recurred with greater insistence. Both painters kept to their theme: Braque, a man with a guitar; Picasso, a man with a pipe, writing at a table in a *bistrot*...."

Edward Fry (1981) has drawn attention to one of the most significant results of Daix's new chronology for an understanding of the collaborative efforts of the two artists at Céret. The evolution of Picasso's work from the spring of 1910 through late 1912 arises, according to Fry's analysis, out of the fundamentally divergent response of the two artists to the art of Cézanne during 1908 and 1909. Braque's "response was to mimic the skin — Cézanne's brushwork and certain of his formal devices — even as he reduced the Cézannian lesson to the harmonious, surface-bound idiom of his own pictorial sensibility." His Cubist achievement is likewise characterized by a fundamentally two-dimensional sensibility. In Picasso's case, Fry argues, it is the dialectical power of intellect and the invention of an entirely new draftsmanship to deal with the "tensions of simultaneous plasticity and flatness" that leads to the full achievement of Cubism. The centrality of the issue of drawing (or *disegno*) is critical to Fry's analysis, and he reasons convincingly that in the juxtaposition of these 1911 Céret works, the contrast between Braque's "two-dimensional pictorial sensibility" and Picasso's "intellect attempting to unite surface and volume through a new kind of *disegno*" is considerably illuminated.

EXHIBITIONS:

Zurich, Kunsthalle, *Picasso*, Sept. 11-Oct. 30, 1932 (extended to Nov. 13), no. 67, repr. pl. IX (lent by Alfred Flechtheim, Berlin); New York, MoMA, *Cubism and Abstract Art*, 1936, no. 214, repr. fig. 30 (lent by G.L.K. Morris); New York, Marie Harriman Gallery, *Figure Paintings: Picasso*, Jan. 30-Feb. 18, 1939, no. 6 (lent by George L.K. Morris); New York, MoMA, *Art in Our Time*, May 10-Sept. 30, 1939, no. 158, repr.; New York, Art of This Century, 1942-47, p. 38, repr. p. 39; Venice, *P.G.*, 1948, (Biennale), no. 103; Florence, *P.G.*, 1949, no. 109; Venice, XXV Biennale, June 8-Oct. 15, 1950, *Quatro maestri del cubismo*, no. 33; Amsterdam, *P.G.*, 1951, no. 125; Zurich, *P.G.*, 1951, no. 121; London, *P.G.*, 1964-65, no. 1, repr.; Stockholm, *P.G.*, 1966-67, no. 1, repr.; New York, *P.G.*, 1969, p. 49, repr. p. 48; Paris, *P.G.*, 1974-75, no. 1, repr. p. 38; Torino, *P.G.*, 1975-76, no. 1; Rome, *Guggenheim: Venezia-New York*, 1982, no. 3, repr. color; New York, *P.G.*, 1982-83, no. 1, repr.

REFERENCES:

T. Däubler, *Der Neue Standpunkt*, Dresden, 1916, p. 158; W. Uhde, *Picasso et la tradition française*, Paris, 1928, repr. p. 12; *Documents*, 2ᵉ année, no. 3, 1930, p. 181; P. Guggenheim, *Art of*

This Century, 1942, p. 38, repr. p. 39; C. Zervos, *Pablo Picasso: Œuvres de 1906 à 1912*, vol. 2*, Paris, 1942, no. 285; R. Penrose, *Picasso: His Life and Work*, London, 1958, p. 164; G. Habasque, *Le cubisme*, Geneva, 1959, repr. color p. 48; A. R. Solomon, "Pablo Picasso: Symbolism in the Synthetic Cubist Still Life. A Study of His Iconography from 1911-1927," unpublished Ph.D. dissertation, Harvard University, 1961, pp. 135, 143; Calas, 1966, pp. 20-21, repr. color p. 29 (identifies the figure as Apollinaire); P. Daix, *La Vie de peintre de Pablo Picasso*, Paris, [1977], p. 109; P. Daix and J. Rosselet, *Picasso: The Cubist Years 1907-1916*, Boston, 1979, pp. 89, 269, no. 423, repr. p. 90; M. M. Gedo, *Picasso: Art as Autobiography*, Chicago and London, 1980, n.p.; E. F. Fry, review of Daix and Rosselet, *The Art Journal*, vol. 41, no. 1, spring 1981, p. 93; P. Daix, *Cubists and Cubism*, Geneva, N.Y., 1982, p. 63, repr. color p. 65; idem, "Braque et Picasso au temps des papiers collés," in *Georges Braque: Les Papiers Collés*, exh. cat., MNAM, Paris, 1982, p. 16, repr.

---

138 Pipe, verre, bouteille de Vieux Marc.

Paris, spring 1914.
(*Pipe, glass, bottle of Vieux Marc*; *Lacerba*).

Color plate p. 36.

76.2553 PG 2

Block-printed paper, white laid paper, green wove paper, newspaper, light and dark brown wood-pulp papers, charcoal, india ink, printer's ink, graphite, and white gouache on fine linen unprimed canvas (unvarnished), $28^{13}/_{16}$ x $23^{3}/_{8}$ (73.2 x 59.4).

Not signed or dated.

PROVENANCE:

Galerie Kahnweiler, Paris, 1914 (photo no. 362);[1] probably sequestered Kahnweiler stock, 1914-21; 2e *Vente Kahnweiler*, Hôtel Drouot, Paris, November 17-18, 1921, no. 201? (*Nature morte*, 73 x 53, purchased by Ozenfant, 1150 francs);[2] purchased by Sally Lewis, Oregon;[3] purchased from Sally Lewis by Pierre Matisse, New York; purchased from Pierre Matisse, December 6, 1941.

1. The photo is labeled "*pipe, verre, bouteille de vieux marc*, papier collé avec dessin, 1913-14." M. Raynal, in his 1921 book, credits the photograph to Galerie Simon.
2. It has not been possible to establish with certainty whether the present still life in fact corresponds to this lot number in the Kahnweiler *Ventes*, the only lot that corresponds approximately, though not exactly, in dimensions and other details. It is doubtful that a work of this scale on canvas would have been placed in a miscellaneous grouped lot, and the possibility of its identification with lot 201 is thus presented as a hypothesis. Ozenfant's identity as purchaser and the price were supplied by Gary Tinterow.
3. Sally Lewis began collecting, with apparently modest means, at the time of the 1913 Armory Show. She was also a purchaser at the Kahnweiler *Ventes* (see. D. Cooper, *The Essential Cubism*, exh. cat., The Tate Gallery, London, 1983, p. 28), and knew Ozenfant. It has not been possible to establish that she purchased this work from Ozenfant, but it would be plausible. Pierre Matisse did not recall where or when she had acquired the Picasso or when he purchased it from her (conversation with the author, Mar. 1978).

CONDITION:

In 1964 (Tate Report) some mold or water stains on the canvas upper right were noted, but the condition was otherwise described as excellent.

In 1978 (New York) the mold (attributable to framing directly against glass) was observed again, combined with overall foxing. The fine linen canvas had been stretched and tacked to a wood strainer; mold growth and foxing on verso had penetrated the obverse. The work was removed from the strainer leaving the entire linen support intact. The surface was cleaned recto and verso. Foxing stains were successfully removed and the work fumigated in thymol. It was mounted with linen tabs on a 100% rag board mount. Some light lifting of collage elements was consolidated. Though the papers have darkened to some extent through overexposure to light, the condition is stable. (Venice, Nov. 1982.)

Pierre Daix (1979) has argued convincingly that Picasso's *papiers collés* can be divided into three distinct groups: the first dating from October 1912 to early 1913 and made in Paris; the second from early 1913 in Paris to the spring and summer of the same year in Céret; and the third from the beginning of 1914 in Paris to early summer in Avignon.[4] The Peggy Guggenheim still life belongs to the third group and was completed in Paris during the spring.

138

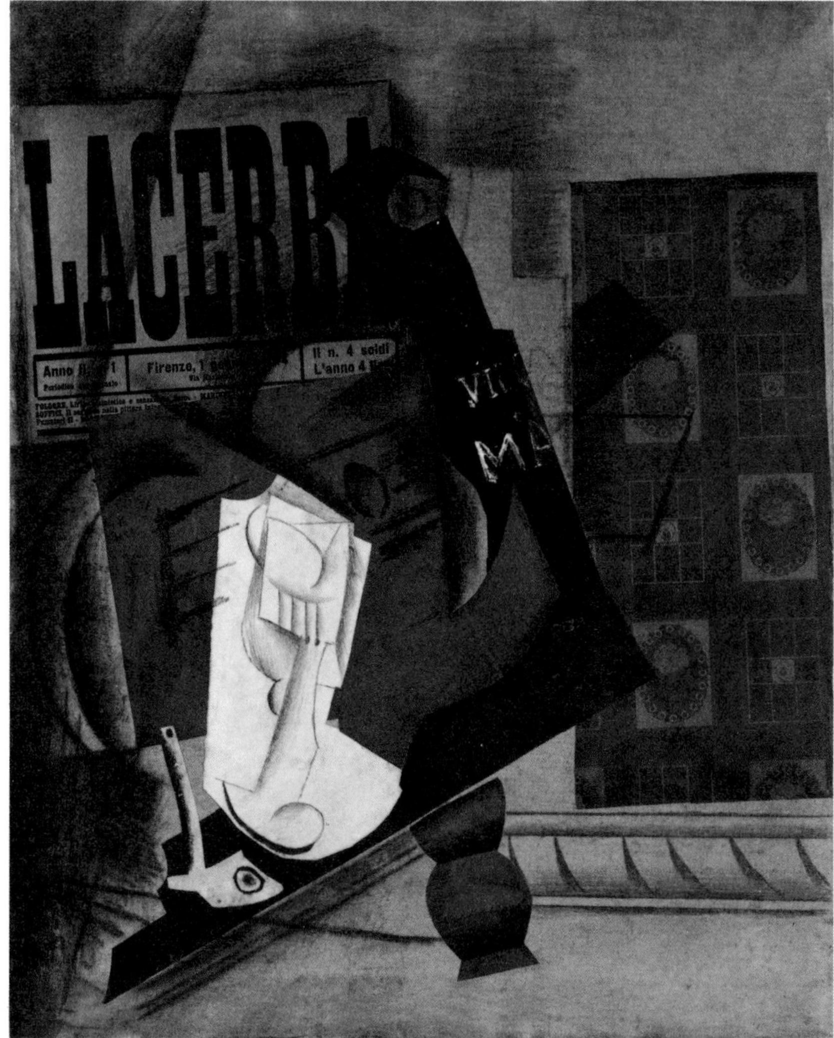

Daix has identified more than forty *papiers collés* belonging to this latter period; however, only six of these, including the Peggy Guggenheim piece, are on canvas.[5] One of these is in several respects closely related to Peggy Guggenheim's, although it is clearly less intricate and complex (Daix and Rosselet, no. 669, repr. color pl. xlii, 11 1/16 x 13 3/4 in., 28 x 35 cm., Národní Galerie, Prague). It includes the same block-printed wallpaper (which occurs in no other located examples); an almost identical pipe and a similarly articulated glass, cut from the same white laid paper; and examples of the same green wove paper and brown wood-pulp paper. Black oil, charcoal, and graphite are used to similar effect in both works, and the inclusion of a printed matchbox cover in the Prague work[6] is comparable in its pictorial function to the "Lacerba" clipping in the larger, more ambitious Venice still-life.[7]

Daix assigns both canvases to Paris, but he places the Prague one very early in the entire sequence and the Venice piece considerably later, with thirty works intervening between them. The much greater complexity of the Peggy Guggenheim work indicates a later date. Nonetheless, the close relationship between the two canvases — in their materials, the objects depicted, and certain aspects of their pictorial resolution — suggests that the Prague still life may have been executed slightly later in the sequence, at a time somewhat closer to the Venice work.

4. As Robert Rosenblum first noted in 1960 (*Cubism and Twentieth-Century Art*, New York, p. 94), the chronology of the *papiers collés* could be clarified to a considerable extent if the date of each of the newspaper fragments were observed and treated as a firm *terminus post quem* for the work under study. Rosenblum subsequently led the way in resolving a considerable number of these dating problems. See "Picasso and the Coronation of Alexander III: A Note on the Dating of Some *Papiers Collés*," *Burlington Magazine*, vol. 113, Oct. 1971, pp. 604-7; and "Picasso and the Typography of Cubism," *Picasso in Retrospect*, R. Penrose and J. Golding, eds., New York and Washington, 1973, pp. 49-75. See also E. F. Fry, *Cubism*, New York, 1966, p. 193, fns. 20, 21; P. Daix, "Des bouleversements chronologiques dans la révolution des papiers collés, 1912-1914," *Gazette des Beaux-Arts*, vol. lxxxii, Oct. 1973, pp. 217-27. In this article, Daix developed an initial set of guidelines for an overall chronology of the 3 groups of *papiers collés*, which was subsequently revised and incorporated into his 1979 catalogue raisonné of the Cubist years. In that volume, see pp. 111-18, 123-28, 131-38, 147-48 for discussions of the characteristics of each phase.

5. A number of the supports, including that of the Peggy Guggenheim picture, are not identified by Daix and Rosselet (1979). The 5 other examples of canvas supports cited by them are: 669 (Národní Galerie, Prague), 690 (John Hay Whitney Collection), 759 and 760 (The Picasso Estate), and 785 (Private Collection, Basel).

6. An identical *ALLUMETTES FRANÇAISES* matchbox was used by Juan Gris in his almost exactly contemporary *papier collé*, cat. no. 74.

7. The printed clipping used by Picasso in this work is taken from the front page of *Lacerba*, dated January 1, 1914. (The Italian review was founded in Florence—in 1913—by Giovanni Papini and Ardengo Soffici, and appeared at irregular intervals until 1915.) Picasso's only other "quotation" from *Lacerba* occurs in *Verre de vin, journal, assiette, couteau* (Daix and Rosselet, 1979, no. 702). As Isabelle Monod-Fontaine has pointed out, Braque at almost exactly the same time (although working in a different place) also made a *papier collé* using clippings from *Lacerba*, in his case the issue of January 15, 1914 (see I. Monod-Fontaine, ed., *Georges Braque: Les papiers collés*, exh. cat., MNAM, Paris, 1982, p. 154, repr. color.)

As Daix has noted, the *papiers collés* of 1914 exhibit an extraordinary range of materials, techniques, and virtuosity. They also demonstrate a continuous effort to explore increasingly complex problems of space: "Whereas the spectacular achievements of the second generation of *papiers collés* aimed at demonstrating the power of paint, these later ones attempted to come to grips with establishing systems of spatial syntax, structured systems which ensured the fabrication of space, without which painting and *papiers collés* alike were no more than ornamental" (Daix and Rosselet, 1979, p. 147).

In the 1914 *papiers collés* Picasso combined, for the first time in a sustained manner, two entirely different approaches to space: those of Cubism and of traditional perspective. In the Peggy Guggenheim still life, for example, a continuous series of intricately devised contradictions serves to establish and hold in equilibrium these two spatial conceptions. Thus the lower edge of the table is drawn with perspective shading, but the table's *papier-collé* surface is tipped to coincide with the picture plane; the glass and pipe are partially drawn in trompe l'oeil but are also cut from paper in such a way as to appear flat; and the fragment of wall molding is drawn and shaded entirely in perspective, but the background wall itself — partly shaded with charcoal, and then abruptly flattened through the application at a slight diagonal of the literal "sign" of the wallpaper — is of an indeterminate depth. Most striking in their virtuosity are the central configurations of the guitar, glass, and bottle: the objects are rendered in three-dimensional and in flattened form; indeed they overlap and interlock in such a way as to establish — and, simultaneously, to undermine — their solidity, transparency, and location in space.

Although spatial ambiguities and contradictions occur at every significant point in the composition, the interrelationships among the objects, and their integration with the surrounding space, remain fundamentally legible. In this respect, the particular achievement of the 1914 works (as Daix suggests) surely owes something to Picasso's exploration of similar problems in the sculpture and constructions of the immediately preceding period. The "constructed" character of these works which clearly is integral to them, contributes significantly to their spatial effects.

EXHIBITIONS:

Venice, *P.G.*, 1948 (Biennale), no. 104; Florence, *P.G.*, 1949, no. 110; Venice, XXV Biennale, *Quattro maestri del cubismo*, June 8-Oct. 15, 1950, no. 38; Amsterdam, *P.G.*, 1951, no. 126; Zurich, *P.G.*, 1951, no. 122; London, *P.G.*, 1964-65, no. 2, repr.; Stockholm, *P.G.*, 1966-67, no. 2, repr.; New York, *P.G.*, 1969, p. 50, repr. p. 51; Paris, *P.G.*, 1974-75, no. 2, repr.; Torino, *P.G.*, 1975-76, no. 2, repr. pl. 2.

REFERENCES:

M. Raynal, *Picasso*, Munich, 1921, Paris, 1922, repr. pl. XIX ("*Nature-morte*, 1913"; no owner listed, photo supplied by Galerie Simon); C. Zervos, *Pablo Picasso: Œuvres de 1912 à 1917*, vol. 2**, Paris, 1942, no. 461 (as "*Pipe, verre, bouteille de Vieux Marc*, winter, 1913-14"); P. Guggenheim, *Art of This Century*, 1942, p. 38, repr. p. 41; P. Daix and J. Rosselet, *Picasso: The Cubist Years 1907-1916*, Boston, 1979, no. 701 ("*Pipe, verre, journal, guitare, bouteille de Vieux Marc ['Lacerba']*, Spring, 1914"); L. Flint, *Handbook*, 1983, p. 12, repr. color p. 13.

139 L'Atelier. 1928.
(*The Studio*).

Color plate p. 397.

76.2553 PG 3

Oil and black crayon on canvas, 63⅝ x 51⅛ (161.6 x 129.9).

Signed and dated u.l. (incised into paint): *Picasso / XXVIII*; apparently originally inscribed on stretcher: *XXVIII* (Zurich, 1932, exhibition catalogue).

PROVENANCE:

Purchased from the artist by D.-H. Kahnweiler, January 22, 1929 (stockbook no. 10699); reacquired by Picasso, July 1934, in exchange for five paintings;[1] retained by the artist until 1942 (lent by him to MoMA exhibition, 1939-42);[2] Valentine Dudensing;[3] purchased from Valentine Dudensing, 1942.

CONDITION:

In 1964 (Tate Report) some branched crackle with elevated edges was observed at the top edge, and in 2 other small locations near the right edge, center. A tiny area of cleavage was consolidated and retouched with Paraloid B-72 in xylene. The condition was described as good. There was some uncertainty about the presence of varnish.

In 1968 (New York) the painting was described as extremely dirty with discolored varnish rendering the white areas yellow. In areas of heavy impasto, scattered groups of pressure cracks had developed, with lifting of the paint layer along the edges of these cracks. (Examination of the 1968 raking light photographs indicates that these were present in the lower left quadrant of the painting, and 1 small area lower right.) The thinly painted vertical rectangle, bordered in yellow, contrasted strongly with the more thickly painted adjacent areas.

Since lining would accentuate the differences between the thinly and thickly painted areas, Magna Medium color, followed by a thin layer of gesso, were applied to the thinly painted areas from the reverse. The painting was treated with water and chemicals on a vacuum table to minimize pressure cracks; it was then lined with wax resin adhesive. The surface was cleaned to remove discolored varnish and soil. Synthetic resin varnish was sprayed over the surface.

In 1982 (Venice) some wax stains and other soil were removed from the surface. The extensive crackle now visible in the paint layer has occurred since the 1968 lining.

Study of the painting itself, and comparision of its present surface with that of the early photographs (see fig. a), as well as with that of other works by the artist from this period, indicates that the subtle differentiations in texture and brushwork have been substantially lost and the surface considerably flattened. The present condition of the paint film, in spite of extensive crackle throughout, appears stable. (New York, Mar. 1983.)

1. The Kahnweiler records include the entry for this (extremely unusual if not unique) exchange, which apparently took place in response to Picasso's insistent desire to repossess the painting. The 5 works he was forced to release in exchange were (Zervos, vol. 7) no. 65: *La Guitare accrochée au mur*, 1927, 81 x 81 cm.; no. 72: *Femme endormie dans un fauteuil*, 1927, 92 x 73 cm.; no. 237: *Tête de femme*, 1929, 69 x 56 cm.; no. 290: *Monument: tête de femme*, 1929, 65 x 54 cm.; no. 309: *Le Peintre*, 1930, 50 x 65 cm.
2. MoMA records for this exhibition are fragmentary. Though the exhibition traveled until 1943, some works, including the present picture, were withdrawn at various points during the travel schedule owing to their fragility.
3. Peggy Guggenheim clearly recalled buying the painting from Valentine Dudensing not long before the opening of her gallery; it has not been possible to establish how or when Dudensing acquired it. Max Ernst later told Robert Motherwell that he had persuaded Peggy Guggenheim to buy the painting (Motherwell, in conversation with the author, Aug. 27, 1982).

139

fig. a.
Photograph of cat. no. 139 from Kahnweiler archives, taken in 1929. Changes in the composition had already been made by the time Kahnweiler bought it.

Detailed examination of *L'Atelier* (with the naked eye, under ultraviolet light, and with infra-red reflectography[4]) reveals extensive *pentimenti* and radical alterations throughout the compositional and coloristic structure of the painting (see fig. b). First (and this is not indicated on the diagram, fig. b), the entire background of the painting was originally dark in tone, although it has not been possible to establish the exact color (or colors) used. Picasso clearly conceived the composition against a rather darkly colored wall. On the left, he then drew and painted either a window or paneled door, and beneath it a table with a red tablecloth. On the right, the extension upward of the bright red area of the present table, beyond the top of the long rectangular "painting-within-the-painting," suggests that this may have been originally conceived as an easel. The edges of the entire composition were also enclosed by a margin (2). The margin is now to some extent confused with a stretcher mark but is nonetheless clearly legible as a drawn margin when examined with the aid of infra-red reflectography. The outer edges (beyond this drawn line) are more thinly painted than the immediately adjacent areas within: the thickly applied white paint layer of the interior space was obviously required in order to cover the dark color of the wall beneath; the outer edges had apparently been painted in a much lighter hue.

4. Maryan Ainsworth, Research Investigator, Paintings Conservation, The Metropolitan Museum of Art, kindly undertook an infra-red reflectography examination of the work March 14, 1983, in the laboratory of the Metropolitan and collaborated with the author and Lucy Flint in reaching the conclusions outlined here. Owing to shortness of time available it was not possible to make photographs of the earlier stages of the composition. The present analysis and diagram are based on notes taken during a 2-hour study of the picture.

fig. b.
Diagram of cat. no 139 based on ultra-violet, naked eye, and infra-red reflectography examinations. Black lines indicate original composition. Shaded areas: brilliant red in original conception. (1) Line incised into lower paint layer, probably indicating trial position of table leg. (2) Margin around all four sides. (3) Original color beige-yellow. (4) Gray underpainting in upper section of this "painting-within-painting." (5) Pale blue underpainting. (6) Traces of yellow pigment near the surface; original tone of entire background dark.

fig. c.
Picasso, *The Studio*, 1927-28, oil on canvas, 59 x 91 in., 149.9 x 231.2 cm., The Museum of Modern Art, New York, Gift of Walter P. Chrysler, Jr.

The drawing of the composition onto the prepared canvas was executed largely in wax crayon. Incising and additional reinforcement of some of the lines (with a wooden brush end and crayon) strengthened certain aspects of the drawing after the white paint had been applied; other linear elements (the table legs, the three eyes of the sculptured bust left) were painted in after the white was dry.

Comparison of the Peggy Guggenheim painting as originally conceived (fig. b) with MoMA's *The Studio* of 1927-28 (fig. c) reveals at once that the two works were initially much more closely related. The intricate linear complexities of the earlier horizontal composition were adapted to the new vertical format, and certain fundamental changes in content were introduced, but many aspects of the physical environment were transferred to the new work with relatively little alteration.

The central juxtaposition in the MoMA work is of the artist and his subject —in this case, a still-life. The artist stands at the left in front of his large yellow canvas, preparing to paint the still-life (at the right) of fruit bowl, green apple, and plaster bust arranged on a table with a red tablecloth. The artist's head, and the counterbalancing sculptured head, are major focal points of the composition as a whole.

Robert Rosenblum has cogently characterized the way in which this painting (related as it is to Velázquez's *Las Meninas*) acts to complicate our view of the relationship between art and reality (*Cubism and Twentieth-Century Art*, New York, 1960, pp. 289-90): "to the right are the realities which [the artist] must translate into art.... framed images ... evoke varying degrees of reality and illusion — pictures, mirrors, doors, windows.... the inventive potentialities of Cubism permit Picasso to describe the artist's superior visual perception by the addition of a third eye, which becomes, with similar physiological fantasy, a mouth in the sculptured head at the right, thereby producing, with familiar Cubist paradox, a work of art more real than the real artist who copies it. And as a comparable ambiguity.... Picasso encloses the entire painting within a narrow white margin which, like the use of trompe-l'oeil or collage, further complicates the interplay of art and reality by suggesting that this is a picture within a picture."

In the Venice picture, the first major change is the elimination of the artist (although the echo of his presence is retained in the triple-eyed sculptured bust). Two works of art now confront one another: the bust on a pedestal transferred to the left and a female portrait, which now fills the previously empty large canvas (at the right). The original version of the Venice painting (fig. b) included doors, windows, and maybe pictures, as well as a clearly delineated outer margin, creating — as in the MoMA instance — the paradox of a picture within a picture; in the Venice painting this multiple allusion to the art of painting is carried one step further by the inclusion of the completed "portrait" of a woman prominently placed within the composition.

William Rubin has aptly described the MoMA picture, with its strong linear emphasis, as the "two-dimensional counterpart of the pioneering rod and wire sculptures that Picasso completed in the same year" (*Picasso in The Museum of Modern Art*, New York, 1972, p. 128). Although a similar point can be made about the initial version of the Venice picture, this emphasis was significantly altered when Picasso made the decision to paint out the complex linear articulation of the doors and/or windows, the intricate table at the left (with its bright red tablecloth), and the dark tones of the background. In eliminating much of the rectilinear emphasis of the earlier version, and its implied references to his sculpture of the time, he also radically altered the picture's actual surface by introducing the pervasive, unifying field of white paint. This field acts, moreover, not as a background, but as a total environment coinciding with the picture plane, shared by the composition depicted on it. The white paint, when first applied, was highly expressive and painterly in its texture and *facture*; the completed picture—with its stark simplifications, greatly reduced number of forms, and emblematic canvas (or mirror?)[5] leaning against the pedestal at the left—

5. For an interpretation of the picture's iconography, which focuses heavily on the presence of the "mirror-and-painting" image and its implications for the understanding of Picasso's art as a whole, see Gasman, 1981.

therefore focused special attention on its own inherently pictorial qualities, especially the texture, substantiality, and presence of the paint itself.

The Peggy Guggenheim picture, even with its fundamental revisions and unusually sparse composition, remains closely related in meaning to other works on the studio theme. But the emphasis is new: two single works of art (embodiments of sculpture and painting) emerge as the dominating presences. The studio as an explicitly delineated physical milieu has all but vanished. Instead, Picasso seems to assert the nature of painting itself as the fundamental environment for his forms.

Picasso himself clearly had a deep sense of the work's personal meaning: having sold it to Kahnweiler soon after it was painted, he went to extraordinary — indeed possibly unprecedented — lengths to repossess it in 1934. When he lent it several years later to Alfred Barr's important exhibition *Picasso: Forty Years of his Art*, he apparently had no intention of selling it. It seems possible that he later decided, at the height of World War II, that it would be difficult to retrieve the work safely.[6]

EXHIBITIONS:

Paris, Galerie Georges Petit, *Exposition Picasso*, June 16-July 30, 1932, no. 180, repr. p. 67; Zurich, Kunsthaus, *Picasso*, Sept. 11-Oct. 30, 1932, no. 174; New York, MoMA, *Picasso: Forty Years of His Art*, Nov. 15, 1939-Jan. 7, 1940, no. 215 (lent by the artist); traveled to The Art Institute of Chicago, Feb. 1-Mar. 3, 1940; New York, MoMA, *Masterpieces of Picasso*, July 16-Sept. 7, 1941 (no cat.); New York, Art of This Century, 1942-47, p. 38; Venice, *P.G.*, 1948 (Biennale), no. 105; Florence, *P.G.*, 1949, no. 111; Amsterdam, *P.G.*, 1951, no. 127; Zurich, *P.G.*, 1951, no. 123; London, *P.G.*, 1964-65, no. 3, repr.; Stockholm, *P.G.*, 1966-67, no. 3, repr.; New York, *P.G.*, 1969, p. 52, repr. color; Paris, *P.G.*, 1974-75, no. 3, repr. color; Torino, *P.G.*, 1975-76, no. 3, repr. pl. 3; Rome, *Guggenheim: Venezia-New York*, 1982, no. 5, repr. color; New York, *P.G.*, 1982-83, no. 2, repr.

REFERENCES:

C. Einstein, "Pablo Picasso: quelques tableaux de 1928," *Documents*, vol. 1, Apr. 1929, p. 38; idem, *Die Kunst des 20. Jahrhunderts*, Berlin, 1931, pp. 95-96; A. Breton, *Le Surréalisme et la peinture*, New York, 1945, repr. betw. pp. 24 and 25; C. Zervos, *Pablo Picasso: Œuvres de 1926 à 1932*, vol. 7, Paris, 1955, no. 136, repr. pl. 59; L. Gasman, "Mystery, Magic and Love in Picasso, 1925-38," unpublished Ph.D. dissertation, Columbia University, 1981, pp. 1042, 1080, 1085, 1099, 1121, 1144-51.

6. It has not been established whether the Picasso estate contains any documents on the nature of the transaction with Dudensing, or clues about Picasso's reasons for parting with the painting.
It is interesting to note that Robert Motherwell recalls the painting as "perhaps the most important influence on my life in those first ten years in New York. That incredible white.... The painting was surely one of the most austere and powerful works since the height of Cubism... unquestionably one of the masterpieces of the 20th century" (in conversation with the author Aug. 23 and 27, 1982).

140 La Baignade. February 12, 1937.
(*On the beach*; *Girls with a Toy Boat*).

Color plate p. 398.

76.2553 PG 5

Oil, conté crayon, chalk, on primed (gray) canvas (unvarnished), 50 13/16 x 76 3/8 (129.1 x 194.0).

Signed l.c.: *Picasso*; formerly dated on reverse (recorded but not photographed before lining): *12.2.37*.

PROVENANCE:

Mary Callery, purchased either from the artist, or from Christian Zervos by 1939;[1] purchased from Mary Callery, New York, by 1947.[2]

CONDITION:

In 1964 (Tate Report) the unvarnished, thinly painted, delicate surface, and the extreme fragility of crayon and chalk areas, were noted. Four tears in the canvas were repaired and 4 scratches from the back, which had cracked the ground and paint film, were consolidated. It was decided that cleaning was not possible, and relining would only be practicable with a cold system and a non-staining adhesive. This was not attempted. No varnish was applied.

In 1968 (New York) extensive cracks in the gray priming were noted; retouching from previous restoration (date and place unknown) had discolored.

In order to protect the chalk and crayon areas from wax penetration, the back of the canvas was coated with Magna Medium color. Areas where stress cracks had developed were treated with chemicals and water on a vacuum table. The painting was lined on a vacuum table using wax resin adhesive and Fiberglas lining fabric, and mounted on a Lebron stretcher. The surface was cleaned to remove excess lining adhesive, which had penetrated cracks in the priming, and old varnish. (It has not been possible to establish when between 1964 and 1968 this varnish was applied.) Old retouchings were removed; gesso filling was used to compensate for paint losses. Damages were retouched with dry color in synthetic resin medium. The surface was sprayed with synthetic resin varnish.

In 1982 (Venice) the above discolored retouchings were removed. Varnish colors and watercolors were used to repaint the damages. No varnish was removed or applied. The condition is fragile. (New York, Mar. 1983.)

Picasso's persistent use of the seashore as an important mis-en-scène has been frequently discussed in the literature. As Robert Rosenblum has written: "The beach had been a recurrent setting in Picasso's work, evoking in his earliest years a kind of social wasteland to which his beggars and circus figures were exiled; in his Neoclassic mode, a pagan idyll of Mediterranean calm and freedom ... and in his Surrealist years, a natural environment that permitted a maximum of animal liberty to the human species. Figures swimming and cavorting on the sand were a common theme in the twenties, but this playful mood could sometimes turn into a kind of grotesquerie familiar to the beach scenes of Miró and Dalí, where the water's edge often becomes a metaphor of the fringe of con-

1. Mary Callery was a close friend of Picasso and together with her companion, the collector Frua de Angeli, assembled a large and important collection of his work. Frua de Angeli, who supported Zervos's gallery and his publication of the catalogue of Picasso's oeuvre, also acquired many paintings through Zervos. It has thus far not been possible to establish the precise provenance of this picture.

2. Callery still owned the picture in 1945 (see EXHIBITIONS). Peggy Guggenheim remembered buying it sometime before her gallery closed in 1947.

sciousness" (*Picasso and Man*, exh. cat., The Art Gallery of Toronto, 1964, pp. 16-17).

Such undercurrents also complicate many of the seashore pictures of the 1930s, and the erotic energy which is at the center of these images occasionally erupts into actual violence (see, for example, *Baigneuses, sirènes, femme nue et minotaure*, Zervos, vol. 9, no. 97, March 1937). More often it expresses itself — as Rosenblum suggested — through the distortion of human anatomy, "which moves backwards down the evolutionary ladder to its often frightening biological roots" (*Picasso from the Musée Picasso, Paris*, exh. cat., Walker Art Center, Minneapolis, 1980, p. 50).

La Baignade is revealing in this respect, particularly when considered in conjunction with two preparatory studies and some closely related drawings and paintings of the preceding and immediately following days.

In one of two known preparatory drawings executed on the same day as the painting (fig. a), the grotesque head of a male figure, peering over the horizon line, enters the scene as a disturbing, potentially violent, but perhaps merely voyeuristic intruder. A second drawing of that same day (present whereabouts unknown, Zervos, vol. 8, no. 343) includes — in the upper and lower margins — several rapid sketches for this same male head, two of which are heavily and decisively crossed out. In the center, a full sketch for the painting presents the

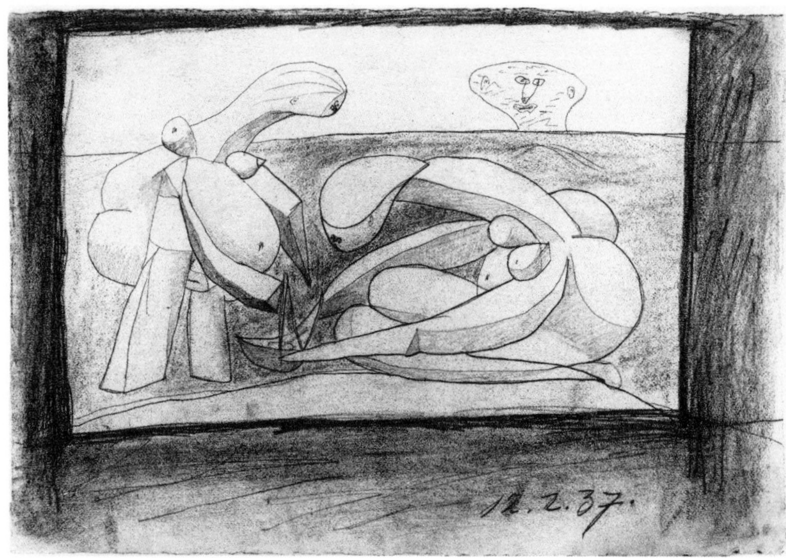

fig. a.
Picasso, *La Baignade*, pencil and pastel on paper, 13⅝ x 19⅞ in., 34.5 x 50.5 cm., dated l. r.: 12.2.37, Musée Picasso, Paris.

male onlooker in a wholly different guise. As in the final painting, his ovoid "sculptured" head, comparable in form to those of the main female protagonists, bears a neutral expression, possibly that of intent curiosity but essentially lacking in menace. Picasso has suppressed the more overtly disruptive implications of the figure in the earlier drawing and replaced it with an enigmatic presence. Nonetheless, the very appearance of this oversize male head, in an ambiguous spatial relationship to the foreground women, and curiously out of scale with them, adds an element of disquiet to the scene. Leo Steinberg has also pointed to the way in which this observer functions dramatically to extend the viewer's perception of the "huge little heroines in the foreground.... The all-sidedness of the foreground figures depends not on their modeled openwork fabric alone, but almost as much on the inquisitive rover peering from beyond the high sea" (1972, pp. 182-83).

The delicacy of the female bathers is accomplished virtually in spite of the profound anatomical distortions and fundamental ungainliness of their bodies. An atmosphere of subtle tension is intrinsic to the balance between human and nonhuman, physical grace and biological explicitness, seaside idyll and latent erotic drama.

Several related drawings and paintings reinforce such a reading of *La Baignade*. Figures in Picasso's oeuvre that share some of the anatomical characteristics of the *Baignade* women include the highly predatory *Baigneuse assise* of 1930 (MoMA, Zervos, vol. 7, 306) and the much more lyrical *Femme assise sur la plage* (Zervos, vol. 8, 345) executed on February 10 — just two days before the Venice picture. Meanwhile several drawings of February 9-10 (Zervos, vol. 8, 346-49) suggest that Picasso was simultaneously exploring two utterly different figural types and hence two distinctive tones for the painting: the one grotesquely biomorphic, the other curvaceous and in repose. The monstrous figures of February 9, bizarrely equipped with skipping ropes (Zervos, vol. 8, nos. 336, 337), are transposed and transformed three days later into the left bather of *La Baignade*. Meanwhile, the much more lyrical forms of the drawing *Femme assise* (Zervos, vol. 8, no. 338) or the painting *Femme assise sur la plage* (both of February 10) are incorporated into the figure of the right bather in the Venice picture. Thus in working through a wide range of possibilities in a very brief period of time, Picasso ultimately purged *La Baignade* of the most grotesque elements of its many "sources," retaining, nonetheless, a trace of disquietude.[3]

More than one commentator has suggested a connection between the bather scenes of 1937 and the highly charged political works of the same year, but the analogies are hard to sustain. Werner Spies (1981, 1982) has suggested, on the other hand, that a work such as *La Baignade* (which he feels is of exaggerated horizontal dimensions) should be considered in connection with Picasso's earliest pre-*Guernica* ideas for the Spanish pavilion. Citing the existence of a series of drawings discovered by Dominique Bozo in the Picasso estate, Spies implies that the artist's first concepts for the pavilion were in no sense political: they arose, on the contrary, directly out of Picasso's persistent interest in the subject of the artist and his model. The drawings in question remain unpublished, and the argument (including its possible implications regarding the original focus or inspiration of *La Baignade*) is therefore difficult to evaluate.

EXHIBITIONS:

New York, MoMA, *Picasso: Forty Years of His Art*, Nov 15, 1939-Jan. 7, 1940, no. 279 (lent by Mary Callery),[4] traveled to The Art Institute of Chicago, Feb. 1-Mar. 3, 1940; New York, MoMA, *Masterpieces of Picasso*, July 16-Sept. 7, 1941 (no cat.); Venice, *P.G.*, 1948 (Biennale), no. 108; Florence, *P.G.*, 1949, no. 112, repr.; Amsterdam, *P.G.*, 1951, no. 128, repr.; Zurich, *P.G.*, 1951, no. 124, repr.; London, *P.G.*, 1964-65, no. 5, repr. color p. 2; Stockholm, *P.G.*, 1966-67, no. 5, repr. frontispiece; New York, *P.G.*, 1969, p. 53, repr.; Paris, *P.G.*, 1974-75, no. 4; Torino, *P.G.*, 1975-76, no. 5; Madrid, Museo Español de Arte Contemporáneo, *Picasso*, Nov.-Dec. 1981, no. 103, repr. color, traveled to Barcelona, Museu Picasso, Jan.-Feb., 1982; New York, *P.G.*, 1982-83, no. 3, repr. color.

3. Picasso's use of the observer beyond the horizon recurs in several works later in 1937. For example, in *Baigneuses, sirènes, femme nue et minotaure* of March 1937 (Zervos, vol. 9, no. 97), the observer's flying hair and gathered brow suggest concerned involvement in the violent and erotic drama unfolding before him. In 2 drawings of December 30, 1937 (Musée Picasso, nos. 1199, 1200), each depicting a fulsome reclining nude on the beach, the watching figure has once again become an inquisitive voyeur, accompanied in each case by a prominently resplendent sun-vagina image. Two other drawings in this series are apparently in the collections of members of the Picasso family. Michèle Richet drew these latter 4 works to the author's attention.

4. According to the fragmentary records of this exhibition, the painting was removed from the travel portion after the 1940 Art Institute of Chicago appearance because of its fragility (information supplied by M. Frost, Registrar's Office, MoMA).

REFERENCES:

"The Callery Collection: Picasso–Leger," *Philadelphia Museum of Art Bulletin*, vol. 40, no. 204, Jan. 1945, checklist p. 37, repr. [p. 42]; A. H. Barr, Jr., *Picasso: Fifty Years of His Art*, New York, 1946, p. 198, repr. p. 199; C. Zervos, *Pablo Picasso: Œuvres de 1932 à 1937*, vol. 8, Paris, 1957, no. 344, repr. pl. 161; R. Penrose, *Picasso: His Life and Work*, London, 1958, p. 265, repr. pl. 15; J. Berger, *Success and Failure of Picasso*, Baltimore, 1965, pp. 146-47, repr. p. 146; R. Passeron, *Histoire de la Peinture Surréaliste*, Paris, 1968, p. 113, repr. p. 108; A. Fermegier, *Picasso*, Paris, 1969, pp. 205-8, repr. p. 207; J. Leymarie, *Picasso: Metamorphoses et unité*, Geneva, 1971, p. 64, repr.; L. Steinberg, "The Algerian Women and Picasso at Large," *Other Criteria*, New York, 1972, pp. 182-83, repr.; P. O'Brian, *Pablo Ruiz Picasso*, New York, 1976, p. 319; P. Cabanne, *Pablo Picasso: His Life and Times*, New York, 1977, p. 291; P. Daix, *La vie de peintre de Pablo Picasso*, Paris, [1977], p. 272; M. M. Gedo, *Picasso: Art as Autobiography*, Chicago and London, 1980, pp. 172-73; W. Spies, "Picasso und seine Zeit," in *Pablo Picasso: Sammlung Marina Picasso*, exh. cat., Haus der Kunst, Munich, 1981, pp. 21-22; idem, "Picasso: L'Histoire dans l'Atelier," *Cahiers du Musée National d'Art Moderne*, no. 9, Paris, 1982, p. 63.

---

141 Buste d'homme en tricot rayé.

Royan, September 14, 1939.
(*Half-length portrait of a man in a striped jersey*).

76.2553 PG 6

Gouache on wove (Ingres) paper (unvarnished), 24⅞ x 17 15/16 (63.1 x 45.6).

Signed and dated u.l.: *14 Septembre 39 Picasso.*

PROVENANCE:

Collection Mlle. Dupuis, Relais-Bisson, Paris, by January 1961;[1] purchased from Mlle. Dupuis by M. Knoedler and Co., New York, jointly with T. Schemp, January 1961; purchased from M. Knoedler and Co., Inc., March 16, 1961.

CONDITION:

In 1964 (Tate Report) the support was buckling, but the condition of the unvarnished surface was otherwise described as good.

In 1978 (New York) the work was removed from direct contact with the glass and acidic masonite backboard, which had caused mold and overall foxing. Some scattered losses (lower right edge and corner; upper right corner) and tears near lower left edge and upper right corner were repaired and inpainted. The foxing was successfully mitigated and the work flattened, fumigated in thymol, and hinged to 100% rag mount. The condition is stable. (Venice, Nov. 1982.)

1. Information supplied by M. Knoedler and Co. It has proved impossible to trace Mlle. Dupuis and to establish the earlier history.

141

On September 2, just before the outbreak of World War II, Picasso moved to Royan — a small harbor town at the mouth of the Gironde, seventy-five miles north of Bordeaux. He remained there almost a year, returning several times to Paris, for short periods, but not moving back to the city until August 24, 1940.

Between September 13 and 17 he produced ten known versions of the *homme en tricot rayé*, six gouaches, three oils on paper, and one ink drawing (Zervos, vol. 9, nos. 320, 321, 323-30).

EXHIBITIONS:

London, *P.G.*, 1964-65, no. 6; Stockholm, *P.G.*, 1966-67, no. 6; Paris, *P.G.*, 1974-75, no. 5; Torino, *P.G.*, 1975-76, no. 6.

REFERENCE:

C. Zervos, *Pablo Picasso: Œuvres de 1937 à 1939*, vol. 9, Paris, 1958, no. 326.

Jackson Pollock

Born January 1912, Cody, Wyoming.
Died August 1956, The Springs, New York.

NOTE: *The Moon Woman* (cat. no. 142), *Two* (cat. no. 144), *Direction* (cat. no. 145), *Circumcision* (cat. no.146), and *Alchemy* (cat. no. 152) have all to a greater or lesser extent been used during the past dozen years to illustrate extensive and controversial attempts to interpret Pollock's iconography from a specifically Jungian point of view.[1] Since detailed analyses of the imagery in these particular paintings have served to buttress some of the central arguments of the Jungian position, a summary of the issues seems appropriate here.

Psychological interpretations of Jackson Pollock's work have been built upon the following biographical facts.

Sometime in January 1937 Pollock embarked on an eight-month period of psychiatric treatment for chronic alcoholism. In June 1938, with the support of a friend, Helen Marot, he committed himself to the Westchester Division of New York Hospital for four months of treatment. In 1939 he began an eighteen-month course of treatment with a Jungian analyst, Dr. Joseph Henderson, who was then in his first year of practice. Following Henderson's departure from New York, Pollock continued Jungian therapy with Dr. Violet Staub de Laszlo, from the fall of 1940 through most of the winter of 1942-43.[2] In 1970 Henderson, who had retained a group of eighty-three drawings which Pollock had produced during the period of his analysis, sold them to a commercial gallery;[3] the Whitney Museum exhibited them, and C. L. Wysuph's book was published, providing the stimulus for much of the ensuing iconographic speculation about the psychological content of Pollock's art.

1. The main bibliographical sources for the Jungian controversy are as follows: C. L. Wysuph, *Jackson Pollock: Psychoanalytic Drawings*, New York, 1970; J. Wolfe, "Jungian Aspects of Jackson Pollock's Imagery," *Artforum*, vol. 11, no. 3, Nov. 1972, pp. 65-73; D. Freke, "Jackson Pollock: a symbolic self-portrait," *Studio International*, vol. 184, no. 950, Dec. 1972, pp. 217-21; Langhorne, 1977; idem, "Jackson Pollock's 'The Moon Woman Cuts the Circle'," *Arts Magazine*, vol. 53, no. 7, Mar. 1979, pp. 128-37; J. Welch, "Jackson Pollock's 'The White Angel' and the Origins of Alchemy," ibid., pp. 138-41; W. Rubin, "Pollock as Jungian Illustrator: The Limits of Psychological Criticism," Part I, *Art in America*, vol. 67, no. 7, Nov. 1979, pp. 104-22; idem, "Pollock as Jungian Illustrator: The Limits of Pychological Criticism," Part II, ibid., vol. 67, no. 8, Dec. 1979, pp. 72-91; D. E. Gordon, "Pollock's 'Bird,' or How Jung Did Not Offer Much Help in Myth Making" (Department of Jungian Amplification, Part I), ibid., vol. 68, no. 8, Oct. 1980, pp. 43-53; I. Sandler, D. Rubin, E. Langhorne, and W. Rubin, Letters to the Editor, "More on Rubin on Pollock" (Department of Jungian Amplification, Part II), ibid., pp. 57-67.
2. Two other main sources for Pollock's possible access to Jungian ideas have been suggested: his friendships with Helen Marot and John Graham. On this point see Gordon, loc. cit., 1980, pp. 47-48 and p. 51 fns. 13, 14. William Rubin, meanwhile, has argued that "any important influence Graham might have had on Pollock's Jungianism would *not* have been through his writing, but in conversation—and would have occurred after Pollock was already in analysis. We have, however, no facts regarding this" (loc. cit., 1980, pp. 66-67).
3. W. Rubin has cogently argued that these were not specifically "psycho-analytic" drawings (i.e. done for the sessions) but more likely just examples of Pollock's current work (loc. cit., vol. 67, no. 7, Nov. 1979, p. 107).

Meanwhile, Pollock's own recorded comments on the role or influence of Jung (or Freud) on his art are few. Only one (oft-quoted) statement on the subject is documented: "I'm very representational some of the time, and a little all of the time. But when you are painting out of your unconscious, figures are bound to emerge. We're all of us influenced by Freud, I guess. I've been a Jungian for a long time" (S. Rodman, *Conversations with Artists*, New York, 1957, p. 82). In one other case, Pollock made a much more general comment: "The source of my paintings is the unconscious" (cited by F. V. O'Connor, *Jackson Pollock*, exh. cat., MoMA, New York, 1967, p. 40).

Pollock owned none of Jung's principal texts, and the only book by Jung known to have been in his library was published in 1949 — three years after Pollock had abandoned the kind of pictorial imagery that might be susceptible of explicit psychological interpretation.

Whether his two analysts ever really explored Jung's theories with Pollock in any detail is not entirely clear, although the evidence seems to indicate they did not. In a letter of November 11, 1969, to B. H. Friedman, Henderson wrote: "Most of my comments centered around the nature of the archetypal symbolism in his drawings" (*Jackson Pollock: Energy Made Visible*, New York, 1972, p. 4). In correspondence with Donald E. Gordon, Henderson was considerably more precise: "My treatment was supportive and I did not consciously discuss Jung or Jungian theories with him" (Gordon, loc. cit., 1980, p. 44). De Laszlo, likewise, told Gordon that "we rarely discussed abstract concepts; nor do I recollect discussing archetypes since I wished to avoid intellectualization.... Alchemy did not become a topic" (Gordon, loc. cit., 1980). Though both analysts apparently discussed with Pollock the general Jungian concept of "a psychic birth-death-rebirth cycle" and " 'the symbol-ordering' device of the circular mandala" (Wolfe, loc. cit., 1972, p. 67; Gordon, loc. cit., 1980, p. 44), no evidence has so far come to light to suggest that these discussions ever developed into a more extensive explication of Jungian symbols and myths.

Common to all those who have proposed Jung's writings as a key intellectual source for Pollock's iconography during this period of analysis is the assumption that certain images were consciously chosen by the artist to illustrate certain themes — that the "referential character" of the imagery was specific and lent "itself to quite precise interpretation in light of Jungian psychology" (Langhorne, loc. cit., 1979, p. 128). Judith Wolfe, for example, begins her discussion by stating that, "While Jackson Pollock's interest in his art was paramount, the theories of Carl Gustave Jung were also important as a means of realizing an expression that was both individual and universal in its implications" (loc. cit., 1972, p. 65). She sees Pollock "consciously borrowing specific Jungian [motifs] and welding [them] into more complex situations" (p. 70).

Elizabeth Langhorne, meanwhile, suggests that the "archetypal nature of Pollock's symbols and of the individuation process they describe was probably due to his saturation in Jungian thought while under analysis" (loc. cit., 1979, p. 31). She interprets Pollock's use of particular "symbols" (female moon, male sun, plumed serpent, etc.) as a conscious process of illustrating the notion of a union of opposites. The symbols express archetypes of the anima and the self, and were used by Pollock, in effect, to "paint the schema for [his own] psychological growth."

Rubin and Gordon have both argued, in different ways, that there are major problems inherent in the effort to apply Jungian concepts in a systematic way to Pollock's art. Rubin — as he stated in his earlier articles of 1967 (see below, cat. no. 148, fn. 4) — agrees that myth played an important role in Pollock's early work. Pollock, like other members of his generation, had a strong interest in ethnic and primitive art, and he was, in Rubin's view, almost certainly influenced in a very general way by Jungian and Freudian ideas: "Signs and symbols drawn from [primitive] sources — and filtered through an awareness of Jung — alternate in Pollock's [early] work with iconographies suggested by classical mythology in surreal, Freudianized form" (1979, loc. cit., Part I, p. 106).

In this connection Rubin cites Lawrence Alloway in his 1961 essay and Francis V. O'Connor in his 1965 dissertation, who make allowance for a very general infiltration of psychological symbolism in some of Pollock's early work. Alloway had written: "Psychology, clinically experienced or as part of the 20th-century history of ideas, has reduced the distance between archaic gods and heroes and ourselves.... Myth in Pollock's hands was never an exercise in classical allusion but kept that enigmatic center which it is the function of myth to preserve ... the figurative works are not pre-planned but improvised. They are images invented and found in the act of painting."[4] And he refers to O'Connor's statement of a few years later that "where recognizable motifs are utilized, their context is usually deliberately mysterious — deliberately poetic — and never dictated by theoretical considerations or a desire for legible meaning."[5]

While Rubin acknowledges a very restricted debt on Pollock's part to psychological concepts or ideas generally current amongst artists in the late 1930s and early 1940s, he takes serious issue with the Jungians on a great many specific counts. First, and perhaps most important from an art-historical point of view, he criticizes their fundamental analysis for the particular way it isolates imagery and iconography and concentrates on the presumed psychological content, to the exclusion of all consideration of the paintings as paintings. In this respect, the Jungians show "virtually no awareness of the way in which the problems and choices of the painting process bear upon the determination of the forms and colors that they interpret only iconographically" (loc. cit., 1979, Part I, p. 106). In addition, Rubin argues, whereas Pollock may well have been receptive

4. L. Alloway, *Jackson Pollock: Paintings, Drawings and Watercolors from the Collection of Lee Krasner Pollock*, Malborough Fine Art Ltd., London, 1961. Alloway, in reviewing Peggy Guggenheim's exhibition at the Guggenheim Museum in 1969, returned to some of these issues, but did not fundamentally change his mind (*The Nation*, Feb. 17, 1969, p. 221).

5. F. V. O'Connor, "The Genesis of Jackson Pollock: 1912-1943," unpublished Ph.D. dissertation, Johns Hopkins University, 1965, p. 101, cited by Rubin, 1979, Part 1, fn. 5, who raises the possibility that O'Connor may no longer entirely subscribe to this view.

to some of Jung's more general concepts, including the theory of the "collective unconscious," and may even have included occasional specific Jungian images and symbols in his paintings, he did not do so in a consistent or programmatic way. The paintings, consequently, do not lend themselves to the kind of detailed, literal Jungian explication proposed by critics such as Wolfe and Langhorne.

Gordon's discussion of the Jungian approach to Pollock and Rubin's response to it was based on an informed analysis of the actual implications a direct Jungian influence on Pollock might have had. He outlined three alternative hypotheses for consideration: "(1) Pollock consciously *illustrated* Jungian notions he had previously read in Jung or had explained to him by Jungians; (2) Pollock consciously examined his own conscious imagery and *elaborated* it in Jungian directions; (3) Pollock's unconscious symbolism was truly archetypal and disjunctive—susceptible to Jungian explication, but not by Pollock himself, who merely *accepted* it as artistic raw material without intellectual examination.... Options (1) and (2) presuppose the presence of an explicit Jungian 'influence' on Pollock's art... defined broadly by the psychological interpreters and limited narrowly by Rubin. Option (3) would, if present, be explainable not by the artist himself, but only by an informed observer" (loc. cit., 1980, p. 43).

With these hypotheses in mind, Gordon proceeded to examine the relevant biographical and pictorial evidence. He concluded that, during the early 1940s, Pollock experienced a largely unconscious and wholly archetypal personal crisis, but that as a result there was no consistent or specific Jungian "influence" on his iconography, either at that or any other time. According to Gordon's persuasive argument, "the psychological and symbolic contexts of individual Pollock pictures suggest that Jung was even *less* of an iconographic influence than Rubin has claimed."

The Moon Woman (cat. no. 142):

In discussing the iconography of individual pictures, the Jungian critics all touch on Peggy Guggenheim's *The Moon Woman*, which—together with *The Moon Woman Cuts the Circle*—is seen as playing a central role in the iconography of Pollock's work of this period.

Taking the title as the point of departure for her analysis, Wolfe points out that for Jung the moon was in general a symbol of periodic creation, death, and recreation. In Pollock's case, she argues, however, the moon probably carried a meaning that was even more specific, representing the dualism between two Jungian archetypes: "the young girl anima complex contrasted with the all-devouring Terrible Mother." In *The Moon Woman* Wolfe sees Pollock depicting the anima-spirit (loc. cit., 1972, pp. 68, 73 fn. 25).

David Freke shares Wolfe's general views, but places the picture in a series with *Male and Female, The Moon Woman Cuts the Circle, She Wolf*, and others. These are seen as constituting a symbolic narrative: the Jungian hero undergoes a mythic journey from birth through life to death, and—later—to rebirth. This journey is interpreted as a metaphor for Pollock's own experience and particularly his quest for artistic independence.

Langhorne's far lengthier analysis of *The Moon Woman* offers an excellent example of her own methodology. She focuses attention primarily on the figure's large third eye, which intersects with a crescent shape. This intersection is viewed as a symbol of the promised union of opposites—the male "conscious" principle joining with the female "unconscious" principle. The moon becomes, as it does in Wolfe's analysis, Pollock's own anima (the creative, female side of his psyche); the agitated lines around the third eye indicate inner conflict and reveal that the union of opposites has not yet been achieved. The hieroglyphs on the left side of the painting are also seen as "variations on the theme of wholeness and its possible divisions" (op. cit., 1977, p. 154). In the later picture, *The Moon Woman Cuts the Circle* (O'Connor and Thaw, no. 90), Langhorne sees a successful resolution of the psychic struggle represented in *The Moon Woman.*

Rubin disagrees with the thrust of the Jungian analyses. He argues convincingly that Pollock's titles should not be viewed as keys to unlock a very explicit set of meanings. He sees them as representing "*an ex post facto association to the artist's 'inexplicable' depicted image rather than an a priori program for its iconography* [his italics].... The link between title and image is almost certainly a memory, association or private fantasy." Rubin further suggests that Pollock, who is known to have been interested in American Indian folklore and art, may well have known of Indian Moon Woman legends, of which there are several, and would have needed no Jungian inspiration to arrive at such purely associational titles (loc. cit., 1979, Part II, pp. 72, 90 fn. 7). In her response to Rubin (loc. cit., 1980, pp. 59-63), Langhorne argues even more strongly that Pollock's *The Moon Woman* represents his search for higher consciousness and self-realization.[6]

In this context it is interesting to note that Lee Krasner, who readily acknowledged that Pollock had "a special sensitivity to the moon," found it impossible to detect symbolic meaning in the painting: "He did [title] *The Moon Woman, The Moon Woman Cuts the Circle*, and he also did *The Mad Moon Woman*, so that it in itself would indicate his preoccupation with the moon as such." But when asked whether this would suggest a metaphorical or symbolic content in the paintings, Krasner responded: "No. All we can make of it really is that he relegates [the moon] to female; so it goes back to an old mythology of the sun being male and the moon being female.... I would not venture to go beyond that" (conversation with the author, Mar. 6, 1981).

Circumcision (cat. no. 146):

Two of the Jungian critics, Wolfe and Langhorne, have paid particular attention to *Circumcision.* They view the idea of circumcision in the broader context of an initiation rite and draw on the writings of Joseph Henderson in interpreting the theme as an important stage in the individual's progression to psychological maturity.

6. For a reading of *The Moon Woman* that has much in common with Rubin's—suggesting a generalized mythic quality—see L. Alloway, *The Nation*, Feb. 17, 1969, pp. 221-22.

Wolfe focuses her analysis on the recumbant figure beneath the "ground line" (lower left), whom she identifies as the subject of the circumcision. She also distinguishes the figure of a man, center, "in a snow-shovelling posture," who inflicts the wound; and an owl (possibly evocative of darkness and death), which may be perched on the "post" to the man's right. Finally, Wolfe identifies two great cult figures in the outer sections of the canvas: "a seated tattoed man smoking a pipe" (on the right) and a "standing woman" (on the left), whose eye focuses on the boy's head. These cult figures may represent "the parent archetypes or the future grown-up life or both" (loc. cit., 1972, p. 71).

Langhorne differs radically with Wolfe in her reading of the figures in the composition. She identifies the initiate as the small standing white figure with a black head, lower left. Three large figures are identified as Jungian archetypes: the white circular form with four smaller circles (upper center) is the Great Mother with four eyes; between this figure and the child is a menacing figure with a birdlike beaked red head (Wolfe's figure in snow-shovelling posture) who represents the Terrible Male. On the extreme left is the Spirit Mother.

Langhorne interprets the picture—as already suggested—within the context of a symbolic narrative representing the artist's own psychological growth. The mythical hero is engaged in a struggle toward selfhood: he has achieved "male consciousness," but must undergo further trials. The recumbent figure is seen as a totem animal, symbolic of *instinctual* masculinity; the boy, meanwhile, represents a form of higher *spiritual* masculinity; finally, the owl and other bird (right) are viewed as "higher" totem animals, indicating that the boy's mode of spiritual masculinity is in the ascendancy.

The wide disparity in the readings of Wolfe and Langhorne suggests some of the difficulties inherent in a Jungian approach to Pollock. In pictorial terms, *Circumcision* is an intensely crowded, restless composition with a complex integration of turbulent forms, overlapping images, and vibrant colors. Its surface is so dense that the individual forms and figures are impossible to "decipher" with any specificity. It seems clear that Pollock intended to convey a sense of a generalized mythographic drama. Moreover, several important facts about the picture have hitherto not been taken into account. For example, Pollock himself called this painting *Ritual*, not *Circumcision*, in two different sections of a 1947 résumé he prepared in connection with a John Simon Guggenheim Foundation application (reproduced in O'Connor & Thaw, vol. 4, pp. 239, 240). Equally significant, Krasner — in a wide-ranging discussion concerning Pollock's titles — when asked about the unusually specific nature of the title, *Circumcision*, responded: "When he asked me to come in and look at the painting with him, he said 'What does it suggest to you?' And I said 'I honestly don't know, Jackson. The only thing that comes clearly to me is that it's a ritual of some sort.' It was following that, not instantly, but sometime later, that Pollock said: 'What do you think of *Circumcision*?' 'Gee, that's fine.' That's how the painting got titled" (conversation with the author, Mar. 6, 1981).

Krasner's clear recollection of this episode reveals that Pollock—in this case, as in others — adopted an *ex post facto* title, very much in response to the suggestion of another person. Krasner's term "ritual" obviously struck a sympathetic chord in Pollock, and he was led from that rather general and evocative characterization to the more specific *Circumcision*, as if finally selecting one particular ritual from among several possibilities. It may also be that Pollock's 1947 references to this painting as *Ritual* had their origin in this conversation with Krasner; from the evidence available, it is simply not clear whether those later references were purely inadvertent, or whether Pollock was actively considering a new title for the canvas.

Alchemy (cat. no. 152):

Alchemy provides suggestive material for Jungian analysis mainly because of Jung's own interest in alchemical processes and their meaning. Wolfe assumes a direct relationship between Pollock's title and Jung's alchemical theories, and she interprets the painting with this relationship in mind (loc. cit., 1972, pp. 71-72). She sees the dominant colors of the picture as black, white, red, and yellow, and she relates these to the four stages of the alchemical process (black, white, red, and gold). She observes that Pollock had substituted yellow for gold and added aluminum "to mediate between the light-dark contrasts." From among the many thick white markings (where paint has been squeezed directly from the tube) scattered over the surface of the composition, she selects three for discussion: the "figure" of an asterisk-star (at the left); a numeral "4" (left of center); and a numeral "6" (right). These images are then related to a system of Jungian and alchemical number-symbolism: "4," for example, represents completeness, "6" (in hermaphroditic form), the fusion of male and female. The painting as a whole is seen as the achievement of a resolution of the personal and artistic crisis Pollock had been experiencing.

Jonathan Welch for the most part reinforces Wolfe's view of the symbolic content of *Alchemy*, although he expands some aspects of her argument (loc. cit., 1979, pp. 140-41). He suggests a symbolic, as well as a pictorial, significance in the use of aluminum paint, arising out of Jung's statement (in his essay "The Idea of Redemption in Alchemy") that "quicksilver is analogous to and sometimes identical with *materia prima*." He also expands on the notion, initially implied by Wolfe, that Pollock's move in 1947 into a nonfigurative mode may suggest a specific analogy between the alchemical process and the act of painting. He proposes a parallel between the alchemist's quest and the artist's struggle to transform mere paint and canvas into art.

Langhorne does not offer an analysis of *Alchemy*, but she believes that Pollock's relationship with Matta and John Graham, among others, would have given him ample opportunity to learn about alchemical theories. The Surrealists in particular had a strong interest in alchemical processes and their symbolic meaning, and Langhorne makes a persuasive argument for Pollock's absorption of such ideas from the intellectual environment in which he lived (op. cit., 1977, pp. 170ff.).

Rubin disagrees fundamentally with Wolfe and Welch's interpretation of *Alchemy*. He establishes that the title was *not* determined by Pollock in advance, and cannot therefore be taken as a key to the work's iconographical program. Indeed the title was invented, together with others at the time, by the artist's neighbor Ralph Manheim.[7]

In addition to matters concerning the title, Rubin focuses on the precise color scheme for the painting. He draws attention — accurately — to the extensive use of orange, blue, green, and ocher in the painting, and the fact that any effort to read the picture in terms of a color symbolism based mainly on white, black, red, and yellow is highly selective and arbitrary. Rubin also stresses — again accurately — that there are not three dominant figures (the asterisk, the "4," and the "6") painted in thick white on the surface of the canvas, but twelve markings of roughly equal pictorial value. Their significance, moreover, relates to the aesthetic or pictorial role which they play, rather than to any symbolic content: "in the picture's hierarchy of size, paint-thickness and luminescence, [they] function as big structured accents setting off the filigree web in a manner adumbrating the 'elbow joints' of *Autumn Rhythm* and the 'hooks' of *Mural on Indian Red Ground*" (1979, Part II, p. 82).

Within the context of the Jungian debate, *The Moon Woman, Circumcision*, and *Alchemy* have all played an important part.[8] Critics turning to these works, among others, in order to try to demonstrate that Pollock's early work reveals a consistent iconographic program, have suggested that the psychology of Jung offers the most promising conceptual framework for explicating this iconography (Langhorne, op. cit., 1980, p. 63). Rubin, by contrast (together with critics such as Alloway and Gordon), acknowledges the presence of a personal/psychological dimension in these works, as well as references to myth and symbol, but sees the paintings as allusive and suggestive—indeed, poetic—rather than programmatic. He finds a wide range of reference in the material (including American Indian folklore) rather than a concentration on a single set of symbols or theories. Rubin's emphasis on pictorial issues reinforces his more general approach to Pollock's work; it operates against too selective a reading of particular images, symbols, or colors, stressing the need to include all aspects of the works in any effort to characterize their meaning.

A brief evaluation of these various arguments is bound to result in some oversimplification, but since there is now a substantial body of criticism on the question of Jung's influence, and a good deal of it focuses on works in the Peggy Guggenheim Collection, such an evaluation is important.

7. Wolfe acknowledged in her 1972 article that the titles for all the works in the Betty Parsons 1948 exhibition were given to the pictures shortly before the opening (p. 72). Mary and Ralph Manheim had been invited over to help in the titling of these works in preparation for the exhibition. Wolfe nonetheless remained persuaded that *Alchemy* was essentially different in style from the other works in the group and that it must have been completed earlier and titled by Pollock himself. Rubin, however, subsequently confirmed, in conversation with Manheim, that *Alchemy* was one of the titles Manheim proposed (1979, Part II, p. 90, fn. 14).

8. *Direction* (cat. no. 145), *Two* (cat. no. 144), *Untitled* (cat. no. 143) are also discussed by Langhorne and others. See the REFERENCES in these catalogue entries for specific citations.

The Jungian approach has, in general, served to focus attention on Pollock's imagery and his use of myth and symbol. It has offered suggestive readings of particular passages in some of the paintings, and it has stimulated additional research into Pollock's sources, his working methods, and his approach to titles.

The preponderence of evidence, however, argues in favor of much less programmatic, and, in effect, monolithic, analyses. Several points — all mutually reinforcing — seem especially relevant in this regard. First, essentially no evidence exists to suggest Pollock ever developed a strong interest in Jung's theories or methods. Moreover, although Krasner did not discuss these issues in detail, it is clear from various remarks that she did not believe Pollock was specifically influenced in his painting by Jungian concepts or symbols. She had recently stated (in conversation with the author) that she herself had felt a real "resistance to breaking down the exact meanings [of the images] the way the Jungians do."

Second, nothing that is known about Pollock's working methods, or his more general approach to art, would lead one to expect that he worked — even in the early years — in a theoretical or programmatic way. The evidence concerning titles is revealing in this respect: Pollock behaved in a highly intuitive, spontaneous fashion in accepting or rejecting proposed titles. Krasner's recollection of the titling of *Circumcision ("Ritual")* is consistent with the process used by Pollock and the Manheims before the 1948 Parsons exhibition. The titles emerged from the work, post hoc, through a process of suggestion.

Finally, there is the evidence — however ambiguous and difficult to interpret — of the paintings themselves. In all instances, figures and objects are impossible to identify with precision. The canvases, by their very nature, resist the assumption that they are intended to be legible or decipherable in symbolic or theoretical terms. From this point of view, the more pointedly pictorial analyses of Rubin or Alloway, which nevertheless include a recognition of the mythic dimensions of the works, seem clearly more faithful to Pollock's enterprise.

142 The Moon Woman. 1942.

Color plate p. 670.

76.2553 PG 141

Oil on canvas (unvarnished),[1] 69 x 43 1/16 (175.2 x 109.3).

Signed and dated l.r.: *Jackson Pollock 42.*

PROVENANCE:

Gift of the artist, 1946.[2]

CONDITION:

In 1964 (Tate Report) the fact that the work had been originally mounted on a smaller stretcher, leaving tack holes visible along the entire left edge, was noted. The canvas was wrinkled and buckled in the upper right corner due to poor stretching. Scattered drying cracks were apparent, but the unvarnished paint film was described as in good condition with no losses.

There appears to have been no restoration. The condition is stable. (Venice, Nov. 1982.)

For a discussion of the iconography of this painting, see above NOTE, pp. 632-633.

EXHIBITIONS:

New York, Art of This Century, *Jackson Pollock (First Exhibition)*, Nov. 9-27, 1943, no. 4 (*The Moon Woman*); Chicago, The Arts Club of Chicago, *Jackson Pollock*, Mar. 5-31, 1945, no. 1 *(Moon Woman)*, traveled to San Francisco Museum of Art, Aug. 7-26, 1945; Venice, *P.G.*, 1948 (Biennale), no. 110; Florence, *P.G.*, 1949, no. 115; Venice, Museo Correr, *Jackson Pollock*, July 22-Aug. 15, 1950, no. 2; Amsterdam, *P.G.*, 1951, no. 132; Bordighera, *11^A Mostra Internazionale Pittura Americana*, Mar. 1-31, 1953, no. 4; Bern, Kunsthalle, *Tendances actuelles*, Jan. 29-Mar. 6, 1955, no. 52; London, *P.G.*, 1964-65, no. 116, repr. color; Stockholm, *P.G.*, 1966-67, no. 111; New York, *P.G.*, 1969, p. 146, repr. p. 147; Paris, *P.G.*, 1974-75, no. 119; Torino, *P.G.*, 1975-76, no. 133.

REFERENCES:

View, 3rd ser., no. 4, Dec. 1943, repr. inside cover (Art of This Century announcement of forthcoming exhibitions, which states role as Pollock's sole agent); L. Alloway, *The Nation*, Feb. 17, 1969, pp. 221-22; D. Freke, "Jackson Pollock: a symbolic self-portrait," *Studio International*, vol. 184, no. 950, Dec. 1972, pp. 217-19; J. Wolfe, "Jungian Aspects of Jackson Pollock's Imagery," *Artforum*, vol. 11, no. 3, Nov. 1972, p. 68, repr. p. 69; Langhorne, 1977, pp. 143, 153, 154, 160, 161, 162, 208, repr.; *Pollock Painting*, interview with Lee Krasner, ed. Barbara Rose, New York, 1978, n.p.; O'Connor and Thaw, vol. 1, no. 86, repr. color pl. 13, vol. 4, p. 229 (photo of Pollock in his 46 East Eighth St. studio, 1943, completed *The Moon Woman* visible in background); E. L. Langhorne, "Jackson Pollock's 'The Moon Woman Cuts the Circle'," *Arts Magazine*, vol. 53, no. 7, Mar. 1979, pp. 128-37, repr. fig. 2; W. Rubin, "Pollock as Jungian Illustrator: The Limits of Psychological Criticism," Part I, *Art in America*, vol. 67, no. 7, Nov. 1979, pp. 104-23; idem, "Pollock as Jungian Illustrator: The Limits of Psychological Criticism," Part II, ibid., vol. 67, no. 8, Dec. 1979, p. 72; E. Langhorne, Letter to the Editor, ibid., vol. 68, no. 8, Oct. 1980, pp. 61-64; H. Lassalle, "Jackson Pollock: La femme-lune coupe le cercle ou Pollock et Jung," *Cahiers du Musée National d'Art Moderne*, no. 4, Apr.-June 1980, pp. 292-93, 296, repr. p. 293; L. Flint, *Handbook*, 1983, repr. color p. 179.

1. All the Pollock paintings in the Peggy Guggenheim Collection were unvarnished when she acquired them. According to Lee Krasner, he did not varnish his paintings. The issue never arose between them and she did not recall whether or not he had a strong aversion to varnish; but she was certain that he did not use it (conversation with the author, May 24, 1983).
2. Peggy Guggenheim was unable to remember precisely when Pollock gave her the painting; it is recorded among her possessions for the first time in 1946.

143 Untitled. 1944.
(*Don Quixote*).[1]

76.2553 PG 142

Oil on canvas (unvarnished), 28 13/16 x 17 15/16 (73.2 x 45.6).

Signed l.l.: *Jackson Pollock*. Not dated.

PROVENANCE:

Gift of the artist.[2]

CONDITION:

In 1964 (Tate Report) the unvarnished canvas was described as in good condition. A few minute losses at the left edge were noted. Some crackle with flaking in the beard of the figure is visible, and scattered flaking exists elsewhere. Restoration of the gray at the left is of unknown date. There is general soil and the condition is fragile. (Venice, June 1983.)

EXHIBITIONS:

Venice, *P.G.*, 1948 (Biennale), no. 114; Florence, *P.G.*, 1949, no. 117; Venice, Museo Correr, *Jackson Pollock*, July 22-Aug. 15, 1950, no. 4; Amsterdam, *P.G.*, 1951, no. 134 (dated 1941); Zurich, *P.G.*, 1951, no. 127 (dated 1941); London, *P.G.*, 1964-65, no. 117; Stockholm, *P.G.*, 1966-67, no. 112; New York, *P.G.*, 1969, p. 148, repr.; Paris, 1974-75, no. 120, repr.; Torino, *P.G.*, 1975-76, no. 134.

REFERENCES:

Langhorne, 1977, pp. 239, 240, 241, 256, 305; O'Connor and Thaw, no. 117.

1. The title *Don Quixote* was given to the picture by Peggy Guggenheim. Lee Krasner stated, in conversation with the author (Mar. 6, 1981), that she had never heard this title and was certain Pollock had not either. Its anecdotal nature would have been entirely alien to him: "Pollock always said 'Painting is *not* illustration' " (Krasner's emphasis).
2. Peggy Guggenheim was unable to recall precisely when Pollock gave her the painting, but felt certain that it was not at the time of his first one-man show.

144 Two. 1943-45.

Color plate p. 671.

76.2553 PG 143

Oil on canvas (unvarnished), 76 x 43¼ (193 x 110).

Signed l.r.: *Jackson Pollock*; on stretcher in blue pencil: *(43 x 76) (TWO)*. Not dated.

PROVENANCE:

Acquired under contract with Jackson Pollock, 1945.[1]

CONDITION:

In 1964 (Tate Report) the unvarnished surface was described as in good condition. Two minute losses were inpainted, and some bulges in the canvas were noted. A graphite number "2" scribbled in pencil near the right edge was noted. It is unlikely that this is in Pollock's hand.

The unpainted canvas is visible in many areas and appears to have only unevenly applied sizing. There are extensive drying cracks in the blacks, and some small pigment and ground losses, but the overall condition is stable. (New York, Feb. 1983.)

This work was originally dated 1943 in Peggy Guggenheim publications but was later changed to 1945 (see EXHIBITIONS and REFERENCES); the evidence for the change is not clear.

The work includes calligraphic elements suggesting a parallel to the paintings of 1943. Nonetheless, the overall pictorial structure, especially in the treatment of the two figures and of the gray field, closely resembles dated 1945 works such as *Totem Lesson 2* (O'Connor and Thaw, no. 122). Started a year or two earlier, this latter canvas was substantially reworked by Pollock in 1945.[2] It seems very likely that Pollock followed a similar process in *Two*: large areas of the gray field, although functioning pictorially as "background," were applied after many of the calligraphic (and figural) elements. In certain instances, calligraphic details were then added on top of this freshly applied gray. On the basis of this evidence, and by analogy with other works of this period, a date of 1943-45 is the most plausible.

1. In July 1943 Peggy Guggenheim signed a 1-year contract with Pollock. Under the initial terms, he was to receive $150 a month. At the end of the year, if more than $2700 worth of paintings had been sold, he would get an additional settlement, the gallery retaining one-third of the profit in excess of that total. If less than $2700 were realized, Peggy Guggenheim would select paintings to make up the difference. In April 1944 Pollock and Peggy Guggenhiem agreed on a second year's contract similar in terms to the first. In 1945 a 2-year contract was signed, the stipend being raised to $300 a month. Since she had lent him $2000 as a down payment on a house (Fireplace Road in The Springs, Long Island), she deducted monthly installment payments from the $300 until the loan was repaid. Under the terms of this new contract, Pollock's entire output was to go to her.

   In May 1947, preparing to move to Venice, she persuaded Betty Parsons to take over Pollock's work until her contract with him expired (early in 1948). During this period, Peggy Guggenheim would receive the proceeds from the sale of paintings she still owned, and would continue to pay him his monthly allowance. The paintings produced by Pollock until the expiration of the contract were to become her property, though she allowed him to keep one painting a year. (Information supplied by Peggy Guggenheim, in conversation with the author, 1978, and further substantiated by O'Connor and Thaw, vol. 4, pp. 228, 234-35, 238.)

2. Francis V. O'Connor supplied the information regarding the reworking of *Totem Lesson 2*.

144

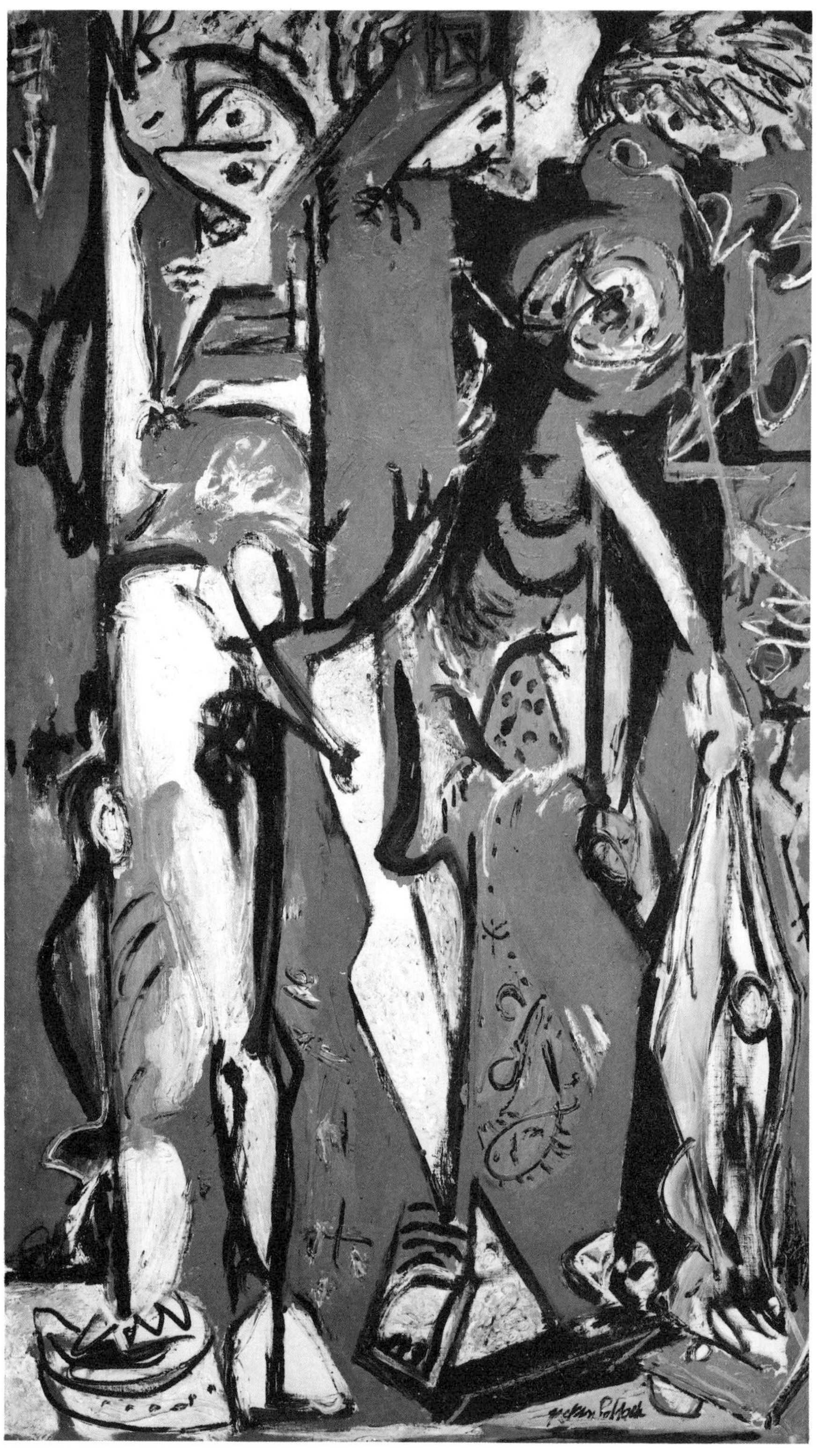

EXHIBITIONS:

New York, Art of This Century, *Jackson Pollock*, Mar. 19-Apr. 14, 1945, no. 10; New York, Whitney Museum of American Art, *Annual Exhibition of Contemporary American Painting*, Dec. 10, 1946-Jan. 16, 1947, no. 121 (Pollock's first participation in the Whitney annuals); Venice, *P.G.*, 1948 (Biennale), no. 111 (dated 1943, the date attributed to it in all *P.G.* publications until 1969); Florence, *P.G.*, 1949, no. 116; Venice, Museo Correr, *Jackson Pollock*, July 22-Aug. 15, 1950, no. 3; Amsterdam, *P.G.*, 1951, no. 133; Bern, Kunsthalle, *Tendances actuelles*, Jan. 29-Mar. 6, 1955, no. 53; London, *P.G.*, 1964-65, no. 118, repr.; Stockholm, *P.G.*, 1966-67, no. 113; New York, *P.G.*, 1969, p. 150, repr. p. 151 (dated 1945); Paris, *P.G.*, 1974-75, no. 121; Torino, *P.G.*, 1975-76, no. 135; Rome, *Guggenheim: Venezia-New York*, 1982, no. 58, repr. color; New York, *P.G.*, 1982-83, no. 53, repr.

REFERENCES:

C. Greenberg, *The Nation*, Dec. 28, 1946, p. 768 (review of Whitney exhibition); B. Robertson, *Jackson Pollock*, London, 1960, p. 140, repr. pl. 125 (dated 1945); Calas, 1966, p. 165, repr. color p. 168; L. Alloway, *The Nation*, Feb. 17, 1969, p. 222; D. Freke, "Jackson Pollock: a symbolic self-portrait," *Studio International*, vol. 184, no. 950, Dec. 1972, p. 218; Langhorne, 1977, pp. 239 (dated ca. 1944-45), 240, 241, 242, 255, 261, 263, 302, 305; O'Connor and Thaw, no. 123, repr. (dated ca. 1945).

---

145 Direction. October 1945.

Color plate p. 672.

76.2553 PG 144

Oil on canvas (unvarnished), 31¾ x 21 15/16 (80.6 x 55.7).

Signed l.l.: *Jackson Pollock*; signed and dated on stretcher (replaced by Peggy Guggenheim after 1969, but inscription recorded before): *10.45 Pollock.*

PROVENANCE:

Acquired under contract with Jackson Pollock, 1945. (See above, cat. no. 144, fn. 1.)

CONDITION:

In 1964 (Tate Report) the unvarnished surface was described as in generally good condition apart from a small dent near the left edge, approximately at the center, and some minute areas of flaking at the center.

In 1977 (Venice) 2 repaired tears in the canvas, ca. ⅝ in., 1.5 cm., with corresponding losses of pigment and ground, were noted: 5⅛ in., 13 cm., from the bottom and 2 in., 5 cm., from the left; 5½ in., 14 cm., from the bottom, 2 in., 5 cm., from the right. A further paint loss was noted 6 11/16 in., 17 cm., from the right, 12 9/16 in., 32 cm., from the top.

In 1982 (Venice) the patches, which had been applied with wax, were removed and the tears repaired with rice paper and Paraloid B-72 (at 20%) in acetone. The surface was cleaned with water and ammonia and sprayed with Lefranc retouching varnish. The painting was mounted on an ICA spring stretcher (untensioned).

There has been some retouching at the edges but almost none elsewhere. Considerable scattered breaks and losses in the impasto brushstrokes are visible. Marks from the rabbet of a previous frame can be seen along the edges. The condition is stable. (Venice, Nov. 1982.)

EXHIBITIONS:

New York, Art of This Century, *Jackson Pollock: Exhibition Paintings*, Apr. 2-20, 1946, no. 8; Venice, *P.G.*, 1948 (Biennale), suppl. to catalogue, no. 175; Venice, Museo Correr, *Jackson Pollock*, July 22-Aug. 15, 1950, no. 7; Amsterdam, *P.G.*, 1951, no. 141; London, *P.G.*, 1964-65, no. 119; Stockholm, *P.G.*, 1966-67, no. 114; New York, *P.G.*, 1969, p. 150, repr. p. 151; Paris, *P.G.*, 1974-75, no. 122, repr.; Torino, *P.G.*, 1975-76, no. 136; New York, *P.G.*, 1982-83, no. 52, repr. color.

145

REFERENCES:

Langhorne, 1977, pp. 257, 258, 259, 263; O'Connor and Thaw, no. 131; W. Rubin, "Pollock as Jungian Illustrator: The Limits of Psychological Criticism," Part II, *Art in America*, vol. 67, no. 8, Dec. 1979, p. 83, repr.

---

146 Circumcision. January 1946.
(*Ritual*).[1]

Color plate p. 673.

76.2553 PG 145

Oil on canvas (unvarnished), 56 1/16 x 66 1/8 (142.3 x 168).

Signed l.l.: *Jackson Pollock*; signed and dated on stretcher: *1.46 Pollock*; *Jackson Pollock 66 x 56.*

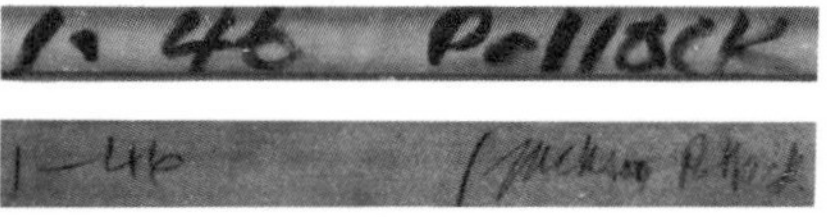

1. For discussion of this title, see above NOTE, pp. 634-35.

PROVENANCE:

Acquired under contract with Jackson Pollock, 1946. (See above, cat. no. 144, fn. 1.)

CONDITION:

In 1964 (Tate Report) a tendency toward flaking of the thinly applied paint and in some areas of the thick impasto was noted. Cleavage was consolidated and losses inpainted.

In 1978 (New York) extensive flaking of the impasto was noted, showing red beneath in several places. The entire surface was cleaned with 5% Soilax solution and rinsed with distilled water; areas of flaking and cleavage were consolidated with Lucite 44; the canvas was removed from the stretcher and a tear in the top right corner mended with epoxy. The canvas was lined on Mylar 1400 with BEVA, strip-lined with Lucite 44-treated linen strips attached with Plus-Ten contact cement, and stapled to a new stretcher. Inpainting in a few small areas was carried out and the surface lightly sprayed with Lucite 44. The condition is fragile. (Rome, May 1982.)

146

The flaking of some of the impasto, which reveals red underpainting, raises a number of questions about the artist's working method in *Circumcision.*

It is possible, for example, that Pollock had begun a different composition on the canvas and that he then abandoned it. Alternatively, he may have worked on *Circumcision* over a considerable period, changing the composition and color from time to time.

Lee Krasner spoke about the way Pollock often "reentered" a canvas, after having set it aside. He rarely abandoned (or destroyed) pictures that proved difficult to resolve, but he returned to them, sometimes painting them over almost entirely, sometimes reworking certain sections.

In the case of *The Moon Woman* (cat. no. 142), for example, the picture's fluency of composition and execution suggested to Krasner that the painting probably "came through directly, upon first contact." *Circumcision*, on the other hand, shows evidence of struggle. Though unable to recall precisely Pollock's experience with the work, she thought that the painting probably caused him difficulty and that he made substantial alterations to it before it was fully resolved (conversation with the author, May 24, 1983).

For further discussion of this work, see above NOTE, pp. 633-35.

EXHIBITIONS:

New York, Art of This Century, *Jackson Pollock: Exhibition Paintings*, Apr. 2-20, 1946, no. 1 (*circumcision*); Venice, *P.G.*, 1948 (Biennale), no. 112 (dated 1946); Florence, *P.G.*, 1949, no. 118 (dated 1945); Venice, Museo Correr, *Jackson Pollock*, July 22-Aug. 15, 1950, no. 5; Amsterdam, *P.G.*, 1951, no. 135 (dated 1945); Zurich, *P.G.*, 1951, no. 129 (dated 1945); London, *P.G.*, 1964-65, no. 120, repr. (dated 1946, the date attributed to it in all subsequent publications); Stockholm, *P.G.*, 1966-67, no. 115, repr.; New York, *P.G.*, 1969, p. 152, repr.; Paris, *P.G.*, 1974-75, no. 123, repr.; Torino, *P.G.*, 1975-76, no. 137; Rome, *Guggenheim: Venezia-New York*, 1982, no. 59, repr. color.

REFERENCES:

B. Robertson, *Jackson Pollock*, New York, 1960, repr. pl. 129 (dated 1945); W. Rubin, "Notes on Masson and Pollock," *Arts Magazine*, vol. 34, no. 2, Nov. 1959, p. 41, repr. p. 40; idem, "Jackson Pollock and the Modern Tradition," Part I, *Artforum*, vol. 5, no. 6, Feb. 1967, p. 17, repr.; F. O'Connor, 1967, pp. 54-55; H. Rosenberg, *Artworks and Packages*, New York, 1969, p. 67; L. Alloway, *The Nation*, Feb. 17, 1969, p. 222; J. Wolfe, "Jungian Aspects of Jackson Pollock's Imagery," *Artforum*, vol. 11, no. 3, Nov. 1972, pp. 70-72, repr.; E. Johnson, "Jackson Pollock and Nature," *Studio International*, vol. 185, no. 956, June 1973, p. 259; Langhorne, 1977, pp. 278-86, 295, 306, 319, 323; O'Connor and Thaw, vol. 1, no. 142, repr., vol. 4, pp. 239, 240 (as *Ritual*); L. Flint, *Handbook*, 1983, p. 180, repr. color p. 181.

147 Untitled. ca. 1946.

76.2553 PG 147

Gouache and pastel on wove paper, 22⅞ x 31½ (58 x 80).

Signed l.r.: *Jackson Pollock*. Not dated.

PROVENANCE:

Acquired under contract with Jackson Pollock, 1945. (See above, cat. no. 144, fn. 1.)

CONDITION:

In 1964 (Tate Report) the work was described as in good condition, though in direct contact with the glass and highly acidic wood pulpboard. The unvarnished surface was well preserved though the paper support was considerably buckled, a natural result of the variations in thickness of paint.

In 1982 (Venice) the orange and blue pastel had powdered and offset onto the glass, which was very moldy on the interior. Nonetheless, the design remained in good condition. As a temporary measure, the acidic secondary support was replaced with 100% ragboard and the glass cleaned. The condition is stable. (Venice, Nov. 1982.)

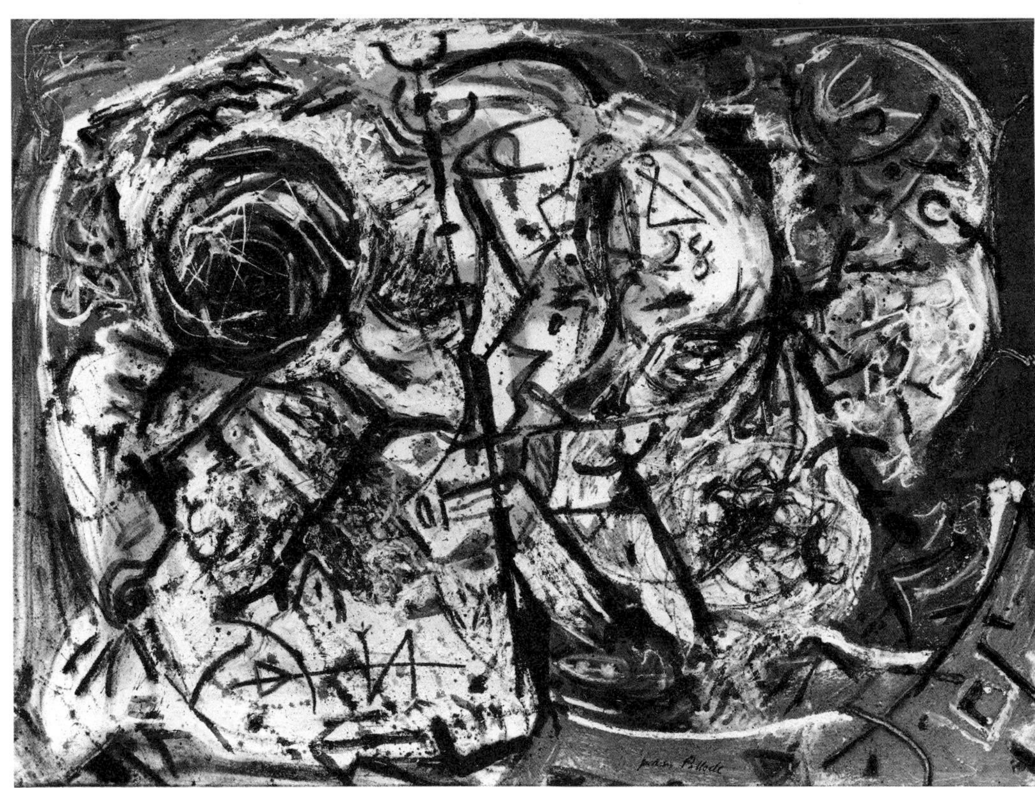

EXHIBITIONS:

Venice, *P.G.*, 1948 (Biennale), no. 114; Florence, *P.G.*, 1949, no. 121; Venice, Museo Correr, *Jackson Pollock*, July 22-Aug. 15, 1950, no. 12 or 13 (both "*Guazzo*, 1946"); Amsterdam, *P.G.*, 1951, no. 137 or 138 (both "gouache, 1946"); Zurich, *P.G.*, 1951, no. 131; Bordighera, *11ᴬ Mostra Internazionale Pittura Americana*, Mar. 1-31, 1953, no. 3; London, *P.G.*, 1964-65, no. 122; Stockholm, *P.G.*, 1966-67, no. 117; New York, *P.G.*, 1969, p. 154, repr.; Paris, *P.G.*, 1974-75, no. 125; Torino, *P.G.*, 1975-76, no. 139.

REFERENCES:

S. Hunter, "Contributi alla conoscenza dell'opera Jackson Pollock," *Soli*, 4, no. 1, Jan.-Feb. 1957, p. 5; Calas, 1966, repr. p. 171; L. Alloway, *The Nation*, Feb. 17, 1969, p. 222; O'Connor and Thaw, vol. 4, no. 1008, repr.

148 Bird Effort (Accabonac Creek Series). 1946.

Color plate p. 672.

76.2553 PG 146

Oil on canvas (unvarnished), 24 x 20$^{1}/_{16}$ (61 x 51).

Signed u.c.: *Jackson Pollock*; signed and dated on reverse (barely visible, but photographed before lining): *Jackson Pollock 46*.

PROVENANCE:

Acquired under contract with Jackson Pollock, 1946. (See above, cat. no. 144, fn. 1.)

CONDITION:

In 1964 (Tate Report) the unvarnished surface applied on a white oil ground was described as in excellent condition.

By 1982 (Venice) the reverse had been heavily coated with wax, apparently in an attempt to consolidate the paint layer. The wax was heated and partially drawn off into a blotter. A Fieux contact lining and ICA spring stretcher (untensioned) were applied. The edges were retouched with watercolors.

There are some breaks in the thick impasto resulting in loss. The top edge of the canvas is torn along much of its length (and is held in place by the lining). There is considerable wear at all edges and drying cracks elsewhere. The condition is fairly stable. (New York, Mar. 1983.)

Pollock and Lee Krasner moved to East Hampton in November 1945. During 1946 he completed fifteen new paintings that were divided into two groups and shown in the January 1947 exhibition at Art of This Century: the Sounds in the Grass Series and the Accabonac Creek Series.[1] The latter group, to which *Bird*

Effort belongs, was named after the body of water near the Pollocks' East Hampton property and included *Magic Light* (O'Connor and Thaw, no. 141); *The Water Bull* (ibid., no. 149); *The Tea Cup* (ibid., no. 150); *Yellow Triangle* (ibid., no. 151); *Gray Center* (ibid., no. 152); *Constellation* (ibid., no. 154); and *The Key* (ibid., no. 156). The Sounds in the Grass Series included *The Blue Unconsciousness* (ibid., no. 158); *The Dancers* (ibid., no. 159); *Something of the Past* (ibid., no. 160); *Croaking Movement* (cat. no. 149); *Eyes in the Heat* (cat. no. 150); *Earth Worms* (ibid., no. 163); and *Shimmering Substance* (ibid., no. 164).

Like *Bird Effort*, all the works in the Accabonac Creek Series contained clearly discernible figurative (if not always representational) elements. Describing the style of *Bird Effort*, in which he saw both "mythic" elements and a new pictorial freedom, Lawrence Alloway in 1969 captured some of the characteristics of this entire group of paintings: the "smeared Cubism of 'Circumcision' has been turned into a subtle interplay of color and line across the flat surface. White canvas intercedes continually between black contours and scabby color patches, so that line and color seem to be pried apart."

The decisive change that occurred in Pollock's style late in 1946 (and which is reflected in both the Accabonac Creek Series and the Sounds in the Grass Series) is attributable to a number of factors, among them his continued preoccupation with the pictorial issues raised by late Cubism. Ellen Johnson (1973) has pointed to another ingredient that should be taken into account, namely Pollock's direct and daily experience of the natural environment of East Hampton.[2] Johnson suggested that this continual contact with nature ultimately helped to transform both the subject matter and the style of Pollock's work. The titles of many of the pictures in the 1947 Art of This Century exhibition, all of which were chosen by Pollock,[3] suggest a new relationship to nature, although in

1. See Appendix, p. 794, for the catalogue of this exhibition.

2. "Jackson Pollock and Nature," *Studio International*, vol. 185, no. 956, June 1973, pp. 257-62.

3. Ibid., p. 259, fn. 24, quoting Lee Krasner.

B. H. Friedman, *Jackson Pollock: Energy Made Visible*, New York, 1972, pp. 94-95, did not regard the titles as Pollock's own. Bruno Alfieri also rejected the notion that any title of Pollock's had significance: "Do not, therefore, be deceived by suggestive titles such as 'Eyes in the Heat' or 'Circumcision': these are phony titles, invented merely to distinguish the canvases and identify them rapidly" (*L'Arte Moderna*, 1950). In a conversation with the author (Mar. 6, 1981), Lee Krasner confirmed, however, that all these titles were Pollock's own.

Judith Wolfe also suggested that the move into natural surroundings was important for Pollock, though she concentrated her attention on a Jungian interpretation of his art ("Jungian Aspects of Jackson Pollock's Imagery," *Artforum*, vol. 11, no. 3, Nov. 1972, p. 72). Harold Rosenberg, on the other hand, saw the 1946 East Hampton paintings, such as *Eyes in the Heat* and *Blue Poles*, as less a response to nature than an evocation of an interior landscape: "Pollock's procedure is not a translation by nature into abstraction, as it is supposed by those who cannot rid themselves of the 'objective' fixation; it is, rather, the artist bringing to the canvas an inner landscape that is part of himself and that is awakened in the activity of painting. Since style determines visual reality, he has been able to reach the scene through favoring the canvas over the cornfield. Pollock painted as if he had penetrated the landscape and was working inside it" (*The Anxious Object: Art Today and Its Audience*, New York, 1964, p. 83).

themselves they were, in Johnson's view, merely a reflection of the more profound pictorial changes that were taking place. Pollock began to feel himself and his art become one with "nature's constant movement, beat and change as he discovered and absorbed it" (ibid., p. 260). In Johnson's view, it was only after a full year (or four full seasons) of residence in East Hampton that Pollock began to abandon his "faintly surrealist imagery" and acquire the freedom that allowed him to develop his characteristic all-over style.

Bird Effort is one of the first examples of Pollock's new mode; like other works of the first part of 1946, it remains rooted in the figurative past. But by the time Pollock had painted *Croaking Movement* (cat. no. 149), *Eyes in the Heat* (cat. no. 150), and *Shimmering Substance* (MoMA, O'Connor and Thaw, no. 164), there was clear evidence that a major change had taken place.

In his important series of articles on Pollock's place in the modern tradition,[4] William Rubin pointed out that the works of 1946 represented a significant transitional moment in Pollock's development. The expressionist-figural style of Pollock's immediately preceding canvases (see above, cat. nos. 144, 145) was still to some extent present in these paintings. *Bird Effort* (which Rubin did not discuss) clearly belongs to this new group. Its style, like that of other related works, shows a certain plastic "violence" in its "compositional discontinuities, convolutions, truncations, angularities and frequent asperity of color" (Rubin, Part I, p. 15).

By the winter of 1946-47, however, Pollock had already begun to develop a more lyrical and "choreographically rhythmic art." This important shift can be more fully appreciated if the style of *Croaking Movement* (cat. no. 149) is compared to that of *Eyes in the Heat* (cat. no. 150) or *Shimmering Substance*. The dense, thick, all-over pattern of *Croaking Movement* (which was imposed on a thinly painted base coat) clearly lacks representational figurative content but nonetheless conveys a strongly linear quality. This derives partly from the painting's scratched and incised markings, but even more from the overlaid thick white lines, which were created by squeezing paint from the tube and manipulating it with sticks or knives. By contrast, *Eyes in the Heat* and *Shimmering Substance* manifest new qualities; the paint is still extremely dense (and it is still squeezed from the tube), but the result is now an all-over pattern that presents an integrated surface. Greenberg instantly recognized the originality of these works when they were exhibited in January 1947: "Pollock ... tends to handle his canvas with an over-all evenness; ... [he] has gone beyond the stage where he needs to make his poetry explicit in ideographs. What he invents instead has perhaps, in its very abstractness and absence of assignable definition, a more reverberating meaning" (see Appendix, p. 794).

In these canvases of late 1946, there are no distinct articulating lines incised with the end of the brush or applied on top of the dense field. Rather, as Rubin

4. W. Rubin, "Jackson Pollock and the Modern Tradition," Part I, *Artforum*, vol. 5, no. 6, Feb. 1967, pp. 14-22; Part II, ibid., vol. 5, no. 7, Mar. 1967, pp. 28-37; Part III, ibid., vol. 5, no. 8, Apr. 1967, pp. 18-31; Part IV, ibid., vol. 5, no. 9, May 1967, pp. 28-33. References to these articles will indicate the Parts and page nos.

wrote, "Pollock's line forms a series of looped and arabesqued patterns all *roughly similar in character and in approximate size* and *more or less even in density* over the *whole surface of the picture*."[5] Rubin also detected "fragments of Pollock's earlier totemistic presences"[6] underneath the "rhythmical linear pattern which dominates" the surface of these transitional works: "These presences have not been wholly 'painted out' but lurk mysteriously in the interstices of the white lines, taking the form in *Eyes in the Heat* that the title suggests. Much less of the 'underpicture'... is so literally visible in *Shimmering Substance*" (Part I, p. 18).

In *Eyes in the Heat* and *Shimmering Substance*, therefore, Pollock created a new all-over style that was free from the limitations of description. The success of this development, moreover, raised important new issues that Pollock felt compelled to confront in the immediately following works (see below, cat. no. 151).

EXHIBITIONS:

New York, Art of This Century, *Jackson Pollock*, Jan. 14-Feb. 1, 1947, Accabonac Creek (Series), no. 10;[7] Florence, *P.G.*, 1949, no. 119 (dated 1945); Venice, Museo Correr, *Jackson Pollock*, July 22-Aug. 15, 1950, no. 6; Amsterdam, *P.G.*, 1951, no. 136 (dated 1945); Zurich, *P.G.*, 1951, no. 130 (dated 1946); London, *P.G.*, 1964-65, no. 121; Stockholm, *P.G.*, 1966-67, no. 116; New York, *P.G.*, 1969, p. 153, repr.; Paris, *P.G.*, 1974-75, no. 124, repr.; Torino, *P.G.*, 1975-76, no. 138; New York, *P.G.*, 1982-83, no. 54, repr. color.

REFERENCES:

T. Hess, *Abstract Painting*, New York, 1951, p. 155, repr. fig. 93; Calas, 1966, pp. 165-66, repr. p. 170; L. Alloway, *The Nation*, Feb. 17, 1969, p. 222; E. Johnson, "Jackson Pollock and Nature," *Studio International*, vol. 185, no. 956, June 1973, p. 259; Langhorne, 1977, p. 277, 296-99, 302, 305, 328; O'Connor and Thaw, no. 153, repr.

5. For a discussion of related developments in the contemporary work of Lee Krasner, see E. G. Landau, "Lee Krasner's Early Career, Part Two: The Early 1940's," *Arts Magazine*, vol. 56, no. 3, Nov. 1981.
6. L. Alloway (*The Nation*, Feb. 17, 1969, p. 222) also saw residual "mythic imagery" in *Eyes in the Heat*: "... there is... what we might call the pulverizing of mythic imagery but not its abandonment. The iconography is present in these later works not as figures but as atmosphere, as rhythm; it is as if somebody had demolished a pagan idol in the room and its dust had settled on everything. Hence, a pulverized but not absent mythology, with meanings—tidal, seasonal, labyrinthine—evoked by rhythm."

   Langhorne, 1977 (pp. 335-39), implausibly drew a Jungian analogy between the "outline of many eyes" and symbols of masculinity and patriarchal castration. For the argument against her Jungian interpretation of paintings such as *Shimmering Substance*, see W. Rubin, "Pollock as Jungian Illustrator: The Limits of Psychological Criticism," Part I, *Art in America*, vol. 67, no. 7, Nov. 1979, pp. 113-15.
7. An untitled work of ca. 1947, posthumously titled *Eyes in the Heat II* at the time of the 1958 Sidney Janis Gallery exhibition, is painted with a much heavier, thicker surface texture (O'Connor and Thaw, no. 167, oil and aluminum paint on canvas, 24 x 20 in., 60.9 x 50.8 cm.). According to Lee Krasner it may have dated from later than the Art of This Century exhibition, though O'Connor and Thaw see it as similar in style to *Shimmering Substance*. The existence of this work has led some critics to designate Peggy Guggenheim's painting *Eyes in the Heat I*.

149 Croaking Movement (Sounds in the Grass Series). 1946.

Color plate p. 674.

76.2553 PG 148

Oil on canvas (unvarnished), 54 x 44 1/8 (137 x 112).

Signed l.l.: *J. Pollock*; signed and dated on reverse: *Jackson / Pollock / 46*.

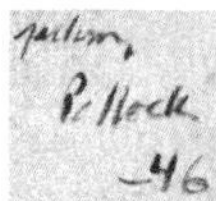

PROVENANCE:

Acquired under contract with Jackson Pollock, 1946. (See above, cat. no. 144, fn. 1.)

CONDITION:

In 1964 (Tate Report) the heavily painted unvarnished surface was described as in excellent condition with only one small loss noted.

Large parts of the composition consist of thick pigment squeezed directly from the tube onto the prepared canvas. Passages of *sgraffito*, in which the lines were scratched into the heavy pigment with the tip of the brush handle, create most of the linear effect.

There is considerable evidence of cleavage and loss in the heavy impasto. The overall condition of the thickly painted surface is fragile. (Venice, Nov. 1982.)

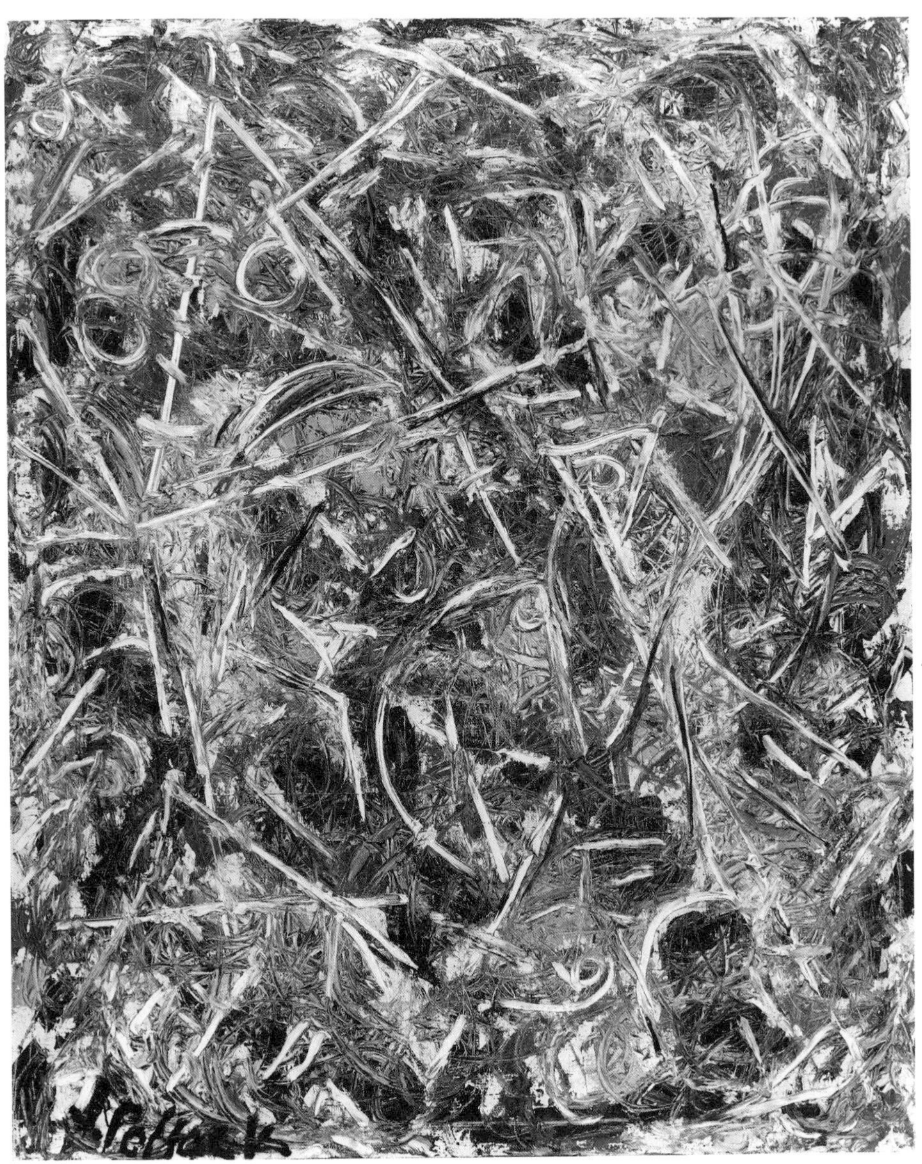

In discussing *Croaking Movement* in a review of the 1969 Peggy Guggenheim Collection exhibition in New York, Lawrence Alloway (1969) drew attention to the carefully calculated relationship between the picture's overall thickly painted surface and the narrow edge of unpainted canvas surrounding it: "The density of paint is constant and ceases just within the edges of the picture, a device which has the effect of making the picture edge subservient to the display of paint. The edges do not break or interrupt any images or shapes. The canvas is only slightly larger than the area of the paint field it carries, a principle of organization which replaces internal subdivisions by a holistic definition of area, a kind of space developed superbly in later drip paintings."

In light of Alloway's comments, it seems possible that the present outer dimensions of the canvas have been slightly altered. Certain "breaks and interruptions" in the "images and shapes," which to Alloway were so notably absent in 1969, are now visible, and the paint field in some places extends beyond the edge. Although there is no existing record of the restretching of *Croaking Movement*, additional nail holes on three sides of the painting's tacking margin provide possible evidence that such restretching has occurred. *Shimmering Substance* of ca. 1946 (MoMA, O'Connor and Thaw, no. 164) and *Eyes in the Heat* (cat. no. 150) are both fully "contained" compositions: neither has a margin of unpainted canvas surrounding it, but the edge in each is strongly defined by the way in which prominent swirls or lines of paint approach the very edge of the canvas and then double back upon themselves into the painted field. These loops or arcs cause the eye to return to the center of the canvas rather than leading it outward "over the edge."

In view of the deliberateness with which Pollock calculated the edges of these and other compositions, it is important to bear in mind that the current outer margins of *Croaking Movement* may not precisely accord with Pollock's original intentions.

EXHIBITIONS:

New York, Art of This Century, *Jackson Pollock*, Jan. 14-Feb. 1, 1947, Sounds in the Grass (Series), no. 1 *(Croaking Movement)*; Florence, *P.G.*, 1949, no. 122 (as *Sounds in the Grass*, the title under which the work was published in *P.G.* exhibitions until 1982); Venice, Museo Correr, *Jackson Pollock*, July 22-Aug. 15, 1950, no. 10; Amsterdam, *P.G.*, 1951, no. 139; Zurich, *P.G.*, 1951, no. 132; Bordighera, *1ª Mostra Internazionale Pittura Americana*, Mar. 1-31, 1953, no. 5; Bern, Kunsthalle, *Tendances actuelles*, Jan. 29-Mar. 6, 1955, no. 55; London, *P.G.*, 1964-65, no. 123; Stockholm, *P.G.*, 1966-67, no. 118; New York, *P.G.*, 1969, p. 155, repr.; Paris, 1974-75, no. 126, repr.; Torino, *P.G.*, 1975-76, no. 140; Rome, *Guggenheim: Venezia-New York*, 1982, no. 60, repr. color.

REFERENCES:

F. O'Connor, 1967, p. 40; L. Alloway, *The Nation*, Feb. 17, 1969, p. 222; S. Hunter, *American Art of the Twentieth Century*, New York, 1972, p. 169, repr. color pl. 306; O'Connor and Thaw, no. 161.

150 Eyes in the Heat (Sounds in the Grass Series). 1946.

Color plate p. 674.

76.2553 PG 149

Oil (and enamel?)[1] on canvas (unvarnished), 54 x 43 (137.2 x 109.2).

Signed and dated l.r.: 46 / *J. Pollock*: titled on stretcher: *Sounds in the Grass Series (Eyes in the Heat)*.

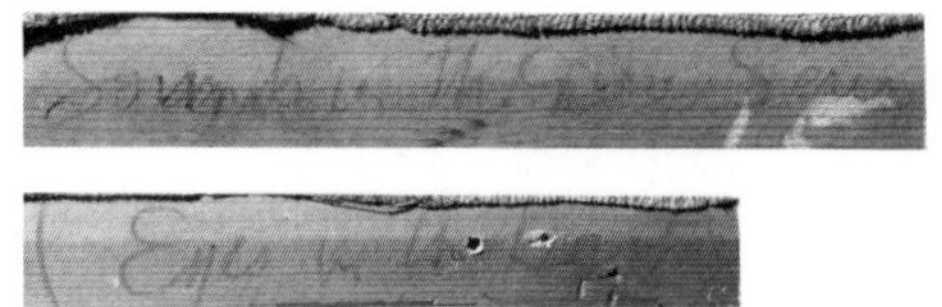

PROVENANCE:

Acquired under contract with Jackson Pollock, 1946. (See above, cat. no. 144, fn. 1.)

CONDITION:

In 1964 (Tate Report) the unvarnished surface was described as in excellent condition. The richness of the medium has resulted in seepage through to the back of the canvas in some places. The wrinkled skin surface of some of the shiny areas may be attributable to the use of enamel in parts of the composition (see fn. 1). There is some scattered breakage and loss of heavy impasto brushstrokes, but the overall condition is stable. (New York, Mar. 1983.)

For a discussion of this picture, see above, cat. no. 149.

EXHIBITIONS:

New York, Art of This Century, *Jackson Pollock*, Jan. 14-Feb. 1, 1947, *Sounds in the Grass (Series)*, no. 3 (*Eyes in the Heat*); Venice, *P.G.*, 1948 (Biennale), no. 109 (dated 1948); Florence, *P.G.*, 1949, no. 123 (dated 1948); Venice, Museo Correr, *Jackson Pollock*, July 22-Aug. 15, 1950, no. 11; Amsterdam, *P.G.*, 1951, no. 140; Bordighera, *11^A Mostra Internazionale Pittura Americana*, Mar. 1-31, 1953, no. 2; Bern, Kunsthalle, *Tendances actuelles*, Jan. 29-Mar. 6, 1955, no. 54; London, *P.G.*, 1964-65, no. 124, repr.; Stockholm, *P.G.*, 1966-67, no. 119, repr.; New York, *P.G.*, 1969, p. 156, repr.; Paris, *P.G.*, 1974-75, no. 127, repr. color; Torino, *P.G.*, 1975-76, no. 140; Paris, MNAM, *Jackson Pollock*, Jan. 21-Apr. 19, 1982, repr. color p. 139; New York, *P.G.*, 1982-83, no. 55, repr.

REFERENCES:

J. Pollock, "My Painting," *Possibilities*, vol. 1, no. 1, winter 1947-48, p. 78, repr.; T. B. Hess, *Abstract Painting*, New York, 1951, p. 156, repr. pl. 94; F. O'Hara, *Jackson Pollock*, New York, 1959, pp. 23, 115, 116, repr. pl. 24; B. Robertson, *Jackson Pollock*, New York, 1960, pp. 139, 144, repr. color pl. 50; F. O'Connor, 1967, pp. 54-55; D. Judd, "Jackson Pollock," *Arts Magazine*, vol. 41, no. 6, Apr. 1967, p. 34; W. Rubin, "Jackson Pollock and the Modern Tradition," Part I, *Artforum*, vol. 5, no. 6, Feb. 1967, pp. 17-19, repr.; I. Tomassoni, *Pollock*, New York, 1968, p. 23, repr. color pl. 35; B. H. Friedman, *Energy Made Visible*, New York, 1972, pp. 94-97, 100, 121; J. Wolfe, "Jungian Aspects of Jackson Pollock's Imagery," *Artforum*, vol. 11, no. 3, Nov. 1972, pp. 71, 73; E. Johnson, "Jackson Pollock and Nature," *Studio International*, vol. 185, no. 956, June 1973, p. 259; Langhorne, 1977, pp. 335-39; C. E. Johannes, "The Relationship Between Some Abstract Expressionist Painting and Samuel Beckett's Writing," unpublished Ph.D. dissertation, University of Georgia, Athens, 1974, pp. 50-51, 52, 54; O'Connor and Thaw, no. 162; W. Rubin, "Pollock as Jungian Illustrator: The Limits of Psychological Criticism," Part II, *Art in America*, vol. 67, no. 8, Dec. 1979, p. 83; E. Landau, "Lee Krasner's Early Career, Part Two: The Early 1940's," *Arts Magazine*, vol. 56, no. 3, Nov. 1981, pp. 82, 83, 89.

1. Pollock used enamel extensively in his later work, often in combination with oil and aluminum paints on the same canvas. It has not thus far been possible to conduct medium analyses of this work, or of others in the Peggy Guggenheim Collection. The nature of the surface in parts of this painting would suggest, however, that enamel is present (see CONDITION).

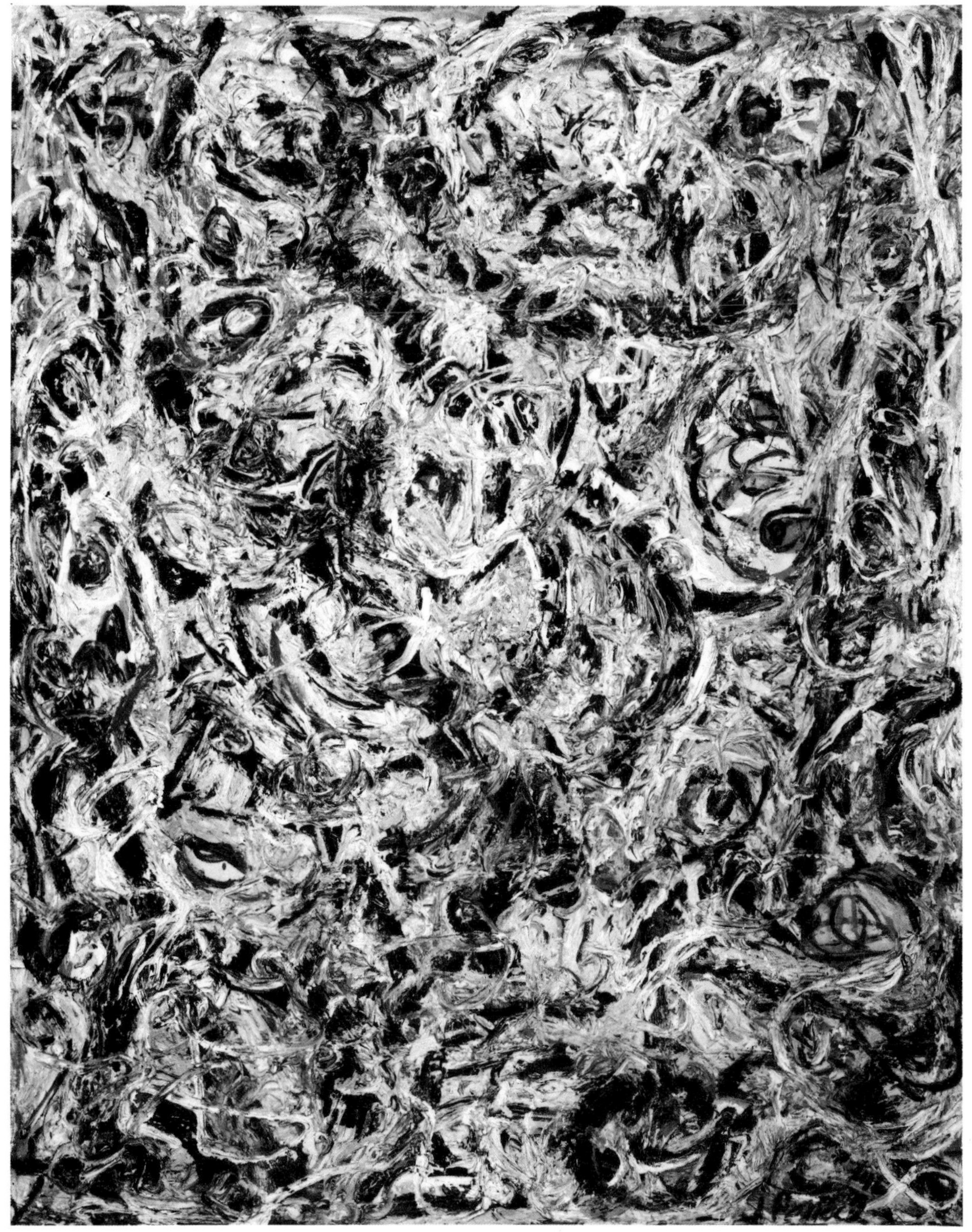

151 Enchanted Forest. 1947.

Color plate p. 675.

76.2553 PG 151

Oil on canvas, (unvarnished), 45 1/8 x 87 1/8 (114.6 x 221.3).

Signed and dated l.c.: *47 Jackson Pollock;* on stretcher (partially visible): *47 Jackson Pollock.*

PROVENANCE:

Acquired under contract with Jackson Pollock, 1948. (See above, cat. no. 144, fn. 1.)

CONDITION:

In 1964 (Tate Report) the unvarnished surface was described as in excellent condition apart from a triangular puncture in the upper left quadrant and a pierced hole in the upper right quadrant.

The work has received no treatment and the condition remains stable. (Paris, Mar. 1982.)

Enchanted Forest and *Alchemy* (cat. no. 152) were both shown in Pollock's first one-man show at the Betty Parsons Gallery in January 1948. The pictures in this show were all painted with Pollock's newly developed pouring technique.

As suggested above (p. 651), *Eyes in the Heat* (cat. no. 150) and *Shimmering Substance* represented a stage in Pollock's career in which he managed to free line from the limitations of description, and this achievement in turn presented him with a new set of issues and possibilities. *Enchanted Forest* and *Alchemy* (cat. no. 152)—together with the other works of 1947—constituted a response to these opportunities and define a further point in Pollock's development.

In some of these works, Pollock eliminated all trace of the expressionist-figural underpainting that persisted in his 1946 paintings; and he demonstrated a use of line which is free not only of figural description but of all suggestion of planar definition.

Michael Fried was the first critic to define this critical shift in Pollock's style:

Pollock's all-over drip paintings refuse to bring one's attention to a focus anywhere. This is important. Because it was only in the context of a style entirely homogeneous, all-over in nature and resistant to ultimate focus that the different elements in the painting — most important, line and color — could be made, for the first time in Western painting, to function as wholly autonomous pictorial elements.

At the same time, such a style could be achieved only if line itself could somehow be pried loose from the task of figuration (Three American Painters, exh. cat., Fogg Art Museum, Cambridge, 1965, p. 14).

In this passage, Fried characterized the achievement of the finest of Pollock's 1947-50 poured paintings, and focused the discussion on *Number One*, 1948 (MoMA). But many of the elements he described are already evident in *Enchanted Forest*. Thus:

[*Pollock's*] *all-over line does not give rise to positive and negative areas: We are not made to feel that one part of the canvas demands to be read as figure, whether abstract or representational, against another part of the canvas read as ground. There is no inside or outside to Pollock's line or to the space*

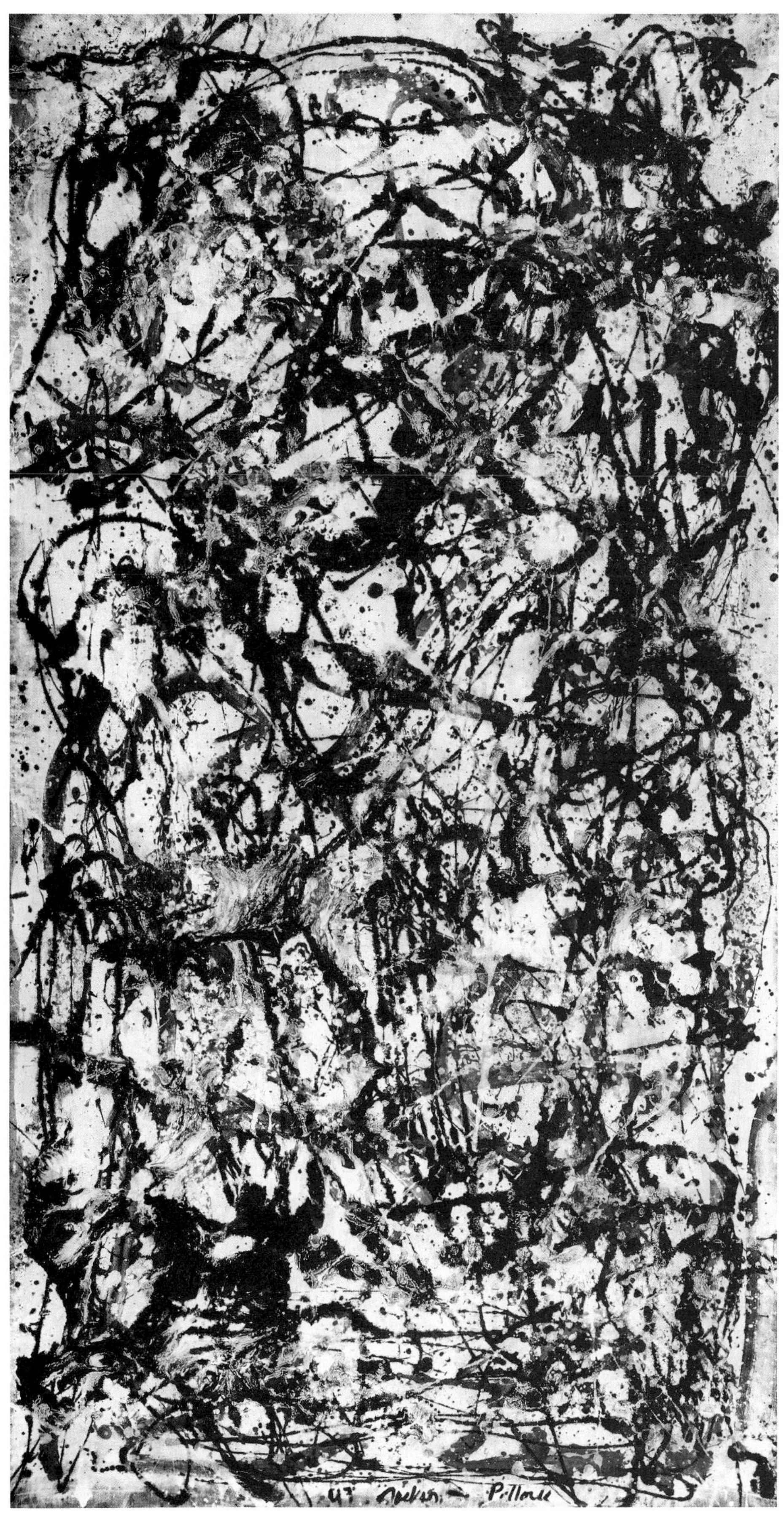

through which it moves. And this is tantamount to claiming that line, in Pollock's all-over drip paintings of 1947-50, has been freed at last from the job of describing contours and bounding shapes.... Line, in these paintings, is entirely transparent both to the non-illusionistic space it inhabits but does not structure, and to the pulses of something like pure, disembodied energy that seem to move without resistance through them ... line is used in such a way as to defy being read in terms of figuration (ibid., p. 14).

Although Fried's characterization accurately describes *Enchanted Forest,* it does not entirely apply to *Alchemy*, where a complete integration of all elements in this particular sense is not fully achieved, and other pictorial issues seem to take precedence (see below, cat. no. 152).

EXHIBITIONS:

New York, Betty Parsons Gallery, *Jackson Pollock*, Jan. 5-23, 1948 (no cat.);[1] Venice, Museo Correr, *Jackson Pollock*, July 22-Aug. 15, 1950, no. 15; Amsterdam, *P.G.*, 1951, no. 144; Bern, Kunsthalle, *Tendances actuelles*, Jan. 29-Mar. 6, 1955, no. 56; London, *P.G.*, 1964-65, no. 126, repr.; Stockholm, *P.G.*, 1966-67, no. 121, repr.; New York, *P.G.*, 1969, p. 159, repr. p. 158; Paris, *P.G.*, 1974-75, no. 129, repr.; Torino, *P.G.*, 1975-76, no. 143; Paris, MNAM, *Jackson Pollock*, Jan. 21-Apr. 19, 1982, repr. color p. 147.

REFERENCES:

R. Coates, review of Parsons exhibition, *New Yorker*, Jan. 17, 1948; C. Greenberg, *The Nation*, Jan. 24, 1948, p. 108; Calas, 1966, pp. 165-66, repr. p. 174; A. Bowness, "The American Invasion and the British Response," *Studio International*, vol. 173, no. 890, June 1967, p. 289, repr. p. 286; O'Connor and Thaw, no. 173.

1. See cat. no. 152, fn. 4.

Clement Greenberg, in his review of the 1948 Betty Parsons exhibition (*The Nation*, Jan. 24, 1948, p. 108), made a connection between the new poured paintings and Picasso's and Braque's late Cubist works of 1912-15. In his 1955 essay "American Type Painting," Greenberg elaborated on this point and altered it, drawing a parallel between the poured paintings and aspects of Analytical (rather than Synthetic) Cubism (revised in 1958, *Art and Culture*, Boston, 1961, pp. 208-29). Fried rejected the Cubist analogy. For William Rubin's analysis and elaboration of the issue, see "Jackson Pollock and the Modern Tradition," Part III, *Artforum*, vol. 5, no. 8, Apr. 1967, pp. 18-31.

152 Alchemy. Completed by September 1947.

Color plate p. 676.

76.2553 PG 150

Oil, aluminum (and enamel?[1]) paint and string on canvas (unvarnished), 45⅛ x 87⅛ (114.6 x 221.3).

Signed and dated l.r.: 47 *Jackson Pollock*; on stretcher (partially visible): *Jackson Pollock*.

PROVENANCE:

Acquired under contract with Jackson Pollock, 1948. (See above, cat. no. 144, fn. 1.)

CONDITION:

In 1964 (Tate Report) the unvarnished paint film (characterized as "generously but thinly painted on unprimed canvas") was described as in good condition. One small puncture through the canvas was noted.

In 1982 (Venice) some mold on the surface was successfully removed. The heavy impasto is on the whole well preserved with minimal loss. The condition is, however, extremely fragile. (Venice, Nov. 1982.)

1. See above, cat no. 150, CONDITION and footnote 1. *Alchemy's* surface shows similar signs of the use of enamel.

fig. a.
Pollock in his studio with *Alchemy* attached to quilting frame, September 1947. Photographer unknown.

A well-known photograph of Pollock shows him crouching on the floor, apparently working on the canvas *Alchemy*, which is attached to a quilting frame (fig. a). On September 3, 1947, Pollock wrote to his mother: "I have a painting stretched on the quilting frame — hope to have it finished in another week — and then send the frame on to you. American Express I think will be best" (O'Connor and Thaw, vol. 4, p. 240).

Lee Krasner indicated that Pollock must have completed the picture before this card was written. Had he still been actively working on the painting, he would not have known when he might finish it. It would have been normal for him, however, to allow approximately one week for a painting of this density to dry completely. Thus he probably finished *Alchemy* on (or shortly before) September 3 and felt that he could safely predict when the picture would be ready for removal from the frame.[2]

2. Krasner, in conversation with the author, March 6, 1981. Stella Pollock had brought the frame with her when she came to visit, in order to do some quilting. Pollock had decided to experiment with it in order to give his canvas a slight distance from the floor. Krasner said that it was unusual for him to work this way, and she was not certain if he did so in other instances. Stella Pollock apparently requested the frame's return, and after *Alchemy* was totally dry, Pollock indeed sent it back. In other cases, as is well known, he laid the canvas directly onto the flat hard surface of the floor itself.

In pictorial terms, *Alchemy* represents an important development in Pollock's work: it is one of the very first pictures in which he used aluminum paint. As Eugene V. Thaw observed:

> *If any coloristic device can be said to be unique to Pollock, the use of aluminum silver paint, with its surface sheen and changing properties in differing light, would have to be the most marked. Pollock continued to use it to the end of his life but not relentlessly.*
>
> *It should be noted in connection with this expressive and highly personal color tactic that its roots go back into this early work. F. V. O'Connor has noted that in early gouaches and pencil drawings Pollock occasionally uses a heavy graphite technique, pressing down hard on the pencil in certain areas to achieve a metallic sheen.... The indentation of the paper serves also to make these accented areas of graphite catch the changing light. Pollock was thus, from a very early moment, seeking experimentally the means of enlivening his surfaces with effects similar to those produced by aluminum paint* (O'Connor and Thaw, p. xv.).

The actual sequence of the nineteen poured paintings that are definitely dated 1947 (O'Connor and Thaw, nos. 167-85) is difficult to establish with certainty. Pollock rarely dated his works by the month (except in the case of *Direction* [cat. no. 145] and *Circumcision* [cat. no. 146]); if he did so (on the stretchers of other works), the information has so far not been published.

The complexity of Pollock's working method, moreover, makes it difficult to arrive at an exact sequence on purely stylistic grounds. On some occasions, he completed a painting in a relatively short time; on others, he set a canvas aside and "reentered it" later; on still others, he "worked it through" easily, or else with much more difficulty.[3] William Rubin has, on stylistic grounds, assigned *Alchemy* to an early position within the sequence of poured pictures, particularly because the white, almost figurative accents on the surface are not always successfully integrated into the "more diaphanous web" ("Pollock as Jungian Illustrator: The Limits of Psychological Criticism," Part II, *Art in America*, vol. 67, no. 8, Dec. 1979, pp. 82, 83). Rubin's distinction between *Alchemy* and the later poured pictures clearly is valid. At the same time, Pollock seemed to have had a set of pictorial aims in *Alchemy* that differed from those of both the earlier and later poured compositions. The string, which he integrated into the fabric of the composition, the aluminum paint, and the thick white calligraphic markings all contribute to a differentiation in texture and levels of articulation that is distinct in its intended effect from the "homogeneous visual fabric" of paintings such as *Enchanted Forest*, also of 1947 (cat. no. 151), or *Number One* of 1948. In this sense *Alchemy* shares certain qualities with *Full Fathom Five*, also of 1947 (MoMA, O'Connor and Thaw, no. 180), in which Pollock used nails, tacks, buttons, keys, combs, cigarettes, and matches mixed into the densely poured surface; but it also shares these same qualities with *Number 4*, of 1949

3. See *Circumcision*, cat. no. 146, for Krasner's comments on this point.

(Private Collection, O'Connor and Thaw, no. 249), in which pebbles are mixed into the oil, enamel, and aluminum pigments. Thus while he was at various times exploring different ways of handling the density of surface texture, he was also — in other works — dealing with transparency and homogeneity.

This simultaneous exploration of somewhat different pictorial problems makes the establishment of a systematic chronology all the more difficult. But the fact that *Alchemy* can with certainty now be given a *terminus ante quem* of September 3, 1947, may be helpful in the construction of a more detailed chronology for the works of this crucial year, during which Pollock produced his first large group of poured paintings.

EXHIBITIONS:

New York, Betty Parsons Gallery, *Jackson Pollock*, Jan. 5-23, 1948 (no. cat.);[4] Venice, Museo Correr, *Jackson Pollock*, July 22-Aug. 15, 1950, no. 19; Bern, Kunsthalle, *Tendances actuelles*, Jan. 29-Mar. 6, 1955, no. 57; London, *P.G.*, 1964-65, no. 125; Stockholm, *P.G.*, 1966-67, no. 120; New York, *P.G.*, 1969, p. 159, repr. p. 158; Paris, *P.G.*, 1974-75, no. 129, repr.; Torino, *P.G.*, 1975-76, no. 142.

REFERENCES:

O'Connor, 1967, p. 53, repr. (Pollock working on *Alchemy* in his East Hampton studio); B. H. Friedman, *Energy Made Visible*, New York, 1972, p. 120; J. Wolfe, "Jungian Aspects of Jackson Pollock's Imagery," *Artforum*, vol. 11, no. 3, Nov. 1972, pp. 71-72, repr.; O'Connor and Thaw, no. 179, repr.; J. Welch, "Jackson Pollock's 'The White Angel' and the Origins of Alchemy," *Arts Magazine*, vol. 53, no. 7, Mar. 1979, pp. 139-41, repr.; D. Rubin, "A Case for Content: Jackson Pollock's Subject was Automatic Gesture," ibid., pp. 108-9, repr.; W. Rubin, "Pollock as Jungian Illustrator: The Limits of Psychological Criticism," Part II, *Art in America*, vol. 67, no. 8, Dec. 1979, pp. 75-77, 82, 83, 90, repr. color; D. E. Gordon, "Pollock's 'Bird,' or how Jung did not offer much help in myth-making," *Art in America*, vol. 68, no. 8, Oct. 1980, p. 47.

4. The list of works exhibited is in the Betty Parsons Gallery records.

Arnaldo Pomodoro

Born June 1926, Morciano, Romagna.
Lives in Milan.

153 Studio N° 1 (Tavola dei segni). 1961.
(*Study No. 1 [Tablet of signs]*).

76.2553 PG 213

Bronze relief (lost wax) with original light silvery patina.

Dimensions of relief: 20⅙ x 12⅛ (51 x 30.9); dims. of mount without base: 20 9/16 x 13 1/16 (52.3 x 33.2); dims. of mount (including base): 22¾ x 13 1/16 (57.8 x 33.2).[1]

Signed on the rear surface (scratched into the bronze): *Arnaldo*. Not dated.

Edition of one.

Foundry: Unknown.

PROVENANCE:

Purchased from the artist after the *IV Concorso Internazionale del Bronzetto di Padova*, December 1961.

CONDITION:

There are small red spots of ink or varnish on the bronze. The sheet-iron mount, which is somewhat oxidized, has a black varnish. There is a crack in the bronze, which occurred during casting and was soldered on the reverse at that time. (Venice, Nov. 1982.)

1. The mount, which was made by an iron craftsman at the artist's request, is not considered an integral part of the work.

In creating this relief, Pomodoro worked in the negative on a piece of damp clay about 2 in., 5 cm., thick.[2] Knives and various other tools (some of which he fashioned himself out of fragments of iron or brass) were used to incise the carefully worked-out design. Liquid wax or plaster was poured over the clay image and the bronze was then cast by the lost-wax method.

The series of *Tavola dei segni* was conceived by Pomodoro as a form of calligraphic image, suggestive or reminiscent of Egyptian tablets. Thus the "signs" operate as a species of indecipherable hieroglyphics, which, nonetheless, are evocative and apparently rational in their organization.

After working for a period of time in this tablet-relief format, Pomodoro became increasingly interested in the more complex possibilities that seemed to be latent in this personal language. He proceeded to develop his columns and, subsequently, his spheres, retaining the "hieroglyphic" element but incorporating it within the interior spaces of a far more intricate structure.

EXHIBITIONS:

Padua, Biennale d'Arte Triveneta, *IV Concorso Internazionale del Bronzetto di Padova*, Oct.-Nov. 1961, no. 82 (*Studio 1*); London, *P.G.*, 1964-65, no. 177; Torino, *P.G.*, 1975-76, no. 198.

2. Much of the information published here was supplied by Pomodoro in correspondence and conversation with the author, Venice, June-July 1983, and in conversation with Lucy Flint, New York, August 1983. The artist was unable to recall the name of the foundry where the piece had been cast.

---

154 Sfero N° 4. 1963-64 (cast 1964).
(*Sphere No. 4*).

76.2553 PG 214

Bronze (lost wax), part polished, part dark brown patina. Circumference: 72⅞ (185).

Not signed or dated.

Edition of three.[1]

Foundry: Battaglia, Milan.

PROVENANCE:

Purchased from the Marlborough Gallery, Rome, after the Biennale, Venice, October 1964.

CONDITION:

In Venice (1984) the green corrosion and residue of cleaning substances that had built up in the interior spaces and on the surface were removed with surgical instruments, but without the use of solvents. The outer surface was polished with a fine buffing liquid. The piece was degreased with trichloroethylene, and washed with distilled water, then with distilled water and neutral detergent; it was rinsed with distilled water and dried with alcohol and acetone. A protective coating of Incralac (acrylic resin containing benzotriazole) was applied.

1. Peggy Guggenheim's cast was the first. The second is in the collection of the Museo Civico Revoltella di Trieste; the third, formerly in the Gerling Collection, Cologne, is now in a private collection in New York.

Pomodoro has explained the complex technical and conceptual procedures he follows in the creation of the *Spheres*, each of which is initially made in two halves and then cast as a single piece.[2]

The first step is a "mental process of invention" in the course of which he evolves the basic concept of the piece and develops its elements, without the aid of preliminary sketches. He then proceeds to draw, in rough outline, the major characteristic element of the piece, indicating on paper whether it will be, for example, a horizontal gash breaking the sphere or a deep hole driving through its surface with irregular breaks and cracks branching out from the incision.

He prepares a semi-spherical bed in a hollow cube made either of wood (as in the case of the Peggy Guggenheim *Sfero*) or plaster. Sufficient clay to mold one half of the sphere is placed in this semi-spherical space. The upper exterior surface of the clay is concave in shape; this surface is excavated and worked by the artist with a variety of tools—creating cracks, fissures, incisions, etc.—until the entire design for the "interior" fabric of the bronze sphere has been made in negative. Plaster is then poured over the clay, producing, as it hardens, the mold for one half of the sphere. The second half is developed in the same manner, and the two semi-spherical plasters are then joined. The complete sphere, with all its "etched" interior detail, is finally cast in bronze by the lost-wax method.

Because its interior is far more deeply excavated and extensively worked than others in the series, the Peggy Guggenheim *Sfero* presented the artist with particularly complex problems. The interior spaces are proportionately greater, and the consistency of the outer "skin" was technically more difficult to create and sustain when so much of the work was deeply and irregularly hollowed.

EXHIBITIONS:

Venice, XXXII Biennale, June 20-Oct. 18, 1964, Italian Pavilion, no. 9 (*Sfero N° 4*); London, *P.G.*, 1964-65, no. 178, repr. (as *Sphere No. 1*, the title attributed to it in *P.G.* publications until 1983), New York, *P.G.*, 1969, p. 173, repr.; Paris, *P.G.*, 1974-75, no. 168; Torino, *P.G.*, 1975-76, no. 199, repr. pl. 68.

REFERENCES:

G. Dorfles, "Arnoldo Pomodoro, Sculptor of the Cosmos," *Studio International*, vol. 167, no. 852, Apr. 1964, repr. p. 140; L. Flint, *Handbook*, 1983, p. 206, repr. color p. 207.

2. Much of the information published here was supplied by Pomodoro in correspondence and conversation with the author, Venice, June-July 1983, and in conversation with Lucy Flint, New York, August 1983.

COLOR PLATES

fig. a.
Gorky, preparatory drawing for cat. no. 73, pencil and wax crayon on paper, 19¼ x 25⅜ in., 48.9 x 64.4 cm., Private Collection.

Cat. no. 73, p. 371.
Gorky, *Untitled*, summer 1944.

Cat. no. 142, p. 638.
Pollock, *The Moon Woman*, 1942.

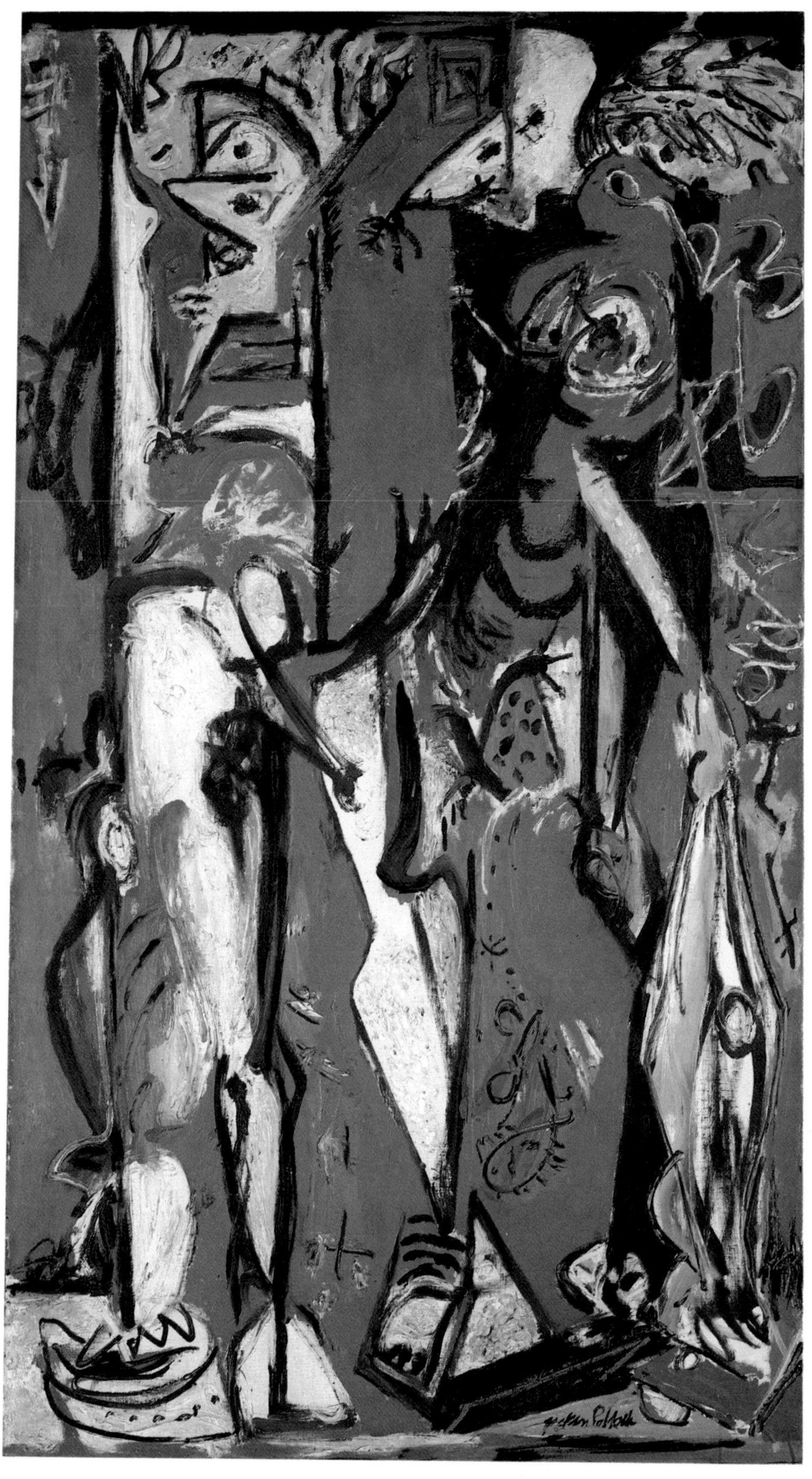

Cat. no. 144, p. 641.
Pollock, *Two*, 1943-45.

Cat. no. 145, p. 643.
Pollock, *Direction*, October 1945.

Cat. no. 148, p. 648.
Pollock, *Bird Effort (Accabonac Creek Series)*, 1946.

Cat. no. 151, p. 656.
Pollock, *Enchanted Forest*, 1947.

Cat. no. 152, p. 659.
Pollock, *Alchemy*, completed by September 1947.

Cat. no. 89, p. 431.
De Kooning, *Untitled*, 1958.

Cat. no. 88, p. 429.
De Kooning, *Untitled*, 1958.

Cat. no. 15, p. 96.
Baziotes, *The Room*, 1945.

Cat. no. 163, p. 707.
Still, *Jamais*, May 1944.

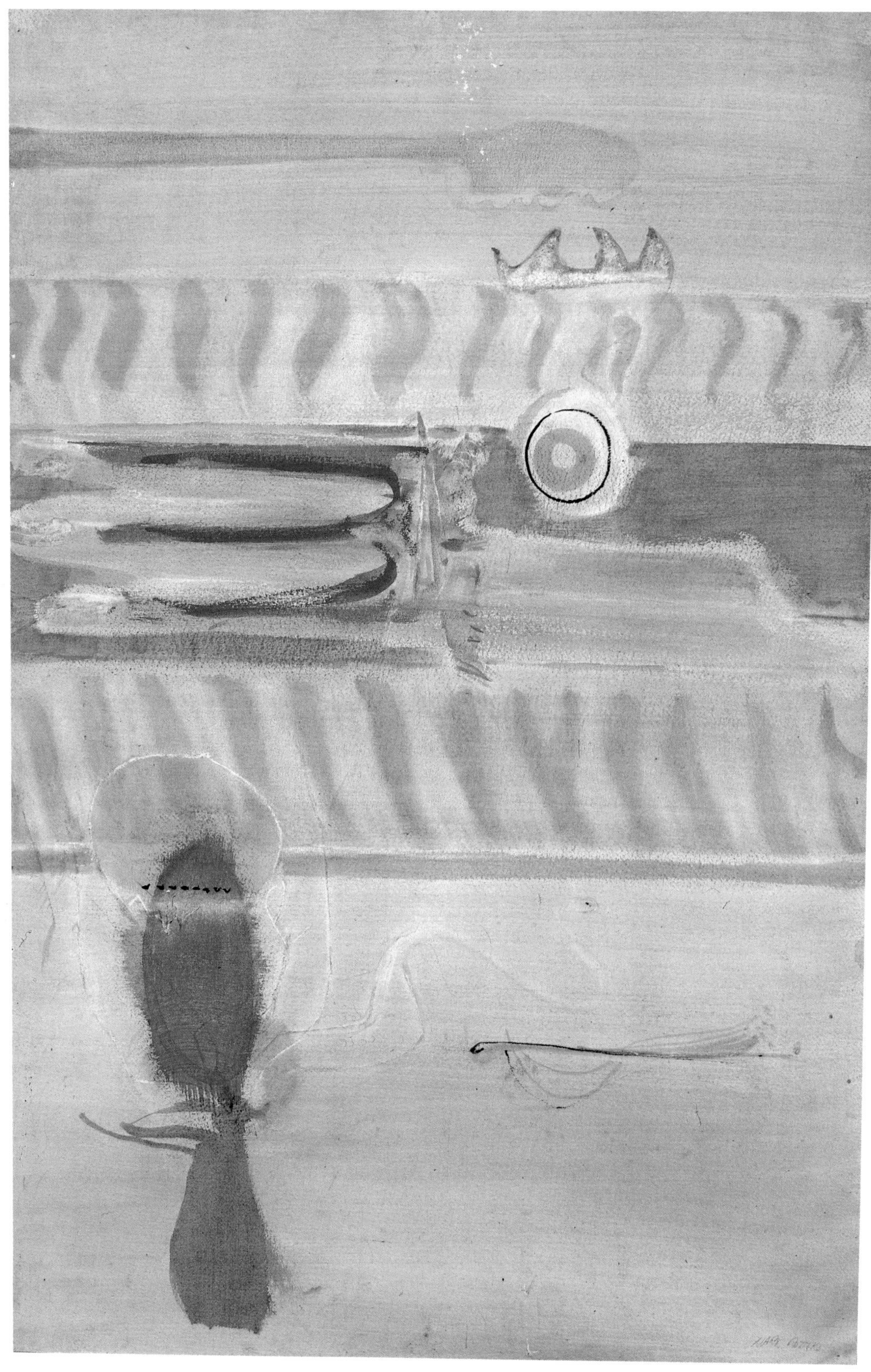

Cat. no. 157, p. 690.
Rothko, *Sacrifice*, April 1946.

Cat. no. 128, p. 583.
Motherwell, *Personage (Autoportrait)*, December 9, 1943.

Cat. no. 48, p. 236.
Dubuffet, *Chataine aux Hautes Chairs*, August 1951.

Cat. no. 114, p. 530.
Matta, *Le Dénommeur renommé*, 1952-53.

Germaine Richier

Born September 1902, Grans, Bouches-du-Rhone.
Died July 1959, Montpellier.

155 Tauromachie. 1953.
(*Tauromachy*).

76.2553 PG 205

Bronze (lost wax, cast in three pieces). Height of figure: 43⅞ (111.5); height of bull's head: 18½ (47); dimensions of base: 37¹¹⁄₁₆ x 20⅝ (95.7 x 52.5).

Edition of ten.[1]

Foundry: Susse.

Not numbered, signed or dated. No foundry mark.

PROVENANCE:

Purchased from the artist by Martha Jackson, ca. 1957; purchased from Martha Jackson, November 14, 1960.[2]

CONDITION:

The copper alloy used by the foundry in making the *Tauromachie* was 75% copper, 22.5% zinc, 1.25% tin, 1.25% lead. The natural appearance of such an alloy when polished is gold/yellow. After the piece emerged from the foundry, the artist allowed it to weather in the atmosphere for several weeks, intermittently rubbing it with fine steel wool. Those portions of the bronze beyond the reach of the steel wool (crevices, indentations, etc.) gradually darkened through exposure to air and humidity; the raised surfaces, meanwhile, maintained their original gold tone. When the desired combination of gold and dark patina had been achieved, the piece, considered finished, was brought indoors, thus arresting the natural patination process (fig. a).

In 1974, when the sculpture was on exhibition at the Grand Palais, Guiter observed that the entire sculpture, long exhibited outdoors in Venice, had become black. The base was also bent and the figure inclined sideways, so that it no longer stood at the intended 90° angle to the base. With the consent of Peggy Guggenheim, the sculpture was taken to the Fonderie Susse for restoration. The figure and base were first restored to their original positions. The bronze was then treated with nitric acid (38°-40°) to remove the accumulated black and green corrosion products; repeated immersion and washing in water

fig. a.
Detail of another cast of *Tauromachie* with the artist's original patina. Photograph courtesy François Guiter.

1. Four (or possibly 5) casts were made during the artist's lifetime, Peggy Guggenheim's apparently being the third; casts made during the artist's lifetime were not always numbered. Four further casts (unnumbered but recorded as 6/6, Hc_1, Hc_2, Hc_3) were posthumously cast and numbered under the supervision of the artist's executor and former assistant, F. Guiter. The author is indebted to Guiter for much of the information published here. She is presently preparing a catalogue raisonné of Richier's work.
2. Peggy Guggenheim was persuaded by Alfred H. Barr, Jr., to purchase the work when they saw it on exhibition at the Palazzo Grassi.

followed to remove all traces of acid. The surface was extensively rubbed with fine steel wool. No varnish was applied, since the artist was opposed to its use. The surface was, however, coated with wax *(cire des antiquaires)*.[3] A crack in the left leg, 5 3/4 in., 14.5 cm., from the base, may date from the time of the Paris restoration.

The sculpture was, after its return to Venice in 1975, reinstalled in the open air; pollution and salt in the atmosphere caused the bronze to blacken again.

In February 1984 (Venice) the piece was cleaned. The surface was degreased with trichloroethylene, and washed with distilled water, then with distilled water and neutral detergent; it was rinsed with distilled water, and dried with alcohol and acetone. The surface was treated for 30 minutes with a 3% solution of benzotriazole in pure alcohol. A protective coating of Incralac (acrylic resin containing benzotriazole) was applied (for outdoor exhibition).

The condition is stable. However, the blackened surface of the bronze is clearly antithetical to the artist's intention (see below). Various approaches to this problem are currently under study.

3. The above information was supplied, in conversation with the author and Guiter, by M. Neyret and M. Dintillac of the Fonderie Susse (Sept. 1982).

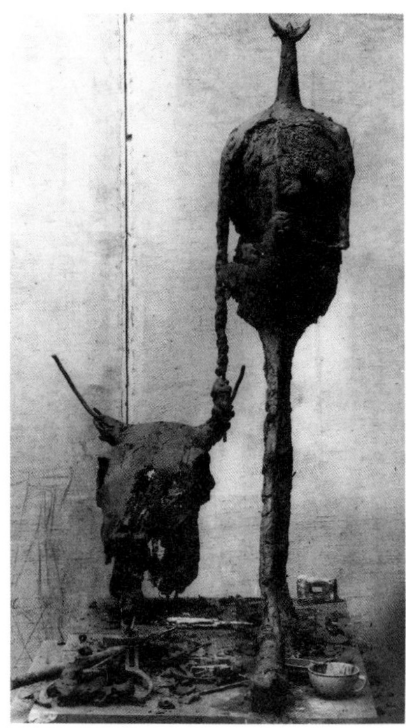

fig. b.
Cat. no. 155 in process. Portions of the iron armature are still visible, although the modeling in clay is almost complete. As in other works by Richier, the armature served as a fully articulated skeleton for the sculpture. Photograph by Bernes-Marouteau.

The technique and procedure followed by Richier in *Tauromachie* were consistent with her normal practice. The figure, based on a posed human model, and the bull's head, based on an actual skeleton, were conceived and executed directly in clay on elaborately constructed iron armatures (fig. b). The composition and precise stance of the figure (including plumb-line measurements) were gradually refined until the precise articulation of all the elements was achieved. The plaster was made (by Maurice Gallimard) from the artist's clay original, and the piece then cast in bronze (lost wax). Existing drawings for the sculpture followed, rather than preceded, the fully articulated conception in clay. In this—as in other instances—Richier's method was to work directly in the sculptural medium rather than developing her ideas in drawing first.

Richier's intense identification with her native Provence, with its folklore and its traditions, emerges in various aspects of her work. In the case of *Tauromachie*, the literal subject matter makes direct reference to the bullfights (or *corridas*),

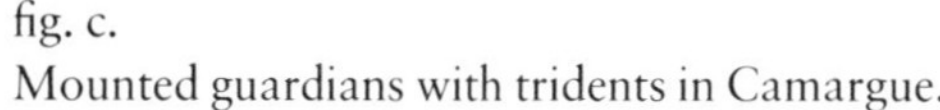

fig. c.
Mounted guardians with tridents in Camargue.

fig. d.
The trident from Camargue used by the artist for the head of the figure in cat. no. 155. Photograph courtesy François Guiter.

which she regularly attended in Camargue in her youth, as well as to the so-called *courses libres*, which involved heroic exploits on the part of the men who participated in the races, but no killing of the wild bulls. The trident, which serves as the head for Richier's figure, carries more oblique associations. Nailed to long sticks, tridents traditionally functioned as ceremonial "scepters" and as "weapons" for the local guardians of the horses and the wild bulls (fig. c). The weathered relic of such a trident was found in Carmargue by F. Guiter and sent by her to Richier in Paris as part of a Christmas package (fig. d). Moved by the gift's rich associations, the artist adapted it as the metaphorical "center" of her depiction of the *Tauromachie*.[4] Thus while the matador and the bull's head suggest the *corridas*, which in Camargue involved the importation of Spanish bulls and matadors, the trident makes direct reference to the more indigenous guardians and the *courses libres*.

Finally, the golden surface of the sculpture clearly carried for Richier a metaphorical significance of its own. Though no written documentation survives that articulates the role of gold in the conceptual language of the *Tauromachie*, Guiter has indicated that for Richier — as for other natives of Provence and Camargue—"*le symbole de la Tauromachie, c'est l'or*," and that this idea would

4. Guiter kindly made available the contents of a letter written by Richier upon receipt of the "trident."

have functioned on several different levels in her work. The golden surface of many of her sculptures was a continual preoccupation for Richier, and she repeatedly instructed her assistants in rubbing techniques developed specifically to her own aesthetic requirements.

On the basis of available evidence, it seems clear that the original golden surface of *Tauromachie* played a significant role in the sculpture's aesthetic. (See above, CONDITION.)

EXHIBITIONS:

New York, Martha Jackson Gallery, *The Sculptures of Germaine Richier,* Nov. 27-Dec. 27, 1957, no. 10, repr.; Minneapolis, Walker Art Center, *Richier*, Sept. 28-Nov. 9, 1958, no. 12; Boston, Boston University School of Fine and Applied Arts, *Sculpture by Germaine Richier*, Jan. 10-Feb. 7, 1959, no. 1; Houston, Contemporary Arts Museum, *The Romantic Agony: From Goya to de Kooning*, Apr. 23-May 31, 1959, repr. p. 13; Venice, Palazzo Grassi, *Dalla Natura all'Arte*, summer 1960 (cat. with unnumbered checklist); London, *P.G.*, 1964-65, no. 171, repr.; New York, *P.G.*, 1969, p. 137, repr. p. 136; Paris, *P.G.*, 1974-75, no. 163, repr.; Torino, *P.G.*, 1975-76, no. 193, repr. pl. 56.

REFERENCES:

J. Cassou, *Germaine Richier*, London, 1961, repr. pl. 27; Calas, 1966, p. 186, repr. p. 201.

Jean-Paul Riopelle

Born October 1923, Montreal, Canada.
Lives in Paris.

156 Peinture. 1955.
(*Painting*; *Composition*).

76.2553 PG 187

Oil on canvas, 45⅜ x 28⁹⁄₁₆ (115.2 x 72.5).

Signed l.r.: *riopelle*; on reverse: *Riopelle / 55*.

PROVENANCE:

Purchased from the artist's studio, Paris, by Gimpel Fils, 1955; purchased from Gimpel Fils, London, February 1966.

CONDITION:

In 1978 (New York) extensive and severe cleavage and cupping of the paint film required treatment. The painting was removed from the stretcher and flattened at 135° and at 5% pressure. The most seriously affected areas were softened with solvent and when supple flattened and resecured with polyvinyl acetate emulsion (PVAE, Union Carbide Corp.) and BEVA. The canvas was lined on Mylar 1400 with BEVA, strip-lined with Lucite 44-treated linen strips, attached with Plus-Ten contact cement and stapled to a new stretcher. There was some filling of losses and inpainting with watercolors. The surface was lightly sprayed with Lucite 44.

The condition is stable. (Venice, Nov. 1982.)

Riopelle's earliest paintings executed entirely with the palette knife date from 1953. During the following half dozen years, he produced an extensive series of paintings closely related to the Peggy Guggenheim work in both composition and technique. All of them are densely patterned nonobjective works in which the bright, thickly applied paint covers the entire field. The heavy applications of pigment were squeezed directly from the tube onto the canvas. Riopelle then modeled the thick substance with a scraper and knife into sharp-edged overlapping strips. Layers of paint were often applied, one upon the other, while not quite dry. Owing to this technique, which allowed for only minimal bonding between layers, the paintings (as in this instance) frequently pose significant conservation problems. (See above, CONDITION.)

EXHIBITIONS:

London, The Commonwealth Institute, *Commonwealth Art Today*, Nov. 1962-Jan. 1963 (no cat.); Lausanne, Musée Cantonal des Beaux-Arts, *Ier Salon International de Galeries-pilotes*, June 20-Sept. 22, 1963, no. H 11 (*Composition*); Stockholm, *P.G.*, 1966-67, no. 144; New York, *P.G.*, 1969, p. 168, repr.; Paris, *P.G.*, 1974-75, no. 144, repr.; Torino, *P.G.*, 1975-76, no. 177.

Mark Rothko

(Marcus Rothkowitz).

Born September 1903, Dvinsk, Russia.
Died February 1970, New York.

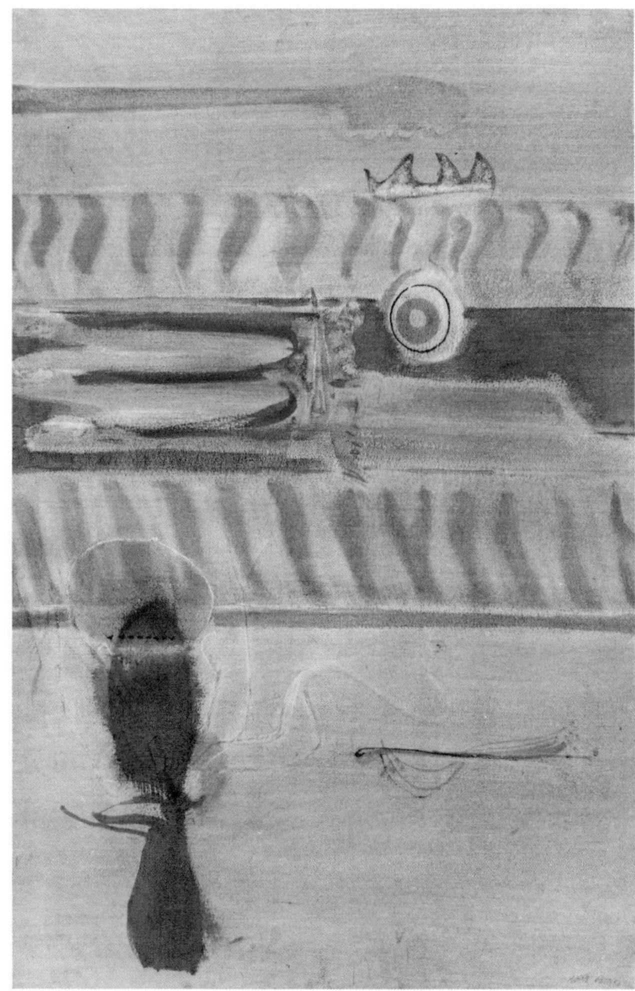

157 Sacrifice. April 1946.

Color plate p. 680.

76.2553 PG 154

Watercolor, gouache, india ink, on Whatman paper, 39 7/16 x 25 7/8 (100.2 x 65.8).

Signed in pencil l.r.: *Mark Rothko*. Not dated.

PROVENANCE:

Purchased from the artist, New York, 1946.[1]

CONDITION:

In 1964 (Tate Report) scattered abrasions with losses near the upper edge (center) were noted. The condition was described as otherwise good.

1. Peggy Guggenheim could not recall precisely when she purchased the work, but she was certain that she had purchased nothing of Rothko's before his Art of This Century exhibition of January 1945. It seems likely in light of the 1947 letter from Rothko published here (see below) that *Sacrifice* was shown in the Mortimer Brandt watercolor exhibition, and that she purchased it afterward. It is recorded among her possessions for the first time in 1946. (Much later she bought another work by Rothko, *Untitled*, 1960, which she gave to the San Francisco Museum of Art in 1962.)

In 1983 (New York) the work was removed from its framing (held between acid backboard and glass). The remains of brown paper tape at the lower left corner and at the left side of the lower edge (probably used by the artist to attach the support to the working surface) were removed with water and alcohol. Extensive foxing (first noted by the author in 1978) over the entire surface was reduced with buffered hydrogen peroxide. Abrasions were repaired and inpainted with Windsor and Newton watercolors: at the lower center (vertical scratch, ca. 2⅜ in., 6 cm.) and at the left edge and upper center edge (scattered circular abrasions, which had disrupted fibers of paper, as noted in 1964). A loss at the lower right corner was replaced with wove paper (attached with rice paste and fibers of Japanese tissue). The verso was deacidified with calcium hydroxide. The support was flattened.

The condition is stable. (New York, Feb. 1983.)

Sacrifice was initially dated 1945 by Peggy Guggenheim (Biennale catalogue of 1948), but she otherwise consistently dated it 1943. A recently discovered letter, however, written by Rothko to The Brooklyn Museum on May 21, 1947, firmly establishes the date of the work as April 1946.

Rothko's letter concerns *Vessels of Magic* (38¾ x 25½ in., 98.5 x 64.8 cm.), a watercolor at that time just acquired by the museum:

> *it was one of five paintings of the same size and shape which were painted almost on the eve of my watercolor exhibition in April 1946. I have looked upon them as a sort of culmination of a period of concerted painting in this medium, and am happy that it is one of those which you have acquired. It occurs to me that the fate of the other four might be of interest [to] you. One of them is in the possession of the Betty Parsons Gallery. The other three have been acquired by Peggy Guggenheim of the Art of this Century, Wm. Folger of San Francisco and J. Draper in Massachusetts.*
>
> *Sincerely hoping that the picture wears well with you,*
>
> *I remain cordially,*
>
> *Mark Rothko*

Most of Rothko's works painted during the early and mid-1940s were not dated by the artist at the time of their execution, and it is therefore difficult to establish a satisfactory chronology for these years. A relatively clear development is nonetheless discernible, and the evidence contained in Rothko's letter provides helpful corroboration. The calligraphic and rather crisply linear forms of the early 1940s were gradually softened by the middle of the decade. Rothko began to use a more fluid, thinly applied painterly wash, and his colors became paler and more luminous. Brian O'Doherty aptly described this tendency: "The forms, half-translucent, filled with light, partake of the atmosphere around them. They are often brushed and stained so lightly on the surface that they are almost not there" (*Art International*, vol. 14, no. 8, Oct. 1970, p. 32).

Vessels of Magic, Sacrifice, and an untitled watercolor of exactly the same size in the collection of Mr. and Mrs. Donald Blinken, which must surely belong to the same group, are not only similar in imagery and scale but characterized by the same quality of painterly freedom. It is interesting that Rothko himself regarded these works as "the culmination of a period of concerted painting in this medium."

Many of Rothko's automatist works from the 1940s were—according to his own testimony—inspired by his reading of Greco-Roman myths, although the actors and situations of these mythic dramas were not meant to be specifically recognizable as such in his paintings (see his essay, "The Romantics were Prompted," *Possibilities*, I, no. I, winter 1947-48, p. 84). The images and the titles of the paintings were intended to be suggestive of a "mythic content ... a pantheism in which man, bird, beast and tree—the known as well as the unknowable merge into a single tragic idea." (Rothko quoted by S. Janis, *Abstract and Surrealist Art in America*, New York, 1944, p. 118. On this point see also I. Sandler, *The Triumph of American Painting*, New York, 1970, pp. 175-81.) Rothko's 1945 text, "A Personal Statement: A Painting Prophecy—1950," suggests the extent to which figurative elements continued to play an integral part in works such as *Sacrifice*: "The Surrealist has uncovered the glossary of the myth and has established a congruity between the phantasmagoria of the unconscious and the objects of everyday life. This congruity constitutes the exhilarated tragic experience which for me is the only source book for art."[2] And the unidentified author of the preface to Rothko's 1945 Art of This Century catalogue was clearly alluding to the same tenuous relationship between image and abstraction, between "mythic" title and elusive content, between "the objects of everyday life" and the "phantasmagoria of the unconscious," when he wrote: "Rothko's painting... occupies a middle ground between abstraction and surrealism. In these paintings the abstract idea is incarnated in the image.... Rothko's symbols, fragments of myth, are held together by a free, almost automatic calligraphy that gives a peculiar unity to his paintings—a unity in which the individual symbol acquires its meaning."[3]

EXHIBITIONS:

New York, Mortimer Brandt Gallery, *Mark Rothko: Watercolors*, Apr. 22-May 4, 1946;[4] Venice, *P.G.*, 1948 (Biennale), no. 117 (dated 1945); Florence, *P.G.*, 1949, no. 128 (described as oil on canvas, dated 1943); Amsterdam, *P.G.*, 1951, no. 156; Zurich, *P.G.*, 1951, no. 145; Bordighera, *II^A Mostra Internazionale Pittura Americana*, Mar. 1-31, 1953, no. 15; London, *P.G.*, 1964-65, no. 129, repr.; Stockholm, *P.G.*, 1966-67, no. 125, repr.; New York, *P.G.*, 1969, p. 129, repr. p. 128; Paris, *P.G.*, 1974-75, no. 131, repr.; Torino, *P.G.*, 1975-76, no. 146, repr. pl. 59; New York, *P.G.*, 1982-83, no. 59, repr.

REFERENCE:

L. Flint, *Handbook*, 1983, p. 190, repr. color p. 191.

2. Exh. cat., David Porter Gallery, Washington, D.C., 1945. See also in this context Robert Rosenblum's convincing suggestion that Rothko would have found powerful sources for his mid-1940s Surrealist imagery in Masson's *Anatomy of My Universe*, published in New York in an English translation in 1943 (*Mark Rothko: The Surrealist Years*, exh. cat., Pace Gallery, New York, 1981, p. 8). On this subject see also L. Alloway, "The Biomorphic 40s," *Artforum*, vol. 4, no. 1, Sept. 1965, pp. 18-22.
3. For full text, see Appendix, p. 782.
4. There was no catalogue; the presumption that *Sacrifice* was included is based on the letter from Rothko published here.

Giuseppe Santomaso

Born September 1907, Venice.
Lives in Venice.

158 Vita Segreta. 1958.
(*Secret Life*; *Hidden Life*).

76.2553 PG 161

Oil on canvas, 28 13/16 x 19 11/16 (73.1 x 49.9).

Signed and dated l.l.: *Santomaso '58*.

PROVENANCE:

Purchased from the artist, ca. 1962.

CONDITION:

The work has received no treatment and the condition is stable. (Venice, June 1983.)

EXHIBITIONS:

London, *P.G.*, 1964-65, no. 135; Paris, *P.G.*, 1974-75, no. 150, repr.; Torino, *P.G.*, 1975-76, no. 153.

REFERENCES:

[Alley], *Peggy Guggenheim Foundation*, 1968, no. 161; L. Flint, *Handbook*, 1983, p. 194, repr. color p. 195.

Kurt Schwitters

Born June 1887, Hannover.
Died January 1948, Kendal, near Ambleside, England.

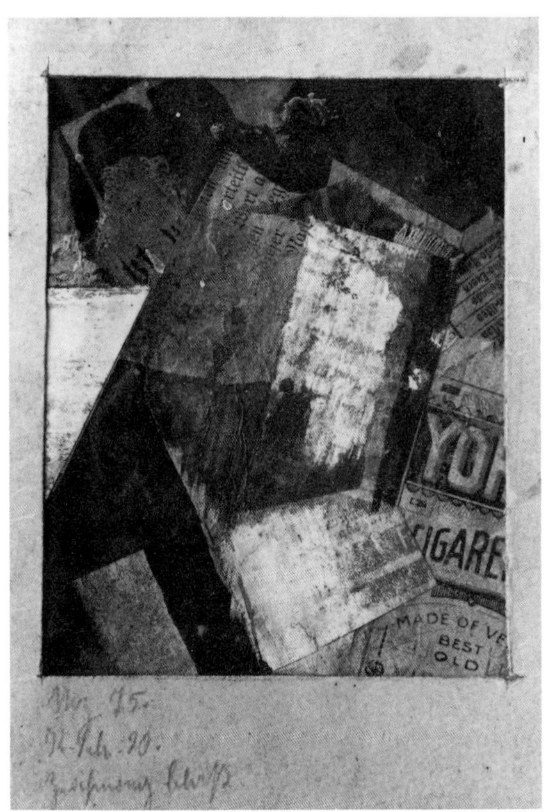

159 Merzzeichnung 75. 1920.
(*Merz drawing 75*).

76.2553 PG 85

Collage, gouache, red and black printer's ink, graphite on wood-pulp papers (newsprint, cardboard), and fabric, 5¾ x 3¹⁵⁄₁₆ (14.6 x 10).

Signed, dated, and titled l.l.: *Mz 75 / K. Sch. 20 / Zeichnung blass.*

PROVENANCE:

Acquired by Käthe Steinitz as a gift from the artist, ca. 1920;[1] purchased from Käthe Steinitz, in Venice, late 1950s.

CONDITION:

In 1964 (Tate Report) some small losses and slight buckling were noted, but the condition was described as otherwise good.

The primary support is pasted directly onto a poor quality board, which has severely photo-oxidized. The border of the primary support has darkened unevenly and shows evidence of scattered stains and creases. The overall condition is otherwise stable. (Venice, Nov. 1982.)

Schwitters created his first *Merz* assemblage in the spring of 1919 (*Das Merzbild*, now lost, repr. W. Schmalenbach, *Kurt Schwitters*, Cologne, 1967, p. 85).[2] The invented term *Merz* became the generic subtitle for his entire subsequent oeuvre, in which he consistently rejected on the one hand all forms of representation and on the other the practice of pure painting as a medium. In his 1919 statement of aesthetic intention, he emphasized the essential abstraction of *Merz*, but his main focus was upon the materials: paint, canvas, brush, and palette would be used in combination with objects such as wire netting, string, cotton wool, box tops, playing cards, newspaper clippings, train tickets, visiting cards, pieces of wood, fragments of broken china and glass, and indeed any objects (such as perambulator wheels) or materials that the artist could endow with aesthetic value. In disassociating such materials from their original context and function, the artist would create new, entirely pictorial roles for them. New concepts of space, surface, line, and plasticity would be created through the imaginative juxtaposition and distribution of materials rather than through conventional techniques:

> *Die Bilder Merzmalerei sind abstrakte Kunstwerke. Das Wort Merz bedeutet wesentlich die Zusammenfassung aller erdenklichen Materialen für künstlerische Zwecke und technisch die prinzipiell gleiche Wertung der einzelnen Materialien. Die Merzmalerei bedient sich also nicht nur der Farbe und der Leinwand, des Pinsels und der Palette, sondern aller vom Auge wahrnehmbaren Materialien und aller erforderlichen Werkzeuge. Dabei ist es unwesentlich, ob die verwendeten Materialien schon für irgendwelchen Zweck geformt waren oder nicht. Das Kinderwagenrad, das Drahtnetz, der Bindfaden und die Watte sind der Farbe gleichberechtigte Faktoren. Der Künstler schafft durch Wahl, Verteilung und Entformung der Materialien.*
>
> *Das Entformeln der Materialien kann schon erfolgen durch ihre Verteilung auf der Bildfläche. Es wird noch unterstützt durch Zerteilen, Verbiegen, Überdecken oder Übermalen. Bei der Merzmalerei wird der Kistendeckel, die Spielkarte, der Zeitungsausschnitt zur Fläche, Bindfaden, Pinselstrich oder Bleistiftstrich zur Linie, Drahtnetz, Übermalung oder aufgeklebtes Butterbrotpapier zur Lasur, Watte zur Weichheit.* ("Die Merzmalerei," *Der Sturm*, vol. x, July 1919, p. 61; also published in *Der Zweemann*, vol. 1, no. 1, Nov. 1919, p. 10; and in *Der Cicerone*, vol. xi, no. 18, 1919.)

The aesthetic validity of the individual materials lay entirely, as Schwitters emphasized, in the artist's capacity to deprive them of their original associations and endow them with new meaning. (See also "Merzzeichnung," *Merz 1, Holland Dada*, Hannover, Jan. 1923.)

Schwitters' *Merz* collages, the earliest of which probably date from the winter of 1918-19, continued to play a significant role in his work until the end of his life. Each collage was usually given the generic subtitle *Mz* [*Merzzeichnung*],

1. Peggy Guggenheim recalled that Käthe Steinitz, a close friend of Schwitters, sold her this work in Venice. She could not remember the exact date, but suggested the late 1950s as a possibility. Ernst Schwitters, the artist's son, confirmed that the work had been acquired by Steinitz as a gift. It is impossible to know when Schwitters gave her the work, but plausible that he would have done so shortly after completing it.

2. The actual word *Merz* derives from Schwitters' original assemblage, which contained (in a prominent position) a collage fragment of typography clipped from a letterhead or label of the KOMMERZ- UND PRIVAT BANK. The arbitrary nature of the source, its isolation from its original context and meaning, and the strong pictorial function which it performed, all combined to provide Schwitters with the emblematic designation he sought for his art. (See his description in *Merz 20. Kurt Schwitters. Katalog*, Hannover, 1927; and a shorter version in "Imitatoren watch step!" *Merz 6*, Hannover, Oct. 1923.)

followed by a number, an individual title, and a date. In the early years (until about 1923) the numbering appears to have been systematic; Peggy Guggenheim's small collage would, thus, almost certainly have been the seventy-fifth in the series.

The *Merz* collages were almost always vertical in orientation and small in size. They incorporated papers and fabrics of innumerable types often combined (as in the present instance) with both drawing and overpainting. Schwitters' designation of these collages as "drawings" was, by his own admission, arbitrary and even misleading, since he intended them to be seen as "paintings":

> *Merzzeichnungen nenne ich kleine, geklebte und manchmal übermalte Kompositionen. Eigentlich ist der Ausdruck "Zeichnungen" nicht gut, denn es handelt sich um dem Wesen nach gemalte, dass heisst flächig-farbig gestaltete kleine Arbeiten. Aber durch irgendein Versehen hat sich schon früh der Ausdrucksfehler eingeschlichen, und nun ist die Bezeichnung nicht mehr zu ändern. Aber bitte, betrachten Sie die kleinen Merzzeichnungen nur als Gemälde. (Merz 20, Kurt Schwitters, Katalog, 1927.)*

EXHIBITIONS:

London, *P.G.*, 1964-65, no. 75 (inscription recorded as *12 Juli 1920*); Stockholm, *P.G.*, 1966-67, no. 73 (inscription recorded as *12 Juli 1920*); Paris, *P.G.*, 1974-75, no. 65; Torino, *P.G.*, 1975-76, no. 83, repr. pl. 37.

---

160 Blau in Blau. 1926-29.
(Blue in Blue).

76.2553 PG 86

Collage, lithographic crayon on wood-pulp paper, 14 7/16 x 11 3/4 (36.7 x 29.9).

Not signed or dated.

PROVENANCE:

Gift of the artist to Jean Arp or Theo van Doesburg;[1] purchased from Arp or Nelly van Doesburg, London, 1939.

CONDITION:

In 1964 (Tate Report) some foxing stains on the right side were noted. The paper had already photo-oxidized and lost its blue tone, the medium being described as "black and white chalk on brown paper."

In 1978 (New York) extensive brown foxing and a white accretion (mold?) were successfully treated. Tape and adhesives were removed, and the work was fumigated in thymol, flattened, and hinged to ragboard.

Overexposure to light has darkened the paper support considerably, and the blue lithographic crayon that originally characterized the composition has entirely changed in tone. Traces of blue can still be found, but the darkening process has altered the relative values of the entire work. The condition is stable. (New York, Mar. 1983.)

1. Peggy Guggenheim recalled that the work belonged to either Arp or van Doesburg, who would have acquired it as a gift from Schwitters. She was unable to remember whether she purchased it from Arp or through Nelly van Doesburg after the Guggenheim Jeune exhibition of May 1939.

During the late 1920s, Schwitters was employed by the City of Hannover to design posters for the city theater. These were printed by the Druckerei Molling. Thin absorbent cardboard was used to create the mottled surfaces, which were printed in a lithographic process. Schwitters collected the discarded fragments of paper coated with lithographic crayon and made a small group of collages, restricting himself to the colors already applied, some of which were blues, some reds. The titles of the works in the group reflect the dominant color, or colors, of the crayon.[2]

Three of these works are in the collection of the artist's son, one dated 1926, the other two 1929. Schwitters worked on the group during these three years, and it has not been possible to establish with certainty when the present example was made.

EXHIBITIONS:

London, Guggenheim Jeune, *Exhibition of Collages, Papiers collés, and Photomontages*, Nov. 3-26, 1938, no. 79 ("*Blue in Blue*, 1929"); London, Guggenheim Jeune, *Abstract and Concrete Art*, May 1939, no. 36 ("*Blau in Blau*, 1929"); New York, Art of This Century, 1942-47, p. 108; Venice, *P.G.*, 1948 (Biennale), no. 119; Florence, *P.G.*, 1949, no. 130 ("*Blu su blu*"; the work was erroneously entitled *Blue on blue* in all subsequent *P.G.* publications); Amsterdam, *P.G.*, 1951, no. 158; Zurich, *P.G.*, 1951, no. 147; London, *P.G.*, 1964-65, no. 76; Stockholm, *P.G.*, 1966-67, no. 74; Paris, *P.G.*, 1974-75, no. 66; Torino, *P.G.*, 1975-76, no. 84; New York, *P.G.*, 1982-83, no. 34, repr.

2. Ernst Schwitters, the artist's son, supplied the information about this series of collages. Schwitters' extensive use of the detritus from the Molling print shop has been recorded by several commentators.

161 *Maraak, Variation 1.* 1930.
(*Merzbild*).

Color plate p. 504.

76.2553 PG 87

Oil and assemblage of rusted steel with blue laminate, enameled tin butterfly, paper, cork, and china on 4 mm. pulp board, 18⅛ x 14⁹⁄₁₆ (46 x 37).

Signed, dated, and titled l.r. (incised into paint): *MVI / K. SCHWITTERS 30*; on reverse in pencil: *Maraak, Var. 1*.

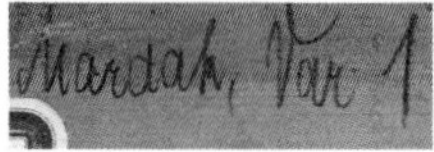

PROVENANCE:

Jean Arp, gift of the artist, ca. 1930; purchased from Arp, Paris, 1940.

CONDITION:

In 1964 (Tate Report) the large fragment of white china at the center of the composition and the 2 small cork balls just below the butterfly (fig. a) were already missing. A fragment of brown paper attached to the right of the cork balls was also missing, and some fragments of the blue laminate were chipped. Apart from a scratch in the lower left corner, the condition was described as good.

The 4 rusted iron nails that secure the circular rusted steel plate to the board penetrate the reverse, where they are covered with gauze. Three nail holes in the impasto area to the right of this plate indicate the method of attachment of the lost china element. Residual fragments of cork in the oil impasto below the butterfly establish that the 2 balls visible in the early photo (fig. a) were made of cork. Fragments of paper and china in that same area indicate the materials of other small losses there. There are abrasions and losses at the edges, some of which are due to the rabbet of the previous frame. The green rectangles were apparently painted by the artist in 2 stages, the second coat probably applied considerably after the first. There are extensive drying cracks in the brown area near the lower edge, and scattered inpainting of losses elsewhere. The paint surface is otherwise in generally stable condition. (New York, Feb. 1983.)

fig. a.
Cat. no. 161 in 1942. The central piece of white china and the two cork balls were apparently lost ca. 1951.

Maraak was a village in western Norway (now called Geiranger). Schwitters lived and worked there on an old farm for several weeks every summer between 1930 and 1940.[1] It was not unusual for him to name works after the locations

1. Information supplied by Ernst Schwitters in conversation with the author, June 1983.

161

in which they were made. The designation *Variation 1* indicates that he made or intended to make further works in the same series. Only one of these has thus far been traced by the present author: *Thema Maraak*, oil on plywood, 1930, 18 x 14½ in., 45.7 x 36.8 cm., Marlborough Gallery, London (repr. *Schwitters*, exh. cat., Galerie Gmurzynska, Cologne, 1978, no. 38).

For a brief note on the origin of Schwitters' *Merz* aesthetic, within the context of which *Maraak, Variation I* must be seen, see above, cat. no. 159.

EXHIBITIONS:

New York, Art of This Century, 1942-47, p. 108, repr. p. 109 (dated 1915, the date attributed to it in all *P.G.* publications until Alley, 1964); Florence, *P.G.*, 1949, no. 129; Amsterdam, *P.G.*, 1951, no. 157, repr.; Zurich, *P.G.*, 1951, no. 146; London, *P.G.*, 1964-65, no. 77, repr. (after losses, dated 1930); Stockholm, *P.G.*, 1966-67, no. 75, repr.; New York, *P.G.*, 1969, p. 75, repr.; Paris, *P.G.*, 1974-75, no. 67; Torino, *P.G.*, 1975-76, no. 85; Rome, *Guggenheim: Venezia-New York*, 1982, no. 43, repr. color; New York, *P.G.*, 1982-83, no. 41, repr. color.

REFERENCES:

P. Guggenheim, *Art of This Century*, 1942, repr. p. 109 (before losses); W. Rubin, *Dada and Surrealist Art*, London, 1969, p. 109, repr. p. 108, no. 102; L. Flint, *Handbook*, 1983, p. 116, repr. color p. 117.

Gino Severini

Born April 1883, Cortona, Italy.
Died February 1966, Paris.

162 Mare = Ballerina.
Anzio, January 1914.
(*Danseuse = Mer*; *Sea = Dancer*).

Color plate p. 47.

76.2553 PG 32

Oil on canvas (unvarnished). Dimensions, including artist's painted frame, 41 1/2 x 33 13/16 (105.3 x 85.9); canvas only, 39 3/8 x 31 11/16 (100 x 80.5).

Signed and dated l.r. (after 1947):[1] *G. Severini 1913*; signed, dated, and titled on reverse (photographed before lining): *„MER = DANSEUSE" / GINO SEVERINI / TABLEAU / 1914.*

PROVENANCE:

Sold to M. Bianchedi of Buenos Aires, 1914, but apparently returned to the artist;[2] acquired from the artist, possibly as a gift or exchange, by Theo van Doesburg (or Nelly van Doesburg), ca. 1928;[3] purchased from Nelly van Doesburg, Paris, 1940.

fig. a.
Cat. no. 162 before addition of signature and date. Photograph ca. 1942.

1. A photograph taken ca. 1942 in New York shows that the work had not at that point been signed or dated on the front (fig. a). Severini obviously added this inscription sometime after Peggy Guggenheim's 1947 move to Venice. On the basis of published sources (see EXHIBITIONS) it is probable that this occurred about 1951. The inscriptions on the reverse would, however, date from not long after the painting's execution. A note in the conservation file at the SRGM states that upon removal of the label immediately adjacent to the word *TABLEAU*, a *No. 1* was found. The inscription would thus apparently have read *TABLEAU NO. 1/1914*. No photograph was made of this and the author was not aware of this additional factor until after the picture had been lined. It is impossible to say whether this part of the inscription was in the same hand or paint as the rest. A probable reference to the frame is to be found in a letter from Severini in Anzio to Giuseppe Sprovieri in Rome (*Archivi del Futurismo*, vol. I, p. 314), dated February 6, 1914: "*La cornice per mare = Danzatrice, bisognerebbe che fosse uguale a quella del quadro 'Tango' che è da Balla—(lasciala del colore del legno)—.*" This would suggest, incidentally, that his extension of the composition onto the frame dates from sometime after the completion (and exhibition) of the picture. He lists both "*Tango argentino*" and "*Mare = Danzatrice*" as priced at "800-1000" lire (presumably for the purposes of the forthcoming exhibition). See fn. 2 for evidence that the picture mentioned in this letter is, in all probability, that of Peggy Guggenheim.

CONDITION:

In 1964 (Tate Report) some slight cleavage of pigment in a few places was noted and secured. Test cleaning revealed that the pale yellow, red, and blue were very vulnerable to water. Some water stains in areas where the ground was not covered with pigment were noted. Because of the danger of possible darkening of the ground, wax lining was discouraged by the conservator.

In 1978 (New York) examination of the work revealed the following conditions: the reverse of the linen had at some point been treated, probably with a coat of colletta, which had penetrated the porous ground in some places. Apart from the resulting discoloration, the top and bottom of the painting had been exposed to severe moisture, if not actually to water, and they were much discolored and stained. There were considerable losses of pigment, and the surface had been coated with a water-soluble substance containing a resinous component.

The surface was partially cleaned, but some areas (mainly ochers and yellows) proved too vulnerable to treat (a finding confirmed by the Tate Report of 1964). Cleaving paint was consolidated with Lucite. The canvas was flattened and lined on Mylar 1400 with BEVA. The edges were strip-lined with Lucite 44-treated linen strips and attached with Plus-Ten contact cement. A coat of Lucite 44 was brushed on in order to avoid any penetration of the exposed ground. The work was mounted on a new stretcher.

The original color balance created by the artist has changed somewhat, owing largely to the darkening of the ground but partly to the fact that certain areas could not be cleaned. Some of the ochers, for example, were of extreme fragility and were not cleaned, and the color transitions from light to dark in those areas are more abrupt than originally intended. The pale yellows have suffered considerable losses, leaving a darker, oil-saturated brush print in their place. Since cleaning was almost impossible in the yellows, a certain brilliance is lacking throughout. Other areas have suffered some color distortion. The condition of the surface is fragile. (New York, Mar. 1983.)

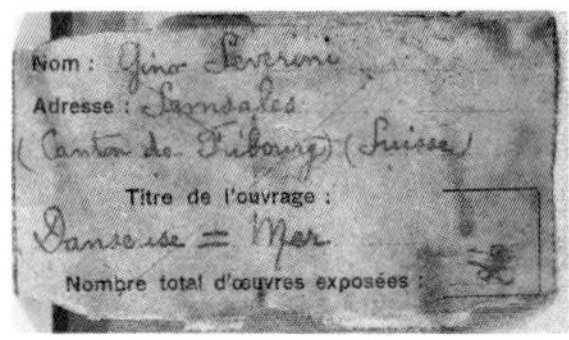

2. The provenance of this picture poses several problems. At the time of the April 1914 Doré Galleries exhibition, the picture still belonged to Severini. A letter from him to Marinetti dated April 26, 1914 (preserved in the Marinetti archives, Yale University) lists the works he is sending to England and their prices; he hopes for a much-needed sale: "*No. 3, Mare = Ballerina £35 . . . Speriamo una vendita di cui ho tanto bisogno.*"

By the time the picture was shown at the 1926 Paris exhibition it was lent by a certain "M. Bianchedi" (see EXHIBITIONS). Moreover, in a letter from Sprovieri to Severini of March 14, 1920, Sprovieri speaks of the picture as follows: "*6 e 7* Mare = ballerina *e* Tango argentino *(due quadri di formato quasi uguali fatti ad Anzio ed esposti nella mia Galleria Futurista. La ballerina era stata acquistata dal Sig. Bianchedi*)" (letter published by Pacini, 1970). The curious fact is, however, that in the 1920 letter Sprovieri is offering to purchase this (and 3 or 4 other works) on behalf of an avant-garde collector who "moves in Italian-American circles" and could therefore offer Severini further sales at higher prices. The implication is that although Bianchedi purchased it and probably took possession of it sometime earlier, he may never have paid for it, and the work thus would have eventually been returned to Severini. This hypothesis—advanced by Pacini in correspondence with the author—is supported by the presence of a label on the reverse (see illustration) giving the address of Severini as *Semsales (Canton de Fribourg) (Suisse)*, where the artist worked only during the years 1924-26. The fact that the painting appeared in the 1926 Paris exhibition as a "loan" from Bianchedi remains unexplained; Pacini has suggested that the dealer Sprovieri might have included the name for "public relations" purposes—in order to give the impression that paintings by Severini had been acquired by important private collectors.

3. It seems likely that the van Doesburgs acquired the picture in 1928. They lived at 2 rue d'Arceuil July 19, 1928-December 1930, and this address had been squeezed in at the bottom of the Doré Galleries label of 1914 (see illustration). The information already written on the label at the time of the exhibition included only the title (in English and French) and Severini's name. Nelly van Doesburg apparently added her own name and address at the bottom after she acquired the work.

162

The development of Severini's style in 1912-14 has been lucidly analyzed and documented by both Marianne Martin (*Futurist Art and Theory, 1909-1915*, Oxford, 1968, pp. 138-47) and Piero Pacini (see especially 1977, pp. 3-8). The dancer as subject matter had already become a central preoccupation for Severini by 1910, but during the critical years when he created what he called a "plastic analogy of dynamism," the dancer became probably his most important vehicle of expression.

As Martin has written, the *Mare = danzatrice* images produced at the very end of 1913 and early in 1914 offered the most explicit demonstration of Severini's notion of a dynamic relationship between complementary images: "The quality of the glistening, rippling movement superimposed upon a steady inexorable rhythm, which is common to both the sea and the dance, was caught by an intricate play of complementary forms, lines and colours, opposed to each other either as single units or as composite groups or else by a combination of both" (op. cit., pp. 144-45).

In a manifesto written at approximately the same time,[4] Severini described the nature of his aesthetic aims in these paintings, drawing a distinction between what he saw as "real analogies" and "apparent analogies":

> *Analogie reali: il mare con la sua danza sul posto, movimenti di zig-zag e contrasti scintillanti di argento e smeraldo, evoca nella mia sensibilità plastica la visione lontanissima di una danzatrice coperta di pagliettes smaglianti, nel suo ambiente di luce, rumori e suoni. perciò mare = danzatrice.*
>
> *Analogie apparenti: l'espressione plastica dello stesso mare, che per analogia reale evoca in me una danzatrice, mi dà, al primo sguardo, per analogia apparente, la visione d'un gran mazzo di fiori. Queste analogie apparenti, superficiali, concorrono ad intensificare il valore espressivo dell'opera plastica. Si giunge così a questa realtà: mare = Danzatrice + mazzo di fiori.*

Severini fell ill late in the winter 1913 and went to the seaside at Anzio to recover. He arrived there in December and stayed until May 1914.[5] Although it is difficult to trace the chronology of the sea = dancer pictures painted at Anzio with certainty, a development toward a gradually increasing degree of abstraction is discernible. Among the early examples in which the movement of the dancer's arms and the corresponding ripple of the waves is still legible is a

4. The manifesto was not published until 1961 and the date of its completion is unclear. (The full text is to be found in *Gino Severini*, exh. cat., Palazzo Venezia, Rome, 1961; also in *Archivi del Futurismo*, vol. I. pp. 76-80.) The manuscript itself apparently bears the date "*Settembre-ottobre 1913*." It seems likely, however, that Severini did most of his work on it during the winter 1913-14, and even later, since it would appear that certain passages (including those quoted here) would have been developed simultaneously with—if not after—the completion of the paintings done at Anzio early in 1914. Indeed, in a letter to Sprovieri dated February 6, 1914 (see above, fn. 1), Severini mentions the manifesto and says it will come out ("*uscirà*") in a month, implying that it is a new document. On April 24, Marinetti wrote to Severini saying "*Aspetto il manoscritto definitivo del tuo manifesto*" (*Archivi del Futurismo*, vol. I, p. 329).

5. A published letter from Severini to Herwarth Walden establishes that the former was still in Pienza on November 26, 1913 (*Archivi del Futurismo*, vol. I, p. 306). The entire development of the Sea = Dancer theme almost certainly followed Severini's arrival at Anzio. Sprovieri's 1920 letter (see fn. 2), in which he specifically connects a *Mare = Danzatrice* with Anzio, with his own exhibition, and with Bianchedi's purchase, makes it possible to establish here for the first time that Peggy Guggenheim's picture was indeed the subject of his query and is datable to early 1914 in Anzio. The probability that the Winston-Malbin examples were also completed at Anzio is very great. The author is indebted to Piero Pacini (who concurs with the chronology presented here) for illuminating discussions regarding the dating and sequence of the dancer paintings and drawings.

fig. b.
Severini, Study for a *Mare = ballerina*, charcoal on paper, 27⅞ x 19⅞ in., 70.8 x 50.5 cm., The Lydia and Harry Lewis Winston Collection (Dr. and Mrs. Barnett Malbin, New York).

charcoal drawing in the Winston-Malbin collection (fig. b). Following closely upon it is the oil with sequins, in the same collection (repr. color in *Futurism: A Modern Focus*, exh. cat., SRGM, New York, 1973, p. 191). In this literally sparkling work, there is a striking translation into pictorial terms of Severini's verbal description of the actual analogies that exist between the sea, with its "scintillating contrasts of silver and emerald," and the dancer, "covered with sparkling sequins."

A slightly later and more abstract stage — even though residual figural elements are still discernible — is represented by the painting formerly in the collection of Romana Severini, Rome (repr. Pacini, 1970, p. 33). By the time Severini painted the Peggy Guggenheim picture, however, he had reached a degree of abstraction almost equal to that of the immediately following group of *Espansione sferica della luce* (see the example in the Jucker collection, Milan, repr. Martin, op. cit., pl. 103).[6]

In the opening passages of his manifesto, Severini indicated the direction he felt his work was taking: "*Noi vogliamo rinchiudere l'universo nell'opera d'arte. Gli oggetti non esistono più.*" In the *Espansione sferica* and, to a slightly lesser extent, Peggy Guggenheim's *Mare = Danzatrice*, he achieved this almost total suppression of the observed object, but retained its visual echo. As Martin has pointed out, "the picture's non-representational content had now become an

6. In his February 6 letter to Sprovieri (see fn. 1 above), following his reference to Peggy Guggenheim's picture, Severini mentions 2 small and apparently experimental works bearing the titles *Espansione sferica della luce (centrifuga)* and *Espansione sferica della luce (centripeda)*. He priced both at 300-400 lire and implied that he recently completed them by adding: "*Questi due ultimi quadretti che porterò io stesso sono venuti di una grande bellezza e trasparenza di colore.*"

analogy to, or an abstract recreation of, the universal dynamism" (op. cit., p. 145).

The fragmentation of the form and substance of the dancer into a series of light-color effects is achieved through, on the one hand, the introduction of stronger centrifugal motion and, on the other, the elimination of all chiaroscuro. As he described this process in the manifesto, Severini wrote:

> Danzatrice = mare *avrà preferibilmente irradiazioni luminose (forme e colori-luce) partente dal centro e andanti verso lo spazio (centrifughe) ... è essenzialmente importante di distruggere il principio di luce, tono locale e ombre ... per dare l'azione della luce sui corpi e che appartiene alla relatività di fenomeni luminosi momentanei, accidentali. Noi chiameremo questa nuova espressione plastica della luce: espansione sferica della luce nello spazio. Avremo così una espansione sferica del colore in perfetto accordo con l'espansione sferica delle forme.*

It is interesting to note that in his February 1914 letter to Sprovieri (see fn. 1), Severini wrote of the Peggy Guggenheim picture: "*Con questo si inizia la pittura e scultura delle analogie plastiche — (ma parlare il meno possibile di analogie, altrimento il manifesto non farà più alcun effetto).*"

The manifesto was almost certainly being written (or completed) while these latter pictures were being painted, and Severini's aims — as expressed in the passages above — correspond to a considerable extent with the visual evidence offered by the pictures themselves. Coming to the very threshold of abstraction by the early months of 1914, Severini accomplished in the Peggy Guggenheim painting (and a very few others) the form of a "plastic analogy" described in his writings of the same time. Using color as a means of depicting light rather than of defining form, he arrived at what he called "*un complementarismo di immagine*" — although, not long afterward, he returned to a far more literal and descriptive form of representation. (For a discussion of the important issues related to *Danse de l'ours = barques à voile + vase de fleurs*, see Pacini, 1977.)

EXHIBITIONS:

Rome, Galleria Futurista, *Esposizione di pittura futurista*, Feb.-Mar. 1914, no. 3, p. 27 (*Mare = Ballerina*);[7] London, Doré Galleries, *Exhibition of the Works of the Italian Futurist Painters and Sculptors*, Apr. 1914, no. 48 (*Sea = Dancer*); San Francisco, The Palace of Fine Arts, *Panama-Pacific International Exhibition*, 1915, no. 1166 (*Sea Dancer*); Paris, Palais des Bois, *Société des artistes indépendants*, Mar. 20-May 2, 1926, no. 3318 ("*Danseuse = Mer*. Appartient à M. Bianchedi de Buenos-Ayres"); Amsterdam, Stedelijk Museum, *Expositions selectes d'art contemporain* (organisées par Mme. Petro van Doesburg), Oct. 1-31, 1929, no. 65 (*danseuse-la mer*); New York, MoMA, *Cubism and Abstract Art*, 1936, p. 223, no. 261, repr. p. 59 (*Sea-Dancer*,

7. The appearance of the painting here, in London, and in San Francisco is established through the evidence cited in fn. 2.

1914); New York, Art of This Century, 1942-47, p. 81, repr. ("*Sea Dancer*, 1914"); San Francisco Museum of Art, *Art of our Time*, Jan. 18-Feb. 5, 1945, no. 45; Venice, *P.G.*, 1948 (Biennale), no. 122 ("*Ballerina di mare*, 1914"); Florence, *P.G.*, 1949, no. 134 ("*La Ballerina marina*, 1914"); Venice, XXV Biennale, *I firmatori del primo manifesto futurista*, June 8-Oct. 15, 1950, no. 38; Amsterdam, *P.G.*, 1951, no. 163 ("*La danseuse marine*, 1914"); Zurich, *P.G.*, 1951, no. 151 ("*Meertänzerin*, 1913"); London, *P.G.*, 1964-65, no. 24 ("*Dancer = Sea*, 1913," the title and date by which it has since been known); Stockholm, *P.G.*, 1966-67, no. 24, repr.; New York, *P.G.*, 1969, p. 60, repr. color p. 61; Paris, *P.G.*, 1974-75, no. 23, repr; Torino, *P.G.*, 1975-76, no. 31, repr. pl. 17; Rome, *Guggenheim: Venezia-New York*, 1982, no. 14, repr. color ("*Ballerina = Mare*, 1913-14"); New York, *P.G.*, 1982-83, p. 16, repr. color; Florence, Palazzo Pitti, Sala Bianca, *Gino Severini*, June 25-Sept. 25, 1983, cat. no. 36, repr. color p. 85 (dated 1913-14).

REFERENCES:

P. Guggenheim, *Art of This Century*, 1942, p. 81, repr. ("*Sea Dancer*, 1914"); M. D. Gambillo and T. Fiori, *Archivi del Futurismo*, Rome, 1962, vol. II, cat. no. 57, repr. p. 327; P. Pacini, *Gino Severini*, Florence, 1966, repr. color no. 27 (dated 1913); idem, "Lettera di Giuseppe Sprovieri a Gino Severini," *Critica d'Arte*, xvii, fasc. iii, June 1970, p. 54; P. Pacini, *Severini 1913*, Prato, 1977, p. 6, repr. pl. 1.

Clyfford Still

Born November 1904, Grandin, North Dakota.
Died June 1980, Baltimore, Maryland.

163 Jamais. Richmond, Virginia, May 1944.
(*PH-739*).

Color plate p. 679.

76.2553 PG 153

Oil on canvas (unvarnished), 65 1/16 x 32 1/4 (165.2 x 82).

Signed and dated l.l.: *Clyfford S. 44*; on stretcher, in artist's hand, in ink: *Jamais $450⁰⁰ Clyfford S. 1944.*

PROVENANCE:

Purchased from the artist after the exhibition at Art of This Century, March 1946.

CONDITION:

In 1964 (Tate Report) the unvarnished oil surface was described as in good condition, but the stretcher was somewhat warped. A backboard was fitted to correct the unevenness of the support.

In 1982 (Venice) a Fieux contact lining and an ICA spring stretcher (untensioned) were applied. In the area around the red circle and in certain other areas where pigment has been lost the unprepared canvas is visible. At the top of the slender black form 2 heavy impasto green dots (eyes?) have cracked and partially flaked. The yellow impasto area to the right shows deep pigment cracks and some loss. Some flaking and incipient cleavage are visible in other yellow and ocher sections. The overall surface, applied in an extremely dry oil medium, is free of drying cracks, though scattered areas of abrasion and minor loss are visible. The condition is in general fragile. (New York, Mar. 1983.)

The titles of this and other works of the early and mid-1940s by Still pose problems that must be taken into account in attempts to arrive at an understanding of the subject matter and meaning of these paintings.

By the late 1950s, Still's commitment to the notion of abstraction led him to reject all the titles for his earlier work, and indeed to deny that he had ever provided any.[1] It is not certain, however, that the statements of his later years are an entirely satisfactory guide to the actual complexities of his own development. It seems more likely that as his views consolidated in the late 1950s he adopted certain positions ex post facto.

In 1959, Still's wife compiled a biography of her husband for the catalogue of the Albright-Knox Art Gallery retrospective. Referring to the titles ascribed to the paintings in the Art of This Century exhibition of 1946, she noted that they had been invented by the Art of This Century gallery staff and that Still had repudiated the titles in an "open letter" to the gallery at the time, unequivocally rejecting these inventions and all interpretations of his work by "myth-makers."[2]

The introduction to the 1946 Art of This Century exhibition catalogue, written by Mark Rothko, contained the following paragraph:

> *It is significant that Still, working out West and alone, has arrived at pictorial conclusions so allied to those of the small band of Myth Makers who have emerged here during the war.... Bypassing the current preoccupation with genre and the nuances of formal arrangements, Still expresses the tragic-religious drama which is generic to all Myths at all times, no matter where they occur. He is creating new counterparts to replace the old mythological hybrids who have lost their pertinence in the intervening centuries.... For me, Still's pictorial dramas are an extension of the Greek Persephone Myth. As he himself expressed it, his paintings are "of the Earth, the Damned and of the Recreated"* (see Appendix, p. 789).

Still's earliest documented repudiation of Rothko's text and the "mythic" qualities here attributed to his work dates from 1979 (see fn. 1). Since he and Rothko were close friends in 1946, it is difficult to imagine that Rothko would have published such a characterization unless he had believed it to be accurate and faithful to Still's own intentions; moreoever, no contemporary record of a dispute between the two artists survives.[3]

1. See, for example, *Clyfford Still*, exh. cat., The Metropolitan Museum of Art, New York, 1979, p. 24.
2. "Invited to exhibit a group of paintings at Art of This Century. (All titles associated with work were applied by gallery for their personal interests.) Appreciation by 'Myth-makers' group in New York at this time led to misinterpretation of meaning and intent of the painting. Still corrected this identification in an open letter to the Art of This Century Gallery in 1946" (biography of Clyfford Still, by his wife, in *Paintings by Clyfford Still*, exh. cat., The Buffalo Fine Arts Academy, Buffalo, 1959, n.p.). The "open letter" cited by Mrs. Still has never been traced, and Peggy Guggenheim had no memory of it, nor of a controversy about the issue (conversation with the author, 1978).

Three years before the Art of This Century exhibition, Still had had a one-man show at the San Francisco Museum of Art (March 1943). All the works in the exhibition carried titles supplied by the artist himself.[4] When Still supervised the republication, forty-three years later, of the catalogue information for this early exhibition, however, all the original titles had been replaced by numbers. Similarly, catalogue information concerning the Art of This Century exhibition was republished in the same volume and those titles were also replaced by numbers.[5]

Still's earliest experimentation with numerical titles seems to be traceable not to the 1943 era but to the period in 1947 when he was preparing for his exhibition at the Betty Parsons Gallery. In this context, he wrote to Parsons on March 3: "The pictures will be without titles; — only identified by number. Risking the charge of affectation, I am omitting titles because they would inevitably mislead the spectator and delimit the meanings and implications latent in the works" (Betty Parsons papers, AAA, reel N68/72 frame 0651).

This constitutes the clearest evidence available concerning Still's changing attitude toward the use of titles in his work. He was obviously at a point of transition: anxious about the possible charge of affectation, he had nonetheless come to the conclusion that titles constricted — rather than enriched — the meaning of his work.

In the specific case of *Jamais* and hence, presumably, of the other paintings included at Art of This Century the previous year, recently uncovered evidence indicates that the original titles were definitely Still's own. On the discarded original stretcher of the Peggy Guggenheim painting is the inscription *Jamais $450^{00} Clyfford S. 1944*, written in a single hand in pen and blue ink (see illustration p. 707, above). Comparison of this inscription with examples of Still's handwriting, and especially of his signature (fig. a), reveals unmistakable similarities.[6] Given this evidence, it seems certain that, in this instance at least, Still himself gave the picture its title.

Insofar as the titles of the early works offer suggestive clues to their subject matter—whether they are expressive of a residual figurative content or evocative of even the most elliptical associative meaning—Still's responsibility in the titling process up to 1947 should be borne in mind.[7]

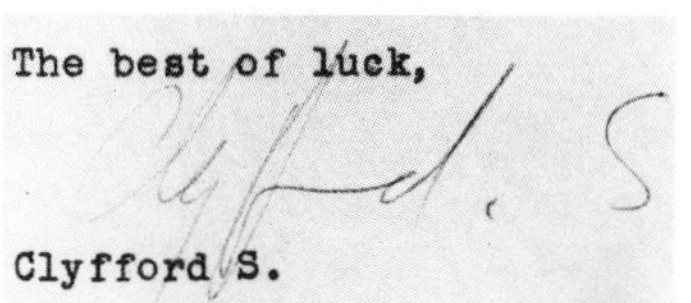

fig. a.
Still's signature on a letter to Edward Dugmore, December 6, 1961. Edward Dugmore Papers, Archives of American Art, Smithsonian Institution.

3. It is interesting to note that Thomas B. Hess recalled being struck by "the vaguely allegorical, probably Jungian subject matter" of Still's work in the 1946 exhibition, and that he especially noted the way in which "the paintings seemed to illustrate their subject" ("The Outsider," *Art News*, vol. 68, no. 8, Dec. 1969, pp. 37, 67). Hess and others have described the early friendship between Still and Rothko as a particularly close one.

4. The accession files of the San Francisco Museum contain Still's original list (S. Polcari, "The Intellectual Roots of Abstract Expressionism, Clyfford Still," *Art International*, vol. 25, nos. 5-6, May-June 1982, p. 31, fn. 12).

5. "Clyfford Still Exhibitions," in *Clyfford Still*, exh. cat., San Francisco Museum of Modern Art, 1976, n.p. *Jamais* appears as *PH-739*, painted in May 1944 in Richmond, Virginia.

6. Steven Polcari concurs that the inscription on the stretcher of *Jamais* is in Still's hand.

7. For a discussion of the content and meaning of Still's early work, see Polcari, loc. cit.

EXHIBITIONS:

New York, Art of This Century, *First Exhibition Clyfford Still*, Feb. 12-Mar. 2, 1946, no. 5 (*Jamais*); Venice, *P.G.*, 1948 (Biennale), no. 125 (dated 1945); Florence, *P.G.*, 1949, no. 137 (dated 1945); Amsterdam, *P.G.*, 1951, no. 166; Zurich, *P.G.*, 1951, no. 154; Bordighera, *11ᴬ Mostra Internazionale Pittura Americana*, Mar. 1-31, 1953, no. 22; London, *P.G.*, 1964-65, no. 128, repr.; Stockholm, *P.G.*, 1966-67, no. 124, repr.; New York, *P.G.*, 1969, p. 138, repr. p. 139; Paris, *P.G.*, 1974-75, no. 132; Torino, *P.G.*, 1975-76, no. 145; London, The Arts Council of Great Britain, *Dada and Surrealism Reviewed*, Jan. 10-Mar. 27, 1978, no. 15.51, repr.; Rome, *Guggenheim: Venezia-New York*, 1982, no. 57, repr. color; New York, *P.G.*, 1982-83, no. 58, repr. color.

REFERENCES:

J. K. R[eed], "Extending a Myth," *Art Digest*, vol. 20, no. 11, Mar. 1, 1946, p. 17 (review of Art of This Century exhibition); W. Rubin, *Dada, Surrealism, and Their Heritage*, exh. cat., MoMA, New York, 1968, p. 179, repr. (not included in exhibition); idem, *Dada and Surrealist Art*, London, 1969, repr. p. 449, D. 267.

Graham Vivian Sutherland

Born August 1903, London.
Died February 1980, London.

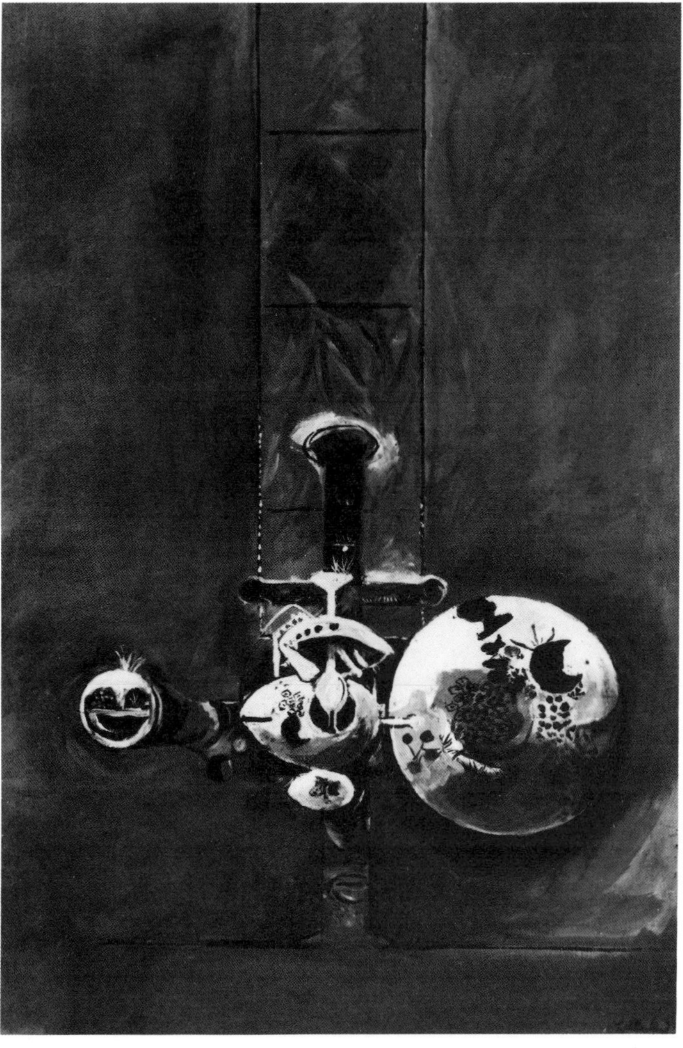

164 Organic Form. 1962-68.

76.2553 PG 120

Oil on canvas, 51¼ x 38⅜ (130.2 x 97.4).

Signed and dated l.r.: *Sutherland 1962 / 1968.*

PROVENANCE:

Acquired from the artist, by exchange, 1968.[1]

CONDITION:

The work has apparently had no restoration and is in stable condition. (Venice, Nov. 1982.)

It has not been possible to establish on stylistic or other grounds whether Sutherland actually worked on this canvas over a six-year period or, having completed it in 1962, only added a few touches and a date before delivering it to Peggy Guggenheim in 1968.

EXHIBITIONS:

Paris, *P.G.*, 1974-75, no. 140, repr.; Torino, *P.G.*, 1975-76, no. 118.

REFERENCE:

L. Flint, *Handbook*, 1983, p. 154, repr. color p. 155.

1. In 1966 Peggy Guggenheim purchased an oil by Sutherland, *Suspended Form*, from the Redfern Gallery in London (£3,150; 38 x 31 in., 96 x 79 cm., Calas, 1966, repr. p. 241). When Sutherland visited her in Venice, he found the work inadequate and insisted that she return it to him, saying that he would paint her a better one. The present work was delivered to her sometime afterward.

Rufino Tamayo

Born August 1899, Oaxaca, Mexico.
Lives in Mexico City.

165 Heavenly Bodies. 1946.

76.2553 PG 119

Oil with sand on canvas (unvarnished), 34 1/8 x 66 15/16 (86.6 x 170).

Signed and dated l.l.: *Tamayo / -46*.

PROVENANCE:

Pierre Matisse (on consignment), 1946-51; returned to the artist; possibly Frank Perls Gallery, Beverly Hills (on consignment), 1951 (see below EXHIBITIONS); M. Knoedler and Co., Inc., New York, October 1958-March 1961; purchased from M. Knoedler and Co., March 1961.

CONDITION:

In 1964 (Tate Report) the work was described as being in excellent condition, and no restoration had been carried out. The condition continues to be stable. (Venice, June 1983.)

EXHIBITIONS:

Venice, XXV Biennale, June 8-Oct. 15, 1950, no. 51; San Francisco, California Palace of the Legion of Honor, *Rufino Tamayo*, May 10-June 10, 1951 (no cat.; the work was shipped by Frank Perls Gallery, Beverly Hills, but it is not clear whether they owned the work or merely shipped it for the artist); London, *P.G.*, 1964-65, no. 104; Stockholm, *P.G.*, 1966-67, no. 98; London, Sotheby and Co., *Twentieth Century Paintings, Drawings and Sculpture presented to the Institute of Contemporary Arts for sale on behalf of the Carlton House Terrace project*, June 23, 1966, lot 69 (withdrawn before the sale); New York, *P.G.*, 1969, p. 115, repr. color; Paris, *P.G.*, 1974-75, no. 139, repr.; Torino, *P.G.*, 1975-76, no. 117.

REFERENCES:

"A Selection on Night. A darkness of the mind or of nature," *Tiger's Eye*, no. 9, Oct. 1949, repr. p. 46 (Collection Pierre Matisse); L. Flint, *Handbook*, 1983, p. 152, repr. color p. 153.

Raymond Georges Yves Tanguy

Born January 1900, Paris.
Died January 1955, Woodbury, Connecticut.

166 Palais promontoire. 1931.
(*Promontory palace*; *Les belles manières* [?]).

Color plate p. 496.

76.2553 PG 94

Oil on canvas (unvarnished?), 28¾ x 23⅜ (73 x 60).

Signed and dated l.r.: *YVES TANGUY 31*;[1] on reverse of canvas (probably not in the artist's hand): *yves tanguy* / *1931* / *"les belles manières"*;[2] on stretcher (possibly not in the artist's hand): *"Palais promontoire"* / *1931*.

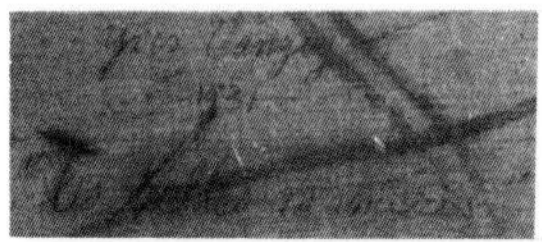

PROVENANCE:

Purchased from Jeanette Tanguy, the artist's wife, Paris, October 1939.

CONDITION:

In 1964 (Tate Report) a horizontal scratch across the center caused by the stretcher, a small hole in the canvas support just below the center, a dark stain above the horizon, and retouching along the top and bottom edges were noted. These conditions were not apparently treated. There was some uncertainty about the presence of varnish.

There is extensive (discolored) inpainting along the lower and upper edges. Ca. ⅝ in., 1.5 cm., up from the center of the lower edge a hole in the canvas has been caused by a nail (visible) penetrating from the reverse. The horizontal scratch along the center of the canvas, noted in the Tate Report, may have been the result of a flaw in the canvas weave. There are extensive paint losses along this line. The starlike rays around the tower upper left and in the sky right were scored by Tanguy into the pigment and ground layer with a sharp instrument. Some additional pinpoint losses have occurred in this area. The overall condition is stable. (Venice, June 1983.)

Upon returning from a journey to Africa, Tanguy painted a series of a half-dozen canvases in 1930-31. As James Thrall Soby was the first to point out, these pictures (of which *Palais promontoire* was one) are closely related to one another, but uncharacteristic of the entire rest of his oeuvre. (See *Yves Tanguy*, exh. cat., MoMA, New York, 1955, pp. 16-17.) All the landscapes contain rather

1. The date on the recto has been variously read as 1930 or 1931. Tanguy's regularity in dating his work at the time of completion has generally provided clarity in the matter of chronology. In the case of *Palais promontoire*, however, the minuteness of his hand in signing and dating the work has presented problems of legibility. The 2 inscriptions on the verso clearly bear the date 1931, but these may not be in the artist's hand or even contemporary with the work's completion. Definitive evidence for the 1931 date remains to be found, but in light of the inscriptions on the work, and of the publication of this date in the 1937 exhibition catalogue, it seems the most plausible alternative.
2. Comparison of the handwriting here with documented examples of Tanguy's handwriting (AAA) suggests that this inscription is not in his hand. The question is rendered more complex by the fact that another composition, dissimilar to *Palais promontoire*, was published in the January 1932 issue of *Nadréalizam Danas I Ovde* (Belgrade, vol. 2, no. 2, n.p.) with the title *Les belles manières*. In view of the potential significance of Tanguy's titles for the understanding of his oeuvre, the possibility that Tanguy, at some stage, considered the title *Les belles manières* for this work, must be borne in mind.

166

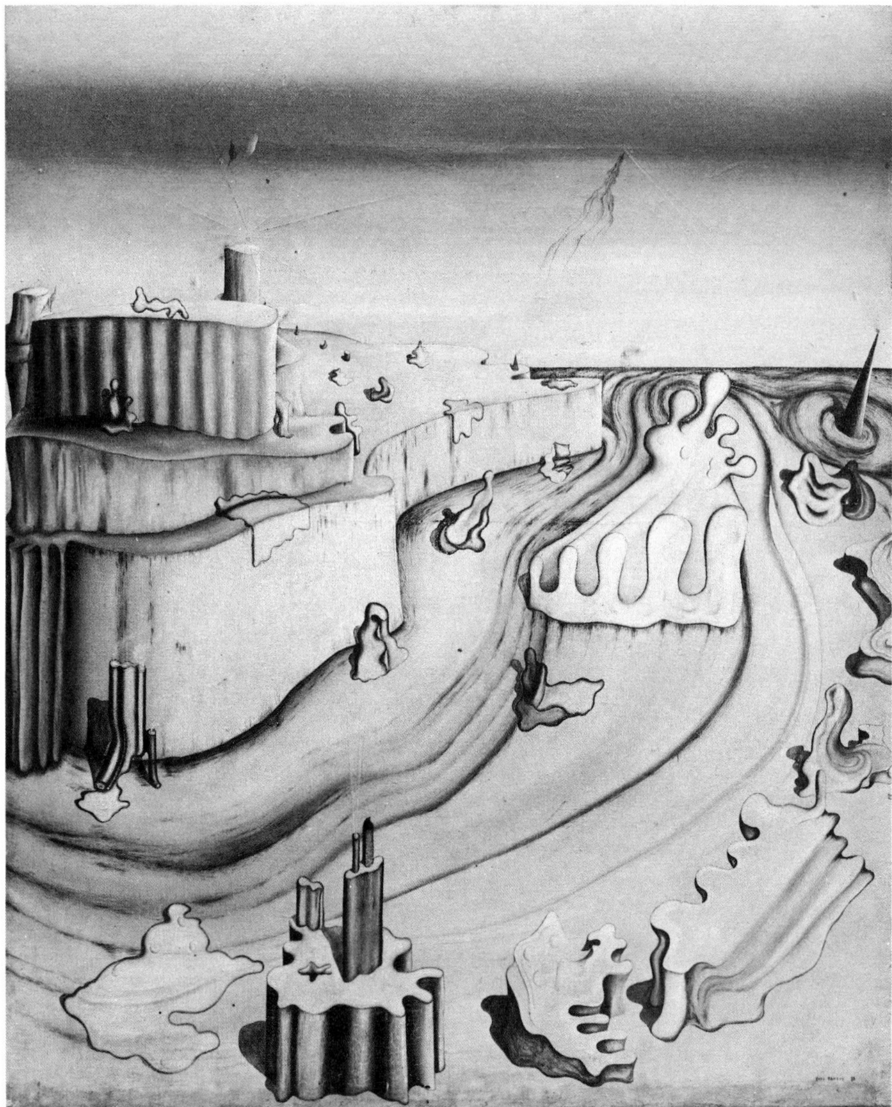

densely "fluted tablelands and jigsaw bastions," which, according to the artist, were inspired by rock formations he saw on his journey. Tanguy had also described to Soby that in this series, for the first and last time, he actually drew his compositions onto the canvas before painting them.

William Rubin characterized the forms in this group of canvases as "more malleable" than those to be found elsewhere in Tanguy's work: "They give the impression of beginning to melt, as if made of candle wax." Rubin — as well as other writers — attributed the crowding of motifs at least partly to Tanguy's testimony that the compositions were in fact drawn onto the canvas first.[3] A detailed examination of *Palais promontoire* under high magnification, however, reveals no trace of any underdrawing, even in those areas where pigment has been lost and the ground is visible. While it is possible that the pencil lines may have been entirely obliterated in the course of Tanguy's meticulous painting of the delicate surface, it may also be the case that he did not use preliminary drawing in every case or, alternatively, that he only partially prepared the canvas in this way.

The titles of Tanguy's paintings pose considerable problems, and, as is well known, he was generally reluctant to attach meanings of any kind to his paintings. In an oft-quoted letter to Emily Genauer, he wrote that "*je ne peux, ni par conséquent ne veux essayer de donner une définition, aussi simple soit elle, de ce que je peint. Si je tentais de le faire je risquerais à tout jamais de m'enfermer dans une définition qui ne tarderai* [sic] *pas à devenir pour moi comme une prison*" (June 20, 1947, Genauer papers, AAA, reel NG1, frame 570).

Tanguy's attitude toward titles was consistent with his attitude toward meaning expressed in the letter to Genauer. In a 1946 interview with James Johnson Sweeney, for example, Tanguy stated that his titles for the works in his 1927 exhibition were entirely arbitrary: "[Breton] wrote the introduction to the catalog of my show. I remember spending a whole afternoon with him before the catalog went to press searching through books on psychiatry for statements of patients which we could use as titles for the paintings" (*The Museum of Modern Art Bulletin*, vol. 13, nos. 4-5, New York, Sept. 1946, p. 23). This position has been widely accepted in the literature (see, for example, S. Alexandrian, 1969). John Ashbery has argued, however, that the fact that most of the pictures carry titles "implies that a choice has been made, and that the purpose of this choice is to extend the range of a picture's meaning by slanting it in a certain direction." Thus, Ashbery suggested, the titles cannot be ignored: they "are like filters which project an oddly appropriate light on a scene that cannot be rationally deduced from them."[4]

Very recent scholarship has been helpful in pursuing Ashbery's line of thought. Jennifer V. Mundy has identified the precise source from which Tanguy and Breton actually derived the titles for works in the 1927 exhibition ("Tanguy, titles and mediums," *Art History*, vol. 6, no. 2, June 1983, pp. 199-213). Mundy does not disagree with the fundamental proposition that for Tanguy a title was not a "necessary complement to a painting." Many of his works — especially the gouaches — remained untitled; others, meanwhile, carry titles that have undoubtedly been added by dealers or collectors. But Mundy — like Ashbery — does attach importance to the titles that can with some confidence be attributed to Tanguy himself or are known to have received his concurrence. Even though the method of bestowing such titles may have been in some sense arbitrary, the very act of making connections between paintings and words clearly involved a process of testing meanings and of making selections.

In addition, the volume used by Tanguy and Breton was a book of considerable significance within the context of Surrealism. It was Charles Robert Richet's *Traité de métapsychique*, published in 1922, a work that was especially important in the development of Breton's thought.[5]

3. W. Rubin, *Dada and Surrealist Art*, New York, 1969, p. 198.

4. "Yves Tanguy, Geometer of Dreams," *Art in America*, vol. 62, Nov. 1974, pp. 71-75; also published in *Yves Tanguy*, exh. cat., Acquavella Galleries, New York, 1974, n.p.

5. This was pointed out some years ago by M. Bonnet, *André Breton*, Paris, 1975, p. 262, and was also acknowledged by Breton himself, *Entretiens*, Paris, 1969, p. 82.

Richet's vast study is an exploration of the unconscious, of paranormal phenomena — "vibrations" from an exterior reality, telepathy, the premonitions and declarations of mediums or spirits, and the possible existence of extrahuman intelligence. As Mundy notes, these were exactly the kinds of subjects that had a major bearing on Breton's — and, she argues, Tanguy's — entire conception of Surrealism. Given this fact, it does not seem surprising (and certainly not arbitrary) that the two artists turned to Richet's volume as the source for the titles they sought for Tanguy's paintings, which depicted a world of dreams and visions, a world beyond reality and consciousness, a world Breton felt was the product of mysticism. That Breton played a strong, perhaps the major, role in this titling process is undeniable. That Tanguy was a willing pupil and partner in this as in other exercises seems equally clear.

Whether similar sources lie behind some of the titles of Tanguy's post-1927 paintings remains to be established. *Palais promontoire* (or *Les belles manières*, see footnote 1), *Le soleil dans son écrin*, and *En lieu oblique* are titles for which no source has so far been found. They require further study and — given the fruitfulness of Mundy's explorations — it may well be that future discoveries will eventually lead to a fuller understanding of Tanguy's imagery and even of the consistency of his content.

EXHIBITIONS:

New York, Julien Levy Gallery, *Yves Tanguy*, Mar. 10-30, 1936, no. 1 (not dated); Brussels, Palais des Beaux-Arts, *E.L.T. Mesens présente trois peintres surréalistes — René Magritte, Man Ray, Yves Tanguy*, Dec. 11-22, 1937, no. 62, (dated 1931); Paris, Galerie des Beaux-Arts, *Exposition internationale du surréalisme*, Jan. 17-Feb. 1938, no. 213 (dated 1930); London, Guggenheim Jeune, *Yves Tanguy*, July 6-16, 1938, no. 6 (dated 1930); New York, Art of This Century, 1942-47, p. 115, repr. p. 116 (dated 1930, the date ascribed to it in all *P.G.* publications until 1964); New York, Pierre Matisse Gallery, *Tanguy*, Nov. 5-30, 1946, no. 4; Venice, *P.G.*, 1948 (Biennale), no. 126; Florence, *P.G.*, 1949, no. 138, repr.; Amsterdam, *P.G.*, 1951, no. 167; Zurich, *P.G.*, 1951, no. 157; London, *P.G.*, 1964-65, no. 84, repr. p. 84 (dated 1930 or 1931; this alternative dating has been ascribed to the work in all subsequent publications); Stockholm, *P.G.*, 1966-67, no. 81, repr.; Torino, Galleria Civica d'Arte Moderna, *Le Muse Inquietanti*, Nov. 1967-Jan. 1968, no. 235, repr. (dated 1930); New York, *P.G.*, 1969, p. 116, repr. p. 117; Paris, *P.G.*, 1974-75, no. 90, repr.; Torino, *P.G.*, 1975-76, no. 92, repr. pl. 41.

REFERENCES:

View (Tanguy and Tchelitchew number), series 2, no. 2, May 1942, repr. n.p. (dated 1930); *London Bulletin*, nos. 4-5, July 1938, p. 37, cat. of Guggenheim Jeune exhibition; P. Guggenheim, *Art of This Century*, New York, 1942, p. 115, repr. p. 116 (dated 1930); R. Renne and C. Serbanne, "Yves Tanguy or the Mirror of Wonders," *View*, 5th ser., no. 5, Dec. 1945, p. 14; A. Breton, *Yves Tanguy*, New York, 1946, p. 31 (dated 1930); J. T. Soby, "Inland in the Subconscious: Yves Tanguy," *Magazine of Art*, vol. 42, Jan. 1949, pp. 4-5, repr. (dated 1930); K. Sage Tanguy, *Yves Tanguy — Un Receuil de ses œuvres*, New York, 1963, repr. no. 115 (dated 1930); Calas, 1966, p. 117, repr. p. 143 (dated 1930 or 1931); R. Lebel, "Il Surrealismo: Tanguy, Dalí, Brauner, Dominguez e Altri," *L'Arte Moderna*, vol. VII, no. 61, 1967, p. 245, repr. color p. 251 (dated 1930); S. Alexandrian, *L'Art Surréaliste*, Paris, 1969, p. 80; J. Pierre, "Le peintre surréaliste par excellence," *Yves Tanguy Retrospective*, exh. cat., MNAM, Paris, 1982, p. 51.

167 **Le soleil dans son écrin.** 1937.
(The sun in its jewel case; The sun in its casket).

Color plate p. 495.

76.2553 PG 95

Oil on canvas (unvarnished?), 45 7/16 x 34 11/16 (115.4 x 88.1).

Signed and dated l.r.: *Yves Tanguy 37.*

PROVENANCE:

Purchased from the artist, London, July 1938, after the exhibition at Guggenheim Jeune.

CONDITION:

In 1964 (Tate Report) the work was described as in excellent condition. There was some uncertainty about the presence of varnish.

In 1982 (Venice) the work was given a Fieux contact lining, and some small losses were inpainted.

Extensive retouching is visible in the lower right corner, the entire lower edge (extending in some places 2¾ in., 7 cm., into the field), and the left corner. Losses at the upper edges and pinpoint losses in the sky are also apparent. There is a fine crackle pattern throughout most of the sky area and some evidence of poor adhesion between ground and canvas, which resulted in pinpoint losses. A stretcher mark is visible along the left edge. The condition in general is stable. (New York, Feb. 1983.)

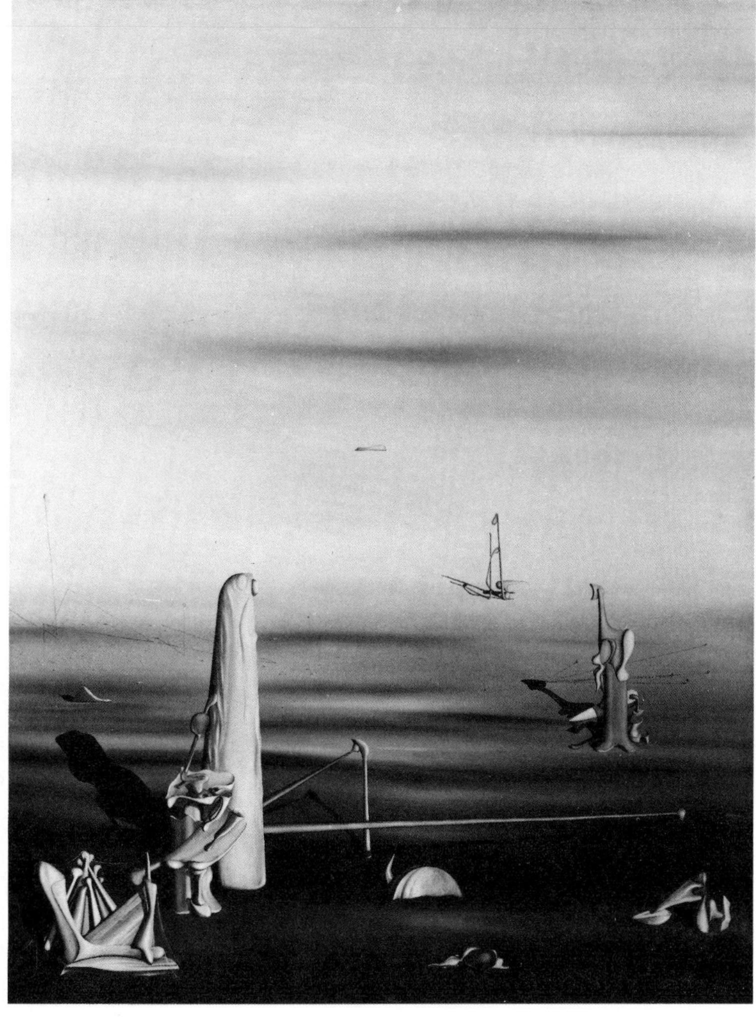

EXHIBITIONS:

Paris, Galerie des Beaux-Arts, *Exposition internationale du surréalisme*, Jan. 17-Feb. 1938, no. 216; London, Guggenheim Jeune, *Yves Tanguy*, July 6-16, 1938, no. 2; New York, Art of This Century, 1942-47, p. 115, repr. p. 117; Venice, *P.G.*, 1948 (Biennale), no. 127; Florence, *P.G.*, 1949, no. 139 (*Il sole sul suo cuscinetto*); Amsterdam, *P.G.*, 1951, no. 168; Zurich, *P.G.*, 1951, no. 158 (*Die Schlafende Sonne*); London, *P.G.*, 1964-65, no. 85, repr.; Stockholm, *P.G.*, 1966-67, no. 82, repr.; Torino, Galleria Civica d'Arte Moderna, *Le Muse Inquietanti*, Nov. 1967-Jan. 1968, no. 236, repr.; New York, *P.G.*, 1969, p. 118, repr. color; Paris, *P.G.*, 1974-75, no. 91, repr.; Torino, *P.G.*, 1975-76, no. 93; New York, *P.G.*, 1982-83, no. 38, repr. color.

REFERENCES:

Minotaure, no. 10, winter 1937, repr. p. 28; *London Bulletin*, nos. 4-5, July 1938, p. 37, cat. of Guggenheim Jeune exhibition; P. Guggenheim, *Art of This Century*, 1942, p. 115, repr. p. 117; R. Renne and C. Serbanne, "Yves Tanguy or the Mirror of Wonders," *View*, 5th ser., no. 5, Dec. 1945, p. 16; J. T. Soby, "In the Subconscious: Yves Tanguy," *Magazine of Art*, vol. 42, Jan. 1949, p. 6; H. Read, *A Concise History of Modern Painting*, New York, 1959, repr. p. 305 (*Sun on Cushion*); K. Sage Tanguy, *Yves Tanguy—Un Receuil de ses œuvres*, New York, 1963, p. 104, cat. no. 207, repr. (*The sun in its splendor*); Calas, 1966, p. 117, repr. p. 145; R. Lebel, "Il Surrealismo: Tanguy, Dalí, Brauner, Dominguez e Altri," *L'Arte Moderna*, vol. VII, no. 61, 1967, p. 246, repr. color p. 253; U. M. Schneede, *Surrealism*, New York, 1973, p. 84, repr. color p. 85 (*The Sun in its shrine*); P. Waldberg, *Yves Tanguy*, Brussels, 1977, repr. p. 162; L. Flint, *Handbook*, 1983, p. 134, repr. color p. 135.

---

168 Untitled. 1938.

76.2553 PG 96

Gouache on paper, 3 11/16 x 9 3/16 (9.3 x 23.3).

Signed and dated l.r.: *Yves Tanguy 38*.

PROVENANCE:

Purchased from the artist, London, July 1938, after his exhibition at Guggenheim Jeune.

CONDITION:

In 1978 (New York) the work was removed from the highly acidic, discolored backboard to which it had been glued, and was remounted on 100% ragboard. Though there was widespread foxing on the verso, this had not penetrated the surface. The paint film remains in stable condition. (New York, Feb. 1983.)

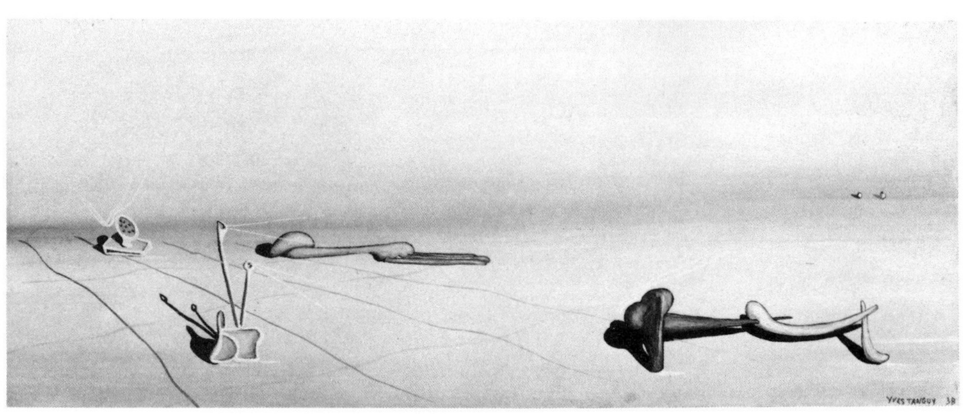

Tanguy painted a large number of small gouaches during this period, all of which were independent works rather than studies for oil paintings. He himself spoke of the extent to which an individual medium, such as pencil, gouache, watercolor, or oil, presented unique and distinct problems that prevented him from using one in the service of another. The particular potential of each medium required and received equal attention, resulting in equally significant statements, irrespective of scale.

EXHIBITIONS:

London, Guggenheim Jeune, *Yves Tanguy*, July 6-16, 1938; Amsterdam, *P.G.*, 1951, no. 172; London, *P.G.*, 1964-65, no. 86; Stockholm, *P.G.*, 1966-67, no. 83; Paris, *P.G.*, 1974-75, no. 92, repr.; Torino, *P.G.*, 1975-76, no. 94; New York, *P.G.*, 1982-83, no. 39, repr.

REFERENCE:

London Bulletin, nos. 4-5, July 1983, p. 37, cat. of the Guggenheim Jeune exhibition. (The works on paper in the catalogue were not listed individually, but Peggy Guggenheim distinctly remembered that this gouache was included.)

---

169 En lieu oblique. March 1941.
(*In an indeterminate place*; *On slanting ground*).

Color plate p. 497.

76.2553 PG 98

Oil on canvas (unvarnished), 16 15/16 x 28 1/8 (43 x 71.4).

Signed and dated l.l.: *Yves Tanguy 41*; on the stretcher in pencil: *YVES TANGUY MARCH 1941 [E]N [LIE]U OBLIQUE.*[1]

PROVENANCE:

Purchased from the artist by Pierre Matisse, 1941; purchased from Pierre Matisse, New York, October 15, 1941.

CONDITION:

In 1964 (Tate Report) the unvarnished oil surface was described as in generally good condition, though a crack near the upper edge (center), a diagonal scratch in the right-hand section of the sky, and some crackle area to the left of this were noted. A stretcher mark was visible along the entire left side.

In 1982 (Venice) attempts were made to ameliorate the discoloration of some inpainting, though this was not removed. A coat of Lefranc retouching varnish was applied.

The support is somewhat buckled owing to uneven tension of the canvas, and the corners of the support are worn through. Stretcher marks are visible on all 4 sides. There is a fine surface crackle and some slight incipient cleavage in 1 or 2 places. The 1964 repair at the top edge and scattered inpainting of pinpoint losses throughout the sky and a few large areas near the edges are visible. The overall condition of the surface is fragile. (New York, Feb. 1983.)

1. This inscription, though now partly obliterated by nail holes and wear, appears to be in the artist's hand. A 1969 transcription of it (before the nails were inserted) indicates that the word "*LIEU*" preceded "*OBLIQUE.*"

169

EXHIBITIONS:

New York, Pierre Matisse Gallery, *Tanguy at View*, Apr. 21-May 8, 1942, no. 4 (*En lieu oblique*); New York, Art of This Century, 1942-47, p. 115; Venice, *P.G.*, 1948 (Biennale), no. 128; Florence, *P.G.*, 1949, no. 140; Amsterdam, *P.G.*, 1951, no. 169 (*sur terrin incliné*); Zurich, *P.G.*, 1951, no. 160 (*Auf schiefem Gelände*); London, *P.G.*, 1964-65, no. 88 (*On Slanting Ground*); Stockholm, *P.G.*, 1966-67, no. 85; Torino, Galleria Civica d'Arte Moderna, *Le Muse Inquietanti*, Nov. 1967-Jan. 1968, no. 240, repr. (*Su un terreno obliquo*); New York, *P.G.*, 1969, p. 119, repr.; Paris, *P.G.*, 1974-75, no. 94; Torino, *P.G.*, 1975-76, no. 96; Rome, *Guggenheim: Venezia-New York*, no. 44, repr. color; New York, *P.G.*, 1982-83, no. 40, repr. (*On slanting ground*).

REFERENCES:

View, 2nd ser., no. 2, May 1942, n.p., cat. of Pierre Matisse exhibition (*En Lieu Oblique*); P. Guggenheim, *Art of This Century*, New York, 1942, p. 115 (*In oblique ground*); K. Sage Tanguy, *Yves Tanguy—Un Receuil de ses œuvres*, New York, 1963, no. 279, repr. (*En lieu oblique*); Calas, 1966, p. 118, repr. color p. 146 (*On slanting Ground*); P. Waldberg, *Yves Tanguy*, Brussels, 1977, repr. p. 110 (*En lieu oblique*).

Mark Tobey

Born December 1890, Centerville, Wisconsin.
Died April 1976, Basel.

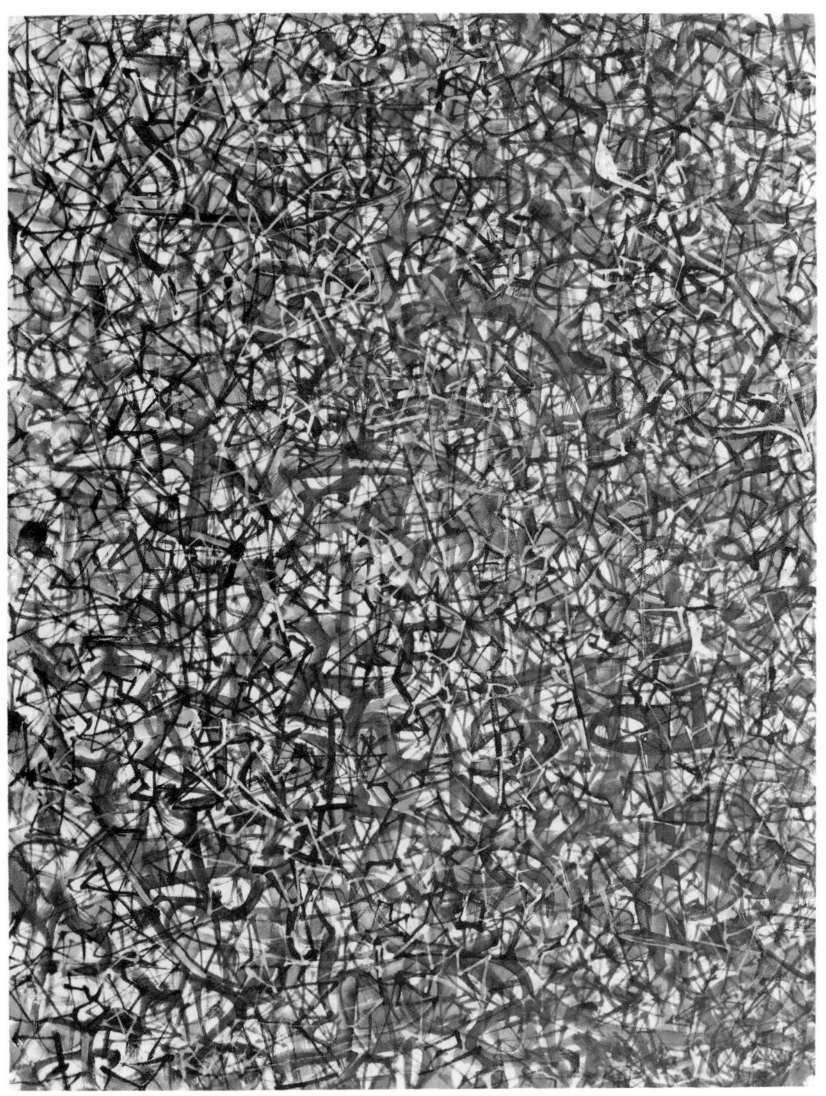

170 Advance of History. 1964.

76.2553 PG 140

Gouache and watercolor on wove paper, glued at corners to acidic mount, 25 5/8 x 19 11/16 (65.2 x 50.1).

Signed l.r.: *Tobey*. Not dated.

PROVENANCE:

Purchased at auction, Sotheby and Co., London, *Twentieth Century Paintings, Drawings and Sculptures*, a sale in support of The Institute for Contemporary Arts, June 23, 1966, lot. no. 72, repr. 93, presented by the artist.[1]

1. Sir Norman Reid, then Director of The Tate Gallery, bid on the work at Peggy Guggenheim's request. The Tate is thus erroneously listed as the buyer.

CONDITION:

In 1983 (New York) the work was removed from its pulpboard acidic mount. Loss at the lower left corner was filled with wove paper. Tears at the lower left and right corners, upper right corner, and center of right edge were repaired with fibers of Japanese tissue and rice paste. The support (pH 5.8) was buffered on the verso with a spray application of calcium hydroxide to achieve pH 6.8. Brown adhesive on verso was removed to some extent, but the softness of the paper rendered total removal impossible. The support was flattened, and hinged to 100% rag. The condition is stable. (New York, Feb. 1983.)

Tobey's characteristic calligraphic style, traditionally described as "white writing," originated in works of 1935, and continued to function as a basic ingredient in his art throughout his lifetime. Clement Greenberg, reviewing a 1944 exhibition in which Tobey showed a number of works in this style, described their effect in the following terms: "the calligraphic, tightly meshed interlacing of white lines which build up to a vertical, rectangular mass reaching almost to the edges of the frame; these cause the picture surface to vibrate in depth—or, better, toward the spectator. Yet this seems little out of which to compose an easel painting. The compensation lies in the intensity, subtlety, and directness with which Tobey registers and transmits emotion usually considered too tenuous to be made the matter of any other art than music" (*The Nation*, Apr. 22, 1944, p. 495).

John Russell, commenting thirty years later on Greenberg, placed Tobey's achievement in a broader historical perspective: "In the year 1944 only a very few people understood what later came to be called action painting (or abstract expressionism). Greenberg wrote on a later occasion that whereas Tobey's white-writing pictures were shown in New York in 1944, Jackson Pollock did not make his own first all over paintings till the late summer of 1946. In other words, Tobey was first with the kind of defocused painting in which motor energy spreads itself across the whole area of the canvas with no concession to conventional ideas of composition" ("The White Writing of Mark Tobey," *Dialogue*, vol. 10, no. 1, 1977, p. 65).

EXHIBITIONS:

Basel, Galerie Beyeler, *Tobey*, Jan. 10-Mar. 1966, no. 10, repr. color.; Stockholm, *P.G.*, 1966-67, no. 122; New York, *P.G.*, 1969, no. 82, repr; Paris, *P.G.*, 1974-75, no. 118, repr.; Torino, *P.G.*, 1975-76, no. 132, repr.; New York, *P.G.*, 1982-83, no. 60, repr.

John Tunnard

Born May 1900, Bedfordshire, England.
Died December 1971, Cornwall, England.

171 ψ Psi. 1938.

76.2553 PG 47

Oil, gesso, gouache, pastel(?), and wax crayon on hardboard (unvarnished), $31\frac{7}{16}$ x $47\frac{3}{16}$ (79.9 x 119.8).

Signed and dated l.r.: Tunnard 38; on reverse: *John Tunnard* / ψ.

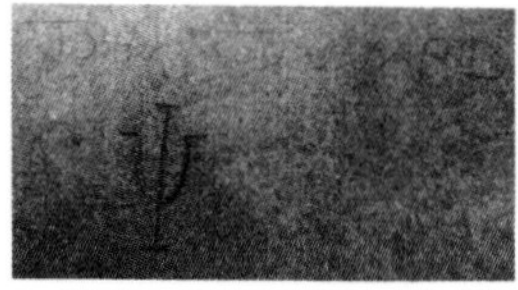

PROVENANCE:

Purchased from the artist, March 1939, London, after exhibition at Guggenheim Jeune.[1]

CONDITION:

In 1964 (Tate Report) a few pinpoint losses were noted, but the overall condition was described as very good.

In 1978 (New York) some minor losses at the lower left, center right margin, and lower left corner were inpainted with watercolor. Chips of flaking paint at the edges were consolidated with Lucite 44. The surface was dirty, but owing to the delicate matte surface and complex combinations of media, no cleaning was attempted. The condition is stable but fragile. (Venice, Nov. 1982.)

1. According to the artist's record book, the work was "sold to Peggy for Museum."

Tunnard's subtle technique, combining a variety of media on a carefully prepared gesso ground and resulting in a smooth, matte "fresco" surface, has not been analyzed or described. Its effects have occasioned comment but not explanation. (See, for example, J. A. Thwaites, who wrote that "the third element in Tunnard's plastic language is his surface texture.... These surfaces are an articulated membrane in themselves..." in *John Tunnard*, exh. cat., The Arts Council of Great Britain, 1977, p. 50.)

The artist touched elliptically on the issue in a 1944 interview in which he acknowledged the influence of both Miró's and Klee's techniques. "I think it is important to have a good technique.... It should come quite naturally to the painter to discover a good technique.... By good technique I don't mean an accepted or academic technique. Klee's was certainly not an accepted technique" (R. Myerscough-Walker, *The Artist*, vol. 27, no. 2, Apr. 1944, p. 42).

A study of Tunnard's working method, which is critical to an understanding of his aesthetic intentions, as well as to the conservation of his delicate surfaces, remains to be undertaken.

Engineers and other scientists have been struck by the apparent references in Tunnard's work of this period to technological tools, compasses, fragments of radar or radio transmission equipment, electrical charges, propellers, rudders, and similar details common to engineering diagrams. The Greek letters that also form a consistent part of Tunnard's imagery (and which in the case of the two Peggy Guggenheim paintings stand as titles for the works) have additional application in calculus. Though Tunnard's interest in the fields of botany and entomology was acknowledged and well known, his use of an engineering vocabulary appears to have been entirely fortuitous (see J. A. Thwaites, "The Technological Eye," *The Art Quarterly*, vol. 9, no. 2, spring 1946, pp. 115-27).

Tunnard's use of the Greek alphabet has also eluded explanation. Elliptical references of this kind, combined with more obviously traceable allusions to the imagery of contemporary artists such as Henry Moore, result in a concept of "invented landscape" which Tunnard himself described as follows: "This world of my own is just as natural to me as your world is to you.... I started as a representational painter ... then I was more interested in the dramatic content of the landscape ... and then with the geometric content.... I got to the stage when, confronted by a landscape, I felt that I could not be bound by the things I saw, and ... the only thing to do was to invent.... and that inventing came gradually into what is called non-representational painting" (R. Myerscough-Walker, loc. cit., p. 41).

EXHIBITIONS:

London, London Gallery, *Living Art in England*, Jan. 18-Feb. 11, 1939, no. 45, repr. (40 gns.); London, Guggenheim Jeune, *Paintings and watercolours by John Tunnard*, Mar. 16-Apr. 18, 1939, no. 1 (40 gns.); New York, Art of This Century, 1942-47, p. 99, repr. (erroneously listed as "*S.P.I.*"); Venice, *P.G.*, 1948 (Biennale), no. 130; Florence, *P.G.*, 1949, no. 142 (as "*P.S.I.* 1939"); Amsterdam, *P.G.*, 1951, no. 173 (1939); Zurich, *P.G.*, 1951, no. 161; London, *P.G.*, 1964-65, no. 40, repr.; Torino, *P.G.*, 1975-76, no. 47.

REFERENCES:

London Bulletin, nos. 8-9, Jan.-Feb. 1939, repr. [p. 41]; P. Guggenheim, *Confessions*, 1960, p. 56; P. Guggenheim, *Art of This Century*, 1942, p. 99, repr. (as "*S.P.I.*"); M. Glazebrook, "John Tunnard: Development and Influences," in *John Tunnard*, exh. cat., The Arts Council of Great Britain, 1977, p. 25, repr. p. 27.

---

172 **Pi.** Spring 1941.

76.2553 PG 48

Gouache, wash, conté crayon, graphite, pastel, black paint (possibly ink?) on wove paper,[1] 15⅜ x 22 (39 x 56).

Signed and dated l.l.: *John Tunnard / 41*; on reverse: "*Pi*" / *D.27 / John Tunnard. / 1941 / 15 gns.* (altered to *45 gns.*)[2] (fig. a).

PROVENANCE:

Purchased from a gallery in New York, February 8, 1944, possibly through Redfern Gallery, London.[2]

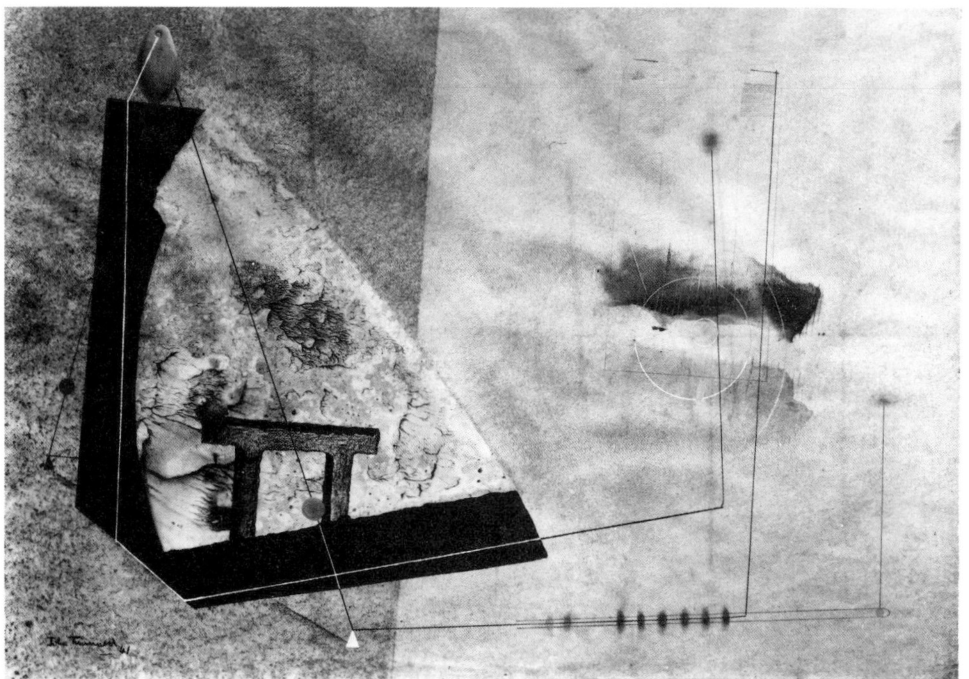

1. The background may have been airbrushed. The technique used in the triangle at the left is decalcomania. For a discussion of this technique, see above, cat. no. 59. Through the influence of Max Ernst, this technique was well known and widely practiced in England by the late 1930s.
2. The artist's record book entry for D[rawing] 27 reads as follows: "Spring 41. D27. Redfern / for U.S.A. 31st Dec. 1941. Sold U.S.A./ 8 Feb. 44 £10.10./Redfern/Peggy Guggenheim." The price, in the right hand column, is listed as 15 gns.

   The precise sequence of events has not been established. Peggy Guggenheim recalled only that she bought the work at a gallery in New York.

CONDITION:

The support, which is laid down on a masonite backing, is cockling slightly throughout. There is a small tear at the lower edge toward the left corner and tack holes at all corners, and elsewhere. A grid pattern drawn with wax substance on the verso (see fig. a) penetrates the obverse. A foxing stain is visible at the lower left, and a light brown scattered foxing (not active) is apparent throughout. Mold is present on the black and brown areas at the left.

In 1982 (Venice) the backboard was replaced as a temporary measure. The overall condition is fairly stable. (Venice, Nov. 1982.)

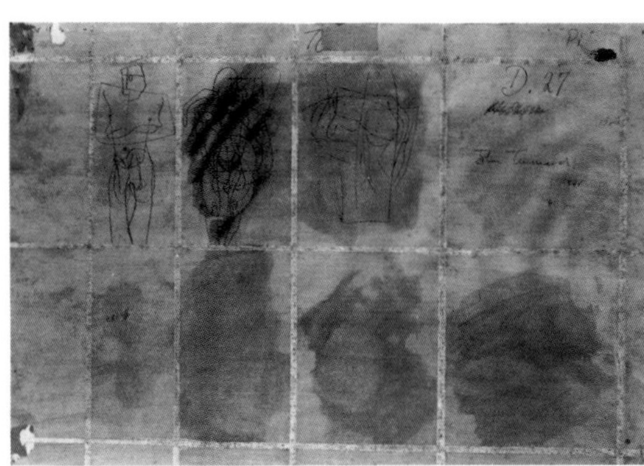

fig. a.
Reverse of cat. no. 172.

EXHIBITIONS:

Venice, *P.G.*, 1948 (Biennale), no. 131; Florence, *P.G.*, 1949, no. 143; Amsterdam, *P.G.*, 1951, no. 174 or 175 (both "gouache, 1941"); Zurich, *P.G.*, 1951, no. 162 or 163 (both "gouache, 1941"); London, *P.G.*, 1964-65, no. 41.

REFERENCE:

[Alley], *Peggy Guggenheim Foundation*, 1968, no. 48.

Günther Uecker

Born March 1920, Mecklenburg.
Lives in Dusseldorf.

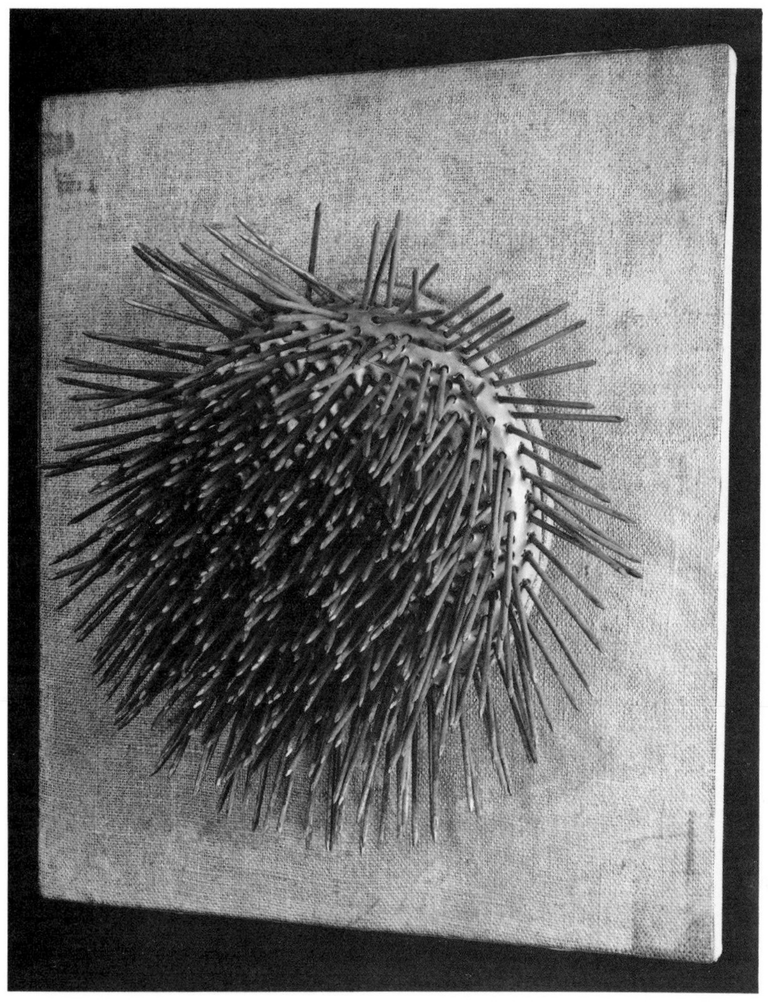

173 Taktile Struktur Rotierend. 1961.
(*Tactile rotating structure*; *Nail construction*).

76.2553 PG 229

Wood conglomerate rectangle covered with painted burlap; foam-filled aluminum; iron nails coated with stove-pipe silver paint (purpurin). Dimensions of rectangular base: 24 x 20¾ (61 x 52.7).

Signed and dated on reverse: *Uecker 61*.

PROVENANCE:

Purchased from McRoberts and Tunnard, Ltd., London, February 6, 1965.

CONDITION:

The nails have oxidized and the silver paint has darkened and flaked in many places. The burlap, also painted silver, is stained. The ball-bearing rotation wheel on which the heavy aluminum structure is mounted has deteriorated and no longer holds the piece at the original, correct angle.

Owing to the deterioration of both the structure and the surface, the artist's primary aesthetic objectives—literal mobility and mobility created through the effects of light—have been seriously compromised.

Conservation measures, to be executed in consultation with the artist, are under active consideration. (Venice, Nov. 1982.)

A member of the Group Zero, Uecker, like Heinz Mack (see above, cat. no. 101) was concerned with problems of light, reflectivity, and motion. In 1958 he discovered that metal nails could function — for his own particular purposes — as ideal carriers of light. Painted white or silver, structures composed of nails (the nails themselves fixed in place or mobile) could be made to absorb or reflect light in such a way as to exploit the aesthetic potential of motion per se.

In order to achieve his intended effects, Uecker made his 1960s nail constructions dependent upon the viewer's participation. The nails themselves (or the rotational surface on which they were mounted) were to be touched, moved, spun, or rippled in order to generate variations in the light playing on them. Uecker wrote in 1961:

> *Wenn Sie meine Arbeiten sehen, werden Sie bemerken, dass diese durch das Licht ihre Wirklichkeit erhalten. Ihre Intensität ist durch das einwirkende Licht wandelbar und vom Standpunkt des Betrachters veränderlich. Diese Objekte fordern Ihre Aktivität heraus und erhalten dadurch ihre Lebendigkeit. Diese Objekte haben eine reale räumliche Beziehung zum Betrachter, der einen Bewegungsprozess verwirklicht. Sie werden zu einem dynamischen Prinzip, das Sie teilnehmen lässt, wo das Licht in seiner Reinheit zu einer Metamorphose des Schönen wird, wo es sich zum menschlichen Theater verwandelt.*[1].

In building his structures, Uecker intentionally sought to avoid any compositional complexity, and, in fact, denied the presence of "composition" as such within the work. Only in conjunction with the surrounding space, and with the participation of the viewer, were the pieces to acquire a compositional dimension: ... "*Sie sind Kompositionen ... wenn man den Raum, in dem sie hängen oder stehen, einschliesst.... Aber in sich selbst enthält es keine Komposition.... ich schaffe keine Assoziationen innerhalb des Bildes, die man ablesen kann.... ich sehe Kompositionen doch als Widerspruch, als Zwiesprache innerhalb des Bildes. Diese Zwiesprache innerhalb des Bildes findet bei mir nicht statt. Es findet nur das Gespräch zwischen dem Betrachter statt.*"[2]

The kinetic effects sought by Uecker inevitably rely on the pristine condition and reflective surfaces of his constructions, factors that must be taken into account in any discussion of the artist's aesthetic and in the evaluation of a particular piece. (See above, CONDITION.)

EXHIBITIONS:

London, McRoberts and Tunnard Gallery, *Group Zero: Mack, Piene, Uecker*, June 23-July 18, 1964 (not in cat.);[3] Torino, *P.G.*, 1975-76, no. 206, repr. pl. 76.

REFERENCE:

Calas, 1966, repr. p. 221.

1. Günther Uecker, *Bildobjekte, 1957-1970*, exh. cat., Moderne Museet, Stockholm, 1971, n.p.
2. *Uecker Zeitung*, No. 4, 1973-74, "Selbstdarstellung," first published by the Museum Folkwang, Essen, April 1971.
3. Uecker recalls that the piece was included in the exhibition, but it corresponds with none of his 8 entries in the catalogue.

Georges Vantongerloo

Born November 1886, Antwerp.
Died October 1965, Paris.

NOTE: Vantongerloo maintained a record of his work in the form of an Oeuvre Catalogue (herein OC). This document is preserved by Max Bill, executor of the artist's estate, and the author is indebted to him for permission to consult and quote from it. The entries include the number, title, dimensions, and date, and, in some cases, the exhibitions or publications in which the work appeared and the name of the collection to which it was sold. In addition there is usually a small sketch, although this does not always correspond exactly to the finished work.

174 **Construction des rapports des volumes émanante du carré inscrit et le carré circonscrit d'un cercle.** 1924.
(Construction of volumetric interrelationships derived from the inscribed square and the square circumscribed by a circle).

OC No. 27, *Construction des rapports des volumes émanante du carré inscrit et le carré circonscrit d'un cercle.*

76.2553 PG 59

Cement cast painted white.[1] Height: 11 13/16 (30); dimensions across center at longest: 10 1/16 (25.5); at shortest: 9 7/8 (25).

Signed with monogram: *GV*. Not dated.

PROVENANCE:

Purchased from the artist, Paris, 1940.

CONDITION:

In 1968 (New York) an upper corner of the topmost element broke off while the piece was being installed. Two large pieces and several small ones were reconstituted with gesso (?) and the corner repaired.

In 1982 (Venice) a broken corner (previously repaired, and possibly the above noted) was repaired again. One other break was repaired at an unrecorded date. Four corners are presently broken. The paint, which has been reapplied several times, shows some losses. (Venice, Nov. 1982.)

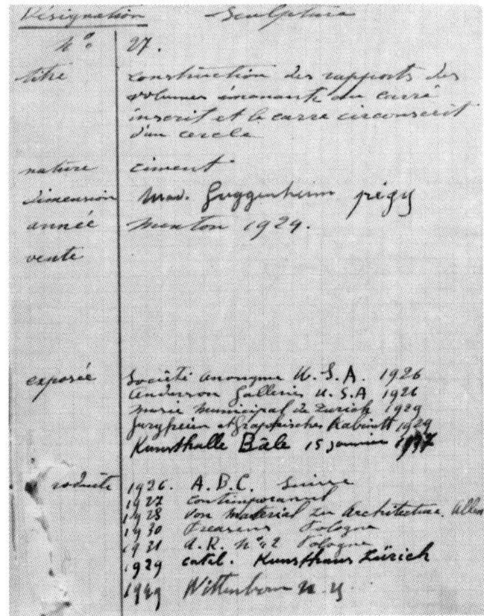
Désignation Sculpture
N° 27.
titre construction des rapports des volumes émanante du carré inscrit et le carré circonscrit d'un cercle
nature ciment
dimension Mad. Guggenheim peggy
année Menton 1924.
vente
exposé Société anonyme U.S.A. 1926
Anderson Gallery U.S.A. 1926
... Zurich 1929
... Kabinett 1929
Kunsthalle Bâle 15 janvier 1947
reproduite 1926. A.B.C. Suisse
1927 ...
1928 ... Architecture ...
1930 ...
1931 ...
1929 catal. Kunsthaus Zürich
1949 Wittenborn N.Y.

fig. a.
Page from Vantongerloo's Oeuvre Catalogue, Estate of the artist.

1. The OC lists the piece as cement; Max Bill, in correspondence with the author, January 1983, confirmed that Vantongerloo painted his cement sculptures white. The piece has been repainted several times since the artist's original coat.

View i.

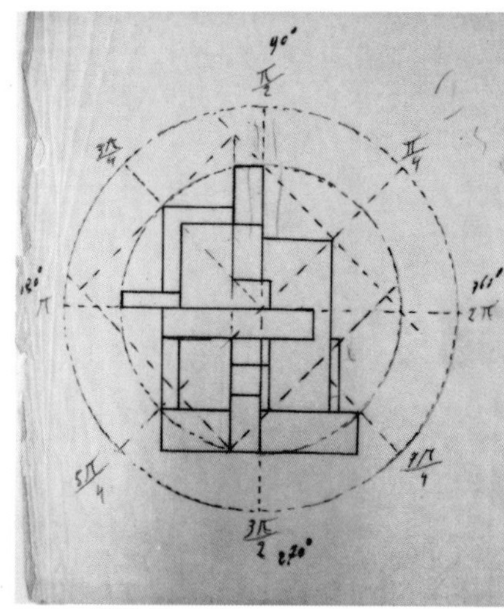

fig. b.
Diagram of View ii, showing 8 equal divisions of the circumference of the outer circle. Sketchbook page, Estate of the artist.

In his 1927 essay (see below REFERENCES), Vantongerloo indicated that the basis for his calculations in creating Peggy Guggenheim's sculpture was to be found in the system governing the construction of the pyramids. He argued that the calculations for the pyramid of Cheops were based on the composition of an inscribed square and a circumscribed square. His own aim was to create a sculpture in which the volumetric relationships were similarly derived.

The relationship of his stated argument to the actual system of proportions generally thought to have governed the construction of the pyramids is difficult to follow, and this part of his exposition remains unexplained.[2]

The diagrams preserved in the estate of the artist (figs. b-d) illuminate to some extent the basic mathematical elements that contributed to Vantongerloo's compositional process.[3]

Vantongerloo's intention was to establish a system of volumetric interrelationships derived from the inscribed square and the square circumscribed by a

2. The author is indebted to Elias M. Stein, Albert Baldwin Dod Professor of Mathematics, Princeton University, for assistance in evaluating Vantongerloo's mathematical indications and for an explanation of those elements of the artist's diagrams that are based on a knowledge of mathematics.

View ii.

View iii (opposite of view i).

circle. In fig. b (showing the narrower elevation of the construction corresponding to View ii), he placed the piece so that four of its outer limits (top, bottom, and two in the upper left quadrant) are in contact with the circumference of the inner circle. Using both a conventional mathematical system (based on the use of π) and an ancient system (based on the use of degrees), he divided the outer circle into eight equal parts according to its overall length (2π or 360°). The ratio of the radius of the inner circle to that of the outer circle is $\sqrt{2} = 1.414$. However, the relationship of this factor to the eight exterior divisions, or to the actual volumes (or planes) of the sculpture, is not indicated.

In fig. c (showing the two opposing elevations of the short sides, corresponding to Views ii and iv), four of the outer limits of the sculpture are again in contact with the circumference of the inner circle (top, bottom, and two in the upper right quadrant). Vantongerloo divided the circumference of the outer circle into a further sequence, in this case of eleven unequal sections. The relationship of these divisions to the sculpture's actual planes or volumes also remains obscure.

3. The author is indebted to Max Bill, the executor of the artist's estate, for permission to study and reproduce the drawings related to Peggy Guggenheim's sculpture.

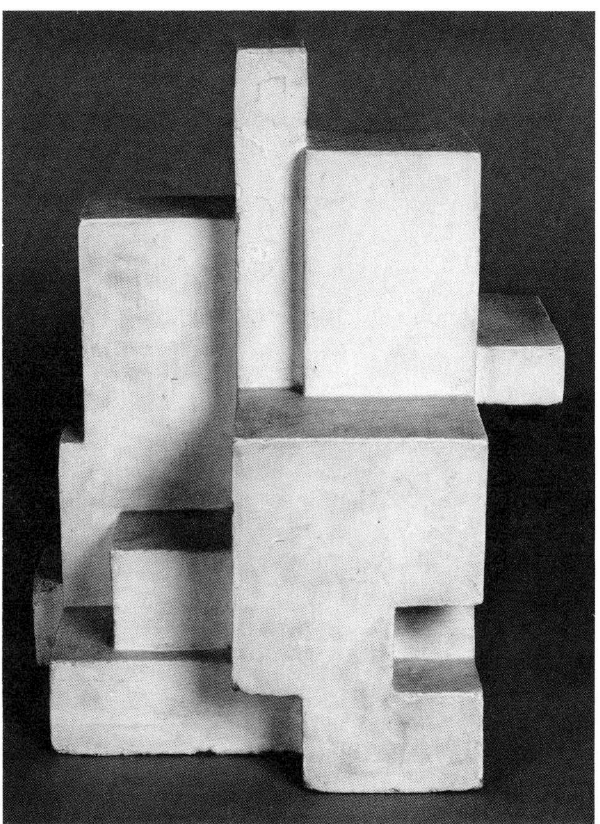

View iv (opposite of view ii).

In fig. d (showing the two opposing elevations of the longer sides, corresponding to Views i and iii), the two circles are — for the first time — brought into relationship with one another: the top and bottom edges of the construction coincide with the circumference of the inner circle; in addition, in View iii, the right bottom corner of the construction meets the circumference of the outer circle. In the opposite instance (View i), the left bottom corner coincides with this latter circumference. In these diagrams (fig. d), an explicit relationship is thus established between the sculpture and both circles. However, the role of the square, and the volumetric (as opposed to planar) implications, are left unclear.

The extensive plotting of lines across the area of the circles' two-dimensional surfaces in figs. c and d do not appear to follow any demonstrable mathematical pattern. It seems, rather, that Vantongerloo was engaged in an exploration of the implications of his basic principle: his desire to circumscribe his construction. In the final analysis, therefore, random and intuitive judgments were probably more decisive in the establishment of the construction's ultimate form and volume than were the mathematical foundations.

Vantongerloo stated in various writings of this period and later that his 1917-36 work was dependent on geometrical analysis (see, for example, A.Z.R. *Guggenheim*, Vol. II, pp. 664-66). Although the diagrams illustrated here suggest

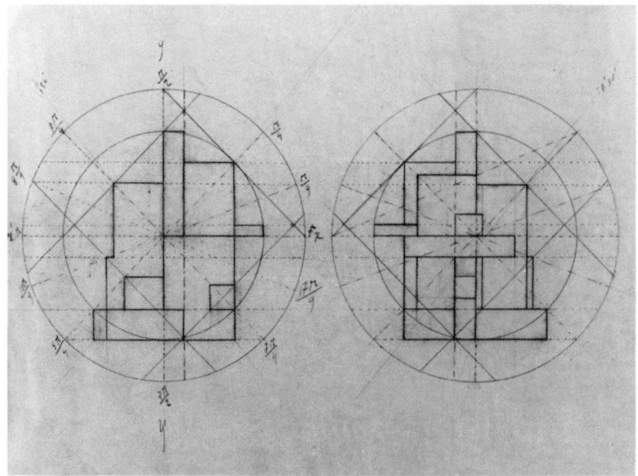

fig. c.
Diagrams of Views iv (left) and ii (right). Sketchbook page, Estate of the artist.

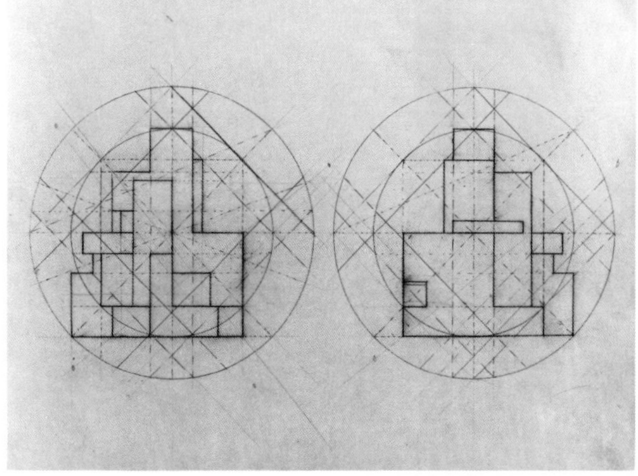

fig. d.
Diagrams of Views i (left) and iii (right). Sketchbook page, Estate of the artist.

that his basic knowledge of mathematics contributed to his calculation of a system of proportions, the precise way in which the calculation affected the fundamental aesthetic decisions remains to be fully established.

EXHIBITIONS:

New York, Société Anonyme, *International Exhibition of Modern Art*, Nov. 19, 1926-Jan. 1, 1927, no. 119 (*Composition in 3 Dimensions in Plaster*);[4] New York, Anderson Galleries, *The International Exhibition of Modern Art: Assembled by the Société Anonyme*, Jan. 25-Feb. 5, 1927, hors catalogue (information from OC, but the work is not listed in the catalogue); Zurich, Kunsthaus, *Ausstellung Abstrakte und Surrealistische Malerei und Plastik*, Oct. 6-Nov. 3, 1929, no. 145, repr. (for sale: 1500 frncs); New York, MoMA, *Cubism and Abstract Art*, 1936, p. 224, repr., p. 145; Basel, Kunsthalle, *Konstruktivisten*, Jan. 16-Feb. 14, 1937, no. 66; New York, Art of This Century, 1942-47, p. 88, repr. ("*Volume construction* plaster, 1918"; the work was so described in *P.G.* exh. cats., until Zurich, 1951); Venice, *P.G.*, 1948 (Biennale), no. 134; Florence, *P.G.*, 1949, no. 150; Amsterdam, *P.G.*, 1951, no. 185; Zurich, *P.G.*, 1951, no. 168 ("*Construction*, 1924, cement"); London, *P.G.*, 1964-65, no. 52, repr. (with full title); Stockholm, *P.G.*, 1966-67. no. 50, repr.; New York, *P.G.*, 1969, p. 66, repr.; Paris, *P.G.*, 1974-75, no. 48, repr.; Torino, *P.G.*, 1975-76, no. 57, repr. pl. 29.

REFERENCES:

Georges Vantongerloo, in *ABC* (Basel), 2nd series, no. 2, [1927], p. 4, repr. (2 views); *i 10*, vol. 1, part 3 (Amsterdam), 1927, repr. p. 96; *Contimporanul*, vol. 6, no. 72 (Bucharest), 1927, repr. p. 8 (information from OC); Allen, "Von Material zu Architektur," 1928 (information from OC, but author and article not otherwise identified); *Praesens* (Poland), 1930 (information from OC, but publication not otherwise located); K. Kobro and W. Strzeminski, "Kompozycja prze strzeni oblicze nia rytmu czaso przestrzennego," *Bibljoteki A.R.*, no. 2, Lodz, 1931, repr., fig. 27; A. H. Barr, Jr., *Cubism and Abstract Art*, New York, 1936, p. 224, repr. p. 145; G. Vantongerloo, *Paintings, Sculptures, Reflections*, New York, 1948, pp. xiv-xv, repr. fig. 8; C. Giedion-Welcker, *Contemporary Sculpture*, New York, 1955, p.145, repr.; H.L.C. Jaffe, *De Stijl*, London, 1970, p. 224, no. 31, repr. p. 34; A. Thomas-Jankowski in *Georges Vantongerloo*, exh. cat., Brussels, 1980, pp. 54-55, repr.

4. The work's appearance in this exhibition is recorded in the OC.

Victor Vasarely

Born April 1908, Pécs, Hungary.
Lives in Paris, Gordes, and Annet-sur-Marne.

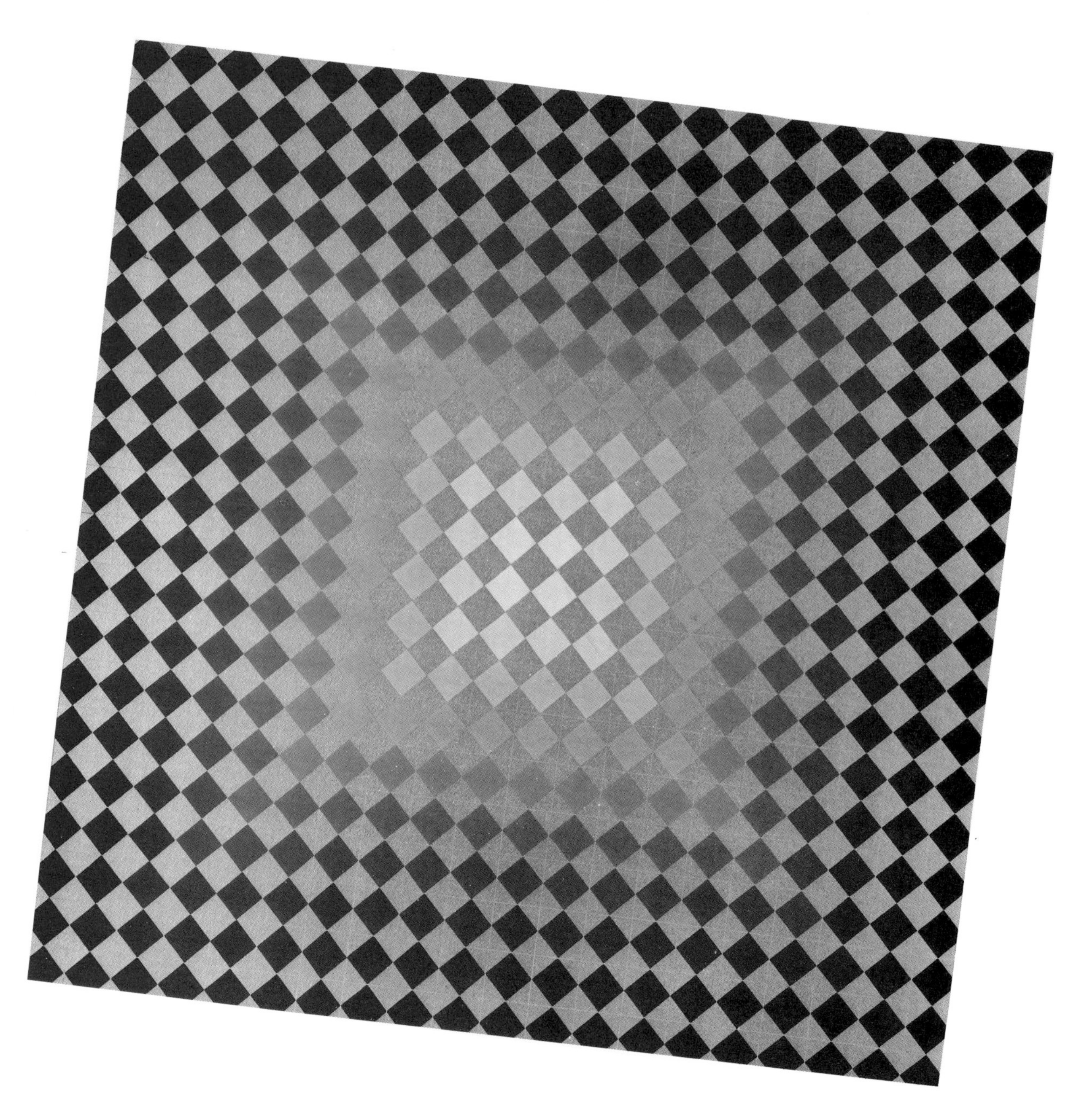

175 JAK. 1965.

76.2553 PG 223

Metallic and acrylic paints on wood panel, with red bole underpainting, 32 7/16 x 32 7/16 (82.3 x 82.3).

Numbered, titled, signed, and dated on reverse: *0586 / "JAK" / 1965 / Vasarely.*

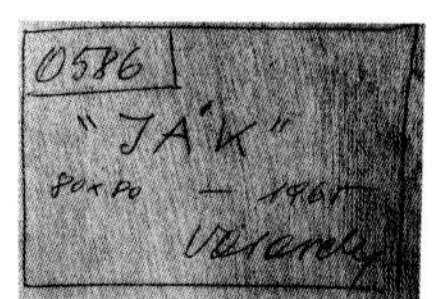

PROVENANCE:

Purchased at auction, Sotheby, London, *Twentieth Century Paintings, Drawings, and Sculptures*, a sale in support of The Institute for Contemporary Arts, June 23, 1966, lot no. 76, repr., presented by the artist.[1]

CONDITION:

The work has received no treatment. The condition is stable. (Venice, Nov. 1982.)

In 1978 a serigraph edition of the composition was made (no. 537 in the artist's inventory, edition of 125, signed and numbered), bearing the title *Yak*. The Peggy Guggenheim painting has erroneously carried the latter title since 1968. The artist's intention in titling the serigraph was apparently to suggest its close relationship to the painting while indicating the subtle differences between the two.

EXHIBITIONS:

Stockholm, *P.G.*, 1966-67, no. 145 ("Jak, gouache"); New York, *P.G.*, 1969, p. 142, repr. ("*Yak*, 1964, tempera"); Paris, *P.G.*, 1974-75, no. 142, repr. ("Yak, 1964, tempera"); Torino, *P.G.*, 1975-76, no. 204 ("*Yak*, 1964, tempera").

REFERENCE:

[Alley], *Peggy Guggenheim Foundation*, 1968, no. 221 ("*Yak*, 1964, tempera").

1. Sir Norman Reid, then Director of The Tate Gallery, bid on the work at Peggy Guggenheim's request. The Tate is thus erroneously listed as the buyer.

Emilio Vedova

Born August 1919, Venice.
Lives in Venice.

176 Immagine del tempo (Sbarramento).
1951.
(*Image of time [Barrier]*).

76.2553 PG 162

Egg tempera on canvas (unvarnished),[1]
51 3/8 x 67 1/8 (130.5 x 170.4).

Signed, dated, and inscribed on reverse:
TITOLO / IMMAGINE / DEL TEMPO /
1951—(SBARRAMENTO) / S.C. /
E. VEDOVA—1951 / VENEZIA.[2]

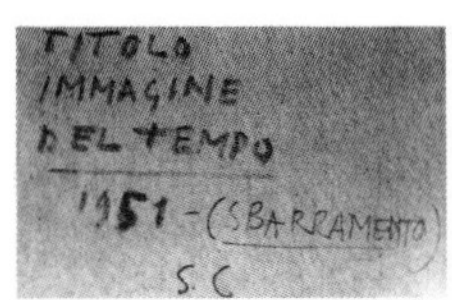

PROVENANCE:
Purchased from the artist, Venice, ca. 1952.

CONDITION:
In 1964 (Tate Report) stretcher marks on the left side and a very small loss near the lower left corner were noted. The condition remains stable. (Venice, June 1983.)

The title of the present work presents problems of interpretation that have hitherto not been addressed; the artist's intended meaning has inadvertently been lost in translation.[3]

Throughout his career, Vedova has been preoccupied with the idea of the barrier (*sbarramento*) in human experience. The implications of the word, which has complex associations for him, are invariably spiritual or intellectual rather than physical. Unlike the term "barricade"—with its inevitable political overtones of revolution, demonstration, or street fighting—Vedova uses the word with only positive connotations, implying protection from spiritual assault: "*Il significato che io dò a questa parola ha piuttosto il senso della diga di difesa contro forze che sopraffano, forze nemiche ma sopratutto in senso spirituale... forze de violenza/ingiusta, forze cattive, forze cieche: forze da cui l'uomo si difende, deve difendersi.*"

To some extent, Vedova traces his preoccupation with this concept to his participation as a very young man in the mountain Resistance during World War II, when he experienced the desperation and apparent hopelessness of warding off threatening forces of evil: "*Un senso di uomo a braccia aperte disperatamente a tenere, trattenere. Trattenere e rigettare indietro quanto le forze umane, le braccia umane, non avrebbero mai la forza.*"

fig. a.
Vedova, preparatory studies for cat. no. 176, 1950-51, ink on paper, 10 13/16 x 8 1/4 in., 27.5 x 21 cm., Collection the artist, Venice. The three sketches are inscribed: *Forze oscure*; *questo senso disperato ossessivo*; *Esprimere questo sbarramento*.

1. Vedova has over the years continued to use an egg tempera prepared in the studio, usually by his wife. The surfaces of his paintings are consistently unvarnished and the resulting matte surface an important element in his aesthetic.
2. The *S.C.* refers to Santa Cristina de Val Gardena, a village in the Alps where Vedova spent several months in a log cabin, painting in the open air. This work was completed there.
3. In response to questions from the author, Vedova supplied the information summarized here. (Letter to L. Flint, May 5, 1983, and conversation with the author, Venice, July 2, 1983.)

The emergence of these issues in the vocabulary of Vedova's nonfigurative paintings was, initially, totally unconscious. It was only later that he began to discern the pattern of meaning suggested by the elliptical titles.

In his use of the concept of time (*Immagine del tempo*), Vedova also draws upon a history of associations. He intends the reference not to be to a specific historical moment but to an abstract concept of time as the medium within which significant human predicaments exist and, indeed, recur. In using the title *Imagine del tempo* for paintings produced throughout his career, he establishes time itself as a dominant presence in the oeuvre, a continuum, in effect, that embraces all the particular images represented by individual paintings.

EXHIBITIONS:

Kassel, *Dokumenta II*, July 11-Oct. 11, 1959, p. 427, repr.; London, *P.G.*, 1964-65, no. 136, repr. ("*Image of our Time [Barricade]*"; the work has been published with this title in all subsequent publications); Stockholm, *P.G.*, 1966-67, no. 132; Torino, *P.G.*. 1975-76, no. 154.

REFERENCES:

G. Marchiori, "Vedova ieri e oggi," *Art International*, vol. 3, no. 8, 1959, repr. p. 48; [Alley], *Peggy Guggenheim Foundation*, 1968, no. 162; L. Flint, *Handbook*, 1983, no. 94, repr. color; G. Celant, *Vedova 1935-1984*, Milan, 1984, no. 68, repr. color (*Sbarramento*).

Jacques Villon

(pseud. of Gaston Duchamp).

Born July 1875, Damville (Eure), Normandy.
Died June 1963, Puteaux.

177 Espaces. 1920.
(*Spaces*).

Color plate p. 40.

76.2553 PG 23

Oil on canvas, $28\frac{3}{4}$ x $36\frac{1}{16}$ (73 x 91.6).

Signed and dated l.r.: *Jacqvues* [sic] *Villon 20*;[1] on reverse in blue: *ESPACES—1920—*; in red: *JACQUES VILLON*.
On a card attached to stretcher: *Toile de M. Villon à porter chez Mme. Guggenheim / 18 Quai d'Orleans—J.V.—*.

PROVENANCE:

Purchased from the artist, 1940, Paris. The sale was arranged by Marcel Duchamp.

1. Villon's paintings of 1920-22 were generally signed in capital letters, *J.V.* The misspelling of the name here and the nature of the handwriting suggest that the signature and date may have been added later by someone other than the artist.

CONDITION:

Drying cracks are extensive throughout. There is some incipient cleavage, but the surface in general is fairly stable.

Extensive pentimenti are visible, partly with the naked eye, partly with the aid of infra-red reflectography (see figs. i-v).

The entire surface appears to have been initially painted bright blue. The ocher brown of the upper background and the yellow areas were applied over this blue, which is still visible at the edges and in many other areas where the upper layer has lost opacity or the pigment has flaked. The red was applied over black in several, though not all, cases. In addition to the changes in color, the extensive compositional adjustments may have been made in several stages—sometime after the canvas had been initially completed. On the other hand, the presence of extensive drying cracks suggests that in some areas color was applied over earlier layers that had not completely dried.

The use of color in *Espaces* poses certain problems. According to his own testimony, Villon by 1920 had begun to use color according to the chromatic system developed by M. A. Rosenstiehl in his *Traité de la couleur*..., Paris, 1913 (for important information on this question, see D. S. Rubin in Robbins, 1976, pp. 102, 116, and Robbins, unpublished manuscript, Société Anonyme, Yale University). Robbins has suggested that the 1920-22 pictures present Villon's understanding of the fundamental color triad, the aesthetic scale, and the law of surfaces. Though he did not apply these principles with equal rigor in all the works of this period, he was concerned with the law of surfaces. Thus he strove to avoid contrary thrusts of color, which would have caused individual elements to advance or retreat and destroy the desired surface harmony. The juxtaposition of the pale brilliant blue with the lower intensity red in *Espaces* is uncharacteristic in this respect. The condition of the painting and the presence of extensive reworking could be responsible for these effects. The state of the surface and the extent of preservation of Villon's original color relationships requires further study. (Venice, June 1983.)

Jacques Villon's canvases of 1919-22, as Walter Pach wrote in his preface to the 1922 one-man exhibition catalogue, represented a new departure for the artist in that they were characterized by a high degree of abstraction and were based on "aesthetic values independent of appearances." But as Pach went on to state, these abstractions were in every case derived from a representational source. The "objects from which the original idea was drawn (the 'Springboard' as

fig. i.
Diagram of cat. no. 177, indicating areas of most extensive *pentimenti.*

fig. ii.
Infra-red reflectogram (by Studio Art System, Venice) of cat. no. 177, showing *pentimenti* in Section A.

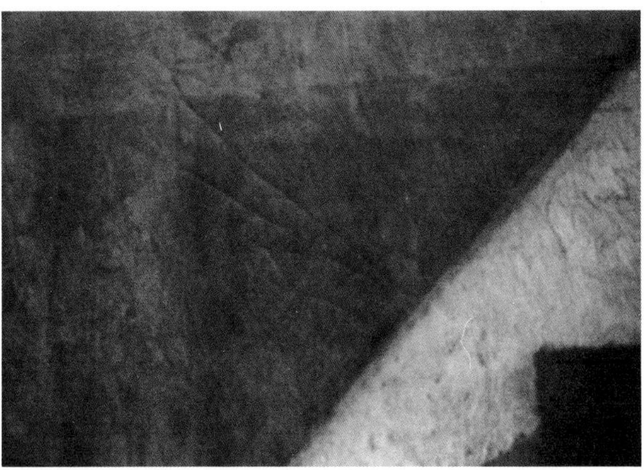

fig. iii.
Infra-red reflectogram (by Studio Art System, Venice) of cat. no. 177, showing *pentimenti* in Section B.

fig. iv.
Infra-red reflectogram (by Studio Art System, Venice) of cat. no. 177, showing *pentimenti* in Section C.

fig. v.
Infra-red reflectogram (by Studio Art System, Venice) of cat. no. 177, showing *pentimenti* in Section D.

Gleizes aptly calls them) are no longer recognizable in the finished work, though the drawings which trace the evolution of each canvas show us the relation of the start and finish of the work" (*Villon*, exh. cat., Société Anonyme, New York, 1922, p. 11). The location of the original source for the abstract imagery thus inevitably determines, to some extent, the response to the final work. Villon described his methodology in part in terms of the etymological roots of the word "*abstrait*": "*C'est à dire que cela consiste à partir d'un objet concret et d'en tirer des éléments éternels*" (quoted in S. Arbois, "Jacques Villon," *Volontés*, Dec. 27, 1944). Whether the specific source was in the external world or in an already extant work of art, Villon's notion of abstraction in these years can be defined as a progressive distillation of objective subject matter until the last traces of "light, chiaroscuro, and depth," as well as of recognizable imagery, are suppressed, but something of the essence of the original idea remains.

The most celebrated instance of this process, and the most extensively documented through surviving preparatory drawings, is the Jockey Series of 1921 (Yale University Art Gallery, Société Anonyme Collection; for a full discussion of this series, see G. H. Hamilton, "The Dialectic of Later Cubism: Villon's Jockey," *Magazine of Art*, vol. XLI, no. 7, Nov. 1948, pp. 268-73, and D. S. Rubin in Robbins, 1976, pp. 105-15). Two years earlier, in 1919, Villon had begun a series of works in which, as he later described it, he used the technique of relief maps, in which the relief is created by superimposed layers of paper or cardboard: "*Plus il y a de couches, plus il y a de relief. C'est ainsi qu'on peut indiquer les moindres dénivellations. Ces cartes m'ont donné l'idée de décomposer les objets par plans de la même façon que les volumes sont décomposés dans les cartes, chaque plan étant l'équivalent d'une couche de carton.... La Table d'échecs est typique de cette méthode*" (Y. Taillander, "Jacques Villon, de la pyramide au carré," *XXe Siècle*, May-June 1959, pp. 21-22). In *La table d'échecs* (fig. a), and the 1919 painting *Jeu* upon which it is based, the origins of the system that led to Villon's pyramidal compositions are clearly displayed. "*Ceci m'a permis d'envisager de diviser et de représenter en plans une figure, un objet, comme on évoque une montagne.... Les différents plans sont superposés et décalés, l'angle est choisi par soi-même*" (quoted in G. de Gnestet et C. Pouillon, *Jacques Villon: Les Estampes et les Illustrations: catalogue raisonné*, Paris, 1979).[2] H. Lassalle, 1975, and D. Robbins et al., 1976, have convincingly demonstrated that several works of 1920-21 follow the same system, with increasingly abstract results. In certain instances, Villon used as his "springboard" a work by his brother Duchamp-Villon. In the case of *Un Buste* (fig. b), and its subsequent evolution in the more abstract *Figure* of 1921 (Albright-Knox Art Gallery), Duchamp-Villon's *Baudelaire* of 1911 clearly served as the source (Lasalle, pp. 96-97, D. S. Rubin in Robbins, pp. 93-97). Specific studies have not been located for *Espaces*, and the precise evolution of the composition remains somewhat problematic. In view of the meticulously calculated studies that exist for the Jockey Series, however, and of Villon's description of a methodology in which every detail of preparation and structure is thought out and drawn onto the canvas in advance, it is likely that a similar series of steps

2. Villon's complete statement on the pyramid concept is as follows: "*Si on réunit tous les plans que j'ai tracés sur la toile au moyen de droites qui partent du centre approximatif de la surface, lequel est situé sur le dernier plan, et qui vont jusqu'au sommet des quatre angles de la toile, on obtient une pyramide. Cette pyramide produit également l'impression de s'avancer vers le regard, la pointe la première, ou de creuser un vide sous lui, la pointe de la pyramide étant au fond du vide. Cette propriété qu'ont les pyramides, quand on les voit d'en haut, de produire deux impressions contradictoires, confère à l'image un mouvement qui est un frémissement, un mouvement sur place, et dont il ne semble pas qu'il y ait de raison qu'il cesse. C'est un* 'perpetuum mobile' " (quoted in Pierre Courthion, "Décomposition et recomposition de l'Espace," *XXe Siècle*, Jan. 1952, p. 29). The use of stacked planes may possibly also owe something to the example of Duchamp's *Tu'M* of 1918 (Société Anonyme Collection, Yale University), where a line of overlapping diamonds arranged as color samples runs across the top of the composition. (This connection has also been pointed out by A. Martin in Robbins, 1976, p.89.)

fig. a.
Villon, *La table d'échecs,* 1920, etching, 8 x 6⅜ in., 20.3 x 15.8 cm., Yale University Art Gallery, The Ernest Steefel Collection of Graphic Art.

fig. b.
Villon, *Un Buste,* 1920, oil on canvas, 31⅞ x 23⅝ in., 81 x 60 cm., Collection Mr. and Mrs. Samuel H. Maslon, Minneapolis.

preceded the Peggy Guggenheim painting. (For Villon's methodological statement, see D. Vallier, *Jacques Villon,* Paris, 1957, p. 114.)

Though these steps are lacking in the present instance, the existence of later prints by the artist, surely themselves based on earlier drawings, offer thematic and structural clues. *Les Lampes* (fig. c) depicts two clearly legible lamps (or possibly globes) in a preliminary stage of "*décomposition constructive*" and suggests a plausible subject for the more highly abstracted cascading planes of Peggy Guggenheim's picture. While these lamps (globes) present the closest analogy and the most likely central source for *Espaces*, echoes of the exactly contemporary distillations of *Baudelaire* suggest an additional possible ingredient in Villon's thinking. (For a discussion of the globe as a perennial subject throughout Villon's career, see D. S. Rubin in Robbins, 1976, pp. 161-62.)

In 1921 Villon developed the composition even further, uniting the two planar groupings into one and arriving at a degree of abstraction that closely approximated Pach's notion of a work in which the "springboard" is no longer recognizable (*Figure par plans*, india ink, 10 x 6⅞ in., 25.5 x 17.5 cm., Galerie Louis Carré, Paris, repr. Robbins, 1976, no. 99). Villon's continued exploration of the image of *Espaces* into the 1950s, using both different color schemes and new titles, is characteristic of his later career when he produced innumerable reworkings of important earlier compositional ideas. (See fig. d and *Livres et mappemondes*, 1959, color lithograph, 6⅛ x 8$\frac{9}{16}$ in., 15.4 x 21.8 cm., repr. Gnestet et Pouillon, op. cit., p. 447, App. 104.)

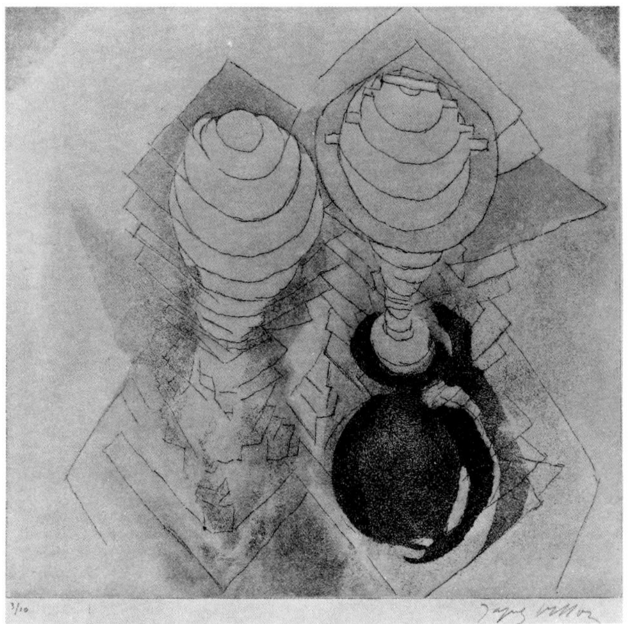

fig. c.
Villon, *Les Lampes*, 1951, etching and aquatint, 9⅝ x 10¾ in., 24.5 x 27.3 cm., The Museum of Modern Art, New York.

fig. d.
Villon, *L'Univers*, 1951, etching and aquatint, 7¼ x 6⅞ in., 18.3 x 17.4 cm. Photograph courtesy Sagot-Le Garrec, Paris.

EXHIBITIONS:

New York, Société Anonyme, *Jacques Villon,* Dec. 16, 1922-Jan. 10, 1923?;[3] New York, Art of This Century, 1942-47, repr. p. 78; Venice, *P.G.*, 1948 (Biennale), no. 135; Florence, *P.G.*, 1949, no. 151; Amsterdam, *P.G.*, 1951, no. 148, repr. n.p.; Zurich, *P.G.*, 1951, no. 169; London, *P.G.*, 1964-65, no. 16, repr. p. 24; Stockholm, *P.G.*, 1966-67, no. 16, repr. p. 18; New York, *P.G.*, 1969, repr. color p. 29; Paris, *P.G.*, 1974-75, no. 16, repr. color n.p.; Torino, *P.G.*, 1975-76, no. 22, repr. pl. 13.

REFERENCES:

P. Guggenheim, *Art of This Century*, 1942, repr. p. 78; Calas, 1966, p. 23, repr. p. 40; H. Lassalle, in O. Popovitch, ed., *Jacques Villon*, exh. cat., Musée des Beaux-Arts, Rouen, 1975, pp. 92, 98, 104; D. S. Rubin, in D. Robbins, ed., *Jacques Villon*, exh. cat., Fogg Art Museum, Cambridge, 1976, pp. 116, 134, repr. p. 117.

3. The Société Anonyme ledger for this exhibition, which lists 16 untitled oils, includes 3 of approximately the correct dimensions (nos. 7, 14, 18). A review of the exhibition published in the *New York Sunday World* (Dec. 24, 1922, Société Anonyme scrapbook, Yale University) stated that "the present selection from his work during the past two years consists of a series of sixteen experimental studies of color perspective and spacing in flat tinted planes of irregular shape but arrangement at various angles." Daniel Robbins has made a detailed analysis of the reviews and of Villon's work of the period in an attempt to reconstruct the contents of the exhibition (unpublished manuscript, Société Anonyme, Yale University). His researches revealed, among other things, that several of the 1920-22 abstract paintings of kaleidoscopically treated flat colored planes received their more descriptive titles only after World War II. It is possible, though not firmly established, that *Espaces* was among this group. The author is indebted to Robbins and to the Beineke Library, Yale University, for making these materials available.

APPENDIX

APPENDIX[1]
GUGGENHEIM JEUNE

Peggy Guggenheim opened her first art gallery—Guggenheim Jeune—at 30 Cork Street, London, W.1, in January 1938. Marcel Duchamp, whom she had met through Mary Reynolds in Paris in the mid-1920s and who remained a close friend, was initially her principal adviser.[2] ("*...he taught me the difference between Surrealism, Cubism and abstract art. Then he introduced me to all the artists. They all adored him and I was well received wherever I went. He planned shows for me and gave me all his best advice.*" *Confessions*, 1960, p. 47.)

Wyn Henderson, a professional typographer, became secretary and assistant to Peggy Guggenheim and designer of all the gallery's publications.

Peggy Guggenheim, Paris, ca. 1924. (Dress by Paul Poiret, headdress by Vera Stravinsky.) Photograph by Man Ray, 19⅛ x 13 in., 48.5 x 33.1 cm. National Portrait Gallery, Smithsonian Institution, Washington, D.C.

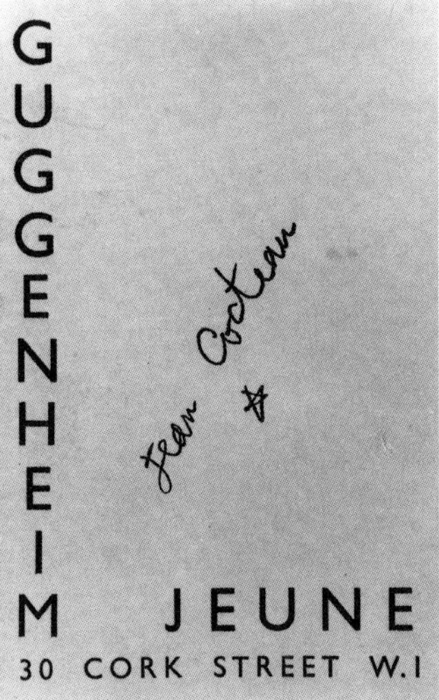

Catalogue cover.

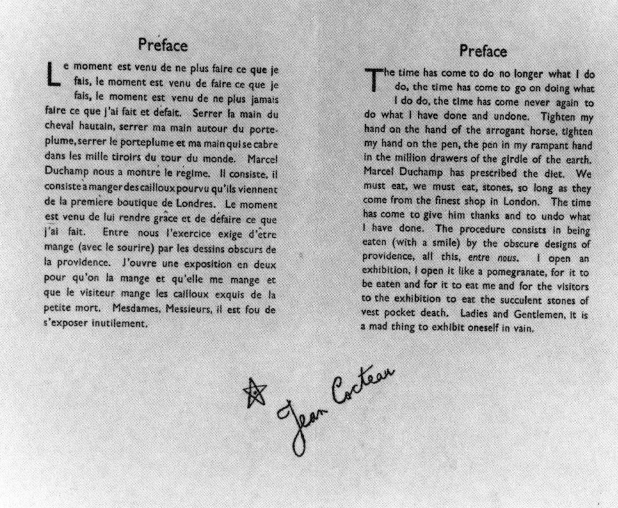

Preface

Le moment est venu de ne plus faire ce que je fais, le moment est venu de faire ce que je fais, le moment est venu de ne plus jamais faire ce que j'ai fait et défait. Serrer la main du cheval hautain, serrer ma main autour du porte-plume, serrer le porteplume et ma main qui se cabre dans les mille tiroirs du tour du monde. Marcel Duchamp nous a montré le régime. Il consiste, il consiste à manger des cailloux pourvu qu'ils viennent de la première boutique de Londres. Le moment est venu de lui rendre grâce et de défaire ce que j'ai fait. Entre nous l'exercice exige d'être mangé (avec le sourire) par les dessins obscurs de la providence. J'ouvre une exposition en deux pour qu'on la mange et qu'elle me mange et que le visiteur mange les cailloux exquis de la petite mort. Mesdames, Messieurs, il est fou de s'exposer inutilement.

Preface

The time has come to do no longer what I do do, the time has come to go on doing what I do do, the time has come never again to do what I have done and undone. Tighten my hand on the hand of the arrogant horse, tighten my hand on the pen, the pen in my rampant hand in the million drawers of the girdle of the earth. Marcel Duchamp has prescribed the diet. We must eat, we must eat, stones, so long as they come from the finest shop in London. The time has come to give him thanks and to undo what I have done. The procedure consists in being eaten (with a smile) by the obscure designs of providence, all this, *entre nous*. I open an exhibition, I open it like a pomegranate, for it to be eaten and for it to eat me and for the visitors to the exhibition to eat the succulent stones of vest pocket death. Ladies and Gentlemen, it is a mad thing to exhibit oneself in vain.

Jean Cocteau

Interior of fold-out.

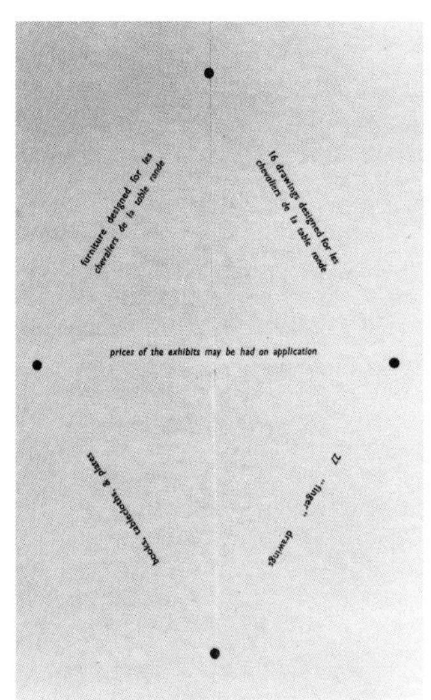

Exhibition of Drawings, also Furniture, designed for "Les Chevaliers de la Table Ronde" by Jean Cocteau. January 24-February 12, 1938.

Catalogue preface by Jean Cocteau, translated from the French by Samuel Beckett. Exhibition proposed and installed by Marcel Duchamp, who was a close friend of Cocteau.

guggenheim jeune
have the pleasure of inviting you
to an exhibition of drawings •
• also furniture designed for
les chevaliers de la table ronde •
by
jean cocteau
january 24th to february 12th—10 to 6
30, cork st., burlington gardens, bond st., w. 1.

Announcement.

1. The information published in this appendix derives, unless otherwise indicated, from Peggy Guggenheim's published memoirs, from the extensive scrapbooks she maintained from 1938 onward, and from conversations between Peggy Guggenheim and the author. (See Introduction, pp. 17-18.) The exhibitions at Guggenheim Jeune and Art of This Century were in most cases widely reviewed. The reviews were regularly sent to Peggy Guggenheim by clipping services, preserved by her in scrapbooks, and, during her lifetime, microfilmed almost in their entirety by the Archives of American Art. Occasional citations included here have been selected from the reviews to suggest the reception to an artist's work at the start of his/her career or when it was shown to a new public, or to indicate something of the press response to the activities of Peggy Guggenheim herself.

2. Peggy Guggenheim lived in Paris during the 1920s and was married there to Laurence Vail in March 1922. In addition to Duchamp, she came to know artists, writers, and collectors such as Brancusi, Kay Boyle, Jean Cocteau, Malcolm Cowley, Nancy Cunard, Janet Flanner, Ernest Hemingway, James Joyce, Ezra Pound, Man Ray, Tristan Tzara, and Virgil Thomson. After her divorce in 1928, she continued to live in Paris for about three years with John Holms; she then moved to England with Douglas Garman, remaining with him until sometime in 1936. It was after the termination of this relationship that she decided to open an art gallery and she turned to her old friend Duchamp for advice and help.

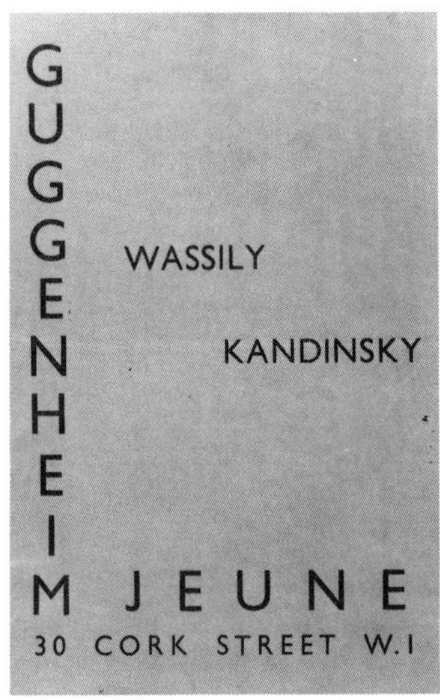

GUGGENHEIM JEUNE

WASSILY KANDINSKY

30 CORK STREET W.1

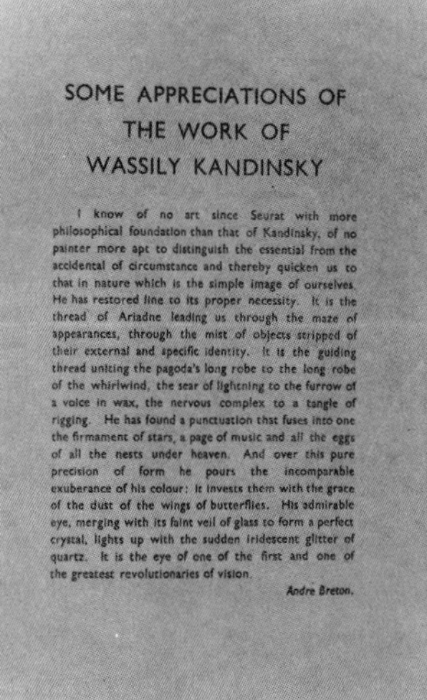

SOME APPRECIATIONS OF THE WORK OF WASSILY KANDINSKY

I know of no art since Seurat with more philosophical foundation than that of Kandinsky, of no painter more apt to distinguish the essential from the accidental of circumstance and thereby quicken us to that in nature which is the simple image of ourselves. He has restored line to its proper necessity. It is the thread of Ariadne leading us through the maze of appearances, through the mist of objects stripped of their external and specific identity. It is the guiding thread uniting the pagoda's long robe to the long robe of the whirlwind, the sear of lightning to the furrow of a voice in wax, the nervous complex to a tangle of rigging. He has found a punctuation that fuses into one the firmament of stars, a page of music and all the eggs of all the nests under heaven. And over this pure precision of form he pours the incomparable exuberance of his colour: it invests them with the grace of the dust of the wings of butterflies. His admirable eye, merging with its faint veil of glass to form a perfect crystal, lights up with the sudden iridescent glitter of quartz. It is the eye of one of the first and one of the greatest revolutionaries of vision.

Andre Breton.

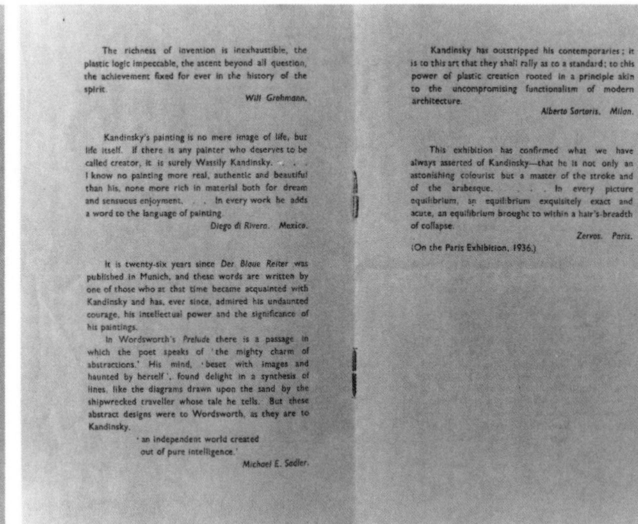

The richness of invention is inexhaustible, the plastic logic impeccable, the ascent beyond all question, the achievement fixed for ever in the history of the spirit.

Will Grohmann.

Kandinsky's painting is no mere image of life, but life itself. If there is any painter who deserves to be called creator, it is surely Wassily Kandinsky. . . . I know no painting more real, authentic and beautiful than his, none more rich in material both for dream and sensuous enjoyment. . . . In every work he adds a word to the language of painting.

Diego di Rivera. Mexico.

It is twenty-six years since *Der Blaue Reiter* was published in Munich, and these words are written by one of those who at that time became acquainted with Kandinsky and has, ever since, admired his undaunted courage, his intellectual power and the significance of his paintings.

In Wordsworth's *Prelude* there is a passage in which the poet speaks of 'the mighty charm of abstractions.' His mind, 'beset with images and haunted by herself', found delight in a synthesis of lines, like the diagrams drawn upon the sand by the shipwrecked traveller whose tale he tells. But these abstract designs were to Wordsworth, as they are to Kandinsky,

'an independent world created
out of pure intelligence.'

Michael E. Sadler.

Kandinsky has outstripped his contemporaries; it is to this art that they shall rally as to a standard; to this power of plastic creation rooted in a principle akin to the uncompromising functionalism of modern architecture.

Alberto Sartoris. Milan.

This exhibition has confirmed what we have always asserted of Kandinsky—that he is not only an astonishing colourist but a master of the stroke and of the arabesque. . . . In every picture equilibrium, an equilibrium exquisitely exact and acute, an equilibrium brought to within a hair's-breadth of collapse.

Zervos. Paris.

(On the Paris Exhibition, 1936.)

Catalogue cover.

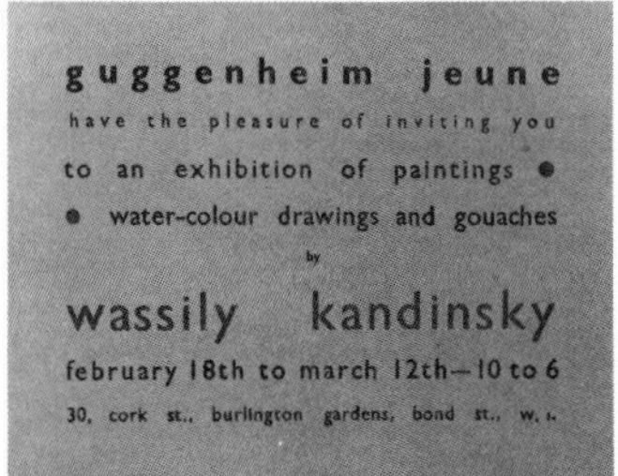

guggenheim jeune
have the pleasure of inviting you
to an exhibition of paintings •
• water-colour drawings and gouaches
by
wassily kandinsky
february 18th to march 12th—10 to 6
30, cork st., burlington gardens, bond st., w. 1.

Announcement.

Exhibition of Paintings, Water-colour Drawings and Gouaches by Wassily Kandinsky. February 18-March 12, 1938.

Catalogue statements by André Breton, Will Grohmann, Diego di Rivera, Michael E. Sadler, Alberto Sartoris, Christian Zervos. Kandinsky's first one-man exhibition in England, proposed by Marcel Duchamp. Kandinsky made the selection and planned the installation, using a scale model of the space. Nothing was sold; Peggy Guggenheim purchased a single work, *Courbe dominante*, which she sold to Karl Nierendorf in New York during World War II. (A friend had persuaded her that the picture was Fascist.) She subsequently greatly regretted the sale; the picture was purchased by Solomon Guggenheim in 1945 and is in the collection of the SRGM.

Review: [unsigned], *The Listener*, 2 March, 1938: "... *Though for the past thirty years one of the foremost leaders of the modern movement, this is the first time that his work has been shown adequately in this country.... In the paintings of 1909 and 1910 we can still find traces of naturalistic subject-matter, but from 1911 onwards Kandinsky has been uncompromisingly abstract, or as he prefers to say, concrete. Whichever word we use—and 'abstract' has perhaps become too firmly established in our critical vocabulary to be discarded—the aim of this kind of art is not in doubt. It involves a complete abandonment of the old relationship between art and the world of nature. The artist relies entirely on his medium, which is colour in some plastic condition (usually oil paint) and with this medium he composes exactly as the musician composes with sound. This musical analogy can be pursued into endless detail, but only a very general comparison is legitimate. An element of composition is, of course, present in traditional representational painting; but Kandinsky has had the courage to isolate it, and to create a pure painting which is directed to our immediate sensations of form and colour.*

"... *There are several... tributes printed in the catalogue, but none is so significant as that which comes from Diego di Rivera, the Mexican artist who is so dear to those young realists who are in full reaction from all forms of abstract art. 'I know of no painting more real, authentic and beautiful than his, none more rich in material both for dream and sensuous enjoyment.' Obviously this is not an exhibition which can be ignored on any plea.*"

CATALOGUE

All the exhibits are for sale and prices may be had on application.

1	" Grilles, et autres "	1937
2	" Environnement "	1936
3	" Deux, etc. "	1937
4	" Pointes noires "	1937
5	" Courbe dominante "	1936
6	" Raye "	1934
7	" Figure verte "	1936
8	" Le noeud rouge "	1936
9	" Succession "	1935
10	" Entre deux "	1934
11	" Tension claire "	1937
12	" Trente "	1937
13	" L'emotion tranquille "	1923
14	" Accompagnement noir "	1924
15	" Tache rouge No. 2 "	1921
16	" Developpement en brun "	1933
17	" La croix bleue "	1926
18	" Signe "	1925
19	" Huit fois "	1929
20	" Volant "	1936
21	" Contrastes "	1937
22	" La durete molle "	1927
23	" Accent en rose "	1926
24	" Lumineux-tranquille "	1929
25	" Quelques pointes "	1925
26	" Sur pointes "	1928
27	" Deux formes en bleu "	1927
28	" Plaisanterie serieuse "	1930
29	" Stabilite "	1931
30	" Un cercle (a) "	1928
31	" Librement accentue "	1930
32	" L'equilibre en rose "	1933
33	" Deux traits noirs "	1930
34	" Attouchement "	1928
35	" Aquarelle mouvementee "	1923
36	" Sur la Plage "	1909
37	" Tache rouge No. 1 "	1914
38	" Improvisation No. 14 "	1910

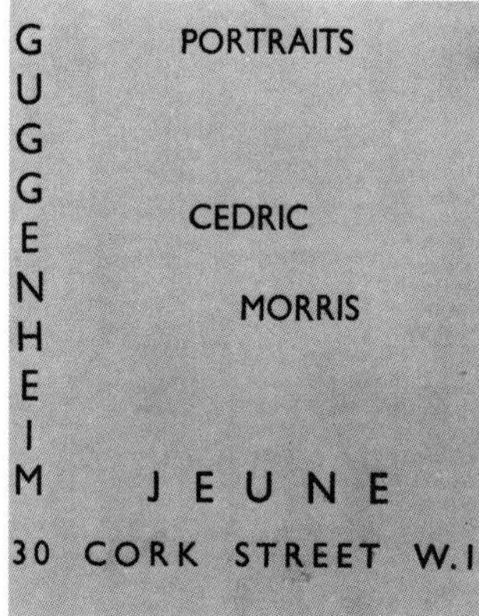

GUGGENHEIM
PORTRAITS
CEDRIC
MORRIS
JEUNE
30 CORK STREET W.1

Catalogue cover.

CATALOGUE

Prices of exhibits may be had on application.

1	Audrey Debenham	1936
2	Helen Lubbock (Lent by Helen Lubbock)	1934
3	Tania Grigorieva	1938
4	Marlene Meyer	1936
5	Vero Pieris	1938
6	Ina Douglas	1937
7	Mother and Child	1919
8	Frances Hodgkins	1928
9	Daphne Bousfield	1937
10	Morwenna Skeaping (Lent by John Skeaping)	1930
11	Mrs. Gorer	1936
12	Achmet Abdulla	1922
13	Barbara Hepworth	1931
14	Frank Daubigny	1924
15	Margaret O'Flaherty	1936
16	Paul Cross	1925
17	Angus Davidson	1927
18	Ian Brinkworth	1933
19	Roma Milla	1935
20	Joe Hopkins	1938
21	Anne Marie Schleger	1935
22	Roma Milla	1936
23	Madame la Concierge	1922
24	Loraine Conran	1933
25	Ralph Banbury	1936
26	Frances Byng Stamper	1935
27	Mary Jewel	1920
28	Scott Macgregor	1937
29	Captain J. R. J. Macnamara, M.P.	1932
30	John Banting	1923
31	Miss Thorpe	1920
32	Denise Broadley	1937
33	Hilaire Hiler	1922
34	Eve Picton-Turbervill	1935
35	Miss Thomas	1936
36	Blossom Hellyer (Lent by Dorothy Hellyer)	1937
37	Elizabeth Addison	1937
38	Rosemary Mavor	1936
39	Kydrich Rhys	1937
40	The late Mary Butts	1924
41	Louise Crowther	1925
42	Frances Byng Stamper & Caroline Byng Lucas	1935
43	Anthony Butts	1937
44	Rupert Doone	1925
45	Milly Gomersall	1936
46	Loraine Conran	1932
47	Rosamond Lehmann	1932
48	Anna Wickham	1922
49	Cecilia Mather-Jackson	1935
50	Brocas Harris	1937

Exhibition of Portraits by Cedric Morris.
March 18-April 7, 1938.
Morris was a friend of Mary Reynolds, who introduced him to Peggy Guggenheim; the exhibition was proposed either by Reynolds or by Duchamp.

GUGGENHEIM JEUNE

have the pleasure of inviting you to an exhibition of* PORTRAITS *by

CEDRIC MORRIS

Private View, March 17th

March 18th to April 7th—10 to 6

30 Cork Street, Bond St., W. 1

Announcement.

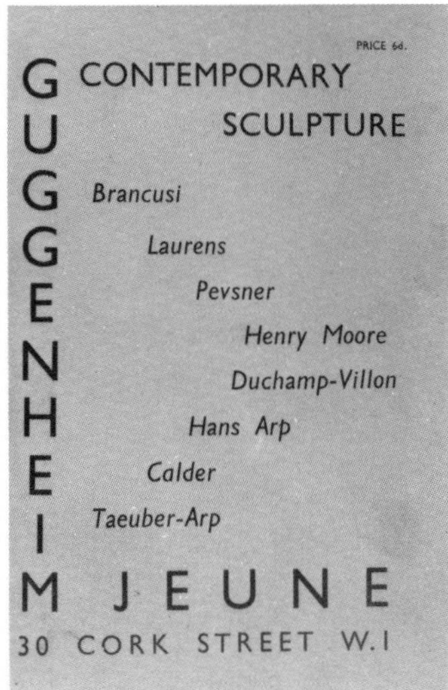

PRICE 6d.

GUGGENHEIM JEUNE

CONTEMPORARY SCULPTURE

Brancusi
Laurens
Pevsner
Henry Moore
Duchamp-Villon
Hans Arp
Calder
Taeuber-Arp

30 CORK STREET W.1

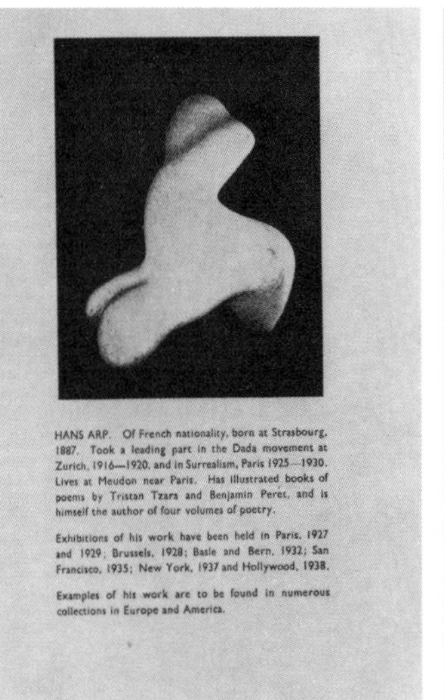

HANS ARP. Of French nationality, born at Strasbourg, 1887. Took a leading part in the Dada movement at Zurich, 1916—1920, and in Surrealism, Paris 1925—1930. Lives at Meudon near Paris. Has illustrated books of poems by Tristan Tzara and Benjamin Peret, and is himself the author of four volumes of poetry.

Exhibitions of his work have been held in Paris, 1927 and 1929; Brussels, 1928; Basle and Bern, 1932; San Francisco, 1935; New York, 1937 and Hollywood, 1938.

Examples of his work are to be found in numerous collections in Europe and America.

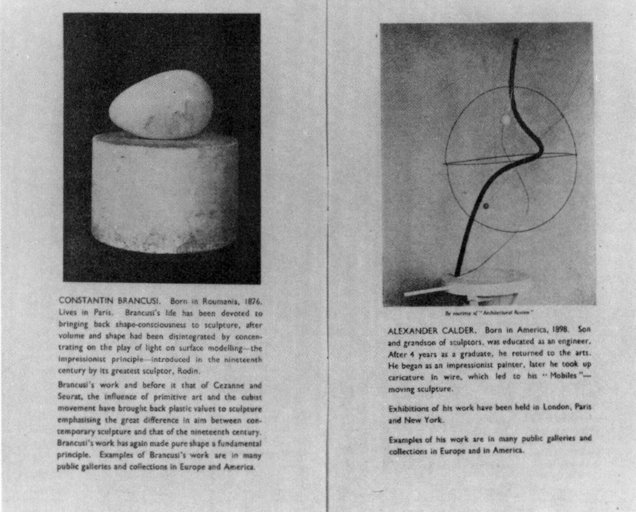

CONSTANTIN BRANCUSI. Born in Roumania, 1876. Lives in Paris. Brancusi's life has been devoted to bringing back shape-consciousness to sculpture, after volume and shape had been disintegrated by concentrating on the play of light on surface modelling—the impressionist principle—introduced in the nineteenth century by its greatest sculptor, Rodin.

Brancusi's work and before it that of Cezanne and Seurat, the influence of primitive art and the cubist movement have brought back plastic values to sculpture emphasising the great difference in aim between contemporary sculpture and that of the nineteenth century. Brancusi's work has again made pure shape a fundamental principle. Examples of Brancusi's work are in many public galleries and collections in Europe and America.

By courtesy of "Architectural Review"

ALEXANDER CALDER. Born in America, 1898. Son and grandson of sculptors, was educated as an engineer. After 4 years as a graduate, he returned to the arts. He began as an impressionist painter, later he took up caricature in wire, which led to his "Mobiles"—moving sculpture.

Exhibitions of his work have been held in London, Paris and New York.

Examples of his work are in many public galleries and collections in Europe and in America.

Catalogue cover.

Exhibition of Contemporary Sculpture. April 8-May 2, 1938.
Catalogue with unsigned text on each artist. Exhibition proposed and selected by Marcel Duchamp; Jean Arp participated in the selection.

Many of the works were shipped from France, but were initially denied access to Great Britain without the payment of a customs fee. On the basis of provisions included in the Import Duties Act and its amendments, all imported manufactured goods were subject to substantial *ad valorem* duty unless specifically certified by the director of the Tate Gallery as works of art. In the case of the sculptures for the Guggenheim Jeune exhibition, the necessary certificates were denied by the director, James B. Manson. Artists, critics, and members of the public, of the press, and of the House of Commons voiced strong objections, and the Manson decision was ultimately reversed.

Letter to *The Daily Telegraph* from the director, H. S. Williamson, and faculty members Robert Medley, Raymond Coxon, Graham Sutherland, Henry Moore of the Chelsea Polytechnic, 22 March, 1938: "*Sir— The report in your paper that under the new Customs regulations the works by the sculptors Brancusi, Duchamp-Villon, Pefsner* [sic] *and Taeuber-Arp have been refused admission to this country as works of art comes as a shock to all artists and art-lovers. It is impossible to regard without cynicism the suggestion that the works of art of these artists were designed to prop up a building, to be converted into sundials or into advertisement stands for a new brand of cigarette. The sculpture of at least one of these artists has been familiar to all serious artists and students in this country for at least 20 years. The question of whether the works are good or bad art cannot, and in the interests of liberty must not, be the issue. Are the new regulations ill-defined and at fault in placing upon one man the responsibility of making the necessary decisions, or is Mr. J. B. Manson ignorant of the international reputations of these artists?*"

Letter to *The Daily Telegraph* from St. John Hutchinson, K.C., 22 March, 1938: "*Sir—To all those interested in art the announcement ...that on the word of Mr. J. B. Manson works of art can be forbidden entry into this country is of the greatest importance.... It may be difficult to tell the difference between works of art and commercial masonry, but it would be fatal if a censorship of this kind were set up and that serious, or even ridiculous, works of art could be excluded from entry. The issue, of course, is not affected by the mere fact that Brancusi is acknowledged throughout Europe to be a serious artist. Let us avoid dictators even if the dictator of taste is the Director of the Tate Gallery.*"

A number of the letters to the newspapers made reference, explicit or implicit, to Hitler's banning of "degenerate art," which was at its height in March 1938. The *Entartete Kunst* auctions were to take place not long afterward.

Letter to *The Daily Telegraph*, 23 March, 1938, from Norman Demuth, Royal Academy of Music: "*Sir — The recent action of forbidding free entrance to this country of certain works of art causes no little anxiety. It is not for the Director of the Tate Gallery or any other individual to decide ex cathedra what is or is not a work of art, nor should such powers be granted.... significant of a danger*

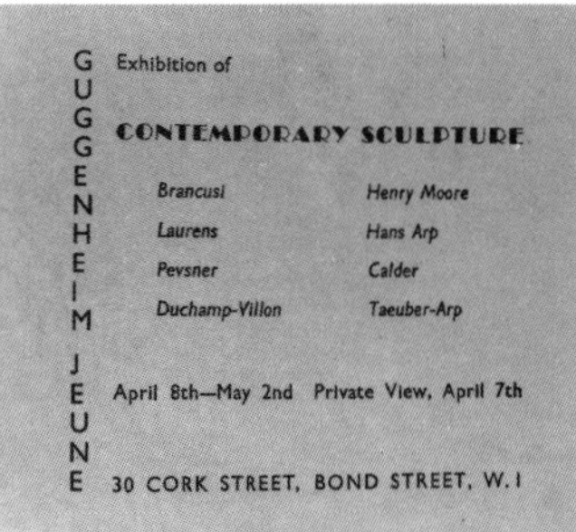

GUGGENHEIM JEUNE

Exhibition of

CONTEMPORARY SCULPTURE

Brancusi	Henry Moore
Laurens	Hans Arp
Pevsner	Calder
Duchamp-Villon	Taeuber-Arp

April 8th—May 2nd Private View, April 7th

30 CORK STREET, BOND STREET, W.1

Announcement.

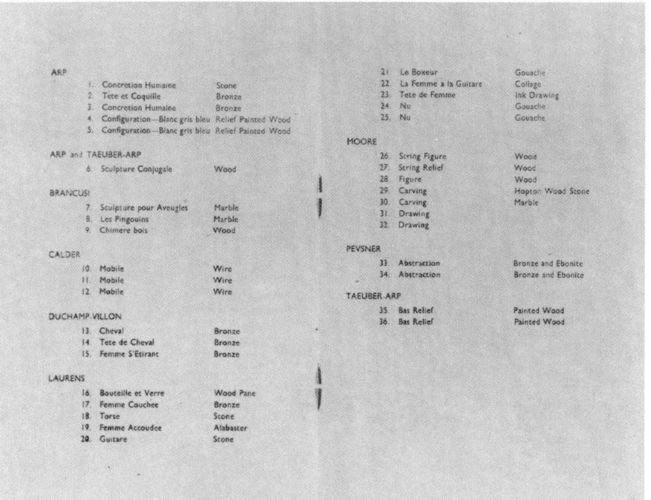

ARP

1.	Concretion Humaine	Stone
2.	Tete et Coquille	Bronze
3.	Concretion Humaine	Bronze
4.	Configuration—Blanc gris bleu	Relief Painted Wood
5.	Configuration—Blanc gris bleu	Relief Painted Wood

ARP and TAEUBER-ARP

6.	Sculpture Conjugale	Wood

BRANCUSI

7.	Sculpture pour Aveugles	Marble
8.	Les Pingouins	Marble
9.	Chimere bois	Wood

CALDER

10.	Mobile	Wire
11.	Mobile	Wire
12.	Mobile	Wire

DUCHAMP-VILLON

13.	Cheval	Bronze
14.	Tete de Cheval	Bronze
15.	Femme S'Etirant	Bronze

LAURENS

16.	Bouteille et Verre	Wood Pane
17.	Femme Couchee	Bronze
18.	Torse	Stone
19.	Femme Accoudee	Alabaster
20.	Guitare	Stone
21.	Le Boxeur	Gouache
22.	La Femme a la Guitare	Collage
23.	Tete de Femme	Ink Drawing
24.	Nu	Gouache
25.	Nu	Gouache

MOORE

26.	String Figure	Wood
27.	String Relief	Wood
28.	Figure	Wood
29.	Carving	Hopton Wood Stone
30.	Carving	Marble
31.	Drawing	
32.	Drawing	

PEVSNER

33.	Abstraction	Bronze and Ebonite
34.	Abstraction	Bronze and Ebonite

TAEUBER-ARP

35.	Bas Relief	Painted Wood
36.	Bas Relief	Painted Wood

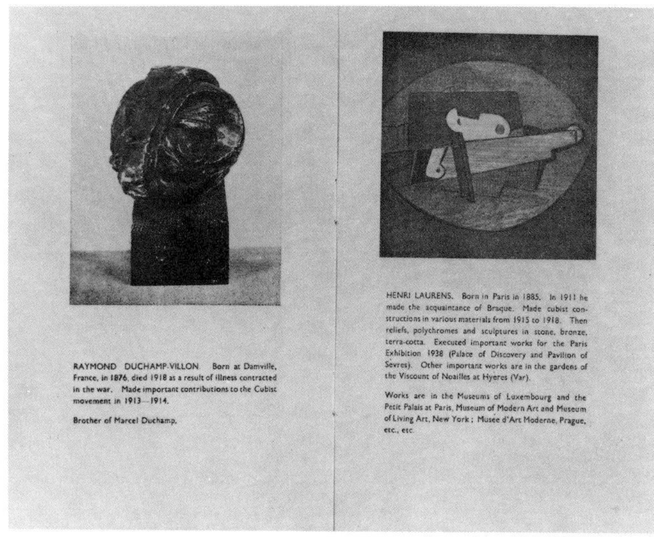

RAYMOND DUCHAMP-VILLON. Born at Damville, France, in 1876, died 1918 as a result of illness contracted in the war. Made important contributions to the Cubist movement in 1913—1914.

Brother of Marcel Duchamp.

HENRI LAURENS. Born in Paris in 1885. In 1911 he made the acquaintance of Braque. Made cubist constructions in various materials from 1915 to 1918. Then reliefs, polychromes and sculptures in stone, bronze, terra-cotta. Executed important works for the Paris Exhibition 1938 (Palace of Discovery and Pavilion of Sevres). Other important works are in the gardens of the Viscount of Noailles at Hyeres (Var).

Works are in the Museums of Luxembourg and the Petit Palais at Paris, Museum of Modern Art and Museum of Living Art, New York; Musée d'Art Moderne, Prague, etc., etc.

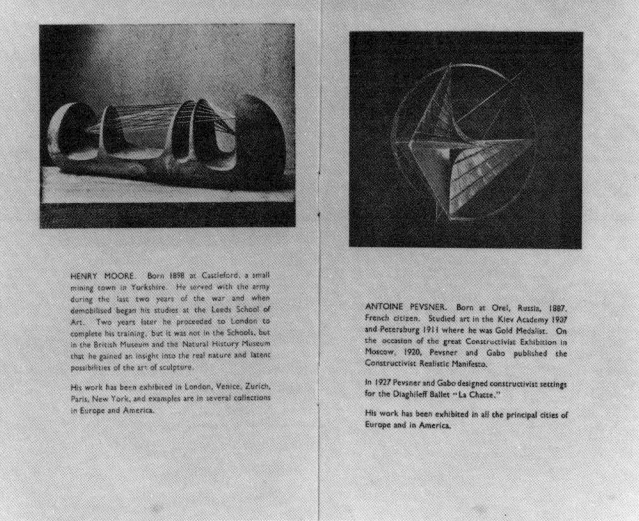

HENRY MOORE. Born 1898 at Castleford, a small mining town in Yorkshire. He served with the army during the last two years of the war and when demobilised began his studies at the Leeds School of Art. Two years later he proceeded to London to complete his training, but it was not in the Schools, but in the British Museum and the Natural History Museum that he gained an insight into the real nature and latent possibilities of the art of sculpture.

His work has been exhibited in London, Venice, Zurich, Paris, New York, and examples are in several collections in Europe and America.

ANTOINE PEVSNER. Born at Orel, Russia, 1887. French citizen. Studied art in the Kiev Academy 1907 and Petersburg 1911 where he was Gold Medalist. On the occasion of the great Constructivist Exhibition in Moscow, 1920, Pevsner and Gabo published the Constructivist Realistic Manifesto.

In 1927 Pevsner and Gabo designed constructivist settings for the Diaghileff Ballet "La Chatte."

His work has been exhibited in all the principal cities of Europe and in America.

is the fact that we are no longer free to judge for ourselves, and can no longer make contact with European ideas unless the Art Dictator of Great Britain sees fit to allow us to do so.... We want no "Nazification of art" in this country."

The extensive publicity generated by the dispute resulted in unprecedentedly high attendance once the exhibition opened; as far as Peggy Guggenheim could recall, however, nothing was sold.

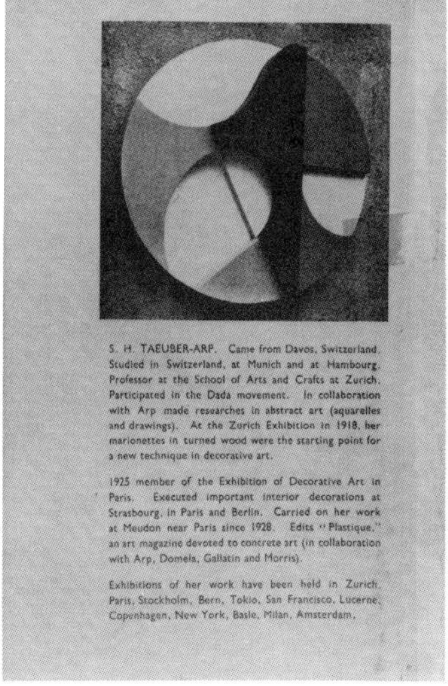

S. H. TAEUBER-ARP. Came from Davos, Switzerland. Studied in Switzerland, at Munich and at Hambourg. Professor at the School of Arts and Crafts at Zurich. Participated in the Dada movement. In collaboration with Arp made researches in abstract art (aquarelles and drawings). At the Zurich Exhibition in 1918, her marionettes in turned wood were the starting point for a new technique in decorative art.

1925 member of the Exhibition of Decorative Art in Paris. Executed important interior decorations at Strasbourg, in Paris and Berlin. Carried on her work at Meudon near Paris since 1928. Edits "Plastique," an art magazine devoted to concrete art (in collaboration with Arp, Domela, Gallatin and Morris).

Exhibitions of her work have been held in Zurich, Paris, Stockholm, Bern, Tokio, San Francisco, Lucerne, Copenhagen, New York, Basle, Milan, Amsterdam.

Back cover.

GUGGENHEIM JEUNE

Exhibition of paintings and gouaches by

GEER VAN VELDE

Private view May 5th — Sherry 5 to 8

Exhibition closes May 26th

30 CORK ST BOND ST W1

Announcement.

Exhibition of Paintings and Gouaches by Geer van Velde. May 5-26, 1938.
No catalogue. Exhibition proposed by Samuel Beckett, a close friend of van Velde.

GUGGENHEIM JEUNE
Exhibition of Paintings
by
BENNO
May 31st
June 18th
Private View
May 30th
30 CORK STREET, W. 1

Announcement.

Exhibition of Paintings by Benno. May 31-June 18, 1938.
No catalogue. Benno was a friend of Picasso's and he took Peggy Guggenheim to Picasso's studio; the latter asked what he could do for her, and she invited him to participate in her collage exhibition, projected for November 1938. He declined.

GUGGENHEIM JEUNE 30 CORK STREET BOND STREET W.1
Exhibition of Surrealist Paintings by
RITA KERNN-LARSEN
May 31-June 18 Private View May 30

Announcement.

Exhibition of Surrealist Paintings by Rita Kernn-Larsen. May 31-June 18, 1938.
No catalogue.

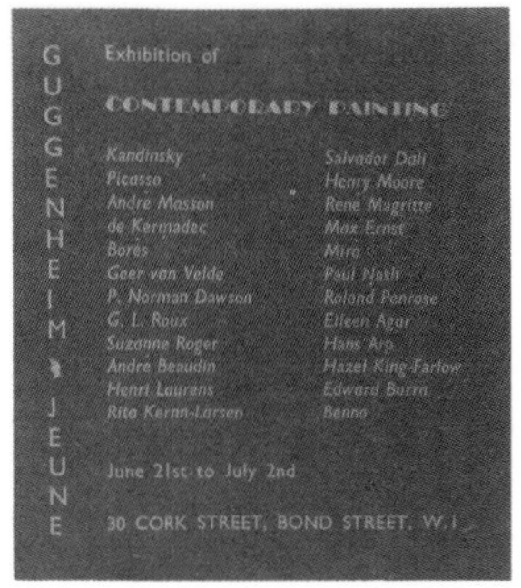
GUGGENHEIM JEUNE
Exhibition of
CONTEMPORARY PAINTING

Kandinsky	Salvador Dali
Picasso	Henry Moore
Andre Masson	Rene Magritte
de Kermadec	Max Ernst
Borès	Miro
Geer van Velde	Paul Nash
P. Norman Dawson	Roland Penrose
G. L. Roux	Eileen Agar
Suzanne Roger	Hans Arp
Andre Beaudin	Hazel King-Farlow
Henri Laurens	Edward Burra
Rita Kernn-Larsen	Benno

June 21st to July 2nd
30 CORK STREET, BOND STREET, W.1

Announcement.

Exhibition of Contemporary Painting and Sculpture. June 21-July 2, 1938.

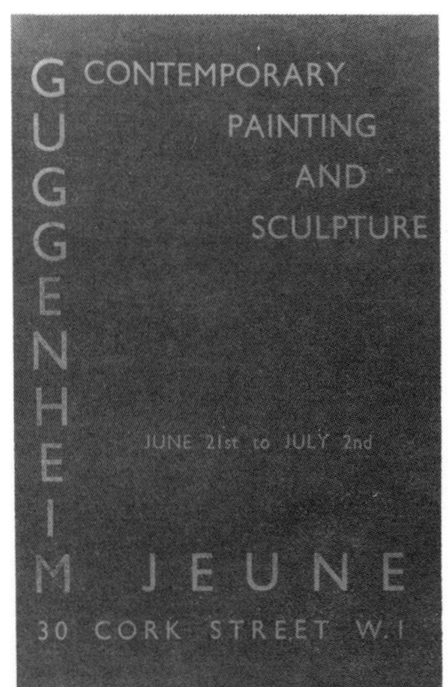
GUGGENHEIM
CONTEMPORARY
PAINTING
AND
SCULPTURE
JUNE 21st to JULY 2nd
JEUNE
30 CORK STREET W.1

Catalogue cover.

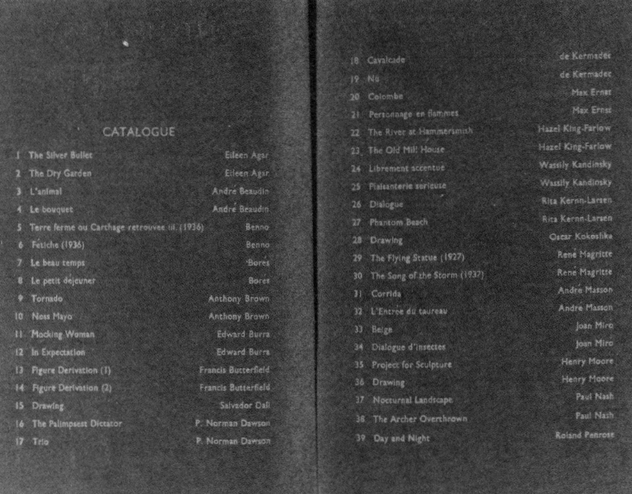
CATALOGUE

1	The Silver Bullet	Eileen Agar
2	The Dry Garden	Eileen Agar
3	L'animal	André Beaudin
4	Le bouquet	André Beaudin
5	Terre ferme ou Carthage retrouvee ill. (1936)	Benno
6	Fétiche (1936)	Benno
7	Le beau temps	Borès
8	Le petit dejeuner	Borès
9	Tornado	Anthony Brown
10	Noss Mayo	Anthony Brown
11	Mocking Woman	Edward Burra
12	In Expectation	Edward Burra
13	Figure Derivation (1)	Francis Butterfield
14	Figure Derivation (2)	Francis Butterfield
15	Drawing	Salvador Dali
16	The Palimpsest Dictator	P. Norman Dawson
17	Trio	P. Norman Dawson
18	Cavalcade	de Kermadec
19	Nu	de Kermadec
20	Colombe	Max Ernst
21	Personnage en flammes	Max Ernst
22	The River at Hammersmith	Hazel King-Farlow
23	The Old Mill House	Hazel King-Farlow
24	Librement accentue	Wassily Kandinsky
25	Plaisanterie serieuse	Wassily Kandinsky
26	Dialogue	Rita Kernn-Larsen
27	Phantom Beach	Rita Kernn-Larsen
28	Drawing	Oscar Kokoshka
29	The Flying Statue (1927)	René Magritte
30	The Song of the Storm (1937)	René Magritte
31	Corrida	André Masson
32	L'Entree du taureau	André Masson
33	Beige	Joan Miro
34	Dialogue d'insectes	Joan Miro
35	Project for Sculpture	Henry Moore
36	Drawing	Henry Moore
37	Nocturnal Landscape	Paul Nash
38	The Archer Overthrown	Paul Nash
39	Day and Night	Roland Penrose

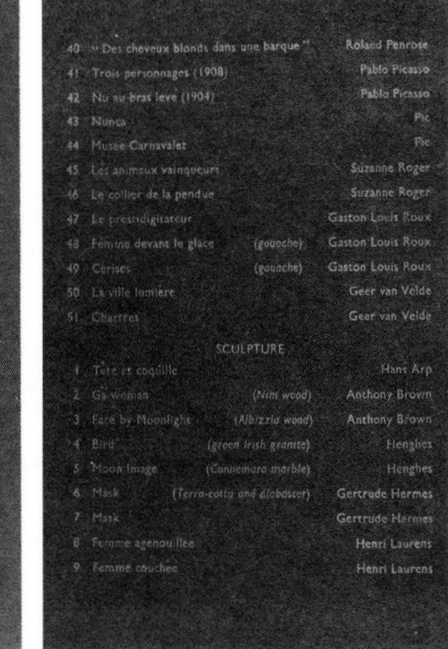

40	"Des cheveux blonds dans une barque"		Roland Penrose
41	Trois personnages (1908)		Pablo Picasso
42	Nu au bras leve (1904)		Pablo Picasso
43	Nunca		Pic
44	Musee Carnavalet		Pic
45	Les animaux vainqueurs		Suzanne Roger
46	Le collier de la pendue		Suzanne Roger
47	Le prestidigitateur		Gaston Louis Roux
48	Femme devant le glace	*(gouache)*	Gaston Louis Roux
49	Cerises	*(gouache)*	Gaston Louis Roux
50	La ville lumière		Geer van Velde
51	Chartres		Geer van Velde

SCULPTURE

1	Tête et coquille		Hans Arp
2	Ga woman	*(Nim wood)*	Anthony Brown
3	Face by Moonlight	*(Albizzia wood)*	Anthony Brown
4	Bird	*(green Irish granite)*	Henghes
5	Moon Image	*(Connemara marble)*	Henghes
6	Mask	*(Terra-cotta and alabaster)*	Gertrude Hermes
7	Mask		Gertrude Hermes
8	Femme agenouillee		Henri Laurens
9	Femme couchee		Henri Laurens

Yves Tanguy and Peggy Guggenheim, July 1938. Photographer unknown.

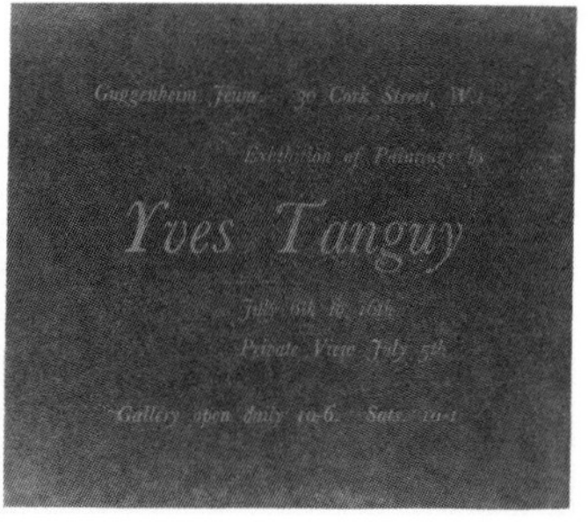

Guggenheim Jeune 30 Cork Street, W.1

Exhibition of Paintings by

Yves Tanguy

July 6th to 16th

Private View July 5th

Gallery open daily 10-6. Sats. 10-1

Announcement.

Exhibition of Paintings by Yves Tanguy. July 6-16, 1938.
No catalogue. Exhibition proposed by Humphrey Jennings; installation by Tanguy. Peggy Guggenheim recalled that many works were sold.

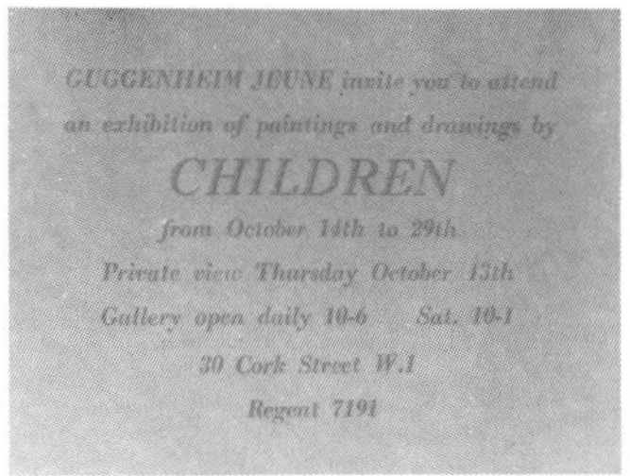

GUGGENHEIM JEUNE invite you to attend

an exhibition of paintings and drawings by

CHILDREN

from October 14th to 29th

Private view Thursday October 13th

Gallery open daily 10-6 Sat. 10-1

30 Cork Street W.1

Regent 7191

Announcement.

Exhibition of Paintings and Drawings by Children. October 14-29, 1938.
No catalogue. Included works by Lucian Freud (submitted by his mother, Anna Freud), Pegeen Vail, and children in various schools contacted by Maria Jolas, Dora Russell, and Peter Dawson.

GUGGENHEIM JEUNE

EXHIBITION OF COLLAGES

PAPIERS-COLLÉS AND

PHOTO-MONTAGES

NOVEMBER 3rd to 26th, 1938

Regent 7191

30 CORK ST. BOND ST. W I

CATALOGUE

Prices of Exhibits may be had on application

1.	Arp (Jean)	Collage	1916
2.	Arp (Jean)	Carton dechire	1937
3.	Arp (Jean)	Dessin dechire	1937
4.	Arp (Jean)	Papier dechire	1937
5.	Arp (Jean)	Papier dechire	1938
6.	Banting (John)	Collage	1936
7.	Banting (John)	Collage	1938
8.	Banting (John)	Collage	1938
9.	Benno	"Venus"	1938
10.	Benno	"L'Amazone"	1938
11.	Braque (Georges)	Collage	
	(Kindly lent by Douglas N. Cooper, Esq.)		
12.	Braque (Georges)	Collage	
13.	Brauner (Victor)	"Faux-Collage"	1938
14.	Breton (Andre)	Collage	
15.	~~Breton (Andre)~~	~~Collage~~	
16.	Brignoni	Collage	
17.	Brignoni	Collage	
18.	Brignoni	Collage	
19.	Brignoni	Collage	
20.	Burn (Guy)	Collage	
21.	Burn (Guy)	Collage	
22.	Cant (James)	The Fisherman	1938
23.	Cant (James)	The Japanese Invasion	1938
24.	~~Cant (James)~~	~~Blackpool week-end~~	1938
25.	Church (Katherine)	Collage	1938
26.	Dawson (P. Norman)	Collage	—
27.	Domela	Collage	1936
28.	Duchamp (Marcel)	"Obligation"	1924
29.	van Doesburg (Theo)	Collage Dada	1921
30.	Eluard	Collage	
31.	Ernst (Max)	Collage	
	(Kindly lent by R. Penrose, Esq.)		
32.	Ernst (Max)	Collage	
33.	Ernst (Max)	Collage	
34.	Freytag von Loringhoven (Baroness)	Collage	1924
	(Kindly lent by Mrs. Reynolds)		
35.	Freytag von Loringhoven (Baroness)	Collage	(pri. coll.) 1924
36.	Gris (Juan)	Papier colle	—
37.	Gris (Juan)	Paquet de cigarettes	
38.	Gris (Juan)	Flacon et verre	—
39.		Le Socialiste	
	(Kindly lent by Miss Valerie Cooper)		
40.	Halicka (Alys)	"La lettre"	
41.	Halicka (Alys)	"H. Matisse"	
42.	Hartung (Hans)	Collage	
43.	Hayter (W.)	Maquette for decoration in concrete	1937
44.	Henderson (Nigel)	Collage	1933
45.	Howard (Charles)	Collage	
46.	Husband (Dalla)	Collage	—
47.	Jennings (Humphrey)	Collage	
48.	Jennings (Humphrey)	Collage	
49.	Kandinsky	Raye	1938
50.	Kernn-Larsen (Rita)	Collage	1938
51.	Kosnick-Kloss (Sophie)	Collage	
52.	Laurens (Henri)	Tete	1917
53.	Laurens (Henri)	Tete	1918
54.	Laurens (Henri)	"Femme au Compotier"	1919
55.	Loy (Mina)	Collage	1924
56.	Maddox (Conroy)	Collage	
57.	Magnelli (Alberto)	"Fer-Collage"	1938
58.	Magnelli (Alberto)	"Zinc-Collage"	1938
59.	Magnelli (Alberto)	"Ardoise"	1938
60.	Man Ray	"Theatre"	1916

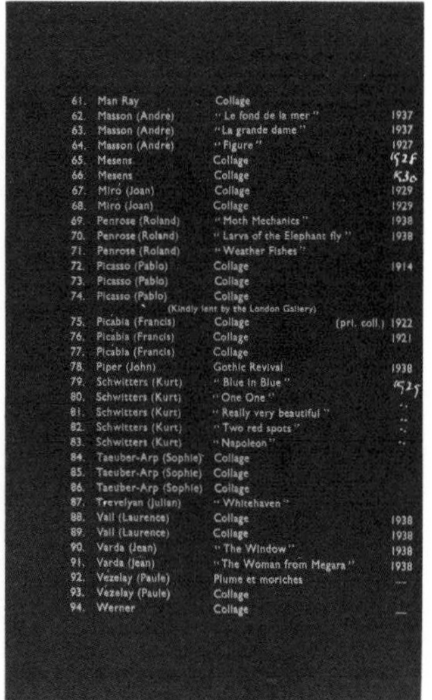
61.	Man Ray	Collage	
62.	Masson (Andre)	"Le fond de la mer"	1937
63.	Masson (Andre)	"La grande dame"	1937
64.	Masson (Andre)	"Figure"	1927
65.	Mesens	Collage	
66.	Mesens	Collage	
67.	Miro (Joan)	Collage	1929
68.	Miro (Joan)	Collage	1929
69.	Penrose (Roland)	"Moth Mechanics"	1938
70.	Penrose (Roland)	"Larva of the Elephant fly"	1938
71.	Penrose (Roland)	"Weather Fishes"	
72.	Picasso (Pablo)	Collage	1914
73.	Picasso (Pablo)	Collage	
74.	Picasso (Pablo)	Collage	
	(Kindly lent by the London Gallery)		
75.	Picabia (Francis)	Collage	(pri. coll.) 1922
76.	Picabia (Francis)	Collage	1921
77.	Picabia (Francis)	Collage	
78.	Piper (John)	Gothic Revival	1938
79.	Schwitters (Kurt)	"Blue in Blue"	
80.	Schwitters (Kurt)	"One One"	〃
81.	Schwitters (Kurt)	"Really very beautiful"	〃
82.	Schwitters (Kurt)	"Two red spots"	〃
83.	Schwitters (Kurt)	"Napoleon"	〃
84.	Taeuber-Arp (Sophie)	Collage	
85.	Taeuber-Arp (Sophie)	Collage	
86.	Taeuber-Arp (Sophie)	Collage	
87.	Trevelyan (Julian)	"Whitehaven"	
88.	Vail (Laurence)	Collage	1938
89.	Vail (Laurence)	Collage	1938
90.	Varda (Jean)	"The Window"	1938
91.	Varda (Jean)	"The Woman from Megara"	1938
92.	Vezelay (Paule)	Plume et moriches	—
93.	Vezelay (Paule)	Collage	
94.	Werner	Collage	—

Catalogue cover.

Exhibition of Collages, Papiers-collés, and Photo-montages. November 4-26, 1938. Roland Penrose installed the exhibition and may well have suggested several of the works to be included as well as arranging for loans. He personally lent the three Picassos (listed as London Gallery).

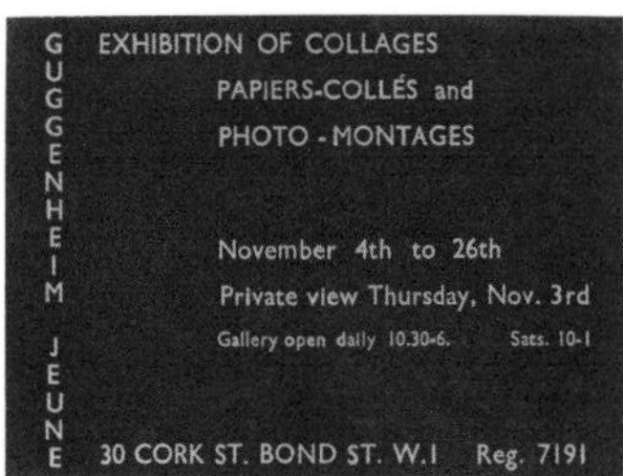
GUGGENHEIM JEUNE

EXHIBITION OF COLLAGES

PAPIERS-COLLÉS and

PHOTO - MONTAGES

November 4th to 26th

Private view Thursday, Nov. 3rd

Gallery open daily 10.30-6. Sats. 10-1

30 CORK ST. BOND ST. W.1 Reg. 7191

Announcement.

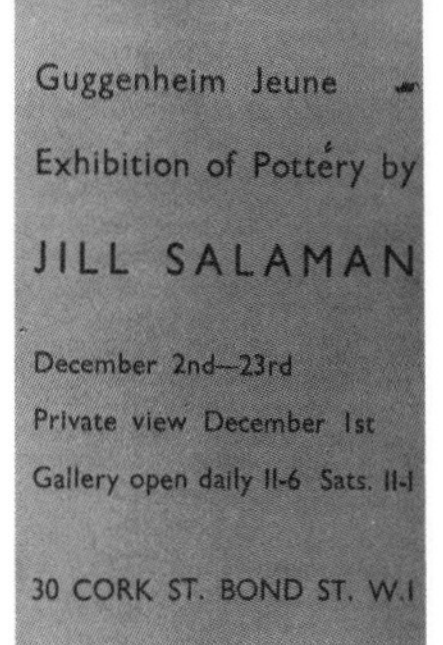
Guggenheim Jeune

Exhibition of Pottery by

JILL SALAMAN

December 2nd—23rd

Private view December 1st

Gallery open daily 11-6 Sats. 11-1

30 CORK ST. BOND ST. W.1

Announcement.

Exhibition of Pottery by Jill Salaman. December 2-23, 1938.
No catalogue.

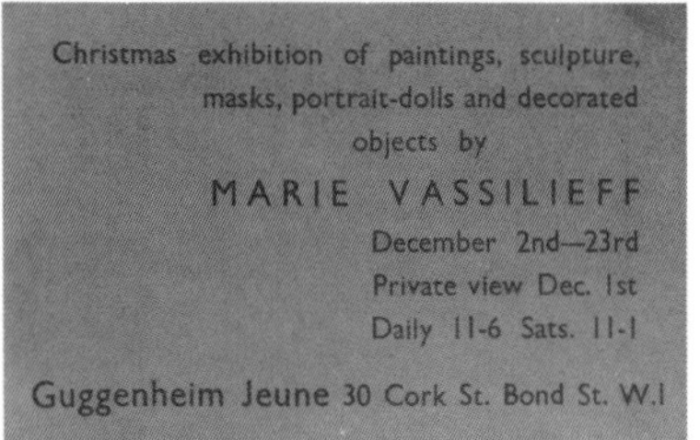
Christmas exhibition of paintings, sculpture, masks, portrait-dolls and decorated objects by

MARIE VASSILIEFF

December 2nd—23rd

Private view Dec. 1st

Daily 11-6 Sats. 11-1

Guggenheim Jeune 30 Cork St. Bond St. W.1

Announcement.

Christmas Exhibition of Paintings, Sculpture, Masks, etc. by Marie Vassilieff. December 2-23, 1938.
No catalogue.

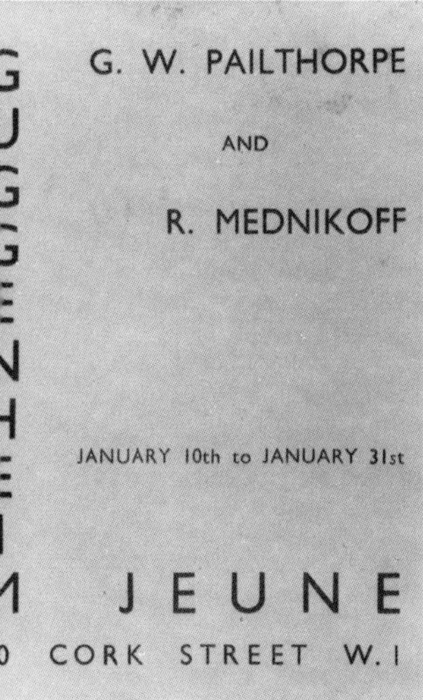

FOREWORD
by
G. W. PAILTHORPE

The paintings and drawings in this exhibition are works created during the progress of a psychological research. Four and a half years ago I asked Reuben Mednikoff to join me in a research along certain psychological lines. At that time I had no idea it was going to lead me into Surrealist art. In fact, I knew practically nothing about any kind of art. It was not until 1936* that we were discovered as Surrealist artists and then only by chance. The paintings and drawings we were producing were part of the psychological experiments we were undertaking and they are an important part of the research material. The findings of the research are of vital consequence educationally, sociologically and therapeutically, and are full of facts that can be scientifically proved.

Although our experiments have led both my colleague and myself to discover, among many things, the real meaning and value of Surrealist art to the world, it was not our intention to exhibit our work (as artists) until after the publication of the history and findings of the research. Unfortunately a force outside our control has compelled us to alter the order of our approach to the public.

The publication of the research work will be extremely costly. It will involve the reproduction in colour and half-tone blocks of a great number of paintings and drawings. It has become necessary, therefore, to try to sell our works in order to raise the money for the expenses of publication.

Surrealist art is a transitional art, or, to be more accurate, an art as yet in its infancy. Because of this it has the quality of childish creations—it is simple, direct and often crude (to a degree according to its nearness to the unconscious objectives†). It is both the art and language of the infantile unconscious. It is my belief, based on the scientific material amassed during these years of research, that Surrealist art will surpass any previous form of art in the richness, quality and vitality of its creations when it reaches its more mature stage of development.

* We were asked to show in the International Surrealist Exhibition in 1936.

† This is demonstrated by the examples given in my article "The scientific aspect of Surrealist art" in the *London Bulletin*, December issue.

We humans are as yet out of tune with our inner selves. When the inner self is fully understood the conscious and unconscious sides of our personality merge to form a unity. When that stage is reached Surrealist art will, I have no doubt, considerably alter the outlook of its critics and astound the world of art.

The quality of *freedom in full expression* can be felt in many Surrealist paintings and drawings. They are vital: they attract or repel: they do not leave the onlooker unmoved. She or he feels the emotion behind them. They tell the spectator a story. It is true the story may not be *consciously* understood by the onlooker; but 'deep speaks to deep'—the unconscious of the spectator responds to that of the artist. For this reason it sometimes becomes difficult to judge the paintings as such for we find ourselves, beyond our wills, controlled by the emotions evoked with regard to them. Our reaction to what is new is always, at first, to drive it away. It is an instinctual reaction to everything which is not understood. We cannot help ourselves.

In respect of Surrealist art, the spectator is often asked to accept, as something of value and worthy of contemplation, a number of pictures that are not only frequently grotesque, but often violent and sometimes repugnant. Less often they are of a type that can be accepted as beautiful, full of palatable interest and without any of the qualities that cause us momentarily to recoil from them. It has become the habit to imagine that all Surrealist art must necessarily be bizarre and devoid of realism. This is not true. The paintings "The Veil of Autumn" and "Ecstasia Purissima" are pure Surrealism or, in other words, the untrammelled expression of the unconscious, just as are the other paintings in this exhibition.

Every true Surrealist (unconscious) creation, whether it be a painting, a piece of sculpture, a poem or a musical composition, is telling a story. Each one of the pictures in this exhibition contains within it a complete story. Every colour, every line is intended; and is an essential part of the story. And, in this respect, there is no over-statement or under-statement.

The full story of these and other works that were done during our experiments will be revealed in the publication of the research findings which will be given to the medical and scientific world when ready. For those interested there is something further written on this subject in my article "The scientific aspect of Surrealist art" in the December issue of the *London Bulletin* which is on sale in the gallery throughout the period of this exhibition.

CATALOGUE

	Guineas
G. W. PAILTHORPE	
1. Differential Calculus, *watercolour*	15
2. The Five Firemen, *watercolour*	15
3. Father's Waistcoat, *watercolour*	15
R. MEDNIKOFF	
4. Fidgeting Digits, *watercolour*	15
G. W. PAILTHORPE	
5. Standbumptious, *watercolour*	15
6. Avaunt! *watercolour*	15
R. MEDNIKOFF	
7. Reluctant Renunciation, *watercolour*	15
8. The Gastronomic Optic, *watercolour*	15
9. A Tale of Mother's Bones, *pen and wash*	8
G. W. PAILTHORPE	
10. The Avenger, *pen*	5
R. MEDNIKOFF	
11. The Awe-inspiring Facade, *pen and wash*	10
G. W. PAILTHORPE	
12. Ancestors II., *pen*	12
13. Ancestors I., *pen*	12
R. MEDNIKOFF	
14. The Ultimate Diversion, *pen*	10
15. Headwaiter, *pen*	7
16. The Whirlpool of Peas, *carbon pencil*	7

talogue cover.

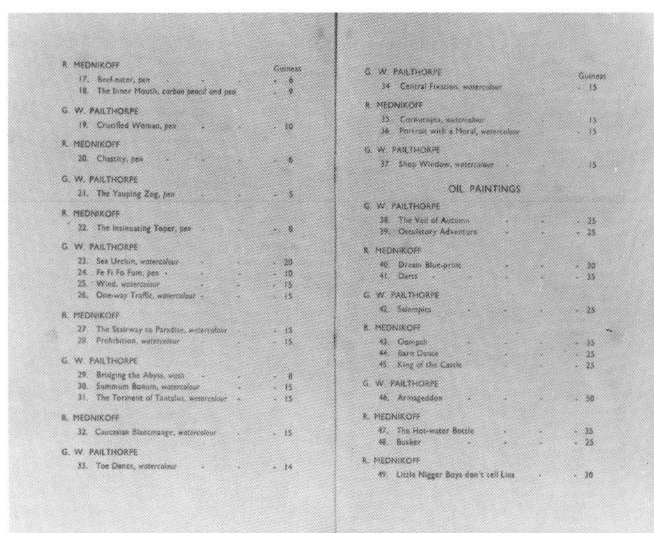

	Guineas
R. MEDNIKOFF	
17. Beef-eater, *pen*	6
18. The Inner Mouth, *carbon pencil and pen*	9
G. W. PAILTHORPE	
19. Crucified Woman, *pen*	10
R. MEDNIKOFF	
20. Chastity, *pen*	6
G. W. PAILTHORPE	
21. The Yauping Zog, *pen*	5
R. MEDNIKOFF	
22. The Insinuating Toper, *pen*	8
G. W. PAILTHORPE	
23. Sea Urchin, *watercolour*	20
24. Fe Fi Fo Fum, *pen*	10
25. Wind, *watercolour*	15
26. One-way Traffic, *watercolour*	15
R. MEDNIKOFF	
27. The Stairway to Paradise, *watercolour*	15
28. Prohibition, *watercolour*	15
G. W. PAILTHORPE	
29. Bridging the Abyss, *wash*	8
30. Summum Bonum, *watercolour*	15
31. The Torment of Tantalus, *watercolour*	15
R. MEDNIKOFF	
32. Caucasian Blancmange, *watercolour*	15
G. W. PAILTHORPE	
33. Toe Dance, *watercolour*	14

	Guineas
G. W. PAILTHORPE	
34. Central Fixation, *watercolour*	15
R. MEDNIKOFF	
35. Cornucopia, *watercolour*	15
36. Portrait with a Moral, *watercolour*	15
G. W. PAILTHORPE	
37. Shop Window, *watercolour*	15
OIL PAINTINGS	
G. W. PAILTHORPE	
38. The Veil of Autumn	25
39. Osculatory Adventure	25
R. MEDNIKOFF	
40. Dream Blue-print	30
41. Darts	35
G. W. PAILTHORPE	
42. Salempics	25
R. MEDNIKOFF	
43. Oompah	35
44. Barn Dance	25
45. King of the Castle	25
G. W. PAILTHORPE	
46. Armageddon	50
R. MEDNIKOFF	
47. The Hot-water Bottle	35
48. Busker	25
R. MEDNIKOFF	
49. Little Nigger Boys don't tell Lies	30

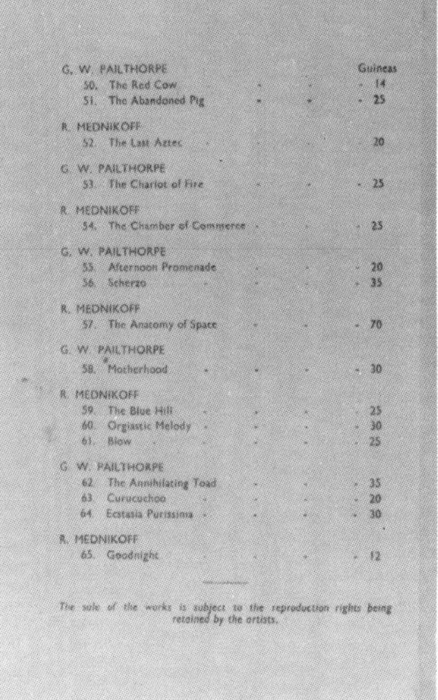

	Guineas
G. W. PAILTHORPE	
50. The Red Cow	14
51. The Abandoned Pig	25
R. MEDNIKOFF	
52. The Last Aztec	20
G. W. PAILTHORPE	
53. The Chariot of Fire	25
R. MEDNIKOFF	
54. The Chamber of Commerce	25
G. W. PAILTHORPE	
55. Afternoon Promenade	20
56. Scherzo	35
R. MEDNIKOFF	
57. The Anatomy of Space	70
G. W. PAILTHORPE	
58. Motherhood	30
R. MEDNIKOFF	
59. The Blue Hill	25
60. Orgiastic Melody	30
61. Blow	25
G. W. PAILTHORPE	
62. The Annihilating Toad	35
63. Curucuchoo	20
64. Ecstasia Purissima	30
R. MEDNIKOFF	
65. Goodnight	12

The sale of the works is subject to the reproduction rights being retained by the artists.

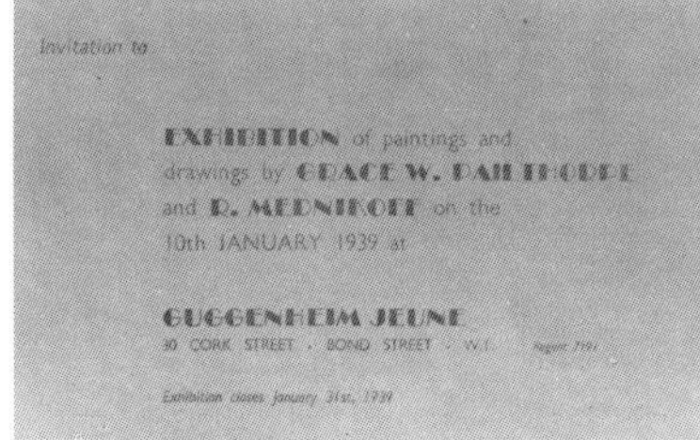

Invitation to

EXHIBITION of paintings and drawings by GRACE W. PAILTHORPE and R. MEDNIKOFF on the 10th JANUARY 1939 at

GUGGENHEIM JEUNE
30 CORK STREET · BOND STREET · W.1

Exhibition closes January 31st, 1939

Announcement.

Exhibition of Paintings and Drawings by Grace W. Pailthorpe and R. Mednikoff. January 10-31, 1939.
Exhibition proposed by Wyn Henderson, who was a friend of the two artists. The exhibition attracted a great deal of press attention, but nothing was sold as far as Peggy Guggenheim could recall.

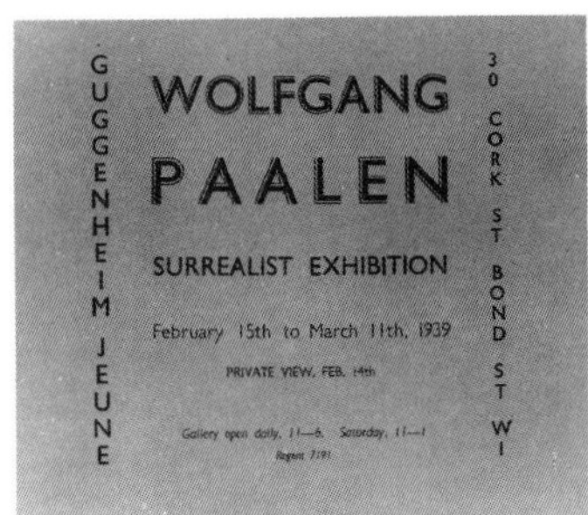

Announcement.

Wolfgang Paalen Surrealist Exhibition. February 15-March 11, 1939.
No catalogue. Peggy Guggenheim met Paalen through Roland Penrose and they became friends. She subsequently gave him another exhibition in New York.

Announcement.

John Tunnard. March 16-April 8, 1939.
No catalogue. Exhibition proposed by the artist.

Announcement.

Exhibition of Sculpture by Henghes. April 14-May 6, 1939.
No catalogue.

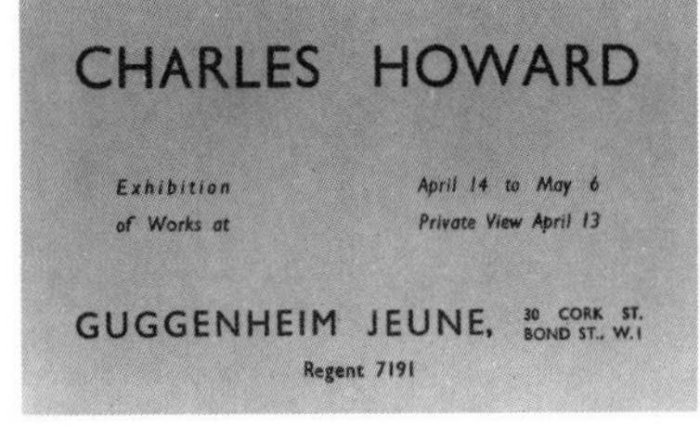

Announcement.

Exhibition of Works by Charles Howard. April 14-May 6, 1939.
No catalogue.

Announcement.

Exhibition of Abstract and Concrete Art. May 11-27, 1939.
No catalogue. Artists included Arp, Baumeister, Calder, Gabo, Hepworth, Kandinsky, Mondrian, Nicholson, Tunnard, Wadsworth.

Announcement.

Announcement.

S. W. Hayter's Studio 17. June 8-23, 1939.
Catalogue preface by Herbert Read. Joint catalogue with *Julian Trevelyan*.

Julian Trevelyan, 1936-37. June 8-22, 1939.
Catalogue preface by Trevelyan. Joint catalogue with *Studio* 17.

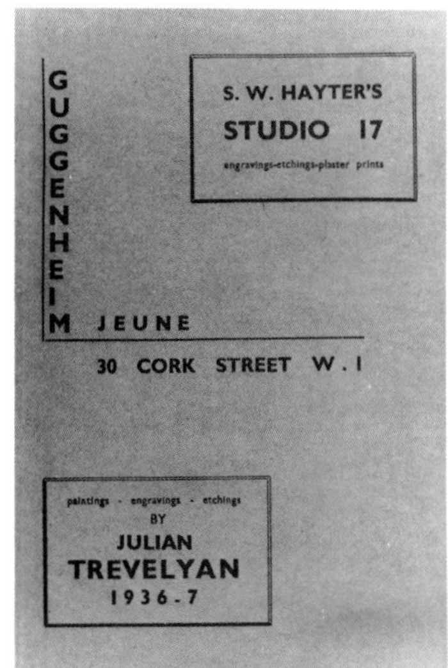

Catalogue cover.

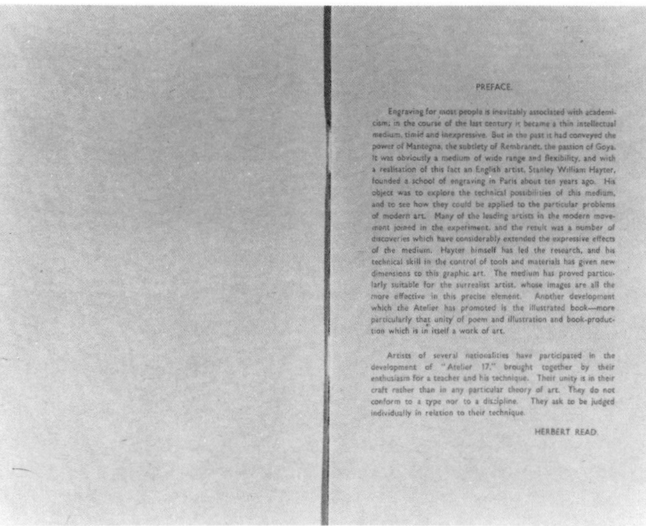

PREFACE.

Engraving for most people is inevitably associated with academicism; in the course of the last century it became a thin intellectual medium, timid and inexpressive. But in the past it had conveyed the power of Mantegna, the subtlety of Rembrandt, the passion of Goya. It was obviously a medium of wide range and flexibility, and with a realisation of this fact an English artist, Stanley William Hayter, founded a school of engraving in Paris about ten years ago. His object was to explore the technical possibilities of this medium, and to see how they could be applied to the particular problems of modern art. Many of the leading artists in the modern movement joined in the experiment, and the result was a number of discoveries which have considerably extended the expressive effects of the medium. Hayter himself has led the research, and his technical skill in the control of tools and materials has given new dimensions to this graphic art. The medium has proved particularly suitable for the surrealist artist, whose images are all the more effective in this precise element. Another development which the Atelier has promoted is the illustrated book—more particularly that unity of poem and illustration and book-production which is in itself a work of art.

Artists of several nationalities have participated in the development of "Atelier 17," brought together by their enthusiasm for a teacher and his technique. Their unity is in their craft rather than in any particular theory of art. They do not conform to a type nor to a discipline. They ask to be judged individually in relation to their technique.

HERBERT READ.

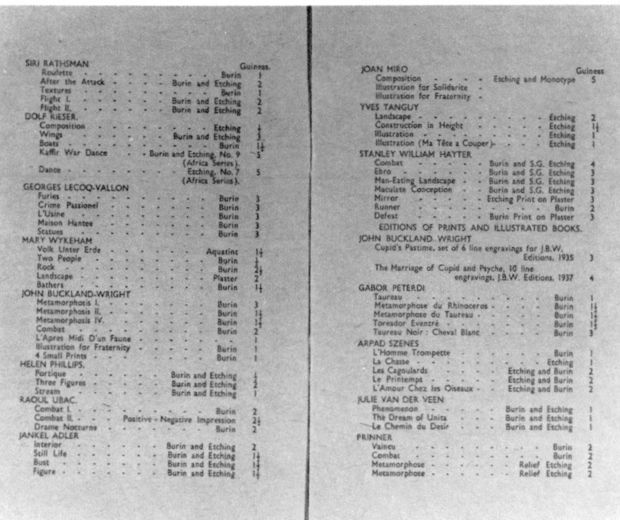

		Guineas.
SIRI RATHSMAN		
Roulette	Burin	1
After the Attack	Burin and Etching	2
Textures	Burin	1
Flight I.	Burin and Etching	2
Flight II.	Burin and Etching	2
DOLF RIESER.		
Composition	Etching	½
Wings	Burin and Etching	½
Boats	Burin	1½
Kaffir War Dance	Burin and Etching, No. 9 (Africa Series).	5
Dance	Etching, No. 7 (Africa Series).	5
GEORGES LECOQ-VALLON		
Furies	Burin	3
Crime Passionel	Burin	3
L'Usine	Burin	3
Maison Hantee	Burin	3
Statues	Burin	3
MARY WYKEHAM		
Volk Unter Erde	Aquatint	1½
Two People	Burin	½
Rock	Burin	2½
Landscape	Plaster	2
Bathers	Burin	1½
JOHN BUCKLAND-WRIGHT		
Metamorphosis I.	Burin	3
Metamorphosis II.	Burin	1½
Metamorphosis IV.	Burin	1½
Combat	Burin	2
L'Apres Midi D'un Faune		1
Illustration for Fraternity	Burin	1
4 Small Prints	Burin	1
HELEN PHILLIPS.		
Portique	Burin and Etching	½
Three Figures	Burin and Etching	½
Stream	Burin and Etching	1
RAOUL UBAC.		
Combat I.	Burin	2
Combat II.	Positive - Negative Impression	2½
Drame Nocturne	Burin	2
JANKEL ADLER		
Interior	Burin and Etching	2
Still Life	Burin and Etching	1½
Bust	Burin and Etching	1½
Figure	Burin and Etching	1½

		Guineas
JOAN MIRO		
Composition	Etching and Monotype	5
Illustration for Solidarite		
Illustration for Fraternity		
YVES TANGUY		
Landscape	Etching	2
Construction in Height	Etching	1½
Illustration	Etching	1
Illustration (Ma Tête a Couper)	Etching	1
STANLEY WILLIAM HAYTER		
Combat	Burin and S.G. Etching	4
Ebro	Burin and S.G. Etching	3
Man-Eating Landscape	Burin and S.G. Etching	3
Maculate Conception	Burin and S.G. Etching	3
Mirror	Etching Print on Plaster	3
Runner	Burin	2
Defeat	Burin Print on Plaster	3

EDITIONS OF PRINTS AND ILLUSTRATED BOOKS.

	Guineas
JOHN BUCKLAND WRIGHT	
Cupid's Pastime, set of 6 line engravings for J.B.W. Editions, 1935	3
The Marriage of Cupid and Psyche, 10 line engravings, J.B.W. Editions, 1937	4

		Guineas
GABOR PETERDI		
Taureau	Burin	1
Metamorphose du Rhinoceros	Burin	1½
Metamorphose du Taureau	Burin	1½
Toreador Eventré	Burin	1½
Taureau Noir : Cheval Blanc	Burin	3
ARPAD SZENES		
L'Homme Trompette	Burin	1
La Chasse	Etching	1
Les Cagoulards	Etching and Burin	2
Le Printemps	Etching and Burin	2
L'Amour Chez les Oiseaux	Etching and Burin	2
JULIE VAN DER VEEN		
Phenomenon	Burin and Etching	1
The Dream of Unita	Burin and Etching	1
Le Chemin du Desir	Burin and Etching	1
PRINNER		
Vaincu	Burin	2
Combat	Burin	2
Metamorphose	Relief Etching	2
Metamorphose	Relief Etching	2

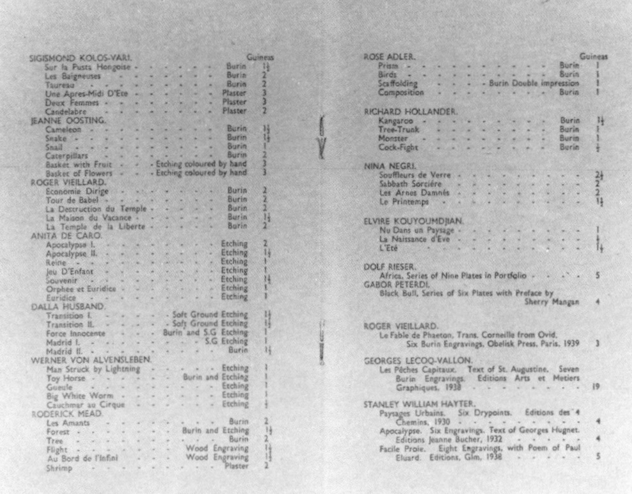

		Guineas
SIGISMOND KOLOS-VARI.		
Sur la Pusta Hongoise	Burin	1½
Les Baigneuses	Burin	2
Taureau	Burin	2
Une Apres-Midi D'Ete	Plaster	3
Deux Femmes	Plaster	3
Candelabre	Plaster	2
JEANNE OOSTING.		
Cameleon	Burin	1½
Snake	Burin	1½
Snail	Burin	1
Caterpillars	Burin	2
Basket with Fruit	Etching coloured by hand	3
Basket of Flowers	Etching coloured by hand	3
ROGER VIEILLARD.		
Economie Dirige	Burin	2
Tour de Babel	Burin	2
La Destruction du Temple	Burin	2
La Maison du Vacance	Burin	1½
La Temple de la Liberte	Burin	2
ANITA DE CARO.		
Apocalypse I.	Etching	2
Apocalypse II.	Etching	1½
Reine	Etching	1
Jeu D'Enfant	Etching	1
Souvenir	Etching	1½
Orphee et Euridice	Etching	1
Euridice	Etching	1
DALLA HUSBAND.		
Transition I.	Soft Ground Etching	1½
Transition II.	Soft Ground Etching	1½
Force Innocente	Burin and S.G Etching	1
Madrid I.	S.G Etching	1
Madrid II.	Burin	1½
WERNER VON ALVENSLEBEN.		
Man Struck by Lightning	Etching	1
Toy Horse	Burin and Etching	1
Gueule	Etching	1
Big White Worm	Etching	1
Cauchmar au Cirque	Etching	½
RODERICK MEAD.		
Les Amants	Burin	2
Forest	Burin and Etching	1½
Tree	Burin	2
Flight	Wood Engraving	1½
Au Bord de l'Infini	Wood Engraving	1½
Shrimp	Plaster	2

		Guineas
ROSE ADLER.		
Prism	Burin	1
Birds	Burin	1
Scaffolding	Burin Double impression	1
Composition	Burin	1
RICHARD HOLLANDER.		
Kangaroo	Burin	1½
Tree-Trunk	Burin	1
Monster	Burin	1
Cock-Fight	Burin	½
NINA NEGRI.		
Souffleurs de Verre		2½
Sabbath Sorciére		2
Les Arnes Damnés		2
Le Printemps		1½
ELVIRE KOUYOUMDJIAN.		
Nu Dans un Paysage		1
La Naissance d'Eve		½
L'Eté		1½

	Guineas
DOLF RIESER.	
Africa, Series of Nine Plates in Portfolio	5
GABOR PETERDI.	
Black Bull, Series of Six Plates with Preface by Sherry Mangan	4
ROGER VIEILLARD.	
Le Fable de Phaeton, Trans. Corneille from Ovid. Six Burin Engravings, Obelisk Press, Paris, 1939	3
GEORGES LECOQ-VALLON.	
Les Pêches Capitaux. Text of St. Augustine. Seven Burin Engravings. Editions Arts et Metiers Graphiques, 1938	19
STANLEY WILLIAM HAYTER.	
Paysages Urbains. Six Drypoints. Editions des 4 Chemins, 1930	4
Apocalypse. Six Engravings. Text of Georges Hugnet. Editions Jeanne Bucher, 1932	4
Facile Proie. Eight Engravings, with Poem of Paul Eluard. Editions, Glm, 1938	5

JULIAN TREVELYAN.

MYTHOS.

(Reprinted from "The Painter's Object," with acknowledgments to Myfawny Evans and Messrs. Gerald Howe).

Every painter shares an intense belief in the moment and its urgency. His urge to create and to continue creating comes from an almost blind faith in the importance of the problem to hand and his personal ability to solve it. Once solved there is always another round the corner. It is the donkey and carrot to the world's end.

But it is sometimes worth his while to take stock of the more permanent sources of his ideas, to value his work on the more horizontal view of output as opposed to the vertical cross-section that the moment to hand affords. Any such valuation must to some extent involve the painter's mythology: he must decide what he is painting about. "Why do you paint?" he might as well ask himself. It is a personal problem, and I can only answer it in a personal way.

When I was a child I shared, I believe with most children, a tremendous capacity for make-believe. A couple of chairs were a railway train: the woods through which I walked became a vast palace with halls, corridors, courtyards, opening out of each other in an endless succession. I even constructed on paper an entire city. First I drew its plan, naming all the streets, and colouring it in neatly, the blocks of houses in red, the public buildings in black. I then wrote a guide to the town, situating it geographically and enumerating all its famous men, its parks, its monuments. Nor was that all. To convince myself yet more fully of its reality and existence, I published its newspaper and its magazine, which followed in the minutest detail the activities of the local mayor and aldermen in their struggles against a quixotic and recalcitrant town council.

To-day there is the same city to paint, but it has become a World City, more all-inclusive yet less precise in its geographic connotation. Mingling in its streets and among its labyrinthine galleries are the mass-desires and individual experiences of its innumerable inhabitants. It is a great squalid metropolis like London, where nothing much would be out of place, and where the houses of every time and place are huddled up, higgledy-piggledy against each other without any objective design. Hence to paint one street is to a certain extent to paint it all. There can be no limit to its vistas, panoramas and air-plans.

Moreover, now and then there is a bit of city, complete with all its inhabitants, that is so organised, so grouped, that the analogy suggests itself to a single nervous system, to a single human being. The line of demarcation between the city and its inhabitants, between houses and people, sometimes almost vanishes. The "Nerves" and "Arteries" of a great town, the "Cells" and "Canals" of our own body: language seems here to have anticipated the painter. It is like one of those postcards which at first sight seem to represent the wrinkled head of an old man, but which on closer inspection turn out to be made up of the nude bodies of hundreds of women. Or an elephant painted in buttons. Here we have suggested a new scale for the city, something by which the painter may measure the size of its units, and hence of the picture he paints of it. The question of scale is of supreme importance to the painter to-day. Why should he voluntarily imprison himself between the four walls of a picture-frame? Why should he confine himself to expounding and developing one single idea at a time (Raphael, Cézanne)? Why should he not, in relating himself to the world, relate himself also to its complexity? Why not paint a hundred thousand shirts, a hundred thousand doves?

It will be becoming obvious that the city is in fact a compound of metaphor and symbol, a new kind of myth. I have stressed it because I believe that such myths in fact form the subject-matter of much contemporary painting. Society in the past provided a continually changing mythology for the artist. To William Blake such a ready-made mythology was already lacking, and he had to create his own. To-day the need for new myths has become far more urgent. The cinema has evolved the Wild West and the paradise of Harpo Marx; but the painter is left high and dry, and has to rely on his own imagination. What we need is a sort of all-round mythological confession, à la Oxford group.

JULIAN TREVELYAN

CATALOGUE

PAINTINGS.

		Guineas.
(1)	A Symposium	15
(2)	Diagram of a City	12
(3)	Picture for a Dining Room	12
(4)	Street Scene in Babylon I.	8
(5)	Street Scene in Babylon II.	8
(6)	Section of a Town with People in Cellars	8
(7)	Symbols of Growth	6
(8)	Two Sgraffiti	6
(9)	Two Studies, I.	6
(10)	Two Studies, II.	6
(11)	See-Saw	10
(12)	Figure No. 1	8
(13)	Figure No. 2	8
(14)	Picture with a Legend	7

COLLAGES.

(15)	The Farm	8
(16)	Le Puy	6
(17)	Coal Mine	8
(18)	Roman Camp at Tisbury	7
(19)	Bolton	6
(20)	Bolton	6
(21)	Whitehaven	8

ETCHINGS.

(22)	Premonitions of Spring, 1938	2
(23)	Two Versions of an Idea	3
(24)	City on Plaster	2½

(And in portfolio.)

Sold for Spanish Refugees—

Solidarite. Poem of Paul Eluard. Translation by Brian Coffey. Engravings by Picasso, Miro, Masson, Tanguy, Hayter, Husband and Buckland-Wright. Editions, Atelier 17, 1938. Last few copies	3
Fraternity. Poem of Stephen Spender. Translation by Louis Aragon. Engravings by Buckland-Wright, Hayter, Hecht, Husband, Kandinsky, Mead, Miro, Rieser, Vargas. Editions, Atelier 17, 1939	2

GUGGENHEIM JEUNE
request the pleasure of your company at

A Farewell Party

on Thursday June 22nd at 9 p.m.
Miss Gisèle Freund of Paris will show
projections of colour-photography of famous
contemporary artists.
R.S.V.P. 30, Cork Street, W.1. Regent 7191

Announcement.

Farewell party for Guggenheim Jeune. June 22, 1939.

Gisèle Freund's color portrait photographs were shown.

Peggy Guggenheim (in conversations with the author) was unable to recall how she met Herbert Read or precisely when; he apparently walked into the gallery one day and introduced himself. She had not known him before, but during the Guggenheim Jeune period, they became close friends and saw each other frequently.

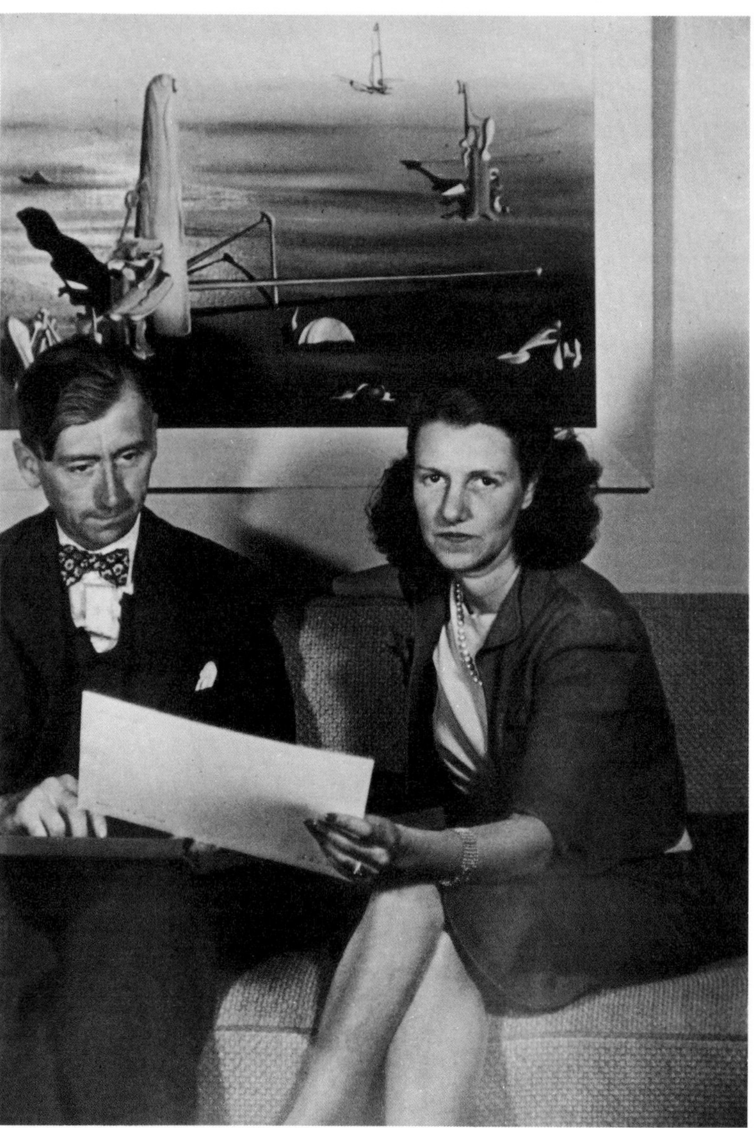

Gisèle Freund, *Herbert Read and Peggy Guggenheim.* Color photograph, Peggy Guggenheim Collection, Venice.

In June 1939 Peggy Guggenheim decided to close her gallery and to open instead a museum of modern art. She persuaded Herbert Read to resign his position as editor of the *Burlington Magazine* and assume the directorship of the museum, which was projected to open in the autumn of 1939.

Sunday Times, 21 May, 1939: "*London has lagged behind New York in providing a permanent exhibition centre for modern art. This state of affairs is shortly to be remedied. At a time when New York's well-known Museum of Modern Art is opening in a bigger and better building comes news that a similar museum is to be established in London.*

"*The promoters of the scheme are Professor Herbert Read and Mrs. Peggy Guggenheim, whose gallery in Cork Street has done much to advance the cause of modernist painting and sculpture. Mrs. Guggenheim, an energetic daughter of a family famous for its benefactions to art and science, is to give up her gallery for the whole-time job of assistant-director of the museum. The director is to be Mr. Read, who for this purpose will shortly relinquish the editorship of the 'Burlington Magazine.'*

"*Professor Read tells me that the new museum, which according to present plans will open in the autumn, will not be limited in its scope by any narrow definition of modern art, though special attention is to be paid to those movements that have grown out of cubism. Nor will it necessarily confine itself to painting, but will aim at showing the interrelation of all the modern arts, including architecture, sculpture, and music. The basis of its activities will be educational in the widest sense of the word. With this in view a permanent collection is to be formed as a background for temporary exhibitions of a special nature, as well as for a regular programme of lectures, recitals, and concerts.*"

Manchester Guardian, 25 May, 1939: "*. . . The proposed Museum of Modern Art in London shows every sign of becoming an established fact in the early autumn. With Mrs. Guggenheim to back it and Mr. Herbert Read to direct it, all it needs now is a collection of works of art and a place to put them in.*

"*Mr. Read finds the latter more difficult to come by than the former. There are one or two powerful champions of post-Cubist modernity like Sir Michael Sadler and Mr. Roland Penrose who could be relied on to interest themselves in helping at the collection, but ideal premises are out of the question, and even moderately suitable premises are not easy to find. The first floor of a new building in Soho Square is at present being considered. That, of course, means putting up with the disadvantages of side lighting, but that is not the only difficulty. What would suit an office building will not necessarily suit an art gallery. On certain occasions, for instance, an art gallery is (one hopes) bound to contain crowds of people, and the London County Council has its own set of regulations about crowds in buildings. But doubtless the difficulties will be overcome. . . . Presumably the inmost shrine of the new collection will be dedicated to Picasso and his French disciples, but one hopes that a corner may be reserved for the English moderns. Certain quarters are beginning to realise that the adjectives 'English' and 'modern' are not after all mutually exclusive.*"

Peggy Guggenheim made preliminary arrangements to rent the Portland Place residence of Kenneth Clark, who planned to move into his Richmond house. Portland Place was to serve primarily as museum premises, Peggy Guggenheim occupying one floor and the Reads another. In August Peggy Guggenheim left for Paris to start locating works that could be borrowed for the first exhibition. But while she was abroad, it became increasingly clear that war would be declared, and she concluded that she would be unable to return to England. Herbert Read was prepared to pursue the museum plan — even in the event of war — but she felt that this would be impracticable. With considerable reluctance she abandoned the project and, in settlement of their contract, paid Read half of the five-year salary she had promised him.

She then decided to use the $40,000 she had set aside for the establishment of the museum to acquire works of art. Herbert Read had prepared a list of works that they should attempt to borrow in Paris for the museum's inaugural exhibition, and Peggy Guggenheim used this list as the basis for her intense acquisition campaign during the ensuing months.[3]

3. The list itself has not, thus far, been located — either among the papers of Herbert Read or among those of Peggy Guggenheim, who believed that the list was lost during World War II. By the 1970s she was unable to recall a single specific work that had been on the list, and it has not been possible to reconstruct it. Indeed, it is not even clear whether the list enumerated individual works or merely artists' names, although the latter seems more likely.

In her search, Peggy Guggenheim was aided and encouraged by Marcel Duchamp and by two new friends of barely a year's standing. The first was Nelly van Doesburg—the widow of Theo van Doesburg—who had met Peggy Guggenheim for the first time when she had visited Guggenheim Jeune in 1938. The second was Howard Putzel, a passionate supporter of modern art who had for several years organized a number of exhibitions in the United States on the West Coast, and had closed his most recent gallery (the Putzel Gallery in Los Angeles) in the summer of 1938.[4] He had then traveled to Paris, where he and Peggy Guggenheim had met at the house of Mary Reynolds. ("*He immediately took me in hand and escorted me, or rather forced me to accompany him to all the artists' studios in Paris. He also made me buy innumerable things that I didn't want, but he found me many paintings that I did need, and usually ones of the highest quality. He used to arrive in the morning with several things under his arm for my approval, and was hurt when I did not buy them. If I found or bought paintings 'behind his back,' as he must surely have considered any independent action on my part, he was even more offended,*" *Confessions*, 1960, pp. 69-70.)

Peggy Guggenheim moved into an apartment at 18, quai d'Orléans and, still determined to open a museum, in April 1940 she rented a large space in the Place Vendôme and commissioned Vantongerloo to make designs for its renovation. But the work progressed too slowly, and she attempted (without success) to organize an exhibition instead. On February 2, 1940, she wrote to Naum Gabo: "*... in the meantime I want to do some exhibitions here to make life less gloomy.*" In April she wrote to him again: "*My collection has grown very quickly, but I still have no gallery.*" During the few months preceding June 1940 she acquired approximately fifty works, thirty-seven of which are still in the collection: four Arps (cat. nos. 4, 5, 8, 9); one Balla (cat. no. 13); two Brancusis (cat. nos. 17, 18); one Braque (cat. no. 19); one de Chirico (cat. no. 31); two Dalís (cat. nos. 40, 41); one Delaunay (cat. no. 43); one van Doesburg (cat. no. 46); one Duchamp-Villon (cat. no. 50); two Ernsts (cat nos. 52, 53); two Giacomettis (cat. nos. 66, 68); one Gleizes (cat. no. 71); one Klee (cat. no. 87); one Léger (cat. no. 97); one Lissitzky (cat. no. 100); one Magritte (cat. no. 102); three Man Rays (cat. nos. 105-7); one Marcoussis (cat. no. 108); one Masson (cat. no. 110); one Miró (cat. no. 117); one Mondrian (cat. no. 121); two Pevsners (cat. nos. 133, 134); one Picabia (cat. no. 136); one Schwitters (cat. no. 161); one Severini (cat. no. 162); one Vantongerloo (cat. no. 174); and a Villon (cat. no. 177). At least twenty of those works were purchased directly from the individual artists, nine from dealers, four from Nelly van Doesburg (the Balla, the *Contra-Compositie* by van Doesburg, the Lissitzky, and the Severini), and two from Duchamp (the Duchamp-Villon and the Gleizes.)[5] Other works bought during this same period were later given away or (in rare cases) sold.[6]

Three days before the fall of Paris on June 14, 1940, Peggy Guggenheim and Nelly van Doesburg fled south to Le Veyrier on the Lac d'Annecy where they rented a house for the summer and were joined by the Arps. Peggy Guggenheim had made arrangements with her friend Maria Jolas to store the collection in the barn of the Jolas château near Vichy. At the end of the summer, the pictures were shipped farther south by yet another friend, James Joyce's son, Giorgio.

4. For extensive unpublished information on the career of Putzel see Hermine Benheim, "Howard Putzel and the Beginnings of Abstract Expressionism," unpublished manuscript, The Howard Putzel Collection, AAA, Washington, D.C.; and Melvin P. Lader, "Peggy Guggenheim's Art of This Century: The Surrealist Milieu and the American Avant-Garde, 1942-47," unpublished Ph.D. dissertation, University of Delaware, 1981, pp. 141-80.

5. With six exceptions, it has not been possible to establish how many of the Paris purchases are directly attributable to the advice of Putzel, Nelly van Doesburg, or Duchamp. The six, as recalled by Peggy Guggenheim, are as follows: the Delaunay was located by Putzel at Léonce Rosenberg's gallery, and she was delighted to acquire it. Duchamp persuaded her, with some difficulty, to purchase the Gleizes, the Marcoussis, and the Villon; Nelly van Doesburg convinced her to acquire the Balla and the Severini. Other purchases from Duchamp (the Duchamp-Villon) and Nelly van Doesburg (the Lissitzky and van Doesburg) resulted from Peggy Guggenheim's own enthusiasm and required no inducement. Nelly van Doesburg introduced her to the Pevsners and the Delaunays, but was apparently not specifically responsible for acquisitions in those cases.

6. A group of works by Paul Klee, acquired in Paris in 1940, were stolen from Art of This Century in about 1943.

Peggy Guggenheim continued to harbor hopes that the collection could be catalogued and publicly exhibited in a French museum. With the help of Nelly van Doesburg, she persuaded André Farcy, director of the museum in Grenoble, to house the collection (although he would not consider exhibiting it), and in the autumn of 1940, she settled in Grenoble. ("*M. Farcy was in a very bad jam himself at this time. Because of the Vichy government he nearly lost his museum directorship and finally ended up in prison. He could not do much for me.... As he was expecting Pétain to visit Grenoble, he had hidden all the museum's modern pictures in the cellar. He gave me perfect freedom in the museum to do anything with my pictures except to hang them. I had a beautiful room where I placed them along the wall and could show them to my friends, photograph them and catalogue them. But he would never fix a date for a show, claiming that he must pave the way with the Vichy government first, so much were they under Hitler's control.*" *Confessions*, 1960, pp. 72-78).

Undaunted, Peggy Guggenheim calmly continued to make her plans for an exhibition with a catalogue. She had persuaded Arp to write a short catalogue essay. She had also commissioned André Breton to provide a lengthy introduction, and she arranged to begin photography of the entire collection for the anticipated publication. As late as January 2, 1941, these plans were apparently still developing, when Breton wrote to Jean Ballard (the editor of *Cahiers du Sud*): "*... Votre lettre commence à reveiller en moi d'autres scrupules. Naturellement mon texte n'est pas prêt, ni même encore entrepris. J'espérais, avant de m'y jeter, pouvoir tenir parole à Madame Guggenheim qui attend de moi une préface à l'exposition de sa collection de tableaux modernes au musée de Grenoble (je n'ai pas encore reçu les photographies).*"[7]

Peggy Guggenheim, second from right, with André Breton, his wife, Jacqueline Lamba, and their daughter, Aube, in Marseilles, March 1941. Photographer unknown.

Toward the end of March, Breton and his family (who had been living as the guests of Varian Fry in Marseilles) sailed for Martinique and thence to America;[8] Peggy Guggenheim paid for their passage. Her own departure (together with Max Ernst, Laurence Vail, Pegeen Vail, Sindbad Vail, Kay Boyle and her four children) took place on July 13 from Lisbon by plane. They arrived in New York on the fourteenth, and the collection (which had been shipped from Grenoble by René Lefebvre-Foinet disguised as "household goods") arrived shortly before them.

7. This letter was brought to the author's attention by Françoise Will-Levaillant. Varian Fry, the head of the Emergency Rescue Committee in Marseilles, had apparently even been under the impression that Peggy Guggenheim had established a museum of modern art in Grenoble. (See his *Surrender on Demand*, New York, 1945, p. 185.)

8. Ibid, p. 185.

Peggy Guggenheim and Berenice Abbott had met for the first time in Paris in about 1925, while Abbott was working as an assistant to Man Ray, developing and printing his photographs. When Abbott subsequently resigned her job and decided to set up a studio of her own, Peggy Guggenheim provided her with a loan to purchase the needed equipment: "*Peggy was a great help in providing a loan to get my first studio started. She offered the money and fortunately I had the good sense to accept it; I would never have thought to ask. There has never been as bad a business person as I was then.*" (Hank O'Neal, *Berenice Abbott: American Photographer*, New York, 1982, pp. 10, 41.) Abbott photographed Peggy Guggenheim and her children in partial repayment of the loan, and in 1942 she made a series of photographs of Frederick Kiesler's installation at Art of This Century (see pp. 764-770).

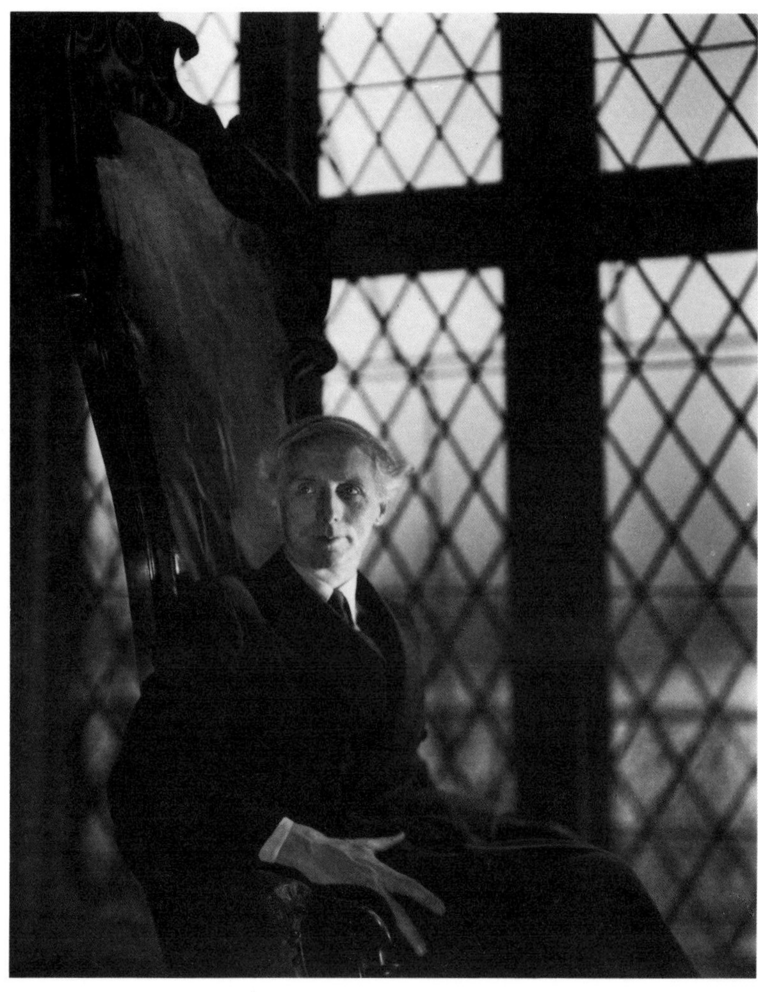

Max Ernst at 440 East Fifty-first Street, 1942. Photograph by Berenice Abbott.

Approximately six months after her return to America, and after travels to California, Arizona, New Mexico, and New Orleans, Peggy Guggenheim and Max Ernst settled into a brownstone at 440 East Fifty-first Street on the East River.[1] Still determined above all else to open a museum, she rented the seventh (top) floor of a building at 30 West Fifty-seventh Street, and — following the suggestion of Howard Putzel — contacted the Viennese architect-designer Frederick Kiesler to make suggestions for the remodeling of the interior.

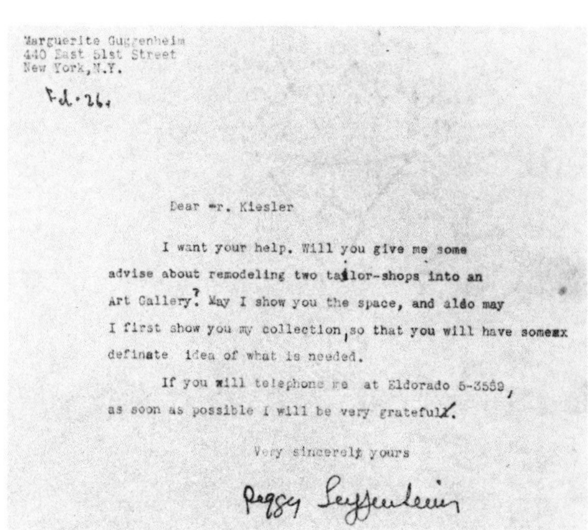

Marguerite Guggenheim
440 East 51st Street
New York, N.Y.

Feb. 26.

Dear Mr. Kiesler

I want your help. Will you give me some advise about remodeling two tailor-shops into an Art Gallery? May I show you the space, and also may I first show you my collection, so that you will have some definate idea of what is needed.

If you will telephone me at Eldorado 5-3559, as soon as possible I will be very grateful.

Very sincerely yours

Peggy Guggenheim

Peggy Guggenheim's first letter to Kiesler, February 26, 1942. Kiesler Archive, New York.

1. Peggy Guggenheim and Max Ernst were married in December 1941. They separated in the spring of 1943 and were divorced not long afterward. That autumn, Peggy Guggenheim moved into a townhouse at 155 East Sixty-first Street.

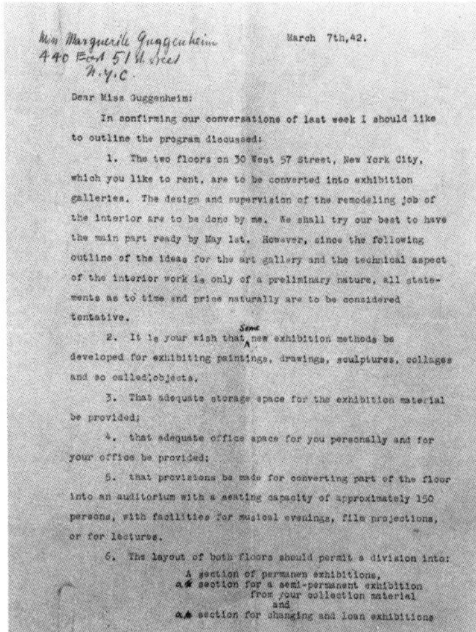

Miss Marguerite Guggenheim
440 East 51th Street
N.Y.C.

March 7th,42.

Dear Miss Guggenheim:

In confirming our conversations of last week I should like to outline the program discussed:

1. The two floors on 30 West 57 Street, New York City, which you like to rent, are to be converted into exhibition galleries. The design and supervision of the remodeling job of the interior are to be done by me. We shall try our best to have the main part ready by May 1st. However, since the following outline of the ideas for the art gallery and the technical aspect of the interior work is only of a preliminary nature, all statements as to time and price naturally are to be considered tentative.

2. It is your wish that some new exhibition methods be developed for exhibiting paintings, drawings, sculptures, collages and so called objects.

3. That adequate storage space for the exhibition material be provided;

4. that adequate office space for you personally and for your office be provided;

5. that provisions be made for converting part of the floor into an auditorium with a seating capacity of approximately 150 persons, with facilities for musical evenings, film projections, or for lectures.

6. The layout of both floors should permit a division into:

A section of permanent exhibitions,
a section for a semi-permanent exhibition from your collection material
and
a section for changing and loan exhibitions

Kiesler's proposal, following discussion with Peggy Guggenheim. Kiesler Archive, New York.

Kiesler's covering letter of March 7, 1942, accompanying his contract proposal. In the first paragraph he makes reference to her only condition regarding the installation — "*that the pictures should be unframed.*" He also provided a detailed estimate for the "*Equipment, Remodeling and Installation of 3 galleries at 30 West 57th St.*"; the total was $4,489. Kiesler and Peggy Guggenheim rapidly reached an agreement and Kiesler began work.

Meanwhile, Peggy Guggenheim continued her vigorous campaign to add to the collection. Max Ernst, André Breton, or Howard Putzel frequently accompanied her to galleries and encouraged her to purchase various works, but with very few exceptions it has not been possible to establish the instances in which their influence, or that of others, may have been exerted. Among the acquisitions made during the few months preceding the publication of her catalogue in May 1942 were the following thirty works: Archipenko's *La Boxe*, cat. no. 3; Calder's *Mobile*, cat. no. 25; Chagall's *La pluie*, cat. no. 29; de Chirico's *La tour rouge*, cat. no. 30, and *Le doux après-midi*, cat. no. 32; Duchamp's *Nu (esquisse)*, *Jeune homme triste dans un train*, cat. no. 49, and *Boîte en valise (no. 1)*, page 806; Ernst's *Von minimax dadamax...*, cat. no. 51, *La mer, le soleil...*, cat. no. 54, *Le Facteur Cheval*, cat. no. 55, *Couple zoomorphe*, cat. no. 56, *Jardin gobe-avions*, cat. no. 57, *La ville entière*, cat. no. 58, and *La toilette de la mariée*, cat. no. 59; Ferren's *Tempora*, cat. no. 64; Giacometti's *Femme qui marche*, cat. no. 67; Kandinsky's *Landschaft mit roten Flecken, No. 2*, cat. no. 82, *Weisses Kreuz*, cat. no. 83, and *Empor*, cat. no. 84; Klee's *Bildnis der Frau P. im Süden*, cat. no. 86; Malevich's *Untitled*, cat. no. 104; Miró's *Peinture*, cat. no. 116, and *Femme assise II*, cat. no. 118; Mondrian's two drawings, cat. nos. 119 and 120; Ozenfant's *Guitare et bouteilles*, cat. no. 131; Picasso's *Le poète*, cat. no. 137, *Pipe, verre, bouteille de Vieux Marc*, cat. no. 138, and *L'Atelier*, cat. no. 139; Tanguy's *En lieu oblique*, cat. no. 169.

By the time the catalogue was published, the collection contained over 170 works, a number of which were later given away or (in rare cases) sold.

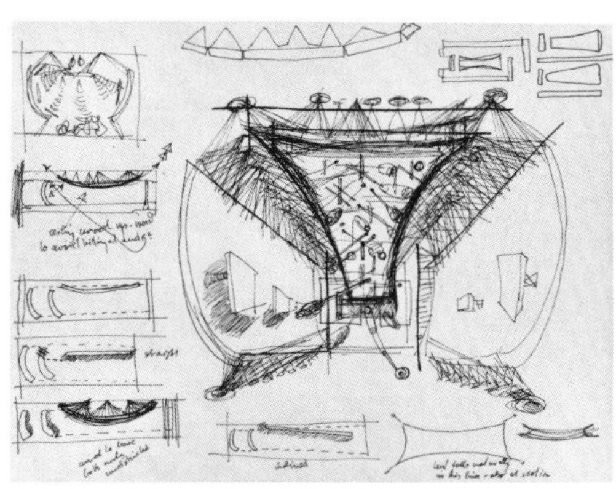

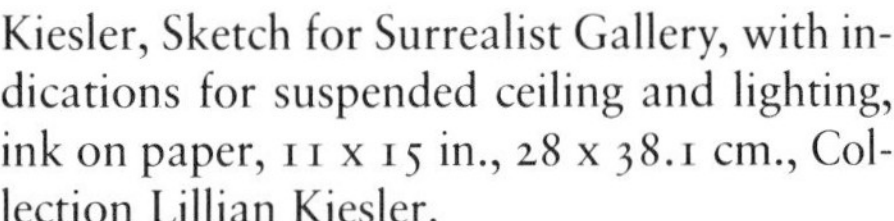

Kiesler, Sketch for Surrealist Gallery, with indications for suspended ceiling and lighting, ink on paper, 11 x 15 in., 28 x 38.1 cm., Collection Lillian Kiesler.

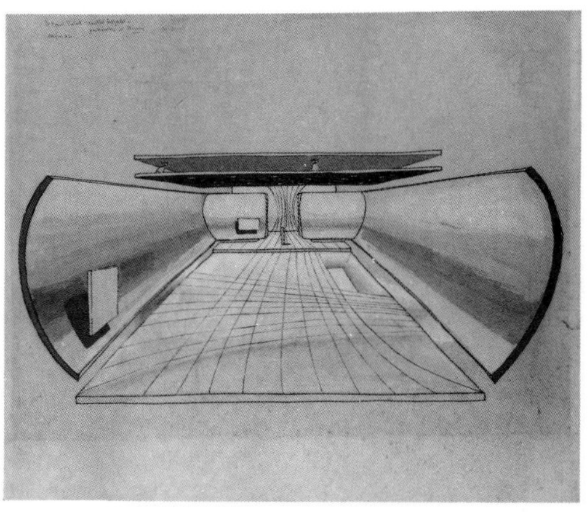

Kiesler, Study for Surrealist Gallery, inscribed to Howard Putzel, gouache on paper, 14¾ x 17⅞ in., 37.5 x 45.5 cm., SRGM, New York, Gift of Peggy Guggenheim.

Completed Surrealist Gallery, Kiesler seated at left. Curved wooden walls; suspended false ceiling (14 x 50 ft., 4.27 x 15.25 m.) hung 15 in., 38.1 cm., below existing ceiling; indirect lighting installed above with spotlights for individual works; unframed paintings mounted on adjustable projecting arms. Photograph by Berenice Abbott, courtesy Lillian Kiesler.

Completed Surrealist Gallery. Removable spotlights have been inserted in two of the ceiling apertures. Photographer unknown, courtesy Lillian Kiesler.

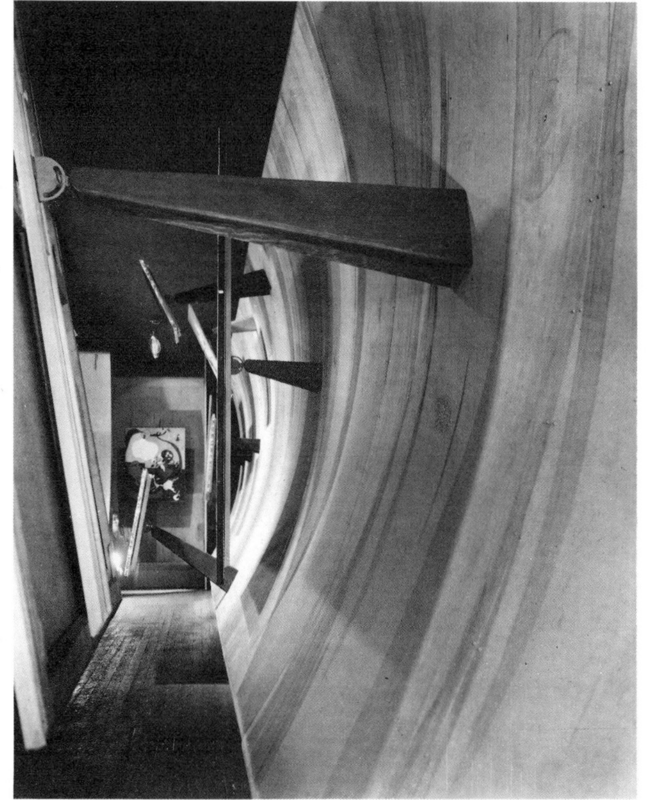

Surrealist Gallery, wooden arms (constructed from sawn-off baseball bats) designed by Kiesler for the installation of paintings at Art of This Century. The flexible hinged mounts allowed for the adjustment of the angle at which each painting would be viewed. Photograph by Berenice Abbott, courtesy Lillian Kiesler.

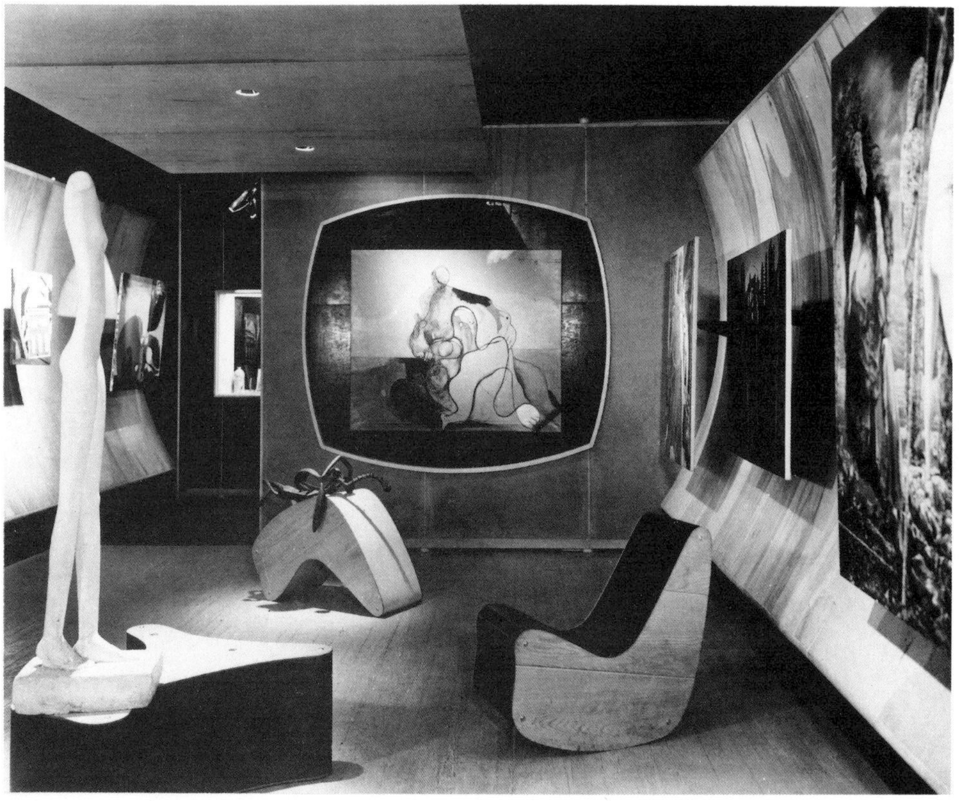

Photograph by Berenice Abbott, courtesy Lillian Kiesler.

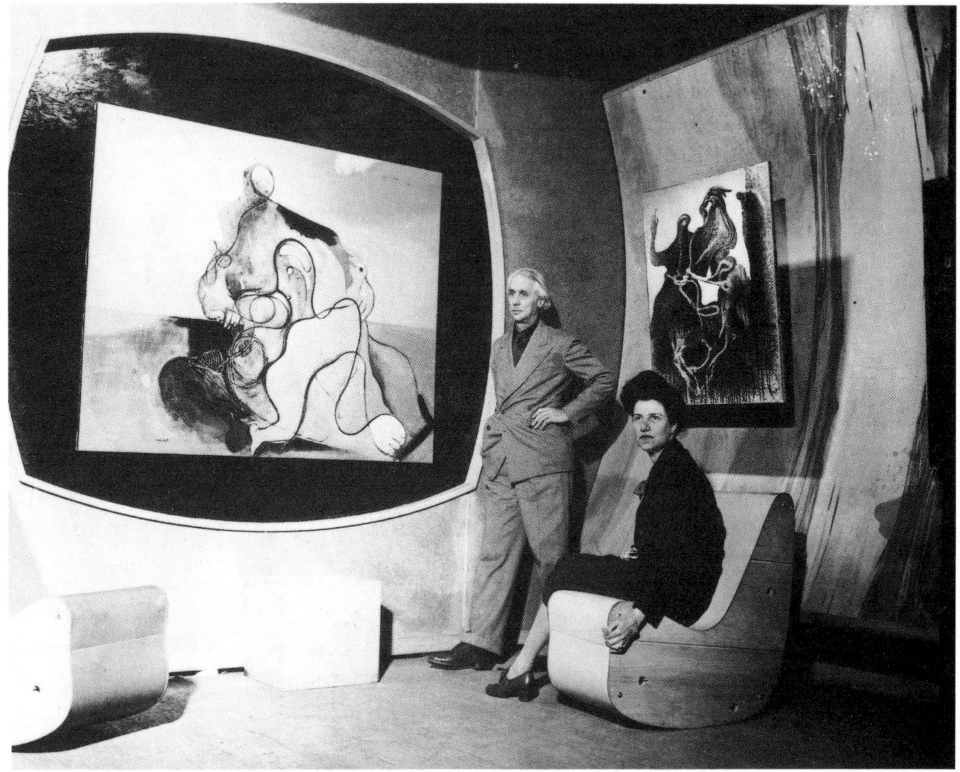

Max Ernst and Peggy Guggenheim in the Surrealist Gallery, shortly after the opening of Art of This Century, October 1942. Photographer unknown.

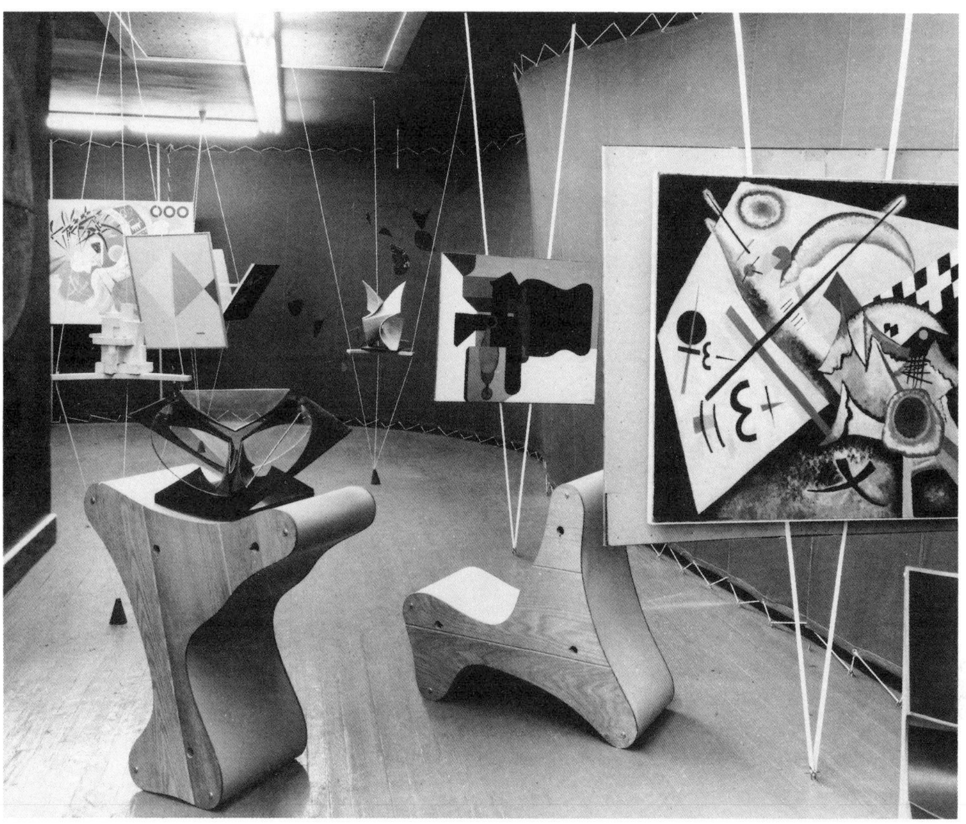

Abstract Gallery. Direct fluorescent lighting; ultramarine, curving canvas walls on two sides attached to ceiling and floor with rope; wooden floor painted turquoise; triangular suspension columns used for display of paintings and sculpture; seven-way wooden stands/chairs intended either for display or for sitting. Photographer unknown.

Abstract Gallery. In the foreground van Doesburg's *Composition in gray (Rag-time)*, cat. no. 45, in the artist's original frame. Photographer unknown, courtesy Lillian Kiesler.

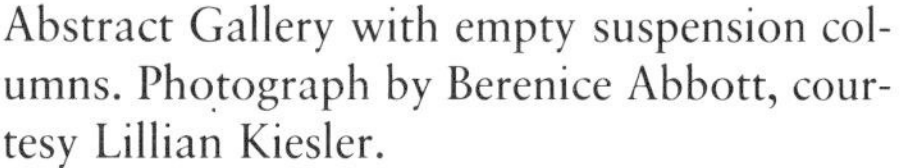

Abstract Gallery with empty suspension columns. Photograph by Berenice Abbott, courtesy Lillian Kiesler.

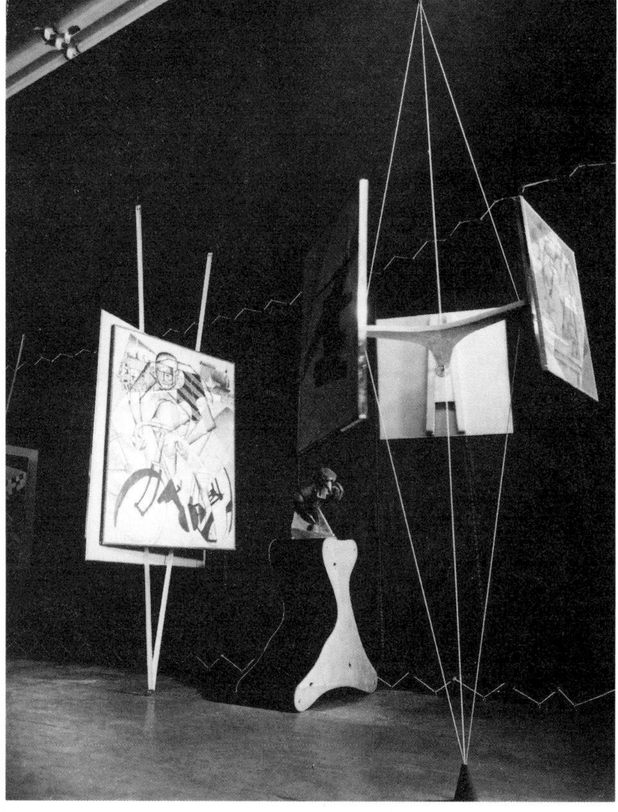

Abstract Gallery with paintings in position on suspension columns. Photograph by Berenice Abbott, courtesy Lillian Kiesler.

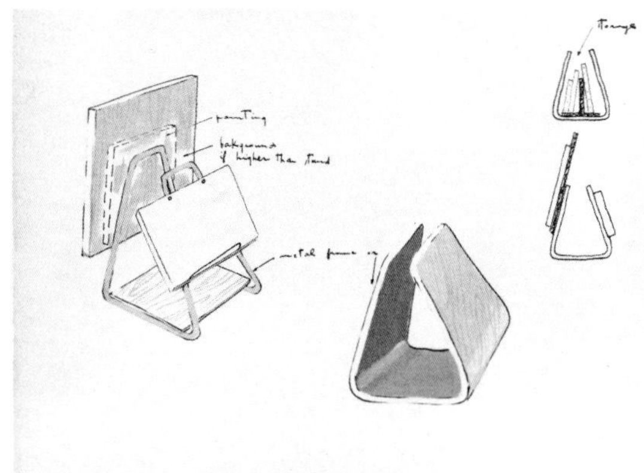

Kiesler, Study for stands and storage bins in painting library, ink and tempera on paper, 10 x 14 in., 25.4 x 35.6 cm., Collection Lillian Kiesler.

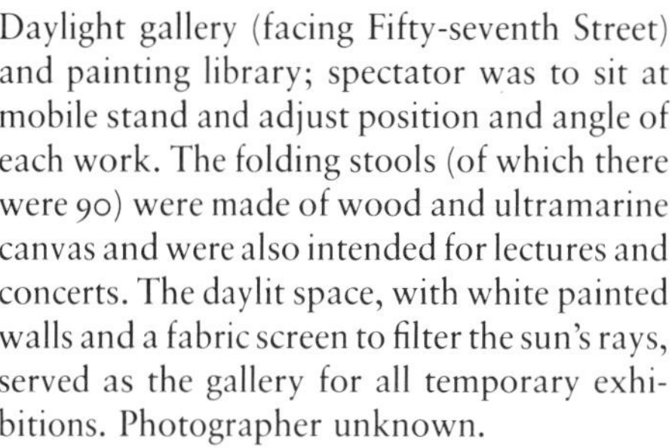

Daylight gallery (facing Fifty-seventh Street) and painting library; spectator was to sit at mobile stand and adjust position and angle of each work. The folding stools (of which there were 90) were made of wood and ultramarine canvas and were also intended for lectures and concerts. The daylit space, with white painted walls and a fabric screen to filter the sun's rays, served as the gallery for all temporary exhibitions. Photographer unknown.

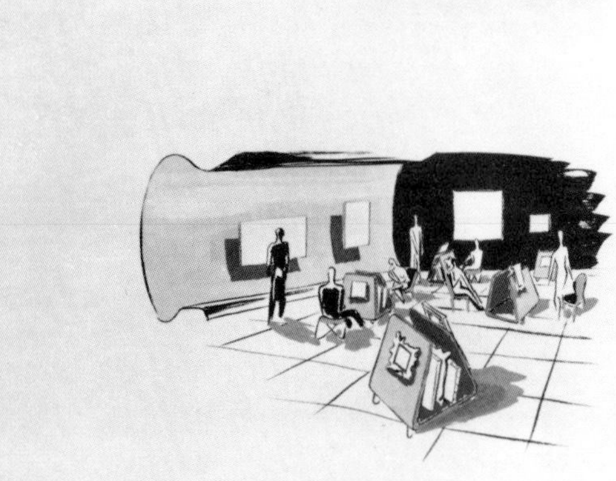

Kiesler, Designs for daylight gallery with painting library, tempera and ink on paper, 11 x 14¾ in., 27.9 x 37.5 cm., Collection Lillian Kiesler.

Photograph by Berenice Abbott, courtesy Lillian Kiesler.

Photograph by Berenice Abbott, courtesy Lillian Kiesler.

Peggy Guggenheim in the kinetic gallery. The visitor turned the large wooden wheel while looking through a small hole; 14 reproductions from the *Boîte-en-valise* of Marcel Duchamp appeared sequentially. Elsewhere in the same gallery was a recessed panel containing a mechanized belt on which original works by Klee were mounted. The spectator standing in front of the panel automatically activated an electric eye that set the belt in motion. The works were visible one by one through a window opening; the progress of the belt could be delayed by pressing a button. Photograph by Berenice Abbott.

Fold-out announcement-order forms for the publication *Art of This Century*, edited by Peggy Guggenheim, New York, May 1942. Edition of 2500 produced under the direction of Inez Chatfield for Art Aid Corporation.

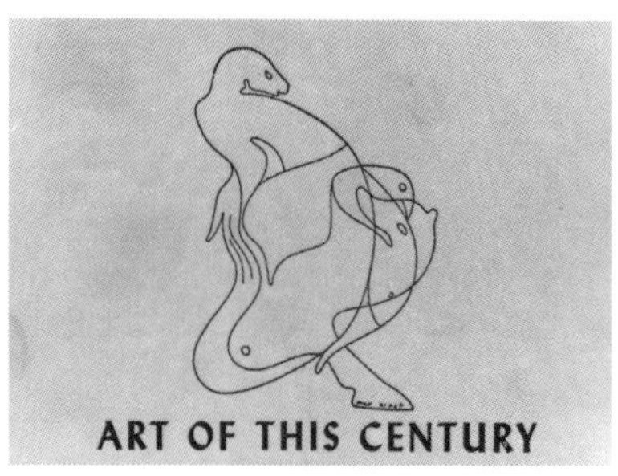

ART OF THIS CENTURY

ART OF THIS CENTURY

Edited by PEGGY GUGGENHEIM

An anthology of non-realistic art from 1910 to 1942, with manifestoes and articles by Breton, Ernst, Arp, Chirico, Pevsner, Gabo, Kandinsky, Mondrian, Nicholson, Braque, Picasso, Balla and others.

This book will also serve as a catalogue to the permanent collection of ART OF THIS CENTURY, a new art center, to be opened to the public in the fall in New York.

The collection represents sixty-seven artists beginning with the early works of Duchamp, Picasso, Kandinsky, Chirico, Ernst, Klee, Mondrian, Chagal, Arp, Brancusi etc. This general survey of the art of the last thirty years also includes the younger Surrealist and Abstract artists.

Cover-design by Max Ernst—Biographies and statements—Various heretofore unpublished material — 68 Halftone reproductions — 160 pages — size: 7⅝ x 10⅛ inches — Price: $3.00 per copy

Publication date: May 15th, 1942

Please send.............copies of ART OF THIS CENTURY ($3.00 post paid in U. S. A.) to:

NAME: ....

ADDRESS: ....

Kindly make checks or money orders payable to:

ART OF THIS CENTURY
PEGGY GUGGENHEIM
440 EAST 51ST STREET
NEW YORK, N. Y.

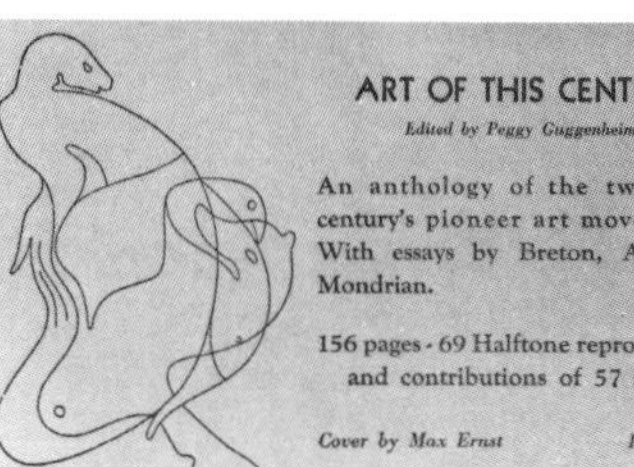

ART OF THIS CENTURY

Edited by Peggy Guggenheim

An anthology of the twentieth century's pioneer art movements. With essays by Breton, Arp and Mondrian.

156 pages - 69 Halftone reproductions and contributions of 57 artists.

Cover by Max Ernst *Price $3.00*

ART OF THIS CENTURY

Edited by Peggy Guggenheim

An anthology of the twentieth century's pioneer art movements.

With essays by Breton, Arp and Mondrian.

156 pages - 69 Halftone reproductions and contributions of 57 artists.

Cover by Max Ernst *Price $3.00*

Peggy Guggenheim had begun working on her catalogue while she was in Grenoble in the winter of 1940-41. Jean Arp had written a preface at that time ("Abstract Art Concrete Art"). André Breton, who had also promised her an introduction (see p. 761), wrote it after his arrival in New York ("Genesis and Perspective of Surrealism"), and he helped to assemble photographs, statements by many of the artists, and other material. Mondrian also contributed a short essay ("Abstract Art"). ("*I was also very busy completing the catalogue I had started in Grenoble. Max did a beautiful cover for it and helped me a lot with the layout. I was rather worried about this catalogue, however, and decided it was very dull. I asked Breton to save it. He was always telling me it was 'catastrophique,' which it probably would have been, had it not been for him. He spent hours of research and found statements by each artist represented in the collection.*" *Confessions*, 1960, p. 94.)

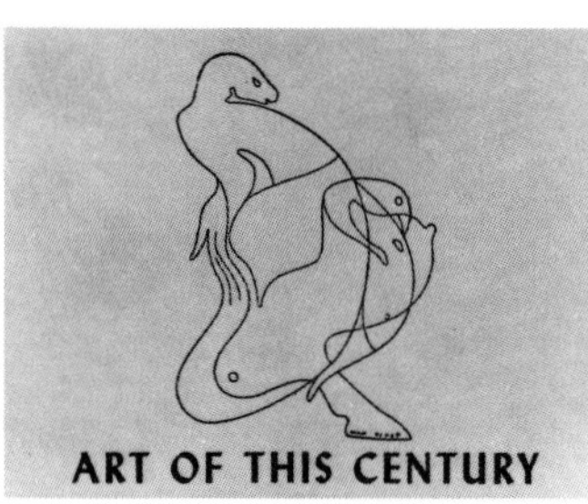

MISS PEGGY GUGGENHEIM
invites you to attend the opening of
ART OF THIS CENTURY
at 30 West 57th Street, New York, N. Y.
TUESDAY, OCTOBER 20th, 1942
From 8.00 P. M. until Midnight

Admission
$1.00 per person

For the Benefit of
The American Red Cross

THIS INVITATON WILL ADMIT TWO (2) PERSONS

Peggy Guggenheim opened her museum on October 20, 1942, with a benefit for The American Red Cross and issued a statement to the press: "*Opening this gallery and its collection to the public during a time when people are fighting for their lives and freedom is a responsibility of which I am fully conscious. The undertaking will serve its purpose only if it succeeds in serving the future instead of recording the past.*" Her initial conception had been that of a museum focusing primarily on its permanent collection and holding occasional loan exhibitions. By the time of the opening, however, she had decided to introduce a gallery dimension, and the planning of exhibitions that would present new artists and sell their work began at once.[2] In the earliest stages of the enterprise, she employed Jimmy Ernst as secretary assistant. Howard Putzel then worked with her until the close of the 1943-44 season; he was followed by Marius Bewley. The opening exhibition of the collection and, in particular, Kiesler's installation, attracted nationwide attention, with articles and syndicated columns appearing in newspapers in, among others, California, Illinois, Indiana, Kansas, Louisiana, Massachusetts, North Carolina, Ohio, Pennsylvania, Texas, Virginia, Washington, and Wisconsin.[3]

Edward A. Jewell, *The New York Times*, 21 October, 1942: "... *Art of This Century has been designed and painstakingly constructed by Frederick J. Kiesler. As a setting contrived for the exhibition of the types of modern art exemplified, it is the last word. One wall of a long room devoted to cubism and other forms of abstract art is of dark blue canvas, and instead of constituting a flat surface it is sinuous and moderately serpentine. The long facing walls of another room, in which surrealist art has been placed, are of wood, and concave.*

"*In most instances paintings are not hung directly on a wall. Instead they are suspended in the air, sometimes close to the wall, again out in the middle of the room, fastened to a neat contrivance that permits their rotating at the will of the spectator. No frames are used, and Mr. Kiesler explains why: 'Today the framed painting on the wall has become a decorative cipher without life and meaning, or else, to the more susceptible observer, an object of interest existing in a world distinct from his. Its frame is at once symbol and agent of an artificial duality of 'vision' and 'reality,' or 'image' and 'environment,' a plastic barrier across which man looks from the world he inhabits to the alien world in which the work of art has its being. That barrier must be dissolved.*"

Henry McBride, *The New York Sun*, 23 October, 1942: "... *Frederick J. Kiesler, who has been called in by Miss Guggenheim to install these amazing pictures and carvings, has made a startling job of it....*

"*'We, the inheritors of chaos,' says Mr. Kiesler, 'must be the architects of a new unity,' and the mere fact that the pictures escape criticism suggests that something of his goal has been achieved....*

"*The surrealist and abstract artists are the ones we know already but Miss Guggenheim has chosen her examples with rare discrimination. The Max Ernst productions are likely to remain his best, as it is now difficult to see how he can go beyond his 'Attainment* [sic] *of the Bride' and his 'Antipope.' Piet Mondrian, 'purest' of all the abstract painters, is at his best in the 'Ocean' drawing, and Man Ray's 'Rope Dancer' is enough to make all Americans regret this artist's expatriation.*

"*So it goes all along the line. Miro, Picasso, Calder, Arp, Brancusi, Chirico, Salvador Dali, Breton, Leger, Juan Gris, Paul Klee, Lipschitz* [sic], *Masson, Matta, Ozenfant, Picabia, Braque, Yves Tanguy, and Kurt Seligman* [sic] *'unite,' as Mr. Kiesler puts it, very easily with the time we live in.*"

Clement Greenberg, *The Nation*, 30 January, 1943: "... *The surrealist pictures, thrust out on rods from tunnel-like walls, seem, because of the dramatic lighting, which switches at intervals from one group of canvases to another, to hang in indefinite space. This is exactly right, because it emphasizes that traditional discontinuity between the specta-*

2. The inclusion of a commercial gallery was originally suggested by Bernard Reis.

3. For an examination of some aspects of Kiesler's work at Art of This Century see E. Kaufmann, jr., "The Violent Art of Hanging Pictures," *Magazine of Art*, vol. 39, March 1946, pp. 108-10; C. Goodman, "Frederick Kiesler: Designs for Peggy Guggenheim's Art of This Century Gallery," *Arts Magazine*, vol. 51, June 1977, pp. 90-95; M. P. Lader, "Peggy Guggenheim's Art of This Century: The Surrealist Milieu and the American Avant-Garde, 1942-1947," unpublished Ph.D. dissertation, University of Delaware, 1981, pp. 113-32. See also the unpublished documents in the Kiesler Archive, Collection Lillian Kiesler: "Outline Specifications," "Note on Designing the Gallery," "Press Release Pertaining to the Architectural Aspects of the Gallery." The author is indebted to Lillian Kiesler for access to these documents.

tor and the space within the picture to which most of the surrealists have returned.

"*Except for the surrealist room, the gallery is, however, a little crowded and scrappy. Mr. Kiesler overdid the functionalism in not providing the other rooms with a more unified background.... Nevertheless, the décor does create a sense of exhilaration and provides a relief from other usually over-upholstered or over-sanitary museums and galleries. And inadequate as it may be in each single department, the collection itself is one of the most comprehensive in this country of cubist, abstract, and surrealist art as a whole. In addition to the very fine Klee in the peep-show, there is a large orange painting by Ernst and a classical view by Chirico which are the best examples of these artists' work I have seen in this country.*"

Objects by Joseph Cornell; Marcel Duchamp: Box Valise; Laurence Vail Bottles. December 1942.
No catalogue.

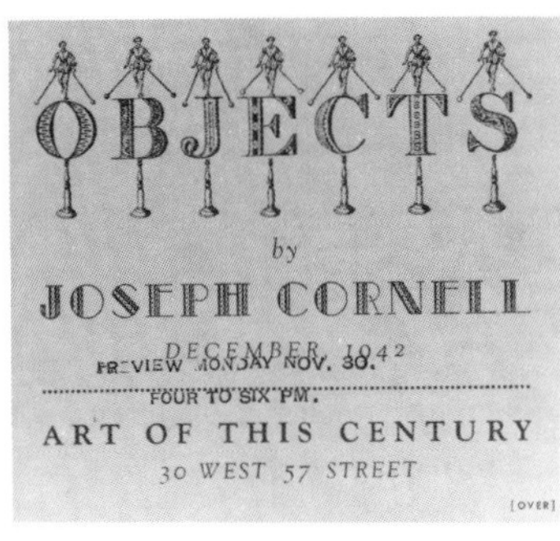

Announcement (recto).

Announcement (verso).

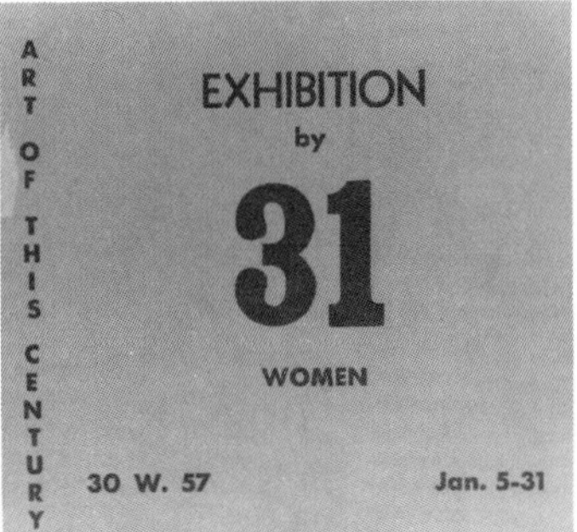

Announcement.

Exhibition by 31 women. January 5-31 [extended to February 6], 1943.
Exhibition proposed by Marcel Duchamp. Selection jury: André Breton, Marcel Duchamp, Jimmy Ernst, Max Ernst, Peggy Guggenheim, Howard Putzel, James Thrall Soby, James Johnson Sweeney. (The press release for the exhibition omitted the names of Jimmy Ernst and Soby.)

Review: [unsigned], *Art News*, vol. 41, January 15-31, 1943: "... *Peggy Guggenheim's new place currently houses one of the more provocative shows.... already this gallery is living up to its promise of uncovering troublesome new talents.... The women... present a chinkless armored front.... Altogether the surprising thing about this show is how solid and serious the accomplishment is.*"

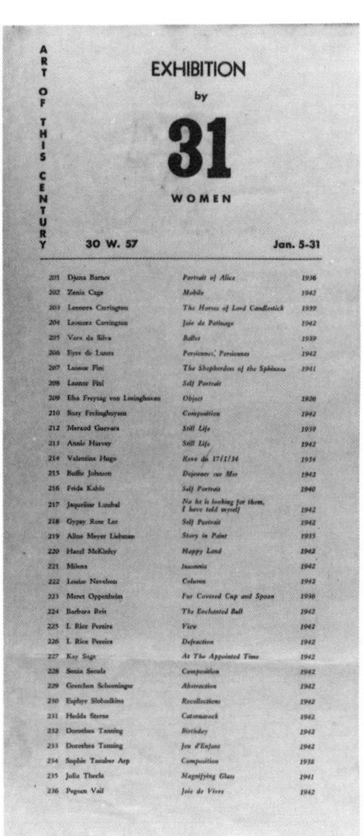

ART OF THIS CENTURY

EXHIBITION
by
31
WOMEN

30 W. 57 — Jan. 5-31

201	Djuna Barnes	*Portrait of Alice*	1936
202	Zenia Cage	*Mobile*	1942
203	Leonora Carrington	*The Horses of Lord Candlestick*	1939
204	Leonora Carrington	*Joie de Patinage*	1942
205	Vera da Silva	*Ballet*	1939
206	Eyre de Lanux	*Persiennes, Persiennes*	1942
207	Leonor Fini	*The Shepherdess of the Sphinxes*	1941
208	Leonor Fini	*Self Portrait*	
209	Elsa Freytag von Loringhoven	*Object*	1920
210	Suzy Frelinghuysen	*Composition*	1942
212	Meraud Guevara	*Still Life*	1939
213	Annie Harvey	*Still Life*	1942
214	Valentine Hugo	*Reve du 17/1/34*	1934
215	Buffie Johnson	*Dejeuner sur Mer*	1942
216	Frida Kahlo	*Self Portrait*	1940
217	Jaqueline Lamba	*No he is looking for them, I have told myself*	1942
218	Gypsy Rose Lee	*Self Portrait*	1942
219	Aline Meyer Liebman	*Story in Paint*	1935
220	Hazel McKinley	*Happy Land*	1942
221	Milena	*Insomnia*	1942
222	Louise Nevelson	*Column*	1942
223	Meret Oppenheim	*Fur Covered Cup and Spoon*	1936
224	Barbara Reis	*The Enchanted Bull*	1942
225	I. Rice Pereira	*View*	1942
226	I. Rice Pereira	*Defraction*	1942
227	Kay Sage	*At The Appointed Time*	1942
228	Sonia Sekula	*Composition*	1942
229	Gretchen Schoeninger	*Abstraction*	1942
230	Esphyr Slobodkina	*Recollections*	1942
231	Hedda Sterne	*Catamarock*	1942
232	Dorothea Tanning	*Birthday*	1942
233	Dorothea Tanning	*Jeu d'Enfant*	1942
234	Sophie Taeuber Arp	*Composition*	1938
235	Julia Thecla	*Magnifying Glass*	1941
236	Pegeen Vail	*Joie de Vivre*	1942

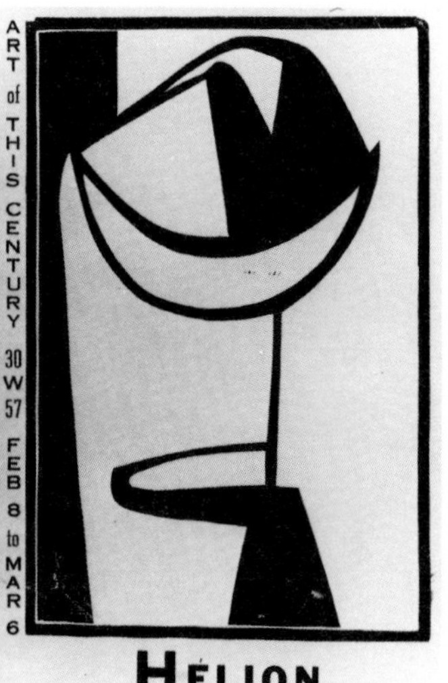

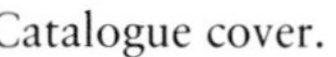

Catalogue cover.

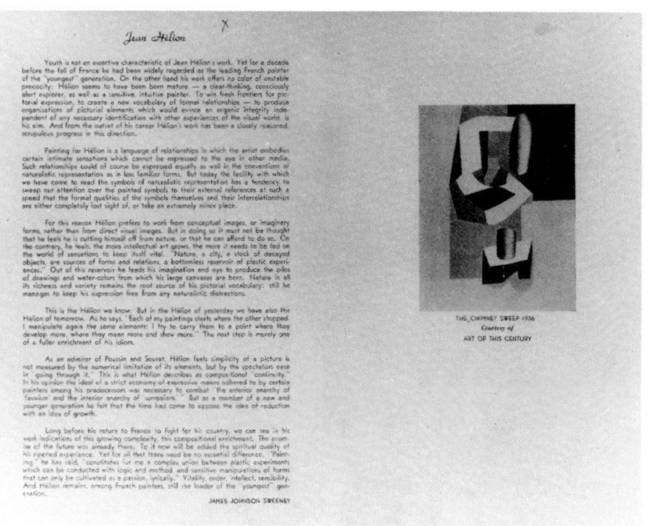

Catalogue

3. PEINTURE VERTICALE	1938-39	Lent By—Passedoit Gallery
4. PEINTURE	1933	Lent By—Mr. Frederick J. Kiesler
5. PEINTURE	1934	Lent By—Museum of Modern Art
6. PEINTURE	1936	Lent By—Museum of Modern Art
7. PEINTURE	1933	Lent By—Valentine Gallery
9. FIGURES JUMELLES	1938	
10. FIGURE TOMBEE	1939	
11. FOND BLEU-VERT	1938	
12. ROUGE BRILLIANT	1938	
13. FIGURE BLEUE	1936	
14. FIGURE CREUSE	1936	
15. BLEU ECLATANT	1938	
16. COMPOSITION COMPLEXE	1937-38	
17. FIGURE ISOLEE	1937	
18. PEINTURE	1937	
19. GRANDE COMPOSITION A PLUSIEURS ETAGES	1939	
20. GRANDE COMPOSITION EN LARGEUR	1939	
21. BANDES JAUNES	1938	
22. BANDES ROSES	1938	
23. FRISE	1938	
24. PETIT TABLEAU	1939	
25. COMPOSITION DRAMATIQUE	1939-43	
26. FIGURE DEBOUT	1935	
27. PEINTURE CLAIRE	1936	
28. EQUILIBRE	1933-34	
29. PETIT TABLEAU	1934	
30-45 FIFTEEN WATERCOLOURS (AQUARELLE)	1937-38-39	
46-47 TWO DRAWINGS (CALLED DESSIN)	1937-38	

Back cover.

Retrospective exhibition of the works of Hélion. February 8-March 6 [extended to March 13], 1943.

Catalogue preface by James Johnson Sweeney.

Review: Robert Coates, *The New Yorker*, 27 February, 1943: "*... His, I think, is a style that derives primarily from Léger's work in the early Dynamist days, but from this beginning Hélion has gone on to develop a design that is strongly personal and that also combines grace, dignity, and deep suggestiveness in a way that few other contemporary abstractionists can equal.*"

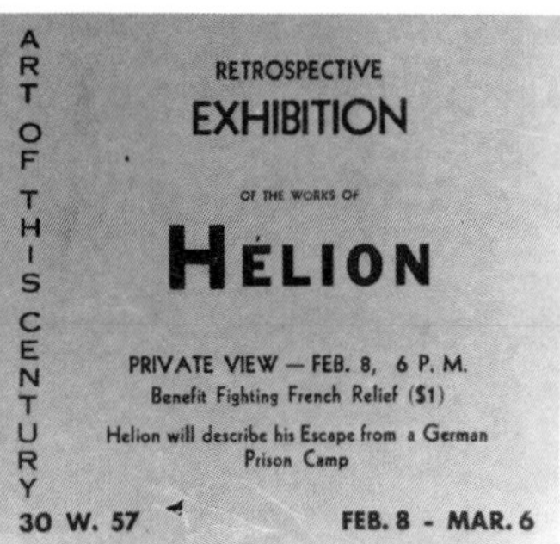

Announcement.

15 Early 15 Late Paintings. March 13-April 10 [extended to April 17], 1943.

Loan exhibition conceived by Jimmy Ernst to take the place of an exhibition organized by André Breton. The latter exhibition, which was a presentation in connection with the review *VVV*, was abruptly cancelled after a disagreement between Breton and Peggy Guggenheim.

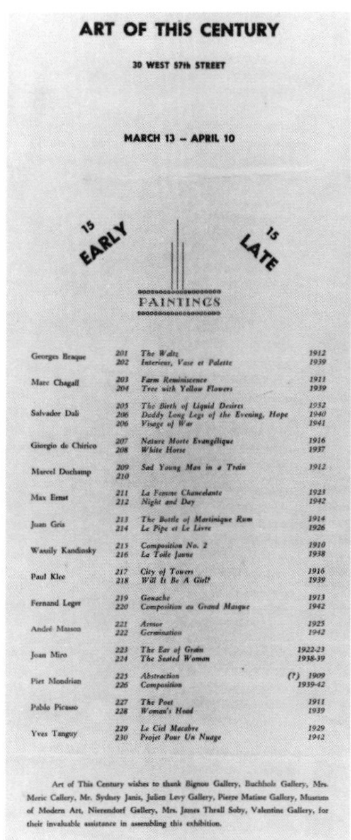

ART OF THIS CENTURY

30 WEST 57th STREET

MARCH 13 – APRIL 10

15 EARLY 15 LATE PAINTINGS

Georges Braque	201	*The Waltz*	1912
	202	*Interieur, Vase et Palette*	1939
Marc Chagall	203	*Farm Reminiscence*	1911
	204	*Tree with Yellow Flowers*	1939
Salvador Dali	205	*The Birth of Liquid Desires*	1932
	206	*Daddy Long Legs of the Evening, Hope*	1940
	206	*Visage of War*	1941
Giorgio de Chirico	207	*Nature Morte Evangélique*	1916
	208	*White Horse*	1937
Marcel Duchamp	209	*Sad Young Man in a Train*	1912
	210		
Max Ernst	211	*La Femme Chancelante*	1923
	212	*Night and Day*	1942
Juan Gris	213	*The Bottle of Martinique Rum*	1914
	214	*Le Pipe et Le Livre*	1926
Wassily Kandinsky	215	*Composition No. 2*	1910
	216	*La Toile Jaune*	1938
Paul Klee	217	*City of Towers*	1916
	218	*Will It Be A Girl?*	1939
Fernand Leger	219	*Gouache*	1913
	220	*Composition au Grand Masque*	1942
André Masson	221	*Armor*	1925
	222	*Germination*	1942
Joan Miro	223	*The Ear of Grain*	1922-23
	224	*The Seated Woman*	1938-39
Piet Mondrian	225	*Abstraction*	(?) 1909
	226	*Composition*	1939-42
Pablo Picasso	227	*The Poet*	1911
	228	*Woman's Head*	1939
Yves Tanguy	229	*Le Ciel Macabre*	1929
	230	*Projet Pour Un Nuage*	1942

Art of This Century wishes to thank Bignou Gallery, Buchholz Gallery, Mrs. Meric Callery, Mr. Sydney Janis, Julien Levy Gallery, Pierre Matisse Gallery, Museum of Modern Art, Nierendorf Gallery, Mrs. James Thrall Soby, Valentine Gallery, for their invaluable assistance in assembling this exhibition.

Exhibition of collage. April 16-May 15, 1943. No catalogue. First international collage exhibition to be held in the United States. The names of participating artists are listed on the announcement, although the list is incomplete (see above, p. 583, fn. 3).

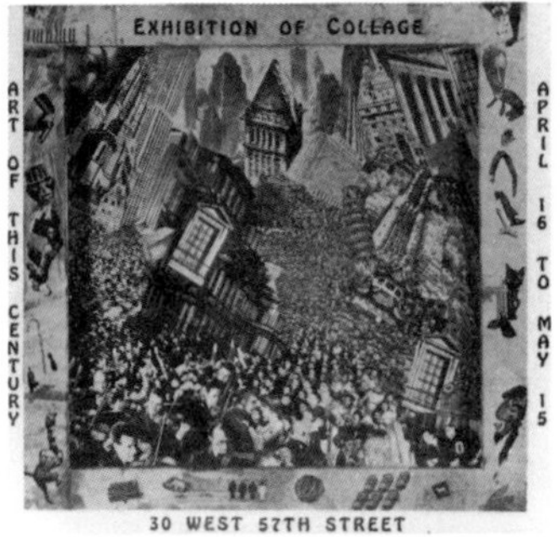

Announcement (recto). Illustration: Detail of a collage screen by Laurence Vail.

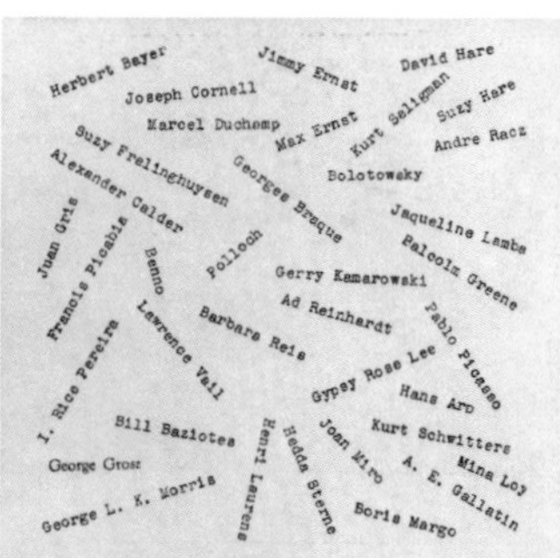

Announcement (verso).

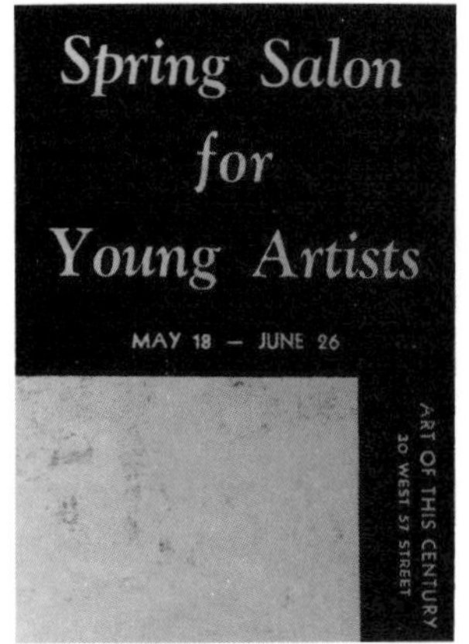

Announcement.

ART OF THIS CENTURY
30 WEST 57th STREET
NEW YORK

LIST OF PICTURES IN THE SPRING SALON FOR YOUNG ARTISTS (UNDER 36 YEARS OLD)

1..Virginia Admiral........Abstraction...........Lent by Robert Duncan
2..William Baziotes........The Mirror at Midnight 1
3..William Baziotes........The Mirror at Midnight 2
4..Ilya Bolotowsky.........Variation with Perpendiculars
5..Ted Bradley.............Private Garden Magic..
6..Peter Busa..............Object-Painting.......
7..Xenia Cage..............Mobile................
8..C. Dilworth.............Object-Collage........
9..C. Dilworth.............Object-Collage........
10..Ronnie Elliott..........A Country of Cockaigne
11..Jimmie Ernst............Translunar Biology....
12..William Pett............Abstraction...........Lent by Kirk Askew
13..Perle Fine..............Gabun.................
14..Perle Fine..............Tensions Dynamique....
15..Sidney Geist............Sculpture.............
16..Morris Graves...........Eagle of the Inner Eye.Lent by the Marion Willard Gallery
17..Morris Graves...........Bird On Rock..........Lent by the Marion Willard Gallery
18..Fannie Hillsmith........Pine Cones............
19..Holtzman................Painting Construction..
20..Kamarowski..............Painting..............
21..Ibram Lassau............Intersecting Rectangle
22..Ibram Lassau............Metal Sculpture.......

page 2

23..Matta...................Coagula Solve.........Collection: Art of This Century
24..Matta...................Omega of Lost Words....Lent by the Pierre Matisse Gallery
25..Azio Martinelli.........Aerials...............
26..Alice Trumbull Mason...Composition............
27..Robert Motherwell......Painting...............
28..Gordon Onslow-Ford.....The Transparent Woman..
29..I. Rice Pereira........Self Portrait..........
30..I. Rice Pereira........Composition............
31..Jackson Pollock........Painting...............
32..Andre Racz.............The Swan...............
33..Ad Reinhardt...........Abstraction............
34..Chris Ritter...........Things On a Table 1....
35..Chris Ritter...........Things On a Table 2....
36..Ralph Rosenberg........Nature 2...............Lent by the Marion Willard Gallery
37..Sonja Sekula...........Construction...........
38..Slobodkina.............Abstraction............
39..Slobodkina.............Abstraction............
40..Hedda Sterne...........Pressed Landscape......
41..Paul Weinstock.........Painting...............Lent by the Julien Levy Gallery
42..Paul Weinstock.........Painting...............Lent by the Julien Levy Gallery
43..Paul Ziff..............Painting...............

Mimeographed checklist.

Spring Salon for Young Artists. May 18-June 26, 1943.

Mimeographed checklist. Exhibition originally proposed for Guggenheim Jeune, London, 1939, by Herbert Read. Selection jury: Alfred H. Barr, Jr., Marcel Duchamp, Peggy Guggenheim, Piet Mondrian, Howard Putzel, James Thrall Soby, James Johnson Sweeney. According to the verbal testimony of Peggy Guggenheim, Jimmy Ernst (who attended the selection) and Sweeney, the members of the jury were especially struck by the promise of Jackson Pollock.

Review: Robert Coates, *The New Yorker*, 29 March, 1943: "... *Despite a faint air of the haphazard about the hanging and a certain amount of dead wood in the paintings, the new show at Art of This Century deserves your attention.... it has attracted a lot of new talent; to most people, I think, at least two-thirds of the thirty-odd artists represented will be totally unknown. A good share of the work is amateurish,... But in Jackson Pollock's abstract 'Painting,' with its curious reminiscences of both Matisse and Miró, we have a real discovery, and I liked, as well, Fannie Hillsmith's 'Pine Cones' and the classically severe 'Abstraction' by Ad Reinhardt....*" (Earliest press mention of Pollock.)

Review: Clement Greenberg, *The Nation*, 29 May, 1943: "...*a show of artists under thirty-five years old. It is a good one, and for once the future reveals a gleam of hope. They are all promising, and some, like I. Rice Pereira, are more than that. Matta copies himself even more superbly than usual.... Robert Motherwell, Fannie Hillsmith, and Ralph Rosenberg, each show small paintings which it would be a pleasure to own.... and there is a large painting by Jackson Pollock which, I am told, made the jury starry-eyed.*"

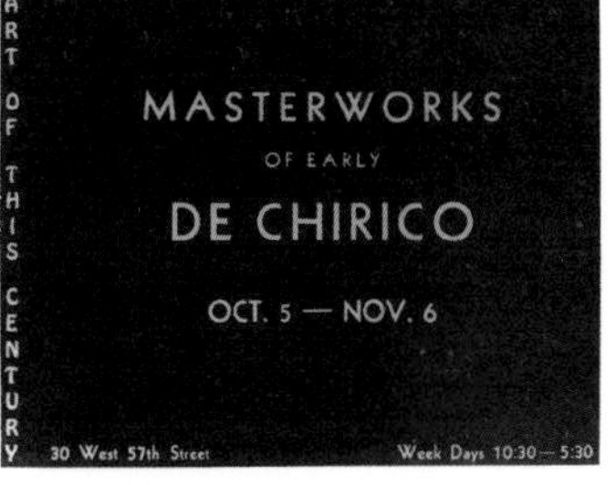

Announcement.

ART OF THIS CENTURY.......30 West 57th Street.......New York

MASTERWORKS OF EARLY DE CHIRICO

1...THE NOSTALGIA OF THE INFINITE (1911).......Lent by the Museum of Modern Art
2...SELF-PORTRAIT (1913).......................Lent by Mr. and Mrs. Gordon Onslow-Ford
3...THE GLASS DOG (c.1913).....................Lent by Mr. and Mrs. Bernard Reis
4...THE TRANSFORMED DREAM (1908)...............Lent by Mr. and Mrs. Joseph Pulitzer, Jr.
5...THE ROSE TOWER (1913)......................Collection Art of This Century
6...THE JOYS AND ENIGMAS OF A STRANGE HOUR (1913)....Lent by Lt. Wright Ludington
7...THE MELANCHOLY OF DEPARTURE (1914).........Lent by Mr. and Mrs. James Thrall Soby
8...THE MELANCHOLY AND MYSTERY OF A STREET (1914)....Lent by Mrs. Stanley Resor
9...THE TORMENT OF THE POET (1914).............Lent by Mr. and Mrs. Gordon Onslow-Ford
10...THE GENERAL'S ILLNESS (1914-1915)..........Lent by the Wadsworth Atheneum, Hartford
11...THE AMUSEMENTS OF A YOUNG GIRL (1915)......Lent by Mr. and Mrs. James Thrall Soby
12...THE SEER (1915)........................... " " " " " " " "
13...THE DOUBLE DREAM OF SPRING (1915).......... " " " " " " " "
14...THE PLAYTHINGS OF THE PRINCE (1915)........Lent by Mr. and Mrs. Matta Echaurren
15...THE DREAM OF THE POET (1915)...............Collection Art of This Century
16...THE GENTLE AFTERNOON (1916)................ " " " " "
17...POLITICS (1916)............................Lent by Mr. and Mrs. Gordon Onslow-Ford
18...GRAND METAPHYSICAL INTERIOR (1917).........Lent by Mr. and Mrs. James Thrall Soby

Typed checklist.

Masterworks of Early De Chirico. October 5-November 6 [extended to November 7], 1943. Loan exhibition. Typed checklist. Exhibition possibly proposed and organized by James Thrall Soby, with whose book *The Early De Chirico* (New York, 1941) the selection closely corresponds.

In July of 1943 Peggy Guggenheim signed a contract with Jackson Pollock. (For the details see above, cat. no. 144, fn. 1). Under the terms he was to receive a monthly stipend in return for paintings. The contract was renewed periodically and remained in effect until after Peggy Guggenheim departed for Europe in 1947. It is not clear who introduced Peggy Guggenheim to Pollock; it is clear, however, that soon after the *Spring Salon* she was encouraged by Matta and by Howard Putzel to give Pollock a contract. They, together with Sweeney and possibly some others, convinced her that Pollock was an artist of unusual promise who deserved her support. She then gave him a commission to paint a mural for her house and signed the contract. Many years later, Lee Krasner Pollock confirmed the importance of Putzel's role, describing his almost nightly visits to their house, his coaching regarding the contract negotiations, and his tireless enthusiasm for Pollock's work. She also emphasized Peggy Guggenheim's ultimate responsibility: Pollock and Krasner lived on the contract payments, having no other source of income, and Peggy Guggenheim thus provided the material and psychological support Pollock needed. ("*When Peggy commissioned that mural and gave him the contract it was enormously helpful; it was terribly important to have that kind of support.*")[4]

4. Krasner, in conversation with the author, March 6, 1981. Clement Greenberg, in conversation with the author, February 26, 1980, also attributed a vital role to Putzel. Peggy Guggenheim herself repeatedly spoke with the author of Putzel's impact on her thinking and planning, especially in relation to her decision to support Pollock. In her last years, she insisted that she had not fully appreciated Pollock's greatness until she saw her own collection of his paintings installed in the Museo Correr, Venice, in July 1950.

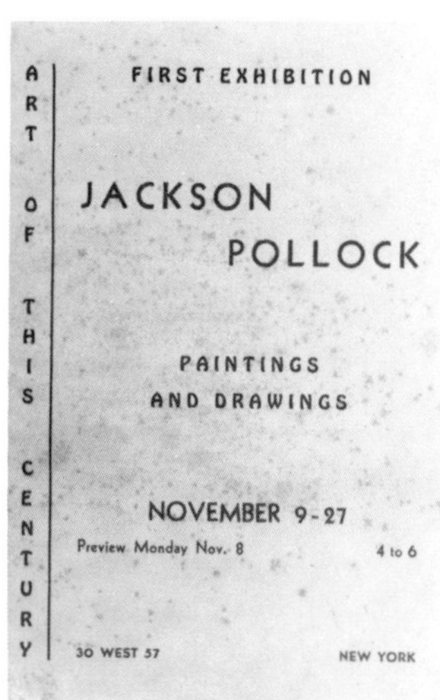

ART OF THIS CENTURY

FIRST EXHIBITION

JACKSON POLLOCK

PAINTINGS AND DRAWINGS

NOVEMBER 9-27

Preview Monday Nov. 8 4 to 6

30 WEST 57 NEW YORK

Catalogue cover.

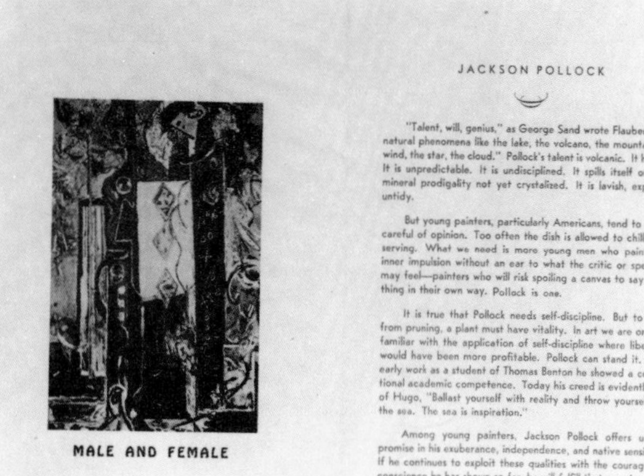

MALE AND FEMALE

JACKSON POLLOCK

"Talent, will, genius," as George Sand wrote Flaubert, "are natural phenomena like the lake, the volcano, the mountain, the wind, the star, the cloud." Pollock's talent is volcanic. It has fire. It is unpredictable. It is undisciplined. It spills itself out in a mineral prodigality not yet crystalized. It is lavish, explosive, untidy.

But young painters, particularly Americans, tend to be too careful of opinion. Too often the dish is allowed to chill in the serving. What we need is more young men who paint from inner impulsion without an ear to what the critic or spectator may feel—painters who will risk spoiling a canvas to say something in their own way. Pollock is one.

It is true that Pollock needs self-discipline. But to profit from pruning, a plant must have vitality. In art we are only too familiar with the application of self-discipline where liberation would have been more profitable. Pollock can stand it. In his early work as a student of Thomas Benton he showed a conventional academic competence. Today his creed is evidently that of Hugo, "Ballast yourself with reality and throw yourself into the sea. The sea is inspiration."

Among young painters, Jackson Pollock offers unusual promise in his exuberance, independence, and native sensibility. If he continues to exploit these qualities with the courage and conscience he has shown so far, he will fulfill that promise.

JAMES JOHNSON SWEENEY

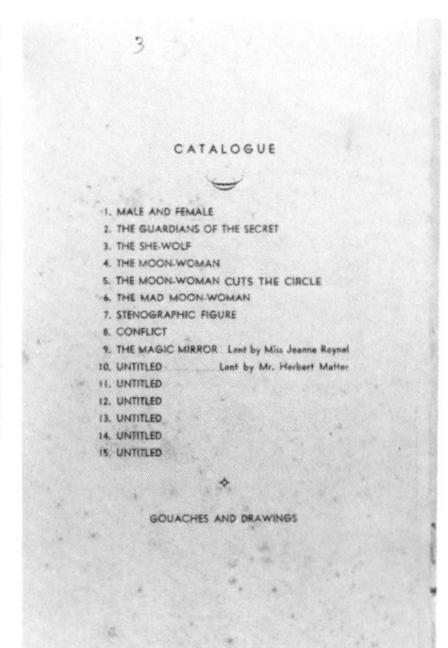

3

CATALOGUE

1. MALE AND FEMALE
2. THE GUARDIANS OF THE SECRET
3. THE SHE-WOLF
4. THE MOON-WOMAN
5. THE MOON-WOMAN CUTS THE CIRCLE
6. THE MAD MOON-WOMAN
7. STENOGRAPHIC FIGURE
8. CONFLICT
9. THE MAGIC MIRROR Lent by Miss Jeanne Reynal
10. UNTITLED Lent by Mr. Herbert Matter
11. UNTITLED
12. UNTITLED
13. UNTITLED
14. UNTITLED
15. UNTITLED

GOUACHES AND DRAWINGS

Back cover.

First Exhibition. Jackson Pollock. Paintings and Drawings. November 9-27, 1943. Catalogue preface by James Johnson Sweeney. Exhibition proposed by Matta and by Howard Putzel.

Review: Robert M. Coates, *The New Yorker*, 20 November, 1943: "*...At Art of This Century, there is what seems to be an authentic discovery—the paintings of Jackson Pollock. ...Mr. Pollock's style, which is a curious mixture of the abstract and the symbolic, is almost wholly individual, and the effect of his one noticeable influence, Picasso, is a healthy one, for it imposes a certain symmetry on his work without detracting from its basic force and vigor....*"

Review: Clement Greenberg, *The Nation*, 27 November, 1943: "*... He is the first painter I know of to have got something positive from the muddiness of color that so profoundly characterizes a great deal of American painting. It is the equivalent, even if in a negative helpless way, of that American chiaroscuro which dominated Melville, Hawthorne, Poe, and has been best translated into painting by Blakelock and Ryder. The mud abounds in Pollock's larger works, and these, though the least consummated, are his most original and ambitious.... 'Conflict,' and 'Wounded animal,' ... are among the strongest abstract paintings I have yet seen by an American.... Pollock has gone through the influences of Miró, Picasso, Mexican painting, and what not, and has come out on the other side at the age of thirty-one painting mostly with his own brush. In his search for style he is liable to lapse into an influence, but if times are propitious it won't be for long.*"

Review: Robert Motherwell, *Partisan Review*, winter 1944: "*Certain individuals represent a young generation's artistic chances. There are never many such individuals in a single field, such as painting — perhaps a hundred to begin with.... The importance of the one-man show of young Jackson Pollock (Art of This Century) lies just in this, that he represents one of the younger generation's chances. There are not three other young Americans of whom this could be said. In his exhibit Pollock reveals extraordinary gifts: his color sense is remarkably fine, never exploited beyond its proper role; and his sense of surface is equally good. His principal problem is to discover what his true subject is. And since painting is his thought's medium, the resolution must grow out of the process of his painting itself.*"

Natural, Insane, Surrealist Art. December 1-31, 1943.
No catalogue. Exhibition proposed by Ladislas Segy. Included were driftwood, petrified tree roots, bones and skeletons; drawings by the insane; Surrealist works by William Baziotes, Alexander Calder, Joseph Cornell, Max Ernst, Paul Klee, André Masson, Matta, Joan Miró, Robert Motherwell, Jackson Pollock, André Racz, Yves Tanguy.

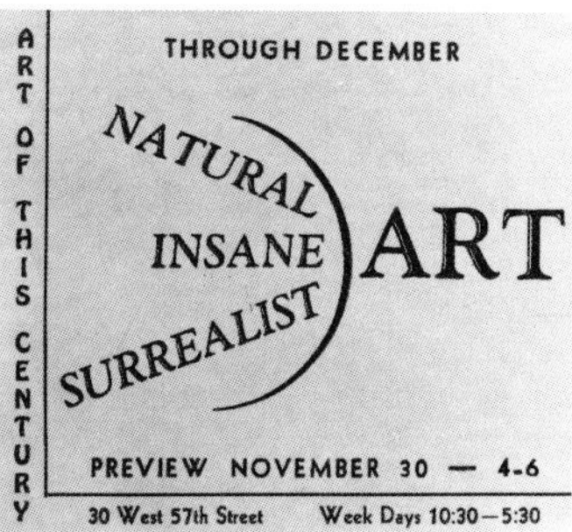

Announcement.

Catalogue cover.

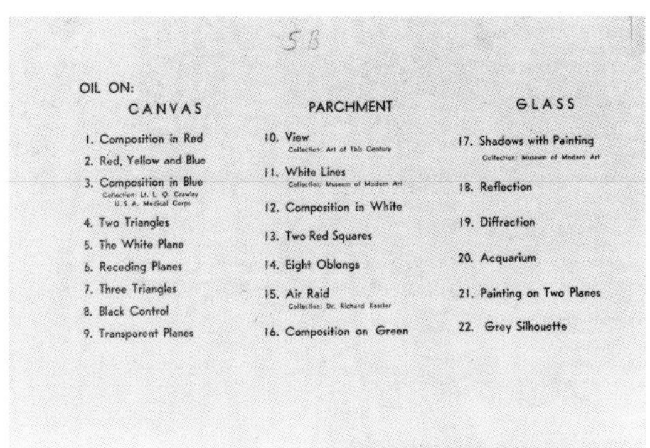

OIL ON:

CANVAS	PARCHMENT	GLASS
1. Composition in Red	10. View Collection: Art of This Century	17. Shadows with Painting Collection: Museum of Modern Art
2. Red, Yellow and Blue	11. White Lines Collection: Museum of Modern Art	18. Reflection
3. Composition in Blue Collection: Lt. L. Q. Crawley U. S. A. Medical Corps	12. Composition in White	19. Diffraction
4. Two Triangles	13. Two Red Squares	20. Acquarium
5. The White Plane	14. Eight Oblongs	21. Painting on Two Planes
6. Receding Planes	15. Air Raid Collection: Dr. Richard Kessler	22. Grey Silhouette
7. Three Triangles	16. Composition on Green	
8. Black Control		
9. Transparent Planes		

Back cover.

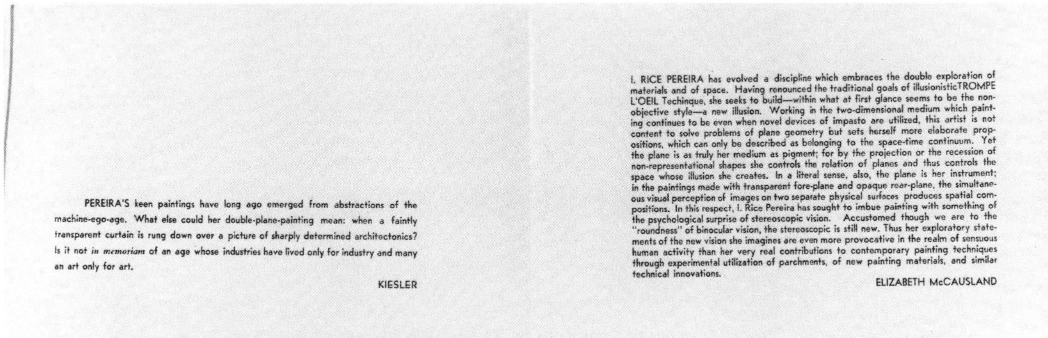

PEREIRA'S keen paintings have long ago emerged from abstractions of the machine-ego-age. What else could her double-plane-painting mean: when a faintly transparent curtain is rung down over a picture of sharply determined architectonics? Is it not *in memoriam* of an age whose industries have lived only for industry and many an art only for art.

KIESLER

I. RICE PEREIRA has evolved a discipline which embraces the double exploration of materials and of space. Having renounced the traditional goals of illusionisticTROMPE L'OEIL Techinque, she seeks to build—within what at first glance seems to be the non-objective style—a new illusion. Working in the two-dimensional medium which painting continues to be even when novel devices of impasto are utilized, this artist is not content to solve problems of plane geometry but sets herself more elaborate propositions, which can only be described as belonging to the space-time continuum. Yet the plane is as truly her medium as pigment; for by the projection or the recession of non-representational shapes she controls the relation of planes and thus controls the space whose illusion she creates. In a literal sense, also, the plane is her instrument; in the paintings made with transparent fore-plane and opaque rear-plane, the simultaneous visual perception of images on two separate physical surfaces produces spatial compositions. In this respect, I. Rice Pereira has sought to imbue painting with something of the psychological surprise of stereoscopic vision. Accustomed though we are to the "roundness" of binocular vision, the stereoscopic is still new. Thus her exploratory statements of the new vision she imagines are even more provocative in the realm of sensuous human activity than her very real contributions to contemporary painting techniques through experimental utilization of parchments, of new painting materials, and similar technical innovations.

ELIZABETH McCAUSLAND

I. Rice Pereira. January 4-22, 1944.
Catalogue prefaces by Frederick Kiesler and Elizabeth McCausland.

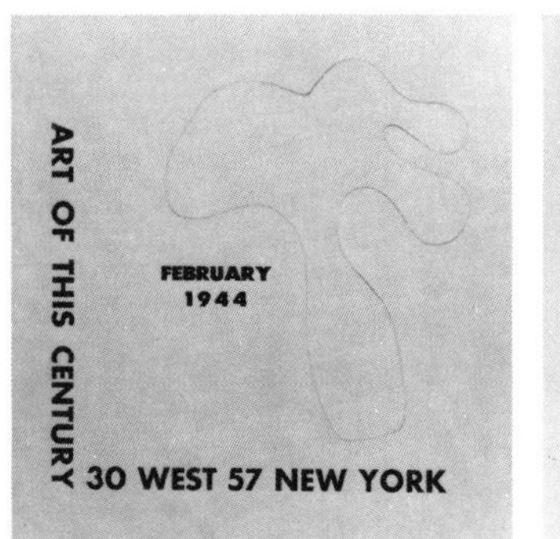

ART OF THIS CENTURY
FEBRUARY
1944
30 WEST 57 NEW YORK

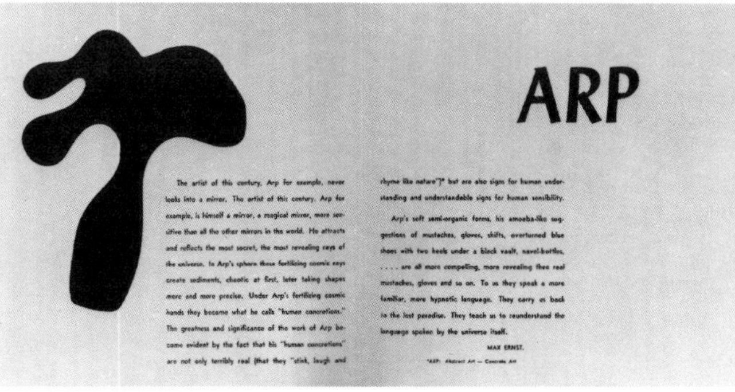

ARP

The artist of this century, Arp for example, never looks into a mirror. The artist of this century, Arp for example, is himself a mirror, a magical mirror, more sensitive than all the other mirrors in the world. He attracts and reflects the most secret, the most revealing rays of the universe. In Arp's sphere these fertilising cosmic rays create sediments, chaotic at first, later taking shapes more and more precise. Under Arp's fertilising cosmic hands they become what he calls "human concretions." The greatness and significance of the work of Arp become evident by the fact that his "human concretions" are not only terribly real (that they "stink, laugh and rhyme like nature")* but are also signs for human understanding and understandable signs for human sensibility.

Arp's soft semi-organic forms, his amoeba-like suggestions of mustaches, gloves, shifts, overturned blue shoes with two heels under a black vault, navel-bottles, ... are all more compelling, more revealing than real mustaches, gloves and so on. To us they speak a more familiar, more hypnotic language. They carry us back to the lost paradise. They teach us to reunderstand the language spoken by the universe itself.

MAX ERNST.

*ARP: Abstract Art — Concrete Art

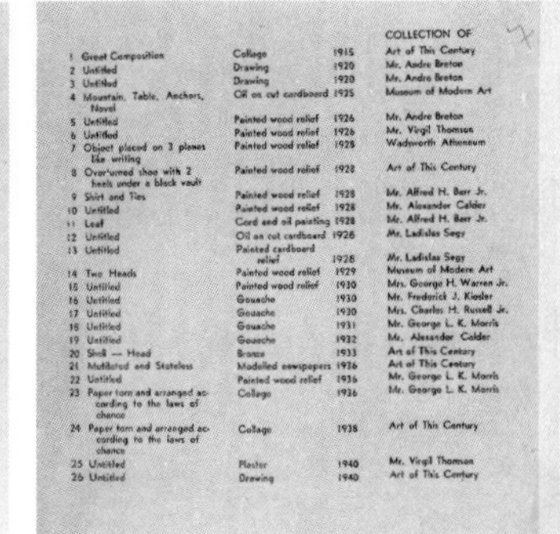

				COLLECTION OF
1	Great Composition	Collage	1915	Art of This Century
2	Untitled	Drawing	1920	Mr. Andre Breton
3	Untitled	Drawing	1920	Mr. Andre Breton
4	Mountain, Table, Anchors, Navel	Oil on cut cardboard	1925	Museum of Modern Art
5	Untitled	Painted wood relief	1926	Mr. Andre Breton
6	Untitled	Painted wood relief	1926	Mr. Virgil Thomson
7	Object placed on 3 planes like writing	Painted wood relief	1928	Wadsworth Atheneum
8	Overturned shoe with 2 heels under a black vault	Painted wood relief	1928	Art of This Century
9	Shirt and Ties	Painted wood relief	1928	Mr. Alfred H. Barr Jr.
10	Untitled	Painted wood relief	1928	Mr. Alexander Calder
11	Leaf	Card and oil painting	1928	Mr. Alfred H. Barr Jr.
12	Untitled	Oil on cut cardboard	1928	Mr. Ladislas Segy
13	Untitled	Painted cardboard relief	1928	Mr. Ladislas Segy
14	Two Heads	Painted wood relief	1929	Museum of Modern Art
15	Untitled	Painted wood relief	1930	Mrs. George H. Warren Jr.
16	Untitled	Gouache	1930	Mr. Frederick J. Kiesler
17	Untitled	Gouache	1930	Mrs. Charles H. Russell Jr.
18	Untitled	Gouache	1931	Mr. George L. K. Morris
19	Untitled	Gouache	1932	Mr. Alexander Calder
20	Shell — Head	Bronze	1933	Art of This Century
21	Mutilated and Stateless	Modelled newspapers	1936	Art of This Century
22	Untitled	Painted wood relief	1936	Mr. George L. K. Morris
23	Paper torn and arranged according to the laws of chance	Collage	1936	Mr. George L. K. Morris
24	Paper torn and arranged according to the laws of chance	Collage	1938	Art of This Century
25	Untitled	Plaster	1940	Mr. Virgil Thomson
26	Untitled	Drawing	1940	Art of This Century

Catalogue cover with cutout biomorphic form. Removal of cutout reveals "ARP" on inside page.

Back cover.

Arp. January 24-February 29, 1944.
Loan Exhibition. Catalogue preface by Max Ernst.

Review: Robert Coates, *New Yorker*, 12 February, 1944: "... *There are few living artists who have had more impact on their contemporaries than Arp has had ... one of the few men — Miró is another — who have managed consistently to straddle the gap between 'classic' Abstraction and 'romantic' Surrealism.*"

First Exhibition, Hans Hofmann. March 7-31, 1944.
No catalogue. Exhibition proposed by Lee Krasner and Jackson Pollock. This was Hofmann's first New York exhibition; 12 oils and 15 gouaches of 1943-44 were shown.

Fold-over announcement.

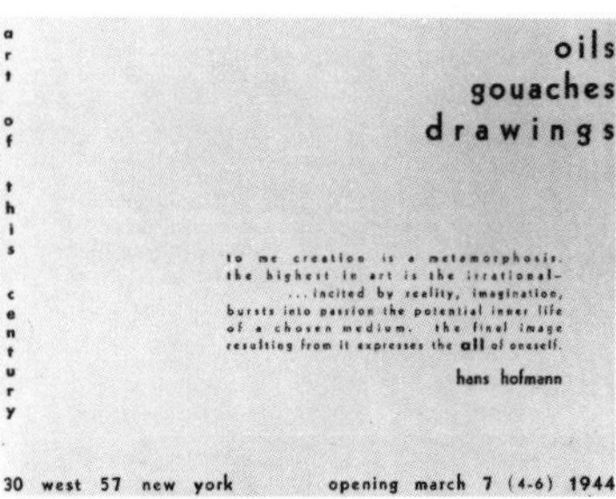

Inside of fold-over announcement.

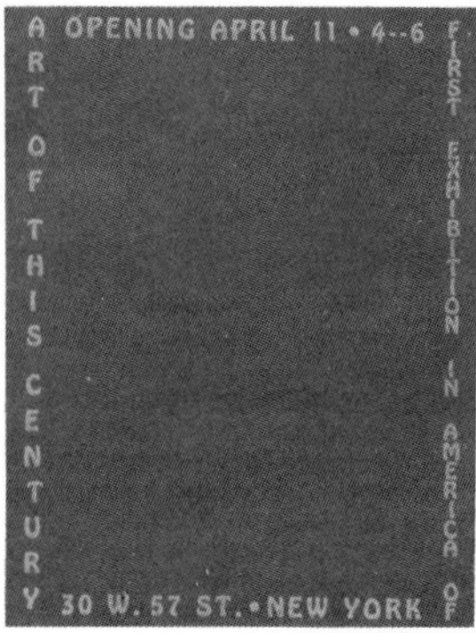

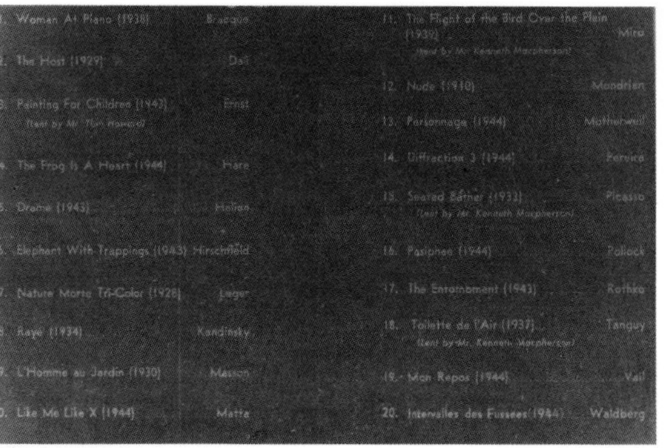

1. Woman At Piano (1938) Braque
2. The Host (1929) Dali
3. Painting For Children (1943) Ernst
4. The Frog Is A Heart (1944) Hare
5. Drame (1943) Hélion
6. Elephant With Trappings (1943) Hirschfeld
7. Nature Morte Tri-Color (1928) Leger
8. Raye (1934) Kandinsky
9. L'Homme au Jardin (1930) Masson
10. Like Me Like X (1944) Matta
11. The Flight of the Bird Over the Plain (1939) Miro (lent by Mr. Kenneth Macpherson)
12. Nude (1910) Mondrian
13. Personnage (1944) Motherwell
14. Diffraction 3 (1944) Pereira
15. Seated Bather (1933) Picasso (lent by Mr. Kenneth Macpherson)
16. Pasiphae (1944) Pollock
17. The Entombment (1943) Rothko
18. Toilette de l'Air (1937) Tanguy (lent by Mr. Kenneth Macpherson)
19. Mon Repos (1944) Vail
20. Intervalles des Fusees (1944) Waldberg

Announcement.

First Exhibition in America of Twenty Paintings. April 11-30, 1944.

Spring Salon for Young Artists. May 2-June 3, 1944.

Mimeographed checklist. Selection jury: Alfred H. Barr, Jr., Marcel Duchamp, Peggy Guggenheim, Kenneth McPherson, Howard Putzel, James Thrall Soby, James Johnson Sweeney. Competition initially restricted to those under 35 years of age, subsequently extended to those under 40.

Review: Maude Riley, *Art Digest*, vol. 18, May 15, 1944: "... *One of the saddest blows to young talent ever dealt was swung by a jury of seven aesthetes last week when it sat in judgment upon submissions by artists under 35 to an 'opportunity' show sponsored by Art of This Century.*

"*The* DIGEST *carried the news of this invitation to young artists painting in the abstract or surrealist forms, with the belief that it was a* bona fide *search for young talent from all around the country. The artists thought so too, it seems, for 300 responded, 50 of them sending in from nearly as many states.*

"*However, instead of extending a hand, the jury of seven, invited by the gallery, played a far more exciting game of 'off with their heads.' The heads they spared were the heads they knew; and they even raised the age limit to 40, as they sat, in order to get twenty-four exhibits they liked.*

"*Of the 24 accepted, four were from out of town and, I believe, unknown to the jury. Of the remaining 20, eleven are well known to me as frequent exhibitors and no doubt the jury was acquainted with the work of still others....*

"*Alfred Barr and James Thrall Soby might make good prize awarders, sitting as they do upon the pinnacles of the supposed highest court in matters of surrealism and abstraction —the directorships of the Museum of Modern Art. But what these gentlemen have never had is training in the judging of formative elements that make up the art of tomorrow, or even the art of this century.*

"*It is clear from the assembled sad little show that this jury looked for duplications or reasonable facsimiles of the things they knew and therefore felt safe about....*

"*What the Modern's men did, in effect, was to put a tourniquet on the blood stream by which they themselves will live or die.*

"*It is bad enough to have the fashionable Museum of Modern Art run its own affairs with the use of mirrors up there in the Big House where it resides. But when it starts running down to the gate of the estate of all art, and turning away visitors it cannot identify, the gate keepers had better drop the cordiality and tend to their jobs themselves.*"

Announcement.

SPRING SALON FOR YOUNG ARTISTS   ART OF THIS CENTURY   30 WEST 57th STREET

PAINTINGS

1...The Balcony....................William Baziotes
2...The Closed Door....................Ronnie Elliott
3...Celestial Object....................Jimmie Ernst
4...Processional....................Aaron Ehrlich
5...Seeds....................Phyllis Goldstein
6...Imprisoned....................Fannie Hillsmith
7...Circus....................Jacqueline Lamba
8...Untitled....................I. Rice Pereira
9...Untitled....................Richard Warren Pousette-Dart
10...The Inescapable Consciousness....................Attilio Salemme
11...Still Life With Violin....................Dick Speyer
12...Memories....................Hedda Sterne
13...Composition #6....................Bonnie Jean Sunderlin

DRAWINGS

14...Red Rose For Rent (crayon)....................Eileen Agar
15...Return From a Journey....................August Casciano
16...Divergations (gouache)....................Perle Fine
17...Pancho Villa Dead and Alive (collage and gouache)......Robert Motherwell
18...Colored Drawing (Pastel and Gouache)....................Jackson Pollock
19...Metaphysician....................Gene Sparks

SCULPTURES

20...Lady-in-Waiting (plaster)....................David Hare
21...Redeemer (wood)....................Azio Martinelli
22...Object (cord and driftwood)....................Gretchen Schoeninger
23...Spider (reed construction)....................Isabelle Waldberg

Mimeographed checklist.

ART OF THIS CENTURY   30 W. 57th ST., N. Y. 19, N. Y.

FOR CITY-WIDE HARLEM WEEK (MAY 29th - JUNE 3rd), ART OF THIS CENTURY, IN CONNECTION WITH THE CITY-WIDE CITIZENS COMMITTEE ON HARLEM AND THE COUNCIL AGAINST INTOLERANCE IN AMERICA, ANNOUNCES A FACTUAL, PHOTOGRAPHIC EXHIBIT.

THE NEGRO IN AMERICAN LIFE

ARRANGED BY JOHN BECKER

Announcement.

The Negro in American Life. Exhibition of Photographs. May 29-June 3, 1944.

No catalogue. Exhibition proposed and organized by John Becker, together with the Council Against Intolerance in America.

Paintings and Drawings by Baziotes. October 3-21, 1944.
Typed checklist. Installation by Baziotes and Robert Motherwell.

Review: Clement Greenberg, *The Nation*, 11 November, 1944: "... *All credit is due Peggy Guggenheim for her enterprise in presenting young and unrecognized artists at her Art of This Century gallery. But even more to her credit is her acumen. Two of the abstract painters she has recently introduced — Jackson Pollock and William Baziotes — reveal more than promise: on the strength of their first one-man shows they have already placed themselves among the six or seven best young painters we possess.*

"*Baziotes, whose show closed last month, is unadulterated talent, natural painter and all painter. He issues in a single jet, deflected by nothing extraneous to painting. Two or three of his larger oils may become masterpieces in several years, once they stop disturbing us by their nervousness, by their unexampled color — off-shades in the intervals between red and blue, red and yellow, yellow and green, all depth, involution, and glow — and by their very originality. Baziotes' gouaches had their own proper quality, which is the intensity of their whites and higher colors.*"

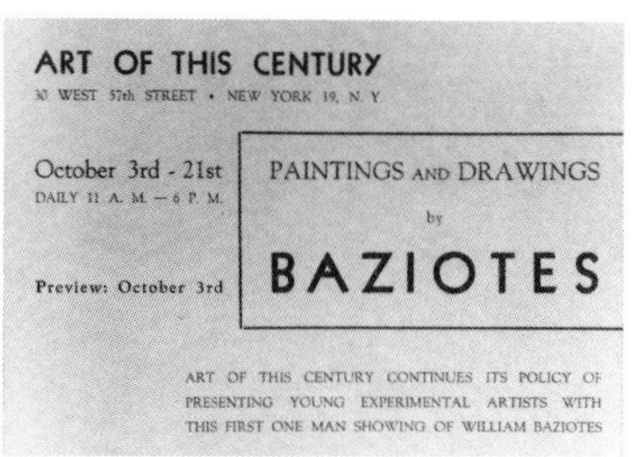
ART OF THIS CENTURY
30 WEST 57th STREET • NEW YORK 19, N. Y.

October 3rd - 21st
DAILY 11 A. M. — 6 P. M.

Preview: October 3rd

PAINTINGS AND DRAWINGS
by
BAZIOTES

ART OF THIS CENTURY CONTINUES ITS POLICY OF PRESENTING YOUNG EXPERIMENTAL ARTISTS WITH THIS FIRST ONE MAN SHOWING OF WILLIAM BAZIOTES

Announcement designed by Jimmy Ernst.

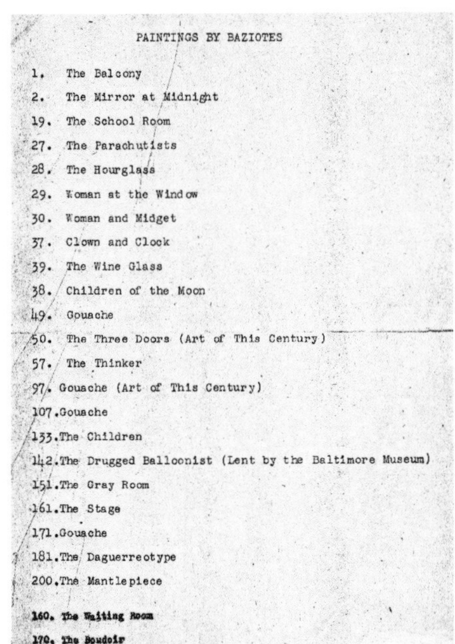
PAINTINGS BY BAZIOTES

1. The Balcony
2. The Mirror at Midnight
19. The School Room
27. The Parachutists
28. The Hourglass
29. Woman at the Window
30. Woman and Midget
37. Clown and Clock
39. The Wine Glass
38. Children of the Moon
49. Gouache
50. The Three Doors (Art of This Century)
57. The Thinker
97. Gouache (Art of This Century)
107. Gouache
133. The Children
142. The Drugged Balloonist (Lent by the Baltimore Museum)
151. The Gray Room
161. The Stage
171. Gouache
181. The Daguerreotype
200. The Mantlepiece
160. The Waiting Room
170. The Boudoir

Typed checklist.

Robert Motherwell. October 24-November 11, 1944.
Catalogue preface by James Johnson Sweeney.

Review: Clement Greenberg, *The Nation*, 11 November 1944: "... *Motherwell's water-color drawings are of an astonishing felicity and that felicity is of an astonishing uniformity. But it owes too much to Picasso, pours too directly from post-cubism. Only in his large oils and collages does Motherwell really lay his cards down. There his constant quality is an ungainliness, an insecurity of placing and drawing, which I prefer to the gracefulness of his water-colors because it is through this very awkwardness that Motherwell makes his specific contribution.... he has already done enough to make it no exaggeration to say that the future of American painting depends on what he, Baziotes, Pollock, and only a comparatively few others do from now on.*"

Review: Manny Farber, *The New Republic*, 13 November, 1944, p. 626: "... *There are a number of qualities that should be mentioned in Motherwell's work as a whole. A nobility of craftsmanship is evident in the crisp, sure manner of brushing on paint, in the brashness*

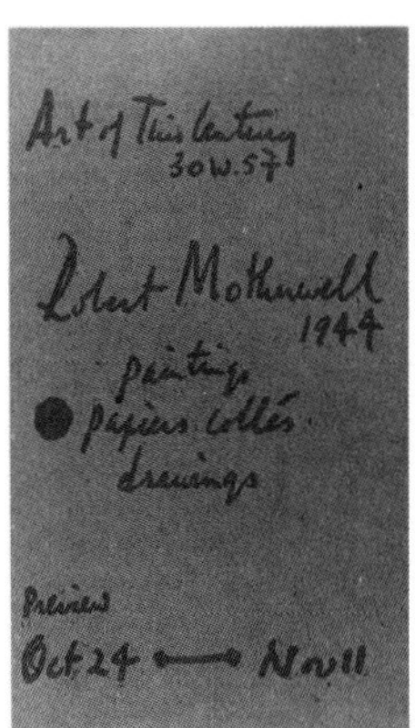
Art of This Century
30 W. 57
Robert Motherwell
1944
paintings
papiers collés
drawings
Preview
Oct 24 → Nov 11

Announcement.

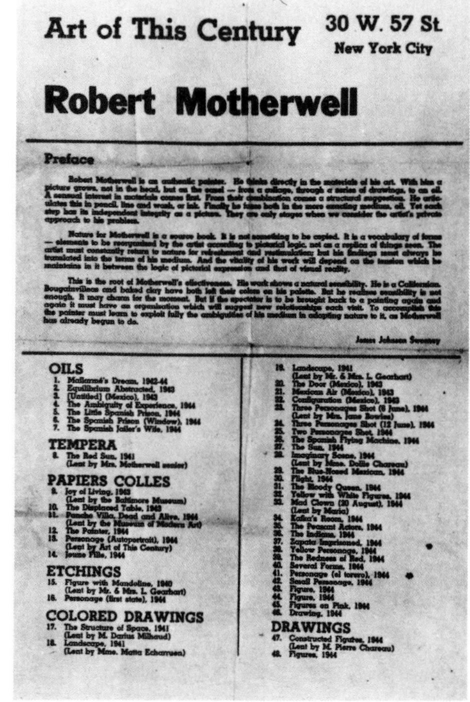
Art of This Century
30 W. 57 St.
New York City

Robert Motherwell

Preface

Robert Motherwell is an authentic painter.

James Johnson Sweeney

OILS
1. Mallarmé's Dream, 1942-44
2. Equilibrium Abstracted, 1943
3. [Untitled] (Mexico), 1943
4. The Ambiguity of Experience, 1944
5. The Little Spanish Prison, 1944
6. The Spanish Prison (Window), 1944
7. The Spanish Jailer's Wife, 1944

TEMPERA
8. The Red Sun, 1941 (Lent by Mrs. Motherwell senior)

PAPIERS COLLES
9. Joy of Living, 1943 (Lent by the Baltimore Museum)
10. The Displaced Table, 1943
11. Pancho Villa, Dead and Alive, 1944 (Lent by the Museum of Modern Art)
12. The Painter, 1944
13. Personage (Autoportrait), 1944 (Lent by Art of This Century)
14. Jeune Fille, 1944

ETCHINGS
15. Figure with Mandoline, 1940 (Lent by Mr. & Mrs. L. Gearhart)
16. Personage (first state), 1944

COLORED DRAWINGS
17. The Structure of Space, 1941 (Lent by M. Darius Milhaud)
18. Landscape, 1941 (Lent by Mme. Matta Echarruen)
19. Landscape, 1941 (Lent by Mr. & Mrs. L. Gearhart)
20. The Door (Mexico), 1943
21. Mexican Air (Mexico), 1943
22. Configuration (Mexico), 1943
23. Three Personages Shot (8 June), 1944 (Lent by Mrs. Jane Bowles)
24. Three Personages Shot (12 June), 1944
25. Two Personages Shot, 1944
26. The Spanish Flying Machine, 1944
27. The Sun, 1944
28. Imaginary Scene, 1944 (Lent by Mme. Dollie Chareau)
29. The Blue-Nosed Mexican, 1944
30. Flight, 1944
31. The Bloody Queen, 1944
32. Yellow with White Figures, 1944
33. Mad Clown (20 August), 1944 (Lent by Maria)
34. Kafka's Room, 1944
35. The Peasant Actors, 1944
36. The Indians, 1944
37. Zapata Imprisoned, 1944
38. Yellow Personage, 1944
39. The Redness of Red, 1944
40. Several Forms, 1944
41. Personage (el torero), 1944
42. Small Personage, 1944
43. Figure, 1944
44. Figure, 1944
45. Figures on Pink, 1944
46. Drawing, 1944

DRAWINGS
47. Constructed Figures, 1944 (Lent by M. Pierre Chareau)
48. Figures, 1944

Catalogue.

of the statements which lack worry, meanness or deadness, and in the willingness to show everything he has done, whether it is good, bad or indifferent ... his 48 pictures exhibited here ... are very exciting pictures and show him to be a robust, improving, serious painter, and a good one."

Review: Jon Stroup, *Art Digest*, vol. 19, November 1, 1944: "*Robert Motherwell ... has titled one of his oils* Equilibrium Abstracted. *He might justly have used it as the title of the exhibition, for the precise and varied equilibrium of his art is its most striking characteristic. Balance is maintained not only within the plastic means themselves, but between subject matter and mode of expression.... His more serious canvases ... are more than mere abstractions of physical reality, they are recreations of aesthetic perceptions generated in the artist by profound intercourse with the world around him....*"

In October 1944, Peggy Guggenheim financed a recording of music by Paul Bowles issued by Art of This Century Recordings, album 1, vol. 1: *Sonata for Flute and Piano*, 1932, played by René Le Roy and George Reeves, and *Two Mexican Dances*, played by duo-pianists Arthur Gold and Robert Fizdale. This was Fizdale's and Gold's first recording and the only record ever issued by Art of This Century. The cover was designed by Max Ernst.

(Not illustrated)

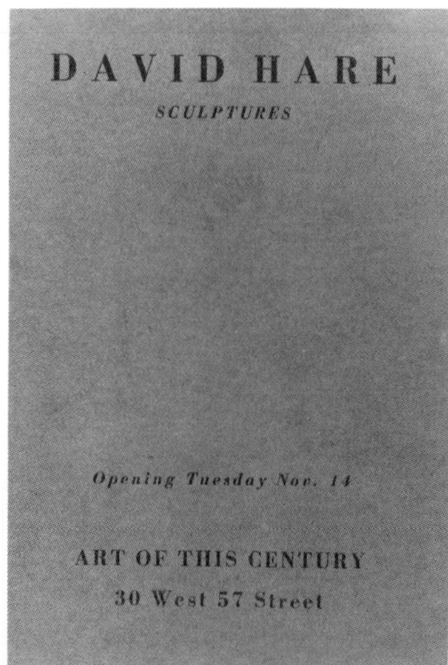

Catalogue cover.

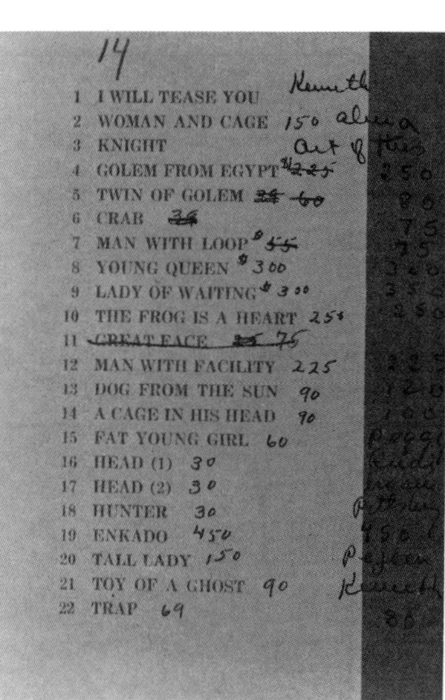

14

1 I WILL TEASE YOU
2 WOMAN AND CAGE 150
3 KNIGHT
4 GOLEM FROM EGYPT
5 TWIN OF GOLEM
6 CRAB
7 MAN WITH LOOP
8 YOUNG QUEEN $300
9 LADY OF WAITING
10 THE FROG IS A HEART
11 GREAT FACE
12 MAN WITH FACILITY 225
13 DOG FROM THE SUN 90
14 A CAGE IN HIS HEAD 90
15 FAT YOUNG GIRL 60
16 HEAD (1) 30
17 HEAD (2) 30
18 HUNTER 30
19 ENKADO 450
20 TALL LADY 150
21 TOY OF A GHOST 90
22 TRAP 69

Back cover.

David Hare Sculptures. November 14-December 2, 1944.

Review: Robert Coates, *The New Yorker*, 2 December, 1944: "*... Hare ... is a newcomer both to the galleries and to this medium, for it seems that until about two years ago he had occupied himself solely with photography. Perhaps the chief charm of his work at the moment is its freshness of attack. All the pieces shown are in plaster, and, unlike most sculptors... he treats it as an end in itself and achieves some unusual effects with it.... Hare has that prime quality that all good sculptors, fantastic or otherwise, must have—a sense of form and balance — and this, coupled with his feeling for the portentous, gives his work a good deal of evocative power.*"

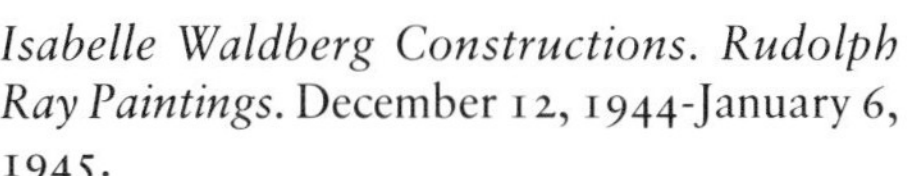

Isabelle Waldberg Constructions. Rudolph Ray Paintings. December 12, 1944-January 6, 1945.

Exhibition proposed by Isabelle Waldberg, who, together with her husband, Patrick Waldberg, was a close friend of Peggy Guggenheim.

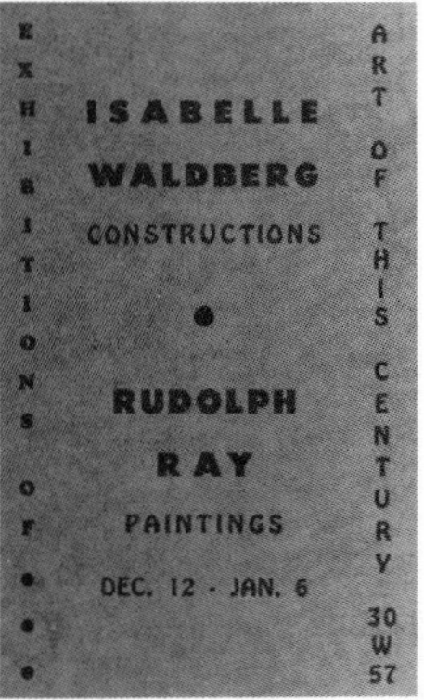

Announcement.

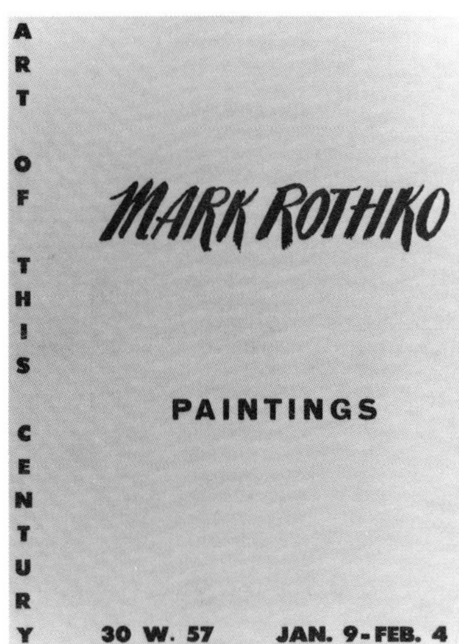
ART OF THIS CENTURY

MARK ROTHKO

PAINTINGS

30 W. 57 JAN. 9-FEB. 4

Catalogue cover.

ENTOMBMENT

Rothko's painting is not easily classified. It occupies a middle ground between abstraction and surrealism. In these paintings the abstract idea is incarnated in the image. Rothko's style has a latent archaic quality which the pale and uninsistent colours enforce. This particular archaization, the reverse of the primitive, suggests the long savouring of human and traditional experience as incorporated in the myth. Rothko's smybols, fragments of myth, are held together by a free, almost automatic calligraphy that gives a peculiar unity to his paintings — a unity in which the individual symbol acquires its meaning, not in isolation, but rather in its melodic adjustment to the other elements in the picture. It is this feeling of internal fusion, of the historical conscious and subconscious, capable of expanding far beyond the limits of the picture space that gives Rothko's work its force and essential character. But this is not to say that the images created by Rothko are the thin evocations of the speculative intellect; they are rather the concrete, the tactual expression of the intuitions of an artist to whom the subconscious represents not the farther, but the nearer shore of art.

ART OF THIS CENTURY

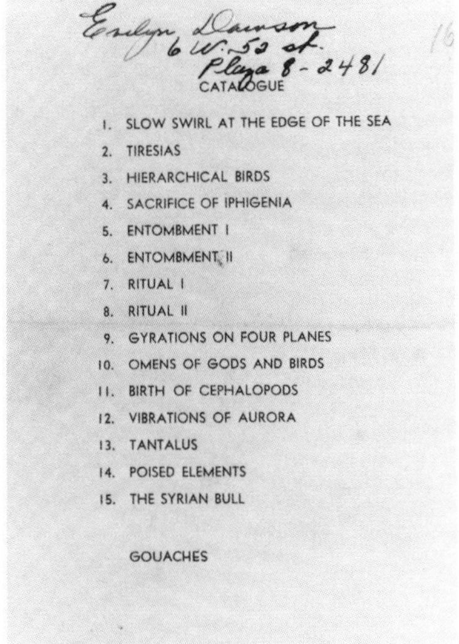
Evelyn Dawson
6 W. 52 st.
Plaza 8-2481

CATALOGUE

1. SLOW SWIRL AT THE EDGE OF THE SEA
2. TIRESIAS
3. HIERARCHICAL BIRDS
4. SACRIFICE OF IPHIGENIA
5. ENTOMBMENT I
6. ENTOMBMENT II
7. RITUAL I
8. RITUAL II
9. GYRATIONS ON FOUR PLANES
10. OMENS OF GODS AND BIRDS
11. BIRTH OF CEPHALOPODS
12. VIBRATIONS OF AURORA
13. TANTALUS
14. POISED ELEMENTS
15. THE SYRIAN BULL

GOUACHES

Back cover.

Mark Rothko Paintings. January 9-February 4, 1945.

Unsigned catalogue preface. Howard Putzel proposed that Rothko should be represented by Art of This Century.

Review: Jon Stroup, *Town and Country*, January 1945: "*The work of Mark Rothko eludes classification so far as we are concerned, although it is generally labeled 'abstract.' But so flat, so dehumanized a term, can never convey the wealth of poetry to be found in his painting, the slow mysterious movement, the quiet spaciousness, the muted philosophical reverberations, and the lyricism at times whimsical and capricious, and again solemn and mystical. In regard to his latest and most original canvases we can think of no artist with whom to compare him. It is strange that though he achieves his effects with strictly painter's terms, the most apt comparison lies outside the field of art. We are reminded of Walt Whitman.... Here is genuine talent definitely worth watching. It is continually expanding, consistently original, and as spacious as our native land.*"

Review: Maude Riley, *Art Digest*, vol. 19, January 15, 1945: "*...Mark Rothko has been a kind of myth in contemporary art for about ten years.... One gathered that he was a determined non-conformist but his personality as a painter has remained veiled.... In the fifteen paintings now on view, Rothko continues to be elusive. His color is subconsciously dictated in most cases, it would seem, and results in subtleties of great beauty now and then....*"

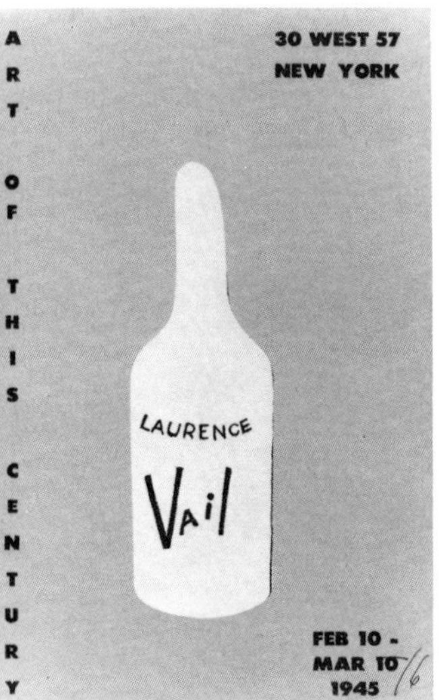

atalogue cover.

ANENT ME, LAURENCE VAIL, BOTTLE MAKER.

Yesterday, my oldest daughter, Pegeen Vail (earring maker) met Kisling (picture maker). Said he: Well, well. Delighted. It's been a long time. And how's your father? I hear he now makes bottles. He used to empty them in the old days. . . . I still occasionally, and quite frequently, and very perpetually, empty a bottle. This is apt to give one a guilty feeling. Is it not possible, I moaned and mooned, that I have neglected, the exterior (of the bottle) for the interior (of the bottle). Why cast away the empty bottle? The spirits, in the bottle are not necessarily the spirit of the bottle. The spirit of the spirits of the bottle are potent, potential, substance that should not be discarded, eliminated in spleen, plumbing and hangover. Why not exteriorise these spirits on the body of the bottle. . . Hence these bottles. The glee in fizz, the melancholy in rouge, the sin in absinthe, the fun in rum, the pain in champagne, should not be relegated to remorse, biliousness, sewer. The soul of sap should flourish on the bark. I will not throw away the skirt of my lost girl. I prefer to embroider.

LAURENCE Vail

1. DIANE DE MEGEVE .... loaned by Jean Helion
2. SEA-SCUM .... loaned by Pegeen Vail
3. WATER GIRL
4. GOD SAVE
5. UN COUP DE PEIGNE
6. LES YEUX D'ELSA
7. CHANGE OF WEATHER .... loaned by Mrs. Eugene Vail
8. BLACKHEAD .... loaned by Pegeen Vail
9. THE YELLOW WIDOW
10. BROWN BETTY
11. JOLLITA .... loaned by Jean Connolly
12. V-DAY
13. ANATOMY .... loaned by Mrs. Malcolm Cowley
14. CHINESE MEASLES
15. PERFECT LADY
16. STRATOSPHERE
17. HOLY BLIZZARD
18. HELLUVA DEATH
19. LA JEUNE GEANTE
20. MLLE. NITOUCHE .... loaned by Peggy Guggenheim
21. FORGETMENOT .... loaned by Peggy Guggenheim
22. PLAINTIVE DEMOISELLE .... loaned by Peggy Guggenheim
23. SQUARE ROOT .... loaned by Peggy Guggenheim
24. VICTORY GARDEN .... loaned by Peggy Guggenheim
25. DIE WACHT AM RHEIN .... loaned by Peggy Guggenheim
26. WOODBINE .... loaned by Peggy Guggenheim
27. FROGSPAWN .... loaned by Peggy Guggenheim
28. WORLD OF THIS CENTURY .... loaned by Peggy Guggenheim
29. CARRIBEAN
30. LES BAISERS
31. WATERY GRAVE
32. ALERTE
33. LA GRANDE MADEMOISELLE
34. LE BON BONBON
35. PERROQUET
36. HANG O VER
37. ESKIMO
38. MME. BOVARY .... loaned by Max Ernst
39. SING SING
40. YELLOW FEVER
41. OPHELIA
42. MON BEBE
43. SUSAN GREY
44. CUT MY THROAT
45. JEZEBEL'S GARTER .... loaned by Jezebel V.
46. SHANGHAI DOWAGER
47. DOWN TO EARTH
48. ECHEC AU ROI .... loaned by Mary Reynolds
49. OUT OF MY WINDOW .... loaned by Mrs. Bernard Reis
50. HE FORGOT TO REMEMBER .... loaned by Mrs. Bernard Reis
51. DANDELION WINE .... loaned by Barbara Reis
52. POKER FACE BLUES .... loaned by Nelda Audibert

AND OTHERS

Back cover.

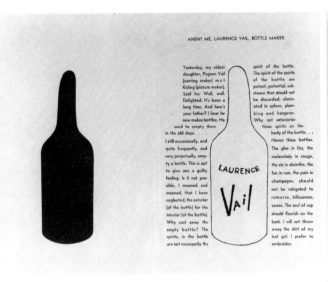

Laurence Vail. February 10-March 10, 1945.
Catalogue preface by Laurence Vail.

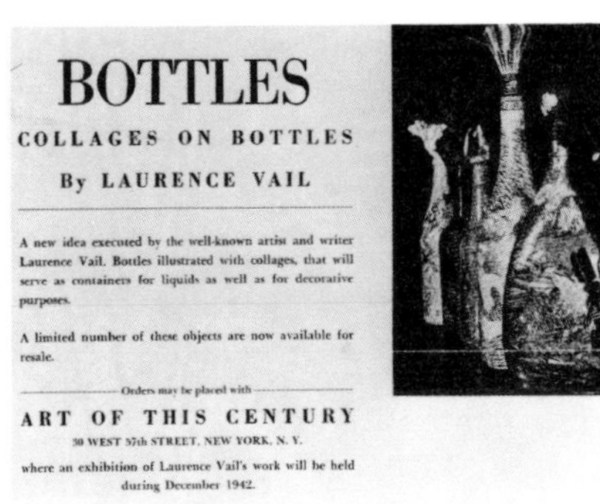

BOTTLES

COLLAGES ON BOTTLES

By LAURENCE VAIL

A new idea executed by the well-known artist and writer Laurence Vail. Bottles illustrated with collages, that will serve as containers for liquids as well as for decorative purposes.

A limited number of these objects are now available for resale.

Orders may be placed with

ART OF THIS CENTURY

30 WEST 57th STREET, NEW YORK, N. Y.

where an exhibition of Laurence Vail's work will be held during December 1942.

Announcement.

Alberto Giacometti. February 10-March 10 [extended to March 16], 1945.
Catalogue statements (all previously published) by André Breton, Julien Levy, Georges Hugnet, Alfred H. Barr, Jr., Alberto Giacometti.

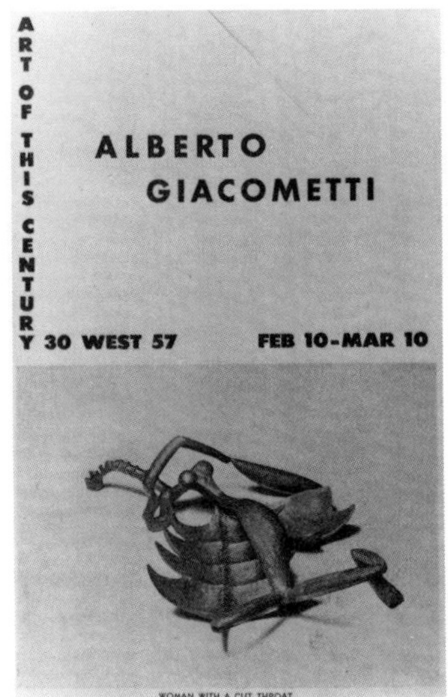

Catalogue cover.

In Giacometti's work—and it is a touching moment, like that in Gothic novels, when the characters walk out of their picture frames—new figures, sprung from the head and heart of man, step to earth with infinite caution, and in the materialization of the burning light that bathes Henri d'Ofterdingen or Aurelia, victoriously brave the test of reality.

Andre Breton, 'Genesis and Perspective of Surrealism, 'Art of This Century

ALBERTO GIACOMETTI . . . at his best has advanced the abstractions of Brancusi into the complicated realm of psychological objects, so that his sculptures are magical and profound fetiches, with all the mystery of a dream, made concreete, the hallucination of inutility. His best work, such as the marble On Ne Joue Plus or the carved wood Palace: 4 o'Clock in the Morning are signposts towards the surrealist "Apotheosis of the object."

JULIEN LEVY
FROM "SURREALISM"
BLACK SUN PRESS, 1936

. . . there appear the marvelous sculpture-objects of Giacometti in wood, stone and plaster, setting of poetic precision, palaces of sleep where mysterious dramas are enacted at daggers drawn, games whose bizarre and lucid rules are derived from dreams. The mobile objects of Giacometti, functioning like dream-machines from the landscapes of Ernst or Tanguy give a new impulse to the creation of Surrealist objects.

GEORGES HUGNET, 1936
FANTASTIC ART DADA AND SURREALISM
ALFRED H. BARR Jr.

I return to the constructions which amuse me and which live in their own superreality: a beautiful palace, a floor of white dice dotted with red and black upon which we walk, high up in the air a laughing ceiling and those pretty mechanical devices that serve no purpose whatsoever. Gropingly I seek to capture in the void the invisible white thread of the miraculous which vibrates and from which facts and dreams escape with the murmur of a brook rolling over lively and precious pebbles.

ALBERT GIACOMETTI
"CHARBON D'HERBE", LE SURREALISM,
A.S.D.L.R., 1933

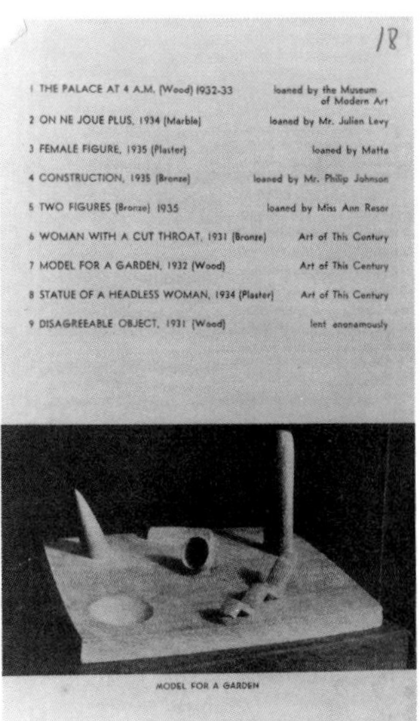

18

1 THE PALACE AT 4 A.M. (Wood) 1932-33 — loaned by the Museum of Modern Art
2 ON NE JOUE PLUS, 1934 (Marble) — loaned by Mr. Julien Levy
3 FEMALE FIGURE, 1935 (Plaster) — loaned by Matta
4 CONSTRUCTION, 1935 (Bronze) — loaned by Mr. Philip Johnson
5 TWO FIGURES (Bronze) 1935 — loaned by Miss Ann Resor
6 WOMAN WITH A CUT THROAT, 1931 (Bronze) — Art of This Century
7 MODEL FOR A GARDEN, 1932 (Wood) — Art of This Century
8 STATUE OF A HEADLESS WOMAN, 1934 (Plaster) — Art of This Century
9 DISAGREEABLE OBJECT, 1931 (Wood) — lent anonamously

MODEL FOR A GARDEN

Back cover.

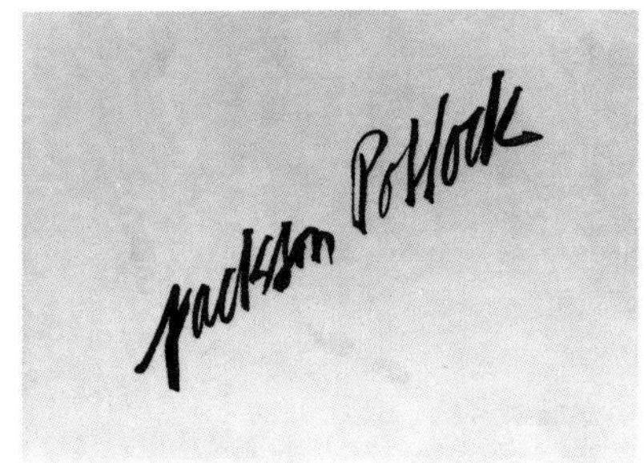

ART

OF

THIS

CENTURY

You are invited to view a Mural on March 19,
from 3 to 6, at 155 East 61st Street • 1st Floor

30 West 57th Street

1. HORIZONTAL ON BLACK
   Lent by Mr. Kenneth Macpherson
2. SQUARE ON BLACK
3. TOTEM LESSON 1
4. TOTEM LESSON 2
5. THE NIGHT DANCER
6. THE FIRST DREAM
7. PORTRAIT OF H. M.
8. NIGHT CEREMONY
9. NIGHT MIST
10. TWO
11. THERE WERE SEVEN IN EIGHT
12. NIGHT MAGIC
13. IMAGE

GOUACHES and DRAWINGS

MARCH 19—APRIL 14

Catalogue cover.

Jackson Pollock. March 19-April 14, 1945. Catalogue includes invitation to view Pollock's mural at Peggy Guggenheim's residence, 155 East Sixty-first Street.

Review: Clement Greenberg, *The Nation*, 7 April, 1944: "*Jackson Pollock's second one-man show at Art of This Century (through April 14) establishes him, in my opinion, as the strongest painter of his generation and perhaps the greatest one to appear since Miró. The only optimism in his smoky, turbulent painting comes from his own manifest faith in the efficacy, for him personally, of art. There has been a certain amount of self-deception in School of Paris art since the exit of cubism. In Pollock there is absolutely none, and he is not afraid to look ugly—all profound original art looks ugly at first.... Among the* [oils] ... *are two — both called Totem Lessons — for which I cannot find strong enough words of praise....*"

Review: Manny Farber, *The New Republic*, 25 June, 1945: "*The painting of Jackson Pollock ... has been, in at least three paintings I have seen, both masterful and miraculous. The three paintings include a wild abstraction, twenty-six feet long, commissioned by Miss Peggy Guggenheim for the hallway of her home.... The mural is voluminously detailed with swirling line and form, painted spontaneously and seemingly without preliminary sketch, and is, I think, an almost incredible success. It is violent in its expression, endlessly fascinating in detail, without superficiality, and so well ordered that it composes the wall in a quiet, contained, buoyant way.... The style is very personal and, unlike that of many painters of this period, the individuality is in the way the medium is used rather than in the peculiarities of subject matter....*"[5]

5. When she left America in 1947, Peggy Guggenheim gave the mural to the University of Iowa.

talogue cover.

OILS

1. LES PREMIERES SPATIALES 1941-44
2. " " "
3. " " "
4. FOCUS ISLAND 1941
5. SOLARISATION 1942
6. PREMIERE APPARITION DU SIGNE DYN 1941
7. GYRA 1943
8. TELLURIN 1943
9. EROUN 1944
10. VISAGES PLANETAIRES 1944
11. TABLEAU BLOND 1944
12. LE SIGNE DYN 1944
13. AEROGYL PRISMATIQUE 1944
14. AEROGYL BLEU 1944
15. LES COSMOGONES 1944-45
16. " (stages) 1943
17. " " 1944
18. " " 1944
19. " " 1944

GOUACHES, WATER-COLORS, BRUSH-DRAWINGS, PASTELS, 1939-45

ENTRE MATIERE ET LUMIERE, PAGES FROM THE PAINTER'S LOG-BOOK AND OTHERS.

DRAWINGS 1941-45

DISCOVERY OF INFRA-SPACE AND OTHERS.

FUMAGES (smoke paintings) 1944-45

VARIOTYPES 1943-44

SPACE-OBJECTS 1944

Wolfgang Paalen, of French and Austrian origin; born Vienna (Austria). Studied in France, Germany, Italy. Travelled widely in Europe, U. S. A., Canada and Mexico. Lived in Paris until May 1939. Living since 1939 in Mexico.

One-man exhibitions: Galerie Vignon, Paris 1934. Galerie Pierre, Paris 1936, Galerie Renou et Colle, Paris 1938, Guggenheim Jeune Gallery, London 1938, Julien Levy Gallery, New York 1940.

His work has been published in: *Cahiers d'Art*, *Abstraction-Création*, *transition*, *London Bulletin*, *Review of Modern Art*, *Surrealism* by Herbert Read, *Dictionnaire Abrégé du Surréalisme*, *Art of this Century*, *Letras de México*, *Dyn*, etc.

His work is represented in France in the collections of: Joe Bousquet, André Breton, Vicomtesse de Noailles, and others.

In England in the collections of: Roland Penrose, John Davenport, E. L. T. Mesens, and others.

In Switzerland in the collections of: Dr. Ramel, Mrs. Reber, Eva Sulzer, and others.

In the U. S. A. in the: Museum of Living Art, New York University, Museum of Modern Art, Art of this Century, and in various private collections.

He has collaborated with the "Surindépendants," "Abstraction-Création" from 1932-35. Belonged to the Surrealist Group from 1936-40. Organized the "Exposición Internacional del Surrealismo," Mexico 1940.

Separated from the Surrealists in 1941 and founded the Art Magazine *Dyn* which he has been editing since then.

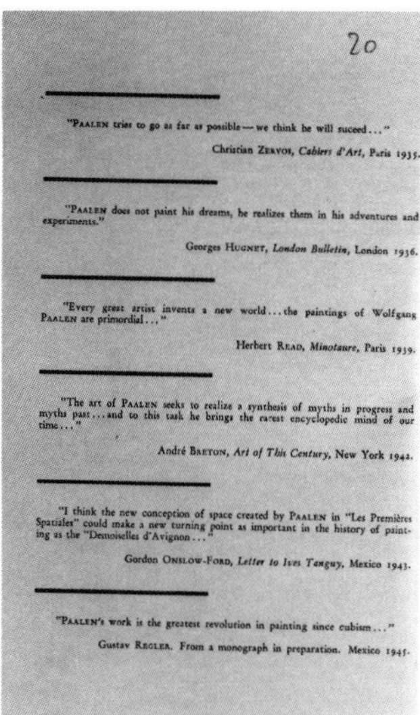

"Paalen tries to go as far as possible—we think he will suceed..."

Christian Zervos, *Cahiers d'Art*, Paris 1935.

"Paalen does not paint his dreams, he realizes them in his adventures and experiments."

Georges Hugnet, *London Bulletin*, London 1936.

"Every great artist invents a new world...the paintings of Wolfgang Paalen are primordial..."

Herbert Read, *Minotaure*, Paris 1939.

"The art of Paalen seeks to realize a synthesis of myths in progress and myths past...and to this task he brings the rarest encyclopedic mind of our time..."

André Breton, *Art of This Century*, New York 1942.

"I think the new conception of space created by Paalen in "Les Premières Spatiales" could make a new turning point as important in the history of painting as the "Demoiselles d'Avignon..."

Gordon Onslow-Ford, *Letter to Ives Tanguy*, Mexico 1943.

"Paalen's work is the greatest revolution in painting since cubism..."

Gustav Regler. From a monograph in preparation. Mexico 1945.

There is no doubt why the tejon is called tejon: one day, some Indians found an unknown animal which looked so much like a tejon and behaved so perfectly like one, that they could not think of any other name for it than "tejon." But in order to know what it really looks like, one has to *see* a tejon. Equally, to know what an "Aerogyl," an "Eroun," or a "Tellurin" is, you have to look at one. There is no reason why the artist should not have the right to give new names to his new beings.

Art created the gods and formed the human prototypes; but, since the end of humanism it has been lacking in a clear definition of its task. Art, in historical development, after its totemic, mythological, humanistic and realistic periods, has arrived at the experimental period which we call "modern art." Historically all these periods are of equal value; each of them has produced great works; especially the last one (the experimental) has prodigiously enriched the plastic language. But it coincides with the *crisis of subject*, with a general disagreement as to what subject-matter or themes are apt for plastic expression.

The plastic analysis of the subject-matter (cubism), which has led to arbitrary deformations in the degeneration of cubism; the poetical revelation of the subject by unexpected juxtapositions (surrealism), which has led to literary academicism; the renunciation of subject-matter (purist abstractivism), which finally reduced painting to simple plays of optic equilibrium — these are the principal aspects of this crisis of subject. It shows that now it is no longer a question of experimenting how to paint, but of finding *what* to paint. The problem is no longer to invent new techniques but to find new themes.

These themes can no longer be either sham-mythologies or interpretations of given things. For the given things (among which I include the social conflicts), interpretations by new technical means have become far more satisfactory — no realistic or semi-realistic painting can match a documentary film.

What, then, could be the new themes of art?

The new directions of physics as much as those of art led me to a potential concept of reality, opposed to any concept of deterministic finality. This concept, which I call *dynatic* (from the Greek word dynaton: the possible) or the Philosophy of the Possible, excludes any kind of mysticism and metaphysics, because it includes the equal necessity of art and of science. (Whereas idealistic metaphysics overrates the importance of art, materialistic metaphysics overrates the importance of science.)

Science and art both have their roots in the imagination; form and sense can not be separated since no mental concept can become intelligible without assuming a form. But it is equally as false to try to poetize science as to try to make a scientific art — too often proposed by people who lack, at least, the understanding of one of them.

It must be understood that art and science are indispensable complementaries; that only their cooperation will be able to create a new ethics.

Art, as far as it accomplished major tasks, has always been concerned with symbolizing the forces of nature (extra-human and human nature); but mere symbolization as well as interpretation has become obsolete.

The new theme will be a *plastic cosmogony*, which means: no longer a symbolization or interpretation but, through the specific means of art, a direct visualization of the forces which move our body and mind. Having nothing to do with metaphysics, this cosmogony does not try to anthropomorphize the universe but to make man universal, making him participate emotionally in the great cosmic polarities.

Thus, it is no longer the task of art to answer naive questions. Now, it is the painting which will look at the spectator and ask him: what do you represent?

Wolfgang Paalen. April 17-May 12, 1945. Catalogue statements (previously published) by Christian Zervos, Georges Hugnet, Herbert Read, André Breton, Gordon Onslow-Ford, Gustav Regler, Wolfgang Paalen. Paalen had been a friend of Peggy Guggenheim since the 1930s and had had an exhibition at Guggenheim Jeune in London.

talogue cover.

ALICE RAHON PAALEN — *PAINTINGS*

TITLES

1. "PEAU DE SOLEIL"
loaned by Mrs. Stoude
2. FETE NATIONALE
loaned by Mr. & Mrs. William Wright
3. PROMENEURS DANS UN PRE
loaned by Institute of Modern Art, Pasadena
4. LA VILLE ORIENTALE
loaned by Mr. & Mrs. Harold English
5. TYPHON
6. BIOGRAPHIE D'UN OISEAU
loaned by Mrs. Windham
7. DANZANTE
8. MARINE
9. RENDEZ-VOUS DE RIVIERES
10. LE BLE
11. EL CASTILLO
12. VICENTE ESCUDERO
13. MEMOIRE DE L'EAU
14. MORAINES
loaned by Mr. & Mrs. W. Davis
15. LA VILLE AZTEQUE AU SOLEIL LEVANT
16. LA CONJURATION DES ANTILOPES
17. SCENE DE CHASSE
18. L'AUBE
19. L'ARBRE
loaned by Mr. & Mrs. Vincent Price
20. LA MAISON DU VENT
21. LA RUEDA DE LA FORTUNA
loaned by Mr. & Mrs. E. Stendahl
22. NAISSANCE D'EMERAUDES
23. ALMORA
24. LA FENETRE MAGIQUE
25. JARDIN DE FEU
26. LA NEIGE
27. SOUVENIR DE PARIS
28. PORTRAIT OF A LADY
29. LA VILLE BYZANTINE
30. LES PHASES DU SOLEIL
31. L'OISELEUR
32. APRES MIDI BOREALE
33. BOITE A MUSIQUE II
loaned by Marquise de Montferrier
34. BOITE A MUSIQUE III
loaned by Mr. & Mrs. J. S. Stein

ART OF THIS CENTURY 30 West 57th Street, N. Y.

Verso of cover.

Alice Rahon Paalen. Paintings. May 15-June 7, 1945.

The Women. June 12-July 7, 1945.
Works by Alice Trumbull Mason, Dolia Lorant, and Patricia Phillips were substituted for those by Gypsy Rose Lee, Loren McIver, and Lenore Krasner.

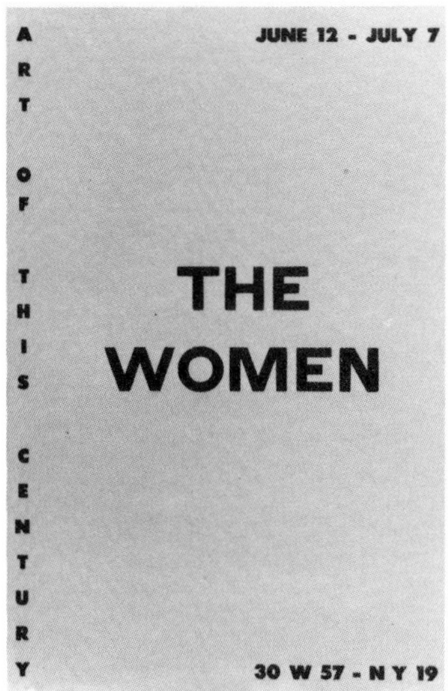
JUNE 12 - JULY 7

ART OF THIS CENTURY

THE WOMEN

30 W 57 - N Y 19

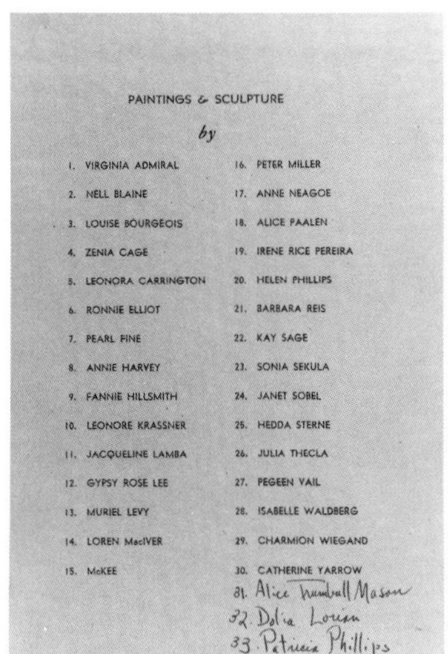
PAINTINGS & SCULPTURE

by

1. VIRGINIA ADMIRAL
2. NELL BLAINE
3. LOUISE BOURGEOIS
4. ZENIA CAGE
5. LEONORA CARRINGTON
6. RONNIE ELLIOT
7. PEARL FINE
8. ANNIE HARVEY
9. FANNIE HILLSMITH
10. LEONORE KRASSNER
11. JACQUELINE LAMBA
12. GYPSY ROSE LEE
13. MURIEL LEVY
14. LOREN MacIVER
15. McKEE
16. PETER MILLER
17. ANNE NEAGOE
18. ALICE PAALEN
19. IRENE RICE PEREIRA
20. HELEN PHILLIPS
21. BARBARA REIS
22. KAY SAGE
23. SONIA SEKULA
24. JANET SOBEL
25. HEDDA STERNE
26. JULIA THECLA
27. PEGEEN VAIL
28. ISABELLE WALDBERG
29. CHARMION WIEGAND
30. CATHERINE YARROW
31. Alice Trumbull Mason
32. Dolia Lorian
33. Patricia Phillips

Catalogue cover.

ART OF THIS CENTURY

Announcement.

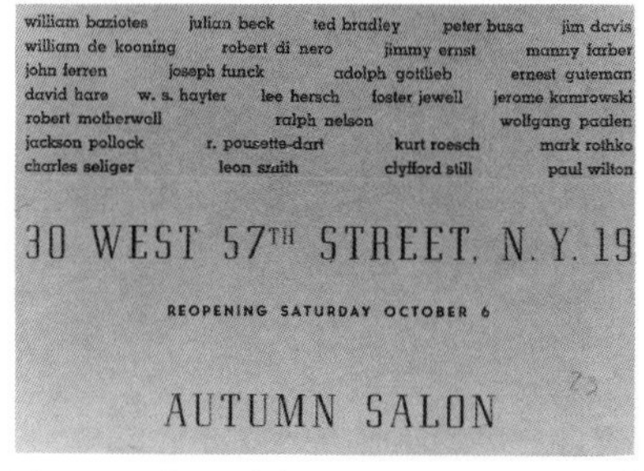
william baziotes julian beck ted bradley peter busa jim davis
william de kooning robert di nero jimmy ernst manny farber
john ferren joseph funck adolph gottlieb ernest guteman
david hare w. s. hayter lee hersch foster jewell jerome kamrowski
robert motherwell ralph nelson wolfgang paalen
jackson pollock r. pousette-dart kurt roesch mark rothko
charles seliger leon smith clyfford still paul wilton

30 WEST 57TH STREET, N. Y. 19

REOPENING SATURDAY OCTOBER 6

AUTUMN SALON

Names of participating artists printed inside fold-over announcement.

Autumn Salon. October 6-29, 1945.

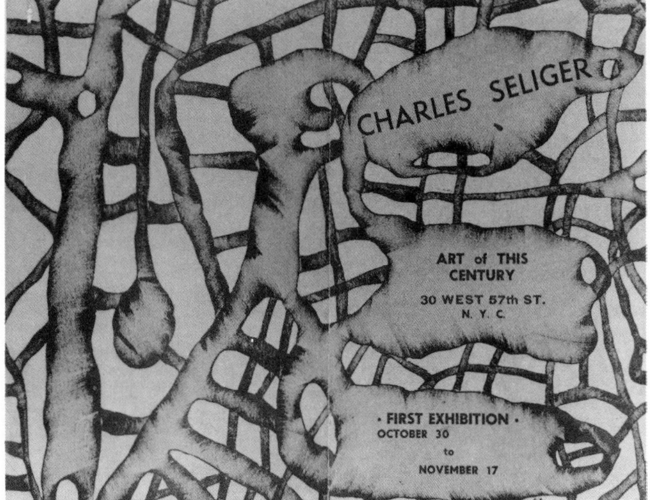

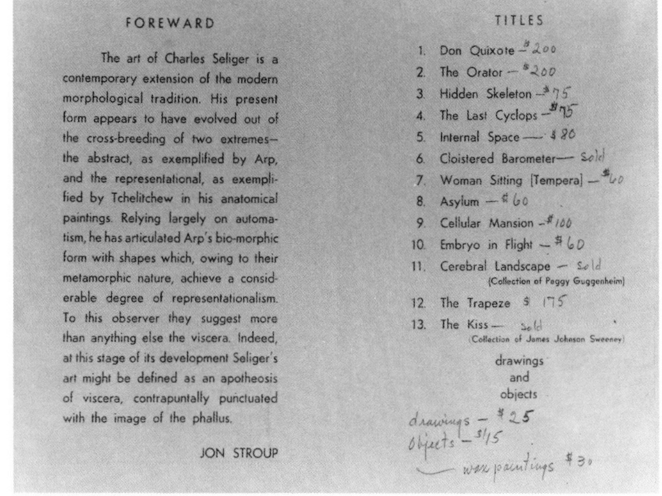
FOREWARD

The art of Charles Seliger is a contemporary extension of the modern morphological tradition. His present form appears to have evolved out of the cross-breeding of two extremes—the abstract, as exemplified by Arp, and the representational, as exemplified by Tchelitchew in his anatomical paintings. Relying largely on automatism, he has articulated Arp's bio-morphic form with shapes which, owing to their metamorphic nature, achieve a considerable degree of representationalism. To this observer they suggest more than anything else the viscera. Indeed, at this stage of its development Seliger's art might be defined as an apotheosis of viscera, contrapuntally punctuated with the image of the phallus.

JON STROUP

TITLES

1. Don Quixote —$200
2. The Orator — $200
3. Hidden Skeleton —$75
4. The Last Cyclops —$75
5. Internal Space — $80
6. Cloistered Barometer— Sold
7. Woman Sitting [Tempera] — $60
8. Asylum — $60
9. Cellular Mansion —$100
10. Embryo in Flight — $60
11. Cerebral Landscape — Sold (Collection of Peggy Guggenheim)
12. The Trapeze $ 175
13. The Kiss — Sold (Collection of James Johnson Sweeney)

drawings
and
objects

drawings — $25
objects — $15
— wax paintings $30

Back and front covers of catalogue (open).

Charles Seliger, First Exhibition. October 30-November 17, 1945.
Catalogue preface by Jon Stroup.

Paul Wilton. First Exhibition. October 30-November 17, 1945.
No catalogue. (A short introductory text by Frank Crowninshield mentioned in the press has not been located.)

Lee Hersch Paintings. November 20-December 8, 1945.
No catalogue.

Announcement.

Catalogue cover.

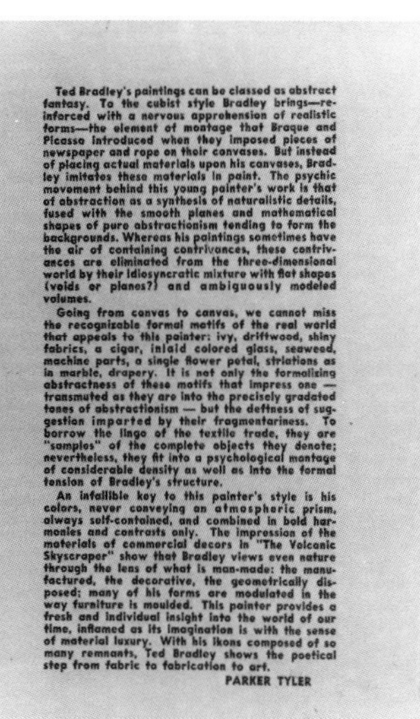

Ted Bradley's paintings can be classed as abstract fantasy. To the cubist style Bradley brings—reinforced with a nervous apprehension of realistic forms—the element of montage that Braque and Picasso introduced when they imposed pieces of newspaper and rope on their canvases. But instead of placing actual materials upon his canvases, Bradley imitates these materials in paint. The psychic movement behind this young painter's work is that of abstraction as a synthesis of naturalistic details, fused with the smooth planes and mathematical shapes of pure abstractionism tending to form the backgrounds. Whereas his paintings sometimes have the air of containing contrivances, these contrivances are eliminated from the three-dimensional world by their idiosyncratic mixture with flat shapes (voids or planes?) and ambiguously modeled volumes.

Going from canvas to canvas, we cannot miss the recognizable formal motifs of the real world that appeals to this painter: ivy, driftwood, shiny fabrics, a cigar, inlaid colored glass, seaweed, machine parts, a single flower petal, striations as in marble, drapery. It is not only the formalizing abstractness of these motifs that impress one — transmuted as they are into the precisely gradated tones of abstractionism — but the deftness of suggestion imparted by their fragmentariness. To borrow the lingo of the textile trade, they are "samples" of the complete objects they denote; nevertheless, they fit into a psychological montage of considerable density as well as into the formal tension of Bradley's structure.

An infallible key to this painter's style is his colors, never conveying an atmospheric prism, always self-contained, and combined in bold harmonies and contrasts only. The impression of the materials of commercial decors in "The Volcanic Skyscraper" show that Bradley views even nature through the lens of what is man-made: the manufactured, the decorative, the geometrically disposed; many of his forms are modulated in the way furniture is moulded. This painter provides a fresh and individual insight into the world of our time, inflamed as its imagination is with the sense of material luxury. With his ikons composed of so many remnants, Ted Bradley shows the poetical step from fabric to fabrication to art.

PARKER TYLER

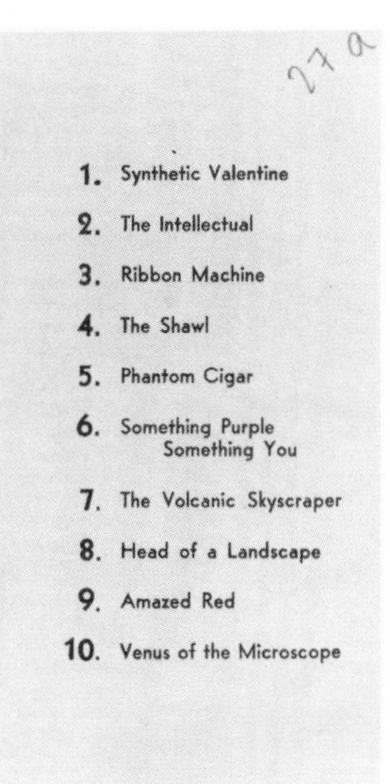

Back cover.

Ted Bradley Paintings. November 20-December 8, 1945.
Catalogue preface by Parker Tyler.

Christmas Exhibition of Gouaches. December 11-29, 1945.
No catalogue. Artists included were Minna Citron, Arshile Gorky, Matta, Jackson Pollock, Mark Rothko, Yves Tanguy, Laurence Vail.

Announcement.

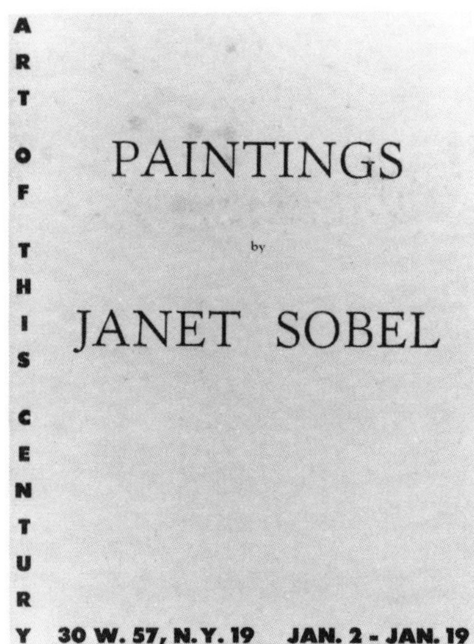

Catalogue cover.

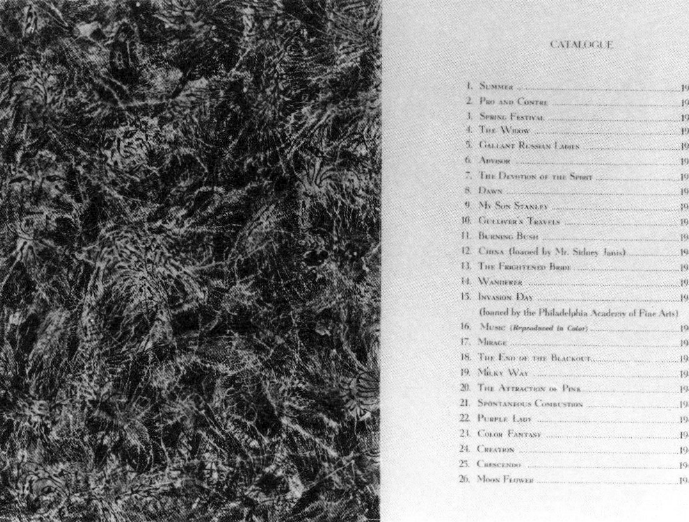

CATALOGUE

1. Summer 1941
2. Pro and Contre 1941
3. Spring Festival 1942
4. The Widow 1942
5. Gallant Russian Ladies 1942
6. Advisor 1943
7. The Devotion of the Spirit 1943
8. Dawn 1943
9. My Son Stanley 1943
10. Gulliver's Travels 1943
11. Burning Bush .... 1944 — 250
12. China (loaned by Mr. Sidney Janis) 1944
13. The Frightened Bride 1944
14. Wanderer .... 1944 — 200
15. Invasion Day 1944
(loaned by the Philadelphia Academy of Fine Arts)
16. Music (Reproduced in Color) .... 1944 — 250
17. Mirage .... 1945 — 250
18. The End of the Blackout .... 1945 — 200
19. Milky Way 1945
20. The Attraction of Pink 1945
21. Spontaneous Combustion .... 1945 — 225
22. Purple Lady 1945
23. Color Fantasy 1945
24. Creation 1945
25. Crescendo 1945
26. Moon Flower 1945

Paintings by Janet Sobel. January 3-19, 1946.
Catalogue preface by Sidney Janis.

JANET SOBEL

In seclusion from art and artists and only after she had become a grandmother did Janet Sobel feel the compelling urge to paint. Her beginnings, fresh as those of a child, were primitive, not in the sense of crude and awkward strivings many believe primitive to mean, but in a truer sense, that of *original, source* inspiration.

The self taught or instinctive-naïve painter is generally expected to develop. Unfortunately this development usually is at the sacrifice of a rare innate quality — his originality. Becoming aware of sophistication in art, he introduces knowing touches and short cuts which are in conflict with his basic style. Although Mrs. Sobel's work is no longer primitive and has taken another direction no such development but rather a metamorphosis takes place. A comparison of her early oils, Nos. 1, 3, and outstanding recent examples, Nos. 11, 12, 16, demonstrate this metamorphosis. Today her paintings are filled with unconscious surrealist phantasy.

The psychological drive of instinctive-naïve painters almost invariably manifests itself in perfection of detail. Mrs. Sobel is an exception. More and more her work is given over to freedom and imaginative play. Her autodidactic techniques in which *automatism* and *chance* effectively predominate, are improvised according to inner demands. Further, *a posteriori* images suggest themselves to her and these she develops. Out of them springs the intense hallucinatory phantasy that often intuitively parallels in concept and spirit the work of leaders of surrealism such as Ernst and Masson.

Unexpected color transpositions and self invented methods for applying pigment are uncanny plastic weapons in Mrs. Sobel's hands. With these the artist is enabled to project psychologically and in various moods her emotive forms which confront the observer as strange new visual experiences.

SIDNEY JANIS

Back cover.

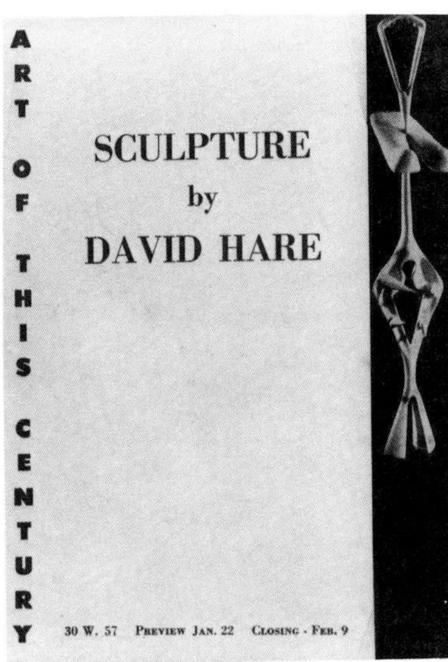

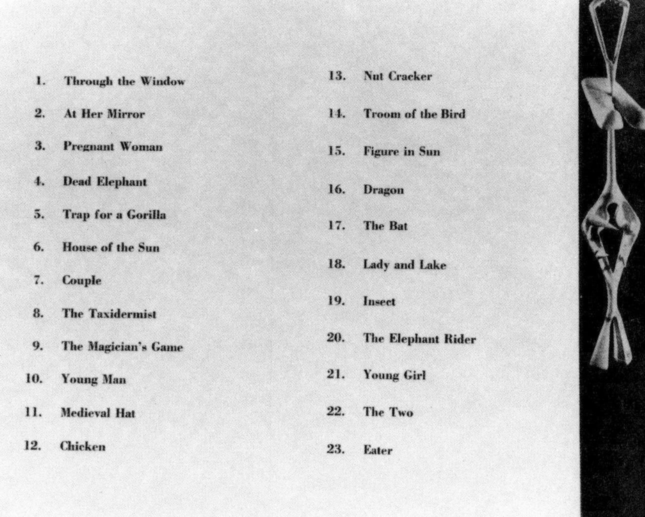

1. Through the Window
2. At Her Mirror
3. Pregnant Woman
4. Dead Elephant
5. Trap for a Gorilla
6. House of the Sun
7. Couple
8. The Taxidermist
9. The Magician's Game
10. Young Man
11. Medieval Hat
12. Chicken
13. Nut Cracker
14. Troom of the Bird
15. Figure in Sun
16. Dragon
17. The Bat
18. Lady and Lake
19. Insect
20. The Elephant Rider
21. Young Girl
22. The Two
23. Eater

Sculpture by David Hare. January 22-February 9, 1946.

Review: Clement Greenberg, *The Nation*, 9 February, 1946: "*...The sculpture in plaster, concrete, and other materials of David Hare, whose second one-man show is now being held at Art of This Century (through February 9), is another instance—a rich, full-blown, open instance—of the contemporary baroque. Hare stands second to no sculptor of his generation, unless it be David Smith, in potential talent. But like Smith in his latest phase and like all those who practice the baroque seriously at this moment, he is overwhelmed by the challenge of what is thought to be the contemporary mood.*

"*Hare's is the most intensely surrealist art I have ever seen—in the sense that it goes all the way in the direction of surrealism and then beyond, developing surrealism's premises with a consistency and boldness the surrealist doctrinaires themselves have hardly envisaged.... Hare has a prodigious amount of talent. The linear inventiveness of his sculpture cannot be denied; it is almost possible, in fact, to argue that he is a great draftsman—which is, perhaps, why he is not a successful sculptor in any final way.... Only when Hare comes to include his surrealism in something larger and outwardly more impassive and controlled, something that scorns to compete with nature in procreation, will he realize the fullness of his unquestionable talent.*"

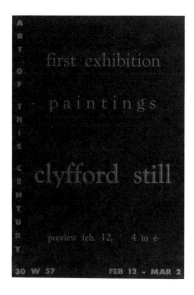

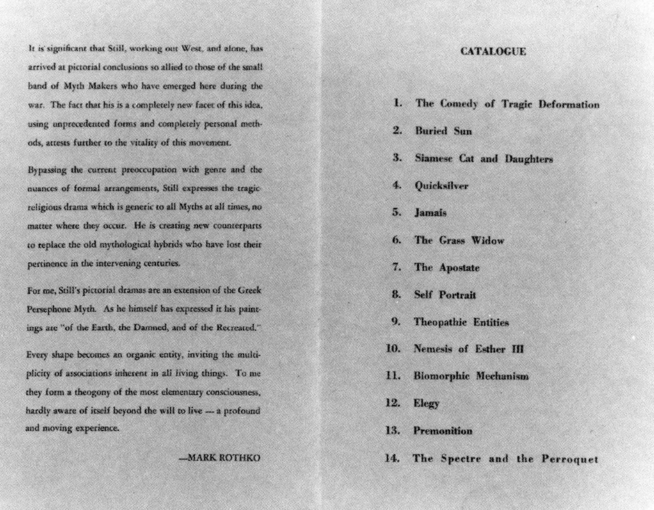

It is significant that Still, working out West, and alone, has arrived at pictorial conclusions so allied to those of the small band of Myth Makers who have emerged here during the war. The fact that his is a completely new facet of this idea, using unprecedented forms and completely personal methods, attests further to the vitality of this movement.

Bypassing the current preoccupation with genre and the nuances of formal arrangements, Still expresses the tragic religious drama which is generic to all Myths at all times, no matter where they occur. He is creating new counterparts to replace the old mythological hybrids who have lost their pertinence in the intervening centuries.

For me, Still's pictorial dramas are an extension of the Greek Persephone Myth. As he himself has expressed it his paintings are "of the Earth, the Damned, and of the Recreated."

Every shape becomes an organic entity, inviting the multiplicity of associations inherent in all living things. To me they form a theogony of the most elementary consciousness, hardly aware of itself beyond the will to live — a profound and moving experience.

—MARK ROTHKO

CATALOGUE

1. The Comedy of Tragic Deformation
2. Buried Sun
3. Siamese Cat and Daughters
4. Quicksilver
5. Jamais
6. The Grass Widow
7. The Apostate
8. Self Portrait
9. Theopathic Entities
10. Nemesis of Esther III
11. Biomorphic Mechanism
12. Elegy
13. Premonition
14. The Spectre and the Perroquet

First Exhibition Paintings Clyfford Still. February 12-March 2 [extended to March 7], 1946.

Catalogue preface by Mark Rothko. Exhibition proposed by Rothko; installed by Clement Greenberg and David Porter.

5 Sculptures. Pamela Bodin. February 12-March 2 [extended to March 7], 1946.
No catalogue.

Announcement.

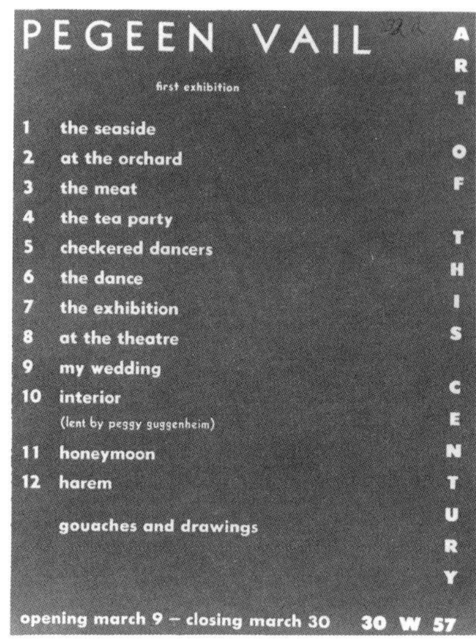

PEGEEN VAIL

first exhibition

1 the seaside
2 at the orchard
3 the meat
4 the tea party
5 checkered dancers
6 the dance
7 the exhibition
8 at the theatre
9 my wedding
10 interior
(lent by peggy guggenheim)
11 honeymoon
12 harem

gouaches and drawings

ART OF THIS CENTURY

opening march 9 – closing march 30 30 W 57

Checklist.

Verso of checklist.

Pegeen Vail. First Exhibition. March 9-30, 1946.

Catalogue cover.

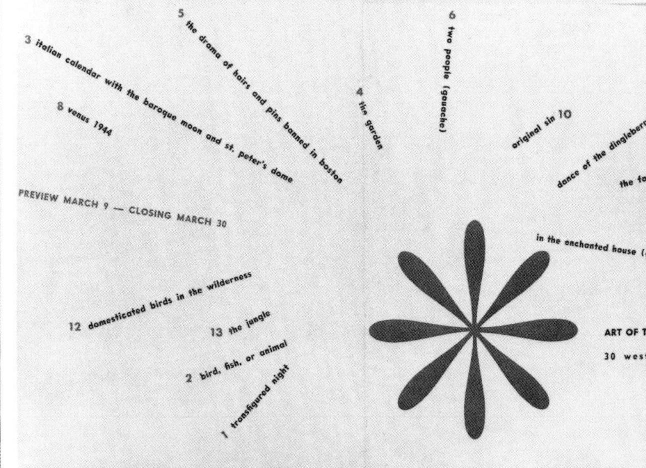

Verso of cover.

Peter Busa. Paintings. March 9-30, 1946.

Jackson Pollock's jacket design for Peggy Guggenheim, *Out of This Century*.

In March 1946, Peggy Guggenheim's memoirs *Out of This Century* were published by Dial Press, New York. 365 pages. Cover designed by Jackson Pollock. She had begun the writing in the summer of 1944 and completed it during 1945.

JACKSON POLLOCK

exhibition paintings

OILS

1 circumcision
2 water figure
3 troubled queen
4 the little king
5 the child proceeds
6 the white angel
7 an ace in the hole
8 direction
9 moon vessel
10 high priestess
11 once upon a time

eight temperas

ART OF THIS CENTURY

preview april 2–closing april 20 30 W 57

Announcement-checklist.

Jackson Pollock. April 2-20, 1946.

Review: Clement Greenberg, *The Nation*, 13 April, 1946: "... *Pollock's superiority to his contemporaries in this country lies in his ability to create a genuinely violent and extravagant art without losing stylistic control. His emotion starts out pictorially; it does not have to be castrated and translated in order to be put into a picture.* [His] *third show in as many years contains nothing to equal the two large canvases, 'Totem I' and 'Totem II,' that he exhibited last year. But it is still sufficient — for all its divagations and weaknesses, especially in the gouaches — to show him as the most original contemporary easel-painter under forty. What may at first sight seem crowded and repetitious reveals on second sight an infinity of dramatic movement and variety. One has to learn Pollock's idiom to realize its flexibility. And it is precisely because I am, in general, still learning from Pollock that I hesitate to attempt a more thorough analysis of his art.*"

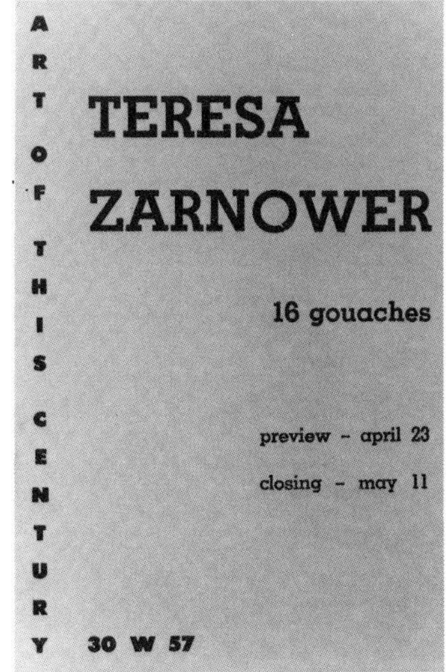
ART OF THIS CENTURY

TERESA ZARNOWER

16 gouaches

preview - april 23
closing - may 11

30 W 57

Catalogue cover.

Teresa Zarnower, leader of the Contructivist movement in Poland, who is well-known throughout the capitals of Europe, has been in this country for only two and a half years. She is perhaps the last important European artist to arrive here during the war, and it is America's pride that having enjoyed its hospitality, she has joined the small but distinguished company of European artists who have chosen to make America their permanent home.

In Warsaw, she initiated the Contructivist revolution in abstract art, and was instrumental, as editor of the avant-garde publication BLOK, in making Poland an important center for the movement. Teresa Zarnower is one of the important figures in the formulation of those functional principles that have profoundly influenced American painters, architects and industrial designers. It is only fitting that the prophet should find her home where her prophecy has been so well fulfilled. ...

She now, in her first exhibition of work done here, feels that purist constructions in a world that she has seen collapse around her into shambles and personal tragedy is not enough, that an insistance on absolute purity may be total illusion. Art must say something. In this she is close to many American painters, who have been no less sensitive to the tragedy of our times.

It is this transition from abstract language to abstract thought, it is this concern with abstract subject matter rather than abstract disciplines that gives her work its strength and its dignity. The truth here is mutually inclusive, for the defense of human dignity is the ultimate subject matter of art. And it is only in its defense that any of us will ever find strength.

B. B. NEWMAN

1 the serpent
2 cataclysm
3 interpenetration of forms
4 bridal day
5 catacombs of sorrow
6 pallas athene
7 walls of force
8 maelstrom
9 europa
10 entombment
11 interpenetration
12 the eye of vanity
13 exile
14 the bridge
15 the shock
16 the prophet

Teresa Zarnower. 16 Gouaches. April 23-May 11, 1946.
Catalogue preface by Barnett Newman.

Robert De Niro. First Exhibition of Painting. April 23-May 11, 1946.

Review: Clement Greenberg, *The Nation*, 18 May, 1946: "*Peggy Guggenheim has discovered another important young abstract painter ... Robert De Niro, whose first show exhibits monumental effects rare in abstract art. In two of De Niro's ten pictures ... the originality and force of his temperament demonstrate themselves under an iron control of the plastic elements such as is rarely seen in our time outside the oldest surviving members of the School of Paris. His other canvases are much less successful but offer at least evidence of great possibilities, especially in their draftsmanship....*"

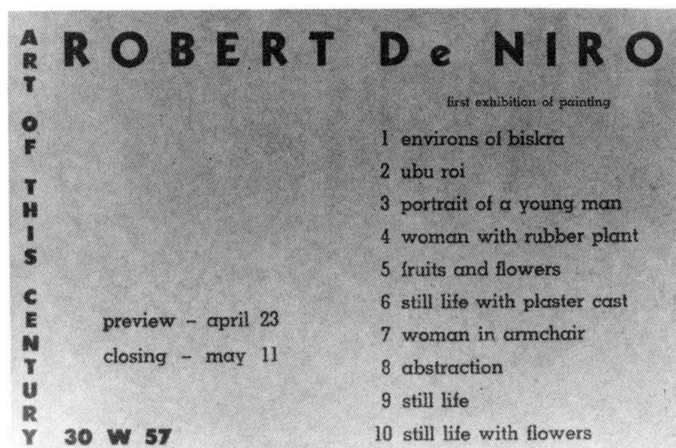

ART OF THIS CENTURY

ROBERT De NIRO

first exhibition of painting

1 environs of biskra
2 ubu roi
3 portrait of a young man
4 woman with rubber plant
5 fruits and flowers
6 still life with plaster cast
7 woman in armchair
8 abstraction
9 still life
10 still life with flowers

preview - april 23
closing - may 11

30 W 57

Announcement-checklist.

Sonja Sekula. First Exhibition of Paintings. May 14-June 1, 1946.

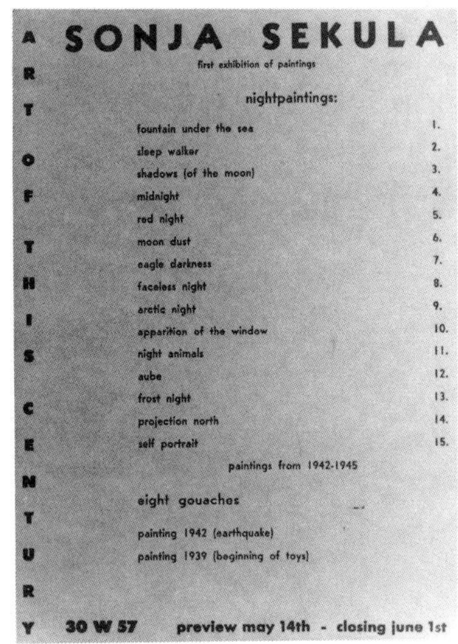

ART OF THIS CENTURY

SONJA SEKULA

first exhibition of paintings

nightpaintings:

fountain under the sea 1.
sleep walker 2.
shadows (of the moon) 3.
midnight 4.
red night 5.
moon dust 6.
eagle darkness 7.
faceless night 8.
arctic night 9.
apparition of the window 10.
night animals 11.
aube 12.
frost night 13.
projection north 14.
self portrait 15.

paintings from 1942-1945

eight gouaches

painting 1942 (earthquake)
painting 1939 (beginning of toys)

30 W 57 preview may 14th - closing june 1st

Announcement-checklist.

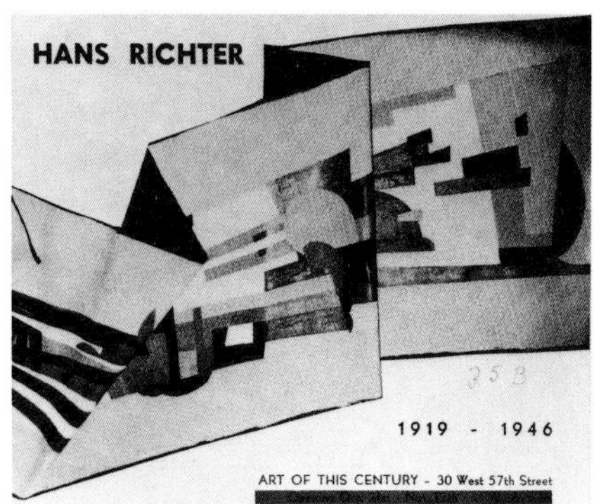

Catalogue cover.

HANS RICHTER

If the artist is an image of his time, then Hans Richter is a true artist; because what else expresses so much the character of our time as the struggle for the secret of CONTINUITY. Has not science entered, finally, into the inner heart of matter and brought forth the nucleus of such knowledge? But the artist, naturally, has done it long ago. (The vision of art precedes that of science.)

As early as 1919 Richter changed the individual presentation of pictures to a continuous one, namely, that of a scroll. And after many years of features, he has now, in 1945, returned to his original scrolling. This, too, is continuity.

One returns to oneself. One is eternally coming home.

Thus we say that he or she has arrived.

Frederick Kiesler

Log of Richter's Work:

1916 Member of Dada-group, Zürich.
1919 Coriginator with Eggeling of abstract (non-objective) paintings for film-scrolls.
1921 First abstract film.
Contrary to Eggeling's two-dimensional presentation, Richter, first introduced spatial depth expressed in a forth-and-from-movement of non-objective forms.
1926 - 1940 Avantgarde-films; design-theoretical work; documentaries and film research.
1943 - 1944 Scroll: Stalingrad.
Combined abstract painting and collage. The composition reels off from left to right. Abstraction of anorganic forces (representing the forward drive) are opposed and intertwined with motifs derived from organic expressions. At the end liberation from the onslaught of the war-machinale. (New York)
1944 Scroll: Liberation of Paris.
A visual poem. Painting and collage (New York).
1945 - 1946 Scroll: Momentum of Invasion.
The composition develops its structure from left to right. (New York)
1942-1946 Paintings in motifs of the
a) organic.
b) anorganic.

Orchestration of organic and inorganic forms

SCROLLS
1 Prelude 1919
2 Stalingrad 1943/44
3 Liberation of Paris 1944
4 Momentum of Invasion 1945/46

FILM-STILLS
RHYTHM 21 1921
DREAMS THAT MONEY CAN BUY feature film in 6 sequences, produced bv Hans Richter for Art Of This Century Films, Inc.—in cooperation with A. Calder, M. Duchamp, M. Ernst, F. Leger, Man Ray. 1945-1946

ORGANIC
5 Organic No. 1
6 Organic No. 2
7 Organic No. 3
8 Theme with four instruments (Tryptichon)
9 Relations between the organic and the inorganic

INORGANIC
10 Linear motive
11 Good government No. 1
12 Good government No. 2

Hans Richter 1919-1946. October 22-November 9, 1946.
Catalogue preface by Frederick Kiesler.

Peggy Guggenheim met Richter through Nelly van Doesburg in New York. She supplied most of the financial backing for his film *Dreams That Money Can Buy,* produced, in collaboration with Alexander Calder, Marcel Duchamp, Max Ernst, Fernand Léger, and Man Ray, for Art of This Century Films, Inc.

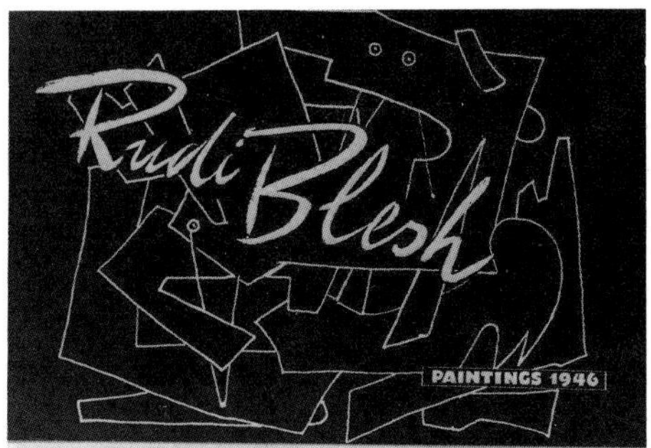

Cover of fold-over catalogue.

Rudi Blesh Paintings 1946. November 12-30, 1946.
Catalogue preface by Harriet Janis.

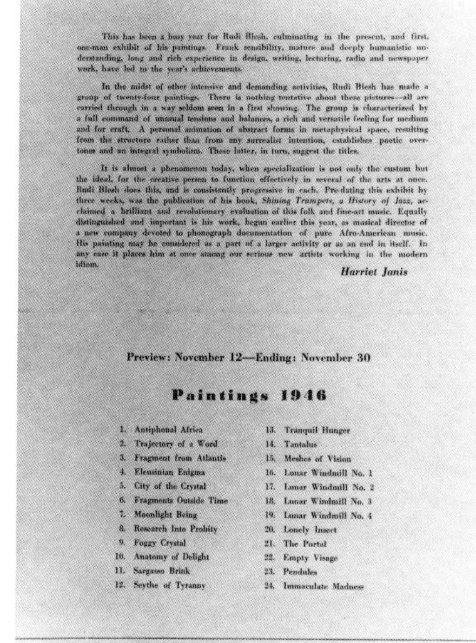

This has been a busy year for Rudi Blesh, culminating in the present, and first, one-man exhibit of his paintings. Frank sensibility, mature and deeply humanistic understanding, long and rich experience in design, writing, lecturing, radio and newspaper work, have led to the year's achievements.

In the midst of other intensive and demanding activities, Rudi Blesh has made a group of twenty-four paintings. There is nothing tentative about these pictures—all are carried through in a way seldom seen in a first showing. The group is characterized by a full command of unusual tensions and balances, a rich and versatile feeling for medium and for craft. A personal animation of abstract forms in metaphysical space, resulting from the structure rather than from any surrealist intention, establishes poetic overtones and an integral symbolism. These latter, in turn, suggest the titles.

It is almost a phenomenon today, when specialization is not only the custom but the ideal, for the creative person to function effectively in several of the arts at once. Rudi Blesh does this, and is consistently progressive in each. Pre-dating this exhibit by three weeks, was the publication of his book, *Shining Trumpets, a History of Jazz*, acclaimed a brilliant and revolutionary evaluation of this folk and fine-art music. Equally distinguished and important is his work, begun earlier this year, as musical director of a new company devoted to phonograph documentation of pure Afro-American music. His painting may be considered as a part of a larger activity or as an end in itself. In any case it places him at once among our serious new artists working in the modern idiom.

Harriet Janis

Preview: November 12—Ending: November 30

Paintings 1946

1. Antiphonal Africa
2. Trajectory of a Word
3. Fragment from Atlantis
4. Eleusinian Enigma
5. City of the Crystal
6. Fragments Outside Time
7. Moonlight Being
8. Research Into Probity
9. Foggy Crystal
10. Anatomy of Delight
11. Sargasso Brink
12. Scythe of Tyranny
13. Tranquil Hunger
14. Tantalus
15. Meshes of Vision
16. Lunar Windmill No. 1
17. Lunar Windmill No. 2
18. Lunar Windmill No. 3
19. Lunar Windmill No. 4
20. Lonely Insect
21. The Portal
22. Empty Visage
23. Pendules
24. Immaculate Madness

ART OF THIS CENTURY • 30 WEST 57th STREET

Virginia Admiral Six Paintings. November 12-30, 1946.
No catalogue.

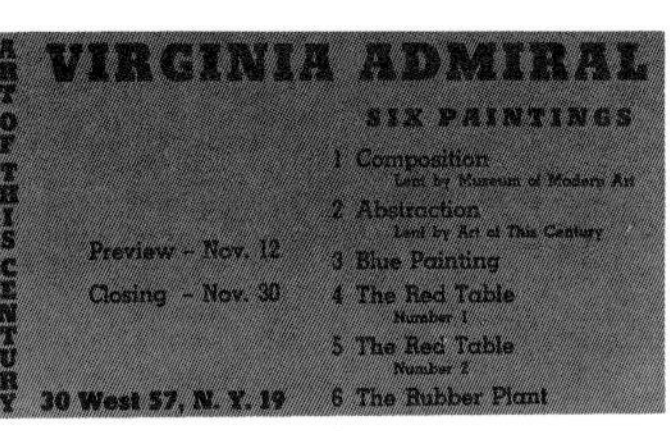

Announcement.

Charles Seliger, Kenneth Scott, Dwight Ripley, John Goodwin, David Hill. December 3-21, 1946.
No catalogue.

Announcement.

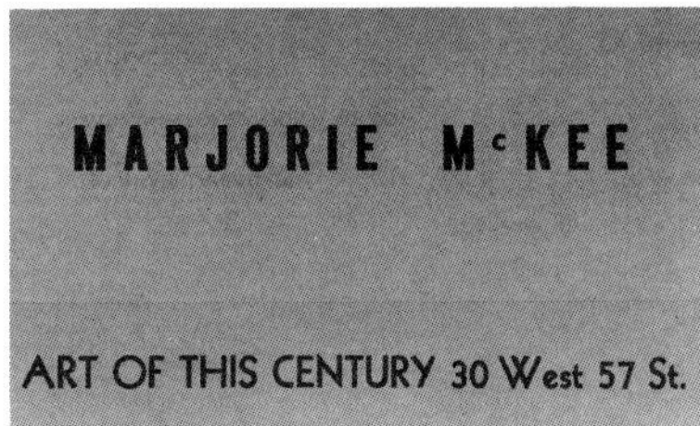

Cover of fold-over catalogue.

Marjorie McKee. December 24, 1946-January 11, 1947.

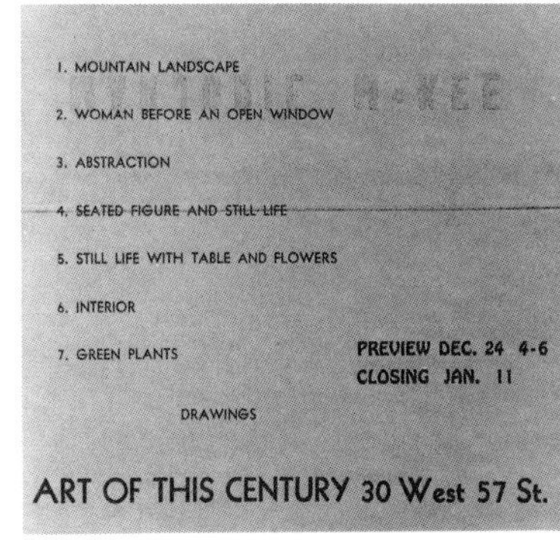

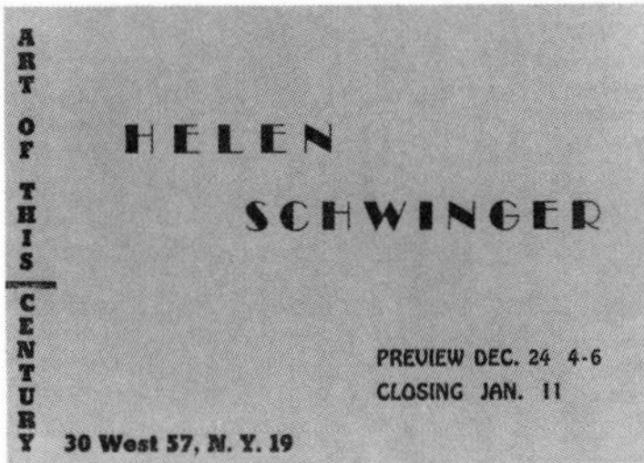

ART OF THIS CENTURY

HELEN SCHWINGER

PREVIEW DEC. 24 4-6
CLOSING JAN. 11

30 West 57, N. Y. 19

Catalogue cover.

Those who know Helen Schwinger will tell you that she's an unusual person. At the University of Arizona she majored in animal husbandry. Born to one of the green valleys of California settled by her relatives, one thinks of her as the familiar spirit of mountain vistas, stretches of citrus groves, live water and reaches of Pacific sky.

For the first time, she brings her intense canvases to New York. Take a surface and with color, create moving patterns of familiar but unrecognizable forms. Now extend that surface three dimensionally to infinity by some uncanny manipulation of perspective. What have you got but a new world, alive as a heart-beat.

Others have captured and imprisoned light, and used it to serve their purpose. Here Ariel is set free and this is his own country.

Everyone has looked into hearth fires burning. Everybody has read his mind in the sky. Flame and clouds, however, lack intention. In these paintings there is uncommon decisiveness. But the mood of reverie is preserved and the peace of understanding.

Edward Newman Horn.

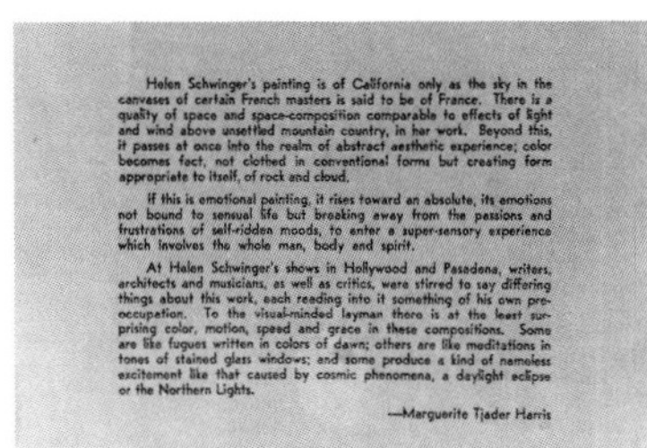

Helen Schwinger's painting is of California only as the sky in the canvases of certain French masters is said to be of France. There is a quality of space and space-composition comparable to effects of light and wind above unsettled mountain country, in her work. Beyond this, it passes at once into the realm of abstract aesthetic experience; color becomes fact, not clothed in conventional forms but creating form appropriate to itself, of rock and cloud.

If this is emotional painting, it rises toward an absolute, its emotions not bound to sensual life but breaking away from the passions and frustrations of self-ridden moods, to enter a super-sensory experience which involves the whole man, body and spirit.

At Helen Schwinger's shows in Hollywood and Pasadena, writers, architects and musicians, as well as critics, were stirred to say differing things about this work, each reading into it something of his own preoccupation. To the visual-minded layman there is at the least surprising color, motion, speed and grace in these compositions. Some are like fugues written in colors of dawn; others are like meditations in tones of stained glass windows; and some produce a kind of nameless excitement like that caused by cosmic phenomena, a daylight eclipse or the Northern Lights.

—Marguerite Tjader Harris

Back cover.

Helen Schwinger. December 24, 1946-January 11, 1947.

The seven oils shown were: *Mountain Landscape, Woman Before an Open Window, Abstraction, Seated Figure and Still Life, Still Life with Table and Flowers, Interior, Green Plants.* Drawings were also included. The exhibition was proposed by the artist, who paid $200 toward the expenses; this was the only instance in Peggy Guggenheim's career when she asked an artist to contribute to the gallery's costs.

Jackson Pollock. January 14-February 1 [extended to February 7], 1947.
Catalogue preface by Nathan M. [Bill] Davis. Davis was a great supporter of Pollock and persuaded Peggy Guggenheim to give him the second, more lucrative contract (see cat. no. 144, fn. 2). He purchased several of Pollock's works during the 1940s.

Review: Clement Greenberg, *The Nation*, 1 February, 1947: "*Jackson Pollock's fourth one-man show in so many years is his best since his first one and signals what may be a major step in his development — which I regard as the most important so far of the younger generation of American painters. He has now largely abandoned his customary heavy black-and-whitish or gunmetal chiaroscuro for the higher scales, for alizarins, cream-whites, cerulean blues, pinks, and sharp greens. Like Dubuffet, however, whose art goes in a similar if less abstract direction, Pollock remains essentially a draftsman in black and white who must as a rule rely on these colors to maintain the consistency and power of surface of his pictures. As is the case with almost all post-cubist painting of any real originality, it is the tension inherent in the constructed, re-created flatness of the surface that produces the strength of his art.... Pollock has gone beyond the stage where he needs to make his poetry explicit in ideographs. What he invents instead has perhaps, in its very abstractness and absence of assignable definition, a more reverberating meaning.... Pollock points a way beyond the easel, beyond the mobile, framed picture, to the mural, perhaps — or perhaps not. I cannot tell.*"

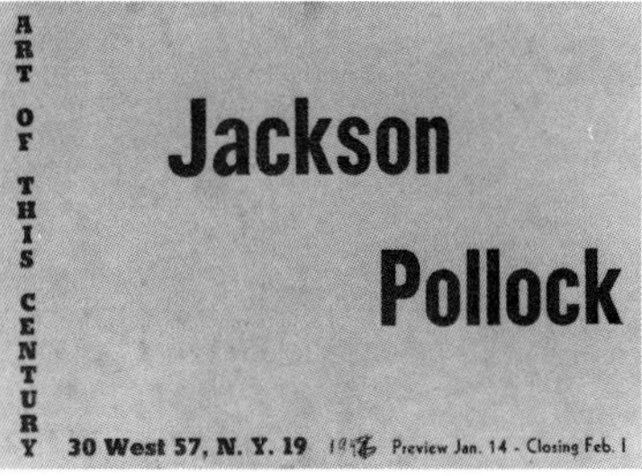

ART OF THIS CENTURY

Jackson Pollock

30 West 57, N. Y. 19 1946 Preview Jan. 14 - Closing Feb. 1

Cover of fold-over catalogue.

SOUNDS IN THE GRASS
(Series)

1. CROAKING MOVEMENT
2. SHIMMERING SUBSTANCE (loaned by Mr. N. M. Davis)
3. EYES IN THE HEAT 1946
4. EARTH WORMS 1946
5. THE BLUE UNCONSCIOUS (loaned by Mr. Schwamm) 1946
6. SOMETHING OF THE PAST
7. THE DANCERS

ACCABONAC CREEK
(Series)

8. THE WATER BULL
9. YELLOW TRIANGLE
10. BIRD EFFORT 1946
11. GREY CENTER
12. THE KEY
13. CONSTELLATION
14. THE TEA CUP (loaned by Mr. N. M. Davis)
15. MAGIC LIGHT
16. MURAL — 1943

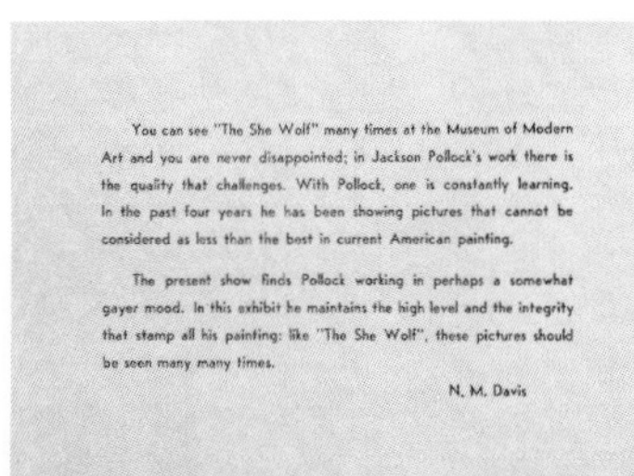

You can see "The She Wolf" many times at the Museum of Modern Art and you are never disappointed; in Jackson Pollock's work there is the quality that challenges. With Pollock, one is constantly learning. In the past four years he has been showing pictures that cannot be considered as less than the best in current American painting.

The present show finds Pollock working in perhaps a somewhat gayer mood. In this exhibit he maintains the high level and the integrity that stamp all his painting: like "The She Wolf", these pictures should be seen many many times.

N. M. Davis

Back cover.

Catalogue cover.

9. Nude with Flowers, 1945*

In painting today, it is generally conceded that while the approach of the sophisticated artist is opposite from that of the "naive", each creates in his own way valid works of art. The schooled painter, continually sharpening his critical perception by virtue of the selection necessary in the process of his own work, is essentially consistent in his appreciation of the work of others. The autodidact on the other hand, relies not so much upon a sense of selection as on his own intuition, sure in creating his own work, uneven in evaluating the work of others. The honest disparity in appreciative viewpoints is pointed up in the following incidents.

Mondrian, despite the restricted regimen of his own art, was noted for his quick response to originality, however different, in other painters. Not long after his arrival from abroad, he selected from a group of paintings by leading international advance-guard artists including his own work, a painting by an artist unknown to him, remarking: "Excepting Picasso, this is the strongest picture here." It was a painting by Morris Hirshfield.

Hirshfield would unquestionably have agreed with this point of view, but he in turn could not prove receptive to Mondrian's art. At the opening of his own exhibition at the Museum of Modern Art, Hirshfield, noticing a picture hanging in the Museum foyer, inquired about it. When he learned it was a painting recently purchased by the Museum (Mondrian's *BROADWAY BOOGIE WOOGIE*), he thought this incredible.

For some reason the two men never actually met. Mondrian came to the Hirshfield opening, and later, when the guests assembled in the garden for refreshments, a chance arrangement around the long narrow table found them sitting at opposite ends. Across the length of the table the two artists, so different in every way, yet each equally great in his own genre, sat facing each other. In little more than two years both were dead.

The present showing of Hirshfield's last works, never before exhibited, is catalogued in the order in which the pictures were painted. He began to paint in 1937 at the age of 65. In his nine years as an artist — painting daily and often so engrossed that he worked far into the night — he made a total of 72 paintings.

Although Morris Hirshfield was the center of a stormy controversy in the press, over half his paintings had been acquired during his lifetime by collectors and museums both here and abroad, persons and institutions who, like Mondrian, found his art to be uncompromising integrity and originality.

SIDNEY JANIS

Memorial Showing of the Last Paintings of Morris Hirshfield. February 1-March 1, 1947. Catalogue preface by Sidney Janis.

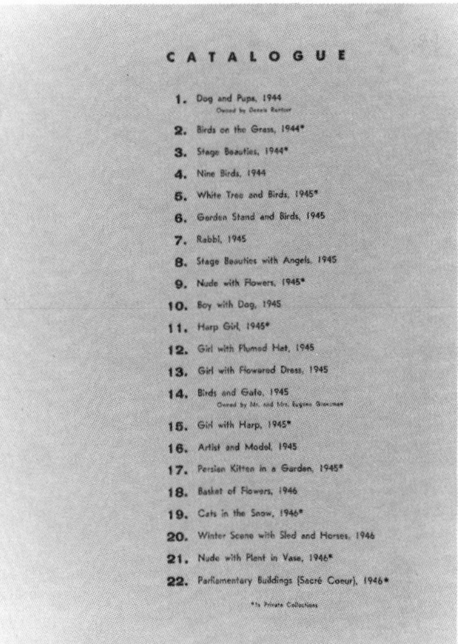

CATALOGUE

1. Dog and Pups, 1944
2. Birds on the Grass, 1944*
3. Stage Beauties, 1944*
4. Nine Birds, 1944
5. White Tree and Birds, 1945*
6. Garden Stand and Birds, 1945
7. Rabbi, 1945
8. Stage Beauties with Angels, 1945
9. Nude with Flowers, 1945*
10. Boy with Dog, 1945
11. Harp Girl, 1945*
12. Girl with Plumed Hat, 1945
13. Girl with Flowered Dress, 1945
14. Birds and Gate, 1945
15. Girl with Harp, 1945*
16. Artist and Model, 1945
17. Persian Kitten in a Garden, 1945*
18. Basket of Flowers, 1946
19. Cats in the Snow, 1946*
20. Winter Scene with Sled and Horses, 1946
21. Nude with Plant in Vase, 1946*
22. Parliamentary Buildings (Sacré Coeur), 1946*

*In Private Collections

Back cover.

Richard Pousette-Dart. March 4-22, 1947. Catalogue statement by the artist. Peggy Guggenheim purchased one work out of the exhibition and later gave it away. In her later years she regretted doing so.

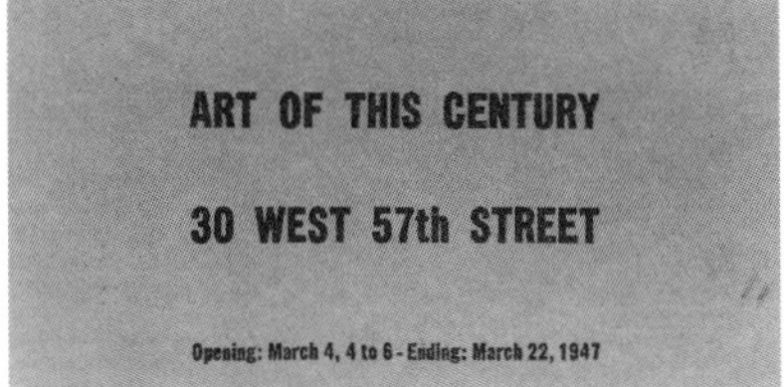

Cover of fold-over catalogue.

I strive to express the spiritual nature of the universe.
Painting is for me a dynamic balance and wholeness of life;
it is mysterious and transcending, yet solid and real.

1. SYMPHONY #1, THE TRANSCENDENTAL
2. COMPREHENSION OF THE ATOM, CRUCIFIXION
3. CATHEDRAL, THE ASCENSION
4. SPIRIT
5. HEAD OF THE MIRACLE
6. FRUIT OF DARKNESS
7. CENTER OF THE CONSCIOUS
8. ANONYMITY
9. ELEMENTAL
10. CIRCLES
11. SUN JEWEL
12. MAGICAL
13. MYRIADS #1
14. MYRIADS #2
15. THE INNER LIFE

ART OF THIS CENTURY

30 WEST 57th STREET

Opening: March 4, 4 to 6 - Ending: March 22, 1947

Back of fold-over.

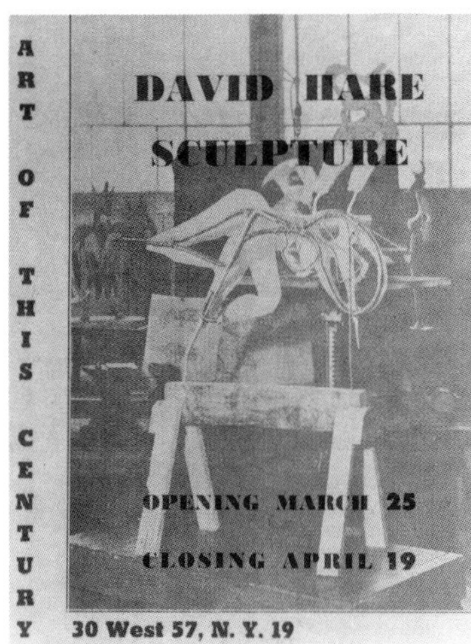

1 TORSO
2 FETISH
3 THE FLOATER
4 THE SUICITE
5 THIRSTY MAN
6 MAN WITH DRUMS
7 THE EARTH WADER
8 THE QUEEN'S GARDEN
9 CHAIR AND OCCUPANT
10 KNEELING DANCER
11 ENTER THE KING
12 THE FISHERMAN
13 YOUNG SHADOW
14 THE DUEL
15 FIGURE

David Hare Sculpture. March 25-April 19, 1947.

Review: Clement Greenberg, *The Nation*, 19 April, 1947: "... *If Smith is baroque, Hare is gothic, more angular and awkward, less closely related to cubism and more directly inspired by surrealism. Although under thirty and working as a sculptor only in the last three or four years, Hare has already shown enough promise to place him in the forefront of what now begins to seem, not a renaissance, but a* naissance *of sculpture in America: sculpture that in its methods and very utensils no less than in its conceptions—which, like our architecture and engineering, tend toward linearism, flat surfaces, and the denial of weight and mass—attaches itself more intimately to industrialism than any other form of art now being practiced. Hare is still somewhat too prone to the self indulgence and whimsey of surrealism to channel his powers into a style.... It is my hope that Hare will confine his surrealism more strictly to the role of stimulant and not let it usurp as many of the functions of aesthetic preceptor as it has in the past.*"

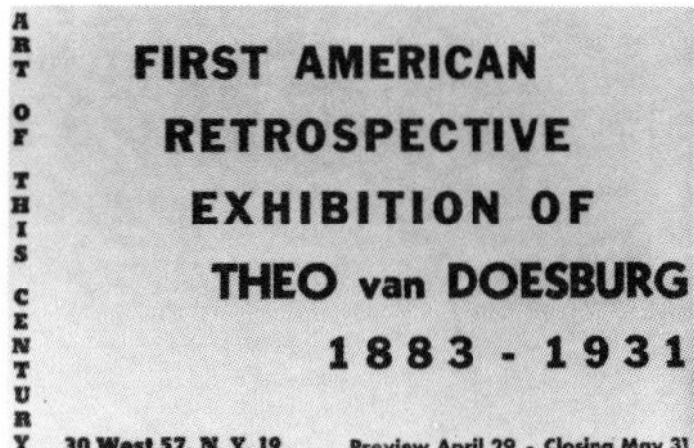

Announcement.

First American Retrospective Exhibition of Theo van Doesburg 1883-1931. April 29-May 31, 1947.
Catalogue preface by James Johnson Sweeney. Chronology and bibliography by Nelly van Doesburg. Loan exhibition organized by Nelly van Doesburg, who brought the works with her from Europe.

Catalogue cover.

COMPOSITION IN BLACK AND WHITE, 1917, Kunst-Museum, Basel.

THEO VAN DOESBURG, 1883-1931.

THEO van DOESBURG

Theo van Doesburg, like his DE STIJL colleague, Piet Mondrian, looked beyond easel-painting. Neither felt there was any longer a justification for easel-painting in its traditional character, either as an illusionistic reproduction of visual experiences, or as a decoration. They felt painting had passed beyond that stage. Easel-painting for Doesburg, as for Mondrian, was almost exclusively an expression of his philosophical view of the world in a vocabularly of forms conscientiously reduced to the strictest pictorial essentials — line, color and space intervals: a concrete analogue of that union of particular and universal which they saw as constituting the harmony of the universe.

Both Doesburg and Mondrian looked beyond easel-painting in the sense that they visualized the total environment of man as a potential work of art once it could be given the order which they were striving to achieve on their canvases. For this reason the easel-painting of both Doesburg and Mondrian must not be looked at in the same way we regard most pictorial representations, but as microcosmic patterns, or as models of the artists' larger visions.

And in Doesburg's work, particularly where it has carried him into the architectural field, we see this character more clearly than in Mondrian's. For Mondrian was by temperament more shy and retiring. His painting as a result has a more private air about it. The environment he was most consistently engaged in organizing was his studio, which, wherever he was, seemed a three—or even four dimensional expansion of his painting: tiny related rectangles of primary color on the walls, larger bold colored rectangles of linoleum on the floor and furniture painted in solid primary tones to relate. — But always with an air of shy intimacy about the whole conception.

On the other hand, in both Theo van Doesburg's own architectural work and in his collaborations with other architects in group housing and city planning, we recognize a broader social application of his philosophy than Mondrian ever achieved. In comparison with Mondrian, Doesburg was a public poet — a poet on a platform — an articulate propagandist of his own ideas. Actually he and Kurt Schwitters together gave several public poetry recitals. And Doesburg's mature painting with its breadth, swing and movement, has the same character in contrast to Mondrian's subtle, quiet, perfectionist calm that their personal characters offer.

In their painting both had turned from naturalistic representation early in the STIJL period. They both saw naturalistic representation as "particularized" representation. "The predominance," as Doesburg puts it, "of individualism as well as that of local character, was always the great obstacle to the birth of a universal art. If the means of expression are liberated from all particularity, they are in harmony with the end of art which is to realize a universal language." This was the STIJL aim. And both Mondrian and Doesburg found a constant equivalent for the universal in the right-angle, while color contrasts, differences of color areas and of space intervals represented the variable particulars.

Yet an essential difference of viewpoint from that of Mondrian becomes evident in the mature work of Doesburg. As early as 1921 Doesburg had turned to an interest in "Elementarism" which, as he described it, "forced into unification in a new form of expression the two principal factors of our creative activity — that is to say repose and movement, time and space." Furthermore, Doesburg's new outlook was opposed to the system of strict right-angle compositions, one of oblique arrangements: "an expression of dynamic equilibrium" in opposition "to static equilibrium." And here we see Doesburg's expression leaving the orthogonal and relatively static base-organizations, which he and Mondrian had both employed, to associate itself more closely with the running forms which characterize north European art, from the zoomorphic art of Scandinavia to the twentieth century abstractions of Malewich, Lizzitsky, or Kandinsky. Yet possibly these two eventual developments could have been anticipated in Mondrian's and Doesburg's De Stijl beginnings. For Mondrian reductions of form in the early years had been simplifications out of cubism, a fundamentally static structural expression while Doesburg on the other hand arrived at his through a stripping stylization of natural forms, as we see in the compositions he subsequently derived from his "Card Players" and "Foxtrot".

Finally, in color, it was the aim of both to wash the eyes of the period. And here they both spoke directly to the senses of the observer — with no other intention. For, as Doesburg put it, "color is the raw material of painting; it has no other significance but itself." And if Mondrian expressed their ideal just as completely on his canvases as his colleague, it was Doesburg, the poet and propagandist of DE STIJL who best put their intentions into words:

"WHITE! There's the spiritual color of our times, the clean-cut attitude that directs all our actions. Not grey, not ivory-white, but pure white.

"WHITE! There's the color of the new age, the color which signifies a whole epoch: ours, that of the perfectionist, of purity and of certainty.

"WHITE! Just that.

"Behind us the 'browns' of decay and of Academicism, the 'blue' of divisionism, the cult of the blue sky, of gods with greenish whiskers and of the spectre.

"White, pure white."

JAMES JOHNSON SWEENEY

"NATURE MORTE", 1915. Rijks Museum Kröller-Müller, Otterloo, The Netherlands.

THEO Van DOESBURG = "I. K. BONSET" = "ALDO CAMINI":

1883—Born August 30, Utrecht, Holland.
School in Holland.
In early years ambition was "to become an actor".

1899—First paintings.

1902—Began to write fables suggested by his dreams and pieces for the theatre.

1908—First one-man exhibition in The Hague.

1912—Articles on Asiatic art, modern art, cubism, futurism and Kandinsky.

1913—Published his first collection of poems "VOLLE MAAN" and started researches towards the unification of pure painting and architecture. Projects; lectures; articles.

1914—Mobilized; wrote his "DE STEM UIT DE DIEPTE".

1916—First collaboration with the architects Oud and Wils. Founded the DE STIJL group and the review of the same name which appeared in October.
Composed a series of poems using only two or three words.

1917—Designed pavements, wall paintings and stained glass windows for the Vacantiehuis at Noordwijkerhout built by the architect Oud. Painted CARD PLAYERS.

1918—Project for a monument in reinforced concrete which was cited for its "architectural qualities" by a jury composed of well-known architects and engineers including Berlage, De Bazel, Holsboer and others. Collaborated with several architects of the DE STIJL group on different undertakings.
In November DE STIJL manifesto issued; signed by all members except Van der Leck.

1920—Began construction of laborers houses and schools in collaboration with the architect de Boer at Dragten, Holland. Set out on a journey to spread DE STIJL ideas through Central Europe. Met the architects Gropius, Adolf Meyer, Erich Mendelsohn, Mies van der Rohe, Le Corbusier and others.

1921—Weimar and Berlin. Edition of review DE STIJL published in Germany.
Foundation of a group at Weimar: courses and lectures: effort to develop the fundamental spirit of a new style. Edited the publication of the dada magazine MECANO in collaboration with Arp, Tzara, Ribemont-Dessaignes, Schwitters, Hausmann, etc.

1922—Dada tour throughout Holland and to Hanover with Kurt Schwitters, Petro van Doesburg at piano. Van Doesburg lectured on Dada movement, both he and Schwitters read poems. Joined in Hanover by Tzara, Arp and Raoul Hausmann.

1923—Paris. Invited by Leonce Rosenberg to organize an exhibition at the GALERIE DE L'EFFORT MODERNE of the architecture and painting of the DE STIJL group.

1924—Studies and first project for a city of circulation (a viaduct city). Exhibition at the "Special School of Architecture", Paris. Lectures on the DE STIJL Movement in Prague, Vienna and Brno, Czechoslovakia. Beginnings of Elementarism.

1925—Exhibition of architecture, Nancy, France.

1926—Published Manifesto on Elementarism in "DE STIJL" no 75/76. Undertook entire internal architectural reconstruction of the cabaret L'Aubette, Strasbourg commissioned by Horn, painting in collaboration with Hans Arp, Sophie Taeuber Arp. The work throughout was done on strict De Stijl principles, all save the facade which was an historical monument. Up to this time the fullest attempt at plastic unity in a building.
Reconstructed a shop in Strasbourg, Maison Meyer, rue de Vieux Marché-aux-Poissons. Made over an apartment in reinforced concrete and rabitz.

1929-1930—Paris. Designed own house at Meudon-val-Fleury near Paris —which was still uncompleted at his death. Lectures on architecture, Madrid and Barcelona. Edited review "ART CONCRET" in collaboration with Carlsund, Tutundjian, Hélion.

1931—January: first meeting for the foundation of Abstraction-Création group in Doesburg's studio in Meudon.

1931—Died, March 7, in Davos, Switzerland.

CATALOGUE

1. NATURE MORTE, 1906
2. PORTRAIT DE L'ARTISTE, 1906
3. PORTRAIT DE MR. L, 1908
4. PORTRAIT DE L'ARTISTE, 1908
5. PORTRAIT, 1908
6. PORTRAIT DE L'ARTISTE, 1911
7. MARINE, 1912
8. DUNES, 1912
9. MARINE, 1912
10. PORTRAIT, 1913
11. PANIER RENVERSE, 1913
12. JEUNE FILLE AUX FLEURS, 1914
13. PAYSAGE, 1916
14. ARBRE AVEC MAISONS, 1916
15. LA DANSE, 1916
16. NATURE MORTE, 1916
17. JOUEURS AUX CARTES, 1916-17
18. MOUVEMENT HEROIQUE, 1917
19. COMPOSITION 7, 1917
20. COMPOSITION 13, 1916
21. ETUDES POUR COMPOSITION 10, 1917
22. COMPOSITION D'UN INTERIEUR, 1917
23. COMPOSITION VARIATION, 1918
24. COMPOSITION, 1918 (Lent by Art of this Century)
25. DANSE RUSSE, 1918 (Lent by Museum of Modern Art)
26. COMPOSITION, 1919-20
27. COMPOSITION, 1924
28. CONTRE COMPOSITION 8, 1924
29. CONTRE COMPOSITION, 1926 (Lent by Art of this Century)
30. COMPOSITION SIMULTANEE, 1929
31. COMPOSITION SIMULTANEE, 1929
32. CONTRE COMPOSITION SIMULTANEE, 1930

Water-Colors, Gouaches, Pastels, Drawings, Photographs and Architectural Drawings.

COMPOSITION EN GRIS, 1918, Art of this Century, New York.

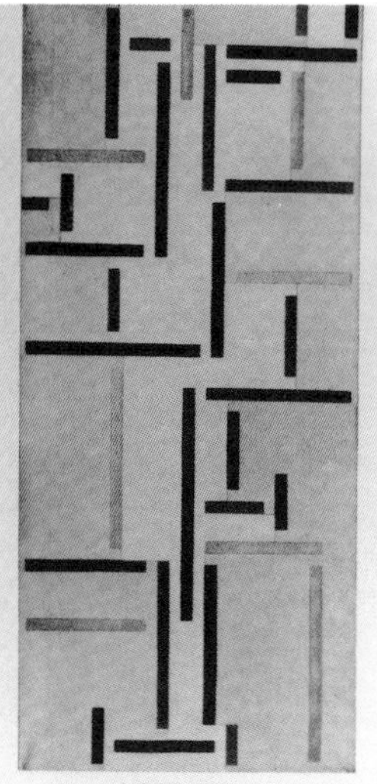

DANSE RUSSE, 1918, Museum of Modern Art, New York.

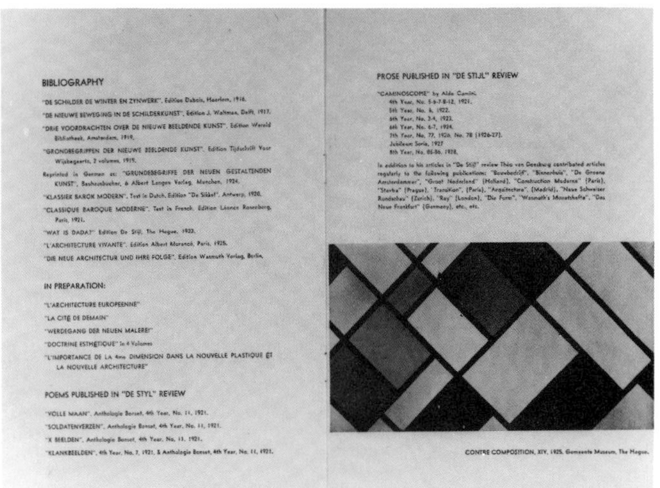
BIBLIOGRAPHY

"DE SCHILDER DE WINTER EN ZYNWERK". Edition Dubois, Haarlem, 1916.

"DE NIEUWE BEWEGING IN DE SCHILDERKUNST". Edition J. Waltman, Delft, 1917.

"DRIE VOORDRACHTEN OVER DE NIEUWE BEELDENDE KUNST". Edition Wereld Bibliotheek, Amsterdam, 1919.

"GRONDBEGRIPPEN DER NIEUWE BEELDENDE KUNST". Edition Tijdschrift Voor Wijsbegeerte, 2 volumes, 1919.

Reprinted in German as: "GRUNDEBEGRIFFE DER NEUEN GESTALTENDEN KUNST", Bauhausbucher, 6 Albert Langen Verlag, Munchen, 1924.

"KLASSIEK BAROK MODERN". Text in Dutch. Edition "De Sikkel", Antwerp, 1920.

"CLASSIQUE BAROQUE MODERNE". Text in French. Edition Léonce Rosenberg, Paris, 1921.

"WAT IS DADA?" Edition De Stijl, The Hague, 1923.

"L'ARCHITECTURE VIVANTE". Edition Albert Morancé, Paris, 1925.

"DIE NEUE ARCHITECTUR UND IHRE FOLGE". Edition Wasmuth Verlag, Berlin.

IN PREPARATION:

"L'ARCHITECTURE EUROPEENNE"

"LA CITÉ DE DEMAIN"

"WERDEGANG DER NEUEN MALEREI"

"DOCTRINE ESTHÉTIQUE" in 4 Volumes

"L'IMPORTANCE DE LA 4me DIMENSION DANS LA NOUVELLE PLASTIQUE ET LA NOUVELLE ARCHITECTURE"

POEMS PUBLISHED IN "DE STYL" REVIEW

"VOLLE MAAN". Anthologie Bonset, 4th Year, No. 11, 1921.

"SOLDATENVERZEN". Anthologie Bonset, 4th Year, No. 11, 1921.

"X BEELDEN". Anthologie Bonset, 4th Year, No. 11, 1921.

"KLANKBEELDEN". 4th Year, No. 7, 1921, & Anthologie Bonset, 4th Year, No. 11, 1921.

PROSE PUBLISHED IN "DE STIJL" REVIEW

"CAMINOSCOPIE" by Aldo Camini.
4th Year, No. 5-6-7-8-12, 1921.
5th Year, No. 6, 1922.
6th Year, No. 3-4, 1923.
6th Year, No. 6-7, 1924.
7th Year, No. 77, 1926, No. 78 (1926-27).
Jubileum Serie, 1927
8th Year, No. 85-86, 1928.

In addition to his articles in "De Stijl" review Théo van Doesburg contributed articles regularly to the following publications: "Bouwbedrijf", "Binnenhuis", "De Groene Amsterdammer", "Groot Nederland" (Holland), "Construction Moderne" (Paris), "Stavba" (Prague), "Transition", (Paris), "Arquitectura", (Madrid), "Neue Schweizer Rundschau" (Zurich), "Ray" (London), "Die Form", "Wasmuth's Monatshefte", "Das Neue Frankfurt" (Germany), etc., etc.

CONTRE COMPOSITION, XIV, 1925. Gemeente Museum, The Hague.

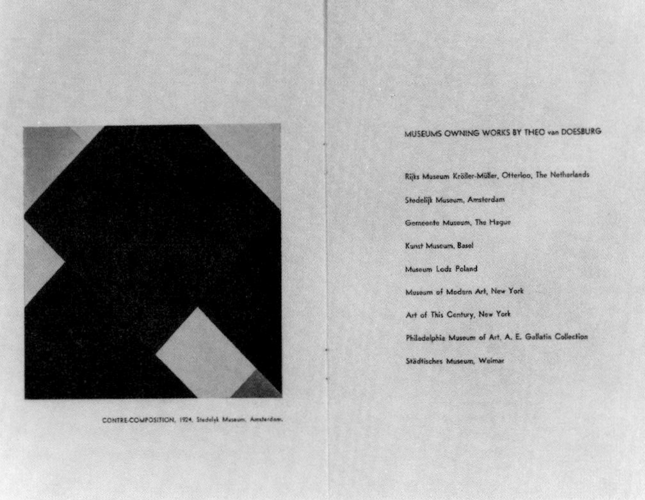
CONTRE-COMPOSITION, 1924. Stedelyk Museum, Amsterdam.

MUSEUMS OWNING WORKS BY THEO van DOESBURG

Rijks Museum Kröller-Müller, Otterloo, The Netherlands

Stedelijk Museum, Amsterdam

Gemeente Museum, The Hague

Kunst Museum, Basel

Museum Lodz Poland

Museum of Modern Art, New York

Art of This Century, New York

Philadelphia Museum of Art, A. E. Gallatin Collection

Städtisches Museum, Weimar

EXHIBITION ARRANGED BY Mme. THEO VAN DOESBURG.

Printed by HIGH GRADE PRESS
New York 22

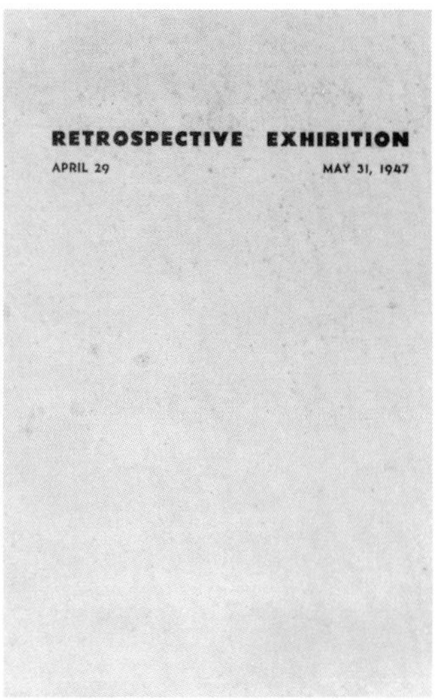
RETROSPECTIVE EXHIBITION
APRIL 29 MAY 31, 1947

Back cover.

Art of This Century closed at the conclusion of the van Doesburg retrospective. In his review (*The Nation*, 31 May, 1947), Clement Greenberg paid tribute to Peggy Guggenheim's achievement: "*[Van Doesburg's] gift for painting was such, in fact, that one regrets that he dispersed that gift in other fields and did not concentrate more exclusively on painting. His first cubist efforts, in 1917, already show a crispness and originality that make them much more than promising apprentice pieces. And no less than six of his seven post-1920 canvases at Art of This Century are actually and sufficiently successful—which, if this is a truly representative show, is a phenomenal rate of success, equaled, perhaps, in the twenties only by Mondrian of all the School of Paris....*

"*The Van Doesburg show, incidentally, is the last to be given at the Art of This Century gallery, which will not reopen next season, since Miss Guggenheim plans to transfer her permanent collection of contemporary art to Italy, where she will make her home. Her departure is in my opinion a serious loss to living American art. The erratic gaiety with which Miss Guggenheim promoted 'non-realistic' art may have misled some people, as perhaps her autobiography did too, but the fact remains that in the three or four years of her career as a New York gallery director she gave first showings to more serious new artists than anyone else in the country (Pollock, Hare, Baziotes, Motherwell, Rothko, Ray, De Niro, Admiral, McKee, and others). I am convinced that Peggy Guggenheim's place in the history of American art will grow larger as time passes and as the artists she encouraged mature.*"[6]

A full evaluation of Peggy Guggenheim's role as a gallery owner remains to be undertaken within another context. But even the slightest selection of reminiscences dating from the late 1970s and early 1980s reveals a strikingly consistent view of her achievement.[7]

Roland Penrose, April 9, 1980: "*Peggy's influence in London was considerable. Cork Street was where the important things were happening (Freddy Mayor's Gallery, The London Gallery, and Peggy's). Everyone came there, and Peggy brought an international flavor to it all. The sculpture show was very important, and she brought Tanguy's work over and Kandinsky, and others. She was a catalyst. Herbert Read had a profound influence on her—he was an extraordinary person. Nelly van Doesburg, Ernst, and Duchamp were surely important too. Duchamp was an eminence grise for her. But she made her own mark.*"

David Hare, June 3, 1977: "*There were only three places in New York during the early 1940s: Julien Levy, Pierre Matisse, and Peggy. She was the only one who showed contemporary Americans: of course she was important. She gave people a chance to show, to see, to be seen. She wasn't a dealer in the conventional sense: she never pushed artists to develop in certain directions thinking that certain things might sell. She left it up to the artist entirely. But she supported you, and it was vital.*"

Lee Krasner Pollock, March 6, 1981: "*Art of This Century was of the utmost importance as the first place where the New York School could be seen. That can never be minimized, and Peggy's achievement should not be underestimated; she did major things for the so-called Abstract-Expressionist group. Her gallery was the foundation, it's where it all started to happen. There was nowhere else in New York where one could expect an open-minded reaction. Peggy was invaluable in founding and creating what she did. That must be kept in the history.*"

James Johnson Sweeney, August 10, 1982: "*Art of This Century had a real impact in New York in those years. None of the other galleries had anything like the character of Peggy's place. It was quite different; everyone went there; it was a gathering place, and it gave young people an opportunity they might never have had. Peggy attracted a good number of people who helped her (Duchamp, Read, Nelly, Matta), but she also had her own views and she acted on them.*"

Robert Motherwell, August 27, 1982: "*I'll be eternally grateful to Peggy and her memory: she suggested that Pollock and Baziotes and I make collages for her collage show. I might never have done it otherwise, and it was here that I found (to use that awful word) my "identity".... The tiny gallery and the museum were one and the same: they were a single enterprise. My haunts, apart from museums, in those days were the Wittenborn book shop, Curt Valentin's, and Peggy's. Peggy's place was unique in several ways. It could be treated as a place to browse, and it was designed to be treated that way. The pictures had a narrow steel frame, just to protect the edges; many of them were hung on a universal joint and screwed to a stainless steel pole. You were invited to take the pictures in your hands — like a print or a book — and move them back and forth so that you could see a line or a surface more clearly in different kinds of light. It was a small place, intimate, and everything was meant to be used, and she felt strongly about that. The works in the permanent collection — especially the Surrealist collection — were masterpieces. If you were having a one-man show as a youngster, and you were having it here flanked by this collection, it was an amazing experience.*"

6. Reminded of these words in an interview with the author, February 26, 1980, Greenberg commented: "I stand by what I wrote. Her place in history has grown in the last thirty-odd years; no question about it."
7. The comments by Roland Penrose, David Hare, Lee Krasner Pollock, James Johnson Sweeney, and Robert Motherwell are taken from interviews with the author.

With the closing of Art of This Century, Peggy Guggenheim's career as a gallery owner came to an end; but her resolve to maintain a museum and to arrange occasional exhibitions continued to govern her activities. Having decided to move to Venice, she took up temporary residence in the Hotel Danieli and began the search for a suitable home. The collection initially remained in storage in New York. Within a few months, however, through the intervention of Giuseppe Santomaso, she was invited by Count Elio Zorzi and Rodolfo Pallucchini to present her holdings in the vacant Greek pavilion at the 1948 Biennale.

The Peggy Guggenheim pavilion attracted enormous interest, and after it closed in September, Carlo Ragghianti proposed that the collection be shown in Florence. Thus, it was exhibited at the Strozzina in Florence (February-March 1949), and from there it traveled to the Palazzo Reale in Milan (June 1949).

Peggy Guggenheim receiving President Luigi Einaudi of Italy at the entrance to her pavilion at the 1948 Biennale.

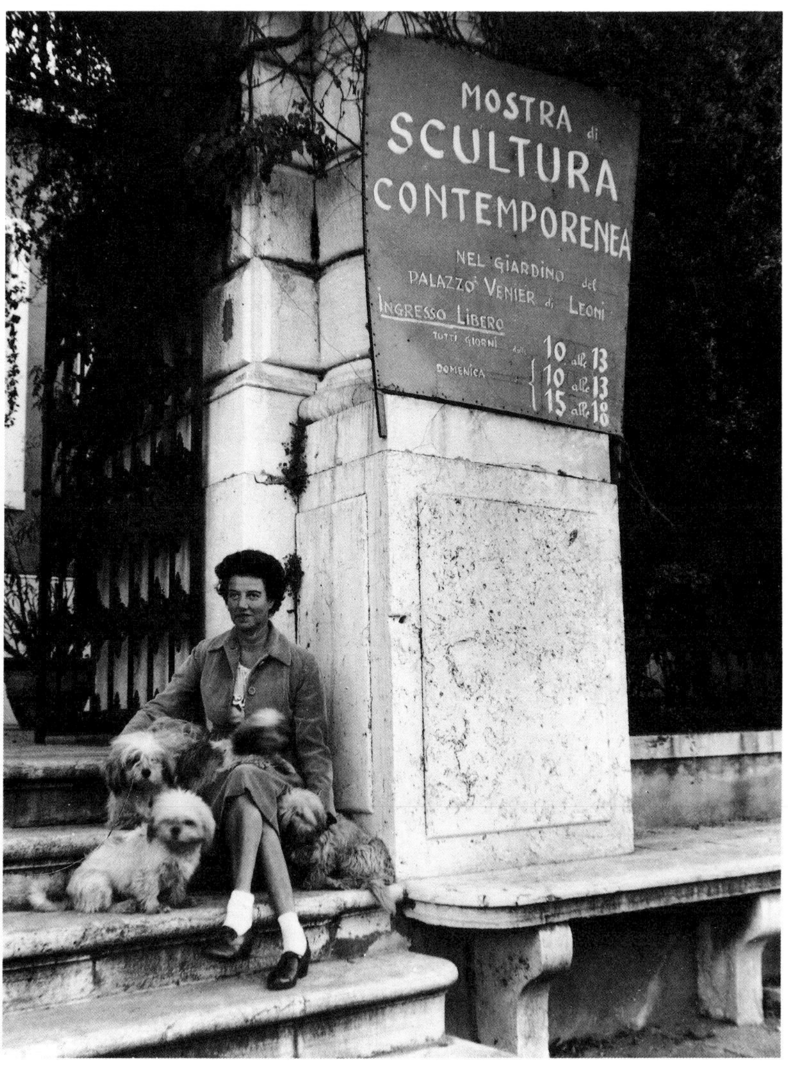

Peggy Guggenheim seated at the entrance to the Palazzo Venier dei Leoni during the *Mostra di scultura contemporanea*, September 1949.

In the spring of 1949 Peggy Guggenheim purchased the Palazzo Venier dei Leoni. Shortly after moving into it, she opened an exhibition of contemporary sculpture in the garden of her new home.

During the years 1949 and 1950, the collection was stored at the Ca' Pesaro in Venice, but plans were already underway for a new exhibition. In January-February 1951 Willem Sandberg invited Peggy Guggenheim to show the collection at the Stedelijk Museum in Amsterdam; it traveled from there to the Palais des Beaux-Arts in Brussels and the Kunsthaus in Zurich. Only after the close of this latter presentation late in the spring of 1951 was Peggy Guggenheim able to install the collection in her newly renovated palazzo on the Grand Canal. Very shortly afterward she opened her "museum" to the public three afternoons a week, a practice she maintained until her death.

PEGGY GUGGENHEIM COLLECTION[1]

Pierre Alechinsky
Peignoir (Dressing Gown). 1972.
Acrylic on wood-pulp paper mounted (with acrylic glue) on canvas, 38 3/16 x 60 7/16 in., 99.5 x 153.5 cm.
76.2553 PG 176a

Marina Apollonio
Rilievo, No. 505 (Relief no. 505). Ca. 1968.
Aluminum and fluorescent paint on masonite, 20 x 20 in., 49.9 x 49.8 cm.
76.2553 PG 230

Karel Appel
The Crying Crocodile Tries to Catch the Sun. 1956.
Oil on canvas, 57 1/4 x 44 1/2 in., 145.5 x 113.1 cm.
76.2553 PG 174

Alexander Archipenko
La Boxe (Boxing). 1935.
Terra cotta. Height: 30 1/8 in., 76.6 cm.
76.2553 PG 26

Arman
Variable et invariable. (Variable and Invariable). 1963.
Metal and wood, 25 1/2 x 33 1/2 in., 24.8 x 85.1 cm.
76.2553 PG 219

Kenneth Armitage
People in a Wind. 1951.
Bronze. Height: 25 5/8 in., 65.2 cm.
76.2553 PG 196

Diarchy. 1957.
Bronze. Height: 11 3/4 in., 29.8 cm.
76.2553 PG 197

Jean Arp (Hans Arp)
Grand collage (Large collage). 1955 reconstruction of an original made in Zurich, ca. 1918.
Papier collé, watercolor wash, metallic paint on pavatex (masonite) painted with gray oil. Dimensions of entire support: 38 3/8 x 30 5/8 in., 97.6 x 77.8 cm.; dims. of image: 31 1/2 x 23 9/16 in., 80 x 59.9 cm.
76.2553 PG 52

Soulier bleu renversé à deux talons, sous une voûte noire (Overturned Blue Shoe With Two Heels Under a Black Vault). Ca. 1925.
Wood, painted, 31 1/4 x 41 1/8 in., 79.3 x 104.6 cm. Depth of mount: 1 in., 2.5 cm.; depth of relief elements: 1 in., 2.5 cm.
76.2553 PG 53

Tête et coquille (Head and shell). Ca. 1933.
Polished brass cast in two pieces (lost wax). Height: 7 3/4 in., 19.7 cm; length: 8 7/8 in., 22.5 cm.
76.2553 PG 54

Couronne de bourgeons I (Crown of buds I). 1936.
Pink limestone (*pierre calcaire*). Height: 19 3/8 in., 49.1 cm.; width: 14 3/4 in., 37.5 cm.; height of base (not original): 6 1/16 in., 15.4 cm.
76.2553 PG 56

Mutilé et apatride (Maimed and stateless). 1936.
Newspaper, papier-mâché. Height (dimensions of piece placed on flat surface): 6 3/4 in., 17.1 cm.; width: 7 3/16 in., 18.3 cm.; depth: 9 13/16 in., 25 cm. Dimensions of wood box (not original): 16 1/16 x 14 x 6 5/16 in., 40.8 x 35.5 x 16.0 cm.
76.2553 PG 55

Untitled. 1940.
Pencil on thin wove paper (watermark: VIDALON), 10 1/2 x 8 3/16 in., 26.7 x 20.8 cm.
76.2553 PG 57

1. This complete list of the collection includes a majority of works which have not been fully studied by the author. The data (titles, media, dimensions, dates, etc.) for works that are not included in the main body of the catalogue are, thus, tentative and subject to further study.

Fruit-amphore (Amphora fruit). 1946? (cast 1951).
Bronze (sand cast). Height: 29⅜ in., 74.5 cm.; length (measured from tip to tip): 38 15/16 in., 99 cm.; length (measured horizontally at ground plane): 29¾ in., 75.6 cm.
76.2553 PG 58

Edmondo Bacci
Avvenimento #247 (Event #247). 1956.
Oil with sand on canvas, 55 3/16 x 55⅛ in., 140.2 x 140 cm.
76.2553 PG 164

Avvenimento #292 (Event No. 292). 1958.
Oil on canvas, 32⅞ x 54 5/16 in., 83.5 x 138 cm.
76.2553 PG 165

Francis Bacon
Study for Chimpanzee. March 1957.
Oil and pastel on canvas (unvarnished), 60 x 46 1/16 in., 152.4 x 117.
76.2553 PG 172

Enrico Baj
Perdu (Lost). 1967.
Oil and collage on fabric, 23¾ x 28⅞ in., 60.2 x 73.2 cm.
76.2553 PG 184a

Giacomo Balla
Velocità astratta + rumore (Abstract speed + sound). 1913-14.
Oil on millboard (unvarnished) with wood frame made and painted by the artist. Dimensions of board: 20 1/16 x 28⅝ in., 50.5 x 72.8 cm.; outer dims. of frame: 21½ x 30⅛ in., 54.5 x 76.5 cm.
76.2553 PG 31

William Baziotes
Untitled. 1943.
Gouache on black-wove construction paper, glued to wood-pulp cardboard, 9 1/16 x 12 in., 23 x 30.5 cm.
76.2553 PG 157

The Room. 1945.
Gouache on pressboard, 17 15/16 x 24 in., 45.6 x 61.0 cm.
76.2553 PG 156

Umberto Boccioni
Dinamismo di un cavallo in corsa + case (Dynamism of a speeding horse + houses). 1914-15.
Gouache and oil on wood, paper collage with gouache on wood, cardboard, copper sheet (*lastra di rame*); iron sheet coated with tin or zinc (*lastra di latta*). Height (including vertical iron support, which is not original): 44½ in., 112.9 cm.; height (including original projecting wood strut, but excluding iron support): 38 3/16 in., 97 cm.; width 45¼ in., 115 cm.
76.2553 PG 30

Martha Boto
Structure optique (Optical structure). 1963.
Plexiglas, 12½ x 12½ x 21¼ in., 31 x 31 x 53 cm.
76.2553 PG 224

Constantin Brancusi
Maiastra. 1912 (?).
Polished brass (lost wax). Height (top of head to top of base): 24¼ in., 61.6 cm.; maximum circumference: 24⅞ in., 63.2 cm.; height of legs: 8 5/16 in., 21.2 cm. Original height of stone saw-tooth base: ca. 6⅜ in., 16.2 cm.; present height of saw-tooth base (partially sunk into wooden pedestal): 4½ in., 11.5 cm.
76.2553 PG 50

L'Oiseau dans l'espace (Bird in Space). 1932-40.
Polished brass (lost wax). Height (plumbline measurement from tip to top of cement base): 53 in., 134.7 cm.; maximum circumference: 13 15/16 in., 35.4 cm.; minimum circumference: 3 1/16 in., 7.8 cm.; height of footing: 9 in., 22.9 cm.; height of cylindrical stone base: 6 11/16 in., 17 cm.
76.2553 PG 51

Georges Braque
La clarinette (The clarinet). Summer-fall 1912.
Oil with sand on fine linen canvas (unvarnished), 36 x 25⅜ in., 91.4 x 64.5 cm.
76.2553 PG 7

Le compotier de raisin (The bowl of grapes). 1926.
Oil with pebbles and sand on fine linen canvas (unvarnished), 39⅜ x 31¼ in., 100 x 80.8 cm.
76.2553 PG 8

Victor Brauner
Untitled. 1941.
Three gouaches mounted on a single sheet. Dimensions of mount, 14 x 13 in., 35.5 x 33 cm.; dimensions of each work: (left): 4¾ x 4¼ in., 12 x 10.4 cm.; (upper right): 5 9/16 x 4⅜ in., 14.2 x 10.7 cm.; (lower right): 5 x 3 3/16 in., 12.8 x 8.2 cm.
76.2553 PG 114.1-.3

Untitled. 1945.
Encaustic on board, $9\frac{3}{16}$ x $5\frac{13}{16}$ in., 23.3 x 14.8 cm. (sight).
76.2553 PG 115

Le Surréaliste (The Surrealist). January 1947.
Oil on canvas, $23\frac{5}{8}$ x $17\frac{3}{4}$ in., 60 x 45 cm.
76.2553 PG 111

Téléventré. 1948.
Wax encaustic on millboard, $28\frac{1}{2}$ x $23\frac{5}{8}$ in., 72.5 x 60.0 cm.
76.2553 PG 112

Consciousness of Shock. April 1951.
Wax encaustic on hardboard, $25\frac{1}{4}$ x $31\frac{1}{2}$ in., 64 x 80 cm.
76.2553 PG 113

Untitled. 1954.
Encaustic on board, $13\frac{9}{16}$ x $9\frac{15}{16}$ in., 34.5 x 25.2 cm.
76.2553 PG 116

René Brô
L'Automne à Courgeron (Autumn at Courgeron). 1960.
Oil on canvas, $73\frac{5}{8}$ x $57\frac{11}{16}$ in., 187 x 146.5 cm.
76.2553 PG 188

Reg Butler
Woman Walking. 1951.
Bronze. Height: 19 in., 48.3 cm.
76.2553 PG 195

Alexander Calder
Mobile. Ca. 1934.
Glass and china fragments, each of which is tied with wire; six iron wire suspension elements painted red; knotted red nylon thread (not original). Height: ca. $65\frac{3}{4}$ in., 167 cm.; width: ca. $46\frac{1}{16}$ in., 117 cm.
76.2553 PG 139

Mobile. 1941.
Sheet aluminum, iron suspension wire, copper rivets, thirteen upper aluminum leaves painted black, one unpainted; thirteen lower leaves unpainted. Height: ca. $84\frac{1}{4}$ in., 214 cm.
76.2553 PG 137

Silver Bed Head. Winter 1945-46.
Silver. Height: 63 in., 160 cm.; width: $51\frac{9}{16}$ in., 131 cm.
76.2553 PG 138

Le grand passage. 1974.
Gouache on paper, $23\frac{7}{8}$ x $30\frac{3}{4}$ in., 58 x 78 cm.
76.2553 PG 139a

Massimo Campigli
Il Gioco a Palla (The Ball Game). 1946.
Tempera with gesso on canvas, $26\frac{1}{4}$ x $23\frac{7}{16}$ in., 66.5 x 59.5 cm.
76.2553 PG 160

Leonora Carrington
Oink (They shall behold thine eyes). 1959.
Oil on canvas, $15\frac{3}{4}$ x $35\frac{13}{16}$ in., 40 x 90.9 cm.
76.2553 PG 117

César (Baldaccini)
L'homme dans la toile d'araignée (Man in spider's web). 1955.
Bronze. Height: $13\frac{9}{16}$ in., 34.4 cm.
76.2553 PG 206

Compression. 1969.
Aluminum. Height: $13\frac{15}{16}$ in., 35.4 cm.; varying width of narrow edges: $4\frac{7}{8}$-$5\frac{1}{2}$ in., 12.5-14 cm.; width of front and back: $14\frac{3}{16}$ in., 36 cm.
76.2553 PG 207

Lynn Chadwick
Maquette for *Teddyboy and Girl.* 1955.
Iron and stolit. Height: $15\frac{3}{16}$ in., 38.6 cm.
76.2553 PG 198

Marc Chagall
La pluie (Rain). 1911.
Oil (and possibly some charcoal) on canvas (unvarnished), $34\frac{1}{8}$ x $42\frac{1}{2}$ in., 86.7 x 108 cm.
76.2553 PG 63

Giorgio de Chirico
La tour rouge (The red tower). 1913.
Oil on canvas, $28\frac{15}{16}$ x $39\frac{5}{8}$ in., 73.5 x 100.5 cm.
76.2553 PG 64

La nostalgie du poète (The nostalgia of the poet). 1914.
Oil and charcoal on canvas, $35\frac{5}{16}$ x 16 in., 89.7 x 40.7 cm.
76.2553 PG 65

Le doux après-midi (The gentle afternoon). Before July 1916.
Oil on canvas, $25\frac{11}{16}$ x $22\frac{15}{16}$ in., 65.3 x 58.3 cm.
76.2553 PG 66

William Congdon
Piazza San Marco #15. 1957.
Oil on board, $47\frac{7}{16}$ x $55\frac{1}{16}$ in., 120.5 x 139.8 cm.
76.2553 PG 180

Venice #1. 1957.
Oil on board, $19\frac{1}{2}$ x $31\frac{7}{16}$ in., 49.5 x 79.7 cm.
76.2553 PG 179

Cambodia. 1960.
Oil on board, 15 13/16 x 23 15/16 in., 40.2 x 60.7 cm.
76.2553 PG 181

Pietro Consagra
Colloquio Mitico (Mythical Conversation). 1959.
Bronze (sandcast and soldered), 33 11/16 x 28 in., 85.5 x 71 cm.
76.2553 PG 204a

Guillaume Corneille
La grande symphonie solaire (The great solar symphony). 1964.
Oil on canvas, 51 1/16 x 63 13/16 in., 129.6 x 162 cm.
76.2553 PG 176

Joseph Cornell
Fortune Telling Parrot. Ca. 1937-38.
Box construction. Height: 16 1/16 in., 40.8 cm.; width: 8 1/4 in., 22.2 cm.; depth: 6 11/16 in., 17 cm.
76.2553 PG 126

Swiss Shoot-the-Chutes. 1941.
Box construction. Height: 21 3/16 in., 53.8 cm.; width: 13 13/16 in., 35.2 cm.; depth: 4 1/8 in., 10.5 cm.
76.2553 PG 127

Setting for a Fairy Tale. 1942.
Box construction. Height: 11 9/16 in., 29.4 cm.; width: 14 3/8 in., 36.6 cm.; depth: 3 7/8 in., 9.9 cm.
76.2553 PG 125

Untitled (Pharmacy). Ca. 1942.
Box construction. Height: 14 in., 35.5 cm.; width: 12 1/16 in., 30.6 cm.; depth: 4 3/8 in., 11.1 cm.
76.2553 PG 128

Soap Bubble Set. 1942.
Box construction. Height: 15 3/4 in., 40 cm.; width: 18 3/8 in., 46.7 cm.; depth: 2 5/8 in., 6.7 cm.
76.2553 PG 129

Toni Costa
Dinamica Visuale (Visual Dynamics). 1964.
Paper and plastic on wood frame, 19 1/8 x 19 1/8 in., 48.6 x 48.6 cm.
76.2553 PG 226

Franco Costalonga
Sfero (Sphere). 1969.
Plexiglas and chrome. Circumference: 49 13/16 in., 126.5 cm.
76.2553 PG 231

Egidio Costantini (Fucina degli Angeli).
23 poured glass figures based upon sketches by Picasso; each dated 1964 and marked *Picasso* and *FA*. Figures vary in height from 3 5/16-12 in., 10 cm.-30.5 cm.
76.2553 PG 294.1-.23

Salvador Dalí
Untitled. 1931.
Oil on canvas, 10 11/16 x 13 3/4 in., 27.2 x 35 cm.
76.2553 PG 99

La Naissance des désirs liquides (Birth of liquid desires). 1931-32.
Oil and collage on canvas (unvarnished), 37 7/8 x 44 1/4 in., 96.1 x 112.3 cm.
76.2553 PG 100

Alan Davie
Peggy's Guessing Box. 1950.
Collage and oil on masonite, 47 15/16 x 59 15/16 in., 121.7 x 152.2 cm.
76.2553 PG 169

Orange Jumper. 1960.
Oil on paper, 14 x 36 in., 35 x 91 cm.
76.2553 PG 170

The Golden Drummer Boy No. 2. 1962.
Oil on canvas, 68 x 84 in., 172.2 x 213.3 cm.
76.2553 PG 171

Robert Delaunay
Fenêtres ouvertes simultanément lère partie 3e motif (Windows open simultaneously 1st part, 3rd motif). 1912.
Oil on canvas, oval, 22 3/8 x 48 3/8 in., 57 x 123 cm.
76.2553 PG 36

Paul Delvaux
L'Aurore (The break of day). July 1937.
Oil on canvas (unvarnished), 47 1/4 x 59 1/4 in., 120 x 150.5 cm.
76.2553 PG 103

Theo van Doesburg
Composition in gray (Rag-time). 1919.
Oil on canvas (unvarnished), 38 x 23 1/4 in., 96.5 x 59.1 cm.
76.2553 PG 40

Contra-Compositie XIII (Counter-Composition XIII). 1925-26.
Oil on canvas (unvarnished), 19 5/8 x 19 5/8 in., 49.9 x 50.0 cm.
76.2553 PG 41

Piero Dorazio
Unitas. 1965.
Oil on canvas, 18 $^{1}/_{16}$ x 30 $^{1}/_{4}$ in., 45.8 x 76.5 cm.
76.2553 PG 168

Jean Dubuffet
Chataine aux Hautes Chairs (Fleshy face with Chestnut Hair). August 1951.
Oil-based mixed media on board (Isorel), 25 $^{9}/_{16}$ x 21 $^{1}/_{4}$ in., 64.9 x 54 cm.
76.2553 PG 121

Henri-Robert-Marcel Duchamp
Nu (esquisse), Jeune homme triste dans un train (Nude [study], Sad young man on a train). 1911-12.
Oil on textured cardboard ($^{1}/_{4}$ in., 0.7 cm., thick), nailed to masonite. Brown paper tape surrounding all edges covers join between cardboard and masonite and serves as $^{3}/_{8}$ in., 2 cm., surround to painting itself. (This is now covered by the frame.) Dimensions of cardboard support: 39 $^{3}/_{8}$ x 28 $^{3}/_{4}$ in., 100 x 73 cm.; visible painted surface within taped edges: 38 $^{9}/_{16}$ x 27 $^{15}/_{16}$ in., 98 x 71 cm.
76.2553 PG 9

Boîte-en-valise (Box in a valise). 1941.
Leather valise containing miniature replicas and color reproductions of works by Duchamp, 16 x 14 $^{5}/_{8}$ x 3 $^{15}/_{16}$ in., 40.7 x 37.2 x 10.1 cm. Inscribed in black ink on inside bottom of box: *Pour Peggy Guggenheim ce No I/de vingt boites-en-valise contenant/chacune 69 items et un original/et par Marcel Duchamp/ Paris janvier 1941*. Stamped on inside edge: PEGGY GUGGENHEIM I/XX. Includes one original: inside lid, under velvet frame, photographic reproduction of *Le roi et la reine entourés de nus vites,* with additions in graphite and watercolor, inscribed in black ink along lower edge: *coloriage original/ Marcel Duchamp/1937*.
76.2553 PG 10

Raymond Duchamp-Villon
Le Cheval (The Horse). 1914 (cast ca. 1930).
Bronze (sand cast) with black-green patina with large areas of pale green. Height: 17 $^{3}/_{16}$ in., 43.6 cm.; depth: 16 $^{1}/_{8}$ in., 41 cm.
76.2553 PG 24

Dušan Džamonja
Totem. 1959.
Wood, nails, glass. Height: 38 $^{5}/_{16}$ in., 97.3 cm.
76.2553 PG 217

Max Ernst
Von minimax dadamax selbst konstruiertes maschinchen (Little machine constructed by minimax dadamax in person). 1919-20.
Handprinting(?), pencil and ink frottage, watercolor and gouache on heavy brown pulp paper, 19 $^{1}/_{2}$ x 12 $^{3}/_{8}$ in., 49.4 x 31.5 cm.
76.2553 PG 70

Le Baiser (The Kiss). 1927.
Oil on canvas (unvarnished), 50 $^{3}/_{4}$ x 63 $^{1}/_{2}$ in., 129 x 161.2 cm.
76.2553 PG 71

La Forêt (The Forest). 1927-28.
Oil on canvas (unvarnished), 37 $^{7}/_{8}$ x 51 in., 96.3 x 129.5 cm.
76.2553 PG 72

La mer le soleil le tremblement de terre (Sea, sun, earthquake). 1931.
Oil, gouache, and collage on canvas (unvarnished), 17 $^{7}/_{8}$ x 14 $^{7}/_{8}$ in., 45.4 x 37.8 cm.
76.2553 PG 73

Le Facteur Cheval (The Postman Cheval). 1932.
Paper and fabric collage with pencil, ink, and gouache on manila paper, 25 $^{3}/_{8}$ x 19 $^{1}/_{4}$ in., 64.3 x 48.9 cm.
76.2553 PG 74

Couple zoomorphe (Zoomorphic couple). 1933.
Oil on canvas (unvarnished), 36 $^{1}/_{4}$ x 28 $^{7}/_{8}$ in., 91.9 x 73.3 cm.
76.2553 PG 75

Jardin gobe-avions (Garden Airplane-Trap). 1935-36.
Oil on canvas (unvarnished), 21 $^{1}/_{4}$ x 25 $^{1}/_{2}$ in., 54 x 64.7 cm.
76.2553 PG 76

La ville entière (The entire city). 1936-37.
Oil on canvas, 38 x 63 $^{1}/_{8}$ in., 96.5 x 160.4 cm.
76.2553 PG 77

La toilette de la mariée (Attirement of the bride). 1940.
Oil on canvas, 51 x 37 $^{7}/_{8}$ in., 129.6 x 96.3 cm.
76.2553 PG 78

'The Antipope.' Ca. 1941.
Oil on thin cardboard mounted on cardboard, 12 $^{3}/_{4}$ x 10 $^{3}/_{8}$ in., 32.5 x 26.5 cm.
76.2553 PG 79

The Antipope. December 1941-March 1942.
Oil on canvas, 63 $^{1}/_{4}$ x 50 in., 160.8 x 127.1 cm.
76.2553 PG 80

Jeune femme en forme de fleur (Young woman in the form of a flower). 1944 (cast 1957).
Bronze (lost wax). Cast in three parts and soldered. Height at back: 12 $^{13}/_{16}$ in., 32.6 cm.;

at front: 13 3/4 in., 35 cm.; width: 14 in., 35.6 cm.; depth: 8 7/16 in., 21.5 cm.
76.2553 PG 81

Dans les rues d'Athènes (In the streets of Athens). 1960 (cast January 1961).
Bronze (sand cast) with dark black-green patina. Height (including base): 38 3/4 in., 98.4 cm.; width (widest point): 19 9/16 in., 49.7 cm.; depth of base: 7 3/16 in., 18.3 cm.
76.2553 PG 82

Claire Falkenstein
Entrance Gates to the Palazzo. 1961.
Iron and colored glass, two parts, 109 1/16 x 35 7/16 in., 109 1/16 x 36 in.; 277 x 90 cm., 277 x 91.2 cm.
76.2553 PG 203

John Ferren
Tempora. 1937.
Plaster print, carved and tinted with ink and tempera. Dimensions of plaster: 15 x 12 5/8 in., 38.1 x 32.1 cm.; dims. of image: 11 13/16 x 9 7/16 in., 30 x 24 cm.; outer dims. of artist's frame: 18 9/16 x 16 3/16 in., 47.1 x 41.1 cm.
76.2553 PG 49

Leonor Fini
The Shepherdess of the Sphinxes. 1941.
Oil on canvas, 18 3/16 x 15 1/16 in., 46.2 x 38.2 cm.
76.2553 PG 118

Sam Francis
Untitled. March 1964.
Acrylic on wove paper mounted on masonite, 40 7/8 x 27 3/8 in., 103.7 x 69.5 cm.
76.2553 PG 185

Alberto Giacometti
Projet pour une place (Model for a square). 1931-32.
Wood. Height without base: 6 3/4 in., 17.1 cm.; height of base: 7/8 in., 2.3 cm.; dims. of base: 12 3/8 x 8 7/8 in., 31.4 x 22.5 cm.
76.2553 PG 130

Femme qui marche (Woman walking). 1932.
Plaster, iron wire armature. Height without base: 54 3/4 in., 139 cm.; height of base along left (viewer's) side: 3 3/4 in., 9.5 cm.; height along right side: 4 5/16 in., 11.0 cm.; depth of base: 14 9/16 in., 37 cm.; width of base: 9 7/16 in., 24 cm.; width across shoulders: 10 11/16 in., 27.2 cm.
76.2553 PG 132

Femme qui marche (Woman walking). 1932 (cast 1961 or 1969).
Bronze. Height: 56 15/16 in., 144.6 cm.
76.2553 PG 133

Femme égorgée (Woman with her throat cut). 1932 (cast 1940).
Bronze solid cast (sand cast) with dark brown-black patina. Width (at greatest diagonal extent): 35 1/16 in., 89 cm.; height: 9 1/8 in., 23.2 cm.
76.2553 PG 131

Femme debout ("Leoni") (Standing woman ["Leoni"]). 1947 (Cast November 1957).
Bronze (sand cast). Height (top of head to ankle): 54 5/16 in., 138 cm.; averge height (at back) of sloping base: 5 15/16 in., 15 cm.; at front 2 5/8 in., 6.7 cm.; depth of base: 13 5/8 in., 34.6 cm.; width of base at front: 5 1/4 in., 13.3 cm.; width of base at back: 5 15/16 in., 13.9 cm.
76.2553 PG 134

Piazza. 1947-48 (cast 1948-49).
Bronze (sand cast), with original dark brown-black patina on base. Wood fills the entire interior of the base, which has an edge of 3/16 in., .4 cm. Height of base: 1 3/4 in., 4.5 cm.; length of base: 24 5/8 in., 62.5 cm.; width of base: 16 7/8 in., 42.8 cm. Height of figures: Figure 1: 5 3/4 in., 14.6 cm.; Figure 2: 5 11/16 in., 15 cm.; Figure 3: 5 5/16 in., 13.6 cm.; Figure 4: 6 1/2 in., 16.5 cm.; Figure 5: 6 1/8 in., 15.5 cm.
76.2553 PG 135

Rosalda Gilardi
Presenze (Presence). Ca. 1967.
Serpentine stone. Height: 77 5/8 in., 197.2 cm.
76.2553 PG 205a

Albert Gleizes
La dame aux bêtes (Madame Raymond Duchamp-Villon) (Woman with animals [Madame Raymond Duchamp-Villon]). 1914.
Oil on canvas, 77 5/16 x 45 15/16 in., 196.4 x 114.1 cm.
76.2553 PG 17

Julio González
"Monsieur" Cactus. 1939 (cast 1953-54).
Bronze with black patina and some greenish areas (lost wax). Height (without wood base, which is not part of the work): 25 5/16 in., 64.3 cm.; width: 9 13/16 in., 25 cm.; depth: 6 11/16 in., 17 cm.
76.2553 PG 136

Arshile Gorky
Untitled. Summer 1944.
Oil on canvas (unvarnished), 65 3/4 x 70 3/16 in., 167 x 178.2 cm.
76.2553 PG 152

Juan Gris
Bouteille de rhum et journal (Bottle of rum and newspaper). June 1914.
Faux-bois paper, patterned wallpaper, white-wove paper, brown paper, printed tobacco and matchbox covers, gouache, conté crayon, pencil, and varnish on newspaper glued to canvas, 21⅝ x 18¼ in., 54.8 x 46.2 cm.
76.2553 PG 11

Alberto Guzmán
Partizione Percuotente (Hammered Partition). 1965.
Bronze. Height: 12⅜ in., 31.5 cm.
76.2553 PG 220

David Hare
Moon Cage. 1955.
Welded steel, brass spray. Height: 30⅛ in., 76.5 cm.
76.2553 PG 201

Grace Hartigan
Ireland. 1958.
Oil on canvas (unvarnished), 78¾ x 106¾ in., 200 x 271 cm.
76.2553 PG 182

Raoul Hausmann
Untitled. 1919.
Watercolor and gouache on paper, 15¼ x 10 13/16 in., 38.8 x 27.5 cm. (sight).
76.2553 PG 88

Stanley William Hayter
Defeat. 1938-39.
Carved plaster cast from intaglio plate, 9½ x 15 in., 24 x 38 cm.
76.2553 PG 105

Jean Hélion
Equilibre (Equilibrium). 1933-34.
Oil on canvas (unvarnished), 38⅜ x 51⅝ in., 97.4 x 131.2 cm.
76.2553 PG 44

Composition. August-December 1935.
Oil on canvas (unvarnished), 57⅛ x 78 13/16 in., 145 x 200.2 cm.
76.2553 PG 45

Morris Hirshfield
Two Women in Front of a Mirror. 1943.
Oil on canvas, 52⅜ x 59⅞ in., 133 x 152 cm.
76.2553 PG 122

Hundertwasser
Casa Che Protegge—Die Schutzhütte (Shelter). May 1960.
Watercolor on wood-pulp, wove wrapping paper, with chalk and polyvinyl ground, 25 3/16 x 19⅜ in., 64 x 49.2 cm.
76.2553 PG 186

Gwyther Irwin
Serendipity 2. 1957.
Collage on canvas, 47 x 33 15/16 in., 119.4 x 86.2 cm. (sight).
76.2553 PG 173

Asger Jorn
Untitled. 1956-57.
Oil on canvas (unvarnished), 55½ x 43⅜ in., 141 x 110.1 cm.
76.2553 PG 175

Vasily Kandinsky
Landschaft mit roten Flecken, No. 2 (Landscape with red spots No. 2). 1913.
Oil on canvas (unvarnished), 46¼ x 55⅛ in., 117.5 x 140 cm.
76.2553 PG 33

Weisses Kreuz (White Cross). January-June 1922.
Oil on canvas (unvarnished), 39 9/16 x 43 9/16 in., 100.5 x 110.6 cm.
76.2553 PG 34

Empor (Upward). October 1929.
Oil on cardboard (unvarnished), 27½ x 19¼ in., 70 x 49 cm.
76.2553 PG 35

Zoltan Kemeny
Mouvement partagé (Divided movement). 1957.
Prefabricated copper elements with copper and iron filings soldered to copper sheet nailed to wood. Copper sheet: 30¾ x 19⅞ in., 78.5 x 50.7 cm.; wood mount: 31⅛ x 20⅛ x 1 in., 79 x 51 x 2.5 cm.
76.2553 PG 208

Paul Klee
Bildnis der Frau P. im Süden (Portrait of Frau P. in the South). 1924.
Watercolor and oil transfer drawing on heavy wove (Whatman) paper mounted by artist on pulpboard, painted with gray gouache borders. Primary support: 14¾ x 10¾ in., 37.6 x 27.4 cm.; secondary support: 16¾ x 12¼ in., 42.5 x 31 cm.
76.2553 PG 89

Zaubergarten (Magic Garden). March 1926.
Oil on gypsum plaster-filled wire mesh mounted in wood frame. Plaster: 20½ x 16⅝ in., 50.2 x 42.1 cm.; exterior of artist's wood frame: 20⅞ x 17¾ in., 52.9 x 44.9 cm.
76.2553 PG 90

Rosemarie Heber Koczÿ
Arbres (Trees). 1972.
Hemp, sisal, linen, jute, raw silk, algae, wool, ca. 37 x 22 7/16 in., 94 x 57 cm.
76.2553 PG 188a

Fritz Koenig
Biga (Chariot). 1957.
Bronze. Height (including base): 20 1/16 in., 51 cm.
76.2553 PG 215

Willem de Kooning
Untitled. 1958.
Pastel and charcoal (fixed) on heavy wove paper, 22 7/16 x 30 1/2 in., 57 x 77.5 cm.
76.2553 PG 159

Untitled. 1958.
Oil on wove paper (Favor-Bristol blind stamp), mounted on masonite mounted on plywood, 23 x 29 1/8 in., 58.5 x 74.0 cm.
76.2553 PG 158

František Kupka
Untitled. ca. 1910?
Pastel on wove paper, 9 1/4 x 8 3/16 in., 23.5 x 20.8 cm.
76.2553 PG 12

Study for *Amorpha, Chromatique chaude* and for *Fugue à deux couleurs* (Study for *Amorpha, Warm Chromatic* and for *Fugue in two colors).* Ca. 1910-11.
Pastel on machine-made laid-line paper, 18 15/16 x 19 in., 46.8 x 48.3 cm.
76.2553 PG 13

Study for *Femme cueillant des fleurs* (Study for *Woman picking flowers*). Ca. 1910?
Pastel on paper, 18 7/16 x 19 1/16 in., 46.8 x 48.3 cm.
76.2553 PG 13a (reverse of 76.2553 PG 13)

Study for *Localisations de mobiles graphiques I* (Study for *Organization of graphic motifs I*). Ca. 1911-12.
Pastel on wove paper (watermark: CANSON), 12 15/16 x 12 7/16 in., 32.9 x 31.6 cm.
76.2553 PG 15

Autour d'un point (Around a point). Ca. 1920-25.
Watercolor, gouache, and graphite on wood-pulp wove paper, 7 15/16 x 9 3/8 in., 20.1 x 23.8 cm.
76.2553 PG 16

Plans verticaux (Vertical planes).
Gouache and watercolor on paper, 22 3/16 x 16 in., 56.3 x 40.6 cm.
76.2553 PG 14

Berto Lardera
Rincontro Dramatico (Dramatic Meeting). 1968.
Iron and copper. Height (including base): 18 13/16 in., 47.8 cm.
76.2553 PG 204

Ibram Lassaw
Corax. December 1953.
Chromium bronze with additional metals. Height: 19 1/2 in., 49.5 cm.; width: 23 in., 58.8 cm.; depth: 10 in., 25.5 cm.
76.2553 PG 202

Henri Laurens
Tête de jeune fillette (Head of a young girl). 1920 (cast 1959).
Terra-cotta cast. Height: 13 1/2 in., 34.2 cm.; width: 6 1/2 in., 16.5 cm.
76.2553 PG 27

Fernand Léger
Study of a nude. Winter 1912-13.
Oil on wood-pulp paper, 25 x 19 1/16 in., 63.6 x 48.5 cm.
76.2553 PG 19

Les hommes dans la ville (Men in the city). 1919.
Oil on canvas (unvarnished), 57 3/8 x 44 11/16 in., 145.7 x 113.5 cm.
76.2553 PG 21

Leonid
Venetian Lagoon.
Oil on canvas, 32 5/16 x 50 1/16 in., 82 x 127.1 cm.
76.2553 PG 221

Jacques Lipchitz
Pierrot assis (Seated Pierrot). 1922.
Lead. Height (including base): 13 5/16 in., 33.5 cm.
76.2553 PG 28

Aurelia. 1946.
Bronze (lost wax, solid cast). Height (without base): 25 3/8 in., 64.5 cm.
76.2553 PG 29

El Lissitzky
Untitled. Ca. 1919-20.
Oil on canvas (unvarnished), 31 5/16 x 19 1/2 in., 79.6 x 49.6 cm.
76.2553 PG 43

Ludovico De Luigi
Parnassus, Apollo and Papileo Macaon. 1970.
Oil on canvas, 39 9/16 x 59 3/16 in., 100.4 x 150.3 cm.
76.2553 PG 181a

Heinz Mack
Cardiogram eines Engels (Cardiogram of an Angel). 1964.
Aluminum foil sheets nailed to masonite on wood; edges secured with plastic strips; 68 1/8 x 39 9/16 in., 173 x 100.5 cm.
76.2553 PG 228

René François Ghislain Magritte
La voix des airs (Voice of space). 1931.
Oil on canvas (unvarnished), 28 5/8 x 21 3/8 in., 72.7 x 54.2 cm.
76.2553 PG 101

L'Empire des lumières (Empire of light). 1953-54.
Oil on canvas (unvarnished), 76 15/16 x 51 5/8 in., 195.4 x 131.2 cm.
76.2553 PG 102

Kazimir Severinovich Malevich
Untitled. Ca. 1916.
Oil on canvas, 20 7/8 x 20 7/8 in., 53 x 53 cm.
76.2553 PG 42

Man Ray
Silhouette. 1916.
India ink, charcoal underdrawing, and white gouache (?) on wood-pulp board (with machine-mold textured imprint), 20 15/16 x 25 1/4 in., 51.6 x 64.1 cm.
76.2553 PG 68

Untitled. 1923.
Rayograph, gelatin silver print, 11 3/8 x 9 1/4 in., 28.8 x 23.5 cm.
76.2553 PG 69a

Untitled. 1927.
Rayograph, gelatin silver print, 11 15/16 x 10 in., 30.4 x 25.4 cm.
76.2553 PG 69b

Louis Marcoussis
L'Habitué (The Regular). 1920.
Oil with sand and pebbles on canvas, 63 3/4 x 38 3/16 in., 161.9 x 97 cm.
76.2553 PG 22

Marino Marini
L'angelo della città (The angel of the city). 1948 (cast 1950?).
Bronze (cast in three pieces, lost wax). Height (to top of base): 65 15/16 in., 167.5 cm.; dimensions of base: 31 5/8 x 20 9/16 x 1 3/4 in., 80.4 x 52.3 x 4.5 cm.; arm span of figure: 41 3/4 in., 106 cm.
76.2553 PG 183

Manfredo Massironi
Ipercubo Plexiglas. 1963.
Plexiglas, 16 1/8 x 14 3/4 x 14 3/4 in., 40.9 x 37.5 x 37.5 cm.
76.2553 PG 227

André Masson
L'Armure (The Armor). January-April 1925.
Oil on canvas (unvarnished), 31 3/4 x 21 1/4 in., 80.6 x 54 cm.
76.2553 PG 106

Two Children. 1942.
Bronze (lost-wax solid cast), with original brown patina. Height: 6 in., 15.3 cm.; length: 4 1/4 in., 10.7 cm.
76.2553 PG 107

Oiseau fasciné par un serpent (Bird fascinated by a snake). 1942.
Tempera on watercolor paper, 22 1/4 x 29 3/4 in., 56.5 x 75.5 cm.
76.2553 PG 108

Matta
The Dryads. 1941.
Pencil and colored crayon on paper, 22 15/16 x 28 15/16 in., 58.2 x 73.4 cm.
76.2553 PG 109

Le Dénommeur renommé (The Un-nominator renominated). 1952-53.
Oil on canvas, 47 3/8 x 68 7/8 in., 120.4 x 175 cm.
76.2553 PG 110

Jean Metzinger
Au Vélodrome (At the cycle-race track). Ca. 1914(?).
Oil and collage on canvas (unvarnished), 51 3/8 x 38 1/4 in., 130.4 x 97.1 cm.
76.2553 PG 18

Luciano Minguzzi
He-Goat. 1956.
Bronze. Height: 6 5/8 in., 16.8 cm.; length: 13 3/8 in., 34 cm.
76.2553 PG 212

Mirko (Basaldella)
Elemento architettonico—Linee forza nello spazio (Architectural element—Lines of force in space). 1953.
Copper, 78 1/2 x 38 3/8 in., 199.3 x 97.5 cm.
76.2553 PG 210

Piccolo chimera (Little chimera). 1956.
Bronze. Height: 6 1/8 in., 15.5 cm.
76.2553 PG 211

Joan Miró
Peinture (Painting). 1925.
Oil on canvas (unvarnished), 45 1/8 x 57 3/8 in., 114.5 x 145.7 cm.
76.2553 PG 91

Intérieur hollandais (Dutch Interior II). Summer 1928.
Oil on canvas (unvarnished), 36 1/4 x 28 3/4 in., 92.0 x 73.0 cm.
76.2553 PG 92

Femme assise II (Seated Woman II). February 27, 1939.
Oil on canvas (unvarnished), 63 3/4 x 51 3/16 in., 162 x 130 cm.
76.2553 PG 93

Piet Mondrian
Untitled (Oval Composition). 1914.
Charcoal on wood-pulp wove paper, glued to Homosote panel. Dimensions of paper: 60 x 39 3/8 in., 152.5 x 100 cm.; dims. of panel: 60 x 40 1/2 x 1/2 in., 152.5 x 102.8 x 1.3 cm.
76.2553 PG 37

The Sea. 1914.
Charcoal and gouache on wood-pulp wove paper glued to Homosote panel. Dimensions of paper: 34 1/2 x 47 3/8 in., 87.6 x 120.3 cm.; dims. of panel: 35 1/2 x 48 3/8 x 1/2 in., 90.2 x 123 x 1.3 cm.
76.2553 PG 38

Composition. 1938-39.
Oil on canvas mounted on painted wood support. Dimensions of canvas: 41 7/16 x 40 5/16 in., 105.2 x 102.3 cm.; outer dims. of wood support: 43 x 41 3/4 in., 109.1 x 106 cm., depth of wood support: 1 in., 2.5 cm.
76.2553 PG 39

Henry Moore
Ideas for Sculpture. 1937.
Black and white chalk, brown crayon on wood-pulp wove paper, laid down on cardboard, 15 x 22 in., 38 x 56 cm.
76.2553 PG 190

Untitled. 1937.
Black chalk, pastel, colored crayon on wood-pulp wove paper glued down on wood-pulp board, 15 x 22 in., 38 x 56 cm.
76.2553 PG 189

Stringed Object (Head). 1938 (cast 1956).
Bronze with original black patina on concave surfaces, polished convex surfaces, and coarse string. Length: 2 15/16 in., 7.5 cm.; width: 2 1/16 in., 5.2 cm.
76.2553 PG 191

Reclining Figure. 1938 (cast 1946).
Polished bronze (lost wax). Height: 5 3/8 in., 13.6 cm.; length: 12 3/8 in., 31.5 cm.
76.2553 PG 192

Family Group. Ca. 1944 (cast 1956).
Bronze (lost wax) with original brown patina. Height at left, with base causing fluctuation of 1/8 in., 4 cm., left to right: 5 5/8 in., 14.2 cm.; at right: 5 3/8 in., 13.8 cm. Dimensions of base: 2 15/16 x 4 3/16 x 5/16 in., 7.5 x 10.7 x 0.8 cm.
76.2553 PG 193

Three Standing Figures. 1953.
Bronze (figures hollow cast, lost wax; base sand cast), black-green patina. Height of left figure: 28 3/16 in., 71.7 cm.; center figure: 28 1/8 in., 72 cm.; right figure: 28 1/16 in., 71.3 cm.; Height of base: 9/16-3/4 in., 1.5-2 cm.; width of base: 26 3/4 in., 68 cm.; depth of base: 11 3/8 in., 29 cm.
76.2553 PG 194

Robert Motherwell
Personage (Autoportrait). December 9, 1943.
Collage of Japanese and western papers, gouache and black ink on thick pulpboard, 40 7/8 x 25 15/16 in., 103.8 x 65.9 cm.
76.2553 PG 155

E. R. Nele
Kollektiv II (Collective II). 1961.
Bronze. Height: 15 3/4 in., 39.9 cm.
76.2553 PG 216

Ben Nicholson
February 1956 (menhir). 1956.
Oil with black ink (?) on carved board, 39 1/8 x 11 13/16 in., 99.4 x 30 cm.
76.2553 PG 46

Richard Oelze
Untitled. Ca. 1933.
Pencil on paper, 10 5/16 x 7 1/4 in., 26.2 x 18.4 cm.
76.2553 PG 104

Kenzo Okada
Above the White. 1960.
Oil on canvas, 50 1/8 x 38 1/16 in., 127.3 x 96.7 cm.
76.2553 PG 184

Amédée Ozenfant
Guitare et bouteilles (Guitar and bottles). 1920.
Oil on canvas, 31 11/16 x 39 5/16 in., 80.5 x 99.8 cm.
76.2553 PG 24

Eduardo Paolozzi
Chinese Dog 2. May 1958.
Bronze (lost wax). Height: 36 3/8 in., 92.3 cm.; width: 25 3/16 in., 64 cm.
76.2553 PG 200

Pegeen (Vail)
Girls in the Arches. Ca. 1936.
Gouache on paper, 15 15/16 x 21 13/16 in., 40.5 x 55.5 cm.
76.2553 PG 178

At the Seaside. 1945.
Oil on canvas, 31 3/4 x 42 3/4 in., 80.7 x 108.7 cm.
76.2553 PG 267

The Exhibition. Ca. 1945.
Pastel on flocked paper, 29 5/16 x 40 7/8 in., 74.5 x 103.7 cm.
76.2553 PG 268

My Wedding. 1946.
Oil on canvas, 29 15/16 x 35 13/16 in., 76.1 x 91 cm.
76.2553 PG 177

Palazzo Venier dei Leoni. 1950s.
Pastel on paper, 9 3/8 x 25 9/16 in., 23.9 x 65 cm. (sight).
76.2553 PG 269

Childbirth. Ca. 1952.
Crayon and gouache on paper, 8 11/16 x 11 in., 22.1 x 28 cm.
76.2553 PG 270

On the Grand Canal. 1950s.
Pastel, gouache, and gold paint on flocked paper, 9 15/16 x 15 15/16 in., 25.3 x 40.5 cm.
76.2553 PG 271

In the Park. 1953.
Oil on canvas, 21 5/8 x 43 3/4 in., 55 x 111.1 cm.
76.2553 PG 177a

Family Portrait. Late 1950s.
Pastel on flocked paper, 20 5/16 x 29 5/16 in., 51.7 x 74.7 cm. (sight).
76.2553 PG 272

In the Bath. Late 1950s.
Pastel on paper, 19 1/4 x 25 1/4 in., 48.9 x 64.2 cm. (sight).
76.2553 PG 273

Palazzo Venier—Grand Canal. 1960s.
Pastel on paper, 12 5/8 x 19 1/4 in., 32 x 49 cm.
76.2553 PG 274

The Sunshade. 1960s.
Pastel on paper, 18 5/16 x 12 3/8 in., 46.6 x 31.5 cm.
76.2553 PG 275

Intimate Conversation. 1960s.
Pastel on flocked paper, 12 9/16 x 19 5/16 in., 31.9 x 49 cm.
76.2553 PG 276

Girls in a Room. 1964.
Pastel on paper, 19 7/8 x 26 7/16 in., 49.3 x 67.1 cm. (sight).
76.2553 PG 277

Pegeen with Egidio Costantini (Fucina degli Angeli).
Clementine. 1966.
12 poured glass figures set in a vitrine. Dimensions of vitrine: 55 1/2 x 37 in., 141 x 94 cm.
76.2553 PG 278

Antoine Pevsner
La Croix Ancrée (Anchored cross). 1933.
Black marble (base), brass sheets painted black, crystal. Dimensions of marble base: 15 3/16 x 13 5/16 in., 38.6 x 33.8 cm.; overall length (diagonal): 33 5/16 in., 84.6 cm.; height of semicircular crystal sheets: 9 15/16 in., 25.2 cm.; height of triangular crystal sheets: 5 9/16 in., 14.2 cm.
76.2553 PG 60

Surface développable (Developable surface). 1938-August 1939.
Bronze and copper. Height (without base): 19 7/8 in., 50.5 cm.; width along longest side: 12 3/16 in., 31 cm.; along shortest side: 11 in., 28 cm.; Copper-edged base, tin soldered: 11 7/16 x 11 7/16 in., 29 x 29 cm.; height of base: 5/8 in., 1.6 cm. Construction screwed into base with eight copper screws (one of which is missing, one of which has been replaced).
76.2553 PG 61

Surface développable (Developable surface). 1941.
Bronze and silver gilt. Height (including double base of bronze on slate): 21 5/8 in., 55 cm.; dimensions of base: 14 1/4 x 19 5/16 in., 36.3 x 49.1 cm.
76.2553 PG 62

François Marie Martinez Picabia
Très rare tableau sur la terre (Very rare picture on the earth). 1915.
Oil and metallic paint on paper board; silver and gold leaf applied to plywood relief cylinders, which are screwed to support from reverse. Wood frame constructed by artist as integral part of the work. Inner dimensions of paper board support: 44 9/16 x 33 1/2 in., 113.2 x 85.2 cm.; inner edge of frame: 46 9/16 x 35 1/2 in., 118.2 x 90.2 cm.; outer dims. of frame: 49 1/2 x 38 1/2 in., 125.7 x 97.8 cm.
76.2553 PG 67

Pablo Ruiz Picasso
Le poète (The poet). August 1911.
Oil on fine linen canvas (unvarnished), 51⅝ x 35¼ in., 131.2 x 89.5 cm.
76.2553 PG 1

Pipe, verre, bouteille de Vieux Marc (Pipe, glass, bottle of Vieux Marc). Spring 1914.
Block-printed paper, white laid paper, green wove paper, newspaper, light and dark brown wood-pulp papers, charcoal, india ink, printer's ink, graphite, and white gouache on fine linen unprimed canvas (unvarnished), 28 13/16 x 23⅜ in., 73.2 x 59.4.
76.2553 PG 2

L'Atelier (The Studio). 1928.
Oil and black crayon on canvas, 63⅝ x 51⅛ in., 161.6 x 129.9 cm.
76.2553 PG 3

La Baignade (On the beach). February 12, 1937.
Oil, conté crayon, chalk on primed (gray) canvas (unvarnished), 50 13/16 x 76⅜ in., 129.1 x 194.0 cm.
76.2553 PG 5

Sueño y Mentira de Franco (The Dream and Lie of Franco). 1937. 56/150.
Etching and aquatint, two parts, each 15 1/16 x 22 7/16 in., 38.2 x 54.5 cm.
76.2553 PG 4a-4b

Buste d'homme en tricot rayé (Half-length portrait of a man in a striped jersey). September 14, 1939.
Gouache on wove (Ingres) paper (unvarnished), 24⅞ x 17 15/16 in., 63.1 x 45.6 cm.
76.2553 PG 6

Jackson Pollock
The Moon Woman. 1942.
Oil on canvas (unvarnished), 69 x 43 1/16 in., 175.2 x 109.3 cm.
76.2553 PG 141

Untitled. 1944.
Oil on canvas (unvarnished), 28 13/16 x 17 15/16 in., 73.2 x 45.6 cm.
76.2553 PG 142

Two. 1943-45.
Oil on canvas (unvarnished), 76 x 43¼ in., 193 x 110 cm.
76.2553 PG 143

Direction. October 1945.
Oil on canvas (unvarnished), 31¾ x 21 15/16 in., 80.6 x 55.7 cm.
76.2553 PG 144

Circumcision. January 1946.
Oil on canvas (unvarnished), 56 1/16 x 66⅛ in., 142.3 x 168 cm.
76.2553 PG 145

Untitled. Ca. 1946.
Gouache and pastel on wove paper, 22⅞ x 31½ in., 58 x 80 cm.
76.2553 PG 147

Bird Effort (Accabonac Creek Series). 1946.
Oil on canvas (unvarnished), 24 x 20 1/16 in., 61 x 51 cm.
76.2553 PG 146

Croaking Movement (Sounds in the Grass Series). 1946.
Oil on canvas (unvarnished), 54 x 44⅛ in., 137 x 112 cm.
76.2553 PG 148

Eyes in the Heat (Sounds in the Grass Series). 1946.
Oil (and enamel?) on canvas (unvarnished), 54 x 43 in., 137.2 x 109.2 cm.
76.2553 PG 149

Enchanted Forest. 1947.
Oil on canvas (unvarnished), 45⅛ x 87⅛ in., 114.6 x 221.3 cm.
76.2553 PG 151

Alchemy. 1947.
Oil, aluminum (and enamel?) paint and string on canvas (unvarnished), 45⅛ x 87⅛ in., 114.6 x 221.3 cm.
76.2553 PG 150

Arnaldo Pomodoro
Studio No I (Tavola dei segni) (Study No. I [Tablet of signs]). 1961.
Bronze relief (lost wax) with original light silvery patina. Dimensions of relief: 20 1/16 x 12⅛ in., 51 x 30.9 cm.; dims. of mount without base: 20 9/16 x 13 1/16 in., 52.3 x 33.2 cm.; dims. of mount (including base): 22¾ x 13 1/16 in., 57.8 x 33.2 cm.
76.2553 PG 213

Sfero No 4, (Sphere No. 4). 1963-64.
Bronze (lost wax), part polished, part dark brown patina. Circumference: 72⅞ in., 185 cm.
76.2553 PG 214

Germaine Richier
Tauromachie (Tauromachy). 1953.
Bronze (lost wax, cast in three pieces). Height of figure: 43⅞ in., 111.5 cm., height of bull's head: 18½ in., 47 cm.; dimensions of base: 37 11/16 x 20⅝ in., 95.7 x 52.5 cm.
76.2553 PG 205

Hans Richter
Dadakopf (Dadahead). 1918.
Ink on paper, 10 11/16 x 6 3/16 in., 27.2 x 15.7 cm.
76.2553 PG 83

Dadakopf (Dadahead). 1923.
Oil on canvas mounted on wood panel, ca. 11 x 6 1/2 in., 28 x 16.6 cm.
76.2553 PG 84

Jean-Paul Riopelle
Peinture (Painting). 1955.
Oil on canvas, 45 3/8 x 28 9/16 in., 115.2 x 72.5 cm.
76.2553 PG 187

Mark Rothko
Sacrifice. April 1946.
Watercolor, gouache, india ink, on Whatman paper, 39 7/16 x 25 7/8 in., 100.2 x 65.8 cm.
76.2553 PG 154

Giuseppe Santomaso
Vita Segreta (Secret Life). 1958.
Oil on canvas, 28 13/16 x 19 11/16 in., 73.1 x 49.9 cm.
76.2553 PG 161

Kurt Schwitters
Merzzeichnung 75 (Merz drawing 75). 1920.
Collage, gouache, red and black printer's ink, graphite on wood-pulp papers (newsprint, cardboard), and fabric, 5 3/4 x 3 15/16 in., 14.6 x 10 cm.
76.2553 PG 85

Blau in Blau (Blue in Blue). 1926-29.
Collage, lithographic crayon on wood-pulp paper, 14 7/16 x 11 3/4 in., 36.7 x 29.9 cm.
76.2553 PG 86

Maraak, Variation I. 1930.
Oil and assemblage of rusted steel with blue laminate, enameled tin butterfly, paper, cork, and china on 4 mm. pulp board, 18 1/8 x 14 9/16 in., 46 x 37 cm.
76.2553 PG 87

Gino Severini
Mare = Ballerina (Sea = Dancer). January 1914.
Oil on canvas (unvarnished). Dimensions including artist's painted frame: 41 1/2 x 33 13/16 in., 105.3 x 85.9 cm.; canvas only: 39 3/8 x 31 11/16 in., 100 x 80.5 cm.
76.2553 PG 32

Francisco Sobrino
Transformation Instable—Superposition—Juxtaposition (Unstable Transformation—Superpostion—Juxtaposition). 1963.
Plexiglas, 32 7/16 x 16 3/4 x 16 3/4 in., 82.3 x 42.5 x 42.5 cm.
76.2553 PG 255

Clyfford Still
Jamais. May 1944.
Oil on canvas (unvarnished), 65 1/16 x 32 1/4 in., 165.2 x 82 cm.
76.2553 PG 153

Graham Vivian Sutherland
Organic Form. 1962-68.
Oil on canvas, 51 1/4 x 38 3/8 in., 130.2 x 97.4 cm.
76.2553 PG 120

Takis
Signal. 1958.
Iron. Height: ca. 141 3/4 in., 360 cm.
76.2553 PG 209

Rufino Tamayo
Heavenly Bodies. 1946.
Oil with sand on canvas (unvarnished), 34 1/8 x 66 15/16 in., 86.6 x 170 cm.
76.2553 PG 119

Tancredi
Untitled. Ca. 1951-52.
Gouache on paper, 27 3/8 x 39 1/4 in., 69.6 x 99.7 cm.
76.2553 PG 279

Paesaggio di spazio. Ca. 1951-52.
Gouache on paper, 27 5/8 x 39 3/16 in., 70.2 x 99.6 cm.
76.2553 PG 280

Untitled. Ca. 1952.
Gouache and crayon on paper, 27 9/16 x 39 1/4 in., 70 x 99.8 cm.
76.2553 PG 281

Untitled. Ca. 1953.
Gouache, graphite, pastel on paper, 27 9/16 x 39 1/4 in., 70 x 99.8 cm.
76.2553 PG 282

Untitled. Ca. 1953.
Gouache and pastel on paper, 27 9/16 x 39 1/4 in., 70.1 x 99.8 cm.
76.2553 PG 283

Untitled. Ca. 1953.
Gouache and pastel on paper, 27 1/4 x 39 1/8 in., 69.2 x 99.5 cm.
76.2553 PG 284

Untitled. Ca. 1954.
Gouache on paper, 29 3/8 x 41 1/4 in., 74.6 x 104.8 cm.
76.2553 PG 285

Untitled. Ca. 1954.
Gouache on paper, 27½ x 39¼ in., x 69.9 x 99.8 cm.
76.2553 PG 286

Composition. 1955.
Oil and tempera on canvas, 51 x 76¾ in., 129.5 x 195 cm.
76.2553 PG 166

Transparenze degli elementi. 1957.
Wax crayon and gouache on paper, 27 x 39 1/16 in., 68.7 x 99.2 cm.
76.2553 PG 287

Composition. 1957.
Tempera on canvas, 51 5/16 x 66 11/16 in., 130.4 x 169.4 cm.
76.2553 PG 167

Raymond Georges Yves Tanguy
Palais promontoire (Promontory palace). 1931.
Oil on canvas (unvarnished?), 28¾ x 23⅝ in., 73 x 60 cm.
76.2553 PG 94

Le soleil dans son écrin (The sun in its jewel case). 1937.
Oil on canvas (unvarnished?), 45 7/16 x 34 11/16 in., 115.4 x 88.1 cm.
76.2553 PG 95

Untitled. 1938.
Gouache on paper, 3 11/16 x 9 3/16 in., 9.3 x 23.3 cm.
76.2553 PG 96

Untitled. July 20, 1938.
Pencil and feather on paper, 21 7/16 x 7 3/16 in., 54.5 x 18.2 cm.
76.2553 PG 97

En lieu oblique (In an indeterminate place). March 1941.
Oil on canvas (unvarnished), 16 15/16 x 28⅛ in., 43 x 71.4 cm.
76.2553 PG 98

Leslie Thornton
Roundabout. 1955.
Bronze. Height: 27⅞ in., 70.8 cm.
76.2553 PG 199

Mark Tobey
Advance of History. 1964.
Gouache and watercolor on wove paper, glued at corners to acidic mount, 25⅝ x 19 11/16 in., 65.2 x 50.1 cm.
76.2553 PG 140

Tomonori Toyofuku
Drifting No. 2. 1959.
Wood. Height of man: 69½ in., 176.5 cm.; length of boat: 119½ in., 303.5 cm.
76.2553 PG 218

John Tunnard
Psi. 1938.
Oil, gesso, gouache, pastel(?), and wax crayon on hardboard (unvarnished), 31 7/16 x 47 3/16 in., 79.9 x 119.8 cm.
76.2553 PG 47

Pi. Spring 1941.
Gouache, wash, conté crayon, graphite, pastel, black paint (possibly ink?) on wove paper, 15⅜ x 22 in., 39 x 56 cm.
76.2553 PG 48

Günther Uecker
Taktile Struktur Rotierend (Tactile rotating structure). 1961.
Wood conglomerate rectangle covered with painted burlap; foam-filled aluminum; iron nails coated with stove-pipe silver paint (purpurin). Dimensions of rectangular base: 24 x 20¾ in., 61 x 52.7 cm.
76.2553 PG 229

Laurence Vail
Screen. 1940.
Gouache and paper collage pasted to canvas on wooden screen; three panels, total ca. 67 x 65 in., 170 x 165 cm.
76.2553 PG 123

Untitled. Ca. 1962.
Assemblage, wire, bones, keys, buttons, etc. Height: 19¾ in., 50 cm.
76.2553 PG 124

Untitled.
Assemblage, wire, brushes, sequins, beads, bottle cap, fabric. Height: 13 9/16 in., 34.5 cm.
76.2553 PG 288

Untitled.
Glass bottle and collage. Height: 8¼ in., 21 cm.
76.2553 PG 289

Untitled.
Glass bottle and collage. Height: 16 15/16 in., 43 cm.
76.2553 PG 290

Untitled.
Glass bottle and collage with light fixture. Height (with fixture): 11⅜ in., 29 cm., (without): 10 in., 25.5 cm.
76.2553 PG 291

Untitled.
Glass bottle with encrusted miniature bottles glued to surface. Height: 17⅛ in., 43.5 cm.
76.2553 PG 292

Untitled.
Glass bottle with paper, fabric, and sequin collage. Height: 11 in., 28 cm.
76.2553 PG 293

Georges Vantongerloo
Construction des rapports des volumes émanante du carré inscrit et le carré circonscrit d'un cercle (Construction of volumetric interrelationships derived from the inscribed square and the square circumscribed by a circle). 1924.
Cement cast painted white. Height: 11 13/16 in., 30 cm.; dimensions across center at longest: 10 1/16 in., 25.5 cm.; at shortest: 9⅞ in., 25 cm.
76.2553 PG 59

Victor Vasarely
JAK. 1965.
Metallic and acrylic paints on wood panel, with red bole underpainting, 32 7/16 x 32 7/16 in., 82.3 x 82.3 cm.
76.2553 PG 223

Emilio Vedova
Immagine del tempo (Sbarramento) (Image of time [Barrier]). 1951.
Egg tempera on canvas (unvarnished), 51⅜ x 67⅛ in., 130.5 x 170.4 cm.
76.2553 PG 162

Città Ostaggio (Hostage City). 1954.
Tempera, india ink, sand, enamel on paper, 27⅝ x 39 7/16 in., 70.2 x 100.1 cm.
76.2553 PG 163

Jacques Villon
Espaces (Spaces). 1920.
Oil on canvas, 28¾ x 36 1/16 in., 73 x 91.6 cm.
76.2553 PG 23

SCULPTURE FROM AFRICA, OCEANIA, THE AMERICAS, JAPAN, AND CORFU.

Africa

Reliquary Figure.
Gabon, Kota.
Wood and brass. Height: 22½ in., 57 cm.
76.2553 PG 245

Mask.
Guinea, Toma.
Wood. Height: 33½ in., 85 cm.
76.2553 PG 246

Yoke Mask (Nimba).
Guinea, Baga.
Wood. Height: 55 in., 138 cm.
76.2553 PG 243

Mask (Gelede)
Nigeria, Yoruba.
Polychrome wood. Height: 29 in., 72 cm.
76.2553 PG 247

Bird (Porpianong).
Ivory Coast, Senufo.
Polychrome wood. Height: 55 in., 140 cm.
76.2553 PG 242

Pair of Male and Female Figures (Rhythm Pounders).
Ivory Coast, Senufo.
Wood. Height: 52 in., 130 cm.
76.2553 PG 250A - B.

Horse and Rider.
Ivory Coast, Senufo.
Wood. Length: 20 in., 50 cm.
76.2553 PG 251

Seat.
Ivory Coast, Senufo.
Wood. 30 x 7 in., 74 x 18 cm.
76.2553 PG 255

Standing Male Figure.
Ivory Coast, Senufo.
Wood. Height: 24½ in., 72 cm.
76.2553 PG 257

Helmet Mask.
Ivory Coast, Senufo.
Wood. 18 x 13 x 27 in., 46 x 33 x 68.5 cm.
76.2553 PG 244

Mask.
Zaire, Salampasu.
Wood, copper, paint, vegetable fiber.
Height: 24 in., 62 cm.
76.2553 PG 258

Wall Panel with Sculptured Face of Owl.
Zaire, Yaka.
Polychrome wood. Height: 19½ in., 48 cm.
76.2553 PG 252

Wall Panel with Sculptured Face of Animal.
Zaire, Yaka.
Polychrome wood. Height: 19½ in., 48 cm.
76.2553 PG 253

Initiation Mask.
Zaire, Yaka.
Polychrome wood, woven raffia, and raffia.
Height: 20½ in., 50 cm.
76.2553 PG 254

Male Antelope Headdress (Chi Wara).
Mali, Bamana.
Wood. Height: 39 in., 98 cm.
76.2553 PG 256A

Female Antelope Headdress (Chi Wara).
Mali, Bamana.
Wood. Height: 33 in., 84 cm.
76.2553 PG 256B

Seated Figure.
Mali, Dogon.
Wood. Height: 27¼ in., 69 cm.
76.2553 PG 241

Lidded Container.
Mali, Dogon.
Wood. Height: 44 in., 110 cm.
76.2553 PG 249

Coffer.
Mali, Dogon.
Wood. Length: 47½ in., 118 cm.
76.2553 PG 248

Oceania

Tatanua Mask.
Northern New Ireland.
Polychrome wood with fringe. Height: 14¾ in., 37.5 cm.
76.2553 PG 232

Funerary Carving (Malanggan).
Northern New Ireland.
Polychrome wood. Length: 63 in., 158 cm.
76.2553 PG 233

Soul Ship.
Irian Jaya (West New Guinea), Asmat.
Polychrome wood. Length: 88⅛ in., 223.9 cm.
76.2553 PG 236

Ancestral Carving.
Papua, New Guinea, East Sepik Province, Southern Abelam.
Polychrome wood. Height: 58 in., 144 cm.
76.2553 PG 240

Ancestral Figure.
Papua, New Guinea, East Sepik Province, Southern Abelam.
Polychrome wood. Height: 65 in., 164 cm.
76.2553 PG 234

Suspension Hook.
Papua, New Guinea, East Sepik Province, Western Iatmul.
Wood. Height: 26 in., 65 cm.
76.2553 PG 235

Figure.
Papua, New Guinea, East Sepik Province, Yamok Village, Sawos.
Wood. Height: 54 in., 134 cm.
76.2553 PG 237

Male Figure.
Papua, New Guinea, East Sepik Province, Murik.
Wood. Height: 31½ in., 78 cm.
76.2553 PG 238

Flute Figure.
Papua, New Guinea, East Sepik Province, Chambri.
Polychrome wood and dog's teeth. Height: 20 in., 50 cm.
76.2553 PG 239

The Americas

Bark Mask.
Amazon River, Brazil.
Fabric and straw. Height: 50 in., 123 cm.
76.2553 PG 261

Three Panels, One with Mask.
North Peru, Chimu.
Wood. 20 x 21 in., 50 x 52 cm.
76.2553 PG 262

Poncho with Llamas.
North Peru, Chimu.
Feathers woven into cotton. 32 x 32 in., 80 x 80 cm.
76.2553 PG 263

Female Figure.
Mexico, Nayarit.
Terra cotta. Height: 17 in., 42 cm.
76.2553 PG 264

Male Figure.
Mexico, Nayarit.
Terra cotta. Height: 19 in., 47 cm.
76.2553 PG 265

Embracing Couple with Baby.
Mexico, Nayarit.
Terra cotta. Height: 12 in., 32 cm.
76.2553 PG 266

Japan

Wagōjin.
Japan.
Wood. 28 x 15 in., 71 x 38 cm.
76.2553 PG 260

Corfu

Two Horses.
Stone. Height: 45¼ in., 115 cm.; Length: 49¼ in., 125 cm.; width: 22 in., 56 cm.
76.2553 PG 259A-B

PHOTOGRAPHIC CREDITS

The photographs of works in the Peggy Guggenheim Collection were made, unless otherwise noted below, by Carmelo Guadagno and David Heald.

Works for which no photographers are listed are reproduced by courtesy of their owners.

Credits not cited in the captions to the individual illustrations are as follows:

Ferruzzi, Venice: cat no. 4, fig. b.

Robert E. Mates: cat. no. 10, fig. b; main black and white photos of cat. nos. 102, 103, 128, 131, 137, 141-46, 148-49, 151-52, 156, 158, 161-69.

Mirko Lion: cat no. 39, figs. a, b, c.

Dienst Verspreide Rijkskollekties, The Hague: cat. no. 45, figs. c, d, e, f.

Musée National d'Art Moderne, Centre Georges Pompidou: cat. No. 50, figs. d, e, f, g, h, j. These drawings by Duchamp-Villon, credited in the captions to the Estate of the artist, Paris, were donated to the MNAM after the present catalogue had gone to press.

Michael J. Pirrocco: cat. no. 55, figs. a, b; cat. no. 61, fig. a.

Carmelo Guadagno and David Heald: cat. no. 72, figs. a, b, i.

Studio Art System, Venice: cat. no. 104, fig. b.

Cameraphoto, Venice: pp. 800, 801.

Camera Press, London: Frontispiece, p. 7.

Berenice Abbott granted permission for reproduction of copy prints made from her originals: Appendix, pp. 762-770.

Molly Murphy: diagram, p. 102.

INDEX*

Numerals in parentheses indicate the catalogue number of the work cited. "PGC" in parentheses indicates a work in the Peggy Guggenheim Collection which is not the subject of an individual catalogue entry.

*References to Peggy Guggenheim are not included in the Index. The EXHIBITIONS and REFERENCES sections of each catalogue entry have not been indexed. Exhibitions and references have been indexed, however, when they are discussed in the text or in footnotes.

3,000 copies of this catalogue, edited by Brenda Gilchrist, designed by Malcolm Grear Designers, typeset by Schooley Graphics/ Harlan Typographic, have been printed in Japan in September 1985 for the Trustees of The Solomon R. Guggenheim Foundation and Harry N. Abrams, Inc.